British Literature

Third Edition

bju press®
Greenville, South Carolina

Note: The fact that materials produced by other publishers may be referred to in this volume does not constitute an endorsement of the content or theological position of materials produced by such publishers. Any references and ancillary materials are listed as an aid to the student or the teacher and in an attempt to maintain the accepted academic standards of the publishing industry.

British Literature

Third Edition

Coordinating Writer
Bethany Harris, MA, MEd

Writers
Jill Blackstock, MEd
Abigail Groves, MA
Michelle Johnson, MA
Lois Oldenburg, MS
Michael Pope, MA
Barbara J. Rooks, MEd
Elizabeth Rose, MEd, MA
Kristin Villalba, MAT
Kelly Walter, MA

Contributing Writers
Dan Gass, MA
Margaret Wooten, PhD

Biblical Worldview
Brian Collins, PhD
Bryan Smith, PhD

Academic Oversight
Jeff Heath, EdD

Editors
Kristin Kowalk, MA
Rebecca S. Moore

Cover Design
Drew Fields

Designer
Sarah Lompe

Digital Content Management
Peggy Hargis

Page Layout
Kelley Moore

Permissions
Tatiana Bento
Sylvia Gass
Carrie Hanna
Ashleigh Schieber

Project Coordinators
Tony Every
Kathy Vasso

Based in part on original materials from *British Literature*, Second Edition, by Ronald A. Horton, PhD.

Acknowledgments begin on page iii, which is an extension of this copyright page. Illustrators and Photo Credits appear on pages 680–84.

ISBN 978-1-62856-256-9

15 14 13 12 11 10 9 8 7 6 5 4 3

ACKNOWLEDGMENTS

Partial definitions of the following vocabulary words are from *OED Online*. Copyright © 2018 Oxford University Press: heinous, prevarication, conceit, trenchant, chide, effectually, immutably, sequestered, circumspection, amiability, indomitable, bludgeoned, infiltrator, adamantly.

The remaining dictionary definitions are from THE AMERICAN HERITAGE DICTIONARY, Fifth Edition. Copyright © 2012 by Houghton Mifflin Harcourt Publishing Company. Reprinted by permission of Houghton Mifflin Harcourt Publishing Company. All rights reserved.

UNIT 1

Penguin Random House Excerpts from BEOWULF translated by Burton Raffel, translation copyright © 1963 by Burton Raffel, renewed 1991 by Burton Raffel. Used by permission of New American Library, an imprint of Penguin Publishing Group, a division of Penguin Random House LLC. All rights reserved. (19–30)

Excerpt from LE MORTE D'ARTHUR: KING ARTHUR AND THE LEGENDS OF THE ROUND TABLE by Thomas Malory, translated by Keith Baines, translation copyright © 1962 by Keith Baines; copyright renewed © 1990 by Francesca Evans. Used by permission of New American Library, an imprint of Penguin Publishing Group, a division of Penguin Random House LLC. All rights reserved. (54–60)

"The Prologue" and "The Nun's Priest Tale" from THE CANTERBURY TALES by Geoffrey Chaucer, translated by Nevill Coghill, translation copyright © 1951, 1958, 1960, 1975, 1977 by Neville Coghill. (Penguin Classics 1951, Fourth revised edition 1977). Used by permission of Penguin Classics, an imprint of Penguin Publishing Group, a division of Penguin Random House LLC (worldwide excluding the UK & Commonwealth) and reproduced by permission of **Penguin Books Ltd.** (UK & Commonwealth). All rights reserved. (89–115)

Any third party use of these materials, outside of this publication, is prohibited. Interested parties must apply directly to Penguin Random House LLC and Penguin Books Ltd. for permission.

Columbia University Press Excerpts from THE PETERBOROUGH CHRONICLE translated by Harry A. Rositzke. Copyright © 1951 Columbia University Press. Reprinted by permission of the publisher. (32–35)

W. W. Norton & Company Excerpts from SIR GAWAIN AND THE GREEN KNIGHT: A NEW VERSE TRANSLATION, translated by Simon Armitage. Copyright © 2007 by Simon Armitage. Used by permission of W. W. Norton & Company, Inc. (worldwide excluding the UK & Commonwealth) and **Faber and Faber Ltd.** (UK & Commonwealth). (38–51)

"Caedmon's Hymn," translated by John C. Pope. Copyright © 1993, 1986, 1979, 1974, 1968, 1962 by W. W. Norton & Company, Inc. from THE NORTON ANTHOLOGY OF ENGLISH LITERATURE, SIXTH EDITION, VOLUME 1, edited by M. H. Abrams. Used by permission of W. W. Norton & Company, Inc. (65–67)

Enitharmon Editions Anglo-Saxon riddles "Shield" and "Iceberg" from THE BATTLE OF MALDON AND OTHER OLD ENGLISH POEMS translated by Kevin Crossley-Holland, edited by Bruce Mitchell. Copyright © Kevin Crossley-Holland and Bruce Mitchell 1965. (London: Macmillan, 1966). Used by permission of Enitharmon Editions Ltd. (70)

Oxford University Press JULIAN OF NORWICH: REVELATIONS OF DIVINE LOVE, a new translation by Barry Windeatt (Oxford World's Classics, 2015): Extracts totalling 3,141 words from pages 40–43, 45–46, 74–75, 160–62. By permission of Oxford University Press. (76–81)

D. C. Heath C. Warren Hollister, ed. *A History of England: The Making of England 55 B.C. - 1339.* Lexington, MA: D. C. Heath & Co., 1971. (116)

UNIT 2

W. W. Norton & Company Excerpts from UTOPIA: A Norton Critical Edition by Sir Thomas More, translated by Robert M. Adams. Copyright © 1975 by W. W. Norton & Company, Inc. Used by permission of W. W. Norton & Company, Inc. (132–39)

British Library Queen Elizabeth's Tilbury speech, 1588 in present-day English. British Library (www.bl.uk) granted permission to edit text. (180)

Penguin Books Ltd. "Farewell, Love, and all thy laws forever" (Sonnet 31) from THE COMPLETE POEMS by Sir Thomas Wyatt, edited by R. A. Rebholz (London: Penguin Classics, 1978). Introduction and notes copyright © R. A. Rebholz, 1978. Reproduced by permission of Penguin Books Ltd. (187)

Oxford University Press Sonnets 31 and 41 from "Astrophil and Stella" in SIR PHILIP SIDNEY: THE MAJOR WORKS edited by Katherine Duncan-Jones (2008), pp. 165, 169. Used by permission of Oxford University Press. (188)

UNIT 3

W. W. Norton & Company Excerpts from OROONOKO, OR THE ROYAL SLAVE: A TRUE HISTORY by Aphra Behn, edited by Joanna Lipking. Copyright © 1997 by W. W. Norton & Company. Used by permission of W. W. Norton & Company, Inc. (395–401)

UNIT 4

W. W. Norton & Company Excerpts from HEART OF DARKNESS: A NORTON CRITICAL EDITION, FIFTH EDITION by Joseph Conrad, edited by Paul B. Armstrong. Copyright © 2017, 2006, 1988, 1971, 1963 by W. W. Norton & Company, Inc. Copyright renewed 1991 by Robert A. Kimbrough. Used by permission of W. W. Norton & Company, Inc. (575–76)

UNIT 5

Simon & Schuster "Sailing to Byzantium" from THE COLLECTED WORKS OF W. B. YEATS, VOLUME 1: THE POEMS, REVISED by W. B. Yeats, edited by Richard J. Finneran. Copyright © 1928 by The Macmillan Company, renewed 1956 by Georgie Yeats. Reprinted with the permission of Scribner, a division of Simon & Schuster, Inc. All rights reserved. (597)

The C. S. Lewis Co. PERELANDRA by C. S. Lewis. Copyright © C. S. Lewis Pte. Ltd. 1944. Extract reprinted by permission. (630–31)

Curtis Brown, London "Be Ye Men of Valor" speech reproduced with permission of Curtis Brown, London on behalf of The Estate of Winston S. Churchill. © The Estate of Winston S. Churchill. (633–35)

Farrar, Straus and Giroux "Aubade" from THE COMPLETE POEMS OF PHILIP LARKIN by Philip Larkin, edited by Archie Burnett. Copyright © 2012 by The Estate of Philip Larkin. Reprinted by permission of Farrar, Straus and Giroux (US) and **Faber & Faber Ltd.** (worldwide excluding the US for print and worldwide for electronic). (640–41)

"The Thought-Fox" from COLLECTED POEMS by Ted Hughes. Copyright © 2003 by The Estate of Ted Hughes. Also published in THE HAWK IN THE RAIN © 1957. Reprinted by permission of Farrar, Straus and Giroux (US) and **Faber & Faber Ltd.** (worldwide excluding the US for print and worldwide for electronic). (645)

"Follower" from OPENED GROUND: SELECTED POEMS 1966–1996 by Seamus Heaney. Copyright © 1998 by Seamus Heaney. Also published in DEATH OF A NATURALIST © 1966. Reprinted by permission of Farrar, Straus and Giroux (US) and **Faber & Faber Ltd.** (worldwide excluding the US). (652)

ACKNOWLEDGMENTS

"The Moment Before the Gun Went Off" from JUMP AND OTHER STORIES by Nadine Gordimer. Reprinted by permission of Farrar, Straus and Giroux (worldwide excluding the UK & Commonwealth) and **Russell & Volkening** as agents for the author (UK & Commonwealth for print and worldwide for electronic). Copyright © 1991 by Felix Licensing, B. V. (654–58)

Grove/Atlantic Excerpt from WAITING FOR GODOT copyright © 1954 by Grove Press, Inc.; copyright © renewed 1982 by Samuel Beckett. Used by permission of Grove/Atlantic, Inc (US & Canada) and **Faber & Faber Ltd.** (worldwide excluding the US & Canada). Any third party use of this material, outside of this publication, is prohibited. (646–47)

New Directions Publishing "Not Waving but Drowning" by Stevie Smith, from COLLECTED POEMS OF STEVIE SMITH, copyright © 1957 by Stevie Smith. Reprinted by permission of New Directions Publishing Corp (worldwide including Canada, excluding the UK & Commonwealth) and **Faber & Faber Ltd.** (UK & Commonwealth excluding Canada). (649)

Rogers, Coleridge & White "A Devoted Son" from *Games at Twilight and Other Stories* by Anita Desai. Published by William Heinemann Ltd., 1978. Copyright © Anita Desai. Reproduced by permission of the author c/o Rogers, Coleridge & White Ltd., 20 Powis Mews, London W11 1JN. (660–67)

CONTENTS

TO THE STUDENT xi

UNIT 1: *The Middle Ages (449–1485)* 1

PART 1: HEROES OF OLD 14

from **BEOWULF** 19

from THE ANGLO-SAXON CHRONICLE 32

PEARL POET 36

from SIR GAWAIN AND THE GREEN KNIGHT 38

THOMAS MALORY 52

from LE MORTE D'ARTHUR 54

PART 2: LITERATURE AND COMMUNITY 63

BEDE 64

from AN ECCLESIASTICAL HISTORY OF THE ENGLISH PEOPLE 65

POPULAR GENRES 68

Anglo-Saxon Riddles 70

Ballads: SIR PATRICK SPENS 70

GET UP AND BAR THE DOOR 72

Medieval Lyrics: THE CUCKOO SONG 73

I SING OF A MAIDEN 73

JULIAN OF NORWICH 74

from REVELATIONS OF DIVINE LOVE 76

MEDIEVAL DRAMA: EVERYMAN 82

PART 3: CHANGING SOCIETY 84

GEOFFREY CHAUCER 86

from THE PROLOGUE *to* THE CANTERBURY TALES 89

from THE NUN'S PRIEST'S TALE 107

PIERS PLOWMAN 116

UNIT 2: *The English Renaissance (1485–1640)* 119

PART 1: RENAISSANCE HUMANISM 128

SIR THOMAS MORE 130

from UTOPIA 132

SIR PHILIP SIDNEY 140

from AN APOLOGY FOR POETRY 141

AMELIA LANIER 143

EVE'S APOLOGY IN DEFENSE OF WOMEN *from* SALVE DEUS REX JUDAEORUM 144

SIR FRANCIS BACON 146

from ESSAYS 148

CONTENTS

MARGARET CAVENDISH 151
from THE PREFACE TO OBSERVATIONS UPON EXPERIMENTAL PHILOSOPHY 152
A WORLD MADE BY ATOMES 155

PART 2: REFORMATION AND NATIONAL IDENTITY 156

from THE BOOK OF COMMON PRAYER 158

JOHN FOXE 160
from Foxe's BOOK OF MARTYRS 161

THE ENGLISH BIBLE 164

EDMUND SPENSER 169
from THE FAERIE QUEENE 171

QUEEN ELIZABETH I 179
SPEECH TO THE TROOPS AT TILBURY 180

PART 3: LYRIC AND METAPHYSICAL POETRY 182

SONNETS AND SONNETEERS 184
Sir Thomas Wyatt: FAREWELL, LOVE, AND ALL THY LAWS FOREVER 187
Sir Philip Sidney: *from* ASTROPHIL AND STELLA 188
Edmund Spenser: *from* AMORETTI 189
William Shakespeare: *from* SONNETS 190

CHRISTOPHER MARLOWE AND SIR WALTER RALEIGH 192
THE PASSIONATE SHEPHERD TO HIS LOVE 194
THE NYMPH'S REPLY TO THE SHEPHERD 195

JOHN DONNE 196
SONG 198
A VALEDICTION FORBIDDING MOURNING 199
HOLY SONNET 14 200

GEORGE HERBERT 201
JORDAN (2) 202
LOVE (3) 202
THE PULLEY 203

BEN JONSON 204
SONG TO CELIA 205
STILL TO BE NEAT 205
ON MY FIRST SON 206

PART 4: RENAISSANCE DRAMA 208

CONVENTIONS OF RENAISSANCE DRAMA 210

WILLIAM SHAKESPEARE 211
MACBETH 214

CONTENTS

UNIT 3: Civil War to Enlightenment (1640–1789) 283

PART 1: CIVIL WAR AND RESTORATION 294

THE CAVALIER POETS 296
Robert Herrick: TO THE VIRGINS, TO MAKE MUCH OF TIME 297
Richard Lovelace: TO LUCASTA: GOING TO THE WARS 297

ANDREW MARVELL 298
TO HIS COY MISTRESS 299

JOHN MILTON 301
from AREOPAGITICA 303
SONNET 19 305
from PARADISE LOST 307

SAMUEL PEPYS 314
from THE DIARY 315

PART 2: EARLY NEOCLASSICAL WRITERS 320

DANIEL DEFOE 322
from ROBINSON CRUSOE 323

THE RISE OF THE NOVEL 332

JOSEPH ADDISON AND RICHARD STEELE 333
from THE TATLER *No. 25*. 334
from THE SPECTATOR *No. 34*. 336

ALEXANDER POPE 338
from AN ESSAY ON MAN 340
from AN ESSAY ON CRITICISM 342

JONATHAN SWIFT 345
from GULLIVER'S TRAVELS 347

PART 3: AGE OF JOHNSON 358

SAMUEL JOHNSON 360
from A DICTIONARY OF THE ENGLISH LANGUAGE 362
from THE RAMBLER *No. 4*. 365

JAMES BOSWELL 367
from THE LIFE OF SAMUEL JOHNSON, LL.D. 368

THOMAS GRAY 374
ELEGY WRITTEN IN A COUNTRY CHURCHYARD 375

PART 4: VOICES FROM THE OUTSIDE 380

JOHN BUNYAN 382
from THE PILGRIM'S PROGRESS 385

CONTENTS

ISAAC WATTS AND CHARLES WESLEY 391
OUR GOD, OUR HELP IN AGES PAST 392
BEHOLD THE MAN! 393

APHRA BEHN 394
from OROONOKO, THE ROYAL SLAVE 395

OLAUDAH EQUIANO AND WILLIAM WILBERFORCE 402
from THE LIFE OF OLAUDAH EQUIANO, OR GUSTAVUS VASSA, THE AFRICAN 404
from 1789 ABOLITION SPEECH 408

UNIT 4: *Romanticism to Victorianism (1789–1901)* 412

PART 1: SIGNS OF CHANGE 426

ROBERT BURNS 428
TO A MOUSE, ON TURNING HER UP IN HER NEST WITH THE PLOUGH 429
A RED, RED ROSE 431

WILLIAM BLAKE 432
THE LAMB 434
THE TYGER 435
LONDON 436

MARY WOLLSTONECRAFT 437
from A VINDICATION OF THE RIGHTS OF WOMAN 438

JANE AUSTEN 444
from PRIDE AND PREJUDICE 446

PART 2: THE MAJOR ROMANTICS 454

WILLIAM WORDSWORTH 456
I WANDERED LONELY AS A CLOUD 458
THE WORLD IS TOO MUCH WITH US 459
LINES COMPOSED A FEW MILES ABOVE TINTERN ABBEY 460

SAMUEL TAYLOR COLERIDGE 464
THE RIME OF THE ANCIENT MARINER 466

GEORGE GORDON, LORD BYRON 479
from CHILDE HAROLD 481
SHE WALKS IN BEAUTY 486

PERCY BYSSHE SHELLEY 487
OZYMANDIAS 489
ENGLAND IN 1819 491
ODE TO THE WEST WIND 492

JOHN KEATS 495
TO AUTUMN 497
ODE ON A GRECIAN URN 498
WHEN I HAVE FEARS THAT I MAY CEASE TO BE 499

FRANKENSTEIN: MARY SHELLEY 500

CONTENTS

PART 3: EARLY VICTORIANS 502

ALFRED, LORD TENNYSON 504
from IN MEMORIAM 506
ULYSSES 509
CROSSING THE BAR 511

ROBERT BROWNING 512
PORPHYRIA'S LOVER 515

ELIZABETH BARRETT BROWNING 517
SONNET 43 518

THOMAS CARLYLE 519
THE CONDITION OF ENGLAND *from* PAST AND PRESENT 521
from SIGNS OF THE TIMES 525

HARD TIMES: CHARLES DICKENS 530

CHARLOTTE BRONTË 532
from JANE EYRE 535

PART 4: LATE VICTORIANS 550

MATTHEW ARNOLD 552
DOVER BEACH 553

THOMAS HARDY 555
THE DARKLING THRUSH 556

GERARD MANLEY HOPKINS 558
PIED BEAUTY 559
GOD'S GRANDEUR 560

OSCAR WILDE 561
from THE IMPORTANCE OF BEING EARNEST 564

RUDYARD KIPLING 569
THE CONVERSION OF AURELIAN MCGOGGIN 571

HEART OF DARKNESS: JOSEPH CONRAD 575

UNIT 5: Modern and Contemporary Literature (1901–Present) 579

PART 1: MODERN LITERATURE 592

WILLIAM BUTLER YEATS 594
THE LAKE ISLE OF INNISFREE 596
SAILING TO BYZANTIUM 597
THE SECOND COMING 598

KATHERINE MANSFIELD 599
A CUP OF TEA 600

CONTENTS

JAMES JOYCE 606
ARABY 608
D. H. LAWRENCE 613
A SICK COLLIER 615
VIRGINIA WOOLF 622
THE MARK ON THE WALL 624
PERELANDRA: C. S. LEWIS 630
SIR WINSTON CHURCHILL 632
BE YE MEN OF VALOR 633

PART 2: POSTWAR AND COMMONWEALTH LITERATURE 636
PHILIP LARKIN 638
AUBADE 640
TED HUGHES 642
THE THOUGHT-FOX 645
WAITING FOR GODOT: SAMUEL BECKETT 646
STEVIE SMITH 648
NOT WAVING BUT DROWNING 649
SEAMUS HEANEY 650
FOLLOWER 652
NADINE GORDIMER 653
THE MOMENT BEFORE THE GUN WENT OFF 654
ANITA DESAI 659
A DEVOTED SON 660
THINGS FALL APART: CHINUA ACHEBE 668

GLOSSARY 671
PUBLIC DOMAIN WORKS 678
ILLUSTRATORS 680
PHOTO CREDITS 681
INDEX 685

British Literature presents the storytelling and writing of England from its beginnings to the present. The textbook covers the historical context, literary movements, and representative authors of a dynamic heritage that remains a vital expression of the heart and soul of the British people.

CULTURAL LITERACY

It is our desire that you will find your study of British literature a personally valuable experience, both pleasurable and educational, as a student of the Bible and of human nature and the cultures that influence it. As you move through these units, you will doubtless recognize authors and stories you have enjoyed in some fashion from your earliest years.

Understanding America's British roots improves understanding of the source of ideas and philosophies that have shaped American culture. As you grow in your understanding of British literature, you will better understand American and world literature of the corresponding period. British literature opens a window into the vista of world literature, and world literature in turn has been powerfully influenced by Great Britain.

An important goal for any British literature textbook is to develop cultural literacy by exposing students to authors and works that have exerted influence on British culture and society. What writers say (their themes) and how they express themselves (their styles) are powerfully dependent upon their times. You will study authors and their works roughly in the order they appeared in history. This approach helps you to track historical trends and influences and see how one period of British literature led to the next. The unit and part openers in this text will provide you with a historical, literary framework before you examine the works themselves. Similarly, background and biography sections provide helpful context for individual pieces and authors.

The study of British literature also gives the opportunity to see the truth of Ecclesiastes played out in the cyclical nature of history: "There is no new thing under the sun" (1:9). Culture changes with time, but human nature remains the same. While you are becoming more culturally literate through your exposure to great works, we hope you will benefit from this literary study of human nature and find enjoyment in the beauty of these works.

READING PROCESS

Each literature lesson is broken down into three stages: Before, During, and After Reading.

The **Before Reading** section highlights some key aspects of the literature selection for you. It identifies and explains important literary concepts, defines some of the challenging vocabulary you will encounter, and helps orient you to the work and how it will be discussed.

The **During Reading** section presents the literature and uses margin questions to draw your attention to the emphases outlined in the Before Reading instruction. These questions encourage you to think about these aspects as you read the work.

The **After Reading** section includes Think and Discuss questions that review and assess your comprehension of the Before and During Reading emphases as well as other prominent features and ideas connected to the literary work. At the end of each part, a test review outlines important concepts to help you prepare for testing.

BIBLICAL WORLDVIEW

Like other literature courses, this study focuses on interpretation (what does the work mean?) and technical analysis (how does the work say what it means?), but it also presents a third focus—biblical evaluation (how good is the work?). Evaluating how good a work is—that is, how it reflects the Truth, Goodness, and Beauty that the Creator has worked into His creation—is essential to a true understanding of literature and a primary purpose of this book. Thus, you will be challenged to evaluate literature in the light of Scripture—especially when authors' philosophies contradict the Word of God. The practice of applying a biblical worldview should help you to become discerning and Christlike in your approach not only to British literature but to life itself.

A CHRISTIAN MOTIVATION

What you learn in this class should lead you to worship God in a richer way. Influenced by the Holy Spirit and Scripture, you can show God's greatness in powerful ways. You can develop a greater ability to worship God verbally by learning about literary expression. We find examples of this application of literary knowledge and skill within British literature.

You can also sharpen your discernment skills through the study of British literature. As you learn to analyze and evaluate works of literature, you will become more skilled at interpreting novels, films, and cultural movements. The creativity and skills fostered by your study of literature will equip you to declare God's glory more effectively through your own writing, private or public, allowing you to reflect another aspect of the Master-Creator, who spoke life into the world.

UNIT OPENERS provide a historical framework and highlight prominent philosophical and cultural movements.

3

NEOCLASSICISM

During the Interregnum, literature had taken a narrower, more serious bent. Puritan leaders closed theaters and frequently censored materials. Prose works (often political or religious) and serious poetry dominated while edgier poems such as Andrew Marvell's "To His Coy Mistress" were written but left unpublished. The Restoration created a broader, more eclectic literature. Charles II reopened theaters, partly as a lover of drama himself and partly to make a political point. In fact, Restoration dramas often included racy elements, partially as a statement on past restrictions. At the same time, deeply religious writings still thrived, as proved by Bunyan's *The Pilgrim's Progress*, while authors such as John Dryden took the poet's public role seriously, writing satirical works commenting on society's ills.

But as Enlightenment thought spread, a new artistic style generally coinciding with it arose to dominate Europe for much of the eighteenth century. Known as **neoclassicism**, this style was based on models from classical Greece and Rome. For example, poets such as Alexander Pope looked to Roman writers from Emperor Augustus's time (27 BC–AD 14) for inspiration and stylistic models, resulting in the era's literature often being termed *Augustan*.

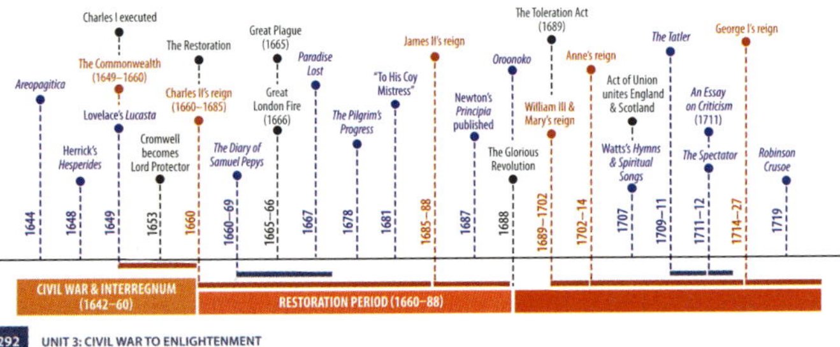

A BIOGRAPHICAL OVERVIEW of each author provides historical context and insight into author purpose and philosophy. Additional features may include an author timeline or interesting fact.

BIOGRAPHY

Jane Austen (1775–1817)

AT A GLANCE

- **1796** Began a draft of what would become *Sense and Sensibility*
- **1800** Moved to Bath, a transition that disrupted her writing habits
- **1809** Moved to Chawton where she finished *Sense and Sensibility* and wrote *Pride and Prejudice*, *Mansfield Park*, and *Emma*
- **1817** Died of an undetermined illness in Winchester; *Persuasion* and *Northanger Abbey* printed later that year
- **1833** First collection of her novels published

Although Jane Austen spent her life within the highly stratified and limited social world of the English country gentry, she wrote timeless novels that transcend their settings through their keen observation of human character and social mores. In doing so, Austen practically invented the realistic novel of manners, shifting the focus of the modern novel from extraordinary or outrageous events to the drama of everyday life.

Early Life

Austen was born in Hampshire, England. Her father, an Anglican rector, had a personal library of more than five hundred volumes, and young Jane was deeply familiar with the works of Richardson, Fielding, and Burney. Austen began writing at an early age, experimenting with various literary forms. By her early twenties she had already produced the first drafts of three of her six complete novels.

In 1800 her father retired and moved his family to the resort town of Bath. In the years both before and after his death in 1805, Austen had little time to write. In 1809, however, her brother Edward arranged for his sisters and mother to live on his estate in Chawton, Hampshire, where Austen was finally able to concentrate on her work.

Literary Success

In Austen's day, public authorship was still considered disreputable for a woman in Austen's position. Austen's name was never attached to her works during her lifetime. In fact, reputation probably influenced Austen's choice to rework and publish *Sense and Sensibility* (1811) first, since its content and themes were most in conformity with the social values of the day. Encouraged that *Sense and Sensibility* was accepted for publication, Austen quickly published *Pride and Prejudice* (1813), which met with widespread popularity.

The year 1814 brought the publication of *Mansfield Park*, Austen's most ambitious novel. This work brought her more income than her other novels during her lifetime, but it has seen the least commercial success to date. By the time *Emma* was published in 1815, Austen's novels had found a devoted fan in the Prince Regent himself, to whom the book is dedicated. By 1816, however, her health was failing, and she died, probably of Addison's disease, in the spring of 1817. Her brother Henry supervised the publication of *Northanger Abbey* and *Persuasion* in 1817, along with the first notice to the world of Austen's identity as an author.

Legacy

Austen's work is characterized by both a careful attention to the details of human life and a concern for the moral uplift of the reader. Thus, while Austen is famous for her realistic, fully rounded characters, many of them (such as Elinor Dashwood in *Sense and Sensibility* and John Knightley in *Emma*) remain exemplary models for behavior. The idealistic portraits of the central male characters in particular have proved influential on the modern romance novel.

Austen's works also reflect the trends in larger society. In her novels, older gentry, whose income traditionally comes from their land, members of the rising middle cla[ss] have made their fortunes i[n] mediocre pursuits such ness. Both groups seek t[o] their status in highly social situations such and personal visits.

This focus on th[e] significance of everyday [behav]ior created the novel of m[anners] and led directly to the realis[tic nov]els of the Victorian period. In time, novels were regarded as frivolous enterta[inment] Austen saw the unique potential for social anal[ysis] moral education in the novel form, and her w[orks re]mains both entertaining and inspiring today.

DID YOU KNOW?

All of Austen's heroines married their true love; however, Jane did not accept her one and only proposal.

BEFORE READING

ANALYZE: *Utopia and Social Satire*

The term ***utopia*** designates a genre of fictional writings about ideal societies. The name comes from More's *Utopia*, a traveler's account of an ideal society organized and administered on principles of reason. More called this imaginary kingdom Utopia based on the Greek word *outopia*, which means "no place," and puns on the word *eutopia*, which means "good place." A utopia differs from other fictional places in that it is vastly superior to the writer's contemporary world. In some cases, however, this supposed superiority can actually be an exaggeration of social ills. Utopian literature can serve as **social satire** (p. 85), using irony to critique a society. The rational standards by which Utopia operates, though unattainable and in some ways undesirable, reveal the shortcomings of English society in More's day. As you read, examine how rational principles govern the organization and operations of the ideal society. Also consider how exaggerated situations reveal *Utopia's* satirical purpose.

READ: *Infer Author's Tone*

How an author says something is as important as *what* he says. An author communicates his **tone** (p. 88) through the details he includes, such as descriptions and characters' words. But inferring an author's tone can be difficult. He or she may seem serious in places but speak ironically or playfully in others. *Utopia* contains such doubleness in tone, presenting readers with a challenge. Is More being serious or playfully ironic? Is *Utopia* a real blueprint for social change, a joke, or maybe both? More has not left us without clues. For instance, the surname of the work's main speaker, Raphael Hythloday, means "purveyor of nonsense." On the other hand, the fact that Utopians rise above personal greed indicates that More views such vices with seriousness. As you read, examine the details closely to determine where More is speaking seriously and where he is speaking ironically.

EVALUATE: *Author's Perspective*

The tone an author uses and the themes he explores are both windows into his perspective. What does Sir Thomas More think about the subjects of greed, personal possessions, and religious tolerance, just to name a few? As you read—and after you have inferred More's tone—begin evaluating his perspective on the themes he addresses. When forming your evaluations, refer to biblical principles and passages such as the following: Psalm 62:10, Proverbs 28:25, Matthew 6:24, Romans 13:9, and Hebrews 13:5–6.

OBJECTIVES

- Identify the characteristics of utopian literature.
- Infer authorial tone to determine meaning in a text.
- Analyze how satire supports an author's social critique.
- Evaluate the author's view of human nature and society in light of a biblical worldview.

VOCABULARY

eminence (ĕm′ə-nəns) *n.* A position of great distinction or superiority.

concoct (kən-kŏkt′) *tr.v.* To devise, using skill and intelligence; contrive.

conspicuous (kən-spĭk′yo͞o-əs) *adj.* Attracting attention, as by being unusual or remarkable; noticeable.

inexplicable (ĭn-ĕk′splĭ-kə-bəl) *adj.* Difficult or impossible to explain or account for.

proselytize [British *proselytise*] (prŏs′ə-lĭ-tīz′) *intr.v.* To attempt to convert someone to one's own religious faith.

What would an **IDEAL COMMUNITY** *be like?*

The answer depends on whom you ask. Most people want everyone in their community to be happy and healthy, but how to reach those goals remains a question. Some cultures emphasize the importance of relationships and family while others especially value freedom of the individual. Some value regulations and certifications to ensure the quality of various services while others think these stifle the dynamism and creativity of a culture. What about you? Write a paragraph describing your ideal community.

BEFORE READING PAGES

Analyze: The Analyze section highlights relevant literary concepts and defines new literary terms.

Read: The Read section provides strategies for approaching the literature selection.

Evaluate/Create: The Evaluate section provides a scriptural or aesthetic context to help you evaluate the work. Alternatively, the Create section provides a motivation for writing under the inspiration of the featured author.

Vocabulary previews and defines some of the challenging words in the literature.

Motivate questions challenge students to consider important ideas related to a selection.

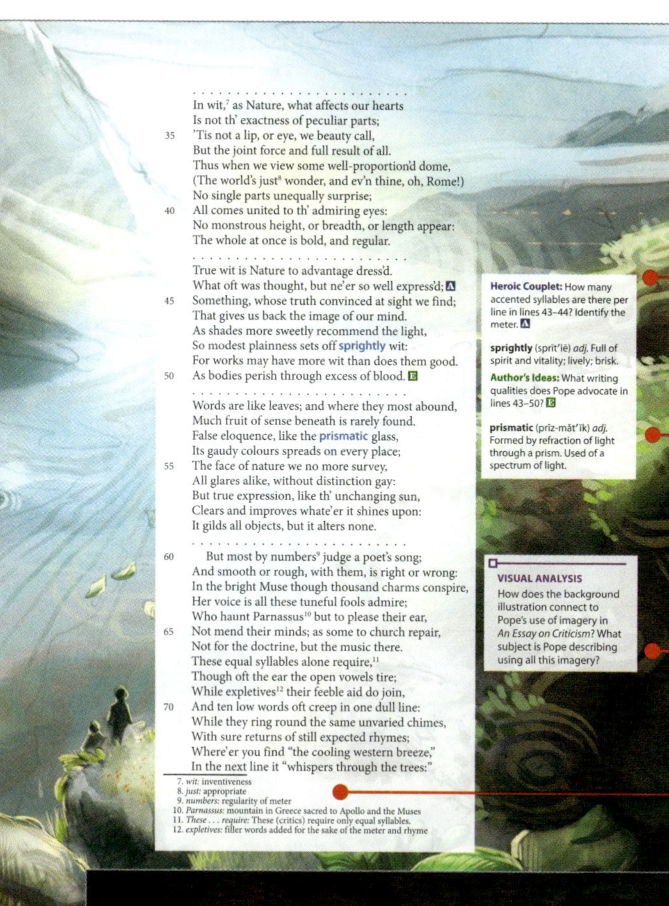

In wit,[7] as Nature, what affects our hearts
Is not th' exactness of peculiar parts;
'Tis not a lip, or eye, we beauty call,
But the joint force and full result of all.
Thus when we view some well-proportion'd dome,
(The world's just[8] wonder, and ev'n thine, oh, Rome!)
No single parts unequally surprise;
All comes united to th' admiring eyes:
No monstrous height, or breadth, or length appear;
The whole at once is bold, and regular.

True wit is Nature to advantage dress'd,
What oft was thought, but ne'er so well express'd; A
Something, whose truth convinced at sight we find;
That gives us back the image of our mind.
As shades more sweetly recommend the light,
So modest plainness sets off **sprightly** wit:
For works may have more wit than does them good,
As bodies perish through excess of blood. B

Words are like leaves; and where they most abound,
Much fruit of sense beneath is rarely found.
False eloquence, like the **prismatic** glass,
Its gaudy colours spreads on every place;
The face of nature we no more survey,
All glares alike, without distinction gay:
But true expression, like th' unchanging sun,
Clears and improves whate'er it shines upon:
It gilds all objects, but it alters none.

But most by numbers[9] judge a poet's song;
And smooth or rough, with them, is right or wrong:
In the bright Muse though thousand charms conspire,
Her voice is all these tuneful fools admire;
Who haunt Parnassus[10] but to please their ear,
Not mend their minds; as some to church repair,
Not for the doctrine, but the music there.
These equal syllables alone require,[11]
Though oft the ear the open vowels tire;
While expletives[12] their feeble aid do join,
And ten low words oft creep in one dull line:
While they ring round the same unvaried chimes,
With sure returns of still expected rhymes;
Where'er you find "the cooling western breeze,"
In the next line it "whispers through the trees:"

7. *wit:* inventiveness
8. *just:* appropriate
9. *numbers:* regularity of meter
10. *Parnassus:* mountain in Greece sacred to Apollo and the Muses
11. *These . . . require:* These (critics) require only equal syllables.
12. *expletives:* filler words added for the sake of the meter and rhyme

Heroic Couplet: How many accented syllables are there per line in lines 43–44? Identify the meter. A

sprightly (sprīt′lē) *adj.* Full of spirit and vitality; lively; brisk.

Author's Ideas: What writing qualities does Pope advocate in lines 43–50? B

prismatic (prĭz-măt′ĭk) *adj.* Formed by refraction of light through a prism. Used of a spectrum of light.

VISUAL ANALYSIS
How does the background illustration connect to Pope's use of imagery in *An Essay on Criticism?* What subject is Pope describing using all this imagery?

DURING READING questions draw attention to material related to emphases from the Before Reading section.

Previously discussed **VOCABULARY WORDS** are shown in bold and reviewed in context.

VISUAL ANALYSIS questions help you interpret art and illustration, aiding your understanding of artists' creative decisions and of the relationship between visual and literary texts.

FOOTNOTES provide definitions or helpful explanations of difficult or unfamiliar terms.

UNIT REVIEWS help you prepare for tests by providing a list of key literary terms and asking questions about background, concepts, and ideas from the chapter.

Speech to the Troops at Tilbury

My loving people,

We have been persuaded by some that are careful of our safety, to take heed how we commit our selves to armed multitudes, for fear of treachery; but I assure you I do not desire to live to distrust my faithful and loving people. Let tyrants fear. I have always so behaved myself that, under God, I have placed my chiefest strength and safeguard in the loyal hearts and good-will of my subjects; and therefore I am come amongst you, as you see, at this time, not for my recreation and **disport**, but being resolved, in the midst and heat of the battle, to live and die amongst you all; to lay down for my God, and for my kingdom, and my people, my honour and my blood, even in the dust. A

I know I have the body but of a weak and feeble woman; but I have the heart and stomach of a king, and of a king of England too, and think foul scorn that Parma or Spain, or any prince of Europe, should dare to invade the borders of my realm: to which rather than any dishonour shall grow by me, I myself will take up arms, I myself will be your general, judge, and rewarder of every one of your virtues in the field. A B

I know already, for your forwardness you have deserved rewards and crowns; and We do assure you in the word of a prince, they shall be duly paid you. In the mean time, my lieutenant general shall be in my stead, than whom never prince commanded a more noble or worthy subject; not doubting but by your obedience to my general, by your **concord** in the camp, and your valour in the field, we shall shortly have a famous victory over those enemies of my God, of my kingdom, and of my people.

disport (dĭ-spôrt′) *n.* Div[…] serious duties; relaxation, entertainment, amuseme[…]

Persuasive Appeal: Wha[…] sentences in this paragra[…] an appeal to pathos? A

Rhetorical Device: What antithesis occurs in this p[…]

Oral Reading: Read this […] yourself, noting the punc[…] its rhythmic effects. What words would you give m[…] to in your voice? B

concord (kŏn′kôrd′) *n.* Ha[…] agreement of interests o[…] accord.

THINK AND DISCUSS

1. Explain how Queen Elizabeth I uses appeals to both pathos and ethos in her speech. Be sure to include specific words and sentences to support your explanations.
2. Identify two instances of general parallelism and one instance of antithesis. What effect does each instance create in the speech?
3. When reading the speech aloud, how wo[…] your rhythm and emphasis? Use specific ex[…] the speech to support your explanation.
4. Imagine that you are an English soldier wh[…] Queen Elizabeth I's speech. Write a letter to […] that expresses your thoughts about the e[…] of the queen's speech and the ideas that s[…] Try to use appeals to pathos or ethos in yo[…]

180 UNIT 2: THE ENGLISH RENAISSANCE

THINK AND DISCUSS questions specifically apply the literary terms and concepts presented in the Before Reading section to the literature and touch on other important ideas.

UNIT 5 REVIEW

What Do You Know?

Understand the Background

1. Identify two authors who were personally affected by the rise of Nazi Germany.
2. Compare and contrast Joyce's and Heaney's attitudes toward Ireland. Use examples from their biographies and writings to support your conclusions.
3. Which Unit 5 author is a representative of postcolonialism?
4. List characteristics of modernism.

Apply the Concepts

5. Choose either "The Lake Isle of Innisfree" or "The Second Coming" and explain how Yeats's use of symbolism points to theme.
6. How does the third-person narrator in "A Cup of Tea" present Rosemary? What value does the use of third-person narrator offer as opposed to first-person?
7. Choose one of the stream-of-consciousness pieces. Use examples to explain how this approach differs from normal story narration and how it reflects modernist attitudes within your chosen work.
8. Identify and give examples of several rhetorical devices Churchill used in "Be Ye Men of Valor."
9. What primary method of rhetorical appeal did Churchill use? Why was this method dominant? Give several examples from his speech.
10. Give examples of how either Lawrence or Woolf is representative of modernism.
11. How do Smith and Larkin exemplify postwar attitudes in their poems?
12. Larkin, Hughes, and Heaney all use enjambment to great effect in their poetry. Choose one of their poems and explain how enjambment affects the poem.
13. Describe how Hughes develops an extended metaphor around his central image in "The Thought-Fox."
14. Identify and analyze the key conflict in "A Devoted Son."

Evaluate the Ideas

15. Evaluate the theme of either "Sailing to Byzantium" or "A Sick Collier" according to a biblical worldview. How are Truth and Beauty reflected?
16. Evaluate Mansfield's attitude toward human nature. Does she present a truthful reflection? How could Scripture inform her point of view?
17. Evaluate Joyce's depiction of religion from a biblical worldview.
18. Why does the speaker in "Aubade" say he is horrified of death but not remorseful for his mistakes? Evaluate his view of death from a biblical worldview.
19. Evaluate the contrasting perspectives of the drowned man and his acquaintances in "Not Waving but Drowning."

Write a Response

20. What is Gordimer's message in "The Moment Before the Gun Went Off"? How does the story interact with domestic and international politics of the day?
21. Compare Heaney's treatment of the father/son relationship with Desai's. Especially consider the development of character and conflict.

Define each term and provide an example of each from a selection in Unit 5.

TERMS
end rhyme
third-person limited point of view
stream of consciousness
epiphany
foreshadowing
interior monologue
aubade
mood
black humor
perfect rhyme
slant rhyme

TEST REVIEW 669

UNIT 1 OBJECTIVES

LITERARY ELEMENTS

- Analyze characteristics of Anglo-Saxon and Middle English genres: epic, romance, ballads, devotional literature, and satire.
- Trace changes in the heroic ideal of Middle Ages England.
- Examine how characters are developed and how they help reveal themes.
- Interpret imagery, symbols, and motifs and their connection to theme.
- Analyze the use of variation, repetition, and rhythm in oral poetry and alliterative verse.

READING STRATEGIES

- Read poetry aloud to understand and appreciate it.
- Summarize a text's key ideas.
- Apply knowledge of a text's historical, social, and philosophical context to interpret it.

TEXT CRITICISM AND CREATION

- Evaluate a culture's conception of heroism and injustice from a biblical worldview.
- Determine whether a text effectively engages an audience and communicates a message.
- Judge whether satire is used appropriately in a text.
- Compose texts for a variety of purposes.

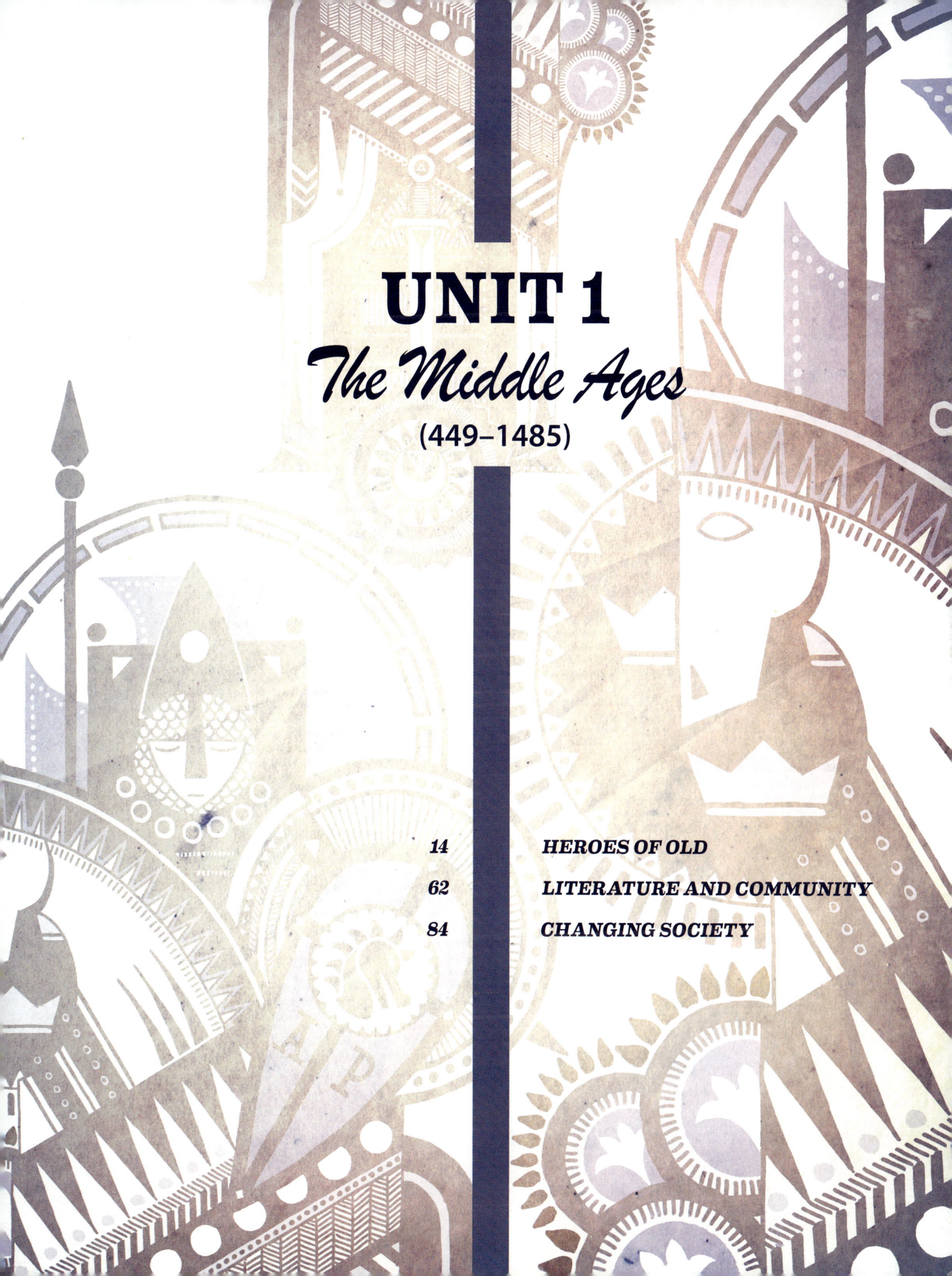

UNIT 1
The Middle Ages
(449–1485)

14 **HEROES OF OLD**
62 **LITERATURE AND COMMUNITY**
84 **CHANGING SOCIETY**

The Middle Ages

THE CELTS AND ROMANS (PREHISTORY–AD 449)

Twenty-first century British literature encompasses cultures across the globe, but its vast tradition began in one small region, Great Britain. The first outside records of the island came when Greek explorers encountered an indigenous Celtic tribe, the Britons (ca. 300s BC). The Britons were only one of many Celtic tribes in the region who, lacking a strong centralized government, succumbed to Roman invasion in AD 43. Rome entitled the province Britannia and created a hybrid Romano-British culture that flourished until the empire, crumbling from within, withdrew (ca. AD 410).

The Roman era strongly influenced Britain geographically and culturally. London—Britain's premier city and now capital for nearly a millennium—began as Rome's administrative center, Londinium. Supply roads and garrisons radiating out from it formed the base for many modern cities and roads, while Roman ruins that dot the countryside have drawn sightseers for centuries. The occupation also generated legends (e.g., the warrior-queen Boadicea) that still inform British national identity and, more importantly, saw the arrival and flourishing of Christianity on British soil.

Shorn of Rome's might, the Celts were left vulnerable to Northern Germanic invaders who drove them into the island's far corners (future Wales, Cornwall, Scotland) and farther (Ireland, Brittany). Later deemed inferior by the English, these Celtic-based cultures would develop their own literature. They did bequeath to the English, however, their mythology's vivid tales and legends. In fact, England's greatest legend, King Arthur, originated in stories of Romano-British warriors who resisted Germanic invasion. In the meantime, the Celts' fall created a profound shift in the region's cultural landscape.

The resulting new era is known as the Middle Ages, or medieval period. Beginning in upheaval with a series of Germanic tribal invasions, the English Middle Ages stretched for a thousand years until the start of the Tudor dynasty (1485). The era spans three cultural eras: the Anglo-Saxon period (449–1066), the High Middle Ages (1066–1300), and the Late Middle Ages (1300–1485). Each contributed significantly to England's emerging national identity.

ANGLO-SAXON BRITAIN (449–1066)

BECOMING A NATION: INVASIONS AND ASSIMILATION

The Anglo-Saxon period was dominated by two waves of invasion. First, beginning in AD 449, the Celts were continually harassed and eventually conquered by Germanic tribes from the Baltic Sea region (e.g., the Jutes, Angles, and Saxons). Later termed Anglo-Saxons, these people were immigrants fleeing conflict, and they came to stay. As the Celts either emigrated or assimilated into Germanic communities, both the land and its peoples took on a Germanic identity and names: *Englaland* (based on *Angles*) and the *Englisc* (*sc* pronounced /sh/).

Often organized around strong leaders rather than hereditary succession, early Anglo-Saxon politics were fragmented; coalitions rose and fell quickly. But by AD 600, seven powerful kingdoms (Northumbria, Mercia, Wessex, East Anglia, Essex, Kent, and Sussex) emerged. Constantly jostling for power, these kingdoms united only when faced with a new and powerful threat, the Scandinavian Vikings.

Viking coastal raids became legendary for their suddenness and brutality. Raiders destroyed and looted wealthy monasteries, sometimes the same ones multiple times, and killed or enslaved many of the English. By the late 800s, Danish raiding parties had ravaged the eastern coast, and an army of Danes was residing year-round in the midlands and much of Wessex, the era's dominant kingdom. Norwegians encroached in the northwest and Ireland too.

Using a series of brilliant military tactics, Alfred, King of Wessex (871–99), forced the Danes to sue for peace in the Treaty of Wedmore (878), which confined them to a northeast region called the Danelaw. Thereafter, Alfred held sway over all the kingdoms. His descendants retook the Danelaw for the English, but their achievement was short-lived. Taking advantage of weak leadership, dissension, and treachery in the ruling class, the Danes annexed all of England to King Canute's Scandinavian empire by 1016.

The Danish presence produced few major cultural changes. Possessing similar northern European roots and language, Danes adapted easily to the English, mingled freely, and developed loyalties to these new communities. Danish kings even upheld English laws and customs. What they did succeed in bringing was a stronger sense of national, rather than tribal, identity. Sharing a language, culture, and government, these communities naturally developed toward a single political system and a common perspective toward the outside world.

WHAT'S IN A NAME?

Europe's Middle Ages were long termed the Dark Ages in popular thinking. The name sprang from intellectuals who thought the era a culturally barren landscape formed by Rome's fall and enlightened by the Renaissance. Reasons cited for this view included the loss of Greco-Roman civilization, the lack of new cultural art and learning, and the dominance (through the Catholic Church) of faith rather than reason. Today many scholars resist these condemnations, citing evidence that vigorous intellectual and cultural life remained. Perhaps ironically, this culture was often fostered by the Church, which preserved classical and Christian learning and even inspired new ideas and art.

CHRISTIANITY AND THE ROMAN CATHOLIC CHURCH

Christianity in England was disrupted by these invaders, who maintained their polytheistic traditions. Christian missionaries (e.g., St. Patrick) had much greater success in Ireland, where the church grew tremendously and was renowned for its monastic centers of learning. The Irish church evangelized its neighbors in northern Britain. In southern Britain, a Roman Catholic missionary expedition arrived in AD 597 and began a long process of official conversions. Whether genuine or just politically expedient (sometimes the case), such conversions spread Christianity throughout Anglo-Saxon England. After wavering between the Irish and Roman churches, the English church chose Rome at the Synod of Whitby (AD 664).

The benefits of integration into Roman Catholic Christendom were many. The Church acted as a stabilizing influence on politics and common life both by providing a unifying worldview and by creating a national structure long before the region unified politically. Eventually, the ecclesiastical and civil hierarchies evolved into overlapping, mutually supporting institutions. Additionally, the Church provided politically and culturally valuable ties with continental Europe.

The Church also preserved and fostered learning and culture in monasteries (e.g., Wearmouth and Jarrow). It inspired and facilitated the spread of learning and literacy, kept historical records, and supported the English vernacular's development into a written language. Meanwhile, Church scribes recorded and preserved many Anglo-Saxon traditional (oral) works for later generations. These traditional works reveal a slow blending of Christian and tribal worldviews.

LANGUAGE AND LEARNING

Old English

Surviving works from Anglo-Saxon England come to us in one of two languages: Medieval Latin or Old English. Unfortunately, the latter is unintelligible to modern English speakers because of naturally occurring changes in grammar, syntax, and vocabulary over time. Old English encompassed multiple Anglo-Saxon and Scandinavian dialects, most mutually understandable at the time. Four regional dialects—Northumbrian, Mercian, West Saxon, and Kentish—eventually dominated, but most extant texts (e.g., *Beowulf*, the jewel of known Anglo-Saxon literature) survive in the West Saxon dialect because of Alfred the Great's work.

Anglo-Saxons possessed a system of runic writing, but it was not well-known, nor was it complex and flexible enough for literary works. Of necessity, church scholars began adapting the Latin alphabet to express Old English as early as the seventh century. As a result, Old English became easier to write in, allowing people to record new and old compositions.

King Alfred: Language and Literacy

Perhaps more than anyone else, Alfred the Great (849–899) deserves credit for advancing learning, literacy, and literature in Anglo-Saxon times. During his reign, Viking raids left many centers of learning in shambles. Priceless books were destroyed, and few scholars of note were left. An outstanding leader, Alfred believed that a Christian king should care for his people both physically and spiritually. To create better leaders and citizens, he promoted increased literacy and study of the liberal arts from a Christian viewpoint.

To begin a program of education and translation, Alfred brought in scholars from around the country and from Europe. The nobility, persons in leadership, and even promising commoners were educated in English, Latin,

Bewcastle Cross (ca. 600s): The remains of an Anglo-Saxon cross in the churchyard of St. Cuthbert's in Bewcastle, Cumbria, UK. The highlighted portion shows the epitaph inscribed in Anglo-Saxon runes on the cross's west side.

and the classics. Alfred also ordered important Latin texts to be translated into Old English and Old English oral compositions to be recorded in his native West Saxon dialect. Moreover, many believe *The Anglo-Saxon Chronicle* (a record of nearly four hundred years of English history) was begun at his behest. His programs helped preserve and grow Anglo-Saxon language and culture.

ANGLO-SAXON LITERATURE

Oral Literature

Most Anglo-Saxon literature was oral literature, a genre with distinct characteristics. Recreated from memory, no two performances of an oral work are exactly the same, though they share core content and traditional patterns of expression. Furthermore, the structure and style of oral works reflect their intended use: live performance. They use repetition and emphasis to draw attention to, elaborate on, or reveal connections between key content. They also add sound devices and rhetorical flourishes purely for audience enjoyment. Finally, literature from oral cultures tends to record important cultural values and history.

The most complex oral works (e.g., epics such as *Beowulf*) were for special occasions. Reciters used formal, elevated language to convey a sense of occasion and of the works' momentous content. In Anglo-Saxon society, bards known as scops (SKŎPS) performed traditional works or their own compositions at important events. Their performances required skilled verbal improvisation and often incorporated a harp to accentuate a piece's mood or important parts. Accomplished performers and custodians of a culture's identity, skillful scops held a place of great honor.

Themes and Genres in Old English Literature

Surviving Old English literature reflects its tribal environment. For generations, continual warfare and violence created tremendous uncertainty. A somber mood and stoic attitude—the idea that little may be expected in this life or the next by those lacking the courage and strength to endure—emerge in the literature. Not surprisingly then, the most common genres include the epic and the elegy. The former displayed the culture's conception of a heroic warrior-leader while the latter mourned life's uncertainty and fleetingness. On the other hand, Anglo-Saxons' fondness for riddles and wry irony shows their resilience despite such pressures.

Additionally, these works show Christian influence. Many include a curious blend of pagan elements with Christian elements juxtaposed against or overlaid on them. Biblical heroes and Catholic saints appear as tribal chiefs and champions while despair at life's fleeting nature is often barely countered by the hope Christ provides. Scholars offer two possible origins for this blend. Church scribes may have woven Christian elements into a piece as they recorded it, or the stories may have gradually acquired these elements as Anglo-Saxon culture was Christianized. Whichever the case, and despite its oft-mysterious origins, Old English poetry remains enjoyable for its vitality and unique charm.

Summary

Though often characterized by conflict and upheaval, the Anglo-Saxon period produced a surprisingly rich store of literature. It also set the template for many aspects of British life today. From the English language to regional government divisions (e.g., the shires) to the concept of common law, England's characteristic features still bear the mark of Anglo-Saxon society.

MEDIEVAL LATIN AND LITERATURE

A page from the Latin Lindisfarne Gospels (ca. 700), the greatest of Britain's medieval illuminated manuscripts.

The other primary language of Anglo-Saxon literature was Medieval Latin (an offshoot of Classical Latin). The language of Europe's educated elite, Medieval Latin was employed in government and diplomacy as well as intellectual pursuits, publications, and amusements. For example, the Venerable Bede (p. 64), an English scholar revered in England and the continent, corresponded in Latin with a wide array of scholars throughout Europe, fostering cultural ties and mutual respect.

Much of the era's available literature was in Latin and often concerned religious topics. For instance, the Latin Vulgate was the standard Bible translation, and Latin biographies of saints' lives abounded. Additionally, scholarly works such as Bede's *Ecclesiastical History of the English People* (ca. 731) were composed in Latin. As Latin was inaccessible to most people, attempts were made to translate important texts into English and circulate these rare copies more widely.

THE HIGH MIDDLE AGES (1066–1300)

THE NORMAN INVASION

When King Edward the Confessor died childless in 1066, a flurry of claimants to the Anglo-Saxon throne arose. One was the ambitious Duke William of Normandy. William believed he had a legitimate claim to the throne through his mother. He also alleged (controversially) that Edward had named him royal heir fifteen years earlier.

His primary opponent was the newly crowned King Harold Godwinson, a powerful Anglo-Saxon nobleman descended from King Canute. Harold had been selected by the Anglo-Saxons' witenagemot, a body of nobles and high clergy who traditionally elected the king. His supporters were strongly opposed to further Norman influence, which had grown under Edward. Harold likewise claimed that Edward had designated him as heir.

The two sides clashed at the Battle of Hastings. Unfortunately for Harold, his militia had just fended off the Norwegians in the North and then marched the length of England to get to the battlefield in the South. They fought courageously, but not at full strength, and the result was a predictable defeat. Harold died, and with him died Anglo-Saxon rule of England.

ANGLO-NORMAN ENGLAND: A NEW ORDER

The Norman Conquest marked a turning point in English history. In general, William simply placed Norman leadership and culture on top of Anglo-Saxon society, leaving its structures in place and ensuring a stable handoff of power. But he also needed loyal leaders. To that end, he confiscated the Anglo-Saxon nobility's titles and lands and distributed them to loyal Norman retainers, forming a new aristocracy. This new nobility spoke Norman French, lived by Norman customs, and had more in common with Continental culture than with their subjects. But as generations passed, each side influenced the other; the resulting Anglo-Norman culture combined features of both.

Feudalism

William's new aristocracy helped him implement the feudal system in England. The core of feudalism was the relationship between a lord and his vassals. The lord accepted oaths of fealty from capable retainers (now vassals) and awarded them new lands (fiefs) and wealth. Theoretically, the king held the right to all the land (vassals were only tenants) and political power, with no official equal (i.e., no witenagemot) to check him. In reality, the nobility and the Church would frequently challenge royal power. This political arrangement dominated Anglo-Norman social structures and economic life and broadly categorized the population into three estates (classes).

The Three Estates The first estate was the clergy (i.e., members of the Church, from friars to archbishops). The spiritual shepherds of the nation, they offered guidance to everyone from peasants to monarchs. The Church could exert great political power, threatening even monarchs with serious spiritual sanctions (e.g., excommunication). Many clergy members enjoyed considerable wealth and a level of immunity from secular powers.

The second estate consisted of knights and nobles owing fealty. In addition to governing and maintaining lands on the king's behalf, they served as royal counselors, military backup, and church patrons, funding monasteries, abbeys, and other works. The vassal relationship was replicated down through the nobility's ranks: the most powerful pledged fealty directly to the king but had their own vassals (gentry and knights) as well.

Finally, the peasantry formed the third and largest estate. Peasants were the backbone of the system and mostly served as agricultural workers (serfs) on manors, owing the lords a portion of their harvest or income. Unfortunately, serfs had the fewest rights and privileges. They were tied to the lord in whose manor they were born and, without permission, could not leave the manor from birth to death. They could buy their freedom, but in reality, few had the means. In England, only a small group of freemen—usually specialized laborers (e.g., blacksmiths) or those who owned some land—operated outside serf restrictions.

The Manor In feudal society, farming and other land-based wealth dominated the economy. Thus the basic social and economic unit became the manor, a self-sufficient estate ruled by a nobleman or an institution such as the Church. A manor produced crops and other goods, generating income through sales and taxes on tenants. The rise of cities and a mercantile class would challenge its position.

Politics and Government

Wars and Royal Decline The political history of Anglo-Norman England involved frequent warring abroad and infighting at home. Lingering Anglo-Saxon resentment led to revolts, and the Normans also fought wars with Scotland, Ireland, and Wales. Internal conflicts over the throne were constant and eventually led to a devastating civil war, the Anarchy (1135–54). Henry II's accession to the throne ended this period and began a new dynasty, the Plantagenets, that would last through the Middle Ages.

The Plantagenet kings suffered a steady attrition of power. Through French incursions, poor leadership, and conflicts with English nobility, they gradually lost their French territories (larger than England), which most considered home. By 1259, they held only a small fiefdom from the French king, while pressures from the Church and nobility challenged royal power at home.

Seeds of Democracy At the same time, small seeds of democracy were already forming in England. For example, Henry II's expansion of royal influence through the courts introduced several important legal rights (e.g., the right to a speedy trial by one's peers), saw the rise of common law, and curtailed the influence of the clergy by removing them as judges in secular courts and allowing them authority only on canon (church) law.

Additionally, a power struggle between King John and his nobles in 1215 produced one of the world's most influential legal documents, the Magna Carta (or "Great Charter"). John's signing of the Magna Carta established several key precedents. First, the king was subject to written laws; second, freemen had the right to a fair and speedy trial by their peers; and third, the king had limited ability to tax the nobility without their consent. Eventually, these principles would extend to all citizens.

Finally, John's yielding to his barons edged England closer to a monarchy limited by Parliament. Within the next fifty years, the nobles forced Henry III to give them administrative—not just advisory—functions, foreshadowing the English Parliament's House of Lords. Then, in a precursor to its House of Commons, they called a general assembly in 1265 that included the gentry below the nobility ("the commons"). Over the years, these assemblies would solidify into a feature of English life and accrue actual power.

The Roman Catholic Church

The Roman Catholic Church of the High Middle Ages formed a long-standing and vital presence of English life. Its dogma defined the medieval view of the world and of mankind's place in it, and its influence extended from the lowest serfs to the king himself. Individual adherence was assumed, beginning with a child's christening. The entire country was divided into church parishes who presided over and kept official records of births, marriages, and deaths. The Church also collected from the population a tithe for itself, and amassed extensive wealth and lands. Even the yearly calendar and annual holidays proceeded from and were celebrated with the Church. Its presence was inescapable.

THE BECKET CONTROVERSY

In medieval Europe, the "benefit of clergy" provision allowed any accused person who could show he was a clergy member to be tried by canon law, whose punishments were less severe than criminal law. But when Henry II attempted to withdraw this privilege, Thomas à Becket, archbishop of Canterbury (Henry's former friend and a man who took his responsibilities seriously), stubbornly resisted the reform. Enraged, Henry bemoaned that none of his followers would "avenge [him] of this turbulent priest"— a comment that led to the murder of Becket by four of Henry's knights in Canterbury Cathedral itself. Disgraced, Henry was forced by domestic and international pressure to back down. Within three years, Becket was elevated to sainthood (1173), inspiring the Canterbury pilgrimages that Chaucer immortalized in his *Canterbury Tales*.

The Church wielded such power in medieval life for two key reasons. First, doctrine mandated that a person engage in six of seven sacraments (baptism, confirmation, penance, the Holy Eucharist, matrimony, holy orders, and extreme unction) to receive salvation. The sole avenue for engaging in these, the Church claimed power over salvation and damnation. Second, the medieval mindset imposed little difference between the secular and the sacred—all of life was spiritual in nature. As the spiritual authority, the Church thus exercised authority in arenas traditionally reserved for secular government: advising rulers, sharing the nation's administrative functions, operating ecclesiastical courts, and even acting in military conflicts.

Two main branches of clergy served the Church. First, the secular clergy accomplished its everyday work, including administering church services, the sacraments, the clergy themselves, and church properties. Second, the regular clergy lived under regulations as monks and nuns and pursued a variety of lifestyles, from living in secluded, self-reliant communities focused on worship, to scholarly work, service as mendicants (those who took a vow of poverty), or charitable work (e.g., serving in hospitals).

As in Anglo-Saxon times, the Church exerted a stabilizing influence, mediating between enemies, softening conflicts, and promoting scholarship and culture. Additionally, it took on charitable work many would not or could not do, such as the care of the poor, the sick, and the otherwise needy. Its message and traditions provided spiritual solace to many; undoubtedly, people were truly converted to Christ under its ministry. Sadly its power would become increasingly corrupted.

Social Improvements

Life for average citizens in the Middle Ages was grueling, dangerous, uncertain, and monotonous: average life expectancy was about thirty, partially a result of abysmal infant and childhood mortality rates. Feudalism confined most peasants (nearly 95 percent of the population) to rural life at subsistence levels, with few paths to personal betterment. Events conspired, however, to push medieval society toward change.

The Rise of Trade and Towns After Rome fell, trade and the urban centers it fed seriously declined in Europe. But the High Middle Ages saw a rapid influx of trade from the Mediterranean, North Africa, and the Far East. Italian and Flemish merchants traded luxury goods such as silk, spices, gems, and wines for raw materials such as timber, wool, and grain. Trade fairs arose at markets large and small; even peasants could buy and sell goods, perhaps earning enough to buy their freedom. Meanwhile, agricultural advances allowed manors to raise more crops with fewer workers, freeing up laborers for other work.

As the center of this burgeoning trade, towns rose to prominence by providing economic and social opportunities to these workers. For example, town charters (legal agreements between a town and its feudal lord) commonly granted any peasant who lived in the city for a year and a day the status of freeman. The opportunities improved people's daily lives and created wealth to fund cultural growth in art, learning, and literature. But as cities grew in size and prosperity, their vigorous middle class and powerful leaders and guilds diluted the nobility's feudal monopoly on power and challenged Church disapproval of pursuing wealth, causing new tensions.

THE CRUSADES

More than any other Church action in the Middle Ages, the Crusades have captured people's imaginations for centuries. A series of expeditions to the Holy Land from 1095 to 1291, their purpose was initially twofold: to recapture Christendom's sacred sites and pilgrimage routes from Muslim Turk incursions and to defend Christian Europe from the same. Later Crusades expanded the war theater to other groups considered heretical as well.

Though the realities of these conflicts were often brutal and un-Christian, the Crusades and Crusaders took on mythic proportions in Europe. Crusader adventures reinforced feudal warrior culture and created fodder for the literature of chivalry. Furthermore, they reopened Europe to trade from the Mediterranean and beyond. Crusaders brought back new trade items (e.g., spices, silks, weapons, porcelain) and new knowledge from abroad (e.g., Islamic and Greco-Roman scholarship from philosophy to medical knowledge). The latter would lead to the new ideas and scholarship of the Renaissance.

VISUAL ANALYSIS
Examine Émile Signol's *Taking of Jerusalem by the Crusaders, 15th July 1099* (1847) below. Do you think it reflects Crusaders realistically? What tone toward the Crusades does the artist seem to express?

New Ideas and Universities At the same time, new learning and ideas were changing how people viewed the world. Crusaders brought back Islamic learning in medicine, mathematics, and classical studies, adding new dimensions to European knowledge. New Classical Greek writings (or better translations of them) also emerged from the conflict; *humanist* became a term for scholars who studied these new texts on the humanities (subjects dealing with the human experience and culture). Their ideas paved the way for the Renaissance.

The advent of this new learning changed education. Founded in Anglo-Saxon times, cathedral and monastic schools at first offered the most advanced medieval education, preparing clergymen and government workers (e.g., scribes, bureaucrats, and diplomats). However, the rise of universities with an improved curriculum loosened the Church's hold on intellectual life. Growing from self-organized groups of scholar-teachers and their students, universities were recognized by royal charter or license. In medieval England, the result was two major institutions of British life—the University of Oxford and Cambridge University.

Art and Architecture The medieval era produced a great deal of art mostly centered on theological or courtly subjects. Illuminated manuscripts; carvings in stone, ivory, and precious metals and gems; complex tapestries and needlework; and fine jewelry all typified the era. But the most visible art form resided at the community's center: the church. Communities took decades, sometimes centuries, to build magnificent cathedrals designed to point an illiterate population to God. These were littered with artwork depicting saints and Bible characters. Even the basic architecture had meaning: for example, floor plans usually formed a cross. Originating in twelfth-century France, the school of Gothic architecture designed churches whose tall and airy structures lifted viewers' attention to God. Beautiful examples of English Gothic cathedrals exist at Salisbury, Canterbury, and York, among other places.

THE LATE MIDDLE AGES: MEDIEVAL DECLINE (1300–1485)

Unfortunately, a series of disasters in the fourteenth century brought this prosperity crashing down. The rise in both international and domestic conflict that followed colored the final two centuries of the Middle Ages with a more pessimistic brush.

DISASTER AND POPULATION DECLINE

In the twelfth and thirteenth centuries, the population in England nearly doubled because of prolific agricultural production and rising prosperity. Unfortunately, in 1315–17, bad weather led to a series of terrible harvests and the Great Famine. Altogether, millions died of starvation and disease. Poor weather continued, making famine a recurring problem in the early century.

Then came unimaginable disaster: the Black Death, a plague that devastated Europe's population, culture, and psyche. Lasting in England from 1348 to 1349, this outbreak came to Europe by trade routes, entering England through ports such as London and Bristol. Victims often died within hours, and the disease could ravage an area's population within weeks, killing so many people so quickly that the dead were left unburied. In England, historians now agree that the Black Death killed at least 30–45 percent of the population. A few villages experienced 90 percent casualties. The clergy died in greater numbers as some unflaggingly pursued their duty to administer the last rites and care for the sick.

With no idea of what was happening, people attributed the plague to God's wrath, to astronomical events, or even to vulnerable populations (e.g., the Jews or the Romani) while the medical community thought it was spread through "bad air." Unchecked, the plague resulted in several important consequences. First, many lost faith in a church that could not prevent the plague or whose corruption they blamed as the plague's cause. Second, resulting social disruptions caused increases in crime and violence. Finally, the population reduction left fewer serfs to work the land, putting pressure on the feudal system that it would not recover from.

The Pedlar

The Abbess

CHURCH CORRUPTION AND DECLINE

Loss of faith in the Church had been building for quite some time. Church actions too often benefited the Church or its clergy instead of its flocks. And as with all organizations, some members behaved selfishly or maliciously. Some clergy showed little evidence of faith at all, being just as worldly as the laity. The worst victimized their flocks (e.g., demanding bribes) or indulged themselves through Church wealth and influence. Satires such as Chaucer's *Canterbury Tales* reveal clerical corruption as an often-stereotyped fact, a standing joke.

Already under fire, the Church increasingly experienced crises in its leadership and faith. Political machinations undermined it in the Avignon Papacy (1309–77) and the Papal Schism (1378–1417). During the former, seven popes supposedly representative of Christ instead fell under the sway of the French crown, residing in Avignon (a French city) instead of Rome. In the latter, the papacy's return to Rome produced a succession crisis in which two, and then three, rival popes concurrently claimed the office. Additionally, intense rivalry among clergymen of various ranks and affiliations produced internal strife and confusion. These events caused great turmoil and made the Church a laughingstock.

VISUAL ANALYSIS

Parts of Hans Holbein the Younger's *Dance of Death* woodcut series (1523–26) are in the medieval *danse macabre* tradition, in which death (a skeleton) calls individuals from all walks of life. Most historians believe the danse to be a response to the fourteenth century's disasters, especially the plague. What do you think the artist meant to convey to his viewers?

JOHN WYCLIFFE AND LOLLARDY

In England, Oxford theologian John Wycliffe (ca. 1328–84) was the most prominent critic of the Church. He condemned the clergy's worldliness and immorality, called for the Church to give up its vast wealth, and believed that it should not wield political authority or have legal immunity. More radical than other critics, he attacked key Church doctrines (e.g., transubstantiation, the priesthood). At first backed by Oxford University and the powerful John of Gaunt (Duke of Lancaster and patron of Chaucer), Wycliffe lost support after some of his followers endorsed the Peasants' Revolt of 1381 (pp. 85, 116) against his convictions. Now a threat to the social order, the movement he had inspired (Lollardy) was condemned and driven into hiding. Nonetheless, Wycliffe completed the first translation of the Bible into English (ca. 1382), and his work left a rich vein of ideas for Reformation theologians to tap. For this reason, he is often termed the "Morning Star" of the Reformation.

THE HUNDRED YEARS' WAR AND WARS OF THE ROSES

Coinciding with and aggravating these problems was another costly enterprise: the Hundred Years' War (1337–1453). Believing they held a legitimate claim to the French throne through Henry II's wife, Eleanor of Aquitaine, the Plantagenet kings fought over a century of campaigns to acquire the French crown. The war led to memorable victories at Crécy (1346), Poitiers (1356), and Agincourt (1415). But though the English briefly gained nearly complete control of France, their emptied coffers and weakened leadership could not sustain the victory.

The war eroded royal power at home until the rise of a weak king, Henry VI, gave the nobility free rein, and their rivalry erupted into a thirty-year civil war between the dukedoms of Lancaster and York. Named the Wars of the Roses for the red and white rose insignias of these houses, this dark period (1455–85) was rife with political machinations and betrayals. It ended with the ruthless Richard III's death at the Battle of Bosworth Field (1485). The rise of Henry VII (first Tudor king) brought both the civil hostilities and the English Middle Ages to an end. With its social institutions outdated and changing, England was at the threshold of the modern age.

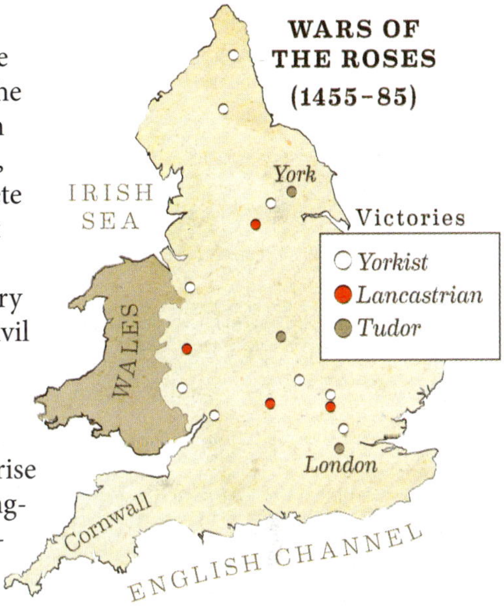

WARS OF THE ROSES (1455–85)

IRISH SEA
York
WALES
London
Cornwall
ENGLISH CHANNEL
Victories
Yorkist
Lancastrian
Tudor

MIDDLE ENGLISH LITERATURE (1066–1485)

ENGLISH AFTER THE CONQUEST

The literary era following the Norman Conquest is known as the Middle English period. It is named for a transitional form of English (between Old and Modern English) that resulted from William's choice to use Latin and Anglo-Norman French as official languages. His action pushed Old English almost entirely out of written use in the business of the church, the crown, and the nobility (and thus in literature).

While French and Latin dominated written language on the surface, English was roiling underneath in common life. With no written standard for usage, multiple dialects coexisted on equal footing, resulting in two major changes. First, in the Great Vowel Shift (1350–1600), all English long vowels rapidly shifted to their modern pronunciations. Second, Middle English lost many inflections (i.e., varied word forms used to express tense, person, number, etc.).

Furthermore, many citizens out of necessity became bilingual, encouraging vocabulary transfers; Middle English acquired from Norman French many loan words for everything from legal concepts (*crown, reign, parliament, justice, judge, jury, court*) to terms for cuisine and art (*boil, toast, sauce, pastry, beauty, paint*). By the time English reemerged in writing in the 1300s, it had undergone tremendous changes and was rapidly approaching its modern structure and basic vocabulary. Though short-lived, Middle English remains important for the great treasures of English literature written during its heyday.

LITERATURE AFTER THE CONQUEST

Anglo-Norman Literature

Directly after the Norman Conquest, most literature was upper-class French or Latin texts. Many works retold stories from Greek and Roman classic literature or followed Continental (French and Italian) literary fashions of content and form (e.g., the use of rhyme). This era's contribution to English literature is twofold. First, the French popularized English Arthurian legends, crafting literary versions that highlighted chivalry and courtly love. Second, English writers acquired skill in Continental poetic forms and features that they then transferred to their English writing.

God Speed (1900) by Edmund Leighton.

The Rise of Middle English Poetry

By the mid-fourteenth century, English had regained upper-class respect. It resurged in everyday prose, and many grammar schools were conducted in English rather than Latin and French. As general literacy rose, more prose works were composed in this vernacular. In 1362, for the first time since 1066, Parliament opened with a speech in English and ordered that all lawsuits be argued in English.

Following this official recognition came a flowering of English vernacular poetry under the reign of Richard II (1377–99). During this time, three major poets wrote classic works in Middle English dialects. William Langland authored *Piers Plowman*, the anonymous Pearl poet composed *Gawain and the Green Knight*, and Geoffrey Chaucer composed his *Canterbury Tales*. Chaucer's dialect, the East Midland dialect that formed the vernacular of London where most printing took place, prevailed as the literary standard.

The poets first using English to write literature were very conscious of their choice. Their works often reflect the common man's life and center on native heroes (e.g., Robin Hood, King Arthur). They still drew from more high-flown Continental genres but made these work for Middle English (far different from literary French or Italian) and the concerns of the lower classes. Chaucer especially excelled at this and popularized many such forms.

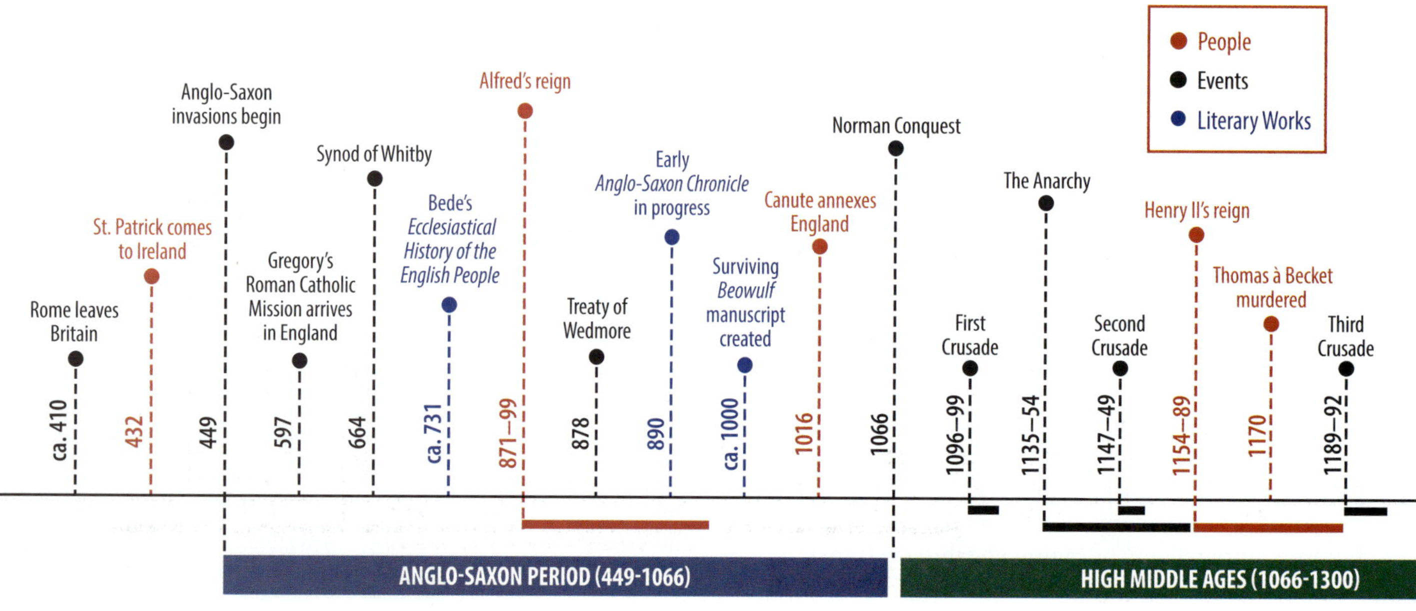

Popular Forms and Themes

Broadly speaking, Continental influences along with the merging of popular and courtly points of view gave Middle English literature greater diversity than Old English in subject matter, genres, styles, and tones. Like most medieval literature, Middle English literature was largely didactic. Just as the Church saw no difference between the secular and sacred in society, so much of medieval society's literature speaks to ethical and spiritual concerns directly or indirectly. Histories moralized, fictional stories had multiple spiritual layers, and devotional literature was common.

The range of genres expanded as well. While religious genres such as hagiographies (p. 64) dominated writings in the vernacular for a time, tales of courtly love (p. 37) and chivalric adventure grew in prominence. Additionally, lyric poetry, the most widespread genre in the last half of the Middle Ages, encompassed many subgenres, from complex French or Italian forms to simple songs and ballads in English vernacular to hymns written by clerics for the masses. While courtly love infused much of the upper-class lyrics, Christ's love was a major theme of religious poetry. Unfortunately, the social unrest and war of the fifteenth century would temporarily slow the flow of literary endeavors. Nonetheless the English language's range and power continued to grow and would blossom anew in the Renaissance.

During the Middle Ages, England was making the leap from oral to literate culture. The availability of written works increased, as did the wealthy class's ability to commission copies. A major boost was the arrival of the printing press (1476), which revolutionized the speed and ease of creating books. The press was brought by wealthy London businessman William Caxton, who proceeded to acquire, sometimes translate, and print a great many materials, including Chaucer's *Canterbury Tales* (one of Caxton's first projects).

PRINTED LITERATURE

SUMMARY

A thousand years of history encompasses a kaleidoscope of cultural realities and changes. For the English, political alliances rose and fell, cultural influences from abroad came and went or were assimilated, and social structures shifted in various ways. Medieval literature often reflects the resulting struggles. But while life was always hard, it was not without joy. And people then, just like people now, put their struggles, joys, and aspirations into songs and stories; they wrote to understand life, to pass along knowledge, and to make their society better for themselves and for others. As a result, we have a treasure trove of literature that reflects the ideals, hopes, and daily lives of medieval people. In this unit, you will be introduced to a small but influential collection of these works.

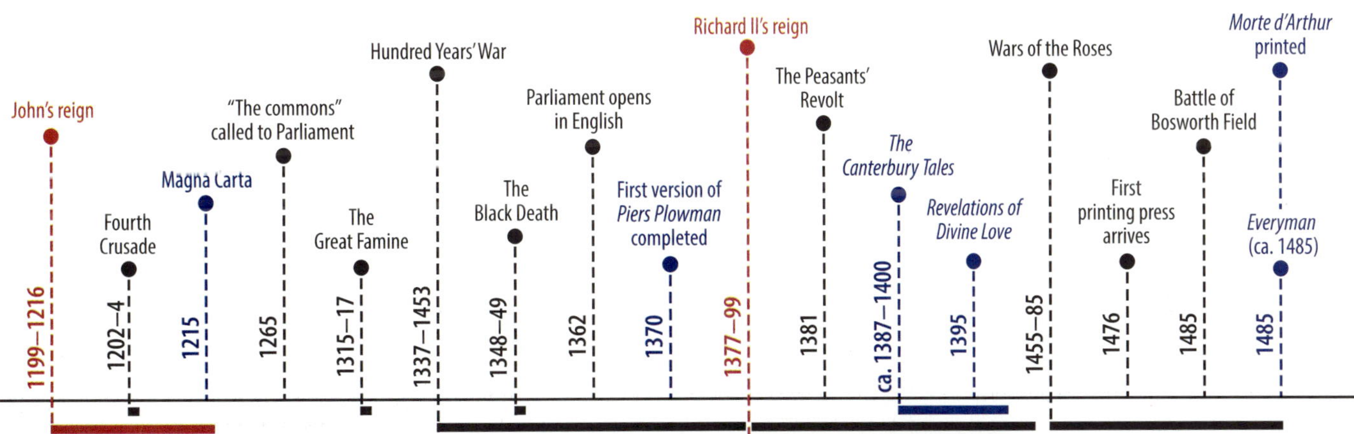

PART 1

Heroes of Old

Heroism is not a static concept. Your own idea of what it means to be a hero has likely changed since you were a child. That is because your values have changed. Likewise, a culture's view of heroism can morph over time, reflecting deep shifts in its values. England in the Middle Ages was no exception. From Old English warrior to Middle English knight, the culture's conception of heroism transformed dynamically throughout the era. As you will see in this section, this gradual shift from war glory to courtly conduct is readily apparent in the literature of the times.

When Germanic tribes invaded England, they brought along their own cultural values, including a heroic ideal. Typified in the warrior-king, Anglo-Saxon heroism lauds a brave leader who assails opposing forces with immense (often superhuman) strength and unwavering courage (*fortitude* in classical literature). The warrior-king's strength and courage achieve personal and national glory. This war glory, a kind of heroic pride, was the paramount aim in the Anglo-Saxons' shame- or honor-driven culture.

To achieve ultimate glory, a warrior would die in battle protecting his people and land. Such a death perpetuated his legacy as scops (see p. 5) celebrated his war-deeds. The epic poem *Beowulf* exemplifies these celebrations of honor in battle. The hero Beowulf embodies the strength and courage of a warrior-king in fighting the monster Grendel. As Beowulf illustrates, such a hero's bravery burned brightest in the heat of battle; in fact, retreating from a fight to preserve one's life was seen as the most shameful of acts.

The ideal Anglo-Saxon hero exhibits more than fortitude, however; he also possesses practical wisdom (classical literature's *prudence*), wisely avoiding reckless or rash acts such as rushing unprepared into battle. Furthermore, he is intensely loyal to and generous with his people, traits embodied in the Anglo-Saxon **comitatus**. Comitatus describes a relationship of mutual respect and friendship in which a tribal leader protected and provided for his followers, who in turn pledged their loyalty and support in battle. The mead-hall (social center of Anglo-Saxon life) formed the stage for expressions of comitatus. There, brave leaders would lavish their generosity on faithful followers, throwing great feasts and bestowing gifts of gold while followers offered boasting praises of their comrades' prowess in battle.

With the rise of feudalism and Norman culture, English heroic ideals gradually transitioned to the knight-courtier of the High Middle Ages. This knightly ideal emphasized a more refined warrior, one guided by the code of chivalry and courtly love. Such warriors excelled in war and in peace, fighting fiercely yet with ethical and social restraints sometimes absent in the Anglo-Saxon tribal ethic. As its terms exemplify, the new ideal fused French and Anglo-Saxon values: *Knight* comes from the Germanic word *knecht*, or "soldier"; and *chivalry* comes from the Old French *chevalerie,* referring to soldiers who fought on horseback (*cheval,* Fr., "horse").

Like the warrior-king, the knight was expected to show bravery and skill in battle and to prize loyalty and generosity. But where comitatus loyalty was a mutual responsibility of a leader and his followers, loyalty in medieval romances emphasized a knight's service to his king, to God, and to his lady. And while the warrior-king showed generosity to his men, the knight might show generosity even to an enemy (e.g., by refusing to fight an unfair battle). For the knight, war glory was an ideal but not the highest one.

These differences sprang in part from Church teachings. During the tenth to twelfth centuries, the Church decreed ethical boundaries for fighting honorably (e.g., defining noncombatants, truce days) in The Peace and Truce of God. Then the Crusades infused fighting with sacred significance, offering spiritual reasons and rewards for it. Gradually knightly ideals took on Christian dimensions. In addition to military prowess, the knight must display piety. He fought for God and the Church, seeking for goodness and justice to triumph. Additionally, knights must show mercy, especially on the weak, whom they were to protect and defend. Courtly love formed an outgrowth of the latter virtue: a knight showed courtesy to all women, but he also went to great lengths to prove fidelity to the lady he loved. Likely patterned on the Church's elevation of Mary, the courtly love behaviors encouraged an idealized view of romantic love.

Just as the knight's rise marked a shift away from the warrior-king, so too the knight gave way to other heroic ideals. As Sir Thomas Malory's *Morte D'Arthur* illustrates, changes in the nature of warfare toward the end of the Middle Ages spelled the end for the age of chivalry. Despite new shifts in the hero's form or identity, many of the era's ideals—including strength, courage, benevolence, and loyalty to comrade and country—would continue throughout English history into the modern period.

Beowulf AT A GLANCE

- **ca. 600–1000** *Beowulf* composed and recorded
- **ca. 1000** Scribes record the earliest surviving manuscript
- **1563** First known owner, Laurence Nowell, labels the manuscript with his name
- **1600s** Manuscript added to Sir Robert Cotton's extensive collection
- **1702** John Cotton wills the manuscript to the English nation

Origin and Author

Among the writings copied into West Saxon by Alfred's scribes was the first complete epic in any Germanic language. Left untitled, the poem came to be known by the name of its protagonist, Beowulf [BAY oh woolf]. Though the only extant manuscript is dated tentatively around AD 1000, uncertainty surrounds the poem's place of origin and date of composition (probably somewhere between the seventh and the eleventh centuries). However, scholars do agree that *Beowulf* forms one of the grand peaks of English literature.

Unsurprisingly then, scholars can only speculate on the *Beowulf* poet's identity. Some believe he may have been an honored churchman associated with a Mercian court or a reclusive scholar-poet in a monastery. Others think he was a professional scop, fluent in the pagan Germanic and Christian traditions, both of which influence the poem. In any case, he was a mature artist, composing for an audience able to appreciate subtle effects. Indeed, the poetic finesse of *Beowulf* argues for a higher degree of civilization present during earlier Anglo-Saxon times than many realize.

Genre

The poem's content and style reflect its origins in tribal, oral literature. First, through its themes, the poem celebrates the Anglo-Saxon culture's heroic tradition, affirming key values such as prudence, fortitude, loyalty, and generosity. Additionally, the poem follows patterns key to oral, not written, literature (see p. 5). Composed in the style a scop might use to quickly improvise an exciting performance, *Beowulf* uses elevated language, highlights outward words and deeds rather than internal thoughts, and incorporates oral stylistic elements such as repetition and rhetorical flourishes of sound and syntax.

In form, *Beowulf* is an **epic**, a long, stylized narrative poem celebrating the deeds of a national hero of legend. Specifically, it is an oral folk epic (as opposed to a literary epic like *Paradise Lost*, pp. 307–13) springing from oral stories of past heroes or significant events and reflecting the customs, rituals, and ideals of its tribal society.

At one time regarded as the chief of genres, the epic poem no longer has a wide audience. But its heroic material lives on. Stories that mirror the sweeping scope and high principles of the epic tale and its hero are still being created. Arguably, Tolkien wrote a modern epic in his *Lord of the Rings* trilogy, while films such as *Star Wars* continue the tradition; even comic-book superheroes similarly reflect the moral aspirations of modern life. However, in an increasingly pluralistic world, it is difficult to find a modern work that so completely embodies a culture's unified view of heroism and heroic virtue as did ancient epics.

Epic Conventions

Epics display certain conventions in their basic content. First, the setting is usually broad in scope. Similarly, the heroes are larger than life, being unusually gifted or historically significant. Next, the story incorporates the supernatural. *Beowulf,* for example, depicts a race of monsters and a dragon. Finally, the plot usually revolves around a necessary journey or battle. Overall, through their character and events, epics address topics central to human existence—life, death, love, war, family, and friendship.

Traditional epics also incorporated certain textual features. They often begin with a clear statement of theme as well as an invocation to a muse or other guiding spirit, soliciting help for the poet's endeavor. Additionally, they jump right into the middle of the story's action, beginning *in medias res* (meaning "in the middle"). Other characteristics include the use of epic catalog, a descriptive list (e.g., of important historical genealogies); epic simile, a kind of simile with extended (sometimes overblown) descriptions; Homeric epithet (see p. 18); and long, formal speeches, which interrupt the action of the poem.

Setting and Hero

Although *Beowulf*'s origin is in Anglo-Saxon England, its setting is Scandinavia, ancient home of the Angles, Saxons, and Jutes. Its supernatural elements hail from Germanic folklore and some passages seem to reference tribal historical knowledge of the late fifth and sixth centuries. Yet the hero Beowulf is evidently uniquely English. While some parallels to the character and his deeds appear in heroic literature around the world, no other story quite matches his. Indeed, some evidence suggests the author may have embellished an essentially true story.

Plot and Themes

The struggles of Beowulf reflect the universal conflict of good and evil as seen through the lens of both

Christian and Germanic tribal ideas. The characters are pagan and the plot and themes consistently elevate and endorse characteristics of traditional Germanic heroes. But some incidents also tease out areas where these values do not quite answer the circumstances of life. Additionally, Christian elements are sprinkled throughout, and the speaker sometimes spins the story's characters and events through specifically Christian values.

The first part of the poem, from which the excerpt included here is taken, contains two incidents—Beowulf's contests with the monster Grendel [GREHN dehl] and with Grendel's dam (mother). According to the speaker, Grendel is an offspring of Cain, and Heaven has allowed him to afflict the Danes because of their pride and their ignorance of the true God. The resolution of these incidents restores traditional Germanic tribal order and affirms Beowulf as a quintessential Germanic hero.

The second part presents Beowulf fifty years later as king of the Geats rather than a subordinate warrior, a significant change in roles from a Germanic perspective. At the time, a dragon is terrorizing and destroying the people after someone stole a goblet from its gold horde. The cause of the people's misery is thus greed, whereas in the case of the Danes it was pride. Beowulf responds by arming himself with shield and weapon and accepting the support of his retainers (the comitatus bond) to fight. But all forsake him except Wiglaf, who helps him defeat the dragon. Sadly, the victory costs Beowulf his life. The poem ends with the flames of his funeral pyre ascending to the sky and with Wiglaf reproaching his countrymen for forsaking their leader in his time of need. The scene is not wholly victorious. While Beowulf heroically dies in battle as a Germanic warrior should do, he also leaves his people kingless and vulnerable. Additionally, the speaker presents an evaluation of events from a more Christian perspective: the morally honorable Beowulf has been defeated by the moral weaknesses—including pride, cowardice, and greed—of the people he committed to protect. The ending reflects the often melancholy nature of Anglo-Saxon literature.

DID YOU KNOW ?

The only existing copy of *Beowulf*, now in the British Museum, was seriously damaged by fire in 1731.

The Selection and Translation

The following selection, recounting the first of Beowulf's three battles with monsters, amounts to about a fourth of the entire poem. It shows the artistry of the original poet, who uses the full gamut of Old English poetic devices in addition to narrative effects such as suspense and foreshadowing.

The translation included here is a lively free-verse version by Burton Raffel, a notable translator of Old-English poetry and prose. One of the translation's goals was to create a text that is as accessible to modern readers as the original version of *Beowulf* was to its readers. Though some of the poem's original stresses and alliteration have been necessarily sacrificed for readability, it nevertheless practices these poetic techniques selectively. Its vivid language and vigorous movement help preserve some of the poem's original momentum, making it enjoyable and appealing for future generations.

ANALYZE: *Epic, Kenning, Litotes, Wyrd*

The **epic** (p. 16) *Beowulf* incorporates some unusual figurative language. First, **kenning**, a device peculiar to Germanic oral poetry, communicates a metaphor by a compound expression (e.g., saying *whale-road* or *swan's road* for "sea"). An indirect metaphor, kenning assumes the reader will infer the metaphor's tenor (what it renames). This feature also illustrates a very old tendency in Germanic languages—the expression of new ideas by creating compound words. Second, the irony prevalent in Anglo-Saxon literature is often conveyed through a type of understatement called **litotes**: the affirmation of something by denying its contrary. For example, the statement "He was not unmindful of his duty" is really affirming that he was mindful (carefully attentive) of it.

Additionally, as noted earlier, *Beowulf* blends Germanic lore and moral codes of conduct with Christian narratives and morals. An example of this blending is the story's use of Germanic ***wyrd*** (translated "fate") alongside the Christian idea of providence as a determiner in human affairs. Look for such disparate elements throughout the poem.

READ: *Oral Poetry*

Understanding several features of Anglo-Saxon poetry can help you navigate it better. First, like many oral works, Old English poetry uses repetition. For example, formulaic expressions such as **stock epithets** (also termed *Homeric epithets*) describe or rename a noun they precede or follow. Using these stock phrases made a poet's job of extemporizing poetry easier. A simple example is the phrase "Beowulf, Higlac's follower." The second half is a common formula that can be retailored for any character.

Stock epithets are a tool to incorporate **variation**. Variation uses new, grammatically parallel phrases to elaborate on something just stated. It allows a poet to emphasize an idea or convey new facets of it. The following phrases, referring to God, illustrate both functions: "the Lord of all life, Ruler / of Glory" (ll. 16–17a). A side benefit of variation is the formal, stately rhythm it creates.

Second, **alliterative verse** is the conventional Old English verse form; it does not employ meter or rhyme but instead uses a complex combination of stresses and alliteration. Each line is divided by a caesura, a natural pause, and includes four heavily stressed syllables (two per half line). The third stressed syllable could alliterate with one or both stresses preceding it but not with the fourth one. This alliteration could include not just initial consonants but also vowel sounds.

EVALUATE: *Heroic Virtues*

Traditional epics are enjoyable but also **didactic** (meant to instruct). They elevate a culture's highest virtues, creating a model for both leaders and citizens to emulate in varying ways. *Beowulf* presents a pattern of heroic conduct (Shild) to the listeners early on as criteria by which to judge the main character's subsequent acts. As you read, locate the places the poem fleshes out the Germanic heroic virtues (pp. 14–15). Are these virtues outdated, or are they valid criteria for judging leaders today?

OBJECTIVES

- Analyze the literary elements and cultural background of an epic.
- Read poetry aloud.
- Evaluate the virtues of the Anglo-Saxon heroic ideal.

CHARACTER LIST

Beo (BAY oh) Mythical Danish king, son of Shild.

Beowulf (BAY oh WOOLF) Son of Higlac; the hero of the poem.

Grendel (GREHN duhl) Monster harassing Herot.

Healfdane (HEH ahlf DEH neh) Historical Danish king; son of Beo.

Hrothgar (ROTH gahr) Historical Danish king; son of Healfdane.

Shild (SHIHLD) Mythical Danish king; legendary founder of the Danish royal line.

Welthow (WAHLKH thayo) Queen of the Danes, wife to Hrothgar.

Wulfgar (WOOLF gahr) Herald and counselor to Hrothgar.

What does it mean to BE A HERO?

Is being a hero simply a matter of being in the right place at the right time, or does heroism require certain character qualities that impel someone to act? What makes any act heroic? We often associate heroes with the battlefield. But in what other spheres can heroism be forged and displayed? Discuss your idea of heroism with your class and share examples.

FROM BEOWULF

Translated by Burton Raffel

Prologue

Hear me! We've heard of Danish heroes,
Ancient kings and the glory they cut
For themselves, swinging mighty swords!
How Shild made slaves of soldiers from every
Land, crowds of captives he'd beaten
Into terror; he'd traveled to Denmark alone,
An abandoned child, but changed his own fate,
Lived to be rich and much honored. He ruled
Lands on all sides: wherever the sea
Would take them his soldiers sailed, returned
With tribute and obedience. There was a brave
King! And he gave them more than his glory,
Conceived a son for the Danes, a new leader
Allowed them by the grace of God. They had lived,
Before his coming, kingless and miserable;
Now the Lord of all life, Ruler
Of glory, blessed them with a prince, Beo,
Whose power and fame soon spread through the world.
Shild's strong son was the glory of Denmark;
His father's warriors were wound round his heart
With golden rings, bound to their prince
By his father's treasure. So young men build
The future, wisely open-handed in peace,
Protected in war; so warriors earn
Their fame, and wealth is shaped with a sword.
When his time was come the old king died,
Still strong but called to the Lord's hands.
His comrades carried him down to the shore,
Bore him as their leader had asked, their lord
And companion, while words could move on his tongue.
Shild's reign had been long; he'd ruled them well.
There in the harbor was a ring-prowed fighting
Ship, its timbers icy, waiting,
And there they brought the belovèd body
Of their ring-giving lord, and laid him near
The mast. Next to that noble corpse
They heaped up treasures, jeweled helmets,
Hooked swords and coats of mail, armor
Carried from the ends of the earth: no ship
Had ever sailed so brightly fitted,
No king sent forth more deeply mourned.
Forced to set him adrift, floating
As far as the tide might run, they refused
To give him less from their hoards of gold
Than those who'd shipped him away, an orphan.
And a beggar, to cross the waves alone.
High up over his head they flew
His shining banner, then sadly let
The water pull at the ship, watched it
Slowly sliding to where neither rulers
Nor heroes nor anyone can say whose hands
Opened to take that motionless cargo.

[The Line of Danish Kings]

Then Beo was king in that Danish castle,
Shild's son ruling as long as his father
And as loved, a famous lord of men.
And he in turn gave his people a son,
The great Healfdane,[1] a fierce fighter
Who led the Danes to the end of his long
Life and left them four children,
Three princes to guide them in battle, Hergar[2]
And Hrothgar, and Halga[3] the Good, and one daughter,
Yrs,[4] who was given to Onela,[5] king
Of the Swedes, and became his wife and their queen.

[The Building of Herot[6] Hall]

Then Hrothgar, taking the throne, led
The Danes to such glory that comrades and kinsmen
Swore by his sword, and young men swelled
His armies, and he thought of greatness and resolved
To build a hall that would hold his mighty
Band and reach higher toward Heaven than anything
That had ever been known to the sons of men.
And in that hall he'd divide the spoils
Of their victories, to old and young what they'd earned
In battle, but leaving the common pastures
Untouched, and taking no lives. The work
Was ordered, the timbers tied and shaped
By the hosts that Hrothgar ruled. It was quickly
Ready, that most beautiful of dwellings, built
As he'd wanted, and then he whose word was obeyed
All over the earth named it Herot.
His boast come true he commanded a banquet,
Opened out his treasure-full hands.
That towering place, gabled and huge,
Stood waiting for time to pass, for war
To begin, for flames to leap as high
As the feud that would light them, and for Herot to burn.

1. *Healfdane:* Means "half-Dane." His mother was a foreigner.
2. *Hergar:* (HEHR gahr)
3. *Halga:* (HAHL guh)
4. *Yrs:* (OORS)
5. *Onela:* (Oh NEH lah)
6. *Herot:* (HAY raht), or Heorot (HAY uh raht); means "Hart Hall"; may mean that antlers hung from its gables, or may refer to hornlike projections from the eaves; often associated with the village Leire, the royal seat of the Danes in ancient times

Reading Check: Who were Hrothgar's father, grandfather, and great-grandfather?

Heroic Virtues: Which comitatus virtue does Hrothgar exhibit here?

[The Threat of a Monster]

A powerful monster, living down
In the darkness, growled in pain, impatient
As day after day the music rang
Loud in that hall, the harp's rejoicing
Call and the poet's clear songs, sung
Of the ancient beginnings of us all, recalling
The Almighty making the earth, shaping
These beautiful plains marked off by oceans,
Then proudly setting the sun and moon
To glow across the land and light it;
The corners of the earth were made lovely with trees
And leaves, made quick with life, with each
Of the nations who now move on its face. And then

As now warriors sang of their pleasure:
So Hrothgar's men lived happy in his hall
Till the monster stirred, that demon, that fiend,
Grendel, who haunted the moors, the wild
Marshes, and made his home in a hell
Not hell but earth. He was spawned in that slime,
Conceived by a pair of those monsters born
Of Cain, murderous creatures banished
By God, punished forever for the crime
Of Abel's death.[7] The Almighty drove
Those demons out, and their exile was bitter,
Shut away from men; they split
Into a thousand forms of evil—spirits
And fiends, goblins, monsters, giants,
A brood forever opposing the Lord's
Will, and again and again defeated.

[Grendel's Ravaging of Herot]

Then, when darkness had dropped, Grendel
Went up to Herot, wondering what the warriors
Would do in that hall when their drinking was done.
He found them sprawled in sleep, suspecting
Nothing, their dreams undisturbed. The monster's
Thoughts were as quick as his greed or his claws:
He slipped through the door and there in the silence
Snatched up thirty men, smashed them
Unknowing in their beds and ran out with their bodies,
The blood dripping behind him, back
To his lair, delighted with his night's slaughter.
At daybreak, with the sun's first light, they saw
How well he had worked, and in that gray morning
Broke their long feast with tears and laments
For the dead. Hrothgar, their lord, sat joyless
In Herot, a mighty prince mourning
The fate of his lost friends and companions,
Knowing by its tracks that some demon had torn
His followers apart. He wept, fearing
The beginning might not be the end. And that night
Grendel came again, so set
On murder that no crime could ever be enough,
No savage assault quench his lust
For evil. Then each warrior tried
To escape him, searched for rest in different
Beds, as far from Herot as they could find,
Seeing how Grendel hunted when they slept.
Distance was safety; the only survivors
Were those who fled him. Hate had triumphed.
So Grendel ruled, fought with the righteous,
One against many, and won; so Herot
Stood empty, and stayed deserted for years,
Twelve winters of grief for Hrothgar, king
Of the Danes, sorrow heaped at his door
By hell-forged hands. His misery leaped
The seas, was told and sung in all
Men's ears: how Grendel's hatred began,
How the monster relished his savage war
On the Danes, keeping the bloody feud
Alive, seeking no peace, offering
No truce, accepting no settlement, no price
In gold or land, and paying the living
For one crime only with another. No one
Waited for reparation from his plundering claws:
That shadow of death hunted in the darkness,
Stalked Hrothgar's warriors, old
And young, lying in waiting, hidden
In mist, invisibly following them from the edge
Of the marsh, always there, unseen. **A**
So mankind's enemy continued his crimes,
Killing as often as he could, coming
Alone, bloodthirsty and horrible. Though he lived
In Herot, when the night hid him, he never
Dared to touch king Hrothgar's glorious
Throne, protected by God—God,
Whose love Grendel could not know. But Hrothgar's
Heart was bent. The best and most noble
Of his council debated remedies, sat
In secret sessions, talking of terror
And wondering what the bravest of warriors could do.
And sometimes they sacrificed to the old stone gods,
Made heathen vows, hoping for Hell's
Support, the Devil's guidance in driving
Their affliction off. That was their way,
And the heathen's only hope, Hell
Always in their hearts, knowing neither God
Nor His passing as He walks through our world, the Lord
Of Heaven and earth; their ears could not hear
His praise nor know His glory. Let them
Beware, those who are thrust into danger,
Clutched at by trouble, yet can carry no solace
In their hearts, cannot hope to be better! Hail
To those who will rise to God, drop off
Their dead bodies and seek our Father's peace!

7. *He was spawned . . . death:* See Genesis 4:11–12; 6:4.

Kennings/Litotes: What kennings and litotes appear in lines 144–63? **A**

[Beowulf's Voyage to Hrothgar's Hall]

So the living sorrow of Healfdane's son
Simmered, bitter and fresh, and no wisdom
Or strength could break it: that agony hung
On king and people alike, harsh
And unending, violent and cruel, and evil.
In his far-off home Beowulf, Higlac's[8]
Follower and the strongest of the Geats[9]—greater
And stronger than anyone anywhere in this world—
Heard how Grendel filled nights with horror
And quickly commanded a boat fitted out,
Proclaiming that he'd go to that famous king,
Would sail across the sea to Hrothgar,
Now when help was needed. None
Of the wise ones regretted his going, much
As he was loved by the Geats: the omens were good,
And they urged the adventure on. So Beowulf
Chose the mightiest men he could find,
The bravest and best of the Geats, fourteen
In all, and led them down to their boat;
He knew the sea, would point the prow
Straight to that distant Danish shore. E
Then they sailed, set their ship
Out on the waves, under the cliffs.
Ready for what came they wound through the currents,
The seas beating at the sand, and were borne
In the lap of their shining ship, lined
With gleaming armor, going safely
In that oak-hard boat to where their hearts took them.
The wind hurried them over the waves,
The ship foamed through the sea like a bird
Until, in the time they had known it would take,
Standing in the round-curled prow they could see
Sparkling hills, high and green,
Jutting up over the shore, and rejoicing
In those rock-steep cliffs they quietly ended
Their voyage. Jumping to the ground, the Geats
Pushed their boat to the sand and tied it
In place, mail shirts and armor rattling
As they swiftly moored their ship. And then
They gave thanks to God for their easy crossing.

. . . .

Then they moved on. Their boat lay moored,
Tied tight to its anchor. Glittering at the top
Of their golden helmets wild boar heads gleamed,
Shining decorations, swinging as they marched,
Erect like guards, like sentinels, as though ready
To fight. They marched, Beowulf and his men
And their guide, until they could see the gables
Of Herot, covered with hammered gold
And glowing in the sun—that most famous of all dwellings,
Towering majestic, its glittering roofs
Visible far across the land.
Their guide reined in his horse, pointing
To that hall, built by Hrothgar for the best
And bravest of his men; the path was plain,
They could see their way. R

. . . .

[Beowulf's Reception]

The path he'd shown them was paved, cobbled
Like a Roman road. They arrived with their mail shirts
Glittering, silver-shining links
Clanking an iron song as they came.
Sea-weary still, they set their broad,
Battle-hardened shields in rows
Along the wall, then stretched themselves
On Herot's benches. Their armor rang;
Their ash-wood spears stood in a line,
Gray-tipped and straight: the Geats' war-gear
Were honored weapons.

8. *Higlac's:* (HEEY lahks), or Hygelac (HEE yeh lahk)
9. *Geats:* (YAY ahts) Beowulf's nation, which inhabited Gotland, off the coast of southern Sweden

Heroic Virtues: What heroic virtues does Beowulf already exhibit? E

Oral Poetry: Read lines 229–43 aloud. What characteristics of alliterative verse appear in these lines? R

A Danish warrior
Asked who they were, their names and their fathers':
"Where have you carried these gold-carved shields from,
These silvery shirts and helmets, and those spears
Set out in long lines? I am Hrothgar's
Herald and captain. Strangers have come here
Before, but never so freely, so bold.
And you come too proudly to be exiles: not poverty
But your hearts' high courage has brought you to Hrothgar."
He was answered by a famous soldier, the Geats'
Proud prince:
"We follow Higlac, break bread
At his side. I am Beowulf. My errand
Is for Healfdane's great son to hear, your glorious
Lord; if he chooses to receive us we will greet him,
Salute the chief of the Danes and speak out
Our message."
Wulfgar replied—a prince
Born to the Swedes, famous for both strength
And wisdom:
"Our warmhearted lord will be told
Of your coming; I shall tell our king, our giver
Of bright rings, and hurry back with his word,
And speak it here, however he answers
Your request."
He went quickly to where Hrothgar sat,
Gray and old, in the middle of his men,
And knowing the custom of that court walked straight
To the king's great chair, stood waiting to be heard,
Then spoke:
"There are Geats who have come sailing the open
Ocean to our land, come far over
The high waves, led by a warrior
Called Beowulf. They wait on your word, bring messages
For your ears alone. My lord, grant them
A gracious answer, see them and hear
What they've come for! Their weapons and armor are nobly
Worked—these men are no beggars. And Beowulf
Their prince, who showed them the way to our shores,
Is a mighty warrior, powerful and wise."

[Hrothgar's Welcome to Beowulf]

The Danes' high prince and protector answered:
"I knew Beowulf as a boy. His father
Was Edgetho,[10] who was given Hrethel's one daughter—
Hrethel,[11] Higlac's father. Now Edgetho's
Brave son is here, come visiting a friendly
King. And I've heard that when seamen came,
Bringing their gifts and presents to the Geats,
They wrestled and ran together, and Higlac's
Young prince showed them a mighty battle-grip,
Hands that moved with thirty men's strength,
And courage to match. Our Holy Father
Has sent him as a sign of His grace, a mark
Of His favor, to help us defeat Grendel
And end that terror. I shall greet him with treasures,
Gifts to reward his courage in coming to us.
Quickly, order them all to come to me
Together, Beowulf and his band of Geats.
And tell them, too, how welcome we will make them!" E
Then Wulfgar went to the door and addressed
The waiting seafarers with soldier's words:
"My lord, the great king of the Danes, commands me
To tell you that he knows of your noble birth

10. *Edgetho:* (EJ eh thoh), or Ecgtheow (EJ thay oh)
11. *Hrethel:* (HRAY thel)

Heroic Virtues: Which heroic virtues does Hrothgar exhibit in this passage? Is he behaving properly as an Anglo-Saxon lord? E

And that having come to him from over the open
Sea you have come bravely and are welcome.
Now go to him as you are, in your armor and helmets,
But leave your battle-shields here, and your spears,
Let them lie waiting for the promises your words
May make."
Beowulf arose, with his men
Around him, ordering a few to remain
With their weapons, leading the others quickly
Along under Herot's steep roof from Hrothgar's
Presence. Standing on that prince's own hearth,
Helmeted, the silvery metal of his mail shirt
Gleaming with a smith's high art, he greeted
The Danes' great lord:
"Hail, Hrothgar!
Higlac is my cousin and my king; the days
Of my youth have been filled with glory. Now Grendel's
Name has echoed in our land: sailors
Have brought us stories of Herot, the best
Of all mead-halls, deserted and useless when the moon
Hangs in skies the sun had lit,
Light and life fleeing together.
My people have said, the wisest, most knowing
And best of them, that my duty was to go to the Danes'
Great king. They have seen my strength for themselves,
Have watched me rise from the darkness of war,
Dripping with my enemies' blood. I drove
Five great giants into chains, chased
All of that race from the earth. I swam
In the blackness of night, hunting monsters
Out of the ocean, and killing them one
By one; death was my errand and the fate
They had earned. Now Grendel and I are called
Together, and I've come. Grant me, then,
Lord and protector of this noble place,
A single request! I have come so far,
Oh shelterer of warriors and your people's loved friend,
That this one favor you should not refuse me—
That I, alone and with the help of my men,
May purge all evil from this hall. I have heard,
Too, that the monster's scorn of men
Is so great that he needs no weapons and fears none.
Nor will I. My lord Higlac
Might think less of me if I let my sword
Go where my feet were afraid to, if I hid
Behind some broad linden[12] shield: my hands
Alone shall fight for me, struggle for life
Against the monster. God must decide
Who will be given to death's cold grip.
Grendel's plan, I think, will be
What it has been before, to invade this hall
And gorge his belly with our bodies. If he can,
If he can. And I think, if my time will have come,
There'll be nothing to mourn over, no corpse to prepare
For its grave: Grendel will carry our bloody
Flesh to the moors, crunch on our bones
And smear torn scraps of our skin on the walls
Of his den. No, I expect no Danes
Will fret about sewing our shrouds, if he wins.
And if death does take me, send the hammered
Mail of my armor to Higlac, return
The inheritance I had from Hrethel, and he
From Wayland.[13] Fate will unwind as it must!" **A**

[The Feasting and Customs of Herot]

Hrothgar replied, protector of the Danes:
"Beowulf, you've come to us in friendship, and because
Of the reception your father found at our court.
. . . .
My tongue grows heavy,
And my heart when I try to tell you what Grendel
Has brought us, the damage he's done, here
In this hall. You see for yourself how much smaller
Our ranks have become, and can guess what we've lost
To his terror. Surely the Lord Almighty
Could stop his madness, smother his lust!
How many times have my men, glowing
With courage drawn from too many cups
Of ale, sworn to stay after dark
And stem that horror with a sweep of their swords.
And then, in the morning, this mead-hall glittering
With new light would be drenched with blood, the benches
Stained red, the floors; all wet from that fiend's
Savage assault—and my soldiers would be fewer
Still, death taking more and more.
But to table, Beowulf, a banquet in your honor:
Let us toast your victories, and talk of the future."

12. *linden:* a kind of tree whose lightweight but resilient wood was used for shields
13. *Wayland:* famous blacksmith of Danish legend

Wyrd: Reread lines 351–71. How do these lines reflect a blending of pagan and Christian beliefs regarding destiny? **A**

Then Hrothgar's men gave places to the Geats,
Yielded benches to the brave visitors
And led them to the feast. The keeper of the mead
Came carrying out the carved flasks,
And poured that bright sweetness. A poet
Sang, from time to time, in a clear
Pure voice. Danes and visiting Geats
Celebrated as one, drank and rejoiced.

. . . .

Hrothgar, gray-haired and brave, sat happily
Listening, the famous ring-giver sure,
At last, that Grendel could be killed; he believed
In Beowulf's bold strength and the firmness of his
spirit.

There was the sound of laughter, and the cheer-
ful clanking
Of cups, and pleasant words. Then Welthow,
Hrothgar's gold-ringed queen, greeted
The warriors; a noble woman who knew
What was right, she raised a flowing cup
To Hrothgar first, holding it high
For the lord of the Danes to drink, wishing him
Joy in that feast. The famous king
Drank with pleasure and blessed their banquet.

Reading Check: What feelings are fostered by the people's time in Herot?

Then Welthow went from warrior to warrior,
Pouring a portion from the jeweled cup
For each, till the bracelet-wearing queen
Had carried the mead-cup among them and it was Beowulf's
Turn to be served. She saluted the Geats'
Great prince, thanked God for answering her prayers,
For allowing her hands the happy duty
Of offering mead to a hero who would help
Her afflicted people. He drank what she poured
Edgetho's brave son, then assured the Danish
Queen that his heart was firm and his hands
Ready:
"When we crossed the sea, my comrades
And I, I already knew that all
My purpose was this: to win the good will
Of your people or die in battle, pressed
In Grendel's fierce grip. Let me live in greatness
And courage, or here in this hall welcome
My death!"
Welthow was pleased with his words,
His bright-tongued boasts; she carried them back
To her lord, walked nobly across to his side.
The feast went on, laughter and music
And the brave words of warriors celebrating
Their delight. Then Hrothgar rose, Healfdane's
Son, heavy with sleep; as soon
As the sun had gone, he knew that Grendel
Would come to Herot, would visit that hall
When night had covered the earth with its net
And the shapes of darkness moved black and silent
Through the world. Hrothgar's warriors rose with him.
He went to Beowulf, embraced the Geats'
Brave prince, wished him well, and hoped
That Herot would be his to command. And then
He declared:
"No one strange to this land
Has ever been granted what I've given you,
No one in all the years of my rule.
Make this best of all mead-halls yours, and then
Keep it free of evil, fight
With glory in your heart! Purge Herot
And your ship will sail home with its treasure-holds full."

[Beowulf's Watch in Herot]

Then Hrothgar left that hall, the Danes'
Great protector, followed by his court; the queen
Had preceded him and he went to lie at her side,
Seek sleep near his wife. It was said that God
Himself had set a sentinel in Herot,
Brought Beowulf as a guard against Grendel and a shield
Behind whom the king could safely rest.
And Beowulf was ready, firm with our Lord's
High favor and his own bold courage and strength.
He stripped off his mail shirt, his helmet, his sword
Hammered from the hardest iron, and handed
All his weapons and armor to a servant,
Ordered his war-gear guarded till morning.
And then, standing beside his bed,
He exclaimed:
"Grendel is no braver, no stronger
Than I am! I could kill him with my sword; I shall not,
Easy as it would be. This fiend is a bold
And famous fighter, but his claws and teeth
Scratching at my shield, his clumsy fists
Beating at my sword blade, would be helpless. I will meet him
With my hands empty—unless his heart
Fails him, seeing a soldier waiting
Weaponless, unafraid. Let God in His wisdom
Extend His hand where He wills, reward
Whom He chooses!"
Then the Geats' great chief dropped
His head to his pillow, and around him, as ready
As they could be, lay the soldiers who had crossed the sea
At his side, each of them sure that he was lost
To the home he loved, to the high-walled towns
And the friends he had left behind where both he
And they had been raised. Each thought of the Danes
Murdered by Grendel in a hall where Geats
And not Danes now slept. But God's dread loom
Was woven with defeat for the monster, good fortune
For the Geats; help against Grendel was with them,
And through the might of a single man
They would win. Who doubts that God in His wisdom

Oral Poetry: Reread lines 401–33. What stock epithets occur in these lines?

And strength holds the earth forever
In His hands? Out in the darkness the monster
Began to walk. The warriors slept
In that gabled hall where they hoped that He
Would keep them safe from evil, guard them
From death till the end of their days was determined
And the thread should be broken. But Beowulf lay wakeful,
Watching, waiting, eager to meet
His enemy, and angry at the thought of his coming.

[Beowulf's Fight with Grendel]

Out from the marsh, from the foot of misty
Hills and bogs, bearing God's hatred,
Grendel came, hoping to kill
Anyone he could trap on this trip to high Herot.
He moved quickly through the cloudy night,
Up from his swampland, sliding silently
Toward that gold-shining hall. He had visited Hrothgar's
Home before, knew the way—
But never, before nor after that night,
Found Herot defended so firmly, his reception
So harsh. He journeyed, forever joyless,
Straight to the door, then snapped it open,
Tore its iron fasteners with a touch
And rushed angrily over the threshold.
He strode quickly across the inlaid
Floor, snarling and fierce: his eyes
Gleamed in the darkness, burned with a gruesome
Light. Then he stopped, seeing the hall
Crowded with sleeping warriors, stuffed
With rows of young soldiers resting together.
And his heart laughed, he relished the sight,
Intended to tear the life from those bodies
By morning; the monster's mind was hot
With the thought of food and the feasting his belly
Would soon know. But fate, that night, intended
Grendel to gnaw the broken bones
Of his last human supper. Human
Eyes were watching his evil steps,
Waiting to see his swift hard claws.
Grendel snatched at the first Geat
He came to, ripped him apart, cut
His body to bits with powerful jaws,
Drank the blood from his veins and bolted
Him down, hands and feet; death
And Grendel's great teeth came together,
Snapping life shut. Then he stepped to another
Still body, clutched at Beowulf with his claws

Oral Poetry: How do the caesuras and stresses in lines 499–518 add to the text's meaning?

VISUAL ANALYSIS
How does the artist's rendering of this moment in the story reflect the proper mood? What does it communicate about the two main characters depicted?

Grasped at a strong-hearted wakeful sleeper
—And was instantly seized himself, claws
Bent back as Beowulf leaned up on one arm.
That shepherd of evil, guardian of crime,
Knew at once that nowhere on earth
Had he met a man whose hands were harder;
His mind was flooded with fear—but nothing
Could take his talons and himself from that tight
Hard grip. Grendel's one thought was to run
From Beowulf, flee back to his marsh and hide there:
This was a different Herot than the hall he had emptied.
But Higlac's follower remembered his final
Boast and, standing erect, stopped
The monster's flight, fastened those claws
In his fists till they cracked, clutched Grendel
Closer. The infamous killer fought
For his freedom, wanting no flesh but retreat,
Desiring nothing but escape; his claws
Had been caught, he was trapped. That trip to Herot
Was a miserable journey for the writhing monster!
The high hall rang, its roof boards swayed,
And Danes shook with terror. Down
The aisles the battle swept, angry
And wild. Herot trembled, wonderfully
Built to withstand the blows, the struggling
Great bodies beating at its beautiful walls;
Shaped and fastened with iron, inside
And out, artfully worked, the building
Stood firm. Its benches rattled, fell
To the floor, gold-covered boards grating
As Grendel and Beowulf battled across them.
Hrothgar's wise men had fashioned Herot
To stand forever; only fire,
They had planned, could shatter what such skill had put
Together, swallow in hot flames such splendor
Of ivory and iron and wood. Suddenly
The sounds changed, the Danes started
In new terror, cowering in their beds as the terrible
Screams of the Almighty's enemy sang
In the darkness, the horrible shrieks of pain
And defeat, the tears torn out of Grendel's
Taut throat, hell's captive caught in the arms
Of him who of all the men on earth
Was the strongest.

[Grendel's Defeat]

That mighty protector of men
Meant to hold the monster till its life
Leaped out, knowing the fiend was no use
To anyone in Denmark. All of Beowulf's
Band had jumped from their beds, ancestral
Swords raised and ready, determined
To protect their prince if they could. Their courage
Was great but all wasted: they could hack at Grendel
From every side, trying to open
A path for his evil soul, but their points
Could not hurt him, the sharpest and hardest iron
Could not scratch at his skin, for that sin-stained demon
Had bewitched all men's weapons, laid spells
That blunted every mortal man's blade.
And yet his time had come, his days
Were over, his death near; down
To hell he would go, swept groaning and helpless
To the waiting hands of still worse fiends.
Now he discovered—once the afflictor
Of men, tormentor of their days—what it meant
To feud with Almighty God: Grendel
Saw that his strength was deserting him, his claws
Bound fast, Higlac's brave follower tearing at
His hands. The monster's hatred rose higher,
But his power had gone. He twisted in pain,
And the bleeding sinews deep in his shoulder
Snapped, muscle and bone split
And broke. The battle was over, Beowulf
Had been granted new glory: Grendel escaped,
But wounded as he was could flee to his den,
His miserable hole at the bottom of the marsh,
Only to die, to wait for the end
Of all his days. And after that bloody
Combat the Danes laughed with delight.
He who had come to them from across the sea,
Bold and strong-minded, had driven affliction
Off, purged Herot clean. He was happy,
Now, with that night's fierce work; the Danes
Had been served as he'd boasted he'd serve them; Beowulf,
A prince of the Geats, had killed Grendel,
Ended the grief, the sorrow, the suffering
Forced on Hrothgar's helpless people
By a bloodthirsty fiend. No Dane doubted
The victory, for the proof, hanging high
From the rafters where Beowulf had hung it, was the monster's
Arm, claw and shoulder and all. **R**

Oral Poetry: What stock epithets for Beowulf and Grendel appear in lines 579b–624? Which of Grendel's stock epithets illustrate variation? **R**

[The Celebration of Victory and Song About Beowulf]

And then, in the morning, crowds surrounded
Herot, warriors coming to that hall
From faraway lands, princes and leaders
Of men hurrying to behold the monster's
Great staggering tracks. They gaped with no sense
Of sorrow, felt no regret for his suffering,
Went tracing his bloody footprints, his beaten
And lonely flight, to the edge of the lake
Where he'd dragged his corpselike way, doomed
And already weary of his vanishing life.
The water was bloody, steaming and boiling
In horrible pounding waves, heat
Sucked from his magic veins; but the swirling
Surf had covered his death, hidden
Deep in murky darkness his miserable
End, as hell opened to receive him.
Then old and young rejoiced, turned back
From that happy pilgrimage, mounted their hard-hooved
Horses, high-spirited stallions, and rode them
Slowly toward Herot again, retelling
Beowulf's bravery as they jogged along.
And over and over they swore that nowhere
On earth or under the spreading sky
Or between the seas, neither south nor north,
Was there a warrior worthier to rule over men.
(But no one meant Beowulf's praise to belittle
Hrothgar, their kind and gracious king!)
And sometimes, when the path ran straight and clear,
They would let their horses race, red
And brown and pale yellow backs streaming
Down the road. And sometimes a proud old soldier

Who had heard songs of the ancient heroes
And could sing them all through, story after story,
Would weave a net of words for Beowulf's
Victory, tying the knot of his verses
Smoothly, swiftly, into place with a poet's
Quick skill, singing his new song aloud. E

Heroic Virtues: How do lines 655b–61 fulfill the didactic role of epics? E

THINK AND DISCUSS

1. Identify the four Anglo-Saxon heroic virtues discussed in the introduction (pp. 14–15).
2. Name and describe the characteristics of Anglo-Saxon oral poetry involving rhythm, pauses, and sound devices.
3. Define *litotes* and give an example from *Beowulf*.
4. Reread lines 617b–21a. Other than the characteristics of alliterative verse, what features of Anglo-Saxon oral poetry do these lines illustrate?
5. What epic convention (p. 16) does the genealogy in *Beowulf* (ll. 4–63) illustrate, and what effect does it have?
6. How do Shild, Hrothgar, Wulfgar, and Grendel exhibit or lack the heroic virtues?
7. Citing specifics from the poem, justify Beowulf as an epic hero.
8. What is the author's purpose for telling this story? Defend your answer from the text.
9. How well do the following lines from Raffel's translation capture the original characteristics of Anglo-Saxon alliterative verse? Explain your answer. "Out from the marsh, from the foot of misty / Hills and bogs, bearing God's hatred, / Grendel came, hoping to kill / Anyone he could trap on this trip to high Herot."
10. In line 402, the kenning "ring-giver" refers to Hrothgar. Create two original kennings, one for Beowulf and one for Grendel.

The Anglo-Saxon Chronicle

Around the year 890, King Alfred the Great ordered scholars to combine any available earlier historical accounts of national events (e.g., from Roman documents and Bede's *Ecclesiastical History*) into one history of the English. Alfred's purpose was to raise the historical, literary, and religious awareness of his subjects. On his orders, contemporary chronicles were compiled yearly thereafter to update the official account. After his death, accounts were maintained in various locations (usually monasteries) by generations of anonymous scribes. These have come down to modern scholars in seven surviving manuscripts, which together are known as *The Anglo-Saxon Chronicle*.

One of the most important surviving historical records from the Middle Ages, the *Chronicle* serves as a timeline of British history from the invasions of Julius Caesar (60 BC) to the end of the reign of King Stephen (AD 1154). In their entirety, they paint an invaluable picture of what actually happened in Britain over a thousand years ago. In fact, scribes often incorporated historical accounts from other sources that no longer survive, increasing the *Chronicle*'s value for historians.

Additionally, they reveal the linguistic evolution taking place in English. For instance, *The Peterborough Chronicle* (the most recent manuscript and the source of the excerpts that follow) includes entries in Old English, Medieval Latin, and Middle English.

Individual entries vary in their scope and nature; some are extremely brief summaries of a year's most important events (anything from omens to battles to severe weather). Others tell full stories in great detail. Chroniclers related these events as facts, but their sources may well have varied from firsthand knowledge to second- or thirdhand news. Additionally, some were not averse to adding interpretations of an event's significance. Sometimes these evince clear bias toward the Anglo-Saxon perspective. Nonetheless, the *Chronicle* offers an interesting and invaluable perspective on the Middle Ages in England.

BEFORE READING

ANALYZE: *Chronicles, Perspective, and Bias*

A **chronicle** records a place's or group's history chronologically by year, listing significant facts and events and often weaving all into an overall narrative. It uses a variety of sources, from firsthand witnesses to written materials (e.g., letters, earlier chronicles). Like other writers, a chronicler views facts through his own **perspective** (the mental view or outlook influencing an account of a story), using his judgment to decide which facts to include and what they mean. If this perspective is not controlled, however, it can become **bias** (i.e., thinking that precludes fairness in judgment). As you read these entries, note any points that might reveal a writer's personal perspective or even cross into bias.

READ: *Summarize Key Ideas*

Summarizing is a core reading strategy. If you can't summarize a text's contents, you likely don't remember its key points. To acquire this skill, you must learn to recognize a text's main ideas. These are often found in topic sentences or concluding statements. Most nonfiction texts also cue main ideas and supporting points or show how these relate using **transitional phrases** (e.g., *first, second, third, additionally, in contrast, most importantly*, etc.). As you read each entry, look for these important details. Try to summarize each entry with a classmate.

EVALUATE: *Evaluate Leaders*

The *Chronicle*'s records of historical rulers offer insights into and evaluations of each man's character and actions. Inevitably, the writers' perspectives affect such conclusions. Review the Anglo-Saxon heroic ideal (see pp. 14–15). How might these values have affected the writers' judgments? For instance, how do the actions of King Ethelred or William the Conqueror measure up to or transgress the Anglo-Saxon heroic ideal? What did the chroniclers see as the consequences? Might bias have affected these conclusions, or are they legitimate?

OBJECTIVES

- Identify the purpose of historical narratives.
- Summarize the key ideas of a passage.
- Analyze how a character exhibits or lacks Anglo-Saxon heroic virtues.
- Evaluate a historical narrative for writer bias.

VOCABULARY

besiege (bĭ-sēj′) *tr.v.* To surround with hostile forces.

resolute (rĕz′ə-lo͞ot′) *adj.* Firm or determined.

bequeath (bĭ-kwēth′) *tr.v.* To pass (something) on to another; hand down.

depose (dĭ-pōz′) *tr.v.* To remove from office or power.

ingenuity (ĭn′jə-no͞o′ĭ-tē) *n.* Inventive skill or imagination; cleverness.

FROM

The Anglo-Saxon Chronicle

[The Victory of Canute]

This entry tells the end of Danish King Canute's three-year campaign against England. Begun under his father, Sweyn Forkbeard, Canute's successful invasion positioned him to succeed his brother as the Danish king. Though he was ambitious and brutal, historians judge Canute to have been a very capable ruler. His rule brought England great prosperity. The Anglo-Saxon kings mentioned here, Æthelred and Edmund, have a more mixed legacy. Æthelred had already been defeated and exiled once by Canute, and he struggled with complex problems throughout his reign. In contrast, the leadership skills of Edmund (known as Ironsides) shone in the brief time he had to exercise them.

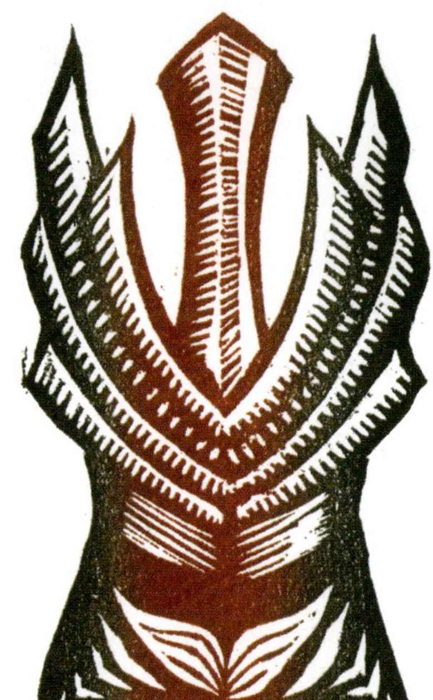

1016. Here in this year Canute with his army of one hundred and sixty ships [crews], and Alderman[1] Eadric with him, crossed the Thames at Cricklade into Mercia, and then went to Warwickshire at Christmas time and ravaged and burned and killed everything they came upon. Then Atheling[2] Edmund began to assemble a fyrd.[3] When the fyrd was assembled, they would not be satisfied unless the king was there, and [unless] they had the help of the townsmen of London. Then they gave up the expedition and each man went home. Then after that time the fyrd was again ordered out on pain of the full penalty [of the law], that each man who was fit for service should go out; and they sent to the king at London and prayed him to come to meet the fyrd with such help as he could gather. When they had all come together, it did no more good than it had often done before. **A** The king was then informed that those who should have helped him planned to betray him. Then he left the fyrd and returned to London.

Perspective: What perspective on Æthelred does the chronicler's comment about the king communicate? Could this be an example of bias? **A**

Then Atheling Edmund rode into Northumbria to Earl Uhtred, and everyone imagined that they would assemble a fyrd against King Canute. They then went into Staffordshire and into Shropshire and to Chester, and they ravaged on their part and Canute on his. And he [Canute] went out through Buckinghamshire into Bedfordshire and from there to Huntingdonshire and along the fens[4] to Stamford and then into Lincolnshire, from there to Nottinghamshire and so to Northumbria towards York. When Uhtred learned this, he abandoned his raiding and hurried north, and then of necessity submitted, and all the Northumbrians with him, and he gave hostages; and nevertheless they killed him, and with him Thurcytel, son of Nafen. And then after that King Canute appointed Eric earl of Northumbria just as Uhtred had been. And afterwards they went south by another route, quite [far] to the west, and then before Easter the whole Scandinavian army took to their ships. And Atheling Edmund went to London to his father; and then after Easter King Canute went with all his ships toward London. **R**

Summarize Key Ideas: Historical narratives often use transitional words to indicate a sequence of events. What transitional word is frequently used in paragraphs 1 and 2 to achieve this result? (Hint: It usually occurs near the beginning of sentences.) **R**

Then it happened that King Æthelred died before the ships came—he ended his days on St. George's Day [April 23] after the great labor and hardships of his life. And then after his death all the witan[5] who were in London and the townsmen elected Edmund king, and while he lived, he sturdily defended his kingdom.

Then the ships came to Greenwich at the Rogation days [the three days before Ascension] and within a short time went to London, and there they dug a big ditch on the south side and brought their ships to the west side of

1. *Alderman:* a noble serving the king as a chief officer
2. *Atheling:* an Anglo-Saxon prince, usually the crown prince
3. *fyrd:* national army
4. *fens:* a low and marshy or frequently flooded area of land
5. *witan:* king's council

the bridge, and afterwards they built a dike around the town on the outside so that no man could go in or out; and they constantly attacked the town, but they [the townsmen] sturdily resisted them. King Edmund had left [London] before that, and he overran Wessex, and all the people submitted to him; and shortly after that he fought against the Scandinavian army at Pen Pits near Gillingham. And he fought a second battle after midsummer [June 24] at Sherston, and a great number was killed there on both sides, and the armies voluntarily abandoned the fight, and Alderman Eadric and Ælfmær Darling were helping the Scandinavians against King Edmund. And then for the third time he [Edmund] assembled a fyrd and went to London and delivered the townsmen and chased the Scandinavian army to the ships. And then two days later the king crossed [the Thames] at Brentford and then fought against the Scandinavian army and routed them, and many of the English people—those who went in front of the fyrd and wanted to get booty—were drowned there through their own carelessness. And after that the king went into Wessex and assembled his fyrd. Then the Scandinavian army at once went to London and **besieged** the town from the outside and fought strongly against it both by water and by land, but Almighty God delivered it. E

After that the Scandinavians then went from London with their ships into the *Arwe* and went up it and proceeded into Mercia and killed and burned whatever they came upon, as their custom was; and they provided themselves with food and brought both their ships and their cattle into the Medway. Then for the fourth time King Edmund assembled the whole English nation and crossed the Thames at Brentford and went into Kent, and the Scandinavians fled in front of him with their horses to the Isle of Sheppey, and the king killed as many of them as he could overtake. And Alderman Eadric went there to [submit to] the king at Aylesford—no worse advice than that was ever given.[6] A

The Scandinavian army again turned inland into Essex and went into Mercia and destroyed everything it came upon. When the king learned that the Scandinavian army was inland, he for the fifth time assembled the whole English nation and followed them and overtook them in Essex at the hill called Assa's hill [now Ashingdon], and there they **resolutely** engaged. Then Alderman Eadric did as he had often done before. He, with the people of the Maund district, first began the retreat and so betrayed his royal lord and the entire nation. There Canute won the victory and conquered all England for himself. . . . E

After this battle King Canute then went inland with his army into Gloucestershire, where he had heard that King Edmund was. Then Alderman Eadric and the witan who were there advised the kings to make peace between themselves; and they gave hostages to each other, and then the kings met at *Olanig* and there confirmed their friendship with both pledge and oath and arranged the tribute for the Scandinavian army; and then on this agreement they separated, and King Edmund took possession of Wessex and Canute of Mercia.

Then the Scandinavians went to the ships with the things they had seized, and the men of London made a truce with the Scandinavian army and bought themselves peace; and the Scandinavians brought their ships into London and set up their winter quarters there.

Then on St. Andrew's Day [Nov. 30] King Edmund died, and he is buried with his grandfather, Edgar, in Glastonbury. . . . R

6. *no . . . given:* i.e., advice to accept Eadric's submission

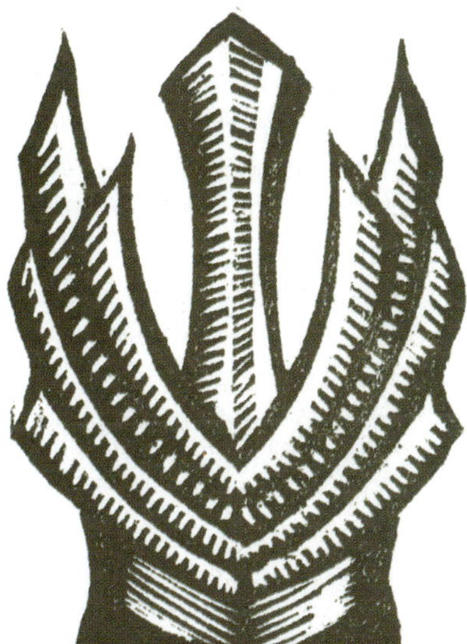

besiege (bĭ-sēj′) *v.* To surround with hostile forces.

Evaluate Leaders: What heroic quality does Edmund repeatedly display in this paragraph? E

Perspective: What perspective on the narrative does the chronicler's comment here reveal? Does he exhibit any bias? A

resolute (rĕz′ə-lo͞ot′) *adj.* Firm or determined.

Evaluate Leaders: What heroic quality does Eadric lack? E

Summarize Key Ideas: What event turned the tide of the war? Summarize the consequences that followed. R

[The Character and Reign of William the Conqueror]

This entry records the death of William and then delivers a retrospective on his reign, including its broad consequences and impact on England. This selection illustrates a growing trend in the Chronicle: *entries increasingly moralize the events they describe.*

1086 [1087]. Alas, how false and how unstable are this world's riches! He[7] who had previously been a powerful king and lord of many a land, he had of the whole land but a seven-foot measure. And he who was once clothed with gold and with jewels, he lay then covered with earth. **A**

He left behind him three sons. The eldest was named Robert, who was duke of Normandy after him. The second was named William, who wore the royal crown in England after him. The third was named Henry, to whom his father **bequeathed** innumerable treasures.

If anyone wishes to know what kind of man he was or what honor he had or how many countries he was lord of, we will write of him just as we knew him, we who have looked upon him and at one time lived in his court. King William, about whom we are speaking, was a very wise and very powerful man, and more distinguished and stronger than any of his predecessors were. He was mild to the good men who loved God and inordinately stern to the men who opposed his will. On the very site where God had granted him that he might conquer England, he built a splendid monastery [Battle Abbey, Sussex] and placed monks there and endowed it well. In his day the splendid church in Canterbury was built and also very many others over all England. This country was also plentifully filled with monks, and they lived their life according to the rule of St. Benedict; and Christendom was such in his day that every man who wished followed what fitted his rank. He was also very distinguished: three times each year he wore his royal crown, as often as he was in England. At Easter he wore it in Winchester, at Pentecost in Westminster, at Christmas in Gloucester, and then there were with him all the prominent men over all England, archbishops and suffragan[8] bishops, abbots and earls, thegns[9] and knights. **A**

So, too, he was a very stern and fierce man, so that no one dared do anything against his will. Earls who had acted against his will he had in bonds; he **deposed** bishops from their bishoprics and abbots from their abbacies; and he put thegns in prison. And finally he did not spare his own brother, named Odo. The latter was a very powerful bishop in Normandy—his bishop's see[10] was in Bayeux; and he was the most prominent man besides the king; and he had an earldom in England, and when the king [was] in Normandy, he was master in this country. And he [William] put him in prison. Among other things not to be forgotten is the good peace which he made in his country, so that a man who was of any importance could travel unmolested over his kingdom with his bosom full of gold; and no man dared kill another, even if he had done ever so great an injury to him. . . . **R**

He reigned over England, and by his craft so surveyed it that there was not one hide[11] of land in England but that he knew who owned it and what it was worth; and afterwards he set [it] down in his writing [Domesday

Perspective: What personal perspective on life does the narrator reveal in this paragraph? **A**

bequeath (bĭ-kwēth′) *v.* To pass (something) on to another; hand down.

Perspective: This paragraph reveals two other important facts affecting the scribe's personal perspective on William. What are they? **A**

depose (dĭ-pōz′) *v.* To remove from office or power.

Summarize Key Ideas: Examine paragraphs 2–4. Does each paragraph state its main idea? If so, where does it usually occur? **R**

7. *He:* William the Conqueror
8. *suffragan:* subordinate
9. *thegns:* thanes
10. *bishop's see:* the seat of a bishop's authority, a cathedral town
11. *hide:* "a measure of land in Old English times" (*OED Online.* June 2018. Oxford University Press. http://www.oed.com [hereafter acknowledged by *OED*])

Survey].[12] Wales was in his power, and he built castles there and completely controlled that people. So also he subjected Scotland to himself by his great strength. The country of Normandy was his by right of inheritance, and he reigned over the countship called Maine, and if he had lived two years more, he would have conquered Ireland by his **ingenuity**, and without any arms. Truly in his time men suffered great hardship and very many wrongs. E

ingenuity (ĭn′jə-no͞o′ĭ-tē) *n.* Inventive skill or imagination; cleverness.

Evaluate Leaders: What heroic virtues has William exhibited so far? E

He caused castles to be built
And poor men to be greatly oppressed.
The king was very severe
And took from his subjects many a mark
Of gold and more hundreds of pounds of silver.
He took this by weight and with great injustice
From his people, for little need.
He fell into covetousness,
And he loved greediness very much.
He set up many deer preserves and also enacted laws
That whoever killed a hart or hind
Should be blinded.
He placed a ban on harts, also on boars.
He loved the stags as much
As if he were their father.
He also made laws concerning hares that they should run free.
His great men complained of it and the poor men bewailed it,
But he [was] so stern that he did not care for all their hate.
But they had to follow the king's will
If they wanted to live or hold land,
Land or property, or particularly his favor. A
Alas! that any man should be so proud,
Should raise himself up and account himself above all men.
May Almighty God show mercy to his soul
And grant him forgiveness of his sins.

Bias: Having read the full entry, do you think that the writer is biased? Why or why not? A

We have written these things about him, both good and bad, so that good men may take to virtue and shun evil and go in the way that leads us to the heavenly kingdom.

12. *Domesday Survey:* a written census and property records made by order of William the Conqueror

THINK AND DISCUSS

1. Define *historical narrative*. Using text examples, explain why *The Anglo-Saxon Chronicle* fits the definition.
2. How does the content of the 1086 entry fulfill all three qualities of a chronicle (p. 31)?
3. Describe the broad perspective that both chroniclers share in common.
4. Examine paragraphs 1–2 of the 1016 entry. Then summarize their contents in four sentences. Focus not on the individual facts but on their combined message.
5. Choose one of paragraphs 3–5 from the 1086 entry. State the paragraph's main idea and list three details the writer includes to support that idea.
6. Which chronicle entry is easier to summarize? What text features mentioned in the Read section (p. 31) make this entry more digestible for readers?
7. Summarize the characteristics the second chronicler attributes to William. Which ones seem to contradict each other? Do the contradictions seem realistic or could bias be affecting the writer's opinion? Use details from the text to develop your answer.
8. Analyze King Edmund, Alderman Eadric, King Æthelred, Canute, and William the Conqueror for the presence or absence of the four heroic virtues.
9. Identify a contemporary leader and describe how that person exhibits or does not exhibit one or more of the four heroic virtues.

Pearl Poet

AT A GLANCE

- **Mid to late 1400s** The Pearl Poet writes *Sir Gawain and the Green Knight* and *Pearl*.
- **1701** Sir John Cotton donates the Cotton Library (including the *Gawain* manuscript) to the English nation.
- **1839** Sir Frederic Madden publishes the first print edition of *Sir Gawain and the Green Knight*.
- **1898** Jessie L. Weston publishes her translation of the poem, the first in Modern English.

The Gawain Poet (or Pearl Poet)

Questions surround the identity of this anonymous poet, who likely made his home in the Northwest Midlands of England, an area bordering Wales. The Pearl Poet and Gawain Poet monikers, by which he is known today, come from his authorship of two of the most important works of Middle English poetry, *Pearl* and *Sir Gawain and the Green Knight*, both written in the late fourteenth century. The works are written in the Northwest Midlands dialect of Middle English, which differs significantly from the dialect standardized by Chaucer (p. 86): the Pearl Poet's language is closer to Old English and also heavily influenced by Welsh.

DID YOU KNOW ?

Lud's Church, a deep chasm in northwest Staffordshire, England, has been suggested as the location that inspired the Green Chapel.

These poems (along with two others by the same poet, *Purity* and *Patience*) come to modern readers through one remaining manuscript, Cotton Nero, A.x. As its name indicates, this manuscript was acquired by Sir Robert Cotton, who also possessed the only surviving manuscript of *Beowulf*. After Cotton obtained the manuscript, it went unnoticed for over two hundred years, only to be rediscovered in 1824 and published in 1839. The manuscript is currently housed in the British Library.

Sir Gawain and the Green Knight

Like *Beowulf*, *Sir Gawain and the Green Knight* is **alliterative verse**, unrhymed poetry that uses alliteration to structure its lines. The following excerpt of the poem, for example, opens with "This kyng lay at Camylot upon Krystmasse." *Sir Gawain* and several other late fourteenth-century poems formed an alliterative revival, deliberately imitating the alliterated rhythms of Old English poetry.

The poem does differ from Old English oral poetry in a few ways: it has a longer line length and does not contain a fixed number of stresses per line (note only three in the previously quoted line). Additionally, the poem's stanzas vary in length, and each ends with five short lines rhyming *ababa*. The first line, called the *bob*, is very short, usually two syllables long. The remaining four lines, called the *wheel*, are three stresses in length.

In addition to being alliterative verse, *Sir Gawain and the Green Knight* is also a romance. A romance is a kind of narrative that came out of twelfth-century France. Initially named after the language of its origin (French, a Romance language descended from Latin, the Roman tongue), the medieval **romance** was a poetic narrative that focused on courtly life and the knightly code of chivalry rather than the heroism of a tribal warrior found in the epic (which it overtook in popularity). Usually, romances involved a knightly quest and incorporated fantastical elements of magic.

Because the poem draws upon the tales of King Arthur and his knights, it may also be called an Arthurian romance. But *Sir Gawain* differs in focus from other Arthurian romances such as Thomas Malory's *Le Morte d'Arthur* (p. 54). Rather than emphasizing King Arthur himself or his famed knight Sir Launcelot, the central character of this tale is Sir Gawain, Arthur's nephew. The story's plot follows Sir Gawain on a quest to fulfill his promise to the mysterious Green Knight.

A view of the Peak District in Staffordshire, part of the English Midlands where the Pearl Poet likely resided.

ANALYZE: *Symbol*

A **symbol** is something in a story—usually an object, character, or setting—that carries meaning or significance in addition to itself. For instance, the cross, an instrument of punishment and torture, now represents to many people salvation from sin through Christ's death.

Sir Gawain and the Green Knight contains multiple symbols, but three are especially significant. The first and most obvious is the color green. What objects, characters, or settings are green? Are any of these linked? What are some ideas often associated with green? How might these associations develop the story's message? Obviously, the Green Knight plays a significant role in this symbol. His and the symbol's meaning interact and develop throughout the story. A second significant symbol is the pentangle (five-pointed star) on Sir Gawain's shield. Read descriptions of it closely, and consider what the pentangle communicates about the moral virtue of Sir Gawain. Finally, the green girdle in Part 3 should also be viewed as a symbol. What does it at first seem to represent? How does that meaning change? Pay attention to how these symbols help develop the work's themes.

READ: *Apply Cultural Context*

Sir Gawain and the Green Knight emphasizes the code of conduct known as chivalry (p. 15). The chivalric code demanded that knights exhibit both bravery in battle and moral character; qualities such as honesty and prudence were to temper their passionate spirit. This story emphasizes Gawain's virtues at the start, presenting him as an ideal example of chivalry. Does Gawain continue to fulfill this role as the story unfolds?

Intertwined with chivalry was the courtly love tradition, which prescribed formal ways a knight and lady could exhibit their love. Regarded as the grandest of earthly passions, courtly love was spiritual (not physical); thus a knight could pursue such a relationship with a married lady. The knight performed deeds of valor (e.g., winning a tournament prize, embarking on a quest) in his lady's name with a kind of idolizing devotion. In turn, the lady bestowed on him tokens of love. Courtly love traditions figure prominently in the excerpt of Part 3.

EVALUATE: *Chivalric Code and Courtly Love*

Christianity's influence on chivalry required a truly noble knight to exhibit piety and love for his fellow man; these were thought to produce the Christian fruits of generosity, honesty, gentleness, and service. Does the poem emphasize Christian virtues? Evaluate the idea of adhering to a code of conduct. Is one's outward conduct important? How so? Can such a code of conduct produce righteous living? Assess courtly love as part of this code. What might be its advantages and pitfalls in a society of politically contracted marriages?

OBJECTIVES

- Identify the characteristics of a romance.
- Analyze how symbols contribute to theme.
- Apply historical context to understand a text.
- Evaluate the chivalric code through a biblical worldview.

VOCABULARY

mettle (mĕt′l) *n.* The ability to meet a challenge or persevere under demanding circumstances; determination or resolve.

consort (kŏn′sôrt′) *n.* A companion or partner.

carp (kärp) *intr.v.* To complain or find fault in a petty or disagreeable way.

brandish (brăn′dĭsh) *tr.v.* To wave or flourish (something, often a weapon) in a menacing, defiant, or excited way.

heinous (hā′nəs) *adj.* Hateful, odious; highly criminal or wicked.

flummox (flŭm′əks) *tr.v.* To confuse; perplex.

What does it mean to have INTEGRITY?

Maintaining integrity is not easy. When things we value are threatened—reputation, wealth, perhaps life itself—it is easy to lay aside our principles. And sometimes we discount the small things too—cheating on a test, lying to a friend or parent, gossiping about someone. But all these things, big or small, test the limits of our integrity. Describe a situation in which you felt tempted to or maybe did lay aside your principles under pressure. What did you learn from the situation?

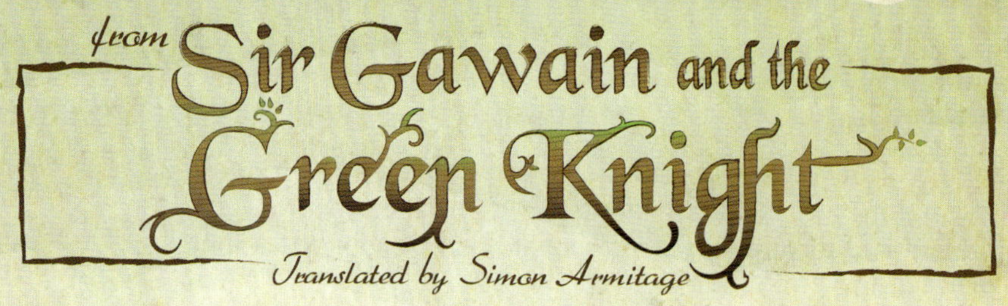

FROM PART 1

The tale begins at "Christmas at Camelot—King Arthur's court." The whole court is gathered for the Yuletide feast. Seated by Queen Guinevere is the king's nephew Sir Gawain, the tale's hero. Suddenly, an unexpected sound disrupts the festivities, and "a fearful form appear[s], framed in the door." The immense man is thought "to be half giant"; unlike anything the crowd has ever seen, he is "entirely emerald green."

The fellow in green was in fine fettle.[1]
The hair of his head was as green as his horse,
fine flowing locks which fanned across his back,
plus a bushy green beard growing down to his breast,
and his face hair along with the hair of his head
was lopped in a line at elbow length
so half his arms were gowned in green growth,
crimped at the collar, like a king's cape.
The mane of his mount was groomed to match,
combed and knotted into curlicues
then tinseled with gold, tied and twisted
green over gold, green over gold. . . .
The fetlocks[2] were finished in the same fashion
with bright green ribbon braided with beads,
as was the tail—to its tippety-tip!
And a long, tied thong lacing it tight
was strung with gold bells which resounded and shone.
No waking man had witnessed such a warrior
or weird warhorse—otherworldly, yet flesh
and bone.
A look of lightning flashed
from somewhere in his soul.
The force of that man's fist
would be a thunderbolt.

Yet he wore no helmet and no hauberk[3] either,
no armored apparel or plate was apparent,
and he swung no sword nor sported any shield,
but held in one hand a sprig of holly—
of all the evergreens the greenest ever—
and in the other hand held the mother of all axes,
a cruel piece of kit[4] I kid you not:
the head was an ell in length[5] at least
and forged in green steel with a gilt finish;
the skull-busting blade was so stropped[6] and buffed
it could shear a man's scalp and shave him to boot. A

Symbol: What green objects does the Green Knight hold? What might each object represent or connect him to? A

1. *fettle:* physical condition or state
2. *fetlock:* a tuft of hair on the projection on the lower part of a horse's leg above and behind the hoof
3. *hauberk:* "a long tunic made of chain mail" (*The American Heritage Dictionary.* June 2018. Houghton Mifflin Harcourt. https://ahdictionary.com. [hereafter acknowledged by *AHD*])
4. *kit:* equipment
5. *ell in length:* length from the elbow to the tip of the middle finger
6. *stropped:* sharpened

The crowd was stunned by the fearsome appearance of their green guest. He seemed to be a thing of magic. He proceeded to the head table and spoke boldly, addressing the one in charge of the feast, King Arthur.

Then the king acknowledged this curious occurrence,
cordially addressed him, keeping his cool.
"A warm welcome, sir, this winter's night.
My name is Arthur, I am head of this house.
Won't you slide from that saddle and stay awhile,
and the business which brings you we shall learn of later."
"No," said the knight, "it's not in my nature
to idle or allack about[7] this evening.
But because your acclaim is so loudly chorused,
and your castle and brotherhood are called the best,
the strongest men to ever mount the saddle,
the worthiest knights ever known to the world,
both in competition and true combat,
and since courtesy, so it's said, is championed here,
I'm intrigued, and attracted to your door at this time.
Be assured by this hollin[8] stem here in my hand
that I mean no menace. So expect no malice,
for if I'd slogged here tonight to slay and slaughter
my helmet and hauberk wouldn't be at home
and my sword and spear would be here at my side,
and more weapons of war, as I'm sure you're aware;
I'm clothed for peace, not kitted out for conflict. **A**
But if you're half as honorable as I've heard folk say
you'll gracefully grant me this game which I ask for
by right."
Then Arthur answered, "Knight
most courteous, you claim
a fair, unarmored fight.
We'll see you have the same."

Symbol: What additional meaning does the holly branch have? **A**

"I'm spoiling for no scrap, I swear. Besides,
the bodies on these benches are just bum-fluffed bairns.[9]
If I'd ridden to your castle rigged out for a ruck[10]
these lightweight adolescents wouldn't last a minute.
But it's Yuletide—a time of youthfulness, yes?
So at Christmas in this court I lay down a challenge:
if a person here present, within these premises,
is big or bold or red blooded enough
to strike me one stroke and be struck in return,
I shall give him as a gift this gigantic cleaver
and the axe shall be his to handle how he likes.
I'll kneel, bare my neck and take the first knock.
So who has the gall? The gumption? The guts?
Who'll spring from his seat and snatch this weapon?
I offer the axe—who'll have it as his own?
I'll afford one free hit from which I won't flinch,
and promise that twelve months will pass in peace,
then claim

7. *allack about:* Yorkshire slang for "larking about" (i.e., playing)
8. *hollin:* holly
9. *bairns:* children
10. *ruck:* fight

the duty I deserve
in one year and one day.
Does no one have the nerve
to wager in this way?"

Reading Check: What challenge does the Green Knight wish to make? Does this seem like a game to you?

Flustered at first, now totally foxed
were the household and the lords, both the highborn and the low.
Still stirruped, the knight swiveled round in his saddle
looking left and right, his red eyes rolling
beneath the bristles of his bushy green brows,
his beard swishing from side to side.
When the court kept its counsel he cleared his throat
and stiffened his spine. Then he spoke his mind:
"So here is the House of Arthur," he scoffed,
"whose virtues reverberate across vast realms.
Where's the fortitude and fearlessness you're so famous for?
And the breathtaking bravery and the big-mouth bragging?
The towering reputation of the Round Table,
skittled[11] and scuppered[12] by a stranger—what a scandal!
You flap and you flinch and I've not raised a finger!"
Then he laughed so loud that their leader saw red.
Blood flowed to his fine-featured face and he raged
inside.
His men were also hurt—
those words had pricked their pride.
But born so brave at heart
the king stepped up one stride.

"Your request," he countered, "is quite insane,
and folly finds the man who flirts with the fool.
No warrior worth his salt would be worried by your words,
so in heaven's good name hand over the axe
and I'll happily fulfil the favor you ask."
He strides to him swiftly and seizes his arm;
the man-mountain dismounts in one mighty leap.
Then Arthur grips the axe, grabs it by its haft[13]
and takes it above him, intending to attack.
Yet the stranger before him stands up straight,
highest in the house by at least a head.
Quite simply he stands there stroking his beard,
fiddling with his coat, his face without fear,
about to be bludgeoned, but no more bothered
than a guest at the table being given a goblet
of wine.
By Guinevere, Gawain
now to his king inclines
and says, "I stake my claim.
This moment must be mine."
"Should you call me, courteous lord," said Gawain to his king,
"to rise from my seat and stand at your side,
politely take leave of my place at the table
and quit without causing offence to my queen,
then I shall come to your counsel before this great court.

11. *skittled:* knocked down
12. *scuppered:* defeated
13. *haft:* handle

For I find it unfitting, as my fellow knights would,
when a deed of such daring is dangled before us
that you take on this trial—tempted as you are—
when brave, bold men are seated on these benches,
men never matched in the **mettle** of their minds,
never beaten or bettered in the field of battle.
I am weakest of your warriors and feeblest of wit;
loss of my life would be grieved the least.
Were I not your nephew my life would mean nothing;
to be born of your blood is my body's only claim.
Such a foolish affair is unfitting for a king,
so, being first to come forward, it should fall to me.
And if my proposal is improper, let no other person
    stand blame."
  The knighthood then unites
  and each knight says the same:
  their king can stand aside
  and give Gawain the game.

mettle (mĕt'l) n. The ability to meet a challenge or persevere under demanding circumstances; determination or resolve.

Cultural Context: How does this scene reflect the code of chivalry?

. . . .

In the standing position he prepared to be struck,
bent forward, revealing a flash of green flesh
as he heaped his hair to the crown of his head,
the nape of his neck now naked and ready.
Gawain grips the axe and heaves it heavenwards,
plants his left foot firmly on the floor in front,
then swings it swiftly towards the bare skin.
The cleanness of the strike cleaved the spinal cord
and parted the fat and the flesh so far
that the bright steel blade took a bite from the floor.
The handsome head tumbles onto the earth
and the king's men kick it as it clatters past.
Blood gutters[14] brightly against his green gown,
yet the man doesn't shudder or stagger or sink
but trudges towards them on those tree-trunk legs
and rummages around, reaches at their feet
and cops[15] hold of his head and hoists it high,
and strides to his steed, snatches the bridle,
steps into the stirrup and swings into the saddle
still gripping his head by a handful of hair.
Then he settles himself in his seat with the ease
of a man unmarked, never mind being minus
    his head!
And when he wheeled about
  his bloody neck still bled.
  His point was proved. The court
  was deadened now with dread.

For that scalp and skull now swung from his fist;
towards the top table he turned the face
and it opened its eyelids, stared straight ahead
and spoke this speech, which you'll hear for yourselves:
"Sir Gawain, be wise enough to keep your word
and faithfully follow me until I'm found

14. *gutters:* flows in channels or rivulets
15. *cops:* grabs, catches

as you vowed in this hall within hearing of these horsemen.
You're charged with getting to the Green Chapel,
to reap what you've sown. You'll rightfully receive
the justice you are due just as January dawns.
Men know my name as the Green Chapel knight
and even a fool couldn't fail to find me.
So come, or be called a coward forever."
With a tug of the reins he twisted around
and, head still in hand, galloped out of the hall,
so the hooves brought fire from the flame in the flint.
Which kingdom he came from they hadn't a clue,
no more than they knew where he made for next.
And then?
Well, with the green man gone
they laughed and grinned again.
And yet such goings-on
were magic to those men.

Cultural Context: Why is it important for Gawain to keep his word to the Green Knight? What would violating his vow to the Green Knight say about Gawain?

Reading Check: What is supernatural, or magical, about the events immediately after the beheading?

Nearly a year later, Sir Gawain prepares to embark on his quest to find the Green Chapel. In keeping with his knightly station, he is dressed in stunning apparel, including a fine suit of armor.

FROM PART 2

Fastened in his armor he seemed fabulous, famous,
every link looking golden to the very last loop.
Yet for all that metal he still made it to mass,
honored the Almighty before the high altar.
After which he comes to the king and his **consorts**
and asks to take leave of the ladies and lords;
they escort and kiss him and commended him to Christ.

. . . .

Then he holds up his helmet and kisses it without haste;
it was strongly stapled and its lining was stuffed,
and sat high on his head, fastened behind
with a colorful cloth to cover his neck
embroidered and bejeweled with brilliant gems
on the broad silk border, and with birds on the seams
such as painted parrots perched among periwinkles[16]
and turtle doves and true lover's knots,[17] tightly entwined
as if women had worked at it seven winters
at least.
The diamond diadem
was greater still. It gleamed
with flawless, flashing gems
both clear and smoked, it seemed.

Then they showed him the shining scarlet shield
with its pentangle painted in pure gold.
He seized it by its strap and slung it round his neck;
he looked well in what he wore, and was worthy of it.
And why the pentangle was appropriate to that prince
I intend to say, though it will stall our story.

consort (kŏn'sôrt') *n.* A companion or partner.

16. *periwinkle:* a trailing evergreen plant that has bluish-purple flowers
17. *true lover's knot:* An herb with four or more leaves and a single green, starlike flower accented with golden stamens and a purple berry in the center. The quatrefoil pattern of its leaves resembles the pattern of a true-love knot.

It is a symbol that Solomon once set in place
and is taken to this day as a token of fidelity,
for the form of the figure is a five-pointed star
and each line overlaps and links with the last
so is ever eternal, and when spoken of in England
is known by the name of the endless knot.
So it suits this soldier in his spotless armor,
fully faithful in five ways five times over.
For Gawain was as good as the purest gold—
devoid of vices but virtuous, loyal
                and kind,
    so bore that badge on both
    his shawl and shield alike.
    A prince who talked the truth.
    A notable. A knight. A

Symbol: What does the pentangle generally represent? What do its gold paint and overlapping lines represent respectively? A

First he was deemed flawless in his five senses;
and secondly his five fingers were never at fault;
and thirdly his faith was founded in the five wounds
Christ received on the cross, as the creed recalls.
And fourthly, if that soldier struggled in skirmish
one thought pulled him through above all other things:
the fortitude he found in the five joys
which Mary had conceived in her son, our Savior.
For precisely that reason the princely rider
had the shape of her image inside his shield,
so by catching her eye his courage would not crack.
The fifth set of five which I heard the knight followed
included friendship and fraternity with fellow men,
purity and politeness that impressed at all times,
and pity, which surpassed all pointedness. Five things
which meant more to Gawain than to most other men.
So these five sets of five were fixed in this knight,
each linked to the last through the endless line,
a five-pointed form which never failed,
never stronger to one side or slack at the other,
but unbroken in its being from beginning to end
however its trail is tracked and traced. A
So the star on the spangling shield he sported
shone royally, in gold, on a ruby red background,
the pure pentangle as people have called it
                for years.
    Then, lance in hand, held high,
    and got up in his gear
    he bids them all good-bye
    one final time, he fears.

Symbol: Reread lines 223–65. What do the pentangle's five points represent? A

On his journey Sir Gawain faces many dangers: violent giants, wild animals, harsh weather, and treacherous terrain. Wherever he goes, he asks about the chapel's location, but no one knows where it is. Eventually, at Christmastime, he comes to a grand castle, where he is greeted warmly by the king and queen of that realm. When Gawain asks about the Green Chapel, the king reveals that it is nearby but insists that Gawain remain at their court until his appointment with the Green Knight. As Part 2 of the tale closes, the king is going away to hunt, but he and Sir Gawain first make a pact: whatever the king wins from the hunt he will give to Gawain, and Gawain, in exchange, will give the king whatever he gains during the king's absence.

FROM PART 3

The tale continues with three hunts. Before each, Gawain and the king renew their agreement to exchange winnings. And each time the king is away, the queen visits Gawain in his bedchamber and entices him with her beauty. The king's hunts increase in difficulty (deer, a wild boar, a wily fox) while the queen's advances become more difficult to resist. But being honorable, Gawain behaves virtuously. During the first hunt, the knight receives one kindly kiss from the queen and gives it to the king upon his return; during the second, Gawain receives two more and likewise returns both to the king. But during the third hunt, the queen instead asks Gawain for a token of affection. When he admits he has none to give her, she gives him a token of her own.

She offers him a ring of rich, red gold,
and the stunning stone set upon it stood proud,
beaming and burning with the brightness of the sun;
what wealth it was worth you can well imagine.
But he would not accept it, and said straight away,
" . . . [N]o tokens will I take at this time;
I have nothing to give, so nothing will I gain."
She insists he receives it but still he resists,
and swears, on his name as a knight, to say no.
Snubbed by his decision, she said to him then,
"You refuse my ring because you find it too fine,
and don't dare to be deeply indebted to me;
so I give you my girdle, a lesser thing to gain."
From around her body she unbuckled the belt
which tightened the tunic beneath her topcoat,
a green silk girdle trimmed with gold,
exquisitely edged and hemmed by hand.
And she sweetly beseeched Sir Gawain to receive it,
in spite of its slightness, and hoped he would accept.
But still he maintained he intended to take
neither gold nor girdle, until by God's grace
the challenge he had chosen was finally achieved.
"With apologies I pray you are not displeased,
but I must firmly refuse you, no matter how flattered I am.
For all your grace I owe
a thousand thank-you's, ma'am.
I shall through sun and snow
remain your loyal man."

"And now he sends back my silk," the lady responded,
"so simple in itself, or so it appears,
so little and unlikely, worth nothing, or less.
But the knight who knew of the power knitted in it
would pay a high price to possess it, probably.
For the body which is bound within this green belt,
as long as it is buckled robustly about him,
will be safe against those who seek to strike him,
and all the slyness on earth wouldn't see him slain."
The man mulled it over, and it entered his mind
that this girdle being given could be just the job
to save him from the strike in his challenge at the chapel.
With luck, it might let him escape with his life. **A**
So relenting at last he let her speak,
and promptly she pressed him to take the present,
and he granted her wish, gave in with good grace,
though the woman begged him not to whisper a word
of this gift to her husband, and Gawain agreed;
those words of theirs within those walls
should stay.
His thanks are heartfelt, then.
No sooner can he say
how much it matters, when
three kisses come his way. **R**

Symbol: What magical power does Gawain believe the green girdle possesses? **A**

Cultural Context: What details in this scene reflect or contrast with the courtly love tradition? **R**

When the king returns, Sir Gawain gives him the queen's three kisses but keeps the girdle, believing that it might save him from the Green Knight. Gawain says his good-byes and retires for the night; the next morning he is to depart for the Green Chapel.

FROM PART 4

Gawain arrays himself in fine clothes and armor for his trip, tying his most prized apparel, the green girdle, tightly around his waist. A guide leads him across the countryside but, terrified, turns back from the wilderness where the Green Knight resides. Gawain journeys on alone and upon arriving at the Green Chapel is surprised to find it unlike any chapel he has ever seen—an earthen, cave-like structure covered in grass. He enters the place to the sounds of an axe being sharpened on a grindstone and calls for the giant to reveal himself. The Green Knight emerges, axe in hand, to greet his guest and recall the vow they made a year ago. Gawain remembers its terms and kneels down to receive one strike from the knight's axe.

VISUAL ANALYSIS
How does the artist capture Gawain's feelings about this confrontation in the way he portrays it?

Suddenly the green knight summons up his strength,
hoists the axe high over Gawain's head,
lifts it aloft with every fiber of his life
and begins to bring home a bone-splitting blow.
Had he seen it through as thoroughly as threatened
the man beneath him would have met with his maker.
But glimpsing the axe at the edge of his eye
bringing death earthwards as it arced through the air,
and sensing its sharpness, Gawain shrank at the shoulders.
The swinging axman swerved from his stroke,
and reproached the young prince with piercing words:

"Call yourself good Sir Gawain?" he goaded,
"who faced down every foe in the field of battle
but now flinches with fear at the foretaste of harm.
Never have I known such a namby-pamby knight.
Did I budge or even blink when you aimed the axe,
or **carp** or quibble in King Arthur's castle,
or flap when my head went flying to my feet?
But entirely untouched, you are terror struck.
I'll be found the better fellow, since you were so feeble
and frail."
Gawain confessed, "I flinched
at first, but will not fail.
Though once my head's unhitched
it's off once and for all!"

carp (kärp) *intr.v.* To complain or find fault in a petty or disagreeable way.

So be brisk with the blow, bring on the blade.
Deal me my destiny and do it out of hand,
and I'll stand the stroke without shiver or shudder
and be wasted by your weapon. You have my word."
"Take this then," said the other, throwing up the axe,
menacing the young man with the gaze of a maniac.
Then he launches his swing but leaves him unscathed,
withholds his arm before harm could be done.
And Gawain was motionless, never moved a muscle,
but stood stone-still, or as still as a tree stump
anchored in the earth by a hundred roots.
Then the warrior in green mocked Gawain again:
"Now you've plucked up your courage I'll dispatch you properly.
May the honorable knighthood heaped on you by Arthur—
if it proves to be powerful—protect your pretty neck."
That insulting slur drew a spirited response:
"Get hacking, then, head-banger, your threats are hollow.
Such huffing and fussing—you'll frighten your own heart."
. . . [T]he green man[said], "[S]ince you speak so grandly
there'll be no more shilly-shallying, I shall shatter you
right now."
He stands to strike, a sneer
from bottom lip to brow.
Who'd fault Gawain if fear
took hold. All hope is down.

Hoisted and aimed, the axe hurtled downwards,
the blade baring down on the knight's bare neck,
a ferocious blow, but far from being fatal
it skewed to one side, just skimming the skin
and finely snicking the fat of the flesh
so that bright red blood shot from body to earth.
Seeing it shining on the snowy ground
Gawain leapt forward a spear's length at least,
grabbed hold of his helmet and rammed it on his head,
brought his shield to his side with a shimmy of his shoulder,
then **brandished** his sword before blurting out brave words,
because never since birth, as his mother's babe,

brandish (brăn′dĭsh) *tr.v.* To wave or flourish (something, often a weapon) in a menacing, defiant, or excited way.

was he half as happy as here and now.
"Enough swiping, sir, you've swung your last swing.
I've borne one blow without backing out,
go for me again and you'll get some by return,
with interest! Hit out, and be hit in an instant,
and hard.
One axe attack—that's all.
Now keep the covenant
agreed in Arthur's hall
and hold the axe in hand."

The warrior steps away and leans on his weapon,
props the handle in the earth and slouches on the head
and studies how Gawain is standing his ground,
bold in his bearing, brave in his actions,
armed and ready. In his heart he admires him.
With volume but less violence in his voice, he replied
with reaching words which rippled and rang:
"Be a mite less feisty, fearless young fellow,
no insulting or **heinous** incident has happened
beyond the game we agreed on in the court of your king.
One strike was promised—consider it served!
From any lingering loyalties you are hereby released.
Had I mustered all my muscles into one mighty blow
my axe would have dealt you your death, without doubt.
But my first strike fooled you—a feint, no less—
not fracturing your flesh, which was only fair
in keeping with the contract we declared that first night,
for with truthful behavior you honored my trust
and gave up your gains as a good man should.
Then I missed you once more, and this for the morning
when you kissed my pretty wife then kindly kissed me.
So twice you were truthful, therefore twice I left
no scar.
The person who repays
will live to feel no fear.
The third time, though, you strayed,
and felt my blade therefore."

"Because the belt you are bound with belongs to me;
it was woven by my wife so I know it very well.
And I know of your courtesies, and conduct, and kisses,
and the wooing of my wife—for it was all my work!
I sent her to test you—and in truth it turns out
you're by the far the most faultless fellow on earth.
As a pearl is more prized than a pea which is white,
so . . . is Gawain, amongst gallant knights.
But a little thing more—it was loyalty that you lacked:
not because you're wicked, or a womanizer, or worse,
but you loved your own life; so I blame you less."
Gawain stood speechless for what seemed like a century,
so shocked and ashamed that his stomach churned
and the fire of his blood brought flames to his face

Cultural Context: How do Gawain's responses to each axe swing reflect or contrast with his code of conduct?

heinous (hā'nəs) *adj.* Hateful, odious; highly criminal or wicked.

Reading Check: How many axe swings does the Green Knight attempt when fulfilling the challenge? To what other set of three does he connect these attempts?

Courtly Love: What potential pitfalls of courtly love are alluded to in lines 426–31 of this stanza? Does Gawain succumb to these according to the king's report?

and he wriggled and writhed at the other man's words.
Then he tried to talk, and finding his tongue, said:
"A curse upon cowardice and covetousness.
They breed villainy and vice, and destroy all virtue."
Then he grabbed the girdle and ungathered its knot
and flung it in fury at the man in front.
"My downfall and undoing; let the devil take it.
Dread of the death blow and cowardly doubts
meant I gave in to greed, and in doing so forgot
the fidelity and kindness which every knight knows.
As I feared, I am found to be flawed and false,
through treachery and untruth I have totally failed," said Gawain.
"Such terrible mistakes,
and I shall bear the blame.
But tell me what it takes
to clear my clouded name."

Cultural Context: How does Gawain describe his failing? How is it a violation of the code of chivalry?

The green lord laughed, and leniently replied:
"The harm which you caused me is wholly healed.
By confessing your failings you are free from fault
and have openly paid penance at the point of my axe.

I declare you purged, as polished and as pure
as the day you were born, without blemish or blame.
And this gold-hemmed girdle I present as a gift,
which is green like my gown. It's yours, Sir Gawain,
a reminder of our meeting when you mix and mingle
with princes and kings. And this keepsake will be proof
to all chivalrous knights of your challenge in this chapel.
But follow me home. New Year's far from finished—
we'll resume our reveling with supper and song.
What's more
my wife is waiting there
who **flummoxed** you before.

flummox (flŭm′əks) *tr.v.* To confuse; perplex.

This time you'll have in her
a friend and not a foe."
"Thank you," said the other, taking helmet from head,
holding it in hand as he offered his thanks.
"But I've loitered long enough. The Lord bless your life
and bestow on you such honor as you surely deserve."
. . . .

Before leaving, Gawain swears to wear the girdle as "a sad reminder" of his sin. When he is tempted to pride in his virtue, it will keep him humble, reminding him of possible future failure. He also asks for the king's name, which is Bertilak. Bertilak in turn reveals that the sorceress Morgan le Fay (Arthur's half sister who studied with Merlin) created this green enchantment to test the Round Table's worth.

So they clasped and kissed and made kindly commendations
to the Prince of Paradise, and then parted in the cold,
that pair.
Our man, back on his mount
now hurtles home from there.
The green knight leaves his ground
to wander who-knows-where.

So he winds through the wilds of the world once more,
Gawain on Gringolet, by the grace of God,
under a roof sometimes and sometimes roughing it,
and in valleys and vales had adventures and victories
but time is too tight to tell how they went.

Gawain returns to Camelot and recounts his adventure, including his "breach of faith" regarding the girdle. He relives the shame of the moment and reveals the nick on his neck left by the Green Knight's axe. Thereafter, every Round Table knight wears a green sash in honor of Sir Gawain and as a reminder of both the frailty of their human hearts and the virtue of humility.

THINK AND DISCUSS

1. What "game" is the backbone of the plot of this tale? Trace its key happenings and final outcome.
2. What is the Green Knight's true identity? What additional challenge does he give Gawain? Summarize the key events of this second test.
3. Identify three instances (situations or choices) prior to the tale's conclusion that reflect or violate the chivalric code (including courtly love). Briefly explain your answers.
4. Why does the Green Knight use beheading to test Gawain? What is each test meant to ascertain about Gawain, and how do both connect thematically? Why doesn't the Knight strongly condemn Gawain's failing?
5. Identify instances of the color green in the story. From these examples, infer what the color might symbolize.
6. What does the pentangle represent? How does it connect to the chivalric code and to Christianity?
7. What does the green girdle illustrate before and then after Gawain's failing? Why is it appropriate that all of the knights of Camelot choose to wear a green girdle?
8. How does the story's resolution reflect a biblical worldview? Does it portray an idealized or realistic view of the hero? Support your answer with evidence from the text.
9. How might the story have turned out differently if Gawain had given in to the queen or if Gawain had not responded as he did when the Green Knight pointed out Gawain's failing?

Thomas Malory (ca. 1408–1471)

AT A GLANCE

- **1451** Began period of legal trouble
- **1468, 1470** Excluded from general pardon of Lancastrians
- **ca. 1469–70** Writes *Le Morte d'Arthur* while imprisoned
- **1485** *Le Morte d'Arthur* published by William Caxton

Historical research has not solved the puzzle of Thomas Malory. The few facts available reveal a man of strange contradictions. Though viewed by many as a criminal (he spent years in prison), Malory produced prose romances that show great concern for proper behavior and moral responsibility in society.

DID YOU KNOW ?

Malory escaped from prison at least twice, once by swimming a moat and another time by executing an impressive display with sword, dagger, and halberd (a spear with an axe blade).

Accused Criminal

A gentleman of Warwickshire in the Earl of Warwick's service during the Wars of the Roses, Malory was caught up in the turmoil of his times. Contemporary records picture him as a flagrant disrupter of community peace (although, in fairness, he lived in an era notorious for trumped-up charges based on political allegiances). From 1451 on, he was charged with a variety of offenses, ranging from cattle raiding, land theft, house and church breaking, and extortion to attempted ambush and malicious assault. For the next twenty years of his life, he was in and out of prisons. Having switched allegiances from the House of York to the House of Lancaster, he was excluded from two general pardons of Lancastrians (1468, 1470) and was released shortly before his death only because a Lancastrian king returned briefly to the throne.

Romance Writer

For the last decade of his life, Malory's residence was London's Newgate Prison. The prison stood near the well-stocked Grey Friars library, to which prisoners were allowed access. It was there that Malory likely found many of the source materials that inspired his work. In these surroundings, he began the cycle of prose romances on which his literary reputation rests. These describe the world of King Arthur and his knights of the Round Table, a world of seeming honor and virtue that was long past and far different from the one in which Malory lived. The work's genre matched its nostalgic content as by this time the romance was falling out of favor.

Published in 1485 by William Caxton as *Le Morte d'Arthur* ("the death of Arthur"), the final work was massive, including eight separate romances divided into twenty-one books altogether. It knit together a multiplicity of Arthurian legends found in French and English sources and gave them a thematic shape; Malory recreated an exciting narrative of the rise and fall of Arthur and his knights but also infused it with an examination of ethical and moral issues.

Arthurian Legends

The legend of Arthur stems from fifth-century battles between the native Celts and invading Anglo-Saxons. The Anglo-Saxons experienced a series of military setbacks at the hands of a Romano-British chieftain named Ambrosius. Once the Celts were driven from central England, stories of this great military leader lived on. As the tales migrated to other cultures, new adventures and new trappings were added. In Wales, Cornwall, and Brittany, Arthurian lore picked up supernatural additions: the magician Merlin, the sorceress Morgan le Fay, and the fairy underworld. As the legend spread from Brittany throughout France, it also acquired aristocratic embellishments. Arthur became a king rather than a chieftain. His retinue became knights holding their lands in fealty to him. Eventually, his behavior and the atmosphere of his court summed up the social ideal of chivalry. An important character, the French knight Launcelot du Lac, was added to the Round Table and became nearly as prominent as Arthur. When the legend, thus enriched, returned to Britain, it took on patriotic meaning for the English. Malory likely saw in the Arthur story the reflection of an ideal English past, a past all the more radiant when viewed against the violence and corruption of his present.

ANALYZE: *Legend, Prose Romance, Christ Figure*

In most cultures, the earliest literature springs from oral traditions. One kind of oral tradition is the **legend**, an ostensibly historical story that is popularly believed but that lacks factual evidence. The Arthur tales were originally legends. Intrigued by these stories, twelfth-century medieval French writers developed them further in a series of medieval romances.

Malory borrowed heavily from these romances but wrote his own in Middle English as a **prose romance**, without the lines and other conventions of poetry but with the usual romance content (p. 36). His writing style is simple and direct and incorporates realistic dialogue. The following excerpt is a retelling, but it features the same straightforward manner. As you read, note how the style of the narration and dialogue help to move the plot along quickly.

Many consider Arthur to be a **Christ figure**, a character who resembles Jesus Christ in characterization or function (e.g., His sacrificial act). The resemblance appears especially strong in the story of Arthur's death. How are the deaths of Arthur and Jesus Christ similar? How are they different?

READ: *Summarize, Apply Historical Context*

Summarizing a text's ideas is a great deal easier when the author provides clear organization. Malory did just that in his romance. His sources were classic medieval narratives that tended to shift between many plot threads at once. Taking a more modern approach, Malory concentrated on one story at a time and rearranged the stories into a chronological sequence. In doing so, he gave these Arthurian legends the feel of reality, like a historical narrative. As you read this portion of *Le Morte d'Arthur*, note the text's clear chronological progression and the way each new incident propels the next forward. Use the skills you have already practiced to recognize and summarize the excerpt's key ideas.

Additionally, you have read about the intermingling of military virtues and Christian elements within the chivalric code (p. 15). As you read, try to distinguish Christianity's influence on the thoughts and behavior of the characters.

CREATE: *A Reflective Paragraph*

Chivalry especially emphasized virtues such as bravery and skill in battle, honor, piety, dedication to women, and the correction of injustice. As you read, note how these abstract ideas play out in reality. If Arthur (the epitome of chivalry) returned to rule Britain today, what would he think of contemporary society? Do you see in your society any actions motivated by similar principles? At the end of your reading, you will be asked to write a paragraph describing how the principles behind chivalry do or do not inspire real people today.

OBJECTIVES

- Summarize a text's key information.
- Apply historical context to understand a text and its themes.
- Justify a text's genre as a romance or a legend or both.
- Analyze a character as a Christ figure and its connection to the work's themes.

VOCABULARY

assail (ə-sāl′) *tr.v.* To attack verbally, as with ridicule or censure.

stint (stĭnt) *n.* A limitation or restriction.

succor (sŭk′ər) *n.* Assistance in time of distress; relief.

adder (ăd′ər) *n.* Any of several nonvenomous snakes, such as the hognose snake, often believed to be harmful.

dauntless (dônt′ lĭs) *adj.* Incapable of being intimidated or discouraged; fearless.

copse (kŏps) *n.* A thicket of small trees or shrubs; a coppice.

Why do people follow LEADERS?

Why do people choose one leader over another? Is personal well-being the key factor, or are other principles at stake? Does it depend on the situation? Do you personally know people who are natural leaders? Why do people follow them? Consider a past leader notable for his or her many followers. Write a short paragraph explaining why you think people followed this person. Or write the same about someone you know who is a leader.

from Le Morte d'Arthur

THE DAY OF DESTINY

One of King Arthur's most trusted knights, Sir Launcelot, had pursued an adulterous relationship with Queen Guinevere. Outraged by his betrayal of Arthur, Sir Gawain, Arthur's nephew, encourages Arthur to travel to France to attack Launcelot in his French lands. While Arthur is away from Britain, however, his illegitimate son, Modred, schemes to usurp the throne. As moral deterioration threatens to rip apart the society that Arthur and his knights have built, Arthur returns to Britain to try to save his throne and his kingdom.

During the absence of King Arthur from Britain, Sir Modred, already vested with sovereign powers, had decided to usurp the throne. Accordingly, he had false letters written—announcing the death of King Arthur in battle—and delivered to himself. Then, calling a parliament, he ordered the letters to be read and persuaded the nobility to elect him king. The coronation took place at Canterbury and was celebrated with a fifteen-day feast.

Sir Modred then settled in Camelot and made overtures to Queen Gwynevere to marry him. The queen seemingly acquiesced, but as soon as she had won his confidence, begged leave to make a journey to London in order to prepare her trousseau. Sir Modred consented, and the queen rode straight to the Tower which, with the aid of her loyal nobles, she manned and provisioned for her defense.

Sir Modred, outraged, at once marched against her, and laid siege to the Tower, but despite his large army, siege engines, and guns, was unable to effect a breach. He then tried to entice the queen from the Tower, first by guile and then by threats, but she would listen to neither. Finally the Archbishop of Canterbury came forward to protest:

"Sir Modred, do you not fear God's displeasure? First you have falsely made yourself king; now you, who were begotten by King Arthur on his aunt, try to marry your father's wife! If you do not revoke your evil deeds I shall curse you with bell, book, and candle." A

Prose Romance: What stylistic features of Malory's prose romance do the previous paragraphs already illustrate? A

"Fie on you! Do your worst!" Sir Modred replied.

"Sir Modred, I warn you take heed! or the wrath of the Lord will descend upon you."

"Away, false priest, or I shall behead you!"

The Archbishop withdrew, and after excommunicating Sir Modred, abandoned his office and fled to Glastonbury. There he took up his abode as a simple hermit, and by fasting and prayer sought divine intercession in the troubled affairs of his country.

Sir Modred tried to assassinate the Archbishop, but was too late. He continued to **assail** the queen with entreaties and threats, both of which failed, and then the news reached him that King Arthur was returning with his army from France in order to seek revenge.

assail (ə-sāl′) *tr.v.* To attack verbally, as with ridicule or censure.

Sir Modred now appealed to the barony to support him, and it has to be told that they came forward in large numbers to do so. Why? it will be asked. Was not King Arthur, the noblest sovereign Christendom had seen, now leading his armies in a righteous cause? The answer lies in the people of Britain, who, then as now, were fickle. Those who so readily transferred their allegiance to Sir Modred did so with the excuse that whereas King Arthur's reign had led them into war and strife, Sir Modred promised them peace and festivity.

Hence it was with an army of a hundred thousand that Sir Modred marched to Dover to battle against his own father, and to withhold from him his rightful crown.

As King Arthur with his fleet drew into the harbor, Sir Modred and his army launched forth in every available craft, and a bloody battle ensued in the ships and on the beach. If King Arthur's army were the smaller, their courage was the higher, confident as they were of the righteousness of their cause. Without **stint** they battled through the burning ships, the screaming wounded, and the corpses floating on the bloodstained waters. Once ashore they put Sir Modred's entire army to flight. R

The battle over, King Arthur began a search for his casualties, and on peering into one of the ships found Sir Gawain, mortally wounded. Sir Gawain fainted when King Arthur lifted him in his arms; and when he came to, the king spoke:

"Alas! dear nephew, that you lie here thus, mortally wounded! What joy is now left to me on this earth? You must know it was you and Sir Launcelot I loved above all others, and it seems that I have lost you both."

"My good uncle, it was my pride and my stubbornness that brought all this about, for had I not urged you to war with Sir Launcelot your subjects

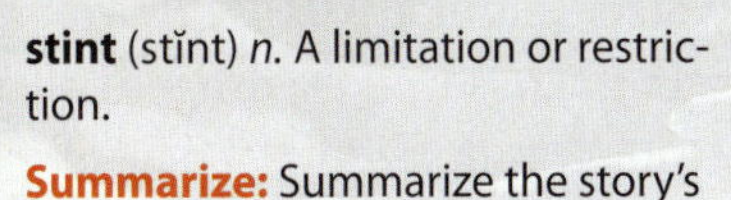

stint (stĭnt) *n.* A limitation or restriction.

Summarize: Summarize the story's events so far. How do the author's organization and style ease this task? R would not now be in revolt. Alas, that Sir Launcelot is not here, for he would soon drive them out! And it is at Sir Launcelot's hands that I suffer my own death: the wound which he dealt me has reopened. I would not wish it otherwise, because is he not the greatest and gentlest of knights?

"I know that by noon I shall be dead, and I repent bitterly that I may not be reconciled to Sir Launcelot; therefore I pray you, good uncle, give me pen, paper, and ink so that I may write to him."

A priest was summoned and Sir Gawain confessed; then a clerk brought ink, pen, and paper, and Sir Gawain wrote to Sir Launcelot as follows:

"Sir Launcelot, flower of the knighthood: I, Sir Gawain, son of King Lot of Orkney and of King Arthur's sister, send you my greetings!

"I am about to die; the cause of my death is the wound I received from you outside the city of Benwick; and I would make it known that my death was of my own seeking, that I was moved by the spirit of revenge and spite to provoke you to battle.

"Therefore, Sir Launcelot, I beseech you to visit my tomb and offer what prayers you will on my behalf; and for myself, I am content to die at the hands of the noblest knight living.

"One more request: that you hasten with your armies across the sea and give **succor** to our noble king. Sir Modred, his bastard son, has usurped the throne and now holds against him with an army of a hundred thousand. He would have won the queen, too, but she fled to the Tower of London and there charged her loyal supporters with her defense.

succor (sŭk′ər) *n.* Assistance in time of distress; relief.

"Today is the tenth of May, and at noon I shall give up the ghost; this letter is written partly with my blood. This morning we fought our way ashore, against the armies of Sir Modred, and that is how my wound came to be reopened. We won the day, but my lord King Arthur needs you, and I too, that on my tomb you may bestow your blessing." R

Apply Context: Review Gawain's thoughts from his first words to Arthur until here. What Christian virtues are evident in his ideas? R

Sir Gawain fainted when he had finished, and the king wept. When he came to he was given extreme unction, and died, as he had anticipated, at the hour of noon. The king buried him in the chapel at Dover Castle, and there many came to see him, and all noticed the wound on his head which he had received from Sir Launcelot.

Then the news reached Arthur that Sir Modred offered him battle on the field at Baron Down. Arthur hastened there with his army, they fought, and Sir Modred fled once more, this time to Canterbury.

When King Arthur had begun the search for his wounded and dead, many volunteers from all parts of the country came to fight under his flag, convinced now of the rightness of his cause. Arthur marched westward, and Sir Modred once more offered him battle. It was assigned for the Monday following Trinity Sunday, on Salisbury Down.

Sir Modred levied fresh troops from East Anglia and the places about London, and fresh volunteers came forward to help Arthur. Then, on the night of Trinity Sunday, Arthur was vouchsafed a strange dream:

He was appareled in gold cloth and seated in a chair which stood on a pivoted scaffold. Below him, many fathoms deep, was a dark well, and in the water swam serpents, dragons, and wild beasts. Suddenly the scaffold tilted and Arthur was flung into the water, where all the creatures struggled toward him and began tearing him limb from limb.

Arthur cried out in his sleep and his squires hastened to waken him. Later, as he lay between waking and sleeping, he thought he saw Sir Gawain, and with him a host of beautiful noblewomen. Arthur spoke:

"My sister's son! I thought you had died; but now I see you live, and I thank the lord Jesu! I pray you, tell me, who are these ladies?"

"My lord, these are the ladies I championed in righteous quarrels when I was on earth. Our lord God has vouchsafed that we visit you and plead with you not to give battle to Sir Modred tomorrow, for if you do, not only will you yourself be killed, but all your noble followers too. We beg you to be warned, and to make a treaty with Sir Modred, calling a truce for a month, and granting him whatever terms he may demand. In a month Sir Launcelot will be here, and he will defeat Sir Modred." R

Summarize: Summarize the contents of Arthur's dream. R

Thereupon Sir Gawain and the ladies vanished, and King Arthur once more summoned his squires and his counselors and told them his vision. Sir Lucas and Sir Bedivere were commissioned to make a treaty with Sir Modred. They were to be accompanied by two bishops and to grant, within reason, whatever terms he demanded. A

Prose Romance: How do Arthur's dreams and their meaning reflect the typical content of a prose romance? A

The ambassadors found Sir Modred in command of an army of a hundred thousand and unwilling to listen to overtures of peace. However, the ambassadors eventually prevailed on him and in return for the truce granted him suzerainty of Cornwall and Kent, and succession to the British throne when King Arthur died. The treaty was to be signed by King Arthur and Sir Modred the next day. They were to meet between the two armies, and each was to be accompanied by no more than fourteen knights.

Both King Arthur and Sir Modred suspected the other of treachery, and gave orders for their armies to attack at the sight of a naked sword. When they met at the appointed place the treaty was signed and both drank a glass of wine.

Then, by chance, one of the soldiers was bitten in the foot by an **adder** which had lain concealed in the brush. The soldier unthinkingly drew his sword to kill it, and at once, as the sword flashed in the light, the alarums were given, trumpets sounded, and both armies galloped into the attack. R

adder (ăd'ər) *n.* Any of several nonvenomous snakes, such as the hognose snake, often believed to be harmful.

Apply Context: What Bible passage does this incident hark back to? How are the situations similar? R

"Alas for this fateful day!" exclaimed King Arthur, as both he and Sir Modred hastily mounted and galloped back to their armies. There followed one of those rare and heartless battles in which both armies fought until they were destroyed. King Arthur, with his customary valor, led squadron after squadron of cavalry into the attack, and Sir Modred encountered him unflinchingly. As the number of dead and wounded mounted on both sides, the active combatants continued **dauntless** until nightfall, when four men alone survived. A

dauntless (dônt' lĭs) *adj.* Incapable of being intimidated or discouraged; fearless.

Prose Romance: What chivalric virtue do both armies exhibit? How does Malory's description of the fighting add a realistic note to the story? A

King Arthur wept with dismay to see his beloved followers fallen; then, struggling toward him unhorsed and badly wounded, he saw Sir Lucas the Butler and his brother, Sir Bedivere.

"Alas!" said the king, "that the day should come when I see all my noble knights destroyed! I would prefer that I myself had fallen. But what has become of the traitor Sir Modred, whose evil ambition was responsible for this carnage?"

Looking about him King Arthur then noticed Sir Modred leaning with his sword on a heap of the dead.

"Sir Lucas, I pray you give me my spear, for I have seen Sir Modred."

"Sire, I entreat you, remember your vision—how Sir Gawain appeared with a heaven-sent message to dissuade you from fighting Sir Modred. Allow this fateful day to pass; it is ours, for we three hold the field, while the enemy is broken."

"My lords, I care nothing for my life now! And while Sir Modred is at large I must kill him: there may not be another chance."

"God speed you, then!" said Sir Bedivere.

When Sir Modred saw King Arthur advance with his spear, he rushed to meet him with drawn sword. Arthur caught Sir Modred below the shield and drove his spear through his body; Sir Modred, knowing that the wound was mortal, thrust himself up to the handle of the spear, and then, brandishing his sword in both hands, struck Arthur on the side of the helmet, cutting through it and into the skull beneath; then he crashed to the ground, gruesome and dead. **A**

Christ Figure: How does Arthur's thinking and conduct in this passage qualify him as a literary Christ figure? **A**

King Arthur fainted many times as Sir Lucas and Sir Bedivere struggled with him to a small chapel nearby, where they managed to ease his wounds a little. When Arthur came to, he thought he heard cries coming from the battlefield.

"Sir Lucas, I pray you, find out who cries on the battlefield," he said.

Wounded as he was, Sir Lucas hobbled painfully to the field, and there in the moonlight saw the camp followers stealing gold and jewels from the dead, and murdering the wounded. He returned to the king and reported to him what he had seen, and then added:

"My lord, it surely would be better to move you to the nearest town?"

"My wounds forbid it. But alas for the good Sir Launcelot! How sadly I have missed him today! And now I must die—as Sir Gawain warned me I would—repenting our quarrel with my last breath."

Sir Lucas and Sir Bedivere made one further attempt to lift the king. He fainted as they did so. Then Sir Lucas fainted as part of his intestines broke through a wound in the stomach. When the king came to, he saw Sir Lucas lying dead with foam at his mouth.

"Sweet Jesu, give him succor!" he said. "This noble knight has died trying to save my life—alas that this was so!"

Sir Bedivere wept for his brother.

"Sir Bedivere, weep no more," said King Arthur, "for you can save neither your brother nor me; and I would ask you to take my sword Excalibur to the shore of the lake and throw it in the water. Then return to me and tell me what you have seen."

"My lord, as you command, it shall be done."

Sir Bedivere took the sword, but when he came to the water's edge, it appeared so beautiful that he could not bring himself to throw it in, so instead he hid it by a tree and then returned to the king.

"Sir Bedivere, what did you see?"

"My lord, I saw nothing but the wind upon the waves."

"Then you did not obey me; I pray you, go swiftly again, and this time fulfill my command."

Sir Bedivere went and returned again, but this time too he had failed to fulfill the king's command.

"Sir Bedivere, what did you see?"

"My lord, nothing but the lapping of the waves."

"Sir Bedivere, twice you have betrayed me! And for the sake only of my sword: it is unworthy of you! Now I pray you, do as I command, for I have not long to live." **R**

Apply Context: How does Sir Bedivere's behavior violate the code of chivalry as well as Christian virtue? **R**

This time Sir Bedivere wrapped the girdle around the sheath and hurled it as far as he could into the water. A hand appeared from below the surface, took

Nyneve, the Lady of the Lake, who gave Excalibur to Arthur and now takes it back.

the sword, waved it thrice, and disappeared again. Sir Bedivere returned to the king and told him what he had seen.

"Sir Bedivere, I pray you now help me hence, or I fear it will be too late."

Sir Bedivere carried the king to the water's edge, and there found a barge in which sat many beautiful ladies with their queen. All were wearing black hoods, and when they saw the king, they raised their voices in a piteous lament.

"I pray you, set me in the barge," said the king.

Sir Bedivere did so, and one of the ladies laid the king's head in her lap; then the queen spoke to him:

"My dear brother, you have stayed too long: I fear that the wound on your head is already cold."

Thereupon they rowed away from the land and Sir Bedivere wept to see them go.

"My lord King Arthur, you have deserted me! I am alone now, and among enemies."

"Sir Bedivere, take what comfort you may, for my time is passed, and now I must be taken to Avalon for my wound to be healed. If you hear of me no more, I beg you pray for my soul."

The barge slowly crossed the water and out of sight while the ladies wept. Sir Bedivere walked alone into the forest and there remained for the night.

In the morning he saw beyond the trees of a **copse** a small hermitage. He entered and found a hermit kneeling down by a fresh tomb. The hermit was weeping as he prayed, and then Sir Bedivere recognized him as the Archbishop of Canterbury, who had been banished by Sir Modred.

copse (kŏps) *n.* A thicket of small trees or shrubs; a coppice.

"Father, I pray you, tell me, whose tomb is this?"

"My son, I do not know. At midnight the body was brought here by a company of ladies. We buried it, they lit a hundred candles for the service, and rewarded me with a thousand bezants."

"Father, King Arthur lies buried in this tomb."

Sir Bedivere fainted when he had spoken, and when he came to he begged the Archbishop to allow him to remain at the hermitage and end his days in fasting and prayer.

"Father, I wish only to be near to my true liege."

"My son, you are welcome; and do I not recognize you as Sir Bedivere the Bold, brother to Sir Lucas the Butler?"

Thus the Archbishop and Sir Bedivere remained at the hermitage, wearing the habits of hermits and devoting themselves to the tomb with fasting and prayers of contrition.

Such was the death of King Arthur as written down by Sir Bedivere. By some it is told that there were three queens on the barge: Queen Morgan le Fay, the Queen of North Galys, and the Queen of the Waste Lands; and others include the name of Nyneve, the Lady of the Lake who had served King Arthur well in the past, and had married the good knight Sir Pelleas.

In many parts of Britain it is believed that King Arthur did not die and that he will return to us and win fresh glory and the Holy Cross of our Lord Jesu Christ; but for myself I do not believe this, and would leave him buried peacefully in his tomb at Glastonbury, A where the Archbishop of Canterbury and Sir Bedivere humbled themselves, and with prayers and fasting honored his memory. And inscribed on his tomb, men say, is this legend:

HIC IACET ARTHURUS, REX QUONDAM REXQUE FUTURUS.[1] A

1. *Hic . . . Futurus:* Here lies Arthur, the once and future king.

Legend: How do Malory's final comments on the story reflect its status as a legend? A

Christ Figure: How do the ambiguous end of Arthur and the legends surrounding his death further solidify Arthur as a Christ figure? A

THINK AND DISCUSS

1. What problem distracts Arthur's attention and allows Modred to usurp the throne?
2. Why does Arthur seek a truce with Modred? What ruins his plans?
3. Summarize the story from Modred's death to the end.
4. What parts of the story seem to indicate its status as a legend? How does the story qualify as a romance?
5. Point out realistic touches in the story that show how Malory (a participant in the Wars of the Roses) had experience with battles and treacherous behavior.
6. As in *Sir Gawain and the Green Knight*, Arthur's knights are imperfect here. Indeed, several regret their actions during the story. Name two and tell what choices they turn away from.
7. What Christian or chivalric values are these regrets based on? How do they seek to redeem themselves? What other actions are lauded in the story?
8. Explain why Arthur qualifies as both a romance hero and a literary Christ figure.
9. What do you think Malory meant to say by depicting Arthur as a Christ figure and by the moral struggles of his knights? Note what led to the ruin of the kingdom and speculate on what people might hope Arthur's return would bring back to Britain.
10. Write a paragraph describing Arthur's imagined response to the twenty-first century and its response to him. Consider especially how people today would view the code of chivalry. Which parts of this story do you think might appeal to people today, and which would seem foreign?

What Do You Know?

Understand the Background

1. Identify the four traditional Anglo-Saxon heroic virtues. Describe *comitatus* and the virtues associated with it.
2. Why is the *Anglo-Saxon Chronicle* so valuable to modern scholars?
3. What features make *Sir Gawain and the Green Knight* part of the alliterative revival? How do these differ from the original alliterative verse form?
4. What is the source of the legend of King Arthur? How does Malory's version specifically differ from previous versions?

Apply the Concepts

5. Which of the following lines from *Beowulf* do(es) not meet the standard alliteration of Anglo-Saxon oral poetry?

   So Grendel waged his lonely war,
   inflicting constant cruelties on the people,
   atrocious hurt. He took over Heorot,
   haunted the glittering hall after dark,
   but the throne itself, the treasure-seat,
   he was kept from approaching; he was the Lord's outcast.

6. Explain how these lines illustrate a blend of tribal and Christian thinking:

   My household-guard / are on the wane, fate sweeps them away / into Grendel's clutches— / but God can easily / halt these raids and harrowing attacks!

7. List two characteristics of chronicles and give a brief example of each from the *Anglo-Saxon Chronicle*.
8. Identify two symbols from *Sir Gawain and the Green Knight*. Explain the significance of each using evidence from the text.
9. Explain how Malory's *Le Morte d'Arthur* fits the characteristics of a romance.

Evaluate the Ideas

10. In the *Anglo-Saxon Chronicle*, how might the writer's perspective color his readers' understanding of events? Cite textual details in your answer.
11. Exemplify each of the four heroic virtues (or their obvious lack) with a character from the unit selections. Characters can be used only once.
12. Answer one of the following question sets assessing the two heroic codes covered in the unit. Support your ideas with biblical references.

    How do the Anglo-Saxon heroic virtues measure up against scriptural principles? What biblical virtues might they overlook or even contradict in their traditional applications?

    Evaluate the idea of adhering to a code of conduct such as chivalry. Are its suggested virtues biblically sound? Is outward conduct an important aspect of virtuous living? What else might be important to virtuous living?

Write a Response

13. Describe the change in medieval England's cultural conception of the hero. Explain the ideals important to each type, and illustrate each with examples from the selections.
14. Compare and contrast the deaths of Arthur and Christ. Justify viewing Arthur as a literary Christ figure.

Define each term and provide an example of each from a selection in Unit 1, Part 1.

TERMS

comitatus
epic
kenning
litotes
wyrd
stock epithet
variation
alliterative verse
didactic
chronicle
perspective
bias
transitional phrase
symbol
legend
prose romance
Christ figure

UNIT 1

PART 2

Literature and Community

Have you ever thought about what literature contributes to a community? For people in the Middle Ages, community was the key to a stable life. For the common man especially, life was often brutally tough and insecure: death stalked people daily in the form of war, famine, or disease. Furthermore, in a time when power, rather than the democratic rule of law, held sway, having a place in the community was safer than not. Altogether, community provided a buffer against insecurities such as crop failure, loss of family or health, exploitation by greedy nobles or clergy, and more. Literature might seem superfluous in such a precarious environment, but in fact, it was not.

Many people today tend to think of literature as a solitary experience. That's because print works are often read silently and alone. But medieval communities existed before high literacy and cheap printing characterized most societies. In that environment, literature was more often a shared experience. Many works were oral, meant to be told and heard by more than one person. If they were written, the very scarcity of information and works in print meant that people read them together and discussed them. Furthermore, the few who could write often had a keen sense that their works would serve a constructive purpose in their community. Otherwise they would not have gone to the great effort and expense that writing demanded. As a result, much of medieval literature shows deep awareness of the community.

In fact, literature actively served to strengthen medieval communities in two main ways. One of these you studied in the previous section: literature could help a community preserve and reinforce its cultural values and sense of identity. But literature, especially oral literature, also brought people together, creating shared experiences that strengthened personal relationships. While heroic literature very clearly illustrates the former function, other sorts of literature contributed to and reflected the community too, in both similar and different ways. As this next group of selections illustrates, a wide variety of works—both fiction and nonfiction, serious and playful, communal and individual, print and oral—explored the community's values and sense of identity and contributed to its spiritual and emotional well-being.

The selections in this section of Unit 1 either reminded medieval English inhabitants of their common values and identity, created shared experiences for them, or combined both. For example, Bede's *Ecclesiastical History of the English People* records the English community's biography for posterity. Bede sought to shape a sense of English identity by reminding readers of their shared values and history of God's working in their community. Meanwhile, songs, ballads, and riddles were oral genres meant for a popular audience; they reached the broadest segment of the community. They offered an enjoyable chance to rest and relax together and often affirmed shared cultural values too. On the other hand, Julian of Norwich's *Revelations of Divine Love* exemplifies the era's abundant devotional literature, meant to spiritually strengthen its readers and the community as a whole. Finally, medieval dramas were corporate affairs in which the entire community participated. The dramas affirmed cultural values while community members' shared work and celebration strengthened their sense of common identity.

As you read, ask the following questions: What does this literature say about medieval community life? What did English society value? How did people entertain themselves in the midst of their tough lives? Perhaps even more interesting, explore what literature contributes to your society in similar or dissimilar ways. What kind of literature does your personal community create and share? Does that literature reflect your common values? Does the experience of sharing it strengthen your relationships? How might literature make life better for your community?

Bede (673–735)

The Northumbrian monk and scholar named simply Bede is primarily known for his great work *An Ecclesiastical History of the English People*. About Bede himself we know very little save for his life's basic outline. At seven he went to live in the monastery at Jarrow to become a Benedictine monk. A center of Anglo-Saxon learning, Jarrow boasted one of the greatest libraries in Europe at the time; in this environment, Bede thrived. At nineteen he was ordained as a deacon, and at thirty, a priest. During his sixty-two years, he corresponded with many scholars abroad and at home and gained a reputation as the greatest scholar of the early medieval era. Well-versed in Latin, Greek, and Hebrew as well as his native Old English, Bede wrote more than fifty works covering a broad spectrum of subjects: natural history, biography, poetry, grammar, astronomy, history, and theology. "The Venerable" was added to his name in recognition of his piety and outstanding scholarship.

Written in Medieval Latin, the *Ecclesiastical History* was translated by Alfred's scholars into Old English; the translation's content informed the earliest sections of *The Anglo-Saxon Chronicle*. Bede's five-book history describes England's political and church history beginning with Julius Caesar's raids in 55–54 BC, through Saint Augustine's successful missionary expedition (begun 597), and ending in 731, the time of Bede's writing. Bede carefully collected his information from a variety of sources, from ancient Roman accounts to contemporary eyewitnesses. For his painstaking and rigorous work, he is often called the Father of English History.

Bede had two main purposes for writing his history. First, he sought to trace God's working in England in order to glorify God and to instruct readers. Second, he wanted to show a unified identity for the English peoples, one based on shared history guided by God Himself. The following excerpt, taken from the work's fourth book, tells the origin story of the monk Caedmon, the oldest known English poet. In it, Bede accomplished a literary first, recording one of the oldest existing—if not the oldest—Old English poems.

DID YOU KNOW?

Bede is credited with popularizing the use of *AD* (*anno Domini*, "in the year of the Lord") to signify years after the traditional date of the birth of Christ.

BEFORE READING

ANALYZE: *Hagiography*

Bede's historical narrative incorporates one of his era's most popular genres, **hagiography** (biographies of saints). Hagiographies instruct readers with stories of pious protagonists who do or experience miracles enabling them to overcome trials by God's grace. In his history of the English, Bede demonstrates God's providential work in the community's life by telling of saints and pious kings and describing miracles great and small. How might his overall story and purpose resemble a hagiography? How does Caedmon's tale specifically qualify as hagiography?

READ: *Apply Historical Context*

Known for his beautiful Latin prose, Bede handily used rhetorical flourishes while preserving a clear and simple delivery. Unsurprisingly then, he was one of the first to note English poetry's beauty and to record an example. How does his rendition of Caedmon's hymn reflect Anglo-Saxon culture? Reference conventions of Anglo-Saxon poetry such as **epithets**, **variation**, **kenning**, and **alliterative verse** (p. 18).

EVALUATE: *Aesthetic Effectiveness*

Many short lyric poems rely on two principles of aesthetics (artistic beauty): unity and progression. Unity of ideas ensures a poem's main idea is clear; unity of imagery provides emphasis and attractive symmetry. Progression signifies that a poem develops its ideas (or images) in a way that unfolds logically and coherently. Both principles help poets convey a well-developed theme briefly but effectively. Consider these principles as you read Caedmon's hymn. Look for progression in the poem's imagery and ideas, and examine how its content projects a unified message.

OBJECTIVES

- Identify conventions of Anglo-Saxon oral poetry in a text.
- Apply historical context to understand a text.
- Analyze how a text exhibits characteristics of hagiographies.
- Assess a text's effectiveness using the criteria of unity and progression.

VOCABULARY

expound (ĭk-spound′) *tr.v.* To explain in detail; elucidate.

commission (kə-mĭsh′ən) *tr.v.* To authorize or engage (someone to do something).

incarnation (ĭn′kär-nā′shən) *n.* The doctrine that the Son of God was conceived in the womb of Mary and that Jesus is true God and true man.

advent (ăd′vĕnt′) *n.* The coming or arrival of something or someone that is important or worthy of note.

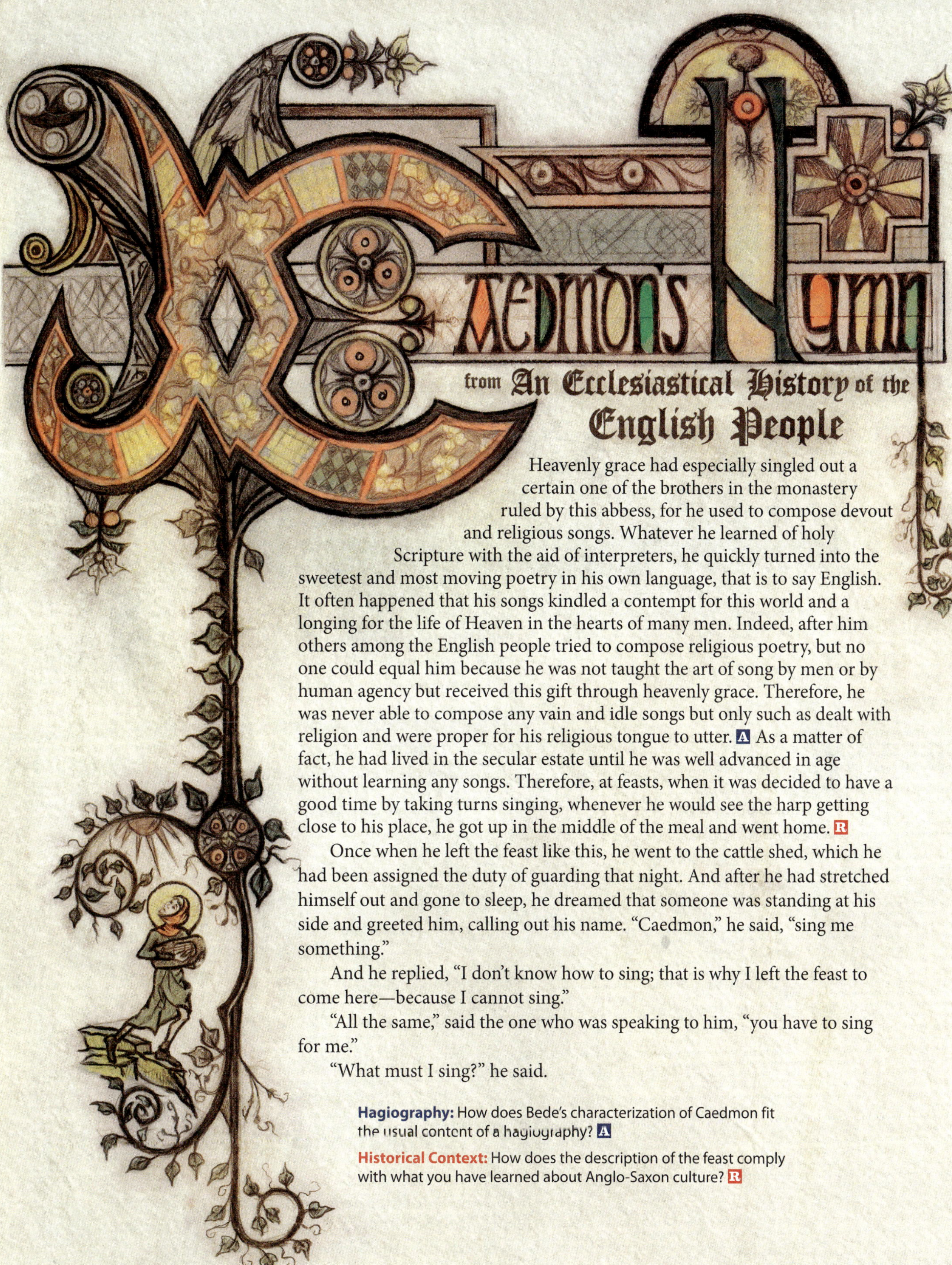

Caedmon's Hymn

from *An Ecclesiastical History of the English People*

Heavenly grace had especially singled out a certain one of the brothers in the monastery ruled by this abbess, for he used to compose devout and religious songs. Whatever he learned of holy Scripture with the aid of interpreters, he quickly turned into the sweetest and most moving poetry in his own language, that is to say English. It often happened that his songs kindled a contempt for this world and a longing for the life of Heaven in the hearts of many men. Indeed, after him others among the English people tried to compose religious poetry, but no one could equal him because he was not taught the art of song by men or by human agency but received this gift through heavenly grace. Therefore, he was never able to compose any vain and idle songs but only such as dealt with religion and were proper for his religious tongue to utter. A As a matter of fact, he had lived in the secular estate until he was well advanced in age without learning any songs. Therefore, at feasts, when it was decided to have a good time by taking turns singing, whenever he would see the harp getting close to his place, he got up in the middle of the meal and went home. R

Once when he left the feast like this, he went to the cattle shed, which he had been assigned the duty of guarding that night. And after he had stretched himself out and gone to sleep, he dreamed that someone was standing at his side and greeted him, calling out his name. "Caedmon," he said, "sing me something."

And he replied, "I don't know how to sing; that is why I left the feast to come here—because I cannot sing."

"All the same," said the one who was speaking to him, "you have to sing for me."

"What must I sing?" he said.

Hagiography: How does Bede's characterization of Caedmon fit the usual content of a hagiography? A

Historical Context: How does the description of the feast comply with what you have learned about Anglo-Saxon culture? R

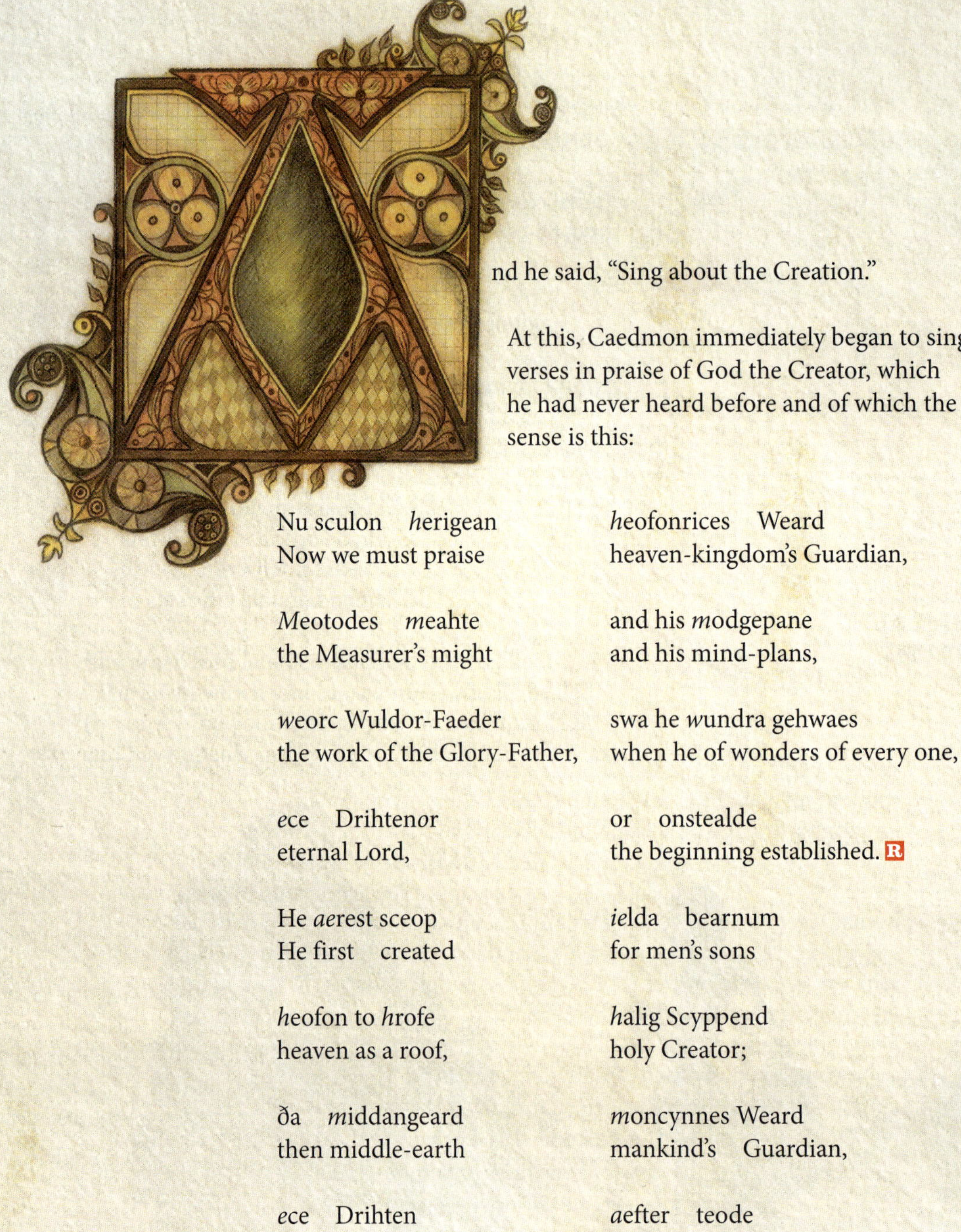

A nd he said, "Sing about the Creation."

At this, Caedmon immediately began to sing verses in praise of God the Creator, which he had never heard before and of which the sense is this:

Nu sculon *h*erigean *h*eofonrices Weard
Now we must praise heaven-kingdom's Guardian,

*M*eotodes *m*eahte and his *m*odgepane
the Measurer's might and his mind-plans,

*w*eorc Wuldor-Faeder swa he *w*undra gehwaes
the work of the Glory-Father, when he of wonders of every one,

*e*ce Drihten*or* or onstealde
eternal Lord, the beginning established. **R**

He *ae*rest sceop *ie*lda bearnum
He first created for men's sons

*h*eofon to *h*rofe *h*alig Scyppend
heaven as a roof, holy Creator;

ða *m*iddangeard *m*oncynnes Weard
then middle-earth mankind's Guardian,

*e*ce Drihten *a*efter teode
eternal Lord, afterwards made—

*f*irum *f*oldan *F*rea *a*elmihtig
for men earth, Master almighty. **E**

This is the general sense but not the exact order of the words that he sang in his sleep; for it is impossible to make a literal translation, no matter how well-written, of poetry into another language without losing some of the beauty and dignity. When he woke up, he remembered everything that he had sung in his sleep, and to this he soon added, in the same poetic measure, more verses praising God.

Historical Context: What feature of Anglo-Saxon poetry do the italicized letters in the Old English lines point out? Do you see any other conventions present? **R**

Aesthetic Effectiveness: Where does the process of Creation begin? Where does it move to? **E**

The next morning he went to the reeve, who was his foreman, and told him about the gift he had received. He was taken to the abbess and ordered to tell his dream and to recite his song to an audience of the most learned men so that they might judge what the nature of that vision was and where it came from. It was evident to all of them that he had been granted the heavenly grace of God. Then they **expounded** some bit of sacred story or teaching to him, and instructed him to turn it into poetry if he could. He agreed and went away. And when he came back the next morning, he gave back what had been **commissioned** to him in the finest verse.

Therefore, the abbess, who cherished the grace of God in this man, instructed him to give up secular life and to take monastic vows. And when she and all those subject to her had received him into the community of brothers, she gave orders that he be taught the whole sequence of sacred history. He remembered everything that he was able to learn by listening, and turning it over in his mind like a clean beast that chews the cud, he converted it into sweetest song, which sounded so delightful that he made his teachers, in their turn, his listeners. He sang about the creation of the world and the origin of the human race and all the history of Genesis; about the exodus of Israel out of Egypt and entrance into the promised land; and about many other stories of sacred Scripture, about the Lord's **incarnation**, and his passion, resurrection, and ascension into Heaven; about the **advent** of the Holy Spirit and the teachings of the apostles. He also made many songs about the terror of the coming judgment and the horror of the punishments of hell and the sweetness of the heavenly kingdom; and a great many others besides about divine grace and justice in all of which he sought to draw men away from the love of sin and to inspire them with delight in the practice of good works.

expound (ĭk-spound′) *tr.v.* To explain in detail; elucidate.

commission (kə-mĭsh′ən) *tr.v.* To authorize or engage (someone to do something).

incarnation (ĭn′kär-nā′shən) *n.* The doctrine that the Son of God was conceived in the womb of Mary and that Jesus is true God and true man.

advent (ăd′vĕnt′) *n.* The coming or arrival of something or someone that is important or worthy of note.

THINK AND DISCUSS

1. What was the setting for Caedmon's dream? Why was Caedmon there?
2. What did Caedmon see and hear in his dream? Who else was in it?
3. Compare and contrast Caedmon before and after his dream. How does he remain the same? How does he change?
4. How does Caedmon's story reflect the genre of hagiography?
5. Identify the poem's seven epithets. How do they develop the theme of the story?
6. Choose two other conventions of Old English oral poetry noted on page 18. Cite examples of each from the text.
7. Evaluate the reliability of this story. Might a miracle have occurred? If it did not, does that discount the whole story? Why or why not?
8. Why might Caedmon have employed so many epithets and kennings in the poem? What does their use of metaphor and variation contribute to a reader's experience of the poem? How might the poem and its imagery follow the principles of unity and progression?
9. How might this story have helped Bede fulfill his overall purpose for his history? What responses might its content have produced in his audience?
10. Explain how the poem illustrates at least one of these three elements of quality literature: Truth, Beauty, and Goodness. Briefly cite details from the text to support your answer.

Popular Genres

Much of the literature you have studied so far was enjoyed only by England's elite because most people of the era were illiterate. Oral genres, however, flourished among the general populace. The riddle, the ballad, and simple songs were among the most common of these popular genres (i.e., genres enjoyed by the general populace). Interestingly, all three are still alive and well in contemporary cultures.

Anglo-Saxon Riddles

The riddle is a form of guessing game present in most cultures' folklore since ancient times. A speaker presents a series of images or scenarios describing a person, place, object, or event. These images are meant to mislead as much as they are to inform. Purposes for riddles vary. In many traditional stories they can be a test of a person's wisdom and worthiness. In ordinary life, they are used as a form of communal entertainment, delighting and confounding audiences by the riddler's cleverness. Anglo-Saxons loved riddles, and many from that time still survive. The origins of these vary; some are anonymous, while others came from Latin riddles composed by Anglo-Saxon churchmen. The topics they cover range widely, including the sacred and the secular, common and unusual, animate and inanimate, and more. Stylistically, some are aimed at broad audiences and make their answers fairly obvious while others aimed at the learned are deliberately obscure. To modern audiences, many are still decipherable and illuminate facets of Anglo-Saxon life. But some are baffling and probably unsolvable today given the cultural gap.

Medieval Songs

Much like today, one of the most common forms of literature in medieval culture was song lyrics. With no musical notation or literate community, songs were mostly passed along by singing them. They could be sung alone or as a community to worship, to while away an evening, or to make work more fun. Lyrics encompassed a wide variety of topics from the secular to the sacred.

A purely secular song, "The Cuckoo Song" (p. 73; also known as "Sumer is icumen in") celebrates summer's arrival. The song exemplifies a round, in which singers begin the melody one by one in succession as the previous singer reaches a specific point in the song. Other common secular song themes included war, chivalry, and courtly love; satirical songs, even ones aimed at the Church, were not uncommon.

On the other hand, "I sing of a maiden" is a medieval hymn. Most popular hymns were written by literate clergy and taught to the illiterate masses. They were fairly simple and memorable and could be sung for enjoyment as much as for worship. The topic of this hymn was a very common one: the virgin Mary. The veneration of Mary was prevalent in common life, partially because, to many, she was a much more relatable, less intimidating figure than many other saints or Church figures. Perhaps for similar reasons, Christ's love was also a common theme in medieval hymns.

Folk Ballads

Oral storytelling has long been used to preserve accounts of interesting historical events and personages, to exemplify a culture's values and point of view, or simply to entertain. During the Middle English era, such stories were combined with song into a new form, the folk ballad. Folk **ballads** are narrative poems of folk origin, intended to be sung and consisting of simple stanzas usually with a refrain. They present dramatic, engaging stories (e.g., tragic accidents, heroic deeds, unrequited love, murderous acts, and sudden disasters) in compressed form using broad strokes. Though often performed by traveling minstrels, anyone could easily sing them. Medieval folk ballads provide valuable glimpses into everyday life and attitudes of the time.

DID YOU KNOW ?

A favorite target of medieval humor or satire was married life.

ANALYZE: *Oral Genre Features and Folk Ballads*

These three genres—riddles, songs, and folk ballads—possess characteristics common to oral literature. To begin with, the author or speaker is anonymous; his or her identity and feelings are in the background. This personal distance allows a work to be presented by a variety of performers in their own way. Also, the genres are brief and concentrated: the riddles are very short but packed with ideas, for example. Finally, they use repetition for ease in remembering and retelling and for pure enjoyment. For instance, songs (including ballads) often incorporate a **refrain** (i.e., a line, part of a line, or group of lines repeated throughout).

Songs have additional requirements such as using stanza form, incorporating sound devices (e.g., rhyme), and developing their topics with imagery and figurative language. The **folk ballad** has its own specific characteristics. It must be a narrative, and the story must be condensed. Thus, sudden shifts—in setting, action, or dialogue—are frequent, making audiences fill in details themselves. Also, many ballads follow a specific form, the ballad stanza. **Ballad stanzas** are quatrains; the first and third lines contain four stresses and no rhyme while the second and fourth have three stresses as well as rhyme. As you read, notice how the pieces reflect characteristics common to oral literature or unique to their specific genres.

READ: *Read Poetry Aloud, Infer Meaning*

Read the following pieces aloud as they were meant to be enjoyed. Notice how their compression keeps listeners' attention or how other genre requirements enhance audience enjoyment. For example, how does ballad stanza add excitement to a story performed aloud? Next, focus on each text's details, inferring what they contribute to overall meaning. Pose questions to discover the purpose of certain details: What double meanings could a riddle's images suggest? Who (or what) speaks in a work, and what actions do characters take? How is the audience encouraged to view these facts?

EVALUATE: *Theme*

Ballads treat a variety of subjects (serious and otherwise), but many concern some kind of injustice—societal, domestic, or romantic. With well-chosen details, ballads raise strong feelings toward their subjects. Ballads often work to rally popular opinion in behalf of a point of view, and they still sometimes serve as vehicles of social criticism today. As you read, determine what expressions of injustice these ballads address.

OBJECTIVES

- Analyze ballads, songs, and riddles for characteristics of these genres.
- Read a work aloud to appreciate its craft.
- Infer a work's meanings from its details.
- Evaluate a theme of injustice from a biblical perspective.

VOCABULARY

grievous (grē′vəs) *adj.* Causing grief, pain, or anguish.

gape (gāp, găp) *intr.v.* To be or become open or wide.

resound (rĭ-zound′) *intr.v.* To be filled with sound; reverberate.

baleful (bāl′fəl) *adj.* Harmful or malignant in intent or effect.

How can LITERATURE *bring us together?*

Literature is rarely a solitary affair: plays require an audience, people share books they enjoy with others, and most of us have told ghost stories or sung songs around a campfire surrounded by friends. Imagine a medieval scop similarly holding listeners spellbound. How do experiences like these build a sense of community? Working with a partner, list several ways in which people can bond over literature, giving examples for each. Share these with your class.

Popular Genres

Anglo-Saxon Riddles

1

I'm by nature solitary, scarred by spear
And wounded by sword, weary of battle.
I frequently see the face of war, and fight
Hateful enemies; yet I hold no hope
Of help being brought to me in the battle,
Before I'm eventually done to death.
In the stronghold of the city the sharp-edged
 swords,
Skilfully forged in the flame by smiths,
Bite deeply into me. I can but await
A more fearsome encounter; it is not for me
To discover in the city any of those doctors
Who heal **grievous** wounds with roots and herbs.
The scars from sword wounds **gape** wider and
 wider;
Death blows are dealt me by day and by night. R

grievous (grē′vəs) *adj.* Causing grief, pain, or anguish.

gape (gāp, găp) *intr.v.* To be or become open or wide.

Infer Meaning: Make a list of the personal details that the speaker shares. What do they tell you about what the speaker is, or perhaps cannot be? R

2

A curious, fair creature came floating on the
 waves,
Shouting out to the distant shores,
Resounding very loudly; her laughter was terrible
And fearsome to all. Sharp were her edges.
She is slow to join battle but severe in the fray,
Smashing great ships with savagery.
She binds them with **baleful** charm,
And speaks with characteristic cunning:
'My mother, one of the beloved maidens,
Is my daughter also, swollen and strong,
Known by all people as she falls on the earth,
Welcomed with love through the width of all
 lands.' R

resound (rĭ-zound′) *intr.v.* To be filled with sound; reverberate.

baleful (bāl′fəl) *adj.* Harmful or malignant in intent or effect.

Infer Meaning: Reread the riddle. Is this a human, an object, or an animal? Try restating the clues without the poetic imagery attached. R

Ballads

Sir Patrick Spens

I. The Sailing.

The king sits in Dunfermline town°
 Drinking the blude°-red wine;
'O whare will I get a skeely° skipper
 To sail this new ship o' mine?'

O up and spak an eldern knight,
 Sat at the king's right knee:
'Sir Patrick Spens is the best sailor
 That ever sail'd the sea.' A

Our king has written a braid° letter,
 And seal'd it with his hand,
And sent it to Sir Patrick Spens,
 Was walking on the strand.°

. . . .

'The first word that Sir Patrick read
 So loud, loud laugh'd he;
The neist° word that Sir Patrick read
 The tear blinded his e'e.°

1 **Dunfermline town:** a town several miles inland from the Firth of Forth opposite Edinburgh; capital of Scotland for six centuries

2 **blude:** blood

3 **skeely:** "skillful" (*OED*)

9 **braid:** broad (on a large sheet of paper: i.e., a royal decree)

12 **strand:** "land, typically a beach, bordering a body of water" (*AHD*)

15 **neist:** next

16 **e'e:** eye

Ballad: Count the number of stresses in each line of stanzas 1 and 2. Which lines in each stanza end in rhyming words? A

'O wha is this has done this deed
And tauld the king o' me,
To send us out, at this time o' year,
To sail upon the sea?

'Be it wind, be it weet, be it hail, be it sleet,
Our ship must sail the faem;°
The king's daughter o' Noroway,
'Tis we must fetch her hame.'

. . . .

II. The Return.

'Mak ready, mak ready, my merry men a'! **R**
Our gude ship sails the morn.'—
'Now ever alack, my master dear,
I fear a deadly storm.

'I saw the new moon late yestreen°
Wi' the auld moon in her arm;
And if we gang to sea, master,
I fear we' ll come to harm.'

They hadna sail'd a league, a league, **A**
A league but barely three,
When the lift° grew dark, and the wind blew loud,
And gurly° grew the sea.

The ankers brak, and the topmast lap,°
It was sic a deadly storm:
And the waves cam owre the broken ship
Till a' her sides were torn.

. . . .

'O laith,° laith were our gude Scots lords
To wet their cork-heel'd shoon;°
But lang or a'° the play was play'd
They wat their hats aboon.°

And mony was the feather bed
That flatter'd° on the faem;
And mony was the gude lord's son
That never mair cam hame.

O lang, lang may the ladies sit,
Wi' their fans into their hand,
Before they see Sir Patrick Spens
Come sailing to the strand!

And lang, lang may the maidens sit
Wi' their gowd kames° in their hair,
A-waiting for their ain° dear loves!
For them they' ll see nae mair. **R**

Half-owre,° half-owre to Aberdour,°
'Tis fifty fathoms deep;
And there lies gude Sir Patrick Spens,
Wi' the Scots lords at his feet!

22 **faem:** foam

VISUAL ANALYSIS
What qualities of ballad narratives does the artist illustrate in the way he has constructed his image?

29 **yestreen:** last night

35 **lift:** sky

36 **gurly:** "boisterous, stormy, rough" (*OED*)

37 **lap:** sprang

41 **laith:** loath, reluctant

42 **shoon:** shoes

43 **lang or a':** long before all

44 **aboon:** above (them)

46 **flatter'd:** tossed afloat

54 **gowd kames:** gold combs

55 **ain:** own

57 **Half-owre:** halfway over / **Aberdour:** coastal town on the Firth of Forth opposite Edinburgh several miles from Dunfermline.

Read Aloud: What effect does the repetition in lines 13–15, 21, and 25 create when read aloud? **R**

Ballad: What shift owing to ballads' compression occurs between lines 32 and 33? **A**

Infer Meaning: How does the speaker convey that people died in the wreck? **R**

Get Up and Bar the Door

It fell about the Martinmas° time,
And a gay time it was then,
When our goodwife got puddings to make,°
And she's boil'd them in the pan.

The wind sae cauld° blew south and north,
And blew into the floor;
Quoth our goodman° to our goodwife,
'Gae out and bar the door.'—°

'My hand is in my hussyfskap,°
Goodman, as ye may see;
An' it shou'dna° be barr'd this hundred year,
It's no be barr'd for° me.' R

They made a paction 'tween them twa,°
They made it firm and sure,
That the first word whae'er° shou'd speak,
Shou'd rise and bar the door.

Then by there came two gentlemen,
At twelve o' clock at night,
And they could neither see house nor hall,
Nor coal nor candle-light.

'Now whether is this a rich man's house,
Or whether is it a poor?'
But ne'er a word wad ane o'° them speak,
For barring of the door.

And first they ate the white puddings,
And then they ate the black.
Tho' muckle° thought the goodwife to hersel'
Yet ne'er a word she spake.

Then said the one unto the other,
'Here, man, tak ye my knife;
Do ye tak aff the auld man's beard,°
And I'll kiss the goodwife.'—

'But there's nae water in the house,
And what shall we do than?'—
'What ails ye at the pudding-broo,°
That boils into the pan?'

O up then started our goodman,
An angry man was he:
'Will ye kiss my wife before my een,
And sca'd° me wi' pudding-bree?'°

Then up and started our goodwife,
Gied° three skips on the floor:
'Goodman, you've spoken the foremost word!
Get up and bar the door.' R

1 **Martinmas:** feast of St. Martin, Nov. 11

3 **goodwife . . . make:** The mistress of the house was making sausages.

5 **sae cauld:** so cold

7 **goodman:** master of the house

8 **Gae . . . the door:** Go out and latch the door.

9 **My hand . . . hussyfskap:** I'm busy with housewifery.

11 **An' it shou'dna:** If it should not

12 **It's . . . for:** It won't be barred by

13 **paction . . . twa:** an agreement between the two

15 **whae'er:** whoever

23 **wad ane o':** would one of

27 **muckle:** much

31 **tak . . . beard:** take off the old man's beard

35 **What . . . pudding broo:** What's wrong with the pudding broth?

40 **sca' d:** scald / **bree:** -broth

42 **Gied:** gave

Infer Meaning: Note that this stanza contains dialogue. What mood or tone does the dialogue in this ballad usually enhance? R

Infer Meaning: What do you think is the ballad's topic? What message does the writer seem to imply about that topic? R

Medieval Lyrics

The Cuckoo Song

Summer is[1] come in,
Loud sing, cuckoo![2]
Groweth seed, and bloweth mead,[3]
And spring'th the wood now,
Sing cuckoo.

Ewe bleateth after lamb,
Loweth after calf [the] cow;
Bullock starteth,[4] buck verteth,[5]

Merry sing, cuckoo,
Cuckoo, cuckoo!
Well sing'st thou, cuckoo,
Nor cease thou never now.

Sing, cuckoo, now; sing, cuckoo;
Sing, cuckoo; sing, cuckoo, now! **A**

1. *is:* has
2. *cuckoo:* a migrant bird associated with the return of warm weather
3. *bloweth mead:* the meadow blooms
4. *starteth:* leaps, jumps
5. *verteth:* Some sources have translated this word "turneth," as in "turning and darting about." Most sources, however, translate it "farteth."

Genre Characteristics: What common feature of songs do these two lines illustrate? **A**

I sing of a maiden

I sing of a maiden
That is makeless;[1]
King of all kings
To her son she ches.[2]

He came al so[3] still
There his mother was,
As dew in April
That falleth on the grass.

He came al so still
To his mother's bower,
As dew in April
That falleth on the flower.

He came al so still
There his mother lay,
As dew in April
That falleth on the spray.[4] **A**

Mother and maiden
Was never none but she;
Well may such a lady
Goddes[5] mother be.

1. *makeless:* matchless
2. *ches:* chose
3. *also:* as
4. *spray:* "small or slender twigs of trees or shrubs" (*OED*)
5. *Goddes:* possessive, as in "God's mother"

Genre Characteristics: What kind of figurative language do stanzas 2–4 contain? What do these images convey about the subject they describe? **A**

THINK AND DISCUSS

1. For what purpose were ballads written? Why do riddles, ballads, and songs all belong with the literature of community?
2. Define *ballad stanza*.
3. What formal feature do many ballads and songs share?
4. Choose one of the riddles and explain one or two ways its details led you astray. Which detail helped you finally understand the answer?
5. Choose one of the songs and explain its simple message. Cite details from the text to support your answer.
6. Does "Sir Patrick Spens" reflect the typical characteristics of the ballad genre? Cite details from the text in your answer.
7. What is the overall tone of "Get Up and Bar the Door"? List and illustrate from the text two techniques that help create that tone.
8. What were the husband's and wife's reasons for their refusal to bar the door? Was either justified in refusing? What was the potential consequence? Which side does the ballad seem to favor?
9. Briefly trace how one or the other ballad deals with the theme of injustice.
10. Choose one song and one ballad and analyze how each measures up to the criteria of Truth, Goodness, and Beauty. How can the literature of community help reinforce and develop biblical values?

Julian of Norwich (ca. 1342–1416)

AT A GLANCE

- **1370s** Entered her cell as an anchoress
- **1373** Received her revelation or "showings" at age 30
- **1393** Completed the Long Text

Anonymous Anchoress

The given name of the first woman to write a book in English (that survived) has been lost to us. An anchoress, she adopted solitary seclusion for a life of prayer and devotion to God. Like most anchoresses, she lived closed in a cell attached to the outside wall of her church, the Church of St. Julian in Norwich. For this reason she is called Julian of Norwich or Lady Julian, referring to the church's saint.

Julian entered her cell in the early 1370s around age thirty. Historians are unsure whether she was single or a widow, perhaps having lost her family to plague, which was rampant in Norwich at the time. We do know, however, that Julian developed a reputation as a spiritual adviser to the community and was sought out. If Julian's anchorhold (an anchorite's cell) was typical, she would have had at least two openings or windows in the church wall: one through which to see Mass and another to talk with those who sought advice. Unfortunately, Julian's original cell was destroyed and the church badly damaged in World War II. Only the church was rebuilt.

Mystic and Writer

Julian's sole work stemmed from a serious illness in May of 1373 when she was thirty. Everyone, including Julian herself, thought it would take her life. Consequently, the last rites were administered to her. During the sacrament, with her eyes fixed on the crucifix held in the air, Julian reported that Christ's body appeared to bleed. Thus began the first of sixteen mystic "showings" or revelatory visions of Christ's sufferings she purported to experience.

Julian recovered from her illness and wrote about her visions soon afterward. Because she had previously prayed to be more conscious of Christ's sufferings, she meditated on the lessons she had gleaned about sin and God's love. By at least twenty years later she had expanded her original writing to the longer version known today as *Revelations of Divine Love*. This work uses her visions as a springboard for a theological exploration of her main themes. Julian called herself "unlettered," perhaps meaning she had a limited formal education. Nonetheless, she wrote stylistically beautiful and clear Middle English prose that she enlivened with apt and unpretentious imagery. Julian revised this version several times, and in the end, produced a classic of British literature that still resonates with readers today.

A view of the reconstructed St. Julian's Church in Norwich.

DID YOU KNOW ?

Before entering her cell, an anchoress was often symbolically laid on a funeral bier and given last rites. The cell might also contain an open grave in which the anchoress would be buried upon her actual death.

ANALYZE: *Devotional Literature and Imagery*

Revelations of Divine Love is an example of Christian **devotional literature**. Unlike theological or doctrinal treatises intended for professionally trained readers, devotional literature addresses church laity. Its main purpose is not to expound doctrines or explicate passages (though it can do both) but rather to encourage individuals to deepen their devotion to God. Like much devotional literature, Julian's *Revelations* is reflective in mode, contemplating her past visions.

To make spiritual ideas concrete, Julian uses a variety of images. Broadly defined, **imagery** refers to descriptions based on sense perceptions (visual, tactile, auditory, etc.). It can also more narrowly refer to the figurative language used to convey these images. Julian's images are usually either biblical or "homely" (i.e., familiar, unpretentious) analogies of her own. Christ himself used homely images—simple, concrete images from daily life. For example, his Parable of the Sower uses farming imagery. Many of Julian's images possess a similar profound simplicity. Some also allude to biblical imagery (e.g., using blindness to represent sin). As you read, note the text's imagery as well as characteristics of devotional literature. Consider how the imagery contributes to Julian's devotional purpose.

READ: *Nonfiction Text Structures*

Examining **text structures** reveals how a writer has chosen to organize the information in a text. Five common patterns for structuring nonfiction texts are (1) description/list, (2) sequence/time order, (3) compare/contrast, (4) cause/effect, and (5) problem/solution. These reflect how a text's ideas relate to each other. To create or reinforce the pattern, writers use **signal words**, verbal cues that guide readers through the writer's train of thought. For instance, a compare/contrast text might use *similarly* or *on the other hand*. The following selections from *Revelations of Divine Love* use two of these structures: sequence/time order and problem/solution. As you read, look for signal words (e.g., *first, second, after* or *problem, question, why, answer,* respectively). Determine which chapter follows a sequence/time order structure and which follows a problem/solution structure.

EVALUATE: *Sin and God's Love*

The title *Revelations of Divine Love* reveals Julian's subject matter: the love of God. As you have read, she says that she received sixteen visions that dealt with various aspects of God's love. After she received the visions, she wrestled with their meaning and tried to reconcile what she had been shown about the love of God with basic Christian doctrine. In particular, she struggled to understand how a loving God could allow sin. Chapters 27 and 82 address the topics of the purpose of sin and the view of the sinner from God's perspective as opposed to mankind's. As you read these chapters, try to identify the dilemmas she felt and the conclusions she came to. Do you think her conclusions are biblically sound? Read these passages before forming your evaluations: Deuteronomy 32:4; Job 42:2–3; Habakkuk 1:13, 3:17–19; Ephesians 1:11; Romans 3:21–26, 11:33.

OBJECTIVES

- Analyze a text's imagery, themes, and characteristics of devotional literature.
- Identify a passage's organizational structure.
- Evaluate an author's theological views on sin and God's love.

VOCABULARY

contrition (kən-trĭsh′ən) *n.* Sincere remorse for wrongdoing; repentance.

rite (rīt) *n.* The prescribed or customary form for conducting a religious or other solemn ceremony.

assent (ə-sĕnt′) *intr.v.* To express agreement or acceptance.

abnegation (ăb′nĭ-gā′shən) *n.* Self-denial.

tribulation (trĭb′yə-lā′shən) *n.* Great affliction, trial, or distress; suffering.

inestimably (ĭn-ĕs′tə-mə-blē) *adv.* In an *inestimable* (*adj.* Impossible to estimate or compute) manner or degree.

What can SUFFERING *teach us?*

We often feel sympathy for someone going through a difficult circumstance—a relative recovering from a car accident, a friend with divorcing parents, a teammate battling cancer—or perhaps experiencing painful consequences for his or her own actions. But we usually don't want the suffering for ourselves. In fact, the idea of suffering scares us. Nevertheless, sometimes we can learn from hardships small and large, even ones we have brought on ourselves. And sometimes they teach us lessons we cannot learn any other way. Briefly write down some practical life lessons you have learned through suffering.

FROM

REVELATIONS OF DIVINE LOVE

from Chapter 2

Concerning the time of [her] revelations, and how she made three petitions.

These revelations were shown to a simple, uneducated creature[1] in the year of our Lord 1373, on the eighth day of May. This person had already asked for three gifts by the grace of God. The first was to relive his Passion in her mind;[2] the second was bodily sickness; the third was that God would give her three wounds.

As for the first gift, it seemed to me that I had some feeling for the Passion of Christ but I still wanted more, by God's grace. It seemed to me I wished I had been there at that time with Mary Magdalene[3] and with others who loved Christ, so that I might have seen with my own eyes the Passion which our Lord suffered for me, and so that I might have suffered with him as others did who loved him. And so I longed for a vision of him in the flesh, by which I might have more knowledge of the bodily sufferings of our Saviour and of the fellowsuffering of our Lady[4] and of all those who truly loved him and saw his sufferings at that time, for I wanted to be one of them and suffer with him. . . .

The second gift came to my mind with **contrition**, freely and without any seeking: a willing desire to be given a bodily sickness by God. I wanted that sickness to be severe enough as to seem mortal, so that in that illness I might receive all the rites of Holy Church, myself believing that I was to die, and that all who saw me might suppose the same, for I wanted to have no hopes of any fleshly or earthly life. In this sickness I wanted to have every kind of suffering in body and spirit that I would have if I were to die, with all the turbulent terrors and tumults caused by devils, and every other kind of pain, short of the soul's leaving the body. And this was my intention because I wanted to be purged by the mercy of God, and afterwards live more to the glory of God because of that sickness. . . . **R**

contrition (kən-trĭsh'ən) *n.* Sincere remorse for wrongdoing; repentance.

Text Structure: What signal words occur in the first paragraph of Chapter 2 and establish the structure of the paragraphs that follow? **R**

I expressed my two requests about the Passion and the sickness with a condition, for it seemed to me that this was not the usual practice of prayer. So I said, 'Lord, you know what I want, if it is your will that I should have it; and if it is not your will, good Lord, do not be displeased, for I only want what you want.'[5] I asked for this illness in my young days, that I should have it when I was thirty years old.[6]

As for the third gift, by the grace of God and the teaching of Holy Church, I conceived a strong desire to receive three wounds in my life:[7] that is to say, the wound of true contrition, the wound of kind compassion, and the wound of purposeful longing for God. Just as I asked for the other two with a condition, so I asked for this third one urgently without any condition.

The first two of these desires just mentioned passed from my mind, and the third remained with me continually.

---

1. *a simple, uneducated creature:* This may refer to her inability to read and write in Latin, the language of the church and part of formal education of the day. However, it does not mean that she was completely uneducated or unable to read and write in English. In either case, the expression is one of humility.
2. *relive his Passion in his mind:* A practice of medieval religious devotion was to meditate on the Passion of Christ by imagining that one is participating with Christ in His suffering.
3. *there . . . with Mary Magdalene:* See Matthew 27:55–56, 61; Mark 15:40–41, 47; and John 19:25.
4. *our Lady:* Mary, the mother of Jesus
5. *'Lord . . . what you want':* See Matthew 26:39.
6. *thirty years old:* Because Christ started his earthly ministry at age thirty, this was seen as the perfect age.
7. *a strong desire . . . in my life:* Lady Julian is identifying here with St. Cecilia, who was sentenced to be beheaded. The executioner tried three times but failed to end her life. She survived the beheading only to die three days later.

Chapter 3

Concerning the sickness obtained from God by petition.

And when I was thirty and a half years old, God sent me a bodily sickness in which I lay for three days and three nights; and on the fourth night I received all the rites of Holy Church and did not expect to live until morning. And after this I lingered on for two days and two nights. And on the third night I often thought I was about to die, and so did those who were with me. R

rite (rīt) *n.* The prescribed or customary form for conducting a religious or other solemn ceremony.

Text Structures: What signal words appear in the first paragraph? What do they tell you about the structure of the narrative to follow? R

And being still young, I thought it was a great pity to die, but this was not because of anything on earth that I wanted to live for, nor because I was afraid of any pain, for I trusted in God's mercy. But it was because I wanted to live so as to have loved God better and for longer, in order that I might, through the grace of that living, have more knowledge and love of God in the bliss of heaven. For all the time that I had lived here seemed to me so little and so brief in comparison with that unending bliss—I thought it as nothing. So I thought, 'Good Lord, may my living no longer be to your glory!' And I understood in my reason and through the sensation of my pains that I was going to die. And with the will of my heart I fully **assented** to be at God's will.

assent (ə-sĕnt′) *intr.v.* To express agreement or acceptance.

So I lasted till day, and by then my body was dead from the waist down, as it felt to me. Then I wanted to be propped up, leaning back and supported, so that my heart could be more freely at God's will, and so that I could think of God while my life should last. My curate[8] was sent for to be present at my end, and by the time he came my eyes were fixed and I could not speak. He set the cross before my face and said, 'I have brought you the image of your maker and Saviour. Look at it and take comfort from it.'

It seemed to me that I was all right as I was, for my gaze was fixed upwards into heaven where I trusted I was going, by God's mercy. But nevertheless I consented to fix my eyes on the face of the crucifix if I could, and so I did, for it seemed to me that I could manage to look straight ahead of me for longer than I could look upwards. After this my sight began to fail, and all grew dark around me in the room, as though it had been night, except for the image of the cross in which I saw a light for all mankind—I did not know how. Everything apart from the cross was ugly to me, as if much crowded with fiends.

After this the upper part of my body began to die to such an extent that I hardly had any sensation. My greatest pain was my shortness of breath and the ebbing away of life. And then I truly believed that I was at the point of death. And suddenly, at that moment, all my pain was taken from me and I was as well, especially in the upper part of my body, as I ever was before. I was astonished at this sudden change, for it seemed to me a mysterious act of God, not of nature. And yet I had no more confidence that I would live because I felt this relief; nor did feeling more comfortable in this way fully comfort me, for it seemed to me I would rather have been released from this world, because my heart was willingly set upon that.

Then it suddenly came to mind that I ought to wish for the second wound, as a gift and a grace from our Lord, so that my body might be filled with recollection and feeling of his blessed Passion, as I had prayed before; for I wanted his pains to be my pains, with compassion, and then longing for God. So it seemed to me that, through his grace, I might have the wounds which I had wanted before. But in this I never asked for any bodily vision or any kind of revelation from God, but for compassion, such as it seemed to me a naturally sympathetic soul might feel for our Lord Jesus, who for love was willing to become a mortal man. And I longed to suffer with him, while living in my mortal body, as God would give me grace.

8. *curate:* the religious leader of a parish

from Chapter 5

How God is to us everything that is good, tenderly enfolding us; and everything that is made is as nothing, compared with almighty God; and how a man has no rest until he counts himself and everything as nothing for the love of God.

Our Lord showed me spiritually in a vision how intimately he loves us. I saw that he is to us everything that is good and comforting for our help. He is our clothing that out of love enwraps us and enfolds us, embraces us and wholly encloses us, surrounding us for tender love, so that he can never leave us. And so in this vision I saw that he is everything that is good, as I understand it. **A**

Imagery: What imagery appears in this paragraph? What does it illustrate? **A**

And in this vision he also showed a little thing, the size of a hazelnut, lying in the palm of my hand, as it seemed to me, and it was round as a ball. I looked at it with my mind's eye and thought, 'What can this be?' And the answer came in a general way, like this, 'It is all that is made.' I wondered how it could last, for it seemed to me so small that it might have disintegrated suddenly into nothingness. And I was answered in my understanding, 'It lasts, and always will, because God loves it; and in the same way everything has its being through the love of God.'

In this little thing I saw three properties: the first is that God made it; the second is that God loves it; the third is that God cares for it. But what is that to me? Truly, the maker, the carer, and the lover. For until I am of one substance with him I can never have complete rest nor true happiness; that is to say, until I am so joined to him that there is no created thing between my God and me. It seemed to me that this little thing that is made might have disintegrated into nothing because of its smallness. We need to know about this so as to delight in setting at nought everything that is made in order to love and possess God who is unmade.[9] For this is the reason why we are not entirely at ease in heart and soul: because we seek rest here in these things which are so small and in which there is no rest, and do not know our God who is almighty, all wise, all good; for he is true rest. God wishes to be known, and is pleased that we should rest in him; for all that is beneath him is not enough for us; and this is the reason why no soul is at rest until it counts as nothing all that is created. When a soul has willingly made itself as nothing for love, in order to have him who is all, then he is able to receive spiritual rest. **A**

Imagery: What image is introduced in the second paragraph and developed in this paragraph? What does the image illustrate? **A**

. . . This is the natural yearnings of the soul touched by the Holy Spirit: 'God, of your goodness, give me yourself; for you are enough for me, and I cannot ask for anything less that would fully honour you. And if I do ask for anything less, I shall always be in want, but in you alone I have everything.'

. . . He has made us only for himself, and restored us by his blessed Passion, and sustains us in his blessed love, and all this is out of his goodness.

Chapter 27

The thirteenth revelation is that our Lord God wishes us to have great regard to all his deeds that he has done in creating all things with great nobility; and how sin is recognized only by the suffering.

After this, the Lord brought to mind the longing that I had for him before;[10] and I saw that nothing held me back except sin, and I saw that this is so with all of us in general. And it seemed to me that if there had been no sin, we should all have been pure and like our Lord, as he made us; and so, in my folly, I had often wondered before this time why, through the great foreseeing wisdom of God, the beginning of sin was not prevented; for then, it seemed to

9. *setting at nought . . . unmade:* See the theme of abnegation in Chapter 27.
10. *the longing . . . before:* i.e., the purposeful longing for God; see the third wound in Chapter 2.

me, all would have been well. I should have given up such thoughts, yet I grieved and sorrowed over this, unreasonably and without discretion. But Jesus, who in this vision informed me of everything needful to me, answered with these words and said, 'Sin is befitting, but all shall be well, and all shall be well, and all manner of things shall be well.'[11] **R**

Text Structure: What problem, or question, is mentioned in this first paragraph? Is an answer to the problem introduced? **R**

In this unadorned word 'sin', our Lord brought to mind everything in general which is not good, and the shameful scorn and the uttermost abnegation that he bore for us in this life, and his dying, and all the pains and sufferings in body and spirit of all his creatures—for we are all in part set at nought, and we shall be set at nought,[12] following the example of our master Jesus, until we are fully purged: that is to say, until our mortal flesh is made as nothing, and all our inward feelings which are not truly good. And in contemplating this, together with all the sufferings that ever were or ever shall be, I understand Christ's Passion as the greatest and most surpassing suffering. And all this was shown in an instant and quickly turned into consolation; for our good Lord did not wish the soul to be frightened by this ugly sight.

abnegation (ăb′nĭ-gā′shən) *n.* Self-denial.

But I did not see sin, for I believe it has no kind of substance nor share of being, nor could it be recognized except by the suffering it causes. And, as it seems to me, this suffering is something that exists for a while, because it purges us and makes us know ourselves and ask for mercy, for the Passion of our Lord is a comfort to us against all this, and that is his blessed will. And because of the tender love which our good Lord has for all who shall be saved, he comforts us readily and sweetly, meaning this, 'It is true that sin is cause of all this suffering, but all shall be well, and all shall be well, and all manner of things shall be well.' **E**

Sin and God's Love: What comforts the Christian who is troubled by the suffering of sin? **E**

These words were said very tenderly, indicating no kind of blame for me or for anyone who will be saved. So it would be most unkind to blame God or marvel at him because of my sin, since he does not blame me for sin.[13]

And in these same words I saw a marvellous and exalted mystery hidden in God, a mystery which he will make openly known to us in heaven, in which knowledge we shall truly see the reason why he allowed sin to come about; and in the sight of this we shall rejoice in our Lord God forever.

Chapter 82

God regards the lamenting of the soul with pity and not with blame, and yet we do nothing but sin, and in this we are kept in joy and in fear; for he wants us to turn to him, clinging readily to his love, seeing that he is our medicine; and so we must love, in longing and in rejoicing, and anything contrary to this comes not from God but from the enemy.

But here our courteous Lord showed the lamenting and the mourning of the soul, with this meaning: 'I am well aware that you wish to live for love of me, cheerfully and gladly bearing all the suffering that may come to you; but in as much as you do not live without sin, you are therefore depressed and sorrowful, and if you could live without sin you are willing to suffer for love of me all the misery, and all the tribulation and distress that could come to you. And it is true. But do not be upset too much by sin that you commit against your will.'

tribulation (trĭb′yə-lā′shən) *n.* Great affliction, trial, or distress; suffering.

11. *Sin is befitting . . . shall be well:* The word *befitting* means "appropriate," or "suitable." God's grace to humanity in the incarnation was not caused by Adam's fall, as if it caught Him by surprise, but was actually part of His plan from eternity (1 Peter 1:18–20, Ephesians 3:7–12, Romans 8:28). His eternal plan and its redemptive purpose do indeed make sin "suitable."

12. *we are all . . . set at nought:* The "set at nought" phrase is a reiteration of the concept of self-denial (abnegation), of which Christ is the best example. As Christ denied himself in the incarnation, so too Christians should deny themselves in this life.

13. *These words . . . blame me for sin:* See the reference to blame in Chapter 82 (footnote 14).

And here I understood that the Lord regards the servant with pity and not with blame, for in this passing life we are not asked to live entirely free of sin and blame.[14] He loves us without end, and we sin habitually, and he reveals this to us most gently; and then we sorrow and mourn appropriately, turning to the contemplation of his mercy, holding fast to his love and goodness, seeing that he is our medicine, knowing that we do nothing but sin.

And so by the humility that we gain through seeing our sin, faithfully recognizing his everlasting love, thanking and praising him, we please him. 'I love you and you love me; and our love shall not be divided in two, and it is for your benefit that I suffer.' And all this was shown in spiritual understanding, these blessed words being said: 'I am keeping you very safe.'

And through the great desire that I saw in our blessed Lord that we should live in this way—that is to say, in longing and rejoicing, as all this lesson of love shows—I understood that all that is against us comes not from him but from our enemy, and he wants us to know this through the sweet, gracious light of his kind love.

If there be any such lover of God on earth who is continually kept from falling, I do not know of it, for it was not revealed to me. But this was revealed: that in falling and in rising we are always **inestimably** protected in one love; for in the sight of God we do not fall, and in our own view we do not remain standing, and both of these are true, as I see it, but the sight of our Lord God is the highest truth. So we are much indebted to God that he wishes to reveal this high truth to us in this life. And I understood that while we are in this life, it is most advantageous to us to see both of these at once; for the higher view keeps us in spiritual solace and true delight in God; the other, that is the lower view, keeps us in fear and makes us ashamed of ourselves. But our good Lord always wants us to regard ourselves much more in accordance with the higher view, and yet not to relinquish our recognition of the lower one, until the time when we are brought up above, where we shall have our Lord Jesus for our reward, and be filled full of joy and bliss without end. E

inestimably (ĭn-ĕs′tə-mə-blē) *adv.* In an *inestimable* (*adj.* Impossible to estimate or compute) manner or degree.

Sin and God's Love: How does God's view of us when we sin differ from our own view? E

14. *And here I understood . . . and blame:* See the reference to blame in Chapter 27 (footnote 13).

THINK AND DISCUSS

1. What three gifts does Lady Julian ask God for in Chapter 2?
2. What object does Lady Julian fix her eyes upon before she is mysteriously healed of her condition?
3. Why is Lady Julian grateful to God for sending her physical suffering? What does she want it to teach her?
4. Using your knowledge of nonfiction text structures (see p. 75), outline the structure of Chapters 2 and 27 respectively. Be sure to include the signal words that alerted you to each structure as well as any key ideas revealed in the structure.
5. What text structure is used in the first part of the third paragraph of Chapter 5? What signal words were clues for you?
6. What two images does Lady Julian use in Chapter 5? How do they support the theme of the chapter?
7. What image does Lady Julian use briefly in Chapter 82 that is similar to the imagery in Jeremiah 8:22? Explain the image's meaning.
8. How does it benefit a person to consider both God's and his own views of his sin according to Chapter 82? Do these ideas agree with the teaching of passages such as Romans 3:10–12, 5:19; 2 Corinthians 5:21; Ephesians 2:1–10; and Philippians 3:9? Explain your answer, referencing two or more of these passages.
9. Julian struggled with why God would allow sin and all the suffering it brings. How does her answer (that sin is "befitting") balance with the facts that sin is evil and God is good and loving?
10. Chapter 27 highlights the suffering caused by sin. Of what advantage can our own suffering be to us? How did Christ's suffering on the cross cause all things to be well for the world?

Medieval Drama

The history of drama in the Middle Ages is one of death and rebirth. At the dawn of the era, Church officials suppressed the Roman Empire's thriving theatrical community, objecting both to its pagan origins and suspected moral corruption, as well as to acting in general. Theaters were closed and actors made objects of social contempt. Then with Rome's fall, drama all but died out as a cultural force.

Perhaps ironically then, it was the Roman Catholic Church that revived the genre. As early as the tenth century, the Church began using liturgical dramas (short scenes of key biblical or historical Church events acted out with very little dialogue) to reach its mostly illiterate flock. From this seed eventually grew the major genres of medieval theater: the morality, mystery, and miracle plays.

In 1633 the people of Oberammergau, Germany, asked God to protect the town from an outbreak of the plague. In return, they pledged to put on an Easter Passion Play every ten years. These images are from the 2010 community production of this ongoing tradition.

Purpose and Genres

Most surviving medieval plays come from the fourteenth and fifteenth centuries when drama again flourished. The authors are unknown, but their purposes and themes were clearly religious. Furthermore, their primary audience was not the wealthy, educated elite; they wrote in English (not Latin) so that everyone could understand.

The resulting plays generally fall into three genres, each an outgrowth of Church teaching. Closest to liturgical dramas were the **miracle** and **mystery plays**. The former portrayed stories from Church saints' lives; the latter were cycles of short plays depicting biblical stories and meant to be performed together. Most scholars agree that *mystery* refers not to the plays' content but rather to their production. The word's Medieval Latin root, *ministerium,* denoted a kind of work or trade; its use reflected that the plays were usually produced by a city's guilds (medieval trade associations organized around particular vocations, such as goldsmiths, butchers, or merchants).

A morality play told an allegorical story representing a spiritual theme or truth. Characters in morality plays were usually stock representations of man or abstract ideas. Commonly called *Everyman*, the protagonist encountered characters such as Vice, Death, Good Deeds, Justice, or even God. Their interactions explored a common human problem and presented a clear moral lesson for the audience.

Drama and Community

More than any other genre at the time, medieval dramas demanded broad community involvement. Performed on important Church holidays (Whitsuntide or Corpus Christi), they were acted by a combination of volunteers and professional entertainers, produced by community members, and attended by the entire community. As dedicated theater buildings were impractical, the plays were staged outside in amphitheaters or public squares around which audiences would gather.

Because of their scope, mystery plays demanded the most community involvement. Usually, they were performed by cities, the only communities with the necessary wealth and manpower. Frequently, the plays in a cycle were staged at different locations around the city. In such cases, each play was enacted on a movable stage called a pageant wagon. Beginning at first light in the lengthier cycles, pageant wagons would move from station to station, reenacting their portion of the drama cycle for the town. Actors and other townspeople would create the sets, props, and costumes for each pageant wagon. These could be extremely elaborate, clever, and costly, especially once guilds were involved. Usually, guilds took responsibility for one pageant wagon and chose to perform a story that could incorporate the skills or products of their trade. Their production would then both celebrate and advertise their expertise.

Notable extant drama cycles include ones from York, Chester, and Wakefield. The Wakefield *Second Shepherds' Play* has particularly gained notice for its hilarious mixture of **farce** (a type of broad, highly exaggerated comedy) with a serious retelling of the shepherds' visit to the newborn Jesus. Farce was a common addition to plays, adding pure entertainment value and sometimes a bit of social criticism on the side.

EVERYMAN

Written in the late 1400s, *Everyman* is the most widely known and best medieval morality play. It begins with God ordering Death to retrieve the main character, Everyman. Informed of his impending death, Everyman seeks to avoid it, appealing to characters such as Fellowship, Goods, Knowledge, Beauty, and Strength to save him or go with him. But all abandon him. Finally, stripped of all his outer and inner resources, Everyman is left with only Good Deeds to go with him and speak to God in his favor. The play reminds the audience that earthly life is temporary; in a final accounting of one's life, only the spiritual matters. It also reveals how even people who know better are never quite ready for Death to visit.

Take example, all ye that this do hear or see, / How they that I loved best do forsake me, / Except my Good Deeds that bideth truly.

In the following passage, the characters Fellowship, Cousin, Kindred, Goods, Beauty, Strength, Discretion, and Five Wits have forsaken Everyman, who finally realizes that he cannot take them with him into Death.

EVERYMAN. O Jesu, help! All hath forsaken me!
GOOD DEEDS. Nay, Everyman; I will bide with thee,
I will not forsake thee indeed;
Thou shalt find me a good friend at need.
EVERYMAN. Gramercy, Good Deeds! Now may I true friends see.
They have forsaken me, every one;
I loved them better than my Good Deeds alone.
Knowledge, will ye forsake me also?
KNOWLEDGE. Yea, Everyman, when ye to death shall go;
But not yet, for no manner of danger.
EVERYMAN. Gramercy, Knowledge, with all my heart.
KNOWLEDGE. Nay, yet I will not from hence depart
Till I see where ye shall be come.
EVERYMAN. Methink, alas, that I must be gone
To make my reckoning and my debts pay,
For I see my time is nigh spent away.
Take example, all ye that this do hear or see,
How they that I loved best do forsake me,
Except my Good Deeds that bideth truly.
GOOD DEEDS. All earthly things is but vanity.
Beauty, Strength, and Discretion do man forsake,
Foolish friends and kinsmen, that fair spake,
All fleeth save Good Deeds, and that am I.
EVERYMAN. Have mercy on me, God most mighty;
And stand by me, thou Mother and Maid, holy Mary!
GOOD DEEDS. Fear not, I will speak for thee.
EVERYMAN. Here I cry God mercy!
GOOD DEEDS. Short our end, and 'minish our pain.
Let us go and never come again.
EVERYMAN. Into thy hands, Lord, my soul I commend.
Receive it, Lord, that it be not lost.
As thou me boughtest, so me defend,
And save me from the fiend's boast,
That I may appear with that blessed host
That shall be saved at the day of doom.

. . . .

[EVERYMAN and GOOD DEEDS descend into the grave.]

KNOWLEDGE. Now hath he suffered that we all shall endure;
The Good Deeds shall make all sure.
Now hath he made ending.
Methinketh that I hear angels sing
And make great joy and melody
Where Everyman's soul received shall be.

UNIT 1

PART 3

Changing Society

The title of this section—“Changing Society”—can be read two ways. First, it is a descriptive phrase. Societies are always changing, sometimes slowly, sometimes quickly. Look around and you will see your society in the midst of all sorts of variations and transformations, from fashion trends to construction projects, from demographic shifts to great sea changes in morals. Obviously, some are more important than others, but all are facts of life in a time-bound and, unfortunately, broken world.

While *changing society* can be a descriptive phrase, it can also be an expression of action. Every society should be asking, how can we change to be better? As long as we live in a world broken by sin, change will be necessary; no culture or society will be perfect until Christ returns.

Literature offers a number of tools for writers to help change their world. One of these is the mode of **satire**. Satire entails the ridiculing of a person, group, or institution in order to provoke corrective change in the beliefs and behaviors of those involved. It is often an uncomfortable genre, but it wields unquestionable power when done well.

Medieval English society was in one sense no different from any other: it had problems. Near the close of the fourteenth century, several pressures forced these to a boiling point. First, the Black Death's casualties had created a serious labor shortage. High demand for labor gave peasants power to bargain for higher wages, and some even left their manors (often illegally) to work for a landlord who paid better or to enter urban occupations formerly closed to them. Second, as post-plague trade picked back up, the commercial class profited immensely; some merchants and trade guilds exercised considerable power, even over the aristocracy. They also challenged traditional mores by pursuing financial profit (which the Church thought greedy) and enjoying some luxuries previously available only to the upper classes. Finally, the Church's extensive corruption and internal strife led to widespread disillusionment with the institution as a whole. These broad societal shifts undermined the feudal system's economic base, strict social hierarchy, and basic worldview.

The ruling class's response to these changes was to attempt to reverse them. They reinforced geographic constraints on peasants, pushed wages back down to pre-plague levels, and passed sumptuary laws limiting luxury goods and services to the upper classes. At the same time, King Richard II began levying increasingly higher taxes to fund the Hundred Years' War. Finally, peasants had had enough. In 1381, widespread revolt ensued. Beginning in Essex and spreading to London, protestors caused property damage to feudal and Church manors and executed some people they perceived as the main culprits of their oppression. Their demands included lower taxes, the abolishment of serfdom, and the disbanding and redistribution of Church properties. Eventually quashed (with many executions following), the Peasants' Revolt of 1381 showed the rising power of the lower classes and had at least one tangible effect: no king ever tried to tax the people to such high levels again.

This tumultuous time produced two great satirical works. The first, written by William Langland in the years leading up to the revolt, was *Piers Plowman*. A long narrative poem, *Piers* was partly an allegory of the Christian's spiritual journey and partly a satire of Langland's social environment. The second, written by Geoffrey Chaucer in the years after the revolt, was *The Canterbury Tales*, a sprawling collection of tales touching on every sector of English society and satirizing most. Both are numbered among the great classics of British literature. Their authors both documented societal change and encouraged it through their works.

Like Chaucer and Langland, most of us today do not have to sit back and watch change happen; we can effect change ourselves. A good satirist is someone who has not given up, someone who hopes to communicate a message and affect people's actions so that his or her world becomes a better place. For the believer, there is a guide in pursuing that goal—the Bible. Believers also have an indispensable help in the Holy Spirit, who transforms God's people from within. We can advocate for biblical change in our society, but we must always remember that lasting change comes from a heart transformed by God's grace. In the end, more than satire or any other tool, the gospel's power to change individual lives is our greatest hope for true change.

Geoffrey Chaucer (ca. 1343–1400)

AT A GLANCE

- **1359–60** Captured in war in France but ransomed by Edward III
- **1360** Published *The Book of the Duchess*, his first major work
- **1368–78** Served on diplomatic missions to France and Italy
- **1369–72** Completed his translation of the *Roman de la Rose*
- **1387–1400** Wrote *The Canterbury Tales*
- **1400** Died and was buried in Westminster Abbey

DID YOU KNOW?

Chaucer is often called the Father of English Poetry.

Poet in the Making

Born in London, Geoffrey Chaucer was the son of a middle-class master vintner, the deputy to King Edward III's butler. He was educated in French, Latin, and general medieval knowledge (as gentlemen were) and through his father's connections gained a position as a page and later squire in the household of the Countess of Ulster (wife of Edward III's son Lionel). His work exposed him early on to courtly literature, sowing seeds for his later writing career. Eventually, Chaucer entered the service of John of Gaunt (Duke of Lancaster and son of Edward III), the most powerful man in Britain for decades. He also married one of the queen's ladies-in-waiting, whose sister eventually married John of Gaunt. By 1368 Chaucer was part of the royal household, engaged in diplomatic service for the king. With patronage from these sources, his writing career was assured.

Poet in Society

Chaucer's nonliterary career acquainted him with almost every area of England's social and political life. Employment as a soldier in the Hundred Years' War taught him something of the military, while participation in diplomatic missions to Flanders, Spain, France, and Italy acquainted him with wider Europe (especially its literature). His tenures as Controller of Customs for the port of London (1374–86) and Clerk of the King's Works (1389–91) involved him in urban London and its mercantile class. His term as justice of the peace and a member of parliament in Kent (1386) familiarized him with village life and the political realm, and an appointment as deputy forester of a royal game preserve in Somerset (1391–ca. 1396) gave him experience in manor life. These varied posts introduced him to nearly every type of person found in medieval England. Chaucer's careful observation of the attitudes and concerns of these social classes would form the material for his key work.

Father of English Poetry

Chaucer's poetic career is often divided into three phases: the French (1361–71), Italian (1372–85), and English (1385–1400) periods. His early compositions worked within French literary traditions. Key works include his translation of the *Roman de la Rose*, a French poem of the 1200s, and *The Book of the Duchess*, an elegiac poem modeled on contemporary French modes that Chaucer created in honor of John of Gaunt's deceased wife. Then his diplomatic missions introduced him to Italian Renaissance poetry, which influenced works such as his longest poem, *Troilus and Criseyde*. His final and most significant phase found Chaucer composing the culminating work of his career, *The Canterbury Tales*.

The leading poet of his age, Chaucer is still ranked among the best literary craftsmen in English literature. His chief achievement was successfully bringing vernacular English into the realm of literary works. He did so by successfully employing European literary genres and topics in English and by turning these genres to reflect the attitudes and concerns of late medieval England. These skills are most clearly exhibited in *The Canterbury Tales*. In this seminal work, Chaucer utilized a plethora of literary genres. But far from being derivative, the work offered a fresh view of its genre's tropes through Chaucer's skillful writing and insights. Its combination of lively narration, subtle characterization, and vigorous social satire remains unsurpassed among English narrative poets.

The Canterbury Tales

The product of Chaucer's fertile imagination, *The Canterbury Tales* traces the religious journey of thirty pilgrims on their way to Saint Thomas à Becket's shrine at Canterbury Cathedral. To pass the time, each pilgrim is tasked with telling four tales, two on the way and two as they return home, making a total of 120 tales. But Chaucer's complete plans were never realized. After fourteen years of work on this masterpiece, he died, leaving behind only twenty-four tales, two incomplete. The pilgrims never reach their destination, and not all of the twenty-eight pilgrims described in "The Prologue" (not counting the innkeeper and narrator) get to share their tales. Nevertheless, Chaucer left behind an immense accomplishment, a rich tableau of stories from a socially diverse cast of characters.

Because the pilgrimage itself serves as the unifying situation, or frame, for the various tales, *The Canterbury Tales* is referred to as a **frame tale**. Frame tales were quite popular in the late Middle Ages. Chaucer had already used one in his *Legend of Good Women* and was likely familiar with others (e.g., Boccaccio's *Decameron*). But his configuration of the genre in *The Canterbury Tales* is unique in that the frame brings together characters from all three estates, or classes, of English society. A common English activity, the Canterbury pilgrimage, forms the ostensible reason for this unlikely social microcosm, but the fact that these diverse characters would not, historically, have traveled together points to Chaucer's larger purpose: the tales together form an example of estates satire, a genre critiquing the medieval classes.

The pilgrims begin as stereotypes from English society. While Chaucer reinforces these at times, he also subtly expands the characters beyond their set roles. In fact, the pilgrims represent a veritable parade of general humanity; they differ not only in social class and vocation but also in their worldviews, their preoccupations in life, and their individual strengths and flaws. Their personal interactions often suggest class distinctions and conflicts contemporary to Chaucer. For example, the first tale is told by the Knight, the pilgrim of highest rank, but then the middle-class Miller violates the social order by telling his story next, before others of higher rank. A few pilgrims even squabble and use their tales to take potshots, subtle or overt, at each other. The tales themselves tend to reflect an individual teller's character and perspective. The many genres Chaucer incorporates (e.g., hagiographies, courtly love tales, fables) thus allow him to show his literary prowess and to offer a wide variety of human perspectives.

The speech of the narrator, who introduces the pilgrims, speaks with them, and loosely ties their tales together, is written as if Chaucer himself were speaking; however, he is just a persona, a fictional version of Chaucer's voice. For example, the narrator is frequently omniscient, knowing more than a new acquaintance should about each pilgrim. He also shifts between overt irony and extreme naiveté in his conversation and commentary. While both approaches usually serve to highlight what is ridiculous, contradictory, or improper in a character, this gap between what the narrator says and Chaucer's actual views can make his exact tone toward certain characters difficult to ascertain, even for scholars. He seems to move between relishing the ridiculous and quirky in humanity and condemning the more egregious flaws of certain characters. As the work illustrates, Chaucer believed he had much to ridicule in late medieval English society. Between the new middle class's disruption of traditional order and the clergy's moral compromise and hypocrisy, his wit finds many targets. The critical force of that wit (so often humorous) is one reason the work has remained an important piece of British literature. Together with its elaborate structural scheme, unique use of established genres, and rich characterization, these characteristics make *The Canterbury Tales* the masterpiece in which English literature truly came of age.

A modern view of the North Downs Way National Trail in Southern England, along which medieval pilgrims to Canterbury sometimes traveled.

ANALYZE: *Characterization, Tone, and Irony*

In "The Prologue," Chaucer's narrator, who characterizes himself as gregarious and inquisitive, introduces the reader to the pilgrims. According to him, he has talked with all twenty-nine pilgrims and is, therefore, able to tell the reader the condition, rank, position, and array of each one. This gallery of portraits presents human as well as social types and offers satiric commentary on each. Chaucer's deft touch with **characterization** (the act of portraying a character in a narrative) gives his satire much of its power. He uses both **direct characterization** (using explicit statements to tell the reader about the character) and **indirect characterization** (using dialogue, description, or action to reveal the character to the reader) to sketch out the general and individual traits of each character in an engaging way. As you read, examine what Chaucer reveals about his characters.

No less engaging than the characterization is Chaucer's ever-present humor, sometimes subtle, sometimes slapstick. Irony often helps convey Chaucer's **tone**, the attitude an author has toward his subject that readers are meant to share. Look for instances of **verbal irony** (when a speaker means something other than what he says) and **situational irony** (when a situation violates reader expectations) in the descriptions of each character.

READ: *Apply Historical/Social Context*

To understand *The Canterbury Tales*, you must understand something of the medieval society in which Chaucer lived. Review the upheavals in society (e.g., the emerging middle class and corrupt Church) that weakened the feudal system and led to the Peasants' Revolt (p. 85). Chaucer's pilgrims illustrate such social changes.

Thus, one way to examine the pilgrims is as examples of traditional and nontraditional roles. The former fulfill clearly defined social roles that have associated ideals (e.g., the Knight, the Squire, the Prioress, the Monk, the Friar). The latter (e.g., the Merchant, the Franklin, the Tradesmen, the Wife of Bath) are often experiencing new privileges as a result of the new opportunities afforded them and tend to upset normal societal order in some way. As you read, consider how the pilgrims with traditional social roles have diverged from their ideal and how Chaucer characterizes the pilgrims with nontraditional social identities. Do any characters escape the satiric edge of Chaucer's pen?

CREATE: *A Satirical Character Sketch*

The satire of "The Prologue" rests on how Chaucer describes his characters. Chaucer uses description and ironic commentary to show how well or ill the pilgrims fulfill their roles and conform to societal expectations. Much of this is indirectly conveyed. For example, when Chaucer describes the Prioress's tender-heartedness toward small creatures, his inability to say that she cares similarly for humans becomes glaringly obvious. The Prioress thus fails to measure up to her religious office by default. After you read "The Prologue," you will be asked to create a satirical character sketch, using descriptions. Pay attention as you read so that you can model Chaucer's characterizations.

OBJECTIVES

- Identify the characteristics of a frame tale.
- Analyze a work's characterization.
- Analyze a work's irony (verbal and situational) and overall tone.
- Apply historical and social context to understand a text.
- Create a satirical character sketch based on a textual model.

VOCABULARY

engender (ĕn-jĕn′dər) *intr.v.* To come into existence; originate.

burnish (bûr′nĭsh) *tr.v.* To make smooth or glossy by rubbing; polish.

accrue (ə-kro͞o′) *intr.v.* To come to one as a gain, addition, or increment.

motley (mŏt′lē) *adj.* Having many colors; variegated; parti-colored.

encumber (ĕn-kŭm′bər) *tr.v.* To cause to have difficulty in moving or in accomplishing something; burden.

duress (do͝o-rĕs′) *n.* Compulsion by threat or violence; coercion.

prevarication (prĭ-văr′ĭ-kā′shən) *n.* Avoidance of straightforward statement of the truth; equivocation, evasiveness, misrepresentation; deceit; an instance of this.

How do you JUDGE SOMEONE?

We tend to judge people's appearances first even though we know that appearances rarely reveal the important facts about a person. What else do you want to know when you first meet people? Their vocation or hobbies? What music or movies they like? Whom you know in common? We tend to judge others based on what we ourselves think is important. Consider some of your first meetings with people. What about them made you respond positively or negatively? What do those judgments suggest you value?

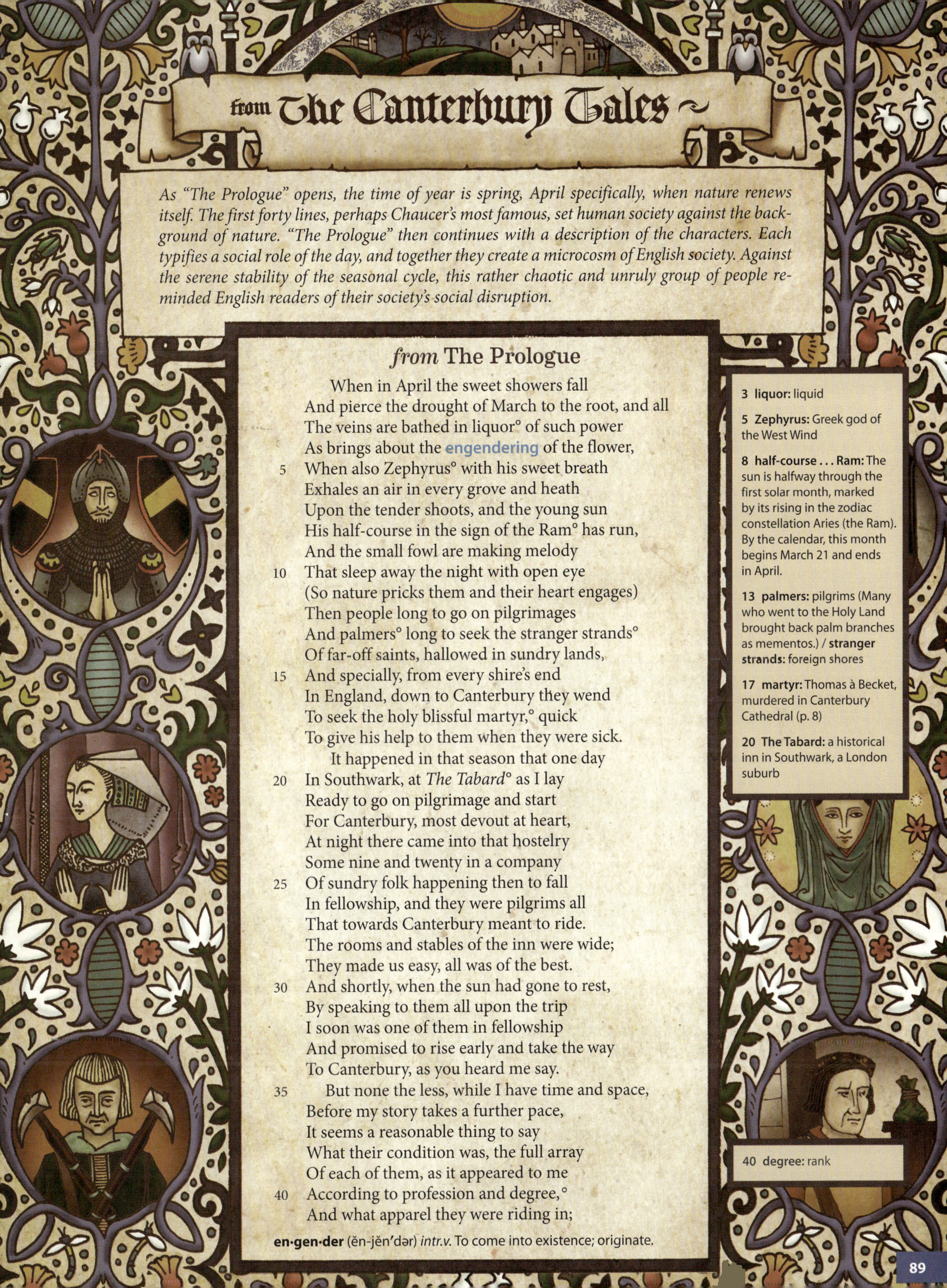

from The Canterbury Tales

As "The Prologue" opens, the time of year is spring, April specifically, when nature renews itself. The first forty lines, perhaps Chaucer's most famous, set human society against the background of nature. "The Prologue" then continues with a description of the characters. Each typifies a social role of the day, and together they create a microcosm of English society. Against the serene stability of the seasonal cycle, this rather chaotic and unruly group of people reminded English readers of their society's social disruption.

from The Prologue

When in April the sweet showers fall
And pierce the drought of March to the root, and all
The veins are bathed in liquor° of such power
As brings about the **engendering** of the flower,
When also Zephyrus° with his sweet breath
Exhales an air in every grove and heath
Upon the tender shoots, and the young sun
His half-course in the sign of the Ram° has run,
And the small fowl are making melody
That sleep away the night with open eye
(So nature pricks them and their heart engages)
Then people long to go on pilgrimages
And palmers° long to seek the stranger strands°
Of far-off saints, hallowed in sundry lands,
And specially, from every shire's end
In England, down to Canterbury they wend
To seek the holy blissful martyr,° quick
To give his help to them when they were sick.
It happened in that season that one day
In Southwark, at *The Tabard*° as I lay
Ready to go on pilgrimage and start
For Canterbury, most devout at heart,
At night there came into that hostelry
Some nine and twenty in a company
Of sundry folk happening then to fall
In fellowship, and they were pilgrims all
That towards Canterbury meant to ride.
The rooms and stables of the inn were wide;
They made us easy, all was of the best.
And shortly, when the sun had gone to rest,
By speaking to them all upon the trip
I soon was one of them in fellowship
And promised to rise early and take the way
To Canterbury, as you heard me say.
But none the less, while I have time and space,
Before my story takes a further pace,
It seems a reasonable thing to say
What their condition was, the full array
Of each of them, as it appeared to me
According to profession and degree,°
And what apparel they were riding in;

en·gen·der (ĕn-jĕn′dər) *intr.v.* To come into existence; originate.

3 liquor: liquid

5 Zephyrus: Greek god of the West Wind

8 half-course . . . Ram: The sun is halfway through the first solar month, marked by its rising in the zodiac constellation Aries (the Ram). By the calendar, this month begins March 21 and ends in April.

13 palmers: pilgrims (Many who went to the Holy Land brought back palm branches as mementos.) / **stranger strands:** foreign shores

17 martyr: Thomas à Becket, murdered in Canterbury Cathedral (p. 8)

20 The Tabard: a historical inn in Southwark, a London suburb

40 degree: rank

And at a Knight I therefore will begin.
There was a *Knight*, a most distinguished man,
Who from the day on which he first began
To ride abroad had followed chivalry,
Truth, honour, generousness and courtesy.
He had done nobly in his sovereign's war
And ridden into battle, no man more,
As well in christian as in heathen places,
And ever honoured for his noble graces.
When we took Alexandria,° he was there.
He often sat at table in the chair
Of honour, above all nations, when in Prussia.
In Lithuania he had ridden, and Russia,°
No christian man so often, of his rank.
When, in Granada, Algeciras° sank
Under assault, he had been there, and in
North Africa, raiding Benamarin;°
In Anatolia he had been as well
And fought when Ayas and Attalia° fell,
For all along the Mediterranean coast
He had embarked with many a noble host.
In fifteen mortal battles he had been
And jousted for our faith at Tramissene°
Thrice in the lists,° and always killed his man.
This same distinguished knight had led the van°
Once with the Bey of Balat,° doing work
For him against another heathen Turk; A
He was of sovereign value in all eyes.
And though so much distinguished, he was wise
And in his bearing modest as a maid.
He never yet a boorish thing had said
In all his life to any, come what might;
He was a true, a perfect gentle-knight. A
Speaking of his equipment, he possessed
Fine horses, but he was not gaily dressed.
He wore a fustian tunic stained and dark
With smudges where his armour had left mark;
Just home from service, he had joined our ranks
To do his pilgrimage and render thanks.
He had his son with him, a fine young *Squire*,
A lover and cadet, a lad of fire
With locks as curly as if they had been pressed.
He was some twenty years of age, I guessed.
In stature he was of a moderate length,
With wonderful agility and strength.
He'd seen some service with the cavalry
In Flanders and Artois and Picardy°
And had done valiantly in little space

51 Alexandria: Alexandria, Egypt, sacked by Crusaders in 1365

54 Prussia . . . Russia: where Crusades against the Tartars took place in the 1380s

56 Algeciras: a city in Granada that saw fighting against the Moors in the 1340s

58 Benamarin: a Moorish kingdom in North Africa

60 Anatolia . . . Attalia: areas in Asia Minor, modern-day Turkey, where Crusaders fought

64 Tramissene: Moorish kingdom in North Africa

65 lists: an arena used for formal martial contests

66 van: the vanguard or front section of an armed force

67 Bey of Balat: ruler in Asia Minor

88 Flanders . . . Picardy: sites of battles (1383) in the Hundred Years' War (p. 11)

Irony: Note the glosses in lines 51–67. How might Chaucer's description of the Knight's feats include a bit of irony? A

Characterization/Tone: What characteristics does Chaucer give the Knight? Do these show him measuring up to his traditional role? What tone does Chaucer seem to express toward him? A

Of time, in hope to win his lady's grace.
He was embroidered like a meadow bright
And full of freshest flowers, red and white.
Singing he was, or fluting all the day;
He was as fresh° as is the month of May.
Short was his gown, the sleeves were long and wide;
He knew the way to sit a horse and ride.
He could make songs and poems and recite,
Knew how to joust and dance, to draw and write.
. . . .
Courteous he was, lowly and serviceable,
And carved to serve his father at the table. A
There was a *Yeoman*° with him at his side,
No other servant; so he chose to ride.
This Yeoman wore a coat and hood of green,
And peacock-feathered arrows, bright and keen
And neatly sheathed, hung at his belt the while
—For he could dress his gear in yeoman style,
His arrows never drooped their feathers low—
And in his hand he bore a mighty bow.
His head was like a nut, his face was brown.
He knew the whole of woodcraft up and down.
A saucy brace° was on his arm to ward
It from the bow-string, and a shield and sword
Hung at one side, and at the other slipped
A jaunty dirk,° spear-sharp and well-equipped.
A medal of St Christopher° he wore
Of shining silver on his breast, and bore
A hunting-horn, well slung and **burnished** clean,
That dangled from a baldrick of bright green.
He was a proper forester I guess.
There also was a *Nun*, a *Prioress*,°
Her way of smiling very simple and coy.
Her greatest oath was only 'By St Loy!'
And she was known as Madam Eglantyne.°
And well she sang a service, with a fine
Intoning through her nose, as was most seemly,
And she spoke daintily in French, extremely,
After the school of Stratford-atte-Bowe;°
French in the Paris style she did not know.
At meat her manners were well taught withal;
No morsel from her lips did she let fall,
Nor dipped her fingers in the sauce too deep;
But she could carry a morsel up and keep
The smallest drop from falling on her breast.
For courtliness she had a special zest,
And she would wipe her upper lip so clean
That not a trace of grease was to be seen
Upon the cup when she had drunk; to eat,
She reached a hand sedately for the meat.
She certainly was very entertaining,
Pleasant and friendly in her ways, and straining

94 fresh: full of vigor

101 Yeoman: independent land-owning farmer

111 brace: leather wrist guard

114 dirk: dagger

115 St Christopher: patron saint of travelers

120 Prioress: head of a group of nuns, ranked right below an abbess

123 Madam Eglantyne: "Lady Rosebud"

127 in French . . . Stratford-atte-Bowe: She spoke Anglo-Norman French (a hybrid) rather than Parisian French.

Characterization: How does the Squire's behavior comply with the chivalric code? How does his character compare with the Knight's? A

burnish (bûr′nĭsh) *tr.v.* To make smooth or glossy by rubbing; polish.

To counterfeit a courtly kind of grace,
A stately bearing fitting to her place,
And to seem dignified in all her dealings. E
As for her sympathies and tender feelings,
She was so charitably solicitous
She used to weep if she but saw a mouse
Caught in a trap, if it were dead or bleeding.
And she had little dogs she would be feeding
With roasted flesh, or milk, or fine white bread.
And bitterly she wept if one were dead
Or someone took a stick and made it smart;
She was all sentiment and tender heart.
Her veil° was gathered in a seemly way,
Her nose was elegant, her eyes glass-grey;
Her mouth was very small, but soft and red,
Her forehead, certainly, was fair of spread,°
Almost a span° across the brows, I own;
She was indeed by no means undergrown.°
Her cloak, I noticed, had a graceful charm.
She wore a coral trinket on her arm,
A set of beads,° the gaudies tricked in green,
Whence hung a golden brooch of brightest sheen
On which there first was graven a crowned A,
And lower, *Amor vincit omnia.*° A
Another *Nun*, the chaplain at her cell,
Was riding with her, and *three Priests* as well.
A *Monk* there was, one of the finest sort
Who rode the country; hunting was his sport.

153 veil: wimple; a nun's cloth headdress wound about the head, revealing only the face

156 fair of spread: A broad forehead, a well-shaped nose, gray (e.g., blue) eyes, and small red mouth were typical of medieval heroines, but a nun should have been veiled.

157 span: hand's breadth

158 She was . . . undergrown: Fatness in Chaucer's time, when food was scarce, was a sign of prosperity. (cf. the Monk)

161 beads: her rosary

164 *Amor vincit omnia*: "Love conquers all."

A manly man, to be an Abbot° able;
Many a dainty horse he had in stable.
His bridle, when he rode, a man might hear
Jingling in a whistling wind as clear,
Aye, and as loud as does the chapel bell
Where my lord Monk was Prior of the cell.
The Rule of good St Benet or St Maur°
As old and strict he tended to ignore;
He let go by the things of yesterday
And took the modern world's more spacious way.

169 Abbot: head of an abbey, the first rank of a monastery (cf. a priory, the second rank)

175 Rule . . . St Maur: guides (written by St. Benedict, founder of Western monasticism, and his disciple St. Maurus) for monastic communities, usually outlining virtues to pursue and vices to avoid

Satirical Character Sketch: What social role is the Prioress imitating? What does Chaucer think of her behavior? Consider how you might use a character's actions to offer a critique. E

Tone: What is Chaucer's overall tone toward the Prioress? What details (other than her attitude toward animals) support this tone? A

He did not rate that text at a plucked hen
Which says that hunters are not holy men°
And that a monk uncloistered° is a mere
Fish out of water, flapping on the pier,
That is to say a monk out of his cloister.
That was a text he held not worth an oyster;
And I agreed and said his views were sound;
Was he to study till his head went round
Poring over books in cloisters? Must he toil
As Austin° bade and till the very soil?
Was he to leave the world upon the shelf?
Let Austin have his labour to himself.
This Monk was therefore a good man to horse;
Greyhounds he had,° as swift as birds, to course.
Hunting a hare or riding at a fence
Was all his fun, he spared for no expense.
I saw his sleeves were garnished at the hand
With fine grey fur, the finest in the land,
And on his hood, to fasten it at his chin
He had a wrought-gold cunningly fashioned pin;
Into a lover's knot it seemed to pass.
His head was bald and shone like looking-glass;
So did his face, as if it had been greased.
He was a fat and personable priest;
His prominent eyeballs never seemed to settle.
They glittered like the flames beneath a kettle;
Supple his boots, his horse in fine condition.
He was a prelate fit for exhibition,
He was not pale like a tormented soul.°
He liked a fat swan best, and roasted whole.
His palfrey° was as brown as is a berry. R
There was a *Friar*, a wanton one and merry,
A Limiter,° a very festive fellow.
In all Four Orders° there was none so mellow
So glib with gallant phrase and well-turned speech.
He'd fixed up many a marriage, giving each
Of his young women what he could afford her.°
He was a noble pillar to his Order. A
Highly beloved and intimate was he
With County folk within his boundary,
And city dames of honour and possessions;
For he was qualified to hear confessions,
Or so he said, with more than priestly scope;
He had a special license from the Pope.
Sweetly he heard his penitents at shrift
With pleasant absolution, for a gift.
He was an easy man in penance-giving
Where he could hope to make a decent living;
It's a sure sign whenever gifts are given
To a poor Order that a man's well shriven,°

180 hunters . . . men: Gen. 10:9

181 uncloistered: living outside a monastic cloister, where monks undertook quiet, secluded lives according to their order's regulations

188 Austin: Saint Augustine of Hippo (354–430)

192 Greyhounds he had: Keeping hounds violated monastical rules.

207 He . . . soul: Stereotypical monks were pale and thin from staying indoors and fasting.

209 palfrey: saddle horse

211 Limiter: "a friar licensed to preach, hear confessions, and beg within a defined area" (*OED*)

212 Four Orders: the four mendicant orders (Franciscan, Dominican, Carmelite, Augustinian), who took a vow of poverty and often begged for their living

215 He'd fixed . . . afford her: He found husbands and supplied dowries for girls he had seduced.

228 well shriven: has fulfilled the requirements of penance

Social Context: Regular clergy (p. 8) took vows of poverty, chastity, and obedience and often lived secluded lives to focus on spiritual matters. How does Chaucer's characterization of the Monk comply or not comply with those expectations? R

Irony: What type of irony does line 216 illustrate? A

And should he give enough he knew in verity
The penitent repented in sincerity.
For many a fellow is so hard of heart
He cannot weep, for all his inward smart.
Therefore instead of weeping and of prayer
One should give silver for a poor Friar's care.
He kept his tippet° stuffed with pins for curls,
And pocket-knives, to give to pretty girls.
And certainly his voice was gay and sturdy,
For he sang well and played the hurdy-gurdy.
At sing-songs he was champion of the hour.
His neck was whiter than a lily-flower
But strong enough to butt a bruiser down.
He knew the taverns well in every town
And every innkeeper and barmaid too
Better than lepers, beggars and that crew,°
For in so eminent a man as he
It was not fitting with the dignity
Of his position, dealing with a scum
Of wretched lepers; nothing good can come
Of dealings with the slum-and-gutter dwellers,
But only with the rich and victual-sellers.
But anywhere a profit might **accrue**
Courteous he was and lowly of service too.
Natural gifts like his were hard to match.
He was the finest beggar of his batch,
And, for his begging-district, payed a rent;
His brethren did no poaching where he went.
For though a widow mightn't have a shoe,
So pleasant was his holy how-d'ye-do
He got his farthing from her just the same
Before he left, and so his income came
To more than he laid out. And how he romped,
Just like a puppy! He was ever prompt
To arbitrate disputes on settling days°
(For a small fee) in many helpful ways,
Not then appearing as your cloistered scholar
With threadbare habit hardly worth a dollar,
But much more like a Doctor° or a Pope.
Of double-worsted was the semi-cope°
Upon his shoulders, and the swelling fold
About him, like a bell about its mould
When it is casting, rounded out his dress.
He lisped° a little out of wantonness
To make his English sweet upon his tongue.
When he had played his harp, or having sung,
His eyes would twinkle in his head as bright
As any star upon a frosty night.°
This worthy's name was Hubert, it appeared. **A**
    There was a *Merchant* with a forking beard

235 tippet: hood

244 lepers . . . crew: Mendicant orders were founded to minister to the poor.

263 settling days: originally "love-dayes," days officially designated for the settling of differences

267 Doctor: an academic doctor

268 semi-cope: a short cloak

272 lisped: Both lisping and a white neck were considered marks of sensuality.

276 His eyes . . . night: Cf. the Monk's eyes. Heat traditionally implied sins of passion; cold, sins of malice.

accrue (ə-kro͞o') *intr.v.* To come to one as a gain, addition, or increment.

Tone: What is Chaucer's overall tone toward the Friar? List three characteristics that help contribute to this tone. **A**

And **motley** dress; high on his horse he sat,
Upon his head a Flemish beaver hat
And on his feet daintily buckled boots.
He told of his opinions and pursuits
In solemn tones, and how he never lost.
The sea should be kept free at any cost
(He thought) upon the Harwich-Holland range,
He was expert at currency exchange.°
This estimable Merchant so had set
His wits to work, none knew he was in debt,
He was so stately in negotiation,
Loan, bargain and commercial obligation.
He was an excellent fellow all the same;
To tell the truth I do not know his name.
An *Oxford Cleric*, still a student though,
One who had taken logic° long ago,
Was there; his horse was thinner than a rake,
And he was not too fat, I undertake,
But had a hollow look, a sober stare;
The thread upon his overcoat was bare.
He had found no preferment° in the church
And he was too unworldly to make search
For secular employment. By his bed
He preferred having twenty books in red
And black, of Aristotle's° philosophy,
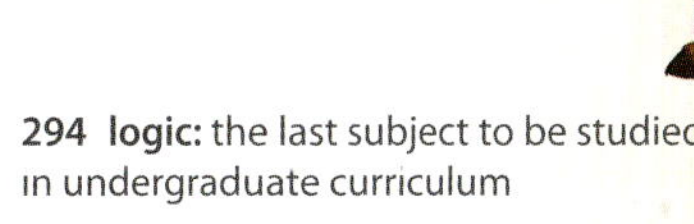
To having fine clothes, fiddle or psaltery.
Though a philosopher, as I have told,
He had not found the stone for making gold.
Whatever money from his friends he took
He spent on learning or another book
And prayed for them most earnestly, returning
Thanks to them thus for paying for his learning.
His only care was study, and indeed
He never spoke a word more than was need,
Formal at that, respectful in the extreme,
Short, to the point, and lofty in his theme.
The thought of moral virtue filled his speech
And he would gladly learn, and gladly teach. **A**
A *Serjeant at the Law*° who paid his calls,

286 He was . . . exchange: Only the royal moneychangers could legally profit in foreign exchange.

294 logic: the last subject to be studied in undergraduate curriculum

299 preferment: ecclesiastical position providing an income

303 Aristotle's: Greek philosopher (384–322 BC) and the medieval authority on nontheological subjects

317 Serjeant at the Law: lawyer appointed by the king

motley (mŏt′lē) *adj*. Having many colors; variegated; parti-colored.

Characterization: Chaucer tells the reader that the Cleric's "only care was study." Does his indirect characterization support or contradict this direct statement? **A**

Wary and wise, for clients at St Paul's
There also was, of noted excellence.
Discreet he was, a man to reverence,
Or so he seemed, his sayings were so wise.
He often had been Justice of Assize°
By letters patent, and in full commission.
His fame and learning and his high position
Had won him many a robe and many a fee.
There was no such conveyancer° as he;
All was fee-simple to his strong digestion,
Not one conveyance could be called in question.
Nowhere there was so busy a man as he;
But was less busy than he seemed to be.
He knew of every judgement, case and crime
Recorded, ever since King William's time.
He could dictate defences or draft deeds;
No one could pinch a comma from his screeds,°
And he knew every statute off by rote.
He wore a homely parti-coloured coat
Girt with a silken belt of pin-stripe stuff;
Of his appearance I have said enough.
There was a *Franklin* with him, it appeared;
White as a daisy-petal was his beard.
A sanguine° man, high-coloured and benign,
He loved a morning sop of cake in wine.
He lived for pleasure and had always done,
For he was Epicurus'° very son,
In whose opinion sensual delight
Was the one true felicity in sight.
As noted as St Julian° was for bounty
He made his household free to all the County.
His bread, his ale were finest of the fine
And no one had a better stock of wine.
His house was never short of bake-meat pies,
Of fish and flesh, and these in such supplies
It positively snowed with meat and drink
And all the dainties that a man could think.
According to the seasons of the year
Changes of dish were ordered to appear.
He kept fat partridges in coops, beyond,
Many a bream and pike were in his pond.
Woe to the cook whose sauces had no sting
Or who was unprepared in anything!
And in his hall a table stood arrayed
And ready all day long, with places laid.
As Justice at the Sessions° none stood higher;
He often had been Member for the Shire.°
A dagger and a little purse of silk
Hung at his girdle, white as morning milk.
As Sheriff he checked audit, every entry.
He was a model among landed gentry. **A**
A *Haberdasher*, a *Dyer*, a *Carpenter*,

322 Justice of Assize: He was one of the few judges appointed to the royal circuit courts (of Assize).

326 conveyancer: one who transfers a property title from one party to another

334 screed: a long piece of writing, often tedious

341 sanguine: personality type tending toward optimism

344 Epicurus: Greek philosopher who advocated pursuing pleasure as the absence of pain (emotional or physical), stereotyped here as promoting self-indulgent pleasures

347 St. Julian: patron saint of hospitality

363 Justice at the Sessions: justice of the peace

364 Member for the Shire: member of the House of Commons

Characterization: What is the Franklin's most prominent characteristic? **A**

A *Weaver* and a *Carpet-maker* were
Among our ranks, all in the livery
Of one impressive guild-fraternity.°
They were so trim and fresh their gear would pass
For new. Their knives were not tricked out with brass
But wrought with purest silver, which avouches
A like display on girdles and on pouches.
Each seemed a worthy burgess, fit to grace
A guild-hall with a seat upon the dais.
Their wisdom would have justified a plan
To make each one of them an alderman;
They had the capital and revenue,
Besides their wives declared it was their due.
And if they did not think so, then they ought;
To be called '*Madam*' is a glorious thought,
And so is going to church and being seen
Having your mantle carried like a queen. **R**
They had a *Cook* with them who stood alone
For boiling chicken with a marrow-bone
Sharp flavouring-powder and a spice for savour.
He could distinguish London ale by flavour,
And he could roast and seethe and broil and fry,
Make good thick soup and bake a tasty pie.
But what a pity—so it seemed to me,
That he should have an ulcer° on his knee.
As for blancmange,° he made it with the best.
There was a *Skipper* hailing from far west;
He came from Dartmouth, so I understood.
He rode a farmer's horse as best he could,
In a woollen gown that reached his knee.
A dagger on a lanyard falling free
Hung from his neck under his arm and down.
The summer heat had tanned his colour brown,
And certainly he was an excellent fellow.
Many a draught of vintage, red and yellow,
He'd drawn at Bordeaux,° while the trader snored.
The nicer rules of conscience he ignored.
If, when he fought, the enemy vessel sank,
He sent his prisoners home; they walked the plank. **A**
As for his skill in reckoning his tides,
Currents and many another risk besides,
Moons, harbours, pilots, he had such dispatch
That none from Hull to Carthage° was his match.
Hardy he was, prudent in undertaking;
His beard in many a tempest had its shaking,
And he knew all the havens as they were
From Gottland° to the Cape of Finisterre,°
And every creek in Brittany and Spain;°
The barge he owned was called *The Maudelayne.*°
A *Doctor* too emerged as we proceeded;

372 guild-fraternity: parish fraternity organized for religious and social service

394 ulcer: an open sore

395 blancmange: a medieval dish of chicken, rice, almonds, almond milk, and spices

405 Bordeaux: a region of France known for excellent wine

412 Hull to Carthage: ports in England and Spain or North Africa

416 Gottland: island off Sweden's southern coast / **Cape of Finisterre:** area of Spain's western coast

417 And every . . . Spain: valuable knowledge for smugglers

418 *The Maudelayne*: possible reference to a ship docked in Dartmouth, a port notorious for piracy

Historical Context: What roles do these pilgrims represent, traditional or nontraditional? What might Chaucer's characterization of them imply about his view of this class? Consider medieval attitudes toward wealth. **R**

Irony: What kind of irony is illustrated in lines 406–8? **A**

No one alive could talk as well as he did
On points of medicine and of surgery,
For, being grounded in astronomy,
He watched his patient's favourable star
And, by his Natural Magic, knew what are
The lucky hours and planetary degrees
For making charms and magic effigies.°
The cause of every malady you'd got
He knew, and whether dry, cold, moist or hot;
He knew their seat, their humour and condition.°
He was a perfect practising physician.
These causes being known for what they were,
He gave the man his medicine then and there.
All his apothecaries in a tribe
Were ready with the drugs he would prescribe,
And each made money from the other's guile;°
They had been friendly for a goodish while.
He was well-versed in Esculapius too
And what Hippocrates and Rufus knew
And Dioscorides, now dead and gone,
Galen and Rhazes, Hali, Serapion,
Averroes, Avicenna, Constantine,
Scotch Bernard, John of Gaddesden, Gilbertine.°
In his own diet he observed some measure;
There were no superfluities for pleasure,
Only digestives, nutritives and such.
He did not read the Bible very much.
In blood-red garments, slashed with bluish-grey
And lined with taffeta, he rode his way;
Yet he was rather close as to expenses
And kept the gold he won in pestilences.
Gold stimulates the heart, or so we're told.
He therefore had a special love of gold. **A**
    A worthy *woman* from beside *Bath* city
Was with us, somewhat deaf, which was a pity.
In making cloth she showed so great a bent
She bettered those of Ypres and of Ghent.°
In all the parish not a dame dared stir
Towards the altar steps in front of her,
And if indeed they did, so wrath was she
As to be quite put out of charity.
Her kerchiefs were of finely woven ground;
I dared have sworn they weighed a good ten pound,
The ones she wore on Sunday, on her head.
Her hose were of the finest scarlet red
And gartered tight; her shoes were soft and new.
Bold was her face, handsome, and red in hue.
A worthy woman all her life, what's more
She'd had five husbands, all at the church door,
Apart from other company in youth;
No need just now to speak of that, forsooth.
And she had thrice been to Jerusalem,

426 He watched . . . effigies: Medieval physicians consulted astrology (prevalent in medieval times) to decide when best to treat each patient.

429 whether dry . . . condition: The qualities of dry, cold, moist, and hot reflected the four humours of the body (black bile, yellow bile, blood, phlegm), which, according to popular medieval theory, must stay in equilibrium for good health.

435 All his . . . guile: Physicians over-prescribed; pharmacists overcharged; both got a cut of the proceeds.

442 He was . . . Gilbertine: medical authorities from Ancient Greece, Persia, and medieval Europe

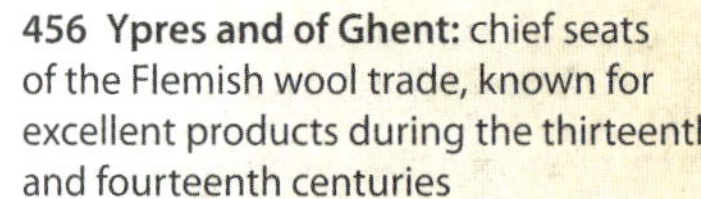

456 Ypres and of Ghent: chief seats of the Flemish wool trade, known for excellent products during the thirteenth and fourteenth centuries

Irony/Tone: What kind of irony do the last two lines exhibit? How do they summarize Chaucer's tone toward the Doctor? **A**

Seen many strange rivers and passed over them;
She'd been to Rome and also to Boulogne,
St James of Compostella and Cologne,°
And she was skilled in wandering by the way.
She had gap-teeth, set widely,° truth to say.
Easily on an ambling horse she sat
Well wimpled up,° and on her head a hat
As broad as is a buckler or a shield;
She had a flowing mantle that concealed
Large hips, her heels spurred sharply under that.
In company she liked to laugh and chat
And knew the remedies for love's mischances,
An art in which she knew the oldest dances. A

474 Rome . . . Cologne: sites of famous shrines in Italy, France, Spain, and Germany respectively

476 She had . . . widely: a mark of assertiveness and sensuality

478 Well wimpled up: having a cloth wimple wrapped around her neck, head, and the sides of her face

A holy-minded man of good renown
There was, and poor, the *Parson* to a town,
Yet he was rich in holy thought and work.
He also was a learned man, a clerk,
Who truly knew Christ's gospel and would preach it
Devoutly to parishioners, and teach it.
Benign and wonderfully diligent,
And patient when adversity was sent
(For so he proved in great adversity)
He much disliked extorting tithe or fee,
Nay rather he preferred beyond a doubt
Giving to poor parishioners round about
From his own goods and Easter offerings.
He found sufficiency in little things.
Wide was his parish, with houses far asunder,
Yet he neglected not in rain or thunder,
In sickness or in grief, to pay a call
On the remotest, whether great or small,
Upon his feet, and in his hand a stave.
This noble example to his sheep he gave,
First following the word before he taught it,
And it was from the gospel he had caught it.
This little proverb he would add thereto
That if gold rust, what then will iron do?
For if a priest be foul in whom we trust
No wonder that a common man should rust;
And shame it is to see—let priests take stock—
A shitten shepherd and a snowy flock.
The true example that a priest should give
Is one of cleanness, how the sheep should live.
He did not set his benefice to hire°
And leave his sheep **encumbered** in the mire
Or run to London to earn easy bread
By singing masses for the wealthy dead,°
Or find some Brotherhood and get enrolled.
He stayed at home and watched over his fold
So that no wolf should make the sheep miscarry.

515 He did . . . to hire: pay a vicar to perform his parish duties

518 singing . . . wealthy dead: The rich endowed chantries where monks sang daily masses for their souls after death.

Characterization: What is the Woman of Bath's physical appearance and dress meant to tell the reader about her? A

encumber (ĕn-kŭm′bər) *tr.v.* To cause to have difficulty in moving or in accomplishing something; burden.

He was a shepherd and no mercenary.
Holy and virtuous he was, but then
Never contemptuous of sinful men,
Never disdainful, never too proud or fine
But was discreet in teaching and benign.
His business was to show a fair behaviour
And draw men thus to Heaven and their Saviour,
Unless indeed a man were obstinate;
And such, whether of high or low estate,
He put to sharp rebuke to say the least.
I think there never was a better priest.
He sought no pomp or glory in his dealings,
No scrupulosity had spiced his feelings.
Christ and His Twelve Apostles and their lore
He taught, but followed it himself before.
    There was a *Plowman* with him there, his brother.
Many a load of dung one time or other
He must have carted through the morning dew.
He was an honest worker, good and true,
Living in peace and perfect charity,
And, as the gospel bade him, so did he,
Loving God best with all his heart and mind
And then his neighbour as himself, repined
At no misfortune, slacked for no content,
For steadily about his work he went
To thrash his corn, to dig or to manure
Or make a ditch; and he would help the poor
For love of Christ and never take a penny
If he could help it, and, as prompt as any,
He paid his tithes in full when they were due
On what he owned, and on his earnings too.
He wore a tabard smock° and rode a mare.
    There was a *Reeve*, also a *Miller*, there,
A College *Manciple* from the Inns of Court,°
A papal *Pardoner* and, in close consort,
A Church-Court *Summoner*, riding at a trot,
And finally myself—that was the lot.
    The *Miller* was a chap of sixteen stone,°
A great stout fellow big in brawn and bone.
He did well out of them, for he could go
And win the ram at any wrestling show.
Broad, knotty and short-shouldered, he would boast
He could heave any door off hinge and post,
Or take a run and break it with his head.
His beard, like any sow or fox, was red
And broad as well, as though it were a spade;
And, at its very tip, his nose displayed
A wart on which there stood a tuft of hair
Red as the bristles in an old sow's ear.
His nostrils were as black as they were wide.

553 tabard smock: a short, coarse coat

555 Inns of Court: four law associations in London to which all British lawyers (barristers) must belong

559 stone: British unit of weight, about 14 pounds

Historical Context: How does the Parson differ from the Monk and the Friar? What social problem is Chaucer clearly taking aim at with these characters?

He had a sword and buckler at his side,
His mighty mouth was like a furnace door.°
A wrangler and buffoon, he had a store
Of tavern stories, filthy in the main.
His was a master-hand at stealing grain.
. . . .
He wore a hood of blue and a white coat.
He liked to play his bagpipes up and down
And that was how he brought us out of town. A

573 like a furnace door: i.e., like pictures of the entrance of hell in medieval art

The *Manciple*° came from the Inner Temple;°
All caterers might follow his example
In buying victuals; he was never rash
Whether he bought on credit or paid cash.
He used to watch the market most precisely
And got in first, and so he did quite nicely.
Now isn't it a marvel of God's grace
That an illiterate fellow can outpace
The wisdom of a heap of learned men?
His masters—he had more than thirty then—
All versed in the abstrusest legal knowledge,
Could have produced a dozen from their College
Fit to be stewards in land and rents and game
To any Peer° in England you could name,
And show him how to live on what he had
Debt-free (unless of course the Peer were mad)
Or be as frugal as he might desire,
And they were fit to help about the Shire
In any legal case there was to try;
And yet this Manciple could wipe their eye.°

580 Manciple: purchasing agent of a college / **Inner Temple:** one of the four Inns of Court

593 Peer: nobleman

599 wipe their eye: cheat them

The *Reeve*° was old and choleric° and thin;
His beard was shaven closely to the skin,
His shorn hair came abruptly to a stop
Above his ears, and he was docked on top
Just like a priest in front; his legs were lean,
Like sticks they were, no calf was to be seen.
He kept his bins and garners very trim;
No auditor could gain a point on him.
And he could judge by watching drought and rain
The yield he might expect from seed and grain.
His master's sheep, his animals and hens,
Pigs, horses, dairies, stores and cattle-pens
Were wholly trusted to his government.
And he was under contract to present
The accounts, right from his master's earliest years.
No one had ever caught him in arrears.
No bailiff,° serf or herdsman dared to kick,
He knew their dodges, knew their every trick;°

600 Reeve: manager of one of a nobleman's manors, in this case directly responsible to the lord / **choleric:** personality type prone to anger

616 bailiff: under-steward

617 dodges . . . trick: their ways of cheating and shirking

Characterization: Chaucer's physical description of the Miller is particularly vivid. What figurative language does Chaucer employ to describe the Miller's beard, the hair on his wart, his nostrils, and his mouth? What personal character trait does Chaucer share about the Miller? A

Feared like the plague he was, by those beneath. A
He had a lovely dwelling on a heath,
Shadowed in green by trees above the sward.°
A better hand at bargains than his lord,
He had grown rich and had a store of treasure
Well tucked away, yet out it came to pleasure
His lord with subtle loans or gifts of goods,
To earn his thanks and even coats and hoods.
When young he'd learnt a useful trade and still
He was a carpenter of first-rate skill.
The stallion-cob he rode at a slow trot
Was dapple-grey and bore the name of Scot.
He wore an overcoat of bluish shade
And rather long; he had a rusty blade
Slung at his side. He came, as I heard tell,
From Norfolk, near a place called Baldeswell.
His coat was tucked under his belt and splayed.
He rode the hindmost of our cavalcade.

There was a *Summoner*° with us in the place
Who had a fire-red cherubinnish face,
For he had carbuncles.° His eyes were narrow,
He was as hot and lecherous as a sparrow.
Black, scabby brows he had, and a thin beard.
Children were afraid when he appeared.
No quicksilver, lead ointments, tartar creams,
Boracic, no, nor brimstone,° so it seems,
Could make a salve that had the power to bite,
Clean up or cure his whelks° of knobby white
Or purge the pimples sitting on his cheeks.
Garlic he loved, and onions too, and leeks,
And drinking strong wine till all was hazy.
Then he would shout and jabber as if crazy,
And wouldn't speak a word except in Latin
When he was drunk, such tags as he was pat in;
He only had a few, say two or three,
That he had mugged up° out of some decree;
No wonder, for he heard them every day.
And, as you know, a man can teach a jay
To call out 'Walter' better than the Pope.
But had you tried to test his wits and grope
For more, you'd have found nothing in the bag.
Then '*Questio quid juris*'° was his tag.
He was a gentle varlet° and a kind one,
No better fellow if you went to find one. . . .
And if he found some rascal with a maid
He would instruct him not to be afraid
In such a case of the Archdeacon's curse°
(Unless the rascal's soul were in his purse)
For in his purse the punishment should be.
'Purse is the good Archdeacon's Hell,' said he.
But well I know he lied in what he said;

620 sward: grassy land

636 Summoner: one who summoned violators of canon law to an ecclesiastical court

638 carbuncles: severe sores created by bacterial infection in the skin, usually reddened and oozing; in the medieval period, denoted lechery

643 No quicksilver . . . brimstone: medieval treatments for skin infections

645 whelks: swellings

653 mugged up: memorized

659 *Questio quid juris*: legal jargon; translated "The question is, what part of the law [applies]?"

660 varlet: rascal

664 Archdeacon's curse: excommunication, presided over by an archdeacon in ecclesiastical courts

Characterization/Irony: What does the rest of the description imply is the reason that the Reeve knows the workers' every trick for cheating and shirking? What kind of irony do lines 621–25 especially illustrate? A

A curse should put a guilty man in dread,
For curses kill, as shriving brings, salvation.
We should beware of excommunication.
Thus, as he pleased, the man could bring **duress**
On any young fellow in the diocese.
He knew their secrets, they did what he said.
He wore a garland set upon his head
Large as the holly-bush upon a stake
Outside an ale-house, and he had a cake,
A round one, which it was his joke to wield
As if it were intended for a shield. R

He and a gentle *Pardoner*° rode together,
A bird from Charing Cross° of the same feather,
Just back from visiting the Court of Rome.
He loudly sang '*Come hither, love, come home!*'°
The Summoner sang deep seconds to this song,
No trumpet ever sounded half so strong.
This Pardoner had hair as yellow as wax,
Hanging down smoothly like a hank of flax.
In driblets fell his locks behind his head
Down to his shoulders which they overspread;
Thinly they fell, like rat-tails, one by one.
He wore no hood upon his head, for fun;
The hood inside his wallet° had been stowed,
He aimed at riding in the latest mode;
But for a little cap his head was bare
And he had bulging eye-balls, like a hare.
He'd sewed a holy relic on his cap;
His wallet lay before him on his lap,
Brimful of pardons come from Rome all got.
He had the same small voice a goat has got.
His chin no beard had harboured, nor would harbour,
Smoother than ever chin was left by barber.
I judge he was a gelding,° or a mare.
As to his trade, from Berwick down to Ware°
There was no pardoner of equal grace,
For in his trunk he had a pillow-case
Which he asserted was Our Lady's° veil.
He said he had a gobbet of the sail
Saint Peter had the time when he made bold
To walk the waves, till Jesu Christ took hold.
He had a cross of metal set with stones
And in a glass, a rubble of pigs' bones.
And with these relics,° any time he found
Some poor up-country parson to astound
On one short day, in money down, he drew
More than the parson in a month or two,
And by his flatteries and **prevarication**

680 Pardoner: a person who sold papal indulgences waiving some of the buyer's punishment for sins

681 Charing Cross: area of London

683 Come . . . home!: from a popular love song

692 wallet: knapsack

702 gelding: a castrated animal (usually a horse)

703 Berwick . . . Ware: English towns in the north and south respectively

706 Our Lady's: the virgin Mary's

712 relics: objects considered sacred by association with a religious figure; often physical remains

duress (dŏŏ-rĕs′) *n.* Compulsion by threat or violence; coercion.

Historical Context: Chaucer has nothing good to say about the Summoner. What about his vices are so toxic? R

prevarication (prĭ-văr′ĭ-kā′shən) *n.* Avoidance of straightforward statement of the truth; equivocation, evasiveness, misrepresentation; deceit; an instance of this.

Made monkeys of the priest and congregation.
But still to do him justice first and last
In church he was a noble ecclesiast.
How well he read a lesson or told a story!
But best of all he sang an Offertory,
For well he knew that when that song was sung
He'd have to preach and tune his honey-tongue
And (well he could) win silver from the crowd.
That's why he sang so merrily and loud. **C**

The remaining 144 lines of "The Prologue" tell how the innkeeper himself becomes a pilgrim. At supper he proposes a plan to award the winner of a storytelling contest with a free dinner at the others' expense on the return from Canterbury. Obviously a business scheme, it will bring the entire company back to his inn for another meal and presumably for another night's lodging.

Satirical Character Sketch: Review Chaucer's characterization of the Pardoner. Does Chaucer end with mild or strong satire? What kind of characterizations does he use to convey his thoughts? **C**

THINK AND DISCUSS

1. What broad genre and purpose does Chaucer pursue in *The Canterbury Tales*?
2. How does "The Prologue" qualify as a frame tale? What purpose unites its characters?
3. What are some common flaws that Chaucer points out in his characters? Do any characters escape his satire?
4. Choose two characters and list three examples each of direct characterization from their descriptions.
5. Choose two characters and list three examples each of indirect characterization from their descriptions.
6. The Pardoner states that greediness is evil. How does this statement illustrate irony? Briefly explain.
7. Chaucer often conveys his tone by creating irony, sometimes through indirect characterization or direct statements that violate readers' expectations for a character based on his or her role. Choose a character and cite several such details conveying Chaucer's tone.
8. Describe how Chaucer has already satirized religious professionals. Support your ideas with textual details.
9. Chaucer uses figures such as the Franklin, Man of Law, Cleric, Cook, Shipman, Physician, and Wife of Bath to represent middle-class influence in society. What does his point of view on that influence seem to be so far? Cite details from the text to support your answer.
10. How has Chaucer already used satire to affirm goodness and condemn wrong? Do you disagree with any of his points so far?
11. Choose a public person or perhaps a societal stereotype that you want to comment on (positively or negatively) for a constructive purpose. Compose a brief satirical description of that person or stereotype that might help a reader recognize and understand the problems you see, and then seek to correct the problems. Remember that your constructive purpose should be clear.

ANALYZE: *Beast Fable and Mock Epic*

The **beast fable** (or bestiary) is a brief, fanciful tale that embodies a moral and in which animals act like humans. In Europe, the genre was long influenced by the *Physiologus*, a second-century Greek work that drew Christian lessons from various "facts" about animals, plants, and stones. Large collections of such fables were available in Chaucer's day for entertainment as well as instruction. "The Nun's Priest's Tale" was adapted out of a French collection, *Roman de Renard*, which told stories of a fox named Reynard.

The potential for satire in a beast fable is obvious: the very notion that animals can behave in human ways is deflating to human pride. "The Nun's Priest's Tale" adds to that potential through its role as a **mock epic**, a tale that treats a trivial subject in heroic terms. As you read, consider how the characters themselves, the ways in which they express themselves, and the nature of the plot give comic significance to the activities of the animal kingdom, thus poking fun at human folly. What aspects of human behavior might Chaucer be satirizing through these elements of the story?

READ: *Compare Text to Text*

Comparing Chanticleer's story to other texts can help reveal Chaucer's satirical point. First, remember what you have learned about medieval epics and romances. As you read, notice how Chaucer riffs off the idealized characters, flowery language, and courtly love themes of these genres. Additionally, the narrating Priest suggests an analogy between his story and the fall of man. As you examine the character and actions of the story's main participants, compare them with the narrative of Adam and Eve in the Bible. What similarities does the Priest draw between Chanticleer and Adam, Pertelote and Eve, and the fox and Satan? Are these similarities biblically accurate or inaccurate? How so? What might the Priest intend them to mean?

EVALUATE: *Use of Satire*

Remember that satire uses ridicule to correct behavior. Among its tools are mild mockery, irony, caricature (an exaggerated depiction of a person that makes him appear ridiculous), and **parody** (imitating another author's style for comic effect). Depending on the context and seriousness of its target, its intensity can vary from gentle correction to harsh invective. In any case, the intention ought to be primarily constructive rather than destructive, self-indulgent, or self-righteous. Consider the biblical examples of 1 Kings 18:27 and 2 Kings 2:23. Why did Elijah speak to the prophets of Baal as he did? How does Elijah's communication compare with that of the young people who mocked Elisha? Why do you think the outcome in each situation was different? As you continue reading from *The Canterbury Tales*, consider whether Chaucer's satire is appropriate. What does the purpose of his satire seem to be? Does he achieve that purpose? Be prepared to use specific examples to support your opinions.

OBJECTIVES

- Identify the characteristics of beast fables and mock epics.
- Compare two or more texts.
- Analyze the use of satire to critique society.
- Evaluate the effectiveness and appropriateness of Chaucer's use of satire.

VOCABULARY

debonair (dĕb′ə-nâr′) *adj.* Sophisticated; urbane.

rhetorician (rĕt′ə-rĭsh′ən) *n.* An expert in or teacher of *rhetoric* (*n.* the art or study of using language effectively and persuasively).

stringent (strĭn′jənt) *adj.* Imposing rigorous standards of performance; severe.

contingent (kən-tĭn′jənt) *adj.* Dependent on other conditions or circumstances; conditional.

emulate (ĕm′yə-lāt′) *tr.v.* To strive to equal or excel, especially through imitation.

sycophant (sĭk′ə-fənt, sī′kə-) *n.* A person who attempts to gain advantage by flattering influential people or behaving in a servile manner.

Have you ever learned something the HARD WAY?

We constantly get advice on everything from simple matters such as shopping to complex ones such as relationships. Sometimes this advice is good and we follow it; other times we think it is safe to ignore. Have you ever ignored advice that could have prevented trouble? Did you want to go back and change the past? Or was the experience valuable because you learned a useful lesson? Write about your experience and its effect on you.

VISUAL ANALYSIS
What qualites of the mock epic does the artist illustrate in the way he constructed his image?

FROM The Nun's Priest's Tale

Once, long ago, there dwelt a poor old widow
In a small cottage, by a little meadow
Beside a grove and standing in a dale.
This widow-woman of whom I tell my tale
Since the sad day when last she was a wife
Had led a very patient, simple life.
Little she had in capital or rent,
But still, by making do with what God sent,
She kept herself and her two daughters going.
Three hefty sows—no more—were all her showing,
Three cows as well; there was a sheep called Molly.
Sooty her hall,° her kitchen melancholy,
And there she ate full many a slender meal;
There was no *sauce piquante*° to spice her veal,
No dainty morsel ever passed her throat,
According to her cloth she cut her coat.°
Repletion never left her in disquiet
And all her physic° was a temperate diet,
Hard work for exercise and heart's content.
And rich man's gout° did nothing to prevent
Her dancing, apoplexy° struck her not;
She drank no wine, nor white nor red had got.
Her board was mostly served with white and black,
Milk and brown bread, in which she found no lack;
Broiled bacon or an egg or two were common,
She was in fact a sort of dairy-woman.
She had a yard that was enclosed about
By a stockade and a dry ditch without,
In which she kept a cock called Chanticleer.
In all the land for crowing he'd no peer;
His voice was jollier than the organ blowing
In church on Sundays, he was great at crowing.
Far, far more regular than any clock
Or abbey bell the crowing of this cock.
The equinoctial wheel° and its position
At each ascent he knew by intuition;
At every hour—fifteen degrees of movement—
He crowed so well there could be no improvement.
His comb was redder than fine coral, tall
And battlemented like a castle wall,
His bill was black and shone as bright as jet,
Like azure° were his legs and they were set
On azure toes with nails of lily white,
Like burnished gold his feathers, flaming bright.
This gentlecock was master in some measure
Of seven hens, all there to do his pleasure. A
They were his sisters and his paramours,°
Coloured like him in all particulars;

12 her hall: referring to a nobleman's hall, a comic reference in context

14 sauce piquante: a spicy brown sauce; French in origin

16 According . . . coat: idiom, to live within one's means

18 physic: medicine

20 gout: inflammation of the joints traditionally associated with a rich diet

21 apoplexy: stroke

35 equinoctial wheel: an imaginary circle around the earth's equator that rotates 360 degrees in a day; used for telling time, as Chanticleer does in line 37

42 azure: sky blue

47 paramours: lovers

Beast Fable/Mock Epic: Reread the descriptions of the widow and Chanticleer. Which description is more modest? Explain your answer with details. What human trait do you think the Priest is using Chanticleer to critique? A

She with the loveliest dyes upon her throat
Was known as gracious Lady Pertelote.
Courteous she was, discreet and **debonair**,
Companionable too, and took such care
In her deportment,° since she was seven days old
She held the heart of Chanticleer controlled,
Locked up securely in her every limb;
O such happiness his love to him!
And such a joy it was to hear them sing,
As when the glorious sun began to spring,
In sweet accord *My Love is far from land*
—For in those far off days I understand
All birds and animals could speak and sing. **A**

Now it befell, as dawn began to spring,
When Chanticleer and Pertelote and all
His wives were perched in this poor widow's hall
(Fair Pertelote was next him on the perch),
This Chanticleer began to groan and lurch
Like someone sorely troubled by a dream,
And Pertelote who heard him roar and scream
Was quite aghast and said, 'O dearest heart,
What's ailing you? Why do you groan and start?
Fie,° what a sleeper! What a noise to make!'
'Madam,' he said, 'I beg you not to take
Offence, but by the Lord I had a dream
So terrible just now I had to scream;
I still can feel my heart racing from fear.
God turn my dream to good and guard all here.
And keep my body out of durance vile!°
I dreamt that roaming up and down a while
Within our yard I saw a kind of beast,
A sort of hound that tried or seemed at least
To try and seize me . . . would have killed me dead!
His colour was a blend of yellow and red,
His ears and tail were tipped with sable fur
Unlike the rest; he was a russet cur.°
Small was his snout, his eyes were glowing bright.
It was enough to make one die of fright.
That was no doubt what made me groan and swoon.' **✓**

'For shame,' she said, 'you timorous poltroon!°
. . . .
How dare you say for shame, and to your love,
That anything at all was to be feared?
Have you no manly heart to match your beard?
And can a dream reduce you to such terror?
Dreams are a vanity, God knows, pure error.' **A**
. . . .

53 deportment: behavior, conduct

71 Fie: an interjection used to express disgust or disapproval

77 durance vile: evil traps or snares

84 russet cur: red-haired dog

88 timorous poltroon: timid or fearful coward

debonair (dĕb′ə-nâr′) *adj.* Sophisticated; urbane.

Mock Epic: What is comical about the way in which Lady Pertelote and Lord Chanticleer are portrayed? What genre that you have already studied do you think Chaucer is satirizing in these portrayals? **A**

Reading Check: What is the gist of Chanticleer's dream? **✓**

Mock Epic: How does Pertelote respond to Chanticleer regarding the dream? What trait, sometimes stereotyped in wives, is the Priest using Pertelote to satirize? **A**

For most of the next 265 lines, Pertelote and Chanticleer debate the significance of dreams. Pertelote attributes them to natural causes (indigestion) and Chanticleer to supernatural. Pertelote prescribes an herb remedy, showing wifely concern for her husband's health. His dignity offended, Chanticleer counters with a long string of instances, drawn from learned "authorities," in which disregard of dreams proved ruinous. This tour de force of classical knowledge from a rooster adds to the story's comedy. Finally, to be certain that he has silenced Pertelote once and for all on the matter of dreams, he flatters her, saying, "When I look on the beauty of your face, / And see those scarlet circles round your eyes, / Then all the terror that affrights me dies." His self-assurance restored, he flies from his perch and begins his daily routine without the slightest concern for what had troubled him. At last the Priest picks up the thread of the story.

    Now when the month in which the world began,
March, the first month, when God created man,°
Was over, and the thirty-second day
Thereafter ended, on the third of May
It happened that Chanticleer in all his pride,
His seven wives attendant at his side,
Cast his eyes upward to the blazing sun,
Which in the sign of *Taurus*° then had run
His twenty-one degrees and somewhat more,
And knew by nature and no other lore
That it was nine o'clock. With blissful voice
He crew triumphantly and said, 'Rejoice,
Behold the sun! The sun is up, my seven.
Look, it has climbed forty degrees in heaven,
Forty degrees and one in fact, by this.
Dear Madam Pertelote, my earthly bliss,
Hark to those blissful birds and how they sing!
Look at those pretty flowers, how they spring!
Solace and revel° fill my heart!' He laughed.
    But in that moment Fate let fly her shaft;
Ever the latter end of joy is woe,
God knows that worldly joy is swift to go.
A **rhetorician** with a flair for style
Could chronicle this maxim in his file
Of Notable Remarks with safe conviction.
Then let the wise give ear; this is no fiction
My story is as true, I undertake,
As that of good Sir Lancelot du Lake
Who held all women in such high esteem.
Let me return full circle to my theme.
    A coal-tipped fox of sly iniquity
That had been lurking round the grove for three

95 Now when . . . God created man: Medieval tradition dated Creation at the spring equinox (then March 12 rather than the modern March 21 because of differences in the calendar).

101 Taurus: constellation of the bull

112 revel: celebration, delight

Text to Text: What lines from this passage (lines 94–115) point to a comparison with the biblical narrative of Genesis?

rhetorician (rĕt′ə-rĭsh′ən) *n.* An expert in or teacher of *rhetoric* (*n.* the art or study of using language effectively and persuasively).

Long years, that very night burst through and passed
Stockade and hedge, as Providence forecast,
Into the yard where Chanticleer the Fair
Was wont,° with all his ladies, to repair.
Still, in a bed of cabbages, he lay
Until about the middle of the day
Watching the cock and waiting for his cue,
As all these homicides so gladly do
That lie about in wait to murder men.
O false assassin, lurking in thy den!
O new Iscariot, new Ganelon!°
And O Greek Sinon,° thou whose treachery won
Troy town and brought it utterly to sorrow!
O Chanticleer, accursed be that morrow
That brought thee to the yard from thy high beams!
Thou hadst been warned, and truly, by thy dreams
That this would be a perilous day for thee.
    But that which God's foreknowledge can foresee
Must needs occur, as certain men of learning
Have said. Ask any scholar of discerning;
He'll say the Schools are filled with altercation
On this vexed matter of predestination°
Long bandied by a hundred thousand men.
How can I sift it to the bottom then?
The Holy Doctor St Augustine shines
In this, and there is Bishop Bradwardine's
Authority, Boethius'° too, decreeing
Whether the fact of God's divine foreseeing
Constrains me to perform a certain act
—And by 'constraint' I mean the simple fact
Of mere compulsion by necessity—
Or whether a free choice is granted me
To do a given act or not to do it
Though, ere it was accomplished, God foreknew it,
Or whether Providence is not so **stringent**
And merely makes necessity **contingent**.
    But I decline discussion of the matter;
My tale is of a cock and of the clatter
That came of following his wife's advice
To walk about his yard on the precise
Morning after the dream of which I told.
    O woman's counsel is so often cold!
A woman's counsel brought us first to woe,
Made Adam out of Paradise to go
Where he had been so merry, so well at ease.
But, for I know not whom it may displease
If I suggest that women are to blame,

129 wont: accustomed, used

136 Ganelon: knight who betrayed Roland, legendary prince and nephew of Charlemagne, to the Saracens at the battle of Roncesvalles in 778

137 Sinon: Greek soldier who deceived the Trojans to bring about the fall of Troy

147 predestination: "the doctrine that God has foreordained all things, especially that God has elected certain souls to eternal salvation" (*AHD*)

152 St Augustine . . . Boethius': St. Augustine (354–430), Roman philosopher Boethius (ca. 480–524), and Archbishop of Canterbury, Bradwardine (1290–1349), all debated God's sovereignty and man's free will. In context, the Priest is displaying his learning, while Chaucer is ridiculing vain theological wrangling.

Text to Text: In what ways does the fox resemble Satan in Genesis? (Consider lines 124–29.) What part of the Genesis narrative do lines 139–42 mirror?

stringent (strĭn′jənt) *adj.* Imposing rigorous standards of performance; severe.

contingent (kən-tĭn′jənt) *adj.* Dependent on other conditions or circumstances; conditional.

Pass over that; I only speak in game.°
Read the authorities to know about
What has been said of women; you'll find out.
These are the cock's words, and not mine, I'm giving;
I think no harm of any woman living. R
    Merrily in her dust-bath in the sand
Lay Pertelote. Her sisters were at hand
Basking in sunlight. Chanticleer sang free,
More merrily than a mermaid in the sea
(For *Physiologus*° reports the thing
And says how well and merrily they sing).
And so it happened as he cast his eye
Towards the cabbage at a butterfly
It fell upon the fox there, lying low.
Gone was all inclination then to crow.
'Cok cok,' he cried, giving a sudden start,
As one who feels a terror at his heart,
For natural instinct teaches beasts to flee
The moment they perceive an enemy,
Though they had never met with it before.
    This Chanticleer was shaken to the core
And would have fled. The fox was quick to say
However, 'Sir! Whither so fast away?
Are you afraid of me, that am your friend?
A fiend, or worse, I should be, to intend
You harm, or practise villainy upon you;
Dear sir, I was not even spying on you!
Truly I came to do no other thing
Than just to lie and listen to you sing.
You have as merry a voice as God has given
To any angel in the courts of Heaven;
To that you add a musical sense as strong
As had Boethius° who was skilled in song.
My Lord your Father (God receive his soul!),
Your mother too—how courtly, what control!—
Have honoured my poor house, to my great ease;
And you, sir, too, I should be glad to please.
For, when it comes to singing, I'll say this
(Else may these eyes of mine be barred from bliss),
There never was a singer I would rather
Have heard at dawn than your respected father. R
All that he sang came welling from his soul
And how he put his voice under control!
The pains he took to keep his eyes tight shut
In concentration—then the tip-toe strut,
The slender neck stretched out, the delicate beak!
No singer could approach him in technique
Or rival him in song, still less surpass.
I've read the story in *Burnel the Ass*,°
Among some other verses, of a cock

173 in game: in jest, jokingly

182 *Physiologus*: an ancient collection of beast fables (p. 92)

205 Boethius: author of the standard medieval textbook on music theory

221 *Burnel the Ass*: from *A Mirror of Fools*, a Latin verse satire of the religious orders

Text to Text: What lines explicitly connect this tale to the Genesis narrative? Do you think the Priest is being serious in his discussion of women? Explain. R

Text to Text: How does the fox in lines 194–213 resemble Satan in Eden? R

Whose leg in youth was broken by a knock
A clergyman's son had given him, and for this
He made the father lose his benefice.°
But certainly there's no comparison
Between the subtlety of such an one
And the discretion of your father's art
And wisdom. Oh, for charity of heart,
Can you not **emulate** your sire and sing?'
This Chanticleer began to beat a wing
As one incapable of smelling treason,
So wholly had this flattery ravished reason. A
Alas, my lords! there's many a **sycophant**
And flatterer that fill your courts with cant°
And give more pleasure with their zeal forsooth
Than he who speaks in soberness and truth.
Read what Ecclesiasticus° records
Of flatterers. 'Ware° treachery, my lords! E
This Chanticleer stood high upon his toes,
He stretched his neck, his eyes began to close,
His beak to open; with his eyes shut tight
He then began to sing with all his might.
Sir Russel Fox then leapt to the attack,
Grabbing his gorge he flung him o'er his back
And off he bore him to the woods, the brute,
And for the moment there was no pursuit.
O Destiny that may not be evaded!
Alas that Chanticleer had so paraded!
Alas that he had flown down from the beams!
O that his wife took no account of dreams!

. . . .

Sure never such a cry or lamentation
Was made by ladies of high Trojan station,
When Ilium° fell and Pyrrhus° with his sword
Grabbed Priam by the beard, their king and lord,
And slew him there as the *Aeneid*° tells,
As what was uttered by those hens. Their yells
Surpassed them all in palpitating° fear
When they beheld the rape of Chanticleer.
Dame Pertelote emitted sovereign shrieks
That echoed up in anguish to the peaks
Louder than those extorted from the wife
Of Hasdrubal,° when he had lost his life
And Carthage all in flame and ashes lay.
She was so full of torment and dismay
That in the very flames she chose her part
And burnt to ashes with a steadfast heart.
O woeful hens, louder your shrieks and higher

225 benefice: A church office that comes with a fixed income. In other words, the cock failed to wake the boy on his ordination, thus forfeiting the right to such an office.

235 cant: pious but hypocritical speech about religious, moral, or political values

238 Ecclesiasticus: reference to Ecclesiasticus, a book in the Apocrypha

239 'Ware: beware

254 Ilium: Troy / **Pyrrhus:** Greek prince, son of Achilles

256 *Aeneid*: epic by the Roman poet Virgil (70–19 BC) recounting the adventures of the Trojan hero Aeneas and his founding of Rome

258 palpitating: trembling, shaking

263 Hasdrubal: ancient king of Carthage

emulate (ĕm'yə-lāt') *tr.v.* To strive to equal or excel, especially through imitation.

Beast Fable/Mock Epic: What human trait is the Priest using Chanticleer's response to the fox to satirize? A

sycophant (sĭk'ə-fənt, sī'kə-) *n.* A person who attempts to gain advantage by flattering influential people or behaving in a servile manner.

Use of Satire: Do you think Chaucer's use of satire here is appropriate from a biblical perspective? E

Than those of Roman matrons when the fire
Consumed their husbands, senators of Rome,
When Nero burnt their city and their home,
Beyond a doubt that Nero was their bale!°
Now let me turn again to tell my tale;
This blessed widow and her daughters two
Heard all these hens in clamour and halloo°
And, rushing to the door at all this shrieking,
They saw the fox towards the covert streaking
And, on his shoulder, Chanticleer stretched flat.
'Look, look!' they cried, 'O mercy, look at that!
Ha! Ha! the fox!' and after him they ran,°
And stick in hand ran many a serving man,
Ran Coll our dog, ran Talbot, Bran and Shaggy,
And with a distaff° in her hand ran Maggie,
Ran cow and calf and ran the very hogs
In terror at the barking of the dogs;
The men and women shouted, ran and cursed,
They ran so hard they thought their hearts would burst,
They yelled like fiends in Hell, ducks left the water
Quacking and flapping as on point of slaughter,
Up flew the geese in terror over the trees,
Out of the hive came forth the swarm of bees;
So hideous was the noise—God bless us all,
Jack Straw and all his followers in their brawl
Were never half so shrill, for all their noise,
When they were murdering those Flemish boys,°
As that day's hue and cry upon the fox.
They grabbed up trumpets made of brass and box,
Of horn and bone, on which they blew and pooped,°
And therewithal they shouted and they whooped
So that it seemed the very heavens would fall. ✓
And now, good people, pay attention all.
See how Dame Fortune quickly changes side
And robs her enemy of hope and pride!
This cock that lay upon the fox's back
In all his dread contrived to give a quack
And said, 'Sir Fox, if I were you, as God's
My witness, I would round upon these clods
And shout, "Turn back, you saucy bumpkins all!
A very pestilence upon you fall!
Now that I have in safety reached the wood
Do what you like, the cock is mine for good;
I'll eat him there in spite of everyone."'
The fox replying, 'Faith, it shall be done!'
Opened his mouth and spoke. The nimble bird,
Breaking away upon the uttered word,

272 bale: misfortune, woe, misery

275 halloo: long cries intended to be heard at a distance, usually to draw attention

280 after . . . ran: The fox chase is a stock incident in medieval poetry.

283 distaff: a stick around which unspun fibers, such as wool or flax, are wound for spinning

295 Jack Straw . . . Flemish boys: Jack Straw was a leader of the Peasants' Revolt of 1381, in which English cloth workers killed many of their Flemish competitors.

298 pooped: made a short blast

Reading Check: What common event of English country life is being portrayed in the preceding lines on this page? ✓

Flew high into the tree-tops on the spot. A
And when the fox perceived where he had got,
'Alas,' he cried, 'alas, my Chanticleer,
I've done you grievous wrong, indeed I fear
I must have frightened you; I grabbed too hard
When I caught hold and took you from the yard.
But, sir, I meant no harm, don't be offended,
Come down and I'll explain what I intended;
So help me God I'll tell the truth—on oath!
'No,' said the cock, 'and curses on us both,
And first on me if I were such a dunce
As let you fool me oftener than once.
Never again, for all your flattering lies,
You'll coax a song to make me blink my eyes;
And as for those who blink when they should look,
God blot them from his everlasting Book!'°
'Nay, rather,' said the fox, 'his plagues be flung
On all who chatter that should hold their tongue.'
    Lo, such it is not to be on your guard
Against the flatterers of the world, or yard,
And if you think my story is absurd,
A foolish trifle of a beast and bird,
A fable of a fox, a cock, a hen,
Take hold upon the moral, gentlemen.
    St Paul himself, a saint of great discerning,
Says that all things are written for our learning;°
So take the grain and let the chaff be still.°
And, gracious Father, if it be thy will
As saith my Saviour, make us all good men,
And bring us to his heavenly bliss. E
Amen.

331 everlasting Book: the Book of the Living (Psalm 69:28)

341 St Paul . . . learning: Romans 15:4

342 So take . . . be still: standard medieval terminology for distinguishing the doctrinal and fictional elements of a poetic narrative

Mock Epic: How does Chanticleer's tricking of the fox compare to the fox's tricking of Chanticleer? What human trait is this reversal satirizing? A

Use of Satire: What preceding lines speak explicitly of the use of this satire? Is this use appropriate biblically? E

THINK AND DISCUSS

1. Using specific examples from the tale, explain why "The Nun's Priest's Tale" can be categorized as a mock epic.
2. How is Chanticleer described directly? Indirectly?
3. How is the fox described directly? Indirectly?
4. How does Chaucer use the animals' behavior to satirize human behavior?
5. How does Chaucer use the animals' conversation to satirize human conversation?
6. Compare the character and actions of Chanticleer and Pertelote to those of Adam and Eve, and compare the fox to Satan.
7. Using specific examples from the tale, explain what you think Chaucer's purpose for this satire was. Do you think his purpose was constructive? Destructive?
8. Out of the three qualities of Truth, Beauty, and Goodness, which is most prominent in this story? Defend your answer using examples from the text.

PIERS PLOWMAN

During the fourteenth century, recurring war, plague, famine, and unrest caused England, especially its poorest citizens, much misery. At the same time, wealthy elites resisted social change that would surrender their favored position, and corrupt Church officials seemed more interested in material than spiritual wealth. This context prompted the writing of one of the great masterworks of Middle English, *Piers Plowman,* a combination of social satire and devotional allegory.

The Author and Text

Not much is known about the work's author except what scholars can deduce from the manuscript and the research it prompts. Evidence from the poem and one manuscript (ca. 1400) strongly suggests the author to be William Langland. The poem's narrator cryptically alludes to Langland's name, saying, "I have lived in land. . . . My name is Long Will" (15.152). The dialect and opening location of the poem (Malvern Hills) suggest that Langland grew up in the West Midlands; but the narrator's great familiarity with London society indicates Langland spent much time there. He may have been a clergyman, though one from the lower orders since he was likely married. If so, his calling could have familiarized him with society's worst conditions and motivated his satirical yet spiritual response.

Three versions of the work exist. The first was probably completed by 1370; the second, revised during the 1370s, added significantly to the first; and the last, not much longer but almost completely rewritten, was finished in the 1380s.

Allegory and Satire

Written in unrhymed alliterative verse, *Piers Plowman* is framed as a dream vision, a story presented as if the author were dreaming it. The work comprises a series of visions divided into sections (called *passus*). These are seen and recalled by the narrator, Will. In his visions, Will seeks answers to many questions, especially how he can find truth. Much of the story is allegorical, but interwoven is strong social criticism.

Probably the best example of this dual nature is the first passus, in which Will sees a tower on a hill, a fortress in a valley below, and people wandering in a field between the two. Allegorically, the tower represents heaven; the fortress, hell; and the folk, people passing through life toward one or the other destination. But Langland also uses the setting to describe and critique many in the crowd, highlighting those who used their positions to prey on the poor. Unlike similar passages from Chaucer, whose satire is relatively lighthearted, Langland scathingly denounces the wealthy and corrupt.

Prompted by this first vision, Will begins a quest for truth. Along the way he interacts with various personified things or qualities (e.g., Kynde Wit, Holy Church, Conscience, and Reason) that give him direction. The key character who helps Will and other pilgrims is Piers Plowman, a simple farmer who at times is identified with Adam, Moses, the Good Samaritan, and Christ. The quest for truth seems to climax in Passus 18, which describes Jesus' death and resurrection and discusses His sufficiency to pay for sin. However, the poem does not end there, and Will continues searching. The clearest conclusion of the poem seems to be the importance of doing truly good works.

An artist's depiction of William Langland dreaming the story that became *Piers Plowman*.

The poor may plead and pray in doorways, / They may quake for cold and thirst and hunger. / None receives them rightfully and relieves their suffering; / They are hooted at like hounds and ordered away.

Influence

The existence of more than fifty manuscripts and at least three versions suggests the significant influence of *Piers Plowman*. Its strong support for the common man led to widespread reading of the work and, in fact, prompted leaders of the Peasants' Revolt of 1381 (p. 85) to use its language to justify their rebellion. Though Langland himself was probably basically conservative (and the third revision of *Piers Plowman* was likely meant to distance it from the revolt), his work continued to insert a voice for change well beyond the lifetime of its author. Moreover, his allegorical journey for truth is mirrored in such later devotional masterworks as *The Pilgrim's Progress*.

What Do You Know?

Understand the Background

1. What was Bede's purpose in writing *An Ecclesiastical History of the English People*? Why is Caedmon's hymn in particular significant to English literature?
2. Identify three characteristics of folk ballads.
3. List two common kinds of text structures. Why is it helpful to examine a text's structure?
4. Which kind of medieval drama typically took the most community involvement? Why?
5. What is the main purpose of satire?
6. How does the nature of mock epics and parodies help fulfill the purpose of satire?

Apply the Concepts

7. List two Anglo-Saxon oral poetry conventions that Caedmon used in his hymn. Cite an example from the text for each.
8. Give three different examples of repetition from one of the ballads in the unit. Briefly explain how each contributes to the poem dramatically or thematically.
9. Choose one of the songs on page 73 and explain how its images help convey its message.
10. Identify one of the text structures Julian used in *Revelations of Divine Love*. Cite details from the chapters to support your answer.
11. Choose one major character from "The Prologue" of *The Canterbury Tales* and show how Chaucer used both direct and indirect characterization to develop the character. Cite details from the text to support your answer.
12. Cite two examples each of verbal and situational irony from Chaucer's text and explain what each contributes to the meaning of the surrounding text or the selection as a whole.

Evaluate the Ideas

13. Analyze the effectiveness of Caedmon's artistry in his hymn. Reference the principles of unity and progression as well as Anglo-Saxon artistic techniques.
14. Choose one of the ballads and show how its creator used both engaging content and artful techniques to effectively communicate his message to listeners.
15. Evaluate Julian of Norwich's thoughts on sin and God's love from a biblical perspective.
16. Chaucer heavily critiques the clergy in *The Canterbury Tales*. Choose two of the religious characters, explain Chaucer's critique of each, and evaluate the biblical truthfulness of his opinions.

Write a Response

17. What are three ways that literature can strengthen a community? Develop these ideas fully using examples from the texts in Unit 1.
18. Explain the worth and proper parameters for satire from a biblical perspective. Use Scripture to establish these criteria, and cite details from the texts in this unit to exemplify good or bad approaches to satire.

Define each term and provide an example of each from a selection in Unit 1, Part 2 or 3.

TERMS

hagiography
refrain
folk ballad
ballad stanza
devotional literature
imagery
text structures
signal words
miracle, mystery, and morality plays
farce
satire
frame tale
characterization: direct and indirect
tone
verbal irony
situational irony
beast fable
mock epic
parody

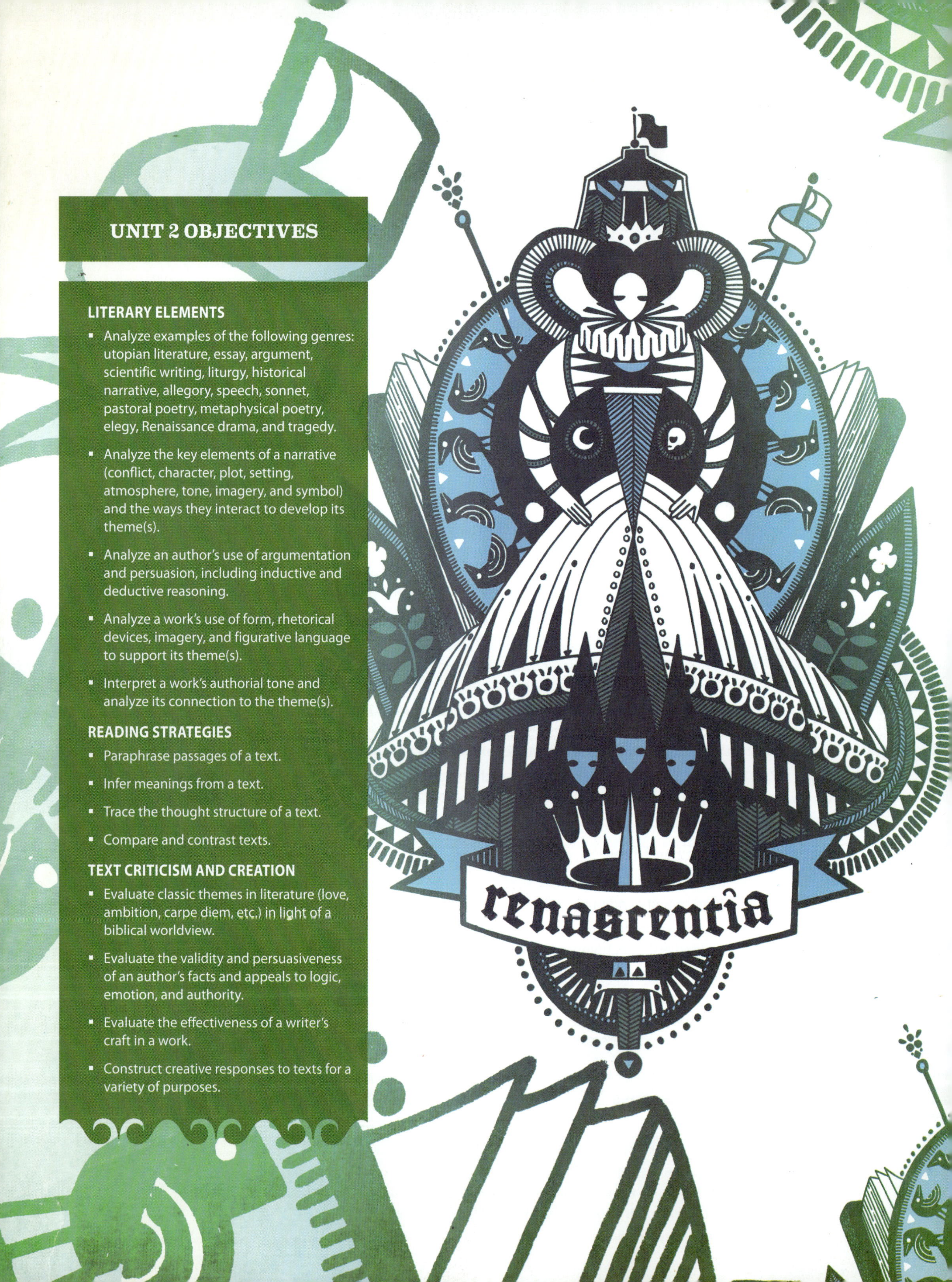

UNIT 2 OBJECTIVES

LITERARY ELEMENTS

- Analyze examples of the following genres: utopian literature, essay, argument, scientific writing, liturgy, historical narrative, allegory, speech, sonnet, pastoral poetry, metaphysical poetry, elegy, Renaissance drama, and tragedy.
- Analyze the key elements of a narrative (conflict, character, plot, setting, atmosphere, tone, imagery, and symbol) and the ways they interact to develop its theme(s).
- Analyze an author's use of argumentation and persuasion, including inductive and deductive reasoning.
- Analyze a work's use of form, rhetorical devices, imagery, and figurative language to support its theme(s).
- Interpret a work's authorial tone and analyze its connection to the theme(s).

READING STRATEGIES

- Paraphrase passages of a text.
- Infer meanings from a text.
- Trace the thought structure of a text.
- Compare and contrast texts.

TEXT CRITICISM AND CREATION

- Evaluate classic themes in literature (love, ambition, carpe diem, etc.) in light of a biblical worldview.
- Evaluate the validity and persuasiveness of an author's facts and appeals to logic, emotion, and authority.
- Evaluate the effectiveness of a writer's craft in a work.
- Construct creative responses to texts for a variety of purposes.

UNIT 2
The English Renaissance
(1485–1640)

128 RENAISSANCE HUMANISM
156 REFORMATION AND NATIONAL IDENTITY
182 LYRIC AND METAPHYSICAL POETRY
208 RENAISSANCE DRAMA

Renaissance England

The Renaissance, literally "rebirth," refers to the extraordinary era of achievement in science and the arts that displaced the Middle Ages and planted the seeds of modern society. Beginning around 1300 in Italy, rediscovered or newly imported texts ignited an intellectual revolution. At the same time, disruptive social forces (e.g., the continued rise of the middle class, the expansion of trade) created opportunities for new Renaissance thought to influence society. One result, the Reformation, would send shock waves through Europe, breaking its oldest and strongest allegiances.

In England, as in much of northern Europe, Renaissance forces flowered later than in Italy. Amidst the political chaos of the fifteenth century, particularly the Wars of the Roses, the Renaissance had little opportunity to flourish. However, the rise of a new dynasty, the Tudors, led to a century of relative political stability, which allowed English culture, especially English literature, to thrive.

THE TUDORS

Henry VII Henry Tudor began the Tudor dynasty by defeating Richard III at the Battle of Bosworth Field (1485). A Lancastrian with a shaky claim to the throne, Henry VII (1485–1509) cemented his claim with his marriage to Elizabeth of York (the opposing house). With the nobility weakened in the conflict's aftermath, Henry drew the nation's power to himself. Indeed, Tudor rule is marked by the royal court's being the absolute center of the nation's social and political power.

Henry VIII Henry VII's oldest son, Arthur, died early and left Henry, the second son, sole heir. An attractive and charismatic man, Henry VIII (1509–47) was also willful, capricious, proud, and pleasure-seeking. Believing firmly in the divine right of kings, he ruled with a despotic disposition, though capably in many ways. Unfortunately, his marriage with Catherine of Aragon (also briefly wife of Arthur, in a political alliance) produced only a daughter, Mary. This inability to produce a male heir threatened England's political stability.

Citing the fact that Catherine was his brother's widow (usually a marriage forbidden by the church but here allowed by papal dispensation), Henry sought a papal annulment to his marriage. His request was denied. Nonetheless, in 1532 Henry secretly married Anne Boleyn, whom he had long courted. His councilors annulled his marriage to Catherine in May 1533 (making Mary illegitimate), and Henry officially remarried.

Anne soon gave birth to a daughter, Elizabeth, but no son; eventually earning Henry's disfavor, she was charged with adultery and executed in 1536. After her would come four more wives, the next of which (Jane Seymour) produced Henry's longed-for heir, Edward.

Having defied the Pope publicly, Henry, formerly a devout Catholic, broke ties with Rome. In the Act of Supremacy (1534), he had Parliament declare him the Supreme Head of the Church in England. Dissenters were punished or, as with Sir Thomas More, executed. Furthermore, Henry dissolved many of the regular orders in the Dissolution of the Monasteries (ca. 1536–41), and confiscated their wealth and lands, enriching the monarchy. By the time of his death, Henry had drawn to the monarch more power than ever before, holding sway over both the nobility and the Church.

Edward VI Edward VI (1547–53), a minor when he ascended the throne, ruled through regents who favored Protestantism and steered England toward reformation. Always sickly, Edward died at fifteen but not before naming as his heir his cousin Lady Jane Grey (Protestant daughter-in-law of his powerful chief minister). His sister Mary, enjoying more popular support, overcame the new government in only nine days. The sixteen-year-old Lady Jane, a reluctant queen, was executed shortly after.

Mary I A devout Catholic, Mary I (1553–58) set out to reverse the Reformation in England. She returned the country to the Catholic fold and married Philip II of Spain (a devoted Catholic). Additionally, she prosecuted vocal Protestant scholars, churchmen, and laypeople for heresy. Many Protestant leaders left for a time while others were killed, among them Archbishop Cranmer, who had approved her parents' annulment. Mary's harsh policies alienated even her supporters, while economic and agricultural difficulties undermined confidence in her reign. After only five years, she died in an influenza epidemic.

Elizabeth I Mary's successor, Elizabeth I (1558–1603), was Protestant by upbringing and personal conviction. She quickly restored the Church of England and once again united all political and religious authority in the monarch. Though many, even her close counselors, at first thought a woman incapable of reigning, she proved them wrong. Under her governance, England grew as a nation and enjoyed a cultural golden age.

Elizabeth was physically attractive, vivacious, and witty; she was also a humanist and extremely erudite for a woman of the time (reading widely in Latin and Greek and speaking fluent French, Italian, and Spanish). More practically, she was keenly perceptive and surrounded herself with loyal and brilliant advisers. Though she could sometimes be blind to her favorites' flaws, her administration was unusually capable and committed.

Politically shrewd and skilled in the art of self-preservation, Elizabeth cultivated an image that both endeared her to her citizens and left them in awe of her. Abroad and at home, she used her intelligence, charm, and even her marital eligibility to keep England's powerful enemies at bay and hold the nation on a moderate course in foreign and domestic policy (her *via media* or "middle way"). She expanded England's influence abroad and united the nation as never before.

THE RENAISSANCE

The English Renaissance (ca. 1485–1640) was part of a broader Northern Renaissance that focused less on art (though much was created) and more on the movement's intellectual side, humanism. Renaissance humanism redirected scholarship toward investigating man in his earthly environment—for example, studying human society and natural philosophy (philosophical inquiry into nature and the material world). Experts in classical languages and learning such as Agricola (German), Erasmus (Dutch), and Montaigne (French) exerted huge influence. English universities changed their curriculum to reflect the humanities while young nobles routinely traveled to southern Europe to pick up Italian, French, and Spanish; firsthand experience with Renaissance learning and art; and sophistication and polish.

VISUAL ANALYSIS
Examine the objects represented in *The Ambassadors* (1533) by Hans Holbein the Younger. How do these objects represent areas of Renaissance scholarship?

As a result, the Tudor court became a hotbed not only of cutthroat political intrigue but also of Renaissance learning and literature. The most privileged men in English society were often extremely well educated in Renaissance humanism. Even some noblewomen received a good education; for instance, the ill-fated Lady Jane Grey was said to be one of the best-educated women in the kingdom. Courtiers used their learning for everything from innocuous amusements to the Machiavellian pursuit of power. Some even contributed positively to governing. Humanists such as John Colet, Sir Thomas More, and Sir Francis Bacon all tried to use their considerable learning and skills to improve society.

The Renaissance primarily affected the upper class, but it did trickle down to the masses in some ways. To create an educated leadership, humanists established grammar schools teaching Latin and the classics to even commoners who could afford it. The success of the grammar schools along with increased university enrollment reflected a broader interest in learning. With the printing press making print materials more widely and cheaply available, further increases in literacy followed. Together, these forces spread Renaissance ideas to an ever-broader audience.

Altogether, the Renaissance focus on man and his environment created a new energy in English society. This was pointed in various new directions—from linguistics and philosophy, to science and technology, to exploration and colonization, and, most significantly, toward reformation. Allied, these forces would expand England's spiritual, intellectual, and cultural horizons.

THE REFORMATION

By the sixteenth century, Church abuses had worsened. The sale of indulgences, the Church's vast wealth, clerical politicking, and worldly (or overtly sinful) living had created widespread disgust. Renaissance scholars newly investigating ancient biblical texts and interested in earthly society found the problems they saw in doctrine and practice hard to overlook. These catalysts sparked the movement known as the Reformation.

By the time Martin Luther published his Ninety-Five Theses (1517), Reformation ideas had already existed in England for over a century. Wycliffe's Lollardy (p. 11) was suppressed but not dead: the forerunner of the English Reformation, it paved the way for Lutheran influences, which attracted the educated. Reformation thought was especially strong at Cambridge, which would produce many of England's Protestant leaders.

In the official sphere, Reformation began with Henry's split with Rome. However, Henry did not advocate for changes in doctrine or practice other than those that gave him, and England, full autonomy (e.g., denying papal authority, dissolving the monasteries). Only with Edward VI did Protestant doctrine receive the monarchy's full support. Encouraged by a strong Protestant faction, Edward took the English church further from Rome than ever before in actions such as the Act of Uniformity (1549), imposing a new, more Protestant liturgy (*The Book of Common Prayer*).

However, Protestantism had not yet taken hold, so Mary I's reversal of such changes was at first widely approved. But her persecution of Protestants (around three hundred died during her brief reign) and seeming capitulation to papal and Spanish authority undid this sympathy. At her death, the country was exhausted by religious turmoil, wary of foreign interference, and ready for change. Elizabeth chose a path acceptable to a broad spectrum of society. She reinstated England's autonomy from papal jurisdiction and its use of the *Prayer Book* in worship, without embracing the Puritans' stricter Protestantism. Pressed by Puritans and Catholic traditionalists on either side, she walked a fine line, keeping England firmly in the Protestant camp.

ENGLAND ABROAD: CONFLICT AND EXPLORATION

The Reformation coincided with the rapid expansion of European trade and power known as the Age of Exploration (1400s–1700s). While many people sincerely embraced Protestant doctrine, growing nations such as England also had self-interested reasons for escaping the politics of Catholic unity. Royalty and commoners alike wanted to further English interests abroad unhindered by papal politics. Both sincere and self-interested motives were encapsulated in England's conflict with Spain.

The era's most powerful nation, Spain, under Philip II (1556–98) extended to Portugal, the Netherlands, Naples, and Milan, as well as to its wealthy new-world colonies. Philip, a devout Catholic, sought to maintain the Church's crumbling power. Thus, he repeatedly clashed with Protestant England in religious battlegrounds such as the Netherlands. But just as important to the two nations' conflict were their competing colonial and mercantile aspirations.

Spain led in the race to trade and colonize and gained enormous wealth from sources abroad, especially its colonies in South America. In fact, the papacy favored Spain, endorsing its claim (highly arrogant in hindsight) to the Philippines and half the Western Hemisphere. England came late to the frenzied competition and ignored papal dictum to get its foot in the door. Further, from the 1570s to the 1590s, English privateers led by skilled captains such as John Hawkins and Sir Francis Drake harassed and plundered Spanish shipping and ports. Their raids, approved but not officially acknowledged by Elizabeth, weakened their colonial rival. In fact, their success very nearly destroyed Spain's financial credit in Europe. Meanwhile they were claiming territory for England in the New World and exploring sea routes for trade.

SPANISH ARMADA

In 1588, Philip made an all-out attempt to end the English threat. Against his military leaders' advice, he gathered a massive naval expedition of 130 ships (the Spanish Armada) and sent them to ferry an invading army from Spanish-held Flanders to England. Sir Francis Drake, vice-admiral of the English fleet, found himself outnumbered and outgunned.

Cleverly, Drake attacked preemptively, using fire ships to flush the Spanish galleons from anchorage at Calais and break their battle formation. In disarray, the heavily armed but unwieldy ships were at the mercy of England's lighter, more maneuverable ships. Capitalizing on enemy panic and favorable winds (called by the English "Protestant" winds), the English harried the diminished Armada north of Britain and down the rocky, treacherous North Sea coasts of Ireland and Scotland. There, terrible storms foundered nearly a third of the vessels. This spectacular victory was hailed by the Protestant English as a special sign of divine favor.

ENGLAND AT HOME: SOCIAL PROSPERITY

During the Tudor period, the steady accumulation of wealth begun in the fourteenth century continued. The wool trade, a pillar of Elizabethan England's economy, brought great wealth. Additionally, early sixteenth century Portuguese explorers broke the Arabian-Venetian trade monopoly with Asia by discovering a sea route around Africa. The result was lower commodity prices throughout Europe. Finally, raids on Spanish settlements and shipping brought gold flowing into the royal treasuries. The resulting currency increases improved commercial capabilities: money transactions replaced barter and allowed for modern credit and capital investment. By the century's end, England's average standard of living had increased.

The middle class was both engine and beneficiary of this success. As the profit-making segment of society, it earned royal recognition and support. Indeed, the policy of mercantilism that dominated late sixteenth-century Europe favored powerful merchant companies as drivers of national expansion. For instance, Elizabeth I preserved the wool exports monopoly held by the Merchant Adventurers (founded in 1407), while colonization efforts were often led by private companies (some begun by nobles) given royal charters.

Additionally, growing middle-class influence in society and politics could not be ignored. An increase in landed gentry and wealthy commoners with estates expanded the size and influence of the House of Commons. Furthermore, the middle class administered burgeoning industrial centers. The greatest of these, London, had by 1563 almost doubled in population from Chaucer's time and would double again during Elizabeth's reign, becoming one of the largest and wealthiest urban areas in Europe. As cities grew in size, wealth, and power, their commercial class wielded more weight in national concerns. Now better educated than ever and with fewer ties to tradition, merchants and artisans were likelier conveyers of new ideas. For example, the majority took to Protestantism, tipping the balance toward its overall success in England.

Nonetheless, middle-class wealth did cause some consternation. The Renaissance worldview endorsed the idea that the hierarchy of human society and of the natural world was ordained by God. Violations of one's given place in society were officially frowned on. Sumptuary laws limiting consumption of luxury goods based on one's class returned or were strengthened. Interestingly, these laws sometimes limited upper-class consumption of goods too, as increased wealth at society's peak led to unseemly extravagances.

Sadly, the lowest classes were often left out of this prosperity. Rural laborers struggled as their upper-class landlords enclosed lands formerly used for tenant farming to raise sheep for wool (a more lucrative investment). Many left for cities such as London, which sometimes provided work but also carried risks. Both vagrancy through lack of work and devastating poverty were acknowledged problems throughout the country. Indeed, a poor rate levied on wealthier members of society and the creation of workhouses (later objects of dread in Victorian England) were attempts to alleviate these onerous conditions.

THE RISE OF A NEW SCIENCE

The early Renaissance saw the recovery of ancient texts (from Archimedes, Pythagoras, etc.) dealing with a variety of scientific fields, including medicine, botany, physics, mathematics, astronomy, and more. Renaissance scholars turned this new knowledge toward practical ends. New discoveries and technological inventions in areas such as metallurgy, firearms, navigation, and engineering (e.g., machinery, building projects) drove developments in industry, exploration, and general society.

Additionally, outstanding scholars promoted new ideas that shook the traditional medieval worldview. For example, cosmologists debated the medieval geocentric theory (embodied in astrology's view of zodiacal constellations and planets circling the earth) and the seemingly new (actually ancient) heliocentric theory supported by scholars such as Copernicus, Galileo, and Kepler. Termed *natural philosophers*, the investigators of such phenomena introduced a new approach to studying the natural world.

Scholastics of medieval universities had focused their efforts on confirming accepted truths and resolving seeming contradictions among classical authorities (e.g., Aristotle, Cicero) and between these sources and the Bible. Scholars would ask questions and present opposing arguments, all with the goal of confirming the established truth. This style of learning operated in a predefined field of knowledge and relied heavily on deductive logic, reasoning from ancient premises.

Renaissance scholars still trusted these ancient authorities, but new advancements were showing that contemporary scholars could contribute something entirely new to a field, changing its scope or nature. The preferred method for these investigations was inductive reasoning based on one's personal observations. Promoted in particular by Sir Francis Bacon, this experimental approach would form the basis for modern science. While adoption of the new science lagged for a time, the early seventeenth century saw important developments, including Gilbert's treatise on magnetism (1600), the invention of the microscope and telescope (1608), and Harvey's demonstration of the circulation of the blood (1628).

Kepler's model of the solar system.

TECHNOLOGY FOR THE AGE OF EXPLORATION

Today, it is hard to imagine not knowing general world geography, but Renaissance Europeans did not even know how many continents exist. Exploration required navigating into the unknown. But intrepid sailors and curious Renaissance inventors worked with rediscovered principles of science (e.g., of astronomy, geometry), resulting in inventions such as the mariner's compass, which allowed sailors to track directions more easily from a moving deck. Also, the rediscovery and refinement of ancient instruments such as the astrolabe, quadrant, and cross-staff helped sailors find their latitude (distance from the equator) and chart new courses and land masses on maps. Finally, Renaissance engineering advances led shipbuilders to design vessels better suited to oceangoing expeditions. The printing press allowed many of these discoveries to rapidly become known.

Map of the world (1608).

THE STUARTS

The Stuarts, the dynasty following the Tudors, now seem ill-fated. They experienced setbacks from the beginning, given a populace largely unsympathetic to their vision of England. In this clash of values, the monarchy lost; the Stuart line contained three deposed kings and ended as a constitutional monarchy. The first two Stuarts would see out the Renaissance in England.

James I Elizabeth never married and died heirless. Fearing a succession crisis on her death, she chose James VI of Scotland as the next monarch, peacefully ending the Tudor dynasty. James I of England (1603–25) had high hopes for his reign, desiring to unite the British Isles. Unfortunately, the delicate balance of church and state preserved by Elizabeth required a political intelligence he lacked; he had her shrewdness but not her sensitivity to popular feeling.

Like most of his descendants, James experienced pushback from his English subjects on intertwined issues of royal absolutism and religious conformity. He made alliances with Spain and France (both Catholic) and committed England to neutrality in the Protestant-Catholic struggle, but many of his subjects disapproved, suspecting he was biased in favor of Catholic interests. These fears would frustrate Stuart monarchs throughout the century.

Meanwhile, the Puritans, who wanted to remove Catholic remnants from the Anglican church, advocated for greater tolerance of nonconformist views (as they had under Elizabeth I), sometimes with broader political implications. James, like many of the time, viewed political and religious nonconformity as one and the same threat and vigorously suppressed both. Within the next few decades, thousands left to settle in America or northern Ireland.

Charles I Upon James's death, his son Charles I (1625–49) took the throne. Sadly, Charles was even less attuned to his people than his father was. A firm believer in his divine right, he antagonized Parliament by ignoring its will in foreign policy, exacting forced loans from promi-

nent men to pay for these foreign endeavors, increasing taxes on imports and property, and discouraging political and religious dissent. To suppress the latter, he assumed the right to arrest, try, and punish subjects without normal judicial procedures and enforced these measures with the royal courts. For eleven years, he refused to call Parliament into session at all.

Additionally, Charles reinforced public fears by seeking to infuse greater formality and ritual into Anglican worship. When he tried to force Scottish Presbyterians to use the Anglican liturgy, their army invaded northern England. Parliament, sympathetic to them, refused to finance a military campaign unless Charles yielded some of his power. In response, he left London to gather troops in York. Thus began a civil war that would end with the execution of Charles and the formation of a government without a king.

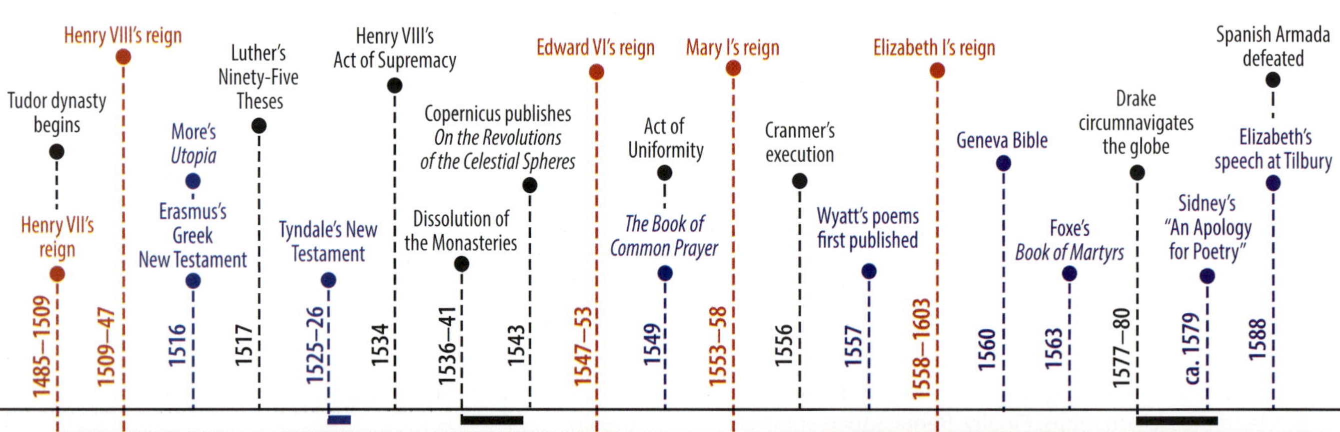

RENAISSANCE LITERATURE

The political and social context of the Renaissance helped prepare the way for some of the most brilliant achievements of English literature. Peace and prosperity created leisure for cultural pursuits and wealth for the patronage of writers. Growing social mobility encouraged personal ambition, and some writers sought fame and fortune, or at least a decent living, through their work. The thriving court offered privileged authors a chance to use their word skills for play, prestige, and even power. In addition, both humanist and Reformation thinking saw in literature an opportunity for improving readers in mind and spirit.

At the same time, the printing press and higher literacy increased the number and types of readers, giving writers a broader audience. Many created literature that could appeal to a wider range of tastes and life experiences. Elizabethan dramas, for example, show the influence of both court and town, university and marketplace. Authors drew on multiple literary traditions from the classical, medieval, and humanist to the academic, courtly, and popular. The resulting body of work is extremely eclectic. For instance, *The Faerie Queene* is an epic, a romance, and an allegorical moral treatise all in one, while Shakespeare's plays use comedy to lighten tragedy, and tragic elements to give weight to comedy. This creative synthesis of varied materials forms part of the genius and originality of the era's literary giants and contributes to their continued popularity.

LANGUAGE

The Tudors' arrival marks the beginning of Early Modern English (ca. 1485–1800). The shift was smaller than that between Old and Middle English but still significant. The Great Vowel Shift (see p. 11) continued to play out, and personal pronouns changed again (e.g., losing *th-* forms *thou*, *thee*, *thy*, *thine* and their verb endings *-est*, *-st*, and *-t*). Printers started to standardize spellings, helped along by the first dictionaries. At the same time, humanist borrowings, widening trade, and diplomatic contacts vastly enriched the English word stock, importing words from ancient Latin and Greek and contemporary Spain, Portugal, Italy, and more. In literature, the flexibility and lack of prescriptive rules for English made innovation less risky than today; writers could exploit and expand the language with little reproach. Thus, Spenser chose to revive archaic words, while Shakespeare coined new ones.

Elizabethan theater.

SUMMARY

By the end of the Renaissance, the European view of and influence in the world had changed and expanded markedly. England's individual identity shifted to become more urbanized and sophisticated, uniquely Protestant, confidently expansionist, and decidedly independent of its Continental counterparts. Its society was bustling with energy turned to political, religious, philosophical, scientific, and commercial ends. Though the coming decades would be marked by internal turmoil, English society would continue to develop on this strong foundation.

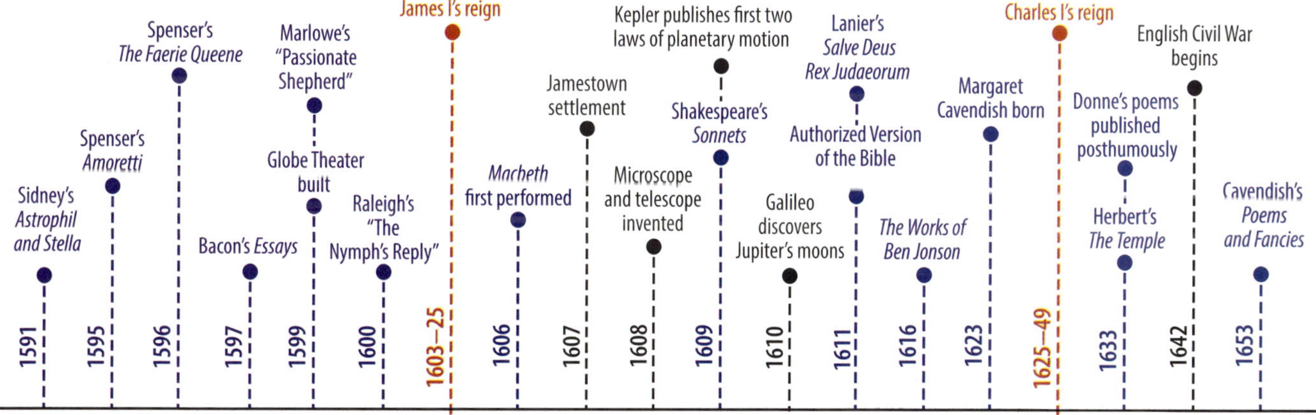

UNIT 2

PART 1

Renaissance Humanism

You have likely felt the influence of Renaissance humanism every year of your school career. Have you learned a foreign language? Do you consider yourself an artist or a musician? Have you studied the history of the world and of your country? All of these, and even the literature book you are currently reading, are part of a field of studies known as the humanities. The humanities help us make sense of our shared human experiences. Their place in the standard curriculum originated in large part with Renaissance humanists.

Renaissance humanists changed the focus and methods of European culture and learning (pp. 122, 125). In the Middle Ages, the Catholic Church's pervasive influence had produced a society focused on the community and on the immaterial, spiritual world. Humanists did not abandon Christianity; in fact, those in northern Europe were frequently known as Christian humanists. They did, however, revive the classical (and biblical) ideas that people have great worth and potential as individuals and that earthly life is worth studying. The ideal Renaissance man developed his knowledge and skills in many areas, far exceeding the often narrow focus of medieval scholars.

These changes heavily influenced the content and style of English literature. Renaissance works intensely examine earthly man, his inner life, his outer relationships in society, and his natural surroundings. For example, academic literature took on new subjects (e.g., science) and brought new ways of thinking to old ones (e.g., government). One of the era's premiere prose works, Sir Thomas More's *Utopia*, examined human nature, government, and society. Similarly, drama broadened to focus on man's earthly life, presenting personal and societal relationships as well as spiritual truths, and lyric poetry delved deeper into inner, psychological realities.

Additionally, the humanists of the Renaissance wanted to produce citizens who could express themselves clearly and persuasively, not just for service in the church, as in the Middle Ages, but for service to the community as a whole. Renaissance scholars thus chose to focus on the classical tradition of rhetoric, the effective use of language for persuasive purposes. Cicero, an often-studied Roman politician and orator, identified five canons of rhetoric—invention, arrangement, style, memory, and delivery—as steps for creating, organizing, and presenting an argument.

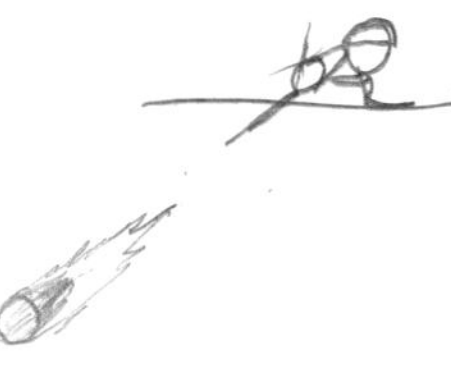

To improve their writing style, humanists looked to various rhetorical strategies and tools that in ancient times had been employed in the production of polished public persuasion. Since they considered all literature to be a form of moral persuasion (an idea promoted by the Roman poet Horace), they applied these strategies to literature in general. **Rhetorical appeals** to logic, emotion, and credible authorities (i.e., logos, pathos, ethos) infused Renaissance literature while analogies (p. 140) fleshed out these ideas. Additionally, **figurative language** (language that departs from standard or literal usage for meaning or effect) littered works, especially **rhetorical devices** (deviations from the standard use of language—mainly in syntactical arrangement—to achieve a special effect) such as parallelism.

Another prevalent tool, **allusion** (indirect references to ideas outside a work of literature, usually from history or another literary work, with which authors assume their audience will be familiar), took advantage of a body of classical knowledge shared by a growing segment of readers. Today, readers are often befuddled by these obscure references to classical mythology and history. In earlier times, however, everyone knew about Hector and Achilles, Ulysses and the Sirens, Cupid and Psyche, Hercules and Alcestis, and the Greco-Roman pantheon of gods and goddesses. Such references helped universalize the situations and themes an author examined.

The writers that you will study in the first part of Unit 2 illustrate these new emphases and approaches. More, Bacon, and Sidney all spent significant portions of their lives in public service and displayed a wide range of interests and abilities. They tried to encourage the public to better living through their writings. More's *Utopia* follows the trend of several Renaissance works to use another place (i.e., Utopia) to say something about one's own place (perhaps England). Bacon's essays offer concise formulations of fact that have practical value to mankind. Sidney's *In Defense of Poesy* seeks to prove the value of imaginative literature in compelling people to virtue. Both Bacon and Sidney made skillful use of numerous stylistic devices and organizational structures to craft their arguments. Finally, Amelia Lanier's work illustrates the ongoing debate over gender roles, while Margaret Cavendish's work shows how some women were able to practice Renaissance scholarship. Though women were not always included in the new emphasis on the worth of the individual (many writings of this period, in fact, stated their inferiority), both Cavendish and Lanier entered the male-dominated world of professional writing to defend their sex and to tackle subjects (like science) that were typically the province of males.

Sir Thomas More (1478–1535)

AT A GLANCE

- **1492–93** Studied at Oxford
- **1499** Met Erasmus
- **1516** Published *Utopia* in its complete form
- **1529–32** Served as Lord Chancellor
- **1534** Refused to take an oath supporting the Act of Succession
- **1535** Was executed by beheading
- **1935** Was canonized by the Roman Catholic Church

Thomas More was a controversial figure in his day, and, some would say, still is. Catholics revere him for his piety and reasonableness. Protestants condemn him for his antagonism toward evangelical truth and his religious bigotry. Though a naturally reticent man, he was drawn into the turbulence of his times, and his virulent and intemperate attacks against reformers such as Tyndale are difficult to reconcile with his otherwise urbane and devout character.

Student of Law and Literature

The son of a London judge, Thomas More received the best education his age could offer. From St. Anthony's School he proceeded to Oxford, where he studied under classical scholars who prepared the way for the growth of humanism in England. Leaving the university without graduating, he studied law at the Inns of Court in London and soon distinguished himself as both teacher and practitioner of the legal profession.

Meanwhile, More did not neglect his literary interests but acquired a reputation as the most learned layman of his day. His friend Erasmus introduced him to the leading continental humanists, whom he delighted with his publication of *Utopia* in 1516. Unlike his scholarly friends, More was in a position to bring his ideas to bear on the world of political realities. A series of diplomatic and political appointments, climaxing with the office of Lord Chancellor (1529–32), made More one of the most powerful men in England. As familiar friend and counselor of Henry VIII, More fulfilled the humanist's ideal of the philosopher-orator advising his prince.

Defender of Catholicism

Although More declined the priesthood for law, Catholicism has never had a more determined defender. As a page to a cardinal and a boarder with monks for several years, More was exposed to the worldly-hedonistic and the mystical-ascetic sides of Renaissance Catholicism and felt drawn toward both. He was a lover of courtly entertainments and witty conversation but was also an austere man, who throughout his life wore a haircloth shirt next to his skin and flagellated his body with knotted cords. His humanism placed him among the progressive Catholic thinkers, who took exception to many of the practices of the Church. But his fierce loyalty to the Catholic religion set him resolutely against the Protestants, whom he suppressed with a rigor that he had not represented as permissible in *Utopia*.

Such zeal did he show against the Reformed views in a reply to Martin Luther, that he was officially commissioned by the bishop of London to refute the writings of the reformers. The contrast between More's religious intolerance and religious toleration in the kingdom of Utopia may be due to the fact that *Utopia* was published a year before the outbreak of the German Reformation.

Unable to support Henry in his divorce of Catherine and break with Rome, More resigned his chancellorship in 1532. When he refused to take an oath required by the Act of Succession (1534), which established the children of Anne Boleyn as heirs to the throne, More was accused of high treason and sentenced to death. With his execution Protestantism lost an enemy, Catholicism gained a saint (More was canonized in 1935 on the four-hundredth anniversary of his death), and the world was given another example of the fickleness of political favor.

DID YOU KNOW ?

Climbing the flimsy scaffold to his death, More is said to have quipped, "I pray you, Master Lieutenant, see me safe up, and for my coming down let me shift for myself."

ANALYZE: *Utopia and Social Satire*

The term ***utopia*** designates a genre of fictional writings about ideal societies. The name comes from More's *Utopia*, a traveler's account of an ideal society organized and administered on principles of reason. More called this imaginary kingdom Utopia based on the Greek word *outopia*, which means "no place," and puns on the word *eutopia*, which means "good place." A utopia differs from other fictional places in that it is vastly superior to the writer's contemporary world. In some cases, however, this supposed superiority can actually be an exaggeration of social ills. Utopian literature can serve as **social satire** (p. 85), using irony to critique a society. The rational standards by which Utopia operates, though unattainable and in some ways undesirable, reveal the shortcomings of English society in More's day. As you read, examine how rational principles govern the organization and operations of the ideal society. Also consider how exaggerated situations reveal *Utopia*'s satirical purpose.

READ: *Infer Author's Tone*

How an author says something is as important as *what* he says. An author communicates his **tone** (p. 88) through the details he includes, such as descriptions and characters' words. But inferring an author's tone can be difficult. He or she may seem serious in places but speak ironically or playfully in others. *Utopia* contains such doubleness in tone, presenting readers with a challenge. Is More being serious or playfully ironic? Is *Utopia* a real blueprint for social change, a joke, or maybe both? More has not left us without clues. For instance, the surname of the work's main speaker, Raphael Hythloday, means "purveyor of nonsense." On the other hand, the fact that Utopians rise above personal greed indicates that More views such vices with seriousness. As you read, examine the details closely to determine where More is speaking seriously and where he is speaking ironically.

EVALUATE: *Author's Perspective*

The tone an author uses and the themes he explores are both windows into his perspective. What does Sir Thomas More think about the subjects of greed, personal possessions, and religious tolerance, just to name a few? As you read—and after you have inferred More's tone—begin evaluating his perspective on the themes he addresses. When forming your evaluations, refer to biblical principles and passages such as the following: Psalm 62:10, Proverbs 28:25, Matthew 6:24, Romans 13:9, and Hebrews 13:5–6.

OBJECTIVES

- Identify the characteristics of utopian literature.
- Infer authorial tone to determine meaning in a text.
- Analyze how satire supports an author's social critique.
- Evaluate the author's view of human nature and society in light of a biblical worldview.

VOCABULARY

eminence (ĕm′ə-nəns) *n.* A position of great distinction or superiority.

concoct (kən-kŏkt′) *tr.v.* To devise, using skill and intelligence; contrive.

conspicuous (kən-spĭk′yo͞o-əs) *adj.* Attracting attention, as by being unusual or remarkable; noticeable.

inexplicable (ĭn-ĕk′splĭ-kə-bəl) *adj.* Difficult or impossible to explain or account for.

proselytize [British *proselytise*] (prŏs′ə-lĭ-tīz′) *intr.v.* To attempt to convert someone to one's own religious faith.

What would an IDEAL COMMUNITY *be like?*

The answer depends on whom you ask. Most people want everyone in their community to be happy and healthy, but how to reach those goals remains a question. Some cultures emphasize the importance of relationships and family while others especially value freedom of the individual. Some value regulations and certifications to ensure the quality of various services while others think these stifle the dynamism and creativity of a culture. What about you? Write a paragraph describing your ideal community.

The following excerpts from Utopia*'s Book 2 require context from Book 1 to be understood. Book 1 is set during a real event, More's 1515 diplomatic mission to the Low Countries in Europe, and incorporates fictional versions of actual persons (e.g., More, Peter Giles) and places (e.g., Antwerp). More's friend Peter Giles introduces him to Raphael Hythloday, a (fictional) scholar and world traveler who becomes the work's main speaker. Hythloday sailed with Amerigo Vespucci to the New World (another touch of realism) and relates his visit to a land whose customs sharply differ from Europe's. Book 1 offers his scathing criticism of European society and contrasts with his glowing descriptions of Utopia in Book 2. This structure forms a dialogue, a genre used for classical philosophical and satirical discussion (e.g., Plato's* Republic*) and revived in the Renaissance. A dialogue often begins with a situation inciting a discussion by two or more characters, one of whom emerges as spokesman of the author's ideas. More's part in the discussion falls mostly in Book 1, but Book 2 also conveys his ideas through the mouthpiece of Hythloday.*

from The Discourse of Raphael Hythloday on the Best State of a Commonwealth, Book 2: As Recounted by Thomas More, Citizen and Undersheriff of London

[Geography]

The island of the Utopians is two hundred miles across in the middle part, where it is widest, and nowhere much narrower than this except towards the two ends, where it gradually tapers. These ends, curved round as if completing a circle five hundred miles in circumference, make the island crescent shaped, like a new moon. Between the horns of the crescent, which are about eleven miles apart, the sea enters and spreads into a broad bay. Being sheltered from the wind by the surrounding land, the bay is not rough, but placid and smooth instead, like a big lake. Thus nearly the whole inner coast is one great harbour, across which ships pass in every direction. . . . What with shallows on one side and rocks on the other, the mouth of the bay is perilous. Near mid-channel, there is one reef that rises above the water, and so presents no danger in itself; a tower has been built on top of it, and a garrison is kept there. Since the other rocks lie under the water, they are very dangerous. The channels are known only to the Utopians, so hardly any strangers enter the bay without one of their pilots; and even they themselves could not enter safely if they did not direct their course by some landmarks on the coast. Should these landmarks be shifted about, the Utopians could easily lure to destruction an enemy fleet, however big it was. . . .

There are fifty-four cities on the island, all spacious and magnificent, entirely identical in language, customs, institutions and laws. So far as the location permits, all of them are built on the same plan and have the same appearance. The nearest are twenty-four miles apart, and the farthest are not so remote that a person cannot travel on foot from one to another in a day.

Once a year each city sends three of its old and experienced citizens to Amaurot[1] to consider affairs of common interest to the island. Amaurot lies at the navel of the land . . . so it acts as a capital. Every city has enough ground assigned to it so that at least twelve miles of farmland are available in every direction, though where the cities are farther apart, their territories are much more extensive. No city wants to enlarge its boundaries, for the inhabitants consider themselves cultivators rather than landlords. A

Utopia: What geographical characteristics of Utopia make the island ideal? How do its general customs already seem idealistic? A

1. *Amaurot:* Greek etymology implies "dark city," perhaps in humorous ironic contrast to the enlightenment More attributes to their deliberations.

[The Country]

At proper intervals all over the countryside they have houses furnished with farm equipment. These houses are inhabited by citizens who come to the country by turns. No rural household has fewer than forty men and women in it, besides two slaves bound to the land. A master and mistress, serious and mature persons, are in charge of each household, and over every thirty households is placed a single phylarch.[2] Each year twenty persons from each household move back to the city after completing a two-year stint in the country. In their place, twenty substitutes are sent out from town, to learn farm work from those who have already been in the country for a year and are therefore better skilled in farming. They, in turn, will teach those who come the following year. If all were equally untrained in farm work and new to it, they might harm the crops out of ignorance. This custom of alternating farm workers is the usual procedure, so that no one has to perform such heavy labour unwillingly for too long; but many of them who take a natural pleasure in farm life are allowed to stay extra years. . . . **R**

Infer Tone: How does the description of Utopian society so far contrast with More's English society? What do you think More's tone is toward these differences? **R**

Their Cities, Especially Amaurot

If you know one of their cities you know them all, for they're exactly alike, except where geography itself makes a difference. So I will describe one of them, and no matter which. But what one rather than Amaurot, the most worthy of all?—since its **eminence** is acknowledged by the other cities that send representatives to the senate there; besides which, I know it best because I lived there for five full years.

eminence (ĕm′ə-nəns) *n.* A position of great distinction or superiority.

Well, then, Amaurot lies up against a gently sloping hill; the town is almost square in shape. From a little below the crest of the hill, its shorter side runs down about two miles to the river Anyder,[3] its length along the river bank is somewhat greater. . . .

The town is surrounded by a thick, high wall, with many towers and battlements. On three sides it is also surrounded by a dry ditch, broad and deep and filled with thorn hedges; on its fourth side the river itself serves as a moat. The streets are conveniently laid out both for use by vehicles and for protection from the wind. Their buildings are by no means shabby. Long unbroken rows of houses face each other down the whole block. The house-fronts along each block are separated by a street twenty feet wide. Behind the houses, a large garden—as long on each side as the block itself—is hemmed in on all sides by the backs of the houses.

Every house has a front door to the street and a back door to the garden. The double doors, which open easily with a push of the hand and close again automatically, let anyone come in—so there is nothing private anywhere. Every ten years they exchange the houses themselves by lot. . . . **R**

Infer Tone: Private versus common ownership of property is a key issue in *Utopia*. How realistic does this brief description seem? **R**

Their Occupations

The chief and almost the only business, of the syphogrants[4] is to take care and see to it that no one sits around in idleness, and to make sure that everyone works hard at his trade. But no one has to be exhausted with endless toil from early morning to late at night like a beast of burden. Such wretchedness, really worse than slavery, is the common lot of workmen almost everywhere except in Utopia. Of the twenty-four equal hours into which they divide the day and the night, the Utopians devote only six to work. They work three hours before

2. *phylarch:* "a high-ranking magistrate" (*OED*, specific to *Utopia*)
3. *Anyder:* (Gk.) "waterless"
4. *syphogrants:* another name for phylarchs

noon, when they go to lunch. After lunch, they rest for two hours, then go to work for another three hours. Then they have supper, and about eight o'clock (counting the first hour after noon as one) they go to bed, and sleep eight hours. . . .

But at this point you may get a wrong impression if we don't go back and consider one matter more carefully. Because they allot only six hours to work, perhaps you might think the necessities of life would be in scant supply. This is far from the case. Their working hours are ample to provide not only enough but more than enough of the necessities and even the conveniences of life. You will easily appreciate this if you consider how large a part of the population in other countries lives without doing any work at all. . . .

And now consider how few of those who do work are doing really essential things. For where money is the measure of everything, many vain and completely superfluous trades are bound to be carried on simply to satisfy luxury and licentiousness. Suppose the multitude of those who now work were limited to a few trades and set to producing just those commodities that nature really requires. They would be bound to produce so much that prices would drop and the workmen would be unable to make a living. But suppose again that all the workers in useless trades were put to useful ones, and that the whole crowd of languid idlers (each of whom consumes as much as any two of the workmen who provide what he consumes) were assigned to productive tasks—well, you can easily see how little time would be enough and more than enough to produce all the goods that human needs and conveniences call for—yes, and human pleasure too, as long as it's true and natural pleasure. . . .

Since there is an abundance of everything—as a result of everyone working at useful trades and the trades requiring less work—they sometimes assemble great numbers of people to work on the roads, if any need repairs. And when there is no need even for this sort of work, then they very often proclaim a shorter work day, since the magistrates never force their citizens to perform useless labour. The chief aim of their constitution is that, as far as public needs permit, all citizens should be free to withdraw as much time as possible from the service of the body and devote themselves to the freedom and culture of the mind. For in that, they think, lies the happiness of life. **A**

Social Satire: List some customs and attitudes of European society that More seems to be criticizing in this passage by contrast with Utopian customs. **A**

Social Relations

. . . The oldest of every household, as I said, is the ruler. Wives act as servants to their husbands, children to their parents, and generally the younger to their elders. Every city is divided into four equal districts, and in the middle of each district is a market for all kinds of commodities. Whatever each household produces is brought here and stored in warehouses, each kind of goods in its own place. Here the head of each household looks for what he or his family needs, and carries off what he wants without any sort of payment or compensation. Why should anything be refused him? There is plenty of everything, and no reason to fear that anyone will claim more than he needs. For why would anyone be suspected of asking for more than is needed, when he knows there will never be any shortage? Fear of want, no doubt, makes every living creature greedy and rapacious, and man, besides, develops these qualities out of sheer pride, which glories in getting ahead of others by a superfluous display of possessions. But this sort of vice has no place whatever in the Utopian scheme of things. . . . **E**

Author's Perspective: What does More believe causes greed? Does it seem likely that a society will be able to eliminate these issues? **E**

[Gold and Silver]

. . . They treat gold and silver quite differently from the way we do. After all, they never do use money among themselves, but keep it only for a contingency that may or may not actually arise. So in the meanwhile they keep gold and silver (of which money is made) in such a way that no one will value them beyond what the metals themselves deserve. . . . But Nature granted to gold and silver no function with which we cannot easily dispense. Human folly has made them precious because they are rare. In contrast, Nature, like a most indulgent mother, has placed her best gifts out in the open, like air, water and the earth itself; vain and unprofitable things she has hidden away in remote places.

And so, if in Utopia gold and silver were kept locked up in some tower, smart fools among the common people might **concoct** a story that the governor and senate were out to cheat ordinary folk and get some advantage for themselves. . . . To avoid these problems they thought of a plan which conforms with the rest of their institutions as sharply as it contrasts with our own. Unless one has actually seen it working, their plan may seem incredible, because we prize gold so highly and are so careful about guarding it. While they eat from earthenware dishes and drink from glass cups, finely made but inexpensive, their chamber pots and their humblest vessels, for use in the common halls and even in private homes, are made of gold and silver. Moreover, the chains and heavy shackles of slaves[5] are also made of these metals. Finally, criminals who are to bear the mark of some disgraceful act are forced to wear golden rings in their ears and on their fingers, golden chains around their necks, and even gold headbands. Thus they hold up gold and silver to scorn in every conceivable way. As a result, if they had to part with their entire supply of these metals, which other people give up with as much agony as if they were being disembowelled, no one would feel it any more than the loss of a penny. . . .

concoct (kən-kŏkt′) *tr.v.* To devise, using skill and intelligence; contrive.

These customs so different from those of other people also produce a quite different cast of mind: this never became clearer to me than it did in the case of the Anemolian[6] ambassadors, who came to Amaurot while I was there. Because they came to discuss important business, the national council had assembled ahead of time, three citizens from each city. The ambassadors from nearby nations, who had visited Utopia before and knew the local customs, understood that fine clothing was not respected in that land, silk was despised, and gold a badge of contempt; therefore they always came in the very plainest of their clothes. But the Anemolians, who lived farther off and had had fewer dealings with them, had heard only that they all dressed alike and very simply; so they took for granted that their hosts had nothing to wear that they didn't put on. Being themselves rather more proud than wise, they decided to dress as elegantly as the very gods, and dazzle the eyes of the poor Utopians with the splendour of their garb.

And so the three ambassadors made a grand entry with a suite of a hundred attendants, all in clothing of many colours, and most in silk. Being noblemen at home, the ambassadors were arrayed in cloth of gold, with heavy gold chains round their necks, gold earrings, gold rings on their fingers and sparkling strings of pearls and gems hanging on their caps. In fact, they were decked out in all the articles which in Utopia are used to punish slaves, shame

5. *slaves:* Hythloday later reports that slaves were prisoners of war, extremely offensive criminals, or foreigners facing death sentences in their own countries, not people stolen from other countries.
6. *Anemolian:* (Gk.) "windy people"

wrongdoers or entertain infants. It was a sight to see how they strutted when they compared their finery with the dress of the Utopians, who had poured out into the streets. But it was just as funny to see how wide they fell of the mark, and how far they were from getting the consideration they thought they would get. Except for a very few Utopians who for some good reason had visited foreign countries, all the onlookers considered this splendid pomp a mark of disgrace. They therefore bowed to all the humblest of the party as lords, and took the ambassadors, because of their golden chains, to be slaves, passing them by without any reverence at all. . . .

But after the ambassadors had spent a couple of days among the Utopians, they saw the immense amounts of gold which were as thoroughly despised there as they were prized at home. They saw too that more gold and silver went into making chains and shackles for a single runaway slave than into costuming all three of them. Somewhat ashamed and crestfallen, they put away all the finery in which they had strutted so arrogantly—especially after they had talked with the Utopians enough to learn their customs and opinions. . . . **A**

Social Satire: Who wears gold in Utopia? Whose values might More be poking fun at in this passage? **A**

The Religions of the Utopians

There are different forms of religion not only throughout the island but even within the individual cities. Some worship as a god the sun, others the moon, still others one of the planets. There are some who worship a man of past ages, **conspicuous** either for virtue or glory; they consider him not only a god but the supreme god. But the vast majority, and those by far the wiser ones, believe nothing of the kind: they believe in a single divinity, unknown, eternal, infinite, **inexplicable**, beyond the grasp of the human mind, and diffused throughout the universe, not physically, but in influence. Him they call their parent, and to him alone they attribute the origin, increase, progress, changes and ends of all things; they do not offer divine honours to any other. . . .

conspicuous (kən-spĭk′yo͞o -əs) *adj.* Attracting attention, as by being unusual or remarkable; noticeable.

inexplicable (ĭn-ĕk′splĭ-kə-bəl) *adj.* Difficult or impossible to explain or account for.

But after they heard from us the name of Christ, and learned of his teachings, his life, his miracles and the no less marvellous constancy of the many martyrs whose blood, freely shed, has drawn so many nations far and near into their religion, you would not believe how eagerly they assented to it, either through the secret inspiration of God or because Christianity seemed very like the sect that most prevails among them. . . .

Those who have not accepted Christianity make no effort to restrain others from it, nor do they criticise new converts to it. . . . For it is one of their oldest rules that no one should suffer for his religion.

Utopus[7] had heard that before his arrival the natives were continually squabbling over religious matters, and he had observed that it was easy to conquer the whole country because the different sects were too busy fighting one another to oppose him. And so at the very beginning, after he had gained the victory, he prescribed by law that everyone may cultivate the religion of his choice, and strenuously **proselytise** for it too, provided he does so quietly, modestly, rationally and without insulting others. If persuasion fails, no one may resort to abuse or violence; and anyone who fights wantonly about religion is punished by exile or slavery.

proselytize [British *proselytise*](prŏs′ə-lĭ-tīz′) *intr.v.* To attempt to convert someone to one's own religious faith.

Utopus laid down these rules not simply for the sake of peace, which he saw was being completely undermined by constant quarrels and implacable hatreds, but he also thought such decrees would benefit religion itself. In such matters

7. *Utopus:* King Utopus

he was not at all quick to dogmatize, because he was uncertain whether God likes diverse and manifold forms of worship and hence inspires different people with different views. On the other hand, he was quite sure that it was arrogant folly for anyone to enforce conformity with his own beliefs on everyone else by threats or violence. . . . So he left the whole matter open, allowing each person to choose what he would believe. The only exception was a solemn and strict law against anyone who should sink so far below the dignity of human nature as to think that the soul perishes with the body, or that the universe is ruled by blind chance, not divine providence. . . . R

Infer Tone: Does More's tone seem serious in this passage? How do these ideas about religious tolerance compare with what you know of his life? R

[Conclusion]

Now I have described to you as accurately as I could the structure of that commonwealth which I consider not only the best but indeed the only one that can rightfully claim that name. In other places men talk all the time about the commonwealth, but what they mean is simply their own wealth; here, where there is no private business, every man zealously pursues the public business. And in both places people are right to act as they do. For elsewhere, even though the commonwealth may flourish, there are very few who do not know that unless they make separate provision for themselves, they may perfectly well die of hunger. Bitter necessity, then, forces them to think that they must look out for themselves rather than for the people, that is, for other people. But here, where everything belongs to everybody, no one need fear that, so long as the public warehouses are filled, anyone will ever lack for anything for his own use. For the distribution of goods is not niggardly;[8] no one is poor there, there are no beggars, and though no one owns anything, everyone is rich.

8. *niggardly:* stingy

THINK AND DISCUSS

1. What are the characteristics of utopian literature?
2. Note the geographical features of Utopia. With what is the island meant to be compared? What about Amaurot? Anyder?
3. Name three ways Utopia qualifies as an idealistic society. Support your answers from the text.
4. In *Utopia*, what part might names play in the satire?
5. Describe two facets of English society that More seems to be satirizing. Support your ideas with textual details.
6. How might More's description of Utopian practices concerning work exhibit his Renaissance humanist beliefs?
7. Discuss the Utopians' view of gold. What does More's story point out about intrinsic value versus societally determined values? What should a society value more than gold, according to More?
8. Summarize the Utopians' approach to religion and proselytizing in society. In what key way do modern American attitudes tend to differ? Compare and contrast both with the biblical approach. How are Christians to live and spread the gospel in a pluralistic society?
9. Ancient dialogues (see p. 132) were meant to provoke discussion. Do the excerpts included here, including the satirical portions, succeed in that goal? How might that goal explain More's notoriously ambiguous tone in some sections?
10. A common thread through *Utopia* concerns how people value goods, property, and wealth. Does More seem to admire some of these ideas? Does he think they are achievable? Write a paragraph examining how More's Christian background might affect his answers to both questions. Why might such ideals be worth discussing?

Sir Philip Sidney (1554–86)

At once athletic, intellectual, artistic, eloquent, and popular, Sir Philip Sidney epitomized the ideal humanist gentleman from Castiglione's popular Italian text *The Book of the Courtier*. Born in 1554 to an eminent family with political and noble connections, Sidney was trained to enter government service. After traveling Europe for three years, polishing his languages and manners and making valuable political connections, he was appointed cupbearer to Queen Elizabeth in 1575. The queen sent him abroad to test interest in a Protestant league but was disappointed in his performance of the mission. After he wrote a letter challenging her marriage plans, he was banished from court for a year.

Following his punishment, Sidney attended the queen at court, participating in court tournaments, sitting in Parliament for Kent, and writing literature for the consumption of court friends. He continued diplomatic work in England, entertaining foreign dignitaries and nurturing contacts abroad. As he expressed keen interest in everything from literature to science to exploration and patronized many individuals in these fields, he gained a vast array of contacts and friends who held him in great respect.

Sidney eventually gained a long-desired goal, a military command in the Netherlands. His troops engaged in a fierce but futile skirmish with a Spanish convoy. Outnumbered, the English troops failed, but not before Sidney was seriously wounded. The wound became gangrenous and caused his death three weeks later at the young age of thirty-one. His body was laid to rest in St. Paul's Cathedral with great ceremony and widespread grief and eulogies. Sidney's writings were published posthumously and are his most lasting accomplishment. His three works *Arcadia* (prose fiction), *An Apology for Poetry* (literary criticism), and *Astrophel and Stella* (a sonnet sequence) are considered among the most significant works of the English Renaissance.

BEFORE READING

ANALYZE: *Literary Criticism, Parallelism, Analogy*

Sidney's seminal essay, *An Apology for Poetry,* falls into the genre of **literary criticism,** the practice of establishing criteria for and engaging in the analysis, interpretation, and evaluation of works of literature. Sidney employs two prominent **rhetorical devices** (p. 129). First, **parallelism** creates similarity in the structure of two or more phrases, clauses, or sentences (e.g., Julius Caesar's famous "I came, I saw, I conquered"). Second, **analogy**, detailed comparisons of one thing to another dissimilar thing, helps clarify his message. Look for examples of both as you read.

READ: *Rhetorical Appeals*

In the following excerpt, Sidney uses two kinds of **rhetorical appeals** (p. 129) to persuade readers, winning their assent to or sympathy for his ideas. Rhetorical appeals are classically divided into three categories: appeals to facts and reason (**logos**), to emotions (**pathos**), or to credible authorities (**ethos**), whether individuals, institutions, or authoritative works. As you read, determine which paragraphs mainly appeal to your reason, to your emotions, or to an authority of some kind.

CREATE: *Literary Criticism*

Prepare to create a piece of literary criticism of your own. After you read and analyze Sidney's work, use Bible truths and examples (e.g., 2 Sam. 12:1–4, Judg. 9:8–15, Phil. 4:8, the parables of Jesus) to define your own criteria for literary excellence. Then apply this set of criteria to evaluating a story you have read or viewed.

OBJECTIVES

- Identify characteristics of literary criticism in an essay.
- Analyze a work's use of parallelism, analogy, and rhetorical appeals to develop its message.
- Evaluate an author's message from a biblical worldview.

VOCABULARY

precept (prē′sĕpt′) *n.* A rule or principle prescribing a particular course of action or conduct.

abstract (ăb′străkt′) *n.* Something *abstract* (*adj.* Denoting something that is immaterial, conceptual, or nonspecific, as an idea or quality).

conceit (kən-sēt′) *n.* Something conceived in the mind; a notion, conception, idea, or thought.

FROM

An Apology for Poetry

For these [right poets] be they which most properly do imitate to teach and delight; and to imitate borrow nothing of what is, hath been, or shall be; but range, only reined with learned discretion, into the divine consideration of what may be and should be. . . . For these, indeed, . . . delight to move men to take that goodness in hand, which without delight they would fly as from a stranger; and teach to make them know that goodness whereunto they are moved:—which being the noblest scope to which ever any learning was directed, yet want there not idle tongues to bark at them. . . . ✓

This purifying of wit, this enriching of memory, enabling of judgment, and enlarging of conceit, which commonly we call learning, under what name soever it come forth or to what immediate end soever it be directed, the final end is to lead and draw us to as high a perfection as our degenerate souls, made worse by their clay lodgings, can be capable of. This, according to the inclination of man, bred many-formed impressions. . . . But when by the balance of experience it was found that the astronomer, looking to the stars, might fall into a ditch, that the inquiring philosopher might be blind in himself, and the mathematician might draw forth a straight line with a crooked heart; then lo! did proof, the overruler of opinions, make manifest, that all these are but serving sciences, which, as they have each a private end in themselves, so yet are they all directed to the highest end of the mistress-knowledge, . . .which stands, as I think, in the knowledge of a man's self, in the ethic and politic consideration, with the end of well-doing, and not of well-knowing only: —even as the saddler's next end is to make a good saddle, but his further end to serve a nobler faculty, which is horsemanship; so the horseman's to soldiery; and the soldier not only to have the skill, but to perform the practice of a soldier. So that the ending end of all earthly learning being virtuous action, those skills that most serve to bring forth that have a most just title to be princes over all the rest; wherein, if we can show, the poet is worthy to have it before any other competitors. . . . A

Sidney next identifies the moral philosopher and the historian as chief rivals of poets to this princely position over all other modes of learning. In the following excerpt, he responds to their challenge.

The philosopher, therefore, and the historian are they which would win the goal, the one by **precept**, the other by example. But both not having both, do both halt.[1] For the philosopher, setting down with thorny arguments the bare rule, is so hard of utterance and so misty to be conceived, that one that hath no other guide but him shall wade in him till he be old, before he shall find sufficient cause to be honest.[2] For his knowledge standeth so upon the **abstract** and general, that happy is that man who may understand him, and more happy that can apply what he doth understand. On the other side, the historian, wanting[3] the precept, is so tied, not to what should be but to what is, to the particular truth of things, and not to the general reason of things, that his example draweth no necessary consequence, and therefore a less fruitful doctrine. ✓

1. *halt:* walk lamely
2. *honest:* virtuous
3. *wanting:* lacking

Reading Check: According to Sidney, what is a poet's purpose? ✓

Analogy: What does Sidney say is the highest purpose of learning? Identify one of the analogies he uses in the previous paragraph to clarify that idea. A

precept (prē′sĕpt′) *n.* A rule or principle prescribing a particular course of action or conduct.

abstract (ăb′străkt′) *n.* Something *abstract* (*adj.* Denoting something that is immaterial, conceptual, or nonspecific, as an idea or quality).

Reading Check: In Sidney's view, what disqualifies the historian and the philosopher as the best at achieving learning's primary purpose? ✓

Now doth the peerless poet perform both; for whatsoever the philosopher saith should be done, he giveth a perfect picture of it in some one by whom he presupposeth it was done, so as[4] he coupleth the general notion with the particular example. A perfect picture, I say, for he yieldeth to the powers of the mind an image of that whereof the philosopher bestoweth but a wordish description, which doth neither strike, pierce, nor possess the sight of the soul so much as that other doth. For as in outward things, to a man that had never seen an elephant or a rhinoceros, who should tell him most exquisitely all their shapes, colour, bigness, and particular marks, or of a gorgeous palace the architecture, with declaring the full beauties, might well make the hearer able to repeat, as it were by rote, all he had heard, yet should never satisfy his inward **conceit** with being witness to itself of a true lively knowledge; but the same man, as soon as he might see those beasts well painted, or that house well in model, should straightways grow, without need of any description, to a judicial comprehending of them: so no doubt the philosopher with **A** his learned definitions—be it of virtues, vices, matters of public policy or private government—replenisheth the memory with many infallible grounds of wisdom, which, notwithstanding, lie dark before the imaginative and judging power, if they be not illuminated or figured forth by the speaking picture of poesy. . . .

Now therein of all sciences[5] (I speak still of human, and according to the human conceit) is our poet the monarch. For he doth not only show the way, but giveth so sweet a prospect[6] into the way, as will entice any man to enter into it. Nay, he doth, as if your journey should lie through a fair vineyard, at the very first give you a cluster of grapes, that full of that taste, you may long to pass further. He beginneth not with obscure definitions, which must blur the margent[7] with interpretations, and load the memory with doubtfulness. But he cometh to you with words set in delightful proportion, either accompanied with, or prepared for, the well enchanting skill of music; and with a tale, forsooth, he cometh unto you, with a tale which holdeth children from play, and old men from the chimney corner. And, pretending no more, doth intend the winning of the mind from wickedness to virtue—even as the child is often brought to take most wholesome things, by hiding them in such other as have a pleasant taste, which, if one should begin to tell them the nature of the aloes or rhubarb[8] they should receive, would sooner take their physic at their ears[9] than at their mouth. So is it in men (most of which are childish in the best things, till they be cradled in their graves): glad they will be to hear the tales of Hercules, Achilles, Cyrus, Æneas; and, hearing them, must needs hear the right description of wisdom, valour, and justice; which, if they had been barely, that is to say philosophically, set out, they would swear they be brought to school again. **R**

4. *so as:* in so doing
5. *sciences:* branches of learning excluding theology
6. *prospect:* foreview
7. *margent:* margin
8. *aloes . . . rhubarb:* herbs commonly used as medicine
9. *take . . . ears:* i.e., be boxed on the ears for not taking their medicine

conceit (kən-sēt′) *n.* Something conceived in the mind; a notion, conception, idea, or thought.

Analogy: What two analogies does Sidney use to illustrate the superiority of poetry to philosophy? **A**

Rhetorical Appeal: What kind of rhetorical appeal does Sidney both explain and use most in this final paragraph? **R**

THINK AND DISCUSS

1. What does Sidney say poets are trying to do when they "imitate" life?
2. Determine Sidney's main idea in this excerpt.
3. Explain two main supporting ideas that Sidney develops to persuade readers of this thesis.
4. Why is Sidney's *Apology for Poetry* considered literary criticism? Cite two supporting details from the text.
5. Describe and interpret two analogies that Sidney uses in the final paragraph.
6. Find two examples of rhetorical appeals in the text and label each as an example of logos, pathos, or ethos.
7. Identify two examples of parallelism in Sidney's writing. How might these make Sidney's style more effective?
8. Does Scripture address the issue of imaginative literature? How might Sidney's ideas about literature reflect biblical ideas about Truth, Goodness, and Beauty? Consider passages such as 2 Samuel 12:1–4, Judges 9:8–15, Philippians 4:8, and the parables of Jesus in your answer.
9. As described in the Create paragraph (p. 140), write two paragraphs defining criteria for judging literature and applying this set of criteria to a story of your choice.

Amelia Lanier (1569–1645)

Amelia Lanier pioneered the way for women in the world of English literature. In a time when women writing professionally was unheard of, she was the first English female poet to publish poems for the public and call herself a poet. Though her body of work was small and long forgotten, it rivals in literary skill that of her more famous male contemporaries.

Born to a court musician, Baptiste Bassono, Amelia was brought up by the Countess Dowager of Kent after her parents died. A part of court society but with little social standing of her own, Amelia became the mistress of Henry Carey, who was the Lord Chamberlain, Queen Elizabeth's cousin, and patron of the arts. After she became pregnant, Amelia was married off to Alfonso Lanier, a struggling court musician. It was not a happy marriage: Alfonso ran through much of her wealth and left her with little financial support after his death. She unsuccessfully pursued rights to a lucrative patent he had held and, as her poetry received no patronage, had to support herself by teaching for a while. The few remaining records suggest her final years were spent with her son, also a court musician, and his family.

The Countess of Kent believed women had as much right to education as men and so trained Lanier in humanist and Protestant learning. Lanier read many classics and was adept in Latin, rhetoric, poetry, and Bible knowledge. Sadly, her volume *Salve Deus Rex Judaeorum* is all that remains of her work. It includes poems dedicated to famous women of the time (which no other poet had done), "The Description of Cooke-ham" (the first published country house poem, a popular genre in the seventeenth century), and the book's titular poem, which tells of Christ's Passion. The latter was the first long religious poem written by an Englishwoman. It offered a unique perspective, being told mostly by the women who followed Christ. As they tell the story, these women frequently comment satirically on contemporary Renaissance ideas about and treatment of women.

BEFORE READING

ANALYZE: *Argumentation*

The excerpt from Lanier's *Salve Deus Rex Judaeorum*, referred to as "Eve's Apology in Defense of Women," responds to certain ideas about women commonly accepted in the Renaissance. Some are biblical, but some are not. Lanier's poetry here amounts to **argumentation**, the process of presenting a claim and providing reasons to support it. Her use of poetry to make her case exemplifies how Renaissance humanists often used verse for a wider range of purposes than modern writers, a trend that you will also see in Cavendish's work (pp. 152–55).

READ: *Summarize*

Lanier offers evidence to support the claim that she proposes. Evidence, essential to establishing a claim's validity, can be logical reasons, data, or even personal testimony (for examples of kinds of logos appeals, see p. 140). What evidence does Lanier offer? Summarize her supporting reasons as you read.

EVALUATE: *The Fall and Women*

Take some time to reread the narrative of the Fall in Genesis 3 and revisit related New Testament passages (Rom. 5:12, 1 Cor. 15:21–22, Eph. 5:23, 1 Tim. 2:12–14). Evaluate Lanier's claims against Scripture. Do the accounts of Eve differ in any way? If so, how? Lanier's poetry implies certain widespread ideas about women through the Renaissance perspective. Evaluate the views she is responding to by what Scripture says about the relationship between men and women.

OBJECTIVES

- Summarize an author's line of reasoning.
- Apply knowledge of historical context to understand a text's message.
- Analyze an author's main premise, supporting reasons, and conclusion.
- Evaluate Renaissance views on women from a biblical worldview.

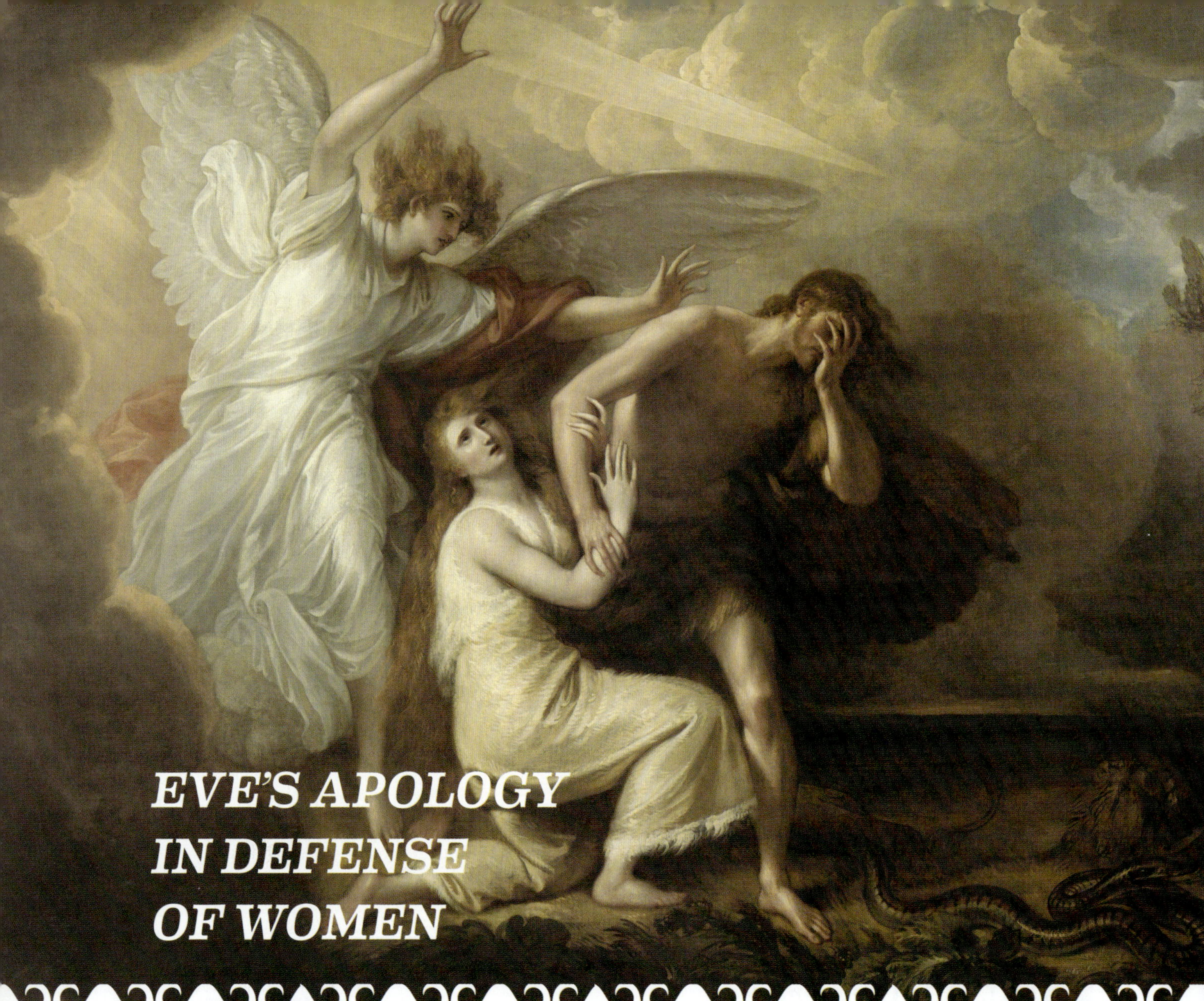

EVE'S APOLOGY IN DEFENSE OF WOMEN

from *SALVE DEUS REX JUDAEORUM*[1]

But surely Adam cannot be excused.
Her [Eve's] fault, though great, yet he was most to blame;
What weakness offered, strength might have refused.
Being Lord of all, the greater was his shame.
Although the serpent's craft had her abused,
God's holy word ought all his actions frame:
For he was Lord and King of all the earth,
Before poor Eve had either life or breath. A

Who being framed by God's eternal hand,
The perfectest man that ever breathed on earth,
And from God's mouth received that straight command,
The breach whereof he knew was present death.
Yea, having power to rule both sea and land,
Yet with one apple won to lose that breath,
Which God hath breathed in his beauteous face,
Bringing us all in danger and disgrace.

VISUAL ANALYSIS
What emotions does the artist seem to attribute to Adam and Eve as they leave the Garden of Eden?

Argumentation: What is Lanier's major argumentative claim? A

1. *Salve Deus Rex Judaeorum:* Latin for "Hail, God, King of the Jews"

And then to lay the fault on patience' back,
That we (poor women) must endure it all;
We know right well he did discretion lack,
Being not persuaded thereunto at all;
If Eve did err, it was for knowledge sake,
The fruit, being fair, persuaded him to fall:
No subtle serpent's falsehood did betray him,
If he would eat it, who had power to stay him? R

Summarize: Examine the preceding stanzas and summarize two of Lanier's supporting reasons for her claim. R

Not Eve, whose fault was only too much love,
Which made her give this present to her dear,
That which she tasted, he likewise might prove,
Whereby his knowledge might become more clear;
He never sought her weakness to reprove,
With those sharp words which he of God did hear:
Yet men will boast of knowledge, which he took
From Eve's fair hand, as from a learned book.

If any evil did in her remain,
Being made of him, he was the ground of all;
If one of many worlds could lay a stain
Upon our sex, and work so great a fall
To wretched man, by Satan's subtle train;
What will so foul a fault amongst you all?
Her weakness did the serpent's word obey,
But you in malice God's dear Son betray.[2]

Whom, if unjustly you condemn to die,
Her sin was small, to what you do commit;
All mortal sins that do for vengeance cry,
Are not to be compared unto it:
If many worlds would altogether try,
By all their sins the wrath of God to get;
This sin of yours, surmounts them all as far
As doth the sun, another little star. R

Summarize: Summarize Lanier's reasoning in stanza six. R

Then let us have our liberty again,
And challenge to yourselves no sovereignty;
You came not in the world without our pain,
Make that a bar against your cruelty;
Your fault being greater, why should you disdain
Our being your equals, free from tyranny? E
If one weak woman simply did offend,
This sin of yours hath no excuse, nor end.

The Fall and Women: What do lines 49–54 indicate about the Renaissance view of women? E

2. *you . . . betray:* At this point in the poem's rendering of Christ's Passion, the women speaking are reproving the men (particularly Pilate) who are condemning Christ to die.

THINK AND DISCUSS

1. As evidenced by Amelia Lanier, how did Renaissance humanism benefit women at times?
2. "Eve's Apology in Defense of Women" illustrates argumentation. For what claim is Lanier arguing? Cite the lines in which she makes this claim.
3. Summarize Lanier's reasons and facts supporting her claim. Is her reasoning valid?
4. How is Lanier's account of the Fall similar to Scripture's? How might it differ from Scripture?
5. What view of women held by her Renaissance audience does Lanier's writing here imply? How do those attitudes agree or disagree with Scripture?
6. What is Lanier's conclusion? Is it biblically valid?

Sir Francis Bacon (1561–1626)

AT A GLANCE

- **1618** Appointed Lord Chancellor
- **1620** Published *Novum Organum*
- **1621** Charged with accepting bribes
- **1625** Published the final version of his *Essays*

If Sir Thomas More towers as a humanist at the start of the English Renaissance, then Sir Francis Bacon shows the end results of humanist education and thought. An important figure in early seventeenth-century history, philosophy, and literature, Bacon is perhaps best remembered for recognizing and codifying a new approach to pursuing knowledge. His work provided the impetus for a whole new generation of thinkers to push beyond the limitations of Renaissance scholarship.

A Rising (and Falling) Star

A man of brilliant intellect and keen observation, Bacon rose quickly under James I. His roles included Solicitor General (1607), Attorney General (1613), member of the Privy Council (1616), Lord Keeper of the Great Seal (1617), and Lord Chancellor (1618). Knighted in 1603, he was named Baron Verulam in 1618 and Viscount St. Alban in 1621. His political fall in 1621 was as sudden as his rise was spectacular. Charged with taking bribes, Bacon, pleading guilty, was fined £40,000, banished from court, imprisoned in the Tower of London, and barred from holding public office. Though the fine and prison sentence were remitted, Bacon's career was ruined, and he retired to St. Albans, Hertfordshire, to pursue his private interests.

A Student of Knowledge

Bacon was a classic humanist both in the breadth of his interests and in his chief concern, the "advancement of learning." This "learning," according to Bacon, was the practical knowledge that man uses to subdue the earth in obedience to God (Gen. 1:28) and with benefit to himself. As Bacon surveyed the past, three inventions—the printing press, gunpowder, and the compass—seemed to him to have done more for the world than two thousand years of philosophy. What is needed, he concluded, is more direct observation of external phenomena and less dependence on ancient authorities such as Aristotle and Galen for information about the physical world. His *Novum Organum* (1620) explains the "new instrument"—scientific induction—by means of which this observation should proceed.

Bacon is often called the Father of Modern Science for his recommending the scientific method—inductive investigation that uses experiments to verify a hypothesis. This view of Bacon is appropriate, not because he originated the scientific method or achieved spectacular results with it, but because his writings produced a climate favorable to scientific progress. Bacon proposed a vast program of scientific inquiry that would bring a new physical prosperity for man. His program called for a survey of present knowledge by disciplines, separating genuine from erroneous knowledge and preserving this knowledge as the starting point of further investigation. His *Advancement of Learning* (1605) states his objections to traditional philosophy and then gives a preliminary overview of the kingdoms of knowledge.

A Writer of Aphorisms

His *Essays* (1597; revised 1612, 1625) exemplifies what he recommended to be undertaken in all realms of knowledge: concise formulations of fact that have practical value to man. "Of Studies" (1597) states the value of book learning, of which Bacon himself was proof. "Of Atheism" (1612) challenges atheism in light of common evidence and examines several of its causes. The style of Bacon's essays shows balance and extreme compression. Many include a series of aphorisms, or sayings, likely modeled on the memorable "commonplaces" (striking statements of general truths) that Renaissance schoolboys would cull from their classical readings and record in their "commonplace books."

ANALYZE: *Essay, Aphorism, and Tricolon*

Bacon introduced to the English language the **essay**, a brief prose composition with a single topic. The form quickly gained popularity because, as Bacon's essays exemplified, its brevity and flexibility allowed scholars to briefly examine any topic through the application of authorities and their own reason.

In his essays, Bacon frequently relies on **aphorisms**—short, pithy statements that express serious truths. Perhaps you have heard your parent or teacher use an aphorism such as "A job worth doing is worth doing well" to make a point. Bacon similarly used these statements to crystalize his ideas and make them memorable.

To assist in that goal, Bacon also employed the rhetorical device of parallelism (p. 140). Indeed, the first sentence of "Of Studies" shows Bacon's reliance on parallel structures, especially **tricolon**, the repetition of three parallel phrases or clauses of equal length that often build in emphasis. Unsurprisingly, the sentence also happens to be an aphorism. As you read, look for such examples of parallelism and aphorism that highlight Bacon's key thoughts.

READ: *Inductive and Deductive Reasoning*

Bacon was deeply interested in the proper uses of reason to produce reliable knowledge and was especially interested in **inductive reasoning**, in which a person observes multiple details about a topic or situation and draws from this evidence the general truth(s) it most logically suggests. These conclusions are, however, open to change based on new evidence. In contrast, a person using **deductive reasoning** offers general premises which, if true, must logically result in his conclusion(s). He frequently offers specific evidence to convince his audience to accept these premises but is himself fully convinced of their veracity. As you read each essay, decide which kind of reasoning Bacon is using. Use your conclusion to help determine Bacon's main ideas and purpose for these essays.

EVALUATE: *Knowledge and Humanity*

A true Renaissance man, Bacon had a thirst for knowledge and a spirit of rational inquiry in both temporal and religious matters. Like many Christian humanists of the northern Renaissance, he sought to use knowledge to improve humanity's material condition. Additionally, Bacon believed that in the Fall mankind lost both innocence and dominion over the world. God made it possible for innocence to be restored through the incarnation of Christ. Bacon believed that God would allow mankind's dominion to be restored by great advances in human knowledge. How do his ideas and use of reason in the following essays pursue these goals? For example, how convincing are his rational arguments against atheism? Is his belief in the power of knowledge biblically sound? Consider Ephesians 4:17–18 in your answer.

OBJECTIVES

- Identify examples of inductive and deductive reasoning.
- Determine an essay's main ideas.
- Analyze a text's use of rhetorical devices to support its message.
- Evaluate an author's hopes for knowledge against a biblical worldview.

VOCABULARY

disposition (dĭs′pə-zĭsh′ən) *n.* The power or liberty to control, direct, or dispose.

affectation (ăf′ĕk-tā′shən) *n.* A mannerism or habit that is assumed rather than natural, especially to impress others.

mutable (myo͞o′tə-bəl) *adj.* Capable of or subject to change or alteration.

dissemble (dĭ-sĕm′bəl) *intr. v.* To disguise or conceal one's real nature, motives, or feelings behind a false appearance.

magnanimity (măg′nə-nĭm′ĭ-tē) *n.* The quality of being *magnanimous* (*adj.* Highly moral, especially in showing kindness or forgiveness, as in overlooking insults or not seeking revenge).

WHAT TOPICS *have you thought through carefully?*

When a controversial topic comes up in conversation, we often chime in without much thought. But some topics deserve deeper consideration. What topics have you thoroughly examined and reached your own opinion on? Sometimes writing can force you to discover what you think on such issues. Working with a partner, assign each other a topic. Write a thesis statement expressing your opinion, one that could be developed into a full essay.

From Essays

Of Studies

Studies serve for delight, for ornament, and for ability. Their chief use for delight is in privateness and retiring; for ornament, is in discourse;[1] and for ability, is in the judgment and **disposition** of business. For expert men can execute, and perhaps judge of particulars, one by one; but the general counsels, and the plots and marshalling of affairs, come best from those that are learned. To spend too much time in studies is sloth; to use them too much for ornament, is **affectation**; to make judgment wholly by their rules, is the humor[2] of a scholar. They perfect nature, and are perfected by experience: for natural abilities are like natural plants, that need proyning,[3] by study; and studies themselves, do give forth directions too much at large, except they be bounded in by experience. Crafty men contemn[4] studies, simple men admire them, and wise men use them; for they teach not their own use; but that is a wisdom without[5] them, and above them, won by observation.

Read not to contradict and confute; nor to believe and take for granted; nor to find talk and discourse; but to weigh and consider. Some books are to be tasted, others to be swallowed, and some few to be chewed and digested; that is, some books are to be read only in parts; others to be read, but not curiously;[6] and some few to be read wholly, and with diligence and attention. Some books also may be read by deputy,[7] and extracts made of them by others; but that would be only in the less important arguments, and the meaner[8] sort of books, else distilled[9] books are like common distilled waters, flashy[10] things.

Reading maketh a full man; conference[11] a ready man; and writing an exact man. And therefore, if a man write little, he had need have a great memory; if he confer little, he had need have a present wit:[12] and if he read little, he had need have much cunning, to seem to know that he doth not. Histories make men wise; poets witty; the mathematics subtile; natural philosophy deep; moral grave; logic and rhetoric able to contend. *Abeunt studia in mores.*[13] Nay, there is no stond[14] or impediment in the wit, but may be wrought out by fit studies; like as diseases of the body, may have appropriate exercises. Bowling is good for the stone and reins;[15] shooting for the lungs and breast; gentle walking for the stomach; riding for the head; and the like. So if a man's wit be wandering, let him study the mathematics; for in demonstrations, if his wit be called away never so little, he must begin again. If his wit be not apt to distinguish or find differences, let him study the School men; for they are *cymini sectores.*[16] If he be not apt to beat over matters, and to call up one thing to prove and illustrate another, let him study the lawyers' cases. So every defect of the mind, may have a special receipt.

1. *discourse:* "reasoned argument or thought" (*OED*)
2. *humor:* eccentricity
3. *proyning:* pruning
4. *Crafty men contemn:* men who work at a craft despise
5. *without:* separate from
6. *curiously:* carefully
7. *deputy:* an assistant
8. *meaner:* lesser in quality
9. *distilled:* abridged, condensed
10. *flashy:* "insipid, tasteless, vapid" (*OED*)
11. *conference:* conversation; consulting sources
12. *present wit:* quick mind
13. *Abeunt . . . mores:* (L.) "Studies pass into and influence character."
14. *stond:* "stoppage" (*OED*)
15. *reins:* kidneys
16. *cymini sectores:* (L.) figurative for *hair-splitters*

disposition (dĭs′pə-zĭsh′ən) *n.* The power or liberty to control, direct, or dispose.

affectation (ăf′ĕk-tā′shən) *n.* A mannerism or habit that is assumed rather than natural, especially to impress others.

Reading Check: What three uses for studies has Bacon already identified? What must be added to these studies to make them most useful?

Reading Check: What three ways to approach a book does Bacon outline here?

Rhetorical Devices: This final section of the essay contains one of Bacon's most famous aphorisms, which also forms an example of tricolon. What sentence illustrates both of these devices?

OF

ATHEISM

I had rather believe all the fables in the Legend,[1] and the Talmud, and the Alcoran,[2] than that this universal frame is without a mind. And therefore God never wrought miracle to convince[3] atheism, because his ordinary works convince it. It is true, that a little philosophy inclineth man's mind to atheism; but depth in philosophy bringeth men's minds about to religion. For while the mind of man looketh upon second causes scattered, it may sometimes rest in them, and go no further; but when it beholdeth the chain of them, confederate and linked together, it must needs fly to Providence and Deity. Nay, even that school which is most accused of atheism doth most demonstrate religion; that is, the school of Leucippus and Democritus and Epicurus.[4] For it is a thousand times more credible, that four **mutable** elements, and one immutable fifth essence, duly and eternally placed, need no God, than that an army of infinite small portions or seeds unplaced, should have produced this order and beauty without a divine marshal. R

The Scripture saith, *The fool hath said in his heart, there is no God*;[5] it is not said, *The fool hath thought in his heart*; so as he rather saith it, by rote to himself, as that he would have, than that he can thoroughly believe it, or be persuaded of it. For none deny there is a God, but those, for whom it maketh[6] that there were no God. It appeareth in nothing more, that atheism is rather in the lip than in the heart of man, than by this; that atheists will ever be talking of that their opinion, as if they fainted in it within themselves, and would be glad to be strengthened by the consent of others. Nay more, you shall have atheists strive to get disciples, as it fareth with other sects. And, which is most of all, you shall have of them that will suffer for atheism, and not recant; whereas if they did truly think that there were no such thing as God, why should they trouble themselves?

Epicurus is charged that he did but **dissemble** for his credit's sake, when he affirmed there were blessed natures, but such as enjoyed themselves without having respect to the government of the world. Wherein they say he did temporize;[7] though in secret he thought there was no God. But certainly he is traduced;[8] for his words arc noble and divine: *Non deos vulgi negare profanum; sed vulgi opiniones diis applicare profanum.*[9] Plato could have said no more. And although he had the confidence to deny the administration, he had not the power to deny the nature. The Indians of the West have names for their particular gods, though they have no name for God: as if the heathens should have had the names Jupiter, Apollo, Mars, etc., but not the word *Deus*;[10] which shows that even those barbarous people have the notion, though they have not the latitude and extent of it. So that against atheists the very savages take part, with the very subtlest philosophers. . . . R

The causes of atheism are: divisions in religion, if they be many; for any one main division addeth zeal to both sides; but many divisions introduce atheism.

1. *the Legend:* a medieval collection of saints' lives
2. *Talmud . . . Alcoran:* the body of Jewish traditional law and the Koran
3. *convince:* refute
4. *the school . . . Epicurus:* Leucippus originated the idea that the universe consists of atoms and voids, a concept known as the atomic theory, of which Democritus and Epicurus were students.
5. *The fool . . . no God:* Psalm 14:1.
6. *maketh:* profiteth
7. *temporize:* avoid an argument
8. *traduced:* maligned
9. *Non . . . profanum:* (L.) "There is no profanity in refusing to believe in the gods of the people: the profanity is in believing of the gods what the people believe of them."
10. *Deus:* (L.) "God"

mutable (myo͞o′tə-bəl) *adj.* Capable of or subject to change or alteration.

Reasoning: Summarize Bacon's line of thought in this passage. Is his purpose for the essay clear yet? R

dissemble (dĭ-sĕm′bəl) *intr. v.* To disguise or conceal one's real nature, motives, or feelings behind a false appearance.

Reasoning: Summarize Bacon's ideas in the previous two paragraphs. Does his reasoning in these and the previous paragraph follow a deductive or inductive pattern so far? R

Another is, scandal of priests; when it is come to that which St. Bernard saith, *Non est jam dicere, ut populus sic sacerdos; quia nec sic populus ut sacerdos.*[11] A third is, custom of profane scoffing in holy matters; which doth by little and little deface the reverence of religion. And lastly, learned times, specially with peace and prosperity; for troubles and adversities do more bow men's minds to religion.

They that deny a God destroy man's nobility; for certainly man is of kin to the beasts by his body; and, if he be not of kin to God by his spirit, he is a base and ignoble creature. It destroys likewise **magnanimity**, and the raising of human nature; for take an example of a dog, and mark what a generosity and courage he will put on when he finds himself maintained by a man; who to him is instead of a God, or *melior natura*;[12] which courage is manifestly such as that creature, without that confidence of a better nature than his own, could never attain. So man, when he resteth and assureth himself upon divine protection and favor, gathered a force and faith which human nature in itself could not obtain. Therefore, as atheism is in all respects hateful, so in this, that it depriveth human nature of the means to exalt itself above human frailty. . . . E

11. *non est . . . up sacerdos:* (L.) "One cannot now say the priest is as the people, for the truth is that the people are not so bad as the priest."

12. *melior natura:* (L.) "better nature"

magnanimity (măg′nə-nĭm′ĭ-tē) *n.* The quality of being *magnanimous* (*adj.* Highly moral, especially in showing kindness or forgiveness, as in overlooking insults or not seeking revenge).

Knowledge: How convincing are Bacon's arguments here? Do you think they might change an atheist's mind? E

THINK AND DISCUSS

1. According to Bacon, what are the three general uses of personal studies? Which does he emphasize in the essay? Cite textual details to support your answer.
2. How do the ideas in "Of Studies" reflect the interests of Renaissance humanists (see pp. 128–29)?
3. Other than the first line, find three examples of tricolon or general parallelism in "Of Studies."
4. Identify an aphorism from one of the essays. Explain its meaning and why it qualifies as an aphorism.
5. What is the main point of Bacon's "Of Atheism"? What kind of reasoning did Bacon use to support that point? Support your answer from the text.
6. Review the three types of rhetorical appeals (p. 140). Identify an example of two types in "Of Atheism."
7. Briefly explain how Bacon's use of parallelism and aphorisms makes his essays more memorable for you. Cite examples from the text
8. Examine Bacon's arguments in "Of Atheism." Which is stated directly in the Bible? Which do you find most convincing? Are any logically or factually flawed?
9. How do these essays reflect Bacon's hopes for knowledge (p. 147)? What does the Bible indicate about the power of knowledge in Ephesians 4:17–18? Do these essays reflect or exemplify that perspective in any way?
10. How might Bacon's essays fulfill the goals of Truth, Goodness, and Beauty?

Margaret Cavendish (1623–73)

Born near the Renaissance's end, Margaret Cavendish showed in her career some of humanism's effects on science and social roles. A woman of the gentry, she received a typical young lady's formal education (e.g., reading, writing, dancing) but, informally, read widely using her family's access to scholarly works. After becoming a lady-in-waiting to Queen Henrietta, she joined the queen's exile in Paris (1644), where she met her husband, William Cavendish (later Duke of Newcastle), a widower and scholar thirty years her senior. William encouraged her studies and writing, introducing her to his "Newcastle Circle" of influential intellectuals such as Thomas Hobbes and René Descartes.

Cavendish was an oddity in her intellectual pursuits as well as in her cultivated eccentricities of mannerism and fashion, earning her the nickname "Mad Madge." More importantly, she was one of the first Englishwomen to write for publication, a gift afforded by her own real talent plus her husband's rank and wealth. Her first works (the 1653 poetic volumes *Philosophical Fancies* and *Poems and Fancies*) led to many other works in various genres; for example, her utopian novel, *The Blazing World*, is considered one of the first science-fiction works. Most of her works, even the poems, tackled natural philosophy (p. 125), a subject considered beyond women's capabilities. In 1667, she achieved another first when she was invited to observe a meeting of the Royal Society of London, England's premiere (and male-only) scientific body.

Despite contradicting modern science at times, Cavendish's work popularized some of the scientific revolution's most important ideas. Her only chance to respond to scientists who refused to debate a woman, these works tackled the same difficult topics others were grappling with, trying to navigate the shift from dependence on authorities to investigating new ways of thinking about the natural world. *Observations upon Experimental Philosophy* (1666) is one of her later works in which she debated the proper approach to science and discussed specific theories of her own. She controversially laid out an early version of naturalism (which views the world as operating purely by natural properties and causes, not supernatural or spiritual ones), but also expressed belief in God as operating in a separate realm altogether. By her death, her reputation and fame had far outgrown traditional female roles. She is buried next to her husband in Westminster Abbey.

BEFORE READING

ANALYZE: *Analogy and Metaphor*

Cavendish used **analogies** (p. 140) and **metaphors** (imaginative comparisons consisting of the stated or implied equivalence of two dissimilar things) in her prose and verse to clarify ideas or lend force to her reasoning. Her poem relies on an **extended metaphor** (a metaphor developed beyond a single sentence or comparison) to clarify her main idea. What broad image does she use and how does she extend it throughout the poem?

READ: *Identifying Arguments*

In both selections that follow, Cavendish addresses a scholarly argument (p. 125). For example, in her preface to *Observations upon Experimental Philosophy* she sets up the claims she will make regarding experimental philosophy. Look for her main ideas and identify the ways she explains and supports them. Note how her comparisons usually develop broader appeals (i.e., logos, pathos, or ethos, p. 140).

EVALUATE: *Renaissance Philosophy*

Many classically educated scholars defaulted to Latin or used a very complex rhetorical style in their English writings. Cavendish opposed these approaches because they created a barrier to those who lacked a privileged education. Instead, she proposed writing in English using a simple, direct style that most literate people could understand. Consider her preface. In comparison to other Renaissance writers (e.g., Bacon and Sidney), did she fulfill her goals of clarity and simplicity?

OBJECTIVES

- Identify examples of inductive and deductive reasoning.
- Determine an essay's main ideas.
- Analyze a text's use of rhetorical devices to support its message.
- Evaluate an author's hopes for knowledge against a biblical worldview.

VOCABULARY

superfluous (so͞o-pûr′flo͞o-əs) *adj.* Being beyond what is required or sufficient.

confound (kən-found′) *v.* To fail to distinguish; mix up

fallacy (făl′ə-sē) *n.* Incorrectness of reasoning or belief; erroneousness.

from the Preface to OBSERVATIONS UPON EXPERIMENTAL PHILOSOPHY

Tis probable, some will say, that my much writing is a disease; but what disease they will judge it to be, I cannot tell; I do verily believe they will take it to be a disease of the Brain. . . . But I hope they will rather call it a disease of wit. But, let them give it what name they please, yet of this I am sure, that if much writing be a disease, then the best philosophers, both moral and natural, as also the best divines,[1] lawyers, physicians, poets, historians, orators, mathematicians, chemists, and many more have been grievously sick; I and Seneca, Plinius, Aristotle, Cicero, Tacitus, Plutarch, Euclid, Homer, Virgil, Ovid, St. Augustin[2]. . . have been at death's door with the disease of writing; but to be infected with the same disease, which the devoutest, wisest, wittiest, subtlest, most learned and eloquent men have been troubled withal, is no disgrace, but the greatest honour. . . . It is also a great delight and pleasure to me, as being the only pastime which employs my idle hours; in so much, that, were I sure nobody did read my works, yet I would not quit my pastime for all this; for although they should not delight others, yet they delight me; and if all women that have no employment in worldly affairs, should but spend their time as harmlessly as I do, they would not commit such faults as many are accused of. R

I confess, there are many useless and **superfluous** books, and perchance mine will add to the number of them; especially is it to be observed, that there have been in this latter age, as many writers of Natural Philosophy, as in former ages there have been of Moral Philosophy;[3] which multitude, I fear, will produce such a confusion of truth and falsehood, as the number of moral

Arguments: Read between the lines in this paragraph. What idea can you infer Cavendish is countering through her arguments? How does she defend her position? R

superfluous (sōō-pûr′flōō-əs) *adj.* Being beyond what is required or sufficient.

1. *divines:* clerics; theologians
2. *Seneca . . . St. Augustin:* a list of well-respected classical authorities
3. *writers . . . Moral Philosophy:* Cavendish likely refers to medieval scholastics, often lampooned as arguing over how many angels can dance on the head of a pin.

call it a disease of wit.
But, let them give it what name they please, yet of this I am sure, that if much writing be a disease, then the best philosophers, both moral and natural, as also the best divines, lawyers, physicians, ~~orators~~ poets, historians, orators, mathematicians, chemists, and many more have been grievously sick and Seneca, Plinius, Aristotle, Cicero, Tacitus, Plutarch, Euclid, Homer, Virgil, Ovid, St. Augustine have all been at death's door with the disease of writing;
But to be infected with the same disease, which the devoutest, wisest, wittiest, subtlest, most learned and eloquent men have been troubled withal, it is no disgrace, but the greatest honour

will produce such a confusion

Reason and Truth

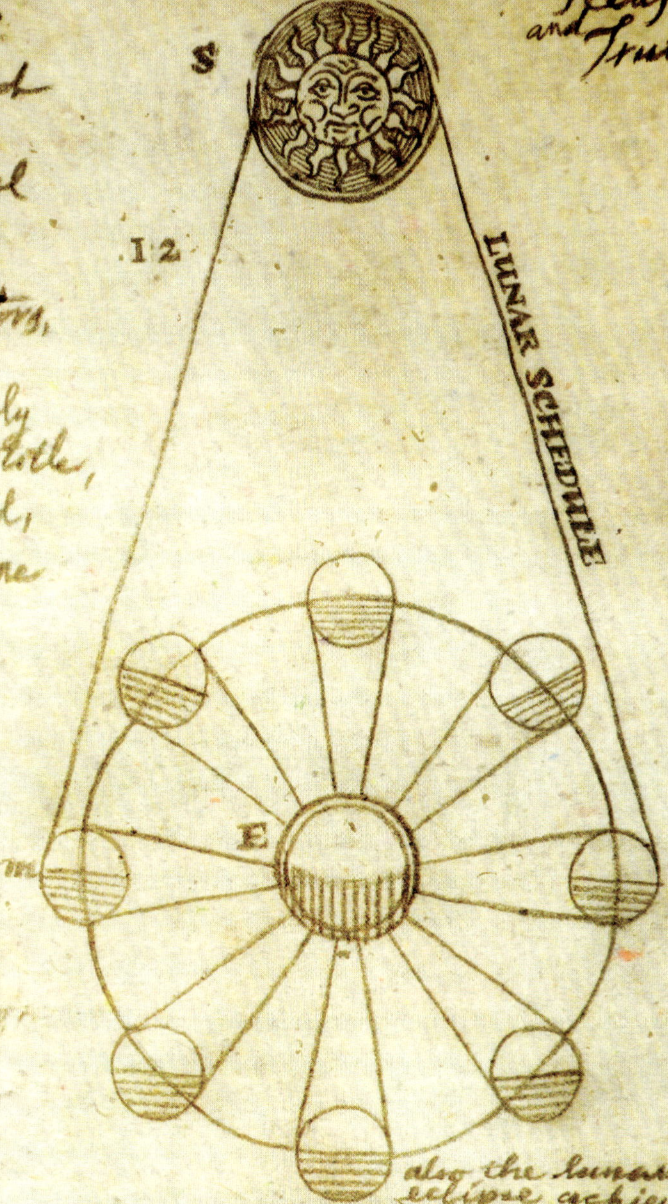

S

12

LUNAR SCHEDULE

E

m

and what of observation

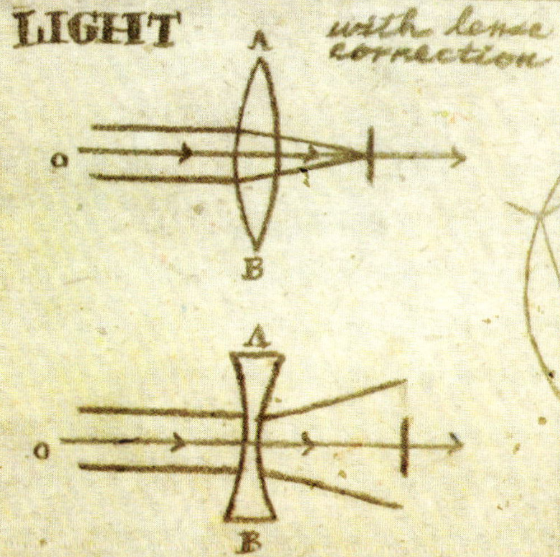

also the lunar eclipse achieved

LIGHT

with lense correction

A

O

B

A

O

B

neither will the inspection of dusty atoms, and reflections of light, teach painters how to make and mix colours

Truly, the art of augury was far more ben than the lately invented art of microgra for I cannot perceive any great advanta this art doth bring us. Also the well- eclipse of the Sun and moon was not fou out by telescopes, nor the motions of the lodestone, nor the ~~printing of the~~ art of the card, nor the art of guns and gunpowder

Fig. 21.

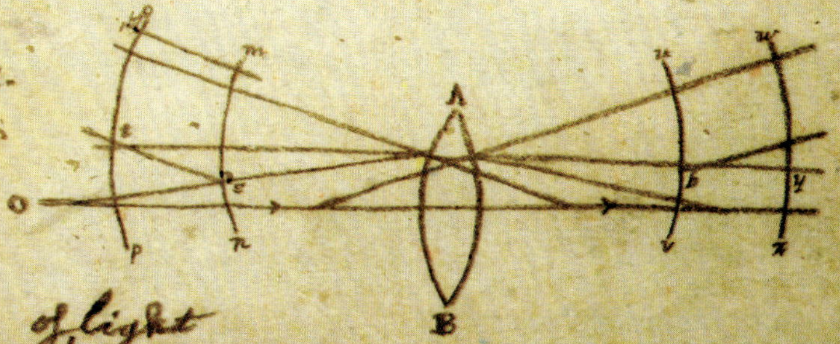

A

O

B

of light

writers formerly did, with their over-nice divisions of virtues and vices, whereby they did puzzle their readers so, that they knew not how to distinguish between them. The like, I doubt, will prove amongst our natural philosophers, who by their extracted, or rather distracted arguments, **confound** both divinity and natural philosophy, sense and reason, nature and art, so much as in time we shall have rather a chaos, than a well-ordered universe by their doctrine: . . . Nor do I think their weak works will be able to overcome the strong wits of the ancient; for setting aside some few of our moderns, all the rest are but like dead and withered leaves, in comparison to R lovely and lively plants. . . . Truly, the art of augury[4] was far more beneficial than the lately invented art of micrography;[5] for I cannot perceive any great advantage this art doth bring us. Also the eclipse of the sun and moon was A not found out by telescopes, nor the motions of the lodestone,[6] nor the art of the card, nor the art of guns and gun-powder, nor the art of printing, and the like, by microscopes; nay, if it be true, that telescopes make appear the spots in the sun and moon, or discover some new stars, what benefit is that to us? Or if microscopes do truly represent the exterior parts and superficies[7] of some minute creatures, what advantages it our knowledge? . . . Wherefore, in my opinion, it is both time and labour lost; for the inspection of the exterior parts of vegetables, doth not give us any knowledge how to sow, set, plant, and graft; so that a gardener or husbandman will gain no advantage at all by this art: The inspection of a bee, through a microscope, will bring him no more honey, nor the inspection of a grain more corn; neither will the inspection of dusty atoms, and reflections of light, teach painters how to make and mix colours. . . . The truth is, most of these arts are **fallacies**, rather than discoveries of truth; for sense deludes more then it gives a true information, and an exterior inspection through an optic glass, is so deceiving, that it cannot be relied upon: Wherefore regular reason is the best guide to all arts, as I shall make it appear in this following treatise. R

confound (kən-found′) *v.* To fail to distinguish; mix up

Arguments: What worries Cavendish about the current science? How does her reasoning in this passage exhibit early Renaissance values? R

Comparisons: What device does Cavendish use to develop her argument in the passage that follows? A

fallacy (făl′ə-sē) *n.* Incorrectness of reasoning or belief; erroneousness.

Arguments: Summarize Cavendish's opinion of "experimental philosophy" (e.g., scientific observation using one's senses). What does she suggest here as an alternative? R

It may be the world will judge it a fault in me, that I oppose so many eminent and ingenious writers, but I do it not out of a contradicting or wrangling nature, but out of an endeavour to find out truth, or at least the probability of truth, according to that proportion of sense and reason nature has bestowed upon me; for as I have heard my noble lord say, that in the art of riding and fencing, there is but one truth, but many falsehoods and fallacies: So it may be said of natural philosophy and divinity; for there is but one fundamental truth in each, and I am as ambitious of finding out the truth of nature, as an honourable dueler is of gaining fame and repute; . . . so have I taken upon me in this present work, to make some reflections also upon some of our modern experimental and dioptrical[8] writers. They will perhaps think myself an inconsiderable opposite, because I am not of their sex, and therefore strive to hit my opinions with a side stroke, rather covertly, then openly and directly; but if this should chance, the impartial world, I hope, will grant me so much justice as to consider my honesty, and their fallacy, and pass such a judgment as will declare them to be patrons, not only to Truth, but also to Justice and Equity; for which heaven will grant them their reward, and time will record their noble and worthy actions in the register of fame, to be kept in everlasting memory.

4. *augury:* skill in divining from omens
5. *micrography:* "examination by means of the microsope" (*OED*)
6. *lodestone:* a piece of black iron oxide mineral that has magnetic properties
7. *superficies:* the outer surface of an area or body
8. *dioptrical:* relating to the refractive power of a lens

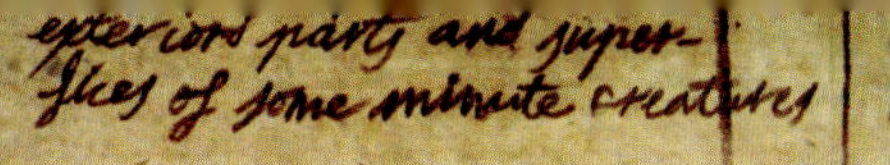

A WORLD MADE BY ATOMES

Renaissance writers used verse form for a broader range of content than modern audiences are used to. Here, as in many of her works of natural philosophy, Cavendish turns to verse to present a scientific idea, in this case atomic theory. While Observations upon Experimental Philosophy *is a later, mature work, this poem is from one of her first,* Poems and Fancies, *published in 1653. Cavendish would later amend her view of the theory.*

Small *Atoms* of themselves a *World* may make,
As being subtle,[1] and of every shape:
And as they dance about, fit places find,
Such *Forms* as best agree, make every kind.
For when we build a house of Brick, and Stone,
We lay them even, every one by one:
And when we find a gap that's big, or small,
We seek out Stones, to fit that place withal.[2]
For when not fit, too big, or little be,
They fall away, and cannot stay we see.
So *Atoms*, as they dance, find places fit,
They there remain, lie close, and fast will stick.
Those that unfit, the rest that rove about,
Do never leave, until they thrust them out.
Thus by their several *Motions*, and their *Forms*,
As several work-men serve each other's turns.
And thus, by chance, may a New *World* create:
Or else predestined to work my *Fate*. **A**

Comparison: What broad image does Cavendish use to unify the various descriptions in this poem? What kind of device does it exemplify? **A**

1. *subtle:* "involving distinctions that are fine or delicate, esp. to such an extent as to be difficult to analyse or describe" (*OED*)
2. *withal:* "along with the rest; in addition" (*OED*)

THINK AND DISCUSS

1. Using details from the preface to *Observations upon Experimental Philosophy,* identify Cavendish's two main purposes for her preface.
2. What main idea does Cavendish develop in the first paragraph of the preface? Describe her arguments in favor of this idea. Identify the kind of rhetorical appeal each utilizes.
3. Cavendish criticizes two scientific advancements in her preface. What are her two main arguments against their use?
4. Summarize Cavendish's arguments against experimental philosophy. What alternative approach does she promote?
5. Describe one way in which Cavendish's approach to science reflects earlier Renaissance thinking.
6. Identify and explain the metaphor Cavendish uses in the first few sentences of the preface.
7. What rhetorical technique does Cavendish use to develop her arguments in the second paragraph of the preface?
8. What type of figurative language unifies "A World Made by Atomes"? Describe and interpret its imagery.
9. Evaluate Cavendish's writing style by her own criteria (see p. 151). Does she achieve her goals? Support your conclusions from her texts.
10. Create a metaphor to describe a physical thing or process. Write a poem or paragraph extending your metaphor.

UNIT 2

PART 2

Reformation and National Identity

What is your identity? On an individual level, you might equate it with a special skill or interest that you have. You might think of yourself, for example, as a pianist, a cyclist, or a mathematician. On a broader level, your identity is likely to come from a group of people who are similar to you in some way. You likely identify with your family because of genetic similarities and shared experiences. You might identify with people who live around you because you share a common culture (foods, expressions, pastimes, etc.). If you know Jesus Christ as your Savior, you identify with other Christians because of your shared faith.

Many of us consider our national origin to be a significant part of our identity. The English in the Renaissance did too; moreover, religious and political developments helped create a stronger and more distinct sense of English identity, one increasingly tied to the Protestant faith. The selections in Unit 2, Part 2 either contributed to or reflected that development.

England's changing identity was influenced greatly by two often interwoven movements: the Reformation and rising nationalism. The former officially broke apart any cultural or political unity Catholicism provided Europe. In many states, religious power was removed from the pope and given to princes or kings. In the north, several countries established Protestant state churches based on the choice of each country's head of state. The end result was that religion became a distinctive of national identity in a way it had not been. At the same time, the Age of Exploration brought to bear forces (e.g., the race for colonies and trade) that heightened nations' competing economic and political interests and contributed further to nationalist feeling.

In England, Tudor rule developed and strengthened English identity. Henry VIII's break with Rome showed England's growing willingness to defend its national interests against outside interference and put the country on a path toward its own unique religious heritage. The latter result produced long-term changes in England's culture and literature. For instance, most churchmen wanted a new liturgy specifically for the English church, a need met by *The Book of Common Prayer*. As church membership was mandated, its familiar phrases thereafter directed the country in personal devotion, public worship, and special occasions (e.g., weddings, funerals), creating a distinct and unified English cultural experience.

Additionally, the Reformation encouraged the need for individual reading of the Scriptures in vernacular languages. This desire produced rising literacy and further developed English language and literature. Bible translation in England (a tumultuous saga) produced two authorized versions of the Scriptures: Henry VIII's Great Bible of 1539 and James I's 1611 version (the KJV), one of English literature's great masterworks. Both were translated for public reading, helping unify the English church and familiarize the public with the Scriptures as never before.

Mary's attempt to restore Catholicism seemed likely to halt the Reformation; the general public was not yet solidly Protestant and might not have posed strong objections. Instead, her reign pushed the English to identify their national concerns with Protestant ones because of two factors—her marriage to Philip II of Spain and her persecutions of Protestants. Philip was a foreigner, the ruler of Spain (England's chief rival abroad), and one of the main defenders of the Catholic Church. His presence in the country, together with Mary's unexpectedly deadly persecutions, provoked a response that was both nationalistic and Protestant. John Foxe's record of the persecutions in his *Book of Martyrs* continued to fan the flames of this response even after Mary's death.

The greatest changes to English identity came under Elizabeth I's reign; over forty years long, it solidified England's status as a powerful and vibrant country. Repeated attempts by Catholic foreigners (e.g., Mary, Queen of Scots, and Philip again) to intervene in English affairs only strengthened support for Elizabeth and her Protestant *via media,* while her strong and capable personality inspired a bold, new national identity. The English embraced their national interests abroad (p. 123) and confirmed the connection between Protestant and English identity. Elizabethan literature often reflects this nationalism and the normalization of Protestant ideas in England. For example, Elizabeth's speech at Tilbury (p. 180) reveals her unusual status as a visible symbol of her country and uses highly nationalist rhetoric. Meanwhile Edmund Spenser's magnificent epic, *The Faerie Queene*, paints England as a mythically great nation and ties that status to its Protestant journey. As the sixteenth century passed, more literature was written in the English vernacular, and that literature reflected a pointedly Protestant perspective and spoke to specifically English contexts and concerns.

THE BOOK OF COMMON PRAYER

After Henry VIII formally broke with the Papacy, the Church of England continued to use Latin liturgies to prescribe the structure and content of worship. Although a practice adapted from the Catholics, liturgies in English were deemed necessary for the church by virtually all church reformers. So when Edward VI ascended the throne, he commissioned Thomas Cranmer, the Archbishop of Canterbury, to write the first English liturgy, which eventually became *The Book of Common Prayer*. Rendered in English rather than Latin, it absented key Catholic doctrines (e.g., transubstantiation) and common rituals deemed unnecessary or unbiblical. It also added many more Scripture readings to everyday worship. Used everywhere in England, it gradually changed the prevailing view of Christianity to a Protestant one.

This collection was central to the common man's daily life. It provided public prayers, exhortations, and Scripture readings for regular weekday and Sunday services, for holy days in the church calendar, and for personal events (e.g., baptism, confirmation, marriage, sickness, and death). The designated Scripture readings, from Coverdale's Great Bible, took the worshiper through the Old Testament once a year, the New Testament three times a year, and Psalms once a month. The language of its prayers and exhortations, repeated regularly and passed down generationally, shaped the religious and social environment of England.

For four centuries *The Book of Common Prayer* provided a service structure for the Anglican Church and, in modified forms, for some other Protestant groups, such as Methodists. In 1965 it was officially replaced by Parliament with a version that unfortunately reflects the doctrinal drift that has more recently characterized Anglicanism. Yet the *Prayer Book* still holds some forgotten splendors of Britain's spiritual and cultural heritage. *The Book of Common Prayer*'s influence extends beyond church custom into English literature, which often alludes to it or incorporates its language. As you read the excerpt from "The Form of Solemnization of Matrimony," see whether you notice any familiar phrases.

FROM
THE FORM OF SOLEMNIZATION OF MATRIMONY

From the Invocation

Dearly beloved, we are gathered together here in the sight of God, and in the face of this congregation, to join together this man and this woman in holy matrimony; which is an honourable estate, instituted of God in the time of man's innocency, signifying unto us the mystical union that is betwixt Christ and his church: which holy estate Christ adorned and beautified with his presence, and first miracle that he wrought, in Cana of Galilee; and is commended of Saint Paul to be honourable among all men: and therefore is not by any to be enterprised, nor taken in hand, unadvisedly, lightly, or wantonly, to satisfy men's carnal lusts and appetites, like brute beasts that have no understanding; but reverently, discreetly, advisedly, soberly, and in the fear of God; duly considering the causes for which matrimony was ordained. . . .

From the Vows

M. Wilt thou have this woman to thy wedded wife, to live together after God's ordinance in the holy estate of matrimony? Wilt thou love her, comfort her, honour, and keep her, in sickness and in health; and, forsaking all other, keep thee only unto her, so long as ye both shall live? . . .

N. Wilt thou have this man to thy wedded husband, to live together after God's ordinance in the holy estate of matrimony? Wilt thou obey him, and serve him, love, honour, and keep him, in sickness and in health; and, forsaking all other, keep thee only unto him, so long as ye both shall live? . . .

> *The minister, receiving the woman at her father's or friend's hands, shall cause the man with his right hand to take the woman by her right hand, and to say after him as followeth:*

I *M.* take thee *N.* to be my wedded wife, to have and to hold, from this day forward, for better for worse, for richer for poorer, in sickness and in health, to love and to cherish, till death us do part, according to God's holy ordinance; and thereto I plight thee my troth. . . .

I *N.* take thee *M.* to my wedded husband, to have and to hold from this day forward, for better for worse, for richer for poorer, in sickness and in health, to love, cherish, and to obey, till death us do part, according to God's holy ordinance; and thereto I give thee my troth.

From the Dedication

O Eternal God, creator and preserver of all mankind, giver of all spiritual grace, the author of everlasting life; send thy blessing upon these thy servants, this man and this woman, whom we bless in thy name; that, as Isaac and Rebecca lived faithfully together, so these persons may surely perform and keep the vow and covenant betwixt them made, (whereof this ring given and received is a token and pledge) and may ever remain in perfect love and peace together, and live according to thy laws; through Jesus Christ our Lord. Amen. . . . Those whom God hath joined together let no man put asunder. . . .

Forasmuch as *M.* and *N.* have consented together in holy wedlock, and have witnessed the same before God and this company, and thereto have given and pledged their troth either to other, and have declared the same, by giving and receiving of a ring, and by joining of hands; I pronounce that they be man and wife together, in the name of the Father, and of the Son, and of the Holy Ghost. Amen.

John Foxe (ca. 1516–87)

John Foxe, English minister and historian, owes his modern reputation to one work, *The Acts and Monuments of the English Martyrs*. Of a scholarly turn, he entered Oxford in 1534, earning a fellowship by 1539. Influenced by Scripture and reformers, he converted to Protestantism. Once university authorities began suspecting his beliefs, he resigned (1545) and moved to London. There he began to write first Protestant tracts and then a history of Christian martyrs.

With Mary I's Catholic restoration and her persecution of Protestants, Foxe left for France, publishing there a partial Latin version of his martyrology. Returning home after Elizabeth's accession, he continued the work and published his English version in 1563. It focused mostly on the Marian martyrs, many of whom he knew. His 1570 revision corrected problems critics had noted and added more on earlier martyrs, extending back to first-century Rome.

Foxe meant his work to inspire the Protestant cause by showing God's hand elevating the true faith despite, and even through, injustices. Often placed in churches next to the Bible, his book was very popular (particularly with Puritans) and played an integral role in making England's developing identity Protestant. In Foxe's time and later generations, its portrayal of martyrs and persecutors galvanized support for Protestantism and left lingering suspicions toward Catholicism.

Foxe's work has since weathered accusations of poor research and intense bias. While he did select material that best suited his purpose and tended not to critique his martyrs, what he chose to write has generally been found to be accurate. In fact, historians agree that his use of primary sources (e.g., legal documents, trial reports, eyewitness statements) was ahead of his time. For the discerning reader, Foxe's *Book of Martyrs* remains instructive and inspirational.

BEFORE READING

ANALYZE: *Historical Narrative*

A **historical narrative** is an account of a real event and real people. The author may give a firsthand account or may construct the story from other sources. Historical narratives rely on objective facts (e.g., dates, settings) and on less certain types of evidence (e.g., human accounts, hearsay) that historians handle as objectively as possible, without preconceived judgments (biases, p. 31). Still, no historian will be perfectly neutral about his or her subject; conflicting worldviews may legitimately lead historians to interpret or evaluate agreed-upon facts differently.

READ: *Infer Tone, Purpose, and Bias*

As you read the excerpt from Foxe, consider both of these scales of judgment. What nonneutral intent does Foxe, like any other historian, bring to his story? Look for direct interpretive commentary that implies Foxe's **purpose** for his work. Does this purpose interfere with his objectivity? To make this judgment, pay attention to his **tone** as you read. Whose actions does he approve of and why? Does he distort facts or use unnecessarily inflammatory language in judging people or their actions? Does he seem unbiased, able to see the situation clearly?

EVALUATE: *Author's Worldview*

Foxe's evaluation of his materials reveals his own values and perspective on the world. How does his interpretation of the people and events reveal his underlying worldview? What does he think should be their significance to his audience? Compare the results of your evaluation to Scripture to see whether Foxe's judgments align with it.

OBJECTIVES

- Identify characteristics of historical narrative in a text.
- Infer meaning from a text.
- Analyze how an author's tone, purpose, and bias interact in a text.
- Evaluate the worldview underlying an author's interpretation of historical events.

What are you willing **TO DIE** *for?*

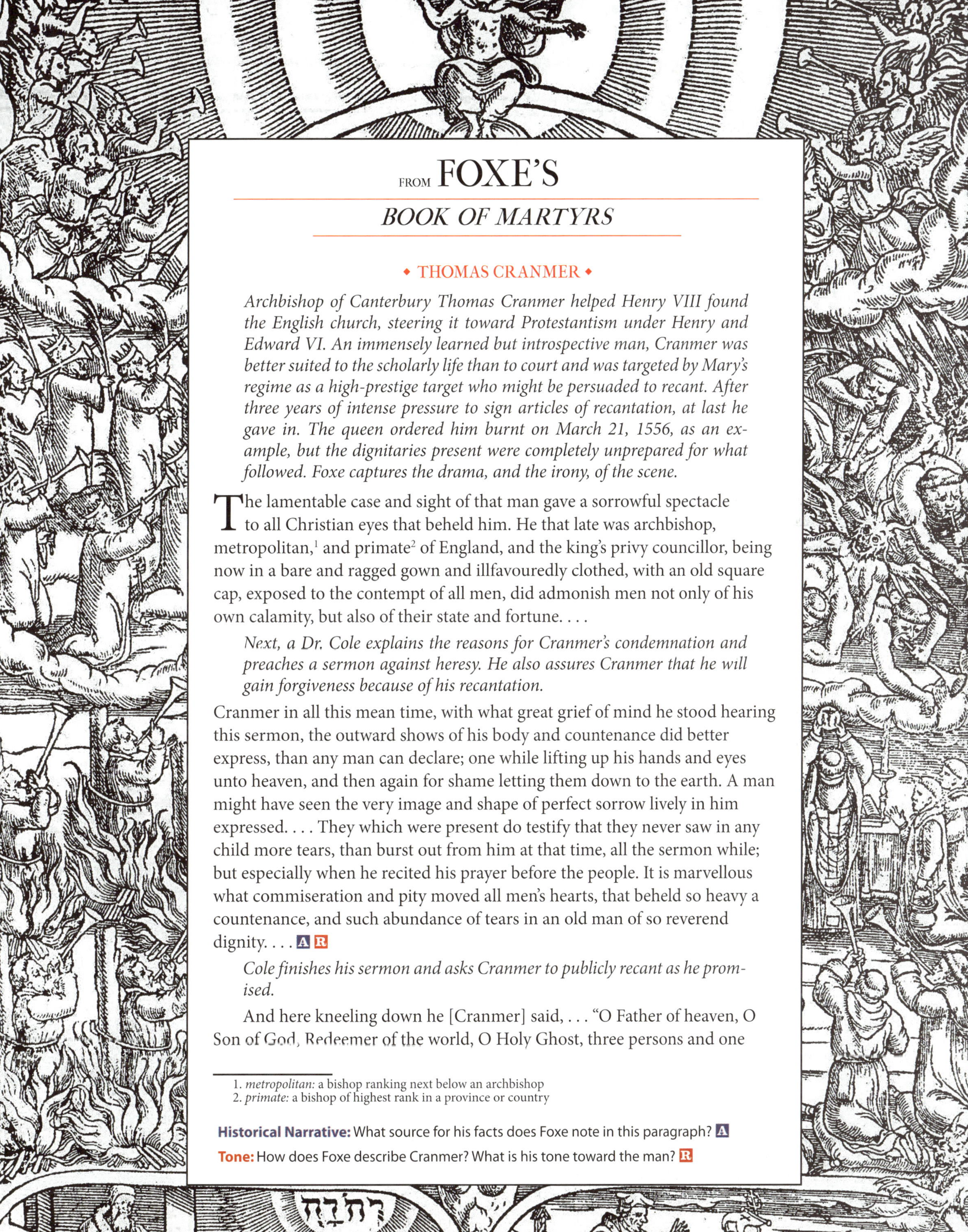

FROM

FOXE'S

BOOK OF MARTYRS

◆ THOMAS CRANMER ◆

Archbishop of Canterbury Thomas Cranmer helped Henry VIII found the English church, steering it toward Protestantism under Henry and Edward VI. An immensely learned but introspective man, Cranmer was better suited to the scholarly life than to court and was targeted by Mary's regime as a high-prestige target who might be persuaded to recant. After three years of intense pressure to sign articles of recantation, at last he gave in. The queen ordered him burnt on March 21, 1556, as an example, but the dignitaries present were completely unprepared for what followed. Foxe captures the drama, and the irony, of the scene.

The lamentable case and sight of that man gave a sorrowful spectacle to all Christian eyes that beheld him. He that late was archbishop, metropolitan,[1] and primate[2] of England, and the king's privy councillor, being now in a bare and ragged gown and illfavouredly clothed, with an old square cap, exposed to the contempt of all men, did admonish men not only of his own calamity, but also of their state and fortune. . . .

Next, a Dr. Cole explains the reasons for Cranmer's condemnation and preaches a sermon against heresy. He also assures Cranmer that he will gain forgiveness because of his recantation.

Cranmer in all this mean time, with what great grief of mind he stood hearing this sermon, the outward shows of his body and countenance did better express, than any man can declare; one while lifting up his hands and eyes unto heaven, and then again for shame letting them down to the earth. A man might have seen the very image and shape of perfect sorrow lively in him expressed. . . . They which were present do testify that they never saw in any child more tears, than burst out from him at that time, all the sermon while; but especially when he recited his prayer before the people. It is marvellous what commiseration and pity moved all men's hearts, that beheld so heavy a countenance, and such abundance of tears in an old man of so reverend dignity. . . . A R

Cole finishes his sermon and asks Cranmer to publicly recant as he promised.

And here kneeling down he [Cranmer] said, . . . "O Father of heaven, O Son of God, Redeemer of the world, O Holy Ghost, three persons and one

1. *metropolitan:* a bishop ranking next below an archbishop
2. *primate:* a bishop of highest rank in a province or country

Historical Narrative: What source for his facts does Foxe note in this paragraph? A

Tone: How does Foxe describe Cranmer? What is his tone toward the man? R

God, have mercy upon me most wretched caitiff[3] and miserable sinner. I have offended both against heaven and earth, more than my tongue can express. Whither then may I go, or whither shall I flee? To heaven I may be ashamed to lift up mine eyes, and in earth I find no place of refuge or succour.[4] To thee therefore, O Lord, do I run; to thee do I humble myself, saying, O Lord my God, my sins be great, but yet have mercy upon me for thy great mercy. The great mystery that God became man, was not wrought for little or few offences. Thou didst not give thy Son, O heavenly Father, unto death for small sins only, but for all the greatest sins of the world, so that the sinner return to thee with his whole heart, as I do here at this present. Wherefore have mercy on me, O God, whose property is always to have mercy; have mercy upon me, O Lord, for thy great mercy. I crave nothing for mine own merits, but for thy name's sake, that it may be hallowed thereby, and for thy dear Son Jesus Christ's sake. And now therefore, Our Father of heaven, hallowed be thy name," &c. E

Cranmer addresses the crowd with some brief reminders to live righteously.

"And now, forasmuch as I am come to the last end of my life, whereupon hangeth all my life past, and all my life to come, either to live with my Master Christ for ever in joy, or else to be in pain for ever with wicked devils in hell, and I see before mine eyes presently either heaven ready to receive me, or else hell ready to swallow me up: I shall therefore declare unto you my very faith how I believe, without any colour of dissimulation: for now is no time to dissemble, whatsoever I have said or written in times past.

"First, I believe in God the Father Almighty, maker of heaven and earth, &c. And I believe every article of the catholic faith, every word and sentence taught by our Saviour Jesus Christ, his apostles and prophets, in the New and Old Testament.

"And now I come to the great thing, which so much troubleth my conscience, more than any thing that ever I did or said in my whole life, and that is the setting abroad of a writing contrary to the truth: which now here I renounce and refuse, as things written with my hand, contrary to the truth which I thought in my heart, and written for fear of death, and to save my life if it might be; and that is, all such bills and papers which I have written or signed with my hand since my degradation; wherein I have written many things untrue. And forasmuch as my hand offended, writing contrary to my heart, my hand shall first be punished therefore; for, may I come to the fire, it shall be first burned.

"And as for the pope, I refuse him, as Christ's enemy, and antichrist, with all his false doctrine. . . ."

Here the standers-by were all astonied, marvelled, were amazed, did look one upon another, whose expectation he had so notably deceived. Some began to admonish him of his recantation,[5] and to accuse him of falsehood. Briefly, it was a world[6] to see the doctors beguiled of so great a hope. I think there was never cruelty more notably or better in time deluded and deceived; for it is not to be doubted but they looked for a glorious victory and a perpetual triumph by this man's retractation; who, as soon as they heard these things, began to let down their ears,[7] to rage, fret, and fume; and so much the more, because they could not revenge their grief—for they could now no longer threaten or hurt him. For the most miserable man in the world can die but once; . . . And so, when they could do nothing else unto him, yet, lest they should say nothing, they ceased not to object unto him his falsehood and dissimulation.[8]

Unto which accusation he answered, "Ah! my masters," quoth he, "do not you take it so. Always since I lived hitherto, I have been a hater of falsehood, and a lover of simplicity, and never before this time have I dissembled:" and in saying this, all the tears that remained in his body appeared in his eyes. And when he began to speak more of the sacrament and of the papacy, some of them began to cry out, yelp, and bawl, and specially Cole cried out upon him, "Stop the heretic's mouth, and take him away."

And then Cranmer, being pulled down from the stage, was led to the fire, accompanied with those friars, vexing, troubling, and threatening him most cruelly. "What madness," say they, "hath brought thee again into this error, by which thou wilt draw innumerable souls with thee into hell?" To whom he answered nothing, but directed all his talk to the people, saving that to one troubling him in the way, he spake, and exhorted him to get him home to his study, and apply his book diligently; saying, if he did diligently call upon God, by reading more he should get knowledge. But the other Spanish barker, raging and foaming, was almost out of his wits, always having this in his mouth, "Didst thou it not?"

But when he came to the place where the holy bishops and martyrs of God, Hugh Latimer and Nicholas

3. *caitiff:* "a captive, a prisoner: a wretched, miserable person" (*OED*)
4. *succour:* assistance in time of distress; relief

Worldview: What reason does Cranmer use to request forgiveness of God? Is his reasoning scriptural? E

5. *recantation:* to make a formal retraction of a statement or belief
6. *it was a world:* it was a great thing
7. *let down their ears:* to have expectations
8. *dissimulation:* the act of concealing what really is

Ridley, were burnt before him for the confession of the truth, kneeling down, he prayed to God; and not long tarrying in his prayers, putting off his garments to his shirt, he prepared himself to death. His shirt was made long, down to his feet. His feet were bare; likewise his head, when both his caps were off, was so bare, that one hair could not be seen upon it. His beard was long and thick, covering his face with marvellous gravity. Such a countenance of gravity moved the hearts both of his friends and of his enemies.

Then the Spanish friars, John and Richard, of whom mention was made before, began to exhort him, and play their parts with him afresh, but with vain and lost labour. Cranmer, with stedfast purpose abiding in the profession of his doctrine, gave his hand to certain old men, and others that stood by, bidding them farewell. . . .

Then was an iron chain tied about Cranmer, whom when they perceived to be more stedfast than that he could be moved from his sentence, they commanded the fire to be set unto him.

And when the wood was kindled, and the fire began to burn near him, stretching out his arm, he put his right hand into the flame, which he held so stedfast and immovable, (saving that once with the same hand he wiped his face,) that all men might see his hand burned before his body was touched. His body did so abide the burning of the flame with such constancy and stedfastness, that standing always in one place without moving his body, he seemed to move no more than the stake to which he was bound; his eyes were lifted up into heaven, and oftentimes he repeated "his unworthy right hand," so long as his voice would suffer him; and using often the words of Stephen, "Lord Jesus, receive my spirit," in the greatness of the flame he gave up the ghost.

This fortitude of mind, which perchance is rare, and not used among the Spaniards, when Friar John saw, thinking it came not of fortitude, but of desperation, although such manner of examples, which are of like constancy,[9] have been common here in England, ran to the Lord Williams of Thame, crying that the archbishop was vexed in mind, and died in great desperation. But he, which was not ignorant of the archbishop's constancy, being unknown to the Spaniards, smiled only, and (as it were) by silence rebuked the friar's folly. And this was the end of this learned archbishop, whom, lest by evil-subscribing[10] he should have perished, by well-recanting God preserved; and lest he should have lived longer with shame and reproof, it pleased God rather to take him away, to the glory of his name and profit of his church. So good was the Lord both to his church, in fortifying the same with the testimony and blood of such a martyr; and so good also to the man with this cross of tribulation, to purge his offences in this world.

9. *constancy:* steadfastness, as in purpose
10. *evil-subscribing:* approving of evil

Tone: Compare the behavior of Cranmer and his opponents throughout the previous events. Who comes across as more admirable? Why so?

Purpose: Summarize Foxe's evaluation of the significance of these events. Which comment in the paragraph may be said to show some bias?

THINK AND DISCUSS

1. How does Foxe's *Book of Martyrs* qualify as a historical narrative?
2. What source(s) does Foxe mention in this excerpt?
3. To readers unfamiliar with Foxe's sources, what features of his text might on their own convey a certain level of reliability?
4. Compare and contrast the behavior of Cranmer and his accusers, citing three similarities or differences. Which side do you find more admirable and why?
5. What is Foxe's tone toward his topic, both its background conflict and the characters present? Support your answer clearly from the text.
6. Determine Foxe's purpose for Cranmer's story, supporting your answer with three details from the text.
7. Foxe has been accused of blatant bias. Do you find in the text any evidence of bias toward Cranmer or the Catholic Church? Support your opinion from the text.
8. Identify where Foxe slips into cultural bias. Might this moment interfere with his overall purpose in any way? Briefly explain.
9. How might Foxe's work fulfill the criteria of Truth, Goodness, or Beauty? Which of these are most prominent in his work?

The English Bible

AT A GLANCE

- **ca. 405** Jerome's Latin Vulgate completed
- **1380s** First English Bible translated by Wycliffe
- **1516** Erasmus's Greek New Testament published
- **1525–26** Tyndale's English New Testament printed
- **1535** Coverdale's first English Bible printed
- **1539** The Great Bible authorized by Henry VIII and printed
- **1560** The Geneva Bible printed
- **1611** The King James Version authorized by James I

Today, the Bible is the best-selling book in the world and has been translated into over 2,500 languages. But it has not always been so accessible; for centuries in Europe St. Jerome's Vulgate, a Church-sanctioned Latin translation, was the only full version of the Scriptures. Once reformers began arguing that people needed to read the Bible for themselves, translators risked their very lives to create vernacular versions. Their combined work produced in 1611 a lasting legacy, the official Authorized (King James) Version of the Bible.

Beginnings and Controversy

The first complete English translation arrived in 1382, courtesy of John Wycliffe (p. 11) and his followers. Unfortunately, Wycliffe's version was banned (1408) by church and political leaders frightened of Lollardy's potential influence. The penalty for its use was death. Ironically, many clergy members continued to use his manuscripts, unaware of their origins.

The arrival of the Renaissance then brought increased knowledge of Greek and Hebrew. Erasmus's Greek edition of the New Testament, published in 1516, gave translators a scholarly standard from which to work. And while England maintained a ban (unique in Europe) on vernacular translations, the Reformation call of *sola scriptura* created an ever-stronger desire for them.

William Tyndale, English theologian, scholar, and linguist, answered this need. Refused sanction for his work, he fled to the Continent, where in 1525 he began printing the first English New Testament translated from the original Greek. This printed Bible, completed by 1526, reached an unprecedented audience, despite dire consequences for reading it. Sadly, Tyndale was persecuted fiercely by figures such as Sir Thomas More. He was eventually betrayed and executed for heresy in 1536.

Further Translations

In 1535, Miles Coverdale (who had assisted Tyndale) published the first complete printed English Bible. He borrowed heavily from earlier versions, especially Tyndale's, and played to Henry VIII's ego by dedicating the Bible to him as "defender of the faith." In 1539, Henry authorized Coverdale's second edition, called the Great Bible for its size. It was chained to every state pulpit and officially sanctioned to be read aloud.

Mary I's persecutions drove reformers to the Continent but resulted in another significant translation, the Geneva Bible. Supervised by scholar William Whittingham in Germany, the translation was based on Tyndale's work and the Great Bible. A scholarly, readable version, it included verse numbers and doctrinal commentary and soon became a favorite, especially of Puritans. The English church countered with the Bishop's Bible (1568), a well-done version that never became as popular as the Geneva Bible.

An English Masterwork

When James I ascended the throne (1603), he tasked the English bishops with compiling a new translation to unite the nation. About fifty able scholars were recruited and told to use the Bishop's Bible as a starting point. They also consulted the original Greek and Hebrew manuscripts and previous translations (Tyndale's contributed over fifty percent of the text). Published in 1611, the first Authorized Version emerged as not only the best translation to date but also an English masterpiece.

The influence of the King James Version on English language and literature should not be underestimated. Though at first resisted by many, its polished and incisive use of English earned the love of many laymen and set a powerful precedent for English authors, many of whom grew up listening to its stories, ideas, and cadences and in turn used these in their own writing. Allusions to its content and phrases abound in English literature, some becoming part of the common vernacular. Although its language challenges modern readers, it has left an indelible mark on the consciousness of the English-speaking world.

The first English Bible printed in America was the King James Version, by printer Robert Aitken in 1782.

ANALYZE: *Paradox and Rhetorical Devices*

In His Beatitudes, Jesus describes key character qualities that identify His followers. These are delivered as a series of literary **paradoxes**, statements that seem self-contradictory yet actually make sense when understood in the right context. Paradoxes are valuable because they provoke thought. For example, English poet John Donne famously used a paradox in his sonnet "Death, be not proud": in celebrating God's promise of eternal life, he paradoxically but truthfully declares, "Death, thou shalt die."

In addition to paradox, Christ used two rhetorical devices—parallelism (p. 140) and anaphora—to make His sermon beautiful and memorable. **Anaphora** is the repetition of words or phrases at the beginnings of lines or grammatical units. Both devices connect equal or similar ideas and draw attention to their content. As is often seen in poetry, they can create pleasing rhythms and sounds. Look for these three devices in the passages that follow and consider what they contribute to each.

OBJECTIVES

- Interpret a text's use of paradox, parallelism, and anaphora.
- Compare translations to observe linguistic changes.
- Analyze a text's structure and its connection to the major ideas.
- Compose a brief personal essay.

READ: *Compare Texts; Examine Text Structures*

The Beatitudes appear here in four translations, ranging from Middle to Early Modern English. The first two include spelling and grammar foreign to modern readers but typical of their time. As you read, compare the translations to determine how the words and grammar changed over the years (e.g., *seynge* [Wycliffe] becomes *seeing* [KJV]). Do the passages reflect any broader changes in English?

Additionally, examine the structures of both passages. Authors structure their texts to help readers easily understand their train of thought and remember their main ideas. Rhetorical devices such as anaphora and parallelism can help visibly tie ideas together. The Beatitudes are a stellar example of a simple, progressing line of thought that is clearly unified by rhetorical details. Though less compact, 1 Corinthians 13 also exhibits solid organization. It progresses through three different sections while examining its topic. Read carefully to see if you can identify them.

CREATE: *A Personal Essay*

Phrases from 1 Corinthians 13:1–13 have entered into the common knowledge even of unbelievers. Perhaps this is true because the subject, love (not just romantic), is one all humans are interested in. We all want to receive the beautiful love the passage describes. But we also fail, frequently and spectacularly, at showing its qualities to others. As you read the passage, consider whether you have encountered such love. At the end of the lesson, you will be asked to write a short essay about how you have been shown three of the qualities it describes.

What is MOST IMPORTANT in life?

All of us identify certain nonnegotiable parts of life—goals, possessions, relationships, for example—that we consider most important. These are things we invest a lot of time, effort, and resources in. God also has ideas about what is most important. And as our Creator, He might have a few good insights into the matter! Look at your day-to-day life. What do your choices reveal that you value most? Does your system of values match what God says is most important?

THE BEATITUDES
MATTHEW 5:1-12

WYCLIFFE VERSION (1388 EDITION)

And Jhesus, seynge[1] the puple, wente up in to an hil; and whanne he was set, hise disciplis camen to hym. And he openyde his mouth, and tauȝte[2] hem[3], and seide, Blessed ben pore men in spirit, for the kyngdom of heuenes[4] is herne. Blessid ben mylde men, for thei schulen welde[5] the erthe. Blessid ben thei that mornen, for thei schulen be coumfortid. Blessid ben thei that hungren and thristen riȝtwisnesse, for thei schulen be fulfillid. Blessid ben merciful men, for thei schulen gete merci. Blessid ben thei that ben of clene herte, for thei schulen se God. Blessid ben pesible men, for thei schulen be clepid Goddis[6] children. Blessid ben thei that suffren persecusioun for riȝtfulnesse, for the kingdam of heuenes is herne. Ȝe schulen be blessed, whanne men schulen curse ȝou, and schulen pursue ȝou, and shulen seie al yuel[7] aȝens ȝou liynge, for me. Ioie[8] ȝe, and be ȝe glad, for ȝoure meede[9] is plenteuouse in heuenes; for so thei han pursued also profetis that weren bifor ȝou. A

1. *seynge:* The -e endings on this and many other words in Wycliffe's translation would often have been pronounced, not silent as in later English.
2. *tauȝte:* The symbol yogh (ȝ) in Middle English represented certain sounds (such as *y*) that closed off the back of the throat.
3. *hem:* For this and other third-person pronouns, Wycliffe used the Old English *he*, *here*, and *hem*, which were gradually being replaced by the Old Norse *they*, *their*, and *them* used today.
4. *heuenes;* In Middle English, *u* could also represent the *v* sound.
5. *welde:* from Middle English *welden*, from Old English *wealdan*, to rule, and *wieldan*, to govern (*AHD*)
6. *clepid Goddis:* i.e., called God's
7. *yuel:* evil
8. *Ioie:* i.e., joy; originally borrowed from medieval French, in which the *i* could be pronounced as a *j*
9. *meede:* archaic, "a merited reward or recompense" (*AHD*)

Rhetorical Devices: What recurring phrase forms an example of anaphora throughout the passage? A

TYNDALE BIBLE (1534 EDITION)

When he sawe the people, he went vp into a mountayne, and when he was set, his disciples came to hym, and he opened hys mouthe, and taught them sayinge: Blessed are the povre in sprete: for theirs is the kyngdome of heven. Blessed are they that morne: for they shalbe conforted. Blessed are the meke: for they shall inheret the erth. Blessed are they which honger R and thurst for rightewesnes: for they shalbe filled. Blessed are the mercifull: for they shall obteyne mercy. Blessed are the pure in herte: for they shall se God. Blessed are the peacemakers: for they shalbe called the chyldren of God. Blessed are they which suffre persecucion for rightwesnes sake: for theirs ys the kyngdome of heuen. Blessed are ye when men reuyle you, and persecute you, and shall falsly say all manner of yvell sayinges agaynst you for my sake. Reioyce, and be glad, for greate is youre rewarde in heven. For so persecuted they the Prophetes which were before youre dayes. R

Compare Texts: Which phrases in the first half of the passage have been switched in order as compared to Wycliffe's translation? R

Compare Texts: What are several differences in grammar, usage, and spelling between Tyndale's Early Modern English translation and Wycliffe's Middle English version? Find several changes that are still in use today. R

GENEVA BIBLE (1560 EDITION)

1 And when he sawe the multitude, he went up into a
mountaine: and when he was set, his disciples came to
him. R
2 And he opened his mouthe and taught them, saying,
3 Blessed *are* the poore in spirit, for theirs is the
kingdome of heaven.
4 Blessed *are* they that mourne, for they shalbe comforted.
5 Blessed *are* the meke, for they shal inherite the
earth.
6 Blessed *are* they which honger and thirst for righ-
teousnes, for they shal be filled.
7 Blessed *are* the merciful, for thei shall obteine
mercie.
8 Blessed *are* the pure in heart: for they shal se God.
9 Blessed *are* the peace makers, for they shalbe called
the children of God.
10 Blessed *are* they which suffer persecution for righ-
teousnes sake, for theirs is the kingdome of heaven.
11 Blessed are ye when men revile you, and persecute
you, and say all maner of evil against you for my sake,
falsely.
12 Reioice and be glad, for great is your rewarde in
heaven, for so persecuted they the Prophets which were
before you. A

Compare Texts: What structural feature has been added to this translation? Do you think it helps or hinders the readability of the passage? R

Rhetorical Devices: What rhetorical device is used to structure the series of key sentences in this passage? A

AUTHORIZED VERSION (1611)

1 And seeing the multitudes, he went up into a
mountaine: and when he was set, his disciples came
unto him:
2 And he opened his mouth, and taught them, saying,
3 Blessed *are* the poore in spirit: for theirs is the
kingdome of heaven. A
4 Blessed *are* they that mourne: for they shall be
comforted.
5 Blessed *are* the meeke: for they shall inherit the
earth.
6 Blessed *are* they which doe hunger and thirst after
righteousnesse: for they shall be filled.
7 Blessed *are* the mercifull: for they shall obtain
mercie.
8 Blessed *are* the pure in heart: for they shall see God.
9 Blessed *are* the peacemakers: for they shall bee
called the children of God.
10 Blessed *are* they which are persecuted for righteousnesse sake: for theirs is the kingdome of heaven.
11 Blessed *are* ye, when men shall revile you, and persecute you, and shal say all manner of evill against you
falsly, for my sake.
12 Reioice, and be exceeding glad: for great is your
reward in heaven: for so persecuted they the Prophets
which were before you.

Paradox: How is this verse an example of paradox? What truth does it highlight? A

1 Though I speak with the tongues of men and of angels, and have not charity, I am become as sounding brass, or a tinkling cymbal.

2 And though I have the gift of prophecy, and understand all mysteries, and all knowledge; and though I have all faith, so that I could remove mountains, and have not charity, I am nothing.

3 And though I bestow all my goods to feed the poor, and though I give my body to be burned, and have not charity, it profiteth me nothing. A

4 Charity suffereth long, and is kind; charity envieth not; charity vaunteth not itself, is not puffed up,

5 Doth not behave itself unseemly, seeketh not her own, is not easily provoked, thinketh no evil;

6 Rejoiceth not in iniquity, but rejoiceth in the truth;

7 Beareth all things, believeth all things, hopeth all things, endureth all things.

8 Charity never faileth: but whether there be prophecies, they shall fail; whether there be tongues, they shall cease; whether there be knowledge, it shall vanish away.

9 For we know in part, and we prophesy in part.

10 But when that which is perfect is come, then that which is in part shall be done away.

11 When I was a child, I spake as a child, I understood as a child, I thought as a child: but when I became a man, I put away childish things.

12 For now we see through a glass, darkly; but then face to face: now I know in part; but then shall I know even as also I am known.

13 And now abideth faith, hope, charity, these three; but the greatest of these is charity. R

Rhetorical Devices: What rhetorical devices do these three verses exhibit in their structure and content? A

Text Structure: This passage can be divided into several broad sections of content. The second section begins with verse 4. Based on the content and the rhetorical structures in the subsequent verses, where does the second section end? R

THINK AND DISCUSS

1. List two ways in which the Beatitude translations significantly differ from each other.
2. Identify three examples of anaphora, parallelism, and paradox from both Authorized Version excerpts.
3. Identify the broad sections of 1 Corinthians 13. What main idea does each develop?
4. Summarize the main idea of both passages. List one or two ideas used to support or develop that idea, citing details from the text.
5. Compare the paradoxes in both passages. Broadly speaking, what do they all communicate about the difference between human values and God's values?
6. Make a list of the qualities assigned to love in 1 Corinthians 13. Choose one and describe several ways in which people commonly fail to exhibit it. What are three ways you can show this quality today?
7. Consider your analysis of the two Authorized Version passages. How do the two rhetorical devices you studied here help clarify meaning in each passage? How do they highlight important ideas for readers?
8. Briefly explain how both passages reflect the qualities of Truth, Goodness, and Beauty. Reference details from the text to support your ideas.
9. Consider the qualities listed in 1 Corinthians 13:4–8. As described on page 165, write a short essay telling how you have been shown three of these qualities by one or more people. Summarize your accounts by explaining the impact these incidents have had on your life.

Edmund Spenser (ca. 1552–99)

AT A GLANCE

- **1569–76** Attended Cambridge (BA, 1573; MA, 1576)
- **1579–80** Published *The Shepherd's Calendar* (1579); began *The Faerie Queene*
- **1590** Published books I–III of *The Faerie Queene*
- **1595–96** Published *Amoretti*, "Epithalamion," and books I–VI of *The Faerie Queene*

Few poets loom larger than Edmund Spenser over the landscape of English literature. Acknowledged as one of its greatest poets both in his own day and since, Spenser helped spark a new phase in English language and literature that took flight in the Elizabethan era.

DID YOU KNOW ?

C. S. Lewis said in *Allegory of Love*, "To read [Spenser] is to grow in mental health."

Education and Early Career

Born in 1552 to poor London relations of a noble family, Spenser attended both grammar school and Cambridge through financial aid. Already showing promise, he became secretary to his former teacher, Dr. Young, when Young became bishop of Rochester (1578).

In 1579 Spenser was married and also published his first major work, *The Shepherd's Calendar*. He also left his secretary position to work for the Earl of Leicester, at whose home he met Philip Sidney, Leicester's nephew. The poets deeply admired each other's work, and Spenser joined Sidney's literary circle. It was likely Sidney's influence that gained him his next position, secretary to Arthur Grey, the current Lord Deputy of Ireland (i.e., leader of English forces subduing Ireland by force and colonization). Further governmental positions kept Spenser in Ireland until the last months of his life.

Life in Ireland

In Ireland, Spenser, an ambitious man, raised his social status, acquiring Kilcolman Castle (1586) and lands in county Cork. In 1588 he became a friend of Sir Walter Raleigh, whose land was only thirty miles away. Impressed with the portion of *The Faerie Queene* he saw (Books I–III), Raleigh brought Spenser with him to London (1590) to present the book to the queen and have it published. The queen granted Spenser an annuity of £50 for life, netting him a larger audience as well.

In 1594 Spenser, a widower, married again and bestowed on his second bride the wedding gift of a sonnet sequence (*Amoretti*, see p. 189) ending with his "Epithalamion," or marriage song, celebrating marriage in general (and his in particular). These were published in 1595. A year later, he brought to London the second installment of *The Faerie Queene*. The resulting edition, containing Books I–VI, was the last during his lifetime. Unfortunately, an Irish rebellion in 1598 destroyed his home. Three months later, having come to London with dispatches from Ireland to the queen's council, Spenser died, likely of an illness. He was buried in Westminster Abbey not far from Chaucer in Poet's Corner.

Literary Achievements

Like his predecessor Chaucer, Spenser mastered a broad variety of sources and integrated them into English language and culture. His works weave together aspects of Classical Latin and Greek works (e.g., myths, philosophy, rhetoric); French, Italian, and English literary traditions (both medieval and contemporary); and even works of folklore (e.g., legends, oral history). As important was his strongly Protestant perspective, one that was not just a creed but a deeply felt reality. Using these building blocks, he shaped unique works that spoke to his times and audience.

Spenser's four masterpieces are without doubt *The Shepherd's Calendar*, *The Faerie Queene*, *Amoretti*, and "Epithalamion." *The Shepherd's Calendar* was designed to launch his poetic career. Composed of twelve pastoral poems corresponding to each month, it displayed a virtuoso command of a variety of poetic forms and established Spenser's reputation as a superior poet. It was also a step toward his greatest task, writing an epic.

The Faerie Queene was the work of a lifetime. Tackling an epic, then considered the highest of poetic modes, was a legacy-defining move for a Renaissance poet. Technically proficient (he created a unique stanza form, Spenserian stanza, just for the work), Spenser's efforts produced an epic unprecedented in complexity; it tied together a spiritual handbook of virtues with a vision of England's past, present, and hoped-for future that was Protestant and mythological, fortifying and celebratory. Immediately a success, it has thrilled and challenged readers since and is justly considered one of British literature's great masterpieces.

ANALYZE: *Literary Epic, Romance, Allegory*

Spenser's *The Faerie Queene*, one of English literature's more complex texts, embodies three major genres—literary epic, romance, and allegory. **Literary epics** are written in imitation of oral folk epics (p. 16), fulfilling the same content conventions (e.g., a hero representing cultural virtues) and using epic stylistic features such as **catalogs** (formal lists) and **epic similes** (similes in which the comparison is extended and elaborate). *The Faerie Queene* adds to these features **romance** elements (p. 36), such as the questing knight, the code of chivalry, and courtly love.

More important to its themes is *The Faerie Queene*'s use of **allegory**, a story with both a literal and an implied level of meaning that are closely tied together. Spenser's tale is an exciting and intriguing adventure but also an unusually complex allegory encompassing not just one layer, but several layers of allegory. These include historical allegories to Tudor court life and ongoing religious wars, spiritual allegories exploring the development of virtues, and mythological allegories defining England's national ideals and aspirations. In the literal story, the main characters are all on a journey, a romantic quest, but the places, obstacles, and choices they encounter all represent aspects of these three allegories. While the historical parallels are hard for casual readers to grasp, the spiritual and nationalistic allegories can more easily be inferred. As you read, note the epic and romance conventions but also try to discern possible allegorical meanings.

READ: *Infer Meaning from Details*

Spenser's work is replete with details and allusions that convey deeper meaning. For example, he uses classic light and dark imagery to suggest good and evil. Additionally, his contemporaries would easily recognize in Red Cross Knight (the main character here) an allegory to St. George, the patron saint of England. Representative of England, Red Cross Knight is both a warrior and a Christian saint. Meanwhile the "lovely lady" with him (identified later as Una) represents truth on the spiritual level, and on the historical level, true religion, particularly the Anglican Church. Knowing their allegorical identities, what can you infer about the nationalistic and spiritual ideas represented by their journey? Stay alert to descriptive details and pay attention to how the characters' thoughts and choices might convey meaning related to their allegorical identities.

EVALUATE: *Truth, Goodness, and Beauty*

With the first installment of *The Faerie Queene*, Spenser included a letter to Sir Walter Raleigh setting forth the purpose and plan of his projected epic. Spenser claimed a desire "to fashion a gentleman . . . in virtuous and gentle discipline" (moral-educational purpose) through the method of "doctrine by ensample" (teaching truth by example). Sidney, to whom the work was dedicated, similarly argued that imaginative literature should teach by delighting. As you read, consider whether Spenser accomplishes this goal in his work and, if so, how. How well do his purposes and methods stack up against the biblically based criteria of pursuing Truth, Goodness, and Beauty?

OBJECTIVES

- Identify features of literary epic (e.g., catalog, epic simile), romance, and allegory in a text.
- Infer meaning from textual details in order to interpret a text's themes.
- Analyze a work's allegorical messages.
- Evaluate a work's purpose and methods from a biblical perspective.

VOCABULARY

wield (wēld) *tr.v.* To handle (a weapon or tool, for example) with skill and ease.

covert (kō′vərt) *n.* A covered place or shelter.

labyrinth (lăb′ə-rĭnth′) *n.* An intricate structure of interconnecting passages through which it is difficult to find one's way; a maze.

disdain (dĭs-dān′) *n.* A feeling or show of contempt and aloofness; scorn.

trenchant (trĕn′chənt) *adj.* Cutting, adapted for cutting; having a keen edge, sharp.

How do I grow MORALLY?

Remember the children's lyrics "Read your Bible, pray every day, and you'll grow, grow, grow"? These actions are in fact only the first steps to spiritual growth; for believers, growth takes a combination of Bible knowledge, Spirit empowerment, virtuous actions, and developed discernment. With a partner, use Scripture (John 14:23; 15:4–5, 10; Col. 1:9–11; 3:1–17; Heb. 5:12–14) to describe these steps. How can you experience each in your spiritual journey?

The Faerie Queene

Spenser envisioned twelve books for his epic, each describing a knight sent out on a quest by Gloriana, Queen of Faerie (and representative of Elizabeth I). On the level of spiritual allegory, Spenser uses each knight to represent one of twelve virtues. Imperfect examples of these, the knights will learn them better as they journey, fully embodying each virtue by the quest's end (along with the invested reader, Spenser hoped).

The story that ties them all together stars King Arthur before his legendary reign. He quests to find Gloriana by assisting the knights of her court. The ideal gentleman-warrior, Arthur demonstrates the virtues they less fully represent as he aids them. A part of English myth, he ties the tale to Spenser's national allegory, which evokes a mythological past to create a path forward for England. Spenser strongly identifies this path with preserving a Protestant identity in order to combat Catholic error.

Completing only six books before his death, Spenser treats, in order, holiness, temperance (self-control), chastity (chaste love), friendship, justice, and courtesy. Book 1's virtue, holiness, begins a believer's journey toward moral maturity. Red Cross Knight (the believer) is accompanied by Una (truth or true faith) and a dwarf (reason). Note where their journey takes them and whom or what they encounter. What might these elements represent about the quest for holiness? What might Spenser have meant this quest to convey about his vision for England's path to greatness?

from Book 1: Of Holiness

A gentle° knight was pricking° on the plain,
Y-clad° in mighty arms and silver shield,
Wherein old dints of deep wounds did remain,
The cruel marks of many a bloody field;
Yet arms till that time did he never **wield**.
His angry steed did chide° his foaming bit,
As much disdaining to the curb° to yield.
Full jolly° knight he seemed and fair did sit,
As one for knightly jousts and fierce encounters fit.

And on his breast a bloody cross he bore, **R**
The dear remembrance of his dying Lord,
For whose sweet sake that glorious badge he wore,
And dead as living ever him adored.
Upon his shield the like° was also scored°
For sovereign hope, which in his help he had.
Right faithful true he was in deed and word,
But of his cheer° did seem too solemn sad;°
Yet nothing did he dread, but ever was y-drad.°

Upon a great adventure he was bond°
That greatest Gloriana to him gave,
That greatest glorious queen of Faerielond,
To win him worship° and her grace° to have,
Which of all earthly things he most did crave.
And ever as he rode, his heart did earn°
To prove his puissance° in battle brave
Upon his foe, and his new force to learn—
Upon his foe, a dragon horrible and stern.

A lovely lady rode him fair beside,
Upon a lowly ass more white than snow,
Yet she much whiter, but the same° did hide
Under a veil, that wimpled° was full low,
And over all a black stole she did throw,
As one that inly mourned. So was she sad,
And heavy sat upon her palfrey° slow;
Seemed in heart some hidden care she had,
And by her in a line° a milk-white lamb she lad.°

1 **gentle:** noble / **pricking:** spurring, galloping

2 **Y-clad:** clad; *y* pronounced as short *i*

6 **chide:** resist

7 **curb:** restraint

8 **jolly:** gallant

14 **like:** same / **scored:** inscribed, delineated; painted

17 **cheer:** facial expression / **sad:** serious

18 **y-drad:** dreaded by others

19 **bond:** bound, headed

22 **worship:** honor / **grace:** favor

24 **earn:** yearn

25 **puissance:** might

30 **same:** i.e., her whiteness

31 **wimpled:** hanging in folds

34 **palfrey:** woman's saddle horse; here, a donkey

36 **in a line:** on a leash / **lad:** led

wield (wēld) *tr.v.* To handle (a weapon or tool, for example) with skill and ease.

Infer Meaning: What meaning can you infer from the bloody cross on Red Cross Knight's breast and shield? What significance does the armor, which has seen battle when Red Cross Knight has not, have? **R**

So pure and innocent as that same lamb
She was in life and every virtuous lore,°
And by descent from royal lineage came
Of ancient kings and queens that had of yore
Their scepters stretched from east to western shore,
And all the world in their subjection held,
Till that infernal fiend° with foul uproar
Forwasted° all their land and them expelled;
Whom to avenge, she had this knight from far compelled.° A

Behind her far away a dwarf did lag,
That lazy seemed in being ever last,
Or wearièd with bearing of her bag
Of needments at his back. Thus as they passed,
The day with clouds was sudden overcast,
And angry Jove° an hideous storm of rain
Did pour into his leman's° lap so fast,
That every wight° to shroud° it did constrain,
And this fair couple eke° to shroud themselves were fain.°

Enforced to seek some **covert** nigh at hand,
A shady grove not far away they spied
That promised aid the tempest to withstand.
Whose lofty trees y-clad with summer's pride°
Did spread so broad that heavens light did hide,
Not pierceable with power of any star.
And all within were paths and alleys wide,
With footing worn and leading inward far.
Fair harbor that them seems,° so in they entered are.

And forth they pass, with pleasure forward led,
Joying to hear the birds' sweet harmony,
Which therein shrouded from the tempest dread
Seemed in their song to scorn the cruel sky.
Much can they praise the trees so straight and high:
The sailing pine,° the cedar proud and tall,
The vine-prop elm,° the poplar never dry,
The builder oak, sole king of forests all,
The aspen good for staves, the cypress funeral.

38 lore: teaching

43 fiend: i.e., the dragon

44 Forwasted: devastated

45 compelled: summoned

51 Jove: god of the sky

52 leman's: mistress's; i.e., the earth's

53 wight: creature / **shroud:** take cover

54 eke: also / **fain:** eager

58 Whose . . . pride: pun: (1) foliage, (2) arrogance (cf. Ps. 37:35)

63 them seems: seems to them

69 sailing pine: used for masts

70 vine-prop elm: used for staking grapes

Genre: What genre is represented by a knight on a quest for a lady? A

covert (kō′vərt) *n.* A covered place or shelter.

The laurel, meed° of mighty conquerors
And poets sage,° the fir that weepeth still,°
The willow worn of° forlorn **paramours**, °
The yew° obedient to the bender's will,
The birch for shafts,° the sallow° for the mill,
The myrrh sweet bleeding in the bitter wound,
The warlike beech,° the ash for nothing ill,
The fruitful olive, and the platan° round,
The carver holm,° the maple seldom inward sound. [A]

Led with delight, they thus beguile° the way
Until the blustering storm is overblown;
When weening° to return whence they did stray,
They cannot find that path which first was shown,
But wander to and fro in ways unknown,
Furthest from end then when they nearest ween,°
That makes them doubt their wits be not their own.
So many paths, so many turnings seen,
That which of them to take in diverse doubt they been.°

At last resolving forward still to fare
Till that some end they find or° in or out,
That path they take that beaten seemed most bare
And like to lead the **labyrinth** about;°
Which when by tract they hunted had throughout°
At length it brought them to a hollow cave
Amid the thickest woods. The champion stout
Eftsoons° dismounted from his courser° brave,
And to the dwarf awhile his needless spear he gave.

"Be well aware," quoth then that lady mild,
"Lest sudden mischief ye too rash provoke.
The danger hid, the place unknown and wild,
Breeds dreadful doubts. Oft fire is without smoke,
And peril without show. Therefore your stroke,
Sir Knight, withhold till further trial° be made."
"Ah, Lady," said he, "shame were to revoke
The forward footing for a hidden shade.
Virtue gives herself light through darkness for to wade."°

"Yea, but," quoth she, "the peril of this place
I better wot° than you, though now too late
To wish you back return with° foul disgrace;
Yet wisdom warns, whilst foot is in the gate,
To stay° the step, ere forcéd to retreat.
This is the Wandering Wood, this Error's den,
A monster vile, whom God and man does hate.
Therefore I read° beware." "Fly, fly," quoth then
The fearful dwarf, "this is no place for living men."

73 **meed:** prize

74 **sage:** wise / **still:** constant

75 **of:** by / **paramours:** lovers

76 **yew:** tree used to make bows

77 **shafts:** arrows / **sallow:** willow growing along streams

79 **beech:** tree reputedly used for making ancient war chariots

80 **platan:** plane tree

81 **holm:** evergreen oak used for carving

82 **beguile:** make pleasant

84 **weening:** thinking

87 **nearest ween:** think themselves nearest

90 **been:** be

92 **or:** either

94 **like . . . about:** most likely to lead out of the maze

95 **by tract . . . throughout:** They had followed the tracks to the end.

98 **Eftsoons:** immediately / **courser:** steed

105 **trial:** investigation

108 **through . . . wade:** to walk through darkness

110 **wot:** know

111 **back return with:** to return back without

113 **stay:** halt

116 **read:** advise

labyrinth (lăb′ə-rĭnth′) *n.* An intricate structure of interconnecting passages through which it is difficult to find one's way; a maze.

Literary Epic: Identify the epic convention found in lines 68–81. [A]

But full of fire and greedy hardiment,°
The youthful knight could not for aught be stayed,°
But forth unto the darksome hole he went **R**
And lookéd in. His glistering armor made
A little glooming light, much like a shade,
By which he saw the ugly monster plain,
Half like a serpent horribly displayed;
But the other half did woman's shape retain,
Most loathesome, filthy, foul, and full of vile **disdain**. **E**

And as she lay upon the dirty ground,
Her huge long tail her den all overspread,
Yet was in knots and many boughts° upwound,
Pointed with mortal sting. Of her there bred
A thousand young ones, which she daily fed,
Sucking upon her poisonous dugs, each one
Of sundry shapes, yet all ill-favoréd. **R**
Soon as that uncouth° light upon them shone,
Into her mouth they crept, and sudden all were gone.

Their dam upstart, out of her den affrayed,°
And rushéd forth, hurling her hideous tail
About her curséd head, whose folds displayed
Were stretched now forth at length without entrail.°
She looked about, and seeing one in mail
Armed to point,° sought back to turn again;
For light she hated as the deadly bale,
Aye wont° in desert darkness to remain,
Where plain none might her see, nor she see any plain.

118 greedy hardiment: eager boldness

119 for . . . stayed: be stopped for anything

129 boughts: coils

134 uncouth: unaccustomed

136 dam . . . affrayed: mother jumped up from her den frightened

139 entrail: coils

141 to point: completely

143 Aye wont: always accustomed

Infer Meaning: Describe Error's cave. What might the description symbolize? **R**

disdain (dĭs-dān′) *n.* A feeling or show of contempt and aloofness; scorn.

Truth, Goodness, and Beauty: In what way is Spenser applying his moral-educational purpose here? How was this strategy applied earlier in the epic in regard to Una? **E**

Infer Meaning: Name a principle taught in lines 130–33. **R**

Which when the valiant elf° perceived, he leapt
As lion fierce upon the flying prey,
And with his **trenchant** blade her boldly kept
From turning back and forcéd her to stay.
Therewith enraged she loudly gan to bray,
And turning fierce, her speckled tail advanced,
Threatening her angry sting, him to dismay.
Who nought aghast,° his mighty hand enhanced;°
The stroke down from her head unto her shoulder glanced.

Much daunted with that dint,° her sense was dazed,
Yet kindling rage, herself she gathered round,
And all at once her beastly body raised
With doubled forces high above the ground.
Tho° wrapping up her wreathéd stern° around,
Leapt fierce upon his shield, and her huge train
All suddenly about his body wound,
That hand or foot to stir he strove in vain.
God help the man so wrapped in Error's endless train.°

His lady, sad to see his sore constraint,
Cried out, "Now, now, Sir Knight, show what ye be;
Add faith unto your force and be not faint!
Strangle her, else she sure will strangle thee."
That when he heard, in great perplexity,
His gall did grate° for grief and high disdain,
And knitting all his force got one hand free,
Wherewith he gripped her gorge° with so great pain
That soon to loose her wicked bands did her constrain.

Therewith she spewed out of her filthy maw
A flood of poison horrible and black,

145 elf: fairy (Spenser has not yet revealed that Red Cross is a human rather than a native of Fairyland.)

152 nought aghast: not afraid / **enhanced:** raised

154 dint: stroke

158 Tho: then / **wreathéd stern:** coiled tail

162 train: pun: (1) tail, (2) deceit

168 gall did grate: anger welled up

170 gorge: throat

trenchant (trĕn′chənt) *adj.* Cutting, adapted for cutting; having a keen edge, sharp.

Full of great lumps of flesh and gobbets raw,
Which stunk so vilely that it forced him slack
His grasping hold and from her turn him back.
Her vomit full of books and papers° was,
With loathly frogs and toads which eyes did lack,
And creeping sought way in the weedy grass.
Her filthy parbreak° all the place defiléd has. E

As when old Father Nilus° gins° to swell
With timely° pride above the Egyptian vale,
His fatty° waves do fertile slime outwell,
And overflow each plain and lowly dale.
But when his later spring° gins to avale,°
Huge heaps of mud he leaves, wherein there breed
Ten thousand kinds of creatures, partly male
And partly female, of his fruitful seed;
Such ugly monstrous shapes elsewhere may no man
read.° A

The same so sore annoyéd has the knight,
That well-nigh chokéd with the deadly stink,
His forces fail, ne° can no lenger° fight.
Whose courage when the fiend perceived to shrink,
She pouréd forth out of her hellish sink°
Her fruitful° curséd spawn of serpents small,
Deforméd monsters, foul and black as ink;
With swarming all about his legs did crawl,
And him encumbered sore, but could not hurt at all.

As gentle shepherd in sweet eventide,
When ruddy Phoebus gins to welk° in west,
High on a hill, his flock to viewen wide,°
Marks which do bite their hasty supper best,
A cloud of cumbrous° gnats do him molest,
All striving to infix their feeble stings,
That from their noyance° he nowhere can rest,
But with his clownish° hands their tender wings
He brusheth oft, and oft doth mar their murmurings. A

Thus ill bestead,° and fearful more of shame
Than of the certain peril he stood in,
Half furious° unto his foe he came,
Resolved in mind all suddenly to win
Or soon to lose before he once would lin;°
And struck at her with more than manly force,
That from her body full of filthy sin
He reft her hateful head without remorse.
A stream of coal-black blood forth gushéd from her
corse.° R

177 papers: heretical writings in general and Catholic propaganda in particular

180 parbreak: vomit

181 Father Nilus: Nile / **gins:** begins

182 timely: seasonal

183 fatty: rich

185 later spring: last flooding / **avale:** recede

189 read: see

192 ne: nor / **lenger:** longer

194 sink: sewage pit, gathering place of corruption

195 fruitful: prolific

200 Phoebus . . . welk: the sun fades

201 flock . . . wide: widely spread flock to view

203 cumbrous: bothersome

205 noyance: annoyance

206 clownish: rough, coarse

208 bestead: situated

210 Half furious: enraged almost to madness

212 lin: cease

216 corse: body

Truth, Goodness, and Beauty: How do lines 172–80 fulfill Spenser's moral-educational purpose of the epic? E

Literary Epic: What epic convention is illustrated in lines 181–89? What is being described? A

Genre: Do lines 199–207 illustrate a characteristic of epic, romance, or allegory? Can Error's brood of monsters harm Red Cross Knight? Explain. A

Infer Meaning: What does the serpent symbolize? What is the significance of Red Cross Knight's defeating Error with a blow to the head? See Genesis 3:14–15. R

Her scattered brood, soon as their parent dear
They saw so rudely° falling to the ground,
Groaning full deadly, all with troublous fear,
Gathered themselves about her body round,
Weening° their wonted° entrance to have found
At her wide mouth; but being there withstood,
They flockéd all about her bleeding wound
And suckéd up their dying mother's blood,
Making her death their life and eke her hurt their good.

That detestable sight him much amazed,
To see the unkindly imps of° heaven accursed
Devour their dam. On whom while so he gazed,
Having all satisfied their bloody thirst,
Their bellies swollen he saw with fullness burst,
And bowels gushing forth. Well worthy end
Of such as drunk her life the which them nursed.
Now needeth him no longer labor spend;
His foes have slain themselves with whom he should
contend. R

His lady seeing all that chanced from far
Approached in haste to greet° his victory
And said, "Fair Knight, born under happy° star,
Who see your vanquished foes before you lie,
Well worthy be you of that armory°
Wherein ye have great glory won this day,
And proved your strength on a strong enemy,
Your first adventure. Many such I pray,
And henceforth ever wish that like succeed it may."°

218 rudely: roughly

221 Weening: thinking / **wonted:** accustomed

227 of: by

236 greet: hail

237 happy: favorable (the astrological reference is metaphoric for "divinely blessed")

239 armory: armor

243 like . . . may: more of the same may follow it

Infer Meaning: During the Renaissance ingratitude was considered the most despicable of sins. Where is this sin depicted in this passage, and what spiritual principle is being illustrated? R

THINK AND DISCUSS

1. Define the genres of epic, romance, and allegory.
2. What is the difference between a folk epic and a literary epic?
3. What epic conventions (p. 16) does the excerpt from *The Faerie Queene* illustrate? Explain their functions in the narrative.
4. Defend *The Faerie Queene*'s status as a romance and as an allegory.
5. Good in *The Faerie Queene* is associated with light, height, and order. With what, conversely, is evil associated? Find two examples from the text to support your answer.
6. Una, representing Truth, is carried by a donkey, "a lowly ass." What earthly institution might the donkey represent? What does its color imply?
7. How does *The Faerie Queene* fulfill the purpose of poetry according to Sir Philip Sidney?
8. Consider the purpose of the spiritual allegory. In addition to St. George, whom or what might Red Cross Knight represent? Why is this representation appropriate for Book I?
9. Analyze the allegorical meanings of Error in the story. First note the biblical parallels. Why is she depicted as a serpent, and how might the manner of her death reflect Genesis 3:15? What spiritual principles do her offspring and their behavior illustrate for the reader?
10. Interpret the symbolism at play in Red Cross Knight's progression by stages to his encounter with Error.
11. Invent a short scenario involving Red Cross Knight and Una following their encounter with Error, one that illustrates a symbol for good or evil. Write in prose rather than poetry.

Queen Elizabeth I (1533–1603)

Elizabeth, only child of Henry VIII and Anne Boleyn, was born in 1533. Her father, who wanted a male heir, was disappointed but gave her the position of heir (held previously by Mary, now deemed illegitimate). When Elizabeth was only two, Anne was executed on charges of adultery, and Henry married Jane Seymour. Elizabeth, like Mary, was declared illegitimate, and Jane's son, Edward (b. 1537), became heir. The sisters were restored to the succession only in 1544.

In her youth Elizabeth benefited from the tutelage of England's brightest humanists. Her studies included classical and modern languages, penmanship, rhetoric, and more. Additionally, Elizabeth received Protestant teaching from Roger Ascham, one of England's premier scholars. But she was not typical: she favored the use of the Catholic crucifix, used Catholic oaths in her speech, and disliked preaching, preferring personal prayer. Elizabeth's religion, like her rule, straddled two highly contentious spheres.

Despite a turbulent relationship, Mary (who once imprisoned Elizabeth) recognized her sister as heir eleven days before her death, and in 1559, Elizabeth commenced one of English history's most significant reigns. Succeeding beyond anyone's wildest predictions, she became a figure both revered and adored and helped to define a sense of English identity. Throughout her reign, Elizabeth struggled to balance opposing forces within her kingdom and within her person: Catholicism and Protestantism, rebellion and unity, diplomacy and autonomy, sovereignty and femininity. Her struggle ended on March 24, 1603, after a steady decline in health. She was interred at Westminster Abbey.

BEFORE READING

ANALYZE: *Persuasive Appeals, Rhetorical Devices*

Elizabeth I's Tilbury speech exemplifies persuasion. Given to troops preparing to battle the Spanish Armada, it leans heavily on Elizabeth's figurative role as England's head to motivate the troops. But Elizabeth also employs skillful rhetoric, appealing to both **pathos** and **ethos** (p. 140). To heighten the effects of these appeals, she employs the rhetorical devices of **parallelism** (p. 140) and **antithesis** (parallelism in two adjacent phrases or clauses that emphasizes their contrasting meanings). As you read, locate both Elizabeth's appeals and the rhetorical devices adorning them.

READ: *Practice Oral Reading*

An oral form, speeches are best appreciated when read aloud. To prepare to read orally, first read the speech quietly to yourself. Listen for the pacing, rhythm, and emphasis created by its punctuation and by the positioning of certain words to give them more oratorical force. If you analyze the rhetorical devices beforehand, how might your understanding of these features affect your oral reading? Once you have practiced, read the text aloud with clarity and understanding.

CREATE: *A Character's Response*

To better understand the persuasive power of Elizabeth I's speech, assume the perspective of an English soldier as you read. Imagine that you are preparing to fend off the invading Spaniards. Which of the queen's appeals are most persuasive? How could you use the same appeals to comfort your loved ones, whom you may never see again? After reading the speech, compose a letter from this same perspective and remark on the queen's ideas and effectiveness.

OBJECTIVES

- Analyze the speech for its persuasive appeals and rhetorical devices.
- Read the speech aloud with attention to text features, rhythm, pacing, and emphasis.
- Compose a letter from the perspective of one of Elizabeth's soldiers.

VOCABULARY

disport (dĭ-spôrt′) *n.* Diversion from serious duties; relaxation, recreation; entertainment, amusement.

concord (kŏn′kôrd′) *n.* Harmony or agreement of interests or feelings; accord.

Speech to the Troops at Tilbury

My loving people,

We have been persuaded by some that are careful of our safety, to take heed how we commit our selves to armed multitudes, for fear of treachery; but I assure you I do not desire to live to distrust my faithful and loving people. Let tyrants fear. I have always so behaved myself that, under God, I have placed my chiefest strength and safeguard in the loyal hearts and good-will of my subjects; and therefore I am come amongst you, as you see, at this time, not for my recreation and **disport**, but being resolved, in the midst and heat of the battle, to live and die amongst you all; to lay down for my God, and for my kingdom, and my people, my honour and my blood, even in the dust. A

I know I have the body but of a weak and feeble woman; but I have the heart and stomach of a king, and of a king of England too, and think foul scorn that Parma or Spain, or any prince of Europe, should dare to invade the borders of my realm: to which rather than any dishonour shall grow by me, I myself will take up arms, I myself will be your general, judge, and rewarder of every one of your virtues in the field. A R

I know already, for your forwardness you have deserved rewards and crowns; and We do assure you in the word of a prince, they shall be duly paid you. In the mean time, my lieutenant general shall be in my stead, than whom never prince commanded a more noble or worthy subject; not doubting but by your obedience to my general, by your **concord** in the camp, and your valour in the field, we shall shortly have a famous victory over those enemies of my God, of my kingdom, and of my people.

disport (dĭ-spôrt′) *n.* Diversion from serious duties; relaxation, recreation; entertainment, amusement.

Persuasive Appeal: What words and sentences in this paragraph indicate an appeal to pathos? A

Rhetorical Device: What instance of antithesis occurs in this paragraph? A

Oral Reading: Read this paragaph to yourself, noting the punctuation and its rhythmic effects. What significant words would you give more emphasis to in your voice? R

concord (kŏn′kôrd′) *n.* Harmony or agreement of interests or feelings; accord.

THINK AND DISCUSS

1. Explain how Queen Elizabeth I uses appeals to both pathos and ethos in her speech. Be sure to include specific words and sentences to support your explanations.
2. Identify two instances of general parallelism and one instance of antithesis. What effect does each instance create in the speech?
3. When reading the speech aloud, how would you vary your rhythm and emphasis? Use specific examples from the speech to support your explanation.
4. Imagine that you are an English soldier who has heard Queen Elizabeth I's speech. Write a letter to a loved one that expresses your thoughts about the effectiveness of the queen's speech and the ideas that she includes. Try to use appeals to pathos or ethos in your letter.

What Do You Know?

Understand the Background

1. How do *Utopia*'s subject and purpose show the effects of humanist thought?
2. What genre did Bacon popularize in English writing?
3. Name and define three rhetorical devices studied in Unit 2, Parts 1 and 2.
4. What two major works of literature (other than the KJV Bible) helped solidify British national identity as culturally Protestant? Briefly explain your choices.
5. What historic event prompted Elizabeth I's "Speech to the Troops at Tilbury"?

Apply the Concepts

6. Name one literary genre that More's *Utopia* represents. Provide details from the text to support this categorization.
7. Do Bacon's essays (pp. 148–150) use deductive or inductive reasoning? Cite two examples from the text to support your answer.
8. Both Sidney and Cavendish used analogies to develop their prose arguments. Describe one from each writer's selections and explain its meaning in context.
9. Label and explain the figures of speech Cavendish employed to structure "A World Made by Atomes."
10. Give an example (from Parts 1 and 2) for each of the three devices you listed in question 3. How does each one heighten the effectiveness of the piece it is in?
11. What two kinds of persuasive appeals did Elizabeth I use in her speech? Describe an example of each from the text.
12. What three major genres are represented by Spenser's *Faerie Queene*? Briefly support your answers with details from the text.

Evaluate the Ideas

13. Describe one of the topics More critiques in *Utopia*. Evaluate whether his stance on the topic conforms to a biblical worldview.
14. What attitude did Lanier refute in *Eve's Apology*? Describe her supporting arguments and ideas. Then evaluate them in light of scriptural truth.
15. Foxe has often been accused of bias in his historical narrative. Is this accusation just? Support your answers from background materials and the text.
16. Choose one of the Bible passages in Part 2 and examine the effectiveness of its rhetorical devices. Explain your conclusions, citing textual details.

Write a Response

17. More's *Utopia* describes someone's version of an ideal society. How does this ideal view succeed or fail? In your opinion, what might an ideal society look like?
18. What purposes did Sidney believe literature should pursue? Choose one selection from Part 1 or 2 and critique the selection based on this criteria. Support your answer with textual details.
19. In *The Faerie Queene* excerpt, Spenser uses allegory to flesh out his view of how a person progresses toward moral growth. Evaluate his picture in light of scriptural truth (for examples, see John 14:23; 15:4–5, 10; Col. 1:9–11; 3:1–17; Heb. 5:12–14).

Define each term and provide an example of each from a selection in Unit 2, Part 1 or 2.

TERMS

utopia
social satire
literary criticism
rhetorical device
parallelism
analogy
rhetorical appeal
logos
pathos
ethos
argumentation
aphorism
tricolon
inductive reasoning
deductive reasoning
extended metaphor
purpose
paradox
anaphora
literary epic
catalog
epic simile
allegory
antithesis

PART 3

Lyric and Metaphysical Poetry

Poetry often deeply affects readers' feelings, but it is also the most technically complex literary genre. From your studies, what technical aspects of poetry do you remember? Consider the simple nursery rhyme "Mary had a little lamb, / Its fleece was white as snow, / And everywhere that Mary went / The lamb was sure to go." Do you recognize its technical features? It is a quatrain (a four-line stanza), whose second and fourth lines exhibit end rhyme. It maintains a **meter** (a rhythmic pattern of accented and unaccented syllables in a line) known as trochaic tetrameter and exhibits figurative language, using the simile "white as snow."

Such devices are foundational elements of most poetic forms, patterns that are based on technical and content requirements. Renaissance poets were great innovators of forms, refining and extending diverse technical and content-based elements beyond their use in previous eras. In so doing, they created fresh, powerful, and often lasting forms for English poetry.

On the technical side, linguistic developments affected poetic form. Ongoing changes included the Great Vowel Shift (p. 11) as well as an influx of new words from Renaissance learning. The former had affected writers' use of sound devices as different regional pronunciations could ruin the rhyme or meter of a poem. As linguistic change settled down and standardized (p. 127), sixteenth-century poets could refine poetic sound devices. Courtier poets revived and developed metrical emphasis in verse, turning the technical structuring of poems into a highly-polished art form. Meanwhile, the flood of new words lent elasticity to poets' diction: Shakespeare tended to coin words while Spenser revived archaic ones.

Additionally, like the era's prose (p. 129), Renaissance poetry was influenced by new learning, exhibiting content and features from classical texts or Continental works (e.g., French, Italian) influenced by the same. For example, the bold wit, extravagant claims, and technical virtuosity of most court poets showed influences from humanist education and Italian Renaissance poetry. Elements such as figurative expressions (e.g., metaphor, simile) were prominent. Ranging from extravagant to unlikely comparisons, they adorned a poem and further developed its topic (frequently human or divine love).

Another classical influence on Renaissance poetry's content was the pastoral mode. The **pastoral** takes as its basic material shepherds and shepherdesses engaged in leisurely activities (e.g., singing contests). A versatile tool, the pastoral provided a platform for a wide variety of themes. Its key virtue was that, like serious science fiction or fantasy today, it removed problems or ideas from their familiar societal bounds so that readers could see them more clearly and objectively. This new perspective exposed the roots of or solutions to a problem or revealed the worth of an idea. Renaissance writers extended the pastoral mode from poetry to plays, romances, elegies, and novels as well.

Most Renaissance forms can be broadly classified as **lyric poetry**. Originally denoting verse to be sung accompanied by a lyre, the term refers to poems that are typically brief, personal, and emotional, presenting the speaker's thoughts and feelings from his own perspective. Often poems that are not *narrative* (telling a story) or *dramatic* (meant to be acted out) are grouped under lyric poetry. As Renaissance thinking focused more on humanity and as printed literature made reading a more individual experience, poetry expressing or investigating inward struggles or states naturally increased. The most famous Tudor form, the sonnet, is classically lyrical. Additionally, its strict demands in structure, meter, rhyme, and thought often served as a display of technical skill, sometimes even more than as a vehicle of deep personal feeling.

By the end of the sixteenth century, some thought the Tudor style was becoming overdone. Reacting to its flowery language and often unrealistic viewpoint, the metaphysical poets, a new school, strove for a more realistic viewpoint and use of sounds and syntax as well as more intellectually vigorous content. The quintessential metaphysical poet John Donne wrote with a rough meter that mimicked normal conversation and presented a view of life and love that was realistic and frank. Also known for the cleverness of its language, metaphysical poetry commonly featured puns and paradoxes and metaphors so unusual that they led to a new category called the *metaphysical conceit* (p. 197). These drew on imagery from a variety of intellectual sources (showing the poets' Renaissance learning), which were often strikingly dissimilar from the objects or ideas being described.

In the following section, you will read examples of these strains of Renaissance poetry. Although they diverge widely in content and style, their variety and vigor show the strength of the era's literary innovations. That their content often still appeals to readers today reveals poetry's ability to speak to the human heart's deepest concerns.

Sonnets and Sonneteers

The Form

The word *sonnet* comes from the Italian *sonnetto* ("little song"), reflecting the form's lyric nature. Originally an Italian form, the sonnet was brought back to England by courtiers who had traveled abroad. After adapting the form to English, Tudor writers continued developing it, producing some of England's finest poetry in the process.

In its original state, the **sonnet** comprised a single, fourteen-line stanza in iambic pentameter. Its content is classically lyric in nature: compressed in length, multilayered in its ideas and expressions, and intensely personal. The form has never fallen out of use since the Renaissance and is undoubtedly one of the era's greatest contributions to literature. Modern sonnets may dispense with some of its stricter demands, but they stay remarkably true to the requirements for length and content structure.

The History

The sonnet was originally popularized by the Italian poet Petrarch (1304–74). Inspired by a beautiful girl, he wrote *To Laura,* a sonnet sequence (i.e., series) telling of frustrated romantic desire. His treatment of the relationship borrows from medieval courtly love (p. 15) the aloof lady; the suffering, submissive lover; and the celestial beauty shining through the beloved. But he combined these elements with a new attention to inner thoughts and personal feelings. Toward the end of the sequence, when Laura has died, the disappointed lover renounces earthly love for the love of God.

Petrarch's elaborate comparisons, known as *conceits* (p. 197), became standard and eventually trite. Classic Petrarchan sentiments—the lady whose eyes are like stars or suns, the lover whose sighs are like a tempestuous wind and who trembled like an earthquake—were parodied at length by later poets. The plot of frustrated love also became conventional—so much so that Edmund Spenser's sonnet sequence celebrating a successful courtship and Shakespeare's sequence idealizing a friendship would appear striking innovations in topic. Though his practices eventually wore thin, Petrarch set the direction for the sonnet to come. In English poetry, the courtier-poet Sir Thomas Wyatt was the first to develop that potential.

The English Poets

A Renaissance man, Wyatt (1503–42) was an accomplished linguist, musician, and poet who used his skills to serve his country and advance his standing. He had conducted diplomatic missions to France and Italy by age twenty-five, was knighted in 1536, and held several important positions, including serving in the king's privy council and Parliament. Somehow among these responsibilities he found time to write the best lyric poetry of the early English Renaissance.

A trip to Italy in 1527 exposed him to Petrarch's poetry. On returning home, he wrote English imitations of Petrarch's poems, especially his sonnets. Wyatt borrowed both the structure and theme of the Italian sonnet in his own compositions, ninety-seven of which were published in 1557.

While Wyatt introduced the sonnet into English, his technique was not especially innovative. A higher-ranking gentleman-poet, Henry Howard, Earl of Surrey, developed the poem's technical aspects. Wyatt's work was more imaginative, but Surrey's lines flowed more smoothly. He smoothed out English meter and invented **blank verse** (unrhymed lines in iambic pentameter) while also improving the sonnet structure with a four-part form known as the English sonnet (p. 185). The latter became the most widely used sonnet form in Tudor England, while blank verse became a classic feature later used by Shakespeare and Milton.

In any case, the contributions of both enabled English Renaissance poets to establish a national literature that could rival continental Europe's. Subsequent great poets have almost universally tried their hand at the sonnet, some experimenting with and further developing the form. Thus the era's great sonnet sequences that followed—Sidney's *Astrophil and Stella*, Spenser's *Amoretti*, and Shakespeare's *Sonnets*—are in no small measure due to the labors of Wyatt and Surrey, even as the later sonnets exceeded the accomplishments of both.

ANALYZE: *Sonnet Structure*

Examining a sonnet's structure can help unlock its meaning. In English sonnets, two major patterns evolved: (1) the **Italian (Petrarchan) sonnet**, containing an *octave* (eight lines) and a *sestet* (six lines), and (2) the **English (Shakespearean) sonnet**, containing three *quatrains* (four lines each) and a *couplet* (two lines). Typically, the Italian sonnet's octave and sestet division corresponds to a shift, or "turn," in thought. The octave presents a problem, raises a question, or poses a possibility that the sestet answers or resolves. The English sonnet structures its content more flexibly. It typically uses the three quatrains to develop a topic and the couplet to resolve or comment on it in the fashion of an epigram (p. 204).

Meter and rhyme are also important in classic sonnets. **Iambic pentameter** (ten-syllable lines consisting of five iambic feet, an unstressed followed by a stressed syllable) is a very common meter, being akin to the spoken rhythms of English. In rhyme, both English and Italian sonnets generally exhibit a specific **rhyme scheme**, the pattern of rhyming sounds that appear at the ends of lines (each identified with letters). The rhyme scheme of an Italian sonnet is typically *abbaabba* in the octave and *cdecde* (or any variation of two or three new rhymes) in the sestet. The rhyme scheme of the English sonnet's quatrains is *abab cdcd efef,* while the couplet's is *gg.*

READ: *Paraphrase Poetry*

Paraphrasing complex poetry is difficult but very useful. Use the following steps to support your understanding of the sonnets that follow. Be aware as you unpack the layered meanings of a poem that such paraphrases will likely be longer than the poem itself.

- Read the poem multiple times for general understanding.
- Break the poem into manageable portions—sentences, phrases, or even words.
- Write the meanings of the portions in regular prose. Change unusual words or figurative language into everyday language that reflects the original meaning.
- Combine the explanations of smaller portions to form complete sentences that explain the poet's ideas for an entire section, such as an octave or a quatrain.

EVALUATE: *Genuine Love*

The sonnets in this lesson address the subject of love in some way. To develop a biblical mindset about the subject, read 1 Corinthians 13, 2 Corinthians 12:15, and Song of Solomon 6:1–10 and 8:5–7. Compare what each poem says about love with what the Scriptures say. Which of the poems align closely with the scriptural view of love? Which deviate from it? Which do both?

OBJECTIVES

- Describe the Italian and English sonnet forms.
- Paraphrase poetry to understand its meaning.
- Trace a poem's structure and progression of thought.
- Determine the theme of a poem.
- Evaluate a poem's view of love from a biblical worldview.

VOCABULARY

trifle (trī′fəl) *n.* Something of little importance or value.

wan (wŏn) *adj.* Unnaturally pale, as from physical or emotional distress.

impute (ĭm-pyo͞ot′) *tr.v.* To relate to a particular cause or source; place the fault or responsibility for.

awry (ə-rī′) *adv.* Away from the correct course; amiss.

felicity (fĭ-lĭs′ĭ-tē) *n.* Great happiness; bliss.

assay (ă-sā′) *tr.v.* To attempt; try.

impediment (ĭm-pĕd′ə-mənt) *n.* Something that *impedes* (retards or obstructs the progress of); a hindrance or obstruction

What does TRUE LOVE *look like?*

When you think about true love, what images or ideas come to mind? Do you think of an elderly couple who have been in a committed marriage for most of their adult lives? Do you think of the tender affection that a mother shows to her baby? How would you characterize true love? Revisit this question of true love periodically throughout the lesson to determine what the poets included here have to say about it.

Sir Thomas Wyatt

Farewell, Love, and all thy laws forever

Farewell, Love, and all thy laws forever.
Thy baited hooks shall tangle me no more.
Senec and Plato[1] call me from thy lore
To perfect wealth my wit for to endeavour.[2]
In blind error when I did persever,[3]
Thy sharp repulse[4] that pricketh ay so sore
Hath taught me to set in **trifles** no store
And scape forth since liberty is lever.[5] **A**
Therefore farewell. Go trouble younger hearts
And in me claim no more authority.
With idle youth go use thy property[6]
And thereon spend thy many brittle darts:
For hitherto though I have lost all my time,
Me lusteth[7] no longer rotten boughs to climb.

trifle (trī′fəl) *n.* Something of little importance or value.

Sonnet Structure: What is the rhyme scheme of lines 1–8? What does it tell you about the structure of this sonnet? **A**

1. *Senec and Plato:* Seneca and Plato, respectively classical Roman and Greek philosophers
2. *my . . . endeavor:* to exert my mind for
3. *persever:* (pûr-sĕv′ər) now archaic; persevere, persist
4. *repulse:* jerking back (setting the hook)
5. *lever:* preferable
6. *property:* "a distinctive, essential, or special quality" (*OED*)
7. *Me lusteth:* I desire

VISUAL ANALYSIS

John Keats's poem "La Belle Dame sans Merci" tells of a knight mysteriously captivated and destroyed by a beautiful woman. How does this painting's depiction of that relationship imply its troubled nature? How does Wyatt's sonnet strike a similar thematic note?

Sidney's Astrophil and Stella *("Star-lover and Star"), published posthumously in 1591, sparked a vogue for sonnet sequences that inspired even Spenser and Shakespeare. Many believe the work's origin to be a missed love relationship between Sidney and Penelope, the Earl of Essex's daughter. A formal betrothal plan fell through, and Penelope married elsewhere (and unhappily). Sidney later met and was attracted to her at court. Too late for marriage, he instead idealized her as Stella in his sonnets.*

31

With how sad steps, O moon, thou climb'st the skies;
How silently, and with how **wan** a face.
What, may it be that even in heav'nly place
That busy archer his sharp arrows tries?
Sure, if that long-with-love-acquainted eyes
Can judge of love, thou feel'st a lover's case;
I read it in thy looks; thy languished grace
To me, that feel the like, thy state descries.[1]
Then even of fellowship, O moon, tell me,
Is constant love deemed there but want of wit?[2]
Are beauties there as proud as here they be?
Do they above love to be loved, and yet
Those lovers scorn whom that love doth possess?
Do they call virtue there ungratefulness?

Reading Check: Who is being addressed in this poem?

wan (wŏn) *adj.* Unnaturally pale, as from physical or emotional distress.

Paraphrase: How would you paraphrase the question in lines 3–4?

1. *descries:* reveals
2. *wit:* intelligence

41

Having this day my horse, my hand, my lance,
Guided so well, that I obtained the prize,
Both by the judgement of the English eyes
And of some sent from that sweet enemy, France;
Horsemen my skill in horsemanship advance;[1]
Town-folks my strength; a daintier[2] judge applies
His praise to sleight,[3] which from good use doth rise;
Some lucky wits **impute** it but to chance;
Others, because of both sides[4] I do take
My blood from them, who did excel in this,
Think nature me a man of arms did make.
How far they shoot **awry**! The true cause is,
Stella looked on, and from her heavenly face
Sent forth the beams, which made so fair my race.[5]

impute (ĭm-pyo͞ot′) *tr.v.* To relate to a particular cause or source; place the fault or responsibility for.

Paraphrase: Reread lines 5–11. What reason does each group of people (five groups total) give for why the speaker has won the tournament?

awry (ə-rī′) *adv.* Away from the correct course; amiss

1. *advance:* offer as explanation
2. *daintier:* more precise
3. *sleight:* dexterity (skillful use of one's body or hands), agility
4. *both sides:* both his mother's and father's families
5. *race:* passage down the jousting course

Edmund Spenser

from Amoretti

Spenser's sonnet sequence differs from Sidney's and many previous sequences by celebrating a courtship ending in marriage. Though the lover suffers the usual misgivings and frustrations, an undercurrent of joyful assurance never leaves the outcome very much in doubt. He also, like Shakespeare, at times addressed other kinds of love, not just romantic love, as one of the following sonnets will illustrate.

68

Most glorious Lord of life! that, on this day,
Didst make thy triumph over death and sin;
And, having harrowed[1] hell, didst bring away
Captivity thence captive, us to win:[2]
This joyous day, dear Lord, with joy begin;
And grant that we, for whom thou didst die,
Being with thy dear blood clean washed from sin,
May live forever in **felicity**!
And that thy love we weighing worthily,[3]
May likewise love thee for the same again;
And for thy sake, that all like dear didst buy,
With love may one another entertain![4]
So let us love, dear love, like as we ought:
Love is the lesson which the Lord us taught.

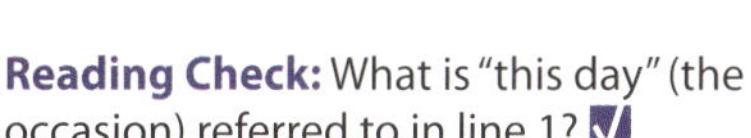

Reading Check: What is "this day" (the occasion) referred to in line 1?

felicity (fĭ-lĭs′ĭ-tē) *n.* Great happiness; bliss.

Genuine Love: According to lines 9–14, what should be the motivation for genuine brotherly love?

1. *harrowed:* plundered
2. *Captivity . . . win:* Ephesians 4:8–10
3. *worthily:* according to its true value, accurately
4. *entertain:* receive, treat

75

One day I wrote her name upon the strand;[1]
But came the waves, and washèd it away:
Again, I wrote it with a second hand;
But came the tide, and made my pains his prey.
Vain man, said she, that doest in vain **assay**
A mortal thing so to immortalize;
For I myself shall like to this decay,
And eek[2] my name be wiped out likewise.
Not so, quod I; let baser things devise[3]
To die in dust, but you shall live by fame:
My verse your virtues rare shall eternize,
And in the heavens write your glorious name.
Where, whenas[4] death shall all the world subdue,
Our love shall live, and later life renew.

assay (ă-sā′) *tr.v.* To attempt; try.

Sonnet Structure: Who is speaking in lines 5–8? Who is speaking in lines 9–12? What does this change in speaker tell you about the structure of the sonnet?

1. *strand:* shore
2. *eek:* also
3. *devise:* (archaic) "to suppose; imagine" (*AHD*)
4. *whenas:* seeing that; although

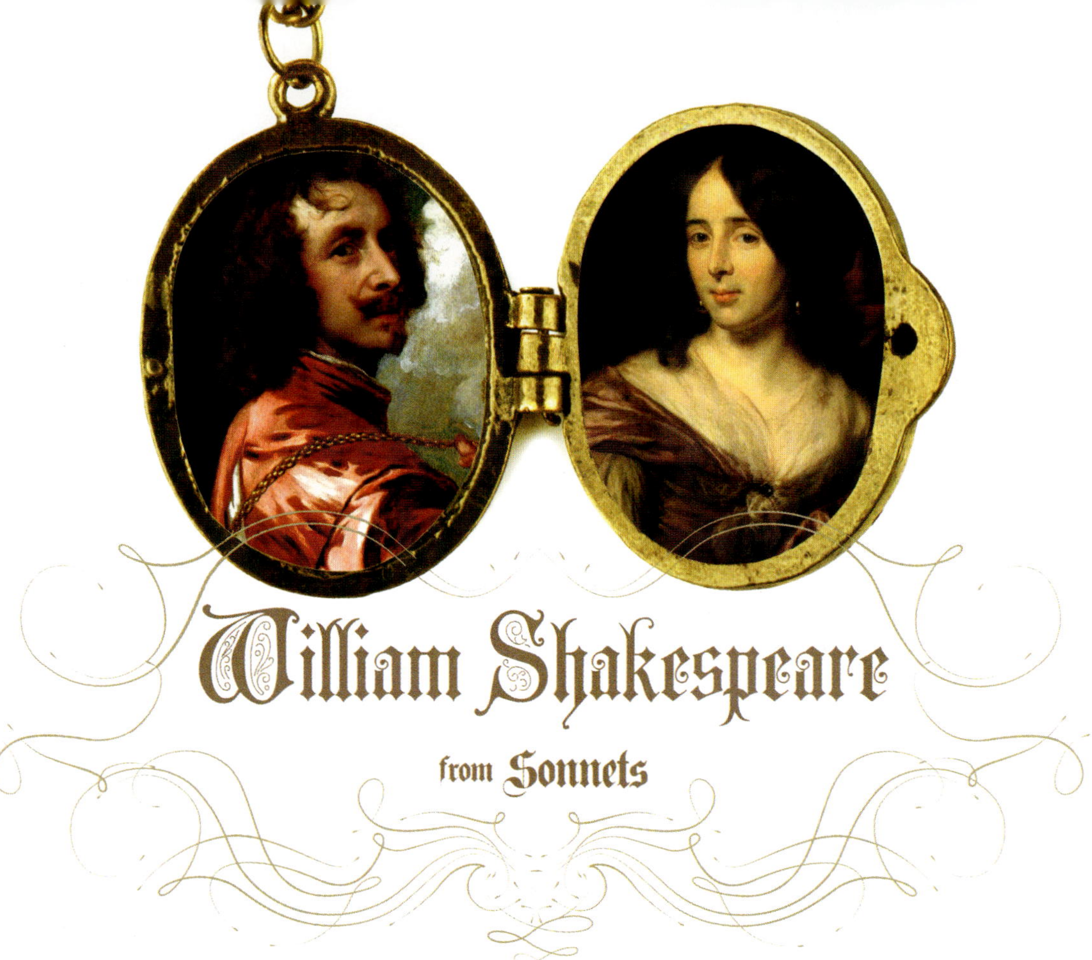

William Shakespeare

from Sonnets

Shakespeare's sonnets were, at their publication (1609), unique in subject, style, and sometimes structure. While still addressing young romantic love, Shakespeare also explored friendship's platonic love and set his characters in different life stages. In style, he often avoided Petrarchan tropes and used the sonnets' language and imagery to create a less idealized, less upperclass voice than other sonneteers. Finally, in structure, he employed both sonnet forms but sometimes blended them. Shakespeare's mastery of the form, fresh approach, and insightful themes established him as a preeminent sonneteer of the era; his sonnets have since been even more widely read than his contemporaries'.

73

That time of year thou mayst in me behold
When yellow leaves, or none, or few, do hang
Upon those boughs which shake against the cold,
Bare ruin'd choirs,[1] where late the sweet birds sang.
In me thou seest the twilight of such day
As after sunset fadeth in the west,
Which by and by black night doth take away,
Death's second self, that seals up all in rest.
In me thou seest the glowing of such fire
That on the ashes of his youth doth lie,
As the death-bed whereon it must expire,
Consum'd with that which it was nourish'd by.
  This thou perceiv'st, which makes thy love more strong,
  To love that well which thou must leave ere long.

Reading Check: What "time of year" is the speaker referring to in this poem? What phase of life does it represent?

1. *choirs:* wooden choir lofts in a cathedral

116

Let me not to the marriage of true minds
Admit[1] **impediments**. Love is not love
Which alters when it alteration finds,
Or bends with the remover[2] to remove.
O, no! it is an ever-fixèd mark[3]
That looks on tempests and is never shaken; E
It is the star to every wandering bark,[4]
Whose[5] worth's unknown, although his height be taken.
Love's not Time's fool, though rosy lips and cheeks
Within his bending sickle's compass come;
Love alters not with his brief hours and weeks,
But bears it out even to the edge of doom.
If this be error and upon me prov'd,
I never writ, nor no man ever lov'd.

impediment (ĭm-pĕd′ə-mənt) *n.* Something that *impedes* (retards or obstructs the progress of); a hindrance or obstruction

Genuine Love: How is true love described in lines 2–6? Do you agree with this description? E

1. *Admit:* grant the existence of
2. *the remover:* the inconstant one
3. *mark:* navigational landmark for sailors
4. *bark:* ship
5. *Whose:* refers to "star"

130

My mistress' eyes are nothing like the sun;
Coral is far more red than her lips' red;
If snow be white, why then her breasts are dun;[1]
If hairs be wires, black wires grow on her head.
I have seen roses damask'd,[2] red and white,
But no such roses see I in her cheeks;
And in some perfumes is there more delight
Than in the breath that from my mistress reeks. A
I love to hear her speak, yet well I know
That music hath a far more pleasing sound;
I grant I never saw a goddess go;
My mistress, when she walks, treads on the ground;
And yet, by heaven, I think my love[3] as rare
As any she belied with false compare![4]

Sonnet Structure: What is the rhyme scheme of lines 1–8? How does Shakespeare develop the description of the mistress within the sonnet's structure? A

1. *dun:* dull, dingy brown
2. *damask'd:* decorated with a rich pattern
3. *my love:* my beloved
4. *As. . . compare:* as any woman misrepresented by exaggerated comparisons

THINK AND DISCUSS

1. To whom or what does the speaker of Sonnet 41 attribute his winning of the tournament prize?
2. According to Sonnet 68, what is the lesson that believers should learn? Who is the teacher of that lesson?
3. What image does Sonnet 75 use to illustrate impermanence?
4. What are three main metaphors of Sonnet 73? How are they related? What do they tell you about the speaker?
5. Is it accurate to call Sonnet 130 an anti-love poem? Support your answer with evidence from the text.
6. Which sonnets in this lesson are Italian in form? Which are English?
7. Choose any two sonnets and write a paraphrase of a quatrain, octave, or sestet of each.
8. Choose two of the three sonnets listed and trace the progression of thought in each: Sonnet 31, Sonnet 75, and Sonnet 73. Reference each sonnet's structural divisions as you trace the development of its ideas.
9. How do Sonnets 68 and 116 portray genuine love? Compare the views of love in these sonnets with the biblical view in the passages listed on page 185.
10. Choose one additional sonnet and evaluate its view of love from a biblical perspective, as you did in the previous question. Support your answer with specific details from the sonnet and the Scriptures.

Christopher Marlowe (1564–93)

The son of a Canterbury shoemaker, Christopher Marlowe attended King's School, known for solid academics, on a scholarship. Again by scholarship, he entered Cambridge, receiving a BA (1584) and an MA (1587). The masters was almost withheld because of rumors regarding his character, but the Queen's Privy Council intervened with a letter attesting to his character and referencing unspecified service to the queen. Combined with his unexplained absences during the academic year, the letter has led to speculations that Marlowe served as a spy at a time when assassination plots were swirling around Elizabeth.

In 1587 Marlowe experienced his first success with his play *Tamburlaine,* a work whose high-quality style and content revolutionized English drama. Having become a credible dramatist, Marlowe continued writing in London, producing major works such as *The Jew of Malta*, *The Massacre at Paris*, and *Dr. Faustus,* the last a masterpiece of English drama that has been adapted for opera and film. His use of blank verse heavily influenced Shakespeare, and recent study strongly suggests that the two playwrights collaborated on Shakespeare's three Henry VI plays.

Meanwhile, Marlowe continued to travel for the government, and his several brushes with the law have further fueled speculation about spy activities. The circumstances of his death only add to suspicions: he was stabbed above the eye with a dagger, ostensibly after a disagreement over the bill at a public house. Sadly, Marlowe's promising life ended at age twenty-nine.

Sir Walter Raleigh (ca. 1554–1618)

Raleigh was born to a gentry family in Devon. After briefly attending Oxford, he fought in France in support of the Huguenots. Back in England, his connections brought him to the royal court, where his personal charm and ambition gained notice. There he advanced steadily and was knighted and given land in Ireland. He reached his pinnacle in 1587 with an appointment as Captain of the Queen's Guard.

Raleigh was one of the daring mariners on whom Elizabeth depended for the safety and prosperity of her realm. From 1578 until his death, Raleigh was mostly occupied with ventures in exploration, colonization, and harassment of Spanish shipping. He helped organize expeditions to the New World, tried twice to plant a settlement on Roanoke Island, and took part in botched expeditions against the Spanish fleet. Twice he sailed vainly up the Orinoco River looking for gold.

Raleigh soared high but ended low. Having survived Elizabeth's anger for secretly marrying her maiden of honor, he could not recover his standing under James. In 1603 he was found guilty, on weak evidence, of plotting against James. He was sentenced to death but was granted an indefinite reprieve as a prisoner in the Tower of London. After thirteen years, he was given a chance to redeem himself by conducting another search for gold in South America on condition that he not offend Spanish colonizers. When his lieutenant attacked a Spanish town, Raleigh's doom was sealed. Upon his return, he was beheaded, an action decried by many contemporaries as a great injustice.

ANALYZE: *Pastoral Poetry and Carpe Diem*

The Renaissance devotion to the **pastoral** mode (p. 183) resulted in its appearance in many genres or forms, including lyric poetry, as the following two poems illustrate. Themes for pastoral works also varied widely; typical ones included critiques of society (especially politics), contemplations on the great human themes of love and death, and the idealization of the simple (rural) life. This last theme was a favorite of the court, often seen in its lyric poetry and in its pageantry: for example, even the queen herself would join the court in dressing up as shepherds for fun.

Pastorals that idealized rural life tended to imply either that life in nature is good because it is easier or that life in nature is good because it is harder (i.e., that physical adversity brings moral prosperity). The former attitude preferred rural to urban life as a temporary and idyllic escape from the pressures and complexities of city dwelling. This attitude dovetailed nicely with the classical theme known as **carpe diem**. Latin for "seize the day," the phrase emphasizes that life is short and urges people to make the most of its gifts while they can. As you read, consider with which of the above perspectives and themes each poem best fits.

OBJECTIVES

- Identify pastoral characteristics in a text.
- Analyze a poem's use of imagery and sound devices to support its theme.
- Compare and contrast the themes of two texts.
- Evaluate the theme of carpe diem in light of biblical truth.

READ: *Compare Text to Text*

Christopher Marlowe's pastoral lyric (p. 194) generated many poetic responses (e.g., from John Donne [p. 196]). None were more effective than that of his friend Sir Walter Raleigh (p. 195). As you read the two poems that follow, compare them in content and form. To begin, note both poems' copious imagery (p. 75). Then consider their structure and sounds, including stanzas, meter, and rhyme. For example, **alliteration**, repetition of initial consonant sounds, is a feature in both. Finally, determine the overall tone and theme of each work. In what ways does Raleigh echo the poem he's responding to? In what ways does his poem differ from Marlowe's? How might these similarities and differences emphasize Raleigh's purpose and theme in his poem? With whose perspective would you personally identify more?

EVALUATE: *Carpe Diem*

Consider the theme of carpe diem. Is its beginning premise—that life is short—valid? In James 4:14, the Scripture concurs that earthly life is fleeting, stating that life is "a vapor, that appeareth for a little time, and then vanisheth away." But what about the attitude's suggested response—to grasp life's joys while we can? How might that response conform to or diverge from God's Word? What factors could make the difference? Consider both what you know of human nature and the truths in the following passages as you contemplate an answer: Luke 12:16–34; 1 Corinthians 15:32; and Ecclesiastes 2:10–11, 16–17, 24–26; and 3:12–13.

Is it good to be an IDEALIST?

Idealists tend to see the world as it ought to be. Their opposites, the realists, prefer to see the world as it is. Both types are generalizations, but people do tend to see the world more through one or the other perspective. Undoubtedly, you know people from both groups. In your opinion, what are the advantages of being an idealist? What might be some pitfalls of this perspective? Write a short paragraph explaining your answer.

The Passionate Shepherd to His Love

Christopher Marlowe

Come live with me and be my love,
And we will all the pleasures prove,[1]
That valleys, groves, hills, and fields,
Woods, or steepy mountain yields.

And we will sit upon the rocks,
Seeing the shepherds feed their flocks,
By shallow rivers, to whose falls
Melodious birds sing madrigals.

And I will make thee beds of roses,
And a thousand fragrant posies,
A cap of flowers and a kirtle[2]
Embroider'd all with leaves of myrtle;[3] R

A gown made of the finest wool,
Which from our pretty lambs we pull;
Fair lined slippers for the cold,
With buckles of the purest gold;

A belt of straw and ivy buds,
With coral clasps and amber studs;
And if these pleasures may thee move,
Come live with me and be my love.

The shepherd swains[4] shall dance and sing
For thy delight each May morning;
If these delights thy mind may move,
Then live with me and be my love. A

1. *we will all the pleasures prove:* try all the pleasures
2. *kirtle:* gown
3. *myrtle:* an aromatic evergreen shrub native to the Mediterranean region, symbolic (like the ivy and the laurel) of poetic achievement
4. *swains:* youths (shepherd boys)

Compare Texts: What sound devices has the poem used so far? R

Pastoral Poetry: What overall attitude toward rural life does this poem express, especially through its imagery? How might the speaker's ideas touch on the theme of carpe diem? A

The Nymph's Reply to the Shepherd

Sir Walter Raleigh

If all the world and love were young,
And truth in every shepherd's tongue,
These pretty pleasures might me move,
To live with thee and be thy love.

Time drives the flocks from field to fold,[1]
When rivers rage, and rocks grow cold;
And Philomel[2] becometh dumb;
The rest complains of[3] cares to come. R

The flowers do fade, and wanton[4] fields
To wayward Winter reckoning[5] yields;
A honey tongue, a heart of gall,
Is fancy's[6] spring, but sorrow's fall.

Thy gowns, thy shoes, thy beds of roses.
Thy cap, thy kirtle, and thy posies.
Soon break, soon wither, soon forgotten,
In folly ripe, in reason rotten.

Thy belt of straw and ivy buds,
Thy coral clasps and amber studs,
All these in me no means can move,
To come to thee and be thy love.

But could youth last, and love still breed,[7]
Had joys no date,[8] nor age no need,
Then these delights my mind might move,
To live with thee and be thy love. A

1. *Time . . . fold:* i.e., winter puts sheep in the sheepfold (pen for sheep)
2. *Philomel:* literary name for the nightingale
3. *The rest complains of:* i.e., the other enticements mentioned give evidence of
4. *wanton:* luxurious
5. *reckoning:* payment
6. *fancy's:* love, usually infatuation
7. *breed:* continually be nurtured
8. *date:* termination

Compare Texts: Compare these beginning stanzas to Marlowe's first two. How are their images and sounds similar? How are they different? R

Pastoral Poetry: What attitude does this poem express toward nature and the simple life? What does the speaker seem to imply about a carpe diem approach to life? A

VISUAL ANALYSIS
Compare and contrast this painting with the one on page 194. How does each reflect the imagery and reinforce the theme of the poem it illustrates?

THINK AND DISCUSS

1. Explain the core features of the pastoral mode.
2. Justify "The Passionate Shepherd to His Love" and "The Nymph's Reply" as examples of pastoralism.
3. Identify the stanza form, meter, and rhyme scheme of each poem.
4. Describe three images from each poem.
5. Analyze and briefly state the message of each poem. Compare the two and explain which offers a carpe diem view of life.
6. Compare and contrast both poems' use of imagery, structure, and sound devices. How might Raleigh's similar or different choices support his message?
7. Review the Scripture passages listed on page 193. According to their truths, what is a biblical view of carpe diem? Which of these poems comes closer to a biblical view of life? Briefly explain your answer.
8. Write a modern-day scenario (e.g., a short scene in a play) that features two characters who conflict over a carpe diem approach to life. Use natural dialogue and actions to flesh out each character's philosophy. Show by your resolution of their conflict which view you believe is correct.

John Donne (1572–1631)

AT A GLANCE

- **1583** Admitted to Oxford University
- **1590s** Wrote much of his early poetry
- **1609–11** Probably wrote much of *Holy Sonnets*
- **1615** Ordained as an Anglican minister
- **1621** Became Dean of St. Paul's Cathedral
- **1623** Wrote *Devotions upon Emergent Occasions*
- **1631** Gave his "Death's Duel" sermon before King Charles I

John Donne is considered one of seventeenth-century England's leading poets and its foremost preacher. His insights into human nature and elaborate, eloquent, and inventive writing style made him a highly influential presence in London.

Years of Struggle

Donne was born to a Catholic family in anti-Catholic England. At age eleven, he began his years of study at Oxford and Cambridge; however, he refused to take a degree as he would not take the Oath of Supremacy (pledging his allegiance to Elizabeth as head of the English Church). Planning to pursue a diplomatic career, he studied law at Lincoln's Inn and traveled widely, even fighting against the Spanish abroad. His work earned him a position as secretary to Sir Thomas Egerton, an officer of the English Crown. Just as he was beginning a promising career, Donne secretly married Egerton's niece against her uncle's and father's wishes, effectively committing career suicide. On a meager lawyer's salary, the couple struggled to support their five children until his wife's father reconciled and paid her dowry.

Years of Ministry

At some point in the late 1590s or early 1600s, Donne converted to the Anglican faith. With encouragement from his friends and under the pressure of James I, he was ordained an Anglican priest and awarded a doctor of divinity degree from Cambridge in 1615. His sermons attracted a wide range of audiences, making him one of the most eminent preachers of his time. However, just as his fortunes seemed to be improving, Anne died in 1617 after giving birth to their twelfth child; grief-stricken, Donne remained faithful to his duties but physically began to wane. In 1621 he was appointed to one of the most prestigious positions in the Church of England, the dean of St. Paul's Cathedral in London, which he held until his death. On February 25, 1631, leaving his sickbed, he preached "Death's Duel," called by some his own funeral sermon, before Charles I. He died March 31, 1631.

Literary Career

The majority of Donne's poems were published posthumously, so identifying their composition dates is difficult. Nevertheless, his forty-year literary career broadly divides into two parts. Usually credited to his early years are several poetic collections, including *Elegies*, *Satires*, and *Songs and Sonnets*. These range from societal critiques to religious thoughts, love lyrics, and erotic verse. His conversion to Protestantism likely brought an end to this phase. According to friend and biographer Izaak Walton, Donne was thereafter "crucified to the world," turning his imaginative powers fully toward his *Holy Sonnets*, sermons, and personal meditations. The latter, published as *Devotions upon Emergent Occasions*, along with his sermons, marked him as a great prose writer as well.

Although Donne was admired by peers, his style—witty, subtle, complex, and abstract—greatly contrasted with the rational style of the seventeenth century, and his works did not gain wide recognition in the centuries that followed. While later poets such as Pope (1700s) and Browning (1800s) greatly admired Donne, it was not until the twentieth century that T. S. Eliot's 1920s study of his works brought him to the public's attention. Now widely acclaimed, Donne, along with his fellow metaphysical poets, is rightfully considered a major author in the British pantheon.

DID YOU KNOW ?

St. Paul's Cathedral in London houses a statue of Donne on his deathbed. The statue replicates a drawing that Donne commissioned as he lay dying.

ANALYZE: *Conceits and Paradoxes*

Metaphysical poets (p. 183) dealt with many themes that previous poets had (love, death, etc.), but they explored them differently. Their approach is characterized by playful wit, clever and unconventional arguments, and unusual imagery that often drew on Renaissance learning and inventions. These references (and other comparisons) were frequently framed as **conceits**, extended metaphors that draw a parallel between highly dissimilar objects or concepts (see *metaphysical conceits*, p. 183). For example, in Donne's poem "Hymn to God, My God, in My Sickness," he compares his physicians to cartographers (mapmakers) and his body to their map. Also characterizing Donne's style are **paradoxes** (p. 165)—statements that seem to contradict themselves and thus draw readers' attention to their underlying truth. As you read the following poems, look for both devices: they often carry important meaning. Additionally, consider why metaphysical poets chose to use them. How might they make each poem more effective?

READ: *Paraphrase Poetry*

Metaphysical poems pose a threefold challenge to readers' understanding. First, they often address complex, abstract concepts. Second, their language is older and in some cases quite different from modern vernaculars. Finally, the figurative devices (e.g., conceits) they use often complicate the text.

To overcome these challenges, use the steps for paraphrasing given in the sonnet lesson (p. 185). In the last step (combining a text's smaller portions), remember to consider each poem's structural divisions as an indicator of how its ideas work together and progress. For instance, figuring out which sonnet structure "Holy Sonnet 14" follows is a step toward understanding how its ideas link into a train of thought. Paraphrasing well takes work, but as you use the strategy more frequently, it will be easier and will become a natural part of your reading.

EVALUATE: *Human Nature*

Donne often struggled with his own faith and sense of unworthiness and sometimes experienced deep depression. These realities are reflected in many of his later poems. "Holy Sonnet 14" reflects some of his struggles as a human being who greatly desired to be near to God but keenly felt his failure to reach that goal. As you read the poem, consider whether Donne's view of his own situation and nature is consistent with a biblical view.

OBJECTIVES

- Define *metaphysical poetry*.
- Paraphrase poetry to clarify syntax and sense.
- Analyze a poem's use of conceit and paradox.
- Evaluate the theme of man's constancy in light of God's constancy.

VOCABULARY

virtuous (vûr′cho͞o-əs) *adj.* Having or showing virtue, especially moral excellence.

laity (lā′ĭ-tē) *n.* The body of the people as opposed to the clergy.

obliquely (ō-blēk′lē) *adv.* In an oblique direction or position; diagonally; slantwise

enthrall (ĕn-thrôl′) *tr.v.* To hold spellbound; captivate.

Have you ever been hurt by someone's INCONSTANCY?

Constancy, the quality of being faithful or dependable, is very often taken for granted in people we know and love. But a person who lacks constancy sticks out like a sore thumb. Why do you think this quality is so important to people? If you have ever had a person be inconstant toward you, how did you respond? In a brief paragraph, describe such an experience. How would you have handled the situation if the tables were turned?

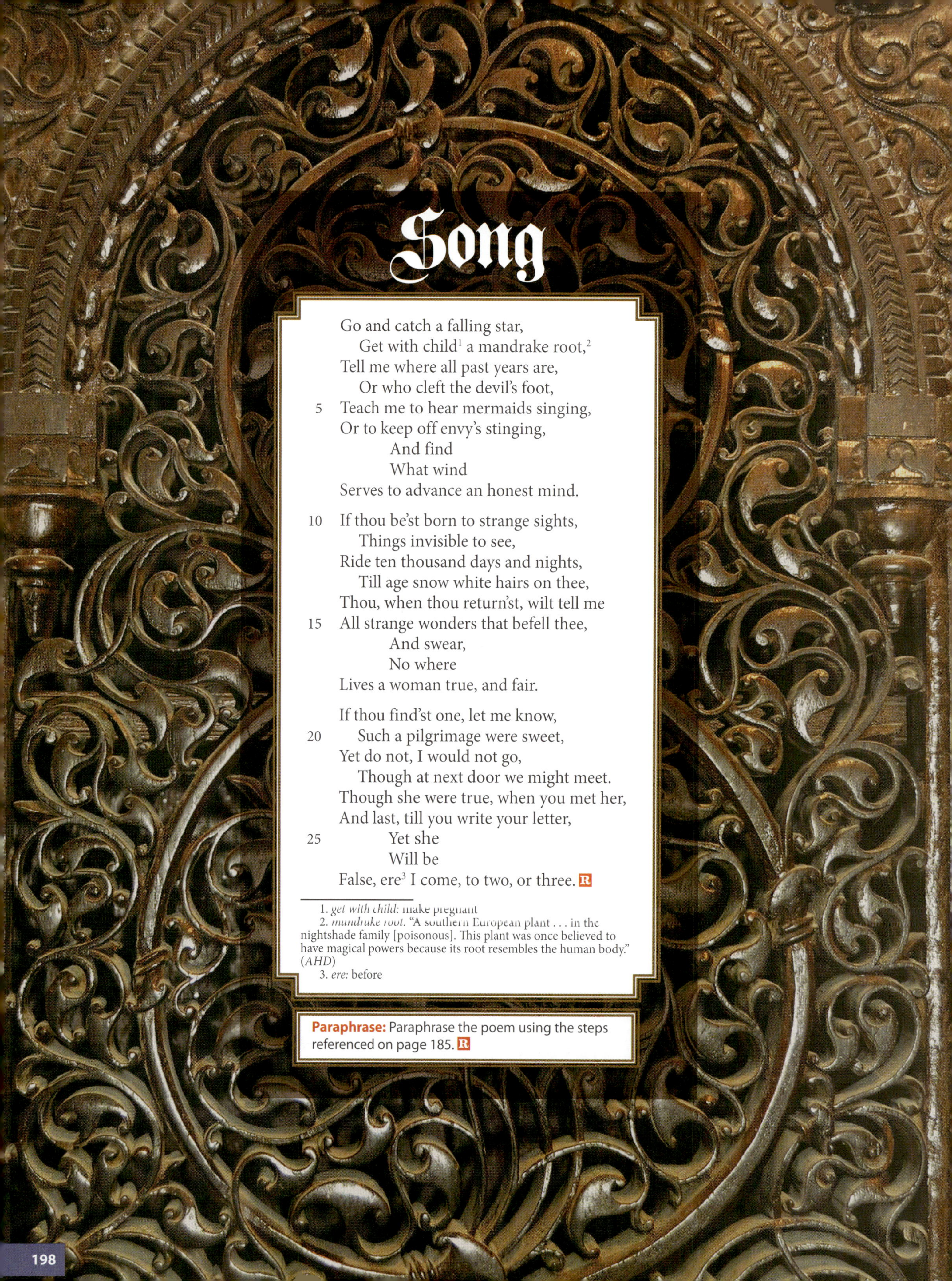

Song

Go and catch a falling star,
Get with child[1] a mandrake root,[2]
Tell me where all past years are,
Or who cleft the devil's foot,
Teach me to hear mermaids singing,
Or to keep off envy's stinging,
And find
What wind
Serves to advance an honest mind.

If thou be'st born to strange sights,
Things invisible to see,
Ride ten thousand days and nights,
Till age snow white hairs on thee,
Thou, when thou return'st, wilt tell me
All strange wonders that befell thee,
And swear,
No where
Lives a woman true, and fair.

If thou find'st one, let me know,
Such a pilgrimage were sweet,
Yet do not, I would not go,
Though at next door we might meet.
Though she were true, when you met her,
And last, till you write your letter,
Yet she
Will be
False, ere[3] I come, to two, or three. R

1. *get with child:* make pregnant
2. *mandrake root:* "A southern European plant . . . in the nightshade family [poisonous]. This plant was once believed to have magical powers because its root resembles the human body." (*AHD*)
3. *ere:* before

Paraphrase: Paraphrase the poem using the steps referenced on page 185. R

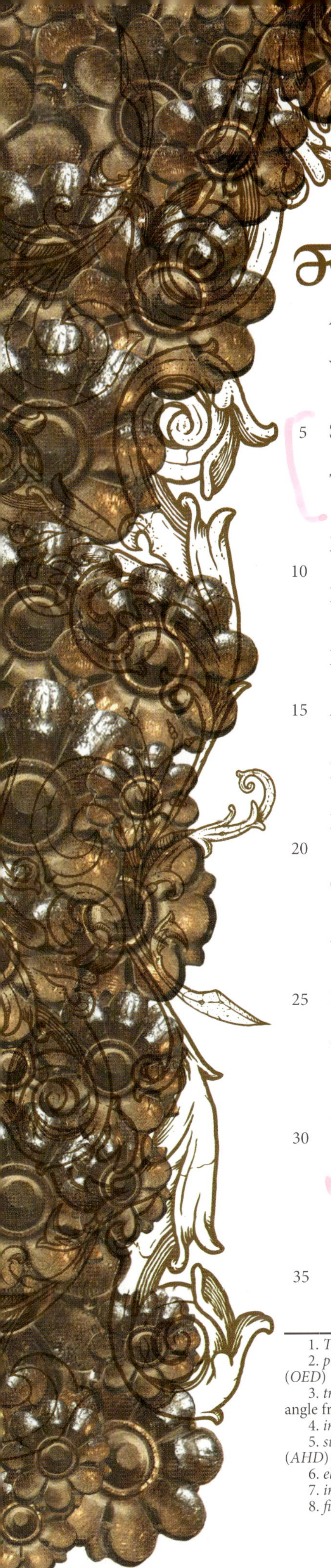

A Valediction Forbidding Mourning

As **virtuous** men pass mildly away,
And whisper to their souls to go,
Whilst some of their sad friends do say,
The breath goes now, and some say, no.

So let us melt, and make no noise,
No tear-floods, nor sigh-tempests move;
T'were[1] profanation[2] of our joys
To tell the **laity** our love. R

Moving of th' earth brings harms and fears;
Men reckon what it did, and meant;
But trepidation of the spheres,[3]
Though greater far, is innocent.[4]

Dull sublunary[5] lovers' love
(Whose soul is sense) cannot admit
Absence, because it doth remove
Those things which elemented[6] it.

But we by a love so much refined,
That ourselves know not what it is,
Inter-assurèd of the mind,[7]
Care less, eyes, lips, and hands to miss.

Our two souls therefore, which are one,
Though I must go, endure not yet
A breach, but an expansion,
Like gold to airy thinness beat.

If they be two, they are two so
As stiff twin compasses are two;
Thy soul, the fixed foot,[8] makes no show
To move, but doth, if th' other do.

And though it in the center sit,
Yet when the other far doth roam,
It leans, and hearkens after it,
And grows erect, as that comes home. A

Such wilt thou be to me, who must,
Like th' other foot, **obliquely** run;
Thy firmness makes my circle just,
And makes me end where I begun.

virtuous (vûr′cho͞o-əs) *adj.* Having or showing virtue, especially moral excellence.

laity (lā′ĭ-tē) *n.* The body of the people as opposed to the clergy.

Paraphrase: Paraphrase these first two stanzas using the steps referenced on page 185. R

Conceit: What does Donne compare to a compass? Who or what is represented by each leg of the compass? A

obliquely (ō-blēk′lē) *adv.* In an oblique direction or position; diagonally; slantwise.

1. *T'were:* contraction of "it were"
2. *profanation:* "desecration or violation of that which is held to be sacred" (*OED*)
3. *trepidation . . . spheres:* when a planet appears to oscillate because of the angle from which its orbit is viewed from earth
4. *innocent:* unseen or unnoticed
5. *sublunary:* literally, "beneath the moon"; also, "of this world; earthly" (*AHD*)
6. *elemented:* began
7. *inter-assured . . . mind:* of the same mind
8. *fixed foot:* the one that stays planted in the center of the circle

Holy Sonnet 14

Batter my heart, three person'd God; for, you
As yet but knock, breathe, shine, and seek to mend;
That I may rise, and stand, o'erthrow me, and bend
Your force, to break, blow, burn, and make me new.
I, like an usurp'd town, to another due,
Labour to admit you, but Oh, to no end.
Reason, your viceroy in me, me should defend,
But is captiv'd, and proves weak or untrue. A
Yet dearly I love you, and would be loved fain,
But am betroth'd unto your enemy;
Divorce me, untie, or break that knot again,
Take me to you, imprison me, for I,
Except you **enthrall** me, never shall be free,
Nor ever chaste, except you ravish me. E

Conceits: What comparisons does Donne use to characterize himself and God in this sonnet's first two stanzas? A

enthrall (ĕn-thrôl′) *tr.v.* To hold spellbound; captivate.

Human Nature: What do Donne's pleas to God reveal of his view of his own human nature? E

THINK AND DISCUSS

1. List two main characteristics of metaphysical poetry.
2. Select one of Donne's poems and paraphrase it using the steps given for paraphrasing on page 185.
3. Explain an example of a paradox from "A Valediction Forbidding Mourning" and "Holy Sonnet 14."
4. Identify and explain a conceit from each poem.
5. Choose one of the paradoxes you explained in question 3 and explain how it supports its poem's theme.
6. Explain how two of the conceits you gathered for question 4 contribute to their poems' themes.
7. Outline the speaker's attitude toward women in "Song." Given Donne's biography, would you expect this poem to have been written earlier or later in his life? Explain your reasoning.
8. Choose either "A Valediction Forbidding Mourning" or "Holy Sonnet 14" and explain how conceits might contribute to the poem's effectiveness. Cite examples from the text.
9. In "Holy Sonnet 14" Donne describes his own view of himself and God. Is his perspective biblical? Consider the truths of John 8:44–45, I Corinthians 2:14, Romans 7:14–25, Galatians 4:8–9, and Philippians 3:4–9.

George Herbert (1593–1633)

The poetry of George Herbert, unlike that of his contemporary John Donne, has always enjoyed critical acclaim. Herbert's poems demonstrate both sophisticated artistry and spiritual fervor. His life demonstrated both as well.

The fifth son of an aristocratic Welsh family, George Herbert had a privileged childhood. His mother kept a watchful eye on his education, providing him with the best tutors and even traveling to Cambridge to influence his education there. Upon his graduation with distinction from Cambridge (BA, 1613; MA, 1616), Herbert collected a number of honors, climaxing with his appointment in 1620 as Public Orator of the University.

During the next eight years, Herbert composed and delivered Latin orations, wrote formal letters and commendatory poems, and enjoyed the prospects of governmental promotion. But he was divided. His mother's desires for him and his own inclinations were toward a career in the church. His mother's death only heightened this conflict. By 1625 the deaths of his major patrons had nearly destroyed his secular prospects. Herbert eventually resigned his oratorship, married, and entered the Anglican ministry. In 1630 he was installed as rector of Bemerton, a small village near Salisbury. Three years later he was dead of tuberculosis.

During the three years at Bemerton, Herbert pursued his ministry so earnestly that he became a model of his profession. He also worked on a volume of poems arranged to suggest the structure of the Hebrew temple. By limiting the scope of his ministry—to a small village parish and a small volume of poems—Herbert increased its spiritual impact, both through his personal example and preaching and through perhaps the finest devotional poetry in English.

BEFORE READING

ANALYZE: *Personification and Apostrophe*

A follower of Donne, Herbert was also a metaphysical poet and made use of conceits (p. 197). Additionally, he employed figurative expressions such as **personification**, the giving of personal characteristics to something that is not a person, and **apostrophe**, the addressing of some nonpersonal (or absent) object as if it were able to reply. First Corinthians 15:55 illustrates the latter: "O death, where is thy sting? O grave, where is thy victory?" Note Herbert's effective use of all three.

READ: *Trace Progression of Thought*

Herbert's poems are usually less convoluted than Donne's. Many present a short imagined scenario or moment of meditation that reveals Herbert's message. Paraphrasing can be helpful to understanding difficult portions, and summarizing each stanza helps condense his overall line of thought and reveal his theme. Make sure to interpret his figurative language and comparisons as you go.

CREATE: *A Poem Using Personification*

Herbert, mimicking Christ's teaching method, often employed the everyday, familiar object to convey his message. Christ used salt, sparrows, coins, seed, candles, and more to teach spiritual lessons. The familiar elucidated the unfamiliar, and the concrete explained the abstract. After reading Herbert's poetry, you will be asked to write a poem in which you personify an everyday object in order to teach a spiritual truth. Use Herbert's poetry as models for your own.

OBJECTIVES

- Trace a poem's progression of thought.
- Infer a poem's meaning from textual details.
- Interpret a poem's figurative language (conceit, personification, and apostrophe).
- Compose a poem based on textual models.

What does it mean to **KNOW GOD** *personally?*

Jordan (2)

When first my lines of heav'nly joys made mention,
Such was their luster, they did so excel,
That I sought out quaint[1] words and trim[2] invention;
My thoughts began to burnish,[3] sprout, and swell,
Curling with metaphors a plain intention,
Decking the sense as if it were to sell.

Thousands of notions in my brain did run,
Off'ring their service, if I were not sped: **A**
I often blotted what I had begun—
This was not quick enough, and that was dead;
Nothing could seem too rich to clothe the sun,
Much less those joys which trample on his head.

As flames do work and wind when they ascend,
So did I weave myself into the sense;
But while I bustled I might hear a friend
Whisper, 'How wide is all this long pretense!
There is in love a sweetness ready penn'd;
Copy out only that, and save expense.' **R**

Figurative Language: What kind of figurative language does line 8 illustrate? **A**

Trace Thought: Briefly summarize each stanza of "Jordan (2)." What is Herbert's main thought? **R**

1. *quaint:* "cunning, ingenious; elaborate, elegant" (*OED*)
2. *trim:* "suitable; hence, fine or beautiful" (*OED*)
3. *burnish:* improve or make more impressive

Love (3)

Love bade me welcome; yet my soul drew back,
Guilty of dust and sin.
But quick-ey'd Love, observing me grow slack
From my first entrance in,
Drew nearer to me, sweetly questioning
If I lack'd anything.

'A guest,' I answer'd, 'worthy to be here':
Love said, 'You shall be he.'
'I, the unkind, ungrateful? Ah, my dear,
I cannot look on Thee.'
Love took my hand, and smiling did reply,
'Who made the eyes but I?'

'Truth, Lord; but I have marr'd them; let my shame
Go where it doth deserve.'
'And know you not,' says Love, 'Who bore the blame?'
'My dear, then I will serve.'
'You must sit down,' says Love, 'and taste My meat.'
So I did sit and eat. **A**

Figurative Language: What kind of figurative language does Herbert use throughout this poem? **A**

VISUAL ANALYSIS
How does the biblical story of the prodigal son reflect the relationship between God and man described in Herbert's poem?

The Pulley

When God at first made man,
Having a glass of blessings standing by,
'Let us,' said He, 'pour on him all we can;
Let the world's riches, which dispersèd lie,
Contract into a span.'[1]

So strength first made a way;
Then beauty flow'd, then wisdom, honor, pleasure;
When almost all was out, God made a stay,[2]
Perceiving that, alone of all His treasure,
Rest in the bottom lay.

'For if I should,' said He,
'Bestow this jewel also on My creature,
He would adore My gifts instead of Me,
And rest in Nature, not the God of Nature:
So both should losers be.

'Yet let him keep the rest,
But keep them with repining restlessness;
Let him be rich and weary, that at least,
If goodness lead him not, yet weariness
May toss him to My breast.' R

1. *span:* "a very small extent or space" (*OED*)
2. *made a stay:* halted

Trace Thought: What scenario does the poem present, and what problem does God identify? How does He solve it? R

THINK AND DISCUSS

1. Define *conceit*, *personification*, and *apostrophe*.
2. Which of the types of figurative language listed on page 201 appear in each of these poems? Give an example for each answer.
3. Summarize the comparison that extends throughout "Love (3)." How does it support the poem's theme?
4. Identify and interpret the main comparison in "The Pulley." How does it illustrate the poem's theme?
5. Summarize Herbert's philosophy of writing as he explains it in "Jordan (2)." List two ways in which one of these poems illustrates the style he described.
6. Both Donne and Herbert are metaphysical poets, but their styles differ somewhat. Using one poem from each poet, compare and contrast how each poet chose to communicate Truth, Goodness, or Beauty.
7. Write a poem in which you personify an everyday object. The purpose of the poem should be to teach a spiritual truth. Model Herbert's poetry.

Ben Jonson (1572–1637)

Ben Jonson, friend and rival of Shakespeare and Donne, became a literary giant in his day. His plays and poetry became so popular with King James I that he was awarded a lifetime pension, making him England's first poet laureate.

As a young man, Jonson gained fame with audiences and contemporary critics for his satiric drama poking fun at the human vices of his day. *Volpone* ("The Fox"), scrutinizing the rising merchant classes, is often regarded as his masterpiece. His popularization of this "new" literary form put it on par with the familiar literature of the day—poetry, historical writing, and essays. In 1616, emboldened by the public's response, Jonson was the first English author to publish his own complete works (complete up to that time, at least).

Although his reputation rests on drama, Jonson was one of the most important of the seventeenth-century poets. He is well-known for mentoring the Sons of Ben, a group of younger poets later called the Cavalier poets. His poetry, unlike Donne's, embraced classical ideals of simplicity, restraint, and precision.

Jonson's recognition by King James I would turn out to be one of his last career successes. At the age of forty-five, Jonson journeyed by foot to his ancestral home of Scotland. Upon his return, he was recognized with an honorary master of arts degree from Oxford but was unable to reclaim his former prominence in literary circles. Upon his death, Jonson was buried upright in Westminster Abbey's Poet's Corner.

BEFORE READING

ANALYZE: *Style, Epigram*

Jonson was well-known for his classical style emphasizing simplicity, concision, balance, and precision. Consider how each poem here pursues these goals in structure and wording. For example, which of these qualities are supported by the use of repetition and parallelism (p. 140) in syntax and sound? Additionally, "On My First Son" is a seventeenth-century **epigram**, a type of short poem from classical poetry that dealt with one subject and was noted for its wit, pithiness, and balanced, polished style. How does the form dovetail well with Jonson's style choices?

READ: *Infer Theme*

A literary work's overriding point is to convey a theme (p. 229). Themes are usually indirectly communicated ideas that readers must infer from a work's significant details (e.g., imagery, structure of ideas, tone). For example, tone (p. 88) can arise from a writer's word choices, use of irony, sympathy for a character, plot resolution, and more. As you read, consider each poem's details, from how its ideas connect or contrast, to what attitude the speaker conveys toward his subjects.

EVALUATE: *Compare Text to Text*

Jonson's "Still to be neat" uses an analogy to describe his approach to writing. What criteria for pleasing and successful writing does he set up in the poem? Use this criteria set to evaluate the other two poems included here. Does Jonson succeed on his own terms? Perhaps compare Jonson's aesthetic approach to Herbert's in "Jordan (2)" (p. 202) or to Donne's as represented by "A Valediction Forbidding Mourning." How might these great artists agree or disagree in their aesthetic values?

OBJECTIVES

- Recognize characteristics of an epigram.
- Infer a work's theme from its details.
- Analyze a poet's stylistic choices.
- Compare two writers' approaches to style based on their texts.

Song to Celia

Drink to me only with thine eyes,
And I will pledge with mine;
Or leave a kiss but in the cup,
And I'll not look for wine.
The thirst, that from the soul doth rise,
Doth ask a drink divine:
But might I of Jove's nectar sup,[1]
I would not change for thine. R

I sent thee late a rosy wreath,
Not so much honouring thee
As giving it a hope, that there
It could not wither'd be.
But thou thereon didst only breathe,
And sent'st it back to me:
Since when it grows, and smells, I swear,
Not of itself, but thee.

1. *Jove's nectar sup:* i.e., drink Jove's nectar, *nectar* meaning ambrosia, a substance supposedly drunk by gods in the Greek and Roman pantheons and believed to give the drinker immortality

Still to be neat

Still to be neat, still to be drest,
As you were going to a feast;
Still to be powdered, still perfumed:
Lady, it is to be presumed,
Though art's hid causes are not found,
All is not sweet, all is not sound. E
Give me a look, give me a face;
That makes simplicity a grace;
Robes loosely flowing, hair as free:
Such sweet neglect more taketh me,
Than all the adulteries[1] of art;
They strike mine eyes, but not my heart. A

1. *adulteries:* debasement, corruption

Infer Theme: What do the speaker's statements here imply about his feelings for Celia? R

Compare Texts: Jonson uses a woman's formal dress to represent his writing style. What difference does he point out between the description in lines 1–6 and the one that follows? E

Style: Give some examples of repetition or parallelism in "Still to be neat." A

On My First Son

An epigram in form, this poem is an elegy in content. An ***elegy*** *is a poem lamenting a death (usually of a loved one) or death and loss in general. Elegies written after the death of a loved one, especially a child as in this case, are truly heartbreaking; readers can feel the writer's pain. How does Jonson attempt to comfort himself in his loss?*

FAREWELL, thou child of my right hand, and joy;
My sin was too much hope of thee, lov'd boy:
Seven years thou wert lent to me, and I thee pay,
Exacted[1] by thy fate, on the just day.
Oh, could I lose all father, now! for why,
Will man lament the state he should envy?
To have so soon 'scaped world's, and flesh's rage,
And, if no other misery, yet age!
Rest in soft peace, and ask'd, say here doth lie
BEN JONSON his best piece of poetry:
For whose sake henceforth all his vows be such,
As what he loves may never like too much.

1. *Exacted:* demanded and obtained by force or authority

Infer Theme: What two truths does Jonson remind himself of in lines 3–4 and 5–8? What does he decide as a result in lines 11–12?

THINK AND DISCUSS

1. Define both a seventeenth-century *epigram* and an *elegy*.
2. Cite two examples of parallelism or repetition (in sounds or syntax) from each of the three poems.
3. Choose two of the three poems and briefly state their themes. Support your answers with at least three pieces of evidence from the texts in question.
4. Explain how "On My First Son" qualifies as both an epigram and an elegy.
5. In "On My First Son," what ideas does Jonson use to try to make sense of his young son's death? Do his attempts give him hope?
6. Explain Jonson's basic approach to poetic style as stated in "Still to be neat." Does he succeed at reaching this goal in these three poems? Cite textual evidence in your answer.
7. Compare Jonson's poetic philosophy to Herbert's in "Jordan (2)" or to Donne's as evidenced in "A Valediction Forbidding Mourning." Give two ways in which your poet is similar to Jonson in style and two ways in which he is different. Cite textual evidence in your answer.

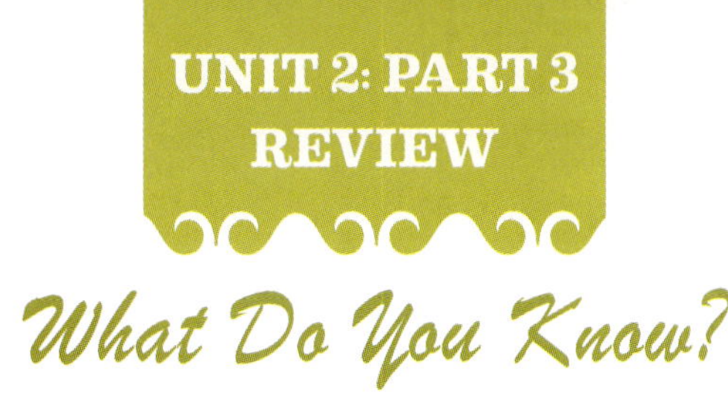

What Do You Know?

Understand the Background

1. What are the differences between lyric, narrative, and dramatic poetry?
2. How did the sonnet form come into English?
3. What is the typical theme of a pastoral poem? Define the theme and give an example of it.
4. Compare and contrast the Petrarchan and Shakespearean sonnet sequences.
5. What literary elements contributed to the clever language of metaphysical poetry?

Apply the Concepts

6. Choose six to nine lines from a poem in Part 3 and paraphrase them.
7. Choose a sonnet from Part 3 and indicate its rhyme scheme. Based on its rhyme scheme, determine whether it is an Italian or English sonnet.
8. Choose a sonnet from Part 3 and explain how its structure and form support its ideas and meaning.
9. How is Shakespeare's Sonnet 130 atypical for a love poem? Would you classify it as such? Support your answer with evidence from the text.
10. How does Raleigh's "The Nymph's Reply to the Shepherd" exhibit the characteristics of a pastoral poem? How does it differ from a traditional pastoral poem? Support your answer with evidence from the text.
11. Choose two images, each from a separate poem in Part 3, and explain their significance to the poem's meaning.
12. Using an example from either "A Valediction Forbidding Mourning" or "Holy Sonnet 14," explain how a conceit supports a poem's overall theme.
13. Choose a poem from Part 3 that is not a sonnet and trace its progression of thought.
14. How do personification and apostrophe advance theme in Herbert's poems? Use examples from his poems to explain your answer.

Evaluate the Ideas

15. Evaluate carpe diem according to Scripture. Consider relevant verses such as Ecclesiastes 2:10–11, 24; 3:12–13 as you form your evaluation.
16. Does the view of love expressed in Shakespeare's Sonnet 116 align with a biblical view of love? Support your evaluation with textual evidence as well as biblical evidence.

Write a Response

17. Compare and contrast Herbert's description of love in "Love 3" with Wyatt's in "Farewell, Love, and all thy laws forever." What does Herbert say about God's love? Compare it with human love, especially as described by Wyatt.
18. Compare and contrast the pastoral poem "The Passionate Shepherd to His Love" to the metaphysical poem "Holy Sonnet 14." How does each exhibit the characteristics of its genre?

Define each term and provide an example of each from a selection in Unit 2, Part 3.

TERMS

meter
pastoral
lyric poetry
sonnet
blank verse
Italian (Petrarchan) sonnet
English (Shakespearian) sonnet
iambic pentameter
rhyme scheme
carpe diem
alliteration
conceit
paradox
personification
apostrophe
epigram

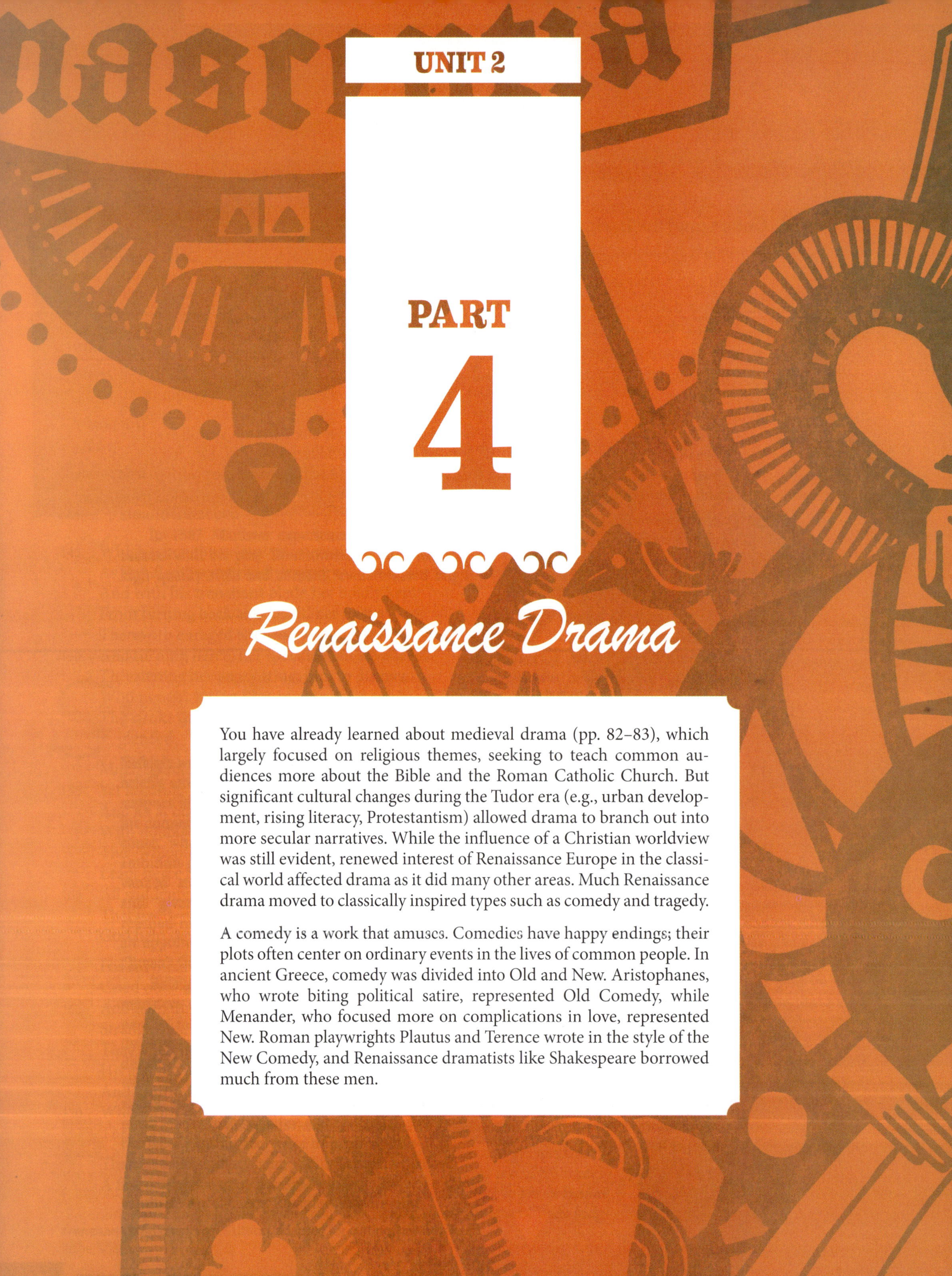

UNIT 2

PART 4

Renaissance Drama

You have already learned about medieval drama (pp. 82–83), which largely focused on religious themes, seeking to teach common audiences more about the Bible and the Roman Catholic Church. But significant cultural changes during the Tudor era (e.g., urban development, rising literacy, Protestantism) allowed drama to branch out into more secular narratives. While the influence of a Christian worldview was still evident, renewed interest of Renaissance Europe in the classical world affected drama as it did many other areas. Much Renaissance drama moved to classically inspired types such as comedy and tragedy.

A comedy is a work that amuses. Comedies have happy endings; their plots often center on ordinary events in the lives of common people. In ancient Greece, comedy was divided into Old and New. Aristophanes, who wrote biting political satire, represented Old Comedy, while Menander, who focused more on complications in love, represented New. Roman playwrights Plautus and Terence wrote in the style of the New Comedy, and Renaissance dramatists like Shakespeare borrowed much from these men.

Another type of classical drama, the **tragedy**, was considered a higher form than comedy. Renaissance tragedy contrasted with comedy not just in its ending but also in its scope. Comedy often dealt with trivial happenings of common people, but tragedy told the stories of kings and nobles whose actions affected the destinies of nations.

Renaissance tragedy also showed classical influence. From Aristotle came the concepts of the tragic hero, the tragic flaw, and the tragic plot. A **tragic hero** is a character who is not inherently bad but who makes a bad decision as the result of a tragic flaw. The **tragic flaw** can range from lack of knowledge to poor judgment to arrogance. The **tragic plot** describes the action surrounding this regrettable decision. The tragic hero, who is a person of importance at the beginning, experiences a reversal of fortunes that leaves him ruined. The audience is meant to pity his fall and fear the possibility of a similar fate.

In addition to types of drama, the classical world also influenced dramatic conventions. Aristotle's descriptions of classical drama were modified to conform to the Renaissance concept of the unities. According to this concept, a play should have *unity of action* (only one major plot line), *unity of place* (only one location), and *unity of time* (action takes place in one day). French writers insisted on strict observation of these unities, but Shakespeare and his English contemporaries treated them more flexibly. For instance, though a drama might have just one major plot, locations and times frequently shifted.

Shifting attitudes toward the theater affected the production of Renaissance drama. Medieval actors had been mostly nonprofessionals. Though there were a few traveling actors in the early Renaissance period, professional actors were more likely to be regarded as public nuisances than celebrities. In fact, a statute written in 1545 made them subject to arrest as vagrants. To avoid prosecution, actors became servants of noblemen. They performed in London and on tour under the protection of such names as the Earl of Worcester's Men. The members of these acting companies performed all parts of each play, acted as shareholders for their companies, and sometimes included playwrights like Shakespeare.

The staging of plays in the early sixteenth century was typically in temporary locations (e.g., the yard of an inn). But in 1576 actor James Burbage built the Theatre, the first building erected in London solely for staging plays. The Theatre was circular, with galleries of seats facing an open-air yard into which a portable, raised wooden peninsula jutted. This tapered stage was about forty-three feet across at its widest point, twenty-eight feet deep, and five feet high, permitting viewing from the "pit" (the area around the stage where members of the lower classes stood). Behind the stage was the tiring (from *attiring*) house, where costumes were kept and changed between scenes and from which the actors could make their entrances.

In 1594 Burbage's son Richard became a member of the Lord Chamberlain's Men, of which Shakespeare was also a member, and the company began to perform at the Theatre. Because of a dispute with the landlord in 1598, the Theatre was dismantled and its materials used for the construction of a new theater, the Globe, on land across the Thames. Some of Shakespeare's greatest plays were written for performance at this 3,000-seat theater, whose name implied metaphorically that "all the world's a stage" and that the stage, conversely, is a little world. The Globe burned to the ground in 1613 but was rebuilt the following year. Its permanent closure by the Puritans in 1642 marked the end of an era and showed the continued disagreement over the appropriateness of the theater in England.

The modern reconstruction of the Globe Theatre.

Conventions of Renaissance Drama

With the renewed interest in classical and medieval literary forms and structures, the Renaissance enabled the spread of profitable public playhouses all over Europe. Live productions kept audiences coming back. As performances increased, playwrights and actors began to develop certain common practices for both the stage and the drama that took place on it. Eventually, through repeated use, these practices became widely accepted by both playwrights and audiences. Some of these common practices, or conventions, were necessary for the era and have since fallen out of use; others, however, became standard to the genre and are still practiced today.

Stage Conventions

The most common Elizabethan stage design was a *thrust* stage, which protruded out into an open-air courtyard from the thatch-roofed backstage area. The well-to-do spectators in the three-storied galleries that surrounded the stage had a definite feeling of involvement. For a penny, the "groundlings" could stand on the rush-strewn floor on three sides of the stage. The *proscenium* stage, common today in many auditoriums, dominated in the late seventeenth century. Its three-walled stage at one end of a room separated the audience from the action by an arched invisible "wall" behind which a curtain was often hung. A third design, *theater-in-the-round*, with its roots in Greece and Rome, became popular again in the twentieth century. In this design, the audience completely surrounds an open stage and is on the same level or slightly elevated. This arrangement gives the audience a feeling of engagement with the actors.

To tantalize his audience's senses, the playwright ingeniously used the spectacle of his day, including all aspects of costumes, props, scenery, and special effects. Early on, stages were often bare; roles were communicated by the use of minimal props, such as daggers, torches, bones, armor, and costumes. Costumes always reflected a character's social status but did not always reflect the time period portrayed. Often the costume colors were symbolic: black for evil or mourning, white for purity, and so on. Props eventually graduated to larger objects such as thrones, canons, furniture, and live animals. Blood always grabbed audience attention. Wounds and injuries were often mimicked with blood-soaked dummies or sacs of blood concealed by clothing that would "bleed" when pierced by a sword. To add to the visual interest, general-purpose scenery (painted on muslin or canvas and known as theatre flats) was dropped or hung behind the actors.

Today, technology has transformed theater, but in Shakespeare's day, special effects required audience imagination. For instance, characters would "appear" from trap doors leading to "hell," the area below the stage. Gods would "fly" from "heaven," the area above the ceiling, attached to wires or ropes rigged overhead. Originating from these spaces, sounds made by fireworks, trumpets, chimes, bells, drums, cannons, and so on, would accompany action and supply realism. Hidden actors mimicked such sounds as hounds howling, roosters crowing, or ghosts moaning.

Dramatic Conventions

Dramatic conventions are accepted practices that structure the writing and performing of plays. Playwrights typically separate the plot of a drama into major units called acts. Acts are further subdivided into scenes, single situations within an act, usually without gaps in time or changes in setting, marked by the entrance or exit of actors. Scripts begin with a list of characters in the play, or *dramatis personae*, followed by actors' parts with stage directions for lighting, movement, and action. In general, actors deliver their lines in dialogues and monologues (long speeches typically to another character). Conventions unique to drama are speeches in which characters express their thoughts directly to the audience. A **soliloquy** is spoken by an actor who is alone or thinks he is alone on stage. An **aside** is a brief disclosure made by one actor in the presence of other actors who, by convention, are thought not to hear him.

As you read the five acts of *Macbeth*, follow the stage directions, imagining the stage props and costumes. What special effects would make the plot come alive? Where do you picture the characters as they give their soliloquies and asides? Imagine all this in the bright daylight of the Globe —no electricity then!

William Shakespeare (1564–1616)

AT A GLANCE

- **ca. April 23, 1564** Born in Stratford-upon-Avon
- **ca. 1588** Began his career as actor-playwright
- **ca. 1589–99** Wrote mainly history plays and comedies
- **1592** Had become a playwright of recognized success
- **1600–1611** Wrote the great tragedies and the later comedies
- **ca. 1610** Retired to Stratford (continued writing for a short while)

His Education and Family

Shakespeare was born in Stratford-upon-Avon to John, a prosperous glover (dealer in leather goods and wool), and his wife, Mary, daughter of a wealthy landowner. John, an influential citizen, was eventually elected mayor, then termed *bailiff*, and acquired a gentleman's coat of arms. As a result of his family's social standing, Shakespeare received a strong education in Latin, writing, and even acting at Stratford's grammar school. When Shakespeare was eighteen (1582), he married Anne Hathaway, and in 1583, the Shakespeares' first child, Susanna, was born. Twins Hamnet and Judith followed in 1585, but Hamnet died at age eleven.

His Theatrical Profession

Exactly when and how Shakespeare entered the theatrical profession is unknown. Perhaps he joined one of the traveling player groups that frequented Stratford-upon-Avon. But by the late 1580s, he had moved to London, and by 1595, he was an actor, writer, and shareholder with the Lord Chamberlain's company, later known as the King's Men. Highly successful, his company owned the Theatre. As a result, Shakespeare was also able to buy the second-largest house in Stratford, New Place, where he retired in 1610 as a wealthy writer of popular plays.

DID YOU KNOW ?

According to tradition, Thomas Lucy prosecuted the boy William for stealing a deer. Will later caricatured him in a play.

His Creative Legacy

One reason Shakespeare's plays are still performed is that they address a diverse audience. Shakespeare's writing appealed to both upper- and lower-class sensibilities with elements as accessible as comic relief and as elevated as speeches that followed rules of classical rhetoric. Now, four hundred years later, the plays are still relevant because Shakespeare wove into them his incredible understanding of human nature.

Since the plays are widely studied, one might expect the survival of standard, finely edited copies. Actually, multiple versions of many of the plays exist, with variations ranging from minor textual differences to the addition or omission of entire scenes. The plays' use accounts for such discrepancies: Shakespeare created them as scripts, not literary texts. A company owned a play, and actors altered it to fit their circumstances. Not until six years after Shakespeare's death were his plays collected and published as the First Folio (1623).

Shakespeare was also an accomplished poet and preeminent sonneteer of the English Renaissance. His collection of 154 sonnets popularized the English sonnet. Additionally, when theaters closed during bubonic plague outbreaks (1593 and 1594), Shakespeare composed two long narrative poems, *Venus and Adonis* and *The Rape of Lucrece*. Unlike his plays, these poems were printed for preservation.

His Debated Authorship

Although the literary community generally attributes thirty-eight plays to Shakespeare, debates about his authorship emerged in the late 1700s. These speculations arose primarily from critics' disbelief that a man of Shakespeare's class and education could write such masterful works. As time passed, others, intrigued by the idea of secret authorship, furthered the debate. At various times, people have argued that the plays were written secretly by such writers as Christopher Marlowe, Sir Francis Bacon, Edward de Vere (Earl of Oxford), the Earl of Southampton, and even Queen Elizabeth I. Most recently, in 2015, the plays once again were attributed to William Stanley, sixth Earl of Derby.

The anti-Stratfordian (i.e., not Shakespeare) arguments are usually easily dismissed based on historical evidence. Most scholars agree that it is unreasonable to conceive that a secret playwright fooled theatergoers and Shakespeare's friends into believing Shakespeare wrote the plays. Furthermore, many of Shakespeare's contemporaries, including some of his fellow actors, attested that he wrote the plays and poetry attributed to him. Combined with the fact that no one questioned the authorship of the plays until over a century after his death, these reasons reinforce William Shakespeare as the author of the plays.

A portrait by John Singer Sargent of actress Ellen Terry as Lady Macbeth from an 1888 production.

His "Scottish Play"

Macbeth portrays the tragic fall of a man, basically noble, ensnared by lawless ambition. Having yielded to evil solicitation, Macbeth commits to his path, hardening as he descends. His fall resembles Adam's: it originates in a deliberate choice that results in spiritual death. Temptation stems from both Satan (the witches) and a woman (Lady Macbeth). The belief that Shakespeare used actual spells has fostered the superstition that saying the play's name in a theater invites a curse. For this reason, *Macbeth* is often called "The Scottish Play." Whether or not one indulges the superstition, the audience in Shakespeare's day believed witches to be animated by Satan and to have supernatural power.

Macbeth's treason springs from ingratitude, a sin greatly despised in the Renassaince. Act 1 shows Duncan heaping honor on Macbeth—an "earnest" of what Macbeth may expect to receive later. Macbeth's response is to plot Duncan's death. The heinousness of the murder is compounded by the circumstance that the victim is the murderer's guest. Duncan's assassination thus violates the duty of subject to ruler, beneficiary to benefactor, and host to guest. The first scenes stress these sacred obligations. The rest of the play shows the terrible results of disregarding them, one of which is that life loses its meaning. Macbeth's moving soliloquy "Tomorrow, and tomorrow, and tomorrow" expresses the despair of a rebel.

His Purpose and Sources

Through this anatomy of rebellion, Shakespeare not only entertains but also accomplishes the moral mission of poetry as defined by Sidney and Spenser: to draw men to virtue by fictional example. Macbeth and other characters, however, are not purely fictional. They represent historical people. The action of the play takes place in Scotland at a time when Scandinavian invaders were still harassing the Scottish. Deviating from his source, Richard Holinshed's *Chronicles of Scotland*, Shakespeare combined two military campaigns and two assassinations. He made Duncan old and venerable and Banquo honorable, unlike their historical originals. James I, the ruling monarch during the writing of *Macbeth*, was believed to have descended from Banquo. Wishing to compliment the king, Shakespeare made Banquo a noble character. (In Holinshed's account Banquo was complicit in Duncan's murder.) With this change and others, Shakespeare tailored history for didactic advantage—consistency of moral character, conduct, and consequences—while increasing narrative pace and focus. Historical truth is not the issue.

Macbeth numbers among Shakespeare's four great tragedies, the others being *Hamlet*, *Othello*, and *King Lear*. Though scholars disagree that 1606 was the year of composition, *Macbeth* is known to have been written late in Shakespeare's career and definitely demonstrates mature artistry. The play's climactic progression allows readers to follow the process of evil from thought to words to action before witnessing its consequences. The scenes move ironically from the horrors of war and demon-haunted wilds to the civilities and comforts of domestic life, which conceal worse barbarities than those beyond the edge of civilization.

His Skill with Language

Macbeth is written in blank verse (p. 184), a form that Shakespeare perfected in his later plays. His linguistic flexibility extended to his coining words and changing them, often turning them into different parts of speech. Such changes often enhanced meaning. Shakespeare's frequent allusions (p. 129) make his plays difficult for modern audiences, but these references were readily understood in his day when writers and readers shared a Latin-based education.

Figurative language also enriches the play. Shakespeare often uses *metaphor* to state or imply the equivalence of two dissimilar things. With *similes* he compares two things using the words *like*, *as*, or *as if*. For example, Lady Macbeth says to her husband, "Your face, my Thane, is as a book" (1.5.60). Later Macbeth responds, "False face must hide what the false heart doth know" (1.7.82). This rhetorical device, *antithesis*, uses parallelism in two phrases or clauses to reinforce their contrast in meaning. The witches' statement "Fair is foul, and foul is fair" (1.1.11) is paradoxical. It also illustrates another rhetorical device, *chiasmus*, a reversal in word order of the second of two parallel phrases, clauses, or sentences. These and other figurative expressions demonstrate Shakespeare's skill with language. *Macbeth* is indeed a work of mature artistry that still has relevance for audiences today.

ANALYZE: *Setting, Atmosphere, Character, Conflict*

In complex stories like *Macbeth*, many fictional elements interact to support the author's ideas and purposes. Some foundational ones are setting, atmosphere, character, and conflict. The general **setting** (time and place) of *Macbeth* is medieval Scotland during Scandinavian invasions. Each scene also inhabits a specific place and time (of day). For instance, act 1, scene 1 opens the play on a Scottish moor during a violent storm. Setting in turn can help create **atmosphere**, the mood or emotion pervading a work, specifically when it is enhanced by a work's setting. As you read, consider these connections. What atmosphere might the setting of scene 1 create? What might the story's overall atmosphere imply about its likely outcome?

Both elements form a backdrop for a work's **characters** and **conflicts** (the opposition of two or more characters or forces). The play's broad setting shrouds the entire play in national conflict while the stormy moor of scene 1 reveals and enhances other conflicts (i.e., in nature, within Macbeth). Similarly, major characters (e.g., the Macbeths) can create an atmosphere through their actions or feelings, primarily because a work's major conflicts hinge on their choices. But even minor characters, such as the three witches, can contribute to atmosphere. As you read, analyze the characterization and purpose of characters both major and minor. What might a character's words or actions contribute to atmosphere or reveal about important conflicts (internal or external)?

READ: *Apply Historical Context*

Shakespeare's age was preoccupied with order in every realm of life (natural, political, social, etc.). Many believed God had ordained hierarchies in creation, links in a Great Chain of Being, ranging down to the basest minerals and up to the angels and God Himself. To perform its God-intended function, each link had to adhere to its position within that great chain. In the natural world, humans (capable of reasoning) ruled over animals; in the social realm, the husband ruled over his wife and children; in the political realm, the king ruled as God's earthly regent to dispense justice. Anyone disrupting this hierarchy was rebelling against God's divine plan. As you read, look for violations of this Renaissance order, especially in the social and political realms as that order relates to Macbeth and his wife.

EVALUATE: *Characters' Words and Actions*

The idea that God created an ordered world is scriptural, but other ideas related to the Great Chain of Being are not. As you read act 1, consider what Macbeth's and Lady Macbeth's words and actions suggest about truthfulness versus deception, one's relationship to civil authorities, and expected social behaviors. Read Genesis 1:26–28; 1 Kings 2:2–4; Proverbs 11:3, 12:22, 31:10–12; Romans 13:1–5; 1 Corinthians 16:13–14; and 1 Peter 3:1–2. Use these verses (or others that apply) to evaluate characters' words and actions from a biblical worldview.

OBJECTIVES

- Examine a text's setting and the way it creates atmosphere and reveals conflict.
- Analyze a text's characters and the way they contribute to atmosphere and reveal conflict.
- Apply historical context when interpreting a text.
- Evaluate a text's ideas from a biblical worldview.

VOCABULARY

plight (plīt) *n.* A situation, especially a bad or unfortunate one.

deign (dān) *tr.v.* To condescend to give or grant; vouchsafe.

prologue (prō′lôg′) *n.* An introductory act, event, or period.

wanton (wŏn′tən) *adj.* Unrestrainedly excessive.

impede (ĭm-pēd′) *tr.v.* To retard or obstruct the progress of.

mettle (mĕt′l) *n.* The ability to meet a challenge or persevere under demanding circumstances; determination or resolve.

What would you SACRIFICE *to get what you want?*

Olympic athletes sacrifice time and energy to achieve their goals. Sacrifice of this sort is commendable; it requires strength and determination. But some things are too dear to sacrifice. One's honesty, for instance, is too valuable to sacrifice by cheating on a test to get a good grade. What are your goals—both short- and long-term? What might they require you to sacrifice? Have you thoroughly considered the cost?

MACBETH

DRAMATIS PERSONAE

MALCOLM

MACBETH

BANQUO

Duncan, *king of Scotland*
Malcolm, *a son of the king*
Donalbain, *a son of the king*
Macbeth, *a general of the king's army*
Banquo, *a general of the king's army*
Macduff, *a nobleman of Scotland*
Lennox, Ross, Menteith, Angus, Caithness, *other noblemen of Scotland*
Fleance, *son to Banquo*
Siward, *Earl of Northumberland, English general*
Young Siward, *his son*
Seyton, *an officer attending on Macbeth*
Boy, *son to Macduff*
English Doctor

MACDUFF

LADY MACBETH

Scottish Doctor
Sergeant
Porter
Old Man
Three Murderers
Lady Macbeth
Lady Macduff
Gentlewoman attending on Lady Macbeth
Three Witches, the Weird Sisters
Three other Witches
Hecate
Apparitions
Lords, Gentlemen, Officers, Soldiers, Attendants, and Messengers

Scene: Scotland, England

A heath°

heath: a wild, treeless tract of land; a moor

(Thunder and lightning. Enter three WITCHES.*)*

FIRST WITCH. When shall we three meet again?
In thunder, lightning, or in rain?
SECOND WITCH. When the hurly burly's° done,
When the battle's lost and won.
THIRD WITCH. That will be ere the set of sun.
FIRST WITCH. Where the place?
SECOND WITCH. Upon the heath.
THIRD WITCH. There to meet with Macbeth.
FIRST WITCH. I come, Graymalkin.°
SECOND WITCH. Paddock° calls.
THIRD WITCH. Anon.°
ALL. Fair is foul, and foul is fair,
Hover through the fog and filthy air. **A**

(Exeunt.°)

3 **hurly burly:** tumult, confusion, uproar

8 **Graymalkin:** "gray cat," the name of the spirit that possesses the First Witch

9 **Paddock:** "toad," the Second Witch's spirit

10 **Anon:** at once; spoken to her spirit, Harpier, identified at 4.1.3

Exeunt: stage direction for a group of actors (two or more) to leave the stage

A camp in Scotland

(Alarum° within. Enter KING DUNCAN, MALCOLM, DONALBAIN, LENNOX, *with* ATTENDANTS, *meeting a bleeding* SERGEANT.*)*

Alarum: trumpet call to arms

DUNCAN. What bloody man is that? He can report,
As seemeth by his **plight**, of the revolt
The newest state.
MALCOLM. This is the sergeant,
Who like a good and hardy soldier fought
'Gainst my captivity. Hail, brave friend!
Say to the King the knowledge of the broil°
As thou didst leave it.
SERGEANT. Doubtful it stood,
As two spent° swimmers that do cling together
And choke their art.° The merciless Macdonwald
(Worthy to be a rebel, for to that°
The multiplying villainies of nature
Do swarm upon him) from the Western Isles°
Of kerns and gallowglasses° is supplied,
And Fortune, on his damnèd quarrel smiling,
Show'd like a rebel's whore.° But all's too weak;
For brave Macbeth (well he deserves that name),
Disdaining Fortune, with his brandish'd steel,
Which smok'd with bloody execution,°
Like Valor's minion° carv'd out his passage

6 **broil:** conflict

8 **spent:** exhausted

9 **choke . . . art:** render their swimming skill ineffective

10 **for . . . that:** to that purpose

12 **Western Isles:** Hebrides

13 **kerns . . . gallowglasses:** untrained foot soldiers drawn from the poor class and better-armed retainers

15 **rebel's whore:** i.e., with a fickle countenance

18 **execution:** pronounced as five syllables

19 **minion:** favorite

Setting/Atmosphere: Based on the details of the setting, how would you describe the atmosphere of scene 1? What might the atmosphere suggest about future events? **A**

plight (plīt) *n.* A situation, especially a bad or unfortunate one.

Till he fac'd the slave;
Which nev'r shook hands, nor bade farewell to him,
Till he unseam'd him from the nave° to th' chops,°
And fix'd his head upon our battlements.

DUNCAN. O valiant cousin,° worthy gentleman!

SERGEANT. As whence the sun 'gins his reflection
Skipwrecking storms and direful thunders break,
So from that spring whence comfort seem'd to come
Discomfort swells. Mark, King of Scotland, mark!
No sooner justice had, with valor arm'd,
Compell'd these skipping kerns to trust their heels,°
But the Norweyan lord, surveying vantage,°
With furbish'd° arms and new supplies of men,
Began a fresh assault.

DUNCAN. Dismay'd not this
Our captains, Macbeth and Banquo?

SERGEANT. Yes,
As sparrows eagles, or the hare the lion.
If I say sooth,° I must report they were
As cannons overcharg'd with double cracks,° so they
Doubly redoubled strokes upon the foe.
Except they meant to bathe in reeking wounds,
Or memorize another Golgotha,°
I cannot tell—
But I am faint, my gashes cry for help.

DUNCAN. So well thy words become thee as thy wounds,
They smack of honor both. Go get him surgeons.

(Exit SERGEANT, attended. Enter ROSS and ANGUS.)

Who comes here?

MALCOLM. The worthy Thane of Ross.

LENNOX. What a haste looks through his eyes! So should he look
That seems to speak things strange.

ROSS. God save the King!

DUNCAN. Whence cam'st thou, worthy Thane?

ROSS. From Fife, great King,
Where the Norweyan banners flout the sky
And fan our people cold.°
Norway° himself , with terrible numbers,
Assisted by that most disloyal traitor,
The Thane of Cawdor, began a dismal conflict
Till that Bellona's bridegroom,° lapp'd in proof,°
Confronted him with self-comparisons,°
Point against point, rebellious arm 'gainst arm,
Curbing his lavish spirit; and, to conclude,
The victory fell on us. A

DUNCAN. Great happiness!

ROSS. That now
Sweno, the Norways' king, craves composition;°
Nor would we **deign** him burial of his men
Till he disbursèd at Saint Colme's Inch°
Ten thousand dollars to our general use.

22 nave: navel / **chops:** jaws

24 cousin: Any relative except a sibling. Macbeth and Duncan are the former King Malcolm's grandsons.

30 kerns . . . heels: soldiers to retreat

31 surveying vantage: seeing his advantage or superiority in the conflict

32 furbish'd: polished

36 sooth: truthfully

37 cracks: charges

40 memorize . . . Golgotha: make the place memorable as a site of slaughters, like Golgotha, "the place of skulls"

50 fan . . . cold: make our people fearful

51 Norway: the king of Norway

54 Bellona's bridegroom: Macbeth, poetically described as being wed to Bellona, the Roman goddess of war / **lapp'd . . . proof:** clad in armor that has been tested

55 self-comparisons: deeds as valiant as his own

59 composition: terms of peace

61 Saint . . . Inch: Inchcomb, a small island near Edinburgh

Conflict: What external, national conflict is mentioned in scene 2? A

deign (dān) *tr.v.* To condescend to give or grant; vouchsafe.

DUNCAN. No more that Thane of Cawdor shall deceive
Our bosom interest. Go pronounce his present death,
And with his former title greet Macbeth.
ROSS. I'll see it done.
DUNCAN. What he hath lost, noble Macbeth hath won.

(Exeunt.)

SCENE 3

A heath

(Thunder. Enter the three WITCHES.)

FIRST WITCH. Where hast thou been, sister?
SECOND WITCH. Killing swine.
THIRD WITCH. Sister, where thou?
FIRST WITCH. A sailor's wife had chestnuts in her lap,
And munch'd, and munch'd, and munch'd. "Give me!"
quoth I.
"Aroint° thee, witch!" the rump-fed ronyon° cries.
Her husband's to Aleppo° gone, master o' th' Tiger;°
But in a sieve° I'll thither sail,
And like a rat without a tail,
I'll do, I'll do, and I'll do.
SECOND WITCH. I'll give thee a wind.
FIRST WITCH. Th' art kind.
THIRD WITCH. And I another.
FIRST WITCH. I myself have all the other,
And the very ports they blow,
All the quarters that they know
I' th' shipman's card.°
I'll drain him dry as hay:
Sleep shall neither night nor day
Hang upon his penthouse lid;°
He shall live a man forbid;
Weary sev'nnights,° nine times nine,
Shall he dwindle, peak,° and pine;
Though his bark cannot be lost,
Yet it shall be tempest-toss'd.
Look what I have.
SECOND WITCH. Show me, show me.
FIRST WITCH. Here I have a pilot's thumb,
Wrack'd° as homeward he did come.

(Drum within.)

THIRD WITCH. A drum, a drum!
Macbeth doth come.
ALL. The weird° sisters, hand in hand,
Posters of° the sea and land,
Thus do go, about, about,
Thrice to thine, and thrice to mine,
And thrice again, to make up nine.°
Peace, the charm's wound up.

6 aroint: be gone / **ronyon:** fat, scabby creature

7 Aleppo: an industrial city in northwest Syria / **Tiger:** a favorite name for Elizabethan ships

8 sieve: In Shakespeare's day witches were believed to have special powers to sail in wire mesh utensils.

17 shipman's card: compass

20 penthouse lid: eyelid, which slants like the root of a penthouse, or lean-to

22 sev'nnights: weeks

23 peak: become thin

29 Wrack'd: wrecked

32 weird: supernatural, eerie, manipulators of fate

33 Posters of: quick riders over

36 thrice . . . nine: Three is a magic number in religion; thus three times three, or nine, is triply sacred.

Historical Context: What two people violate the political order in scene 2? What are they called as a result? Who corrects this disorder?

(Enter MACBETH *and* BANQUO.*)*

MACBETH. So foul and fair a day I have not seen. ✓
BANQUO. How far is't call'd to Forres? What are these
So wither'd and so wild in their attire,
That look not like th' inhabitants o' th' earth,
And yet are on't? Live you? or are you aught°
That man may question? You seem to understand me,
By each at once her choppy° finger laying
Upon her skinny lips. You should be women,
And yet your beards forbid me to interpret
That you are so.
MACBETH. Speak, if you can: what are you?
FIRST WITCH. All hail, Macbeth, hail to thee, Thane of Glamis!
SECOND WITCH. All hail, Macbeth, hail to thee, Thane of Cawdor!
THIRD WITCH. All hail, Macbeth, that shalt be King hereafter!
BANQUO. Good, Sir, why do you start, and seem to fear
Things that do seem so fair?—I' th' name of truth,
Are ye fantastical,° or that indeed
Which outwardly ye show? My noble partner
You greet with present grace, and great prediction
Of noble having and of royal hope,
That he seems rapt° withal; to me you speak not.
If you can look into the seeds of time,
And say which grain will grow, and which will not,
Speak then to me, who neither beg nor fear
Your favors nor your hate.
FIRST WITCH. Hail!
SECOND WITCH. Hail!
THIRD WITCH. Hail!

42 **aught:** anything

44 **choppy:** chapped

53 **fantastical:** imaginary creatures

57 **rapt:** enraptured, distracted in thought

Reading Check: How does Macbeth describe the day? To whose words is his description similar? ✓

FIRST WITCH. Lesser than Macbeth, and greater.
SECOND WITCH. Not so happy,° yet much happier.
THIRD WITCH. Thou shalt get° kings, though thou be none.
So all hail, Macbeth and Banquo!
FIRST WITCH. Banquo and Macbeth, all hail!
MACBETH. Stay, you imperfect speakers, tell me more:
By Sinel's° death I know I am Thane of Glamis,
But how of Cawdor? The Thane of Cawdor lives
A prosperous gentleman; and to be king
Stands not within the prospect of belief,
No more than to be Cawdor. Say from whence
You owe° this strange intelligence, or why
Upon this blasted° heath you stop our way
With such prophetic greeting? Speak, I charge you.

(WITCHES vanish.)

BANQUO. The earth hath bubbles, as the water has,
And these are of them. Whither are they vanish'd?
MACBETH. Into the air; and what seem'd corporal° melted,
As breath into the wind. Would they had stay'd!
BANQUO. Were such things here that we do speak about?
Or have we eaten on the insane root°
That takes the reason prisoner?
MACBETH. Your children shall be kings.
BANQUO. You shall be king.
MACBETH. And Thane of Cawdor too; went it not so?
BANQUO. To th' self-same tune and words. Who's here?

(Enter ROSS and ANGUS.)

ROSS. The King hath happily receiv'd, Macbeth,
The news of thy success; and when he reads
Thy personal venture in the rebels' fight,
His wonders and his praises do contend
Which should be thine or his.° Silenc'd with that,°
In viewing o'er the rest o' th' self-same day,
He finds thee in the stout Norweyan ranks,
Nothing afeard of what thyself didst make,
Strange images of death.° As thick as hail
Came post with post,° and every one did bear
Thy praises in his kingdom's great defense,
And pour'd them down before him.
ANGUS. We are sent
To give thee from our royal master thanks,
Only to herald thee into his sight,
Not pay thee.
ROSS. And for an earnest° of a greater honor,
He bade me, from him, call thee Thane of Cawdor;
In which addition,° hail, most worthy Thane,
For it is thine.
BANQUO. What, can the devil speak true?

66 happy: fortunate

67 get: beget

71 Sinel's: Macbeth's father

76 owe: own

77 blasted: barren

81 corporal: having a physical or material substance

84 insane root: root that causes insanity; probably either hemlock, henbane, or nightshade

93 His . . . his: He cannot decide whether to wonder at you or praise you. / **that:** the conflict in his own mind

97 Nothing . . . death: not at all afraid of death

98 post . . . post: messenger after messenger

104 earnest: pledge, down payment

106 addition: title

Reading Check: What predictions do the witches make about Macbeth?

Character/Atmosphere: How would you characterize the witches, based on their actions, appearance, and words in this scene and scene 1? How do they contribute to atmosphere and reveal conflict?

MACBETH. The Thane of Cawdor lives; why do you dress me
In borrowed robes?
ANGUS. Who was° the thane lives yet,
But under heavy judgment bears that life
Which he deserves to lose. Whether he was combin'd°
With those of Norway, or did line° the rebel°
With hidden help and vantage,° or that with both
He labor'd in his country's wrack,° I know not;
But treasons capital,° confess'd and prov'd,
Have overthrown him.
MACBETH. *(Aside.°)* Glamis, and Thane of Cawdor!
The greatest is behind.° *(To ROSS and ANGUS.)* Thanks for your pains.
(Aside to BANQUO.) Do you not hope your children shall be kings,
When those that gave the Thane of Cawdor to me
Promis'd no less to them?
BANQUO. *(Aside to MACBETH.)* That, trusted home,°
Might yet enkindle you unto° the crown,
Besides the Thane of Cawdor. But 'tis strange;
And oftentimes, to win us to our harm,
The instruments of darkness tell us truths,
Win us with honest trifles, to betray 's
In deepest consequence.—
Cousins,° a word, I pray you.
MACBETH. *(Aside.)* Two truths are told,
As happy **prologues** to the swelling act°
Of the imperial theme,°—I thank you, gentlemen.
(Aside.) This supernatural soliciting
Cannot be ill, cannot be good. If ill,
Why hath it given me earnest of success,
Commencing in a truth? I am Thane of Cawdor.
If good, why do I yield to that suggestion°
Whose horrid image doth unfix my hair
And make my seated heart knock at my ribs,
Against the use° of nature? Present fears
Are less than horrible imaginings:
My thought, whose murder yet is but fantastical,
Shakes so my single state of man° that function°
Is smother'd in surmise,° and nothing is
But what is not.°
BANQUO. Look how our partner's rapt.
MACBETH. *(Aside.)* If chance will have me king, why, chance may
crown me
Without my stir.
BANQUO. New honors come° upon him,
Like our strange° garments, cleave not to their mould°
But with the aid of use.
MACBETH. *(Aside.)* Come what come may,
Time and the hour runs through° the roughest day.
BANQUO. Worthy Macbeth, we stay upon° your leisure.
MACBETH. Give me your favor;° my dull brain was wrought

109 Who was: he who was

111 combin'd: allied

112 line: support / **rebel:** Macdonwald

113 vantage: assistance

114 wrack: ruin

115 treasons capital: treasons deserving capital punishment

116 Aside: spoken in the presence of others but not heard by them

117 behind: to come

120 home: fully

121 enkindle . . . unto: cause you to hope for

127 Cousins: fellow lords

128 swelling act: climactic, dramatic action

129 imperial theme: of kingliness

134 suggestion: temptation

137 use: custom

140 single . . . man: weak nature / **function:** action

141 surmise: imagined action

142 nothing . . . not: Nothing is real to me except that which I imagine.

144 come: that are come

145 strange: new / **mould:** the forms of persons who wear them

147 runs through: comes to the end of

148 stay upon: await

149 favor: pardon

prologue (prō'lôg') *n.* An introductory act, event, or period.

Reading Check: Read lines 130–42a several times. Paraphrase them to help you understand what Macbeth is saying.

Conflict: What internal conflict does Macbeth first experience in this scene? What lines support your answer?

With things forgotten. Kind gentlemen, your pains
Are regist'red where every day I turn
The leaf to read them.° Let us toward° the King.
(Aside to BANQUO.*)* Think upon what hath chanc'd; and at
more time,
The interim having weigh'd it, let us speak
Our free hearts each to other.

152 regist'red . . . them: uppermost in my mind / **toward:** go to

BANQUO. *(Aside to* MACBETH.*)* Very gladly.
MACBETH. *(Aside to* BANQUO.*)* Till then, enough.—Come friends. ✓
(Exeunt.)

SCENE 4

The palace at Forres

(Flourish.° Enter KING DUNCAN, LENNOX, MALCOLM, DONALBAIN, *and* ATTENDANTS.*)*

Flourish: trumpet fanfare

DUNCAN. Is execution done on Cawdor? Are not
Those in commission° yet return'd?
MALCOLM. My liege,°
They are not yet come back. But I have spoke
With one that saw him die; who did report
That very frankly he confess'd his treasons,
Implor'd your Highness' pardon, and set forth
A deep repentance. Nothing in his life
Became him like the leaving it. He died
As one that had been studied° in his death,
To throw away the dearest thing he own'd,
As 'twere a careless trifle.

2 in commission: assigned to carry out the execution / **liege:** lord or sovereign

9 studied: deliberate

DUNCAN. There's no art
To find the mind's construction in the face:
He was a gentleman on whom I built
An absolute trust.
(Enter MACBETH, BANQUO, ROSS, *and* ANGUS.*)*

Reading Check: Based on the witches' prophecy and the events that followed, what do you think lies ahead for Macbeth? ✓

O worthiest cousin!
The sin of my ingratitude even now
Was heavy on me. Thou art so far before,°
That swiftest wing of recompense is slow
To overtake thee. Would thou hadst less deserv'd
That the proportion both of thanks and payment
Might have been mine!° Only I have left to say,
More is thy due than more than all can pay.

MACBETH. The service and the loyalty I owe,
In doing it, pays itself. Your Highness' part
Is to receive our duties;° and our duties
Are to your throne and state children and servants,
Which do but what they should, by doing every thing
Safe toward° your love and honor. R

DUNCAN. Welcome hither!
I have begun to plant thee, and will labor
To make thee full of growing. Noble Banquo,
That hast no less deserv'd, nor must be known
No less to have done so, let me infold thee
And hold thee to my heart.

BANQUO. There if I grow,
The harvest is your own.

DUNCAN. My plenteous joys,
Wanton in fullness, seek to hide themselves
In drops of sorrow. Sons, kinsmen, thanes,
And you whose places are the nearest, know,
We will establish our estate upon
Our eldest, Malcolm, whom we name hereafter
The Prince of Cumberland;° which honor must
Not unaccompanied invest him only,
But signs of nobleness, like stars, shall shine
On all deservers. From hence to Inverness,
And bind us further to you.

MACBETH. The rest is labor, which is not us'd for you.°
I'll be myself the harbinger,° and make joyful
The hearing of my wife with your approach;
So humbly take my leave.

DUNCAN. My worthy Cawdor!

MACBETH. *(Aside.)* The Prince of Cumberland! that is a step
On which I must fall down, or else o'erleap,
For in my way it lies. Stars, hide your fires,
Let not light see my black and deep desires;
The eye wink at° the hand; yet let that be
Which the eye fears, when it is done, to see. A

(Exit.)

DUNCAN. True, worthy Banquo! he is full so valiant,
And in his commendations I am fed;
It is a banquet to me. Let's after him,
Whose care is gone before to bid us welcome:
It is a peerless kinsman.

(Flourish. Exeunt.)

16 before: ahead

20 That . . . mine: so that I could have thanked and repaid you sufficiently

24 duties: acts of obedience and love

27 Safe toward: with a sure regard for

39 Prince of Cumberland: official title of the heir to the Scottish throne; cf. Prince of Wales in England

44 The . . . you: Time other than that spent in your service is toilsome.

45 harbinger: an officer of the household who traveled ahead of the king and made the arrangements for his lodging

52 wink at: be blind to

Historical Context: Do Macbeth's words (ll. 22–27) violate or honor the Great Chain of Being? Explain. R

wanton (wŏn′tən) *adj.* Unrestrainedly excessive.

Conflict: What more does this aside (ll. 48–53) tell you about Macbeth's internal conflict? A

SCENE 5

Macbeth's castle at Inverness

(Enter LADY MACBETH *alone, with a letter.)*

LADY MACBETH. *(Reads.)* "They met me in the day of success; and I have learn'd by the perfect'st report, they have more in them than mortal knowledge. When I burnt in desire to question them further, they made themselves air, into which they vanish'd. Whiles I stood rapt in the wonder of it, came missives° from the King, who all hail'd me 'Thane of Cawdor,' by which title, before, these weird sisters saluted me, and referr'd me to the coming on of time with 'Hail, King that shalt be!' This have I thought good to deliver thee, my dearest partner of greatness, that thou mightst not lose the dues of rejoicing by being ignorant of what greatness is promis'd thee. Lay it to thy heart, and farewell."

5 **missives:** messengers

Glamis thou art, and Cawdor, and shalt be
What thou art promis'd. Yet do I fear thy nature,
It is too full o' th' milk of human kindness
To catch the nearest way. Thou wouldst be great,
Art not without ambition, but without
The illness° should attend it. What thou wouldst highly,
That wouldst thou holily; wouldst not play false,
And yet wouldst wrongly win. Thou'ldst have, great Glamis,
That° which cries, "Thus thou must do," if thou have it;°
And that which rather thou dost fear to do
Than wishest should be undone. Hie thee hither,
That I may pour my spirits in thine ear,
And chastise thee with the valor of my tongue
All that **impedes** thee from the golden round,°
Which fate and metaphysical° aid doth seem
To have thee crown'd withal.° E

18 **illness:** scheming, plotting

21 **That:** the crown / **Thus . . . it:** "You must do this" in order to have the crown.

26 **round:** crown

27 **metaphysical:** supernatural

28 **withal:** with

(Enter MESSENGER.*)*

What is your tidings?

MESSENGER. The King comes here tonight.

LADY MACBETH. Thou'rt mad to say it!
Is not thy master with him? who, were't so,
Would have inform'd for preparation.

impede (ĭm-pēd′) *tr.v.* To retard or obstruct the progress of.

Character's Words: What does Lady Macbeth claim Macbeth possesses that is keeping him from becoming a great leader? What does she say a great leader should possess? E

MESSENGER. So please you, it is true; our Thane is coming.
One of my fellows had the speed of° him,
Who, almost dead for breath, had scarcely more
Than would make up his message.
LADY MACBETH. Give him tending,
He brings great news.

(Exit MESSENGER.)

The raven himself is hoarse
That croaks the fatal entrance of Duncan
Under my battlements. Come, you spirits
That tend on mortal° thoughts, unsex me here,
And fill me from the crown to the toe topful
Of direst cruelty! Make thick my blood,
Stop up th' access and passage to remorse,
That no compunctious visitings of nature°
Shake my fell° purpose, nor keep peace between
Th' effect and it!° Come to my woman's breasts,
And take my milk for gall, you murd'ring ministers,
Wherever in your sightless° substances
You wait on nature's mischief! Come, thick night,
And pall thee° in dunnest° smoke of hell,
That my keen knife see not the wound it makes,
Nor heaven peep through the blanket of the dark
To cry, "Hold, hold!"° A

(Enter MACBETH.)

Great Glamis! worthy Cawdor!
Greater than both, by the all-hail hereafter!
Thy letters have transported me beyond
This ignorant present, and I feel now
The future in the instant.
MACBETH. My dearest love,
Duncan comes here tonight.
LADY MACBETH. And when goes hence?
MACBETH. Tomorrow, as he purposes.
LADY MACBETH. O never
Shall sun that morrow see!
Your face, my Thane, is as a book, where men
May read strange matters. To beguile the time,°
Look like the time; bear welcome in your eye,
Your hand, your tongue; look like th' innocent flower
But be the serpent under't. He that's coming
Must be provided for; and you shall put
This night's great business into my dispatch,°
Which shall to all our nights and days to come
Give solely sovereign sway° and masterdom.° E
MACBETH. We will speak further.
LADY MACBETH. Only look up clear:°
To alter favor° ever is to fear.
Leave all the rest to me.

(Exeunt.)

33 had . . . of: overtook

39 mortal: murderous

43 compunctious . . . nature: natural human sympathy

44 fell: inhumanly cruel

45 it: my purpose and its accomplishment

47 sightless: invisible

49 pall thee: cover yourself / **dunnest:** darkest

52 "Hold, hold!": an allusion to Abraham's foiled sacrifice of Isaac (Gen. 22:10–12)

61 beguile . . . time: deceive the age

66 dispatch: management

68 sway: royal power / **masterdom:** rulership

69 clear: tranquil

70 alter favor: look afraid

Atmosphere/Character: What atmosphere do Lady Macbeth's words create? Is it similar or dissimilar to the atmosphere created by the witches? How so? A

Character's Words: What "art" is Lady Macbeth trying to teach her husband (ll. 60–68)? What do you think of her advice? E

Before Macbeth's castle

(Hautboys° and torches. Enter KING DUNCAN, MALCOLM, DONALBAIN, BANQUO, LENNOX, MACDUFF, ROSS, ANGUS, *and* ATTENDANTS.*)*

DUNCAN. This castle hath a pleasant seat,° the air
Nimbly and sweetly recommends itself
Unto our gentle senses.

BANQUO. This guest of summer,
The temple-haunting martlet,° does approve,°
By his lov'd masonry, that the heaven's breath
Smells wooingly here; no jutty,° frieze,°
Buttress, nor coign of vantage,° but this bird
Hath made his pendent° bed and procreant° cradle.
Where they most breed and haunt, I have observ'd
The air is delicate. **A**

(Enter LADY MACBETH.*)*

DUNCAN. See, see, our honor'd hostess!
The love that follows us sometime is our trouble,
Which still° we thank as° love. Herein I teach you
How you shall bid God 'ield us for your pains,°
And thank us for your trouble.

LADY MACBETH. All our service
In every point twice done, and then done double,
Were poor and single business to contend
Against those honors deep and broad wherewith
Your Majesty loads our house. For those of old,
And the late dignities heap'd up to them,
We rest your hermits.°

DUNCAN. Where's the Thane of Cawdor?
We cours'd° him at the heels, and had a purpose
To be his purveyor;° but he rides well,
And his great love, sharp as his spur, hath holp° him
To his home before us. Fair and noble hostess,
We are your guest tonight.

LADY MACBETH. Your servants ever
Have theirs, themselves, and what is theirs, in compt°
To make their audit at your Highness' pleasure,
Still° to return° your own.

DUNCAN. Give me your hand.
Conduct me to mine host, we love him highly,
And shall continue our graces towards him.
By your leave, hostess.

(Exeunt.)

Hautboys: (HO boyz) oboes, used to announce the entrance of royalty

1 **seat:** location

4 **martlet:** martin, a bird resembling the swallow that builds its nest of mud under the eaves of a roof / **approve:** show

6 **jutty:** part of a building that juts out beyond the rest / **frieze:** sculpted horizontal band above the columns of a building

7 **coign . . . vantage:** convenient corner

8 **pendent:** suspended / **procreant:** fertile

12 **still:** nevertheless / **thank as:** are grateful for as arising from

13 **How . . . pains:** Duncan jokingly expresses his gratitude to his hostess by suggesting that God will reward "him" for the trouble that "she" has taken to entertain him.

20 **hermits:** recluses who will continually pray for thee

21 **cours'd:** chased

22 **be . . . purveyor:** arrive before him to make arrangements for his accommodations

23 **holp:** helped

26 **in compt:** subject to account

28 **Still:** always / **return:** give back

Setting/Atmosphere: What atmosphere does the setting of scene 6 create, according to King Duncan and Banquo (ll. 1–10a)? How does it support Lady Macbeth's intentions? **A**

Inner court of Macbeth's castle at Inverness

(Hautboys, torches. Enter a SEWER° *and divers* SERVANTS *with dishes and service, [pass] over the stage, [and] then enter* MACBETH.*)*

MACBETH. If it were done when 'tis done, then 'twere well
It were done quickly. If th' assassination
Could trammel up° the consequence, and catch
With his surcease,° success; that but this blow
Might be the be-all and the end-all—here,
But here,° upon this bank and shoal° of time,
We'd jump° the life to come. But in these cases
We still have judgment here, that we but teach
Bloody instructions, which being taught, return
To plague th' inventor. This even-handed justice
Commends th' ingredience° of our poison'd chalice
To our own lips. He's here in double trust:
First, as I am his kinsman and his subject,
Strong both against the deed; then, as his host,
Who should against his murderer shut the door,
Not bear the knife myself. Besides, this Duncan
Hath borne his faculties° so meek, hath been
So clear in his great office, that his virtues
Will plead like angels, trumpet-tongu'd, against
The deep damnation of his taking-off;
And pity, like a naked new-born babe,
Striding° the blast, or heaven's cherubin, hors'd
Upon the sightless couriers° of the air,
Shall blow the horrid deed in every eye,
That tears shall drown the wind. I have no spur
To prick the sides of my intent, but only
Vaulting ambition, which o'erleaps itself,°
And falls on th' other—° R E

(Enter LADY MACBETH.*)*

How now? what news?

LADY MACBETH. He has almost supp'd. Why have you left the chamber?
MACBETH. Hath he ask'd for me?
LADY MACBETH. Know you not he has?
MACBETH. We will proceed no further in this business:
He hath honor'd me of late, and I have bought°
Golden opinions° from all sorts of people,
Which would be worn now in their newest gloss,
Not cast aside so soon.
LADY MACBETH. Was the hope drunk
Wherein you dress'd yourself? Hath it slept since?
And wakes it now to look so green and pale
At what it did so freely? From this time
Such I account thy love. Art thou afeard
To be the same in thine own act and valor
As thou art in desire? Wouldst thou have that

Sewer: butler

3 **trammel up:** entangle as in a net

4 **his surcease:** Duncan's death

6 **But here:** even in this mortal life / **shoal:** sandbar

7 **jump:** risk

11 **Commends . . . ingredience:** presents the contents

17 **faculties:** royal powers

22 **Striding:** bestriding

23 **sightless couriers:** invisible runners; i.e., the wind

27 **which . . . itself:** which, vaulting into the saddle, leaps too far

28 **other:** other side

32 **bought:** won

33 **Golden opinions:** glowing commendations

Historical Context: What two violations of social order does Macbeth consider as he ponders Duncan's "double trust" (l. 12)? R

Character's Words: What biblical truths or commands does Macbeth risk violating as he considers his situation? E

Which thou esteem'st the ornament of life,°
And live a coward in thine own esteem,
Letting "I dare not" wait upon "I would,"
Like the poor cat i' th' adage?°

MACBETH. Prithee peace!
I dare do all that may become° a man;
Who dares do more is none.

LADY MACBETH. What beast was't then
That made you break° this enterprise to me?
When you durst do it, then you were a man;
And to be more than what you were, you would
Be so much more the man. Nor time nor place
Did then adhere,° and yet you would° make both:
They have made themselves, and that their° fitness now
Does unmake you. I have given suck, and know
How tender 'tis to love the babe that milks me;
I would, while it was smiling in my face,
Have pluck'd my nipple from his boneless gums,
And dash'd the brains out, had I so sworn as you
Have done to this. E

MACBETH. If we should fail?

LADY MACBETH. We fail?
But screw your courage to the sticking place,°
And we'll not fail. When Duncan is asleep
(Whereto the rather shall his day's hard journey
Soundly invite him), his two chamberlains
Will I with wine and wassail° so convince,°
That memory, the warder° of the brain,
Shall be a fume,° and the receipt° of reason
A limbeck° only. When in swinish sleep
Their drenchèd natures lie as in a death,
What cannot you and I perform upon
Th' unguarded Duncan? what not put upon
His spongy° officers, who shall bear the guilt
Of our great quell?° R

VISUAL ANALYSIS
What does the actors' portrayal of this scene between Macbeth and Lady Macbeth suggest about the relationship between these characters?

42 **ornament . . . life:** i.e., the crown

45 **Like . . . adage:** an allusion to the proverb "the cat would eat fish but would not wet her feet"

46 **become:** adorn, be suitable to

48 **break:** reveal

52 **Did . . . adhere:** was then suitable for the murder / **would:** wanted to

53 **their:** their very

60 **to . . . place:** as in cocking a crossbow

64 **wassail:** carousing / **convince:** overcome

65 **warder:** guard

66 **fume:** alcohol fume / **receipt:** receptacle

67 **limbeck:** part of a still to which the fumes rise

71 **spongy:** drunken

72 **quell:** murder

Character's Actions: In Macbeth's view, what distinguishes man from beast? How does Macbeth's view compare with Lady Macbeth's? E

Historical Context: How does Lady Macbeth violate her place in the social order, according to Renaissance ideals? R

MACBETH. Bring forth men-children only!
For thy undaunted **mettle** should compose
Nothing but males. Will it not be receiv'd,
When we have mark'd with blood those sleepy two
Of his own chamber, and us'd their very daggers,
That they have done't?

LADY MACBETH. Who dares receive it other,
As° we shall make our griefs and clamor roar
Upon his death? **E**

MACBETH. I am settled, and bend up
Each corporal agent° to this terrible feat.
Away, and mock the time with fairest show;
False face must hide what the false heart doth know.

(Exeunt.)

78 As: when

80 bend . . . agent: call up every ounce of my bodily strength; perhaps also extends the crossbow metaphor in line 60

mettle (mĕt'l) *n.* The ability to meet a challenge or persevere under demanding circumstances; determination or resolve.

Character's Words/Actions: What biblical truths does Lady Macbeth transgress in her words and actions? **E**

THINK AND DISCUSS

1. Identify two instances in which setting contributes to the atmosphere of act 1. Explain how each supports the scene's purpose or meaning. Support your answers with details from the text.
2. Based on their characterization, how do the witches contribute to act 1's atmosphere? What do they represent? Note Banquo's words in scene 3, lines 122–26.
3. What other character(s) contribute(s) in a similar way to the atmosphere or perform(s) the function that Banquo expresses? Support your answers with textual details.
4. What paradoxical statement do the witches make in scene 1 that Macbeth reiterates when he first meets them? What does this statement communicate about Macbeth's situation?
5. Which of the witches' two prophecies concerning Macbeth is not fulfilled by the end of act 1? What is the third prophecy? Do you expect it to come true?
6. What external conflict provides the historical and political setting for act 1? What two people are seen as traitors to Scotland? What becomes of them?
7. At what point does Macbeth first experience internal conflict? How does he respond to it? Why does he say that "This supernatural soliciting / Cannot be ill, cannot be good" (1.3.130–31)?
8. To whom is Duncan referring in scene 4, lines 13–14a? What does he mean when he says, "There's no art / To find the mind's construction in the face" (ll. 11b–12)? What is ironic about Macbeth's entrance at that particular time?
9. How does Lady Macbeth's initial reaction to the witches' prophecy differ from that of Macbeth? What traits does she consider weaknesses in her husband? What does her reaction to the news that Duncan is coming tell you about her character?
10. What misgivings (internal conflict) does Macbeth reveal in his soliloquy at the beginning of scene 7 (ll. 1–28a)? How does Lady Macbeth convince him that he should proceed with the murder? How does he react to her plan? Is her influence greater than the witches'?
11. Identify three violations of the Great Chain of Being in act 1. Indicate who violates the order, how it is violated, and which sphere has been violated (social, political, etc.). Support your answers with textual details.
12. Evaluate two instances of characters' words and actions in the areas of deception, responsibility to civil authority, and male and female roles. Draw upon evidence from the play as well as from the Scriptures to support your evaluations.

ANALYZE: *Imagery and Symbol*

In *Macbeth*, as in his other works, Shakespeare used vibrant **imagery** (p. 75) to ignite audiences' imaginations and evoke ideas beyond the printed text or performed line. For instance, the following quotation uses a series of images to illustrate various beneficial aspects of sleep, which itself is a recurring image in *Macbeth*: "Sleep that knits up the ravell'd sleave of care, / The death of each day's life, sore labor's bath, / Balm of hurt minds, great nature's second course, / Chief nourisher in life's feast" (2.2.34–37a). In visualizing each image, listeners or readers deepen their understanding of sleep.

Additionally, Shakespeare infuses deeper meaning into specific images to create symbols (p. 37). For example, in context of the play's themes, sleep suggests more than just rest. Note how Macbeth's statement in act 2 that he "heard a voice cry, 'Sleep no more! / Macbeth does murder sleep'—the innocent sleep" (2.32–33) clearly describes more than the literal fact that he has murdered the sleeping King Duncan. What does Macbeth imply by saying he has killed sleep? Why can he himself no longer sleep? What might sleep symbolize for him? As you read, try to infer how Shakespeare uses sleep and other images as symbols to point out something beyond their literal meaning.

READ: *Trace Theme*

All elements, including symbols and imagery, point to **themes**, recurring or emerging ideas that provide coherence as they embody and emphasize a work's message. As you read, look for themes by noting common threads and dramatic contrasts. For instance, the characterization of Macbeth repeatedly references and illustrates ambition. His thoughts revolve around the witches' prophecy of his kingship and his resulting choice to kill Duncan. In fact, Macbeth uses the imagery of horse and rider to picture his "vaulting ambition, which o'erleaps itself / And falls on th' other [side]" (1.7.27–28). Dramatic contrasts highlight another theme encapsulated in the witches' statement that "fair is foul, and foul is fair" (1.1.11). Duncan's betrayal by the Thane of Cawdor illustrates one aspect of this theme: as he says, "There's no art / To find the mind's construction in the face" (1.4.11b–12). What does Duncan mean by this statement? How else does this theme surface in the play?

CREATE: *Psychological Profiles of Characters*

At this point in the play, the Macbeths are plotting to kill Duncan. To help you follow the couple as they proceed, you will be asked to create a psychological profile at the end of act 2. Imagine that you are a criminal psychologist analyzing Macbeth and Lady Macbeth as suspects of Duncan's murder. As you read, carefully observe the characters' motivations and states of mind before, during, and after the crime. Your profile should include a summary of your investigation into their minds, based on textual evidence. Next, write a conclusion based on your findings, describing their development as criminals. What has their ambition done to them? Finally, make predictions, proposing the future trajectory of each. At the end of the play, you will be asked to review your initial assessment and write a revised conclusion that includes any additional evidence you have gathered.

OBJECTIVES

- Identify and interpret key imagery in a work.
- Analyze a work's use of symbol.
- Trace a work's developing theme.
- Evaluate a character's choices in light of Scripture.
- Evaluate an author's worldview from a biblical perspective.

VOCABULARY

husbandry (hŭz′bən-drē) *n.* Careful management or conservation of resources; economy.

largess (lär-zhĕs′) *n.* Money or gifts bestowed.

augment (ôg-mĕnt′) *tr.v.* To make (something already developed or well under way) greater, as in size, extent, or quantity.

prate (prāt) *intr.v.* To talk idly and at length; chatter.

equivocate (ĭ-kwĭv′ə-kāt′) *intr.v.* To use *equivocal* (*adj.* Open to two or more interpretations and often intended to conceal the truth) language in an attempt to mislead.

suborn (sə-bôrn′) *tr.v.* To induce (a person) to commit an unlawful or evil act.

ACT 2

(Enter BANQUO *and* FLEANCE *with a torch [bearer] before him.)*

BANQUO. How goes the night, boy?
FLEANCE. The moon is down; I have not heard the clock.
BANQUO. And she goes down at twelve.
FLEANCE. I take't, 'tis later, sir.
BANQUO. Hold, take my sword. There's **husbandry** in heaven,
Their candles are all out. Take thee that too.
(Gives him his belt and dagger.)
A heavy summons° lies like lead upon me,
And yet I would not sleep. Merciful powers,
Restrain in me the cursèd thoughts that nature
Gives way to in repose!
(Enter MACBETH *and a* SERVANT *with a torch.)*
Give me my sword.
Who's there?
MACBETH. A friend.
BANQUO. What, sir, not yet at rest? the King's a-bed.
He hath been in unusual pleasure, and
Sent forth great **largess** to your offices.°
This diamond he greets your wife withal,
By the name of most kind hostess, and shut up
In measureless content.
MACBETH. Being unprepar'd,
Our will became the servant to defect,
Which else should free have wrought.°
BANQUO. All's well.
I dreamt last night of the three weird sisters:
To you they have show'd some truth.
MACBETH. I think not of them;

6 heavy summons: i.e., of sleep

13 great . . . offices: generous gifts of money to your household officers

18 Our . . . wrought: We would have entertained him more lavishly had we known earlier that he was coming.

husbandry (hŭz′bən-drē) *n.* Careful management or conservation of resources; economy.

largess (lär-zhĕs′) *n.* Money or gifts bestowed.

Yet when we can entreat an hour to serve,
We would spend it in some words upon that business,
If you would grant the time.

BANQUO. At your kind'st leisure.

MACBETH. If you shall cleave to my consent, when 'tis,°
It shall make honor for you.

BANQUO. So I lose none
In seeking to **augment** it, but still keep
My bosom franchis'd° and allegiance clear,
I shall be counsell'd.°

MACBETH. Good repose the while!

BANQUO. Thanks, sir; the like to you!

(Exit BANQUO with FLEANCE.)

MACBETH. Go bid thy mistress, when my drink is ready,
She strike upon the bell. Get thee to bed.

(Exit SERVANT.)

Is this a dagger which I see before me,
The handle toward my hand? Come, let me clutch thee:
I have thee not, and yet I see thee still.
Art thou not, fatal vision, sensible°
To feeling as to sight? or art thou but
A dagger of the mind, a false creation,
Proceeding from the heat-oppressèd° brain?
I see thee yet, in form as palpable
As this which now I draw.
Thou marshal'st me the way that I was going,
And such an instrument I was to use.
Mine eyes are made the fools o' th' other senses,
Or else worth all the rest. I see thee still;
And on thy blade and dudgeon° gouts° of blood,
Which was not so before. There's no such thing:
It is the bloody business which informs
Thus to mine eyes. Now o'er the one half-world °
Nature seems dead, and wicked dreams abuse
The curtain'd sleep; witchcraft celebrates
Pale Hecate's° off'rings;° and wither'd Murder,
Alarum'd by his sentinel, the wolf,
Whose howl's his watch, thus with his stealthy pace,
With Tarquin's° ravishing strides, towards his design
Moves like a ghost. Thou sure and firm-set earth,
Hear not my steps, which way they walk, for fear
Thy very stones **prate** of my whereabout,
And take the present horror from the time,
Which now suits with° it. Whiles I threat, he lives:
Words to the heat of deeds too cold breath gives.

(A bell rings.)

I go, and it is done; the bell invites me.
Hear it not, Duncan, for it is a knell
That summons thee to heaven or to hell. R

(Exit.)

24 cleave . . . 'tis: support my cause at the appropriate time

27 bosom franchis'd: conscience clear

28 be counsell'd: listen to your proposal

35 sensible: perceptible

38 heat-oppressed: feverish

45 dudgeon: handle / **gouts**: drops

48 half-world: hemisphere

51 Hecate: goddess of the underworld and witchcraft / **off'rings**: rites

54 Tarquin: legendary Roman prince who ravished Lucrece

59 suits with: matches

augment (ôg-mĕnt') *tr.v.* To make (something already developed or well under way) greater, as in size, extent, or quantity.

prate (prāt) *intr.v.* To talk idly and at length; chatter.

Theme: How do lines 32–63 touch on the two themes mentioned in the Read paragraph (p. 229)? How might Macbeth's hallucinations reflect one of these themes? R

(Enter LADY MACBETH.*)*

LADY MACBETH. That which hath made them drunk hath made me bold;
What hath quench'd them hath given me fire. Hark! Peace!
It was the owl that shriek'd, the fatal bellman°
Which gives the stern'st good-night. He is about it:
The doors are open; and the surfeited grooms°
Do mock their charge° with snores. I have drugg'd their possets,°
That death and nature do contend about them,
Whether they live or die.

MACBETH. *(Within.)* Who's there? What ho?

LADY MACBETH. Alack, I am afraid they have awak'd,
And 'tis not done; th' attempt, and not the deed,
Confounds us. Hark! I laid their daggers ready,
He could not miss 'em. Had he not resembled
My father as he slept, I had done't.

(Enter MACBETH.*)*

My husband!

MACBETH. I have done the deed. Didst thou not hear a noise?

LADY MACBETH. I heard the owl scream and the crickets cry.
Did not you speak?

MACBETH. When?

LADY MACBETH. Now.

MACBETH. As I descended?

LADY MACBETH. Ay.

MACBETH. Hark! Who lies i' th' second chamber?

LADY MACBETH. Donalbain.

MACBETH. *(Looking on his hand[.])* This is a sorry sight.

LADY MACBETH. A foolish thought, to say a sorry sight.

MACBETH. There's one did laugh in's sleep, and one cried, "Murder!"
That they did wake each other. I stood and heard them;
But they did say their prayers, and address'd them
Again to sleep.

3 fatal bellman: allusion to the custom of a bellman's ringing a bell at midnight outside the cell of a condemned man as a grim bidding to repentance

5 surfeited grooms: drunken chamberlains

6 charge: assigned duty; i.e., guarding the sleeping king / **possets:** hot alcoholic drinks taken just before bedtime

LADY MACBETH. There are two lodg'd together.

MACBETH. One cried, "God bless us!" and "Amen!" the other,
As they had seen me with these hangman's hands.°
List'ning their fear, I could not say "Amen,"
When they did say "God bless us!"

LADY MACBETH. Consider it not so deeply.

MACBETH. But wherefore could not I pronounce "Amen"?
I had most need of blessing, and "Amen"
Stuck in my throat.

LADY MACBETH. These deeds must not be thought
After these ways; so, it will make us mad.

MACBETH. Methought I heard a voice cry, "Sleep no more!
Macbeth does murder sleep"—the innocent sleep,
Sleep that knits up the ravell'd sleave° of care,
The death of each day's life, sore labor's bath,
Balm of hurt minds, great nature's second course,°
Chief nourisher in life's feast.

LADY MACBETH. What do you mean?

MACBETH. Still it cried, "Sleep no more!" to all the house;
"Glamis hath murd'red sleep, and therefore Cawdor
Shall sleep no more—Macbeth shall sleep no more."

LADY MACBETH. Who was it that thus cried? Why, worthy thane,
You do unbend° your noble strength, to think
So brainsickly of things. Go get some water,
And wash this filthy witness from your hand. **A**
Why did you bring these daggers from the place?
They must lie there. Go carry them, and smear
The sleepy grooms with blood.

MACBETH. I'll go no more.
I am afraid to think what I have done;
Look on't again I dare not.

LADY MACBETH. Infirm of purpose!
Give me the daggers. The sleeping and the dead
Are but as pictures; 'tis the eye of childhood
That fears a painted devil. If he do bleed,
I'll gild the faces of the grooms withal,
For it must seem their guilt.

(Exit. Knock within.)

MACBETH. Whence is that knocking?
How is't with me, when every noise appalls me?
What hands are here? Hah! they pluck out mine eyes.
Will all great Neptune's° ocean wash this blood
Clean from my hand? No; this my hand will rather
The multitudinous seas incarnadine,°
Making the green one red.

(Enter LADY MACBETH.)

LADY MACBETH. My hands are of your color; but I shame
To wear a heart so white. *(Knock.)* I hear a knocking
At the south entry. Retire we to our chamber.
A little water clears us of this deed;
How easy is it then! Your constancy

25 **hangman's hands:** an allusion to the symbolic red gloves worn by the actor playing Herod in the medieval mystery plays

34 **ravell'd sleave:** tangled skein as of yarn

36 **second course:** the main part of a meal

42 **unbend:** relax

57 **Neptune:** the Roman god of the sea

59 **incarnadine:** make the color of blood

Symbol: What are some indicators from lines 14–44 that Macbeth is feeling guilty? What two images help symbolize his guilt? **A**

Hath left you unattended.° *(Knock.)* Hark, more knocking.
Get on your nightgown, lest occasion call us
And show us to be watchers. Be not lost
So poorly in your thoughts.

MACBETH. To know my deed, 'twere best not know myself. *(Knock.)*
Wake Duncan with thy knocking! I would thou couldst! **E**

(Exeunt.)

66 left . . . unattended: deserted you

SCENE 3

(Enter a PORTER. *Knocking within.)*

PORTER. Here's a knocking indeed! If a man were porter of Hell Gate, he should have old° turning the key. *(Knock.)* Knock, knock, knock! Who's there, i' th' name of Belzebub?° Here's a farmer, that hang'd himself on th' expectation of plenty.° Come in time!° Have napkins° enow about you, here you'll sweat for't. *(Knock.)* Knock, knock! Who's there, in th' other devil's name? Faith, here's an equivocator, that could swear in both the scales against either scale, who committed treason enough for God's sake, yet could not **equivocate** to heaven. O, come in, equivocator. *(Knock.)* Knock, knock, knock! Who's there? Faith, here's an English tailor come hither for stealing out of a French hose.° Come in, tailor, here you may roast your goose.° *(Knock.)* Knock, knock! Never at quiet! What are you? But this place is too cold for hell. I'll devilporter it no further. I had thought to have let in some of all professions that go the primrose way to th' everlasting bonfire. *(Knock.)* Anon, anon! *(Opens the gate.)* I pray you remember the porter.

2 have old: become an old man

3 Belzebub: the chief of the angels who fell with Satan

4 farmer . . . plenty: one who had hoarded his grain, hoping for a bad harvest and higher prices, but who despaired when the harvest proved plentiful

5 Come . . . time: You've arrived at an opportune moment. / **napkins:** handkerchiefs

12 hose: Breeches. The tailor stole some of his customer's cloth.

13 roast . . . goose: heat your iron

(Enter MACDUFF *and* LENNOX.*)*

MACDUFF. Was it so late, friend, ere you went to bed,
That you do lie so late?

PORTER. Faith, sir, we were carousing till the second cock.°

MACDUFF. I believe drink gave thee the lie last night.

PORTER. That it did, sir, i' the very throat on me; but I requited him for his lie, and, I think, being too strong for him, though he took up my legs sometime, yet I made a shift to cast him.°

MACDUFF. Is thy master stirring?

21 second cock: i.e., 3:00 a.m.

25 That . . . him: Here the Porter describes his bout with drink as a wrestling match.

(Enter MACBETH.*)*

Our knocking has awak'd him; here he comes.

LENNOX. Good morrow, noble sir.

MACBETH. Good morrow, both.

MACDUFF. Is the King stirring, worthy Thane?

MACBETH. Not yet.

MACDUFF. He did command me to call timely° on him.
I have almost slipp'd the hour.

MACBETH. I'll bring you to him.

MACDUFF. I know this is a joyful trouble to you;
But yet 'tis one.

MACBETH. The labor we delight in physics° pain.
This is the door.

30 timely: early

34 physics: cures

Profile: What details from lines 47–71 reveal how Macbeth has already been affected psychologically by murdering Duncan? **E**

equivocate (ĭ-kwĭv'ə-kāt') *intr.v.* To use *equivocal* (*adj.* Open to two or more interpretations and often intended to conceal the truth) language in an attempt to mislead.

MACDUFF. I'll make so bold to call,
For 'tis my limited service.°

(*Exit* MACDUFF.)

LENNOX. Goes the King hence today?
MACBETH. He does; he did appoint so.
LENNOX. The night has been unruly. Where we lay,
Our chimneys were blown down, and as they say,
Lamentings heard i' th' air, strange screams of death,
And prophesying, with accents terrible,
Of dire combustion,° and confus'd events
New hatch'd to th' woeful time. The obscure bird°
Clamor'd the livelong night. Some say, the earth
Was feverous, and did shake.
MACBETH. 'Twas a rough night.
LENNOX. My young remembrance cannot parallel
A fellow to it.

(*Enter* MACDUFF.)

MACDUFF. O horror, horror, horror! Tongue nor heart
Cannot conceive nor name thee!
MACBETH, LENNOX. What's the matter?
MACDUFF. Confusion now hath made his masterpiece!
Most sacrilegious murder hath broke ope
The Lord's anointed temple,° and stole thence
The life o' th' building! R
MACBETH. What is't you say—the life?
LENNOX. Mean you his Majesty?
MACDUFF. Approach the chamber, and destroy your sight
With a new Gorgon.° Do not bid me speak;
See, and then speak yourselves.

(*Exeunt* MACBETH *[and]* LENNOX.)

Awake, awake!
Ring the alarum-bell! Murder and treason!
Banquo and Donalbain! Malcolm, awake!
Shake off this downy sleep, death's counterfeit,
And look upon death itself! Up, up, and see
The great doom's image!° Malcolm! Banquo!
As from your graves rise up, and walk like sprites,°
To countenance° this horror! Ring the bell.

(*Bell rings.*)

(*Enter* LADY MACBETH.)

LADY MACBETH. What's the business,
That such a hideous trumpet calls to parley°
The sleepers of the house? Speak, speak!
MACDUFF. O gentle lady,
'Tis not for you to hear what I can speak:
The repetition in a woman's ear
Would murder as it fell.

(*Enter* BANQUO.)

O Banquo, Banquo,
Our royal master's murder'd!
LADY MACBETH. Woe, alas!
What, in our house?

36 limited service: duty

42 combustion: tumult

43 obscure bird: the owl, bird of darkness

52 The . . . temple: the body of the king

56 Gorgon: one of the three Greek mythological sisters whose hair was entwined with serpents and whose horrible faces turned anyone to stone who looked on them

62 The . . . image: a day like Doomsday

63 sprites: spirits

64 countenance: give approval to

66 parley: a conference for the purpose of establishing a truce among enemies

Theme: How do the images in lines 38–45 and 50–53 support the theme of social disorder? R

BANQUO. Too cruel any where.
Dear Duff, I prithee contradict thyself,
And say it is not so.

(Enter MACBETH and LENNOX.)

MACBETH. Had I but died an hour before this chance,°
I had liv'd a blessèd time; for from this instant
There's nothing serious in mortality:
All is but toys:° renown and grace is dead,
The wine of life is drawn, and the mere lees
Is left° this vault° to brag of.

(Enter MALCOLM and DONALBAIN.)

DONALBAIN. What is amiss?
MACBETH. You are, and do not know't.
The spring, the head, the fountain of your blood
Is stopp'd, the very source of it is stopped.
MACDUFF. Your royal father's murder'd.
MALCOLM. O, by whom?
LENNOX. Those of his chamber, as it seem'd, had done't.
Their hands and faces were all badg'd with blood.
So were their daggers, which unwip'd we found
Upon their pillows. They star'd and were distracted;
No man's life was to be trusted with them.
MACBETH. O, yet I do repent me of my fury,
That I did kill them.
MACDUFF. Wherefore did you so?
MACBETH. Who can be wise, amaz'd, temp'rate, and furious,
Loyal, and neutral, in a moment? No man.
Th' expedition° of my violent love
Outrun the pauser,° reason. Here lay Duncan,
His silver skin lac'd with his golden blood,
And his gash'd stabs look'd like a breach in nature
For ruin's wasteful entrance; there the murderers,
Steep'd in the colors of their trade, their daggers
Unmannerly breech'd° with gore. Who could refrain,
That had a heart to love, and in that heart
Courage to make 's love known?
LADY MACBETH. Help me hence, ho!

[Faints.]

MACDUFF. Look to the lady.
MALCOLM. *(Aside to DONALBAIN.)* Why do we hold our tongues,
That most may claim this argument for ours?
DONALBAIN. *(Aside to MALCOLM.)* What should be spoken here, where our fate,
Hid in an auger-hole,° may rush and seize us?
Let's away,
Our tears are not yet brew'd.
MALCOLM. *(Aside to DONALBAIN.)* Nor our strong sorrow
Upon the foot of motion.°
BANQUO. Look to the lady.

(LADY MACBETH is carried out.)

And when we have our naked frailties hid,°

75 chance: event

78 toys: trifles

80 The . . . left: The pleasures of life are gone and only the unpleasant (lees or dregs) remains. / **vault:** world

94 expedition: haste

95 pauser: restrainer

100 Unmannerly breech'd: inappropriately sheathed; i.e., in blood

106 auger-hole: a very small cranny

109 Upon . . . motion: Moving. It is not yet apparent.

110 frailties hid: bodies clothed

Profile: How many innocent lives has Macbeth's unchecked ambition driven him to take?

That suffer in exposure, let us meet
And question this most bloody piece of work,
To know it further. Fears and scruples° shake us.
In the great hand of God I stand, and thence
Against the undivulg'd pretense° I fight
Of treasonous malice.

MACDUFF. And so do I.

ALL. So all.

MACBETH. Let's briefly° put on manly readiness,
And meet i' th' hall together.

ALL. Well contented.

(Exeunt all but MALCOLM *and* DONALBAIN.*)*

113 scruples: doubts, suspicions

115 undivulg'd pretense: secret contrivance

117 briefly: quickly

MALCOLM. What will you do? Let's not consort with them.
To show an unfelt sorrow is an office
Which the false man does easy. I'll to England.

DONALBAIN. To Ireland, I; our separated fortune
Shall keep us both the safer. Where we are,
There's daggers in men's smiles; the near in blood,
The nearer bloody.°

MALCOLM. This murderous shaft that's shot
Hath not yet lighted, and our safest way
Is to avoid the aim. Therefore to horse,
And let us not be dainty of leave-taking,
But shift away. There's warrant in that theft
Which steals itself,° when there's no mercy left.

(Exeunt.)

125 The . . . bloody: The closer kin to Duncan, the more likely we are to be murdered ourselves.

130 There's . . . itself: To escape stealthily at this point is justifiable.

Theme: Reread lines 91–116. How do the characters' words, especially Macbeth's and Banquo's, reveal that things are not as they appear?

Outside Macbeth's castle

(Enter ROSS *with an* OLD MAN.*)*

OLD MAN. Three score and ten I can remember well,
Within the volume of which time I have seen
Hours dreadful and things strange; but this sore° night
Hath trifled former knowings.

ROSS. Ha, good father,
Thou seest the heavens, as troubled with man's act,
Threatens his bloody stage.° By th' clock 'tis day,
And yet dark night strangles the travelling lamp.°
Is't night's predominance, or the day's shame,
That darkness does the face of the earth entomb,
When living light should kiss it?

OLD MAN. 'Tis unnatural,
Even like the deed that's done. On Tuesday last,
A falcon, tow'ring in her pride of place,°
Was by a mousing owl hawk'd at, and kill'd.

ROSS. And Duncan's horses (a thing most strange and certain),
Beauteous and swift, the minions of their race,
Turn'd wild in nature, broke their stalls, flung out,
Contending 'gainst obedience, as they would make
War with mankind.

OLD MAN. 'Tis said, they eat each other.

ROSS. They did so—to th' amazement of mine eyes
That look'd upon't. A

(Enter MACDUFF.*)*

3 **sore:** miserable

6 **heavens . . . stage:** The "heavens" was the canopy roof that stretched over part of the stage in Shakespeare's theatre; hence this passage puns on act and stage.

7 **travelling lamp:** the sun

12 **tow'ring . . . place:** soaring at the highest point of her flight

Imagery: How does the imagery in lines 1–20 accentuate one of the play's themes? A

Here comes the good Macduff.
How goes the world, sir, now?

MACDUFF. Why, see you not?

ROSS. Is't known who did this more than bloody deed?

MACDUFF. Those that Macbeth hath slain.

ROSS. Alas the day,
What good could they pretend?

MACDUFF. They were **suborned**.
Malcolm and Donalbain, the King's two sons,
Are stol'n away and fled, which puts upon them
Suspicion of the deed.

ROSS. 'Gainst nature still!
Thriftless ambition, that will ravin up°
Thine own life's means! Then 'tis most like
The sovereignty will fall upon Macbeth.

MACDUFF. He is already nam'd, and gone to Scone°
To be invested.

ROSS. Where is Duncan's body?

MACDUFF. Carried to Colmekill,°
The sacred storehouse of his predecessors
And guardian of their bones.

ROSS. Will you to Scone?

MACDUFF. No, cousin, I'll to Fife.

ROSS. Well, I will thither.

MACDUFF. Well, may you see things well done there: adieu,
Lest our old robes sit easier than our new!

ROSS. Farewell, father.

OLD MAN. God's benison° go with you, and with those
That would make good of bad, and friends of foes!

(Exeunt.)

28 ravin up: consume greedily

31 Scone: site of the royal residence of Scotland and place of coronation

33 Colmekill: ancient burial place of Scottish kings

40 benison: blessing

suborn (sə-bôrn′) *tr.v.* To induce (a person) to commit an unlawful or evil act.

THINK AND DISCUSS

1. Define *imagery* and *symbol* and identify an example of each from *Macbeth.*
2. How does Macbeth feel about having murdered Duncan?
3. How does Lady Macbeth tend to affect Macbeth?
4. How has the natural world been upset in act 2?
5. Who do you predict will be held responsible for Duncan's murder? Explain your answer with details from the text.
6. Explain how your example of imagery and your example of symbol (from question 1) support a theme in the play.
7. In scene 2, what keeps Lady Macbeth from murdering Duncan herself? What does this indicate about her character?
8. Review Donalbain's and Malcolm's statements in act 2, scene 3, lines 121–22, 124. What major theme of the work do these lines reflect? Briefly explain your answer.
9. Compare Banquo's attitude in response to the witches' prophecies with Macbeth's response. Do they value the advice differently or similarly? Explain.
10. Identify three ways Lady Macbeth's thoughts, words, or actions reflect or violate the current social and natural order. Briefly explain your answer.
11. List three of the effects of Macbeth's ambition on himself and others. What do these effects illustrate about unchecked ambition?
12. Create a psychological profile, analyzing the suspects Macbeth and Lady Macbeth, according to the instructions in the Create section (p. 229).

ANALYZE: *Verbal and Dramatic Irony*

Situational and verbal irony, two types of irony in *The Canterbury Tales* (p. 88), also occur in act 3 of *Macbeth*. The **verbal irony** in this act takes primarily two forms—sarcasm and hyperbole. Words spoken in **sarcasm**, or mock praise, mean the opposite of what the speaker says. Consider Job's response to poor counsel from his friends: "No doubt but ye are the people, and wisdom shall die with you" (Job 12:1–2). **Hyperbole**, or exaggeration, is an obvious overstatement to make a point or emphasize meaning. If a classmate said, "I died of embarrassment," your response would be sympathy for the humiliation—not horror to be speaking to a ghost. Similarly, in act 2 Macbeth asks, "Will all great Neptune's ocean wash this blood / Clean from my hand?" (2.57). His exaggeration reveals his desperation to take back his actions.

Dramatic irony, a third major type of irony, occurs when a reader or audience is made aware of a plot development that is unknown to a story's characters. The book of Esther provides an example in Haman's plot against the Jewish people. Unaware that Queen Esther and her uncle Mordecai (who saved the king's life) are Jewish, Haman plans to massacre the Jews. In addition, he builds a gallows on which to hang Mordecai. Readers, who *are* aware of these facts, experience tension as they wait for these realities to collide. Similarly, in act 3 of *Macbeth*, the reader is privy to plot developments of which certain characters remain ignorant, creating dramatic irony. Examine instances of both verbal and dramatic irony as you read act 3.

READ: *Trace Plot Development*

Plot is defined as a connected series of events arranged to produce a definite sense of movement toward a specific goal. The **exposition** introduces the setting, characters, and situation, which comes in act 1 of *Macbeth*. The **inciting incident** is the event that introduces the conflict and sets it in motion. Can you determine the inciting incident in act 1? The events that follow the inciting incident and lead up to the crisis compose the **rising action**. The **crisis** is the major turning point for the protagonist, the point at which something happens that affects the outcome of the story and determines the future of the main character. In a tragedy the crisis is often tied to a reversal of fortune for the tragic hero (p. 209). Where in act 3 do circumstances begin to unravel for Macbeth? As you read, decide at what point the plot reaches the moment of highest emotional intensity—the **climax**—which may or may not be the same moment as the crisis. The events that unfold from the crisis and lead to the conclusion form the **falling action**. The final outcome of a story—the last element of the plot in which the major complications are explained or settled—is called the **denouement**, or resolution. In *Macbeth,* what key piece of explanatory information is withheld until the final scene?

EVALUATE: *Results of Characters' Choices*

In a biblical worldview, evil is punished and good is rewarded—if not now, then at least in eternity. Literature that operates on this foundational principle reflects a biblical view of morality. For instance, if a character makes a morally good choice, he or she can expect blessing and prosperity (though perhaps not immediately). If, however, a character makes an immoral choice, he or she can ultimately expect negative consequences (physical, emotional, social, etc.). In act 3 the Macbeths begin experiencing some of the results of their actions. As you read, examine these results and consider what they suggest about Shakespeare's worldview. Do the Macbeths encounter positive or negative results? What do they lose or gain? In your evaluation, consider what Psalm 38:1–7, 32:3–4; 1 Samuel 26:9; and Mark 8:36 reveal about the physical and emotional results of choices. Does Shakespeare's portrayal of the results of characters' choices match that of the Scriptures?

OBJECTIVES

- Identify a work's key plot points.
- Examine how plot intersects with other major elements.
- Analyze a work's use of verbal and dramatic irony.
- Investigate how irony in a work informs tone and theme.
- Evaluate a work's portrayal of morality from a biblical worldview.

VOCABULARY

verity (vĕr′ĭ-tē) *n.* The quality or condition of being true, factual, or real.

parricide (păr′ĭ-sīd′) *n.* 1. The killing of one's father, mother, or other near relative. 2. The killing of the ruler of one's country.

sundry (sŭn′drē) *adj.* Various; miscellaneous.

jocund (jŏk′ənd) *adj.* Sprightly and lighthearted in disposition, character, or quality.

traffic (trăf′ĭk) *intr.v.* To carry on trade or other dealings.

homage (hŏm′ĭj) *n.* Formal acknowledgment by a vassal of allegiance to his lord under feudal law.

The palace at Forres

(Enter BANQUO.*)*

BANQUO. Thou hast it now: King, Cawdor, Glamis, all,
As the weird women promis'd, and I fear
Thou play'dst most foully for't; yet it was said
It should not stand in thy posterity,
But that myself should be the root and father
Of many kings. If there come truth from them—
As upon thee, Macbeth, their speeches shine—
Why, by the **veritie**s on thee made good,
May they not be my oracles as well,
And set me up in hope? But hush, no more.

(Sennet° sounded. Enter MACBETH *as King,* LADY MACBETH *as Queen,* LENNOX, ROSS, LORDS, *and* ATTENDANTS *.)*

Sennet: a trumpet call signaling ceremonial entrances and exits

MACBETH. Here's our chief guest.
LADY MACBETH. If he had been forgotten,
It had been as a gap in our great feast,
And all-thing° unbecoming.
MACBETH. Tonight we hold a solemn supper,° sir,
And I'll request your presence.

13 all-thing: altogether

14 solemn supper: formal banquet

BANQUO. Let your Highness
Command upon me, to the which my duties
Are with a most indissoluble tie
For ever knit.
MACBETH. Ride you this afternoon?
BANQUO. Ay, my good lord.
MACBETH. We should have else desir'd your good advice,
Which still hath been both grave and prosperous,
In this day's council; but we'll take tomorrow.
Is't far you ride?
BANQUO. As far, my lord, as will fill up the time
Twixt this and supper. Go not my horse the better°
I must become a borrower of the night
For a dark hour or twain.
MACBETH. Fail not our feast.

25 Go . . . better: if my horse does not travel faster than I expect him to

verity (vĕr′ĭ-tē) *n.* The quality or condition of being true, factual, or real.

BANQUO. My lord, I will not.
MACBETH. We hear our bloody cousins are bestow'd
In England and in Ireland, not confessing
Their cruel **parricide**, filling their hearers
With strange invention. But of that tomorrow,
When therewithal we shall have cause of state
Craving us jointly.° Hie you to horse; adieu,
Till you return at night. Goes Fleance with you?
BANQUO. Ay, my good lord. Our time does call upon's.
MACBETH. I wish your horses swift and sure of foot;
And so I do commend you to their backs.
Farewell.

(Exit BANQUO.)

Let every man be master of his time
Till seven at night. To make society
The sweeter welcome, we will keep ourself
Till supper-time alone; while° then, God be with you!

(Exeunt [all but] MACBETH and a SERVANT.)

Sirrah,° a word with you. Attend those men
Our pleasure?
SERVANT. They are, my lord, without the palace gate.
MACBETH. Bring them before us.

(Exit SERVANT.)

To be thus is nothing,
But to be safely thus. Our fears in Banquo
Stick deep, and in his royalty of nature°
Reigns that which would be fear'd. 'Tis much he dares,
And to° that dauntless temper of his mind,
He hath a wisdom that doth guide his valor
To act in safety. There is none but he
Whose being I do fear; and under him
My Genius is rebuk'd, as it is said
Mark Antony's was by Caesar. He chid the sisters
When first they put the name of king upon me,
And bade them speak to him; then prophet-like
They hail'd him father to a line of kings.
Upon my head they plac'd a fruitless crown,
And put a barren sceptre in my gripe,°
Thence to be wrench'd with an unlineal hand,
No son of mine succeeding. If't be so,
For Banquo's issue have I fil'd° my mind,
For them the gracious Duncan have I murder'd,
Put rancors in the vessel of my peace
Only for them, and mine eternal jewel°
Given to the common enemy of man,°
To make them kings—the seed of Banquo kings!
Rather than so, come fate into the list,
And champion me to th' utterance!° Who's there?

34 Craving . . . jointly: calling for our joint consideration

43 while: until

44 Sirrah: a contemptuous form of address; fellow

49 royalty . . . nature: regal nature

51 to: in addition to

61 gripe: grip, hold

64 fil'd: defiled

67 mine . . . jewel: i.e., my soul

68 the . . . man: Satan

71 champion . . . utterance: fight me to the death

parricide (păr′ĭ-sīd′) *n.* 1. The killing of one's father, mother, or other near relative. 2. The killing of the ruler of one's country.

Plot: What news is discovered in lines 29–32? Of what plot element is this news a part?

Reading Check: Reread the entire soliloquy (ll. 47–71). What do lines 47–48 mean? What concerns Macbeth?

(Enter SERVANT *and two* MURDERERS.*)*

Now go to the door, and stay there till we call.

(Exit SERVANT.*)*

Was it not yesterday we spoke together?
FIRST MURDERER. It was, so please your Highness.
MACBETH. Well then, now
Have you consider'd of my speeches? Know
That it was he in the times past which held you
So under fortune,° which you thought had been
Our innocent self. This I made good to you
In our last conference, pass'd in probation with° you:
How you were borne in hand,° how cross'd, the instruments,
Who wrought with them, and all things else that might
To° half a soul and to a notion craz'd
Say, "Thus did Banquo."
FIRST MURDERER. You made it known to us.
MACBETH. I did so; and went further, which is now
Our point of second meeting. Do you find
Your patience so predominant in your nature
That you can let this go? Are you so gospell'd,°
To pray for this good man, and for his issue,
Whose heavy hand hath bow'd you to the grave,
And beggar'd yours for ever?
FIRST MURDERER. We are men, my liege.
MACBETH. Ay, in the catalogue ye go for men,
As hounds and greyhounds, mongrels, spaniels, curs,
Shoughs, water-rugs, and demi-wolves ° are clept°
All by the name of dogs; the valued file°
Distinguishes the swift, the slow, the subtle,
The house-keeper,° the hunter, every one
According to the gift which bounteous nature
Hath in him clos'd;° whereby he does receive
Particular addition,° from° the bill
That writes them all alike:° and so of men.
Now if you have a station in the file,°
Not i' th' worst rank of manhood, say't,
And I will put that business in your bosoms,
Whose execution takes your enemy off,
Grapples you to the heart and love of us,
Who wear our health but sickly in his life,°
Which in his death were perfect. A
SECOND MURDERER. I am one, my liege,
Whom the vile blows and buffets of the world
Hath so incens'd that I am reckless what
I do to spite the world.
FIRST MURDERER. And I another,
So weary with disasters, tugg'd with fortune,
That I would set my life on any chance,
To mend, or be rid on't.
MACBETH. Both of you
Know Banquo was your enemy.
BOTH MURDERERS. True, my lord.

77 held . . . fortune: caused your bad fortune

79 pass'd . . . with: proved to

80 borne . . . hand: deceived

82 To: even to

87 gospell'd: under the spell of biblical teachings concerning forgiveness

93 Shoughs . . . demi-wolves: shaggy-haired dogs, water spaniels, and hybrids of dogs and wolves / **clept:** called

94 the . . . file: list of those valued

96 house-keeper: watchdog

98 clos'd: enclosed

99 addition: distinction / **from:** in contrast to

100 writes . . . alike: lumps them all together

101 file: ranks

106 in . . . life: while Banquo lives

Irony: Reread lines 91–107. What is the meaning of lines 106–7 specifically? What type of verbal irony do these lines illustrate? A

MACBETH. So is he mine; and in such bloody distance,°
That every minute of his being thrusts
Against my near'st of life;° and though I could
With barefac'd power sweep him from my sight,
And bid my will avouch° it , yet I must not,
For certain friends that are both his and mine,
Whose loves I may not drop, but wail his fall
Who I myself struck down. And thence it is
That I to your assistance do make love,
Masking the business from the common eye
For **sundry** weighty reasons.

SECOND MURDERER. We shall, my lord,
Perform what you command us.

FIRST MURDERER. Though our lives—

MACBETH. Your spirits shine through you. Within this hour, at most,
I will advise you where to plant yourselves,
Acquaint you with the perfect spy o' th' time,°
The moment on't, for't must be done tonight,
And something° from the palace, always thought°
That I require a clearness;° and with him—
To leave no rubs nor botches in the work—
Fleance his son, that keeps him company,
Whose absence is no less material to me
Than is his father's, must embrace the fate
Of that dark hour. Resolve yourselves apart,°
I'll come to you anon.

BOTH MURDERERS. We are resolv'd, my lord.

MACBETH. I'll call upon you straight; abide within.

(Exeunt MURDERERS.)

It is concluded: Banquo, thy soul's flight,
If it find heaven, must find it out tonight.

(Exit.)

115 distance: enmity

117 near'st . . . life: heart

119 avouch: justify

129 th' . . . time: the exact time most favorable to your purposes

131 something: some distance from / **always thought:** it being

132 require . . . clearness: must remain above suspicion

137 Resolve . . . apart: Decide whether you will assist me.

(Enter LADY MACBETH and a SERVANT.)

LADY MACBETH. Is Banquo gone from court?

SERVANT. Ay, madam, but returns again tonight.

LADY MACBETH. Say to the King, I would attend his leisure
For a few words.

SERVANT. Madam, I will.

(Exit.)

LADY MACBETH. Nought's had, all's spent,
Where our desire is got without content;
'Tis safer to be that which we destroy
Than by destruction dwell in doubtful joy.

(Enter MACBETH.)

How now, my lord, why do you keep alone,
Of sorriest fancies your companions making,
Using° those thoughts which should indeed have died
With them they think on? Things without° all remedy
Should be without regard: what's done is done.

10 Using: entertaining

11 without: beyond

sundry (sŭn′drē) *adj.* Various; miscellaneous.

Reading Check: Whom does Macbeth instruct the murderers to kill in addition to Banquo?

MACBETH. We have scotch'd° the snake, not kill'd it;
She'll close° and be herself, whilest our poor malice
Remains in danger of her former tooth.
But let the frame of things disjoint,° both the worlds° suffer
Ere we will eat our meal in fear, and sleep
In the affliction of these terrible dreams
That shake us nightly. Better be with the dead,
Whom we, to gain our peace, have sent to peace,
Than on the torture of the mind to lie
In restless ecstasy.° Duncan is in his grave;
After life's fitful° fever he sleeps well.
Treason has done his worst; nor steel, nor poison,
Malice domestic, foreign levy, nothing,
Can touch him further. **E**

LADY MACBETH. Come on;
Gentle my lord, sleek o'er your rugged looks,
Be bright and jovial among your guests tonight.

MACBETH. So shall I, love, and so, I pray, be you.
Let your remembrance apply to Banquo,
Present him eminence both with eye and tongue:
Unsafe the while, that we
Must lave our honors in these flattering streams,°
And make our faces vizards° to our hearts,
Disguising what they are. **A**

LADY MACBETH. You must leave this.

MACBETH. O, full of scorpions° is my mind, dear wife!
Thou know'st that Banquo and his Fleance lives.

LADY MACBETH. But in them nature's copy is not eterne.°

MACBETH. There's comfort yet, they are assailable.
Then be thou **jocund**. Ere the bat hath flown
His cloister'd flight, ere to black Hecate's summons
The shard-borne° beetle with his drowsy hums
Hath rung night's yawning peal, there shall be done
A deed of dreadful note.

LADY MACBETH. What's to be done?

MACBETH. Be innocent of the knowledge, dearest chuck,°
Till thou applaud the deed. Come, seeling° Night,
Scarf up° the tender eye of pitiful° day,
And with thy bloody and invisible hand,
Cancel and tear to pieces that great bond
Which keeps me pale!° Light thickens, and the crow
Makes wing to th' rooky° wood;
Good things of day begin to droop and drowse,
Whiles night's black agents to their preys do rouse.
Thou marvel'st at my words but hold thee still:
Things bad begun make strong themselves by ill.
So prithee go with me.

(Exeunt.)

13 **scotch'd:** injured so as to cripple

14 **close:** heal

16 **frame . . . disjoint:** the universe dissolve / **both . . . worlds:** heaven and earth

22 **ecstasy:** frenzy

23 **fitful:** that which comes and goes

33 **Unsafe . . . streams:** We are not safe for the time being, so we must make ourselves look honorable by flattering Banquo and covering up our hatred.

34 **vizards:** masks

36 **scorpions:** symbol of treachery in Shakespeare's age

38 **in . . . eterne:** They are not immortal.

42 **shard-borne:** borne on scaly wings; dungbred

45 **chuck:** "a familiar term of endearment, derived from *chick*" (*OED*)

46 **seeling:** blinding

47 **Scarf up:** cover / **pitiful**: compassionate

50 **that . . . pale:** my conscience, that which restrains me from evil

51 **rooky:** black and full of rooks, or crows

Results of Choices: Reread lines 13–26a. With what does Macbeth associate sleep? Who, according to Macbeth, is in a better position than he and Lady Macbeth? **E**

Irony: Reread lines 27–35a. What type of irony is illustrated in these lines? Explain. **A**

jocund (jŏk′ənd) *adj.* Sprightly and lighthearted in disposition, character, or quality.

SCENE 3

A park near the palace at Forres

(Enter three MURDERERS.*)*

FIRST MURDERER. But who did bid thee join us?
THIRD MURDERER. Macbeth.
SECOND MURDERER. He needs not our mistrust,° since he delivers
Our offices,° and what we have to do,
To the direction just.°
FIRST MURDERER. Then stand with us.
The west yet glimmers with some streaks of day;
Now spurs the lated traveller apace
To gain the timely inn, and near approaches
The subject of our watch.
THIRD MURDERER. Hark, I hear horses.
BANQUO. *(Within.)* Give us a light there, ho!
SECOND MURDERER. Then 'tis he; the rest
That are within the note of expectation°
Already are i' th' court.
FIRST MURDERER. His horses go about.
THIRD MURDERER. Almost a mile; but he does usually,
So all men do, from hence to th' palace gate
Make it their walk.°

(Enter BANQUO *and* FLEANCE *with a torch.)*

SECOND MURDERER. A light, a light!
THIRD MURDERER. 'Tis he.
FIRST MURDERER. Stand to't.
BANQUO. It will be rain tonight.
FIRST MURDERER. Let it come down.

(They assault BANQUO.*)*

BANQUO. O, treachery! Fly, good Fleance, fly, fly, fly!
Thou mayst revenge. O slave! *(Dies.* FLEANCE *escapes.)*
THIRD MURDERER. Who did strike out the light?
FIRST MURDERER. Was't not the way?
THIRD MURDERER. There's but one down; the son is fled.
SECOND MURDERER. We have lost
Best half of our affair.
FIRST MURDERER. Well, let's away, and say how much is done.

(Exeunt.)

Reading Check: What did not go according to plan in this scene?

2 He . . . mistrust: We need not distrust the Third Murderer.

3 offices: duties

4 To . . . just: exactly according to Macbeth's instructions

10 within . . . expectation: expected as guests at the banquet

14 His . . . walk: He is walking his horses for almost the last mile back into the stable, as was customary.

The palace at Forres

(Banquet prepared. Enter MACBETH, LADY MACBETH, ROSS, LENNOX, LORDS, *and* ATTENDANTS.*)*

MACBETH. You know your own degrees,° sit down. At first
And last, the hearty welcome.
LORDS. Thanks to your Majesty.
MACBETH. Ourself will mingle with society,
And play the humble host.
Our hostess keeps her state,° but in best time
We will require her welcome.
LADY MACBETH. Pronounce it for me, sir, to all our friends,
For my heart speaks they are welcome.

(Enter FIRST MURDERER *at the door.)*

MACBETH. See, they encounter° thee with their hearts' thanks.
Both sides are even; here I'll sit i' th' midst.
Be large in mirth; anon we'll drink a measure
The table round.—

*(Goes to [*FIRST MURDERER *at] the door.)*

There's blood upon thy face.
FIRST MURDERER. 'Tis Banquo's then.
MACBETH. 'Tis better thee without than he within.°
Is he dispatch'd?
FIRST MURDERER. My lord, his throat is cut,
That I did for him.
MACBETH. Thou art the best o' th' cut-throats,
Yet he's good that did the like for Fleance.
If thou didst it, thou are the nonpareil.°
FIRST MURDERER. Most royal sir, Fleance is scap'd.
MACBETH. Then comes my fit again. I had else been perfect,
Whole as the marble, founded as the rock,
As broad and general as the casing° air;
But now I am cabin'd, cribb'd,° confin'd, bound in
To saucy doubts and fears. But Banquo's safe?
FIRST MURDERER. Ay, my good lord; safe in a ditch he bides,
With twenty trenchèd gashes on his head,
The least a death to nature.
MACBETH. Thanks for that:
There the grown serpent lies; the worm° that's fled
Hath nature that in time will venom breed,
No teeth for th' present. Get thee gone; tomorrow
We'll hear ourselves again.

(Exit FIRST MURDERER.*)*

LADY MACBETH. My royal lord,
You do not give the cheer. The feast is sold
That is not often vouch'd, while 'tis a-making,
'Tis given with welcome.° To feed were best at home;
From thence, the sauce to meat is ceremony,°
Meeting were bare without it.

1 degrees: ranks and hence order of seating

5 state: chair of state

9 encounter: respond to

14 thee . . . within: on your face than in his body

18 nonpareil: matchless one

22 casing: enveloping

23 cribb'd: shut in a hovel, or a small, miserable dwelling

28 worm: young snake

34 The . . . welcome: When a host omits courtesies that assure his guests that they are welcome, the feast is not better than a meal one buys.

35 From . . . ceremony: When one is away from home, courtesies make the meal more pleasant.

Plot: Reread lines 13–31. Did Macbeth's scheme against Banquo and his son succeed? How or how not? How might this outcome affect his future?

(Enter GHOST OF BANQUO *and sit in Macbeth's place.)*

MACBETH. Sweet remembrancer!
Now good digestion wait on appetite,
And health on both!

LENNOX. May't please your Highness sit.

MACBETH. Here had we now our country's honor° roof'd,
Were the grac'd person of our Banquo present,
Who may I rather challenge for° unkindness
Than pity for mischance.

ROSS. His absence, sir,
Lays blame upon his promise. Please't your Highness
To grace us with your royal company?

MACBETH. The table's full.

LENNOX. Here is a place reserv'd, sir.

MACBETH. Where?

LENNOX. Here, my good lord. What is't that moves your Highness?

MACBETH. *[Seeing* GHOST.*]* Which of you have done this?

LORDS. What, my
good lord?

MACBETH. Thou canst not say I did it; never shake
Thy gory locks at me.

ROSS. Gentlemen, rise, his Highness is not well.

LADY MACBETH. Sit, worthy friends; my lord is often thus,
And hath been from his youth. Pray you keep seat.
The fit is momentary, upon a thought
He will be well again. If much you note him,
You shall offend him and extend his passion.
Feed, and regard him not.— *[*LADY MACBETH *and* MACBETH *speak
apart.]* Are you a man?

MACBETH. Ay, and a bold one, that dare look on that
Which might appall the devil.

LADY MACBETH. O proper stuff!
This is the very painting of your fear;
This is the air-drawn dagger which you said
Led you to Duncan. O, these flaws and starts,
Impostors to true fear, would well become
A woman's story at a winter's fire,
Authoriz'd by° her grandam. Shame itself,
Why do you make such faces? When all's done,
You look but on a stool.°

MACBETH. Prithee see there!
Behold! look! lo! how say you?
Why, what care I if thou canst nod, speak too.
If charnel-houses° and our graves must send
Those that we bury back, our monuments
Shall be the maws of kites.°

*[*GHOST *vanishes.]*

LADY MACBETH. What? quite unmann'd in folly?

MACBETH. If I stand here, I saw him.

LADY MACBETH. Fie, for shame!

MACBETH. Blood hath been shed ere now, i' th' olden time
Ere humane statute purg'd the gentle weal;°
Ay, and since too, murders have been perform'd
Too terrible for the ear. The time has been,

39 honor: nobility

41 challenge for: charge with

65 Authoriz'd by: told on the authority of

67 stool: empty chair

70 charnel-houses: places of storage for the bones of the dead that had been exhumed to make room for new bodies

72 maws . . . kites: stomachs of birds of prey

75 Ere . . . weal: before humane laws civilized the state

That when the brains were out, the man would die,
And there an end; but now they rise again
With twenty mortal murders° on their crowns,°
And push us from our stools. This is more strange
Than such a murder is.

LADY MACBETH. My worthy lord,
Your noble friends do lack you.

MACBETH. I do forget. *(Addressing the* LORDS.*)*
Do not muse at me, my most worthy friends,
I have a strange infirmity, which is nothing
To those that know me. Come, love and health to all,
Then I'll sit down. Give me some wine; fill full.

(Enter GHOST.*)*

I drink to th' general joy o' th' whole table,
And to our dear friend Banquo, whom we miss;
Would he were here! to all, and him, we thirst,°
And all to all.°

LORDS. Our duties, and the pledge.

MACBETH. *[Seeing* GHOST.*]* Avaunt, and quit my sight! let the earth hide thee!
Thy bones are marrowless, thy blood is cold;
Thou hast no speculation° in those eyes
Which thou dost glare with!

LADY MACBETH. Think of this, good peers,
But as a thing of custom. 'Tis no other;
Only it spoils the pleasure of the time.

MACBETH. What man dare, I dare.
Approach thou like the rugged Russian bear,
The arm'd° rhinoceros, or th' Hyrcan° tiger,
Take any shape but that, and my firm nerves
Shall never tremble. Or be alive again,
And dare me to the desert with thy sword;
If trembling I inhabit° then, protest° me
The baby of a girl.° Hence, horrible shadow!
Unreal mock'ry, hence!

*[*GHOST *vanishes.]*

Why, so; being gone,
I am a man again. Pray you sit still. A

LADY MACBETH. You have displac'd the mirth, broke the good meeting,
With most admir'd° disorder.

MACBETH. Can such things be,
And overcome us like a summer's cloud,
Without our special wonder? You make me strange
Even to the disposition that I owe,°
When now I think you can behold such sights,
And keep the natural ruby of your cheeks,
When mine is blanch'd with fear.

ROSS. What sights, my lord?

LADY MACBETH. I pray you speak not; he grows worse and worse.
Question enrages him. At once, good night,
Stand not upon the order of your going,°
But go at once.

80 murders: wounds / **crowns:** heads

90 thirst: drink

91 And . . . all: All drink to all.

94 speculation: sight

100 arm'd: armored / **Hyrcan:** from the ancient Asian province of Hyrcania

104 inhabit: remain indoors / **protest:** proclaim

105 The . . . girl: a baby girl

109 admir'd: wondered at

112 the . . . owe: my own nature

118 the . . . going: ceremonial leave-taking

Irony: Whose ghost does Macbeth first see and then address in lines 44–107? Who else sees the ghost? What type of irony does this double encounter illustrate? A

LENNOX. Good night, and better health
Attend his Majesty.
LADY MACBETH. A kind good night to all!
(Exeunt LORDS *and* ATTENDANTS.*)*

MACBETH. It will have blood, they say; blood will have blood.
Stones have been known to move and trees to speak;
Augures° and understood relations° have
By maggot-pies° and choughs° and rooks brought forth
The secret'st man of blood. What is the night?
LADY MACBETH. Almost at odds with morning,° which is which.
MACBETH. How say'st thou, that Macduff denies his person
At our great bidding?
LADY MACBETH. Did you send to him, sir?
MACBETH. I hear it by the way;° but I will send.
There's not a one of them but in his house
I keep a servant fee'd.° I will tomorrow
(And betimes I will) to the weird sisters. ✓
More shall they speak; for now I am bent to know
By the worst means, the worst. For mine own good
All causes° shall give way. I am in blood
Stepp'd in so far that, should I wade no more,
Returning were as tedious as go o'er.
Strange things I have in head, that will to hand,
Which must be acted ere they may be scann'd.°
LADY MACBETH. You lack the season° of all natures, sleep.
MACBETH. Come, we'll to sleep. My strange and self-abuse°
Is the initiate fear° that wants hard use.°
We are yet but young in deed. E
(Exeunt.)

123 Augures: omens / **understood relations:** the relation between the omen and what it signifies

124 maggot-pies: magpies / **choughs:** birds of the crow family, which, like magpies and rooks, could supposedly be taught to speak

126 at . . . morning: dawn

129 by . . . way: indirectly

131 a . . . fee'd: a spy

135 causes: other considerations

139 scann'd: properly studied

140 season: preservative

141 strange . . . abuse: strange self-delusion

142 initiate fear: novice's fear / **hard use:** the hardened conscience that comes from the repetition of crime

A heath

(Thunder. Enter the three WITCHES. *[*HECATE *descends.])*

FIRST WITCH. Why, how now, Hecate? you look angerly.
HECATE. Have I not reason, beldams° as you are,
Saucy and overbold? How did you dare
To trade and **traffic** with Macbeth
In riddles and affairs of death;
And I, the mistress of your charms,
The close° contriver of all harms,
Was never call'd to bear my part,
Or show the glory of our art?
And which is worse, all you have done
Hath been but for a wayward son,°
Spiteful and wrathful, who as others do,
Loves for his own ends, not for you.
But make amends now. Get you gone,
And at the pit of Acheron°
Meet me i' th' morning; thither he
Will come to know his destiny.

2 beldams: hags

7 close: secret

11 a . . . son: one who does not adhere to our teachings

15 Acheron: the mythological river of woe in hell

Reading Check: Whose absence from the banquet arouses Macbeth's suspicion? ✓

Results of Choices: To what does Macbeth attribute his delusion (seeing the ghost)? E

traffic (trăf′ĭk) *intr.v.* To carry on trade or other dealings.

Your vessels and your spells provide,
Your charms and every thing beside.
I am for th' air; this night I'll spend
Unto a dismal and a fatal end;
Great business must be wrought ere noon.
Upon the corner of the moon
There hangs a vap'rous drop profound;°
I'll catch it ere it come to ground;
And that, distill'd by magic sleights,
Shall raise such artificial sprites°
As by the strength of their illusion
Shall draw him on to his confusion.
He shall spurn fate, scorn death, and bear
His hopes 'bove wisdom, grace, and fear;
And you all know, security°
Is mortals' chiefest enemy.

(Music and a song within.)

Hark, I am call'd; my little spirit, see,
Sits in a foggy cloud, and stays for me.

[HECATE ascends.]

FIRST WITCH. Come, let's make haste, she'll soon be back again.

(Exeunt.)

24 **profound:** ready to drop off

27 **artificial sprites:** spirits produced by magic

32 **security:** overconfidence

The palace at Forres

(Enter LENNOX and another LORD.)

LENNOX. My former speeches have but hit your thoughts,
Which can interpret farther;° only I say
Things have been strangely borne.° The gracious Duncan
Was pitied of Macbeth; marry, he was dead.
And the right valiant Banquo walk'd too late,
Whom you may say, if't please you, Fleance kill'd,
For Fleance fled. Men must not walk too late.
Who cannot want the thought, how monstrous
It was for Malcolm and for Donalbain
To kill their gracious father? Damnèd fact!
How it did grieve Macbeth! Did he not straight
In pious rage the two delinquents tear,
That were the slaves of drink and thralls of sleep?
Was not that nobly done? Ay, and wisely too;
For 'twould have anger'd any heart alive
To hear the men deny't. So that, I say,
He has borne all things well, and I do think
That had he Duncan's sons under his key
(As, and't please heaven, he shall not), they should find
What 'twere to kill a father; so should Fleance.
But peace! for from broad words,° and 'cause he fail'd
His presence at the tyrant's feast, I hear
Macduff lives in disgrace. Sir, can you tell
Where he bestows himself?° A

LORD. The son of Duncan,

2 **My . . . farther:** I have touched upon your own opinions in this matter and now leave you to draw further inferences.

3 **borne:** carried on

21 **broad words:** candor, outspokenness

24 **bestows himself:** dwells

Irony: Consider the tone of scene 6, lines 1–24. What type of verbal irony does Lennox's dialogue illustrate? A

From whom this tyrant holds° the due of birth,
Lives in the English court, and is receiv'd
Of the most pious Edward with such grace
That the malevolence of fortune nothing
Takes from his high respect.° Thither Macduff
Is gone to pray the holy King, upon his aid
To wake Northumberland and warlike Siward,
That by the help of these, with Him above
To ratify the work, we may again
Give to our tables meat, sleep to our nights;
Free from our feasts and banquets bloody knives;
Do faithful homage and receive free° honors;
All which we pine for now. And this report
Hath so exasperate the King° that he
Prepares for some attempt of war.

LENNOX. Sent he to Macduff?

LORD. He did; and with an absolute "Sir, not I,"
The cloudy° messenger turns me back,
And hums,° as who should say, "You'll rue the time
That clogs° me with this answer."

LENNOX. And that well might
Advise him to a caution, t' hold what distance
His wisdom can provide. Some holy angel
Fly to the court of England, and unfold
His message ere he come, that a swift blessing
May soon return to this our suffering country
Under a hand accurs'd.

LORD. I'll send my prayers with him.

Exeunt.

25 holds: withholds

29 That . . . respect: He is held in as high esteem as if he were king.

36 free: freely given

38 the King: i.e., Macbeth

41 cloudy: surly

42 hums: expresses contempt

43 clogs: burdens

homage (hŏm′ĭj) *n.* Formal acknowledgment by a vassal of allegiance to his lord under feudal law.

Reading Check: At this point where is Macduff?

THINK AND DISCUSS

1. Define *verbal irony*, *sarcasm*, and *hyperbole*. Give an example of each type of verbal irony from act 3.
2. Define *dramatic irony*. Give an example of it from act 3.
3. Twice in act 3, scene 4 Macbeth draws attention at the banquet to Banquo's absence, and each time Banquo's ghost appears. What type of irony does the ghost's appearance illustrate? What theme introduced in act 1 does this irony enhance?
4. Identify the seven plot elements in the order in which they come in a story. Review the major events of acts 1–3 in your mind. What incident in the play introduces the conflict and sets it in motion?
5. Where would you locate the major turning point for Macbeth, the point at which his fortune reverses? Support your answer with details from the text.
6. Given the three acts that you have read so far, what is the point of highest emotional intensity?
7. With which plot element would you label Duncan's murder? Malcolm's flight? Macbeth's plan to visit the witches?
8. Has Macbeth's deliberate choice to murder Duncan altered his character? Support your answer with details from the text.
9. How does Macbeth assess his situation in scene 4, lines 135–37? According to the Bible, does Macbeth have a valid motive for his continuation of evil? Support your answer with Scripture.
10. What effects do the Macbeths' actions have on them mentally and spiritually? Does Shakespeare's presentation of these effects agree or disagree with a biblical worldview? Consider Psalm 38:1–7, 32:3–4; 1 Samuel 26:9; and Mark 8:36 in your answer.

ANALYZE: *Motif Development*

Shakespeare develops his themes through **motifs**, collections of repeated elements such as objects, images, or descriptions that support a theme. Weather, for instance, is a common motif used to support such themes as chaos and order or unrest and peace. An author may use storms and frigid temperatures or gentle breezes and sunny days to strengthen his theme. Unchecked ambition—the extent to which characters will go to achieve and sustain power—is a theme found in acts 1–3 of *Macbeth*. One way Shakespeare develops this theme is through a motif that includes battles, killings, and blood. What would you call such a motif in light of these elements? How does Shakespeare continue to develop this motif in act 4? What other motifs support the theme of ambition? As you read, identify other themes and supporting motifs.

READ: *Oral Reading of Drama*

Shakespeare wrote his verse to be performed publicly (not studied privately), so to enjoy reading *Macbeth* to its fullest, you should read it aloud. To do so well, though, you must understand Shakespeare's use of blank verse, prose, and rhymed verse. Shakespeare employs variations of **blank verse** (unrhymed iambic pentameter) to distinguish the verse used by the English nobility in their formal roles (see 1.3.130–33) from the prose speech of commoners, such as the Porter. The blank verse indicates to the reader that the lines should be read with a designated rhythm in a proper, authoritative tone. Prose also appears in the speech of nobility, however, for everyday, informal conversations, such as when Lady Macduff converses with her son. Furthermore, Shakespeare uses trochaic tetrameter with rhymed couplets to distinguish the witches (see 1.1.1–4). What effect does the trochaic tetrameter have in these lines? Read aloud the lines indicated in parentheses, noting the differences in meter and how those differences reflect character and situation. Consider these formal characteristics as you read portions of the play aloud.

EVALUATE: *Character Qualities*

God's plan for His people has always been internal moral transformation, not mere external conformity to His law. Virtue is the term that describes moral excellence that has become so internalized that acting in a morally excellent way becomes natural. If this moral development is important for every person, how much more then should a leader—"God's servant for your good" (Rom. 13:4)—possess strong, virtuous character qualities? As you read, look at the character qualities of Malcolm and Macbeth. Do you think Malcolm would be a better king than Macbeth? Use the following Scripture passages (or others that apply) to guide your evaluation: James 4:10; Matthew 7:12, 20:26.

OBJECTIVES

- Examine a work's motifs and how they develop throughout a work.
- Analyze how a work's motifs support its themes.
- Read drama aloud with attention to its use of verse and prose.
- Evaluate the qualities of characters in a work from a biblical perspective.

VOCABULARY

conjure (kŏn′jər) *tr.v.* To call or bring to mind.

pernicious (pər-nĭsh′əs) *adj.* Causing great harm; destructive.

avaricious (ăv′ə-rĭsh′əs) *adj.* Immoderately desirous of wealth or gain.

voluptuousness (və-lŭp′cho͞o əs nəs) *n.* Indulgence in pleasure and luxury.

credulous (krĕj′ə-ləs) *adj.* Gullible.

abjure (ăb-jo͝or′) *tr.v.* To recant solemnly; to renounce.

ACT 4

SCENE 1

A cave with a boiling cauldron in the middle

(Thunder. Enter the three WITCHES.*)*

FIRST WITCH. Thrice the brinded cat° hath mew'd.
SECOND WITCH. Thrice and once the hedge-pig° whin'd.
THIRD WITCH. Harpier° cries, "'Tis time, 'tis time."
FIRST WITCH. Round about the cauldron go;
In the poison'd entrails throw;
Toad, that under cold stone
Days and nights has thirty-one
Swelt'red venom sleeping got,
Boil thou first i' th' charmèd pot.
ALL. Double, double, toil, and trouble;
Fire burn, and cauldron bubble. R
SECOND WITCH. Fillet of a fenny° snake,
In the cauldron boil and bake;
Eye of newt° and toe of frog,
Wool of bat and tongue of dog,
Adder's fork° and blindworm's° sting,
Lizard's leg and howlet's° wing,
For a charm of pow'rful trouble,
Like a hell-broth boil and bubble.
ALL. Double, double, toil and trouble;
Fire burn, and cauldron bubble.

1 **brinded cat:** brindled; tawny or gray with darker streaks; i.e., Graymalkin

2 **hedge-pig:** Paddock

3 **Harpier:** "owl," the Third Witch's spirit; (cf. 1.1.9–10)

12 **fenny:** found in fens or marshes

14 **newt:** a kind of salamander

16 **fork:** forked tongue / **blindworm:** a lizard, so named because its eyes close after death

17 **howlet:** owlet

Oral Reading: What meter does Shakespeare use in lines 4–11? How does it affect these lines? R

THIRD WITCH. Scale of dragon, tooth of wolf,
Witch's mummy,° maw° and gulf°
Of the ravin'd° salt-sea shark,
Root of hemlock digg'd i' th' dark,
Liver of blaspheming Jew,
Gall of goat, and slips of yew
Sliver'd in the moon's eclipse,
Nose of Turk and Tartar's° lips,
Finger of birth-strangled babe
Ditch-deliver'd by a drab,°
Make the gruel° thick and slab.
Add thereto a tiger's chawdron,°
For th' ingredience of our cau'dron.

ALL. Double, double, toil and trouble;
Fire burn, and cauldron bubble.

SECOND WITCH. Cool it with a baboon's blood,
Then the charm is firm and good.

(Enter HECATE *[with three more]* WITCHES.*)*

HECATE. O, well done! I commend your pains,
And every one shall share i' th' gains.
And now about the cauldron sing,
Like elves and fairies in a ring,
Enchanting all that you put in.

([The other three WITCHES *sing.*

Exeunt HECATE *and the other three* WITCHES.*])*

SECOND WITCH. By the pricking of my thumbs,
Something wicked this way comes. *(Knocking.)*
Open, locks,
Whoever knocks! E

(Enter MACBETH.*)*

MACBETH. How now, you secret, black, and midnight hags?
What is't you do?

ALL. A deed without a name.

MACBETH. I conjure you, by that which you profess°
(How e'er you come to know it), answer me:
Though you untie the winds, and let them fight
Against the churches; though the yesty° waves
Confound and swallow navigation up;
Though bladed corn be lodg'd, and trees blown down;
Though castles topple on their warders'° heads;
Though palaces and pyramids do slope
Their heads to their foundations; though the treasure
Of nature's germens° tumble all together,
Even till destruction sicken;° answer me
To what I ask you. A

FIRST WITCH. Speak.

SECOND WITCH. Demand.

THIRD WITCH. We'll answer.

FIRST WITCH. Say if th' hadst rather hear it from our mouths,
Or from our masters'?

23 mummy: a medicinal substance made from the dried flesh of embalmed human bodies / **maw:** stomach / **gulf:** gullet

24 ravin'd: ravenous

29 Tartar: Mongolian

31 drab: prostitute

32 gruel: a thin, watery porridge

33 chawdron: entrails

50 that . . . profess: i.e., witchcraft

53 yesty: foamy

56 warders: a soldier or person set to guard an entrance

59 germens: Seeds. The *rationes seminales*, or seeds of matter described by the Neoplatonists as visible forms that have the potential of becoming material and spiritual essences. Macbeth is willing to forego his whole future for temporary gratification of his evil desires.

60 sicken: be surfeited, gratified to excess

Character: To whom is the second witch referring in line 45? Why do the witches refer to this person as "wicked"? E

conjure (kŏn′jər) *tr.v.* To call or bring to mind.

Motif: Reread lines 50–61. With what powers is Macbeth crediting the witches? A

MACBETH. Call 'em; let me see 'em.
FIRST WITCH. Pour in sow's blood, that hath eaten
Her nine farrow;° grease that's sweaten
From the murderer's gibbet° throw
Into the flame.
ALL. Come high or low;
Thyself and office° deftly show!

(Thunder. FIRST APPARITION*, an armed Head[, ascends.])*

MACBETH. Tell me, thou unknown power–
FIRST WITCH. He knows thy thought:
Hear his speech, but say thou nought.
FIRST APPARITION. Macbeth! Macbeth! Macbeth! beware Macduff;
Beware the Thane of Fife. Dismiss me. Enough.

(He descends.)

MACBETH. What e'er thou art, for thy good caution, thanks;
Thou hast harp'd° my fear aright. But one word more—
FIRST WITCH. He will not be commanded. Here's another,
More potent than the first.

(Thunder. SECOND APPARITION*, a bloody Child[, ascends.])*

SECOND APPARITION. Macbeth! Macbeth! Macbeth!
MACBETH. Had I three ears, I'ld hear thee.
SECOND APPARITION. Be bloody, bold, and resolute: laugh to scorn
The pow'r of man; for none of woman born
Shall harm Macbeth.

(He descends.)

MACBETH. Then live, Macduff; what need I fear of thee?
But yet I'll make assurance double sure,
And take a bond of fate:° thou shalt not live,
That I may tell pale-hearted fear it lies,
And sleep in spite of thunder. A

(Thunder. THIRD APPARITION*, a Child crowned, with a tree in his hand [ascends].)*

What is this
That rises like the issue° of a king,
And wears upon his baby-brow the round
And top° of sovereignty?
ALL. Listen, but speak not to't.
THIRD APPARITION. Be lion-mettled,° proud, and take no care
Who chafes, who frets, or where conspirers are:
Macbeth shall never vanquish'd be until
Great Birnan wood to high Dunsinane hill°
Shall come against him.

([He] descend[s.])

MACBETH. That will never be.
Who can impress° the forest, bid the tree
Unfix his earth-bound root? Sweet bodements!° Good!
Rebellious dead,° rise never till the wood
Of Birnan rise, and our high-plac'd Macbeth
Shall live the lease of nature,° pay his breath

65 farrow: litter of pigs

66 gibbet: gallows

68 office: function

74 harp'd: hit upon

84 take . . . fate: insure the fate already promised him by the evil spirits by murdering Macduff

87 issue: offspring, children, descendants

89 round . . . top: crown

90 lion-mettled: having the courage and spirit of a lion

93 Great . . . hill: i.e., a distance of twelve miles

95 impress: force into service

96 bodements: prophecies

97 Rebellious dead: Ghost of Banquo

99 the . . . nature: his normal lifespan

Motif: Does Macbeth fear Macduff? Why or why not? What do you think Shakespeare is foreshadowing? A

To time and mortal custom.° Yet my heart
Throbs to know one thing: tell me, if your art
Can tell so much, shall Banquo's issue ever
Reign in this kingdom?

100 mortal custom: death

ALL. Seek to know no more.

MACBETH. I will be satisfied. Deny me this,
And an eterne curse fall on you! Let me know.
Why sinks that cauldron? and what noise is this?

(Hautboys.)

FIRST WITCH. Show!

SECOND WITCH. Show!

THIRD WITCH. Show!

ALL. Show his eyes, and grieve his heart;
Come like shadows, so depart.

(A [dumb] show° of eight KINGS, the eighth with a glass° in his hand, and BANQUO['S GHOST] leading them.])

dumb show: pantomime / **glass:** Mirror. The procession represents the royal lineage of James I of England.

MACBETH. Thou art too like the spirit of Banquo; down!
Thy crown does sear mine eyeballs. And thy hair,
Thou other gold-bound brow, is like the first.
A third is like the former. Filthy hags,
Why do you show me this?—A fourth? Start, eyes!
What, will the line stretch out to th' crack of doom?
Another yet? A seventh? I'll see no more.
And yet the eighth appears, who bears a glass

Which shows me many more; and some I see
That twofold balls and treble sceptres° carry.
Horrible sight! Now I see 'tis true,
For the blood-bolter'd° Banquo smiles upon me,
And points at them for his. A

(APPARITIONS vanish.)

What? is this so?

FIRST WITCH. Ay, sir, all this is so. But why
Stands Macbeth thus amazedly?
Come, sisters, cheer we up his sprites,
And show the best of our delights.
I'll charm the air to give a sound,
While you perform your antic round;°
That this great King may kindly say
Our duties did his welcome pay.° A

(Music. The WITCHES dance and [then] vanish.)

MACBETH. Where are they? Gone? Let this **pernicious** hour
Stand aye accursèd in the calendar!
Come in, without there!

(Enter LENNOX.)

LENNOX. What's your Grace's will?
MACBETH. Saw you the weird sisters?
LENNOX. No, my lord.
MACBETH. Came they not by you?
LENNOX. No indeed, my lord.
MACBETH. Infected be the air whereon they ride,
And damn'd all those that trust them! I did hear
The galloping of horse. Who was't came by?
LENNOX. 'Tis two or three, my lord, that bring you word
Macduff is fled to England.
MACBETH. Fled to England!
LENNOX. Ay, my good Lord.
MACBETH. *(Aside.)* Time, thou anticipat'st my dread exploits:
The flighty purpose never is o'ertook
Unless the deed go with it.° From this moment
The very firstlings° of my heart shall be
The firstlings of my hand. And even now,
To crown my thoughts with acts, be it thought and done.
The castle of Macduff I will surprise,
Seize upon Fife, give to th' edge o' th' sword
His wife, his babes, and all unfortunate souls
That trace° him in his line. No boasting like a fool;
This deed I'll do before this purpose cool.
But no more sights!—Where are these gentlemen?
Come bring me where they are. A

(Exeunt.)

121 twofold . . . sceptres: Symbols of the united kingdoms of England, Scotland, and Ireland, which were joined when James VI of Scotland was crowned James I of England. According to legend, James was a descendant of Banquo.

123 blood-bolter'd: his hair matted with blood

130 antic round: fantastic circular dance

132 Our . . . pay: The attention we gave him has repaid the welcome he gave us.

146 The . . . it: An impulsive deed is never performed unless it is carried out immediately.

147 firstlings: firstborn

153 trace: follow

Motif: Why is Macbeth alarmed by the appearance of Banquo's ghost and eight kings? A

Motif: What clues throughout the witches' scene (ll. 1–133) reveal that evil and unnatural things are occurring? A

pernicious (pər-nĭsh'əs) *adj.* Causing great harm; destructive.

Motif: What does Macbeth's aside in scene 1, lines 144–56 reveal about his future ambitions? A

Macduff's castle at Fife

(Enter LADY MACDUFF, *her* SON, *and* ROSS.*)*

LADY MACDUFF. What had he done, to make him fly the land?
ROSS. You must have patience, madam.
LADY MACDUFF. He had none;
His flight was madness. When our actions do not,
Our fears do make us traitors.
ROSS. You know not
Whether it was his wisdom or his fear.
LADY MACDUFF. Wisdom? to leave his wife, to leave his babes,
His mansion and his titles° in a place
From whence himself does fly? He loves us not;
He wants° the natural touch; for the poor wren,
The most diminutive of birds, will fight,
Her young ones in her nest, against the owl.
All is the fear, and nothing is the love;
As little is the wisdom, where the flight
So runs against all reason.
ROSS. My dearest coz,°
I pray you school° yourself. But for your husband,
He is noble, wise, judicious, and best knows
The fits o' th' season° I dare not speak much further,
But cruel are the times when we are traitors,
And do not know ourselves; when we hold rumor
From what we fear, yet know not what we fear,°
But float upon a wild and violent sea
Each way and move—I take my leave of you;
Shall not be long but I'll be here again.
Things at the worst will cease, or else climb upward
To what they were before. My pretty cousin,°
Blessing upon you!
LADY MACDUFF. Father'd he is, and yet he's fatherless.
ROSS. I am so much a fool, should I stay longer,
It would be my disgrace and your discomfort.°
I take my leave at once.

(Exit ROSS.*)*

LADY MACDUFF. Sirrah, your father's dead,
And what will you do now? How will you live?
SON. As birds do, mother.
LADY MACDUFF. What, with worms and flies?
SON. With what I get, I mean, and so do they.
LADY MACDUFF. Poor° bird, thou'dst never fear the net nor lime,°
The pitfall nor the gin.°
SON. Why should I, mother? Poor birds they are not set for.
My father is not dead, for all your saying. **A**
LADY MACDUFF. Yes, he is dead. How wilt thou do for a father?
SON. Nay, how will you do for a husband?
LADY MACDUFF. Why, I can buy me twenty at any market.
SON. Then you'll buy 'em to sell again.
LADY MACDUFF. Thou speak'st with all thy wit, and yet, i' faith,
With wit enough for thee.

7 **titles:** deeds of property

9 **wants:** lacks

14 **coz:** cousin; i.e., kinswoman

15 **school:** control

17 **fits . . . season:** disturbances of the time

20 **we . . . fear:** when we listen to rumors and thus know not what we actually should fear

25 **cousin:** i.e., Young Macduff

29 **It . . . discomfort:** i.e., I would weep.

34 **Poor:** worthless / **lime:** birdlime, a sticky substance smeared on branches or twigs to capture small birds

35 **gin:** trap

Motif: Reread Lady Macduff's conversations with Ross and her son (ll. 1–37). What references to birds and flying appear throughout? **A**

SON. Was my father a traitor, mother?
LADY MACDUFF. Ay, that he was.
SON. What is a traitor?
LADY MACDUFF. Why, one that swears and lies.
SON. And be all traitors that do so?
LADY MACDUFF. Every one that does so is a traitor, and must be hang'd.
SON. And must they all be hang'd that swear and lie?
LADY MACDUFF. Every one.
SON. Who must hang them?
LADY MACDUFF. Why, the honest men.
SON. Then the liars and swearers are fools; for there are liars and swearers enough to beat the honest men and hang them up.
LADY MACDUFF. Now God help thee, poor monkey! But how wilt thou do for a father?
SON. If he were dead, you'd weep for him; if you would not, it were a good sign that I should quickly have a new father.
LADY MACDUFF. Poor prattler, how thou talk'st! R

(Enter a MESSENGER.*)*

MESSENGER. Bless you, fair dame! I am not to you known,
Though in your state of honor I am perfect.°
I doubt° some danger does approach you nearly.
If you will take a homely° man's advice,
Be not found here. Hence with your little ones.
To fright you thus, methinks I am too savage;
To do worse to you were fell cruelty,
Which is too nigh your person. Heaven preserve you!
I dare abide no longer.

(Exit MESSENGER.*)*

LADY MACDUFF. Whither should I fly?
I have done no harm. But I remember now
I am in this earthly world, where to do harm
Is often laudable, to do good sometime
Accounted dangerous folly. Why then, alas,
Do I put up that womanly defense,
To say I have done no harm?

(Enter MURDERERS.*)*

62 **in . . . perfect:** I am well acquainted with the honor of your position.

63 **doubt:** fear

64 **homely:** simple

Oral Reading: What rhythmic or formal differences occur between Lady Macduff's conversation with Ross and her conversation with her son? R

What are these faces?
FIRST MURDERER. Where is your husband?
LADY MACDUFF. I hope, in no place so unsanctified
Where such as thou mayst find him.
FIRST MURDERER. He's a traitor.
SON. Thou li'st, thou shag-hair'd villain!
FIRST MURDERER. *(Stabbing him.)* What, you egg!
Young fry° of treachery!
SON. He has kill'd me, mother:
Run away, I pray you! *(Dies.)* **A**

(Exit LADY MACDUFF *crying "Murder!" and pursued by the* MURDERERS.*)*

80 **fry:** small fish

SCENE 3

Before King Edward's palace in England

(Enter MALCOLM *and* MACDUFF.*)*

MALCOLM. Let us seek out some desolate shade, and there
Weep our sad bosoms empty.
MACDUFF. Let us rather
Hold fast the mortal sword, and like good men
Bestride our downfall'n birthdom.° Each new morn
New widows howl, new orphans cry, new sorrows
Strike heaven on the face, that it resounds
As if it felt with Scotland, and yell'd out
Like syllable of dolor.°
MALCOLM. What I believe, I'll wail,
What know, believe; and what I can redress,
As I shall find the time to friend,° I will.
What you have spoke, it may be so perchance.
This tyrant, whose sole° name blisters our tongues,
Was once thought honest; you have lov'd him well;
He hath not touch'd you yet. I am young, but something
You may deserve of him through me,° and wisdom
To offer up a weak, poor, innocent lamb
T' appease an angry god.
MACDUFF. I am not treacherous.
MALCOLM. But Macbeth is.
A good and virtuous nature may recoil°
In an imperial charge. But I shall crave your pardon;
That which you are, my thoughts cannot transpose:
Angels are bright still, though the brightest° fell.
Though all things foul would wear the brows of grace,
Yet grace must still look so.°
MACDUFF. I have lost my hopes.
MALCOLM. Perchance even there where I did find my doubts.
Why in that rawness° left you wife and child,
Those precious motives,° those strong knots of love,
Without leave-taking? I pray you,
Let not my jealousies° be your dishonors,
But mine own safeties.° You may be rightly just,
What ever I shall think. **E**

4 **Bestride . . . birthdom:** defend our fallen homeland

8 **syllable . . . dolor:** a cry of pain

10 **to friend:** favorable

12 **sole:** mere

15 **something . . . me:** You may see a way of getting into his good graces by betraying me to him.

19 **recoil:** shrink back in fear

22 **the brightest:** Lucifer

24 **look so:** appear virtuous

26 **rawness:** unprotected state

27 **motives:** those whom you desired to love and protect

29 **jealousies:** suspicions

30 **safeties:** protection

Motif: Whom does the son, with his dying breath, encourage to "fly" (ll. 69, 81)? Why is this flight ironic in light of Lady Macduff's earlier comments about her husband's flight (ll. 1–4)? What other motif does this scene illustrate? **A**

Character: Reread lines 10–31. Why does Malcolm not trust Macduff? What reasons does Malcolm give for questioning Macduff's loyalty? **E**

MACDUFF. Bleed, bleed, poor country!
Great tyranny, lay thou thy basis sure,
For goodness dare not check thee; wear thou thy wrongs,°
The title is affeer'd!° Fare thee well, lord,
I would not be the villain that thou think'st
For the whole space that's in the tyrant's grasp,
And the rich East to boot.°
MALCOLM. Be not offended;
I speak not as in absolute fear° of you.
I think our country sinks beneath the yoke:
It weeps, it bleeds, and each new day a gash
Is added to her wounds. I think withal°
There would be hands uplifted in my right;
And here from gracious England° have I offer
Of goodly thousands. But for all this,
When I shall tread upon the tyrant's head,
Or wear it on my sword, yet my poor country
Shall have more vices than it had before,
More suffer, and more sundry ways than ever,
By him that shall succeed.
MACDUFF. What should he be?
MALCOLM. It is myself I mean; in whom I know
All the particulars of vice so grafted
That, when they shall be open'd, black Macbeth
Will seem as pure as snow, and the poor state
Esteem him as a lamb, being compar'd
With my confineless harms.
MACDUFF. Not in the legions
Of horrid hell can come a devil more damn'd
In evils to top Macbeth. E
MALCOLM. I grant him bloody,
Luxurious,° **avaricious**, false, deceitful,
Sudden, malicious, smacking of every sin
That has a name; but there's no bottom, none,
In my **voluptuousness**. Your wives, your daughters,
Your matrons, and your maids could not fill up
The cistern of my lust, and my desire
All continent impediments° would o'erbear
That did oppose my will. Better Macbeth
Than such an one to reign.
MACDUFF. Boundless intemperance
In nature is a tyranny;° it hath been
Th' untimely emptying of the happy throne,
And fall of many kings. But fear not yet
To take upon you what is yours. You may
Convey your pleasures in a spacious plenty,°
And yet seem cold,° the time you may so hoodwink.°
We have willing dames enough; there cannot be
That vulture in you to devour so many
As will to greatness dedicate themselves,
Finding it so inclin'd.

33 **wrongs:** wrongly acquired powers

34 **affeer'd:** assured, confirmed

37 **rich East to boot:** in addition, also, besides (if I were offered all of Macbeth's kingdom and the wealth of the East as well)

38 **fear:** distrust

41 **withal:** besides

43 **England:** the king of England

58 **Luxurious:** lustful

64 **continent impediments:** chaste restraints

67 **a tyranny:** an absolute controller

71 **Convey . . . plenty:** find plenty of opportunity to indulge your pleasures stealthily

72 **cold:** chaste / **hoodwink:** deceive

Character: To whom does Malcolm compare himself when speaking with Macduff? E

avaricious (ăv′ə-rĭsh′əs) *adj.* Immoderately desirous of wealth or gain.

voluptuousness (və-lŭp′cho͞o əs nəs) *n.* Indulgence in pleasure and luxury.

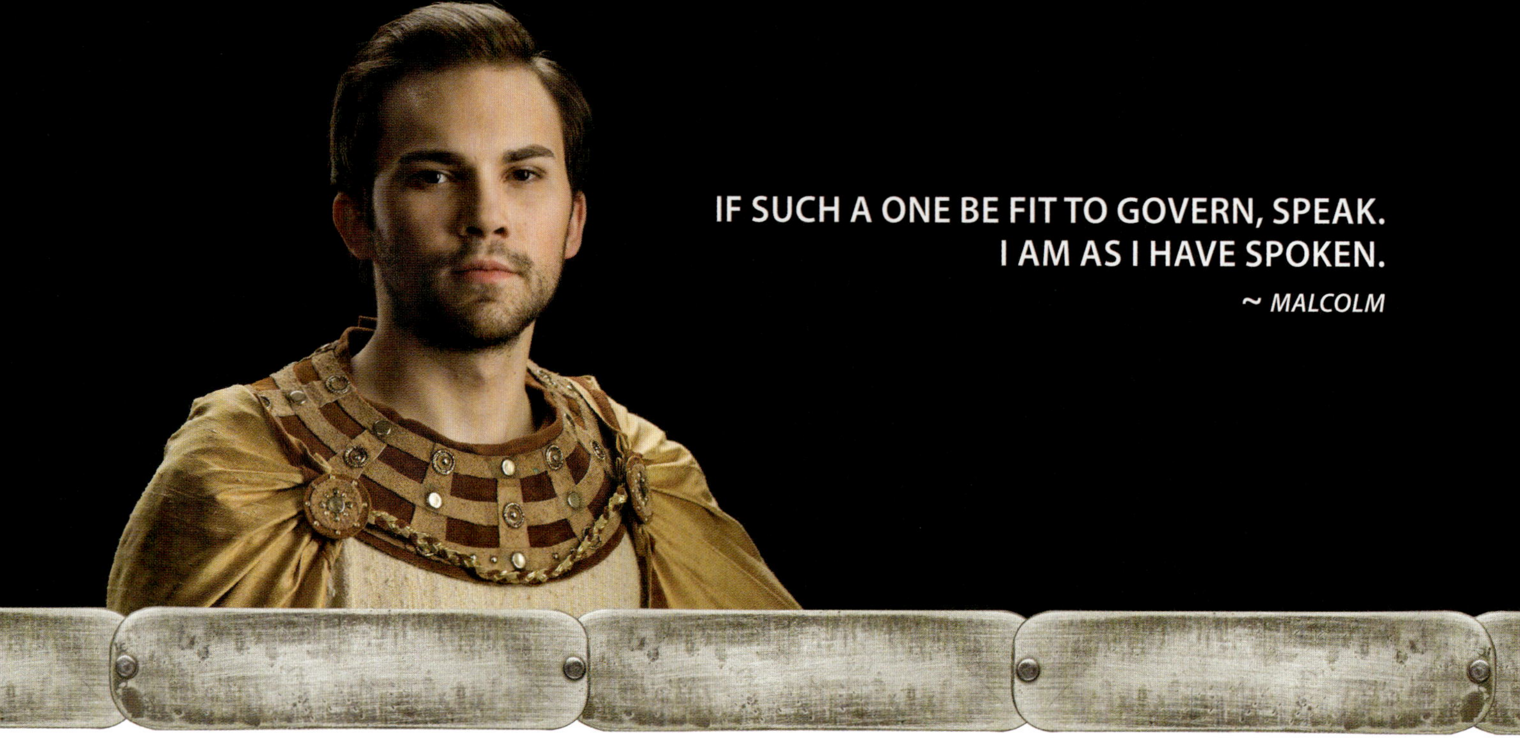

MALCOLM. With this, there grows
In my most ill-compos'd affection such
A staunchless° avarice that, were I King,
I should cut off the nobles for their lands,
Desire his jewels, and this other's house,
And my more-having would be as a sauce
To make me hunger more, that I should forge
Quarrels unjust against the good and loyal,
Destroying them for wealth.
MACDUFF. This avarice
Sticks deeper, grows with more pernicious root
Than summer-seeming° lust; and it hath been
The sword of our slain kings. Yet do not fear,
Scotland hath foisons° to fill up your will
Of your mere own.° All these are portable,°
With other graces weigh'd.
MALCOLM. But I have none. The king-becoming graces,
As justice, verity, temp'rance, stableness,
Bounty, perseverance, mercy, lowliness,
Devotion, patience, courage, fortitude,
I have no relish° of them, but abound
In the division of each several crime,°
Acting it many ways. Nay, had I pow'r, I should
Pour the sweet milk of concord° into hell,
Uproar the universal peace, confound
All unity on earth.
MACDUFF. O Scotland, Scotland!
MALCOLM. If such a one be fit to govern, speak.
I am as I have spoken.
MACDUFF. Fit to govern?
No, not to live. O nation miserable!
With an untitled° tyrant bloody-scept'red,
When shalt thou see thy wholesome days again,
Since that the truest issue of thy throne
By his own interdiction° stands accus'd,

78 **staunchless:** insatiable

86 **summer-seeming:** a young man's

88 **foisons:** abundance

89 **Of . . . own:** i.e., royal property / **portable**: endurable

95 **relish:** appreciation; trace

96 **division . . . crime:** various manifestations of each separate sin

98 **concord:** peace, harmony

104 **untitled:** usurping

107 **interdiction:** confession of weakness

And does blaspheme° his breed? Thy royal father
Was a most sainted king; the queen that bore thee,
Often'r upon her knees than on her feet,
Died° every day she liv'd. Fare thee well,
These evils thou repeat'st upon thyself
Hath banish'd me from Scotland. O my breast,
Thy hope ends here! E

MALCOLM. Macduff, this noble passion,
Child of integrity, hath from my soul
Wip'd the black scruples, reconcil'd my thoughts
To thy good truth and honor. Devilish Macbeth
By many of these trains° hath sought to win me
Into his power, and modest wisdom° plucks me
From over-**credulous** haste. But God above
Deal between thee and me! for even now
I put myself to thy direction, and
Unspeak mine own detraction;° here **abjure**
The taints and blames I laid upon myself,
For strangers to my nature. I am yet
Unknown to woman, never was forsworn,°
Scarcely have coveted what was mine own,
At no time broke my faith, would not betray
The devil to his fellow, and delight
No less in truth than life. My first false speaking
Was this upon myself. What I am truly
Is thine and my poor country's to command:
Whither indeed, before thy here-approach,
Old Siward, with ten thousand warlike men

108 blaspheme: defame

111 Died: an allusion to 1 Corinthians 15:31 ("I die daily.")

118 trains: strategems

119 modest wisdom: prudence; moderation

123 own detraction: self-slander

126 forsworn: a perjurer or breaker of an oath

Character: What is Macduff's response to Malcolm's argument that he is unfit to be king? What causes Macduff's response? E

credulous (krĕj′ə-ləs) *adj.* Gullible.

abjure (ăb-jo͝or′) *tr.v.* To recant solemnly; to renounce.

Already at a point,° was setting forth.
Now we'll together, and the chance of goodness°
Be like our warranted quarrel.° Why are you silent?

MACDUFF. Such welcome and unwelcome things at once
'Tis hard to reconcile. **E**

(Enter [English] DOCTOR.*)*

MALCOLM. Well, more anon.—Comes the King forth, I pray you?

DOCTOR. Ay, sir; there are a crew of wretched souls
That stay his cure.° Their malady convinces
The great assay of art;° but at his touch,
Such sanctity hath heaven given his hand,
They presently° amend.

MALCOLM. I thank you, Doctor.

(Exit DOCTOR.*)*

MACDUFF. What's the disease he means?

MALCOLM. 'Tis call'd the Evil:°
A most miraculous work in this good King,
Which often since my here-remain° in England
I have seen him do. How he solicits heaven,
Himself best knows; but strangely-visited° people,
All swoll'n and ulcerous, pitiful to the eye,
The mere° despair of surgery, he cures,
Hanging a golden stamp° about their necks,
Put on with holy prayers, and 'tis spoken,
To the succeeding royalty he leaves
The healing benediction. With this strange virtue,°
He hath a heavenly gift of prophecy,
And sundry blessings hang about his throne
That speak him full of grace.

(Enter ROSS.*)*

MACDUFF. See who comes here.

MALCOLM. My countryman; but yet I know° him not.

MACDUFF. My ever gentle° cousin, welcome hither.

MALCOLM. I know him now. Good God betimes remove
The means that makes us strangers!

ROSS. Sir, amen.

MACDUFF. Stands Scotland where it did?

ROSS. Alas, poor country,
Almost afraid to know itself. It cannot
Be call'd our mother, but our grave; where nothing,
But who knows nothing,° is once seen to smile;
Where sighs, and groans, and shrieks that rend the air
Are made, not mark'd;° where violent sorrow seems
A modern ecstasy.° The dead man's knell
Is there scarce ask'd for who, and good men's lives
Expire before the flowers in their caps,
Dying or ere they sicken.

MACDUFF. O relation!
Too nice, and yet too true!

MALCOLM. What's the newest grief?

135 at . . . point: prepared for action

136 goodness: success

137 Be . . . quarrel: be as good as the outcome of our present argument

142 stay . . . cure: wait to be cured by him

143 convinces . . . art: defeats the best efforts of medical skill

145 presently: in a short time

146 Evil: scrofula, a disease that was supposedly cured by the touch of a king

148 here-remain: staying here

150 visited: afflicted

152 mere: utter

153 stamp: coin

156 virtue: power

160 know: recognize

161 gentle: noble

167 nothing . . . nothing: no one except the imbecilic

169 mark'd: noticed

170 modern ecstasy: commonplace emotion

Character: Why did Malcolm portray himself as unkingly and compare himself to Macbeth? What does the outcome of the situation reveal about Macduff, Macbeth, and Malcolm? **E**

ROSS. That of an hour's age doth hiss the speaker;°
Each minute teems° a new one.
MACDUFF. How does my wife?
ROSS. Why, well.
MACDUFF. And all my children?
ROSS. Well too.
MACDUFF. The tyrant has not batter'd at their peace?
ROSS. No, they were well at peace when I did leave 'em.
MACDUFF. Be not niggard of° your speech; how goes't?
ROSS. When I came hither to transport the tidings,
Which I have heavily borne, there ran a rumor
Of many worthy fellows that were out,°
Which was to my belief witness'd the rather,°
For that I saw the tyrant's power° afoot.
Now is the time of help; your eye in Scotland
Would create soldiers, make our women fight,
To doff° their dire distresses.
MALCOLM. Be't their comfort
We are coming thither. Gracious England hath
Lent us good Siward, and ten thousand men;
An older and better soldier none
That Christendom gives out. E
ROSS. Would I could answer
This comfort with the like! But I have words
That would be howl'd out in the desert air,
Where hearing should not latch° them.
MACDUFF. What concern they?
The general cause? or is it a fee-grief°
Due to some single breast?
ROSS. No mind that's honest
But in it shares some woe, though the main part
Pertains to you alone.
MACDUFF. If it be mine,
Keep it not from me, quickly let me have it.
ROSS. Let not your ears despise my tongue for ever,
Which shall possess them with the heaviest sound
That ever yet they heard.
MACDUFF. Humh! I guess at it.
ROSS. Your castle is surpris'd; your wife and babes
Savagely slaughter'd. To relate the manner,
Were on the quarry° of these murder'd deer
To add the death of you.
MALCOLM. Merciful heaven!
What, man, ne'er pull your hat upon your brows;
Give sorrow words. The grief that does not speak
Whispers the o'er-fraught° heart, and bids it break.
MACDUFF. My children too?
ROSS. Wife, children, servants, all
That could be found.
MACDUFF. And I must be from thence!
My wife kill'd too?
ROSS. I have said.

175 of . . . speaker: which when only one hour old is stale and thus causes the bearer of it to be hissed at

176 teems: brings forth

180 niggard of: sparing in

183 out: in the field of battle

184 witness'd . . . rather: made more believable

185 power: forces

188 doff: to put off; to turn aside

195 latch: catch

196 fee-grief: private sorrow

206 quarry: heap of slaughtered bodies

210 o'er-fraught: overburdened

Character: What is Malcolm's purpose for returning to Scotland? E

MALCOLM. Be comforted.
Let's make us med'cines of our great revenge,
To cure this deadly grief.
MACDUFF. He has no children.° All my pretty ones?
Did you say all? O hell-kite! All?
What, all my pretty chickens and their dam
At one fell swoop?°
MALCOLM. Dispute it like a man.
MACDUFF. I shall do so;
But I must also feel it as a man:
I cannot but remember such things were
That were most precious to me. Did heaven look on,
And would not take their part? Sinful Macduff,
They were all struck for thee! naught° that I am,
Not for their own demerits, but for mine,
Fell slaughter on their souls. Heaven rest them now!
MALCOLM. Be this the whetstone of your sword, let grief
Convert to anger; blunt not the heart, enrage it.
MACDUFF. O, I could play the woman with mine eyes,
And braggart with my tongue! But, gentle heavens,
Cut short all intermission. Front to front°
Bring thou this fiend of Scotland and myself;
Within my sword's length set him; if he scape,
Heaven forgive him too!°
MALCOLM. This time° goes manly,
Come go we to the King, our power is ready,
Our lack is nothing but our leave.° Macbeth
Is ripe for shaking, and the pow'rs above
Put on their instruments.° Receive what cheer you may,
The night is long that never finds the day.
(Exeunt.)

216 He . . . children: I cannot be properly revenged upon Macbeth, who has no children and who would have never slaughtered mine had he himself been a father.

219 fell swoop: i.e., of the hell-kite, a carnivorous bird of hell

225 naught: wicked

232 Front . . . front: face to face

235 too: i.e., as I will have done if I let him escape / **time:** musical tempo

237 Our . . . leave: We have time only to take our leave of the king.

239 Put . . . instruments: arm themselves

Oral Reading: What verse structure does Shakespeare use to signal the end of act 4?

THINK AND DISCUSS

1. Identify two examples of blank verse in act 4. Explain why each is an example of blank verse. Why is blank verse appropriate in each example's context?
2. Identify a scene in act 4 that switches from blank verse to prose (or vice versa). Explain why Shakespeare switched from one to the other. How does this change inform an oral reading of that scene?
3. Identify two examples of trochaic tetrameter with rhymed couplets in act 4. Why is each example appropriate for that scene and speaker? How does the meter inform an oral reading of those examples?
4. Identify two motifs repeated in act 4. Explain why each qualifies as a motif. For each motif, cite two specific examples from the text and explain how each example contributes to the development of the motif.
5. Pick one of the two motifs (from question 4) and trace it throughout the play thus far. Cite a minimum of three examples from acts 1–4 and explain how each example contributes to the development of the motif. How does this motif support one of Macbeth's themes?
6. Describe Macbeth's character qualities. Do you think he was qualified to be king of Scotland? Support your answer with evidence from act 4.
7. Does Macbeth have the opportunity to do right? How and when does he harden his heart (conscience)? What do you think will be the outcome of his actions? What light does Proverbs 29:1 shed on such actions?
8. Would Malcolm be a better king than Macbeth? Cite at least two pieces of evidence from act 4 to support your answer. Evaluate Malcolm in the light of Romans 13:4; James 4:10; and Matthew 7:12 and 20:26.

ANALYZE: *Tragic Hero*

Review the definitions of *tragic hero*, *tragic flaw*, and *tragic plot* from the Renaissance Drama introduction (p. 209). Ask yourself the following questions (and revisit them as you read) to decide whether Macbeth qualifies as a tragic hero:

1. Was Macbeth initially a good (or at least not distinctively bad) character? (Consider his behavior in act 1 and what Lady Macbeth says about him.)
2. Was Macbeth's decision to kill Duncan prompted by a tragic flaw? (A tragic hero's bad decision is not motivated by malice but by a flaw [e.g., pride that refuses to listen to good advice]. Why did Macbeth kill Duncan?)
3. Did Macbeth experience a reversal of fortunes? (Compare his life at the beginning of the play with his life in the final act.)
4. Would an audience feel pity and fear while watching *Macbeth*? (What is Macbeth's ending? Does he deserve it? Would an audience be likely to fear that something similar could happen to them?)

READ: *Make Thematic Connections*

Reread the Read paragraph on page 229. Remember the importance of a work's themes and how its literary elements (setting, character, imagery, symbol, plot, motif, etc.) intertwine to support its themes. By now you should have identified some of *Macbeth*'s major themes and pointed to textual evidence (details, descriptions, dialogue, etc.) that reveals and supports these themes. As you enter act 5, continue to make (and reinforce) thematic connections between literary elements analyzed thus far in *Macbeth*. For instance, what connections can you make between the witches' prophecy in act 1, Lady Macbeth's role, and the fate of Macbeth in act 5? Has Macbeth been unduly influenced by malevolent forces? Or is his final outcome a product of his own evil design? Making connections like this is vital to a "big picture" understanding of the work's profound messages.

CREATE: *A Character Analysis*

At the end of act 2, you wrote a psychological profile of the Macbeths based on their criminal actions. What direction did their ambition take them in act 2? What predictions did you make about their future trajectory? Now, having read acts 3 and 4, have your predictions changed? After reading act 5, you will write a revised conclusion that incorporates new evidence you have found. Based on your conclusions, what do you think Shakespeare is saying about ambition? Examine both its physical (external) and spiritual (internal) consequences. For instance, what internal, psychological effect does guilt have? Read with these questions in mind and then incorporate your findings into your revision.

OBJECTIVES

- Summarize a text's key events and ideas.
- Analyze a text's literary elements to determine its major themes.
- Determine whether a drama qualifies as a tragedy.
- Evaluate a text's themes from a biblical worldview.
- Revise a character analysis of a work's major characters.

VOCABULARY

avouch (ə-vouch′) *tr.v.* To declare the provable truth or validity of; affirm.

harbinger (här′bĭn-jər) *n.* One that indicates or foreshadows what is to come; a forerunner.

brandish (brăn′dĭsh) *tr.v.* To wave or flourish (something, often a weapon) in a menacing, defiant, or excited way.

vulnerable (vŭl′nər-ə-bəl) *adj.* Susceptible to physical harm or damage; susceptible to attack.

prowess (prou′ĭs) *n.* Superior strength, courage, or daring, especially in battle.

ACT 5

SCENE 1

(Enter [Scottish] DOCTOR *and a* WAITING-GENTLEWOMAN.*)*

DOCTOR. I have two nights watch'd with you, but can perceive no truth in your report. When was it she last walk'd?

GENTLEWOMAN. Since his Majesty went into the field,° I have seen her rise from her bed, throw her night-gown upon her, unlock her closet, take forth paper, fold it, write upon't, read it, afterwards seal it, and again return to bed; yet all this while in a most fast sleep.

DOCTOR. A great perturbation in nature, to receive at once the benefit of sleep, and do the effects of watching.° In this slumb'ry agitation, besides her walking and other actual performances, what, at any time, have you heard her say?

GENTLEWOMAN. That, sir, which I will not report after her.

DOCTOR. You may to me, and 'tis most meet you should.

GENTLEWOMAN. Neither to you nor any one, having no witness to confirm my speech.

(Enter LADY MACBETH *with a taper.)*

Lo you, here she comes. This is her very guise,° and upon my life, fast asleep. Observe her, stand close.°

DOCTOR. How came she by that light?

GENTLEWOMAN. Why, it stood by her. She has light by her continually, 'tis her command.

DOCTOR. You see her eyes are open.

GENTLEWOMAN. Ay, but their sense are shut.°

DOCTOR. What is it she does now? Look how she rubs her hands.

GENTLEWOMAN. It is an accustom'd action with her, to seem thus washing her hands. I have known her continue in this a quarter of an hour.

LADY MACBETH. Yet here's a spot.

DOCTOR. Hark, she speaks. I will set down what comes from her, to satisfy° my remembrance the more strongly.

LADY MACBETH. Out, damn'd spot! out, I say! *[Bell rings without.]*° One—two—why then 'tis time to do't. Hell is murky.° Fie,° my lord, fie! A soldier, and afeard? What need we fear who knows it, when none can call our pow'r to accompt?° Yet who would have thought the old man to have had so much blood in him?

DOCTOR. Do you mark that?

LADY MACBETH. The Thane of Fife° had a wife; where is she now? What, will these hands ne'er be clean? No more o' that, my lord, no more o' that; you mar all with this starting.°

DOCTOR. Go to, go to! You have known what you should not.

GENTLEWOMAN. She has spoke what she should not, I am sure of that; heaven knows what she has known.

LADY MACBETH. Here's the smell of the blood still. All the perfumes of Arabia will not sweeten this little hand. O, O, O!

DOCTOR. What a sigh is there! The heart is sorely charg'd.

GENTLEWOMAN. I would not have such a heart in my bosom for the dignity of the whole body.

3 **field:** i.e., of battle

9 **effects . . . watching:** actions of one who is awake

16 **guise:** custom

17 **close:** concealed

22 **their . . . shut:** They are sightless.

28 **satisfy:** confirm

29 **without:** outside, or offstage

30 **murky:** dark / **Fie:** used to express distaste or disapproval

32 **accompt:** account

36 **Thane . . . Fife:** i.e., Macduff

38 **starting:** startled reaction

DOCTOR. Well, well, well.

GENTLEWOMAN. Pray God it be, sir.

DOCTOR. This disease is beyond my practice; yet I have known those which have walk'd in their sleep who have died holily in their beds.

LADY MACBETH. Wash your hands, put on your nightgown, look not so pale. I tell you yet again, Banquo's buried; he cannot come out on 's grave.

DOCTOR. Even so?

LADY MACBETH. To bed, to bed; there's knocking at the gate. Come, come, come, come, give me your hand. What's done cannot be undone. To bed, to bed, to bed. **R**

(Exit LADY MACBETH.*)*

DOCTOR. Will she go now to bed?

GENTLEWOMAN. Directly.

DOCTOR. Foul whisp'rings are abroad. Unnatural deeds
Do breed unnatural troubles; infected minds
To their deaf pillows will discharge their secrets.
More needs she the divine than the physician.
God, God, forgive us all! Look after her,
Remove from her the means of all annoyance,°
And still keep eyes upon her. So good night.
My mind she has mated,° and amaz'd my sight.
I think, but dare not speak. **E**

GENTLEWOMAN. Good night, good doctor.

(Exeunt.)

VISUAL ANALYSIS
Contrast the actress's portrayal of Lady Macbeth in this scene with her portrayal in the scene pictured on page 227. How do they differ? What do the differences suggest about Lady Macbeth as a character?

65 **annoyance:** injury, harm to herself

67 **mated:** bewildered, confounded

Thematic Connections: What is the spot Lady Macbeth is trying to remove? Is it real or imaginary? What does it symbolize? What do water and washing symbolize? **R**

Character Analysis: Reread lines 60–68. How does the doctor describe Lady Macbeth's state of mind? Can he help her? What do his instructions (ll. 65–66) indicate that he fears? **E**

The country near Dunsinane

(Drum and colors.° Enter MENTEITH, CAITHNESS, ANGUS, LENNOX, SOLDIERS.*)*

MENTEITH. The English pow'r is near, led on by Malcolm,
His uncle Siward, and the good Macduff.
Revenges burn in them; for their dear causes
Would to the bleeding and the grim alarm,°
Excite the mortified° man.

ANGUS. Near Birnan wood
Shall we meet them; that way are they coming.

CAITHNESS. Who knows if Donalbain be with his brother?

LENNOX. For certain, sir, he is not; I have a file°
Of all the gentry. There is Siward's son,
And many unrough° youths that even now
Protest their first of manhood.°

MENTEITH. What does the tyrant?

CAITHNESS. Great Dunsinane he strongly fortifies.
Some say he's mad; others that lesser hate him
Do call it valiant fury; but for certain
He cannot buckle his distemp'red° cause
Within the belt of rule.°

ANGUS. Now does he feel
His secret murders sticking on his hands;
Now minutely° revolts upbraid his faith-breach;
Those he commands move only in command,
Nothing in love. Now does he feel his title
Hang loose about him, like a giant's robe
Upon a dwarfish thief. R

MENTEITH. Who then shall blame
His pest'red° senses to recoil and start,
When all that is within him does condemn
Itself for being there?

CAITHNESS. Well, march we on
To give obedience where 'tis truly ow'd.
Meet we the med'cine of the sickly weal,°
And with him pour we, in our country's purge,
Each drop of us.

LENNOX. Or so much as it needs
To dew° the sovereign flower° and drown the weeds.
Make we our march towards Birnan. A

(Exeunt, marching.)

Drum . . . colors: a drummer and a soldier bearing the flag

4 bleeding . . . alarm: i.e., the battlefield

5 mortified: dead

8 file: list

10 unrough: unbearded

11 Protest . . . manhood: proclaim their manhood for the first time

15 distemp'red: diseased

16 Within . . . rule: under control

18 minutely: those occurring every minute

23 pest'red: tormented

27 med'cine . . . weal: the cure of the state; i.e., Malcolm

30 dew: water / **sovereign flower:** Malcolm

Macbeth's castle at Dunsinane

(Enter MACBETH *and* ATTENDANTS.*)*

MACBETH. Bring me no more reports, let them fly all.
Till Birnan wood remove to Dunsinane
I cannot taint° with fear. What's the boy Malcolm?
Was he not born of woman? The spirits that know

3 taint: be infected

Thematic Connections: How do lines 17–18, which are about Macbeth, relate to Lady Macbeth's "spot" scene? R

Tragic Hero: What evidence in scene 2 shows the results of Macbeth's tragic flaw? A

All mortal consequences° have pronounc'd me thus:
"Fear not, Macbeth, no man that's born of woman
Shall e'er have power upon thee." Then fly, false thanes,
And mingle with the English epicures!°
The mind I sway° by and the heart I bear
Shall never sag with doubt, nor shake with fear.

(Enter SERVANT.*)*

The devil damn thee black, thou cream-fac'd loon!°
Where got'st thou that goose look?°

SERVANT. There is ten thousand—

MACBETH. Geese, villain?

SERVANT. Soldiers, sir.

MACBETH. Go prick thy face, and over-red thy fear,°
Thou lily-liver'd boy. What soldiers, patch?°
Death of thy soul! those linen cheeks of thine
Are counsellors to fear.° What soldiers, whey-face?°

SERVANT. The English force, so please you.

MACBETH. Take thy face hence. *(Exit* SERVANT.*)* Seyton!—I am sick at heart.
When I behold—Seyton, I say!—This push°
Will cheer me ever, or disseat° me now.
I have liv'd long enough: my way of life
Is fall'n into the sear,° the yellow leaf,
And that which should accompany old age,
As honor, love, obedience, troops of friends,
I must not look to have; but in their stead,
Curses, not loud but deep, mouth-honor, breath,
Which the poor heart would fain deny, and dare not.°
Seyton! **A**

(Enter SEYTON *[and Scottish* DOCTOR*].)*

SEYTON. What's your gracious pleasure?

MACBETH. What news more?

SEYTON. All is confirm'd, my lord, which was reported.

MACBETH. I'll fight, till from my bones my flesh be hack'd.
Give me my armor.

SEYTON. 'Tis not needed yet.

MACBETH. I'll put it on.
Send out moe° horses, skirr° the country round,
Hang those that talk of fear. Give me mine armor.
How does your patient, doctor?

DOCTOR. Not so sick, my lord,
As she is troubled with thick-coming fancies,
That keep her from rest.

MACBETH. Cure her of that.
Canst thou not minister to a mind diseas'd,
Pluck from the memory a rooted sorrow,
Raze out° the written° troubles of the brain,
And with some sweet oblivious° antidote
Cleanse the stuff'd bosom of that perilous stuff
Which weighs upon the heart?

DOCTOR. Therein the patient
Must minister to himself. **E**

5 mortal consequences: human destinies

8 epicures: people devoted to sensuous pleasure and luxurious living

9 sway: rule

11 loon: rogue, worthless rascal

12 Where . . . look?: Why do you look like a frightened goose?

14 over-red thy fear: bring some color back into your face

15 patch: fool, clown

17 linen . . . fear: your pale face will influence others to be fearful / **whey face**: pale face

20 push: attack

21 disseat: dethrone

23 sear: withered

27 not . . . not: people who honor me with their words but not in their hearts

35 moe: more / **skirr**: scour

42 Raze out: erase / **written**: permanent, fixed

43 oblivious: causing forgetfulness

Tragic Hero: In what way has Macbeth's fortune reversed? What has he lost? **A**

Character Analysis: What psychological effect does Lady Macbeth's guilt have on her? **E**

MACBETH. Throw physic° to the dogs, I'll none of it.
Come, put mine armor on; give me my staff.
Seyton, send out. Doctor, the thanes fly from me.—
Come, sir, dispatch.°—If thou couldst, doctor, cast
The water° of my land, find her disease,
And purge it to a sound and pristine° health,
I would applaud thee to the very echo,
That should applaud again.—Pull't off, I say.°—
What rhubarb, senna,° or what purgative drug,
Would scour° these English hence? Hear'st thou of them?
DOCTOR. Ay, my good lord; your royal preparation°
Makes us hear something.
MACBETH. Bring it after me.°—
I will not be afraid of death and bane,°
Till Birnan forest come to Dunsinane.
(Exeunt all but the DOCTOR.*)*
DOCTOR. Were I from Dunsinane away and clear,
Profit again should hardly draw me here.
(Exit.)

47 **physic:** medicine

50 **dispatch:** make haste

51 **cast . . . water:** diagnose the ailment

52 **pristine:** uncorrupted

54 **Pull't . . . say:** referring to a part of his armor that has not been put on properly

55 **senna:** a medicinal plant

56 **scour:** make them run swiftly

57 **royal preparation:** preparation for war

58 **Bring . . . me:** referring to the piece of armor alluded to at line 54

59 **bane:** destruction

The country near Birnan Wood

(Drum and colors. Enter MALCOLM, SIWARD, MACDUFF, SIWARD'S SON, MENTEITH, CAITHNESS, ANGUS, LENNOX, ROSS, *and* SOLDIERS, *marching.)*

MALCOLM. Cousins, I hope the days are near at hand
That chambers° will be safe.
MENTEITH. We doubt it nothing.
SIWARD. What wood is this before us?
MENTEITH. The wood of Birnan.
MALCOLM. Let every soldier hew him down a bough,
And bear't before him, thereby shall we shadow
The number of our host, and make discovery
Err in report of us.
SOLDIERS. It shall be done.
SIWARD. We learn no other but the confident tyrant
Keeps still in Dunsinane, and will endure
Our setting down before't.°
MALCOLM. 'Tis his main hope;
For where there is advantage° to be gone,
Both more and less have given him the revolt,°
And none serve with him but constrainèd° things,
Whose hearts are absent too.
MACDUFF. Let our just censures°
Attend the true event,° and put we on
Industrious soldiership.
SIWARD. The time approaches
That will with due decision make us know
What we shall say we have, and what we owe.
Thoughts speculative their unsure hopes relate,
But certain issue strokes must arbitrate,°
Towards which advance the war.
(Exeunt, marching.)

2 **chambers:** bedchambers, or bedrooms

10 **setting . . . before't:** seige of it

11 **advantage:** opportunity

12 **Both . . . revolt:** Both the great and lowly have deserted Macbeth.

13 **constrainèd:** forced

14 **just censures:** judgments

15 **Attend . . . event:** await the actual outcome of the battle

20 **Thoughts . . . arbitrate:** Speculating about the future is dealing merely in hopes, but actions decide the real issue.

Reading Check: Why does Malcolm instruct his soldiers to "hew . . . down a bough"?

SCENE 5

Macbeth's castle at Dunsinane

(Enter MACBETH, SEYTON, *and* SOLDIERS, *with drum and colors.)*

MACBETH. Hang out our banners on the outward walls,
The cry is still, "They come!" Our castle's strength
Will laugh a siege to scorn; here let them lie
Till famine and the ague° eat them up.
Were they not forc'd° with those that should be ours,
We might have met them dareful,° beard to beard,
And beat them backward home.

(A cry within of women.)

What is that noise?

SEYTON. It is the cry of women, my good lord.

(Exit.)

MACBETH. I have almost forgot the taste of fears.
The time has been, my senses would have cool'd°
To hear a night-shriek, and my fell of hair°
Would at a dismal treatise° rouse and stir
As life were in't. I have supp'd full with horrors;
Direness, familiar to my slaughterous thoughts,
Cannot once start° me.

(Enter SEYTON.*)*

Wherefore was that cry?

SEYTON. The Queen, my lord, is dead.

MACBETH. She should have died hereafter;°
There would have been a time for such a word.
Tomorrow, and tomorrow, and tomorrow,
Creeps in this petty pace from day to day,
To the last syllable of recorded time;
And all our yesterdays have lighted fools
The way to dusty death. Out, out, brief candle!
Life's but a walking shadow, a poor player,
That struts and frets his hour upon the stage,
And then is heard no more. It is a tale
Told by an idiot, full of sound and fury,
Signifying nothing. E

4 **ague:** fever

5 **forc'd:** reinforced

6 **dareful:** defiantly

10 **cool'd:** been chilled with fright

11 **my . . . hair:** the hair on my skin

12 **treatise:** story

15 **start:** startle

17 **She . . . hereafter:** She would have died sometime, or death should have occurred at a more opportune time.

Character Analysis: Reread lines 9–28. How have Macbeth's crimes changed him? What kind of attitude does he now possess? Why does he feel this way? E

(Enter a MESSENGER.*)*

Thou com'st to use thy tongue;
Thy story quickly.
MESSENGER. Gracious, my lord,
I should report that which I say I saw,
But know not how to do't.
MACBETH. Well, say, sir.
MESSENGER. As I did stand my watch upon the hill,
I look'd toward Birnan, and anon methought
The wood began to move.
MACBETH. Liar and slave!
MESSENGER. Let me endure your wrath, if't be not so.
Within this three mile may you see it coming;
I say, a moving grove.
MACBETH. If thou speak'st false,
Upon the next tree shall thou hang alive,
Till famine cling° thee; if thy speech be sooth,°
I care not if thou dost for me as much.
I pull in resolution,° and begin
To doubt th' equivocation of the fiend
That lies like truth. "Fear not, till Birnan wood
Do come to Dunsinane," and now a wood
Comes toward Dunsinane. Arm, arm, and out!
If this which he **avouches** does appear,
There is nor flying hence, nor tarrying here.
I 'gin to be a-weary of the sun,
And wish th' estate o' th' world° were now undone.
Ring the alarum-bell! Blow wind, come wrack,°
At least we'll die with harness° on our back. R

(Exeunt.)

39 cling: shrivel / **sooth:** truth

41 pull . . . resolution: check my courage

49 estate . . . world: universe

50 wrack: ruin

51 harness: armor

The plain before Macbeth's castle at Dunsinane

(Drum and colors. Enter MALCOLM, SIWARD, MACDUFF, *and their army, with boughs.)*

MALCOLM. Now near enough; your leavy° screens throw down,
And show like those you are.° You, worthy uncle,
Shall with my cousin, your right noble son,
Lead our first battle.° Worthy Macduff and we
Shall take upon 's what else remains to do,
According to our order.°
SIWARD. Fare you well.
Do we but find the tyrant's power tonight,
Let us be beaten, if we cannot fight.
MACDUFF. Make all our trumpets speak, give them all breath,
Those clamorous **harbingers** of blood and death.

(Exeunt. Alarums continued.)

1 leavy: leafy

2 show . . . are: reveal your true identities

4 battle: battalion

6 order: plan of attack

avouch (ə-vouch') *tr.v.* To declare the provable truth or validity of; affirm.

Thematic Connections: Reread lines 38–50. How does Macbeth respond to the messenger? Why? What theme does this scene support? R

harbinger (här'bĭn-jər) *n.* One that indicates or foreshadows what is to come; a forerunner.

Another part of the plain

([Alarums.] Enter MACBETH.*)*

MACBETH. They have tied me to a stake; I cannot fly,
But bear-like° I must fight the course. What's he
That was not born of woman? Such a one
Am I to fear, or none.

(Enter YOUNG SIWARD.*)*

YOUNG SIWARD. What is thy name?
MACBETH. Thou'lt be afraid to hear it.
YOUNG SIWARD. No; though thou call'st thyself a hotter name
Than any is in hell.
MACBETH. My name's Macbeth.
YOUNG SIWARD. The devil himself could not pronounce a title
More hateful to mine ear.
MACBETH. No; nor more fearful.
YOUNG SIWARD. Thou liest, abhorrèd tyrant; with my sword
I'll prove the lie thou speak'st.

(A fight ensues, and YOUNG SIWARD *is slain.)*

MACBETH. Thou wast born of woman.
But swords I smile at, weapons laugh to scorn,
Brandish'd by man that's of a woman born. R

(Exit.)

(Alarums. Enter MACDUFF.*)*

MACDUFF. That way the noise is. Tyrant, show thy face!
If thou beest slain and with no stroke of mine,
My wife and children's ghosts will haunt me still.
I cannot strike at wretched kerns,° whose arms
Are hir'd to bear their staves;° either thou, Macbeth,
Or else my sword with an unbattered edge
I sheathe again undeeded.° There thou shouldst be;
By this great clatter, one of greatest note
Seems bruited.° Let me find him, Fortune!
And more I beg not.

(Exit. Alarums.)

2 **bear-like:** like a bear chained to a stake and attacked by dogs as in bearbaiting, a favorite sport of Shakespeare's age

17 **kerns:** foot soldiers

18 **staves:** spears

20 **undeeded:** not having performed any deeds

22 **bruited:** announced with a clamor

brandish (brăn′dĭsh) *tr.v.* To wave or flourish (something, often a weapon) in a menacing, defiant, or excited way.

Thematic Connections: How does Macbeth react to having slain Young Siward? R

(Enter MALCOLM *and* SIWARD.*)*

SIWARD. This way, my lord, the castle's gently rend'red:°
The tyrant's people on both sides do fight;
The noble thanes do bravely in the war,
The day almost itself professes yours,
And little is to do.

MALCOLM. We have met with foes
That strike beside us.°

SIWARD. Enter, sir, the castle.

(Exeunt. Alarum.)

24 gently rend'red: easily captured

29 strike . . . us: fight on our side; i.e., those who have deserted Macbeth

SCENE 8

Another part of the plain

(Enter MACBETH.*)*

MACBETH. Why should I play the Roman fool,° and die
On mine own sword? Whiles I see lives, the gashes
Do better upon them.

(Enter MACDUFF.*)*

MACDUFF. Turn, hell-hound, turn!

MACBETH. Of all men else I have avoided thee.
But get thee back; my soul is too much charg'd
With blood of thine already.

MACDUFF. I have no words,
My voice is in my sword, thou bloodier villain
Than terms can give thee out!°

([They] fight. Alarum.)

MACBETH. Thou losest labor.
As easy mayst thou the intrenchant air
With thy keen sword impress as make me bleed.
Let fall thy blade on **vulnerable** crests,°
I bear a charmèd life, which must not yield
To one of woman born.

MACDUFF. Despair thy charm,
And let the angel whom thou still hast serv'd
Tell thee, Macduff was from his mother's womb
Untimely ripp'd.°

MACBETH. Accursèd be that tongue that tells me so,
For it hath cow'd my better part of man!°
And be these juggling fiends no more believ'd,
That palter° with us in a double sense,
That keep the word of promise to our ear,
And break it to our hope. I'll not fight with thee. R

MACDUFF. Then yield thee, coward,
And live to be the show and gaze o' th' time!
We'll have thee, as our rarer monsters are,
Painted upon a pole,° and underwrit,
"Here may you see the tyrant."

MACBETH. I will not yield,
To kiss the ground before young Malcolm's feet,
And to be baited° with the rabble's curse.

1 play . . . fool: commit suicide so as to die nobly

8 terms . . . out: words can describe

11 crests: coat of arms on a helmet; vulnerable crests: a soldier that can be harmed

16 Untimely ripp'd: taken prematurely in a surgical procedure

18 better . . . man: courage

20 palter: shuffle, equivocate

26 Painted . . . pole: i.e., your portrait stuck on a pole

29 baited: ridiculed, insulted

vulnerable (vŭl'nər-ə-bəl) *adj.* Susceptible to physical harm or damage; susceptible to attack.

Thematic Connections: What reality does Macbeth discover that destroys his belief that he "bear[s] a charmed life"? What part did the witches play in this situation? R

Though Birnan wood be come to Dunsinane,
And thou oppos'd, being of no woman born,
Yet I will try the last. Before my body
I throw my warlike shield. Lay on, Macduff,
And damn'd be him that first cries, "Hold, enough!"

(Exeunt, fighting. Alarums.)

([Re-]enter, fighting, and MACBETH *is slain. [Exit* MACBETH*, falling.])* **A**

SCENE 9

Macbeth's castle at Dunsinane

(Retreat and flourish. Enter with drum and colors MALCOLM, SIWARD, ROSS, THANES, *and* SOLDIERS.*)*

MALCOLM. I would the friends we miss were safe arriv'd.
SIWARD. Some must go off;° and yet, by these I see,
So great a day as this is cheaply bought.
MALCOLM. Macduff is missing, and your noble son.
ROSS. Your son, my lord, has paid a soldier's debt.
He only liv'd but till he was a man,
The which no sooner had his **prowess** confirm'd
In the unshrinking station where he fought,
But like a man he died.
SIWARD. Then he is dead?
ROSS. Ay, and brought off the field. Your cause of sorrow
Must not be measur'd by his worth, for then
It hath no end.
SIWARD. Had he his hurts before?
ROSS. Ay, on the front.
SIWARD. Why, then, God's soldier be he!
Had I as many sons as I have hairs,
I would not wish them to a fairer death.
And so his knell is knoll'd.°
MALCOLM. He's worth more sorrow,
And that I'll spend for him.
SIWARD. He's worth no more;
They say he parted° well, and paid his score,
And so God be with him! Here comes newer comfort.

2 **go off:** be killed

16 **knell is knoll'd:** his time has come to die

18 **parted:** departed

Tragic Hero: Does Macbeth deserve to die? Why? **A**

prowess (prou'ĭs) *n.* Superior strength, courage, or daring, especially in battle.

(Enter MACDUFF *with Macbeth's head [on a pole.])*

MACDUFF. Hail, King! for so thou art. Behold where stands
Th' usurper's cursèd head. The time is free.
I see thee compass'd with thy kingdom's pearl,°
That speak my salutation in their minds;
Whose voices I desire aloud with mine:
Hail, King of Scotland!

ALL. Hail, King of Scotland!

(Flourish.)

MALCOLM. We shall not spend a large expense of time
Before we reckon with your several loves,°
And make us even with you.° My thanes and kinsmen,
Henceforth be earls, the first that ever Scotland
In such an honor nam'd. What's more to do,
Which would be planted newly with the time—
As calling home our exil'd friends abroad
That fled the snares of watchful tyranny,
Producing forth° the cruel ministers
Of this dead butcher and his fiend-like queen,
Who, as 'tis thought, by self and violent hands
Took off her life—this, and what needful else
That calls upon us, by the grace of Grace,
We will perform in measure,° time, and place.
So thanks to all at once and to each one,
Whom we invite to see us crown'd at Scone. E

(Flourish. Exeunt.)

22 compass'd . . . pearl: surrounded by the noblemen of your realm

27 reckon . . . loves: reward each of you as your loyalty and service deserves

28 make . . . you: reward you for your services

34 Producing forth: bringing to trial

39 measure: due proportion

Character Analysis: What was the final outcome of Lady Macbeth's sin and subsequent guilt? E

THINK AND DISCUSS

1. To what specific incidents does Lady Macbeth refer in her sleep? Which incident has affected her the most, and why do you think it has done so? Why is it appropriate that Lady Macbeth suffers from a sleep disorder?
2. Why does Lady Macbeth feel a need to continually wash her hands?
3. Although Macbeth washed his hands in act 2, Angus describes Macbeth in act 5 as having "murders sticking on his hands." What does he mean?
4. What reaction does Macbeth display (5.5.17–28) when he learns of his wife's death? What spiritual reality has ultimately caused this emotional state?
5. Trace Macbeth's struggle in act 5 with the fulfillment of the witches' deceptive riddles. How does he attempt to manipulate the results? What do these events suggest about fate and free will?
6. In act 4 Macbeth took the witches' riddles literally. What did the riddles really mean as revealed in act 5? Identify three additional examples of appearance versus reality from acts 1–5. Explain how two of the examples connect thematically.
7. The themes of unchecked ambition and of orderliness (based on the Great Chain of Being) run throughout acts 1–5. Choose one of these themes and provide an example of it from act 5. Connect your example to another instance of that same theme in another act.
8. Does Macbeth qualify as a tragic hero? Read through the numbered list in the Analyze section on page 269, and use the questions listed there to develop your answer. Justify your answer with evidence from acts 1–5.
9. Write a revised conclusion for your psychological profile (p. 229) based on any additional evidence from act 5. Based on your conclusions, what do you think Shakespeare is saying about ambition? Examine both its physical (external) and spiritual (internal) consequences.
10. Evaluate whether Shakespeare's views on ambition, consequences to actions, and nurturing wrong desires align with the Scriptures. Consider what the Bible says about these ideas in the following passages: James 4:1–2, Philippians 2:3, 1 John 2:16, 1 Timothy 6:9, Galatians 6:7–8, Ephesians 4:17–19, and Proverbs 28:13–14.

What Do You Know?

Understand the Background

1. Where were Shakespeare's plays performed during his lifetime? What was the significance of the name of the second theater?
2. Draw a diagram of each of the three Elizabethan stage designs.
3. What source did Shakespeare use for *Macbeth*? Is the play historically accurate?

Apply the Concepts

4. What elements classify *Macbeth* as a tragedy?
5. Which of the unities are evident in *Macbeth*?
6. How does atmosphere in act 3, scene 4, reinforce a theme in *Macbeth*? Use an example from the text as support.
7. List the plot elements and trace them throughout *Macbeth*. Include specific details to support your answer.
8. Explain how and why Shakespeare strategically used prose, blank verse, and trochaic tetrameter with rhymed couplets throughout *Macbeth*.
9. Distinguish between dramatic irony and verbal irony, specifically sarcasm and hyperbole.
10. How does the imagery in *Macbeth* point to a theme? Use an example to explain.
11. Trace a symbol throughout *Macbeth*, providing several examples of it. What is its symbolic meaning?
12. How does a motif in *Macbeth* reinforce a theme (list a different theme from question 10)? Use examples to support your answer.

Evaluate the Ideas

13. Identify several expressions of Macbeth's and Lady Macbeth's guilt. Do the emotional consequences of their actions align with Scripture? Support your answer.
14. How do Macbeth and Lady Macbeth change throughout the play? Justify your answer from the text.

Write a Response

15. Compare the attitude toward actors and playwrights in the early sixteenth century to the modern attitude toward those roles. How has the availability of information on actors and playwrights changed? How does the amount of information available regarding Shakespeare's life and plays affect perspective?

Define each term and provide an example of each from a selection in Unit 2, Part 4.

TERMS

tragedy
tragic hero
tragic flaw
tragic plot
soliloquy
aside
setting
atmosphere
conflict
imagery
theme
verbal irony
sarcasm
hyperbole
dramatic irony
plot
exposition
inciting incident
rising action
crisis
climax
falling action
denouement
motif

UNIT 3 OBJECTIVES

LITERARY ELEMENTS

- Analyze and interpret works in the following genres and modes: lyric poetry, dramatic monologue, literary epic, the novel, eyewitness account, verse epistle, essay, literary criticism, biography, elegy, slave narrative, speech, argumentation, satire, and allegory.
- Determine how a text exhibits neoclassical ideas and style (e.g., heroic couplet).
- Determine how sensory detail, anecdote, imagery, figurative language, symbol, and allegory contribute to a work's purpose or themes.
- Analyze the relationship between a work's characters, speaker/narrator, tone, and themes.
- Examine an argumentative work's main ideas and use of rhetorical appeals and devices to create an effective and valid argument.

READING STRATEGIES

- Ask questions of a text.
- Determine purpose for a text.
- Infer meaning from a text.

TEXT CRITICISM AND CREATION

- Evaluate from a biblical worldview the perspectives of authors on issues such as personal honor, death, race, rationalism, human nature and society, and the connection between virtue and reading.
- Evaluate the use and validity of rhetorical appeals.
- Evaluate and compare critical perspectives on texts.
- Compose texts in a variety of genres based on model works.

UNIT 3
Civil War to Enlightenment
(1640–1789)

294 **CIVIL WAR AND RESTORATION**

320 **EARLY NEOCLASSICAL WRITERS**

358 **AGE OF JOHNSON**

380 **VOICES FROM THE OUTSIDE**

Civil War to Enlightenment

England underwent significant social, religious, and political upheavals in the seventeenth century; these included a protracted civil war and more than one political revolution. Unsurprisingly, then, intellectual leaders of the century that followed favored moderation and restraint while political leaders looked suspiciously on religious enthusiasm as disruptive of a well-ordered society. This new mood favored the rule of reason and knowledge in all areas of life—an attitude known as **rationalism**.

This era of rationalism, spanning the late seventeenth century and most of the eighteenth, is termed the Enlightenment. Educated Europeans saw their society as having emerged from centuries of superstition and crudity into reason's clear light. Combined with scientific, political, and industrial advances, this new attitude would produce an entirely new kind of literature.

POLITICAL DEVELOPMENTS

CIVIL WAR AND THE INTERREGNUM

Civil War In England, the early seventeenth century was characterized by escalating conflicts between the Stuart kings and their people (p. 126). These exploded into the Civil War (1642–51) with two distinct stages. The first ended with traditional institutions generally intact. The second overthrew the monarchy, executed the king, and struggled to create a new kind of government.

In general, the conflict pitted Parliamentarian against Royalist forces. Parliament (i.e., the House of Commons), typically supported by Puritans, Dissenters, and urbanites such as the newly powerful middle class, represented those who feared Charles I's suspected Catholic sympathies and insistence on divine right (the idea that his authority came from God and he answered only to God). Both positions were felt as a threat to English sovereignty, Protestantism, and popular freedoms. In response, Parliament pushed for control in areas long considered royal domain. Royalists, meanwhile, were typically conservative aristocrats and rural inhabitants who valued a traditional monarchy and social hierarchy. With Charles, they pushed back against Parliament's demands.

Parliamentarians dubbed certain Royalists "Cavaliers" for their unseemly eagerness for war and often frivolous, indulgent lifestyle. Royalists (who embraced "Cavalier" as a reference to gallantry and courtliness) mockingly termed Parliamentarians "Roundheads" for sporting short hair instead of fashionable long ringlets.

Tensions finally ignited when Charles I's highhandedness precipitated a Scottish invasion (p. 126). Although the king's forces won some initial victories, a reform of Parliament's army changed the tide. Led by generals Thomas Fairfax and Oliver Cromwell, this New Model Army purged its aristocratic officers and chose leaders by military ability and dedication. Charles's surrender to the Scots in 1646 ended this first stage of the Civil War.

In 1647 the conflict reignited with a radical turn: the army, disenchanted with the lack of reforms, forcibly removed 11 conservative members of Parliament. The king again challenged the army but was forced to surrender in 1648. The army then removed 110 representatives, and 160 more left in protest. The remaining "rump" parliament narrowly voted to give the House of Commons supreme authority and, in 1649, to execute the king as a traitor. Deemed regicide, this was a radical move that sent shock waves across Europe.

Oliver Cromwell One of the New Model Army's key leaders, Oliver Cromwell began as a country gentleman who won a seat in Parliament in the late 1620s. A devoted Puritan, he opposed the king's religious policies but was not yet a strong political reformer. When the Civil War broke out, Cromwell raised troops in his home territory (Cambridge) and vaulted to national attention as a brilliant military commander. By 1644 he was appointed second in command of the army and given the rank of lieutenant general.

In the tense period between the two stages of the Civil War, Cromwell tried repeatedly and unsuccessfully to reconcile the army, Parliament, and the king. Once Charles I fled London and opened talks with the Scots, however, Cromwell began to turn against the king. Though not an instigator of Charles's execution, Cromwell was among those who signed the death warrant. A man of great ability, he would dominate the government during the Interregnum.

The Interregnum Denoting the years between Charles I's and Charles II's reign, the Interregnum encompassed both the Commonwealth (1649–53) and the Protectorate (1654–60). The first was a republican government set up by Parliament after Charles's execution. Heading its executive council, Cromwell spent most of his time crushing uprisings, often brutally, in Ireland and Scotland as the army's supreme commander. Unfortunately, tensions between him and Parliament led to the republic's failure (1653). Its replacement, the Instrument of Government (England's only written constitution), named Cromwell the Lord Protector, to be advised by a council of state and a parliament.

Cromwell's authoritarian leadership was plagued by questions of legitimacy. Without a monarch's historic and divine right to rule, Cromwell held the government together by personal and physical force. When another Royalist uprising occurred, he sent the military to resolve it. Meanwhile, the legality of his authority was routinely questioned by the parliaments he called. Balked in his well-intentioned plans to reform and strengthen England (e.g., he supported religious toleration for many Dissenters), he nonetheless held the government together until his death. However, Richard, his son and successor, could not do the same. Within eighteen months of Oliver's death, a new council of state invited Charles II to reclaim his father's throne.

The Old Royal Naval College, begun in 1696 from designs by architect Sir Christopher Wren, exemplifies neoclassical taste in architecture.

An artist's depiction of the arrival of Charles II in Rotterdam on his return voyage to England in May 1660.

RESTORATION AND REVOLUTION

Restoration Charles II had fought in the Civil Wars, and being exiled, continued attempts to reclaim the throne. When England invited him back in 1660, he was eager to go. Though not of high moral character, he was more politically astute than his father and able to compromise to keep his throne.

Politically, Charles maintained good relations with Parliament. He established a council of royal advisers drawn from Parliament, creating a mechanism for compromise. If representatives questioned royal decisions, they could bring such complaints to the council. Further, Charles's public support for the English Church relieved Parliament, who believed social stability required religious conformity. The resultant Test Acts (1661–78) prohibited non-Anglicans from teaching, preaching, or participating in government. Nearly two thousand Puritans were removed from their congregations.

Unfortunately, two factors triggered old fears of Stuart Catholicism. In 1670 Charles signed a treaty with France promising to promote Catholic Louis XIV's interests in Europe in exchange for financial support. More significantly, he named as his heir his brother James, duke of York, a Catholic. Unlike Charles, James did not pursue compromise and instead ignored the Test Acts and appointed Catholics to governmental posts.

A faction of Parliament tried to exclude him from the throne, birthing two influential political parties, the Whigs (opposing James) and Tories (supporting him). Unwilling to risk civil war and knowing that James's two heirs (daughters) had married Protestant princes, Parliament tolerated James. But when his second wife, a Catholic, gave birth to a boy (legally first in line to the throne), a group of noblemen asked James's older daughter, Mary, and her powerful husband, William of Orange, to challenge James. Lacking sufficient military or political support, he fled to France.

Glorious Revolution The accession of William and Mary became known as the Glorious Revolution: *glorious* for its peacefulness and a *revolution* for its giant step toward constitutional monarchy. William and Mary could make no claim to Stuart-style divine right: taking the throne by invitation strongly implied that Parliament held ultimate sovereignty. In fact, Parliament required them to sign a Bill of Rights whose provisions (e.g., no standing army in peacetime) prevented monarchs from exercising arbitrary power.

Under William and Mary, England saw significant religious, military, and economic change. On religion, their accession settled fears of Catholic incursion, while the Toleration Act of 1689 offered Protestant Dissenters the right to worship previously denied them. Militarily, much of their reign was spent at war in Europe, a challenge that forced the English navy to reform itself into a formidable antagonist. Funding this transformation required the creation of credit instruments that also benefited English industry and trade. Unfortunately, the couple and their successor, Mary's sister Anne, died heirless, leaving Parliament once again to find a new monarch.

House of Hanover James II's son had some support to reclaim the throne, but most would not accept a Catholic king. Instead, the crown was offered to the next Protestant in the line of succession, a great-grandson of James I and prince from the German state of Hanover named George Louis. In 1714 he was crowned George I of England. He, his son George II, and great-grandson George III would lead England through the eighteenth century.

Three key political trends characterize this period. First, power became less centralized in the monarchy. Parliament could pass laws, control the nation's finances, and communicate directly with royal ministers, enabling it to exert great pressure on the king. Moreover, the king's ministers gained considerable power. George I and his son grew up in the German states and were unfamiliar with British politics. George I never even learned English. Both relied heavily on their ministers in setting policy.

Second, the nation's internal unrest continued. Uprisings or invasions for James II's heirs (his son, the "Old Pretender," and grandson, the "Young Pretender") occurred in 1708, 1715, 1719, and 1745–46. More threatening was the continuous struggle between Whigs and Tories and factions within each party. These divisions, both economic (Whig commercial vs. Tory agricultural interests) and social (Whig democratic progressivism vs. Tory aristocratic traditionalism), kept England in a state of unease while also prompting some of the nation's greatest political oratory and satire.

Finally, a worldwide British Empire began to solidify. In 1707 England and Scotland joined together in an official act of union, becoming known collectively as Great Britain. Victory in the Seven Years' War (1756–63) would add to British holdings India, Canada, and all American territory east of the Mississippi. Though George III lost the American colonies, Britain would continue to add to its empire, creating influence that spanned the globe.

Samuel Johnson and James Boswell with other members of the Literary Club in a coffeehouse in London.

SOCIAL CHANGE

SOCIAL LANDSCAPE

Post–Civil War England was predominantly a landscape dotted with small towns or villages and with estates of nobles and gentry. London was its largest city and clear legal, commercial, and industrial capital. Society was similarly divided broadly into agricultural and commercial-professional segments.

In 1688 about five-sixths of the population gained their livelihood from the soil. Among them were both the landed and the landless. The landed included the great nobles with long-established titles and extensive estates as well as the gentry, or lesser aristocracy, whose numbers had grown as the wealthy middle class acquired estates. The landless included tenant farmers and agricultural laborers who, mostly, worked the estates. The commercial and professional segment possessed similar layers. Composing the highest level were the great merchants and governmental officers. Further down were owners of small businesses, artisans, legal solicitors, and physicians. Lowest of all were the petty wage earners and servants in the cities.

Parliament was generally composed of citizens with wealth derived from land or business. Landholders prevailed in numbers, with the great nobles occupying the House of Lords and the gentry controlling the House of Commons. Still, the commercial and professional classes were strongly represented in the lower house. Membership in the upper house depended upon birth; membership in the lower house, upon ability, property ownership, and, frequently, political connections. Because of its increasing wealth and power over taxation, the House of Commons could eventually dominate both the upper house and the king. This rise in the later eighteenth century was assisted by intertwined changes to the British economy.

ECONOMIC UPHEAVAL

Early in the eighteenth century, agricultural advances rapidly increased the amount of agricultural goods the country could produce while lowering the amount of labor needed to produce them. In order to take advantage of new methods for growing and harvesting crops, owners of large estates displaced tenant farmers. Furthermore, the enclosure and transference of traditionally common lands to private ownership accelerated after the Civil War and forced owners of small farms and herds from rural England. From 1760 on, Parliament permitted millions of such acres to be enclosed, signaling the end of an older way of life. The displaced rural folk streamed to cities looking for work.

Simultaneously, other practical conditions for the coming Industrial Revolution were also falling into place. By 1763 England ruled the seas. Her expanding commercial empire crowded out the French, Dutch, and Spanish from the valuable markets and sources of raw materials needed for industry to flourish. At home, trade monopolies were breaking up, increasing competition. Workshops sprang up, forerunners of the factories that would pour out goods in staggering quantities by the century's end. In addition, highway improvements in the 1760s and 1770s made rapid overland transportation of products possible.

Key inventions coincided with these conditions to ensure the success of English industry. James Watt patented the steam engine (1769); James Hargreaves (1764), Richard Arkwright (1768), and Samuel Crompton (1779) contributed to automated spinning, and Edmund Cartwright to automated weaving (1786). These mechanical advances revolutionized textile manufacture, a major source of British wealth. Despite vehement and even violent protests from hand spinners and weavers, textile production shifted from the home to the factory.

The surplus rural population now became the engine of industrial growth. The result was unprecedented productivity, the growth of great manufacturing centers (especially in the Midlands), and an overall increase in the economic power of the lower classes. At the same time, these benefits would bring with them sometimes severe costs. Massed in drab, crowded tenements, the new class of industrial wage earners was often vulnerable to exploitation by both mill owners and labor agitators. Child labor became a concern and, along with the slave trade, would become one of the great reform issues of the century's last quarter.

RELIGIOUS REVOLUTION

In the eighteenth-century Anglican Church, both rationalism (p. 284) and traditionalism unfortunately had a deadening effect. Even many Nonconformists outside the church were losing their original fervency. Sermons were likely to be moral treatises and services merely routine ritual.

Deism In theology, rationalists dependent on the guidance of reason began rejecting certain biblical doctrines. They tended to favor natural theology (truths about God evident to one's reason) over revealed theology (truths about God set forth in the Bible) and minimize the supernatural. Loosely termed *deists*, thinkers with this disposition held widely varying worldviews. The amount of orthodox doctrine rejected by deists varied from person to person, but many deists rejected Christ's deity, His atoning death, and His bodily resurrection, as well as the miracles of Scripture.

Some common beliefs held by deists include these propositions: (1) the existence of a Creator, or "First Cause," who brought the universe into being but left it to operate by its own laws; (2) the potential goodness of man, whose faults may be corrected by education and rational persuasion; and (3) the prospect of an afterlife in which virtue will be rewarded and vice punished. Deism's rationalist approach to morality prevailed throughout the century among intellectuals, even influential clergy. It lent formal religion an intellectual tone and encouraged rational piety rather than religious earnestness.

John Wesley preaching outdoors.

Methodism Onto this scene of religious apathy burst the powerful preaching of John Wesley (1703–91) and George Whitefield (1714–70). They did not intend to found a new denomination or sect but rather desired a spiritual awakening in the Anglican Church. It would begin with the salvation of those who did not know Jesus Christ as their personal Savior and continue with their sanctification by strict "methodic" discipline. This emphasis on the need for a personal relationship with God resulted in preaching that was more personally directed to instruct and transform people. Such earnest engagement drew criticism from more traditional or rationalist critics who believed adherents lacked proper balance, constraint, or reverence.

The influence of Methodism upon England is hard to measure. It brought the transforming power of the gospel to lower classes in dire need of hope. And in teaching otherworldly values and compassion for the downtrodden, Methodism inspired both contentment within life's hardships and a determination to improve the lot of those in need. It awoke the consciences of many to the ill effects of the Industrial Revolution and thus lessened them, prompting reforms that relieved the distressed. It also encouraged the efforts of parliamentary advocates for the abolition of the British slave trade. In the nineteenth century, such effects would continue with the growth of the middle and lower classes and similarly act to counterbalance various intellectual challenges to religious thought.

A view of London (ca. 1630) before the Great Fire of 1666. The old St. Paul's Cathedral is the large church on the left side of the painting.

EIGHTEENTH-CENTURY WORLDVIEW

SCIENCE AND ENLIGHTENMENT

The scientific revolution begun in the seventeenth century continued into the next, bringing great advancements. Henry Cavendish (1731–1810) broke down water into hydrogen and oxygen. Joseph Priestley (1733–1804) isolated oxygen. Both made important discoveries in electricity. Towering above all was the work of mathematician-scientist Isaac Newton (1642–1727). Newton's *Principia* (1687) detailed his work on the universal law of gravitation. His presentation of a single law that explained all motion, great and small, gave the age a logically self-consistent idea of the universe.

Scientific discoveries such as these inspired great faith in the ability of knowledge and reasoning to advance humanity's lot. For instance, the discovery of natural laws governing the operations of the physical universe led to the belief that there must also be natural laws that should be governing human society. It was hoped that if those laws could be discovered and implemented, society could be transformed. The result of such thinking was the intellectual movement known as the Enlightenment. Essentially, Enlightenment thinkers extended a rationalist approach to fields other than science, including religion, philosophy, government, and more.

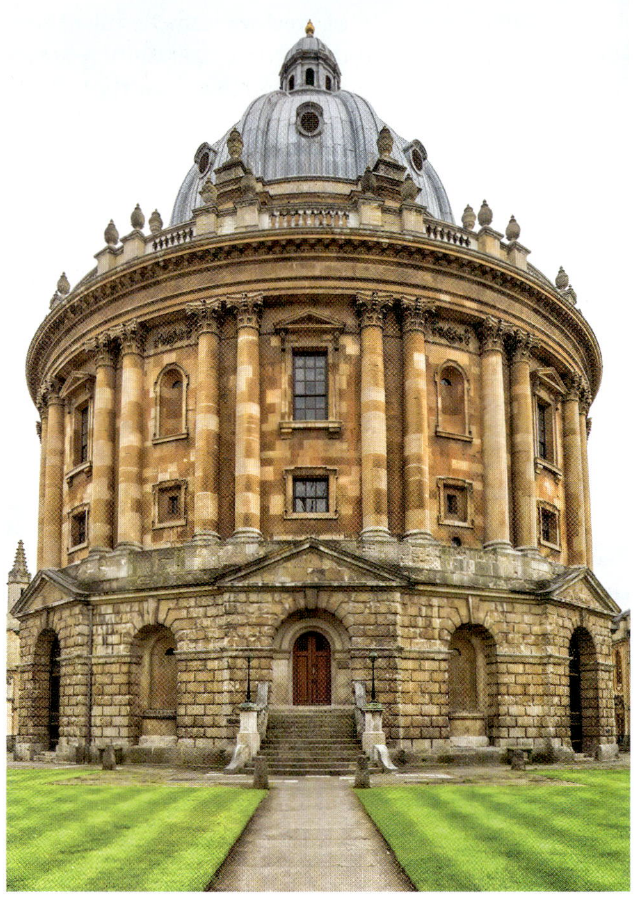

The neoclassical style Radcliffe Camera, begun in 1737 as the Radcliffe Library, in Oxford, England.

The movement had its beginnings in France where, at the time, the king and the Roman Catholic Church held absolute power, strictly censoring any opposition. Rising up to challenge this atmosphere was a group of men known as *philosophes*. Hailing from a variety of professions and backgrounds, they shared the desire to change the current system. To discuss ideas for social reform, they met in the salons (drawing rooms) of private homes and produced ideas such as baron de Montesquieu's separation of governmental powers. This distribution of executive, legislative, and judicial powers (each with specific checks on the others' power) was intended to prevent the absolutism France suffered from.

Similarly, Enlightenment thinkers explored the nature and value of the individual in society. These explorations reinforced political developments toward democracy. They also extended rationalist thought to the principles of established religion (p. 291), which had been central to European conceptions of humanity. Some,

LANGUAGE

When Enlightenment minds contemplated the English language, they saw a logical, or potentially logical, system similar to the universe of eighteenth-century physics. Refining and applying linguistic principles deduced from the Classical Latin grammar taught in respected schools, a series of English grammars systematized English language usage. These used the rules of logic and Latin to define a standard of grammatical correctness that still lingers today.

The same concern for rational refinement of language encouraged the production of dictionaries. Samuel Johnson's two-volume *Dictionary of the English Language* (1755) surpassed its predecessors in the precision and thoroughness of its definitions and in its use of illustrative quotations. Like them, it helped to establish a standard of educated usage in vocabulary and spelling.

such as Voltaire, one of the Enlightenment's key figures, believed in the existence of God but rejected the idea of a personal God as well as Christ's deity. Other *philosophes* rejected the idea of a spiritual world completely, believing there was nothing beyond the material world of molecules. Partly because of this vein, religious toleration for a variety of viewpoints was a common thread of Enlightenment thought.

At the same time, the Enlightenment galvanized the acquisition and organization of new and profitable knowledge. The 1751 publication in France of the twenty-eight-volume *Encyclopedia of the Enlightenment* disseminated ideas more widely, both geographically and socially, than ever before. England, like the rest of Europe, felt the influence of Enlightenment values and goals (e.g., emphasis on human reason, importance of the individual) in its academic, civic, and literary realms.

Voltaire

ENLIGHTENMENT AND THE BIBLE

Many English movers and shakers in the eighteenth century adopted a worldview at the confluence of traditional orthodox and Enlightenment thought. They fundamentally believed that humans were potentially reasonable beings who lived in a logically ordered universe and whose happiness consisted in living reasonably with themselves and their fellow beings. To be ruled by reason was to be ruled by God, for reason had its source in humanity's Creator. Furthermore, as the institutions of society were considered works of both reason and divine order, man in society was man at his best. The reasonable person thus lived prudently among fellow citizens and subjected personal desires to society's overriding interests.

This view of humanity and the world was neither new nor entirely at odds with a Christian worldview. The Bible places humans at the center of the created order (Gen. 1:28). They are responsible to rule both themselves and the earth in accordance with the moral principles taught in Scripture and understood by their reason. Nonetheless, Enlightenment thinkers departed significantly from biblical thought. They often lacked Christianity's more expansive view of the human person, which valued reason and affections as equally important parts of a whole person. They overestimated human capacities, not seeing the pervasive corruption of these resulting from the Fall. Finally, they undervalued the truths of divine wisdom and revelation and the necessity of divine grace to support the rule of reason in the individual or society. Sadly, the biblical portrait of a personal God constantly intervening on behalf of His creation to restore humanity and its sin-cursed environment eluded many.

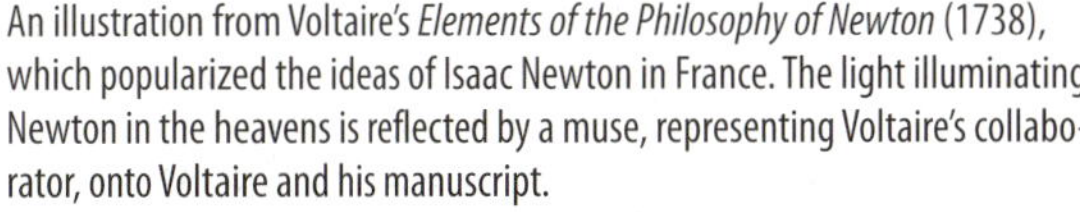

An illustration from Voltaire's *Elements of the Philosophy of Newton* (1738), which popularized the ideas of Isaac Newton in France. The light illuminating Newton in the heavens is reflected by a muse, representing Voltaire's collaborator, onto Voltaire and his manuscript.

NEOCLASSICISM

During the Interregnum, literature had taken a narrower, more serious bent. Puritan leaders closed theaters and frequently censored materials. Prose works (often political or religious) and serious poetry dominated while edgier poems such as Andrew Marvell's "To His Coy Mistress" were written but left unpublished. The Restoration created a broader, more eclectic literature. Charles II reopened theaters, partly as a lover of drama himself and partly to make a political point. In fact, Restoration dramas often included racy elements, partially as a statement on past restrictions. At the same time, deeply religious writings still thrived, as proved by Bunyan's *The Pilgrim's Progress*, while authors such as John Dryden took the poet's public role seriously, writing satirical works commenting on society's ills.

But as Enlightenment thought spread, a new artistic style generally coinciding with it arose to dominate Europe for much of the eighteenth century. Known as **neoclassicism**, this style was based on models from classical Greece and Rome. For example, poets such as Alexander Pope looked to Roman writers from Emperor Augustus's time (27 BC–AD 14) for inspiration and stylistic models, resulting in the era's literature often being termed *Augustan*.

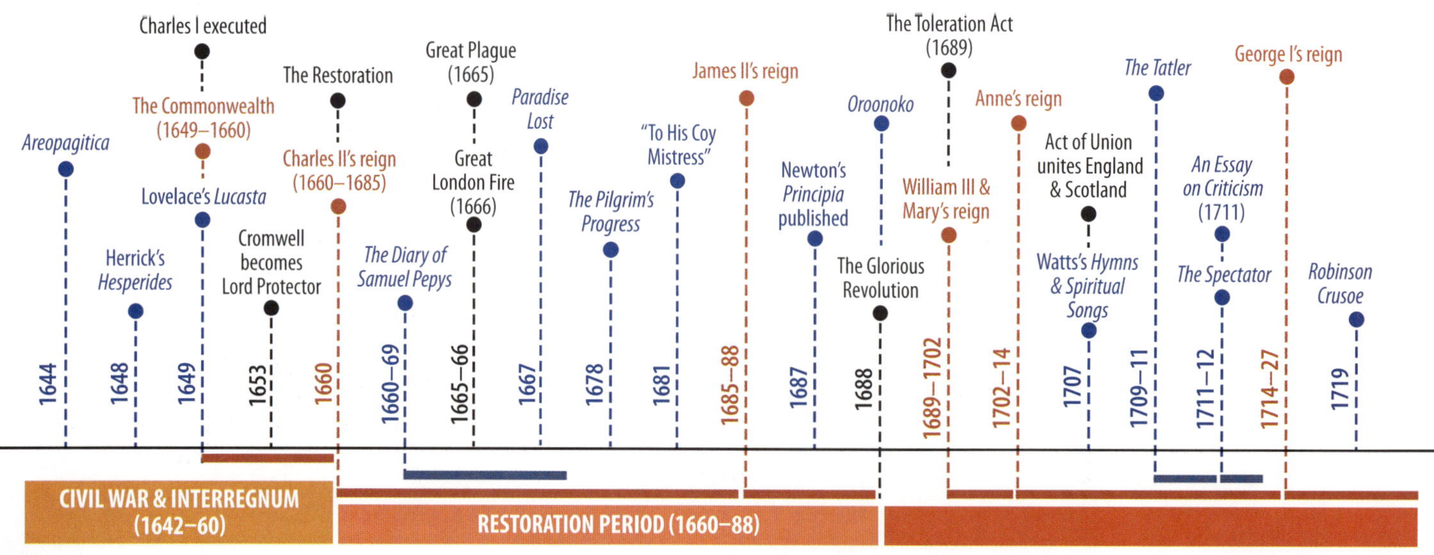

VISUAL ANALYSIS

In this group portrait, Joshua Reynolds depicts the three aristocratic Montgomery sisters decorating a statue of the Roman god of marriage. How does the painting reflect neoclassical ideals?

Consistent with Enlightenment thought, neoclassicists appreciated the idea that clear rules could govern artistic processes and evaluations. Literary critics believed they should directly observe particulars of classic works and form general principles for and classifications of literary elements and genres. As in other fields, these conclusions were regarded as permanently valid rules and became standards of correctness. For example, poetry was classified into ranked types, or genres, descending from the lofty epic to the lowly epigram. These types were considered unchanging, each with its particular governing principles, but all subject to the general obligations of art: to teach and to delight.

Ridiculous Taste or the *Ladies Absurdity* by Matthew Darly.

The dominant literary mode of the neoclassical period—satire—reflected this commitment to constructive purposes. Comedies, odes, epigrams, and verse epistles seethed with the passions of the age as neoclassical satirists adapted the various genres to attack social abuses with ridicule. But poets were also to put general truths into pleasing, memorable form in order to delight readers. This objective required, to neoclassical tastes, the qualities of regularity, exactness, symmetry, neatness, and surface polish. The first four qualities made the heroic couplet, a pair of rhymed lines in iambic pentameter, the dominant verse form of the period. Its simplicity, symmetry, and flexibility made it an effective tool for a variety of genres. The final quality, polish, valued perfection in a lesser genre over imperfection in a greater one. Consequently, neoclassical poets mostly avoided the more demanding genres of tragedy and epic, favoring instead the lesser genres.

SUMMARY

After the midcentury, the rationalist worldview steadily lost traction as the pendulum of societal trends inevitably swung toward new values and emphases. Free thinkers began to question some of the more rigid premises of the rationalists' views, such as a belief in a permanent hierarchy in society. Furthermore, the social ills brought about by the Industrial Revolution began to sour some on the idea that science and urban development were sufficient measures of human progress. Most significantly, some recognized the limits of what pure rationality could perceive and explore in humanity particularly. Literary taste, like political, social, and religious feeling, was in transition. Yet neoclassical writers may justly be valued for often presenting truth and challenging what they believed to be in conflict with reason and the happiness of people. They have left to us works of lasting interest and value.

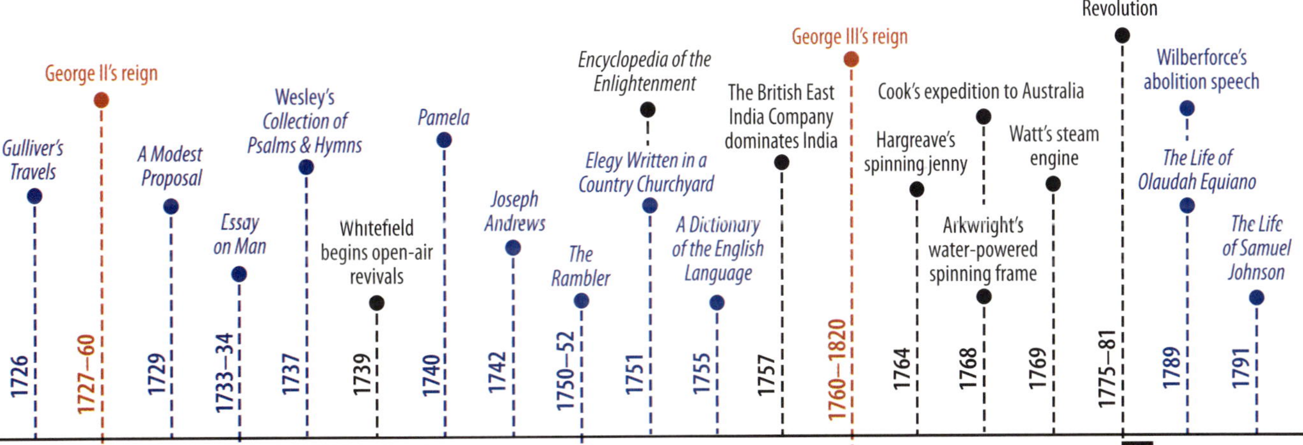

UNIT 3

PART 1

Civil War and Restoration

As world history illustrates, a major event in the life of a people group can change not just their practical circumstances but also their intellectual and emotional lives. The First World War is a good example of such a change. Millions lost their lives, and the spirit of optimism, hope, and progress that had ushered in the twentieth century was shattered. The English Civil War of the seventeenth century had a similar life-changing effect for the English people.

A distinct shift in mindset can be observed between pre- and postwar England. Before the war, literature was centered primarily in the royal court. Writers were supported by generous patrons and wrote to please them. The general tone was fitting for an age of strong monarchy, with emphasis on obedience and conformity to the appointed order. After the war, however, a new world opened up. Temporary lifting of strict censorship controls opened the door to many new voices—religious, political, and social. War weariness caused an increased reluctance to fight for one's own viewpoint. Gradually, England became more characterized by diversity.

The influence of the Civil War can also be seen in the development of a new style of writing and a new style of reader. Postwar writing demonstrated a plain style. This was a clear expression of facts and an absence of highly stylized language. The Puritans, who played a significant role on the parliamentary side of the conflict, were against flowery speech and excessive ornamentation. Their main literary forms were sermons and tracts, and these were written clearly with attention to practical detail. There was also a need for clear speech in the pamphlet wars that characterized the age. Both sides in the conflict tried to win support for their cause through the publishing of arguments in the form of pamphlets. Arguments may have been emotionally charged, but they needed to be clearly understood.

The new readers were different in that they were not so highly educated in the classics as the Renaissance humanists were. They were mostly middle-class tradesmen and professionals. They were not looking for scholarly treatises or flowery poetry but rather sustained arguments that they could follow clearly and use to draw reasonable conclusions. This period saw the beginnings of the intentional shaping of the minds of the public that continues today.

Most of the writers presented in Part 1 of this unit were affected in one way or another by the events of the Civil War. Robert Herrick and Richard Lovelace, both Cavalier poets (see p. 297), supported the king in the conflict. Both evidence the grace and beauty that would be fitting of court literature, and both address themes (carpe diem, love, and honor) that would have been extremely pertinent to the time.

Andrew Marvell and John Milton were on the other side of the conflict. They held positions under Oliver Cromwell's government. (Marvell also held a seat in Parliament after the Restoration.) Marvell gave much of his time and energy to the practical business of his day, but he also composed brilliant lyric poetry and later biting political satire. John Milton's life and writing were strongly connected to his tumultuous times. Though he was highly academic and received extensive training in the classics, he had an active interest in politics too. He wrote provocative pamphlets throughout the period in support of the parliamentary cause. His *Areopagitica,* written in defense of freedom of the press (as Milton conceived of it), was a response to the government's attempt to censor political pamphlets that were produced by unlicensed printers. *Paradise Lost* was written after the Restoration, a quieter though difficult period of Milton's life. It reflected the extent of Milton's classical education yet showed the strong influence of the Civil War. Earlier in his life Milton had shown interest in writing an epic, but his model at that time was Edmund Spenser's *Faerie Queene.* Having experienced the turmoil of many years of violence and upheaval, Milton in his older age turned instead to basic contemplations of what God was doing in the world and took as his subject the grand biblical account of Creation, the Fall, and Redemption.

Samuel Pepys, the youngest of this group, held a position of importance in the Restoration government of Charles II. In the plain prose of a diary, Pepys recorded interesting anecdotal details of public and private events he was witness to in the city of London. In doing so, he provided a treasury of primary source material for the study of Restoration society.

The Cavalier Poets

The Cavalier poets wrote during the tumultuous reign of Charles I, a time when the Roundheads fought to retain parliamentary authority. These men were generally courtiers who embraced their identity as Cavaliers (p. 284), supporting Charles I and the traditional English monarchy. Most were nominally Protestants while a few were Catholics. Well acquainted with the ugliness of war and the brevity of life, the Cavalier poets advocated "seizing the day," often through a licentious lifestyle. However, they did not lack for courage; at least several fought or were imprisoned for their political beliefs.

Noted for composing beautiful, graceful verses, the Cavaliers often wrote lyric poetry to be set to music. They imitated Jonson, who modeled the classical virtues of simplicity, restraint, and precision, and were thus called the "Sons of Ben." Although they wrote in a style generally unlike the metaphysical poets, the Cavaliers did make use of conceits as they covered themes ranging from romance to pastoralism to war and duty.

Despite contrasting vocational backgrounds, both Robert Herrick and Richard Lovelace wrote as Cavaliers. Lovelace, a charming courtier and soldier, was imprisoned at least once for his loyalty to the king. While incarcerated in 1648, he prepared *Lucasta: Epodes, Odes, Sonnets, Songs, etc.* for publication. The compilation includes his poem "To Lucasta: Going to the Wars," which contrasts his conflicting affections: women and honor.

At home in England, Robert Herrick, an amiable Anglican country vicar, was expelled from his parish, Dean Prior, in 1647, after the Puritan victory in the Civil War. He returned from London to his vicarage during the Restoration and continued there until his death fourteen years later. Unrestrained by his church background, his poetry addresses religion as well as typical Cavalier topics. In putting together his volume of poetry *Hesperides: or the Works both Humane and Divine of Robert Herrick, Esq.*, he became the first English poet to carefully organize and compile nearly all of his poetry into a single volume, including instructions for reading the poems ("The Argument of His Book"). Altogether, Herrick, Lovelace, and other Cavalier poets struck a note of determined lightness in an era darkened by burdens of state.

BEFORE READING

ANALYZE: *Rhyme, Ballad Meter, and Alliteration*

In the following lyric poems, Herrick and Lovelace employ **rhyme** and meter (p. 185) for emphasis and beauty. Both use **ballad meter** (see ballad stanza, p. 69), alternating lines of iambic tetrameter and trimeter. Lovelace's meter is rougher, reminiscent of metaphysical poetry, but he augments it with **alliteration**, the repetition of initial consonant sounds. Read the poems aloud, listening for all three elements. Determine how they emphasize ideas or enhance the poems' musicality.

READ: *Annotating a Text*

When a reader interacts with a text thoughtfully—asking questions, noting features, and making connections between ideas or features—it is helpful to annotate the text. Annotations record these responses directly in a text—through questions or comments, circles, underlining, diagrams, arrows, pictures, and more. As you read these poems, try annotating examples of imagery, figurative language, and sound devices, elements that Cavalier poets used to convey their thoughts and feelings. Consider how these elements relate to each poet's purpose and message.

EVALUATE: *Honor*

As you read Lovelace's poem, note the two affections he juxtaposes. How might his underlying conception of these connect to medieval chivalry? What does Scripture say about the nature and value of honor (Prov. 22:1; 29:23; 21:21; Ps. 15:4)? How do Lovelace's thoughts measure up against this biblical view?

OBJECTIVES

- Identify characteristics of Cavalier poetry in a text.
- Explain how sound devices support meaning and beauty in a text.
- Annotate a text to analyze it.
- Evaluate an author's values from a biblical worldview.

Is
LOVE
the most important thing?

Robert Herrick

To the Virgins, To Make Much of Time

Gather ye rosebuds while ye may,
Old Time is still a-flying;
And this same flower that smiles to-day,
To-morrow will be dying.

The glorious lamp of heaven, the sun,
The higher he's a-getting,
The sooner will his race be run,
And nearer he's to setting. A R

That age is best which is the first,
When youth and blood are warmer;
But being spent, the worse and worst
Times still succeed the former.

Then be not coy,[1] but use your time,
And while ye may, go marry;
For having lost but once your prime,
You may for ever tarry.

1. *coy:* "affectedly and often flirtatiously shy or modest" (*AHD*)

Alliteration: What examples of alliteration can you find in the first two stanzas? A

Annotating: Underline the examples of alliteration you found. Also circle two examples of personification in stanzas 1–2. R

Richard Lovelace

To Lucasta: Going to the Wars

Tell me not, (Sweet,) I am unkind,
That from the nunnery
Of thy chaste breast and quiet mind
To war and arms I fly.

True: a new mistress now I chase,
The first foe in the field;
And with a stronger faith embrace
A sword, a horse, a shield. E

Yet this inconstancy is such,
As you too shall adore;
I could not love thee (Dear) so much,
Loved I not honor more.

Honor: What two competing interests does the speaker identify in the first two stanzas? E

THINK AND DISCUSS

1. List three characteristics of Cavalier poetry.
2. Record the meter patterns of each poem's first stanza. Do they perfectly qualify as ballad meter?
3. What conflict does Lovelace address in his poem? How does he use personification to highlight this conflict?
4. What three images does Herrick use to express a sense of urgency? Which exemplify personification?
5. State the themes of Herrick's and Lovelace's poems. Cite textual evidence for your statement.
6. What outstanding example of alliteration does Lovelace use in stanza 2? Why might he have used alliteration so strongly here in light of the stanza's meter?
7. Does the Bible support Herrick's theme? Consult these verses for your answer: James 1:17; Proverbs 31:30; Ecclesiastes 9:7–10; 11:9; 12:1; 13–14; and Ephesians 5:16.
8. Lovelace's honor is "a code of integrity, dignity, and pride, chiefly among men, that was maintained in some societies . . . by force of arms" (*AHD*). Is this conception of honor biblical? For your answer, consult related verses (Prov. 22:1; 29:23; 21:21; Ps. 15:4).

Andrew Marvell (1621–1678)

Andrew Marvell, son of Reverend Andrew and Anne Marvell, was reared in Hull, a prosperous Yorkshire city. His promising career at Cambridge (BA 1639) was interrupted by his father's tragic drowning in 1641. Afterwards, Marvell traveled the Continent (ca. 1642–46) acquiring languages, possibly tutoring, and avoiding the Civil War entirely.

He returned to republican England and, beginning in 1651, tutored the children of several prominent figures, including the daughter of Thomas Fairfax, retired parliamentary commander in chief, and William Dutton, a ward of Oliver Cromwell. Marvell's two years at Fairfax's Yorkshire estate were likely the occasion for many of his popular lyric poems, including "To His Coy Mistress." In 1657 Milton's influence gained Marvell a post as an assistant to the blind poet, then the Commonwealth's Latin Secretary.

In 1659 Marvell was elected a Member of Parliament for Hull. Despite his closeness to Cromwell, he transitioned to Restoration politics with remarkable ease, serving notably as an MP until his death. In fact, his intercession likely saved Milton from execution on Charles II's return. Marvell was better known for his political career than for his poetry, most of which was published posthumously. Only in the twentieth century was he acknowledged as a major poet.

As a poet, he is transitional; various works bear similarities to the style of classical, metaphysical (with whom he is often grouped), and even Cavalier poets. During the reign of Charles II, Marvell wrote satirical verse (anonymously) in the spirit and style of the new age. He also wrote in heroic couplets, the dominant verse form for the next century. Marvell's poetry thus links pre-and post-Restoration poetic styles, assimilating the past and heralding the future.

BEFORE READING

ANALYZE: *Dramatic Monologue and Speaker*

In "To His Coy Mistress," Marvell writes as a metaphysical poet, combining rational argument, wit, and striking imagery to explore a topic. The poem is an early form of a **dramatic monologue**, a poem in which a single character speaks, either to himself or to another character, about a particular topic or incident. As you read, consider who might be the **speaker** of the poem, the character or person who voices it. Whom is he talking to? Imagine two people having this conversation in real life. How would you characterize the speaker?

READ: *Ask Questions of a Text*

This particular text begs the reader to question it. On the surface, the poem's topic is a seduction. As you read, note the arguments the speaker uses to support this intention. What big ideas about human life does he assert while making these arguments? How does he describe these ideas? Next, consider Marvell's tone (p. 88) toward the ideas. How seriously does Marvell seem to take the speaker's purpose? How might he perhaps undercut the speaker's ideas and intentions in his particular choice of images (p. 75) and abundant use of hyperbole (p. 240)?

EVALUATE: *Human Mortality*

In the midst of his argument, the speaker addresses the reality of human mortality. Is there validity to the points of his argument? Read the following Scripture passages: James 4:14, Isaiah 40:8, and 1 Peter 1:24. What realities does he get right? What truths does he not consider? Be prepared to compose a response to the poem's theme.

OBJECTIVES

- Identify a poem's characteristics as a dramatic monologue.
- Examine a poem's speaker, arguments, and imagery for theme.
- Analyze a poet's tone through features such as humor and hyperbole.
- Evaluate a poem's response to human mortality.

VOCABULARY

hue (hyo͞o) *n.* Color.

amorous (ăm′ər-əs) *adj.* Of or associated with love.

languish (lăng′gwĭsh) *intr.v.* To become downcast or pine away in longing.

To His Coy Mistress

Had we but world enough, and time,
This coyness,[1] lady, were no crime. ☑
We would sit down, and think which way
To walk, and pass our long love's day.
Thou by the Indian Ganges'[2] side
Should'st rubies find: I by the tide
Of Humber[3] would complain. I would
Love you ten years before the flood,[4]
And you should, if you please, refuse
Till the conversion of the Jews;[5]
My vegetable love should grow
Vaster than empires and more slow;
An hundred years should go to praise
Thine eyes, and on thy forehead gaze;
Two hundred to adore each breast,
But thirty thousand to the rest;
An age at least to every part,
And the last age should show your heart.
For, lady, you deserve this state,
Nor would I love at lower rate. A

Reading Check: For what "crime" is the lady being reprimanded? ☑

Speaker: What claim does the speaker make and accentuate with hyperbole in this stanza? Does he seem sincere? A

1. *coyness:* here both false or flirtatious shyness and a reluctance to commit
2. *Ganges:* a major river in India
3. *Humber:* a river in Hull, the town in which Marvell was reared; the river in which his father drowned
4. *the flood:* the biblical Flood recorded in Genesis 6:9–9:17
5. *the conversion of the Jews:* Traditionally, Christians have believed the conversion will occur at the Second Coming of Christ.

But at my back I always hear
Time's winged chariot hurrying near,
And yonder all before us lie
Deserts of vast eternity.
Thy beauty shall no more be found,
Nor, in thy marble vault[6], shall sound
My echoing song: then worms shall try
That long preserved virginity,
And your quaint honor turn to dust,
And into ashes all my lust:
The grave's a fine and private place,
But none, I think, do there embrace. R

Ask Questions: List the images the speaker uses in lines 25–30. Do you think his listener would respond positively to them? R

Now therefore, while the youthful **hue**
Sits on thy skin like morning dew,
And while thy willing soul transpires[7]
At every pore with instant fires,
Now let us sport us while we may,
And now, like **amorous** birds of prey
Rather at once our time devour,
Than **languish** in his slow-chapped[8] power.
Let us roll all our strength and all
Our sweetness up into one ball,
And tear our pleasures with rough strife,
Thorough[9] the iron gates of life;
Thus, though we cannot make our sun
Stand still, yet we will make him run. E

hue (hyo͞o) *n.* Color.

amorous (ăm′ər-əs) *adj.* Of or associated with love.

languish (lăng′gwĭsh) *intr.v.* To become downcast or pine away in longing.

Mortality: The speaker seeks to evade the control of whom or what? Does he succeed? E

6. *vault:* "a burial chamber, especially when underground" (*AHD*)
7. *transpires:* breathes
8. *slow-chapped:* slow-jawed, as if time is slowly chewing
9. *Thorough:* through

THINK AND DISCUSS

1. Explain why "To His Coy Mistress" qualifies as a dramatic monologue.
2. Identify two examples of hyperbole in the poem.
3. Whom or what does the speaker personify throughout the last two stanzas?
4. What can you deduce about the character of the poem's speaker? Support your answer from the text.
5. Give two ways in which "To His Coy Mistress" qualifies as an example of metaphysical poetry, supporting your answer from the text.
6. Summarize in one sentence each stanza's main argument offered by the speaker to support his goal.
7. What are the poem's two intertwined themes?
8. Examine Marvell's tone toward the poem's subject as expressed through his images. Which clearly support or develop his themes? Which might undercut the speaker's purpose?
9. Evaluate the speaker's response to encroaching time and mortality. Is there validity to his argument? Is the grave the ultimate reality? Compose a response to the poem's theme incorporating Scripture (James 4:14; Isa. 40:8; 1 Pet. 1:24) into your answer.

John Milton (1608–74)

AT A GLANCE

- **ca. 1617–32** Attended St. Paul's School and Cambridge
- **1638–39** Toured the Continent, mainly Italy
- **1640s** Wrote polemical works supporting Parliament
- **1649–59** Served as secretary for foreign tongues to Cromwell's Council of State
- **1667** Published *Paradise Lost*
- **1671** Published *Paradise Regained*

Like Shakespeare, John Milton towers above the general landscape of English literature. His fierce dedication to his work produced a polished craftsmanship and an unprecedented range of works that have exerted a sustained influence on subsequent writers and thinkers. Indeed, his epic *Paradise Lost* stands unassailed as a great masterwork of English literature. Milton began weighing the challenge of writing such an epic early on, but the immense upheavals of his era would send him on a long and winding path to fulfilling his vision.

Dedicated Student

Milton was born in London to middle-class parents, John and Sara. His father, a scrivener and composer, gave him the best education possible at St. Paul's grammar school and Cambridge (BA 1629 and MA 1632). He found Cambridge intellectually constricting but performed brilliantly, publishing there poems such as the companion pieces *L'Allegro* and *Il Penseroso*.

Milton left school having decided to be a poet, a career he saw as a public vocation contributing to civil society. For six years he stayed at the family home, amassing the intellectual resources he felt he needed through rigorous reading in the humanities. He remains one of England's most-learned poets, fluent in multiple ancient and contemporary languages and very broadly read. Afterward he embarked on a tour of the Continent, interacting with famous intellects (including Galileo) and polishing his skills. But the trip was cut short in 1639 by civil unrest in England.

Civil Servant

For the next two decades Milton prioritized writing in prose, chiefly works contending for religious and political liberty. An independent (sometimes unorthodox) thinker with a libertarian spirit, Milton advocated against state religion and for greater tolerance of religious minorities while resisting absolute monarchy and supporting the new Commonwealth. His most-celebrated treatise, *Areopagitica* (1644), argued against intensifying censorship of ideas. His ideas have heavily informed the modern concept of freedom of the press.

In 1649 Milton accepted the position of secretary for foreign tongues to Cromwell's Council of State. His duties included defending the Commonwealth against detractors. In the next decade, this work gained him fame and influence abroad. On the eve of the Restoration, Milton courageously published *The Ready and Easy Way to Establish a Commonwealth* (1660), presenting a pattern for a workable republic and urging the English not to become slaves once again.

The failure of the Commonwealth was one of a series of personal disappointments in the 1650s. In 1652 Milton lost his infant son, John; his first wife, Mary; and his eyesight, which had been fading for several years. In 1658 he lost his second wife, Katherine, and with Charles II's accession, he was in very real danger of losing his life. Influential friends, including Andrew Marvell and Milton's Royalist brother, Christopher, prevented his exclusion from the general pardon.

Persevering Poet

After the loss of these hopes, Milton, in his fifties—blind, arthritic, ostracized from public life—began a fruitful poetic period. Finally having time to write the epic he long desired (and may have already begun), he now brought his accumulated knowledge, experience, and powers of persuasion to bear on the task. He chose the grandest of subjects, the Fall and Redemption of man, to show how God brings good out of evil. Now blind, he amazingly wrote and revised through dictation, finishing *Paradise Lost* in 1665 and publishing it in 1667. *Paradise Regained*, a shorter epic celebrating the heroic resistance of Christ to Satanic temptation, followed in 1671. A 1674 revised version of *Paradise Lost* divided it into twelve books (a classical conceit) rather than the original ten. That same year he died, having completed his life's work, and was buried next to his father in London at St. Giles, Cripplegate.

ANALYZE: *Text Structure and Argumentation*

Text structures vary depending on an author's purpose. Analyzing structure, therefore, can help you determine a text's purpose and better understand its meaning. The following two texts possess very different structures. The first is a **pamphlet**, a short publication, often stapled together, that includes **arguments** and information on a single (often controversial) subject. As you read, determine Milton's main argument and look for details, evidence, and other arguments that support his main claim. The second text is a **sonnet**, a familiar form (p. 185). As you read, examine the sonnet's structural divisions. Does it take a problem-solution (question-answer) structure? Or does the text's main idea develop as the poem progresses?

READ: *Annotating a Text*

Annotating a text (p. 296) can help you monitor and deepen your comprehension. Annotations can vary widely. A reader may mark unfamiliar words, tag confusing passages for rereading, write synonyms of unknown words or paraphrases of difficult passages, pose questions, or even draw a picture of a concept. Such methods may also be used to analyze a text deeply—highlighting literary features, noting character or plot developments, writing a page number beside a statement or concept that relates to something read previously, or even diagramming how a particular element runs throughout a text. As you read, annotate each text to improve your comprehension and analysis.

EVALUATE: *Moral Maturity Through Reading*

How do you know what is virtuous? And how do you grow in that understanding? Proverbs 2:6 reminds us that moral understanding comes from heeding God's words. One way the Scriptures make goodness clear is by contrasting it with evil. Consider the thieves at Christ's crucifixion: one responds in faith and is welcomed; the other mocks Christ, rejecting him as Lord. Faith is contrasted with rebellion. In *Areopagitica*, Milton recognizes the profit of observing contrasts. He advocates for wide reading so that readers can observe vice and virtue in contrast. As you read, consider Milton's arguments. What does he say about man's freedom to choose and about virtue that goes untested? What does he say is the benefit of wide reading? Evaluate Milton's arguments in light of Moses' studies (Acts 7:22) and Daniel's study of pagan literature and philosophy during his captivity (Dan. 1:1–4, 17).

OBJECTIVES

- Identify a text's structure.
- Annotate a text for better comprehension.
- Trace a writer's arguments and support throughout a text.
- Evaluate an author's arguments from a biblical worldview.

VOCABULARY

aver (ə-vûr′) *tr.v.* To affirm positively; declare.

judicious (jo͞o-dĭsh′əs) *adj.* Having or exhibiting sound judgment; prudent.

temperance (tĕm′pər-əns) *n.* Moderation and self-restraint, as in behavior or expression.

arbitrary (är′bĭ-trĕr′ē) *adj.* Based on or subject to individual judgment or preference.

chide (chīd) *intr.v.* To scold by way of rebuke or reproof; in later usage, often merely, to utter rebuke.

Is CENSORSHIP *good or bad?*

Freedom of speech and freedom of the press are vital to functioning democracies. History shows that authoritarian governments can use censorship to suppress unwanted views—religious, political, or otherwise—often with quiet violence toward citizens. But is censorship always bad? Consider television ratings and bans on pornography, both forms of censorship. Discuss the benefits and dangers of censorship. Are there some clear rules to avoid misuse?

FROM AREOPAGITICA

Milton precedes this passage from Areopagitica *with a history of licensing (i.e., requiring official approval for published works), and then pivots to argue that believers should know their culture's classic literature and current ideas. Finally, he uses the example of Dionysius Alexandrinus, a church sage who was asked why it was fine to read books with unbiblical content. Milton relates Dionysius's answer and moves to his own.*

The worthy man,[1] loth to give offence, fell into a new debate with himself what was to be thought; when suddenly a vision sent from God (it is his own epistle that so **avers** it) confirmed him in these words: "Read any books whatever come to thy hands, for thou art sufficient both to judge aright, and to examine each matter." To this revelation he assented the sooner, as he confesses, because it was answerable to that of the Apostle to the Thessalonians: "Prove all things, hold fast that which is good."

aver (ə-vûr′) *tr.v.* To affirm positively; declare.

And he might have added another remarkable saying of the same author: "To the pure, all things are pure"; not only meats and drinks, but all kind of knowledge whether of good or evil; the knowledge cannot defile, nor consequently the books, if the will and conscience be not defiled. For books are as meats and viands[2] are; some of good, some of evil substance; and yet God in that unapocryphal vision, said without exception, "Rise, Peter, kill and eat," leaving the choice to each man's discretion. Wholesome meats to a vitiated[3] stomach differ little or nothing from unwholesome; and best books to a naughty mind are not unappliable to occasions of evil. Bad meats will scarce breed good nourishment in the healthiest concoction; but herein the difference is of bad books, that they to a discreet and **judicious** reader serve in many respects to discover, to confute,[4] to forewarn, and to illustrate. . . . **A**

judicious (jo͞o-dĭsh′əs) *adj.* Having or exhibiting sound judgment; prudent.

Argument: What main claim does Milton make in the first two paragraphs? What additional argument and evidence does he use to support that claim? **A**

I conceive, therefore, that when God did enlarge the universal diet of man's body, saving ever the rules of **temperance**, he then also, as before, left **arbitrary** the dieting and repasting of our minds; as wherein every mature man might have to exercise his own leading capacity. How great a virtue is temperance, how much of moment through the whole life of man! Yet God commits the managing so great a trust, without particular law or prescription, wholly to the demeanor of every grown man. And, therefore, when he himself tabled the Jews from heaven, that omer, which was every man's daily portion of manna, is computed to have been more than might have well sufficed the heartiest feeder thrice as many meals. For those actions which enter into a man, rather than issue out of him, and therefore defile not,[5] God uses not to captivate under a perpetual childhood of prescription, but trusts him with the gift of reason to be his own chooser; there were but little work left for preaching, if law and compulsion should grow so fast upon those things which heretofore were governed only by exhortation. Solomon informs us, that much reading is a weariness to the flesh; but neither he nor other inspired author tells us that such or such reading is unlawful; yet certainly had God thought good to limit us herein, it had been much more expedient to have told us what was unlawful, than what was wearisome. . . . **E**

temperance (tĕm′pər-əns) *n.* Moderation and self-restraint, as in behavior or expression.

arbitrary (är′bĭ-trĕr′ē) *adj.* Based on or subject to individual judgment or preference.

Moral Maturity: What does Milton say God has given to every mature person? **E**

1. *worthy man:* Dionysius Alexandrinus
2. *viands:* food
3. *vitiated:* corrupted
4. *confute:* prove wrong
5. *actions . . . defile not:* a reference to Mark 7:19

Good and evil we know in the field of this world grow up together almost inseparably; and the knowledge of good is so involved and interwoven with the knowledge of evil, and in so many cunning resemblances hardly to be discerned, that those confused seeds which were imposed upon Psyche[6] as an incessant labor to cull out, and sort asunder, were not more intermixed. It was from out the rind of one apple tasted, that the knowledge of good and evil, as two twins cleaving together, leaped forth into the world. And perhaps this is that doom which Adam fell into of knowing good and evil, that is to say, of knowing good by evil.

As, therefore, the state of man now is; what wisdom can there be to choose, what continence to forbear without the knowledge of evil? He that can apprehend and consider vice with all her baits and seeming pleasures, and yet abstain, and yet distinguish, and yet prefer that which is truly better, he is the true wayfaring Christian. I cannot praise a fugitive[7] and cloistered virtue, unexercised and unbreathed, that never sallies out and sees her adversary, but slinks out of the race, where that immortal garland is to be run for, not without dust and heat. Assuredly we bring not innocence into the world; we bring impurity much rather; that which purifies us is trial, and trial is by what is contrary. That virtue, therefore, which is but a youngling in the contemplation of evil; and knows not the utmost that vice promises to her followers, and rejects it, is but a blank virtue, not a pure; her whiteness is but an excremental[8] whiteness. . . . **R**

Annotating: Reread the three preceding paragraphs, making annotations where helpful. For instance, circle unfamiliar words, underline important statements, write out a few words of explanation, or draw a picture of an image Milton uses. **R**

Since, therefore, the knowledge and survey of vice is in this world so necessary to the constituting of human virtue, and the scanning of error to the confirmation of truth, how can we more safely, and with less danger, scout into the regions of sin and falsity, than by reading all manner of tractates and hearing all manner of reason? And this is the benefit which may be had of books promiscuously[9] read. . . . **E**

Moral Maturity: What does Milton claim will better equip readers to make morally virtuous choices? **E**

. . . Wherefore did [God] create passions within us, pleasures round about us, but that these rightly tempered are the very ingredients of virtue? They are not skilful considerers of human things, who imagine to remove sin by removing the matter of sin. . . . Banish all objects of lust, shut up all youth into the severest discipline that can be exercised in any hermitage, ye cannot make them chaste, that came not thither so: such great care and wisdom is required to the right managing of this point.

Suppose we could expel sin by this means; look how much we thus expel of sin, so much we expel of virtue: for the matter of them both is the same; remove that, and ye remove them both alike. This justifies the high providence of God, who, though he commands us temperance, justice, continence, yet pours out before us, even to a profuseness, all desirable things, and gives us minds that can wander beyond all limit and satiety. Why should we then affect a rigor contrary to the manner of God and of nature, by abridging or scanting those means, which books freely permitted are, both to the trial of virtue, and the exercise of truth? . . . **A**

Argument: What arguments in the two preceding paragraphs are similar to those stated earlier in this excerpt? **A**

. . . And albeit whatever thing we hear or see, sitting, walking, travelling, or conversing, may be fitly called our book, and is of the same effect that writings are; yet grant the thing to be prohibited were only books, it appears that this order hitherto is far insufficient to the end which it intends.

6. *Psyche:* a classical allusion to Cupid's wife, who had to pass impossible tests from Venus (Cupid's mother) before the couple could marry
7. *fugitive:* tending to flee
8. *excremental:* "pertaining to . . . the dregs or baser part of any substance" (*OED*)
9. *promiscuously:* "indiscriminately" (*OED*)

SONNET 19

Milton employed the sonnet for a wider variety of topics than either Shakespeare or Donne. His sonnets include both private reflections and very public declarations, even on political or religious topics. The following sonnet is a famed example of his reflective mode. It captures the poet's internal conversation at what must surely have been one of his most vulnerable moments in life.

When I consider how my light is spent,
Ere half my days, in this dark world and wide,
And that one Talent which is death to hide,[1]
Lodged with me useless, though my soul more bent
To serve therewith my Maker, and present
My true account, lest he returning **chide**;
"Doth God exact[2] day-labour, light denied?"[3]
I fondly[4] ask. But Patience, to prevent
That murmur, soon replies, "God doth not need
Either man's work or his own gifts; who best
Bear his mild yoke, they serve him best. His state[5]
Is kingly. Thousands at his bidding speed
And post o'er land and ocean without rest:
They also serve who only stand and wait." A

1. *Talent . . . hide:* Matthew 25:14–30
2. *exact:* require
3. *light denied:* while withholding daylight
4. *fondly:* foolishly
5. *state:* position, rank

chide (chīd) *intr.v.* To scold by way of rebuke or reproof; in later usage, often merely, to utter rebuke.

Text Structure: Annotate the poem's rhyme scheme as you read. In what line does the poet's line of thought pivot dramatically? A

THINK AND DISCUSS

1. Choose two or three paragraphs from the *Areopagitica* excerpt and annotate them (if you have not done so already). Explain three of the annotations you have made, why you made them, and how the annotation has helped deepen your understanding of the text.
2. Annotate the rhyme scheme of Sonnet 19 and the resulting stanza structure. Based on this structure, what type of sonnet is it, Italian or English?
3. In Sonnet 19, how does the poet initially respond to his problem? How does his response change by the end of the sonnet? Describe both his initial and final responses using details from the poem. At what point in the poem does the poet's shift in response and attitude occur?
4. What is the main idea of this passage from *Areopagitica*? Identify at least two supporting arguments Milton uses in the text.
5. Identify two instances of biblical evidence that Milton uses in this excerpt. Explain how he uses the evidence to support his arguments.
6. Evaluate any two of Milton's supporting arguments from a biblical perspective. Consider using the two arguments you included in your answer to question 4. Be sure to include scriptural evidence (see the Evaluate section on p. 302) as well as evidence from the text to support your evaluations.

ANALYZE: *Literary Epic and Blank Verse*

Paradise Lost is a **literary epic** written in the tradition of classical epics such as Virgil's Latin *Aeneid*. Nonetheless, the work is unique in subject matter, hero, and style, weaving together both classical and Protestant English traditions into a seamless whole. The topic is a distinctly English rendering of the biblical Fall; it incorporates Protestant doctrines and political ideas clearly related to England's state at the time. Furthermore, Milton deviated from the epic's traditional rhyme in favor of English **blank verse** (p. 184, up to that point reserved for drama). As you read, consider what potential advantages blank verse accorded Milton.

At the same time, Milton made copious use of classical allusions (p. 129) and largely conformed to classical **epic conventions** (p. 16). Topical conventions include a hero larger than life, a setting broad in scope, a supernatural element, a necessary journey or battle, and themes addressing topics central to human existence. Specific stylistic features include beginning *in medias res* with a statement of theme and an invocation to a muse (i.e., asking for inspiration), incorporating long, formal speeches that interrupt the poem's actions, and using devices such as epic similes (p. 170), catalogs (p. 170), and epithets (p. 18). Make a checklist of these eight conventions and note whether each occurs in the text as you read.

READ: *Paraphrase Difficult Text*

Because Milton wrote in an elevated style characteristic of Latin classics, portions of *Paradise Lost* can be difficult to understand. To help understand difficult sections, paraphrase them using the steps found in the Sonneteers lesson (p. 185). You will likely need to spend extra time on the second step (breaking the poem into manageable portions); Milton's sentences are quite long and use unusual syntax. To gain clarity, first identify the main subject(s) and verb(s). Then locate the phrases or clauses modifying these core parts. Finally, rearrange them all more conventionally and continue on with step three. For best results, try reading through the poem twice, marking difficult sections the first time through and paraphrasing them the second.

EVALUATE: *Critical Interpretation*

Traditionally, epics center their action on a hero who exemplifies particular cultural virtues. Milton's story does not fit very easily into this mold. It opens with Satan, a character who ought to be the story's villain, but who looks, speaks, and acts much in the style of a heroic figure. In fact, over half of the epic narrates his ongoing rebellion against God. Not until Book IV do readers meet Adam and Eve. In the late eighteenth century, some romantics argued these facts to mean that Satan was in fact the story's hero, struggling against God's arbitrary rule. From what you know of Milton, do you believe this to be the proper interpretation? As you read the following excerpt, look for details in the text that might indicate Milton's opinion of Satan. What do you imagine the remaining eleven books of *Paradise Lost* will conclude about Satan?

OBJECTIVES

- Identify a text's use of epic conventions.
- Paraphrase a text to understand it.
- Analyze the effects of a poem's form (e.g., blank verse).
- Evaluate a critical perspective on a work.

VOCABULARY

guile (gīl) *n.* Treacherous cunning; skillful deceit.

impious (ĭm′pē-əs) *adj.* Lacking reverence.

ethereal (ĭ-thîr′ē-əl) *adj.* Of the celestial spheres; heavenly.

obdurate (ŏb′do͝o-rĭt) *adj.* Hardened in wrongdoing or wickedness; stubbornly impenitent.

suppliant (sŭp′lē-ənt) *adj.* Asking humbly and earnestly.

incumbent (ĭn-kŭm′bənt) *adj.* Lying, leaning, or resting on something else.

What might a Christian EPIC HERO *look like?*

Beginning in Genesis, the Bible paints a picture of epic conflict, clarifying it in the Gospels and bringing it to a prophetic conclusion in Revelation. What are the sides to this conflict according to Ephesians 6:10–18, Deuteronomy 20:4, and 2 Timothy 2:1–5? Is there an epic hero, someone with incredible strength and leadership skills, to fight the war? What virtues does this Christian epic hero embody and model?

FROM
PARADISE LOST
BOOK 1

Of man's first disobedience, and the fruit
Of that forbidden tree whose mortal taste
Brought death into the world, and all our woe,
With loss of Eden, till one greater Man°
Restore us, and regain the blissful seat,
Sing heav'nly Muse,° that on the secret top
Of Oreb, or of Sinai, didst inspire
That shepherd who first taught the chosen seed
In the beginning how the heav'ns and earth
Rose out of Chaos: or if Sion hill
Delight thee more, and Siloa's brook that flowed
Fast by the oracle of God; I thence
Invoke thy aid to my adventrous song,
That with no middle flight intends to soar
Above the Aonian mount,° while it pursues
Things unattempted yet in prose or rhyme.
And chiefly Thou, O Spirit, that dost prefer
Before all temples the upright heart and pure,
Instruct me, for Thou know'st; Thou from the first
Wast present, and with mighty wings outspread
Dove-like sat'st brooding on the vast abyss,
And mad'st it pregnant: what in me is dark
Illumine, what is low raise and support;
That to the height of this great argument
I may assert eternal Providence,
And justify° the ways of God to men. R A

Say first, for Heav'n hides nothing from thy view,
Nor the deep tract of Hell, say first what cause
Moved our grand Parents, in that happy state,
Favored of Heav'n so highly, to fall off
From their Creator, and transgress his will
For one restraint, lords of the world besides?
Who first seduced them to that foul revolt?

The infernal Serpent; he it was, whose **guile**,
Stirred up with envy and revenge, deceived
The mother of mankind, what time his pride
Had cast him out from Heav'n, with all his host
Of rebel Angels, by whose aid aspiring
To set himself in glory above his peers,

4 Man: i.e., Christ

6 heav'nly Muse: i.e., Holy Spirit

15 Aonian mount: Home of the Greek Muses who, according to tradition, inspired the Greek poets. Milton here implies that the subject of his poem is on a higher plane than the traditional topics of the Greek poets.

26 justify: "to show or maintain the justice or reasonableness of (an action, claim, etc.)" [*OED*]

Paraphrase: Reread lines 12b–26. Noting the verbs, identify the help Milton requests of the muse. R

Literary Epic: How does Milton's invocation in this epic quickly mark it as a Christian, not a classical, text? What purpose does Milton state for the epic? A

guile (gīl) *n.* Treacherous cunning; skillful deceit.

He trusted to have equaled the most High,
If he opposed; and with ambitious aim
Against the throne and monarchy of God,
Raised **impious** war in Heav'n and battle proud
With vain attempt. Him the almighty Power
Hurled headlong flaming from the **ethereal** sky,
With hideous ruin and combustion, down
To bottomless perdition, there to dwell
In adamantine° chains and penal fire,
Who durst defy the Omnipotent to arms. **A**
Nine times the space that measures day and night
To mortal men, he, with his horrid crew,
Lay vanquished, rolling in the fiery gulf,
Confounded though immortal: But his doom
Reserved him to more wrath; for now the thought
Both of lost happiness and lasting pain
Torments him; round he throws his baleful eyes,
That witnessed huge affliction and dismay
Mixed with **obdurate** pride and steadfast hate:
At once, as far as Angels ken, he views
The dismal situation waste and wild;
A dungeon horrible on all sides round
As one great furnace flamed, yet from those flames
No light, but rather darkness visible
Served only to discover sights of woe,
Regions of sorrow, doleful shades, where peace
And rest can never dwell, hope never comes
That comes to all; but torture without end
Still urges, and a fiery deluge, fed
With ever-burning sulphur unconsumed.
Such place eternal Justice had prepared
For those rebellious, here their prison ordained
In utter darkness, and their portion set
As far removed from God and light of Heaven,
As from the center thrice to the utmost pole.
O how unlike the place from whence they fell!
There the companions of his fall, o'erwhelmed
With floods and whirlwinds of tempestuous fire,
He soon discerns, and, welt'ring by his side
One next himself in pow'r, and next in crime,
Long after known in Palestine, and named
Beelzebub. To whom the Arch-Enemy,
And thence in Heav'n called Satan, with bold words
Breaking the horrid silence, thus began. **A**
"If thou beest he;° But O how fall'n! how changed
From him, who in the happy realms of light
Clothed with transcendent brightness didst outshine

48 adamantine: unbreakable

84 he: Satan is addressing Beelzebub in hell.

impious (ĭm'pē-əs) *adj.* Lacking reverence.

ethereal (ĭ-thîr'ē-əl) *adj.* Of the celestial spheres; heavenly.

Literary Epic: Reread lines 34–49. What epithets can you find already? **A**

obdurate (ŏb'do͝o-rĭt) *adj.* Hardened in wrongdoing or wickedness; stubbornly impenitent.

Literary Epic: What three topical conventions does this opening scene fulfill? **A**

VISUAL ANALYSIS
How is the style and content of this engraving by Gustave Doré appropriate for an epic?

Myriads though bright! If he whom mutual league,
United thoughts° and counsels, equal hope
And hazard in the glorious enterprise,
Joined with me once, now misery hath joined
In equal ruin: into what pit thou seest
From what height fall'n, so much the stronger proved
He with his thunder: and till then who knew
The force of those dire arms? Yet not for those,
Nor what the potent victor in his rage
Can else inflict, do I repent or change,
Though changed in outward luster, that fixed mind,°
And high disdain from sense of injured merit,
That with the Mightiest raised me to contend,
And to the fierce contention brought along
Innumerable force of Spirits armed,
That durst dislike his reign, and me preferring,

88 United thoughts: joint intentions

97 mind: direct object of "repent" and "change"

Reading Check: Who is "He" in line 93?

His utmost pow'r with adverse° pow'r opposed
In dubious battle on the plains of Heaven,
And shook his throne. What though the field° be lost?
All is not lost; the unconquerable will,
And study° of revenge, immortal hate,
And courage never to submit or yield,
And what is else not to be overcome;
That glory never shall his wrath or might
Extort from me. To bow and sue for grace
With **suppliant** knee, and deify his power,
Who from the terror of this arm so late
Doubted° his empire; that were low indeed,
That were an ignominy° and shame beneath
This downfall;° since by fate the strength of Gods
And this empyreal° substance cannot fail,
Since through experience of this great event°
In arms not worse, in foresight much advanced,
We may with more successful hope resolve
To wage by force or guile eternal war,
Irreconcilable to our grand foe,
Who now triumphs, and in the excess of joy
Sole reigning holds the tyranny of Heaven."
So spake the apostate Angel, though in pain,
Vaunting° aloud, but racked° with deep despair: E
And him thus answered soon his bold compeer.°
"O Prince, O Chief of many thronèd Powers,
That led the embattled Seraphim to war

103 adverse: contrary

105 field: battlefield

107 study: plotting

114 Doubted: feared for

115 ignominy: humiliation

116 downfall: lower than the depths to which we have fallen

117 empyreal: heavenly

118 event: outcome

126 Vaunting: boasting / **racked:** tormented

127 compeer: companion

suppliant (sŭp′lē-ənt) *adj.* Asking humbly and earnestly.

Critical Interpretation: Reread Satan's opening speech (ll. 84–124). What can you discern about his character? Is his view of himself and of God accurate according to the Bible? E

Under thy conduct, and, in dreadful deeds
Fearless, endangered Heav'n's perpetual king,
And put to proof his high supremacy,
Whether upheld by strength, or chance, or fate;
Too well I see and rue the dire event,
That with sad overthrow and foul defeat
Hath lost us Heav'n, and all this mighty host
In horrible destruction laid thus low,
As far as Gods and heav'nly essences
Can perish: for the mind and spirit remains
Invincible, and vigor soon returns,
Though all our glory extinct,° and happy state
Here swallowed up in endless misery.
But what if he our conqu'ror (whom I now
Of force° believe almighty, since no less
Then such could have o'erpow'red such force as ours)
Have left us this our spirit and strength entire
Strongly to suffer and support our pains,
That we may so suffice° his vengeful ire,°
Or do him mightier service as his thralls°
By right of war, whate'er his business be
Here in the heart of Hell to work in fire,
Or do his errands in the gloomy deep;
What can it then avail, though yet we feel
Strength undiminished, or eternal being°
To undergo eternal punishment?" R
    Whereto with speedy words the Arch-Fiend replied.
"Fall'n Cherub, to be weak is miserable
Doing or suffering:° but of this be sure,
To do aught good never will be our task,
But ever to do ill our sole delight,
As being the contrary to his high will
Whom we resist. If then his providence
Out of our evil seek to bring forth good,
Our labor must be to pervert that end,
And out of good still° to find means of evil;
Which ofttimes may succeed, so as perhaps
Shall grieve him, if I fail not, and disturb
His inmost counsels from their destined aim. E
But see the angry victor hath recalled
His ministers of vengeance and pursuit°
Back to the gates of Heav'n: the sulphurous hail
Shot after us in storm, o'erblown hath laid°
The fiery surge that from the precipice
Of Heav'n received us falling; and the thunder,
Winged with red lightning and impetuous° rage,
Perhaps hath spent° his shafts,° and ceases now
To bellow through the vast and boundless deep.
Let us not slip the occasion,° whether scorn,
Or satiate° fury yield it from our foe.

141 **extinct:** extinguished

144 **Of force:** pun: (1) in power, (2) perforce

148 **suffice:** gratify / **ire:** wrath

149 **thralls:** slaves

154 **eternal being:** or our existence to be eternal

158 **Doing . . . suffering:** lines 138–47

165 **still:** continually

170 **ministers . . . pursuit:** angelic troops

172 **laid:** calmed

175 **impetuous:** explosively violent

176 **spent:** used up / **shafts:** arrows

178 **slip . . . occasion:** miss the opportunity

179 **satiate:** satisfied

Paraphrase: Restate Beelzebub's speech in your own words. What is he worried about? R

Critical Interpretation: Reread lines 157–68. Identify Satan's avowed goal. Does Satan exhibit heroic character in this matter? E

Seest thou yon dreary plain, forlorn and wild,
The seat of desolation, void of light,
Save° what the glimmering of these livid° flames
Casts pale and dreadful? Thither let us tend
From off the tossing of these fiery waves,
There rest, if any rest can harbour there,
And re-assembling our afflicted° Powers,
Consult how we may henceforth most offend
Our enemy, our own loss how repair,
How overcome this dire° calamity,
What reinforcement we may gain from hope,
If not what resolution from despair."
   Thus Satan talking to his nearest mate
With head uplift above the wave, and eyes
That sparkling blazed; his other parts besides
Prone on the flood, extended long and large
Lay floating many a rood,° in bulk as huge
As whom the fables name of monstrous size,
Titanian, or Earth-born, that warred on Jove,°
Briareos or Typhon, whom the den
By ancient Tarsus held, or that sea-beast
Leviathan, which God of all his works
Created hugest that swim the ocean-stream:° A
Him haply slumbering on the Norway foam
The pilot of some small night-foundered skiff
Deeming some island, oft, as seamen tell,
With fixèd anchor in his scaly rind
Moors by his side under the lee,° while night
Invests° the sea, and wishèd morn delays.
So stretched out huge in length the Arch-Fiend lay,
Chained on the burning lake, nor ever thence
Had ris'n or heaved his head, but that the will
And high permission of all-ruling Heaven
Left him at large to his own dark designs,
That with reiterated° crimes he might
Heap on himself damnation, while he sought
Evil to others, and enraged might see
How all his malice served but to bring forth
Infinite goodness, grace and mercy, shewn
On Man by him seduced, but on himself
Treble° confusion, wrath and vengeance poured. R
   Forthwith upright he rears from off the pool
His mighty stature; on each hand the flames
Driv'n backward slope their pointing spires, and rolled
In billows, leave i' the midst a horrid vale.°
Then with expanded wings he steers his flight
Aloft, **incumbent** on the dusky air
That felt unusual weight, till on dry land

182 Save: except / **livid:** pale (or, by Latin etymology, bluish)

186 afflicted: struck down

189 dire: disastrous

196 rood: forty square rods, about one-fourth acre

198 Titanian . . . Jove: The war of the Titans (including the hundred-armed Briareos) against the Olympian gods and the rebellion of the Giants (including the serpent Typhon) were associated with Satan's revolt.

202 Created . . . stream: Isaiah 27:1

207 under . . . lee: away from the wind

208 Invests: clothes

214 reiterated: repeated, multiplied

220 Treble: triple

224 In . . . vale: cf. Exodus 14:21–22

Literary Epic: Identify the two epic devices illustrated in lines 196–202. What do they communicate about Satan? A

Paraphrase: Restate the content of lines 209–20 in your own words. How does this information assist Milton in his purpose for the epic (p. 307)? R

incumbent (ĭn-kŭm′bənt) *adj.* Lying, leaning, or resting on something else.

He lights, as if it were land that ever burned
With solid, as the lake with liquid fire;
And such appeared in hue, as when the force
Of subterranean wind transports a hill
Torn from Pelorus,° or the shattered side
Of thund'ring Aetna, whose combustible
And fueled entrails thence° conceiving fire,
Sublimed° with mineral fury, aid the winds,
And leave a singèd bottom all involved
With stench and smoke: Such resting found the sole
Of unblest feet. Him followed his next mate,
Both glorying to have 'scaped the Stygian° flood
As Gods, and by their own recovered strength,
Not by the sufferance of supernal° Power.
"Is this the region, this the soil, the clime,"
Said then the lost Arch-Angel, "this the seat
That we must change for Heav'n, this mournful gloom
For that celestial light? Be it so, since he
Who now is Sovran can dispose and bid
What shall be right: farthest from him is best,
Whom reason hath equaled, force hath made supreme
Above his equals. Farewell happy fields,
Where joy for ever dwells: Hail horrors, hail
Infernal world, and thou profoundest Hell,
Receive thy new possessor; one who brings
A mind not to be changed by place or time.
The mind is its own place, and in itself
Can make a Heav'n of Hell, a Hell of Heav'n.
What matter where, if I be still the same,
And what I should be, all but less than he
Whom thunder hath made greater? Here at least
We shall be free; the Almighty hath not built
Here for his envy, will not drive us hence:
Here we may reign secure; and in my choice
To reign is worth ambition though in Hell:
Better to reign in Hell, than serve in Heaven."

232 Pelorus: Sicilian peninsula, from which rises Mt. Aetna

234 thence: from the wind

235 Sublimed: vaporized

239 Stygian: infernal (Styx is one of the classical rivers of hell)

241 supernal: heavenly

Literary Epic: Satan's climactic speech (ll. 242–63) is in blank verse like the rest of the poem. Does the lack of rhyme diminish its impact on readers? How might this verse form offer Milton some flexibility in constructing his lines?

THINK AND DISCUSS

1. Explain why *Paradise Lost* is a literary epic rather than a folk epic.
2. Cite two characteristics of Milton's work that show its uniquely Christian nature.
3. Using the steps for paraphrasing difficult poetry, paraphrase lines 125–27.
4. Annotate the first ten lines of *Paradise Lost* to show how they fulfill the requirements of blank verse.
5. Pick four epic conventions (see p. 306), and illustrate them from the excerpt of *Paradise Lost*.
6. Based on Milton's tone and the foreshadowing in Book 1 (especially ll. 209–20), what do you predict to be Satan's fate by the conclusion of *Paradise Regained*?
7. How does Milton's choice of poetic form differ from other epics? Describe two advantages that using this form gave the poet.
8. What characteristics of an epic hero might you see in Satan in this excerpt? Perhaps compare his behavior to that of Beowulf (pp. 19–30) to find your answer.
9. Is Satan the epic hero of *Paradise Lost*? Why or why not?

Samuel Pepys (1633–1703)

Pepys's father was a London tailor, and his mother was the daughter of a French Huguenot. Pepys was educated at St. Paul's and Cambridge. In 1660, at age twenty-seven, he accompanied his cousin, the first earl of Sandwich, on the ship bringing Charles II to England. The same year he was appointed clerk to the Navy Board, the agency responsible for equipping, manning, and maintaining the king's ships. Though Pepys initially lacked naval experience, he applied himself diligently and for most of the next eighteen years worked in the navy office, eventually becoming the unofficial ruler of the navy. When James left the throne, Pepys retired and wrote a history of the Royal Navy chronicling the years 1679–88. Through his intelligence, honesty, meticulous concern for details, and years of patient labor, Pepys became known as the main architect of the British navy, laying the administrative foundation for two centuries of British sea power.

Pepys served as a member of Parliament and as president of the Royal Society for two years (1684–86). In addition, he has become an important literary figure. He kept careful financial records and reviewed them annually. He also kept a diary for almost a decade, recording other matters of interest encoded in his own version of a contemporary shorthand. It was finally deciphered in the nineteenth century and is a primary document for historians of the early Restoration. His firsthand accounts of the Great Plague (1665), the Great Fire (1666), and the coronation of Charles II are unforgettable. In addition to Pepys's eyewitness accounts of momentous events, the diary is replete with observations of ordinary ones. In both, he showed a gift for lively and detailed narrative. The entries also reveal an enterprising young man's climb to worldly success, including his flaws, his infidelities, and his complexity. Pepys was divided between moral resolution and dereliction, between disgust with and loyalty to the Crown, between dislike of the Puritans and admiration for their integrity. He laments the degeneracy of the age while pursuing its pleasures. Through his diary, we gain valuable insight into Pepys and his age.

BEFORE READING

ANALYZE: *Diary and Sensory Details*

A **diary** is an informal daily record of a person's life. Many diarists unwittingly leave for historians valuable records of an era (e.g., social norms, everyday objects or routines, firsthand accounts of important historical events). Pepys's diary relates such valuable information. But its place in literary history is due to his keen insights and grasp of how **sensory details** (descriptions appealing concretely to the five senses) bring an event alive for readers. As you read, look for such details.

READ: *Ask Questions of a Primary Source*

When historians read primary sources (e.g., a diary), they ask questions to find historical significance. As you read the diary, ask *who*, *what*, *where*, and *when* questions to establish the broad facts. Note specifics of the fire and plague's extent and results. Consider what a diary might record that a government report might not. How did ordinary people respond to events? How does Pepys's personal experience help us feel the devastation wrought, both personal and national?

CREATE: *An Eyewitness Account*

Note the physical details Pepys includes of plague-ridden London as he walks through its streets. What people, places, and happenings does he specify? Note what a bleak picture he paints from the Tower overlooking burning London. What senses does he employ? Try your own hand at writing an eyewitness account. Be sure to include plenty of sensory details.

OBJECTIVES

- Identify sensory details in an eyewitness account.
- Ask questions of a primary source to determine its historical contributions.
- Analyze how Pepys used sensory details to convey his experience.
- Create an eyewitness account that includes sensory details.

VOCABULARY

apprehension (ăp′rĭ-hĕn′shən) *n.* Fearful or uneasy anticipation of the future; dread.

abate (ə-bāt′) *intr.v.* To fall off in degree or intensity; subside.

lamentable (lə-mĕn′tə-bəl) *adj.* Inspiring or deserving of lament or regret; deplorable or pitiable.

loath (lōth) *adj.* Unwilling or reluctant; disinclined.

THE DIARY

THE PLAGUE OF 1665

June 10th. . . . In the evening home to supper; and there, to my great trouble, hear that the plague is come into the City (though it hath these three or four weeks since its beginning been wholly out of the City); . . . . To the office to finish my letters and then home to bed, being troubled at the sickness, and my head filled also with other business enough, and particularly how to put my things and estate in order, in case it should please God to call me away, which God dispose of to his glory!

August 8th. . . . The streets mighty empty all the way, now even in London, which is a sad sight. . . . And poor Will, that used to sell us ale at the Hall-door, his wife and three children died, all, I think, in a day. So home through the City again, wishing I may have taken no ill in going; but I will go, I think, no more thither. . . . R

Ask Questions: What details in the August 8 entry help you to better understand the plague and its extent and results? R

August 22nd I went away and walked to Greenwich, in my way seeing a coffin with a dead body therein, dead of the plague, lying in an open close[1] belonging to Coome farm, which was carried out last night, and the parish have not appointed anybody to bury it; but only set a watch there day and night, that nobody should go thither or come thence, which is a most cruel thing: this disease making us more cruel to one another than if we are dogs. . . .

September 3rd (Lord's day). . . . Among other stories, one was very passionate, methought, of a complaint brought against a man in the town for taking a child from London from an infected house. Alderman Hooker told us it was the child of a very able citizen in Gracious Street, a saddler,[2] who had buried all the rest of his children of the plague, and himself and wife now being shut up and in despair of escaping, did desire only to save the life of this little child; and so prevailed to have it received stark-naked into the arms of a friend, who brought it (having put it into new fresh clothes) to Greenwich; where upon hearing the story, we did agree it should be permitted to be received and kept in the town. . . . R

Ask Questions: How do the details in this entry affect you differently than statistics in a report would? R

1. *open close:* roofless enclosure beside a house; courtyard, yard
2. *saddler:* "one that makes, repairs, or sells equipment for horses" (*AHD*)

September 14th. . . . [W]hen I come home I spent some thoughts upon the occurrences of this day, giving matter for as much content on one hand and melancholy on another, as any day in all my life. For the first; the finding of my money and plate, and all safe at London, and speeding in my business of money this day. The hearing of this good news to such excess, after so great a despair of my Lord's doing anything this year; adding to that, the decrease of 500 and more, which is the first decrease we have yet had in the sickness since it begun: and great hopes that the next week it will be greater. Then, on the other side, my finding that though the Bill[3] in general is abated, yet the City within the walls is increased, and likely to continue so, and is close to our house there. My meeting dead corpses of the plague, carried to be buried close to me at noon-day through the City in Fanchurch-street. To see a person sick of the sores, carried close by me by Gracechurch in a hackney-coach.[4] My finding the Angell tavern, at the lower end of Tower-hill, shut up, and more than that, the alehouse at the Tower-stairs, and more than that, the person was then dying of the plague when I was last there, a little while ago, at night, to write a short letter there, and I overheard the mistress of the house sadly saying to her husband somebody was very ill, but did not think it was of the plague. To hear that poor Payne, my waiter, hath buried a child, and is dying himself. To hear that a labourer I sent but the other day to Dagenhams, to know how they did there, is dead of the plague; and that one of my own watermen, that carried me daily, fell sick as soon as he had landed me on Friday morning last, when I had been all night upon the water (and I believe he did get his infection that day at Brainford), and is now dead of the plague. To hear that Captain Lambert and Cuttle are killed in the taking these ships; and that Mr. Sidney Montague is sick of a desperate fever at my Lady Carteret's, at Scott's-hall. To hear that Mr. Lewes hath another daughter sick. And, lastly, that both my servants, W. Hewer and Tom Edwards, have lost their fathers, both in St. Sepulchre's parish, of the plague this week, do put me into great **apprehensions** of melancholy, and with good reason. But I put off the thoughts of sadness as much as I can, and the rather to keep my wife in good heart and family also. . . . R

apprehension (ăp′rĭ-hĕn′shən) *n.* Fearful or uneasy anticipation of the future; dread.

Ask Questions: Beyond a list of people who have died, what important ideas about the survivors does this entry convey? How did these deaths affect Pepys? R

September 20th. . . . [W]hat a sad time it is to see no boats upon the River; and grass grows all up and down White Hall court, and nobody but poor wretches in the streets! And, which is worst of all, the Duke showed us the number of the plague this week, brought in the last night from the Lord Mayor; that it is increased about 600 more than the last, which is quite contrary to all our hopes and expectations, from the coldness of the late season. For the whole general number is 8,297, and of them the plague 7,165; which is more in the whole by above 50, than the biggest Bill yet; which is very grievous to us all. . . .

December 31st (Lord's day). . . . It is true we have gone through great melancholy because of the great plague. . . . But now the plague is **abated** almost to nothing. . . . My whole family hath been well all this while, and all my friends I know of, saving my aunt Bell, who is dead, and some children of my cousin Sarah's, of the plague. But many of such as I know very well, dead; yet, to our great joy, the town fills apace, and shops begin to be open again. Pray God continue the plague's decrease! . . .

abate (ə-bāt′) *intr.v.* To fall off in degree or intensity; subside.

3. *Bill:* list of the dead
4. *hackney-coach:* "a four-wheeled coach for hire, typically drawn by two horses and with seating for six passengers" (*OED*)

THE GREAT FIRE OF 1666

September 2nd (Lord's day). Some of our maids sitting up late last night to get things ready against our feast to-day, Jane called us up[5] about three in the morning, to tell us of a great fire they saw in the City. So I rose and slipped on my night-gown, and went to her window, and thought it to be on the backside of Marke-lane at the farthest; but, being unused to such fires as followed, I thought it far enough off; and so went to bed again and to sleep. About seven rose again to dress myself, and there looked out at the window, and saw the fire not so much as it was and further off. . . . By and by Jane comes and tells me that she hears that above 300 houses have been burned down to-night by the fire we saw, and that it is now burning down all Fish-street, by London Bridge. So I made myself ready presently, and walked to the Tower, and there got up upon one of the high places . . . and there I did see the houses at that end of the bridge all on fire, and an infinite great fire on this and the other side the end of the bridge. . . . So down, with my heart full of trouble, to the Lieutenant of the Tower, who tells me that it begun this morning in the King's baker's house in Pudding-lane, and that it hath burned St. Magnus's Church and most part of Fish-street already. So I down to the water-side, and there got a boat and through bridge, and there saw a lamentable fire. Poor Michell's house, as far as the Old Swan, already burned that way, and the fire running further, that in a very little time it got as far as the Steele-yard, while I was there. Everybody endeavouring to remove their goods, and flinging into the river or bringing them into lighters[6] that layoff; poor people staying in their houses as long as till the very fire touched them, and then running into boats, or clambering from one pair of stairs by the water-side to another. And among other things, the poor pigeons, I perceive, were loath to leave their houses, but hovered about the windows and balconies till they were, some of them burned, their wings, and fell down. Having staid, and in an hour's time seen the fire rage every way, and nobody, to my sight, endeavouring to quench it, but to remove their goods, and leave all to the fire, and having seen it get as far as the Steele-yard, and the wind mighty high and driving it into the City; and every thing, after so long a drought, proving combustible, even the very stones of churches. . . . At last met my Lord Mayor in Canningstreet, like a

lamentable (lə-mĕn′tə-bəl) *adj.* Inspiring or deserving of lament or regret; deplorable or pitiable.

loath (lōth) *adj.* Unwilling or reluctant; disinclined.

5. *up:* to get out of bed
6. *lighters:* vessels (usually flatbottomed) used to transport a load to a ship

man spent, with a handkerchief about his neck. To the King's message[7] he cried, like a fainting woman, "Lord! what can I do? I am spent: people will not obey me. I have been pulling down houses; but the fire overtakes us faster than we can do it." That he needed no more soldiers; and that, for himself, he must go and refresh himself, having been up all night. So he left me, and I him, and walked home. . . . Met with the King and Duke of York in their barge, and with them to Queenhithe, and there called Sir Richard Browne to them. Their order was only to pull down houses apace, and so below bridge at

VISUAL ANALYSIS
How does the artist evoke emotions similar to those Pepys evokes in his diary account of the Great Fire of London?

7. *the King's message:* The king had instructed Pepys to find the mayor and tell him to pull down houses in the fire's path in order to stop its spread.

the water-side; but little was or could be done, the fire coming upon them so fast. Good hopes there was of stopping it at the Three Cranes above, and at Buttolph's Wharf below bridge, if care be used; but the wind carries it into the City, so as we know not by the water-side what it do there. River full of lighters and boats taking in goods, and good goods swimming in the water. . . . [W]ith one's face in the wind, you were almost burned with a shower of fire-drops. This is very true; so as houses were burned by these drops and flakes of fire, three or four, nay, five or six houses, one from another. When we could endure no more upon the water, we to a little ale-house on the Bankside, over against the Three Cranes, and there stayed till it was dark almost, and saw the fire grow; and, as it grew darker, appeared more and more, and in corners and upon steeples, and between churches and houses, as far as we could see up the hill of the City, in a most horrid malicious bloody flame, not like the fine flame of an ordinary fire. . . . We stayed till, it being darkish, we saw the fire as only one entire arch of fire from this to the other side the bridge, and in a bow up the hill for an arch of above a mile long : it made me weep to see it. The churches, houses, and all on fire and flaming at once; and a horrid noise the flames made, and the cracking of houses at their ruin. So home with a sad heart. . . . A

Sensory Details: Identify sensory imagery that heightens the vividness of the fire, in effect, putting you at the scene. What senses are used most? A

September 5th . . . [G]oing to the fire, I find by the blowing up of houses, and the great help given by the workmen out of the King's yards,[8] sent up by Sir W. Pen, there is a good stop given to it. . . . I walked into the town, and find Fanchurch-street, Gracious-street, and Lumbard-street all in dust. The Exchange a sad sight, nothing standing there, of all the statues or pillars, but Sir Thomas Gresham's picture in the corner. Walked into Moorefields (our feet ready to burn, walking through the town among the hot coals), and find that full of people, and poor wretches carrying their goods there, and every body keeping his goods together by themselves. . . . And took up (which I keep by me) a piece of glass of Mercers' Chappell in the street, where much more was, so melted and buckled with the heat of the fire like parchment. I also did see a poor cat taken out of a hole in the chimney, joining to the wall of the Exchange, with the hair all burned off the body, and yet alive. So home at night. . . . But it is a strange thing to see how long this time did look since Sunday, having been always full of variety of actions, and little sleep, that it looked like a week or more, and I had forgot almost the day of the week. A

Sensory Details: Identify in this entry an image that vividly appeals to your sight. Find one that describes something perceived by touch. A

September 7th. . . . [S]till both sleeping and waking had a fear of fire in my heart, that I took little rest.

8. *yards:* shipyards

THINK AND DISCUSS

1. What two historical events does Pepys relate in the entries included in the text?
2. Explain why Pepys's diary is considered literature. What time period in history does the diary document?
3. Explain the value of Pepys's diary to historians beyond that of a government report.
4. Find four examples where Pepys incorporates sensory details. Label each by the sense it appeals to.
5. Choose two examples of sensory details and explain how each helps engage readers in Pepys's narrative.
6. Write a paragraph giving a detailed account of an experience you witnessed firsthand. Make sure to include multiple examples of sensory details.

UNIT 3

PART 2

Early Neoclassical Writers

Think about the things that you commonly read. What genre of literature would they likely fall under? If you were to compare answers to this question with a friend or parent, you would likely find one thing: whether it is news reports, fiction, informational texts, or just messages from friends, most twenty-first-century reading, online or in print, is a form of prose. This trend had its beginnings in the first half of the eighteenth century, which saw a proliferation of prose both for political and practical reasons. This age also witnessed the pinnacle of development of the simple, elegant writing of the neoclassicist.

Events of the decades following the Civil War and Glorious Revolution continued to polarize public opinion. Whigs and Tories (p. 286) reflected the growing divide in English society between the traditional holders of power, the landed aristocracy, and the rising commercial class. Whigs favored more power for Parliament; Tories favored the traditional authorities of the monarch and established church. The two parties went in and out of royal approval as events tended to favor the interests of one or the other. Controlling public opinion and arguing persuasively were critical in this heated atmosphere of political strife.

The eighteenth century was also distinguished by a rise in literacy. Key to the rise was an increased emphasis on education. For one thing, education was important to the aims of the Enlightenment. The *philosophes* (see p. 290) wanted to reform society according to its natural laws. They believed that training the senses through education was critical to being able to find and implement those laws. This philosophy was behind some of the eighteenth century's growth of educational systems. Within these systems, a wider span of social classes and a larger number of women received educational training (although views of women's role in society remained largely traditional). Other factors behind increased literacy rates were the continued dominance of Protestantism, which emphasized the need for believers to be able to read the Bible for themselves, and the growth of the commercial class, whose members needed training in business knowledge and skills.

New forms of prose developed in response to the divergent interests of this growing group of readers. The rise of journalism was one significant result as these new readers demanded more information. Newspapers provided practical (and sometimes sensational) accounts of current happenings, while journals served a variety of didactic purposes, many of which were related to civic discussions of politics. In continuation of the pamphlet tradition of the Civil War, journals promoted the political and social ideals of their writers. Daniel Defoe, Joseph Addison, and Richard Steele, all Whigs by conviction (though Defoe was also recruited to write for the Tories), established lasting reputations for the elegant wit and didactic purposes of their journals.

The enlarged audience also created demand for a new genre: the novel. The novel as a long work of prose fiction had predecessors in forms such as the romance of the Middle Ages. One typical difference between the two was that romances often depicted fantastic, perhaps supernatural, events, whereas novels typically described the ordinary lives of common people. The readers of the eighteenth century wanted characters and story lines that they could relate to. Daniel Defoe, for example, used realistic dialogue and details to present middle-class characters who confronted practical problems.

Stylistically, this period was also known for its peak of achievement in the principles of neoclassicism (p. 293). For example, Alexander Pope, known as the most "correct" poet of his age, achieved a brilliant mastery of the heroic couplet and the standard neoclassical genres. He showed exact precision of form but at the same time an elegance and complexity of meaning. Meanwhile, Jonathan Swift, writing mostly in prose, exemplified the plain style of the age. His words were simple and vigorous; his syntax, clear and direct. His style was well suited to the common neoclassical mode of satire (another widely used tool of persuasion). *Gulliver's Travels*, Swift's satire on travel literature, presented a clear and scathing indictment of the hypocrisies and weaknesses of human society.

Daniel Defoe (1660–1731)

In the early 1680s a young Whig named Daniel Foe was making a start in business as a hosier (dealer in knitted wear). A half century later, after two financial failures and frequent appearances in court, Defoe (the name he eventually used) closed a quite different, remarkable career as one of England's first great journalists and a father of the English **novel**, an extended work of fictional prose.

During the 1690s young Foe's talent for writing enabled him to serve Whig leaders through pamphleteering. The coming of Tory extremists into power occasioned Foe's writing of an ironic pamphlet in which he posed as a Tory recommending punishments for nonconformity so severe as to show their absurdity. The scheme backfired, sending Foe to the pillory and then to prison. He was rescued by a moderate Tory who, recognizing his potential value, set him to write for a Tory audience. Foe changed his name to the more genteel Defoe and for ten years single-handedly authored the political publication *A Weekly Review of the Affairs of France*, which blended pamphlet and newspaper and was written from a moderate Tory perspective. With the fall of the Tories, Defoe adapted again, writing for Whig periodicals while continuing to write for Tory periodicals in order to dilute their Toryism. By the time *Robinson Crusoe* appeared in 1719, Defoe was an established author. This novel drew not only from his writing experience but also from his experience with mariners and shopkeepers and with questions of size, texture, durability, cost, and supply. Crusoe lives in a world of physical specifications, sums, and estimates. His success requires calculated risks. Crusoe's stay of twenty-eight years on a remarkably well-stocked island has all the elements of a sojourn in an eighteenth-century fantasy world. In a loose allegory of Defoe's life, Robinson Crusoe "reports" the adventures of a providentially assisted but otherwise self-made man. Though other novels—*Captain Singleton, Moll Flanders, Roxana*—followed, none were as successful as the first. Defoe's formula for life, as for art, was resourceful persistence in a role. His successes, like Crusoe's, grew out of his mishaps.

BEFORE READING

ANALYZE: *Verisimilitude and Journalistic Style*

In his novels, Defoe presents realistic content with a journalistic style drawn from his middle-class background and professional writing experience. Minute, even superfluous, detail creates an illusion of actuality, a concept known as **verisimilitude**. In *Robinson Crusoe,* his journalistic style, which contributes to its realism, emerges in two primary ways: his first-person narration (storytelling with the narrator as one of the characters, who refers to himself or herself throughout the story) and his rambling, conversational narrative in the manner of extemporaneous reporting. As you read, examine Defoe's realistic content and journalistic style.

READ: *Consider Author's Purpose*

Defoe purposed to create a morally worthy hero in *Robinson Crusoe.* Portions of the novel (not included here) delineate Crusoe's path from prodigal to penitent. The excerpt included does, however, showcase certain characteristics that Defoe's Puritan lower-middle-class readership deemed admirable—frugality, resourcefulness, resiliency, and orderliness. As you read, examine the text for evidence of these and other characteristics.

EVALUATE: *Author's Worldview*

Marooned, Crusoe must adjust to adverse circumstances. Does he adapt to nature, or does he try to make nature adapt to him? From the ship and the island he obtains some necessities and uses intelligence and effort to survive. But he makes a grave mistake. How is disaster averted? Evaluate Defoe's portrayal of man as a civilizing animal, and discuss the role of Providence. Consider Genesis 1:28–30.

OBJECTIVES

- Examine the realistic content and journalistic style of a text.
- Consider an author's purpose for a text.
- Evaluate an author's attitude toward nature and Providence.

VOCABULARY

effectually (ĭ-fĕk′cho͞o-əl-lē) *adv.* With absolute effect; with complete fulfilment or success, thoroughly.

venture (vĕn′chər) *intr.v.* To proceed despite possible danger or risk.

desolate (dĕs′ə-lĭt) *adj.* Devoid of inhabitants; deserted.

consternation (kŏn′stər-nā′shən) *n.* A state of great alarm, agitation, or dismay.

reprieve (rĭ-prēv′) *n.* The prevention or suspension of a scheduled or expected punishment.

inter (ĭn-tûr′) *tr.v.* To place in a grave or tomb; bury.

FROM ROBINSON CRUSOE

I had now been here so long, that many things which I brought on shore for my help were either quite gone, or very much wasted and near spent.

My ink, as I observed, had been gone for some time, all but a very little, which I eked out[1] with water a little and a little, till it was so pale it scarce left any appearance of black upon the paper. As long as it lasted, I made use of it to minute down[2] the days of the month on which any remarkable thing happened to me, and first by casting up[3] times past. I remember that there was a strange concurrence of days in the various providences which befell me; and which, if I had been superstitiously inclined to observe days as fatal or fortunate, I might have had reason to have looked upon with a great deal of curiosity.

1. *eked out:* increased, caused to last longer
2. *minute down:* to record exactly
3. *casting up:* calculating

First, I had observed, that the same day that I broke away from my father and my friends, and run away to Hull, in order to go to sea, the same day afterwards I was taken by the Sallee man-of-war, and made a slave. The same day of the year that I escaped out of the wreck of that ship in Yarmouth roads, that same day-year afterwards I made my escape from Sallee in the boat. The same day of the year I was born on, viz: the 30th of September, that same day I had my life so miraculously saved twenty-six years after, when I was cast on shore on this island, so that my wicked life and my solitary life began both on a day.

The next thing to my ink being wasted, was that of my bread, I mean the biscuit which I brought out of the ship; this I had husbanded[4] to the last degree, allowing myself but one cake of bread a day for above a year, and yet I was quite without bread for near a year before I got any corn of my own, and great reason I had to be thankful that I had any at all, the getting it being, as has been already observed, next to miraculous. **R**

Author's Purpose: Describe Crusoe's use of resources in the preceding paragraphs. Would Defoe's readership approve or disapprove? **R**

My clothes began to decay, too, mightily. As to linen, I had none a good while, except some checkered shirts which I found in the chests of the other seamen, and which I carefully preserved, because many times I could bear no other clothes on but a shirt; and it was a very great help to me that I had among all the men's clothes of the ship almost three dozen of shirts. There were also several thick watchcoats[5] of the seamen, which were left indeed, but they were too hot to wear; and though it is true that the weather was so violent hot that there was no need of clothes, yet I could not go quite naked; no, though I had been inclined to it, which I was not, nor could not abide the thoughts of it, though I was all alone.

The reason why I could not go quite naked, was, I could not bear the heat of the sun so well when quite naked, as with some clothes on; nay, the very heat frequently blistered my skin; whereas, with a shirt on, the air itself made some motion, and whistling under that shirt, was twofold cooler than without it. No more could I ever bring myself to go out in the heat of the sun without a cap or a hat; the heat of the sun beating with such violence as it does in that place, would give me the head-ache presently, by darting so directly on my head, without a cap or hat on, so that I could not bear it; whereas, if I put on my hat, it would presently go away. **A**

Verisimilitude: What specific details does Defoe use in paragraphs 2–6? What effect do they have on the story? **A**

Upon those views I began to consider about putting the few rags I had, which I called clothes, into some order. I had worn out all the waistcoats I had, and my business was now to try if I could not make jackets out of the great watchcoats which I had by me, and with such other materials as I had; so I set to work a tailoring, or rather indeed a botching,[6] for I made most piteous work of it. However, I made shift[7] to make two or three new waistcoats, which I hoped would serve me a great while; as for breeches or drawers, I made but a very sorry shift[8] indeed, till afterward.

I have mentioned that I saved the skins of all the creatures that I killed, I mean four-footed ones, and I had hung them up stretched out with sticks in the sun, by which means some of them were so dry and hard that they were fit for little, but others it seems were very useful. The first thing I made of these was a great cap for my head, with the hair on the outside to shoot off the rain; and this I performed so well, that after this I made me a suit of clothes wholly

4. *husbanded:* conserved
5. *watchcoats:* heavy coats worn by seamen when on duty in bad weather
6. *botching:* clumsy patching
7. *made shift:* contrived
8. *shift:* effort

of these skins, that is to say, a waistcoat, and breeches open at knees, and both loose, for they were rather wanting[9] to keep me cool than to keep me warm. I must not omit to acknowledge that they were wretchedly made; for if I was a bad carpenter, I was a worse tailor. However, they were such as I made very good shift with; and when I was abroad, if it happened to rain, the hair of my waistcoat and cap being outermost, I was kept very dry. R

Author's Purpose: Describe Crusoe's use of animal skins. How would you characterize him based on this use? R

After this I spent a great deal of time and pains to make me an umbrella. I was indeed in great want of one, and had a great mind to make one. I had seen them made in the Brazils, where they are very useful in the great heats which are there; and I felt the heats every jot as great here, and greater, too, being nearer the equinox;[10] besides, as I was obliged to be much abroad, it was a most useful thing to me, as well for the rains as the heats. I took a world of pains at it, and was a great while before I could make anything likely to hold; nay, after I thought I had hit the way, I spoiled two or three before I made one to my mind; but at last I made one that answered[11] indifferently well. The main difficulty I found was to make it let down. I could make it to spread, but if it did not let down too, and draw in, it was not portable for me any way but just over my head, which would not do. However, at last, as I said, I made one to answer, and covered it with skins, the hair upwards, so that it cast off the rains like a pent-house,[12] and kept off the sun so **effectually**, that I could walk out in the hottest of the weather with greater advantage than I could before in the coolest, and when I had no need of it, could close it and carry it under my arm.

effectually (ĭ-fĕk′cho͞o-əl-lē) *adv.* With absolute effect; with complete fulfilment or success, thoroughly.

Thus I lived mighty comfortably, my mind being entirely composed by resigning to the will of God, and throwing myself wholly upon the disposal of his Providence.[13] This made my life better than sociable; for when I began to regret the want of conversation, I would ask myself whether thus conversing mutually with my own thoughts, and, as I hope I may say, with even God himself, by ejaculations,[14] was not better than the utmost enjoyment of human society in the world? E

Author's Worldview: How does Crusoe respond to his situation? What might his response suggest about Defoe's worldview? E

I cannot say that after this, for five years, any extraordinary thing happened to me, but I lived on in the same course, in the same posture and place, just as before. The chief things I was employed in, besides my yearly labor of planting my barley and rice, and curing my raisins, of both which I always kept up just enough to have sufficient stock of one year's provisions beforehand; I say, besides this yearly labor, and my daily labor of going out with my gun, I had one labor to make me a canoe, which at last I finished. So that by digging a canal to it of six foot wide, and four foot deep, I brought it into the creek, almost half a mile. As for the first, which was so vastly big, as I made it without considering beforehand, as I ought to do, how I should be able to launch it; so never being able to bring it to the water, or bring the water to it, I was obliged to let it lie where it was, as a memorandum to teach me to be wiser next time. Indeed, the next time, though I could not get a tree proper for it, and in a place where I could not get the water to it, at any less distance than as I have said, near half a mile, yet as I saw it was practicable at last, I never gave it over; and though I was near two years about it, yet I never grudged my labor, in hopes of having a boat to go off to sea at last.

9. *wanting:* needed
10. *equinox:* i.e., the equator
11. *answered:* met the need
12. *pent-house:* lean-to
13. *Providence:* provision, care
14. *ejaculations:* prayers

However, though my little periagua[15] was finished, yet the size of it was not at all answerable to the design which I had in view, when I made the first; I mean, of venturing over to the terra firma,[16] where it[17] was above forty miles broad. Accordingly, the smallness of my boat assisted to put an end to that design, and now I thought no more of it. But as I had a boat, my next design was to make a tour round the island; for as I had been on the other side, in one place, crossing, as I have already described it, over the land, so the discoveries I made in that little journey made me very eager to see other parts of the coast, and now I had a boat, I thought of nothing but sailing round the island. **A**

Journalistic Style: How has the text so far demonstrated Defoe's journalistic narrative style? **A**

For this purpose, that I might do everything with discretion and consideration, I fitted up a little mast to my boat, and made a sail to it, out of some of the pieces of the ship's sail, which lay in store, and of which I had a great stock by me.

Having fitted my mast and sail, and tried the boat, I found she would sail very well; then I made little lockers or boxes, at either end of my boat, to put provisions, necessaries and ammunition, etc., into, to be kept dry, either from the rain or the spray of the sea; and a little long, hollow place I cut in the inside of the boat, where I could lay my gun, making a flap to hang down over it to keep it dry.

I fixed my umbrella, also, in a step at the stern, like a mast, to stand over my head, and keep the heat of the sun off of me like an awning; and thus I every now and then took a little voyage upon the sea, but never went far out, not far from the little creek; but at last, being eager to view the circumference of my little kingdom, I resolved upon my tour, and accordingly I victualled[18] my ship for the voyage, putting in two dozen of my loaves (cakes I should rather call them) of barley bread, an earthen pot full of parched rice, a food I eat a great deal of, a little bottle of rum, half a goat, and powder and shot for killing more, and two large watch-coats of those which, as I mentioned before, I had saved out of the seamen's chests; these I took, one to lie upon, and the other to cover me in the night.

It was the sixth of November, in the sixth year of my reign, or my captivity, which you please, that I set out on this voyage, and I found it much longer

15. *periagua:* dugout canoe
16. *terra firma:* solid land (seen earlier)
17. *it:* i.e., the expanse of water
18. *victualled:* stocked with food

than I expected; for though the island itself was not very large, yet when I came to the east side of it, I found a great ledge of rocks lie out of above two leagues[19] into the sea, some above water, some under it; and beyond that, a shoal of sand, lying dry half a league more; so that I was obliged to go a great way out to sea to double[20] the point.

When first I discovered them, I was going to give over my enterprise, and come back again, not knowing how far it might oblige me to go out to sea; and above all, doubting how I should get back again; so I came to an anchor, for I had made me a kind of an anchor with a piece of a broken graphlin,[21] which I got out of the ship. **A**

Verisimilitude: What details in pages 325–27 help make the story more realistic? **A**

Having secured my boat, I took my gun, and went on shore, climbing up upon a hill, which seemed to over-look that point,[22] where I saw the full extent of it, and resolved to **venture**.

venture (vĕn′chər) *intr.v.* To proceed despite possible danger or risk.

In my viewing the sea from that hill where I stood, I perceived a strong, and indeed, a most furious current, which run to the east, and even came close to the point; and I took the more notice of it, because I saw there might be some danger, that when I came into it, I might be carried out to sea by the strength of it, and not be able to make the island again; and indeed, had I not gotten first up upon this hill, I believe it would have been so; for there was the same current on the other side the island, only, that it set off at a further distance; and I saw there was a strong eddy[23] under the shore; so I had nothing to do but to get in out of the first current, and I should presently be in an eddy.

I lay here, however, two days; because the wind blowing pretty fresh at E. S. E.,[24] and that being just contrary to the said current, made a great breach of the sea[25] upon the point; so that it was not safe for me to keep too close to the shore for the breach, nor to go too far off because of the stream.

The third day, in the morning, the wind having abated over night, the sea was calm, and I ventured; but I am a warning-piece again to all rash and ignorant pilots; for no sooner was I come to the point, when even I was not my boat's length from the shore, but I found myself in a great depth of water, and a current like the sluice of a mill; it carried my boat along with it with such violence, that all I could do could not keep her so much as on the edge of it; but I found it hurried me farther and farther out from the eddy, which was on my left hand. There was no wind stirring to help me, and all I could do with my paddlers signified nothing; and now I began to give myself over for lost; for as the current was on both sides the island, I knew in a few leagues distance they must join again, and then I was irrecoverably gone; nor did I see any possibility of avoiding it; so that I had no prospect before me but of perishing; not by the sea, for that was calm enough, but of starving for hunger. I had indeed found a tortoise on the shore, as big almost as I could lift, and had tossed it into the boat; and I had a great jar of fresh water, that is to say, one of my earthen pots; but what was all this to being driven into the vast ocean, where to be sure, there was no shore, no main land, or island, for a thousand leagues at least.

And now I saw how easy it was for the providence of God to make the most miserable condition mankind could be in, worse. Now I looked back upon my **desolate**, solitary island, as the most pleasant place in the world,

desolate (dĕs′ə-lĭt) *adj.* Devoid of inhabitants; deserted.

19. *two leagues:* six miles
20. *double:* pass around
21. *graphlin:* hook for taking hold of another ship
22. *over-look . . . point:* give a view of that peninsula
23. *eddy:* circular current spinning off a larger current and flowing in an opposite direction
24. *E. S. E.:* east-southeast
25. *breach . . . sea:* breaking of waves

and all the happiness my heart could wish for, was to be but there again. I stretched out my hands to it with eager wishes. O happy desert, said I, I shall never see thee more! O miserable creature, said I, whither am I going! Then I reproached myself with my unthankful temper,[26] and how I had repined at[27] my solitary condition; and now what would I give to be on shore there again. Thus we never see the true state of our condition, till it is illustrated to us by its contraries; nor know how to value what we enjoy, but by the want of it. It is scarce possible to imagine the consternation I was now in, being driven from my beloved island (for so it appeared to me now to be) into the wide ocean, almost two leagues, and in the utmost despair of ever recovering it again. However, I worked hard, till indeed my strength was almost exhausted, and kept my boat as much to the northward, that is, towards the side of the current which the eddy lay on, as possibly I could; when about noon, as the sun passed the meridian, I thought I felt a little breeze of wind in my face, spring-

consternation (kŏn′stər-nā′shən) *n.* A state of great alarm, agitation, or dismay.

26. *temper:* disposition
27. *repined at:* complained about

ing up from the S. S. E.[28] This cheered my heart a little, and especially when in about half an hour more, it blew a pretty small, gentle gale. By this time I was gotten at a frightful distance from the island, and had the least cloud or hazy weather intervened, I had been undone another way, too; for I had no compass on board, and should never have known how to have steered towards the island, if I had but once lost sight of it; but the weather continuing clear, I applied myself to get up my mast again, and spread my sail, standing away[29] to the north, as much as possible, to get out of the current.

Just as I had set my mast and sail, and the boat began to stretch away,[30] I saw, even by the clearness of the water, some alteration of the current was near; for where the current was so strong, the water was foul; but perceiving the water clear, I found the current abate, and presently I found to the east, at about half a mile, a breach of the sea upon some rocks; these rocks I found caused the current to part again, and as the main stress of it ran away more southerly, leaving the rocks to the north-east, so the other returned by the repulse of the rocks, and made a strong eddy, which ran back again to the north-west, with a very sharp stream.

They who know what it is to have a **reprieve** brought to them upon the ladder,[31] or to be rescued from thieves just going to murder them, or who have been in such like extremities, may guess what my present surprise of joy was, and how gladly I put my boat into the stream of this eddy, and the wind also freshening, how gladly I spread my sail to it, running cheerfully before the wind, and with a strong tide or eddy under foot.

reprieve (rĭ-prēv′) *n.* The prevention or suspension of a scheduled or expected punishment.

This eddy carried me about a league in my way back again directly towards the island, but about two leagues more to the northward than the current which carried me away at first; so that when I came near the island, I found myself open to the northern shore of it, that is to say, the other end of the island opposite to that which I went out from.

When I had made something more than a league of way by the help of this current or eddy, I found it was spent and served me no farther. However, I found that being between the two great currents, viz: that on the south side, which had hurried me away, and that on the north, which lay about a league on the other side,— I say, between these two, in the wake of the island, I found the water at least still and running no way; and having still a breeze of wind fair for me, I kept on steering directly for the island, though not making such fresh way[32] as I did before.

About four o'clock in the evening, being then within about a league of the island, I found the point of the rocks which occasioned this disaster, stretching out, as is described before, to the southward, and casting off the current more southwardly, had, of course, made another eddy to the north, and this I found very strong, but not directly setting the way my course lay, which was due west, but almost full north. However, having a fresh gale, I stretched across this eddy, slanting north-west, and, in about an hour, came within about a mile of the shore, where, it being smooth water, I soon got to land.

When I was on shore, I fell on my knees and gave God thanks for my deliverance, resolving to lay aside all thoughts of my deliverance by my boat; and refreshing myself with such things as I had, I brought my boat close to the shore in a little cove that I had spied under some trees, and laid me down to sleep, being quite spent with the labor and fatigue of the voyage. **E**

Author's Worldview: What mistake does Crusoe make (p. 327) that jeopardizes his situation? Whom does Crusoe credit with his deliverance? **E**

28. *S. S. E.:* south-southeast
29. *standing away:* setting the sail
30. *stretch away:* change course
31. *upon . . . ladder:* i.e., at the gallows
32. *fresh way:* rapid progress

I was now at a great loss which way to get home with my boat. I had run so much hazard, and knew too much the case to think of attempting it by the way I went out; and what might be at the other side (I mean the west side) I know not, nor had I any mind to run any more ventures; so I only resolved in the morning to make my way westward along the shore, and to see if there was no creek where I might lay up my frigate[33] in safety, so as to have her again if I wanted her. In about three miles or thereabout, coasting the shore, I came to a very good inlet or bay, about a mile over, which narrowed till it came to a very little rivulet or brook, where I found a very convenient harbor for my boat, and where she lay as if she had been in a little dock made on purpose for her. Here I put in, and having stowed my boat very safe, I went on shore to look about me, and see where I was.

I soon found I had but a little passed by the place where I had been before, when I travelled on foot to that shore; so taking nothing out of my boat, but my gun and my umbrella, for it was exceedingly hot, I began my march. The way was comfortable enough after such a voyage as I had been upon, and I reached my old bower in the evening, where I found everything standing as I left it; for I always kept it in good order, being, as I said before, my country house. R

Author's Purpose: Read the three preceding paragraphs. What can you infer about the kind of character Defoe is depicting based on Crusoe's response to calamity and the condition of his "old bower"? R

I got over the fence, and laid me down in the shade to rest my limbs, for I was very weary, and fell asleep; but judge you, if you can, that read my story, what a surprise I must be in, when I was waked out of my sleep by a voice calling me by my name several times, "Robin, Robin, Robin Crusoe, poor Robin Crusoe! Where are you, Robin Crusoe? Where are you? Where have you been?"

I was so dead asleep at first, being fatigued with rowing or paddling, as it is called, the first part of the day, and with walking the latter part, that I did not wake thoroughly; but dozing between sleeping and waking, thought I dreamed that somebody spoke to me. But, as the voice continued to repeat, "Robin Crusoe, Robin Crusoe," at last I began to wake more perfectly, and was at first dreadfully frightened, and started up in the utmost consternation; but, no sooner were my eyes open, but I saw my Poll sitting on the top of the hedge, and immediately knew that it was he that spoke to me; for just in such bemoaning language I had used to talk to him, and teach him; and he had learned it so perfectly, that he would sit upon my finger, and lay his bill close to my face, and cry, "Poor Robin Crusoe, where are you? Where have you been? How came you here?" and such things as I had taught him.

However, even though I knew it was the parrot, and that indeed it could be nobody else, it was a good while before I could compose myself. First, I was amazed how the creature got thither, and then how he should just keep about the place, and no where else. But, as I was well satisfied it could be nobody but honest Poll, I got it over; and holding out my hand, and calling him by his name Poll, the sociable creature came to me, and sat upon my thumb, as he used to do, and continued talking to me, "Poor Robin Crusoe," and "how did I come here?" and "where had I been?" just as if he had been overjoyed to see me again; and so I carried him home along with me.

I had now had enough of rambling to sea for some time, and had enough to do for many days to sit still and reflect upon the danger I had been in. I would have been very glad to have had my boat again on my side of the island; but I knew not how it was practicable to get it about. As to the east side of the island, which I had gone round, I knew well enough there was no

33. *frigate:* small sailing vessel (a hyperbole)

venturing that way; my very heart would shrink, and my very blood run chill but to think of it. And as to the other side of the island, I did not know how it might be there; but supposing the current ran with the same force against the shore at the east as it passed by it on the other, I might run the same risk of being driven down the stream, and carried by the island, as I had been before, of being carried away from it; so with these thoughts I contented myself to be without any boat, though it had been the product of so many months' labor to make it, and of so many more to get it unto the sea.

In this government of my temper[34] I remained near a year, lived a very sedate, retired life, as you may well suppose; and my thoughts being very much composed as to my condition, and fully comforted in resigning myself to the dispositions of Providence, I thought I lived really very happily in all things, except that of society. . . . E

Author's Worldview: Describe Crusoe's general feelings about his life on the island. Why does he feel as he does? Are there any exceptions to his general disposition? E

It would have made a stoic[35] smile to have seen me and my little family sit down to dinner; there was my majesty, the prince and lord of the whole island. I had the lives of all my subjects at my absolute command. I could hang, draw,[36] give liberty, and take it away, and no rebels among all my subjects.

Then, to see how like a king I dined, too, all alone, attended by my servants. Poll, as if he had been my favorite, was the only person permitted to talk to me. My dog, who was now grown very old and crazy, and had found no species to multiply his kind upon, sat always at my right hand; and two cats, one on one side the table, and one on the other, expecting now and then a bit from my hand, as a mark of special favor.

But these were not the two cats which I brought on shore at first, for they were both of them dead, and had been **interred** near my habitation by my own hand; but one of them having multiplied by I know not what kind of a creature, these were two which I had preserved tame, whereas the rest run wild in the woods, and became indeed troublesome to me at last; for they would often come into my house, and plunder me, too, till at last I was obliged to shoot them, and did kill a great many; at length they left me with this attendance, and in this plentiful manner I lived; neither could I be said to want anything but society, and of that, in some time after this, was I like[37] to have too much.

inter (ĭn-tûr′) *tr.v.* To place in a grave or tomb; bury.

34. *temper:* self-composure
35. *stoic:* member of an ancient philosophical sect advocating contentment with few possessions
36. *draw:* pull apart
37. *like:* almost

THINK AND DISCUSS

1. What did Defoe contribute to the development of English literature?
2. Explain how Defoe uses realistic content and a journalistic style in *Robinson Crusoe.* Provide three examples from the text that demonstrate his usage.
3. What indications does Crusoe give that he considers both his own ingenuity and Providence essential for his survival? Give examples of both elements from the excerpt, and explain why both elements are vital.
4. Would you describe Crusoe as generally happy or unhappy in his situation on the island? Why do you think that is the case? What does Crusoe see as an exception to his general disposition? How does he compensate for this exception?
5. At one critical point in the narrative, Crusoe declares: "Thus we never see the true state of our condition, till it is illustrated to us by its contraries; nor know how to value what we enjoy, but by the want of it" (p. 328). To what specific situation is he referring? What character flaw of his is exposed by this statement and situation?
6. Do you think Crusoe's statement in question 5 is valid? Support your answer with specific reasons.
7. What grave mistake almost occasions Crusoe's death? How is he rescued? Evaluate Defoe's portrayal of this incident according to Scripture.
8. How does Crusoe's response to his island circumstances reveal Defoe's worldview? Is his response biblical?

The Rise of the Novel

The eighteenth century saw the rise of one of the modern era's preeminent genres: the novel. Simply defined, a novel is a long work of narrative prose. While the ancient world had produced generally qualifying works, the form had not caught on in oral cultures. The Anglo-Saxons, for instance, preferred poetry's striking effects on nonliterate audiences. Even as Norman and Renaissance England raised literacy, elites still favored the poet's specialized skills in long narratives (e.g., *The Canterbury Tales, The Faerie Queene*).

Cultural Context

By the 1700s, two significant shifts helped change this status quo. First, literacy rates continued to rise. In fact, various outreaches (e.g., Sunday schools, charity schools) promoted literacy, offering working-class boys a basic education. Also, as printing advanced and living standards rose, more people could afford written works. However, this broader audience often appreciated the intricacies of poetic form less.

Second, prose increased in value as writers realized its flexibility and effectiveness for multiple purposes. Early scientists found it a practical, precise vehicle for their ideas and data, while Civil War–era pamphlet wars proved its effectiveness at exchanging and spreading important ideas and arguments quickly. Weekly newspapers (e.g., Addison's and Steele's) then extended its use to personal essays and human interest stories, fostering appreciation for prose narratives.

Realistic Style

True to these nonfictional origins, the emerging novel took a more realistic approach (see *verisimilitude*, p. 322) than previous long narratives. In fact, the earliest examples were often framed as histories: Behn's *Oroonoko* (1688) was supposedly a true story from a real English colony (a favored topic), and Defoe's *Journal of a Plague Year* (1722) used real historic details to portray the Great Plague of 1665. Then fictional travelogues such as *Robinson Crusoe* (1719) and *Gulliver's Travels* (1726) introduced realistic modern settings, which gradually overtook historical and mythical ones in popularity.

Novelists also increasingly sought to portray characters and their inner lives more realistically (a trend nineteenth-century novelists would bring to fruition). Revolting against neoclassicists' prizing of reason, many instead created characters who felt keenly. Their novels of sensibility (p. 359) infused characters with more emotional aspects of human thoughts and behaviors. On occasion devolving into melodrama, this impulse nonetheless provided balance and wider appeal to novels.

Purpose and Form

Besides entertaining readers, early novels often pursued two enduring purposes: didacticism and satire. For example, Samuel Richardson famously offered a didactic theme in his bestseller *Pamela; or Virtue Rewarded* (1740). But though many readers loved the novel's Cinderella ending, it antagonized Henry Fielding, who responded in two humorous parodies, *Shamela* (1741) and *Joseph Andrews* (1742). These satirized, respectively, Richardson's hollow moral ethic and society in general. Similarly, Fanny Burney, one of the first female novelists to be widely acclaimed, satirized society's conventions on women, marriage, and social status in *Evelina* (1778).

In form, the novel quickly diversified beyond historical fiction and travelogues. *Pamela* and *Evelina* popularized the epistolary novel, composed of letters between characters, a form still used today. Similarly, Laurence Sterne's *Tristram Shandy* prefigured postmodern novels, being compiled of impressions and multiple short genres. Finally, *Joseph Andrews* introduced the popular picaresque novel, made of loosely related episodes featuring an often roguish protagonist and broadly satirizing society (e.g., Mark Twain's *Huckleberry Finn*).

In the nineteenth century, the novel and its potential audience would continue to grow exponentially. As the Industrial Revolution lowered costs, raised the standard of living, and broadened educational opportunities and literacy, stronger markets for the genre arose. More importantly, people recognized its potential. By helping readers understand characters' rich inner lives—perspectives, emotions, and decisions—the genre remains a powerful tool for influencing both individual readers and, in outstanding cases, audiences across cultures.

Joseph Addison and Richard Steele

Following Defoe's *Weekly Review*, two Whig journals appeared in short succession: the *Tatler* (1709–11) and the *Spectator* (1711–12). Both were edited by journalist-playwright Richard Steele (1672–1729) in consultation with his friend, the classicist-statesman Joseph Addison (1672–1719), except during Addison's brief revival of the *Spectator* in 1714.

The *Tatler*, conceived as a kind of newspaper, became a periodical of commentary like Defoe's *Review*. Following the *Review*'s example, it used a chatty style and included amusing trivia. Innovatively, the *Tatler* was organized by sources of information. Steele facetiously arranged his materials under the names of coffeehouses, promising to save the inquisitive businessman from having to make the rounds of his favorite coffeehouses for news and friendly discussion.

Following the *Tatler*, a new genre for the eighteenth century emerged—the periodical essay. This relatively brief informal essay was often humorous or satirical in nature, as seen in the *Spectator*. Though like the *Tatler* in varying its content, the *Spectator* included more literary criticism and virtually no political discussion. Also, whereas the *Tatler* followed a coffeehouse plan as an organizing framework, the *Spectator* utilized a fictitious club, whose members represented the special interests and viewpoints of its readers.

Addressing a cultured middle-class audience, Addison and Steele endeavored to reform society by combining the moral earnestness of the Puritans with the social intelligence of the Cavaliers, thus transforming journalism into serious literature. Though the burden of authorship was shared almost equally by Addison and Steele, the more formal, deliberate essays of Addison gave the *Spectator* a distinctive seriousness. Addison commanded a prose style ideal for calm, rational persuasion. His essays, together with Steele's, show the serious and playful sides of English neoclassicism.

BEFORE READING

ANALYZE: *Horatian Satire*

In *The Screwtape Letters*, C. S. Lewis gently but incisively satirizes the common failings of Christians and the modern man. Similarly, when Addison and Steele created the *Tatler* and the *Spectator*, they chose a humorous, didactic tone for their lighthearted appeals for change. Such gentle mockery, often in the form of verbal irony (p. 88), is known as **Horatian satire** (from the Roman writer Horace). Although congenial, Horatian satire is still aimed at a person or group of people in need of correction and a specific issue or idea, often broadly applicable to society. As you read these social critiques, look for characteristics of Horatian satire.

READ: *Trace Arguments*

To soften their correction, Addison and Steele often use personal, fictional examples to illustrate their thinking. Such anecdotes, though disarming and humorous, can challenge a reader's understanding since the author's line of reasoning and illustrations may be woven together. As you read, trace the author's line of reasoning. What arguments does he construct? What evidence does he use to support them?

CREATE: *A Satirical Piece*

Is there a custom in your culture that should be changed? After reading the selections, which serve as models, choose a cultural practice and write a short piece gently satirizing it. Support your argument with reasons and illustrations.

OBJECTIVES

- Examine a text for instances of Horatian satire.
- Determine a text's satirical target.
- Analyze an essay's arguments to determine its main idea.
- Create a short, satirical piece in the style of Addison and Steele.

VOCABULARY

denominate (dĭ-nŏm′ə-nāt′) *tr.v.* Designate.

want (wŏnt) *n.* The condition or quality of lacking something usual or necessary.

raillery (rā′lə-rē) *n.* Good-natured teasing or ridicule; banter.

Numb. 25

FROM The TATLER.

RICHARD STEELE

Published in the Tatler *on June 7, 1709, the following essay addresses a social ill, the practice of dueling to defend one's honor. The descendant of knightly chivalry and trial by combat, dueling was outlawed in 1571 but survived in the nobility. If a man offended another, the offended party (or the offender himself!) could demand the "satisfaction" of his honor through a duel. A challenged man could not refuse without being labeled a coward or implying that his challenger was not a true gentleman (and thus unworthy of being answered), another offense. Deaths and serious injuries, though not a required outcome, too often resulted. Steele's essay was on the forefront of social forces questioning this practice. What arguments does he make against it?*

from No. 25. Tuesday, June 7, 1709.

WHITE'S CHOCOLATE-HOUSE, JUNE 6.

A letter from a young lady, written in the most passionate terms, wherein she laments the misfortune of a gentleman, her lover, who was lately wounded in a duel, has turned my thoughts to that subject, and inclined me to examine into the causes which precipitate men into so fatal a folly. And as it has been proposed to treat of subjects of gallantry in the article from hence, and no one point in nature is more proper to be considered by the company who frequent this place than that of duels, it is worth our consideration to examine into this chimerical groundless humor,[1] and to lay every other thought aside, until we have stripped it of all its false pretenses to credit and reputation amongst men.

But I must confess, when I consider what I am going about, and run over in my imagination all the endless crowd of men of honor who will be offended at such a discourse; I am undertaking, methinks, a work worthy an invulnerable hero in romance, rather than a private gentleman with a single rapier: but as I am pretty well acquainted by great opportunities with the nature of man, and know of a truth that all men fight against their will, the danger vanishes, and resolution rises upon this subject. For this reason, I shall talk very freely on a custom which all men wish exploded, though no man has courage enough to resist it.

But there is one unintelligible word, which I fear will extremely perplex my dissertation,[2] and I confess to you I find very hard to explain, which is the term "satisfaction." An honest country gentleman had the misfortune to fall into company with two or three modern men of honor, where he happened to be very ill-treated; and one of the company, being conscious of his offence, sends a note to him in the morning, and tells him, he was ready to give him *satisfaction*. "This is fine doing," says the plain fellow; "last night he sent me away cursedly out of humor, and this morning he fancies it would be a *satisfaction* to be run through the body."

1. *chimerical humor:* a vain or fantastical, irrational impulse
2. *dissertation:* thesis

As the matter at present stands, it is not to do handsome actions **denominates** a man of honor; it is enough if he dares to defend ill ones. Thus you often see a common sharper[3] in competition with a gentleman of the first rank; though all mankind is convinced, that a fighting gamester[4] is only a pick-pocket with the courage of a highwayman. One cannot with any patience reflect on the unaccountable jumble of persons and things in this town and nation, which occasions very frequently, that a brave man falls by a hand below that of a common hangman, and yet his executioner escapes the clutches of the hangman for doing it. I shall therefore hereafter consider, how the bravest men in other ages and nations have behaved themselves upon such incidents as we decide by combat; and show, from their practice, that this resentment neither has its foundation from true reason or solid fame; but is an imposture,[5] made of cowardice, falsehood, and **want** of understanding. For this work, a good history of quarrels would be very edifying to the public, and I apply myself to the town for particulars and circumstances within their knowledge, which may serve to embellish the dissertation with proper cuts. Most of the quarrels I have ever known, have proceeded from some valiant coxcomb's persisting in the wrong, to defend some prevailing folly, and preserve himself from the ingenuousness of owning a mistake. R

denominate (dĭ-nŏm′ə-nāt′) *tr.v.* Designate.

want (wŏnt) *n.* The condition or quality of lacking something usual or necessary.

Trace Arguments: What is Steele's main argument against dueling? How does the anecdote of the "honest country gentleman" function in his argument? R

By this means it is called "giving a man satisfaction," to urge your offence against him with your sword; which puts me in mind of Peter's order to the keeper, in "The Tale of a Tub": "if you neglect to do all this, [curse] you and your generation forever: and so we bid you heartily farewell."[6] If the contradiction in the very terms of one of our challenges were as well explained and turned into downright English, would it not run after this manner?

"SIR,

"Your extraordinary behavior last night, and the liberty you were pleased to take with me, makes me this morning give you this, to tell you, because you are an ill-bred puppy, I will meet you in Hyde-park an hour hence; and because you want both breeding and humanity, I desire you would come with a pistol in your hand, on horseback, and endeavor to shoot me through the head, to teach you more manners. If you fail of doing me this pleasure, I shall say, you are a rascal, on every post in town: and so, sir, if you will not injure me more, I shall never forgive what you have done already. Pray, sir, do not fail of getting everything ready; and you will infinitely oblige,

Sir,
Your most obedient,
humble servant, &c." A

VISUAL ANALYSIS
How do these drawings support Steele's tone and message in this essay?

3. *sharper:* "one that deals dishonestly with others, especially a cheating gambler" (*AHD*)
4. *gamester:* "one who plays games, especially a gambler" (*AHD*)
5. *an imposture:* a false claimant to the previous virtues
6. *Peter's order . . . farewell:* In Jonathan Swift's religious satire, "The Tale of a Tub," Peter, representing Catholicism, sells fake pardons (i.e., indulgences) to criminals. The insincerity of the pardon is revealed by its abrupt and illogical turn from drastic threat to polite pleasantry in one sentence.

Horatian Satire: How would you describe the author's tone? How did you come to that conclusion? A

FROM The SPECTATOR.

JOSEPH ADDISON

No. 34. Monday, April 9, 1711.

The club of which I am a member, is very luckily composed of such persons as are engaged in different ways of life, and deputed, as it were, out of the most conspicuous classes of mankind. By this means I am furnished with the greatest variety of hints and materials, and know everything that passes in the different quarters and divisions, not only of this great city, but of the whole kingdom. My readers too have the satisfaction to find that there is no rank or degree among them who have not their representative in this club, and that there is always somebody present who will take care of their respective interests, that nothing may be written or published to the prejudice or infringement of their just rights and privileges.

I last night sat very late in company with this select body of friends, who entertained me with several remarks which they and others had made upon these my speculations, as also with the various success which they had met with among their several ranks and degrees of readers. Will Honeycomb told me, in the softest manner he could, that there were some ladies (but for your comfort, says Will, they are not those of the most wit) that were offended at the liberties I had taken with the opera and the puppet-show; that some of them were likewise very much surprised that I should think such serious points as the dress and equipage of persons of quality proper subjects for **raillery**.

He was going on, when Sir Andrew Freeport took him up short,[1] and told him, that the papers he hinted at had done great good in the city, and that all their wives and daughters were the better for them; and farther added, that the whole city thought themselves very much obliged to me for declaring my generous intentions to scourge vice and folly as they appear in a multitude, without condescending to be a publisher of particular intrigues and cuckoldoms.[2] "In short," says Sir Andrew, "if you avoid that foolish beaten road of falling upon aldermen and citizens, and employ your pen upon the vanity and luxury of courts, your paper must needs be of general use."

Upon this my friend the Templar told Sir Andrew that he wondered to hear a man of his sense talk after that manner; that the city had always been the province for satire; and that the wits of King Charles's time jested upon nothing else during his whole reign. He then showed, by the examples of Horace, Juvenal, Boileau, and the best writers of every age, that the follies of the stage and court had never been accounted too sacred for ridicule, how great soever the persons might be that patronized them. "But after all," says he, "I think your raillery has made too great an excursion in attacking several persons of the Inns of Court; and I do not believe you can show me any precedent for your behavior in that particular."

My good friend Sir Roger de Coverley, who had said nothing all this while, began his speech with a pish! and told us, that he wondered to see so many men of sense so very serious upon fooleries. "Let our good friend," says he, "attack everyone that deserves it: I would only advise you, Mr. Spectator," applying himself to me, "to take care how you meddle with country squires. They are the ornaments of the English nation; men of good heads and sound bodies! and, let me tell you, some of them take it ill of you that you mention fox-hunters with so little respect."

Captain Sentry spoke very sparingly on this occasion. What he said was only to commend my prudence in not touching upon the army, and advised me to continue to act discreetly in that point.

By this time I found every subject of my speculations was taken away from me, by one or other of the club; and began to think myself in the condition of the good man that had one wife who took a dislike to his grey hairs, and another to his black, till, by their picking out what each of them had an aversion to, they left his head altogether bald and naked. R

1. *took . . . short:* stopped him suddenly while he was speaking
2. *cuckoldoms:* "the state or position of a cuckold" (a mocking name for a husband of an unfaithful wife) (*OED*)

raillery (rā'lə-rē) *n.* Good-natured teasing or ridicule; banter.

Trace Arguments: How does the "good man" anecdote contribute to the author's line of reasoning and tone? R

While I was thus musing with myself, my worthy friend the Clergyman, who, very luckily for me, was at the club that night, undertook my cause. He told us, that he wondered any order of persons should think themselves too considerable to be advised: that it was not quality, but innocence, which exempted men from reproof: that vice and folly ought to be attacked wherever they could be met with, and especially when they were placed in high and conspicuous stations of life. He further added, that my paper would only serve to aggravate the pains of poverty, if it chiefly exposed those who are already depressed, and in some measure turned into ridicule, by the meanness of their conditions and circumstances. He afterwards proceeded to take notice of the great use this paper might be of to the public, by reprehending those vices which are too trivial for the chastisement of the law, and too fantastical for the cognizance of the pulpit. He then advised me to prosecute my undertaking with cheerfulness, and assured me, that, whoever might be displeased with me, I should be approved by all those whose praises do honor to the persons on whom they are bestowed.

The whole club pay a particular deference to the discourse of this gentleman, and are drawn into what he says, as much by the candid ingenuous manner with which he delivers himself, as by the strength of argument and force of reason which he makes use of. Will Honeycomb immediately agreed, that what he had said was right; and that, for his part, he would not insist upon the quarter which he had demanded for the ladies. Sir Andrew gave up the city with the same frankness. The Templar would not stand out; and was followed by Sir Roger and the Captain; who all agreed that I should be at liberty to carry the war into what quarter I pleased, provided I continued to combat with criminals in a body, and to assault the vice without hurting the person. **A**

This debate, which was held for the good of mankind, put me in mind of that which the Roman triumvirate were formerly engaged in for their destruction. Every man at first stood hard for his friend, till they found, that by this means they should spoil their proscription: and at length, making a sacrifice of all their acquaintance and relations, furnished out a very decent execution.

Having thus taken my resolutions to march on boldly in the cause of virtue and good sense, and to annoy their adversaries in whatever degree or rank of men they may be found; I shall be deaf for the future to all the remonstrances that shall be made to me on this account. If Punch grows extravagant, I shall reprimand him very freely. If the stage becomes a nursery of folly and impertinence, I shall not be afraid to animadvert[3] upon it. In short, if I meet with anything in city, court, or country, that shocks modesty or good manners, I shall use my utmost endeavors to make an example of it. I must, however, entreat every particular person who does me the honor to be a reader of this paper, never to think himself, or anyone of his friends or enemies, aimed at in what is said: for I promise him never to draw a faulty character which does not fit at least a thousand people; or to publish a single paper, that is not written in the spirit of benevolence and with a love to mankind. **E**

3. *animadvert:* "to comment critically (on, upon), to utter criticism (usually of an adverse kind); to express censure or blame" (*OED*)

Horatian Satire: What phrase in this paragraph best expresses the nature of Horatian satire? According to the club member's conclusion, who qualifies as fit to be satirized? What group should not chiefly be satirized? **A**

Create: What is the function of this last paragraph in the essay's general structure? What might it suggest about how you should end your piece? **E**

THINK AND DISCUSS

1. Using evidence from the text, explain how the *Tatler* and the *Spectator* qualify as Horatian satire.
2. What is Steele's main argument against dueling? How does he soften this argument, making it less offensive to his audience?
3. What is Addison's main argument regarding the use of satire in the *Spectator*? How does his essay itself actually illustrate his main argument and target audience?
4. According to the Clergyman and the Spectator himself, how is the *Spectator's* Horatian satire profitable for readers?
5. Choose a current cultural practice that needs to be changed. Using the *Tatler* and the *Spectator* excerpts as models, write a short piece (one or two paragraphs) that gently satirizes the practice. Support your main argument with reasons and illustrations.

Alexander Pope (1688–1744)

AT A GLANCE

- **1709–14** Published his early works, including *An Essay on Criticism*, *The Rape of the Lock*, and his collected poems
- **ca. 1713** Began meeting with the Scriblerus Club
- **1715–26** Translated the *Iliad* and *Odyssey*; edited Shakespeare
- **1726–44** Wrote moral and satirical poems, including *An Essay on Man* (1733–34)

Chief poet of his age, Alexander Pope was the leading spokesman for early neoclassical values. As Swift did in his prose, Pope combined moral indignation and playful wit and practiced an elegant, conversational, precise style in his poetry. Also like Swift, Pope was a Tory and excelled at writing satire.

A Persevering Young Artist

Pope's life, like his art, was narrow but intense. Two factors, health and religion, significantly shaped his early development. Childhood spinal tuberculosis restricted Pope physically. The disease stunted his height—a mere four feet, six inches—and caused severe curvature of the spine, which eventually crippled him. He also suffered from severe headaches and was highly sensitive to pain. While Pope was physically unable to attend Oxford and Cambridge, his frail constitution was only partly responsible for his limited educational options. Pope's religion, Catholicism, also prevented him from attending these schools, which were closed to non-Anglicans. Despite these hurdles, Pope excelled creatively and intellectually. His poor health gave his artistic energies a powerful focus, helping him concentrate on what he did best. He also received instruction in his home at Twickenham from priests, and he later attended Catholic schools at Twyford and at Hyde Park Corner. Pope studied the standard classical authors and began developing his talent for poetry.

A Pursuer of Perfection

Pope's developing art received further focus from the influence of friends and fellow writers. Poet-critic William Walsh introduced the young artist to literary London and acquainted him with the older generation of satiric poets who held to traditional styles and forms. As a result, Pope set himself the task of achieving perfection in the standard neoclassical verse form, heroic couplets, and in the familiar neoclassical genres. Pope eventually became part of a literary circle, the Scriblerus Club, composed of Swift and other Tory wits. These men engaged in intellectual discussion and planned satires on current literary and social fashions.

DID YOU KNOW?

Because Pope was so thin and sickly, he chose to wear several pairs of stockings.

A Literary Proficient

Pope's career can be divided into three periods. Between the publication of his *Pastorals* in 1709 and his first volume of poems in 1714, Pope, still in his twenties, dazzled London readers with works of genius. Among these were *An Essay on Criticism* (1711), a brilliant distillation of neoclassical literary theory into verse, and *The Rape of the Lock* (1714), a sparkling mock-heroic burlesque involving two estranged Catholic families of high society. During the second period, from 1715 to 1726, Pope translated Homer and edited Shakespeare. His *Iliad* (1715–20) and *Odyssey* (1725–26), translated in heroic couplets, were huge undertakings, rivaled only by his edition of Shakespeare's plays in 1725.

In 1726 a hostile review of Pope's edition of Shakespeare launched him into the last phase of his career, that of satirist and moralist. The reviewer, Lewis Theobald, became the hero of Pope's *Dunciad* (1728, 1729), a mock epic. In the meantime, Pope planned and partially executed a series of philosophical verse epistles (p. 340) as a complete exposition of moral truth. Central among these was *An Essay on Man* (1733–34), which attempts to found a universal system of morality on natural theology (p. 289) and summons man to his moral duty.

Whatever Pope's theological failings, his aim as a poet was admirable: to render truth beautiful and memorable. By the end of his life, Pope, the once-persevering youth, had become a literary dynamo. Through careful study and intense commitment to his craft, he ultimately gained what he sought: the distinction of being the most "correct" poet of his age.

ANALYZE: *Style and Heroic Couplet*

Pope's art is one of conscious, subtle craftsmanship, and he never ceased to revise. His neoclassical **style** illustrates balance, symmetry, and parallelism (p. 140), as seen in these lines (not included in your text) from *An Essay on Man.*

> Vice is a monster of so frightful mien [appearance, countenance]
> As, to be hated, needs but to be seen;
> Yet seen too oft, familiar with her face,
> We first endure, then pity, then embrace.

Note how Pope's style reinforces his content, his artistry giving force to his point. For example, the quick succession of verbs (parallelism) in the last line suggests a rapid collapse of resistance to vice. Note also Pope's use of the period's dominant verse form, the heroic couplet. The **heroic couplet** is a pair of rhymed lines written in iambic pentameter that expresses a complete thought. The two couplets in the lines above are linked as a single sentence and present contrasting halves (fear and familiarity) of a single thought (the progress of temptation). As you read, examine the texts for characteristics of neoclassical style.

READ: *Infer Main Ideas*

While both *An Essay on Man* and *An Essay on Criticism* are philosophical treatises in verse, they focus on different topics for different purposes. In *An Essay on Man,* Pope examines the relationship between man, God, and the world, directly stating that he aims to "vindicate the ways of God to man" (1.16). In *An Essay on Criticism,* however, he offers a general critique of poor writing and critiquing and stresses qualities of good writing. In the following passages, note each text's main ideas. First, pay attention to direct statements, which reveal ideas explicitly. Second, examine specific details (figurative language, descriptions, analogies, etc.), which convey ideas implicitly. A strategic reader makes inferences based on a text's details. Consider how these ideas contribute to Pope's overarching purposes, and identify which ideas connect to neoclassical or Enlightenment principles.

EVALUATE: *Author's Ideas*

Like many Enlightenment thinkers, Pope presumed certain ordering principles of the universe. For instance, he believed that God exists and that He is good. What puzzled many, including Pope, was the question of how God could be good if evil exists in the world. In *An Essay on Man*, Pope, like John Milton, attempts to answer this question. But whereas Milton relied on Christian doctrine and scriptural revelation to answer this question, Pope turned toward reason. He advocated for natural theology as an answer. A natural theologian begins with observations of the natural world and, through reason, draws conclusions about God based on those observations. Reason, therefore, becomes the primary reconciler of divine purpose and human observation. As you read, look for instances of Pope's reliance on reason to explain God's purposes. Is Pope's approach to understanding biblical? What might his approach be missing to give one an accurate picture of the world?

OBJECTIVES

- Identify characteristics of the heroic couplet.
- Infer a text's main ideas from its details.
- Analyze a text for its characteristics of neoclassical style.
- Evaluate an author's rationalist approach from a biblical perspective.

VOCABULARY

candid (kăn′dĭd) *adj.* Characterized by openness and sincerity of expression; unreservedly straightforward.

isthmus (ĭs′məs) *n.* A narrow strip of land connecting two larger masses of land.

intoxicate (ĭn-tŏk′sĭ-kāt′) *tr.v.* To stimulate or excite.

sprightly (sprīt′lē) *adj.* Full of spirit and vitality; lively; brisk.

prismatic (prĭz-măt′ĭk) *adj.* Formed by refraction of light through a prism. Used of a spectrum of light.

fraught (frôt) *adj.* Filled with a specified element or elements; charged.

What can **REASON** *tell me about my place in the world?*

Do you think much about thinking? The ability to reason—to think logically and rationally—sets us apart from animals, whose "intelligence" is limited. Because humans think, we enjoy a position over animal and plant life. Are there, however, limitations to reason? Do limitations position us under anyone or anything? What do you think?

FROM

AN ESSAY ON MAN

Intended as part of a larger work on moral philosophy, An Essay on Man *contains four* ***verse epistles****, a minor neoclassical poetic genre in which a poem, usually of high moral seriousness, takes the form of an address to a friend. This work is addressed to Tory political leader and philosopher Henry St. John, Viscount Bolingbroke, from whose ideas it is largely drawn. The following selections are from Epistles 1 and 2.*

EPISTLE 1

Awake, my St. John! Leave all meaner[1] things
To low ambition and the pride of kings.
Let us, since life can little more supply,
Than just to look about us, and to die,
Expatiate free[2] o'er all this scene of Man;
A mighty maze! but not without a plan;
A wild, where weeds and flowers promiscuous shoot;[3]
Or garden, tempting with forbidden fruit.
Together let us beat[4] this ample field,
Try what the open, what the covert[5] yield;
The latent tracts,[6] the giddy heights explore,
Of all who blindly creep, or sightless soar;[7]
Eye Nature's walks, shoot folly as it flies,
And catch the manners living as they rise;
Laugh where we must, be **candid** where we can;
But vindicate the ways of God to man. R
Say first, of God above, or man below,
What can we reason, but from what we know?
Of man, what see we but his station[8] here,
From which to reason, or to which refer?
Through worlds unnumbered, though the God be known,
Tis ours to trace Him only in our own.
He, who through vast immensity can pierce,
See worlds on worlds compose one universe,
Observe how system into system runs,
What other planets circle other suns,
What varied Being peoples every star,
May tell why Heaven has made us as we are.
But of this frame the bearings and the ties,
The strong connections, nice[9] dependencies,
Gradations just, has thy pervading soul
Looked through? Or can a part contain the whole?
Is the great chain,[10] that draws all to agree,
And drawn supports,[11] upheld by God or thee? E

candid (kăn′dĭd) *adj.* Characterized by openness and sincerity of expression; unreservedly straightforward.

Main Ideas: What line (in lines 1–16) explicitly reveals Pope's purpose in *An Essay on Man*? R

Author's Ideas: Reread lines 17–34. What is man's means for understanding himself and God? What lines support your answer? E

VISUAL ANALYSIS

How does the illustration here help visualize what Pope says about man's nature and place in the universe?

1. *meaner:* baser, more ordinary
2. *Expatiate free:* wander freely
3. *promiscuous shoot:* grow randomly
4. *beat:* hunt through
5. *covert:* sheltered place
6. *latent tracts:* hidden areas
7. *Of . . . soar:* i.e., the ignorant and the presumptuous
8. *station:* position, status
9. *nice:* subtle
10. *great chain:* Great Chain of Being (see p. 213)
11. *And . . . supports:* and, when drawn, supports

EPISTLE 2

Know then thyself, presume not God to scan,
The proper study of mankind is Man.
Placed on this **isthmus** of a middle state,
A Being darkly wise, and rudely great:
With too much knowledge for the Skeptic side,
With too much weakness for the Stoic's pride,
He hangs between; in doubt to act, or rest;
In doubt to deem himself a god, or beast;
In doubt his mind or body to prefer;
Born but to die, and reasoning but to err; A
Alike in ignorance, his reason such,
Whether he thinks too little, or too much:
Chaos of Thought and Passion, all confused;
Still by himself abused or disabused;[12]
Created half to rise, and half to fall;
Great lord of all things, yet a prey to all;
Sole judge of truth, in endless error hurled:
The glory, jest, and riddle of the world!

12. *abused . . . disabused:* deceived or enlightened

isthmus (ĭs′məs) *n.* A narrow strip of land connecting two larger masses of land.

Style: What neoclassical stylistic features (e.g., balance, symmetry, parallelism) can you detect in lines 1–10? Refer to specific lines in your answer. A

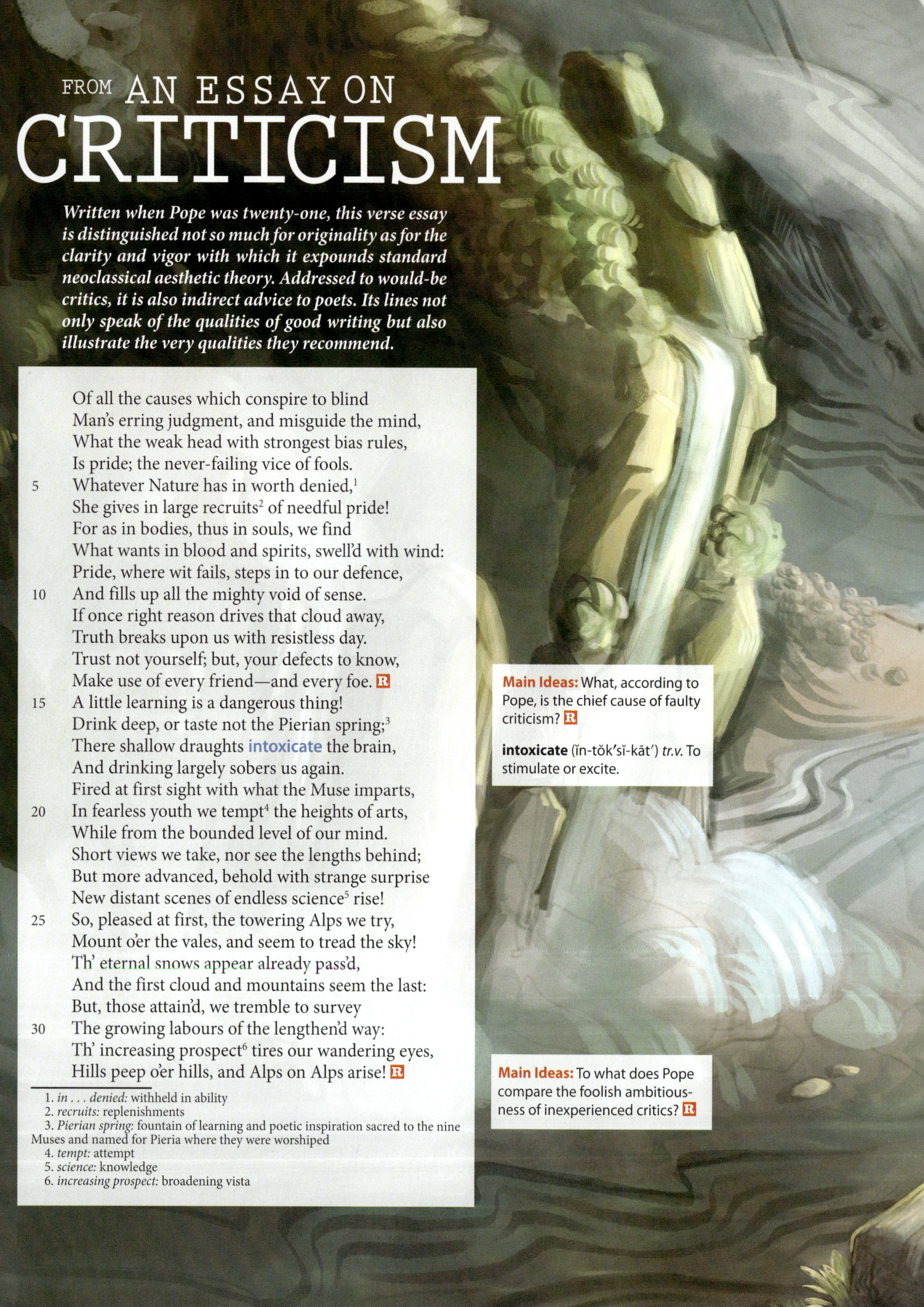

FROM **AN ESSAY ON**

CRITICISM

Written when Pope was twenty-one, this verse essay is distinguished not so much for originality as for the clarity and vigor with which it expounds standard neoclassical aesthetic theory. Addressed to would-be critics, it is also indirect advice to poets. Its lines not only speak of the qualities of good writing but also illustrate the very qualities they recommend.

Of all the causes which conspire to blind
Man's erring judgment, and misguide the mind,
What the weak head with strongest bias rules,
Is pride; the never-failing vice of fools.
Whatever Nature has in worth denied,[1]
She gives in large recruits[2] of needful pride!
For as in bodies, thus in souls, we find
What wants in blood and spirits, swell'd with wind:
Pride, where wit fails, steps in to our defence,
And fills up all the mighty void of sense.
If once right reason drives that cloud away,
Truth breaks upon us with resistless day.
Trust not yourself; but, your defects to know,
Make use of every friend—and every foe. R
A little learning is a dangerous thing!
Drink deep, or taste not the Pierian spring;[3]
There shallow draughts **intoxicate** the brain,
And drinking largely sobers us again.
Fired at first sight with what the Muse imparts,
In fearless youth we tempt[4] the heights of arts,
While from the bounded level of our mind.
Short views we take, nor see the lengths behind;
But more advanced, behold with strange surprise
New distant scenes of endless science[5] rise!
So, pleased at first, the towering Alps we try,
Mount o'er the vales, and seem to tread the sky!
Th' eternal snows appear already pass'd,
And the first cloud and mountains seem the last:
But, those attain'd, we tremble to survey
The growing labours of the lengthen'd way:
Th' increasing prospect[6] tires our wandering eyes,
Hills peep o'er hills, and Alps on Alps arise! R

Main Ideas: What, according to Pope, is the chief cause of faulty criticism? R

intoxicate (ĭn-tŏk'sĭ-kāt') *tr.v.* To stimulate or excite.

Main Ideas: To what does Pope compare the foolish ambitiousness of inexperienced critics? R

1. *in . . . denied:* withheld in ability
2. *recruits:* replenishments
3. *Pierian spring:* fountain of learning and poetic inspiration sacred to the nine Muses and named for Pieria where they were worshiped
4. *tempt:* attempt
5. *science:* knowledge
6. *increasing prospect:* broadening vista

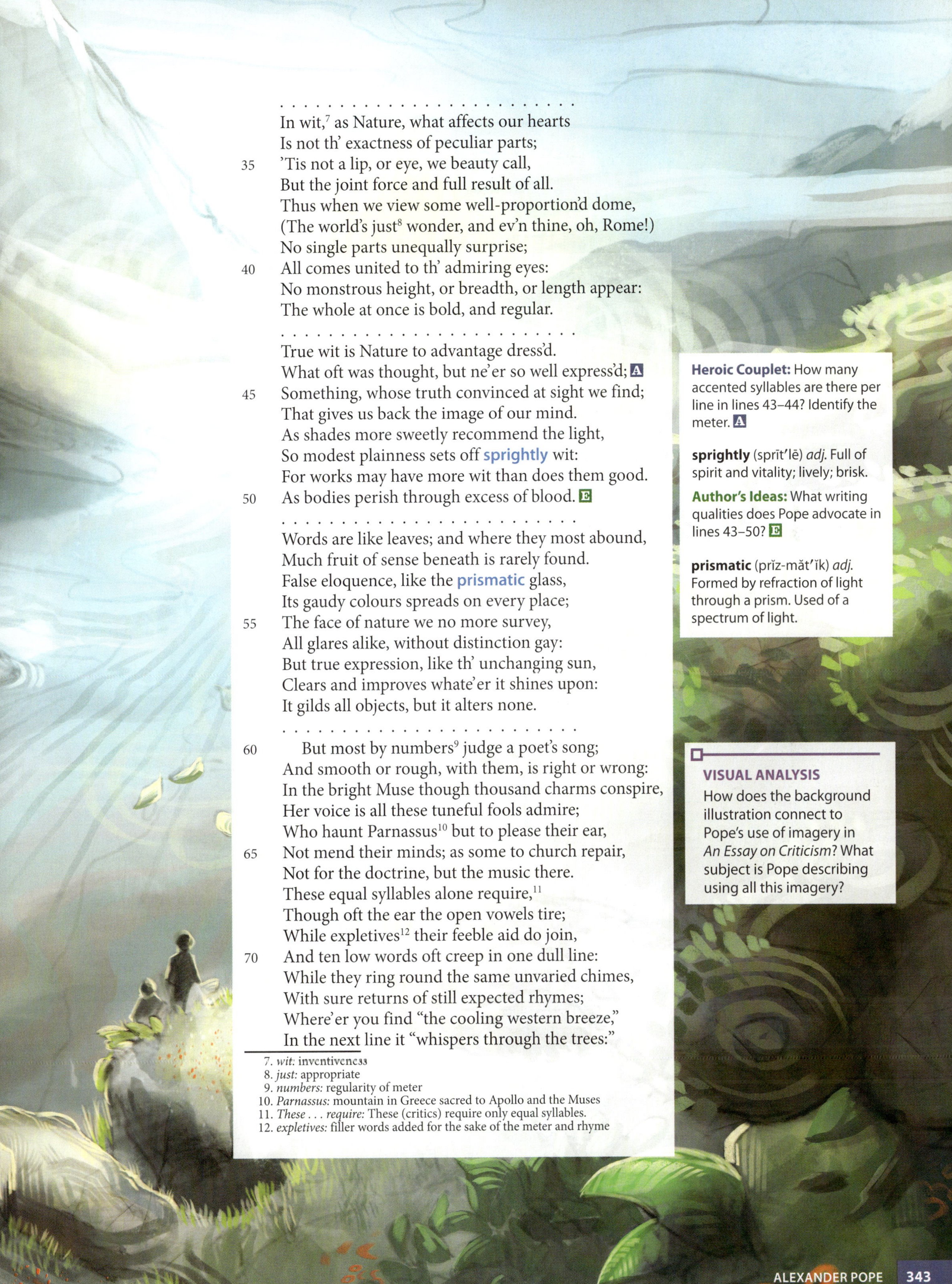

. . . . .

In wit,[7] as Nature, what affects our hearts
Is not th' exactness of peculiar parts;
'Tis not a lip, or eye, we beauty call,
But the joint force and full result of all.
Thus when we view some well-proportion'd dome,
(The world's just[8] wonder, and ev'n thine, oh, Rome!)
No single parts unequally surprise;
All comes united to th' admiring eyes:
No monstrous height, or breadth, or length appear:
The whole at once is bold, and regular.

. . . . .

True wit is Nature to advantage dress'd.
What oft was thought, but ne'er so well express'd; **A**
Something, whose truth convinced at sight we find;
That gives us back the image of our mind.
As shades more sweetly recommend the light,
So modest plainness sets off **sprightly** wit:
For works may have more wit than does them good.
As bodies perish through excess of blood. **E**

. . . . .

Words are like leaves; and where they most abound,
Much fruit of sense beneath is rarely found.
False eloquence, like the **prismatic** glass,
Its gaudy colours spreads on every place;
The face of nature we no more survey,
All glares alike, without distinction gay:
But true expression, like th' unchanging sun,
Clears and improves whate'er it shines upon:
It gilds all objects, but it alters none.

. . . . .

But most by numbers[9] judge a poet's song;
And smooth or rough, with them, is right or wrong:
In the bright Muse though thousand charms conspire,
Her voice is all these tuneful fools admire;
Who haunt Parnassus[10] but to please their ear,
Not mend their minds; as some to church repair,
Not for the doctrine, but the music there.
These equal syllables alone require,[11]
Though oft the ear the open vowels tire;
While expletives[12] their feeble aid do join,
And ten low words oft creep in one dull line:
While they ring round the same unvaried chimes,
With sure returns of still expected rhymes;
Where'er you find "the cooling western breeze,"
In the next line it "whispers through the trees:"

7. *wit:* inventiveness
8. *just:* appropriate
9. *numbers:* regularity of meter
10. *Parnassus:* mountain in Greece sacred to Apollo and the Muses
11. *These . . . require:* These (critics) require only equal syllables.
12. *expletives:* filler words added for the sake of the meter and rhyme

Heroic Couplet: How many accented syllables are there per line in lines 43–44? Identify the meter. **A**

sprightly (sprīt′lē) *adj.* Full of spirit and vitality; lively; brisk.

Author's Ideas: What writing qualities does Pope advocate in lines 43–50? **E**

prismatic (prĭz-măt′ĭk) *adj.* Formed by refraction of light through a prism. Used of a spectrum of light.

VISUAL ANALYSIS

How does the background illustration connect to Pope's use of imagery in *An Essay on Criticism*? What subject is Pope describing using all this imagery?

If crystal streams "with pleasing murmurs creep,"
The reader's threatened (not in vain) with "sleep:"
Then at the last, and only couplet **fraught**
With some unmeaning thing they call a thought,
A needless Alexandrine[13] ends the song,
That, like a wounded snake, drags its slow length
    along.
  Leave such to tune their own dull rhymes, and
    know[14]
What's roundly smooth, or languishingly slow:
And praise the easy vigour of a line,
Where Denham's strength and Waller's sweetness
    join.[15]
True ease in writing comes from art, not chance,
As those move easiest who have learn'd to dance.
'Tis not enough no harshness gives offence,
The sound must seem an echo to the sense:
Soft is the strain when Zephyr gently blows,
And the smooth stream in smoother numbers flows;
But when loud surges lash the sounding shore,
The hoarse, rough verse should like the torrent roar.
When Ajax[16] strives some rock's vast weight to throw,
The line too labours, and the words move slow:
Not so, when swift Camilla[17] scours the plain,
Flies o'er th' unbending corn, and skims along the
    main. R

13. *Alexandrine:* iambic hexameter line
14. *Leave . . . know:* "Know" parallels "Leave," not "tune."
15. *Denham's . . . join:* Sir John Denham (1615–69) and Edmund Waller (1606–87) were forerunners of eighteenth-century neoclassicism.
16. *Ajax:* Greek hero in the Trojan War
17. *Camilla:* legendary Amazon warrior-princess of such swiftness she could run upon a field of grain without bending the stalks and upon the sea ("the main") without wetting her feet

fraught (frôt) *adj*. Filled with a specified element or elements; charged.

Main Ideas: Reread lines 85–96. On what basis, rather than regularity of meter and rhyme, must we judge the expertness of a poem? R

THINK AND DISCUSS

1. Define *verse epistle* and explain why *An Essay on Man* qualifies as one.
2. What request does the speaker in *An Essay on Man* make of Henry St. John in the first stanza? What does he say is the reason for this request, and how is his purpose similar to that of Milton's in *Paradise Lost*?
3. According to the opening lines of *An Essay on Man,* how will Pope and St. John conduct their moral-theological inquiry? What limits do lines 17–20 place on their inquiry, and what is their exclusive means of understanding?
4. Based on Acts 14:15–17, how would you evaluate lines 17–20? What is the "witness" that the apostle Paul refers to in this passage? How is Paul also a witness? What role do the Scriptures themselves play in human understanding?
5. Identify the characteristics of neoclassical style present in Pope's poetry. Provide two examples of these characteristics from *An Essay on Man* and explain your choices.
6. Identify the figurative language Pope uses in lines 15–16 and 51–52 of *An Essay on Criticism*, and tell whether you think they are appropriate. Do you agree or disagree with the ideas expressed in these couplets, and what are your reasons for doing so?
7. In line 88 the poet says, "The sound must seem an echo to the sense." Find specific lines in the poem that illustrate this principle most clearly. How does the poet humorously deride those poets who ignore this principle?
8. Which of the other principles that Pope sets forth for the poet do you think he exemplifies best in his own writing?
9. Choose any two couplets from the two selections by Pope and write them in prose form. After doing so, what observations can you make about the heroic couplet as a verse form and about Pope as a writer?
10. Write an original didactic couplet of your own.

Jonathan Swift (1667–1745)

AT A GLANCE

- **1689–99** Served as secretary to Sir William Temple
- **1695** Ordained as an Anglican priest
- **1704** Published "Battle of the Books" and *A Tale of a Tub*
- **1713** Became dean of St. Patrick's Cathedral in Dublin
- **1726** Published *Gulliver's Travels*
- **1729** Published *A Modest Proposal*

Often named as Britain's best prose satirist, Jonathan Swift advocated a rationalist approach to religion and society. His works were famed for biting but often playful wit and were frequently the talk of London. Characterized by a neoclassical style of simple but exact, powerful language, they offered incisive commentary on the problems of his day.

Preparation

Swift was born in Ireland to English parents. His father died before his birth, and his mother left him to his uncle to raise. Educated very well, he earned a BA (1686, Trinity College, Dublin), an MA (1692, Oxford), and a doctorate (1702, Trinity). In 1689 he moved to England for further education and to work as a secretary for Sir William Temple, a distant relative. Ordained in 1695, Swift lived mostly in England, where he began writing first poetry and then prose satire.

Priest and Writer

After Temple's death (1699), Swift reluctantly returned to Ireland to be the Earl of Berkley's secretary. Instead, given a small vicarage outside Dublin, he used the opportunity to write satirical essays on politics and religion. He also returned multiple times in the next decade to personally engage in London society (e.g., he was a member of Pope's Scriblerus Club) and politics.

In 1704 two works brought the author (officially anonymous, as he would remain) to the public's eye. His playful allegorical fantasy "Battle of the Books" satirized academic tussles between advocates of ancient and modern learning. But *A Tale of a Tub* was his first real masterwork. An allegory about three brothers, it satirized English politics and parodied Catholicism, Anglicanism, and Dissenters. Unfortunately, the work offended as many readers as it intrigued and likely damaged Swift's chances of advancement.

On important issues, Swift wavered between the Whig and Tory parties (p. 286); for instance, he approved of England's developing constitutional monarchy but also supported the traditional dominance of the Anglican Church. By the end of the decade, he was fully invested in the Tory party, editing the Tory *Examiner* and attacking Whig pro-war commercial policies such as enlarging the empire and controlling the seas. When the Tories suffered great defeat in 1713, he lost his hope for an English bishopric, instead being appointed dean of St. Patrick's Cathedral, Dublin.

Disillusioned Reformer

At first gravely disappointed, Swift eventually rallied to propose and support reforms addressing the deep social problems in Ireland. Economically restricted and politically oppressed by England, the Irish suffered from poverty, overpopulation, and starvation. Swift's masterful satirical essay *A Modest Proposal* (1729) was the culmination of a decade of writing reformist literature. Its narrator matter-of-factly recommends a startling proposal—that Irish babies be fattened for the tables of the English to relieve these problems and enhance English trade (a chief concern of Whigs). The savage irony of the work provoked both thoughtful and outraged responses.

Written about the same time was his greatest masterpiece, *Travels into Several Remote Nations of the World* or *Gulliver's Travels* (1726). With multiple targets, including English politics, society, and religion, the work formed a scathing indictment of humanity. It represented Swift's shaken hopes for reason to prevail and for progress in society. He continued his work, but with age and the loss of multiple close friends, his health began to decline. A stroke in 1739, by some accounts, diminished the mental acuity that so defined him, and by 1745 he was dead.

In the Isaac Bickerstaff papers (1708), Swift satirically predicted and confirmed the death of a popular astrologer, despite the latter's indignant protests.

ANALYZE: *Juvenalian Satire and Narrator*

Swift's most famous work, *Gulliver's Travels*, is a combination of satire (p. 85) and travelogue (a popular genre at the time). Swift creates a clearly fantastical travel story in which the narrator's improbable encounters are meant as analogies (p. 140) to real details of English and European history. In context, these fictional analogies satirically comment on society. Swift's work exemplifies **Juvenalian satire**, a type of more biting, savage, and serious corrective ridicule than Horatian (p. 333). As you read, consider Swift's tone toward his satirical targets. If Horatian satire comes alongside the target with gentle ridicule, how might Swift's approach take a full frontal attack instead?

An important feature of Swift's satire is his use of a **narrator** (the individual telling a story to readers) who paints a veneer of verisimilitude (p. 322) over an often ridiculously nonfactual tale. As you read, notice the narrator's character. What character traits does he claim or display? What aspects of his descriptions help create a feeling of verisimilitude and believability? On the satirical level, how might his perspective or tone toward his narrative help heighten Swift's ironic or humorous points about society?

READ: *Apply Historical Background*

The following passages from *Gulliver's Travels* introduce readers to several groups Swift created to represent contemporaries of his. First, the so-called Tramecksans and Slamecksans (or "high heels" and "low heels") represent the Tory and Whig parties. As you read, consider what Swift's presentation of their disagreements says about both parties. Also, two nations in the story, the Lilliputians and Blefuscudians, represent England and France respectively. The narrator shares a part of these fictitious peoples' history, termed the "egg controversy." This conflict parallels a long-standing European division (1500s to Swift's time) that was still causing tension between England and France. What controversy is Swift satirizing? What does his fictionalized version imply or directly state about the value of this real controversy?

EVALUATE: *Misanthropy and Social Reform*

Some critics believe that Swift, disappointed with society near the end of his life, descended into misanthropy (i.e., "hatred or mistrust of humankind" [*AHD*]). Indeed, in a letter to Pope (Sept. 29, 1725), Swift stated that he wrote *Gulliver's Travels* "to vex the world rather than divert it." By the end of the work, he seems to fatalistically predict that, even if rule by reason is the answer to the troubles of humanity, society will never be able to achieve this state. Is this conclusion about human society biblically correct? Is misanthropy a biblical view of man? Consider Psalm 72:1–4; Psalm 139:14–16; Matthew 5:44–45; and Romans 5:8. Additionally, evaluate the following selections in this light. Do they illustrate a misanthropic attitude, or are their observations about humans more balanced? Consider the behavior of all the characters, including Gulliver himself.

OBJECTIVES

- Identify features of Juvenalian satire in a text.
- Analyze a work's narrator and its connection to the theme.
- Apply historical background to understand a text.
- Evaluate an author's perspective on human nature and society from a biblical perspective.

VOCABULARY

conjecture (kən-jĕk′chər) *tr.v.* To judge or conclude by conjecture; guess.

intrepidity (in′-trə-pĭd′ĭ-tē) *n.* Resolutely courageous; fearless.

faction (făk′shən) *n.* A conflict or intrigue involving opposed or mutually hostile groups.

gait (gāt) *n.* A particular way or manner of moving on foot.

expostulate (ĭk-spŏs′chə-lāt′) *intr.v.* To reason earnestly with someone in an effort to dissuade or correct; remonstrate.

encomium (ĕn-kō′mē-əm) *n.* A formal expression of praise.

How can MAKING FUN *of something be constructive?*

As children, we are taught not to make fun of people. Mocking words hurt and are often prideful, unloving, and unfair. Satire can sometimes descend to this level. But it can also be a powerful constructive tool. What do you think makes the difference between helpful and simply hurtful satire? With a partner, write down a few guidelines that satirists should follow to avoid being purely destructive in their criticism.

FROM

GULLIVER'S TRAVELS

FROM BOOK 1

My father had a small estate in Nottinghamshire; I was the third of five sons. He sent me to Emanuel College in Cambridge, at fourteen years old, where I resided three years, and applied myself close to my studies; but the charge of maintaining me (although I had a very scanty allowance) being too great for a narrow fortune, I was bound apprentice to Mr. James Bates, an eminent surgeon in London, with whom I continued four years; and my father now and then sending me small sums of money, I laid them out in learning navigation, and other parts of the mathematics, useful to those who intend to travel, as I always believed it would be some time or other my fortune to do. When I left Mr. Bates, I went down to my father; where, by the assistance of him and my uncle John, and some other relations, I got forty pounds, and a promise of thirty pounds a year to maintain me at Leyden[1]: there I studied physic[2] two years and seven months, knowing it would be useful in long voyages.

1. *Leyden:* Dutch university known for medical studies
2. *physic:* medicine

Soon after my return from Leyden, I was recommended by my good master, Mr. Bates, to be surgeon[3] to the *Swallow*, Captain Abraham Pannell, commander; with whom I continued three years and a half, making a voyage or two into the Levant,[4] and some other parts. When I came back I resolved to settle in London, to which Mr. Bates, my master, encouraged me, and by him I was recommended to several patients. I took part of a small house in the Old Jury;[5] and being advised to alter my condition, I married Mrs. Mary Burton, second daughter to Mr. Edmund Burton, hosier, in Newgate-street, with whom I received four hundred pounds for a portion.[6]

But, my good master Bates dying in two years after, and I having few friends, my business began to fail; for my conscience would not suffer me to imitate the bad practice of too many among my brethren. Having therefore consulted with my wife, and some of my acquaintance, I determined to go again to sea. I was surgeon successively in two ships, and made several voyages, for six years, to the East and West-Indies, by which I got some addition to my fortune. My hours of leisure I spent in reading the best authors, ancient and modern, being always provided with a good number of books; and when I was ashore, in observing the manners and dispositions of the people, as well as learning their language, wherein I had a great facility by the strength of my memory. **A**

The last of these voyages not proving very fortunate, I grew weary of the sea, and intended to stay at home with my wife and family. I removed from the Old Jury to Fetter Lane, and from thence to Wapping, hoping to get business among the sailors; but it would not turn to account. After three years expectation that things would mend, I accepted an advantageous offer from Captain William Prichard, master of the *Antelope*, who was making a voyage to the South-Sea. We set sail from Bristol, May 4, 1699, and our voyage at first was very prosperous.

It would not be proper, for some reasons, to trouble the reader with the particulars of our adventures in those seas: let it suffice to inform him, that in our passage from thence to the East-Indies, we were driven by a violent storm to the north-west of Van Diemen's Land.[7] By an observation, we found ourselves in the latitude of 30 degrees 2 minutes south. Twelve of our crew were dead by immoderate labor, and ill food, the rest were in a very weak condition. On the fifth of November, which was the beginning of summer in those parts, the weather being very hazy, the seamen spied a rock, within half a cable's length[8] of the ship; but the wind was so strong, that we were driven directly upon it, and immediately split. Six of the crew, of whom I was one, having let down the boat into the sea, made a shift[9] to get clear of the ship, and the rock. We rowed, by my computation, about three leagues,[10] till we were able to work no longer, being already spent with labor while we were in the ship. We therefore trusted ourselves to the mercy of the waves, and in about half an hour the boat was overset by a sudden flurry[11] from the north.

What became of my companions in the boat, as well as of those who escaped on the rock, or were left in the vessel, I cannot tell; but conclude they were all lost. For my own part, I swam as fortune directed me, and was pushed forward by wind and tide. I often let my legs drop, and could feel no bottom: but when I was almost gone, and able to struggle no longer, I found myself within my depth; and by this time the storm was much abated. The declivity was so small, that I walked near a mile before I got to the shore, which I **conjectured** was about eight o'clock in the evening. I then advanced forward near half a mile, but could not discover any sign of houses or inhabitants; at least I was in so weak a condition, that I did not observe them. I was extremely tired, and with that, and the heat of the weather, and about half a pint of brandy that I drank as I left the ship,

3. *surgeon:* physician
4. *Levant:* countries bordering the eastern Mediterranean
5. *Old Jury:* Jewry; Jewish section during the Middle Ages
6. *portion:* dowry

7. *Van Diemen's Land:* Tasmania
8. *cable's length:* 304 feet
9. *made . . . shift:* contrived
10. *three leagues:* nine miles
11. *flurry:* gust of wind

Narrator: What do readers learn about Gulliver in these opening paragraphs? Does he seem like a trustworthy source for the story that follows? **A**

conjecture (kən-jĕk′chər) *tr.v.* To judge or conclude by conjecture; guess.

I found myself much inclined to sleep. I lay down on the grass, which was very short and soft, where I slept sounder than ever I remember to have done in my life, and, as I reckoned, about nine hours; for when I awaked it was just daylight. I attempted to rise, but was not able to stir: for as I happened to lie on my back, I found my arms and legs were strongly fastened on each side to the ground; and my hair, which was long and thick, tied down in the same manner. I likewise felt several slender ligatures across my body, from my arm-pits to my thighs. I could only look upwards, the sun began to grow hot, and the light offended my eyes. I heard a confused noise about me, but in the posture I lay, could see nothing except the sky. **A**

In a little time I felt something alive moving on my left leg, which advancing gently forward over my breast, came almost up to my chin; when bending my eyes downwards as much as I could, I perceived it to be a human creature not six inches high, with a bow and arrow in his hands, and a quiver at his back. In the meantime, I felt at least forty more of the same kind (as I conjectured) following the first. I was in the utmost astonishment, and roared so loud, that they all ran back in a fright; and some of them, as I was afterwards told, were hurt with the falls they got by leaping from my sides upon the ground. However, they soon returned, and one of them, who ventured so far as to get a full sight of my face, lifting up his hands and eyes by way of admiration,[12] cried out in a shrill, but distinct voice, "*Hekinah degul*": the others repeated the same words several times, but then I knew not what they meant.

I lay all this while, as the reader may believe, in great uneasiness: at length, struggling to get loose, I had the fortune to break the strings, and wrench out the pegs that fastened my left arm to the ground; for, by lifting it up to my face, I discovered the methods they had taken to bind me, and at the same time with a violent pull, which gave me excessive pain, I a little loosened the strings that tied down my hair on the left side, so that I was just able to turn my head about two inches. But the creatures ran off a second time, before I could seize them; whereupon there was a great shout in a very shrill accent, and after it ceased, I heard one of them cry aloud "*Tolga phonic*"; when in an instant I felt above an hundred arrows discharged on my left hand, which pricked me like so many needles; and besides, they shot another flight into the air, as we do bombs

12. *admiration:* wonder

Narrator: How do Gulliver's descriptions give readers a sense of verisimilitude so far? Consider both his content and his tone. **A**

in Europe, whereof many, I suppose, fell on my body, (though I felt them not) and some on my face, which I immediately covered with my left hand. When this shower of arrows was over, I fell a groaning with grief and pain, and then striving again to get loose, they discharged another volley larger than the first, and some of them attempted with spears to stick me in the sides; but, by good luck, I had on a buff jerkin,[13] which they could not pierce. I thought it the most prudent method to lie still, and my design was to continue so till night, when, my left hand being already loose, I could easily free myself: and as for the inhabitants, I had reason to believe I might be a match for the greatest armies they could bring against me, if they were all of the same size with him that I saw. But fortune disposed otherwise of me. When the people observed I was quiet, they discharged no more arrows; but, by the noise I heard, I knew their numbers increased; and about four yards from me, over-against my right ear, I heard a knocking for above an hour, like that of people at work; when turning my head that way, as well as the pegs and strings would permit me, I saw a stage erected, about a foot and a half from the ground, capable of holding four of the inhabitants, with two or three ladders to mount it: from whence one of them, who seemed to be a person of quality,[14] made me a long speech, whereof I understood not one syllable. But I should have mentioned, that be fore the principal person began his oration, he cried out three times, "*Langro dehul san*": (these words and the former were afterwards repeated and explained to me). Whereupon immediately about fifty of the inhabitants came and cut the strings that fastened the left side of my head, which gave me the liberty of turning it to the right, and of observing the person and gesture of him that was to speak.

He appeared to be of a middle age, and taller than any of the other three who attended him, whereof one was a page that held up his train, and seemed to be somewhat longer than my middle finger; the other two stood one on each side to support him. He acted every part of an orator, and I could observe many periods of threatenings, and others of promises, pity, and kindness. I answered in a few words, but in the most submissive manner, lifting up my left hand, and both my eyes to the sun, as calling him for a witness; and being almost famished with hunger, having not eaten a morsel for some hours before I left the ship, I found the demands of nature so strong upon me, that I could not forbear showing my impatience (perhaps against the strict rules of decency) by putting my finger frequently on my mouth, to signify that I wanted food.

The *Hurgo* (for so they call a great lord, as I afterwards learnt) understood me very well. He descended from the stage, and commanded that several ladders should be applied to my sides, on which above an hundred of the inhabitants mounted and walked towards my mouth, laden with baskets full of meat, which had been provided and sent thither by the King's orders, upon the first intelligence he received of me. I observed there was the flesh of several animals, but could not distinguish them by the taste. There were shoulders, legs, and loins, shaped like those of mutton, and very well dressed, but smaller than the wings of a lark. I ate them by two or three at a mouthful, and took three loaves at a time, about the bigness of musket bullets. They supplied me as fast as they could, showing a thousand marks of wonder and astonishment at my bulk and appetite. I then made another sign that I wanted drink. They found by my eating, that a small quantity would not suffice me; and being a most ingenious people, they slung up with great dexterity one of their largest hogsheads,[15] then rolled it towards my hand, and beat out the top; I drank it off at a draught, which I might well do, for it did not hold half a pint, and tasted like a small wine of Burgundy, but much more delicious. They brought me a second hogshead, which I drank in the same manner, and made signs for more, but they had none to give me.

When I had performed these wonders, they shouted for joy, and danced upon my breast, repeating several

VISUAL ANALYSIS

What key aspect of Swift's satirical setup do this and the previous illustration (p. 349) highlight? How might the different perspective in the second illustration further develop the satirical tone?

13. *jerkin:* vest of soft, undyed leather
14. *quality:* social rank
15. *hogsheads:* barrels

times as they did at first, "*Hekinah degul.*" They made me a sign that I should throw down the two hogsheads, but first warning the people below to stand out of the way, crying aloud, "*Borach mivola,*" and when they saw the vessels in the air, there was an universal shout of "*Hekinah degul.*" I confess I was often tempted, while they were passing backwards and forwards on my body, to seize forty or fifty of the first that came in my reach, and dash them against the ground. But the remembrance of what I had felt, which probably might not be the worst they could do, and the promise of honor I made them, for so I interpreted my submissive behavior, soon drove out these imaginations. Besides, I now considered myself as bound by the laws of hospitality to a people who had treated me with so much expense and magnificence. However, in my thoughts, I could not sufficiently wonder at the **intrepidity** of these diminutive mortals, who durst venture to mount and walk upon my body, while one of my hands was at liberty, without trembling at the very sight of so prodigious[16] a creature as I must appear to them.

After some time, when they observed that I made no more demands for meat, there appeared before me a person of high rank from his Imperial Majesty. His Excellency, having mounted on the small of my right leg, advanced forwards up to my face, with about a dozen of his retinue. And producing his credentials under the Signet Royal, which he applied close to my eyes, spoke about ten minutes, without any signs of anger, but with a kind of determinate resolution; often pointing forwards, which, as I afterwards found, was towards the capital city, about half a mile distant, whither it was agreed by his Majesty in council that I must be conveyed. I answered in few words, but to no purpose, and made a sign with my hand that was loose, putting it to the other (but over his Excellency's head for fear of hurting him or his train[17]) and then to my own head and body, to signify that I desired my liberty. It appeared that he understood me well enough, for he shook his head by way of disapprobation, and held his hand in a posture to show that I must be carried as a prisoner. However, he made other signs to let me understand that I should have meat and drink enough, and very good treatment. Whereupon I once more thought of attempting to break my bonds; but again, when I felt the smart of their arrows, upon my face and hands, which were all in blisters, and many of the darts still sticking in them, and observing likewise that the number of my enemies increased, I gave tokens[18] to let them know that they might do with me what they pleased. Upon this, the *Hurgo* and his train withdrew, with much civility and cheerful countenances. . . . **A**

Gulliver, drugged, is transported a quarter mile toward Mildendo, the capital of Lilliput, on a low, wheeled platform drawn by "fifteen hundred of the Emperor's largest horses, each about four inches and a half high," and chained in an ancient, abandoned temple outside the city walls. In time he gains the confidence of the emperor and citizens and is granted his liberty.

The first request I made after I had obtained my liberty, was, that I might have license to see Mildendo, the metropolis; which the Emperor easily granted me, but with a special charge to do no hurt either to the inhabitants or their houses. The people had notice by proclamation of my design to visit the town. The wall which encompassed it, is two foot and an half high, and at least eleven inches broad, so that a coach and horses may be driven very safely round it; and it is flanked with strong towers at ten foot distance. I stepped over the great Western Gate, and passed very gently, and sideling through the two principal streets, only in my short waistcoat, for fear of damaging the roofs and eaves of the houses with the skirts of my coat. I walked with the utmost circumspection, to avoid treading on any stragglers that might remain in the streets, although the orders were very strict, that all people should keep

16. *prodigious:* awesome
17. *train:* attendants
18. *gave tokens:* made signs

intrepidity (in′-trə-pĭd′ĭ-tē) *n.* Resolutely courageous; fearless.

Satire: What about the story is humorous so far? How might Gulliver's tone make incidents funnier? **A**

in their houses, at their own peril. The garret windows and tops of houses were so crowded with spectators, that I thought in all my travels I had not seen a more populous place. The city is an exact square, each side of the wall being five hundred foot long. The two great streets, which run cross and divide it into four quarters, are five foot wide. The lanes and alleys, which I could not enter, but only viewed them as I passed, are from twelve to eighteen inches. The town is capable of holding five hundred thousand souls. The houses are from three to five stories. The shops and markets well provided.

The Emperor's palace is in the center of the city, where the two great streets meet. It is enclosed by a wall of two foot high, and twenty foot distant from the buildings. I had his Majesty's permission to step over this wall; and the space being so wide between that and the palace, I could easily view it on every side. The outward court is a square of forty foot, and includes two other courts: in the inmost are the royal apartments, which I was very desirous to see, but found it extremely difficult; for the great gates, from one square into another, were but eighteen inches high, and seven inches wide. Now the buildings of the outer court were at least five foot high, and it was impossible for me to stride over them without infinite damage to the pile, though the walls were strongly built of hewn stone, and four inches thick. At the same time the Emperor had a great desire that I should see the magnificence of his palace; but this I was not able to do till three days after, which I spent in cutting down with my knife some of the largest trees in the royal park, about an hundred yards distant from the city. Of these trees I made two stools, each about three foot high, and strong enough to bear my weight. The people having received notice a second time, I went again through the city to the palace, with my two stools in my hands. When I came to the side of the outer court, I stood upon one stool, and took the other in my hand: this I lifted over the roof, and gently set it down on the space between the first and second court, which was eight foot wide. I then stept over the buildings very conveniently from one stool to the other, and drew up the first after me with a hooked stick. By this contrivance I got into the inmost court; and lying down upon my side, I applied my face to the windows of the middle stories, which were left open on purpose, and discovered the most splendid apartments that can be imagined. There I saw the Empress and the young Princes, in their several lodgings, with their chief attendants about them. Her Imperial Majesty was pleased to smile very graciously upon me, and gave me out of the window her hand to kiss.

But I shall not anticipate the reader with farther descriptions of this kind, because I reserve them for a greater work, which is now almost ready for the press, containing a general description of this empire, from its first erection, through a long series of princes, with a particular account of their wars and politics, laws, learning, and religion: their plants and animals, their peculiar manners and customs, with other matters very curious and useful; my chief design at present being only to relate such events and transactions as happened

to the public, or to myself, during a residence of about nine months in that empire. **A**

One morning, about a fortnight[19] after I had obtained my liberty, Reldresal, principal Secretary (as they style him) of private Affairs, came to my house attended only by one servant. He ordered his coach to wait at a distance, and desired I would give him an hour's audience; which I readily consented to, on account of his quality and personal merits, as well as the many good offices he had done me during my solicitations at court. I offered to lie down, that he might the more conveniently reach my ear; but he chose rather to let me hold him in my hand during our conversation. He began with compliments on my liberty; said he might pretend to some merit in it: but, however, added, that if it had not been for the present situation of things at court, perhaps I might not have obtained it so soon. "For," said he, "as flourishing a condition as we may appear to be in to foreigners, we labor under two mighty evils; a violent **faction** at home, and the danger of an invasion by a most potent enemy from abroad. As to the first, you are to understand, that for about seventy moons[20] past there have been two struggling parties in this empire, under the names of *Tramecksan* and *Slamecksan*, from the high and low heels on their shoes, by which they distinguish themselves.

"It is alleged indeed, that the high heels are most agreeable to our ancient constitution: but however this be, his Majesty hath determined to make use of only low heels in the administration of the government, and all offices in the gift of the Crown, as you cannot but observe; and particularly, that his Majesty's Imperial heels are lower at least by a *drurr* than any of his court; (*drurr* is a measure about the fourteenth part of an inch). The animosities between these two parties run so high, that they will neither eat nor drink, nor talk with each other. We compute the *Tramecksan*, or High-Heels, to exceed us in number; but the power is wholly on our side. We apprehend his Imperial Highness, the Heir to the Crown, to have some tendency towards the High-Heels; at least we can plainly discover one of his heels higher than the other, which gives him a hobble in his **gait**. **A** Now, in the midst of these intestine disquiets,[21] we are threatened with an invasion from the Island of Blefuscu, which is the other great empire of the universe, almost as large and powerful as this of his Majesty. For as to what we have heard you affirm, that there are other kingdoms and states in the world inhabited by human creatures as large as yourself, our philosophers are in much doubt and would rather conjecture that you dropped from the moon, or one of the stars; because it is certain, that an hundred mortals of your bulk would, in a short time, destroy all the fruits and cattle of his Majesty's dominions. Besides, our histories of six thousand moons make no mention of any other regions, than the two great empires of Lilliput and Blefuscu. Which two mighty powers have, as I was going to tell you, been engaged in a most obstinate war for six and thirty moons past. It began upon the following occasion. It is allowed on all hands, that the primitive way of breaking eggs before we eat them, was upon the larger end: but his present Majesty's grandfather, while he was a boy, going to eat an egg, and breaking it according to the ancient practice, happened to cut one of his fingers. Whereupon the Emperor his father published an edict, commanding all his subjects, upon great penalties, to break the smaller end of their eggs.

The people so highly resented this law, that our histories tell us there have been six rebellions raised on that account; wherein one Emperor lost his life, and another his crown. These civil commotions were constantly fomented[22] by the monarchs of Blefuscu; and when they were quelled,[23] the exiles always fled for refuge to that empire. It is computed, that eleven thousand persons

19. *fortnight:* two weeks
20. *moons:* months
21. *intestine disquiets:* civil turmoils
22. *fomented:* stirred up
23. *quelled:* suppressed

Satire: If Swift's Lilliputians are meant to represent England, how might Gulliver's descriptions of their capital and palace set the stage for a very pointed satirization of English politics? **A**

faction (făk'shən) *n.* A conflict or intrigue involving opposed or mutually hostile groups.

gait (gāt) *n.* A particular way or manner of moving on foot.

Satire: How does Reldresal's description of the Tramecksan and Slamecksan (or high-heel/low-heel) parties' controversy reflect on the Tories and Whigs it was meant to represent? How does Swift want readers to feel about these parties? **A**

have, at several times, suffered death, rather than submit to break their eggs at the smaller end. Many hundred large volumes have been published upon this controversy: but the books of the Big-Endians have been long forbidden, and the whole party rendered incapable by law of holding employments. During the course of these troubles, the Emperors of Blefuscu did frequently **expostulate** by their ambassadors, accusing us of making a schism in religion, by offending against a fundamental doctrine of our great prophet Lustrog, in the fifty-fourth chapter of the Blundecral (which is their Alcoran[24]). This, however, is thought to be a mere strain upon the text: for the words are these; *That all true believers break their eggs at the convenient end*: and which is the convenient end, seems, in my humble opinion, to be left to every man's conscience, or at least in the power of the chief magistrate to determine. R Now the Big-Endian exiles have found so much credit[25] in the Emperor of Blefuscu's court, and so much private assistance and encouragement from their party here at home, that a bloody war has been carried on between the two empires for six and thirty moons with various success; during which time we have lost forty capital[26] ships, and a much greater number of smaller vessels, together with thirty thousand of our best seamen and soldiers; and the damage received by the enemy is reckoned to be somewhat greater than ours. However, they have now equipped a numerous fleet, and are just preparing to make a descent upon us; and his Imperial Majesty, placing great confidence in your valor and strength, has commanded me to lay this account of his affairs before you."

I desired the Secretary to present my humble duty[27] to the Emperor, and to let him know, that I thought it would not become[28] me, who was a foreigner, to interfere with parties; but I was ready, with the hazard of my life, to defend his person and state against all invaders.

The Empire of Blefuscu is an island situated to the north north-east side of Lilliput, from whence it is parted only by a channel of eight hundred yards wide. I had not yet seen it, and upon this notice of an intended invasion, I avoided appearing on that side of

24. *Alcoran:* Koran (i.e., sacred book)
25. *credit:* acceptance
26. *capital:* chief
27. *duty:* obedience
28. *become:* be appropriate for

expostulate (ĭk-spŏs′chə-lāt′) *intr.v.* To reason earnestly with someone in an effort to dissuade or correct; remonstrate.

Apply Background: What European division is Swift clearly alluding to? What does he seem to believe is the most rational solution to such differences? R

the coast, for fear of being discovered by some of the enemy's ships, who had received no intelligence of me, all intercourse between the two empires having been strictly forbidden during the war, upon pain of death, and an embargo laid by our Emperor upon all vessels whatsoever. I communicated to his Majesty a project I had formed of seizing the enemy's whole fleet: which, as our scouts assured us, lay at anchor in the harbor ready to sail with the first fair wind. I consulted the most experienced seamen, upon the depth of the channel, which they had often plumbed,[29] who told me, that in the middle at high-water it was seventy *glumgluffs* deep, which is about six foot of European measure; and the rest of it fifty *glumgluffs* at most. I walked towards the north-east coast over against[30] Blefuscu; and lying down behind a hillock, took out my small pocket perspective-glass, and viewed the enemy's fleet at anchor, consisting of about fifty men of war, and a great number of transports: I then came back to my house, and gave order (for which I had a warrant) for a great quantity of the strongest cable and bars of iron. The cable was about as thick as packthread, and the bars of the length and size of a knitting-needle. I trebled the cable to make it stronger, and for the same reason I twisted three of the iron bars together, binding the extremities into a hook. Having thus fixed fifty hooks to as many cables, I went back to the north-east coast, and putting off my

29. *plumbed:* measured the depth of
30. *against:* facing

coat, shoes, and stockings, walked into the sea in my leathern jerkin, about half an hour before high water. I waded with what haste I could, and swam in the middle about thirty yards till I felt ground; I arrived at the fleet in less than half an hour. The enemy was so frighted when they saw me that they leaped out of their ships, and swam to shore, where there could not be fewer than thirty thousand souls. I then took my tackling,[31] and fastening a hook to the hole at the prow[32] of each, I tied all the cords together at the end. While I was thus employed, the enemy discharged several thousand arrows, many of which stuck in my hands and face; and besides the excessive smart, gave me much disturbance in my work. My greatest apprehension was for my eyes, which I should have infallibly lost, if I had not suddenly thought of an expedient.[33] I kept among other little necessaries a pair of spectacles in a private pocket, which, as I observed before, had scaped the Emperor's searchers. These I took out and fastened as strongly as I could upon my nose, and thus armed went on boldly with my work in spite of the enemy's arrows, many of which struck against the glasses of my spectacles, but without any other effect, further than a little to discompose them. I had now fastened all the hooks, and taking the knot in my hand, began to pull; but not a ship would stir, for they were all too fast held by their anchors, so that the boldest part of my enterprise remained. I therefore let go the cord, and leaving the hooks fixed to the ships, I resolutely cut with my knife the cables that fastened the anchors, receiving about two hundred shots in my face and hands; then I took up the knotted end of the cables, to which my hooks were tied, and with great ease drew fifty of the enemy's largest men-of-war[34] after me.

The Blefuscudians, who had not the least imagination of what I intended, were at first confounded with astonishment. They had seen me cut the cables, and thought my design was only to let the ships run a-drift, or fall foul on[35] each other: but when they perceived the whole fleet moving in order, and saw me pulling at the end, they set up such a scream of grief and despair, that it is almost impossible to describe or conceive. When I had got out of danger, I stopped awhile to pick out the arrows that stuck in my hands and face; and rubbed on some of the same ointment that was given me at my first arrival, as I have formerly mentioned. I then took off my spectacles, and waiting about an hour, till the tide was a little fallen, I waded through the middle with my cargo, and arrived safe at the royal port of Lilliput.

The Emperor and his whole court stood on the shore, expecting the issue of this great adventure. They saw the ships move forward in a large half-moon, but could not discern me, who was up to my breast in water. When I advanced to the middle of the channel, they were yet in more pain, because I was under water

31. *tackling:* pulling apparatus
32. *prow:* forward point
33. *an expedient:* a remedy
34. *men-of-war:* warships
35. *foul on:* collide with

to my neck. The Emperor concluded me to be drowned, and that the enemy's fleet was approaching in a hostile manner: but he was soon eased of his fears, for the channel growing shallower every step I made, I came in a short time within hearing, and holding up the end of the cable by which the fleet was fastened, I cried in a loud voice, "*Long live the most puissant*[36] *Emperor of Lilliput!*" This great prince received me at my landing with all possible **encomiums**, and created me a *Nardac* upon the spot, which is the highest title of honor among them. **A**

His Majesty desired I would take some other opportunity of bringing all the rest of his enemy's ships into his ports. And so unmeasureable is the ambition of princes, that he seemed to think of nothing less than reducing the whole empire of Blefuscu into a province, and governing it by a viceroy; of destroying the Big-Endian exiles, and compelling that people to break the smaller end of their eggs, by which he would remain the sole monarch of the whole world. But I endeavored to divert him from this design, by many arguments drawn from the topics of policy as well as justice; and I plainly protested, that I would never be an instrument of bringing a free and brave people into slavery. And when the matter was debated in council, the wisest part of the ministry were of my opinion.

This open bold declaration of mine was so opposite to the schemes and politics of his Imperial Majesty, that he could never forgive it; he mentioned it in a very artful[37] manner at council, where I was told that some of the wisest appeared, at least by their silence, to be of my opinion; but others, who were my secret enemies, could not forbear some expressions, which by a side-wind[38] reflected on me. And from this time began an intrigue between his Majesty and a junto[39] of ministers maliciously bent against me, which broke out in less than two months, and had like to have ended in my utter destruction. Of so little weight are the greatest services to princes, when put into the balance with a refusal to gratify their passions. **E**

36. *puissant:* powerful

37. *very artful:* carefully contrived
38. *side-wind:* indirectly
39. *junto:* small, secret group

encomium (ĕn-kō′mē-əm) *n.* A formal expression of praise.

Satire: What details in the narration make this whole incident humorous and further trivialize the issue Swift is satirizing? **A**

Misanthropy: What view of rulers does Swift present in Gulliver's conflict with the emperor? Does he have a point, or is he unnecessarily harsh? **E**

THINK AND DISCUSS

1. Define *Juvenalian satire.*
2. Briefly explain the historical connection between Swift's England and one of the two main controversies in this passage.
3. List two character traits of the narrator in this passage. Support each with a piece of evidence from the text.
4. How do the Lilliputians' general character and behavior contrast with Gulliver's? How does the emperor's character differ from Gulliver's?
5. What is Swift saying about Europe's long-standing controversy through the analogy of the egg controversy?
6. How does Gulliver exhibit verisimilitude in his narration? What is his general tone toward his subject? How do both features enhance Swift's satirical purpose in the story?
7. Name two broad human flaws or social problems that Swift satirizes in the story. Consult question 4 for ideas, and support your answers with textual details.
8. Compare the satirical tone of the *Spectator* to that of *Gulliver's Travels*. Support your comparison using details from the text. Why do you think the authors took different approaches?
9. Does Swift exhibit misanthropy in this passage from the text? How does the Bible view such an attitude? Consult Genesis 1:27; Psalm 139:14–16; Matthew 5:44–45, 22:39; and Romans 5:8 in your answer.
10. Swift despaired of society's improvement through rational means. Does the Bible support his view? Cite the following references in your answer: Psalm 72:1–4, Matthew 5:16, Romans 8:18–23, and Revelation 21:2–5.

What Do You Know?

Understand the Background

1. What corrective mode of writing dominated the neoclassical period? Provide an example of this mode from Unit 3.
2. Which genre of writing was most frequently used politically in the English Civil War era? Identify an example of the genre and an author who used it.
3. What factors contributed to the rise of prose genres such as the novel?
4. What were two common purposes for early novels?
5. What effects did John Wesley and George Whitefield have on society?

Apply the Concepts

6. What did the neoclassical literary critics appreciate in writing? Which characteristics of neoclassicism are evident in Pope's style?
7. Using the text, show how *Robinson Crusoe* demonstrates verisimilitude.
8. Why is ballad meter an appropriate choice for Cavalier poetry?
9. Provide two examples of alliteration, one from Herrick's "To the Virgins" and one from Lovelace's "To Lucasta" (p. 297). What effect does the sound device have in each poem respectively?
10. Explain what it means to annotate a text, including various ways to annotate. Provide an example of an annotated passage (at least eight lines or sentences long) for a selection from Unit 3, Part 1 or 2. Explain how your annotation improved your understanding of the selection.
11. How did Pepys use sensory details to document his experience? Use evidence from the text to explain your answer.
12. List four of the epic conventions and explain how they occur in *Paradise Lost*.

Evaluate the Ideas

13. How does Enlightenment thinking measure up against a biblical worldview? What premises are scriptural? What premises are not?
14. Using Scripture as support, evaluate the responses to God in Sonnet 19.
15. Is Satan the epic hero of *Paradise Lost*? Support your answer with details from the text.
16. Define *natural theology* and show how Pope's *An Essay on Man* reflects this philosophy with textual evidence. Finally, evaluate Pope's ideas biblically.

Write a Response

17. How do Addison's and Steele's essays qualify as Horatian satire? How does the selection from Swift's *Gulliver's Travels* exhibit Juvenalian satire? Which type of satire did you find most effective as a reader? Explain your reasoning.
18. Why does Milton argue in *Areopagitica* that it is profitable for mature readers to read widely, including from books that contain potentially censorable elements? What is one way the Bible supports his position? Can you offer an argument *for* censorship from Proverbs 4:13–27 that Milton does not consider in this excerpt? Explain why this additional argument is necessary biblically.

Define each term and provide an example of each from a selection in Unit 3, Part 1 or 2.

TERMS

rationalism
deism
neoclassicism
ballad meter
dramatic monologue
speaker
pamphlet
sonnet
blank verse
narrator
diary
sensory details
novel
verisimilitude
Horatian satire
heroic couplet
verse epistle
Juvenalian satire

UNIT 3

PART 3

Age of Johnson

Have you ever watched a pendulum swing? As soon as it gets to one side, it starts falling back in the opposite direction. This same pattern occurs frequently in society as well. Trends come and go, and often one trend is a reaction against the trend that came before it. The period known as the Age of Johnson is an example of the pendulum beginning to fall back. Early neoclassical writing had been highly focused on reason, logic, restraint, and an elegant, elevated style. The period of romanticism that followed would place more emphasis on emotions, subjective experience, and a more natural, free-flowing style of writing. The second half of the eighteenth century witnessed the peak of one period and the beginning of movement toward the other. Key writers and scholars of the era continued to emphasize the value of sound logic, moral restraint, and a balanced writing style. But they also broke with the neoclassical tradition on certain points.

The literary era was dominated by scholar-writer-critic Samuel Johnson. Johnson was a devout Anglican who was known for his powerful, scholarly mind, incisive argumentation, and practical wisdom. Like the writings of many neoclassicists, his often focused on the ability of knowledge (including biblical knowledge in his case) to improve the human condition. For instance, his best-known work today, the monumental *A Dictionary of the English Language,* standardized and clarified the English language for two altruistic purposes: (1) its preservation for future generations and (2) increased communicative power through a more precise standard for judging word choices.

Similarly, in his periodical, the *Rambler* (1750–52), Johnson used essays to offer his opinions on a variety of social topics, mostly from a neoclassical perspective and in neoclassical style. Especially key were his explorations in literary criticism. Essays such as *Rambler,* No. 4 (see pp. 365–66), displayed his nuanced theory of literature. Indeed, besides his dictionary, Johnson's role as a critic is often considered his greatest contribution to British literature.

Although Johnson shared earlier neoclassical writers' didactic purposes, he sometimes implemented them in new ways. For example, he advocated a more down-to-earth style of writing than figures such as Pope, a style focused on accurate and precise language that anyone could understand. Similarly, Johnson broke with past theories of biography. Rather than focusing on scandalous information to shock audiences or on glowing information to flatter or promote a particular person, Johnson sought to tell the truth. In his famous *Lives of the Poets,* he presented both good and bad facts about his subjects, often describing their lives in copious detail. By giving a truthful, balanced perspective on poets' lives, he hoped to teach lessons that would lead to better behavior. Appropriately, Johnson's protégé, James Boswell, adopted this concern for details and truth in writing his seminal biography of the great man.

Beneath this final flowering of neoclassicism flowed a new approach to literature, one dependent on the concept of **sensibility** (or *sentimentality*). Writers of this new tradition generally rejected the view of many neoclassicists that people are essentially self-seeking. Instead, they argued that people are naturally good, preferring to recognize humans' tendency to help their fellow man and sympathize with others, sharing joys and sorrows. The ability to sympathize, along with the ability to appreciate beauty (thought an emotional response), was seen as evidence of goodness. As a result, standards of correctness subtly moved from being conceived of as objective laws applied to corporate society to being more subjectively perceived and navigated through the lens of individual experiences.

Sentimental literature reflected this attitude by appealing to emotions rather than to reason, an appeal often meant to encourage goodness. Thus didactic *novels of sensibility*, such as Richardson's *Pamela,* induced audience sympathy for characters who, though placed in difficult situations, won out through their goodness (p. 332). Similarly, in drama, the *sentimental comedy* featured relatable middle-class protagonists who used goodness to defeat vice. These plays often elicited audience tears to create sympathy for their themes.

Additionally, some poetry also showed the influences of sensibility. Instead of being essentially public in nature and didactic in purpose, such works tended to be private and reflective of individual experience. Much like the sentimental comedy, the poetry often tugged on melancholy emotions. Most prominently, an unofficial group known as the Graveyard Poets wrote contemplations on death and life after death. One such poem (possibly the century's greatest), Thomas Gray's *Elegy Written in a Country Churchyard,* focused particularly on the common man in death. Of the works in this section, Gray's poem most clearly prefigured the coming of romanticism as the pendulum swung away from a century of neoclassical thought.

Samuel Johnson (1709–84)

AT A GLANCE

- **1750–52** Authored the *Rambler* (208 issues)
- **1755** Published *A Dictionary of the English Language*
- **1763** Met James Boswell
- **1765** Published *The Plays of William Shakespeare*
- **1781** Published *The Lives of the English Poets*

A Difficult Beginning

Author and lexicographer Samuel Johnson was the son of a Lichfield bookseller. In 1728 he went to Oxford, but the brilliant yet slothful Johnson wasted his opportunity. At his father's death (1731), Johnson returned to Lichfield without a degree. A time of poverty, aimlessness, and depression followed. His marriage in 1735 to a widow, Elizabeth Porter, rescued him from this dark period. Deeply devoted to him, Elizabeth encouraged him to become a professional writer.

Soon Johnson began writing for periodicals and assisting London booksellers (the publishers of the day) with publishing projects. Two early successes, *London* (a Juvenalian satire) and *Life of Mr. Richard Savage* (his first biography), set Johnson on a seemingly favorable path, but the young author still lacked the reputation needed for his next endeavor. In 1745 Johnson published a critical essay on *Macbeth* with proposals for a new edition of Shakespeare. But his recognition as a scholar-critic was insufficient to attract subscriptions (guarantees of purchase). This setback ended a decade of struggle (1736–45) to become a serious writer.

A Scholarly Achievement

From 1746 through 1755, as his abilities reached maturity, Johnson worked on the project for which he is best known—*A Dictionary of the English Language*. Impressively, Johnson completed the work in only nine years. To do so, he contracted six booksellers and employed six copyists. His method was simple, scholarly, and demanding: he began with a list of words from previous dictionaries, leaving spaces between entries for additions. Reading voluminously from English writers past and present, he underlined words he wished included and then gave the books to his copyists, who transcribed the words and their sentences for filing. The result, published in 1755 in two huge volumes, won the praise of learned societies throughout Europe. In England, Johnson's dictionary remained the authority on word meanings for more than a century.

While working on his dictionary, Johnson wrote several other significant works, including the *Rambler* (1750–52), a single-essay periodical that established his reputation as a moral essayist, and his finest poem, *The Vanity of Human Wishes* (1749). By 1755 his reputation as scholar, essayist, and poet was secure. His new prestige encouraged him in 1756 to again publish proposals for an edition of Shakespeare's plays. This time subscribers responded. His long-standing goal culminated in 1765 with the publication of this edition. Three years earlier, Johnson had received a royal pension of £300, assuring his financial security for life.

DID YOU KNOW ?

For most of his life Johnson suffered from poor eyesight, partial deafness, scars from childhood illnesses, and involuntary tics and spasms.

An Enduring Legacy

Along with his improved finances, good company also raised Johnson's spirits after his wife's death in 1752. In 1763 he met James Boswell, a lively young Scottish lord, and in 1764 Johnson and Sir Joshua Reynolds founded the Literary Club, a group of thinkers and writers (see introduction, p. 287) whose minds Johnson could seed with his conservative principles. Boswell's account of Johnson's club conversations reveals a wise, humane eccentric who was at once a tough-minded controversialist and a tenderhearted lover of mankind.

In his final years (1776–84) Johnson completed arguably his greatest literary achievement, fifty-two biographical and critical prefaces for a series of editions of verse by poets of the preceding century. In these prefaces, collected as *The Lives of the Most Eminent English Poets* in 1781, Johnson's penetrating mind and polished style appear at their best.

On December 13, 1784, Johnson left his friends and accomplishments behind. An attending physician reported that "[Johnson] talked often to me about the necessity of faith in the *sacrifice* of Jesus, as necessary . . . for the salvation of mankind." Johnson's long struggle to success climaxed in spiritual victory. In 1791 Johnson's earthly reputation was cemented with the publication of Boswell's great biography. Because of this work and Johnson's own writings, his stature as a person of integrity and deep humanity has continued and even increased.

ANALYZE: *Style and Literary Criticism*

Every author has a **style**, a mode of writing formed by a combination of elements such as syntax (word order), diction (word choice), figurative language, imagery, tone, and voice. Some authors deliberately break with the typical style of their era, but many make stylistic choices reflecting the preferences of their time and place. Although Samuel Johnson did advocate for some changes (p. 359) to the elevated diction and allusions of poets such as Pope, his prose style fulfilled many neoclassical requirements. His writing was very polished, incorporating precise diction and balanced, symmetrical sentences. Parallelism (p. 140) and an associated repetition of words helped create the latter feature. As you read the following selections, consider how this technique might enhance his writing's effectiveness.

But it was Johnson's ideas—as much as or more than his writing skills—that made him the dominant voice of his day. The two selections that follow show evidence of his scholarly mind. In the first, his preface to his *Dictionary*, Johnson defends his work from the criticism he predicts will ensue. How does he mitigate what he supposes people will point out as its flaws? The second passage, excerpted from one of his essays in the *Rambler*, is an example of **literary criticism** (p. 140). What part of literary criticism is he engaging in? Is he laying out criteria for good literature or judging the worth of particular pieces?

READ: *Infer Author's Tone and Voice*

One key part of an author's style is his or her **voice**, the unique imprint of an author's personality on a work. An author's voice is usually an impression the reader infers from the choices the writer makes for literary elements—from theme to characters, from narrative plots to favored poetic images or diction. Particularly important to gaining a sense of an author's personality is inferring his tone (p. 88) toward his content. As you read these selections, particularly the *Dictionary* excerpts, pay close attention to Johnson's tone. What does his attitude toward certain ideas tell you about his perspective on the world? What might his way of talking convey about his sense of self? For example, is his personality confident and forceful or calm and retiring? What can you infer about the man behind the literature?

EVALUATE: *A Critic's Theory of Literature*

Johnson was well respected for his thoughts on literary criticism. In *Rambler,* No. 4 he gives his personal answer to a key moral question authors must address. As you read, ascertain Johnson's key ideas. Then compare the approach Johnson advocates to the contents of popular television shows or movies of recent years. How might his criteria differ from modern approaches to storytelling? More importantly, how well do his ideas conform to the principles and practices of Scripture? Of the three criteria of Truth, Goodness, and Beauty (p. xi), which are Johnson's main ideas in the essay mostly concerned with?

OBJECTIVES

- Examine an author's key ideas in a text.
- Infer authorial tone from textual details.
- Analyze an author's style and voice.
- Evaluate critical approaches to literature.

VOCABULARY

immutably (ĭ-myo͞o′tə-blē) *adv.* Unchangeably.

aggregate (ăg′rĭ-gĭt) *adj.* Constituting or amounting to a whole; total.

insolence (ĭn′sə-ləns) *n.* Impertinently insulting behavior.

veracity (və-răs′ĭ-tē) *n.* Adherence to the truth; truthfulness.

abhor (ăb-hôr′) *tr.v.* To regard with horror or loathing; detest.

How hard can DEFINING WORDS *be?*

Johnson at first seemed to think he could bring complete order to the English language, systematizing it through logic and reason. He did bring more order to the chaos but found that the complex meanings and usages of individual words often eluded simple or final answers. Why might Johnson have had so much trouble pinning words down? Try to list all possible definitions of a common word. Check its entries in a dictionary. How many definitions did you miss?

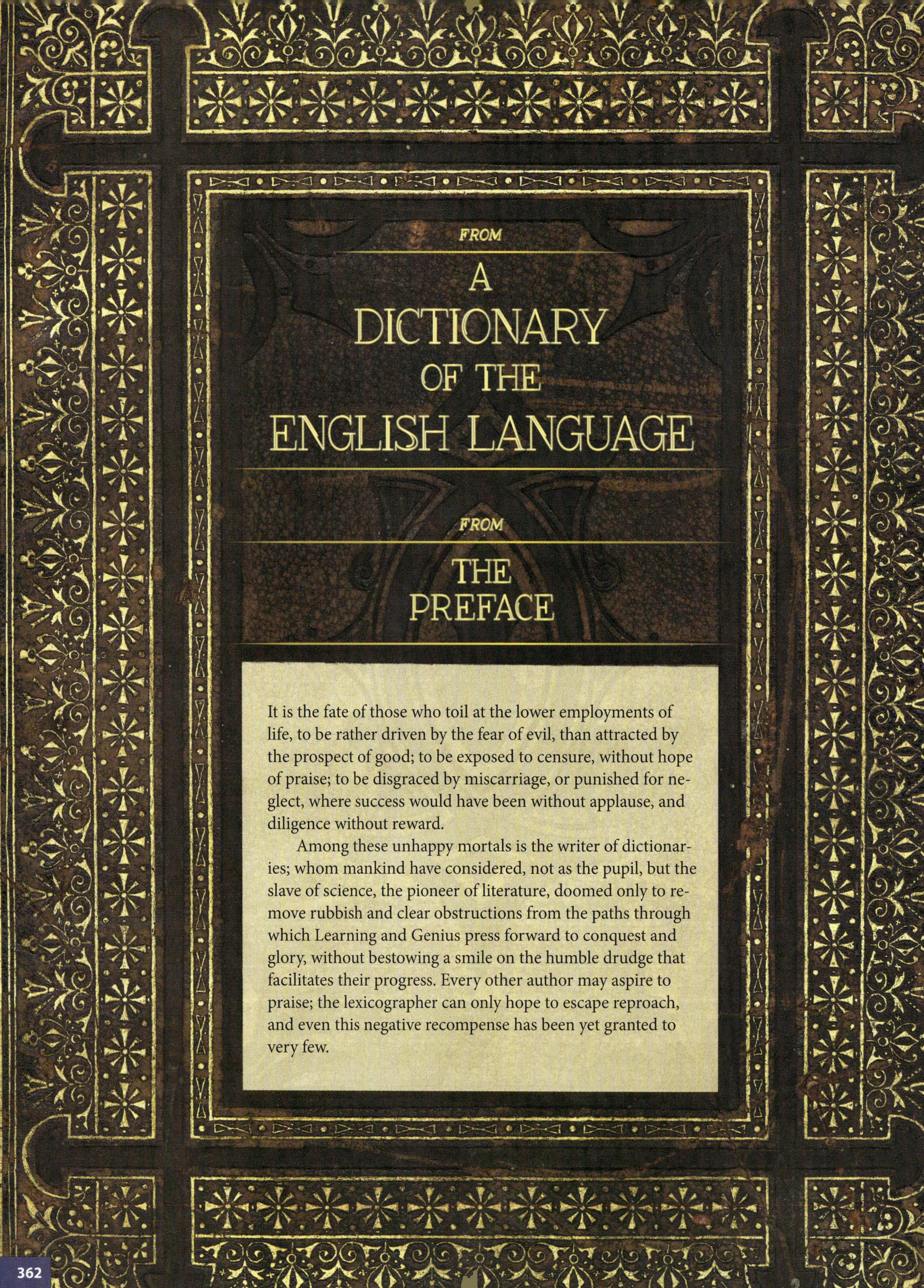

FROM

A DICTIONARY OF THE ENGLISH LANGUAGE

FROM

THE PREFACE

It is the fate of those who toil at the lower employments of life, to be rather driven by the fear of evil, than attracted by the prospect of good; to be exposed to censure, without hope of praise; to be disgraced by miscarriage, or punished for neglect, where success would have been without applause, and diligence without reward.

Among these unhappy mortals is the writer of dictionaries; whom mankind have considered, not as the pupil, but the slave of science, the pioneer of literature, doomed only to remove rubbish and clear obstructions from the paths through which Learning and Genius press forward to conquest and glory, without bestowing a smile on the humble drudge that facilitates their progress. Every other author may aspire to praise; the lexicographer can only hope to escape reproach, and even this negative recompense has been yet granted to very few.

have, notwithstanding this discouragement, attempted a *Dictionary of the English Language*. . . .

In hope of giving longevity to that which its own nature forbids to be immortal, I have devoted this book, the labor of years, to the honor of my country, that we may no longer yield the palm of philology, without a contest, to the nations of the continent. The chief glory of every people arises from its authors: whether I shall add anything by my own writings to the reputation of English literature, must be left to time: . . . but I shall not think my employment useless or ignoble, if by my assistance foreign nations, and distant ages, gain access to the propagators of knowledge, and understand the teachers of truth. . . .

When I am animated by this wish, I look with pleasure on my book, however defective, and deliver it to the world with the spirit of a man that has endeavored well. That it will immediately become popular I have not promised to myself: . . . but useful diligence will at last prevail, and there never can be wanting some who distinguish desert; who will consider that no dictionary of a living tongue ever can be perfect, since while it is hastening to publication, some words are budding, and some falling away; that a whole life cannot be spent upon syntax and etymology, and that even a whole life would not be sufficient; . . . that a writer will sometimes be hurried by eagerness to the end, and sometimes faint with weariness under a task. . . . A

Style: What technique does Johnson use repeatedly in these first few paragraphs to create symmetrical sentences? How might it help communicate his ideas more effectively? A

In this work, when it shall be found that much is omitted, let it not be forgotten that much likewise is performed; and though no book was ever spared out of tenderness to the author, and the world is little solicitous to know whence proceeded the faults of that which it condemns; yet it may gratify curiosity to inform it, that the *English Dictionary* was written with little assistance of the learned, and without any patronage of the great; not in the soft obscurities of retirement, or under the shelter of academic bowers, but amid inconvenience and distraction, in sickness and in sorrow. It may repress the triumph of malignant criticism to observe, that if our language is not here fully displayed, I have only failed in an attempt which no human powers have hitherto completed. If the lexicons of ancient tongues, now **immutably** fixed, and comprised in a few volumes, be yet, after the toil of successive ages, inadequate and delusive; if the **aggregated** knowledge, and cooperating diligence of the Italian academicians, did not secure them from the censure of Beni; if the embodied critics of France, when fifty years had been spent upon their work, were obliged to change its economy, and give their second edition another form, I may surely be contented without the praise of perfection, which, if I could obtain, in this gloom of solitude, what would it avail me? I have protracted my work till most of those whom I wished to please have sunk into the grave, and success and miscarriage are empty sounds; I therefore dismiss it with frigid tranquility, having little to fear or hope from censure or from praise. R

immutably (ĭ-myo͞o′tə-blē) *adv.* Unchangeably.

aggregate (ăg′rĭ-gĭt) *adj.* Constituting or amounting to a whole; total.

Infer Tone/Voice: What tone does Johnson express toward his work throughout his preface? What is your impression of Johnson's personality, his voice, throughout? R

from

A Dictionary of the English

The following definitions are excerpts from entries in Johnson's Dictionary. *Not all of the possible definitions for each word are included here, although most are Johnson's first entries. Note that several include examples of the word used in context. Johnson almost always included such examples, an unusual practice for the time. He rightly thought they could help convey the nuances of various entries. Such examples are now standard practice in dictionaries.*

Dull. *adj.*

1. Stupid; doltish; blockish; slow of understanding.
2. Not exhilarating; not delightful: as *to make dictionaries is* dull *work.*

Lexicographer. *n.* A writer of dictionaries; a harmless drudge, that busies himself in tracing the original, and detailing the signification of words.

Oats. *n.* A grain, which in England is generally given to horses, but in Scotland supports the people.

> It is of the grass leaved tribe, the flowers have no petals, and are disposed in a loose panicle:[1] the grain is eatable. The meal makes tolerable good bread. *Miller.*

> His horse's allowance of *oats* and beans, was greater than the journey required. *Swift.*

Patron. *n.*

1. One who countenances,[2] supports, or protects. Commonly a wretch who supports with **insolence**, and is paid with flattery.

> I'll plead for you, as for my *patron*. *Shakespeare.*

2. A guardian saint.

3. Advocate; defender; vindicator.

1. *panicle:* spray of flowers
2. *countenances:* permits

insolence (ĭn'sə-ləns) *n.* Impertinently insulting behavior.

Infer Voice: What do you learn about Johnson's personality from the first two entries? How might the next three entries also reflect his personal perspectives? R

Pension. *n.* An allowance made to any one without an equivalent. In England it is generally understood to mean pay given to a state hireling for treason to his country. R

> He has lived with the great without flattery, and been a friend to men in power without *pensions*. *Pope.*

Tory. *n.* [A cant term, derived, I suppose, from an Irish word signifying a savage.] One who adheres to the ancient constitution of the state, and the apostolical hierarchy of the Church of England: opposed to a *Whig.*

> The knight is more a *Tory* in the country than the town, because it more advances his interest. *Addison.*

Whig. *n.* The name of a faction.

> Whoever has a true value for church and state, should avoid the extremes of *Whig* for the sake of the former, and the extremes of Tory on the account of the latter. *Swift.*

Wit. *n.*

1. The powers of the mind; the mental faculties; the intellects. This is the original signification.

> For *wit* and pow'r their last endeavors bend
> T' outshine each other. *Dryden.*

2. Imagination; quickness of fancy.

> They never seem to meet but there's a skirmish of *wit* between them. —Alas, in our last conflict, four of his five wits went halting off, and now is the old man govern'd by one. *Shakespeare.*

Youth. *n.* The part of life succeeding to childhood and adolescence; the time from fourteen to twenty-eight.

> But could *youth* last, and love still breed,
> Had joys no date, and age no need;
> Then these delights my mind might move,
> To live with thee, and be thy love. *Raleigh.*

THE RAMBLER.

FROM NUMB. 4 PRICE 2 ¢.

SATURDAY, *March 31, 1750*

The works of fiction, with which the present generation seems more particularly delighted, are such as exhibit life in its true state, diversified only by accidents that daily happen in the world, and influenced by passions and qualities which are really to be found in conversing with mankind. . . .

It is therefore precluded from the machines[1] and expedients of the heroic romance, and can neither employ giants to snatch away a lady from the nuptial rites[2] nor knights to bring her back from captivity; it can neither bewilder its personages in deserts, nor lodge them in imaginary castles. . . .

In the romances formerly written, every transaction and sentiment was so remote from all that passes among men, that the reader was in very little danger of making any applications to himself; the virtues and crimes were equally beyond his sphere of activity; and he amused himself with heroes and with traitors, deliverers and persecutors, as with beings of another species, whose actions were regulated upon motives of their own, and who had neither faults nor excellencies in common with himself.

But when an adventurer is levelled with the rest of the world, and acts in such scenes of the universal drama, as may be the lot of any other man; young spectators[3] fix their eyes upon him with closer attention, and hope, by observing his behavior and success, to regulate their own practices, when they shall be engaged in the like part. . . .

The chief advantage which these fictions have over real life is, that their authors are at liberty, though not to invent, yet to select objects, and to cull from the mass of mankind, those individuals upon which the attention ought most to be employed: as a diamond, though it cannot be made, may be polished by art, and placed in such a situation, as to display that luster which before was buried among common stones.

It is justly considered as the greatest excellency of art, to imitate nature; but it is necessary to distinguish those parts of nature, which are most proper for imitation: greater care is still required in representing life, which is so often discolored by passion, or deformed by wickedness. If the world be promiscuously[4] described, I cannot see of what use it can be to read the account: or why it may not be as safe to turn the eye immediately upon mankind as upon a mirror which shows all that presents itself without discrimination.

It is therefore not a sufficient vindication of a character, that it is drawn as it appears; for many characters ought never to be drawn: nor of a narrative, that the train of events is agreeable to observation and experience; for that observation which is called knowledge of the world, will be found much more frequently to make men cunning than good. The purpose of these writings is surely not only to show mankind, but to provide that they may be seen

1. *machines:* "a literary device used to produce an effect, especially the introduction of a supernatural being to resolve a plot" (*AHD*)
2. *nuptial rites:* marriage ceremony
3. *young spectators:* In another part of his essay, Johnson identifies the typical readers of these works as those who are young, impressionable, and particularly vulnerable to corruption.
4. *promiscuously:* "in a promiscuous manner; without distinction, discrimination, or order; indiscriminately, at random" (*OED*)

hereafter with less hazard; to teach the means of avoiding the snares which are laid by Treachery for Innocence, without infusing any wish for that superiority with which the betrayer flatters his vanity; to give the power of counteracting fraud, without the temptation to practice it; to initiate youth by mock encounters in the art of necessary defense, and to increase prudence without impairing virtue. A

Many writers, for the sake of following nature, so mingle good and bad qualities in their principal personages, that they are both equally conspicuous; and as we accompany them through their adventures with delight, and are led by degrees to interest ourselves in their favor, we lose the abhorrence of their faults, because they do not hinder our pleasure, or, perhaps, regard them with some kindness, for being united with so much merit.

There have been men indeed splendidly wicked, whose endowments threw a brightness on their crimes, and whom scarce any villany made perfectly detestable, because they never could be wholly divested of their excellencies; but such have been in all ages the great corrupters of the world, and their resemblance ought no more to be preserved, than the art of murdering without pain. . . .

In narratives where historical **veracity** has no place, I cannot discover why there should not be exhibited the most perfect idea of virtue; of virtue not angelical, nor above probability, for what we cannot credit, we shall never imitate, but the highest and purest that humanity can reach, which, exercised in such trials as the various revolutions of things shall bring upon it, may, by conquering some calamities, and enduring others, teach us what we may hope, and what we can perform. Vice, for vice is necessary to be shown, should always disgust; nor should the graces of gaiety, or the dignity of courage, be so united with it, as to reconcile it to the mind. Wherever it appears, it should raise hatred by the malignity of its practices, and contempt by the meanness of its stratagems: for while it is supported by either parts or spirit, it will be seldom heartily **abhorred**. The Roman tyrant was content to be hated, if he was but feared; and there are thousands of the readers of romances willing to be thought wicked, if they may be allowed to be wits. It is therefore to be steadily inculcated, that virtue is the highest proof of understanding, and the only solid basis of greatness; and that vice is the natural consequence of narrow thoughts; that it begins in mistake, and ends in ignominy. E

Literary Criticism: What new kind of literature is Johnson critiquing in this passage? How does he believe this approach can be a moral asset? What possible problem can it also result in, according to him? A

veracity (və-răs′ĭ-tē) *n.* Adherence to the truth; truthfulness.

abhor (ăb-hôr′) *tr.v.* To regard with horror or loathing; detest.

Theory of Literature: How does Johnson feel about representing evil? E

THINK AND DISCUSS

1. According to Johnson, what challenges did he face in writing the *Dictionary*?
2. From the preface, what can you infer formed at least part of Johnson's motivation to create a dictionary?
3. Compare Johnson's dictionary entries to modern dictionary entries. How are they different?
4. What kind of literature does Johnson examine in *Rambler,* No. 4? What moral dimension of this genre does he address in his literary critical essay?
5. Summarize Johnson's main conclusion or argument in *Rambler,* No. 4.
6. How would you describe Johnson's style? Use examples to explain your answer.
7. What various tones toward his topics does Johnson express in the excerpts from his dictionary?
8. What sense of Johnson as a person do you get from his writings? How would you describe his voice? Support your answer from the text.
9. Compare Johnson's literary critical argument in *Rambler,* No. 4 with the ideas of either Milton (in *Areopagitica*) or Pope (in *Essay on Criticism*). How are their ideas similar or different?
10. Of Truth, Goodness, and Beauty, which standard does Johnson seem to focus on in *Rambler*, No. 4? How does his perspective on the issue compare with scriptural ideas and practice?

James Boswell (1740–95)

Born to a Scottish nobleman and judge, James Boswell left Edinburgh for London in 1762, escaping what he felt was parental tyranny to seek a military appointment. Unsuccessful, he stayed through the winter, visiting sights and relishing city life. Chief on his list of attractions was the venerable Samuel Johnson, whom he soon contrived to meet. Johnson, then fifty-four, was well established in his career; the twenty-two-year-old Boswell, a brash extrovert full of energy and charm, was quite unlike Johnson. Nonetheless, mutual fascination and affection soon sprung up. Johnson reluctantly parted from his young friend in 1763 when Boswell left to study law. Upon completing his studies and a continental tour (during which he met political and literary figures such as Voltaire and Rousseau), Boswell returned to Great Britain in 1766 and was admitted to the Scottish bar.

Boswell practiced law in Edinburgh but, during the courts' recesses, visited London to expand his friendship with Johnson. In 1773 he achieved two triumphs: (1) admittance to the Literary Club and (2) Johnson's agreement to travel with him through Scotland. In his journal, kept since 1758, he recorded much of this time in minute detail, analyzing his experiences and behavior. The journals, discovered in the 1920s and 1930s, reveal his own complex, unstable personality. They also show a stage in the process of creating his final, published image of Johnson. The journal was the source for many recorded conversations later made famous in Boswell's *Journal of a Tour to the Hebrides* (1785) and *The Life of Samuel Johnson, LL.D.* (1791).

Seven years after Johnson's death, Boswell published his biography. At the time, it was unusual for its mass of firsthand materials, its frank portrayal of Johnson (an approach Johnson himself advocated for), and its artistic worth. Boswell had a journalist's sense for detail, a playwright's ability to dramatize, and a lawyer's concern for accuracy and thoroughness. The result is a monument of scholarship and literary artistry. A fitting tribute from Boswell to his friend, it in many ways defined subsequent perceptions of Johnson.

BEFORE READING

ANALYZE: *Biography, Dialogue, and Anecdote*

Boswell's **biography** (a nonfiction account of the life events of a real person other than the author) helped pioneer the use of meticulous research to paint a full picture of a person's life. Boswell exhausted accessible documents and interviews and drew on his copious correspondence with and personal records of Johnson. He framed this information as **anecdotes**, short narratives of interesting or amusing incidents, incorporating **dialogue** (conversations between characters) from his memory and records. As you read, consider how these explicitly or implicitly characterize Johnson.

READ: *Infer Author's Purpose*

Johnson believed that a truthful biography should present a balanced view of its subject, including the good and the bad. He also wrote biographies as moral examples for readers and felt that people painted as angelically good were impossible to emulate (see *Rambler,* No. 4). How might the following excerpts show Boswell's attempt to follow Johnson's broad approach and didactic purpose for biographies?

EVALUATE: *Perspective on Death*

Johnson was well known for his fear of death and of the possible loss of his mental faculties (he frequently suffered from depression). At the same time, he was a devout Christian. As you read Boswell's passages on Johnson's final days, consider how passages such as Psalm 23:4–5, Isaiah 41:10, John 14:1–6, and 2 Corinthians 5:6–8 can help believers navigate such waters. Did Johnson seem to gain victory over his fears?

OBJECTIVES

- Identify characteristics of biography in a text.
- Analyze a work's characterization through the use of dialogue and anecdote.
- Infer an author's purpose for a work.
- Evaluate a perspective on death.

VOCABULARY

presumptuous (prĭ-zŭmp′cho͞o-əs) *adj.* Going beyond what is right or proper; excessively forward.

sophistry (sŏf′ĭ-strē) *n.* A plausible but misleading or fallacious argument.

alacrity (ə-lăk′rĭ-tē) *n.* Speed or quickness.

assiduity (ăs′ĭ-do͞o′ĭ-tē) *n.* Persistent application or diligence; unflagging effort.

from The Life of Samuel Johnson, LL.D.

1763

This is to me a memorable year; for in it I had the happiness to obtain the acquaintance of that extraordinary man whose memoirs I am now writing; an acquaintance which I shall ever esteem as one of the most fortunate circumstances in my life. Though then but two-and-twenty, I had for several years read his works with delight and instruction, and had the highest reverence for their author, which had grown up in my fancy into a kind of mysterious veneration by figuring to myself a state of solemn elevated abstraction, in which I supposed him to live in the immense metropolis of London. Mr. Gentleman, a native of Ireland, who passed some years in Scotland as a player, and as an instructor in the English language, a man whose talents and worth were depressed by misfortunes, had given me a representation of the figure and manner of Dictionary Johnson! as he was then generally called; and during my first visit to London, which was for three months in 1760, Mr. Derrick the poet, who was Gentleman's friend and countryman, flattered me with hopes that he would introduce me to Johnson, an honor of which I was very ambitious. But he never found an opportunity; which made me doubt that he had promised to do what was not in his power; till Johnson some years afterwards told me, "Derrick, Sir, might very well have introduced you. I had a kindness for Derrick, and am sorry he is dead." . . . **A**

Mr. Thomas Davies the actor, who then kept a bookseller's shop in Russell Street, Covent Garden, told me that Johnson was very much his friend and came frequently to his house, where he more than once invited me to meet him; but by some unlucky accident or other he was prevented from coming to us.

Mr. Thomas Davies was a man of good understanding and talents, with the advantage of a liberal education. Though somewhat pompous, he was an entertaining companion; and his literary performances have no inconsiderable share of merit. He was a friendly and very hospitable man. Both he and his wife (who has been celebrated for her beauty), though upon the stage for many years, maintained an uniform decency of character; and Johnson esteemed them, and lived in as easy an intimacy with them as with any family which he used to visit. Mr. Davies recollected several of Johnson's remarkable sayings, and was one of the best of the many imitators of his voice and manner, while relating them. He increased my impatience more and more to see the extraordinary man whose works I highly valued, and whose conversation was reported to be so peculiarly excellent.

At last, on Monday, the 16th of May, when I was sitting in Mr. Davies's back parlor, after having drunk tea with him and Mrs. Davies, Johnson unexpectedly came into the shop; and Mr. Davies having perceived him through the glass door in the room in which we were sitting, advancing towards us, he announced his aweful approach to me, somewhat in the manner of an actor in the part of Horatio,[1] when he addresses Hamlet on the appearance of his father's ghost, "Look, my Lord, it comes." I found that I had a very perfect idea of Johnson's figure, from the portrait of him painted by Sir Joshua Reynolds[2] soon after he had published his *Dictionary*, in the attitude of sitting in his easy chair in deep meditation, which was the first picture his friend did for him, which Sir Joshua very kindly presented to me, and from which an engraving has been made for this work. Mr. Davies mentioned my name, and respectfully introduced me to him. I was much agitated; and recollecting his prejudice against the Scotch, of which I had heard much, I said to Davies, "Don't tell where I come from." — "From Scotland," cried Davies roguishly. "Mr. Johnson," said I, "I do indeed come from Scotland, but I cannot help it." I am willing to flatter myself that I meant this as light pleasantry to soothe and conciliate him, and not as an humiliating abasement at the expense of my country. But however that might be, this speech was somewhat unlucky; for with that quickness of wit for which he was so remarkable, he seized the expression "come from Scotland," which I used in the sense of being of that country; and, as if I had said that I had come away from it, or left it, retorted, "That, Sir, I find, is what a very great many of your countrymen cannot help." This stroke[3] stunned me a good deal; and when we had sat down, I felt myself not a little embarrassed, and apprehensive of what might come next. He then addressed himself to Davies: "What do you think

1. *Horatio:* Hamlet's most loyal friend throughout Shakespeare's play
2. *Joshua Reynolds:* foremost painter of his generation and cofounder of the Literary Club
3. *stroke:* "an inspired or effective idea or act" (*AHD*)

Biography: According to Boswell, what did he imagine Johnson would be like? **A**

of Garrick?[4] He has refused me an order for the play for Miss Williams, because he knows the house will be full, and that an order would be worth three shillings." Eager to take any opening to get into conversation with him, I ventured to say, "O, Sir, I cannot think Mr. Garrick would grudge such a trifle to you." "Sir," said he, with a stern look, "I have known David Garrick longer than you have done: and I know no right you have to talk to me on the subject." Perhaps I deserved this check; for it was rather **presumptuous** in me, an entire stranger, to express any doubt of the justice of his animadversion[5] upon his old acquaintance and pupil. I now felt myself much mortified, and began to think that the hope which I had long indulged of obtaining his acquaintance was blasted. And, in truth, had not my ardor been uncommonly strong, and my resolution uncommonly persevering, so rough a reception might have deterred me forever from making any further attempts. . . .

I was highly pleased with the extraordinary vigor of his conversation, and regretted that I was drawn away from it by an engagement at another place. I had, for a part of the evening, been left alone with him, and had ventured to make an observation now and then, which he received very civilly; so that I was satisfied that though there was a roughness in his manner, there was no ill-nature in his disposition. Davies followed me to the door, and when I complained to him a little of the hard blows which the great man had given me, he kindly took upon him to console me by saying, "Don't be uneasy. I can see he likes you very well." **A**

A few days afterwards I called on Davies, and asked him if he thought I might take the liberty of waiting on Mr. Johnson at his chambers in the Temple.[6] He said I certainly might, and that Mr. Johnson would take it as a compliment. So upon Tuesday, the 24th of May, after having been enlivened by the witty sallies[7] of Messieurs Thornton, Wilkes, Churchill and Lloyd,[8] with whom I had passed the morning, I boldly repaired to Johnson. His chambers were on the first floor of No. 1, Inner-Temple Lane, and I entered them with an impression given me by the Reverend Dr. Blair of Edinburgh,[9] who had been introduced to him not long before and

4. *Garrick:* renowned actor and producer of Shakespeare who was Johnson's student before the two came to London

5. *animadversion:* "a criticism" (*OED*)

6. *Temple:* region between Fleet Street and the Thames containing schools and living quarters for law students

7. *sallies:* excursions; going forth, setting out

8. *Messieurs . . . Lloyd:* radicals and cynics whose company Boswell enjoyed

9. *Reverend Dr. Blair of Edinburgh:* an admired preacher of Edinburgh known for his published collection of sermons

presumptuous (prĭ-zŭmp′cho͞o-əs) *adj.* Going beyond what is right or proper; excessively forward.

Dialogue/Anecdote: How does Boswell use their first meeting's dialogue to characterize Johnson? What are his conclusions about Johnson's character? **A**

described his having "found the Giant in his den," an expression which, when I came to be pretty well acquainted with Johnson, I repeated to him, and he was diverted at this picturesque account of himself. Dr. Blair had been presented to him by Dr. James Fordyce.[10] At this time the controversy concerning the pieces published by Mr. James Macpherson,[11] as translations of Ossian, was at its height. Johnson had all along denied their authenticity; and, what was still more provoking to their admirers, maintained that they had no merit. The subject having been introduced by Dr. Fordyce, Dr. Blair, relying on the internal evidence of their antiquity, asked Dr. Johnson whether he thought any man of a modern age could have written such poems? Johnson replied, "Yes, Sir, many men, many women, and many children." Johnson, at this time, did not know that Dr. Blair had just published a dissertation not only defending their authenticity but seriously ranking them with the poems of Homer and Virgil; and when he was afterwards informed of this circumstance, he expressed some displeasure at Dr. Fordyce's having suggested the topic, and said, "I am not sorry that they got thus much for their pains. Sir, it was like leading one to talk of a book when the author is concealed behind the door."

He received me very courteously; but, it must be confessed, that his apartment, and furniture, and morning dress, were sufficiently uncouth. His brown suit of clothes looked very rusty; he had on a little old shriveled unpowdered wig, which was too small for his head; his shirt neck and knees of his breeches were loose; his black worsted stockings ill drawn up; and he had a pair of unbuckled shoes by way of slippers. But all these slovenly particularities were forgotten the moment that he began to talk. Some gentlemen, whom I do not recollect, were sitting with him; and when they went away, I also rose; but he said to me, "Nay, don't go." "Sir," said I, "I am afraid that I intrude upon you. It is benevolent to allow me to sit and hear you." He seemed pleased with this compliment, which I sincerely paid him, and answered, "Sir, I am obliged[12] to any man who visits me." . . . R

On Saturday, July 30, Dr. Johnson and I took a sculler at the Temple Stairs and set out for Greenwich.[13] I asked him if he really thought a knowledge of the Greek and Latin languages an essential requisite to a good education. Johnson. "Most certainly, Sir; for those who know them have a very great advantage over those who do not. Nay, Sir, it is wonderful what a difference learning makes upon people even in the common

10. *Dr. James Fordyce:* a popular Presbyterian preacher and writer
11. *Mr. James Macpherson:* A Scottish man who published a successful translation of ancient Scottish verse. Samuel Johnson searched for the original manuscripts, but because he couldn't find them, he denounced them as fakes. Upon Macpherson's death, Johnson was proven right.

12. *obliged:* to be grateful or indebted
13. *Greenwich:* a popular ten-mile boat trip downriver

Author's Purpose: How have Boswell's characterizations of Johnson so far pursued the balanced perspective that Johnson himself recommended for biographies? R

is the natural feeling of mankind; and every human being whose mind is not debauched will be willing to give all that he has to get knowledge."

We landed at the Old Swan, and walked to Billingsgate, where we took oars, and moved smoothly along the silver Thames. It was a very fine day. We were entertained with the immense number and variety of ships that were lying at anchor, and with the beautiful country on each side of the river. . . .

Afterwards he entered upon the business of the day, which was to give me his advice as to a course of study. And here I am to mention with much regret, that my record of what he said is miserably scanty. I recollect with admiration an animating blaze of eloquence, which roused every intellectual power in me to the highest pitch, but must have dazzled me so much that my memory could not preserve the substance of his discourse; for the note which I find of it is no more than this:—"He ran over the grand scale of human knowledge; advised me to select some particular branch to excel in, but to acquire a little of every kind." . . .

We walked in the evening in Greenwich Park. He asked me, I suppose by way of trying my disposition, "Is not this very fine?" Having no exquisite relish of the beauties of nature, and being more delighted with "the busy hum of men," I answered, "Yes, Sir; but not equal to Fleet Street." Johnson. "You are right, Sir." . . .

We stayed so long at Greenwich that our sail up the river, in our return to London, was by no means so pleasant as in the morning; for the night air was so cold that it made me shiver. I was the more sensible of it from having sat up all the night before, recollecting and writing in my journal what I thought worthy of preservation, an exertion, which, during the first part of my acquaintance with Johnson, I frequently made. I remember having sat up four nights in one week, without being much incommoded[15] in the daytime. . . .

We concluded the day at the Turk's Head coffeehouse very socially. He was pleased to listen to a particular account which I gave him of my family, and of its

intercourse of life, which does not appear to be much connected with it." "And yet," said I, "people go through the world very well, and carry on the business of life to good advantage, without learning." Johnson. "Why, Sir, that may be true in cases where learning cannot possibly be of any use; for instance, this boy rows us as well without learning, as if he could sing the song of Orpheus to the Argonauts,[14] who were the first sailors." He then called to the boy, "What would you give, my lad, to know about the Argonauts?" "Sir," said the boy, "I would give what I have." Johnson was much pleased with his answer, and we gave him a double fare. Dr. Johnson then turning to me, "Sir," said he, "a desire of knowledge

14. *Argonauts:* a band of heroes in Greek mythology who in the years before the Trojan War accompanied Jason in his quest to find the golden fleece

15. *incommoded:* disadvantaged

hereditary estate, as to the extent and population of which he asked questions and made calculations, recommending, at the same time, a liberal kindness to the tenantry, as people over whom the proprietor was placed by Providence. He took delight in hearing my description of the romantic seat[16] of my ancestors. "I must be there, Sir," said he, "and we will live in the old castle; and if there is not a room in it remaining, we will build one." I was highly flattered, but could scarcely indulge a hope that Auchinleck would indeed be honored by his presence and celebrated by a description, as it afterwards was, in his *Journey to the Western Islands.* **A**

After we had again talked of my setting out for Holland, he said, "I must see thee out of England; I will accompany you to Harwich." I could not find words to express what I felt upon this unexpected and very great mark of his affectionate regard. . . .

On Friday, August 5, we set out early in the morning in the Harwich stage coach. . . .

Next day we got to Harwich to dinner; and my passage in the packet-boat to Helvoetsluys being secured, and my baggage put on board, we dined at our inn by ourselves. . . .

We went and looked at the church, and having gone into it and walked up to the altar, Johnson, whose piety was constant and fervent, sent me to my knees, saying, "Now that you are going to leave your native country, recommend yourself to the protection of your Creator and Redeemer."

After we came out of the church, we stood talking for some time together of Bishop Berkeley's ingenious **sophistry** to prove the non-existence of matter, and that everything in the universe is merely ideal. I observed that though we are satisfied his doctrine is not true, it is impossible to refute it. I never shall forget the **alacrity** with which Johnson answered, striking his foot with mighty force against a large stone, till he rebounded from it, "I refute it *thus.*" . . .

My revered friend walked down with me to the beach, where we embraced and parted with tenderness and engaged to correspond by letters. I said, "I hope, Sir, you will not forget me in my absence." JOHNSON. "Nay, Sir, it is more likely you should forget me, than that I should forget you." As the vessel put out to sea, I kept my eyes upon him for a considerable time, while he remained rolling[17] his majestic frame in his usual manner: and at last I perceived him walk back into the town, and he disappeared.

16. *romantic seat:* quaint family residence

Anecdote: From the anecdote of the two at the coffeehouse, what development do we see in Boswell's friendship with Johnson? What side of Johnson is Boswell revealing? **A**

sophistry (sŏf′ĭ-strē) *n.* A plausible but misleading or fallacious argument.

alacrity (ə-lăk′rĭ-tē) *n.* Speed or quickness.

1784

Amidst the melancholy clouds which hung over the dying Johnson, his characteristical manner showed itself on different occasions.

When Dr. Warren, in the usual style, hoped that he was better; his answer was, "No, Sir; you cannot conceive with what acceleration I advance towards death."

A man whom he had never seen before was employed one night to sit up with him. Being asked next morning how he liked his attendant, his answer was, "Not at all, Sir: the fellow's an idiot; he is as awkward as a turnspit[18] when first put into the wheel, and as sleepy as a dormouse."

Mr. Windham having placed a pillow conveniently to support him, he thanked him for his kindness, and said, "That will do,—all that a pillow can do." . . .

As he opened a note which his servant brought to him, he said, "An odd thought strikes me: we shall receive no letters in the grave."

He requested three things of Sir Joshua Reynolds:—To forgive him thirty pounds which he had borrowed of him; to read the Bible; and never to use his pencil on a Sunday. Sir Joshua readily acquiesced.

Indeed he shewed the greatest anxiety for the religious improvement of his friends, to whom he discoursed of its infinite consequence. He begged of Mr. Hoole to think of what he had said, and to commit it to writing: and, upon being afterwards assured that this was done, pressed his hands, and in an earnest tone thanked him. Dr. Brocklesby having attended him with the utmost **assiduity** and kindness as his physician and friend, he was peculiarly desirous that this gentleman should not entertain any loose speculative notions, but be confirmed in the truths of Christianity, and insisted on his writing down in his presence, as nearly as he could collect it, the import of what passed on the subject: and Dr. Brocklesby having complied with the request, he made him sign the paper, and urged him to keep it in his own custody as long as he lived. **R**

17. *rolling:* shifting from foot to foot
18. *as . . . turnspit:* a dog placed in a treadmill to turn roasting meat

assiduity (ăs′ĭ-do͞o′ĭ-tē) *n.* Persistent application or diligence; unflagging effort.

Author's Purpose: The previous few anecdotes are meant to illustrate what Boswell calls Johnson's "characteristical manner." What qualities does he use them to illustrate? **R**

Johnson, with that native fortitude, which, amidst all his bodily distress and mental sufferings, never forsook him, asked Dr. Brocklesby, as a man in whom he had confidence, to tell him plainly whether he could recover. "Give me," said he, "a direct answer." The doctor having first asked him if he could bear the whole truth, which way soever it might lead, and being answered that he could, declared that, in his opinion, he could not recover without a miracle. "Then," said Johnson, "I will take no more physic, not even my opiates; for I have prayed that I may render up my soul to God unclouded." In this resolution he persevered and, at the same time, used only the weakest kinds of sustenance. Being pressed by Mr. Windham to take somewhat more generous nourishment, lest too low a diet should have the very effect which he dreaded, by debilitating his mind, he said, "I will take anything but inebriating sustenance." . . .

Mr. Strahan[19] has given me the agreeable assurance that, after being in much agitation, Johnson became quite composed, and continued so till his death.

Dr. Brocklesby, who will not be suspected of fanaticism, obliged me with the following accounts:—

"For some time before his death, all his fears were calmed and absorbed by the prevalence of his faith, and his trust in the merits and *propitiation* of Jesus Christ.

"He talked often to me about the necessity of faith in the *sacrifice* of Jesus, as necessary beyond all good works whatever, for the salvation of mankind. . . ."

Having, as has been already mentioned, made his will on the 8th and 9th of December, and settled all his worldly affairs, he languished till Monday, the 13th of that month, when he expired about seven o'clock in the evening with so little apparent pain that his attendants hardly perceived when his dissolution took place.

19. *Mr. Strahan:* Rev. George Strahan (1744–1824), later publisher of Johnson's *Prayers and Meditations*

Of his last moments, my brother, Thomas David, has furnished me with the following particulars:—

"The doctor, from the time that he was certain his death was near, appeared to be perfectly resigned, was seldom or never fretful or out of temper, and often said to his faithful servant, who gave me this account, 'Attend, Francis, to the salvation of your soul, which is the object of greatest importance': he also explained to him passages in the scripture, and seemed to have pleasure in talking upon religious subjects.

"On Monday, the 13th of December, the day on which he died, a Miss Morris, daughter to a particular friend of his, called, and said to Francis that she begged to be permitted to see the doctor that she might earnestly request him to give her his blessing. Francis went into his room, followed by the young lady, and delivered the message. The doctor turned himself in the bed, and said, 'God bless you, my dear!' These were the last words he spoke. His difficulty of breathing increased till about seven o'clock in the evening, when Mr. Barber and Mrs. Desmoulins, who were sitting in the room, observing that the noise he made in breathing had ceased, went to the bed, and found he was dead." . . . E

I trust, I shall not be accused of affectation, when I declare, that I find myself unable to express all that I felt upon the loss of such a "Guide, Philosopher, and Friend." I shall, therefore, not say one word of my own, but adopt those of an eminent friend, which he uttered with an abrupt felicity, superior to all studied compositions:— "He has made a chasm which not only nothing can fill up, but which nothing has a tendency to fill up. Johnson is dead. Let us go to the next best:—there is nobody; no man can be said to put you in mind of Johnson."

Perspective on Death: Do you see evidence of fear of death in Johnson's last hours? E

THINK AND DISCUSS

1. Why was Boswell so desirous of meeting Johnson?
2. What seems to be Boswell's intent for writing a biography of Johnson? Support your answer broadly from the text.
3. Select a dialogue between Boswell and Johnson and explain how it characterizes Johnson.
4. Select an anecdote and explain how it explicitly and implicitly characterizes Johnson.
5. What do you think is the value of using anecdote and actual dialogue in a biography? What effects do these create in readers that pure description might not?
6. How might passages such as Psalm 23:4–5, Isaiah 41:10, John 14:1–6, and 2 Corinthians 5:6–8 help believers face their fears? Did Johnson seem to have gained such comfort in his final days? How else might he have evidenced his faith near his death?

BIOGRAPHY

Thomas Gray (1716–71)

The son of an abusive London exchange broker, Thomas Gray left London early, seeking a quiet life of scholarly pursuits. He was educated at Eton and Cambridge (1725–38), where he began lifelong friendships with Richard West, Thomas Ashton, and Horace Walpole. After a tour of Europe (1739–41), Gray spent a year with his mother in Buckinghamshire, where he wrote his first serious poetic work, strongly influenced by West's untimely death (1742). In 1743 Gray began a long residence at Cambridge. He lived quietly except when a student prank exploiting his childhood fear of fire made him switch colleges. Officially studying law, he pursued his own interests and became one of the era's most-learned men. With the help of Walpole, Gray's most famous poem, *Elegy Written in a Country Churchyard,* was published in 1751. Gray's fame soared despite his distaste for public notice. He declined the poet laureateship in 1757 but accepted a Cambridge professorship in 1768. Meanwhile, his *Collected Poems* (1768) gave him a reputation surpassing that of any other living English poet. Today he is regarded as the best of the midcentury poets of solitary meditation, often called the Graveyard School (p. 359). Their poetry exhibits a solemnity of style, melancholy spirit, and somber reflectiveness well suited to the elegy (p. 206). Indeed, Gray's *Elegy* is the best of their work.

Gray's enthusiasts did not include Samuel Johnson, who believed his melancholy poetry and love of solitude conducive to poor mental health. Johnson also thought Gray's body of work too small in light of his gifts and knowledge. So it is worth noting that he approved of Gray's *Elegy,* citing its originality, keen images, and expressions of universal feeling. For these and other reasons, *Elegy Written in a Country Churchyard* is often considered the century's finest poem.

BEFORE READING

ANALYZE: *Style, Poetic Diction, and Sensibility*

Gray's *Elegy* reflects key neoclassical traits: universality of thought and the moral contemplation of man's condition. Its **style**, too, is firmly neoclassical, employing rhyme, meter, symmetry (e.g., parallelism), and eighteenth-century **poetic diction**. This diction aimed to elevate important genres by using refined words (archaisms, Latinisms) and elaborately rephrasing ideas to avoid everyday language. Gray also ventured beyond neoclassical bounds. He deliberately appealed to readers' **sensibilities** (p. 359), their emotions and human sympathies. Furthermore, his poem prefigured romantic features, using rural landscapes, generating atmosphere through natural descriptions, idealizing the humble life, and evoking solitary meditation.

READ: *Infer Theme from Textual Details*

A theme (p. 229) may be explicit but is more often implicit, not directly expressed. How, then, does a theme emerge? What tools enable a poet to convey his message without stating it openly? In *Elegy*, Gray frequently used imagery (p. 75) to evoke readers' feelings and personification (p. 201) to highlight images or elevate ideas. To infer Gray's themes, note these details. Pay attention to how he creates contrasts within elements. Finally, try to state an overall theme in one sentence.

EVALUATE: *Author's View of Death*

Meditation on death defines the poem's genre, the *elegy* (p. 206). Examining death may seem morbid. But as Ecclesiastes points out, wisdom for life can be found in contemplating death. As you read, examine what Gray says about death and, conversely, life. What does Gray *not* say about death that should inform a biblical worldview? Use Ecclesiastes 7:1–4, 1 Timothy 6:17–19, and James 2:1–9 in your evaluation.

OBJECTIVES

- Identify appeals to sensibility and romantic elements in a work.
- Analyze a work's neoclassical elements.
- Infer a work's theme.
- Evaluate an author's attitude toward death from a biblical perspective.

VOCABULARY

disdainful (dĭs-dān′fəl) *adj.* Expressive of disdain; scornful and contemptuous.

penury (pĕn′yə-rē) *n.* Extreme want or poverty; destitution.

sequestered (sĭ-kwĕs′tərd) *adj.* Sheltered, retired, secluded.

wonted (wôn′tĭd) *adj.* Accustomed; usual.

array (ə-rā′) *n.* Splendid attire; fine clothing.

Elegy
WRITTEN IN A COUNTRY CHURCHYARD

The curfew[1] tolls the knell of parting day,
  The lowing herd wind slowly o'er the lea,[2]
The plowman homeward plods his weary way,
  And leaves the world to darkness and to me.

Now fades the glimmering landscape on the sight,
  And all the air a solemn stillness holds,
Save where the beetle wheels his droning flight,
  And drowsy tinklings lull the distant folds;

Save that from yonder ivy-mantled tow'r
  The moping owl does to the moon complain
Of such, as wand'ring near her secret bow'r,
  Molest her ancient solitary reign.

1. *curfew:* evening bell (knell) usually tolled (rung slowly and solemnly) at 8:00 or 9:00
2. *lea:* meadow

Beneath those rugged elms, that yew-tree's shade,[3]
Where heaves the turf in many a mould'ring heap,
Each in his narrow cell forever laid,
The rude[4] forefathers of the hamlet sleep. **R**

Infer Theme: Identify sight and sound imagery in lines 5–16 that helps to convey the setting. **R**

The breezy call of incense-breathing Morn,[5]
The swallow twitt'ring from the straw-built shed,
The cock's shrill clarion, or the echoing horn,
No more shall rouse them from their lowly bed.

For them no more the blazing hearth shall burn,
Or busy housewife ply her evening care:
No children run to lisp their sire's return,
Or climb his knees the envied kiss to share.

Oft did the harvest to their sickle yield,
Their furrow oft the stubborn glebe[6] has broke; **A**
How jocund did they drive their team afield!
How bowed the woods beneath their sturdy stroke!

Style: What traits reflecting sentimentalism and foreshadowing romanticism are illustrated in lines 21–26? **A**

Let not Ambition mock their useful toil,
Their homely joys, and destiny obscure;
Nor Grandeur hear with a **disdainful** smile,
The short and simple annals of the poor.

disdainful (dĭs-dān′fəl) *adj.* Expressive of disdain; scornful and contemptuous.

The boast of heraldry, the pomp of pow'r,
And all that beauty, all that wealth e'er gave,
Awaits alike the inevitable hour.
The paths of glory lead but to the grave.

Nor you, ye proud, impute to these the fault,
If Mem'ry o'er their tomb no trophies raise,
Where through the long-drawn aisle and fretted[7] vault
The pealing anthem swells the note of praise.

Can storied urn[8] or animated bust
Back to its mansion call the fleeting breath?
Can Honor's voice provoke the silent dust,
Or Flatt'ry sooth the dull cold ear of Death? **R**

Infer Theme: Reread lines 29–44. Identify instances of personification and imagery. What happens to both rich and poor alike? **R**

Perhaps in this neglected spot is laid
Some heart once pregnant[9] with celestial fire;
Hands, that the rod of empire might have swayed,
Or waked to ecstasy the living lyre.

But Knowledge to their eyes her ample page
Rich with the spoils of time did ne'er unroll;
Chill **Penury** repress'd their noble rage,[10]
And froze the genial current of the soul.[11]

penury (pĕn′yə-rē) *n.* Extreme want or poverty; destitution.

3. *yew-tree's shade:* The yew tree, common in graveyards, is associated with death.
4. *rude:* rustic
5. *incense-breathing Morn:* so called because of Anglican daily morning worship
6. *glebe:* soil
7. *fretted:* Ornamented. Aisle and vault are parts of a cathedral where indoor burial was possible for the rich or famous.
8. *storied urn:* inscribed vase for ashes
9. *pregnant:* infused, filled
10. *noble rage:* creative frenzy; inspiration
11. *current . . . soul:* flow of natural genius

Full many a gem of purest ray serene,
The dark unfathomed caves of ocean bear:
Full many a flower is born to blush unseen,
And waste its sweetness on the desert air.

Some village Hampden,[12] that with dauntless breast
The little tyrant of his fields withstood;
Some mute inglorious Milton here may rest,
Some Cromwell guiltless of his country's blood. A

Style: Identify the meter and number of feet per line of lines 57–60. What other neoclassical stylistic trait is illustrated in these lines? A

The applause of listening senates to command,
The threats of pain and ruin to despise,
To scatter plenty o'er a smiling land,
And read their hist'ry in a nation's eyes,

Their lot forbade: nor circumscribed[13] alone
Their growing virtues, but their crimes confined;
Forbade to wade through slaughter to a throne,
And shut the gates of mercy on mankind,

The struggling pangs of conscious truth to hide,[14]
To quench the blushes of ingenuous[15] shame,
Or heap the shrine of Luxury and Pride
With incense kindled at the Muse's[16] flame. A

Diction: How do the previous two stanzas illustrate eighteenth-century poetic diction? A

Far from the madding[17] crowd's ignoble strife,
Their sober wishes never learned to stray;
Along the cool **sequestered** vale of life
They kept the noiseless tenor[18] of their way.

sequestered (sĭ-kwĕs′tərd) *adj.* Sheltered, retired, secluded.

Yet ev'n these bones from insult to protect
Some frail memorial still erected nigh,
With uncouth rhymes and shapeless sculpture decked,
Implores the passing tribute of a sigh.

Their name, their years, spelt by the unlettered[19] Muse,
The place of fame and elegy supply:
And many a holy text around she strews,
That teach the rustic moralist to die. R

Infer Theme: Reread lines 77–84, noting the imagery. What point is Gray making? R

For who to dumb Forgetfulness a prey,
This pleasing anxious being e'er resigned,[20]
Left the warm precincts of the cheerful day,
Nor cast one longing ling'ring look behind?

On some fond breast the parting soul relies,
Some pious drops the closing eye requires;
Ev'n from the tomb the voice of Nature cries,
Ev'n in our ashes live their **wonted** fires.

wonted (wôn′tĭd) *adj.* Accustomed; usual.

12. *Hampden:* John Hampden (1594–1643), Oxford graduate and member of Parliament, leader of popular resistance to a tax levied by Charles I, mortally wounded in the Civil Wars
13. *circumscribed:* limited the scope of
14. *The . . . hide:* forbade them to suppress their consciences
15. *ingenuous:* innocent
16. *Muse's:* goddess of poetry's
17. *madding:* frenzied
18. *tenor:* course
19. *unlettered:* uneducated
20. *who . . . resigned:* whoever willingly gave up to Forgetfulness this pleasurable but worrisome earthly existence

For thee, who mindful of the unhonored dead
Dost in these lines their artless tale relate;[21]
If chance, by lonely contemplation led,
Some kindred spirit shall inquire thy fate,

Haply some hoary-headed swain[22] may say,
"Oft have we seen him at the peep of dawn
Brushing with hasty steps the dews away
To meet the sun upon the upland lawn.

"There at the foot of yonder nodding beech
That wreathes its old fantastic roots so high,
His listless length at noontide would he stretch,
And pore upon the brook that babbles by.

"Hard by yon wood, now smiling as in scorn,
Mutt'ring his wayward fancies he would rove,
Now drooping, woeful wan, like one forlorn,
Or crazed with care, or crossed in hopeless love.

"One morn I missed him on the customed hill,
Along the heath and near his fav'rite tree;
Another came; nor yet beside the rill,[23]
Nor up the lawn, nor at the wood was he;

VISUAL ANALYSIS
How has the artist chosen to convey the melancholy mood of Gray's poem ?

21. *thee . . . relate:* Gray himself
22. *hoary-headed swain:* white-haired shepherd
23. *rill:* brook

"The next with dirges due in sad **array**
Slow thro' the churchway path we saw him borne.
Approach and read (for thou canst read) the lay,[24]
Grav'd on the stone beneath yon aged thorn." ✓

THE EPITAPH

Here rests his head upon the lap of Earth
A youth to Fortune and to Fame unknown.
Fair Science[25] frowned not on his humble birth,
And Melancholy marked him for her own.

Large was his bounty, and his soul sincere,
Heav'n did a recompence as largely send:
He gave to Misery all he had, a tear,
He gained from Heav'n ('twas all he wished) a friend. E

No farther seek his merits to disclose,
Or draw his frailties from their dread abode,
(There they alike in trembling hope repose,)
The bosom of his Father and his God. A

24. *lay:* poem
25. *Science:* learning

array (ə-rā′) *n.* Splendid attire; fine clothing.

Reading Check: Who has died? ✓

Author's View: What happens to this man after death? What earthly characteristics of his life does Gray mention in these two stanzas? Which, if any, are factors in his ultimate destination, according to Gray? E

Style: How does Gray's choice of topic illustrate key neoclassical traits? A

THINK AND DISCUSS

1. How does Gray's *Elegy Written in a Country Churchyard* demonstrate the characteristics of neoclassical poetry? Justify your answer with examples from the text.
2. How does *Elegy* exemplify the preromantic idea of sentimentality?
3. What makes this poem an elegy?
4. What is the theme of the poem?
5. What effect does the poetic diction have on how audiences perceive Gray's subject matter? How does it support the theme and the author's purpose?
6. How does Gray's use of imagery and figurative language communicate the theme?
7. How might what Gray achieves in *Elegy Written in a Country Churchyard* comply with what Pope advocates in *An Essay on Criticism*? Consider both universality of thought and beauty of expression.
8. How would you evaluate Gray's view on death from a biblical perspective? Discuss both what is biblically accurate about his view and what he may or may not fail to include in his view.
9. What makes your life valuable? Create a short paragraph describing what you would like people to remember about you.

UNIT 3

PART 4

Voices from the Outside

Have you ever gotten advice from an unexpected source? Maybe it was from someone whom you did not know well or who had little in common with you. Perhaps it was even something you did not like hearing. While advice from outsiders is not always perfect, it can often be quite valuable. People standing outside our circumstances can sometimes see them more clearly than we can. Or sometimes another person's differing life experiences can offer us a fresh perspective on perplexing problems.

The authors studied in the following pages provided their culture with fresh perspectives. Each of these writers was outside the circle of voices (whether religious, literary, or social) normally heard in English culture. The opportunity to be heard arose in large part from the expansion of literacy. This trend introduced a diversity of beliefs and life experiences into both writers and their audiences. As canny publishers targeted these new readers' diverse tastes and interests, new opportunities arose for groups outside the mainstream to express their voices.

One new set of voices was that of religious dissenters. Several groups believed that unbiblical doctrines and practices lingered in Anglican worship. The most prominent of these groups, the Puritans (pp. 284, 295), desired to reform the church from within. Less powerful at first was the dissenting group of Nonconformists, who desired to leave the English church altogether. Restoration parliaments passed several acts to suppress these groups (p. 286). The Conventicle Act of 1664, for instance, forbade any non-Anglican religious assembly of more than five people. But Nonconformists persisted, sometimes at great cost, and saw the fruit of their labors throughout the eighteenth century.

In this section, several works represent the perspective Nonconformists brought to English culture. In 1678 John Bunyan, the head of a small Nonconformist congregation in Bedford, published one of English literature's best-loved books, *The Pilgrim's Progress*. Bunyan found time to write while he was imprisoned for twelve years because of the Conventicle Act. Though he had little education, his allegory insightfully and engagingly commented on the Christian life and the spiritual problems of Restoration England. Bunyan's perspective offered a valuable alternative to that of the establishment's church.

Sadly, by the early eighteenth century, spiritual indifference affected both established and dissenting churches. In response, a revival movement focusing on personal holiness arose. Two key figures were the Wesley brothers (p. 391). Both Anglican ministers, they disrupted the calcifying traditions of the state church. While John preached in open-air meetings across Britain, Charles became famous as a hymn writer. He followed in the footsteps of Nonconformist hymnist Isaac Watts, who had sparked a great new age of hymnody. In keeping with revivalism's focus on personal faith, both hymnists wrote texts combining key doctrinal truths with individual experience.

The ideals of the revivalists were carried on by various groups known collectively as evangelicals. Their focus on believers' personal spiritual growth often led them to perceive and interact with society differently than many fellow citizens. As a result, evangelicals were one of the leading forces in major social reforms near the end of the century. No better embodiment of their work can be found than in William Wilberforce, who for decades was a dominant voice in the fight to end slavery. His powerful speech before Parliament in 1789 exemplifies the best that the evangelical voice could bring to society.

Two other voices also became prominent. Although a few privileged women (e.g., Lanier, Cavendish) had privately published works, female writers were still rare. Aphra Behn became one of the first women to publish professionally. A prolific, innovative, and elegant writer, she wrote everything from plays to poems to essays. Her prose narrative *Oroonoko* incorporated several features unusual for the time, among them a female narrator and an enslaved African hero. Both presented an entirely new perspective to English audiences. Turned into a drama, the story became a staple of eighteenth-century theater. The adventures of its protagonist, Oroonoko (an African prince kidnapped and enslaved in the New World), prompted antagonism in Britain against the slave trade.

Another voice was that of African slaves themselves. A little-understood cost of European colonization, the slave trade arose to fuel lucrative products from the New World. Settlers had found conditions ideal for labor-intensive crops (e.g., sugar cane, coffee, cotton) and, the local peoples providing insufficient labor, turned to importing African slaves. A vigorous and dreadful slave trade developed, increasing throughout the eighteenth century. In one of the first slave narratives, Olaudah Equiano, a former slave, brought the terrible costs of slavery to the attention of Britons. His popular and riveting account, *The Interesting Narrative of the Life of Olaudah Equiano*, fueled growing antislavery sentiments, leading to concerted efforts to end the slave trade (1807) and then slavery itself (1833) in the British Empire.

John Bunyan (1628–88)

AT A GLANCE

- **1644–47** Served in the parliamentary army
- **1648** Began a period of spiritual struggle leading to his conversion
- **1653** Joined a group of Bedford Baptists
- **1655** Began to preach
- **1660–72** Imprisoned for preaching; wrote *Grace Abounding to the Chief of Sinners* (1666)
- **1675–76** Imprisoned again for a short time
- **1678** Published *The Pilgrim's Progress*

Dissenters had very little influence on the English literary tradition before the later Stuart period. But when their voice was heard through the writings of John Bunyan, it had a major impact. *The Pilgrim's Progress* is not only a work of immense spiritual value but also, from almost any viewpoint, one of the great books of the world.

Early Life and Conversion

A converted tinsmith of Bedfordshire yeoman descent, John Bunyan had little in the way of preparation for writing a masterwork of English literature. He received only the limited, though sound, education offered by his village's school. Then from 1644 to 1647, he served in a parliamentary regiment garrisoned twelve miles from his village of Elstow, where he came under both spiritual and profane influences.

About 1648 he married a poor, virtuous girl, who brought with her two devotional books: *The Plain Man's Pathway to Heaven* by Arthur Dent (1601) and *The Practice of Piety* by Lewis Bayly (1612). Bunyan read them and became greatly agitated in soul. Soon he was converted and joined a Baptist congregation in Bedford pastored by a Mr. Gifford (on whom he later modeled his character Evangelist). After years of painful struggle with doubts and temptations, Bunyan received lasting assurance of the genuineness of his conversion and accepted an appointment to preach.

DID YOU KNOW ?

Bunyan's first wife died, leaving him with four children under ten, one of whom was blind. During his imprisonment his second wife reared these four and two more born to her and Bunyan.

Imprisonment and Writings

In 1660 Bunyan was arrested as an "irregular" (a dissenting preacher) and sentenced to three months' imprisonment. His release was conditioned on his promise to refrain from preaching and attend the parish church. Because he would not agree to conform, his imprisonment stretched on for almost twelve years—until the Declaration of Indulgence of 1672 relaxed penalties against Dissenters. Meanwhile, his situation offered him plenty of time and quiet, which he constructively turned toward writing. He first wrote his spiritual autobiography, *Grace Abounding to the Chief of Sinners* (1666), and probably began *The Pilgrim's Progress*. In 1675 Bunyan was imprisoned again, though only for several months, and returned to the writing of his most famous work, completing it either while in confinement or soon after his release.

Success and Homegoing

Published in 1678, *The Pilgrim's Progress from This World to That Which Is to Come* featured a protagonist, Christian, who journeys from his home to the Celestial City. The book was an immediate success. Its reception prompted Bunyan to take time from his preaching to write other imaginative works: *The Life and Death of Mr. Badman* (1680); *The Holy War* (1682); *The Pilgrim's Progress, Part Two* (1684), which traces the salvation and journey through life of Christian's family; and *A Book for Boys and Girls* (1686), containing seventy-four poems for children. His voluminous writing, including fifty-eight published works, shows a busy pastor's regard for the ministry of the pen—a ministry largely responsible for his own conversion.

On August 31, 1688, Bunyan, en route to London, reached the Celestial City instead. The year could not have been more appropriate. England had just found political rest and stability in the Glorious Revolution. Nonconformists had received (or were about to receive) liberty to practice and spread their beliefs. Literature had witnessed, in *The Pilgrim's Progress*, the transformation of the epic into the novel. Alexander Pope, the preeminent poet of the new age, had just been born (May 21). The old political, religious, and literary traditions were making way for the new.

ANALYZE: *Allegory, Allusion, and Motif*

The Pilgrim's Progress is a classic spiritual and social **allegory** (a story with both a literal and an implied level of meaning, see p. 170), in the tradition of *Everyman*, *Piers Plowman*, and *The Faerie Queene*. All three works address challenges, both internal and external, that their protagonists face while on a journey. This premise of a life-changing journey has a rich tradition, appearing in literary works so frequently that it qualifies as a **motif**. You previously studied motifs as unifying, recurring elements *within* a work (p. 254). Another kind of motif is one that occurs across many artistic works, sometimes throughout the world (e.g., see journeys in *The Canterbury Tales*, *Huckleberry Finn*, *The Odyssey*, and the book of Exodus). Can you express the meaning of this broad motif in Bunyan's work?

While works such as Spenser's were addressed to an audience well-versed in classical and medieval literary traditions, Bunyan's required no such background knowledge. Instead, his allegorical narrative is steeped in biblical and historical (contemporary for his time) **allusions**, references within a work of literature to something outside it that carries meaning for readers. As you read, see how many allusions you recognize in *The Pilgrim's Progress*. One biblical allusion is in the title itself. Scripture speaks of men of faith as "strangers and pilgrims on the earth" (Heb. 11:13). Interestingly, this allusion foreshadows the work's journey-based plot.

READ: *Determine Author's Purpose*

Bunyan is an unusual author in the British pantheon. With little education, he could not draw upon the resources British writers commonly used—whether classical and medieval philosophers, Renaissance writers, or even contemporary literary figures—to develop his ideas. In fact, these were unnecessary to his purpose. He did not set out to write high literature or to take part in contemporary intellectual discussions. But what was his purpose? As you read the excerpts that follow, interpret the allegory with an eye to Bunyan's contemporary society and readers. At whom specifically are his themes and ideas aimed? How would the truths he represents agree with or contradict elements of British society? What does he imply his readers should understand or do in response to his work? By answering these questions, you will find that a clear purpose begins to emerge.

CREATE: *An Allegorical Scene or Sketch*

Once you have read from Bunyan's work, try your hand at allegory. Create a short allegorical scene or sketch. Your work should include characters, events, or places that function on a literal level (i.e., the story you are telling) and also mirror and comment on a common situation or recognizable event (preferably something most readers will recognize). Or use Bunyan's characters and adapt them to a modern context. For example, what would constitute a modern-day Vanity Fair? What would modern-day martyrdom look like? Both levels of meaning should be clear.

OBJECTIVES

- Infer an author's purpose from textual details.
- Interpret a text's allusions and motifs.
- Analyze a text's allegorical meanings.
- Compose an allegorical sketch.

VOCABULARY

raiment (rā′mənt) *n.* Clothing; garments.

vanity (văn′ĭ-tē) *n.* Something that is vain, futile, or worthless.

rogue (rōg) *n.* An unprincipled, deceitful, and unreliable person; a scoundrel or rascal.

commodity (kə-mŏd′ĭ-tē) *n.* Something useful that can be turned to commercial or other advantage.

remand (rĭ-mănd′) *tr.v.* To send back (a person) into legal custody, as to a jail or prison.

respite (rĕs′pĭt) *n.* Temporary suspension of the execution of a sentence.

What does it mean to be a **PILGRIM** *in the world?*

What does the word pilgrim *conjure up in your mind? Do you think first of those who founded Plymouth Colony in 1620? Do you think of Chaucer's pilgrims journeying to a religious shrine? The word, which means simply "a traveler," is sometimes used to refer to Christians. In what way are Christians strangers (i.e., foreigners) and pilgrims in the world? Write a paragraph to express your thoughts.*

Illustration by Mike Wimmer

The ~~from~~ Pilgrim's Progress

BEGINNING

As I walked through the wilderness of this world, I lighted on[1] a certain place where was a den, and I laid me down in that place to sleep: and as I slept I dreamed a dream. I dreamed, and behold, I saw a man clothed with rags, standing in a certain place, with his face from his own house, a book in his hand, and a great burden upon his back. I looked, and saw him open the book and read therein; and as he read, he wept and trembled; and not being able longer to contain, he brake out with a lamentable cry, saying, "What shall I do?" **A**

In this plight, therefore, he went home and refrained himself as long as he could, that his wife and children should not perceive his distress; but he could not be silent long, because that his trouble increased. Wherefore at length he brake[2] his mind to his wife and children; and thus he began to talk to them: "O my dear wife," said he, "and you the children of my bowels, I, your dear friend, am in myself undone by reason of a burden that lieth hard upon me; moreover, I am for certain informed that this our city will be burned with fire from heaven, in which fearful overthrow both myself, with thee my wife, and you my sweet babes, shall miserably come to ruin, except (the which yet I see not) some way of escape can be found whereby we may be delivered." At this his relations were sore amazed, not for that they believed that what he had said to them was true but because they thought that some frenzy distemper[3] had got into his head; therefore, it drawing towards night and they hoping that sleep might settle his brains, with all haste they got him to bed. But the night was as troublesome to him as the day; wherefore, instead of sleeping, he spent it in sighs and tears. So, when the morning was come, they would know how he did. He told them, "Worse and worse." He also set to talking to them again, but they began to be hardened. They also thought to drive away his distemper by harsh and surly carriages[4] to him; sometimes they would deride, sometimes they would chide, and sometimes they would quite neglect him. Wherefore he began to retire himself to his chamber, to pray for and pity them, and also to condole[5] his own misery; he would also walk solitarily in the fields, sometimes reading, and sometimes praying. And thus for some days he spent his time.

Now I saw, upon a time when he was walking in the fields, that he was, as he was wont, reading in his book, and greatly distressed in his mind; and as he read, he burst out, as he had done before, crying, "What shall I do to be saved?" . . .

I saw also that he looked this way and that way, as if he would run; yet he stood still, because, as I perceived, he could not tell which way to go. I looked then, and saw a man named Evangelist coming to him, who asked, "Wherefore dost thou cry?"

He answered, " Sir, I perceive by the book in my hand that I am condemned to die, and after that to come to judgment, and I find that I am not willing to do the first nor able to do the second."

Then said Evangelist, "Why not willing to die, since this life is attended with so many evils?" The man answered, "Because I fear that this burden that is upon my back will sink me lower than the grave, and I shall fall into Tophet.[6] And, Sir, if I be not fit to go to prison, I am not fit, I am sure, to go to judgment, and from thence to execution; and the thoughts of these things make me cry." **A**

Then said Evangelist, "If this be thy condition, why standest thou still?" He answered, "Because I know not whither to go." Then he gave him a parchment roll, and there was written within, "Fly from the wrath to come."

The man therefore read it, and looking upon Evangelist very carefully, said, "Whither must I fly?" Then said Evangelist, pointing with his finger over a very wide field, "Do you see yonder wicket gate?"[7] The man said, "No." Then said the other, "Do you see yonder shining light?" He said, "I think I do." Then said Evangelist, "Keep that light in your eye, and go up directly thereto; so shalt thou see the gate, at which, when thou knockest, it shall be told thee what thou shalt do." So I saw in my dream that the man began to run. Now he had not run far from his own door, but his wife and children, perceiving it, began to cry after him to return; but the man put his fingers in his ears and ran on, crying, "Life! Life! Eternal life!" So he looked not behind him but fled towards the middle of the plain. . . .

1. *lighted on:* came upon
2. *brake:* expressed
3. *frenzy distemper:* violent emotional disturbance
4. *surly carriages:* rude, ill-humored behavior
5. *condole:* bewail
6. *Tophet:* originally, a place outside Jerusalem where human sacrifices were once made and where city refuse was thrown to be burnt; later, hell
7. *wicket gate:* small gate, especially one built in or near a large one

Allusion: Identify one biblical allusion from paragraph 1. **A**

Allegory: What do the man's book and burden represent allegorically as seen in the first six paragraphs? **A**

En route to the Wicket Gate, Christian falls into the Slough of Despond, representing "the scum and filth that attends conviction for sin." Rescued by Help and again set on the right path, Christian is later "turned out of his way" by Mr. Worldly Wiseman, who directs him to the village of Morality to ease his burden. Redirected by Evangelist, Christian finally arrives at the Wicket Gate, over which is written "'Knock, and it shall be opened unto you.'" Upon knocking, Christian, "a poor burdened sinner," is readily admitted.

Christian . . . Oh, what a favor is this to me that yet I am admitted entrance here!

Good-will. We make no objections against any, notwithstanding all that they have done before they come hither. They "in no wise are cast out." And therefore, good Christian, come a little way with me, and I will teach thee about the way thou must go. Look before thee; dost thou see this narrow way? That is the way thou must go. It was cast up by the patriarchs, prophets, Christ, and his apostles, and it is as straight as a rule can make it. This is the way thou must go.

Christian. But, said Christian, are there no turnings or windings, by which a stranger may lose his way?

Good-will. Yes, there are many ways butt down upon[8] this, and they are crooked and wide. But thus thou mayest distinguish the right from the wrong, the right only being straight and narrow.

Then I saw in my dream that Christian asked him further if he could not help him off with his burden that was upon his back; for as yet he had not got rid thereof, nor could he by any means get it off without help.

He told him, "As to thy burden, be content to bear it until thou comest to the place of deliverance; for there it will fall from thy back of itself." . . . R

Taking leave of Good-will, Christian again commences his journey, eventually arriving at the House of the Interpreter, where the Interpreter, representing the Holy Spirit, shows Christian "rare and profitable" things. Christian expresses gratitude and continues on his way.

8. *butt down upon:* that come into

Author's Purpose: What three important truths about salvation does Bunyan want his readers to understand through this exchange? R

THE CROSS

Now I saw in my dream that the highway up which Christian was to go was fenced on either side with a wall, and that wall was called Salvation. Up this way, therefore, did burdened Christian run, but not without great difficulty, because of the load on his back.

He ran thus till he came at a place somewhat ascending, and upon that place stood a cross, and a little below, in the bottom, a sepulcher. So I saw in my dream that just as Christian came up with[9] the cross, his burden loosed from off his shoulders, and fell from off his back, and began to tumble, and so continued to do, till it came to the mouth of the sepulcher, where it fell in, and I saw it no more. . . .

9. *came up with:* reached

Illustration by Mike Wimmer

Then was Christian glad and lightsome, and said, with a merry heart, "He hath given me rest by his sorrow, and life by his death." Then he stood still awhile to look and wonder; for it was very surprising to him that the sight of the cross should thus ease him of his burden. He looked, therefore, and looked again, even till the springs that were in his head sent the waters down his cheeks. Now, as he stood looking and weeping, behold, three Shining Ones came to him and saluted him with "Peace be to thee." So the first said to him, "Thy sins be forgiven"; the second stripped him of his rags and clothed him "with change of **raiment**"; the third also set a mark on his forehead, and gave him a roll with a seal upon it, which he bade him look on as he ran, and that he should give it in at the Celestial Gate. So they went their way. Then Christian gave three leaps for joy, and went on, singing, A

Thus far did I come laden with my sin;
Nor could aught ease the grief that I was in
Till I came hither: What a place is this!
Must here be the beginning of my bliss?
Must here the burden fall from off my back?
Must here the strings that bound it to me crack?
Blest cross! Blest sepulcher! Blest rather be
The Man that there was put to shame for me! . . .

VANITY FAIR

Then I saw in my dream that when they were got out of the wilderness, they presently saw a town before them, and the name of that town is Vanity; and at the town there is a fair kept called Vanity Fair. It is kept all the year long. It beareth the name of Vanity Fair because the town where it is kept is lighter than **vanity**; and also, because all that is there sold, or that cometh thither, is vanity. As is the saying of the wise, "All that cometh is vanity." A

This fair is no new-erected business, but a thing of ancient standing; I will show you the original of it.

Almost five thousand years agone, there were pilgrims walking to the Celestial City, as these two honest persons are; and Beelzebub, Apollyon, and Legion, with their companions, perceiving by the path that the pilgrims made that their way to the city lay through this town of Vanity, they contrived[10] here to set up a fair, a fair wherein should be sold all sorts of vanity, and that it should last all the year long. Therefore at this fair are all such merchandise sold, as houses, lands, trades, places, honors, preferments, titles, countries, kingdoms, lusts, pleasures, and delights of all sorts, as whores, bawds, wives, husbands, children, masters, servants, lives, blood, bodies, souls, silver, gold, pearls, precious stones, and what not.

And, moreover, at this fair there are at all times to be seen jugglings, cheats, games, plays, fools, apes,[11] knaves, and **rogues**, and that of every kind.

Here are to be seen too, and that for nothing,[12] thefts, murders, adulteries, false swearers, and that of a blood-red color.

And as in other fairs of less moment[13] there are the several[14] rows and streets under their proper[15] names where such and such wares are vended, so here likewise you have the proper places, rows, streets (viz. countries and kingdoms) where the wares of this fair are soonest to be found. Here is the Britain Row, the French Row, the Italian Row, the Spanish Row, the German Row, where several sorts of vanities are to be sold. But as in other fairs some one **commodity** is as the chief of all the fair, so the ware of Rome and her merchandise is greatly promoted in this fair. Only our English nation, with some others, have taken a dislike thereat.

Now, as I said, the way to the Celestial City lies just through this town where this lusty[16] fair is kept; and he that will go to the City, and yet not go through this town, must needs "go out of the world." The Prince of Princes himself, when here, went through this town to his own country, and that upon a Fair-day too; yea, and as I think, it was Beelzebub, the chief lord of this fair, that invited him to buy of his vanities; yea; would have made him lord of the fair, would he but have done him reverence as he went through the town. Yea, because he was such a person of honor, Beelzebub had him from street to street, and showed him all the kingdoms of the world in a little time, that he might, if possible, allure the Blessed One to cheapen[17] and buy some of his vanities; but he had no mind to the merchandise, and

10. *contrived:* schemed

11. *apes:* mimics
12. *for nothing:* without cost
13. *moment:* importance
14. *several:* various
15. *proper:* own particular
16. *lusty:* (1) high-spirited; (2) lustful
17. *cheapen:* (1) bargain for; (2) debase himself

raiment (rā′mənt) *n.* Clothing; garments.

Allegory/Motif: What overall experience does Bunyan clearly allegorize in these excerpts? How does his allegory already exhibit signs of the life-changing journey motif? A

vanity (văn′ĭ-tē) *n.* Something that is vain, futile, or worthless.

Allusion: What well-known Old Testament passage does the title "Vanity Fair" allude to as represented in this final quotation? A

rogue (rōg) *n.* An unprincipled, deceitful, and unreliable person; a scoundrel or rascal.

commodity (kə-mŏd′ĭ-tē) *n.* Something useful that can be turned to commercial or other advantage.

therefore left the town without laying out so much as one farthing[18] upon these vanities. This fair, therefore, is an ancient thing, of long standing, and a very great fair. Now these pilgrims, as I said, must needs go through this fair. Well, so they did: but behold, even as they entered into the fair, all the people in the fair were moved, and the town itself as it were in a hubbub about them; and that for several reasons: for, A

First, the pilgrims were clothed with such kind of raiment as was diverse from the raiment of any that traded in that fair. The people therefore of the fair made a great gazing upon them. Some said they were fools, some they were bedlams,[19] and some, "They are outlandish men."[20]

Secondly , and as they wondered at their apparel, so they did likewise at their speech; for few could understand what they said. They naturally spoke the language of Canaan, but they that kept the fair were the men of this world; so that from one end of the fair to the other they seemed barbarians each to the other.

Thirdly, but that which did not a little amuse the merchandisers was that these pilgrims set very light by all their wares; they cared not so much as to look upon them; and if they called upon them to buy, they would put their fingers in their ears and cry, "Turn away mine eyes from beholding vanity," and look upwards, signifying that their trade and traffic[21] was in heaven.

One chanced mockingly, beholding the carriage[22] of the men, to say unto them, "What will ye buy?" But they, looking gravely upon him, answered, "We buy the truth." At that there was an occasion taken to despise the men the more; some mocking, some taunting, some speaking reproachfully, and some calling upon others to smite them. At last, things came to a hubbub and great stir in the fair, insomuch that all order was confounded.[23] Now was word presently brought to the great one of the fair, who quickly came down and deputed[24] some of his most trusty friends to take these men into examination, about whom the fair was almost overturned. So the men were brought to examination; and they that sat[25] upon them asked them whence they came, whither they went, and

18. *farthing:* coin worth one-fourth of a penny
19. *bedlams:* insane persons
20. *outlandish men:* foreigners
21. *traffic:* purchasing, business
22. *carriage:* behavior

23. *confounded:* disrupted
24. *deputed:* assigned
25. *sat:* sat in judgment

Allegory/Allusion: What is Vanity Fair meant to represent within Bunyan's allegory, both spiritually and perhaps historically? What biblical story does the incident between the Prince of Princes and Beelzebub allude to? A

VISUAL ANALYSIS

In this image, Christian (now in the armor of God) and Faithful walk through Vanity Fair. How does the artist suggest the contrast in thought and attitude between them and the citizens?

Illustration by Mike Wimmer

what they did there in such an unusual garb. The men told them that they were pilgrims and strangers in the world, and that they were going to their own country, which was the heavenly Jerusalem, and that they had given no occasion to the men of the town, nor yet to the merchandisers, thus to abuse them, and to let[26] them in their journey, except it was for that, when one asked them what they would buy, they said they would buy the truth. But they that were appointed to examine them did not believe them to be any other than bedlams and mad, or else such as came to put all things into a confusion in the fair. Therefore they took them and beat them, and besmeared them with dirt, and then put them into the cage, that they might be made a spectacle to all the men of the fair. There therefore they lay for some time and were made the objects of any man's sport, or malice, or revenge, the great one of the fair laughing still at all that befell them. But the men being patient and not rendering railing for railing, but contrariwise blessing, and giving good words for bad and kindness for injuries done, some men in the fair that were more observing and less prejudiced than the rest, began to check[27] and blame the baser sort for their continual abuses done by them to the men; they therefore in angry manner let fly at them again, counting them as bad as the men in the cage, and telling them that they seemed confederates and should be made partakers of their misfortunes. The other replied that for aught they could see, the men were quiet, and sober, and intended nobody any harm; and that there were many that traded in their fair that were more worthy to be put into the cage, yea, and pillory[28] too, than were the men they had abused. Thus after divers[29] words had passed on both sides (the men behaving themselves all the while very wisely and soberly before them) they fell to some blows among themselves and did harm one to another. Then were these two poor men brought before their examiners again, and there charged as being guilty of the late hubbub that had been in the fair. So they beat them pitifully, and hanged irons upon them, and led them in chains up and down the fair, for an example and a terror to others, lest any should speak further in their behalf or join themselves unto them. But Christian and Faithful behaved themselves yet more wisely, and received the ignominy[30] and shame that was cast upon them with so much meekness and patience that it won to their side (though but few in comparison of the rest) several of the men in the fair. This put the other party yet into greater rage, insomuch that they concluded the death of these two men. Wherefore they threatened that neither the cage nor irons should serve their turn,[31] but that they should die for the abuse they had done and for deluding the men of the fair. . . . **R** **A**

Then were they **remanded** to the cage again, until further order should be taken with[32] them. So they put them in and made their feet fast in the stocks.

Here also they called again to mind what they had heard from their faithful friend, Evangelist, and were the more confirmed in their way and sufferings by what he told them would happen to them. They also now comforted each other that whose lot it was to suffer, even he should have the best of it; therefore each man secretly wished that he might have that preferment,[33] but, committing themselves to the all-wise disposal of him that ruleth all things, with much content they abode in the condition in which they were, until they should be otherwise disposed of.

Then a convenient time being appointed, they brought them forth to their trial, in order to their condemnation. When the time was come, they were brought before their enemies and arraigned. The judge's name was Lord Hate-good; their indictment was one and the same in substance, though somewhat varying in form, the contents whereof was this:

That they were enemies to and disturbers of their trade; that they had made commotions and divisions in the town, and had won a party to their own most dangerous opinions, in contempt of the law of their prince. . . .

Then Faithful began to answer, that he had only set himself against that which had set itself against him that is higher than the highest. "And," said he, "as for disturbance, I make none, being myself a man of peace; the parties that were won to us, were won by beholding our truth and innocence, and they are only turned from the worse to the better. And as to the king you talk of, since he is Beelzebub, the enemy of the Lord, I defy him and all his angels." . . .

Accused by false witnesses Envy, Superstition, and Pickthank (Flattering Informer), Faithful gives a brief defense, concluding that the prince

26. *let:* hinder
27. *check:* rebuke
28. *pillory:* stocks
29. *divers:* various
30. *ignominy:* humiliation

31. *serve their turn:* be their lot
32. *with:* concerning
33. *preferment:* advancement, i.e., opportunity to suffer

Author's Purpose: How might this description of how Christian and Faithful are treated in Vanity Fair address issues in Bunyan's society? How does it reflect his personal experiences? **R**

Allegory: What broad truths about the Christian life is Bunyan allegorizing for readers? **A**

remand (rĭ-mănd′) *tr.v.* To send back (a person) into legal custody, as to a jail or prison.

of the town and his attendants "are more fit for a being in hell than in this town and country." Then Judge Hate-good instructs the jury in the precedents pertaining to the case—laws enacted by Pharoah, Nebuchadnezzar, and Darius. Judge Hate-good determines that Faithful "deserves to die the death."

Then went the jury out, whose names were, Mr. Blindman, Mr. No-good, Mr. Malice, Mr. Love-lust, Mr. Live-loose, Mr. Heady, Mr. High-mind, Mr. Enmity, Mr. Liar, Mr. Cruelty, Mr. Hate-light, and Mr. Implacable; who every one gave in his private verdict against him among themselves, and afterwards unanimously concluded to bring him in guilty before the judge. And first, among themselves, Mr. Blindman, the foreman, said, "I see clearly that this man is a heretic." Then said Mr. No-good, "Away with such a fellow from the earth." "Ay," said Mr. Malice, "for I hate the very looks of him." Then said Mr. Love-lust, "I could never endure him." "Nor I," said Mr. Live-loose, "for he would always be condemning my way." "Hang him, hang him," said Mr. Heady. "A sorry scrub," said Mr. High-mind. "My heart riseth against him," said Mr. Enmity. "He is a rogue," said Mr. Liar. "Hanging is too good for him," said Mr. Cruelty. "Let us dispatch him out of the way," said Mr. Hate-light. Then said Mr. Implacable, "Might I have all the world given me, I could not be reconciled to him; therefore let us forthwith bring him in guilty of death." And so they did; therefore he was presently condemned to be had from the place where he was to the place from whence he came, and there to be put to the most cruel death that could be invented.

They therefore brought him out, to do with him according to their law; and first they scourged him, then they buffeted him, then they lanced his flesh with knives; after that they stoned him with stones, then pricked him with their swords; and last of all they burned him to ashes at the stake. Thus came Faithful to his end. . . . Now I saw that there stood behind the multitude a chariot and a couple of horses, waiting for Faithful, who (so soon as his adversaries had dispatched him) was taken up into it, and straightway was carried up through the clouds, with sound of trumpet, the nearest way to the Celestial Gate. **A**

But as for Christian, he had some **respite**, and was remanded back to prison. So he there remained for a space. But he that overrules all things, having the power of their rage in his own hand, so wrought it about that Christian, for that time, escaped them and went his way; and as he went he sang, saying,

Well, Faithful, thou hast faithfully professed
Unto thy Lord, with whom thou shalt be blest,
When faithless ones, with all their vain delights,
Are crying out under their hellish plights.
Sing, Faithful, sing, and let thy name survive;
For though they killed thee, thou art yet alive.

Now I saw in my dream that Christian went not forth alone, for there was one whose name was Hopeful (being made so by the beholding of Christian and Faithful in their words and behavior, in their sufferings at the fair), who joined himself unto him, and entering into a brotherly covenant, told him that he would be his companion. Thus one died to make testimony to the truth, and another rises out of his ashes to be a companion with Christian in his pilgrimage. This Hopeful also told Christian that there were many more of the men in the fair, that would take their time and follow after. **R**

Allusion: To what Old Testament story do the chariot and horses that carried Faithful away allude? **A**

respite (rĕs′pĭt) *n.* Temporary suspension of the execution of a sentence.

Author's Purpose: What biblical truths about persecution does this incident convey? How do you think Bunyan wanted his contemporaries, both his persecutors and his fellow believers, to respond? **R**

THINK AND DISCUSS

1. Define *allegory*, *motif*, and *allusion*.
2. In what ways might *Pilgrim's Progress* be partially autobiographical?
3. *Pilgrim's Progress* is replete with biblical allusion. Identify five allusions found in the excerpts contained in the text.
4. Identify and explain the overarching motif in *Pilgrim's Progress*.
5. Justify *Pilgrim's Progress* as allegory. In your answer, explain what the following details allegorically represent: Christian's book, Christian's burden, the Wicket Gate, the Slough of Despond, the three Shining Ones, and Vanity Fair.
6. Explain two truths that the Vanity Fair incident illustrates. Support your answers with details from the text.
7. Describe two possible purposes Bunyan had for writing *Pilgrim's Progress*. Support your answer with details from the text.
8. Create a short allegorical scene or sketch in which characters or places represent something on another level. You may want to place Bunyan's characters in a modern scenario.

Isaac Watts and Charles Wesley

Just as Bunyan spoke powerfully from outside mainstream English society, so too did other evangelicals. In the realm of church music, one Nonconformist set off a revolution that eventually reached even mainstream Anglicans. While Reformation thinking had encouraged congregations, not just church choirs, to sing, Puritans' convictions had limited English lyrics to biblical texts (e.g., Psalms) awkwardly fitted to meter and rhyme. The result, the Psalter, excluded personal, creative expressions of Bible truths.

In the early 1700s, Isaac Watts (1674–1748), a dissenting minister, became disappointed in the dryness of the Psalter's music, which perforce included nothing directly about Jesus. His father encouraged him to use his poetic talent to produce a new hymn. The result was "Behold, the Glories of the Lamb." Watts began a determined campaign to replace the stiff psalmody with more vigorous and lyrical paraphrases as well as independent poems on biblical themes. His efforts produced classics such as "When I Survey the Wondrous Cross," "I Sing the Mighty Power of God," and "Joy to the World!" Such hymns prompted Protestant appreciation of more personal worship music and created a new norm, allowing congregations to sing hymns. Watts's influence motivated many others to broaden the lyrical variety in worship music, leading modern hymnists to dub him the Father of English Hymnody.

In 1707, the year that Isaac Watts published his collection *Hymns and Spiritual Songs*, another influential hymn writer was born. Charles Wesley (1707–88), brother of John (p. 289) and Anglican evangelist to England and America, was a much more prolific hymnist than Watts, writing about nine thousand hymns and sacred songs. Around 1736 the first Wesley hymnbook was published: *Collection of Psalms and Hymns*. This and subsequent collections included well-known hymns such as "And Can It Be?," "O for a Thousand Tongues to Sing," and "Christ the Lord Is Risen Today."

Eighteenth-century hymnwriters largely wrote in the style of their times, embracing the neoclassical emphasis on conventional forms and the virtues of clarity, simplicity, fluency, and polish. While didactic, reverent in tone, and often beautifully crafted, their hymns were still plain enough for untrained singers to understand and appreciate. Their lyrical representations of Christian doctrine continue to uplift believers today.

BEFORE READING

ANALYZE: *Hymn and Common Meter*

Watts's **hymns**, lyric poems of praise or thanksgiving to God meant to be sung, still used the original meters of the psalters. The best-known meter, **common meter**, employed quatrains of iambic (p. 185) lines. These lines typically alternated between *tetrameter* (four poetic feet per line) and *trimeter* (three feet per line). The rhyme scheme could vary between *abab* and *abcb*. As you read, ascertain how Watts's hymn complies with common meter. Conversely, Wesley usually used greater metrical variety. How does his hymn differ from Watts's in stanza form, meter, and rhyme scheme? How are these differences reflected in the flow of each poem?

READ: *Compare Texts*

Watts's hymn paraphrases Psalm 90, a song written by Moses. Compare these two texts to find similarities in content. Then note differences between the two hymn selections. How does Watts's hymn reflect his contributions to hymnody (e.g., more lyrical paraphrases)? How does Wesley's hymn shift focus to personal holiness and play a more evangelistic function? Note the focus of each hymn. Who is speaking? What experience is being described? What themes are emphasized?

CREATE: *A Hymn*

Consider a Bible story or doctrine that is of personal significance or special value to you. How does the truth affect your relationship with God? What would you like to share with Christians about that truth? Create a prose meditation that alludes to this biblical story or doctrine. Try to translate it into common meter.

OBJECTIVES

- Identify a hymn's stanza form, meter, and rhyme scheme.
- Compare the subjects and purposes of two texts.
- Analyze a hymn's themes.
- Create a hymn in common meter.

Our God, Our Help In Ages Past

ISAAC WATTS

Our[1] God, our help in ages past,
 Our hope for years to come,
Our shelter from the stormy blast,
 And our eternal home.

Under the shadow of Thy throne
 Thy saints have dwelt secure;
Sufficient is Thine arm alone,
 And our defense is sure. A

Before the hills in order stood,
 Or earth received her frame,
From everlasting Thou art God,
 To endless years the same.

Thy Word commands our flesh to dust,
 "Return, ye sons of men":
All nations rose from earth at first,
 And turn to earth again.

A thousand ages in Thy sight
 Are like an evening gone;
Short as the watch that ends the night,
 Before the rising sun.

The busy tribes of flesh and blood,
 With all their lives and cares,
Are carried downwards by the flood,
 And lost in following years.

Time, like an ever-rolling stream,
 Bears all its sons away;
They fly, forgotten, as a dream
 Dies at the opening day.

Like flowery fields the nations stand
 Pleased with the morning light;
The flowers beneath the mower's hand
 Lie withering ere 'tis night. A

Our God, our help in ages past,
 Our hope for years to come,
Be Thou our guard while troubles last,
 And our eternal home.

1. *Our:* John Wesley changed *Our* to *O* when he published the hymn.

Meter: Scan the first two stanzas of the hymn. What stanza form is used? How many feet are in each line? What is the rhyme scheme? A

Hymn: Beginning in stanza 3, Watts elaborates on what particular quality of God? How do stanzas 4–8 further show that this quality is unique to God? A

VISUAL ANALYSIS
How has the illustrator imaginatively captured the hymnists' depiction of the differences between the nature of God and humankind and the relationship between the two?

Behold the Man![1]

CHARLES WESLEY

Arise, my soul, arise,
Shake off thy guilty fears,
The bleeding sacrifice
In my behalf appears:
Before the throne my surety stands,
My name is written on His hands.

He ever lives above,
For me to intercede;
His all-redeeming love,
His precious blood, to plead;
His blood atoned for all our race,
And sprinkles now the throne of grace. **A**

Five bleeding wounds He bears,
Received on Calvary,
They pour effectual prayers,
They strongly plead for me.
Forgive him, oh! forgive, they cry,
Nor let that ransomed sinner die!

The Father hears Him pray,
His dear anointed one;
He cannot turn away
The presence of His Son.
His Spirit answers to the blood,
And tells me, I am born of God.

My God is reconciled,
His pard'ning voice I hear,
He owns me for His child,
I can no longer fear;
With confidence I now draw nigh,
And Father, Abba Father, cry. **R**

1. *Behold the Man!:* more commonly known today as "Arise, My Soul, Arise"

Meter: What stanza form does Wesley use? How many feet are in each line of his stanzas, and what is the rhyme scheme? **A**

Compare Texts: How do the topic of this poem and the speaker's perspective on it reflect Wesley's contributions to hymnody? **R**

THINK AND DISCUSS

1. Define *hymn* and explain why both Watts's and Wesley's poems qualify as examples of the genre.
2. List the key features of common meter.
3. What unique features did Watts and Wesley each contribute to hymnody?
4. Which of these two hymns employs common meter? Copy one stanza of the poem and annotate its meter pattern and rhyme scheme.
5. Compare Watts's hymn to Psalm 90. Identify three similarities in content.
6. How does Wesley's use of meter and rhyme affect the flow of his hymn both within and between stanzas?
7. Compare Watts's and Wesley's hymns. How do they differ in theme and in the speakers' perspectives?
8. Pick a doctrinal or practical application of truth that God has specifically taught you. Write a few stanzas of a hymn of your own conveying this truth in praise of God. Perhaps use common meter in your poem.

Aphra Behn (1640–89)

Although records of her life are minimal, most researchers agree on certain facts about Aphra Behn. Born near Canterbury, England, she married Johan Behn, a Dutch or German merchant, in the late 1660s but was widowed within two years. To provide for herself, Behn, a staunch Royalist, became an English spy in the war with the Dutch over Atlantic trade routes. Alone and destitute after the war, she became one of the first women to depend on her pen for earning a living.

Behn demonstrated impressive versatility, writing plays, poetry, and novels. Like many Restoration writers, she sometimes liberally sprinkled her works with sensational content. Critics often attacked her for coarse language and scandalous themes. Yet she could also be praised for innovation and for satire of political events and social scandal.

Behn launched her career by writing typical Restoration plays full of libertines, harlots, and foolish characters. Her poetry, often spoken by the persona "Astrea," displays diverse conventional literary forms, especially modifications of the ballad stanza and the couplet.

Behn's short novels, for which she is best known today, influenced the development of the English novel. Her novels combine the epistolary form (see "Rise of the Novel," p. 332) with dramatic elements such as themes, conflict, and symbolism. Her plots, told by an omniscient narrator, focus on common people and emphasize realistic details and specific places.

Behn's prolific pen not only won her public praise but also established her as a literary role model for future women authors. Behn died after an extended illness and was buried in the East Cloister of Westminster Abbey with this epitaph: "Here lies a proof that wit can never be defense enough against mortality."

BEFORE READING

ANALYZE: *First- and Third-Person Points of View*

In her work *Oroonoko*, Behn created one of the earliest examples of historical fiction. Her fictional narrative combines an eyewitness account with secondary sources. To distinguish these materials, she uses **first-person point of view** (in which the narrator refers to herself as *I* throughout) and **third-person point of view** (in which the narrator stands outside the story and refers to the characters as *he*, *she*, or *they*). Which point of view occurs naturally in an eyewitness account? Which works best for relating secondary information? Why would the use of such pronouns as *I* and *we* influence the narrative's believability?

READ: *Infer Author's Tone*

In this section of *Oroonoko*, Behn characterizes two groups: English colonizers (slave traders) and African slaves. Pay attention to how she characterizes each group. What is her tone (p. 88) toward each? What is her tone toward her protagonist, Oroonoko, especially? Does she portray him as a **sympathetic character** (one for whom the reader has favorable feelings) or an **unsympathetic character** (one for whom the reader has strong feelings of dislike)? What proof can you give?

EVALUATE: *Cultural Attitudes*

By creating an African hero, Behn departed from European cultural norms of the time. Her contemporaries generally viewed Africans as culturally, physically, and intellectually inferior. Although her work often rises above such views, how does Behn sometimes fall prey to such assumptions? Does she see Oroonoko as characteristic of his people or as exceptional? How does the prevailing view of her day stack up against biblical truths? Consider 1 Samuel 16:7 and James 3:9–10.

OBJECTIVES

- Analyze a work's use of first- and third-person points of view.
- Infer an author's tone from characterization.
- Evaluate how an author reflects or differs from cultural attitudes and biblical truth.

VOCABULARY

feigned (fānd) *adj.* Made-up; fictitious.

divert (dĭ-vûrt′) *tr.v.* To entertain by distracting the attention from worrisome thoughts or cares; amuse.

upbraid (ŭp-brād′) *tr.v.* To reprove sharply; reproach.

forbear (fôr-bâr′) *tr.v.* To restrain oneself from doing something; hold back.

FROM OROONOKO
THE ROYAL SLAVE

The story of Oroonoko begins with the fictional narrator's account of her visit to the British colony of Surinam, South America. While there, she meets Prince Oroonoko, then a slave. The work's primary story then unfolds as she tells of his enslavement, eventual revolt, and subsequent execution. In the following excerpted passages, the narrator shares the first part, Oroonoko's account of how he came to be a slave in Surinam.

I do not pretend, in giving you the history of this royal slave, to entertain my reader with the adventures of a **feigned** hero, whose life and fortunes, fancy[1] may manage at the poet's pleasure; nor in relating the truth, design to adorn it with any accidents but such as arrived in earnest to him. And it shall come simply into the world, recommended by its own proper merits and natural intrigues,[2] there being enough of reality to support it, and to render it diverting, without the addition of invention.

feigned (fānd) *adj*. Made-up; fictitious.

I was myself an eyewitness to a great part of what you will find here set down, and what I could not be witness of, I received from the mouth of the chief actor in this history, the hero himself, who gave us the whole transactions of his youth; and though I shall omit for brevity's sake a thousand little accidents of his life, which, however pleasant to us, where history was scarce and adventures very rare, yet might prove tedious and heavy to my reader, in a world where he finds diversions for every minute, new and strange. But we who were perfectly charmed with the character of this great man were curious to gather every circumstance of his life.

The scene of the last part of his adventures lies in a colony in America called Surinam, in the West Indies.

But before I give you the story of this gallant slave, 'tis fit I tell you the manner of bringing them to these new colonies, for those they make use of there are not natives of the place; for those we live with in perfect amity, without daring to command 'em, but on the contrary caress 'em with all the brotherly and friendly affection in the world, trading with 'em for their fish, venison, buffaloes, skins, and little rarities. . . . We dealt with 'em with beads of all colors, knives, axes, pins and needles, which they used only as tools to drill holes with in their ears, noses, and lips, where they hang a great many little things, as long beads, bits of tin, brass, or silver beat thin, and any shining trinket. The beads they weave into aprons about a quarter of an ell long, and of the same breadth, working them very prettily in flowers of several colors of beads; which apron they wear just before 'em, as Adam and Eve did the fig leaves, the men wearing a long stripe of linen which they deal with us for. They thread these beads also on long cotton threads and make girdles to tie their aprons to, which come twenty times or more about the waist, and then cross , like a shoulder belt, both ways, and round their necks, arms, and legs. This adornment, with their long black hair, and the face painted in little specks or flowers here and there, makes 'em a wonderful figure to behold. . . .

Those then whom we make use of to work in our plantations of sugar are Negroes, black slaves altogether, which are transported thither in this manner. Those who want slaves make a bargain with a master or captain of a ship and contract to pay him so much apiece, a matter of twenty pound a head for as many as he agrees for, and to pay for 'em when they shall be delivered on such a plantation. So that when there arrives a ship laden with slaves, they who have so contracted go aboard and receive their number by lot; and perhaps in one lot that may be for ten, there may happen to be three or four men, the rest women and children. Or be there more or less of either sex, you are obliged to be contented with your lot. **A**

Point of View: What point of view is used throughout the first five paragraphs? How do you know? Does this point of view reflect Behn's purpose? **A**

Coramantien, a country of blacks so called, was one of those places in which they found the most advantageous trading for these slaves, and thither most of our great traders in that merchandise trafficked; for that nation is very warlike and brave, and having a continual campaign, being always in

1. *fancy:* imagination
2. *intrigues:* complexities

hostility with one neighboring prince or other, they had the fortune to take a great many captives; for all they took in battle were sold as slaves, at least those common men who could not ransom themselves. Of these slaves so taken, the general only has all the profit; and of these generals, our captains and masters of ships buy all their freights.

The King of Coramantien was himself a man of a hundred and odd years old, and had no son, though he had many beautiful black wives; for most certainly there are beauties that can charm of that color. In his younger years he had had many gallant men to his sons, thirteen of which died in battle, conquering when they fell; and he had only left him for his successor one grandchild, son to one of these dead victors, who, as soon as he could bear a bow in his hand and a quiver at his back, was sent into the field, to be trained up by one of the oldest generals to war; where, from his natural inclination to arms and the occasions given him, with the good conduct of the old general, he became, at the age of seventeen, one of the most expert captains and bravest soldiers that ever saw the field of Mars. So that he was adored as the wonder of all that world, and the darling of the soldiers. Besides, he was adorned with a native beauty so transcending all those of his gloomy race that he struck an awe and reverence even in those that knew not his quality; as he did in me, who beheld him with surprise and wonder, when afterwards he arrived in our world.

He had scarce arrived at his seventeenth year, when fighting by his side, the general was killed with an arrow in his eye, which the Prince Oroonoko (for so was this gallant Moor called) very narrowly avoided; nor had he, if the general, who saw the arrow shot, and perceiving it aimed at the Prince, had not bowed his head between, on purpose to receive it in his own body rather than it should touch that of the Prince, and so saved him. R

Infer Author's Tone: What was the narrator's impression of Oroonoko when she first met him? What title does she use for him? What types of words does she use to describe him? R

'Twas then, afflicted as Oroonoko was, that he was proclaimed general in the old man's place; and then it was, at the finishing of that war, which had continued for two years, that the Prince came to court, where he had hardly been a month together from the time of his fifth year to that of seventeen; and 'twas amazing to imagine where it was he learned so much humanity; or to give his accomplishments a juster name, where 'twas he got that real greatness of soul, those refined notions of true honor, that absolute generosity, and that softness that was capable of the highest passions of love and gallantry, whose objects were almost continually fighting men, or those mangled or dead; who heard no sounds but those of war and groans. Some part of it we may attribute to the care of a Frenchman of wit and learning, who, finding it turn to very good account to be a sort of royal tutor to this young black, and perceiving him very ready, apt, and quick of apprehension, took a great pleasure to teach him morals, language, and science, and was for it extremely beloved and valued by him. Another reason was, he loved, when he came from war, to see all the English gentlemen that traded thither, and did not only learn their language but that of the Spaniards also, with whom he traded afterwards for slaves. E

Cultural Attitudes: To what does the narrator attribute Oroonoko's refined sense of honor and humanity? By contrast, what is implied about the natural state of Africans? E

I have often seen and conversed with this great man, and been a witness to many of his mighty actions, and do assure my reader the most illustrious courts could not have produced a braver man, both for greatness of courage and mind, a judgment more solid, a wit more quick, and a conversation more sweet and diverting. He knew almost as much as if he had read much. He had heard of and admired the Romans; he had heard of the late civil wars in

divert (dĭ-vûrt′) *tr.v.* To entertain by distracting the attention from worrisome thoughts or cares; amuse.

England, and the deplorable death of our great monarch, and would discourse of it with all the sense and abhorrence of the injustice imaginable. He had an extreme good and graceful mien,[3] and all the civility of a well-bred great man. He had nothing of barbarity in his nature, but in all points addressed himself as if his education had been in some European court.

This great and just character of Oroonoko gave me an extreme curiosity to see him, especially when I knew he spoke French and English, and that I could talk with him. But though I had heard so much of him, I was as greatly surprised when I saw him as if I had heard nothing of him, so beyond all report I found him. He came into the room and addressed himself to me, and some other women, with the best grace in the world. He was pretty tall, but of a shape the most exact that can be fancied. The most famous statuary could not form the figure of a man more admirably turned from head to foot. His face was not of that brown, rusty black which most of that nation are, but a perfect ebony or polished jet. His eyes were the most awful that could be seen, and very piercing, the white of 'em being like snow, as were his teeth. His nose was rising and Roman, instead of African and flat; his mouth the finest shaped that could be seen, far from those great turned lips which are so natural to the rest of the Negroes. The whole proportion and air of his face was so noble and exactly formed that, bating[4] his color, there could be nothing in nature more beautiful, agreeable, and handsome.[5] There was no one grace wanting that bears[6] the standard of true beauty. His hair came down to his shoulders by the aids of art; which was by pulling it out with a quill and keeping it combed, of which he took particular care. Nor did the perfections of his mind come short of those of his person, for his discourse was admirable upon almost any subject; and whoever had heard him speak would have been convinced of their errors, that all fine wit is confined to the white men, especially to those of Christendom, and would have confessed that Oroonoko was as capable even of reigning well, and of governing as wisely, had as great a soul, as politic maxims, and was as sensible of power, as any prince civilized in the most refined schools of humanity and learning, or the most illustrious courts. . . . **E**

Cultural Attitudes: What standard does the narrator use to judge Oroonoko's appearance, intellect, and behavior? What does the phrase "bating his color" say about her judgment? **E**

Oroonoko meets and falls in love with Imoinda, the daughter of the general who has sacrificed his own life to save Oroonoko's. They marry. Before the marriage is consummated, however, the old king, Oroonoko's grandfather, unaware of the marriage but taken with Imoinda's beauty, extends to her "the royal veil," forcing her into his harem. After Oroonoko secretly claims his bride, the king sells Imoinda into slavery but tells his grandson that she is dead. In despair Oroonoko abandons his responsibility to lead in battle. With the army fleeing the enemy, however, he rallies, resumes leadership, and achieves victory.

Oroonoko was no sooner returned from this last conquest, and received at court with all the joy and magnificence that could be expressed to a young victor, who was not only returned triumphant but beloved like a deity, when there arrived in the port an English ship.

This persons had often before been in these countries and was very well known to Oroonoko, with whom he had trafficked[7] for slaves, and had used to do the same with his predecessors.

---

3. *mien:* "bearing or manner" (*AHD*)
4. *bating:* taking away
5. *There . . . handsome:* Oroonoko's qualities do not come short of Behn's standard of true beauty.
6. *bears:* "to sustain, support, uphold; to sustain successfully" (*OED*)
7. *trafficked:* "to carry on trade or other dealings" (*AHD*)

This commander was a man of a finer sort of address and conversation, better bred and more engaging than most of that sort of men are, so that he seemed rather never to have been bred out of a court than almost all his life at sea. This captain therefore was always better received at court than most of the traders to those countries were; and especially by Oroonoko, who was more civilized, according to the European mode, than any other had been, and took more delight in the white nations, and above all men of parts and wit. To this captain he sold abundance of his slaves, and for the favor and esteem he had for him, made him many presents, and obliged him to stay at court as long as possibly he could. Which the captain seemed to take as a very great honor done him, entertaining the Prince every day with globes and maps, and mathematical discourses and instruments; eating, drinking, hunting, and living with him with so much familiarity that it was not to be doubted but he had gained very greatly upon the heart of this gallant young man. And the captain, in return of all these mighty favors, besought the Prince to honor his vessel with his presence, some day or other, to dinner, before he should set sail; which he condescended to accept, and appointed his day. The captain, on his part, failed not to have all things in a readiness, in the most magnificent order he could possibly. And the day being come, the captain in his boat, richly adorned with carpets and velvet cushions, rowed to the shore to receive the Prince with another longboat where was placed all his music and trumpets, with which Oroonoko was extremely delighted; who met him on the shore attended by his French governor, Jamoan, Aboan, and about a hundred of the noblest of the youths of the court. And after they had first carried the Prince on board, the boats fetched the rest off; where they found a very splendid treat, with all sorts of fine wines, and were as well entertained as 'twas possible in such a place to be.

The Prince, having drunk hard of punch and several sorts of wine, as did all the rest (for great care was taken they should want nothing of that part of the entertainment), was very merry, and in great admiration of the ship, for he had never been in one before; so that he was curious of beholding every place where he decently might descend. The rest, no less curious, who were not quite overcome with drinking, rambled at their pleasure fore and aft, as their fancies guided 'em. So that the captain, who had well laid his design before,[8] gave the word, and seized on all his guests; they clapping great irons suddenly on the Prince, when he was leaped down in the hold to view that part of the vessel, and locking him fast down, secured him. The same treachery was used to all the rest; and all in one instant, in several places of the ship, were lashed[9] fast in irons, and betrayed to slavery. That great design over, they set all hands to work to hois[t] sail; and with as treacherous and fair a wind, they made from the shore with this innocent and glorious prize, who thought of nothing less than such an entertainment. **R**

Infer Tone: How does the English governor treat the Africans? Do you think the narrator approves or disapproves of his treatment? How do you know? **R**

Some have commended this act as brave in the captain; but I will spare my sense of it, and leave it to my reader to judge as he pleases.

It may be easily guessed in what manner the Prince resented this indignity, who may be best resembled to a lion taken in a toil; so he raged, so he struggled for liberty, but all in vain; and they had so wisely managed his fetters that he could not use a hand in his defense, to quit himself of a life that would by no means endure slavery, nor could he move from the place where

8. *well . . . before:* The captain had carefully planned this trap ahead of time, apparently with his shipmates' knowledge.
9. *lashed:* "to secure or bind" (*AHD*)

he was tied to any solid part of the ship, against which he might have beat his head, and have finished his disgrace that way. So that being deprived of all other means, he resolved to perish for want of food. And pleased at last with that thought, and toiled and tired by rage and indignation, he laid himself down, and sullenly resolved upon dying, and refused all things that were brought him. A

Point of View: What is the predominant point of view in the preceding paragraphs? At what point does the narrator puncture the narrative with a shift in point of view? A

This did not a little vex the captain, and the more so because he found almost all of 'em of the same humor; so that the loss of so many brave slaves, so tall and goodly to behold, would have been very considerable. He therefore ordered one to go from him (for he would not be seen himself) to Oroonoko, and to assure him he was afflicted for having rashly done so unhospitable a deed, and which could not be now remedied, since they were far from shore; but since he resented it in so high a nature, he assured him he would revoke his resolution, and set both him and his friends ashore on the next land they should touch at; and of this the messenger gave him his oath, provided he would resolve to live. And Oroonoko, whose honor was such as he never had violated a word in his life himself, much less a solemn asseveration,[10] believed in an instant what this man said, but replied, he expected for a confirmation of this to have his shameful fetters dismissed. . . . R

Infer Tone: How does the narrator describe Oroonoko? What is she implying about the British captain and colonizers? R

The captain pondering and consulting what to do, it was concluded that nothing but Oroonoko's liberty would encourage any of the rest to eat, except the Frenchman, whom the captain could not pretend to keep prisoner, but only told him he was secured because he might act something in favor of the Prince, but that he should be freed as soon as they came to land. So that they concluded it wholly necessary to free the Prince from his irons, that he might show himself to the rest; that they might have an eye upon him, and that they could not fear a single man.

This being resolved, to make the obligation the greater, the captain himself went to Oroonoko; where after many compliments, and assurances of what he had already promised, he receiving from the Prince his parole and his hand for his good behavior, dismissed his irons and brought him to his own cabin; where after having treated and reposed[11] him a while, for he had neither eat nor slept in four days before, he besought him to visit those obstinate people in chains, who refused all manner of sustenance, and entreated him to oblige 'em[12] to eat, and assure 'em of their liberty the first opportunity.

Oroonoko, who was too generous not to give credit to his words,[13] showed himself to his people, who were transported with excess of joy[14] at the sight of their darling prince falling at his feet and kissing and embracing 'em, believing, as some divine oracle, all he assured 'em. But he besought 'em to bear their chains with that bravery that became those whom he had seen act so nobly in arms; and that they could not give him greater proofs of their love and friendship, since 'twas all the security the captain (his friend) could have, against the revenge, he said, they might possibly justly take for the injuries sustained by him. And they all with one accord assured him, they could not suffer enough, when it was for his repose and safety.

After this they no longer refused to eat, but took what was brought 'em, and were pleased with their captivity, since by it they hoped to redeem the Prince, who, all the rest of the voyage, was treated with all the respect due to

10. *asseveration:* a serious or positive declaration
11. *reposed:* "to lie while being supported by something" (*AHD*)
12. *oblige 'em:* i.e., to compel or require them to do something
13. *too . . . words:* His noble character makes his words believable.
14. *transported . . . joy:* i.e., overcome with joy

his birth though nothing could divert his melancholy; and he would often sigh for Imoinda, and think this a punishment due to his misfortune, in having left that noble maid behind him that fatal night, in the Otan, when he fled to the camp.

Possessed with a thousand thoughts of past joys with this fair young person, and a thousand griefs for her eternal loss, he endured a tedious voyage, and at last arrived at the mouth of the river of Surinam, a colony belonging to the King of England, and where they were to deliver some part of their slaves. There the merchants and gentlemen of the country going on board to demand those lots of slaves they had already agreed on, and, amongst those, the overseers of those plantations where I then chanced to be, the captain, who had given the word, ordered his men to bring up those noble slaves in fetters whom I have spoken of; and having put 'em some in one and some in other lots, with women and children (which they call pickaninnies), they sold 'em off as slaves to several merchants and gentlemen; not putting any two in one lot, because they would separate 'em far from each other, not daring to trust 'em together, lest rage and courage should put 'em upon contriving some great action, to the ruin of the colony.

Oroonoko was first seized on, and sold to our overseer, who had the first lot, with seventeen more of all sorts and sizes, but not one of quality with him. When he saw this, he found what they meant, for, as I said, he understood English pretty well; and being wholly unarmed and defenseless, so as it was in vain to make any resistance, he only beheld the captain with a look all fierce and disdainful, **upbraiding** him with eyes that forced blushes on his guilty cheeks; he only cried, in passing over the side of the ship, "Farewell, sir. 'Tis worth my suffering, to gain so true a knowledge both of you and of your gods by whom you swear." And desiring those that held him to **forbear** their pains, and telling 'em he would make no resistance, he cried, "Come, my fellow slaves; let us descend, and see if we can meet with more honor and honesty in the next world we shall touch upon." So he nimbly leaped into the boat, and showing no more concern, suffered himself to be rowed up the river with his seventeen companions. R

upbraid (ŭp-brād′) *tr.v.* To reprove sharply; reproach.

forbear (fôr-bâr′) *tr.v.* To restrain oneself from doing something; hold back.

Infer Tone: In the final scene when Oroonoko is sold, is the narrator portraying him as a sympathetic or unsympathetic character? R

THINK AND DISCUSS

1. Define *first-person point of view* and *third-person point of view*. Give an example for each.
2. How does Behn's use of both first-person point of view and third-person point of view fit the varying nature of the story's content?
3. How does Behn characterize the English colonizers and slave traders? What is her tone toward them—sympathetic or unsympathetic? Provide evidence from the text to support your answers.
4. How does Behn characterize Oroonoko? What is her tone toward him—sympathetic or unsympathetic? Provide evidence from the text to support your answers.
5. How does Behn characterize the African slaves in general? What is her tone toward them? Provide evidence from the text to support your answers.
6. How does Behn's attitude toward Africans differ from the prevailing cultural attitudes of her day? How does she succumb to those cultural attitudes? Provide evidence from the text to support your answer.
7. Evaluate the prevailing cultural attitudes of Behn's day from a biblical worldview. Consult the following passages when forming your answer: 1 Samuel 16:7 and James 3:9–10.

Olaudah Equiano (ca. 1745–97)

Much of what is known of Olaudah Equiano's early life is gained from his autobiography, *The Life of Olaudah Equiano, or Gustavas Vassa, the African*. According to this work, Equiano was born to a leader in the Essaka village of Nigeria, and, along with his sister, was abducted and sold when he was only eleven. Traded to various masters, he was gradually moved across Nigeria and eventually across the Atlantic to Barbados and soon after to Virginia, then a British colony.

In Virginia Equiano was purchased by Lieutenant Michael Henry Pascal, a Royal Navy captain and merchant, who took Equiano to England. While serving Pascal during the Seven Years War, Equiano traveled widely and received a simple education, both opportunities unavailable to plantation slaves. Additionally, he officially converted to Christianity, being baptized into the Anglican Church. In 1763 Equiano was sold to a Quaker merchant, Robert King. He primarily served with the ship's crew and as King's personal servant but was also allowed to run a small business. By this means, he raised forty pounds and bought his freedom in 1766.

After gaining independence, Equiano sought ways to improve the situation of enslaved Africans. He promoted the Sierra Leone resettlement project, a sadly ineffective relocation plan for freed slaves in poverty. He advocated freeing the slaves by helping form a group called the Sons of Africa to support the abolition of slavery. Finally, he published his autobiography in 1789.

One of the first and most influential slave narratives, Equiano's work voiced the desperate situation of thousands of suffering slaves. It also related Equiano's personal spiritual journey which, even after conversion, was fraught with struggles often engendered by his experiences as a slave. The book's wide success brought him a measure of fame and financial stability. Equiano married Susannah Cullen in 1792, and the couple had two daughters. Sadly, first Susannah (in 1796) and then Olaudah (in 1797) died while the girls were still quite young. The location of his grave remains unknown.

William Wilberforce (1759–1833)

Born in Hull, William Wilberforce attended Hull Grammar School and eventually St. John's College in Cambridge. In 1780, at age twenty-one, he was elected to the House of Commons. At age twenty-five he experienced a conversion to evangelical Christianity. Mentored by John Newton, among others, Wilberforce purposefully used his political influence to better society. An advocate for a multitude of social reforms, he is best known for his decades-long fight to abolish slavery in Britain and her colonies. His amazing tenacity was fueled by his vibrant evangelical Christianity.

Wilberforce joined forces with various groups (e.g., Quakers, who had been working toward abolition since the early 1780s) and influential leaders like Charles Fox, Edmund Burke, and Hannah More in pursuing the abolition of the slave trade. He and Thomas Clarkson worked closely in this effort, Wilberforce speaking to leaders in politics and Clarkson to the masses through propaganda. As a result, the Slave Trade Act was passed in 1807, bringing an end to Britain's participation in the slave trade, including in the deadly Middle Passage. In 1823 Wilberforce became the vice president of the Anti-Slavery Society, which sought to abolish the institution of slavery in the British colonies.

Sadly, his lifelong health struggles forced him to retire from the House of Commons in 1825. Weak eyesight, ulcerative colitis, opiate treatments, and a curvature of the spine weakened him physically. He had drawn strength from other believers throughout his lifetime of political work, particularly through the Clapham sect, a close group of Christian men involved in business and government. He had fought for the betterment of society in many ways through his philanthropic and political work (i.e., child labor reform, prison reform).

His antislavery labors bore fruit just days before his death on July 29, 1833, by the July 25 passing of the Slavery Abolition Act, which abolished slavery in most of the British Empire.

ANALYZE: *Slave Narrative, Speech, Persuasion*

The texts that follow are excerpts from Equiano's **slave narrative** (an autobiographical account of the author's experience as a slave) and Wilberforce's **speech** (oral, public communication that can be used for various purposes). Both address the realities of slavery, specifically the dreaded transatlantic Middle Passage. Although their genres differ, the purpose of both authors is the same: persuasion.

To achieve this purpose, both authors use their genres to advantage. For example, Equiano taps into the power of an eyewitness's **first-person point of view** (p. 394) to appeal to readers; Wilberforce adorns his ideas with rhetorical devices such as **anaphora** (p. 165) and **rhetorical questions** (questions asked, not to receive an answer, but to achieve an effect). Finally, both incorporate many **sensory details** (pp. 314) into their works. As you read, find examples of such content and techniques in each text. How do they contribute to the authors' persuasive appeals?

READ: *Ask Questions of a Text*

To change their audiences' ideas and actions, persuasive texts use various appeals, including those to **logos**, **pathos**, and **ethos** (i.e., to logic and reason, to emotions, and to moral or intellectual authority, see p. 140). Some are directly stated. Others may be implied. For example, the use of **connotative language** (words that convey not just their dictionary definitions but also the speaker's emotional or evaluative tone toward his subject) is a common way to imply appeals to pathos and ethos.

When you read persuasive works, asking questions of a text can help you recognize these appeals in order to judge their validity. For example, what reasons or facts has an author given to support his claims? Or how do his anecdotes or evaluations of events make you feel as a reader or listener? Additionally, what underlying beliefs or authorities has he relied on in evaluating an idea or advocating a course of action? As you read the following selections, use such questions to identify the appeals these abolitionists make.

EVALUATE: *Persuasive Appeals*

Authors engaged in persuasion can too often disregard the important biblical qualities of Truth (unbiased and accurate representation of reality) and Goodness (the promotion of that which is morally good). Does the Bible support using the full range of logical, ethical, and emotional appeals in persuasion (see Acts 17:16–19, Rom. 12:20–21, and Prov. 25:15)? If so, do Equiano and Wilberforce use these appeals in a way that shows a biblical concern for both Truth and Goodness?

OBJECTIVES

- Identify rhetorical devices and sensory details in a text.
- Ask questions to identify a work's use of rhetorical appeals.
- Analyze an author's use of point of view, sensory details, and rhetorical devices for persuasive purposes.
- Evaluate a text's use of persuasive appeals from a biblical perspective.

VOCABULARY

aggravate (ăg′rə-vāt′) *tr.v.* To make worse or more troublesome.

avarice (ăv′ə-rĭs) *n.* Immoderate desire for wealth; cupidity.

advocate (ăd′və-kĭt) *n.* One that argues for a cause; a supporter or defender.

exculpate (ĕk′skəl-pāt′) *tr.v.* To clear of guilt or blame.

palliate (păl′ē-āt′) *tr.v.* To make (an offense or crime) seem less serious; extenuate.

irremediable (ĭr′ĭ-mē′dē-ə-bəl) *adj.* Impossible to remedy, correct, or repair; incurable or irreparable.

Why is it important to have a **VOICE?**

Everyone has a perspective. Even if one's opinion does not carry the day, his or her perspective can offer a more complete picture from which to work. Most people are more satisfied when they feel their voice has been heard. In what ways do you contribute your voice in your school and community? If you lead, do you also listen? What would it feel like to lack a voice? Write a paragraph to convey your ideas.

from THE LIFE OF OLAUDAH EQUIANO OR GUSTAVUS VASSA, THE AFRICAN

The slave trade operated in a commercial triangle: European traders bought slaves from African middlemen, sold them to colonists in exchange for their crops, brought these goods to European markets, and then returned to start the cycle again. The most notorious leg of this triangle was the Middle Passage, the journey from Africa to the Americas. The selection that follows is Equiano's firsthand account of this journey. It brought widespread attention to the horrors of the slave trade which, although familiar to modern audiences, were new to many of Equiano's contemporaries.

The first object which saluted my eyes when I arrived on the coast, was the sea, and a slave ship, which was then riding at anchor, and waiting for its cargo. These filled me with astonishment, which was soon converted into terror, when I was carried on board. I was immediately handled, and tossed up to see if I were sound, by some of the crew; and I was now persuaded that I had gotten into a world of bad spirits, and that they were going to kill me. Their complexions, too, differing so much from ours, their long hair, and the language they spoke, (which was very different from any I had ever heard) united to confirm me in this belief. Indeed, such were the horrors of my views and fears at the moment, that, if ten thousand worlds had been my own, I would have freely parted with them all to have exchanged my condition with that of the meanest slave[1] in my own country. When I looked round the ship too, and saw a large furnace of copper boiling, and a multitude of black people of every description chained together, every one of their countenances expressing dejection and sorrow, I no longer doubted of my fate; and, quite overpowered with horror and anguish, I fell motionless on the deck and fainted. When I recovered a little, I found some black people about me, who I believed were some of those who had brought me on board, and had been receiving their pay; they talked to me in order to cheer me, but all in vain. I asked them if we were not to be eaten by those white men with horrible looks, red faces, and long hair. They told me I was not: and one of the crew brought me a small portion of spirituous liquor in a wine glass, but, being afraid of him, I would not take it out of his hand. One of the blacks, therefore, took it from him and gave it to me, and I took a little down my palate, which, instead of reviving me, as they thought it would, threw me into the greatest consternation at the strange feeling it produced, having never tasted any such liquor before. Soon after this, the blacks who brought me on board went off, and left me abandoned to despair. **A**

Slave Narrative: How does Equiano's first-person point of view already add force to his descriptions of the slave trade? **A**

1. *meanest slave:* the slave lowest in rank

I now saw myself deprived of all chance of returning to my native country, or even the least glimpse of hope of gaining the shore, which I now considered as friendly; and I even wished for my former slavery in preference to my present situation, which was filled with horrors of every kind, still heightened by my ignorance of what I was to undergo. I was not long suffered to indulge my grief; I was soon put down under the decks, and there I received such a salutation in my nostrils as I had never experienced in my life; so that, with the loathsomeness of the stench, and crying together, I became so sick and low that I was not able to eat, nor had I the least desire to taste anything. I now wished for the last friend, death, to relieve me; but soon, to my grief, two of the white men offered me eatables; and, on my refusing to eat, one of them held me fast by the hands, and laid me across, I think the windlass,[2] and tied my feet, while the other flogged[3] me severely. I had never experienced anything of this kind before, and although not being used to the water, I naturally feared that element the first time I saw it, yet, nevertheless, could I have got over the nettings,[4] I would have jumped over the side, but I could not; and besides, the crew used to watch us very closely who were not chained down to the decks, lest we should leap into the water; and I have seen some of these poor African prisoners most severely cut, for attempting to do so, and hourly whipped for not eating. This indeed was often the case with myself. In a little time after, amongst the poor chained men, I found some of my own nation, which in a small degree gave ease to my mind. I inquired of these what was to be done with us; they gave me to understand, we were to be carried to these white people's country to work for them. I then was a little revived, and thought, if it were no worse than working, my situation was not so desperate; but still I feared I should be put to death, the white people looked and acted, as I thought, in so savage a manner; for I had never seen among any people such instances of brutal cruelty; and this not only shown towards us blacks, but also to some of the whites themselves. One white man in particular I saw, when we were permitted to be on deck, flogged so unmercifully with a large rope near the foremast,[5] that he died in consequence of it; and they tossed him over the side as they would have done a brute. This made me fear these people the more; and I expected nothing less than to be treated in the same manner. I could not help expressing my fears and apprehensions to some of my countrymen; I asked them if these people had no country, but lived in this hollow place (the ship); they told me they did not, but came from a distant one. "Then," said I, "how comes it in all our country we never heard of them?" They told me because they lived so very far off. I then asked where were their women? had they any like themselves? I was told they had. "And why," said I, "do we not see them?" They answered, because they were left behind. I asked how the vessel could go; they told me they could not tell; but that there was cloth put upon the masts by the help of the ropes I saw, and then the vessel went on; and the white men had some spell or magic they put in the water when they liked, in order to stop the vessel. I was exceedingly amazed at this account, and really thought they were spirits. I therefore wished much to be from amongst them, for I expected they would sacrifice me; but my wishes were vain—for we were so quartered that it was impossible for any of us to make our escape. . . . R

Ask Questions: What kind of appeal—logos, pathos, or ethos—is Equiano already making through his narrative? R

2. *windlass:* a device on a ship used to lift or lower heavy objects (i.e., an anchor)
3. *flogged:* beat with a rod or whip
4. *nettings:* a network of small ropes around a ship used for different purposes, including storage
5. *foremast:* the long pole in the bow of a ship that supports the sails and rigging

At last, when the ship we were in, had got in all her cargo, they made ready with many fearful noises, and we were all put under deck, so that we could not see how they managed the vessel. But this disappointment was the least of my sorrow. The stench of the hold while we were on the coast was so intolerably loathsome, that it was dangerous to remain there for any time, and some of us had been permitted to stay on the deck for the fresh air; but now that the whole ship's cargo were confined together, it became absolutely pestilential. The closeness of the place, and the heat of the climate, added to the number in the ship, which was so crowded that each had scarcely room to turn himself, almost suffocated us. This produced copious perspirations, so that the air soon became unfit for respiration, from a variety of loathsome smells, and brought on a sickness among the slaves, of which many died—thus falling victims to the improvident avarice, as I may call it, of their purchasers. This wretched situation was again **aggravated** by the galling[6] of the chains, now become insupportable, and the filth of the necessary tubs, into which the children often fell, and were almost suffocated. The shrieks of the women, and the groans of the dying, rendered the whole a scene of horror almost inconceivable. Happily perhaps, for myself, I was soon reduced so low here that it was thought necessary to keep me almost always on deck; and from my extreme youth I was not put in fetters. In this situation I expected every hour to share the fate of my companions, some of whom were almost daily brought upon deck at the point of death, which I began to hope would soon put an end to my miseries. Often did I think many of the inhabitants of the deep much more happy than myself. I envied them the freedom they enjoyed, and as often wished I could change my condition for theirs. Every circumstance I met with, served only to render my state more painful, and heightened my apprehensions, and my opinion of the cruelty of the whites. **A**

aggravate (ăg′rə-vāt′) *tr.v.* To make worse or more troublesome.

Persuasion: Find several examples of sensory details in Equiano's description of the ship's hold. How many different senses does he appeal to? **A**

One day they had taken a number of fishes; and when they had killed and satisfied themselves with as many as they thought fit, to our astonishment who were on deck, rather than give any of them to us to eat, as we expected, they tossed the remaining fish into the sea again, although we begged and prayed for some as well as we could, but in vain; and some of my countrymen, being pressed by hunger, took an opportunity, when they thought no one saw them, of trying to get a little privately; but they were discovered, and the attempt procured them some very severe floggings. One day, when we had a smooth sea and moderate wind, two of my wearied countrymen who were chained together, (I was near them at the time), preferring death to such a life of misery, somehow made through the nettings and jumped into the sea; immediately, another quite dejected fellow, who, on account of his illness, was suffered to be out of irons, also followed their example; and I believe many more would very soon have done the same, if they had not been prevented by the ship's crew, who were instantly alarmed. Those of us that were the most active, were in a moment put down under the deck, and there was such a noise and confusion amongst the people of the ship as I never heard before, to stop her, and get the boat out to go after the slaves. However, two of the wretches were drowned, but they got the other, and afterwards flogged him unmercifully, for thus attempting to prefer death to slavery. In this manner we continued to undergo more hardships than I can now relate, hardships which are inseparable from this accursed trade. . . . **R**

Ask Questions: Which two kinds of rhetorical appeals underly Equiano's description of these incidents? **R**

6. *galling:* chafing, physically irritating

. . . At last, we came in sight of the island of Barbadoes, at which the whites on board gave a great shout, and made many signs of joy to us. We did not know what to think of this; but as the vessel drew nearer, we plainly saw the harbor, and other ships of different kinds and sizes, and we soon anchored amongst them, off Bridgetown. Many merchants and planters now came on board, though it was in the evening. They put us in separate parcels, and examined us attentively. They also made us jump, and pointed to the land, signifying we were to go there. We thought by this, we should be eaten by these ugly men, as they appeared to us; and, when soon after we were all put down under the deck again, there was much dread and trembling among us, and nothing but bitter cries to be heard all the night from these apprehensions, insomuch, that at last the white people got some old slaves from the land to pacify us. They told us we were not to be eaten, but to work, and were soon to go on land, where we should see many of our country people. This report eased us much. And sure enough, soon after we were landed, there came to us Africans of all languages.

We were conducted immediately to the merchant's yard, where we were all pent up together, like so many sheep in a fold, without regard to sex or age. . . .

We were not many days in the merchant's custody, before we were sold after their usual manner, which is this: On a signal given, (as the beat of a drum), the buyers rush at once into the yard where the slaves are confined, and make choice of that parcel they like best. The noise and clamor with which this is attended, and the eagerness visible in the countenances of the buyers, serve not a little to increase the apprehension of terrified Africans, who may well be supposed to consider them as the ministers of that destruction to which they think themselves devoted. In this manner, without scruple, are relations and friends separated, most of them never to see each other again. I remember, in the vessel in which I was brought over, in the men's apartment, there were several brothers, who, in the sale, were sold in different lots; and it was very moving on this occasion, to see and hear their cries at parting. O, ye nominal Christians! might not an African ask you—Learned you this from your God, who says unto you, Do unto all men as you would men should do unto you? Is it not enough that we are torn from our country and friends, to toil for your luxury and lust of gain? Must every tender feeling be likewise sacrificed to your **avarice**? Are the dearest friends and relations, now rendered more dear by their separation from their kindred, still to be parted from each other, and thus prevented from cheering the gloom of slavery, with the small comfort of being together, and mingling their sufferings and sorrows? Why are parents to lose their children, brothers their sisters, or husbands their wives? Surely, this is a new refinement in cruelty, which, while it has no advantage to atone for it, thus aggravates distress, and adds fresh horrors even to the wretchedness of slavery. **A** **R**

avarice (ăv′ə-rĭs) *n.* Immoderate desire for wealth; cupidity.

Persuasion: What rhetorical device does Equiano use repeatedly in this paragraph? Would his final appeals be as forceful without it? **A**

Ask Questions: Which two kinds of rhetorical appeal does Equiano lean on heavily in this final paragraph? **R**

from 1789 Abolition Speech

William Wilberforce

The following passages are excerpted from Wilberforce's powerful antislavery speech before Parliament in 1789. The abolitionists' campaign had reached its highest pitch of public fervor, and key proponents requested that Wilberforce, well versed in information on the trade, bring the issue before Parliament. In his first public speech on the issue, he advocated convincingly for a halt to the slave trade (a first step toward abolishing slavery).

Unfortunately, opponents diffused his speech's effects by asking for and then delaying an opportunity to present their own side in response. By the time the issue was once again brought to the point in 1791, the French Revolution had induced a general fear of radical change. Reform efforts came crashing to a halt. Nonetheless, the persuasive power of Wilberforce's speech remains clear today.

When I consider the magnitude of the subject which I am to bring before the House—a subject, in which the interests, not of this country, nor of Europe alone, but of the whole world, and of posterity, are involved: and when I think, at the same time, on the weakness of the **advocate** who has undertaken this great cause—when these reflections press upon my mind, it is impossible for me not to feel both terrified and concerned at my own inadequacy to such a task. But when I reflect, however, on the encouragement which I have had, through the whole course of a long and laborious examination of this question, how much candor I have experienced, and how conviction has increased within my own mind, in proportion as I have advanced in my labors; when I reflect, especially, that however adverse any gentleman may now be, yet we shall all, most assuredly, be of one opinion in the end. When I turn myself to these thoughts, I take courage—I determine to forget all my other fears, and I march forward with a firmer step, in the full assurance that my cause will bear me out, and that I shall be able to justify, upon the clearest principles, every resolution in my hand—the avowed end of which, Sir, is—the total abolition of the slave trade. **A**

I wish exceedingly, in the outset, to guard both myself and the House from entering into the subject with any sort of passion. It is not their passions I shall appeal to—I ask only for their cool and impartial reason; and I wish not to take them by surprise, but to deliberate, point by point, upon every part of this question. I mean not to accuse any one, but to take the shame upon myself, in common, indeed, with the whole Parliament of Great Britain, for having suffered this horrid trade to be carried on, under their authority. We are all guilty—we ought all to plead guilty, and not to **exculpate** ourselves, by throwing the blame on others; and I therefore deprecate every kind of reflection, against the various descriptions of people who are more immediately involved in this wretched business. **R**

In opening the nature of the slave trade, I need only observe, that it is found, by experience, to be just such as every man, who uses his reason, would infallibly conclude it to be. For my own part, so clearly am I convinced of the mischiefs inseparable from it, that I should hardly want any further evidence than my own mind would furnish, by the most simple deductions. Facts, however, are now laid before the House. A report[1] has been made by his Majesty's Privy Council, which, I trust, every gentleman has read, and which ascertains the slave trade to be just such in practice as we know, from theory, that it must be. What should we suppose must naturally be the consequence of our carrying on a

1. *A report:* Wilberforce refers to a government report on the slave trade prepared at the behest of Prime Minister William Pitt, Wilberforce's longtime friend and fellow abolitionist.

advocate (ăd′və-kĭt) *n.* One that argues for a cause; a supporter or defender.

Persuasion: What rhetorical device does Wilberforce use throughout this paragraph to help audiences follow his long, complex sentences? **A**

exculpate (ĕk′skəl-pāt′) *tr.v.* To clear of guilt or blame.

Ask Questions: What kind of appeal does Wilberforce begin with? As you continue reading, note places at which the appeal forms the launching point for the other two types of appeals. **R**

slave trade with Africa? With a country, vast in its extent, not utterly barbarous, but civilized in a very small degree? Does anyone suppose a slave trade would help their civilization? That Africa would profit by such an intercourse? Is it not plain, that she must suffer from it? That civilization must be checked; that her barbarous manners must be made more barbarous; and that the happiness of her millions of inhabitants must be prejudiced by her intercourse with Britain? Does not everyone see, that a slave trade, carried on around her coasts, must carry violence and desolation to her very center? That, in a continent, just emerging from barbarism, if a trade in men is established—if her men are all converted into goods, and become commodities that can be bartered, it follows, they must be subject to ravage just as goods are?. . . **A**

The slave trade, in its very nature, is the source of such kind of tragedies, nor has there been a single person, almost, before the Privy Council, who does not add something, by his testimony, to the mass of evidence upon this point. Some, indeed, of these gentlemen, and particularly the delegates from Liverpool, have endeavored to reason down this plain principle; some have **palliated** it, but there is not one, I believe, who does not more or less, admit it. Some, nay most, I believe, have admitted the slave trade to be the chief cause of wars in Africa.[2] . . . It is a trade in its principle most inevitably calculated to spread disunion among the African princes, to sow the seeds of every mischief, to inspire enmity, to destroy humanity; and it is found in practice, by the most abundant testimony, to have had the effect in Africa of carrying misery, devastation, and ruin wherever its baneful influence has extended.

VISUAL ANALYSIS
How does this political cartoon from Wilberforce's era reflect the irony underlying England's involvement in slavery?

Having now disposed of the first part of this subject, I must speak of the transit of the slaves in the West Indies.

This I confess, in my own opinion, is the most wretched part of the whole subject. So much misery condensed in so little room, is more than the human imagination had ever before conceived. I will not accuse the Liverpool merchants: I will allow them—nay, I will believe them to be men of humanity; and I will therefore believe, if it were not for the multitude of these wretched objects, if it were not for the enormous magnitude and extent of the evil which distracts their attention from individual cases, and makes them think generally, and therefore less feelingly on the subject, they never would have persisted in the trade. I verily believe, therefore, if the wretchedness of any one of the many hundred negroes stowed in each ship could be brought before their view, and remain within the sight of the African merchant, that there is no one among them, whose heart would bear it? Let anyone imagine to himself 600 or 700 of these wretches chained two and two, surrounded with every object that is nauseous and disgusting, diseased, and struggling under every kind of wretchedness! How can we bear to think of such a scene as this? One would think it had been determined to heap upon them all the varieties of bodily pain, for the purpose of blunting the feelings of their mind; **R** and yet, in this very point (to show the power of human prejudice) the situation of the slaves has been described by Mr. Norris,[3] one of the Liverpool delegates, in a manner which, I am sure, will convince the House how interest[4] can draw a film over the eyes, so thick, that total blindness could do no more; and

2. *the chief cause of wars in Africa:* Tribes went to war in order to gain captives to sell to traders as slaves.

3. *Mr. Norris:* Posing as an abolitionist, Norris had met Wilberforce's fellow abolitionist Thomas Clarkson. Norris used the relationship to malign Clarkson's credibility and grossly misrepresent the Middle Passage as a joyous, comfortable experience. Wilberforce thus refutes several of Norris's untruths.

4. *interest:* a personal investment in the outcome of a situation

Persuasion: What rhetorical device does Wilberforce use in this paragraph? What effect does it have on you as the reader? **A**

palliate (păl′ē-āt′) *tr.v.* To make (an offense or crime) seem less serious; extenuate.

Ask Questions: What two types of appeals does Wilberforce focus on in these paragraphs? Consider the main reactions you as a reader have. **R**

how it is our duty, therefore, to trust not to the reasonings of interested men, or to their way of coloring a transaction. . . .

What will the House think, when, by the concurring testimony of other witnesses, the true history is laid open. The slaves, who are sometimes described as rejoicing at their captivity, are so wrung with misery at leaving their country, that it is the constant practice to set sail in the night, lest they should be sensible of their departure. The pulse which Mr. Norris talks of are horse beans;[5] and the scantiness, both of water and provision, was suggested by the very legislature of Jamaica, in the report of their Committee, to be a subject that called for the interference of Parliament. Mr. Norris talks of frankincense and lime-juice;[6] when all the surgeons tell you, the slaves are stowed so close, that there is not room to tread among them: and when you have it in evidence from Sir George Yonge,[7] that even in a ship which wanted 200 of her complement,[8] the stench was intolerable. The song and the dance, says Mr. Norris, are promoted. It had been more fair, perhaps, if he had explained that word *promoted*. The truth is, that, for the sake of exercise, these miserable wretches, loaded with chains, oppressed with disease and wretchedness, are forced to dance by the terror of the lash, and sometimes by the actual use of it. . . . It may be observed too, with respect to food, that an instrument is sometimes carried out, in order to force them to eat, which is the same sort of proof how much they enjoy themselves in that instance also. As to their singing; what shall we say, when we are told, that their songs are songs of lamentation upon their departure, which, while they sing, they are always in tears, insomuch that one Captain (more humane, as I should conceive him, therefore, than the rest) threatened one of the women with a flogging because the mournfulness of her song was too painful for his feelings. **A**

In order, however, not to trust too much to any sort of description, I will call the attention of the House to one species of evidence, which is absolutely infallible. Death at least, is a sure ground of evidence, and the proportion of deaths will not only confirm, but, if possible, will even aggravate our suspicion of their misery in the transit. It will be found, upon an average of all the ships of which evidence has been given at the Privy Council, that exclusive of those who perish before they sail, not less than 12.5 per cent perish in the passage. . . .

How then can the House refute its belief to the multiplied testimonies, before the Privy Council, of the savage treatment of the Negroes in the middle passage? Nay, indeed, what need is there of any evidence? The number of deaths speaks for itself, and makes all such inquiry superfluous.

As soon as ever I had arrived thus far in my investigation of the slave trade, I confess to you, Sir, so enormous, so dreadful, so **irremediable** did its wickedness appear that my own mind was completely made up for the abolition. A trade founded in iniquity, and carried on as this was, must be abolished, let the policy be what it might,—let the consequences be what they would, I from this time determined that I would never rest till I had effected its abolition. **R**

5. *horse beans:* fava beans
6. *frankincense and lime-juice:* Mr. Norris had reported that slave-ship holds were "perfumed" with these.
7. *Sir George Yonge:* member of Parliament and later Secretary at War
8. *wanted 200 of her complement:* lacked 200 of her capacity

Persuasion: What sensory details does Wilberforce use in this passage? How do they help refute Mr. Norris's false account of the Middle Passage? **A**

irremediable (ĭr′ĭ-mē′dē-ə-bəl) *adj.* Impossible to remedy, correct, or repair; incurable or irreparable.

Ask Questions: What kind of appeal does Wilberforce end on? How does his choice of connotative words (*wickedness* and *iniquity*) support that appeal? **R**

THINK AND DISCUSS

1. Identify the characteristics of a slave narrative.
2. Define *anaphora* and *rhetorical question*.
3. Define the three types of persuasive appeals.
4. What specific action did Wilberforce hope to impel through his persuasive speech?
5. For both texts, cite one example of three of the five kinds of sensory details (sight, sound, smell, etc.).
6. Give an example of anaphora and rhetorical question from these texts.
7. Using Equiano's narrative and Wilberforce's speech, give two examples of each type of rhetorical appeal.
8. Choose a social issue about which you feel strongly. List two persuasive appeals you would use to defend your position. Identify which type(s) of appeal each is.
9. Do you find Equiano's narrative and Wilberforce's speech credible? Why or why not? Do they seem to adhere to Truth and support Goodness?
10. Does the Bible seem to support the use of rhetorical appeals to persuade? Consult the following passages as you answer: Acts 17:1–3, 16–19; Ephesians 4:14–15; 2 Corinthians 10:3–5; Romans 12:20–21; and Proverbs 25:15.

What Do You Know?

Understand the Background

1. How does the writing of Johnson's time begin a break with the neoclassical tradition?
2. How was Thomas Gray a transitional poet from neoclassicism to romanticism?
3. Why does Bunyan belong in a section entitled "Voices from the Outside"?
4. In what way does the style of hymn written by Watts and Wesley reflect the period of time in which they lived? What did each hymn writer contribute to hymnody?

Apply the Concepts

5. Select an anecdote from *The Life of Samuel Johnson, LL.D.* and explain whether it explicitly or implicitly characterizes Johnson.
6. Select a portion from *Elegy Written in a Country Churchyard* and explain how it ventures beyond the neoclassical style.
7. In what genre is *Pilgrim's Progress* written? Identify and explain at least three elements on the story level with a corresponding meaning on the implied level.
8. What are the characteristics of common meter? Which hymn studied (that of Watts or that of Wesley) employs this meter?
9. How does Behn's use of two different literary points of view in *Oroonoko* help her mimic historical narratives?
10. Using examples, explain what the sensory details accomplish in Equiano's and Wilberforce's texts. What persuasive appeal(s) can you link them to?

Evaluate the Ideas

11. What was Johnson's purpose for his literary criticism in the *Rambler*? Use text examples to defend your answer.
12. How is Boswell's biography a balanced view of Johnson? Use text examples to defend your answer.
13. Does Behn paint Oroonoko as a sympathetic or unsympathetic character? How might her portrayal conform to or deviate from her society's general view of African slaves? Support your answer with textual details.
14. Identify two examples of rhetorical devices in Wilberforce's speech. What persuasive appeal(s) does he make in this instance? How do they increase the effectiveness of his speech?

Write a Response

15. Explain why you think or do not think Johnson evidences victory over his fear of death.
16. Relate the title of Bunyan's work to the experience of Christian and Faithful in Vanity Fair. What truths does their experience still hold for Christians today?
17. Examine the rhetorical appeals Equiano and Wilberforce use in their works. Explain how these conform to or deviate from a scriptural conception of Truth and Goodness.

Define each term and provide an example of each from a selection in Unit 3, Part 3 or 4.

TERMS

- sensibility
- style
- voice
- biography
- anecdote
- dialogue
- poetic diction
- allusion
- hymn
- common meter
- first-person point of view
- third-person point of view
- sympathetic character
- unsympathetic character
- slave narrative
- speech
- rhetorical question
- connotative language

UNIT 4 OBJECTIVES

LITERARY ELEMENTS

- Analyze examples of the following genres: lyric poetry, persuasion, the novel, frame tale, narrative poetry, elegy, dramatic monologue, argumentative essay, psychological realism, comedy, satire, short story.
- Analyze texts for literary philosophies such as neoclassicism, romanticism, naturalism, and aestheticism.
- Examine a poet's stylistic choices, from the use of dialect or rhythm to devices of sound (e.g., alliteration) and syntax (e.g., enjambment), and their effect on his or her message.
- Analyze a text's use of imagery, figurative expression, symbol, wit, and irony to develop its tone and theme.
- Analyze an argumentative work's structure and development of its primary ideas, including its use of rhetorical devices and appeals.
- Examine a narrative's use of character, plot, atmosphere, setting, and narrator to develop its themes.

READING STRATEGIES

- Annotate a text.
- Draw conclusions about a text.
- Compare and contrast texts.
- Use strategies in combination.

TEXT CRITICISM AND CREATION

- Evaluate from a biblical worldview philosophies such as romanticism, aestheticism, and naturalism as well as authors' views on issues such as death, material wealth, science, reason, and religious faith.
- Evaluate the effectiveness and truthfulness of a text's arguments.
- Evaluate the artistic effectiveness of a text's literary elements.
- Compose texts in a variety of genres based on model works.

UNIT 4

Romanticism to Victorianism

(1789–1901)

426 **SIGNS OF CHANGE**

454 **THE MAJOR ROMANTICS**

502 **EARLY VICTORIANS**

550 **LATE VICTORIANS**

Romanticism to Victorianism

The nineteenth century brought England unprecedented prosperity, including better standards of living, availability of consumer goods, and conveniences (e.g., railways, city sanitation). Democracy expanded, offering more freedom and opportunities. But despite a strong sense of their own progress, people in the era experienced a more complicated reality than such achievements convey. The century's myriad changes altered entire ways of life and frequently left people uncertain of the nature and proper workings of the world. Literature was often on the forefront of these new horizons, sometimes challenging the status quo, sometimes defending it, and as always, cataloging the varied responses of individuals to a world in flux.

ROMANTICISM

Toward the end of the eighteenth century, a surge of social change washed through Europe, fueled by old problems and new ideas. In France, the payment for a centuries-long absolute monarchy and oppressive aristocracy was coming due. In England, the Industrial Revolution and the slave trade were taking their toll. Meanwhile, in the philosophical and artistic realms, the downsides of neoclassical thought were increasingly clear. In response to these problems, a new voice would gradually emerge—that of romanticism.

REVOLUTION AT HOME AND ABROAD

The Industrial Revolution Now at full throttle, the Industrial Revolution brought England tremendous wealth. This success was partly produced by a *laissez-faire* (Fr. "allow [them] to do") policy discouraging government interference. But this approach also left workers desperately in need of employment at the mercy of their employers' often unreasonable expectations for work hours and pay. Most controversial was the issue of child labor as stories emerged of children working long hours under grueling conditions.

In politics, the rise of wealthy industrialists and of factory workers created complicated questions. A common theme in the coming century would be their demand for a greater voice in politics. Between these problems and those engendered by crowded industrial cities (in housing, sanitation, industrial pollution, etc.), British society had to find a new equilibrium in addressing social equity. The century's last two decades thus saw the rise of grassroots reform efforts to address both industrialization's effects and Britain's involvement in the slave trade (pp. 381, 402–10).

The French Revolution France had been Europe's cultural center, the source of Enlightenment thought. Yet it had resisted the direly needed political and social reforms suggested by *philosophes*. In 1789, the resulting unrest erupted into the French Revolution. Unfortunately, this movement, begun with great hopes, soon fell into moral disarray. Radical factions embraced violent means to reform, executing Louis XVI and his queen and implementing mass executions in the Reign of Terror (1793–94). This and the republic's declaration of war on the monarchies surrounding it shocked watchers from abroad.

In England, a reactionary climate set in. Reformers found their hopes for change stymied as new ideas were viewed with fear. Public meetings were forbidden (1795), the right of *habeas corpus* suspended, and censors cracked down on publications with even a whiff of radical thought. Prime Minister William Pitt the Younger had come to the office intent on reform, but other than advocating for the abolition of the slave trade (1807), he instead devoted his long ministry (1784–1801, 1804–6) to responding to a new threat—Napoleon.

The Napoleonic Wars (1803–15) The Napoleonic Wars ranged from Egypt and the New World to the Atlantic high seas and throughout the European continent. They were driven by the meteoric rise of a young Corsican artillery officer, Napoleon Bonaparte, to French military commander in 1795 and emperor in 1804. A brilliant tactical and organizational genius, Napoleon meant to conquer Europe and fended off a series of coalitions seeking to stop him.

Key victories gradually turned the tide. Lord Horatio Nelson penned up the French fleet in a series of battles, most famously at Trafalgar (1805). On land, the Duke of Wellington drove north through Portugal and Spain into France in the peninsular campaign of 1813. These victories together with France's disastrous invasion of Russia (1812) resulted in Napoleon's abdication and exile to the island of Elba (1814).

His escape and reinstatement as emperor in 1815 astonished Europe. For one hundred days, the continent once more teetered on the brink of war until the hastily mobilized forces of both sides met on the plains of Waterloo, Belgium. On June 18, in a devastating battle, a final coalition of nations barely defeated Napoleon's forces. Exiled again, Napoleon spent his last years on the island of St. Helena while France returned to a hereditary monarchy.

PEACE AND REFORM

A time of conservative reaction ensued in Europe. At the Congress of Vienna (1814–15), victor nations gathered to put the political pieces of Europe back into place—or, more accurately, to divide the pieces among themselves. England, now Europe's dominant imperial power and sole ruler of the seas, used her influence to block the ambitions of rival powers.

Affairs at home went less smoothly. Britain was largely physically untouched by the war, but it had monopolized the nation's resources and attention for years, taking hundreds of thousands of lives. Furthermore, war had fueled manufacturing, and its end led to a decrease in markets and labor needs. The wages of regular workers were often cut, while many returning veterans found little to no work and were reduced to begging or vagrancy. Then a series of protectionist tariffs called the Corn Laws (1815–46) limited grain imports, increasing food costs. Resulting workers' uprisings (1816, 1819) were forcefully suppressed, and Parliament restricted protests and worker strikes. The general population's anger and anxiety only increased.

An engraving of the Peterloo Massacre (1819).

Parliament was divided over voting reform, the goal of many agitators. The population then eligible to vote was exceedingly small—no more than three percent of the male population. But personal interests and entrenched beliefs related to class and education made change a steep uphill battle. Parliament repeatedly rejected proposed changes throughout the 1820s.

By the early 1830s, with the nation nearly in open conflict, Parliament finally passed the Reform Act of 1832. It gave new large industrial centers representation in Parliament and eliminated overrepresentation of some older boroughs. Additionally, it dealt with bribery issues and extended the vote to include some of the middle class. The act barely passed, and its actual effects on political power were relatively small. But it began the long process of making Britain's government more representative.

NEW WAYS OF THINKING

These tumultuous events intertwined closely with the rise of romanticism. This new movement would revolutionize European thinking in realms from philosophy to religion, politics, and art.

Enlightenment Rationalism Falters

Reactions to Enlightenment rationalism had been building for some time (pp. 358–59). A rationalistic worldview walled out large areas of human experience since much of what enriches and ennobles life (love, joy, peace, goodness, faith, etc.) is not rationally experienced or understood. Nonrational facets of human nature—feelings, imagination, intuition—can produce insights as profound as any scientific observation.

Furthermore, neoclassicism's confidence that a clear natural order to society's hierarchies existed was soon undermined by the very rising literacy and scientific innovations its rationalistic viewpoint supported. These allowed the common man more of a voice, rupturing the old social order. Once broken, their vision of an ideal order to society was difficult to reinstate.

Romantic Philosophy Rises

Four key new strands of thought would shape romanticism to come. First, philosophical **idealism** gained new popularity. Unlike rationalism, idealism asserts that humanity is unable to fully or accurately observe reality. Thus, people can be sure only of their own perceptions, not of objective reality. All knowledge is thus in some ways a creation of the individual's mind.

Next, the philosophy known as **transcendentalism** arose in Germany among disciples of Immanuel Kant (1724–1804). It offered a worldview alternative to deists' mechanistic religion. Whereas the god of deism is separate or absent from creation, the god of transcendentalism is resident within, almost equivalent with, nature and mankind—a World Spirit. Knowledge of him comes not from revelation or reason but from intuition and feeling.

Kant also put his own spin on Enlightenment **progressivism**, the belief that human society can gradually be made better and better through reform. According to German romantics, man had fallen not into sin but into division—from nature, from his fellows, and from himself. The cause of his fall was analytical reason, by which he is now dominated; the agent of his restoration would be creative imagination, especially as expressed in poetry.

Finally, dovetailing with transcendentalists' emphasis on nature was the **primitivism** of Jean Jacques Rousseau (1712–78). According to him, the cause of human misery is not sin but society. Humanity has abandoned its original happy state in nature. To regain this primal happiness, individuals must shed all artificial hindrances to a free and natural life—the customs, institutions, and habits of thought acquired in civilization—and listen to nature's voice speaking through their feelings and intuitions.

Application of these ideas to society tended to support radical (for the time) political change. The romantic emphasis on the individual and dislike of socially enforced conventions made democratic government and society attractive prospects. Indeed, many transcendentalists hoped the French Revolution could be a start toward a final age of lasting peace and perfect freedom.

This dream ended with the Revolution's moral disintegration and Napoleon's imperial ambitions. The romantics' hope for change became internal rather than external, spiritual rather than physical, with political realization only a distant product of gradual, peaceful transformation. To the romantic mind, a primary instrument of this change would be the nation's literature.

Romanticism in Literature

The rising emphasis on feelings, imagination, and intuition had already transferred to art. To a new generation, neoclassical art came to be regarded as spiritless formula and symmetry. It lacked dynamism, the emotional surge of creative expression. It also lacked personality, suppressing individual experience for the sake of universality.

Romantic literature developed in directions meant to amend these artistic problems and offer an alternative worldview to Enlightenment rationalism. From idealism, it gained a focus on writers' subjective experiences of the world. Based on transcendentalism and primitivism, it took nature as its teacher and source of inspiration. Firmly progressivist, it sought to change society by changing individual hearts and minds.

Poetry These changes were particularly seen in the era's poetry. According to transcendental thought, the creative imagination would be humanity's restorer. Its principal speaker would be the poet-prophet, who would illuminate truth for the masses through the power of intuition and imagination. Thus, romantics prized the poet above all other linguistic craftsmen.

Romantic poets distinguished themselves from their predecessors in their subjectivity and imaginative power. Their poetry tended to present private mental experiences, filtered through a highly individual consciousness. Instead of the poetic treatises of Pope, they preferred lyrical meditations. Rather than simply achieving a satisfying arrangement of parts, they aspired to evoke a sense of wonder and awe. Finally, unlike the erudite neoclassicals, romantics meant to reach the broadest audience possible. Thus, they intentionally used the language and imagery of common life.

These characteristics only gradually infused poetry. Early innovators included late eighteenth-century poets Robert Burns and William Blake. But romantic poetry began its fullest flowering with the publication of *Lyrical Ballads* (1798) by William Wordsworth and Samuel Coleridge. Together with poets Byron, Shelley, and Keats, they would forever change the face of English poetry.

VISUAL ANALYSIS
What emphases of romanticism does this painting reflect?

Prose Although poetry was the dominant voice of romanticism, prose genres continued to develop. The essay flourished in politics and public life, and radical romantic thinkers used it to promote revolutionary political thought. For instance, Mary Wollstonecraft's *A Vindication of the Rights of Woman* (1792) became the first feminist treatise in English. After the wars, the urbane Charles Lamb perfected and popularized the informal essay through a series published during the 1820s. Meanwhile, the novel finally gained full acknowledgment as a literary genre through the works of novelists such as Jane Austen, Mary Shelley, and Sir Walter Scott. By the 1830s, it was poised to become a primary genre of the Victorians.

Romanticism and the Bible

The romantics powerfully stated many genuine insights. Christians would agree that reason has its limitations and intuition some validity. While reason is important to moral judgment, God does speak to people through emotional impressions and conscience. A person without well-developed feelings and imagination is incomplete. Additionally, the romantics' concern for the individual's needs and well-being, whatever his or her origins or class, aligns in many ways with a biblical view of all humans as bearers of God's image (Gen. 1:27). Finally, romantics rightly prized the power of literature to change hearts and minds, a power too often forgotten by Christians uninterested in the arts.

In other ways, the movement was dangerously unbiblical. Both primitivism and progressivism transgress scriptural truth. In pointing backward to a mythical age of simple goodness or forward to a secular millennium, they reinterpret the biblical fall and restoration of man by making culture, not sin, the problem to be addressed. Most importantly, the romantic tendency to escape from limits on personal behavior and answer only to one's subjective feelings ignores God's rightful authority as Creator. It also notably failed to produce in the lives of several major romantics the happiness they desired.

VICTORIA Queen Victoria (1819–1901), who came to the throne when she was only eighteen (1837), represented a distinct break from the general cast of previous monarchs. A female, happily married, devoted to her duty, and holding strict (sometimes overly so) ideas of morality and convention, Victoria was a ruler that an increasingly democratic, middle class, and evangelical society could embrace. She and her German prince consort, Albert, strove to make their family of nine children a model of affectionate domesticity, and their conscientious approach to ruling restored dignity to the crown. An extended period of mourning and seclusion after Albert's death in 1862 only burnished her status as the nation's figurehead. Victoria's long reign provided much-needed stability for British society as industrialization continued to upend the old social order. The Golden and Diamond Jubilee years of her reign (fiftieth and sixtieth anniversaries) were marked across the empire with great celebrations showcasing the empire's diversity, innovations, wealth, and power. Her death in 1901 truly marked the end of an era.

VICTORIANISM

Romanticism's normalization of subjective perspectives and break with convention have left a lasting mark on the modern Western mind. But as change in England accelerated, many romantic ideals would be reshaped or discarded under an avalanche of new social and intellectual forces. These arrived during the era of England's longest-reigning monarch, Queen Victoria. Under her rule, Britain experienced a period of driving energy and bounding enthusiasm not seen since Elizabeth I's England.

ECONOMIC EXPANSION

For most of the nineteenth century, Britain, with a sizable jump on other nations in the Industrial Revolution, led the world in economic productivity and trade, out-producing rivals severalfold. Known as "the workshop of the world," she extended her lead over her economic rivals in the two decades following midcentury, more than doubling her coal and iron production, the size of her railroad network, and the value of her exports. British capital built railroads and canals, erected bridges and public buildings, and opened mines all over the world. Not until the 1870s did nations such as Germany and America compete commercially with England on a significant scale.

Socially and economically the nation continued its change from an agricultural to an urban society. By 1851 most of England's population resided in cities and towns. The booming economy created thriving middle-class communities that had disposable income for everything from leisure activities such as sports and tourism to communal projects, from museums to concert halls. London soon replaced Paris as the hub of European civilization. A metropolis of three million inhabitants, the city pulsated with commercial, social, and intellectual activity; visitors marveled at its vitality and beauty.

With a primarily export-based and industrial economy, England was now dependent on trade. She relied upon imports for raw materials and soon also for food to support her growing population. Her dominance in trade meant that London set world prices for major commodities. Inevitably, the pound sterling became the standard of international exchange, and by the end of the nineteenth century, London had become the world's leader in the banking industry, an arena in which she is still dominant today.

SOCIAL REFORM

Attendant with this economic prosperity came numerous social ills. The rapid disintegration of rural communities and shift to urban settings led to unemployment, deep poverty, tenement slums, and increased prostitution, vagrancy, and drunkenness. Additionally, the government's laissez-faire policies permitted labor abuses to arise in various industries.

The question of what to do about such issues permeated Victorian life. Politicians, lecturers, clergymen, writers, and average citizens discussed the issues and possible solutions in a wide variety of forums, from Parliament to newspapers and community halls. Charitable outreach increased, fueled especially by Nonconformists (e.g., Baptists, Quakers) and evangelicals (e.g., Methodists, low-church Anglicans), who were now a major portion of the population.

Two major legal reform goals of the era included the expansion of the vote and the easing of labor inequities such as inadequate wages, unreasonable hours, and poor working conditions. Realizing that the vote was key to having a voice, commoners rallied to this cause. A group known as Chartists organized mass demonstrations and presented Parliament with petitions (charters) signed by millions calling for further reform. The Second and Third Reform Acts of 1867 and 1884, along with the Ballot Act of 1872 (requiring a secret ballot), gradually expanded the voter pool. However, universal franchise was beyond reach until 1928.

Still, with an influx of new, reform-minded voters, the major parties (called Liberal and Conservative) vied for the good will of the lower classes, competing in relieving the distress of those in need. The emancipation of all slaves came in 1833, and the Corn Laws (p. 416) were finally repealed in 1846. Reforms gradually came to prisons (1835), asylums (1842), and public health and sanitation (1848, 1875).

Most importantly, Parliament addressed labor concerns. Liberals (in the classical sense, being resistant to government regulation) opposed labor legislation as a hindrance to industrial productivity. Nevertheless, reports of children being carried asleep before daylight to work twelve-hour shifts in cotton mills or to pull coal carts along three-foot-high mine shafts touched many consciences. Reforms in the 1830s and '40s limited children's work hours to eight hours a day, banned children under nine from working in some industries, and required employers to provide them at least three hours of schooling per day. Eventually, prompted by fear that British industrial workers would underperform because of lack of education, a series of reforms heading toward universal education were enacted (1870–93).

Anti–universal suffrage cartoon from 1865.

Conditions for adults improved as well. In 1847, the work day was limited to ten hours for all workers. The sheer deadliness of mine work (key to industrial success but subject to explosions, flooding, cave-ins, etc.) led to extensive regulations requiring stringent safety procedures and inspections. Throughout the century, trade unions struggled to gain representation and influence for their members to counterbalance the power afforded employers. Meanwhile, "friendly societies" served as avenues of social, financial, and healthcare support for many workers. Additionally, as social attitudes changed, some manufacturers provided an array of services to their employees, from meals to recreational facilities to circulating libraries. Although gradual, these changes began to unravel Britain's traditional class system, a process that would continue to play out in the twentieth century.

SCIENCE AND TECHNOLOGY

Despite the troubles of Victorian England, many Britons experienced the era in a largely positive way, as a time of new opportunities. Political reform and economic expansion accounted for some of this feeling. But another force helped Britons believe that anything might be possible. That force was an explosion of scientific study and innovative technology that changed the social, intellectual, and physical landscape of Victorian Britain.

Technology

At first driven by industrial needs, technological innovation soon revolutionized global society too. Without a doubt the most representative invention of the Victorian era was the railroad, which became the supreme symbol of industrial progress. It dramatically increased the distances raw materials could be practically transported and allowed cities not located near waterways to become industrial centers. The price of England's manufactured goods dropped significantly, helping her to undersell other nations.

The social effects of the steam engine were considerable. A vast network of rail transportation grew and encouraged the amalgamation of England's population, reducing the cultural distinctions, formerly so striking, between England, Scotland, and Wales. British engineers and companies also became the world's premier builders and financiers of railroads, garnering the nation both wealth and influence. Meanwhile, in 1838, the first fully steam-powered vessels crossed the Atlantic. Used to ferry communications and passengers across the nation and the globe, both inventions pulled the global community ever closer together.

An onslaught of further innovation came throughout the century. In communications, the telegraph and the telephone supported British imperial bureaucracy and shrank the world further. In urban areas, the engineering of sewage and water systems (as well as mass-manufactured soap) contributed greatly to urban health efforts. Medical advances in germ theory and surgical techniques were supported by the discovery of antiseptics and anesthesia. Near the century's end, gas and electric power as well as a subway system revolutionized city life. Finally, the rise of photography forever changed how people perceive people and things distant in time or place. Altogether, technology seemed to be making the world a better, safer, more enjoyable place.

A view of the Crystal Palace, erected in London to house the Great Exhibition of 1851.

Science

Along with the rise in technology came an increased interest in the science behind it. More people than ever had the time, money, and interest to pursue scientific inquiry, and advances followed in a broad spectrum of specialized scientific fields. Natural science, the generalized study of the natural world through observation in the field rather than laboratory study, proved particularly suited to European global explorations. British naval expeditions to explore or map new areas (e.g., Australia), coupled with private expeditions, incorporated observations of local geology, flora, and fauna and strengthened British colonial expansion efforts.

The most culturally significant result of popular interest in natural science, however, was the rise of the theory that animal species evolved from common origins. This theory was first revived in *Principles of Geology* (1830–33), in which Charles Lyell concluded that the earth's appearance is the result of present processes working gradually over long periods of time. Its culmination arrived in Charles Darwin's *On the Origin of Species* (1859), which offered a mass of data in support of what came to be known as evolutionary theory.

Darwinist theory set off a cultural bomb. Already undermined by Enlightenment rationalists and romantic individualists, the traditional Christian worldview took a major hit among both intellectuals and average citizens, heightening the struggle between doubt and faith. Darwin's ideas on natural selection were applied across many fields, from philosophy to economics to social theory, and changed the shape of society to come. The scientific establishment largely came to accept his theories, a consequence which, combined with popular faith in science, would lead to the secularizing of it and of public life in the twentieth century.

Mumbai, India, ca. 1900.

The British Empire in 1886.

COLONIALISM AND EMPIRE

Intertwined with Britain's economic expansion and burgeoning technology was the rise of its empire, which, stretching across the globe from Canada to New Zealand, was the largest in history. British naval dominance of the world's seaways was key, enforcing a century of relative peace (the Pax Britannica) that allowed British commerce to flow freely. And indeed, British colonialism was as much about opening up new markets, ensuring trade routes, and sourcing raw materials as it was an exercise in nationalism.

This expansion was also fueled by British emigration. The nation's population growth during this era—17,000,000 to 37,500,000 during Victoria's reign—surpassed the labor needs of home industry. Emigration surged during crop failures in the 1840s and the financial depression of 1873–96. Many emigrants settled in future commonwealth nations such as Canada, Australia, New Zealand, and South Africa, solidifying British cultural presence there.

Britain's key colony, the "jewel in the crown" of the British Empire, was indisputably India. Rich in resources, from jewel mines to textiles to India rubber, the subcontinent had been governed since 1757 by the British East India Company. However, after the 1857 Indian Mutiny (or, from a different perspective, India's First War of Independence), the British government took over, instituting a bureaucracy known as the British Raj and styling Victoria "Empress of India." A complex colonial culture grew up in the region, one most famously recorded in the literature of Rudyard Kipling, himself a British citizen born in India.

India was the empire's base of operations in Asia. To its northern borders, England conducted "the Great Game" with Russia, a complex duel of diplomacy, intelligence operations, and warfare (e.g., 1842 and 1878 in Afghanistan, 1853–54 in the Crimea) meant to push back the Russian Empire. To the East lay China, whose markets Britain desperately wanted, leading to the infamous Opium Wars (1839–42, 1856–60). In the seas to the southeast were island nations raising treasured spices for trade.

The European "Scramble for Africa" (1881–1914) added imperial holdings in Africa. Besides the riches the region provided (e.g., diamond mines), these territories secured British trade routes. For example, the Suez Canal's completion (1869) rapidly shrank shipping routes between Europe and Asia and prompted Britain to occupy both Egypt and the Sudan in 1882 to ensure the route. Similarly, wars with the South African Dutch Boers (1880–81, 1899–1902) secured passage around the Cape of Good Hope. By the defeat of the Boers, however, England was losing enthusiasm for conquest.

British opinion on the empire had always been mixed. For example, the era's two dominant prime ministers, Benjamin Disraeli and William Gladstone, steered the empire alternately toward expansion (Disraeli) and consolidation (Gladstone). Aside from moral qualms, the cost of running the empire was dear in both resources and sons buried on foreign soil. Doubts increased as Britain's global obligations took an ever-rising toll and Britain found herself diplomatically isolated by her aggressive expansionism. Combined with a general loss of hope and certainty in late-Victorian England, the result was a rise in anticolonialist sentiment. The next century would demand that Britain grapple with the issue.

The Bayswater Omnibus (1895) by George William Joy, depicting people from a variety of economic classes.

VICTORIAN LITERATURE

The literature that resulted from this complex and bustling era reflected its expanding opportunities and diverse voices. Literacy was higher, printing was cheaper, and genres were more varied than ever. Writers represented a broader spectrum of society, including more women and people from varying social classes, many with widely differing purposes and worldviews. The romantic optimism of the early era gradually gave way to a more realistic presentation of life as it was rather than how it should be. These differing voices have left a rich legacy often still relevant today.

Prose Without doubt the preeminent genre of Victorian literature was the novel. Finally brought into serious literature by romantic authors Austen and Scott, the genre flourished as the number and diversity of both its practitioners and its readers increased. Subgenres developed throughout the era, from the gothic romance (p. 533) to condition-of-England novels (p. 530) to the rise of realistic novels and detective fiction in the late century. Moreover, authors such as Charles Dickens, the Brontë sisters, Thomas Hardy, and George Eliot mastered the genre and took it to heights since matched but still unsurpassed.

Additionally, the periodical continued its upward trend as a genre category. Reformers used pamphlets to get their message out, and magazines multiplied to reach specific markets, from housewives to trade workers. Meanwhile, newspapers flourished to meet the demand of merchants and a politically aware populace for access to national and world news. Interestingly, periodicals played a key role in the literary scene as well, publishing everything from political essays and speeches to serialized novels (e.g., those of Dickens) and philosophical works.

Essays and treatises on topics from scientific research to public policy to philosophical theory also increased. Such works were frequently meant for a new intellectual leisure class—college-educated sons of gentry or of well-to-do business and professional men who eventually took their place in Parliament or other governmental service—supported by industrial wealth. The essays written for them were not popular writing, instead requiring of readers a close attention to the line of argument and a taste for elegant style. The era produced several masters of such prose, including philosopher-historians Thomas Carlyle and Thomas Babington Macaulay and art critic John Ruskin.

Poetry and Drama Of course, other traditional literary genres still flourished. Lyric and narrative works dominated poetry, as represented in the quintessential Victorian poet, Alfred, Lord Tennyson. Poet laureate for decades, Tennyson gave voice to the era's conflict between faith in progress and loss of faith in traditional religion, a theme that also played out in later poets such as Thomas Hardy and Matthew Arnold. On the other hand, poets Robert Browning and Gerard Manley Hopkins took a more traditional worldview but innovated in ways that influenced modern poets. Women at last achieved a level of parity with their male counterparts in the poetry of Elizabeth Barrett Browning (at the time more popular than her husband, Robert) and Christina Rossetti. Meanwhile, drama flourished near the end of the century, producing the still-beloved musical comedies of Gilbert and Sullivan as well as introducing the sparkling satirical comedies of Oscar Wilde and George Bernard Shaw.

An artist's illustration of "The Lady of Shalott" by Tennyson.

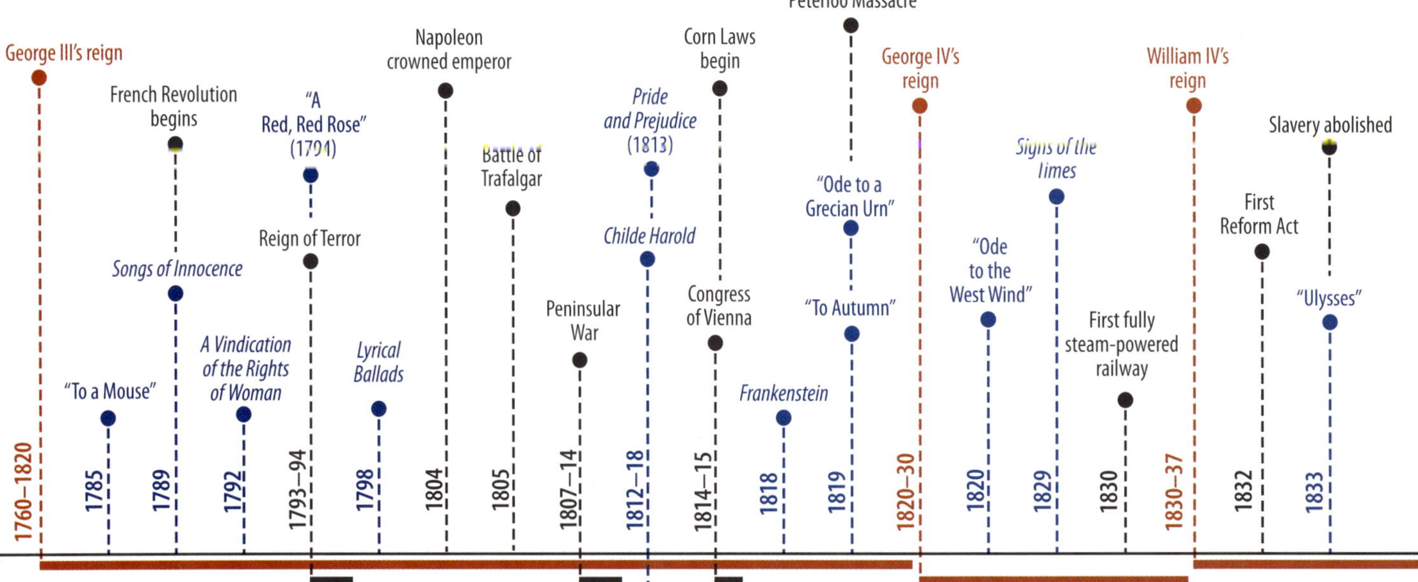

LANGUAGE

The nineteenth century brought changes great and small to English. Grammar and spelling were well standardized by the early century. But in the Victorian era, the homogenizing effect of transportation and communication advances and of a national school system (1870) weakened dialectal differences. London pronunciations prevailed, with students in better schools learning a refined version known as the Received Pronunciation. It remained a marker of one's education and social class well into the twentieth century.

Vocabulary, meanwhile, nearly doubled as writers invented or adapted freely from other languages to keep pace with the rapid expansion of knowledge and trade. Words such as *train*, *car*, and *coach*, originally referring to horse-drawn vehicles, now transferred to railroad travel. Imported words naturally resulted from Britain's imperial connections, and as English spread globally, other nations added their own localisms to the common word stock. But the chief innovators in language were again scientists. In biology, physics, chemistry, and other fields, they constructed words such as *bacteria* and *bacteriology*, *carbohydrate*, *appendicitis*, and *argon* from Greek or Latin word parts. This burgeoning vocabulary was recorded and illustrated in the mammoth *Oxford English Dictionary*. The product of seventy years' labor, it is a linguistic institution that continues to be updated.

SUMMARY

Broadly speaking, this literature reflects in its content and tone the arc of Victorian spirit. Including literature of bold affirmation and painful lament, the era's voice broadly moved from an optimistic faith in the progress of humanity and society to a feeling of creeping social stagnancy. Much of this perception sprang from the loss of traditional worldview and a sense near the century's end that Britain had lost its purpose and drive. The dynamic but troubled period of Victoria's reign, so exemplary in many ways, bequeathed to the twentieth century the unresolved problems and questions that underlie the pessimism of modern thought.

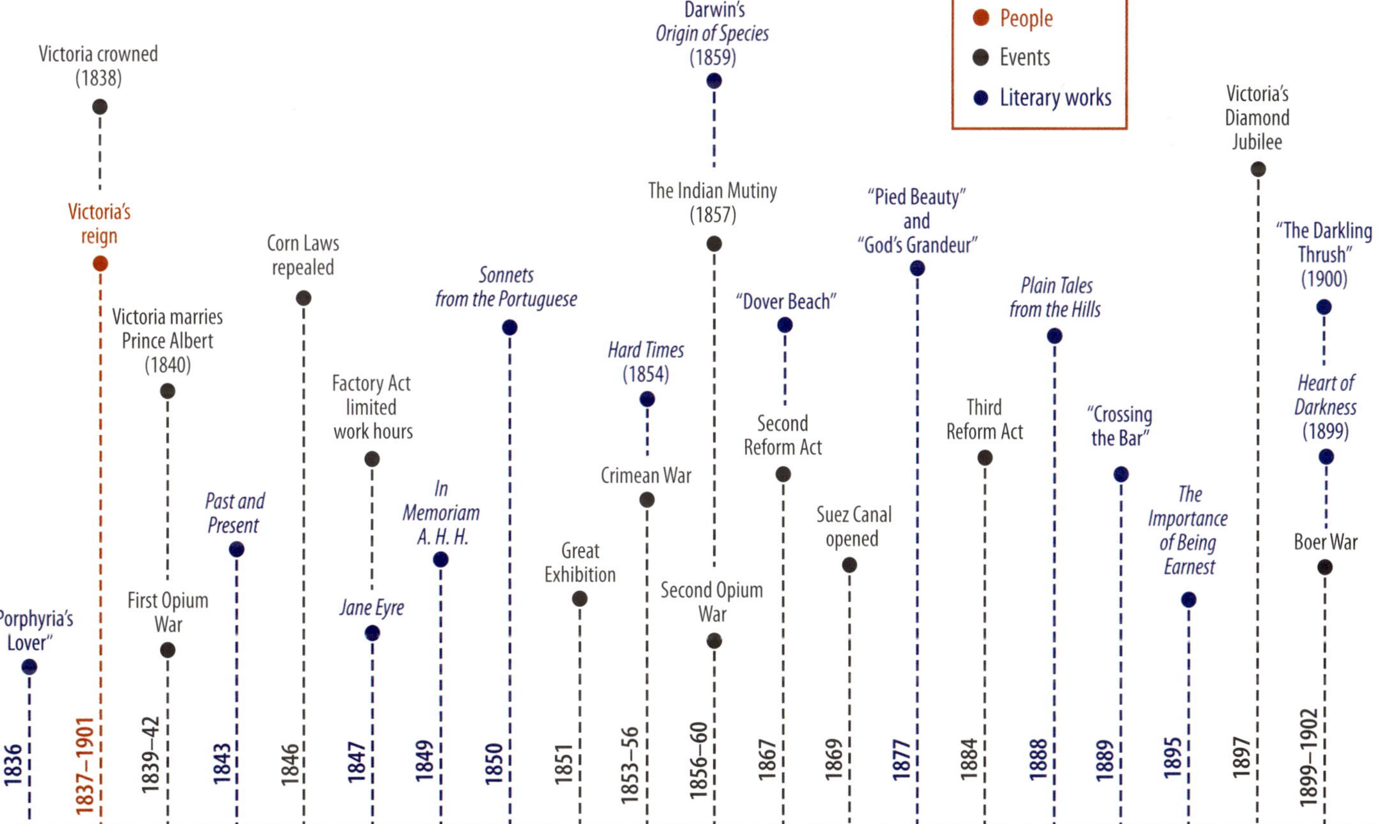

UNIT 4

PART 1

Signs of Change

Life frequently proves true the old saying "Hindsight is better than foresight." In moving from one literary era to the next (a gradual process often unrecognized while it is ongoing), this principle holds true as well. The Age of Johnson with its literature of sensibility had sent the pendulum of literary preferences swinging away from the neoclassicists' rationalism. But what new set of expectations and preferences would emerge was not yet clear. Viewed from the present day, however, significant changes were already clearly taking place, sweeping the mainstream of British literature toward the era of romanticism.

In this section you will read selections from two of the earliest authors who helped define British romanticism. You will also read from two writers who illustrate transitional stages that occurred between neoclassicism and romanticism. Each author highlights a different facet of these literary changes and how they began or played out in real time.

In the mid- to late-eighteenth century, two poets appeared who were quite ahead of their time. It is perhaps not insignificant that both were of the middle class and self-educated. With fewer preconceived notions of what poetry ought to be and with little investment in maintaining the status quo, they exercised their genius in entirely new directions.

The first of these was the Scottish poet Robert Burns, who encapsulated the romantic individualist in his personal life and career. Unique for his time (1759–96), his poems became immensely popular. Instead of employing classical forms, elevated language, and learned allusions, Burns took a simpler approach. He used old forms often from folk literature (e.g., the ballad), employed homely dialect and imagery taken from Scottish rural life, and expressed a more subjective, emotional point of view. In his choices, he presaged four romantic concerns: a love of nature and the truths it could teach, the desire to use common language accessible to all, an interest in one's cultural or ethnic past, and the importance of individual emotions and perceptions.

Next, the poet William Blake was, like Burns, an outlier in his time. Unlike Burns, Blake's poetry was not immediately successful. In fact, it was far more radical in approach and content than Burns's. Instead of harking back to the past and portraying a simpler, rural life, Blake, an urban poet, spoke as a visionary on the political and religious issues of his day. His unorthodox religious views (the natural outgrowth of certain strands of deistic thought), radical social ideas, and almost surreal and prophetic content in his later poetry were for some indigestible. Yet later romantics would find his attempt to return genuine emotion and spirituality to eighteenth-century rationalism, his concern for the individual, his great imaginative power, and his use of simple language undeniably compelling.

The final two writers studied in this section show a transitional stage as neoclassical ideas lingered amidst burgeoning romanticism. First, Mary Wollstonecraft in her *Vindication of the Rights of Woman* evinces the radical (for the time) political impulses of the romantic, advocating for women's right as individuals to a social and legal status up until then denied them. Yet she couched her appeals within neoclassical appeals to reason, society's overall good, and traditional morality and virtue.

Similarly, one of Britain's greatest novelists, Jane Austen, anonymously wrote a small but powerful body of work around the turn of the century. Her immensely popular works reveal a largely neoclassical disposition toward life that was still broadly popular as romanticism began to dominate artistic circles. Key qualities of her sympathetic characters were conformity to social expectations and roles and a personal moral and emotional restraint based on traditional values and reason. As Johnson (whom she much admired) advocated, Austen created realistically good characters whose virtues led to their triumphs. Yet like the romantics, she also valued her characters' emotional happiness as much as their virtuous behavior. Furthermore, her development of the novel took a more romantic direction, using everyday accessible language and developing characters with rich internal lives. Together these artists heralded the thoroughness with which romanticism would change literary expectations across the broad spectrum of writers and readers.

Robert Burns (1759–96)

Robert Burns was a poor tenant farmer whose linguistic ear and passion for traditional culture transformed him into the national poet of Scotland. In his short life, he wrote hundreds of poems and song lyrics in both the English and the Scots language—an output that is even more astonishing given that most of his days were spent working the land. Unlike any poet before or since, Burns's poetry captures the voice of the common Scottish people.

Burns was born into a family of hard-working but unsuccessful tenant farmers in Ayrshire, Scotland. Despite receiving only a few years of formal education, the young Robert was frequently seen with a book in his hand. His most significant literary influences may have been his mother and her relative Betty Davidson, who often recited to him tales of Scottish folklore. His first poem was a love poem written at age thirteen.

When Burns was twenty-five, his father died. Burns responded with several years of loose living, fathering illegitimate children while continuing to write a variety of poems, including satires on the Church of Scotland. In 1786 he submitted his collected poems (*Poems, Chiefly in the Scottish Dialect*) for publication in Edinburgh, where they were an immediate success. Encouraged by their reception, Burns traveled to Edinburgh, where he was entertained by high society and was exposed to current literary trends. There he also met the amateur folklorist James Johnson, who inspired Burns to collect and compose Scottish folk songs. Although Burns would later publish the long poem "Tam o' Shanter" in 1791, he devoted the remainder of his literary life to writing occasional poetry and producing folk songs, among which is the world-famous "Auld Lang Syne."

Exhausted by hard living, Burns died in Dumfries at the age of thirty-seven. Burns remains widely popular to this day, not just because of his skills as a versifier but also because of his deep Scottish nationalism, his love for the common worker, and his strong stance against authority. These traits make him a prototypical romantic poet.

BEFORE READING

ANALYZE: *Dialect, Imagery, Theme*

Burns was well-known for his poetry's musicality, springing partly from his use of **dialect**, the manner of speech—diction, grammar, and pronunciation—characteristic of a certain area or class (in his case, rural Scotland). As you read, pay attention to how this dialect affects a poem's meter and even its mood (p. 213). Additionally, pay attention to Burns's **images** and the **themes** they develop. How might these elements reflect the romantic tendency to value nature, emotion, and the common man?

READ: *Combine Strategies*

To analyze texts, we naturally combine reading strategies. For Burns's poetry, start by reading the poems aloud to understand the dialect and appreciate its sounds. Next, annotate important features (e.g., images, figurative language, repeated words) and jot down any questions you have about elements. Finally, review your notes to begin inferring meaning from the texts' details (e.g., what do the images say about the speaker's feelings?). Finally, compare both poems to recognize romantic elements in Burns's voice and style.

CREATE: *Compose a Poem*

What is a topic that excites you? When you hear it mentioned, what words immediately come to mind? Choose a topic about which you can write enthusiastically. Write a four-stanza poem about this idea using creative comparisons of both simile and hyperbole. Consider using the meter and stanza pattern of Burns's poem "A Red, Red Rose" as a model for your poem.

OBJECTIVES

- Interpret a poem's dialect.
- Combine comprehension strategies to understand a poem's content.
- Analyze a poem's use of sound, imagery, and romantic elements.
- Create a poem based on a model text.

To a Mouse
On Turning Her Up in Her Nest With the Plough

Wee, sleekit, cowrin, tim'rous beastie,°
O, what a panic's in thy breastie!
Thou need na start awa sae hasty,°
Wi' bickerin brattle!°
I wad be laith to rin° and chase thee,
Wi' murd'ring pattle!°

I'm truly sorry man's dominion°
Has broken nature's social union,°
An' justifies that ill opinion,
Which makes thee startle°
At me, thy poor, earth-born companion,
An' fellow-mortal! **A**

1 **Wee . . . beastie:** tiny, sleek, cringing, fearful little creature

3 **Thou . . . hasty:** You need not jump away so hastily.

4 **Wi' . . . brattle:** with hurrying scamper

5 **I . . . rin:** I would be loath (unwilling) to run.

6 **pattle:** "paddle" (plow staff) for cleaning the plow

7 **dominion:** rule (Gen. 1:26)

8 **social union:** sympathetic bond between creatures

10 **startle:** jump away in fear

Dialect: What meter has the dialect created so far? What effect does the dialect have on the poem's mood? Perhaps imagine the poem in standard English and see how it differs. **A**

I doubt na, whyles,° but thou may° thieve;
What then? poor beastie, thou maun° live!
A daimen-icker in a thrave°
'S a sma'° request:
I'll get a blessing wi' the lave,°
And never miss't!

Thy wee bit housie, too, in ruin!
Its silly wa's the win's are strewin!°
An' naething, now, to big a new one,°
O' foggage° green!
An' bleak December's winds ensuin,°
Baith snell and keen.°

Thou saw the fields laid bare an' waste,
An' weary winter comin' fast,
An' cozie here, beneath the blast,
Thou thought to dwell,
Till, crash! the cruel coulter° past
Out thro' thy cell.

That wee bit heap o' leaves an' stibble°
Has cost thee mony° a weary nibble!
Now thou's turned out, for a' thy trouble,
But° house or hald,°
To thole° the winter's sleety dribble,
An' cranreuch° cauld! R

But, Mousie, thou art no thy lane,°
In proving foresight may be vain:
The best-laid schemes o' mice an' men,
Gang aft agley,°
An' lea'e° us nought but grief and pain
For promised joy.

Still thou art blest, compared wi' me!
The present only toucheth° thee:
But, och! I backward cast my e'e°
On prospects drear!
An' forward, tho' I canna see,
I guess an' fear! A

13 whyles: sometimes / **may:** dost

14 maun: must

15 A . . . thrave: an occasional grain ear in a shock

16 'S . . . sma': is a small

17 wi' . . . lave: with what's left

20 Its . . . strewin': pitiful walls the winds are scattering

21 naething . . . one: nothing, now, [exists] to build a new one

22 O' foggage: of grass appearing after harvest

23 ensuin: following

24 Baith . . . keen: both bitter and sharp

29 coulter: plow blade

31 stibble: stubble

32 mony: many

34 But: without / **hald:** hold (home)

35 thole: endure

36 cranreuch: hoarfrost

37 no . . . lane: not alone

40 Gang . . . agley: go oft astray

41 lea'e: leave

44 toucheth: concerns

45 e'e: eye

Combine Strategies: Reread the previous three stanzas. What can you infer about the speaker's feelings toward the mouse? R

Theme: In the final two stanzas, Burns's speaker draws a parallel between the mouse and himself. How are they similar? How do they differ? A

A Red, Red Rose

In this famous poem, Burns deliberately mimicks old folk songs. Notice, for instance, his use of the old ballad stanza (p. 69) throughout. Additionally, pay attention to Burns's use of dialect, figurative expressions, and hyperbole (p. 240). How do they make the poem memorable?

O my luve's like a red, red rose,
That's newly sprung in June:
O my luv's like the melodie
That's sweetly play'd in tune. A

As fair art thou, my bonnie lass,
So deep in luve am I;
And I will luve thee still, my dear,
Till a' the seas gang dry.

Till a' the seas gang dry, my dear,
And the rocks melt wi' the sun;
And I will luve thee still, my dear,
While the sands o' life shall run.

And fare-thee-weel, my only luve!
And fare-thee-weel, a while!
And I will come, again, my luve,
Tho' 'twere ten thousand mile! R

Imagery: What figure of speech does Burns use to describe the speaker's beloved in this stanza? What do you think he means by these images? A

Combine Strategies: Compare this poem to the previous. How do they both reflect romantic preferences in content and style? R

THINK AND DISCUSS

1. Define *dialect*. From Burns's poems, illustrate each of the three aspects of language that dialects reflect.
2. Describe two images from "To A Mouse."
3. Find an example of simile and of hyperbole in "A Red, Red Rose." What does each mean within the poem?
4. Describe the meter of one of the poems. How does Burns's use of sound (e.g., rhythms, dialect) affect the overall mood of that poem?
5. What is the theme of "To a Mouse"? Support your answer from the text.
6. Describe two ways in which both poems reflect romantic preferences. Cite an example from each in support of your answers.
7. In your opinion, what qualities or details of "A Red, Red Rose" make it so memorable? How might it reflect the quality of Beauty?
8. Write a four-stanza poem about a topic of your choice using creative hyperbole and similes. Consider using "A Red, Red Rose" as a model for your poem's meter, stanza, or phrasing.

William Blake (1757–1827)

AT A GLANCE

- **1772** Apprenticed to engraver James Basire
- **1779** Became a student at the Royal Academy of Art
- **1783** Published *Poetical Sketches*
- **1788** Created a new type of etching for his books
- **1789** Wrote *The Book of Thel*
- **1793** Finished *The Marriage of Heaven and Hell*
- **1794** Published *Songs of Innocence and of Experience*
- **1826** Published *Illustrations of the Book of Job*

William Blake was an engraver, painter, and poet whose poetic works, while unappreciated in his time, are now considered among the most imaginative in English literature. His poetry is an eclectic blend of both individualistic and universal themes as well as a creative combination of art forms—he invented his own technique of engraving that allowed him to print colored, beautifully illustrated editions of his own poems. Through his unique art, Blake issued a prophetic call for the romantic return to imagination.

Life

Blake was born in London into a family of religious dissenters with limited means. While he did receive formal schooling first in painting and then in engraving, his literary education was entirely informal. As a teen he was apprenticed to an engraver, and at the age of twenty-one, he set up his own engraver's shop in London. Blake achieved some success during his life with his engravings and watercolor paintings, but for much of his life he lived in near poverty. In 1782 he married Catherine Boucher, with whom he had a childless but fulfilling marriage. Blake taught Catherine to read and write, as well as how to assist him in his professional work. In 1803 Blake was wrongly accused of sedition, and the experience of his arrest and trial jarred him considerably, cementing his already radical social and political views.

In 1809–10 he produced the only exhibition of his paintings during his lifetime, but what little attention it received was damning criticism. By the end of his life, he had finally made a few artistic disciples, but his poetry did not reach a national audience until collected editions were published in the 1860s. He died confident, however, in the artistic and spiritual vision he had developed.

Religion

Blake was devoutly religious. Indeed, Christianity and the Bible formed a core part of his personal beliefs. But his interpretations and religious views were totally unorthodox. He claimed to have seen a vision of angels at the age of four, and spiritual visions accompanied him for the rest of his life. Influenced by these and his own feeling that authentic beliefs and behaviors could not be forced, Blake came to reject all organized religion. Moreover, his mystical, extra-biblical ideas led him to view traditional religion as unable to appreciate the diversity of spiritual experience and the divinity within every person.

Fearing the oppressive power of existing philosophical systems, Blake developed his own complex mythology, which borrows heavily from pagan as well as biblical symbolism. He expressed this mythology in a series of self-published books and personal manuscripts such as *The Marriage of Heaven and Hell* (1790), *The Book of Los* (1795), and *The Four Zoas* (1807). In these works, Blake's art as an engraver interacts with his poetry, both broadening and deepening the implications of the mythology. This mythology is vague and highly allusive, but the effect is intentional. Blake saw it as his mission to counteract the Enlightenment's overemphasis on reason with a more holistic appreciation of the imagination, and his complex mythology serves as a training ground for developing the imagination.

Art

Like his mythology, Blake's poetry demands both careful analysis and a strong imagination. Many of his most famous poems are found in *Songs of Innocence* (1789) and *Songs of Experience* (1794), which Blake also published together as *Songs of Innocence and of Experience: Shewing the Two Contrary States of the Human Soul* in 1794. These companion volumes stress the interrelation of opposites such as good and evil, life and death. Yet his poetry is written in a simple, straightforward style, and this accessibility makes Blake both widely read and influential up to the present day.

ANALYZE: *Symbol, Rhetorical Devices*

Blake chose simple language to reach the everyday person. But his poems cannot be called simplistic. Indeed, their imagery and techniques show great artistry. The imagery of "The Lamb" and "The Tyger" centers on implicit **symbols** (p. 37), which Blake uses to express facets of his worldview. Meanwhile, "London" contains many **sensory details** (p. 314) that suggest the various topics Blake is addressing. As you read, try to infer how these images contribute to each work's themes.

Blake also used poetic techniques to frame or emphasize certain ideas. **Apostrophe** (p. 201) frames the first two poems as conversations in which readers hear only the speaker's side; his commentary and **rhetorical questions** (p. 403) provide the ideas Blake wants readers to receive. Also sprinkled through each poem are other syntactical devices such as **repetition**, **parallelism** (p. 140), and **anaphora** (p. 165). Consider how these contribute to each poem's overall effect. How might they help create its rhythm? What ideas might they group together or emphasize?

OBJECTIVES

- Apply historical context to understand a text.
- Compare and contrast the tone and themes of two texts.
- Analyze how a text's imagery (in its symbols and sensory details) contributes to theme.
- Analyze the effects of apostrophe and rhetorical devices in a text.
- Evaluate an author's dualistic worldview from a biblical perspective.

READ: *Compare Texts, Apply Historical Context*

All three poems hail from Blake's work *Songs of Innocence and of Experience.* Compare the poems to see whether you can determine which are likely to represent innocence and which experience. Ascertaining the underlying **tone** (p. 88) of each will help. Additionally, the poems "The Lamb" and "The Tyger" are often studied as a pair. Record some similarities and differences between the poems' symbols, structures, and themes. As you examine these, consider whether the poems are a pair because of their similarities or because of their differences.

Finally, to best understand "London," remember that Blake was writing in tumultuous times, to which the poem (published in 1794) alludes. First, industrialism and urbanization had profited some people, but they also resulted in public ills (e.g., slums, increased vagrancy, prostitution, child labor). Just as reformers geared up to address these, the initially promising French Revolution devolved into a period of bloody suppression and executions known as the Reign of Terror. The English government reacted by suppressing ideas with even a whiff of radicalism (including reforms). How might "London" reflect and respond to this situation?

EVALUATE: *Dualism*

In *The Marriage of Heaven and Hell*, Blake argues, "Without Contraries is no progression. Attraction and Repulsion, Reason and Energy, Love and Hate, are necessary to Human existence. From these contraries spring what the religious call Good & Evil. Good is the passive. . . . Evil is the active." Behind this comment is the philosophy of dualism, the idea that good versus evil (and man's reason versus his instincts) is a timeless, universal combat and that both sides are necessary. Examine Genesis 1:31, Psalm 92:15, and Isaiah 41:4. Ask yourself whether the Bible and Blake disagree on the source of good and evil. Where does this dualistic view of God surface in the poems that follow?

Why does **EVIL** *exist?*

Evil so pervades earthly life that people learn to accept it as normal. In fact, most of us never seriously consider the why of evil until life circumstances—personal injustices, large-scale oppressions, deaths, crime, war—press evil's reality hard on us. If you have ever wondered the purpose of what's wrong in your life or the world, you have in some part asked this question. The Bible provides the answer, but trusting God in spite of evil is not easy. What circumstances in your life have prompted you to ask God why?

Blake's own illustrations are shown with the three poems included here.

Rhetorical Devices: What rhetorical devices are illustrated in stanza 1? A

Symbol: Who created the lamb? How else is he connected to the lamb and the child? What symbolic meanings might these connections hint at? A

The Tyger

Tyger! Tyger! burning bright
In the forests of the night,
What immortal hand or eye
Could frame thy fearful symmetry?[1]

In what distant deeps or skies
Burnt the fire of thine eyes?
On what wings dared he aspire?
What the hand dare seize the fire?

And what shoulder, and what art,
Could twist the sinews of thy heart?
And when thy heart began to beat,
What dread hand? and what dread feet? A

What the hammer? what the chain?
In what furnace was thy brain?
What the anvil? what dread grasp
Dare its deadly terrors clasp?

When the stars threw down their spears,
And water'd heaven with their tears,
Did he smile his work to see?
Did he who made the Lamb make thee?

Tyger! Tyger! burning bright
In the forests of the night,
What immortal hand or eye,
Dare frame thy fearful symmetry? R E

1. *symmetry:* "in semi-*concr*. sense: (Well-proportioned) figure or form (of a person or animal)" (*OED*)

Symbol: How would you characterize the tiger's nature so far? A

Compare Texts: Compare the form and content of "The Tyger" to that of "The Lamb." Describe several similarities and differences between the poems. R

Dualism: What one word differs between stanzas 1 and 6? What tone does that difference express toward the tiger's creation? Who does Blake imply created the tiger? E

LONDON

I wander through each charter'd[1] street,
Near where the charter'd Thames does flow,
And mark in every face I meet
Marks of weakness, marks of woe.

In every cry of every man,
In every infant's cry of fear,
In every voice, in every ban,[2]
The mind-forg'd manacles I hear.

How the chimney-sweeper's cry
Every black'ning church appalls;[3]
And the hapless[4] soldier's sigh
Runs in blood down palace walls. A

But most through midnight streets I hear
How the youthful harlot's curse
Blasts the new-born infant's tear,[5]
And blights with plagues the marriage hearse. R

1. *charter'd:* "privileged; licensed" (*OED*). This is a reference to how legal documents (e.g., certifications for vocations or grants of rights or property) can evolve into exclusive privilege for the few.
2. *ban:* The word may have multiple meanings here. It may refer to the marriage banns, to a prohibition, to a curse, or to a public condemnation.
3. *appalls:* horrifies
4. *hapless:* unfortunate
5. *Blasts . . . tear:* may refer to blindness caused by venereal disease contracted from the mother during birth (see the previous line)

Sensory Details: Find three sensory details in stanzas 1–3 that you find especially compelling. What images do they contribute to? A

Historical Context: What social ills does Blake allude to in the poem? What social institutions does he reference in stanza 3, and how does he feel about them? R

THINK AND DISCUSS

1. From "The Lamb" or "The Tyger," give an example of each of the following devices: parallelism, repetition, anaphora, and rhetorical question.
2. Identify three examples of sensory details in "London." What historical realities of Blake's time does each help suggest?
3. Compare the content and techniques of "The Lamb" and "The Tyger." List two ways in which the poems are similar. How do they differ in their imagery and mood? Support your answer from the texts.
4. How do "The Lamb" and the "The Tyger" evidence different tones? Which do you think belongs to Blake's *Songs of Experience* and which to *Songs of Innocence*?
5. What are the primary symbols of "The Lamb" and "The Tyger" respectively? Briefly explain the meaning of each in context of the poems' themes.
6. What three social institutions does Blake question in "London"? What is his primary theme? Explain how his image of "mind-forged manacles" relates to that theme.
7. Choose two of the devices listed in question 1. Explain how their use contributes to the meaning or effectiveness of either "The Lamb" or "The Tyger."
8. How do these poems evidence Blake's romantic tendencies?
9. Briefly explain Blake's dualistic worldview. Does this philosophy conform to or diverge from biblical truth? Consult the following passages in your answer: Genesis 1:31, Psalm 92:15, and Isaiah 41:4.

Mary Wollstonecraft (1759–97)

Although Mary Wollstonecraft is famous for issuing the first modern feminist manifesto, *A Vindication of the Rights of Woman*, she played a significant role in the emerging romantic movement. Born into a poor farming family, she received no formal schooling but acquired a great deal of learning on her own. In 1784 she founded a girls' school. She wrote several treatises on education, including *Thoughts on the Education of Daughters* (1787). In 1788 she moved to London and began editing a magazine and writing reviews. There she participated in a radical literary set that included William Blake and William Wordsworth.

When Edmund Burke's *Reflections on the Revolution in France* came out in 1790, Wollstonecraft responded with *A Vindication of the Rights of Man.* The pamphlet decried Burke's more cautious approach to reforming society, advocating for immediate reforms upholding rights established by reason. *Vindication* was quickly followed by *A Vindication of the Rights of Woman* (1791) in which Wollstonecraft argues against women's limited education and political disenfranchisement. While maintaining that women can and should contribute to society through their role as mothers, Wollstonecraft claims that men and women are fundamentally equal and that gender roles are social constructs. She ends her treatise by calling for publicly funded coeducation and property rights for women.

Frustrated with the rigid conservatism of English society, Wollstonecraft traveled to revolutionary France, where she fell in love with American merchant Gilbert Imlay. After she gave birth to a daughter, Imlay abandoned her. This shattered Wollstonecraft, and in depression she attempted suicide three times. At this time she also wrote *Letters Written During A Short Residence in Sweden, Norway, and Denmark*, whose themes were influential on both the romantic movement, and later, travel writing. In 1796 she returned to London, where she married the radical philosopher William Godwin. Only eleven days after she gave birth to the daughter who would become known as Mary Shelley, Wollstonecraft died of childbirth complications.

BEFORE READING

ANALYZE: *Argumentation, Rhetorical Appeals*

Wollstonecraft framed her essay in neoclassical style, based on **argumentation** (p. 143), an exercise in human reasoning. In this way, Wollstonecraft is a product of her age. As you read, identify instances of the three types of **rhetorical appeals** (p. 129) in the text. What facts and logical appeals does Wollstonecraft use to support her ideas? Where do you see emotional appeals (e.g., sarcasm, humor)? Where might Wollstonecraft appeal to a system or source of authority?

Wollstonecraft's purpose, to persuade readers to fix what she saw as an error in society, was a concern shared by neoclassical thinkers and romantics. But romantics felt that the neoclassicals' view of society (rational and focused on general truths) often lost track of individual perspectives. How might the essay's content reflect something of both approaches—a concern for social tradition and stability as well as for the value of individuals' personal happiness?

READ: *Combine Strategies*

You may find it helpful for your understanding to paraphrase sentences or summarize sections as you read. Also, try annotating the text so that you remember Wollstonecraft's main ideas and appeals. As you trace her arguments, can you infer her thesis for this section? What is the main point she is trying to prove?

EVALUATE: *Author's Reasoning*

Finally, evaluate the validity of the author's points and the effectiveness of her persuasion. Are her facts accurate and her reasoning logical? Are her appeals to emotion fair and convincing? Where do her premises and conclusions line up with Scripture or deviate from it? Consult the following passages for your answers: Genesis 1:26–28; 2:20–23; 3:16; Proverbs 31:10–31; Ephesians 5:22–25; and 1 Peter 3:7.

OBJECTIVES

- Identify various kinds of rhetorical appeals in a text.
- Trace an argument throughout a text.
- Analyze how a text's content and style reflect the transition between neoclassicism and romanticism.
- Evaluate the effectiveness and truthfulness of a text's arguments.

VOCABULARY

fastidious (fă-stĭd′ē-əs) *adj.* Difficult to please; exacting.

abrogate (ăb′rə-gāt′) *tr.v.* To abolish, do away with, or annul, especially by authority.

propensity (prə-pĕn′sĭ-tē) *n.* An innate inclination; a tendency.

inculcate (ĭn-kŭl′kāt′) *v.* To impress (something) upon the mind of another by frequent instruction or repetition; instill.

paltry (pôl′trē) *adj.* Lacking in importance or worth.

ignoble (ĭg-nō′bəl) *adj.* Not noble in quality, character, or purpose; base or dishonorable.

After considering the historic page, and viewing the living world with anxious solicitude, the most melancholy emotions of sorrowful indignation have depressed my spirits, and I have sighed when obliged to confess, that either nature has made a great difference between man and man, or that the civilization which has hitherto taken place in the world has been very partial. I have turned over various books written on the subject of education, and patiently observed the conduct of parents and the management of schools; but what has been the result?—a profound conviction that the neglected education of my fellow-creatures is the grand source of the misery I deplore; and that women, in particular, are rendered weak and wretched by a variety of concurring causes, originating from one hasty conclusion. The conduct and manners of women, in fact, evidently prove that their minds are not in a healthy state; for, like the flowers which are planted in too rich a soil, strength and usefulness are sacrificed to beauty; and the flaunting leaves, after having pleased a **fastidious** eye, fade, disregarded on the stalk, long before the season when they ought to have arrived at maturity. One cause of this barren blooming I attribute to a false system of education, gathered from the books written on this subject by men who, considering females rather as women than human creatures, have been more anxious to make them alluring mistresses than affectionate wives and rational mothers; and the understanding of the sex has been so bubbled by this specious homage, that the civilized women of the present century, with a few exceptions, are only anxious to inspire love, when they ought to cherish a nobler ambition, and by their abilities and virtues exact respect. . . . R

fastidious (fă-stĭd′ē-əs) *adj.* Difficult to please; exacting.

Trace Arguments: What social problem discussed in this paragraph does Wollstonecraft identify as her topic? What analogy does she use to describe it? R

Yet, because I am a woman, I would not lead my readers to suppose that I mean violently to agitate the contested question respecting the equality or inferiority of the sex; but as the subject lies in my way, and I cannot pass it over without subjecting the main tendency of my reasoning to misconstruction, I shall stop a moment to deliver, in a few words, my opinion. In the government of the physical world it is observable that the female in point of strength is, in general, inferior to the male. This is the law of nature; and it does not appear to be suspended or **abrogated** in favor of woman. A degree of physical superiority cannot, therefore, be denied—and it is a noble prerogative! But not content with this natural pre-eminence, men endeavor to sink us still lower, merely to render us alluring objects for a moment; and women, intoxicated by the adoration which men, under the influence of their senses, pay them, do not seek to obtain a durable interest in their hearts, or to become the friends of the fellow creatures who find amusement in their society.

abrogate (ăb′rə-gāt′) *tr.v.* To abolish, do away with, or annul, especially by authority.

I am aware of an obvious inference:—from every quarter have I heard exclamations against masculine women; but where are they to be found? If by this appellation men mean to inveigh against their ardor in hunting, shooting, and gaming, I shall most cordially join in the cry; but if it be against the imitation of manly virtues, or, more properly speaking, the attainment of those talents and virtues, the exercise of which ennobles the human character, and which raises females in the scale of animal being, when they are comprehensively termed mankind;—all those who view them with a philosophical eye must, I should think, wish with me, that they may every day grow more and more masculine. . . .

My own sex, I hope, will excuse me, if I treat them like rational creatures, instead of flattering their fascinating graces, and viewing them as if they were in a state of perpetual childhood, unable to stand alone. I earnestly wish to point out in what true dignity and human happiness consists—I wish to persuade women to endeavor to acquire strength, both of mind and body, and to convince them that the soft phrases, susceptibility of heart, delicacy of sentiment, and refinement of taste, are almost synonymous with epithets of weakness, and that those beings who are only the objects of pity and that kind of love, which has been termed its sister, will soon become objects of contempt. . . . A R

Appeals: In this paragraph, what type of rhetorical appeal does Wollstonecraft subtly infuse through her tone? A

Trace Arguments: What misperceptions in her audience does Wollstonecraft address in the last three preceding paragraphs? R

The education of women has, of late, been more attended to than formerly; yet they are still reckoned a frivolous sex, and ridiculed or pitied by the writers who endeavor by satire or instruction to improve them. It is acknowledged that they spend many of the first years of their lives in acquiring a smattering of accomplishments; meanwhile strength of body and mind are sacrificed to libertine notions of beauty, to the desire of establishing themselves,—the only way women can rise in the world,—by marriage. And this desire making mere animals of them, when they marry they act as such children may be expected to act:—they dress; they paint, and nickname God's creatures.[1] Surely these weak beings are only fit for a seraglio![2]—Can they be expected to govern a family with judgment, or take care of the poor babes whom they bring into the world?

If then it can be fairly deduced from the present conduct of the sex, from the prevalent fondness for pleasure which takes place of ambition, and those nobler passions that open and enlarge the soul; that the instruction which women have hitherto received has only tended, with the constitution of civil society, to render them insignificant objects of desire—mere propagators of fools!—if it can be proved that in aiming to accomplish them, without cultivating their understandings, they are taken out of their sphere of duties, and made ridiculous and useless when the short-lived bloom of beauty is over, I presume that rational men will excuse me for endeavoring to persuade them to become more masculine and respectable. A

Argumentation: What weaknesses in women's education existed during Wollstonecraft's time? How does her response reflect neoclassical concerns? A

1. *they dress; . . . creatures:* an allusion to a line spoken by Hamlet to Ophelia in which he accuses women of pretense
2. *seraglio:* haram

Indeed the word masculine is only a bugbear:[3] there is little reason to fear that women will acquire too much courage or fortitude; for their apparent inferiority with respect to bodily strength, must render them, in some degree, dependent on men in the various relations of life; but why should it be increased by prejudices that give a sex to virtue, and confound simple truths with sensual reveries?

Women are, in fact, so much degraded by mistaken notions of female excellence, that I do not mean to add a paradox when I assert, that this artificial weakness produces a **propensity** to tyrannize, and gives birth to cunning, the natural opponent of strength, which leads them to play off those contemptible infantine airs that undermine esteem even whilst they excite desire. Let men become more chaste and modest, and if women do not grow wiser in the same ratio, it will be clear that they have weaker understandings. It seems scarcely necessary to say, that I now speak of the sex in general. Many individuals have more sense than their male relatives; and, as nothing preponderates where there is a constant struggle for an equilibrium, without it has naturally more gravity, some women govern their husbands without degrading themselves, because intellect will always govern.

3. *bugbear:* a cause of fear, anxiety, or irritation

propensity (prə-pĕn′sĭ-tē) *n.* An innate inclination; a tendency.

VISUAL ANALYSIS

William Hogarth's *Marriage A-la-Mode* series of paintings satirized upper-class marriage conventions. This entry, *The Toilette*, depicts the common practice of married aristocratic women entertaining guests (often male) in their bedrooms as they finished dressing for a party. How might it illustrate the kind of marriage Wollstonecraft condemns?

from CHAPTER TWO

To account for, and excuse the tyranny of man, many ingenious arguments have been brought forward to prove, that the two sexes, in the acquirement of virtue, ought to aim at attaining a very different character; or, to speak explicitly, women are not allowed to have sufficient strength of mind to acquire what really deserves the name of virtue. Yet it should seem, allowing them to have souls, that there is but one way appointed by Providence to lead mankind to either virtue or happiness. . . .

. . . For if it be allowed that women were destined by Providence to acquire human virtues, and by the exercise of their understandings, that stability of character which is the firmest ground to rest our future hopes upon, they must be permitted to turn to the fountain of light, and not forced to shape their course by the twinkling of a mere satellite. . . . A

Appeals: What appeal does Wollstonecraft utilize by referring to Providence? A

Consequently, the most perfect education, in my opinion, is such an exercise of the understanding as is best calculated to strengthen the body and form the heart. Or, in other words, to enable the individual to attain such habits of virtue as will render it independent. In fact, it is a farce to call any being virtuous whose virtues do not result from the exercise of its own reason. . . .

Youth is the season for love in both sexes; but in those days of thoughtless enjoyment provision should be made for the more important years of life, when reflection takes place of sensation. But Rousseau, and most of the male writers who have followed his steps, have warmly **inculcated** that the whole tendency of female education ought to be directed to one point:—to render them pleasing. E

inculcate (ĭn-kŭl′kāt′) *v.* To impress (something) upon the mind of another by frequent instruction or repetition; instill.

Author's Reasoning: What seems to be Wollstonecraft's conception of virtue from what she says in these paragraphs? E

Let me reason with the supporters of this opinion who have any knowledge of human nature, do they imagine that marriage can eradicate the habitude of life? The woman who has only been taught to please will soon find that her charms are oblique sunbeams, and that they cannot have much effect on her husband's heart when they are seen every day, when the summer is passed and gone. Will she then have sufficient native energy to look into herself for comfort, and cultivate her dormant faculties? or, is it not more rational to expect that she will try to please other men; and, in the emotions raised by the expectation of new conquests, endeavor to forget the mortification her love or pride has received? When the husband ceases to be a lover—and the time will inevitably come, her desire of pleasing will then grow languid, or become a spring of bitterness; and love, perhaps, the most evanescent of all passions, gives place to jealousy or vanity.

I now speak of women who are restrained by principle or prejudice; such women, though they would shrink from an intrigue with real abhorrence, yet, nevertheless, wish to be convinced by the homage of gallantry that they are cruelly neglected by their husbands; or, days and weeks are spent in dreaming of the happiness enjoyed by congenial souls till their health is undermined and their spirits broken by discontent. How then can the great art of pleasing be such a necessary study? it is only useful to a mistress; the chaste wife, and serious mother, should only consider her power to please as the polish of her virtues, and the affection of her husband as one of the comforts that render her task less difficult and her life happier. But, whether she be loved or neglected, her first wish should be to make herself respectable, and not to rely for all her happiness on a being subject to like infirmities with herself. A E

Appeals: Summarize Wollstonecraft's ideas in the two previous paragraphs. What two types of appeals does she use, and how does each reflect neoclassicism or romanticism? A

Author's Reasoning: What biblical truths about human nature does Wollstonecraft include in her views here? What biblical point does she make about a person's source of happiness? E

The worthy Dr. Gregory fell into a similar error. I respect his heart; but entirely disapprove of his celebrated Legacy to his Daughters. . . .

. . . He actually recommends dissimulation, and advises an innocent girl to give the lie to her feelings, and not dance with spirit, when gaiety of heart would make her feet eloquent without making her gestures immodest. In the name of truth and common sense, why should not one woman acknowledge that she can take more exercise than another? or, in other words, that she has a sound constitution; and why, to damp innocent vivacity, is she darkly to be told that men will draw conclusions which she little thinks of? —Let the libertine draw what inference he pleases; but, I hope, that no sensible mother will restrain the natural frankness of youth by instilling such indecent cautions. Out of the abundance of the heart the mouth speaketh; and a wiser than Solomon hath said, that the heart should be made clean, and not trivial ceremonies observed, which it is not very difficult to fulfil with scrupulous exactness when vice reigns in the heart.

VISUAL ANALYSIS
This painting depicts members of the Blue Stocking Society as the Muses of ancient Greece. This group of well-educated upper-class women promoted the equal participation of women and men in intellectual discussion. Like Wollstonecraft, they supported better education for women, and many of them were writers, artists, and musicians. How does the portrait's style and substance reveal them as transitional figures between neoclassicism and romanticism, just as Wollstonecraft was?

Women ought to endeavor to purify their heart; but can they do so when their uncultivated understandings make them entirely dependent on their senses for employment and amusement, when no noble pursuit sets them above the little vanities of the day, or enables them to curb the wild emotions that agitate a reed over which every passing breeze has power? To gain the affections of a virtuous man, is affectation necessary? Nature has given woman a weaker frame than man; but, to ensure her husband's affections, must a wife, who by the exercise of her mind and body whilst she was discharging the duties of a daughter, wife, and mother, has allowed her constitution to retain its natural strength, and her nerves a healthy tone, is she, I say, to condescend to use art and feign a sickly delicacy in order to secure her husband's affection? Weakness may excite tenderness, and gratify the arrogant pride of man; but the lordly caresses of a protector will not gratify a noble mind that pants for, and deserves to be respected. Fondness is a poor substitute for friendship! . . .

Besides, the woman who strengthens her body and exercises her mind will, by managing her family and practicing various virtues, become the friend, and not the humble dependent of her husband; and if she, by possessing such substantial qualities, merit his regard, she will not find it necessary to conceal her affection, nor to pretend to an unnatural coldness of constitution to excite her husband's passions. . . .

. . . If all the faculties of woman's mind are only to be cultivated as they respect her dependence on man; if, when a husband be obtained, she have arrived at her goal, and meanly proud rests satisfied with such a **paltry** crown, let her grovel contentedly, scarcely raised by her employments above the animal kingdom; but, if, struggling for the prize of her high calling, she look beyond the present scene, let her cultivate her understanding without stopping to consider what character the husband may have whom she is destined to marry. Let her only determine, without being too anxious about present happiness, to acquire the qualities that ennoble a rational being, and a rough inelegant husband may shock her taste without destroying her peace of mind. She will not model her soul to suit the frailties of her companion, but to bear

paltry (pôl'trē) *adj.* Lacking in importance or worth.

with them: his character may be a trial, but not an impediment to virtue. . . . **R**

It is difficult for us purblind[4] mortals to say to what height human discoveries and improvements may arrive when the gloom of despotism subsides, which makes us stumble at every step; but, when morality shall be settled on a more solid basis, then, without being gifted with a prophetic spirit, I will venture to predict that woman will be either the friend or slave of man. We shall not, as at present, doubt whether she is a moral agent, or the link which unites man with brutes. But, should it then appear, that like the brutes they were principally created for the use of man, he will let them patiently bite the bridle, and not mock them with empty praise; or, should their rationality be proved, he will not impede their improvement merely to gratify his sensual appetites. He will not, with all the graces of rhetoric, advise them to submit implicitly their understanding to the guidance of man. He will not, when he treats of the education of women, assert that they ought never to have the free use of reason, nor would he recommend cunning and dissimulation to beings who are acquiring, in like manner as himself, the virtues of humanity. . . .

These may be termed Utopian dreams. Thanks to that Being who impressed them on my soul, and gave me sufficient strength of mind to dare to exert my own reason, till, becoming dependent only on Him for the support of my virtue, I view, with indignation, the mistaken notions that enslave my sex.

I love man as my fellow; but his scepter, real, or usurped, extends not to me, unless the reason of an individual demands my homage; and even then the submission is to reason, and not to man. In fact, the conduct of an accountable being must be regulated by the operations of its own reason; or on what foundation rests the throne of God? **E**

It appears to me necessary to dwell on these obvious truths, because females have been insulated, as it were; and, while they have been stripped of the virtues that should clothe humanity, they have been decked with artificial graces that enable them to exercise a short-lived tyranny. Love, in their bosoms, taking place of every nobler passion, their sole ambition is to be fair, to raise emotion instead of inspiring respect; and this **ignoble** desire, like the servility in absolute monarchies, destroys all strength of character. Liberty is the mother of virtue, and if women are, by their very constitution, slaves, and not allowed to breathe the sharp invigorating air of freedom, they must ever languish like exotics, and be reckoned beautiful flaws in nature. **A**

4. *purblind:* slow to understand

Trace Arguments: Reread the previous three paragraphs. What suggested approach to this female behavior does Wollstonecraft refute? What does she advocate for instead in this and the next paragraph? **R**

Author's Reasoning: Where might Wollstonecraft step past the bounds of scriptural truth in this paragraph? **E**

ignoble (ĭg-nō′bəl) *adj.* Not noble in quality, character, or purpose; base or dishonorable.

Argumentation: How do Wollstonecraft's concluding statements reflect both neoclassical values and romantic concerns? **A**

THINK AND DISCUSS

1. Describe the particular problem(s) Wollstonecraft is responding to in these passages.
2. In your own words, state the thesis for this passage. What solution(s) does she suggest for this problem?
3. List three arguments Wollstonecraft gives in support of her thesis.
4. Consider Wollstonecraft's use of the word *virtue.* How does she seem to define *virtue*?
5. List an example of each kind of rhetorical appeal in Wollstonecraft's work.
6. How does this work show neoclassical and romantic influences in its appeals, values, and approaches?
7. What does Wollstonecraft contend concerning the reasoning, mental ability, and physical strength of women? What does she say about their role in marriage and in society? Evaluate her thinking in light of Scripture (Gen. 1:26–28; 2:20–23; 3:16; Prov. 31:10–31; Eph. 5:22–25; and 1 Pet. 3:7).

Jane Austen (1775–1817)

AT A GLANCE

- **1796** Began a draft of what would become *Sense and Sensibility*
- **1800** Moved to Bath, a transition that disrupted her writing habits
- **1809** Moved to Chawton where she finished *Sense and Sensibility* and wrote *Pride and Prejudice*, *Mansfield Park*, and *Emma*
- **1817** Died of an undetermined illness in Winchester; *Persuasion* and *Northanger Abbey* printed later that year
- **1833** First collection of her novels published

Although Jane Austen spent her life within the highly stratified and limited social world of the English country gentry, she wrote timeless novels that transcend their settings through their keen observation of human character and social mores. In doing so, Austen practically invented the realistic novel of manners, shifting the focus of the modern novel from extraordinary or outrageous events to the drama of everyday life.

Early Life

Austen was born in Hampshire, England. Her father, an Anglican rector, had a personal library of more than five hundred volumes, and young Jane was deeply familiar with the works of Richardson, Fielding, and Burney. Austen began writing at an early age, experimenting with various literary forms. By her early twenties she had already produced the first drafts of three of her six complete novels.

In 1800 her father retired and moved his family to the resort town of Bath. In the years both before and after his death in 1805, Austen had little time to write. In 1809, however, her brother Edward arranged for his sisters and mother to live on his estate in Chawton, Hampshire, where Austen was finally able to concentrate on her work.

All of Austen's heroines married their true love; however, Jane did not accept her one and only proposal.

Literary Success

In Austen's day, public authorship was still considered disreputable for a woman in Austen's position. Austen's name was never attached to her works during her lifetime. In fact, reputation probably influenced Austen's choice to rework and publish *Sense and Sensibility* (1811) first, since its content and themes were most in conformity with the social values of the day. Encouraged that *Sense and Sensibility* was accepted for publication, Austen quickly published *Pride and Prejudice* (1813), which met with widespread popularity.

The year 1814 brought the publication of *Mansfield Park*, Austen's most ambitious novel. This work brought her more income than her other novels during her lifetime, but it has seen the least commercial success to date. By the time *Emma* was published in 1815, Austen's novels had found a devoted fan in the Prince Regent himself, to whom the book is dedicated. By 1816, however, her health was failing, and she died, probably of Addison's disease, in the spring of 1817. Her brother Henry supervised the publication of *Northanger Abbey* and *Persuasion* in 1817, along with the first notice to the world of Austen's identity as an author.

Legacy

Austen's work is characterized by both a careful attention to the details of human life and a concern for the moral uplift of the reader. Thus, while Austen is famous for her realistic, fully rounded characters, many of them (such as Elinor Dashwood in *Sense and Sensibility* and John Knightley in *Emma*) remain exemplary models for behavior. The idealistic portraits of the central male characters in particular have proved influential on the modern romance novel.

Austen's works also reflect the trends in larger society. In her novels, older gentry, whose income traditionally comes from their land, jar with members of the rising middle class, who have made their fortunes in more mediocre pursuits such as business. Both groups seek to assert their status in highly coded social situations such as balls and personal visits.

This focus on the social significance of everyday behavior created the novel of manners and led directly to the realistic novels of the Victorian period. In Austen's time, novels were regarded as frivolous entertainment. Austen saw the unique potential for social analysis and moral education in the novel form, and her work remains both entertaining and inspiring today.

ANALYZE: *Transitional Elements and Character*

Austen's work incorporates both neoclassical and romantic elements. The former shows up in her social satire and subtly didactic characters; she critiques but still values social conventions, upholding class distinctions during a time of social upheaval. Her sympathetic characters model conduct and feelings restrained by common sense, morality, and reason. On the other hand, romanticism surfaces in her focus on rural English life, highly individual characters, a specifically female perspective (unconventional at the time), and realism in elements from setting to language. Consider how the following excerpts reflect this mix of characteristics.

Characters are important to Austen's themes, and she develops them carefully through both **direct** and **indirect characterization** (p. 88). Austen's narrator often directly comments on characters; Austen excels at indirect characterization by revealing characters' thoughts (a new development in the novel) and through their reactions to each other. Indeed, Austen stands out for her ability to realistically capture character traits through **dialogue** (conversations between characters). As you read, pay attention to what characters say, why they say it, and to whom they say it. What do you indirectly learn about each character from conversations?

READ: *Draw Conclusions About Characters*

In the following first chapters of *Pride and Prejudice*, Austen is already shaping readers' responses to her characters. As you read, draw conclusions about Austen's tone toward her characters and their actions. For example, which characters are **sympathetic** and which are **unsympathetic** (p. 394)? Additionally, can you recognize any **foil characters** (characters used to highlight another's opposing traits in connection to the book's themes)?

One helpful way to judge Austen's tone is to pay attention to her use of **wit**, brief verbal expressions that amuse listeners through clever but unexpected turns of phrase or connections between ideas. She frequently relies on verbal irony—for instance, **repartee** (besting another's remark or turning it to one's own advantage in a contest of wits)—to reveal both the foibles and merits of her characters. As you read, note where and how the narrator employs wit. In exchanges of repartee, pay attention to who comes out on top. Consider which characters employ sarcasm (a type of verbal irony, see p. 240) and how it affects or reflects relationships.

CREATE: *Dramatic Scene*

After your reading, you will be asked to write a script based on one scene. Scripts cannot totally reproduce a novel (e.g., usually the narrator must go), but good ones will stay faithful to the essential content and feel of their source, including the key ideas and emotional moments that readers find meaningful. As you read, note scenes or character interchanges that you find particularly enjoyable. Once you choose the scene you want to dramatize, annotate the text for key character traits, emotions, and interchanges to narrow the content of your script. Also, mark any character movements to note in stage directions. Try to recreate the scene as you imagined it while reading.

OBJECTIVES

- Identify both neoclassical and romantic elements in a text.
- Draw conclusions about a text's characters and tone.
- Analyze the connections between a text's characters, wit, and themes.
- Compose a dramatic scene based on a prose text.

VOCABULARY

circumspection (sûr′kəm-spĕk′shən) *n.* Caution, care, heedfulness.

emphatic (ĕm-făt′ĭk) *adj.* Forceful and definite in expression or action.

supposition (sŭp′ə-zĭsh′ən) *n.* An assumption.

mien (mēn) *n.* Bearing or manner, especially as it reveals an inner state of mind.

amiable (ā′mē-ə-bəl) *adj.* Friendly and agreeable in disposition; good-natured and likable.

cordial (kôr′jəl) *adj.* Warm and sincere; friendly.

Are FIRST IMPRESSIONS *reliable?*

When we first meet someone, it is normal to form a first impression. Occasionally first impressions can be scarily accurate; often they can be entirely false. One person's shyness can come across as arrogance while another person's charm might lead people to trust him too much. Have you ever formed a first impression of a person that proved to be quite true? Have you ever made a mistake by relying on a false first impression? What did you learn from your experience?

from PRIDE AND PREJUDICE

Chapter One

It is a truth universally acknowledged, that a single man in possession of a good fortune, must be in want of a wife!

However little known the feelings or views of such a man may be on his first entering a neighborhood, this truth is so well fixed in the minds of the surrounding families, that he is considered as the rightful property of some one or other of their daughters.

"My dear Mr. Bennet," said his lady to him one day, "have you heard that Netherfield Park[1] is let[2] at last?"

Mr. Bennet replied that he had not.

"But it is," returned she; "for Mrs. Long has just been here, and she told me all about it."

Mr. Bennet made no answer.

"Do not you want to know who has taken it?" cried his wife impatiently.

"*You* want to tell me, and I have no objection to hearing it."

This was invitation enough.

"Why, my dear, you must know, Mrs. Long says that Netherfield is taken by a young man of large fortune from the north of England; that he came down on Monday in a chaise and four[3] to see the place, and was so much delighted with it, that he agreed with Mr. Morris immediately; that he is to take possession before Michaelmas,[4] and some of his servants are to be in the house by the end of next week."[5]

"What is his name?"

"Bingley."

"Is he married or single?"

"Oh! single, my dear, to be sure! A single man of large fortune; four or five thousand a year. What a fine thing for our girls!"

"How so? how can it affect them?"

"My dear Mr. Bennet," replied his wife, "how can you be so tiresome! You must know that I am thinking of his marrying one of them."

"Is that his design in settling here?"

"Design! nonsense, how can you talk so! But it is very likely that he *may* fall in love with one of them, and therefore you must visit him as soon as he comcs."

"I see no occasion for that. You and the girls may go, or you may send them by themselves, which perhaps will be still better, for as you are as handsome as any of them, Mr. Bingley might like you the best of the party."

"My dear, you flatter me. I certainly *have* had my share of beauty, but I do not pretend to be anything extraordinary now. When a woman has five grown up daughters, she ought to give over thinking of her own beauty."

"In such cases, a woman has not often much beauty to think of." **R**

Draw Conclusions: What kind of wit does Mr. Bennet employ here? What does this exchange of repartee reflect about the Bennets' relationship? **R**

"But, my dear, you must indeed go and see Mr. Bingley when he comes into the neighborhood."

"It is more than I engage for, I assure you."

1. *Netherfield Park:* the name for a home in the Bennets' neighborhood
2. *let:* rented out
3. *a chaise and four:* a type of enclosed carriage popular for long distances that seats three people
4. *Michaelmas:* September 29; a festival observed in some liturgical calendars
5. *end . . . week:* It was common for servants to precede their masters to prepare for the latter's arrival.

"But consider your daughters. Only think what an establishment[6] it would be for one of them. Sir William and Lady Lucas are determined to go, merely on that account, for in general, you know, they visit no new comers. Indeed you must go, for it will be impossible for *us* to visit him if you do not."

6. *establishment:* marriage

"You are over scrupulous, surely. I dare say Mr. Bingley will be very glad to see you; and I will send a few lines by you to assure him of my hearty consent to his marrying which ever he chooses of the girls; though I must throw in a good word for my little Lizzy."

"I desire you will do no such thing. Lizzy is not a bit better than the others; and I am sure she is not half so handsome as Jane, nor half so good humored as Lydia. But you are always giving *her* the preference."

"They have none of them much to recommend them," replied he; "they are all silly and ignorant like other girls; but Lizzy has something more of quickness[7] than her sisters." **A**

Character: What personality trait of Elizabeth's does Mr. Bennet's response reveal? Why do you think her father relates to her better than to her sisters? **A**

"Mr. Bennet, how can you abuse your own children in such a way? You take delight in vexing me. You have no compassion on my poor nerves."

"You mistake me, my dear. I have a high respect for your nerves. They are my old friends. I have heard you mention them with consideration these twenty years at least."

"Ah! you do not know what I suffer."

"But I hope you will get over it, and live to see many young men of four thousand a year come into the neighborhood."

"It will be no use to us, if twenty such should come since you will not visit them."

"Depend upon it, my dear, that when there are twenty, I will visit them all."

Mr. Bennet was so odd a mixture of quick parts,[8] sarcastic humor, reserve, and caprice, that the experience of three and twenty years had been insufficient to make his wife understand his character. *Her* mind[9] was less difficult to develop. She was a woman of mean understanding,[10] little information,[11] and uncertain temper.[12] When she was discontented, she fancied herself nervous. The business of her life was to get her daughters married; its solace was visiting and news. **A**

Character: Summarize what you can infer so far about Mr. and Mrs. Bennet directly from the narrator and indirectly from their dialogue. **A**

Chapter Two

Mr. Bennet was among the earliest of those who waited on Mr. Bingley. He had always intended to visit him, though to the last always assuring his wife that he should not go; and till the evening after the visit was paid, she had no knowledge of it. It was then disclosed in the following manner. Observing his second daughter employed in trimming a hat,[13] he suddenly addressed her with,

"I hope Mr. Bingley will like it, Lizzy."

"We are not in a way to know *what* Mr. Bingley likes," said her mother resentfully, "since we are not to visit."

"But you forget, mama," said Elizabeth, "that we shall meet him at the assemblies,[14] and that Mrs. Long has promised to introduce him."

"I do not believe Mrs. Long will do any such thing. She has two nieces of her own. She is a selfish, hypocritical woman, and I have no opinion of her."[15]

7. *quickness:* mental sharpness
8. *quick parts:* qualities or attributes
9. *mind:* mental and emotional character
10. *mean understanding:* inferior intelligence or judgment
11. *information:* education or knowledge
12. *uncertain temper:* unsteady temperament
13. *trimming a hat:* decorating a hat with ribbons or feathers, a common practice at that time
14. *assemblies:* general social gatherings with dancing and other amusements
15. *I . . . her:* I have no good opinion of her.

"No more have I," said Mr. Bennet; "and I am glad to find that you do not depend on her serving you."

Mrs. Bennet deigned not to make any reply; but unable to contain herself, began scolding one of her daughters.

"Don't keep coughing so, Kitty, for heaven's sake! Have a little compassion on my nerves. You tear them to pieces."

"Kitty has no discretion in her coughs," said her father; "she times them ill."

"I do not cough for my own amusement," replied Kitty fretfully.

"When is your next ball to be, Lizzy?"

"Tomorrow fortnight."[16]

"Aye, so it is," cried her mother, "and Mrs. Long does not come back till the day before; so, it will be impossible for her to introduce him, for she will not know him herself."

"Then, my dear, you may have the advantage of your friend, and introduce Mr. Bingley to *her*."

"Impossible, Mr. Bennet, impossible, when I am not acquainted with him myself; how can you be so teasing?"

"I honor your **circumspection**. A fortnight's acquaintance is certainly very little. One cannot know what a man really is by the end of a fortnight. But if *we* do not venture, somebody else will; and after all, Mrs. Long and her nieces must stand their chance; and therefore, as she will think it an act of kindness, if you decline the offices[17] I will take it on myself."

circumspection (sûr′kəm-spĕk′shən) *n.* Caution, care, heedfulness.

The girls stared at their father. Mrs. Bennet said only, "Nonsense, nonsense!"

"What can be the meaning of that **emphatic** exclamation?" cried he. "Do you consider the forms of introduction, and the stress that is laid on them, as nonsense? I cannot quite agree with you *there*. What say you, Mary? for you are a young lady of deep reflection I know, and read great books,[18] and make extracts."

emphatic (ĕm-făt′ĭk) *adj.* Forceful and definite in expression or action.

Mary wished to say something very sensible, but knew not how.

"While Mary is adjusting her ideas," he continued, "let us return to Mr. Bingley."

"I am sick of Mr. Bingley," cried his wife.

"I am sorry to hear *that*; but why did not you tell me so before? If I had known as much this morning, I certainly would not have called on him. It is very unlucky; but as I have actually paid the visit, we cannot escape the acquaintance now."

The astonishment of the ladies was just what he wished; that of Mrs. Bennet perhaps surpassing the rest; though when the first tumult of joy was over, she began to declare that it was what she had expected all the while.

"How good it was in you, my dear Mr. Bennet! But I knew I should persuade you at last. I was sure you loved your girls too well to neglect such an acquaintance. Well, how pleased I am! and it is such a good joke, too, that you should have gone this morning, and never said a word about it till now."

"Now, Kitty, you may cough as much as you choose," said Mr. Bennet; and, as he spoke, he left the room, fatigued with the raptures of his wife. R

Draw Conclusions: How might Mr. and Mrs. Bennet function as foils to each other? Which do you find more sympathetic? R

"What an excellent father you have, girls," said she, when the door was shut. "I do not know how you will ever make him amends for his kindness; or me either, for that matter. At our time of life, it is not so pleasant I can tell

16. *Tomorrow fortnight:* two weeks from tomorrow
17. *offices:* duty; service to another
18. *great books:* large, weighty; suggests nothing of the quality of the books

you, to be making new acquaintance every day; but for your sakes, we would do anything. Lydia, my love, though you *are* the youngest, I dare say Mr. Bingley will dance with you at the next ball."

"Oh!" said Lydia stoutly, "I am not afraid; for though I *am* the youngest, I'm the tallest."

The rest of the evening was spent in conjecturing how soon he would return Mr. Bennet's visit, and determining when they should ask him to dinner. **A**

Transition: How might the content of this chapter reflect some of the neoclassical and romantic characteristics listed on page 445? **A**

Chapter Three

Not all that Mrs. Bennet, however, with the assistance of her five daughters, could ask on the subject was sufficient to draw from her husband any satisfactory description of Mr. Bingley. They attacked him in various ways; with barefaced questions, ingenious **suppositions**, and distant surmises; but he eluded the skill of them all; and they were at last obliged to accept the second-hand intelligence of their neighbor Lady Lucas. Her report was highly favorable. Sir William had been delighted with him. He was quite young, wonderfully handsome, extremely agreeable, and to crown the whole, he meant to be at the next assembly with a large party. Nothing could be more delightful! To be fond of dancing was a certain step towards falling in love; and very lively hopes of Mr. Bingley's heart were entertained.

supposition (sŭp′ə-zĭsh′ən) *n.* An assumption.

"If I can but see one of my daughters happily settled at Netherfield," said Mrs. Bennet to her husband, "and all the others equally well married, I shall have nothing to wish for."

In a few days Mr. Bingley returned Mr. Bennet's visit, and sat about ten minutes with him in his library. He had entertained hopes of being admitted to a sight of the young ladies, of whose beauty he had heard much; but he saw only the father. The ladies were somewhat more fortunate, for they had the advantage of ascertaining from an upper window, that he wore a blue coat and rode a black horse.

An invitation to dinner was soon afterwards dispatched; and already had Mrs. Bennet planned the courses that were to do credit to her housekeeping, when an answer arrived which deferred it all. Mr. Bingley was obliged to be in town[19] the following day, and consequently unable to accept the honor of their invitation, etc. Mrs. Bennet was quite disconcerted. She could not imagine what business he could have in town so soon after his arrival in Hertfordshire;[20] and she began to fear that he might be always flying about from one place to another, and never settled at Netherfield as he ought to be. Lady Lucas quieted her fears a little by starting the idea of his being gone to London only to get a large party for the ball; and a report soon followed that Mr. Bingley was to bring twelve ladies and seven gentlemen with him to the assembly. The girls grieved over such a number of ladies; but were comforted the day before the ball by hearing, that instead of twelve, he had brought only six with him from London, his five sisters and a cousin. And when the party entered the assembly room, it consisted of only five altogether; Mr. Bingley, his two sisters, the husband of the eldest, and another young man. **R**

Draw Conclusions: How does the narrator employ verbal irony in the previous few paragraphs? What tone does that irony communicate toward certain characters' concerns? **R**

19. *town:* London
20. *Hertfordshire:* the county in England where the story is taking place

Mr. Bingley was good looking and gentlemanlike; he had a pleasant countenance, and easy, unaffected manners. His sisters were fine women, with an air of decided fashion.[21] His brother-in-law, Mr. Hurst, merely looked the gentleman; but his friend Mr. Darcy soon drew the attention of the room by his fine, tall person, handsome features, noble **mien**; and the report which was in general circulation within five minutes after his entrance, of his having ten thousand a year.[22] The gentlemen pronounced him to be a fine figure of a man, the ladies declared he was much handsomer than Mr. Bingley, and he was looked at with great admiration for about half the evening, till his manners gave a disgust[23] which turned the tide of his popularity; for he was discovered to be proud, to be above his company, and above being pleased; and not all his large estate in Derbyshire[24] could then save him from having a most forbidding, disagreeable countenance, and being unworthy to be compared with his friend.

mien (mēn) *n.* Bearing or manner, especially as it reveals an inner state of mind.

amiable (ā'mē-ə-bəl) *adj.* Friendly and agreeable in disposition; good-natured and likable.

Mr. Bingley had soon made himself acquainted with all the principal people in the room; he was lively and unreserved, danced every dance, was angry that the ball closed so early, and talked of giving one himself at Netherfield. Such **amiable** qualities must speak for themselves. What a contrast between him and his friend! Mr. Darcy danced only once with Mrs. Hurst and once with Miss Bingley, declined being introduced to any other lady, and spent the rest of the evening in walking about the room, speaking occasionally to one of his own party. His character was decided.[25] He was the proudest, most disagreeable man in the world, and everybody hoped that he would never come there again. Amongst the most violent against him was Mrs. Bennet, whose dislike of his general behavior, was sharpened into particular resentment, by his having slighted one of her daughters. **A**

Elizabeth Bennet had been obliged, by the scarcity of gentlemen, to sit down for two dances; and during part of that time, Mr. Darcy had been standing near enough for her to overhear a conversation between him and Mr. Bingley, who came from the dance for a few minutes, to press his friend to join it.

"Come, Darcy," said he, "I must have you dance. I hate to see you standing about by yourself in this stupid[26] manner. You had much better dance."

Character: Summarize what you have learned about Bingley and Darcy so far. How well does each conform to social conventions? **A**

21. *decided fashion:* high social standing; behavior expected of the upper-class society
22. *ten . . .year:* a sum that places him among the one or two hundred wealthiest men in England then
23. *gave a disgust:* produced a distaste or dislike
24. *Derbyshire:* a county in the northern half of England
25. *character . . . decided:* The general opinion of him was established.
26. *stupid:* dull; tiresome

"I certainly shall not. You know how I detest it, unless I am particularly acquainted with my partner. At such an assembly as this, it would be insupportable. Your sisters are engaged, and there is not another woman in the room, whom it would not be a punishment to me to stand up[27] with."

"I would not be so fastidious as you are," cried Bingley, "for a kingdom! Upon my honor, I never met with so many pleasant girls in my life, as I have this evening; and there are several of them you see uncommonly pretty."

"*You* are dancing with the only handsome[28] girl in the room," said Mr. Darcy, looking at the eldest Miss Bennet.[29]

"Oh! she is the most beautiful creature I ever beheld! But there is one of her sisters sitting down just behind you, who is very pretty, and I dare say, very agreeable. Do let me ask my partner to introduce you."

"Which do you mean?" and turning round, he looked for a moment at Elizabeth, till catching her eye, he withdrew his own and coldly said, "She is tolerable; but not handsome enough to tempt *me*; and I am in no humor[30] at present to give consequence[31] to young ladies who are slighted by other men. You had better return to your partner and enjoy her smiles, for you are wasting your time with me." R

Draw Conclusions: How might Bingley and Darcy serve as foils to each other? Which do you find more sympathetic at the moment? R

Mr. Bingley followed his advice. Mr. Darcy walked off; and Elizabeth remained with no very **cordial** feelings towards him. She told the story however with great spirit among her friends; for she had a lively, playful disposition, which delighted in anything ridiculous.

cordial (kôr′jəl) *adj.* Warm and sincere; friendly.

The evening altogether passed off pleasantly to the whole family. Mrs. Bennet had seen her eldest daughter much admired by the Netherfield party. Mr. Bingley had danced with her twice, and she had been distinguished[32] by his sisters. Jane was as much gratified by this, as her mother could be, though in a quieter way. Elizabeth felt Jane's pleasure. Mary had heard herself mentioned to Miss Bingley as the most accomplished girl in the neighborhood; and Catherine and Lydia had been fortunate enough to be never without partners, which was all that they had yet learned to care for at a ball. They returned therefore in good spirits to Longbourn, the village where they lived, and of which they were principal inhabitants.[33] They found Mr. Bennet still up. With a book he was regardless of time; and on the present occasion he had good deal of curiosity as to the event[34] of an evening which raised such splendid expectations. He had rather hoped that all his wife's views[35] on the stranger would be disappointed; but he soon found that he had a very different story to hear.

Oh! my dear Mr. Bennet," as she entered the room, "we have had a most delightful evening, a most excellent ball. I wish you had been there. Jane was so admired, nothing could be like it. Everybody said how well she looked; and Mr. Bingley thought her quite beautiful, and danced with her twice. Only think of *that*, my dear; he actually danced with her twice; and she was the only creature in the room that he asked a second time. First of all, he asked Miss Lucas. I was so vexed to see him stand up with her; but, however, he did not admire her at all: indeed, nobody can, you know; and he seemed quite

27. *stand up:* dance
28. *handsome:* Often used for women, the term had no particular masculine connotation at the time.
29. *eldest Miss Bennet:* Jane
30. *humor:* mood
31. *consequence:* importance or dignity
32. *distinguished:* singled out for notice or attention
33. *principal inhabitants:* the family of the highest social position in the village
34. *event:* outcome
35. *views:* expectations

struck with Jane as she was going down the dance.[36] So, he enquired who she was, and got introduced, and asked her for the two next.[37] Then, the two third he danced with Miss King, and the two fourth with Maria Lucas, and the two fifth with Jane again, and the two sixth with Lizzy, and the Boulanger—"[38]

"If he had had any compassion for *me*," cried her husband impatiently, "he would not have danced half so much! … Say no more of his partners. Oh! that he had sprained his ankle in the first dance!"

"Oh! my dear," continued Mrs. Bennet, "I am quite delighted with him. He is so excessively handsome! and his sisters are charming women. I never in my life saw any thing more elegant than their dresses. I dare say the lace upon Mrs. Hurst's gown—"

Here she was interrupted again. Mr. Bennet protested against any description of finery. She was therefore obliged to seek another branch of the subject, and related, with much bitterness of spirit and some exaggeration, the shocking rudeness of Mr. Darcy. **A**

Transition: Contrast Mrs. Bennet's reaction to Mr. Darcy with Lizzy's reaction. How might Lizzy's response reveal Austen's preference for neoclassical values in her sympathetic characters? **A**

"But I can assure you," she added, "that Lizzy does not lose much by not suiting *his* fancy; for he is a most disagreeable, horrid man, not at all worth pleasing. So high and so conceited that there was no enduring him! He walked here, and he walked there, fancying himself so very great! Not handsome enough to dance with! I wish you had been there, my dear, to have given him one of your set downs. I quite detest the man."

36. *going . . . dance:* a male and a female moving down a row of female dancers and a row of male dancers
37. *two next:* People normally had the same partner for a pair of dances.
38. *Boulanger:* a dance imported from France

THINK AND DISCUSS

1. Define the terms *dialogue*, *wit*, *repartee*, and *foil character*.
2. Describe some of the social conventions and values exhibited in Chapters 1–3 through the characters' thoughts and behaviors. How do the women spend their time? How do the men spend their time? Whose perspective does Austen prioritize, and how does she do so?
3. Note and briefly explain two examples in the text of Austen's use of dialogue to indirectly characterize.
4. Locate three examples of wit (whether verbal irony, sarcasm, or repartee) in the text. How does its use color readers' perspectives on the characters, their motivations and actions, and society at large?
5. Summarize your impression of the following characters: Mr. Bennet, Mrs. Bennet, Lizzy, Mr. Bingley, Mr. Darcy.
6. Which of these characters from the previous question seem sympathetic and which do not? Support your answer from the text.
7. Choose a pair of foil characters from the passage and explain the differences they highlight in each other.
8. How might Austen be subtly critiquing the social customs and values you noted in question 2? Consider her tone toward certain characters and their behaviors.
9. Explain two ways that Austen reveals the neoclassical influences mentioned on page 445 in these excerpts and two in which she shows the romantic influences.
10. Choose a scene from *Pride and Prejudice* and write a script dramatizing it. Begin your scene with a list of characters and a description of the setting. Make sure to follow the correct form for scripts, tagging each section of dialogue with the appropriate character's name and including stage directions as needed (see *Macbeth*, p. 215).

UNIT 4

PART 2

The Major Romantics

Have you ever felt in need of inspiration, whether for a homework assignment, for a personal project, or simply for motivation just to keep going in everyday life? Do you ever feel stress build as assignments, extracurricular activities, and church responsibilities pile up during the school year? Most of us at one point or another experience mental or spiritual burnout and need inspiration to keep going. Many activities, such as reading a book, talking to a mentor, engaging in a sport or hobby, or spending personal time with God, can help you find rejuvenation.

The major romantics considered inspiration extremely important to their personal lives and artistic work. Amidst a rapidly changing and stressful world, they sought inspiration for their writing and tried to inspire readers as well. They saw the poet as a conduit of this inspiration, being a **visionary** who would communicate a new future. Unsurprisingly then, romantic poets can sometimes appear to have inflated egos as they present their ideals about art as truth. Similar to the neoclassicists' goals, their intentions were to access overarching truths and make society better. However, their focus and methods for pursuing this task differed considerably.

Romantics departed from neoclassical thinkers in how they accessed truth. Neoclassicists had prioritized man's rational faculties; romantics insisted on human **imagination** as the appropriate lens through which to see the interconnectedness of the universe and address the world's problems. This emphasis prized knowledge gained through people's emotions and subjective perceptions (the latter the only reliable knowledge according to romantic idealism, p. 416). These served as inspiration and a guide for the visionary poet, whose imaginative "inward eye" (Wordsworth's term) could intuit and powerfully share truth, bringing pleasure and healing.

On a related note, romantics reacted to the neoclassical writers' tendency to stress social hierarchies and to universalize human behavior by elevating the unique needs and perceptions of the **individual**. Socially, many romantics supported more democratic governance and rejected behavioral conventions. In literature, they explored individuals' inner emotional lives. Romantic poetry broadly conveys the subjective experience of individuals, revealing their self-consciousness and ability to judge the world on their own terms. The most extreme examples center on individuals who forged their own paths, often in radical defiance of traditional rules. Such *Byronic heroes* (p. 480) were often used as a stinging critique of society's hypocrisy.

Finally, romantics believed their vision of a better world would be found in **nature**, which exemplified truth more than tradition or human society did. Some even went so far as to see God and nature woven together in a somewhat pantheistic way. According to romantics, civilization muddled man's intuition of truth by separating him from the natural world. Forces of civilization such as industrialization, church, and government were thus corrupting. Instead, a person's living simply and harmoniously with nature was the romantic ideal. Romantics prized contact with nature as the way to rejuvenate one's imagination and intuit overarching truths about humanity. As a result, nature imagery and individual responses to the natural world permeate their poetry.

These emphases intertwined in several characteristic features of romantic poetry. First, most romantic poets sought to realize the potential of human imagination by invoking a sense of wonder—the **sublime**—a momentary emotional experience in which readers transcend everyday living and briefly grasp ultimates of beauty, horror, time, or grandeur. To achieve this effect, romantics used sweeping vistas from nature, mystic or supernatural elements (e.g., ghosts, curses), and macabre or apocalyptic scenes similar to the Gothic. Similarly, romantics frequently employed **the distant** in time or place, sending readers to faraway places such as India, China, or Persia or revisiting past English literature. For example, they invoked the medieval romance for its fantastical content and individualistic heroes. Such exoticized settings lent themselves to the extravagance of emotions romantics expressed.

Romantic poets presented these ideas in genres better suited to them than the ones neoclassical writers had favored. They wrote, almost exclusively, lyric poetry—sonnets, odes, and blank verse compositions that expressed their ideals through subjective personal experiences—and revived older, more relatable, folk forms such as the ballad. Likewise, romantics generally used common language and imagery, believing these could be understood by the broadest audience and so best spread their message to the masses.

In this section you will learn about five poets considered most representative of English romantic literature. First, Wordsworth and Coleridge created the template for romantic poets when they published *Lyrical Ballads* (1798). Then Byron, Shelley, and Keats wrote after the Napoleonic Wars in a very different social context that pushed them in more radical directions. All five revolutionized the literature of their day, and their philosophy still affects the way we view emotion, creativity, and the individual.

William Wordsworth (1770–1850)

AT A GLANCE

- **1791** Moved to France
- **1795** Moved to southwestern England with his sister, Dorothy
- **1798** Published *Lyrical Ballads* with Coleridge
- **1810** Quarreled with Coleridge and parted from him
- **1843** Was appointed poet laureate

William Wordsworth leveraged his rural upbringing to transform English poetry, shifting poetry's focus from the objective truths of society to the subjective experience of the individual. Wordsworth also revolutionized poetic tone. Instead of the aristocratic language and themes of the eighteenth century, Wordsworth treated common life in gracefully unadorned diction.

DID YOU KNOW ?

Wordsworth sometimes used Dorothy's journal to remind himself of scenes from their travels that he wanted to evoke in a poem.

Early Life

Wordsworth was born in the Lake District, a region of northwestern England known for its scenery. In the many hours he spent boating or climbing hills, he developed the intense passion for nature and regard for common life that characterize him as a poet.

His studies at Cambridge were undistinguished, and in 1791 Wordsworth moved to London, where he began to participate in radical politics. The ideals of the French Revolution inspired him, and at the close of 1791 he traveled to France, where he fell in love with a Frenchwoman and fathered an illegitimate daughter. The outbreak of war between England and France, however, forced Wordsworth to return to England alone.

Revolutionary Poetry

In 1794 Wordsworth reunited with his sister, Dorothy, who would remain his lifelong companion. The following year they moved to southwestern England, where they met Samuel Taylor Coleridge. There, with the encouragement of Dorothy and the inspiration of Coleridge, Wordsworth determined to become a poet. In 1798 Wordsworth and Coleridge published a collection of their poems, *Lyrical Ballads,* in which both the preface and the content issued a direct assault on poetic convention. As to be expected, the book was widely panned by critics.

Wordsworth and his sister moved back to the Lake District in 1799. Having provided financial security for his French dependents, Wordsworth married Mary Hutchinson in 1802, with whom he had a long and fulfilling marriage that produced five children. In 1807 Wordsworth published *Poems, in Two Volumes.* This, too, met a furious wave of censure. It was not until he published *The Excursion* (1814) that Wordsworth began to receive general critical acceptance. By this time, however, he had ceased writing his best poetry, and ironically, his romantic contemporaries were largely disappointed by his later work. His friendship with Coleridge, so crucial to his inspiration, had been damaged by a quarrel in 1810.

Later Life and Influence

As Wordsworth aged, he became increasingly conservative, voicing strong opposition to liberal political reforms. He was appointed poet laureate in 1843. In 1850 he died in his beloved Lake District, and that same year his greatest masterpiece, *The Prelude,* was published. This was an autobiographical poem of epic length and ambition, largely written by 1806 but continually revised until his death.

At its most sublime, Wordsworth's poetry celebrates humanity's mysterious relationship with the universe and does so in language that feels natural, not forced. Wordsworth was not merely a poet of nature, however. He was also a poet of internal states. Unlike earlier epics, *The Prelude* is not concerned with great deeds or heroes but with the psychological development of its author. With this new internal focus, Wordsworth permanently shifted the goals of English poetry.

ANALYZE: *Romantic Content, Form, and Style*

In *Lyrical Ballads* Wordsworth codified the break between neoclassical and romantic poetry. Clear changes to perspective and content resulted from the romantic emphasis on imagination, the individual, and nature. As you read his poems, consider how an individual's personal experience and imaginative side permeate his perspectives and themes. Note also how nature imagery dominates. In "Tintern Abbey" Wordsworth describes even himself in terms of the natural world. How does nature imagery help develop each poem's theme?

Wordsworth also developed a new standard for poetic form and style. For example, his term *lyrical ballad* evokes the oral folk poetry that romantics admired. *Lyrical* implies a speaker with a spontaneous, naturalistic voice (like the old bards). *Ballad* adds a sense of loose narrative that neoclassical poets had often neglected. How might his poems combine such elements?

Finally, to achieve a naturalistic style, Wordsworth used common diction of the era and imitated the irregular patterns and rhythms of spoken language. He frequently tried to override readers' natural tendency to pause (even slightly) at each line end. He often extended a line's flow using **enjambment**, in which grammatical units flow seamlessly past the line's end into the next. He also created alternative resting points using **caesura**, a pause in the middle of a poetic line, usually indicated by punctuation. Look for both techniques as you read.

READ: *Compare Texts*

A good way to recognize how Wordsworth's poetry diverged from neoclassical ideals is to compare his works to neoclassical poets'. Notice how different his language choices are from the poetic diction (p. 374) and elevated allusions of poets such as Pope and Gray. Compare his long, flowing lines of thought with the regular rhythms and compact thought of the heroic couplet (p. 339) in Pope's works. Consider how his content favors subjective personal experiences and emotions over Pope's universalized truths and rational discussion (p. 339). Can you see how Wordsworth's poetry was a kind of literary revolution?

EVALUATE: *Romanticism*

Wordsworth calls nature "the guide, the guardian of my heart" ("Tintern Abbey," l. 114). He wanted to reach the transcendent sublime with the help of nature and his own imagination. Christians see in romantic philosophy some points to embrace and others to reject. Consider what Isaiah 24:5–6 says about nature, and contrast that passage to Psalm 19. According to the Bible, how should Christians approach the use of imagination? How does God say the imagination can help man fulfill his mission on earth? Consult Genesis 1:26–27 and 6:5 and Romans 8:18–22.

OBJECTIVES

- Identify examples of enjambment and caesura in a text.
- Compare texts to illustrate differences in poetic styles.
- Analyze how a poem's content, form, and style support romantic themes.
- Evaluate an author's romantic ideas in light of Scripture.

VOCABULARY

pensive (pĕn′sĭv) *adj.* Engaged in deep and serious thought.

repose (rĭ-pōz′) *intr.v.* To lie at rest.

din (dĭn) *n.* A jumble of loud, usually discordant sounds.

corporeal (kôr-pôr′ē-əl) *adj.* Of, relating to, or characteristic of the body.

perchance (pər-chăns′) *adv.* Perhaps; possibly.

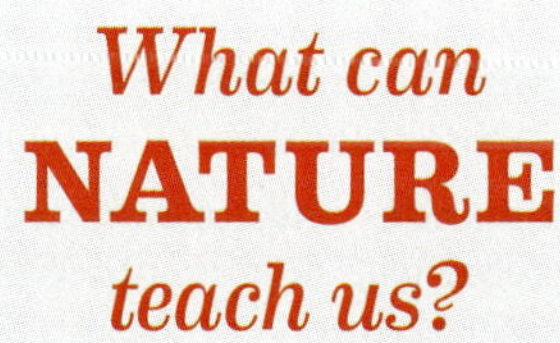

Have you ever experienced that sense of pure bliss on a crisp autumn day or felt the sunshine infusing your whole being, down to your fingertips, as you stretched out on a beach? Have you ever observed an animal or insect busy about its duties or seen the effects of a terrible natural disaster such as a hurricane or wildfire? What emotions did these experiences bring you? What scriptural truths might they have reminded you of?

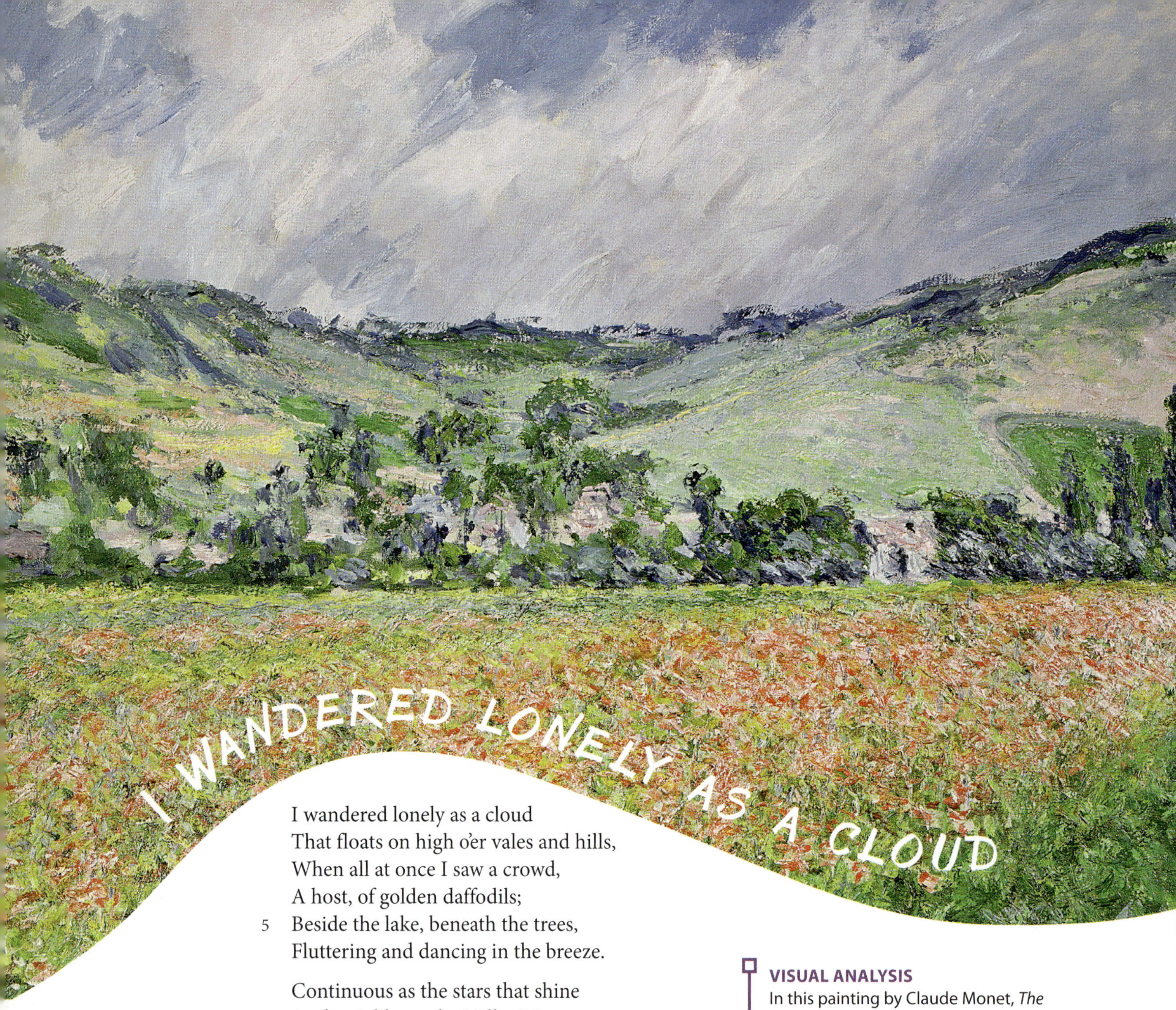

I WANDERED LONELY AS A CLOUD

I wandered lonely as a cloud
That floats on high o'er vales and hills,
When all at once I saw a crowd,
A host, of golden daffodils;
Beside the lake, beneath the trees,
Fluttering and dancing in the breeze.

Continuous as the stars that shine
And twinkle on the Milky Way,
They stretched in never-ending line
Along the margin of a bay:
Ten thousand saw I at a glance,
Tossing their heads in sprightly dance.

The waves beside them danced; but they
Out-did the sparkling waves in glee:
A poet could not but be gay,
In such a jocund company:
I gazed—and gazed—but little thought
What wealth the show to me had brought:

For oft, when on my couch I lie
In vacant or in pensive mood,
They flash upon that inward eye
Which is the bliss of solitude,
And then my heart with pleasure fills,
And dances with the daffodils.

VISUAL ANALYSIS
In this painting by Claude Monet, *The Poppy Field near Giverny* (1885), how does the artist evoke a similar image and mood as Wordsworth does in his depiction of a field of daffodils?

pensive (pĕn′sĭv) *adj.* Engaged in deep and serious thought.

Romantic Content: Wordsworth's poetry is infused with his romantic ideals. Which romantic emphasis does his phrase "inward eye" refer to?

Romantic Content: As you examine the nature images, determine the speaker's response to solitude.

THE WORLD IS TOO MUCH WITH US

The world is too much with us; late and soon,
Getting and spending, we lay waste our powers:
Little we see in nature that is ours;
We have given our hearts away, a sordid boon![1]
The sea that bares her bosom to the moon;
The winds that will be howling at all hours,
And are up-gathered now like sleeping flowers;
For this, for everything, we are out of tune;
It moves us not—great God! I'd rather be
A pagan suckled in a creed outworn;
So might I, standing on this pleasant lea,[2]
Have glimpses that would make me less forlorn;
Have sight of Proteus[3] rising from the sea;
Or hear old Triton[4] blow his wreathèd horn. R

Compare Texts: Compare the selection from Pope's *An Essay on Man* with the poem "The world is too much with us." How do Pope and Wordsworth treat the topic of nature differently? R

1. *sordid boon:* wretched exchange
2. *lea:* meadow
3. *Proteus:* Greek god capable of changing his shape
4. *Triton:* Greek sea god, half man and half fish, usually shown blowing on a shell

Lines Composed a Few Miles Above Tintern Abbey

VISUAL ANALYSIS
How might William Havell's painting of the ruins of Tintern Abbey reflect some characteristics of romantic art (pp. 454–55)? As you read Wordsworth's poem, consider what attitudes the poet and the painter might share.

Five years have past; five summers, with the length
Of five long winters! and again I hear
These waters, rolling from their mountain-springs
With a soft inland murmur.—Once again
Do I behold these steep and lofty cliffs,
That on a wild secluded scene impress
Thoughts of more deep seclusion; and connect
The landscape with the quiet of the sky.
The day is come when I again **repose**
Here, under this dark sycamore, and view
These plots of cottage-ground, these orchard-tufts,[1]
Which at this season, with their unripe fruits,
Are clad in one green hue, and lose themselves
'Mid groves and copses. Once again I see
These hedge-rows, hardly hedge-rows, little lines
Of sportive wood run wild: these pastoral farms,
Green to the very door; and wreaths of smoke
Sent up, in silence, from among the trees!
With some uncertain notice, as might seem
Of vagrant dwellers in the houseless woods,
Or of some Hermit's cave, where by his fire
The Hermit sits alone. **A**

repose (rĭ-pōz′) *intr.v.* To lie at rest.

Romantic Content: Where is the speaker? Would you describe the setting as orderly or wild? Why? **A**

These beauteous forms,
Through a long absence, have not been to me
As is a landscape to a blind man's eye:
But oft, in lonely rooms, and 'mid the **din**
Of towns and cities, I have owed to them,

din (dĭn) *n.* A jumble of loud, usually discordant sounds.

1. *tuft:* a thick group of shrubbery

In hours of weariness, sensations sweet,
Felt in the blood, and felt along the heart;
And passing even into my purer mind,
With tranquil restoration:—feelings too
Of unremembered pleasure: such, perhaps,
As have no slight or trivial influence
On that best portion of a good man's life,
His little, nameless, unremembered, acts
Of kindness and of love. Nor less, I trust,
To them I may have owed another gift,
Of aspect more sublime;[2] that blessed mood,
In which the burthen[3] of the mystery,
In which the heavy and the weary weight
Of all this unintelligible world,
Is lightened:—that serene and blessed mood,
In which the affections gently lead us on,
Until, the breath of this **corporeal** frame
And even the motion of our human blood
Almost suspended, we are laid asleep
In body, and become a living soul:
While with an eye made quiet by the power
Of harmony, and the deep power of joy,
We see into the life of things.
If this
Be but a vain belief, yet, oh! how oft—
In darkness and amid the many shapes
Of joyless daylight; when the fretful stir
Unprofitable, and the fever of the world,
Have hung upon the beatings of my heart—
How oft, in spirit, have I turned to thee,
O sylvan[4] Wye![5] Thou wanderer thro' the woods,
How often has my spirit turned to thee!

And now, with gleams of half-extinguished thought,
With many recognitions dim and faint,
And somewhat of a sad perplexity,
The picture of the mind revives again:
While here I stand, not only with the sense
Of present pleasure, but with pleasing thoughts
That in this moment there is life and food
For future years. And so I dare to hope,
Though changed, no doubt, from what I was when first
I came among these hills; when like a roe[6]
I bounded o'er the mountains, by the sides
Of the deep rivers, and the lonely streams,
Wherever nature led: more like a man
Flying from something that he dreads, than one
Who sought the thing he loved. For nature then **A**
(The coarser pleasures of my boyish days,

corporeal (kôr-pôr'ē-əl) *adj.* Of, relating to, or characteristic of the body.

Romantic Style: What instances of caesura and enjambment can you find in this section of the poem (ll. 58–72)? How many lines does it take Wordsworth to complete a thought? **A**

2. *sublime:* having great spiritual value
3. *burthen:* burden
4. *sylvan:* related to woods or dwelling in a forest
5. *Wye:* the River Wye in England and Wales
6. *roe:* deer

And their glad animal movements all gone by)
To me was all in all.—I cannot paint
What then I was. The sounding cataract[7] A
Haunted me like a passion: the tall rock,
The mountain, and the deep and gloomy wood,
Their colors and their forms, were then to me
An appetite; a feeling and a love,
That had no need of a remoter charm,
By thought supplied, or any interest
Unborrowed from the eye.—That time is past,
And all its aching joys are now no more,
And all its dizzy raptures. Not for this
Faint[8] I, nor mourn nor murmur; other gifts
Have followed; for such loss, I would believe,
Abundant recompense. For I have learned
To look on nature, not as in the hour
Of thoughtless youth; but hearing oftentimes
The still, sad music of humanity,
Nor harsh nor grating, though of ample power
To chasten and subdue. And I have felt
A presence that disturbs me with the joy
Of elevated thoughts; a sense sublime
Of something far more deeply interfused,
Whose dwelling is the light of setting suns,
And the round ocean and the living air,
And the blue sky, and in the mind of man:
A motion and a spirit, that impels
All thinking things, all objects of all thought,
And rolls through all things. Therefore am I still
A lover of the meadows and the woods
And mountains; and of all that we behold
From this green earth; of all the mighty world
Of eye, and ear,—both what they half create,
And what perceive; well pleased to recognize
In nature and the language of the sense,
The anchor of my purest thoughts, the nurse,
The guide, the guardian of my heart, and soul
Of all my moral being. R
                                        Nor **perchance**,
If I were not thus taught, should I the more
Suffer my genial[9] spirits to decay:
For thou art with me here upon the banks
Of this fair river; thou my dearest Friend,
My dear, dear Friend; and in thy voice I catch ✓
The language of my former heart, and read
My former pleasures in the shooting lights
Of thy wild eyes. Oh! yet a little while
May I behold in thee what I was once,
My dear, dear Sister! and this prayer I make,

Romantic Form: How does the poem reflect the qualities of a lyrical ballad? A

Compare Texts: Examine Wordsworth and Pope in light of their poetic styles. How does the lyrical ballad differ from the verse epistle? R

perchance (pər-chăns′) *adv*. Perhaps; possibly.

Reading Check: Who is Wordsworth's "dear, dear Friend"? ✓

7. *cataract:* waterfall
8. *Faint:* to grow weak in spirit
9. *genial:* having to do with creativity or genius

Knowing that Nature never did betray
The heart that loved her; 'tis her privilege,
Through all the years of this our life, to lead
From joy to joy: for she can so inform
The mind that is within us, so impress
With quietness and beauty, and so feed
With lofty thoughts, that neither evil tongues,
Rash judgments, nor the sneers of selfish men,
Nor greetings where no kindness is, nor all
The dreary intercourse of daily life,
Shall e'er prevail against us, or disturb
Our cheerful faith, that all which we behold
Is full of blessings. Therefore let the moon
Shine on thee in thy solitary walk;
And let the misty mountain-winds be free
To blow against thee: and in after years,
When these wild ecstasies shall be matured
Into a sober pleasure; when thy mind
Shall be a mansion for all lovely forms,
Thy memory be as a dwelling-place
For all sweet sounds and harmonies; oh! then,
If solitude, or fear, or pain, or grief,
Should be thy portion, with what healing thoughts
Of tender joy wilt thou remember me,
And these my exhortations! Nor, perchance—
If I should be where I no more can hear
Thy voice, nor catch from thy wild eyes these gleams
Of past existence—wilt thou then forget
That on the banks of this delightful stream
We stood together; and that I, so long
A worshipper of Nature, hither came
Unwearied in that service: rather say
With warmer love—oh! with far deeper zeal
Of holier love. Nor wilt thou then forget,
That after many wanderings, many years
Of absence, these steep woods and lofty cliffs,
And this green pastoral landscape, were to me
More dear, both for themselves and for thy sake! E

Romanticism: What value does the speaker place on nature? Evaluate his view of nature in light of Scripture. E

THINK AND DISCUSS

1. In "I wandered lonely as a cloud," where does the speaker either link himself to or separate himself from nature with the use of nature imagery?
2. To what animal does the speaker in "Tintern Abbey" compare his youthful self? Why do you think this natural image is important to the speaker's development?
3. How do the effects of Pope's heroic couplets and Wordsworth's enjambment differ?
4. In "The world is too much with us," what are people engaged in doing, and how does the poet judge their actions? Why does it matter that they have given their hearts away?
5. Consider the major tenets of British romanticism from the section introduction. Why does Wordsworth mention two Greek gods at the end of "The world is too much with us"?
6. What did Wordsworth expect from his "sublime" experiences that believers can embrace? What expectation should they reject?

Samuel Taylor Coleridge (1772–1834)

AT A GLANCE

- **1791–94** Attended Cambridge
- **1798** Published *Lyrical Ballads* with Wordsworth
- **1799** Studied in Germany
- **1810** Quarreled with Wordsworth
- **1816** Entered treatment for opium addiction
- **1817** Published *Biographia Literaria*

Samuel Taylor Coleridge was the poet, literary critic, and philosopher who, along with William Wordsworth, inaugurated the romantic era in British poetry. His poetry is celebrated for its imaginative power and its radically conversational tone. In addition to his poetic work, Coleridge exerted a strong influence on English literary criticism and philosophy.

Poet and Critic

Coleridge was born to a schoolmaster and vicar in Devon. He was only eight years old when his father suddenly died and he was sent to study at Christ's Hospital School. There he excelled in academics and soon began writing poetry. As a child Coleridge was bookish and dreamy, his vivid imagination helping him cope with the severe physical privation of life at Christ's Hospital. Coleridge entered Cambridge in 1791 but dropped out in 1794 to help found a utopian, egalitarian society. The plan fell through in 1795, but he was already engaged to marry Sara Fricker, a society member. The marriage proved generally unhappy.

Also in 1795 he moved to Somerset, where he published a periodical and sought a position as a Unitarian preacher. Crucially, he also met William and Dorothy Wordsworth, who soon moved to the area. He and the Wordsworths formed a close friendship, Coleridge inspiring William Wordsworth to a more conversational style and Wordsworth in turn challenging Coleridge to a finer attention to nature. Coleridge's famous *The Rime of the Ancient Mariner* was originally suggested by Wordsworth. Together the two published *Lyrical Ballads* (1798), which in its preface and poems broke with poetic tradition. In 1799 Coleridge and the Wordsworths visited Germany, where Coleridge immersed himself in German romanticism and higher criticism (the study of the Bible as a literary and historical text).

As valuable as Coleridge was to Wordsworth as a fellow poet and critic, Coleridge himself was demanding and erratic. In 1799 he fell in love with Wordsworth's future sister-in-law, Sara Hutchinson, and the tension eventually led to the two great friends' falling-out in 1810. Coleridge continued to write poetry afterward, but his great poetry was all behind him.

Coleridge gave us such words as *psychosomatic* and *bipolar*.

Philosopher and Theologian

By this time Coleridge's addiction to opium, which he had begun taking for medicinal purposes in 1796, was overwhelming him. In 1803 his wife and children moved to the home of a brother-in-law, the poet Robert Southey, who eventually assumed financial responsibility for them. In 1816 Coleridge entered a physician's home for treatment. He continued to live there for the rest of his life, frequently experiencing relapses.

By 1813 Coleridge had come to accept Anglicanism and the doctrine of the Trinity, although his theology was interpreted through the lens of German higher criticism. He published *Biographia Literaria* in 1817, a volume that describes his personal poetic development and offers critical insights into Wordsworth's poetry as well. In 1825 he published *Aids to Reflection*, an apology for Christianity and a summary of his theological thought. He died of heart failure in 1834.

Legacy

Immensely influential in his lifetime, Coleridge met and inspired not only Wordsworth but also younger poets such as Keats and Byron. His literary criticism transformed the discipline, and his philosophical and theological writings proved inspirational to early Victorians. As a poet, though, he was widely regarded as not achieving his potential. Nevertheless, Coleridge's great poems—"Kubla Khan," *Christabel*, and the world-famous *Rime*—have an imaginative, sensuous power never replicated in English literature.

ANALYZE: *Ballad, Sound Devices, Imagery*

The Rime of the Ancient Mariner exhibits several characteristics of romantic poetry (p. 417). One such feature is its use of an old form: the **ballad** (pp. 68–69). Much of the poem is in ballad stanza (quatrains of alternating three- and four-stress lines, usually rhyming *abcb*) or a slight variation of it. Similar to old ballads, its story is very dramatic and compressed, shifting suddenly at times between scenes or character voices. Coleridge even deliberately uses archaic words occasionally. What other traits of romantic poetry might the poem feature?

Like many romantics, Coleridge used many sound devices and images in his poetry. *Rime* abounds not only with end rhyme and rhythmic repetition but also with examples of **alliteration**; **onomatopoeia**, the use of words that imitate the sounds being described (e.g., "roared" and "howled"); **internal rhyme**, rhymes within a line (e.g., "The guests are *met*, the feast is *set*"); **assonance**, the repetition of vowel sounds in nearby stressed syllables (e.g., "They gr*oa*n'd, . . . they all upr*o*se"); and **consonance**, the repetition of terminal (more rarely, internal) consonant sounds in words (e.g., "And the goo*d* south win*d* sprung up from behin*d*"). Additionally, many vivid concrete **images** (often of nature) capture readers' imaginations. For example, Coleridge depicts the South Pole with sensory details such as the "mist and snow," the "wondrous cold," and the waves' "loud blast." As you read, find examples of sound devices and images. How do both contribute to the poem's various moods and fantastical feel?

OBJECTIVES

- Identify characteristics of ballad form and romanticism in a work.
- Analyze a work's use of imagery and sound devices.
- Draw conclusions about a work's characters, symbols, and theme.
- Evaluate an author's romantic perspective against biblical truth.

VOCABULARY

ghastly (găst′lē) *adj.* Causing shock, revulsion, or horror.

reek (rēk) *intr.v.* To give off a strong unpleasant odor.

dank (dăngk) *adj.* Disagreeably damp or humid.

READ: *Draw Conclusions About Theme*

Ballads incorporate the usual elements of narratives—setting, plot, character, and so on—all contributing to theme. Central to this poem are two main **characters**, the narrator and his listener (who exists only in the story's frame tale). As you read, draw conclusions about both. What internal conflicts do they feel? How do they act in or react to the story's events? What are the consequences of their choices? Consider whether each is **dynamic** (a character who changes internally) or **static** (one who does not change). How might such changes contribute to the author's intended theme? Finally, Coleridge makes strong use of **symbols** to suggest thematic meaning. For example, consider how the Albatross and Life-in-Death gather symbolic meaning within the story's events.

EVALUATE: *Romanticism and the Fall*

The Mariner's story relates a journey that he has experienced. Journeys are often used in literature to symbolize a process of change or maturity. Coleridge uses both romantic and biblical concepts in depicting the Mariner's journey. From a romantic perspective, the Mariner experiences a fall from unity with nature. What results from this fall? Does he feel guilt or remorse? Is he transformed in any way? Consider where Coleridge incorporates biblical concepts or imagery into this fall as well. Then compare the Mariner's journey to the biblical perspective on humanity's fall and its consequences (including human guilt). How are these narratives similar or different? How does Coleridge's perspective conform to or deviate from Truth?

What are the effects of **GUILT**?

God built into our consciences a knowledge of right and wrong. Often when we do wrong, we feel a gnawing sense of guilt. Describe a time when you felt guilty. How did it affect your actions? How did it affect your relationships? What Bible verses can you cite to explain God's remedy for a guilty conscience?

THE RIME OF THE ANCIENT MARINER

PART I

It is an ancient Mariner,
And he stoppeth one of three.
"By thy long gray beard and glittering eye,
Now wherefore stopp'st thou me?

The Bridegroom's doors are opened wide,
And I am next of kin;
The guests are met, the feast is set:
May'st hear the merry din."

He holds him with his skinny hand,
"There was a ship," quoth he.
"Hold off! unhand me, gray-beard loon!"[1]
Eftsoons[2] his hand dropped he.

He holds him with his glittering eye—
The Wedding Guest stood still,
And listens like a three years' child:
The Mariner hath his will.

The Wedding Guest sat on a stone:
He cannot choose but hear;
And thus spake on that ancient man,
The bright-eyed Mariner.

"The ship was cheered, the harbor cleared,
Merrily did we drop
Below the kirk,[3] below the hill,
Below the lighthouse top.

The sun came up upon the left.
Out of the sea came he!
And he shone bright, and on the right
Went down into the sea.

Higher and higher every day,
Till over the mast at noon—"
The Wedding Guest here beat his breast,
For he heard the loud bassoon.

The bride hath paced into the hall,
Red as a rose is she;
Nodding their heads before her goes
The merry minstrelsy.[4]

The Wedding Guest he beat his breast,
Yet he cannot choose but hear;
And thus spake on that ancient man.
The bright-eyed Mariner.

And now the Storm-Blast came, and he
Was tyrannous and strong:
He struck with his o'ertaking wings,
And chased us south along. A A

With sloping masts and dipping prow,
As who pursued with yell and blow
Still treads the shadow of his foe,
And forward bends his head,
The ship drove fast, loud roared the blast,
And southward aye[5] we fled.

And now there came both mist and snow,
And it grew wondrous cold:
And ice, mast-high, came floating by,
As green as emerald.

1. *loon:* "an ill-bred person" (*OED*)
2. *Eftsoons:* immediately
3. *kirk:* church

4. *minstrelsy:* "a troupe of minstrels" (*AHD*)
5. *aye:* continually

Ballad: What characteristics of the ballad form have you encountered in the text so far? A

Sound Devices: What sound devices can you find in the previous stanzas? What do they add to the poem's overall effect so far? A

And through the drifts the snowy clifts
Did send a dismal sheen:[6]
Nor shapes of men nor beasts we ken—[7]
The ice was all between.

The ice was here, the ice was there,
The ice was all around:
It cracked and growled, and roared and howled,
Like noises in a swound![8] A

At length did cross an Albatross:
Thorough the fog it came;
As if it had been a Christian soul,
We hailed it in God's name.

It ate the food it ne'er had eat,
And round and round it flew.
The ice did split with a thunder-fit;
The helmsman steered us through!

And a good south wind sprung up behind;
The Albatross did follow,
And every day, for food or play,
Came to the mariners' hollo!

In mist or cloud, on mast or shroud,[9]
It perched for vespers[10] nine;
Whiles all the night, through fog-smoke white,
Glimmered the white moon-shine."

"God save thee, ancient Mariner!
From the fiends, that plague thee thus!—
Why look'st thou so?"— With my crossbow
I shot the Albatross. R R

PART II

The Sun now rose upon the right:
Out of the sea came he,
Still hid in mist, and on the left
Went down into the sea.

And the good south wind still blew behind,
But no sweet bird did follow,
Nor any day, for food or play,
Came to the mariners' hollo!

6. *sheen:* shininess
7. *ken:* perceive
8. *swound:* swoon
9. *shroud:* a rope
10. *vespers:* an evening prayer service in formal church liturgies

Imagery: Identify some of the details the poet includes to describe this scene from nature (ll. 51–62). What sound device in line 61 contributes to this description? A

Draw Conclusions: What does the Albatross seem to symbolize for the sailors? Why do they think this? R

Draw Conclusions: What has the Mariner done? Why? How does he seem to feel about it? R

And I had done a hellish thing,
And it would work 'em woe:
For all averred, I had killed the bird
That made the breeze to blow.
Ah, wretch! said they, the bird to slay,
That made the breeze to blow!

VISUAL ANALYSIS

How does this engraving made by Gustave Doré to accompany the poem enhance the imagery and mood in lines 51–70?

Nor dim nor red, like God's own head,
The glorious Sun uprist:[11]
Then all averred, I had killed the bird
That brought the fog and mist.
'Twas right, said they, such birds to slay,
That bring the fog and mist.

The fair breeze[12] blew, the white foam flew.
The furrow followed free:
We were the first that ever burst
Into that silent sea.

Down dropped the breeze, the sails dropped down,
'Twas sad as sad could be;
And we did speak only to break
The silence of the sea!

All in a hot and copper sky,
The bloody Sun, at noon,
Right up above the mast did stand,
No bigger than the Moon.

Day after day, day after day,
We stuck, nor breath nor motion;
As idle as a painted ship
Upon a painted ocean.

Water, water, everywhere,
And all the boards did shrink;
Water, water, everywhere,
Nor any drop to drink.

The very deep did rot: O Christ!
That ever this should be!
Yea, slimy things did crawl with legs
Upon the slimy sea.

About, about, in reel and rout
The death-fires[13] danced at night;
The water, like a witch's oils,
Burnt green, and blue, and white. **A**

And some in dreams assuréd were
Of the spirit that plagued us so:
Nine fathom[14] deep he had followed us
From the land of mist and snow.

11. *uprist:* uprose
12. *fair breeze:* trade winds
13. *death-fires:* phosphorescent gleams in the rigging, electrical in origin, regarded superstitiously by sailors
14. *Nine fathom:* about fifty-four feet

Imagery: List some of the concrete details Coleridge uses to paint his images in lines 107–30. What mood do these images convey? **A**

And every tongue, through utter drought,
Was withered at the root;
We could not speak, no more than if
We had been choked with soot.

Ah! well-a-day! what evil looks
Had I from old and young!
Instead of the cross, the Albatross
About my neck was hung. **R**

PART III

There passed a weary time. Each throat
Was parched, and glazed each eye.
A weary time! a weary time!
How glazed each weary eye!
When looking westward, I beheld
A something in the sky.

At first it seemed a little speck,
And then it seemed a mist:
It moved, and moved, and took at last
A certain shape, I wist.[15]

A speck, a mist, a shape, I wist!
And still it neared and neared:
As if it dodged a water-sprite,[16]
It plunged and tacked[17] and veered.

With throats unslaked,[18] with black lips baked,
We could nor laugh nor wail;
Through utter drought all dumb we stood!
I bit my arm, I sucked the blood,
And cried, A sail! a sail!

With throats unslaked, with black lips baked,
Agape[19] they heard me call:
Gramercy![20] they for joy did grin,
And all at once their breath drew in,
As they were drinking all.

See! see! (I cried) she tacks no more!
Hither to work us weal,—[21]
Without a breeze, without a tide,
She steadies with upright keel!

The western wave was all a-flame,
The day was well-nigh done!

15. *wist:* knew, detected
16. *water-sprite:* spirit
17. *tacked:* changed the set of its sails and hence its direction, zigzagging in the manner of sailing ships angling into a wind
18. *unslaked:* unsatisfied of thirst
19. *Agape:* with the mouth wide open as in wonder or awe
20. *Gramercy:* "an exclamation of surprise or sudden feeling" (*OED*)
21. *weal:* good

Draw Conclusions: What do the sailors mean by hanging the Albatross around the Mariner's neck? What does the Albatross symbolize now? **R**

Almost upon the western wave
Rested the broad bright Sun;
When that strange shape drove suddenly
Betwixt us and the Sun.

And straight the Sun was flecked with bars,
(Heaven's Mother send us grace!)
As if through a dungeon-grate he peered,
With broad and burning face.

Alas! (thought I, and my heart beat loud,)
How fast she nears and nears!
Are those her sails that glance in the Sun,
Like restless gossameres?[22]

Are those her ribs through which the Sun
Did peer, as through a grate?
And is that Woman all her crew?
Is that a Death?[23] and are there two?
Is Death that Woman's mate?

Her lips were red, her looks were free,
Her locks were yellow as gold:
Her skin was as white as leprosy,
The Nightmare Life-in-Death was she,
Who thicks man's blood with cold.

The naked hulk[24] alongside came,
And the twain were casting dice;
"The game is done! I've won! I've won!"
Quoth she, and whistles thrice. ☑

The Sun's rim dips; the stars rush out:
At one stride comes the dark;
With far-heard whisper, o'er the sea,
Off shot the specter-bark.

We listened and looked sideways up!
Fear at my heart, as at a cup,
My life-blood seemed to sip!
The stars were dim, and thick the night,
The steersman's face by his lamp gleamed white;
From the sails the dew did drip—
Till clomb[25] above the eastern bar
The hornéd Moon, with one bright star
Within the nether[26] tip.

22. *gossameres:* floating films of cobweb
23. *Death:* death as represented by a skeleton figure
24. *hulk:* "a heavy, unwieldy ship" (*AHD*)
25. *clomb:* climbed
26. *nether:* lower

Reading Check: What is unusual about the ship that the Mariner sees coming? Which of its crew wins the dice toss? ☑

One after one, by the star-dogged[27] Moon.
Too quick for groan or sigh,
Each turned his face with a **ghastly** pang,
And cursed me with his eye.

Four times fifty living men,
(And I heard nor sigh nor groan)
With heavy thump, a lifeless lump,
They dropped down one by one.

The souls did from their bodies fly—
They fled to bliss or woe!
And every soul, it passed me by,
Like the whizz of my crossbow!" R

PART IV

"I fear thee, ancient Mariner!
I fear thy skinny hand!
And thou art long, and lank, and brown,
As is the ribbed sea-sand.

I fear thee and thy glittering eye,
And thy skinny hand, so brown."—
Fear not, fear not, thou Wedding Guest!
This body dropped not down.

Alone, alone, all, all alone,
Alone on a wide wide sea!
And never a saint took pity on
My soul in agony.

The many men, so beautiful!
And they all dead did lie:
And a thousand thousand slimy things
Lived on; and so did I.

I looked upon the rotting sea,
And drew my eyes away:
I looked upon the rotting deck,
And there the dead men lay.

I looked to Heaven and tried to pray;
But or ever a prayer had gushed
A wicked whisper came, and made
My heart as dry as dust.

I closed my lids, and kept them closed,
And the balls like pulses beat;
For the sky and the sea, and the sea and the sky
Lay like a load on my weary eye,
And the dead were at my feet.

The cold sweat melted from their limbs,
Nor rot nor **reek** did they:
The look with which they looked on me
Had never passed away.

An orphan's curse would drag to Hell
A spirit from on high;
But oh! more horrible than that
Is a curse in a dead man's eye!
Seven days, seven nights, I saw that curse,
And yet I could not die.

The moving Moon went up the sky,
And nowhere did abide:
Softly she was going up,
And a star or two beside—

Her beams bemocked the sultry main,
Like April hoarfrost spread;[28]
But where the ship's huge shadow lay,
The charméd water burnt alway
A still and awful red.

Beyond the shadow of the ship,
I watched the water snakes:
They moved in tracks of shining white,
And when they reared, the elfish light
Fell off in hoary flakes.

"Within the shadow of the ship
I watched their rich attire:
Blue, glossy green, and velvet black,
They coiled and swam; and every track
Was a flash of golden fire.

O happy living things! no tongue
Their beauty might declare:
A spring of love gushed from my heart,
And I blessed them unaware!
Sure my kind saint took pity on me,
And I blessed them unaware!

The selfsame moment I could pray;
And from my neck so free
The Albatross fell off, and sank
Like lead into the sea. R

27. *star-dogged:* star-pursued

28. *Her . . . spread:* The moonbeams paradoxically look like a spring morning's frosted dew spread over the warm sea.

ghastly (găst'lē) *adj.* Causing shock, revulsion, or horror.

Draw Conclusions: What results from the dice game? What does the Mariner imply about these results by mentioning the sound of his crossbow? R

reek (rēk) *intr.v.* To give off a strong unpleasant odor.

Draw Conclusions: Summarize the Mariner's development in Part IV. Symbolically, why does the Albatross fall off his neck? R

VISUAL ANALYSIS
What important moment from the poem does this engraving depict? Do you think Doré captured the emotion and theme of the scene properly?

PART V

Oh sleep! it is a gentle thing,
Beloved from pole to pole!
To Mary Queen the praise be given!
She sent the gentle sleep from Heaven,
That slid into my soul.

The silly[29] buckets on the deck,
That had so long remained,
I dreamt that they were filled with dew;
And when I awoke, it rained.

My lips were wet, my throat was cold,
My garments all were **dank**;
Sure I had drunken in my dreams,
And still my body drank.

I moved, and could not feel my limbs.
I was so light—almost
I thought that I had died in sleep,
And was a blesséd ghost.

And soon I heard a roaring wind:
It did not come anear;
But with its sound it shook the sails
That were so thin and sere.[30]

The upper air burst into life!
And a hundred fire-flags[31] sheen,
To and fro they were hurried about;
And to and fro, and in and out,
The wan[32] stars danced between.

And the coming wind did roar more loud,
And the sails did sigh like sedge;[33]
And the rain poured down from one black cloud;
The Moon was at its edge.

The thick black cloud was cleft, and still
The Moon was at its side:
Like waters shot from some high crag,[34]
The lightning fell with never a jag,
A river steep and wide. E

The loud wind never reached the ship,
Yet now the ship moved on!
Beneath the lightning and the Moon
The dead men gave a groan.

29. *silly:* futile
30. *sere:* withered; dry
31. *fire-flags:* probably the aurora australis (i.e., the southern lights)
32. *wan:* "lacking light, or lustre" (*OED*)
33. *sedge:* stiff, grasslike plants, whose hollow-stemmed leaves rustle in the wind
34. *crag:* "a steep or precipitous rugged rock" (*OED*)

dank (dăngk) *adj.* Disagreeably damp or humid.

Romanticism: Why does the Mariner's natural environment suddenly change? E

They groaned, they stirred, they all uprose,
Nor spake, nor moved their eyes;
It had been strange, even in a dream,
To have seen those dead men rise.

The helmsman steered, the ship moved on;
Yet never a breeze up-blew;
The mariners all 'gan work[35] the ropes,
Where they were wont[36] to do;
They raised their limbs like lifeless tools—
We were a ghastly crew.

35. *all 'gan work:* all began to work
36. *wont:* accustomed

VISUAL ANALYSIS
How did Doré evoke a subtle sense of wrongness in his depiction of the sailors working here?

The body of my brother's son
Stood by me, knee to knee:
The body and I pulled at one rope,
But he said naught to me.

"I fear thee ancient Mariner!"
Be calm, thou Wedding Guest!
'Twas not those souls that fled in pain,
Which to their corses[37] came again,
But a troop of spirits blest:

For when it dawned—they dropped their arms
And clustered round the mast;
Sweet sounds rose slowly through their mouths,
And from their bodies passed.

Around, around, flew each sweet sound,
Then darted to the Sun;
Slowly the sounds came back again,
Now mixed, now one by one.

Sometimes a-dropping from the sky
I heard the skylark sing;
Sometimes all little birds that are,
How they seemed to fill the sea and air
With their sweet jargoning![38]

And now 'twas like all instruments,
Now like a lonely flute;
And now it is an angel's song,
That makes the heavens be mute.

It ceased; yet still the sails made on
A pleasant noise till noon,
A noise like of a hidden brook
In the leafy month of June,
That to the sleeping woods all night
Singeth a quiet tune. **A**

Till noon we quietly sailed on,
Yet never a breeze did breathe:
Slowly and smoothly went the ship
Moved onward from beneath.

Under the keel nine fathom deep,
From the land of mist and snow,
The spirit slid: and it was he
That made the ship to go.
The sails at noon left off their tune,
And the ship stood still also.

37. *corses:* corpses
38. *jargoning:* chattering; singing

The sun, right up above the mast,
Had fixed her to the ocean:
But in a minute she 'gan stir,
With a short uneasy motion—
Backwards and forwards half her length
With a short uneasy motion.

Then like a pawing horse let go,
She made a sudden bound;
It flung the blood into my head,
And I fell down in a swound.

How long in that same fit I lay,
I have not to declare;
But ere my living life returned,
I heard and in my soul discerned
Two voices in the air.

"Is it he?" quoth one "Is this the man?
By him who died on cross,
With his cruel bow he laid full low,
The harmless Albatross.

The spirit who bideth[39] by himself
In the land of mist and snow,
He loved the bird that loved the man
Who shot him with his bow."

The other was a softer voice,
As soft as honey-dew:
Quoth he, "The man hath penance done,
And penance more will do." **E**

PART VI

First Voice

"But tell me, tell me! speak again,
Thy soft response renewing—
What makes that ship drive on so fast?
What is the Ocean doing?"

Second Voice

"Still as a slave before his lord,
The Ocean hath no blast;
His great bright eye most silently
Up to the Moon is cast—

If he may know which way to go;
For she guides him smooth or grim
See, brother, see! how graciously
She looketh down on him."

39. *bideth:* abideth

Imagery: What kind of imagery does Coleridge use to convey the pleasantness of the spirits' singing in lines 354–72? **A**

Romanticism: What sin does the Mariner need to do "penance" for, according to Coleridge? How does this idea differ from the biblical narrative of the Fall and Redemption? **E**

FIRST VOICE
"But why drives on that ship so fast
Without or wave or wind?"

SECOND VOICE
"The air is cut away before,
And closes from behind.

Fly, brother, fly! more high, more high!
Or we shall be belated:[40]
For slow and slow that ship will go,
When the Mariner's trance is abated."[41]

I woke, and we were sailing on
As in a gentle weather:
'Twas night, calm night, the Moon was high;
The dead men stood together.

All stood together on the deck,
For a charnel-dungeon[42] fitter:
All fixed on me their stony eyes
That in the Moon did glitter.

The pang, the curse, with which they died,
Had never passed away:
I could not draw my eyes from theirs,
Nor turn them up to pray.

And now this spell was snapped: once more
I viewed the Ocean green,
And looked far forth, yet little saw
Of what had else been seen—

Like one that on a lonesome road
Doth walk in fear and dread,
And having once turned round, walks on,
And turns no more his head;
Because he knows a frightful fiend
Doth close behind him tread.

But soon there breathed a wind on me,
Nor sound nor motion made:
Its path was not upon the sea,
In ripple or in shade.

It raised my hair, it fanned my cheek
Like a meadow-gale of spring—
It mingled strangely with my fears,
Yet it felt like a welcoming.

Swiftly, swiftly flew the ship,
Yet she sailed softly too:
Sweetly, sweetly blew the breeze—
On me alone it blew.

40. *belated:* left behind
41. *abated:* diminished
42. *charnel-dungeon:* crypt, underground vault for burial

Oh! dream of joy! is this indeed
The lighthouse top I see?
Is this the hill? is this the kirk?
Is this mine own countree?

We drifted o'er the harbor-bar,[43]
And I with sobs did pray—
O let me be awake, my God!
Or let me sleep alway.'

The harbor-bay was clear as glass,
So smoothly it was strewn![44]
And on the bay the moonlight lay,
And the shadow of the Moon.

The rock shone bright, the kirk no less,
That stands above the rock:
The moonlight steeped[45] in silentness
The steady weathercock. **A**

And the bay was white with silent light,
Till rising from the same,
Full many shapes, that shadows were,
In crimson colors came.

A little distance from the prow
Those crimson shadows were:
I turned my eyes upon the deck—
Oh, Christ! what saw I there!

Each corse lay flat, lifeless and flat,
And, by the holy rood![46]
A man all light, a seraph-man,
On every corse there stood.

This seraph-band, each waved his hand:
It was a heavenly sight!
They stood as signals to the land,
Each one a lovely light;

This seraph-band, each waved his hand;
No voice did they impart—
No voice; but oh! the silence sank
Like music on my heart.

But soon I heard the dash of oars,
I heard the Pilot's cheer;
My head was turned perforce away,
And I saw a boat appear.

43. *harbor-bar:* sandbar at the mouth of the harbor
44. *strewn:* spread
45. *steeped:* soaked, saturated
46. *rood:* cross

Sound Devices: What sound devices can you find in lines 452–79? How do they support the content of this passage? **A**

VISUAL ANALYSIS
How does Doré create a sense of high drama in this engraving? How does the image's composition emphasize the men in the boat as the Mariner's saviors?

The Pilot,[47] and the Pilot's boy
I heard them coming fast:
Dear Lord in Heaven! it was a joy
The dead men could not blast.

I saw a third—I heard his voice:
It is the Hermit good!
He singeth loud his godly hymns
That he makes in the wood.
He'll shrieve[48] my soul, he'll wash away
The Albatross's blood.

Part VII

This Hermit good lives in that wood
Which slopes down to the sea:
How loudly his sweet voice he rears!
He loves to talk with mariners
That come from a far countree.

He kneels at morn, and noon, and eve—
He hath a cushion plump:
It is the moss that wholly hides
The rotted old oak-stump.

"The skiff-boat neared: I heard them talk,
"Why this is strange, I trow![49]
Where are those lights so many and fair,
That signal made but now?"

"Strange, by my faith!" the Hermit said—
"And they answered not our cheer!
The planks look warped! and see those sails
How thin they are and sere!
I never saw aught like to them,
Unless perchance it were

Brown skeletons of leaves that lag
My forest brook along;
When the ivy-tod[50] is heavy with snow,
And the owlet whoops to the wolf below
That eats the she-wolf's young." E

"Dear Lord! it hath a fiendish look—
(The Pilot made reply)
I am a-feared"—"Push on, push on!"
Said the Hermit cheerily.

47. *Pilot:* someone who guided ships through hazardous port waters
48. *shrieve:* to hear the confession of and give absolution to (a penitent)
49. *trow:* am sure
50. *ivy-tod:* ivy-bush

Romanticism: Reread lines 508–37. What does the Mariner hope for from the Hermit? What kind of imagery is associated with this man? E

The boat came closer to the ship,
But I nor spake nor stirred;
The boat came close beneath the ship,
And straight a sound was heard.

Under the water it rumbled on,
Still louder and more dread:
It reached the ship, it split the bay;
The ship went down like lead.

Stunned by that loud and dreadful sound,
Which sky and ocean smote,
Like one that hath been seven days drowned
My body lay afloat;
But swift as dreams, myself I found
Within the Pilot's boat.

Upon the whirl, where sank the ship,
The boat spun round and round:
And all was still, save that the hill
Was telling[51] of the sound.

I moved my lips—the Pilot shrieked
And fell down in a fit;
The Holy Hermit raised his eyes
And prayed where he did sit.

I took the oars: the Pilot's boy,
Who now doth crazy go,
Laughed loud and long, and all the while
His eyes went to and fro.
"Ha! ha!" quoth he, "full plain I see,
The Devil knows how to row."

And now, all in my own countree,
I stood on the firm land!
The Hermit stepped forth from the boat,
And scarcely he could stand.

"O shrieve me, shrieve me, holy man!"
The Hermit crossed his brow.
"Say quick," quoth he, "I bid thee say—
What manner of man art thou?"

Forthwith[52] this frame of mine was wrenched
With a woeful agony,
Which forced me to begin my tale:
And then it left me free.

Since then, at an uncertain hour,
That agony returns;
And till my ghastly tale is told,
This heart within me burns.

51. *telling:* echoing
52. *forthwith:* right away

I pass, like night, from land to land;
I have strange power of speech;
That moment that his face I see,
I know the man that must hear me:
To him my tale I teach.

What loud uproar bursts from that door!
The Wedding Guests are there:
But in the garden bower the bride
And bridemaids singing are;
And hark the little vesper bell,[53]
Which biddeth me to prayer!

O Wedding Guest! this soul hath been
Alone on a wide wide sea:
So lonely 'twas, that God himself
Scarce seeméd there to be.

O sweeter than the marriage feast,
'Tis sweeter far to me,
To walk together to the kirk
With a goodly company!—

To walk together to the kirk,
And all together pray,
While each to his great Father bends,
Old men, and babes, and loving friends,
And youths and maidens gay!

Farewell, farewell! but this I tell
To thee, thou Wedding Guest!
He prayeth well, who loveth well
Both man and bird and beast.

53. *vesper bell:* a bell that summons worshipers to a worship service

Romanticism: Is this moral biblically correct? What do you think Coleridge meant by it? E

He prayeth best, who loveth best
All things both great and small;
For the dear God who loveth us,
He made and loveth all. E
The Mariner, whose eye is bright,
Whose beard with age is hoar,[54]
Is gone: and now the Wedding Guest
Turned from the bridegroom's door.

He went like one that hath been stunned,
And is of sense forlorn:[55]
A sadder and a wiser man,
He rose the morrow morn. R

54. *hoar:* white
55. *forlorn:* deprived

Draw Conclusions: Would you call the Wedding Guest a static or dynamic character? R

THINK AND DISCUSS

1. Briefly summarize the Mariner's story. What sin does he commit and what punishments does he receive?
2. Who narrates the frame tale? Who narrates the rest of the story?
3. Choose a stanza and mark where its form qualifies as ballad stanza. Cite an example of one other way in which the poem mimics old ballads.
4. Define *alliteration*, *onomatopoeia*, *internal rhyme*, *assonance*, and *consonance*. Cite an example of each from the poem.
5. Select a passage depicting a striking image from nature. List the sensory details used to construct the image.
6. Briefly describe what you know of both main characters. Explain whether each is static or dynamic, supporting your answer from the text.
7. What theme does Coleridge develop in the Mariner's tale? How does the listener help convey this moral?
8. What does the Albatross symbolize within the story? Support your answer with textual details.
9. How does Coleridge's constant use of sound devices (rhyme, alliteration, etc.) and rhythm (ballad stanza) add to the poem's effects on readers?
10. Besides referencing the distant with ballad form, what romantic traits (p. 455) does Coleridge's poem reflect? Describe three, supporting your answer from the text.
11. How does Coleridge's romantic version of a human's moral fall and redemption conform to or deviate from biblical truths about sin, guilt, and redemption?

George Gordon, Lord Byron (1788–1824)

AT A GLANCE

- **1807** Published *Hours of Idleness*
- **1809–11** Toured southern Europe and the Balkans
- **1812** Published *Childe Harold*, cantos I and II
- **1816** Separated from Lady Byron; left England; published *Childe Harold*, canto III
- **1818** Published *Childe Harold*, canto IV
- **1819–24** Published the unfinished *Don Juan*

George Gordon Byron, generally known as "Lord Byron," was a poet whose public persona and poetry captivated the European imagination. Byron lived a life of uncompromising individualism, one that constantly jarred with social conventions. His most influential literary contribution was the Byronic hero, an antihero who nobly struggles against his interior defects and exterior oppression.

Early Life

Byron was born into an aristocratic family, the son of a rakish English sea captain and a respectable Scottish heiress. In 1798 he became heir to the Byron family estate and fortune. He subsequently attended Harrow School and Cambridge. At nineteen he published his first significant book of poems, *Hours of Idleness*, only to have it attacked in a Scottish literary review. Furious, he responded with a scathing satire of British literature, *English Bards and Scotch Reviewers* (1809).

He then traveled the European continent, whose exotic, war-torn scenes inspired him to write the first two cantos of his narrative poem *Childe Harold's Pilgrimage*. The semiautobiographical work features the first Byronic hero, who, although consumed by dissolute passions, still deeply desires his personal and social renovation. When Byron returned to England in 1811, the book's publication brought him instant international fame, at least partly because it included firsthand accounts of the Continent, which many English had not visited in years due to war. His stay in England also saw the publication of *A Selection of Hebrew Melodies* (1815), which includes some of his most famous short verse and highlights his ability to create graceful lyrics.

DID YOU KNOW?

In 1810 Byron reenacted the Greek legend of Leander by swimming the Hellespont (now known as the Dardanelles).

Life as a Byronic Hero

With his famous good looks, Byron was a notorious womanizer. It was no surprise, then, that his 1815 marriage to Annabella Milbanke quickly collapsed and the two legally separated. When scandalous details of his personal life—including rumors of an affair with his half-sister—became public, Byron felt himself driven from polite society. In response Byron left England for Europe in the spring of 1816, never to return.

Byron first journeyed to Switzerland, where he met Percy Bysshe Shelley and Mary Godwin (later Mary Shelley) and composed the closet drama *Manfred* (1817), a deeper exploration of the Byronic hero. In the fall of 1816 he traveled to Italy, where he fell in love with the profligate lifestyle of the Italian aristocracy. In Venice he began work on his unfinished masterpiece *Don Juan*, a seventeen-canto epic poem written in comic *ottava rima*. Using the legendary character of its protagonist as a springboard, *Don Juan* launches into a broad social satire with a conversational, witty tone.

In 1823, inspired by his political ideals, Byron joined the Greek fight for independence from the Ottoman Empire, providing both financial assistance and his own celebrity. Nine months after his arrival in Greece, however, Byron died from a fever. His death helped unite the Greek resistance movement and inspired the military intervention of the Western powers.

Legacy

Early disillusioned by social hypocrisy, Byron wrote poetry that became a crusade against conventional manners. A deep cynicism also characterizes his work. Byron's poetic persona not only sees evil in others but also suspects it in himself. Both idealism and cynicism characterize the Byronic hero, which became remarkably influential on nineteenth-century literature, appearing in works by the Brontës and Alexandre Dumas.

Like other romantic poets, Byron immortalized everyday experience and common language. In Byron's lifetime, however, his humorous verse was not considered worthy of great poetry. Subsequent generations of critics have rediscovered the poetic craftsmanship in his artfully funny lines.

ANALYZE: *Byronic Hero and Spenserian Stanza*

In his long poem *Childe Harold's Pilgrimage*, Byron created his first rendering of a new type of hero. An individual embodying romanticism's revolutionary extreme, the **Byronic hero** is an emotionally titanic figure. He is deeply sensitive, naturally gifted in intellect and charm. But he also rejects society's conventions and morals as hypocritical and freely indulges his own will and desires. These qualities make him mysterious and fascinating to people and also dangerous; in fact, he is eventually alienated from most of society through his own sins. Perhaps contradictorily, he is deeply torn by his flaws but refuses to yield in spirit to any authority (society, fate, God), believing this defiance frees him. Instead, he continues on into bold adventures, at once idealistic, cynical, and tormented. As you read, consider where the text reveals these qualities in Harold.

Byron also used *Childe Harold* to resurrect an old and complex stanza form created by Edmund Spenser for his epic *The Faerie Queene*. This **Spenserian stanza** consists of nine lines, the first eight in iambic pentameter and the ninth in iambic hexameter (having six iambs), with a rhyme scheme of *ababbcbcc*. Having been neglected in the seventeenth and eighteenth centuries, this form added cachet to the work. Its difficulty also elevated *Childe Harold*, adding, in Byron's perspective, a sense of the sublime. Try annotating this form in several of the work's stanzas.

READ: *Draw Conclusions About the Sublime*

To the romantics, evoking the **sublime** (p. 455) was an important part of engaging their readers' imaginations. Byron is notable for creating a sense of high emotional drama in his poems. As you read, draw conclusions about how his content may achieve the sublime. For example, how might the struggles and passions of a Byronic hero evoke extravagant emotions in readers? Does the poet's nature imagery complement this intention? Additionally, pay attention to how Byron's style shapes reader responses. In *Childe Harold* Byron uses lengthy stanzas and enjambed lines to create long, rolling, declamatory sentences. He also incorporates elevated diction and frequent figurative language (e.g., apostrophe, p. 201). How might these stylistic choices add a sense of significance to his ideas?

EVALUATE: *Character and Moral Goodness*

In *Childe Harold* and "She Walks in Beauty," Byron indirectly or directly describes a person. How would you summarize his characterizations? Considering Byron's own personal character, why do you think he appreciates the lady's moral goodness? As you read, compare Byron's analysis of Harold's despair to the beautiful woman's joy. What causes does Byron attribute to the apparent feelings of each individual? What does Scripture say about the effects of our moral choices in our lives (see Ps. 109:17; Prov. 11:3; 13:15; 2:22; Ps. 24:4–5)?

OBJECTIVES

- Identify figurative language and Spenserian stanza in a poem.
- Draw conclusions about a work's use of the sublime.
- Analyze a text's development of a Byronic hero.
- Evaluate an author's concept of goodness revealed in his characters.

VOCABULARY

quaff (kwŏf) *tr.v.* To drink (a beverage) heartily.

perpetual (pər-pĕch′o͞o-əl) *adj.* Lasting forever; never-ending.

quell (kwĕl) *tr.v.* To put down forcibly; suppress.

intemperate (ĭn-tĕm′pər-ĭt) *adj.* Not temperate or moderate, especially in rhetoric or tone; unrestrained.

arbiter (är′bĭ-tər) *n.* One whose opinion or judgment is considered authoritative or worthy of respect.

fathomless (făth′əm-lĭs) *adj.* Too deep to be fathomed or measured.

What do we IDEALIZE?

Sometimes, a dream is better than reality. What is the best dessert you have ever eaten, the best game you have ever watched, or the most beautiful piece of music you have ever heard? We normally have either a reference point for what we think is the best or a dream of what could be the best. What are some things that you tend to evaluate against your standard of perfection?

from *Childe Harold's Pilgrimage*

Originally based on Byron's travels in southern Europe, Childe Harold *features a protagonist who begins as an exuberant, irreverent young man, reveling in exotic regions of ancient traditions and in his boundless opportunities. The term* Childe *is an archaic title for a young nobleman, a romantic nod to Britain's past. The first two cantos of the poem were written directly after Byron's travels (1811); the last two after his exile from English society (1816). The action of canto III picks up (semiautobiographically) with Harold, shadowed by scandal, departing his country. Publicly condemned and ostracized, he has no home. As you read the following excerpts, consider how Harold's actions and inward thoughts might reflect Byron's romantic perspective.*

VISUAL ANALYSIS
How might Caspar David Friedrich's famous painting *The Wanderer Above the Sea of Fog* (ca. 1818) reflect a romantic point of view, in particular, Byron's point of view?

from Canto III

3

In my youth's summer I did sing of one.
The wandering outlaw of his own dark mind;
Again I seize the theme, then but begun.
And bear it with me, as the gushing wind
Bears the cloud onward: in that tale I find
The furrows of long thought, and dried-up tears,
Which, ebbing, leave a sterile track behind,
O'er which all heavily the journeying years
Plod the last sands of life—where not a flower appears.

8

Something too much of this:—but now 'tis past,
And the spell closes with its silent seal.
Long-absent Harold reappears at last;
He of the breast which fain no more would feel,
Wrung with the wounds which kill not, but ne'er heal;
Yet Time, who changes all, had altered him
In soul and aspect as in age: years steal
Fire from the mind as vigor from the limb;
And life's enchanted cup but sparkles near the brim. [A]

Byronic Hero: What characteristics of the Byronic hero does this metaphor (l. 18) help develop? [A]

9

His had been **quaffed** too quickly, and he found
The dregs were wormwood; but he filled again,
And from a purer fount, on holier ground,
And deemed its spring **perpetual**; but in vain!
Still round him clung invisibly a chain
Which galled forever, fettering though unseen,
And heavy though it clanked not; worn with pain,
Which pined although it spoke not, and grew keen,
Entering with every step he took through many a scene. [A]

quaff (kwŏf) *tr.v.* To drink (a beverage) heartily.

perpetual (pər-pĕch′o͞o-əl) *adj.* Lasting forever; never-ending.

Spenserian Stanza: Mark how stanza 9 complies with Spenserian stanza's meter and rhyme-scheme requirements. [A]

10

Secure in guarded coldness, he had mixed
Again in fancied safety with his kind.
And deemed his spirit now so firmly fixed
And sheathed with an invulnerable mind,
That, if no joy, no sorrow lurked behind;
And he, as one, might 'midst the many stand
Unheeded, searching through the crowd to find
Fit speculation; such as in strange land
He found in wonder-works of God and Nature's hand.

12

But soon he knew himself the most unfit
Of men to herd with Man; with whom he held
Little in common; untaught to submit
His thoughts to others, though his soul was **quelled**
In youth by his own thoughts; still uncompelled,
He would not yield dominion of his mind,
To spirits against whom his own rebelled;
Proud though in desolation; which could find
A life within itself, to breathe without mankind.

quell (kwĕl) *tr.v.* To put down forcibly; suppress.

13

Where rose the mountains, there to him were friends;
Where rolled the ocean, thereon was his home;
Where a blue sky, and glowing clime, extends,
He had the passion and the power to roam;
The desert, forest, cavern, breaker's foam,
Were unto him companionship; they spake
A mutual language, clearer than the tome
Of his land's tongue, which he would oft forsake
For Nature's pages glassed by sunbeams on the lake.

15

But in Man's dwellings he became a thing
Restless and worn, and stern and wearisome,
Drooped as a wild-born falcon with clipt wing,
To whom the boundless air alone were home:
Then came his fit again, which to o'ercome,
As eagerly the barred-up bird will beat
His breast and beak against his wiry dome—
Till the blood tinge his plumage, so the heat
Of his impeded soul would through his bosom eat.

16

Self-exiled Harold wanders forth again,
With naught of hope left, but with less of gloom;
The very knowledge that he lived in vain,
That all was over on this side the tomb,
Had made Despair a smilingness assume,
Which, though 'twere wild—as on the plundered wreck
When mariners would madly meet their doom
With draughts **intemperate** on the sinking deck—
Did yet inspire a cheer, which he forbore to check. A

intemperate (ĭn-tĕm′pər-ĭt) *adj.* Not temperate or moderate, especially in rhetoric or tone; unrestrained.

Byronic Hero: What characteristics of the Byronic hero does Harold exhibit in stanzas 12–13 and 15–16? A

from Canto IV

178

There is a pleasure in the pathless woods,
There is a rapture on the lonely shore,
There is society where none intrudes,
By the deep Sea, and music in its roar:
I love not Man the less, but Nature more,
From these our interviews, in which I steal
From all I may be, or have been before,
To mingle with the Universe, and feel
What I can ne'er express, yet cannot all conceal.

179

Roll on, thou deep and dark blue Ocean—roll!
Ten thousand fleets sweep over thee in vain;
Man marks the earth with ruin—his control
Stops with the shore;—upon the watery plain
The wrecks are all thy deed, nor doth remain
A shadow of man's ravage, save his own,[1]
When for a moment, like a drop of rain,
He sinks into thy depths with bubbling groan,
Without a grave, unknelled, uncoffined, and unknown. R

Sublime: What example of apostrophe begins in this stanza? How might it contribute to the sense of drama in the passage? R

180

His steps are not upon thy paths—thy fields
Are not a spoil for him—thou dost arise
And shake him from thee; the vile strength he wields
For earth's destruction thou dost all despise,

1. *nor . . . own:* On the ocean no trace of man's destructive nature appears. Instead, he is destroyed.

Spurning him from thy bosom to the skies,
And send'st him, shivering in thy playful spray
And howling, to his Gods, where haply lies
His petty hope in some near port or bay,
And dashest him again to earth:—there let him lay.

181

The armaments which thunderstrike the walls
Of rock-built cities, bidding nations quake,
And monarchs tremble in their capitals,
The oak leviathans,[2] whose huge ribs make
Their clay creator the vain title take
Of lord of thee, and **arbiter** of war;
These are thy toys, and, as the snowy flake,
They melt into thy yeast[3] of waves, which mar
Alike the Armada's pride, or spoils of Trafalgar.[4]

arbiter (är′bĭ-tər) *n.* One whose opinion or judgment is considered authoritative or worthy of respect.

182

Thy shores are empires, changed in all save thee—
Assyria, Greece, Rome, Carthage, what are they?
Thy waters washed them power while they were free,
And many a tyrant since; their shores obey
The stranger, slave, or savage; their decay
Has dried up realms to deserts:—not so thou,
Unchangeable save to thy wild waves' play—
Time writes no wrinkle on thine azure brow—
Such as creation's dawn beheld, thou rollest now. R

Sublime: Skim back over stanzas 179–82. Can you find an example of elevated word choice, of figurative language, and of a long, rolling sentence? R

183

Thou glorious mirror, where the Almighty's form
Glasses[5] itself in tempests; in all time,
Calm or convulsed—in breeze, or gale, or storm,
Icing the pole, or in the torrid clime[6]
Dark-heaving;—boundless, endless, and sublime—
The image of Eternity—the throne
Of the Invisible; even from out thy slime
The monsters of the deep are made; each zone
Obeys thee; thou goest forth, dread, **fathomless**, alone.

fathomless (făth′əm-lĭs) *adj.* Too deep to be fathomed or measured.

184

And I have loved thee, Ocean! and my joy
Of youthful sports was on thy breast to be
Borne like thy bubbles, onward: from a boy
I wantoned with[7] thy breakers—they to me
Were a delight; and if the freshening sea
Made them a terror—'twas a pleasing fear,
For I was as it were a child of thee,
And trusted to thy billows far and near,
And laid my hand upon thy mane—as I do here.

2. *leviathans:* huge sea creatures; here a metaphor for battleships (see "oak")
3. *yeast:* froth created by the ocean waters' movement
4. *Armada's . . . Trafalgar:* famous sea battles (in 1588 and 1805) in which storms destroyed many ships
5. *glasses:* reflects
6. *torrid clime:* intensely hot region (in context, the equatorial region)
7. *wantoned with:* sported among

She Walks in Beauty

Byron wrote these lines in praise of Anne Wilmot, a cousin by marriage, shortly after first meeting her at a party. Stanza 1 refers to her black mourning dress, hung with spangles, setting off her loveliness.

She walks in beauty, like the night
Of cloudless climes and starry skies;
And all that's best of dark and bright
Meet in her aspect and her eyes:
Thus mellow'd to that tender light
Which heaven to gaudy day denies

One shade the more, one ray the less,
Had half impair'd the nameless grace
Which waves in every raven tress,
Or softly lightens o'er her face;
Where thoughts serenely sweet express
How pure, how dear their dwelling-place.

And on that cheek, and o'er that brow,
So soft, so calm, yet eloquent,
The smiles that win, the tints that glow,
But tell of days in goodness spent,
A mind of peace with all below,
A heart whose love is innocent!

Sublime: How do Byron's images in this stanza evoke something of the sublime?

THINK AND DISCUSS

1. In *Childe Harold*, what effect has the speaker's suffering had on him since he last wrote? How does he seem similar to Harold himself?
2. In "She Walks in Beauty," the speaker admires a woman's physical beauty. What other qualities does he also admire in her?
3. Define Spenserian stanza. Show how one stanza from *Childe Harold* follows this form.
4. Briefly describe the traits of a Byronic hero.
5. Cite examples from the text proving that Harold shows at least three traits of a Byronic hero.
6. Find and interpret in context an example of three different kinds of figurative language.
7. How did Byron shape the style and content of these texts to evoke the sublime? Cite an example of all five areas discussed in the Read section (p. 480). Do you think his methods provoke greater emotion than, for instance, a neoclassical poem?
8. Evaluate the Byronic hero in light of Scripture.
9. Given Byron's personal lifestyle and conception of a hero, what is odd about his appreciation for the woman in "She Walks in Beauty"? For example, to what does he attribute her sense of peace and joy? Why might he evince this attitude?

Percy Bysshe Shelley (1792–1822)

AT A GLANCE

- **1804–11** Attended Eton and Oxford
- **1811** Eloped with Harriet Westbrook
- **1814** Eloped with Mary Godwin
- **1819** Wrote "Ode to the West Wind"
- **1822** Drowned off the coast of Italy

The life and works of poet and essayist Percy Bysshe Shelley encapsulate the romantic spirit. His poetry depicts in vivid mythological and natural symbols the individual's struggle against social oppression. His life demonstrated both the personal courage and the moral weaknesses of his political radicalism.

Young Radical

Born into an aristocratic family from Sussex, Shelley attended Eton and then enrolled in Oxford in 1810. Already radicalized by the works of philosophers such as his future father-in-law William Godwin, he published an inflammatory pamphlet, *The Necessity of Atheism*, the following year. Oxford required official adherence to Christianity, and when Shelley refused to recant, he was expelled.

Despite his personal belief in free love, he eloped with and married Harriet Westbrook, beginning a fraught marriage. In 1812 they traveled to Ireland, where he agitated for Irish independence and freedom of religion. In 1813 he published *Queen Mab*, a poem sharply satirizing both the government and the established church. That year the couple traveled to London and met Shelley's hero, William Godwin. Shelley and Godwin's daughter Mary quickly fell in love. To the consternation of both families, they eloped to the Continent, returning later to social ostracism.

In 1816 Shelley wrote his next poem, *Alastor*, exploring poetic aesthetics. He and Mary also traveled to Geneva, where they met Lord Byron and where Mary was inspired with the idea for her novel *Frankenstein* (p. 500). They returned to England and, after Harriet's tragic suicide, finally married. Shelley then began work on his allegorical epic, *The Revolt of Islam* (1818), which celebrates love as the true foundation of an ideal society. But facing poor health and financial debts, Shelley moved to Italy in March. He would never return to England.

DID YOU KNOW ?

Shelley drowned when a sudden storm swamped his boat, the *Don Juan*, named for his friend Lord Byron.

Mature Poet

In Italy Shelley was reinvigorated by the climate and friendships with expatriates such as Byron. There he wrote his masterpiece, *Prometheus Unbound* (1820), a closet drama emphasizing the mind's power to free itself from authority. Upon hearing the news of the 1819 Peterloo Massacre, in which many innocent protestors were killed or injured by soldiers, he responded with more political poems, including the *The Mask of Anarchy* (unpublished until 1832), a ballad advocating political protest, and the brilliant satire *Peter Bell the Third* (1839).

By this point, however, Shelley was despairing of seeing political and social revolution in his lifetime. He began to see poetry as a vehicle for change, one in which poets could envision idealistic states that would, in turn, inspire their readers. As he wrote in his influential treatise *A Defence of Poetry* (published in 1840), "Poets are the unacknowledged legislators of the World." This shift in outlook can be seen in *Adonais*, his elegy for Keats, as well as in his final great poem, *The Triumph of Life*. Shelley died in a boating accident on July 8, 1822.

Legacy

Many critics have reacted more strongly to Shelley's controversial life than to his poetry, but Shelley is still widely considered one of the greatest lyric poets of the English language. In particular, he is a master of deploying symbolism. His heavy use of symbols dramatizes an idealistic struggle against oppression while suggesting that this struggle inevitably involves complexity and ambivalence.

ANALYZE: *Ode and Terza Rima*

A favorite genre among romantic poets was the ode. An **ode** is a long lyric poem that is elevated in style, generally serious in theme, and structured with a complex stanza (which can vary from work to work). Romantic odes are usually exaltations or meditations on someone or something. They may, like the sonnet, show the speaker working through a problem in the speaker's mind.

In "Ode to the West Wind," the complex stanza Shelley begins with is **terza rima**, a verse form in which three-line stanzas (tercets) interlock in the following rhyme pattern: *aba*, *bcb*, *cdc*, *ded*, and so on. The end rhyme of the middle line of stanza 1 dictates the end rhyme of lines 1 and 3 in stanza 2. Then the middle line of stanza 2 dictates the end rhyme of the first and third lines of stanza 3. Terza rima works very well for longer poems as its interlocking nature creates a continuous flow.

Shelley also combined terza rima with another formal requirement: the sonnet's (p. 184) fourteen lines of iambic pentameter. The resulting hybrid form comprises four stanzas of terza rima and one couplet, all in iambic pentameter. As you read, consider this complicated verse form. What effect might Shelley have wanted to achieve by linking both structures? Also, note Shelley's frequent use of enjambment (p. 457). How might this trait work well with terza rima stanzas?

READ: *Combine Reading Strategies*

An understanding of historical context can help to unveil important meanings in Shelley's poetry. A political and social radical, Shelley regarded his poetry as an instrument of revolution and reform that could help lead to a golden era of peace and freedom. His flouting of political and social conventions is often expressed directly and indirectly in his poetry. For example, his belief that many contemporary political rulers were tyrants and his disillusionment with conservative postwar British politics are particularly evident in the poems that follow.

Knowing this context, you can also infer certain broader meanings from his poetry. For example, how might his use of irony (verbal, situational, dramatic) and satirical tone in the works that follow speak to broader cultural realities? Additionally, pay attention to his imagery in "Ode to the West Wind." How might Shelley's natural images imply ideas related to his desire to change society? Which images gather associated symbolic meanings through how they are developed in the poem?

EVALUATE: *Perspectives on Human Society*

Shelley's revolutionary ideas and unconventional behavior identify him as a thoroughgoing romantic. Clearly, his personal relationships were often outside the bounds of biblical Goodness. But what about the critiques of and hopes for human government and society that underlie his themes in "Ozymandias," "England in 1819," and "Ode to the West Wind"? Once you finish analyzing the poems, use Scripture to discern what may be Good or True within Shelley's messages and what is not. Apply the following passages: Proverbs 16:18; Psalm 2:10–12; 1 Peter 1:24; Matthew 13:36–43; 2 Peter 3:13; Ecclesiastes 12:13–14; Isaiah 2:1–5 and 9:6–7.

OBJECTIVES

- Identify characteristics of the ode in a work.
- Apply historical context to understand a text.
- Infer an author's tone and meaning from textual details.
- Analyze how a text's structure (e.g., terza rima) supports its theme.
- Evaluate an author's critique of his society against the Bible.

VOCABULARY

visage (vĭz′ĭj) *n.* The face or facial expression of a person; countenance.

colossal (kə-lŏs′əl) *adj.* Of great size, extent, or amount; immense.

zenith (zē′nĭth) *n.* The point on the celestial sphere that is directly above the observer.

dirge (dûrj) *n.* A funeral hymn or lament.

tumult (to͞o′mŭlt′) *n.* A disorderly commotion or disturbance.

What inspires **HOPE**?

Have you ever felt hopeless about a situation or problem? Perhaps you failed to achieve something you really worked for, such as making a team or passing an audition. Maybe you failed a mandatory class and despair of graduating on time. Perhaps you even lost someone very dear to you. What lifts you from the mire at such times? A good night's rest? A broader perspective? Words of encouragement? Your faith? What does it take to renew your sense of hope?

OZYMANDIAS

I met a traveler from an antique[1] land
Who said: "Two vast and trunkless legs of stone
Stand in the desert. Near them, on the sand,
Half sunk, a shattered **visage** lies, whose frown,
And wrinkled lip, and sneer of cold command,
Tell that its sculptor well those passions read
Which yet survive, stamped on these lifeless things,
The hand that mocked them and the heart that fed:[2]
And on the pedestal these words appear:
'My name is Ozymandias,[3] king of kings:
Look on my works, ye mighty and despair!'
Nothing beside remains. Round the decay
Of that **colossal** wreck, boundless and bare
The lone and level sands stretch far away."

visage (vĭz′ĭj) *n.* The face or facial expression of a person; countenance.

colossal (kə-lŏs′əl) *adj.* Of great size, extent, or amount; immense.

Combine Strategies: In context of Shelley's views and the poem's scene, what ironic meaning can you infer from the words on the pedestal?

1. *antique:* ancient
2. *hand . . . fed:* "Hand" and "heart" are direct objects of "survive"; "stamped . . . things" is a participial phrase modifying "passions"; "mocked" can mean merely "imitated" or "mimicked scornfully."
3. *Ozymandias:* Greek name for Ramesses II, a pharaoh who ruled Egypt

ORDER
LOVE
HMP

England in 1819

An old, mad, blind, despised, and dying king,[1] —
Princes,[2] the dregs of their dull race, who flow
Through public scorn,—mud from a muddy spring, —
Rulers who neither see, nor feel, nor know,
But leech-like to their fainting country cling,
Till they drop, blind in blood, without a blow,—
A people starved and staved in the untilled field,[3]—
An army, which liberticide[4] and prey
Makes as a two-edged sword to all who wield:
Golden and sanguine laws which tempt and slay;[5]
Religion Christless, Godless—book sealed;
A Senate,—Time's worst statute unrepealed,[6]—
Are graves, from which a glorious Phantom may
Burst, to illumine our tempestuous day. ✓ R

1. *king:* George III (1760–1820)
2. *Princes:* especially the pleasure-loving Prince Regent, later George IV
3. *A . . . field:* the Peterloo Massacre, in which a cavalry charge broke up a workers' protest meeting in St. Peter's Field, Manchester, 1819
4. *liberticide:* the killing of liberty
5. *Golden . . . slay:* laws both encouraging and punishing political expression
6. *A . . . unrepealed:* a legislative body (Parliament) from which dissenters (both Catholic and Protestant) were excluded by law

Reading Check: This poem is one long sentence. What words make up the compound subject? Where do the verb and the complement for these subjects finally appear? ✓

Combine Strategies: Who or what can you infer that Shelley dislikes in England? What does he think will happen to them and to his country? R

VISUAL ANALYSIS

The illustration across the page was a contemporary depiction of the Peterloo Massacre of 1819 (p. 416). This and other events inspired some of Shelley's poetry. How did the artist convey sympathy for one side of the massacre? How might the action and tone of the art correspond with Shelley's thoughts in "England in 1819"?

Ode to the West Wind

I

O, wild West Wind, thou breath of Autumn's being
Thou, from whose unseen presence the leaves dead
Are driven, like ghosts from an enchanter fleeing,

Yellow, and black, and pale, and hectic red[1]
Pestilence-stricken multitudes: O, thou,
Who chariotest to their dark wintry bed

The wingèd seeds, where they lie cold and low,
Each like a corpse within its grave, until
Thine azure[2] sister of the Spring[3] shall blow

Her clarion[4] o'er the dreaming earth, and fill
(Driving sweet buds like flocks to feed in air)
With living hues and odors plain and hill:

Wild Spirit, which art moving everywhere;
Destroyer and preserver; hear, O, hear! A

Terza Rima: Mark how the stanzas conform to terza rima. Note the section that conforms to sonnet form as well. A

1. *hectic red:* reddened by fever, flushed
2. *azure:* blue
3. *sister . . . Spring:* the south wind
4. *clarion:* "medieval trumpet with a shrill clear tone" (*AHD*)

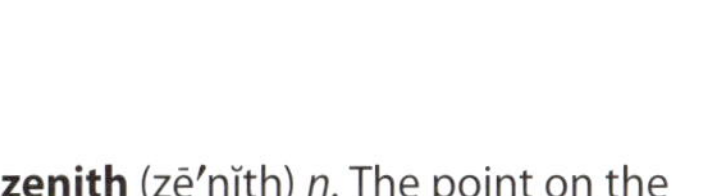

II

Thou on whose stream, 'mid the steep sky's commotion,
Loose clouds like earth's decaying leaves are shed,
Shook from the tangled boughs of Heaven and Ocean,

Angels[5] of rain and lightning: there are spread
On the blue surface of thine airy surge,
Like the bright hair uplifted from the head

Of some fierce Maenad,[6] even from the dim verge
Of the horizon to the **zenith's** height
The locks of the approaching storm. Thou **dirge**

Of the dying year, to which this closing night
Will be the dome of a vast sepulcher,
Vaulted with all thy congregated might

Of vapors, from whose solid atmosphere
Black rain, and fire, and hail will burst: O, hear!

zenith (zē′nĭth) *n.* The point on the celestial sphere that is directly above the observer.

dirge (dûrj) *n.* A funeral hymn or lament.

III

Thou who didst waken from his summer dreams
The blue Mediterranean, where he lay,
Lulled by the coil of his crystalline streams,

Beside a pumice isle in Baiae's bay,[7]
And saw in sleep old palaces and towers
Quivering within the wave's intenser day,

All overgrown with azure moss and flowers
So sweet, the sense faints picturing them! Thou
For whose path the Atlantic's level powers[8]

Cleave themselves into chasms, while far below
The sea-blooms and the oozy woods which wear
The sapless foliage of the ocean, know

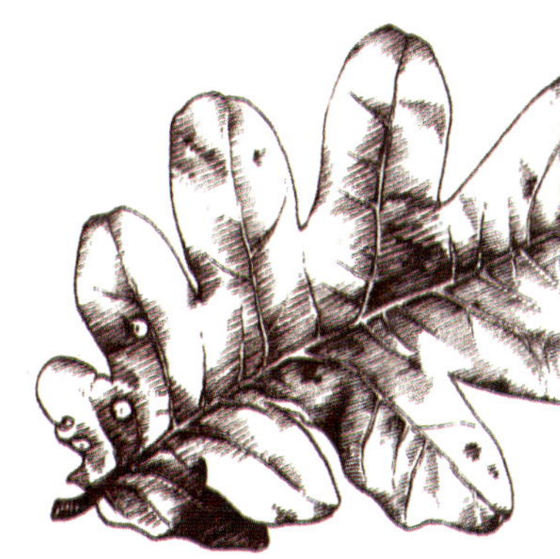

Thy voice, and suddenly grow gray with fear.
And tremble and despoil themselves:[9] O, hear!

IV

If I were a dead leaf thou mightest bear;
If I were a swift cloud to fly with thee;
A wave to pant beneath thy power, and share **A**

The impulse of thy strength, only less free
Than thou, O, uncontrollable! If even
I were as in my boyhood, and could be

The comrade of thy wanderings over heaven,
As then, when to outstrip thy skyey speed
Scarce seemed a vision;[10] I would ne'er have striven

Terza Rima: Section 4 of the ode collects the images of the three previous stanzas. What are these images? What is one effect of the stanza form? **A**

5. *Angels:* messengers
6. *Maenad:* priestess of the wine god Bacchus, known for violent orgies
7. *Baiae's bay:* a bay near Naples, bordered by volcanic hills and ruins of ancient Roman resorts
8. *powers:* expanses
9. *despoil themselves:* plunder themselves; i.e., shed their beauty
10. *vision:* something in view but unattainable

As thus with thee in prayer in my sore need.
Oh! lift me as a wave, a leaf, a cloud!
I fall upon the thorns of life! I bleed!

A heavy weight of hours has chained and bowed
One too like thee: tameless, and swift, and proud.

V

Make me thy lyre,[11] even as the forest is:
What if my leaves are falling like its own!
The **tumult** of thy mighty harmonies

Will take from both a deep, autumnal tone,
Sweet though in sadness. Be thou, Spirit fierce,
My spirit! Be thou me, impetuous[12] one!

Drive my dead thoughts over the universe
Like withered leaves to quicken a new birth!
And, by the incantation[13] of this verse,

Scatter, as from an unextinguished hearth
Ashes and sparks, my words among mankind!
Be through my lips to unawakened earth

The trumpet of a prophecy! O, Wind,
If Winter comes, can Spring be far behind? R

tumult (to͞o′mŭlt′) *n.* A disorderly commotion or disturbance.

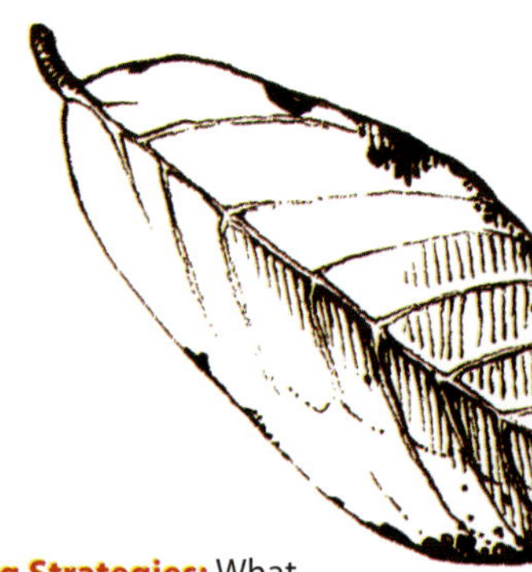

Combine Reading Strategies: What do the wind and its consequences symbolize in the poem? R

11. *lyre:* The Aeolian lyre (named after Aeolus, god of the winds) is a box with strings, open at both ends, that makes musical sounds when the wind blows through it. As a symbol of natural inspiration, it was a favorite image of the romantics.
12. *impetuous:* "having or marked by violent force" (*AHD*)
13. *incantation:* chanting

THINK AND DISCUSS

1. What characteristics of Ozymandias does the sculpture still exhibit? What do they tell you about the man?
2. Identify the type of irony that Shelley uses in "Ozymandias." Analyze the way in which he employs irony to convey theme and purpose.
3. How does an understanding of the historical context of England in 1819 (people and events) shed light on Shelley's poem by that name?
4. How does Shelley use sentence structure and allusion to convey theme in "England in 1819"?
5. What artistic effect does the structure of "Ode to the West Wind" (terza rima, sonnet, enjambment) accomplish?
6. According to parts I–III of "Ode to the West Wind," what three areas of nature are affected by the west wind's awesome power? How is the west wind both "destroyer and preserver" in each of the three areas?
7. How does part IV of "Ode to the West Wind" relate to the first three sections? What personal requests does the speaker make of the wind in parts IV–V, and for what purpose does he make them?
8. Referencing Shelley's imagery and figurative language (similes, metaphors, and personification), analyze how Shelley's references to the wind and its consequences symbolize his ideas and the force of his poetry.
9. Using the following references, evaluate the themes of "Ozymandias" and "England in 1819" from Scripture: Proverbs 16:18, Psalm 2:10–12, 1 Peter 1:24, Matthew 13:36–43, 2 Peter 3:13, and Ecclesiastes 12:13–14.
10. Summarize Shelley's ideas in "Ode to the West Wind," and evaluate his hopes for human society in light of Isaiah 2:1–5 and 9:6–7.

John Keats (1795–1821)

AT A GLANCE

- **1811–16** Studied medicine
- **ca. 1812** Began to read works by Ovid, Milton, Virgil, and Spenser
- **1816** Influenced to write by Leigh Hunt, Shelley, and Wordsworth
- **1817** Published his first collection of poetry
- **1818** Completed his first long poem, *Endymion*
- **1820** Published his final volume of poetry

From the fall of 1818 through September of 1819, John Keats produced some of the finest lyric poetry ever written in English. These poems balance an intensity of imagery and lusciousness of sound with a celebration of the natural life. Yet Keats's life was cut short in 1821, and his legacy is one of both timeless poetry and unrealized potential.

Early Life

Keats was born in London to a father who managed a stable. In 1803 Keats began attending Enfield School, where he would study for seven years. Tragedy, however, soon fell. His father died in 1804, and his mother died five years later. Although their elderly grandmother appointed a guardian for them, Keats felt some responsibility for the family of orphans and remained close to his siblings for the rest of his life. With the family's finances devastated and at the insistence of his guardian, Keats studied to become an apothecary-surgeon, earning his qualifications in London in 1816. By this time, however, he had fallen in love with poetry and was determined to try his hand.

Young Poet

That year he fell in with a young set of London political radicals and romantic poets, meeting and befriending the critic William Hazlitt and Percy Bysshe Shelley. In 1817 Shelley's publisher brought out Keats's first book, *Poems*, which was of uneven quality and generally panned. Undaunted, Keats abandoned his medical work to pursue poetry full-time, publishing his long poem *Endymion* later in the year. This, too, met savage criticism. Although Shelley and Byron later claimed the reviews had crushed his spirit, they actually spurred Keats to more deliberate, self-critical workmanship. He spent the fall of 1818 nursing his dying brother Tom as well as composing his first great poetry, the unfinished epic *Hyperion*.

That December Keats moved to Hampstead, where he met and fell in love with Fanny Brawne. Although they became engaged the following year, they never married, as Keats worried about his career and his health. Nevertheless, he was inspired by his passionate and sometimes obsessive love for Fanny, who served as the muse for the long poem *The Eve of St. Agnes* and the sonnet "Bright star, would I were stedfast as thou art."

The spring and summer of 1819 were marked by a feverish poetic output that included great odes such as "Ode on a Grecian Urn." Keats was desperate to prove himself, and he may also have intuited how short his life would be. By September, when he wrote his celebrated "To Autumn," his health was failing, and the following February he began coughing blood. His newer poems were published to acclaim in *Lamia, Isabella, The Eve of St. Agnes, and Other Poems* (1820), but by then he was too weak to write more poetry. After journeying to Italy on doctor's orders, he died in Rome at the age of twenty-five.

DID YOU KNOW ?

Keats himself wrote the epitaph inscribed on his tombstone in Rome: "Here lies one whose name was writ in water."

Legacy

At his death Keats quickly became a symbol of lost hopes, so much so that Shelley dedicated his elegy *Adonais* to Keats's memory. Within a few decades, critics were comparing Keats with Shakespeare, and Victorian poets were imitating his technique. Since then he has become one of the most widely read English poets.

In his great poems, Keats exhibits what he called negative capability, the power to stand removed from his own intense feelings. He uses his keen eye for nature and his characteristically sensuous language to transfigure his personal emotions into universal themes. A humanistic poet like Shelley, Keats finds tragic beauty in the natural rhythms of life.

ANALYZE: *Poetic Form, Euphony, and Cacophony*

Both "To Autumn" and "Ode on a Grecian Urn" are odes. Analyze how each poem qualifies as an **ode** (p. 488). Then consider how its structure supports Keats's development of ideas and images. For example, pay attention to how stanza breaks and rhyme scheme patterns group specific lines and their content. How might these sections develop particular images or ideas? How might the sections interact (e.g., contrasting or elaborating on each other's ideas) to build themes? Besides the ode, what other familiar lyric form does Keats use in the final poem?

Keats considered beauty of paramount importance to art. This belief extended to his use of sounds in poetry. "To Autumn" shows his skill in creating euphony and cacophony through word choices. **Euphony** refers to agreeable sounds, especially in the phonetic quality of words, while **cacophony** denotes jarring, discordant sounds. Euphony usually arises from a series of words primarily containing the smooth sounds of vowels and soft consonants (e.g., *l, m, r, f, w, s, y, th*). Cacophony often results from words with many hard consonants (*b, d, g, k, p,* and *t*). The effect of these techniques varies in context. Some uses may help project an author's tone toward certain content. Others may affect readers' mood. Identify examples of both techniques in the poem and consider what their intended effect might be.

READ: *Draw Conclusions About Romanticism*

As you read the following poems, draw conclusions about Keats's romanticism. For example, examine how his poems incorporate romanticism's major emphases: the imagination, the individual, and nature. Do his poems evoke the rational or emotional side of readers? Is his perspective in them subjective or objective? How might his images project nature as a source of inspiration and truth? Additionally, look for characteristic features of romanticism such as the distant or the sublime. Finally, more than the other major romantics, Keats perceived a connection between beauty and truth. To him, beauty, in its appeal to the imagination, was a primary (perhaps even *the* primary) marker of the presence of truth. How might the following poems seek to intertwine beauty and truth?

EVALUATE: *Aestheticism*

Keats, as a romantic, believed truth to be accessible through the guidance of human imagination and feelings. He also recognized that beauty (in its broadest sense) evokes human imagination and feelings to an unusual degree. It is perhaps no surprise, then, that he decided the qualities of beauty and truth to be synonymous (or nearly so) and believed the lover of beauty to be a seeker of truth. Such devotion to beauty (and therefore to art) as the highest human concern is known as **aestheticism**, and it is not unique to Keats. But how should a Christian respond to such thinking? Consider how the Scriptures reference beauty in the following passages: Philippians 4:8, 1 Samuel 16:7, James 1:14, and Genesis 3:6. How does the Bible encourage us to value beauty? How might the biblically defined qualities of Beauty and Truth be connected? Are humans capable of creating or accessing either in art?

OBJECTIVES

- Draw conclusions on how romanticism shapes a poet's works.
- Analyze how a text's structure enhances its meaning.
- Analyze a poet's use of sound devices to support his ideas.
- Evaluate an author's aestheticism from a biblical worldview.

VOCABULARY

conspire (kən-spīr′) *tr.v.* To plan or plot secretly.

winnow (wĭn′ō) *tr.v.* To separate the chaff from (grain) by means of a current of air.

sylvan (sĭl′vən) *adj.* Relating to or characteristic of woods or forest regions.

ecstasy (ĕk′stə-sē) *n.* Intense joy or delight.

cloy (kloi) *intr.v.* To be too filling, rich, or sweet.

What is the value of BEAUTY?

Although cultures differ in particulars and in tastes, some universal principles of beauty tend to transcend time. Whether an engaging piece of music, a picturesque watercolor, or a lovely poem, beauty draws us to itself often through artistry, color, or harmonious form or proportion. To be valuable, does such an object need to function beyond the pleasure it brings to our senses, or does it need merely to delight? Write a paragraph expressing your thoughts.

To Autumn

Season of mists and mellow fruitfulness,
Close bosom-friend of the maturing sun;
Conspiring with him how to load and bless
With fruit the vines that round the thatch-eaves run;
To bend with apples the moss'd cottage-trees,
And fill all fruit with ripeness to the core;
To swell the gourd, and plump the hazel shells
With a sweet kernel; to set budding more,
And still more, later flowers for the bees,
Until they think warm days will never cease,
For summer has o'er-brimm'd their clammy cells.

Who hath not seen thee oft amid thy store?
Sometimes whoever seeks abroad may find
Thee sitting careless on a granary[1] floor,
Thy hair soft-lifted by the **winnowing** wind;
Or on a half-reap'd furrow sound asleep,
Drows'd with the fume of poppies, while thy hook[2]
Spares the next swath and all its twined flowers:
And sometimes like a gleaner thou dost keep
Steady thy laden head across a brook;
Or by a cyder-press, with patient look,
Thou watchest the last oozings hours by hours. R

Where are the songs of Spring? Ay, where are they?
Think not of them, thou hast thy music too,—
While barred clouds bloom the soft-dying day,
And touch the stubble-plains with rosy hue;
Then in a wailful choir the small gnats mourn
Among the river sallows,[3] borne aloft
Or sinking as the light wind lives or dies
And full-grown lambs loud bleat from hilly bourn;
Hedge-crickets sing; and now with treble soft
The red-breast whistles from a garden-croft;[4]
And gathering swallows twitter in the skies. A

1. *granary:* where threshed grain is stored
2. *hook:* scythe; an implement made of a long, curved single-edged blade and used for reaping

3. *sallows:* willows
4. *croft:* "a small enclosed field" (*AHD*)

conspire (kən-spīr′) *tr.v.* To plan or plot secretly.

winnow (wĭn′ō) *tr.v.* To separate the chaff from (grain) by means of a current of air.

Draw Conclusions: What major romantic emphases can you find in the poet's treatment of autumn in stanza 2? R

Euphony and Cacophony: Identify one line in the poem with words that exhibit euphony and another line with words that exhibit cacophony. A

ODE ON A GRECIAN URN

Thou still unravish'd bride of quietness,
Thou foster-child of silence and slow time,
Sylvan historian, who canst thus express
A flowery tale more sweetly than our rhyme:
What leaf-fring'd legend haunts about thy shape
Of deities or mortals, or of both,
In Tempe[1] or the dales of Arcady?[2]
What men or gods are these? What maidens
loath?
What mad pursuit? What struggle to escape?
What pipes and timbrels?[3] What wild **ecstasy**?

1. *Tempe:* a valley in Greece known for beauty
2. *Arcady:* Arcadia, a mountainous part of Greece considered idyllic
3. *timbrels:* "an ancient percussion instrument similar to a tambourine" (*AHD*)

sylvan (sĭl′vən) *adj.* Relating to or characteristic of woods or forest regions.

ecstasy (ĕk′stə-sē) *n.* Intense joy or delight.

Draw Conclusions: How do the images depicted on the urn represent truth? R

Heard melodies are sweet, but those unheard
Are sweeter; therefore, ye soft pipes, play on;
Not to the sensual ear, but, more endear'd,
Pipe to the spirit ditties of no tone:
Fair youth, beneath the trees, thou canst not leave
Thy song, nor ever can those trees be bare;
Bold Lover, never, never canst thou kiss,
Though winning near the goal—yet, do not grieve;
She cannot fade, though thou hast not thy bliss,
Forever will thou love, and she be fair! R

Ah, happy, happy boughs! that cannot shed
Your leaves, nor ever bid the Spring adieu;
And, happy melodist, unwearied,
Forever piping songs forever new;
More happy love! more happy, happy love!
Forever warm and still to be enjoy'd,
Forever panting, and forever young;
All breathing human passion far above,
That leaves a heart high-sorrowful and **cloy'd**,
A burning forehead, and a parching tongue. A

Who are these coming to the sacrifice?
To what green altar, O mysterious priest,
Lead'st thou that heifer lowing at the skies,
And all her silken flanks with garlands drest?
What little town by river or sea shore,
Or mountain-built with peaceful citadel,
Is emptied of this folk, this pious morn?
And, little town, thy streets for evermore
Will silent be; and not a soul to tell
Why thou art desolate, can e'er return.

O Attic[4] shape! Fair attitude! with brede[5]
Of marble men and maidens overwrought,[6]
With forest branches and the trodden weed;
Thou, silent form, dost tease us out of thought
As doth eternity: Cold Pastoral![7]
When old age shall this generation waste,
Thou shalt remain, in midst of other woe
Than ours, a friend to man, to whom thou say'st,
"Beauty is truth, truth beauty,"—that is all
Ye know on earth, and all ye need to know. E

4. *Attic:* in the pure, simple style of Attica, the location of Athens, Greece
5. *brede:* braiding
6. *overwrought:* ornate and elaborate
7. *Pastoral:* related to rural life or shepherding

cloy (kloi) *intr.v.* To be too filling, rich, or sweet.

Poetic Form: How does the content of each stanza differ so far? How does the rhyme scheme relate to the content? A

Aestheticism: Consider Keats's philosophy as expressed in lines 49–50. What do these lines mean? E

WHEN I HAVE FEARS THAT I MAY CEASE TO BE

When I have fears that I may cease to be
    Before my pen has glean'd my teeming[1] brain,
Before high-piled books, in charactery,[2]
    Hold like full garners[3] the full-ripen'd grain;
When I behold, upon the night's starr'd race,
    Huge cloudy symbols of a high romance,
And think that I may never live to trace
    Their shadows, with the magic hand of chance;
And when I feel, fair creature of an hour!
    That I shall never look upon thee more,
Never have relish in the faery power
    Of unreflecting love!—then on the shore
Of the wide world I stand alone, and think,
    Till love and fame to nothingness do sink. A E

1. *teeming:* full of things
2. *charactery:* characters or symbols used to express a thought
3. *garners:* storage places for grain

Poetic Form: Note the rhyme scheme. What poetic form does this poem display? A

Aestheticism: What problem does the speaker grapple with in this poem? E

THINK AND DISCUSS

1. Name two odes Keats composed. Explain why each is an ode.
2. Contrast euphony and cacophony. Which one Is predominant in stanza 1 of "To Autumn"? Write one line from the stanza, and explain why it demonstrates your answer.
3. Identify an example of nature imagery in two of Keats's poems. Explain its significance to the overall meaning of the poem.
4. How does the poetic form of "When I have fears" help develop the theme of the poem?
5. How does "When I have fears" reflect the value that Keats places on beauty in art?
6. How does "Ode on a Grecian Urn" exemplify Keats's search for Beauty and Truth? How does the poem reflect other emphases of romanticism?
7. Contrast Keats's view of access to ultimate truth with God's plan. What part do reason and revelation play in accessing ultimate truth?

FRANKENSTEIN

Mary Shelley

Mary Wollstonecraft Shelley (1797–1851) received the inspiration for her most famous work, *Frankenstein: Or, The Modern Prometheus*, on a literary dare. In response, she not only created characters that eventually became pop-culture icons, but she also prophesied the moral dilemmas with which modern science confronts humanity.

The Author

Mary was born into a literary family. Her parents were author Mary Wollstonecraft (1759–97) and radical philosopher William Godwin (1756–1836). At seventeen, she eloped with Percy Bysshe Shelley, who was still married to his first wife. In 1816 the couple traveled to Switzerland to meet Shelley's friend Lord Byron. There on the shores of Lake Geneva, a scene that would feature prominently in *Frankenstein*, the group of friends began a contest to see which of them could write the best ghost story. At first unable to think of a fittingly terrifying tale, Mary eventually found her core material in a nightmare, which she wrote down in short-story form. After some encouragement from Shelley, she developed it into a novel. At its publication in 1818 it received immediate popular success.

The Work

Modern readers who have been introduced to *Frankenstein* by pop-culture adaptations are generally baffled by the original work. To begin with, Victor Frankenstein is the name of the young scientist, not the "creature" to whom he gives life. The monster never receives a name. In many film adaptations, the monster is childish, clumsy, and brutish, whereas in the novel he is highly articulate and possesses superhuman agility and strength.

More, far more, will I achieve; treading in the steps already marked, I will pioneer a new way, explore unknown powers, and unfold to the world the deepest mysteries of creation.

The book and its cultural descendants also differ in their literary genres. *Frankenstein* is not a horror novel—it doesn't wallow in the grotesque. Rather it is a gothic novel, a subgenre of the novel of sensibility, and therefore focuses on Frankenstein's troubled emotional states. Again, while the book is rightly considered the first work of science fiction, it does not detail Frankenstein's scientific techniques. And as with many gothic novels, *Frankenstein* is framed as an epistolary novel. The reader begins the book with a young adventurer who chances upon Frankenstein out on the Arctic ice. It is there that Victor Frankenstein narrates his life story.

Frankenstein begins the novel as a university student from Geneva. Eventually, using processes that go unexplained, he gives life to a "creature." Yet the moment he sees his creation alive—eight feet tall, with "yellow skin" that "scarcely covered the work of muscles and arteries beneath," black hair, and "watery" white eyes—Frankenstein instantly rejects it. Horrified and overwhelmed by the stress of his research, Frankenstein collapses into a feverish delirium, to be later rescued by a friend. His creature is left to discover on his own how to survive. He finds himself persecuted by all human society. His frustrated rage, combined with Frankenstein's repeated rejection, ultimately leads to the deaths of Frankenstein, his dearest family and friends, and the creature himself.

Themes and Cultural Influence

What makes *Frankenstein* so remarkable is its prophetic character. Like her romantic contemporaries, Shelley was skeptical of reason. Unlike her peers, she dramatized the dangers of thoughtless scientific progress in highly prescient ways. As a conscious being, the creature evokes dilemmas strikingly similar to those surrounding human cloning and artificial intelligence. Frankenstein views his creation as inhuman, but his creation considers himself very human. Shelley suggests that we may not want the responsibility that comes with creating new forms of consciousness. She suggests that new technologies, rather than leading to freedom, can enslave us. As the creature states to his maker, "You are my creator, but I am your master; obey!" Frankenstein's end thus serves as a timeless warning against humanity's hubris.

What Do You Know?

Understand the Background

1. Choose one author from Part 1 and explain why he or she is transitional between neoclassicism and romanticism.
2. In Blake's "London" what social ills of the day does he bemoan?
3. What did Austen contribute to the development of the novel?
4. Identify the major characteristics of romanticism.
5. Explain one way that *Frankenstein* reflects romantic thought.

Apply the Concepts

6. Describe three elements of Burns's poetry that reflect a transition to romantic preferences.
7. Choose one rhetorical device found in "The Tyger" and explain how it conveys Blake's message. Use the text to support your answer.
8. Identify two examples of wit in *Pride and Prejudice*. How does Austen's use of wit reflect neoclassicism?
9. Select two characters from *Pride and Prejudice,* and explain through example how each is characterized through his or her dialogue.
10. Using examples from the text, demonstrate how Wollstonecraft uses all three types of rhetorical appeals to enhance her argument.
11. Choose one of Wordsworth's poems and explain how its style and imagery reflect romantic ideals.
12. How does Byron express the sublime in *Childe Harold*? Use examples from the text to explain your answer.
13. How is the imagery in "She Walks in Beauty" expressly romantic?
14. Explain the function of two symbols in *The Rime of the Ancient Mariner.*
15. How does the imagery in "Ode on a Grecian Urn" contribute to theme?
16. How does the structure of "Ode to the West Wind" (terza rima, sonnet, enjambment) contribute to the poem?
17. How does irony in "Ozymandias" contribute to theme?

Evaluate the Ideas

18. How do "The Lamb" and "The Tyger" reflect the philosophy of dualism? Evaluate this idea according to a biblical worldview.
19. Choose two of Wollstonecraft's arguments and explain how they do or do not conform to Scripture.
20. Using Scripture, evaluate Coleridge's treatment of guilt in *The Rime of the Ancient Mariner.*
21. Using the three Wordsworth selections, evaluate the romantic ideal of communion with nature.

Write a Response

22. Describe the major tenets of romanticism and exemplify each from the romantic poets.
23. How does Harold manifest the characteristics of the Byronic hero? Use evidence from the text of *Childe Harold* to support your answer. Evaluate this character type from a biblical worldview.

Define each term and provide an example of each from a selection in Unit 4, Part 1 or 2.

TERMS

dialect
foil character
wit
repartee
the sublime
enjambment
caesura
internal rhyme
assonance
consonance
dynamic character
static character
Byronic hero
Spenserian stanza
ode
terza rima
euphony
cacaphony
aestheticism

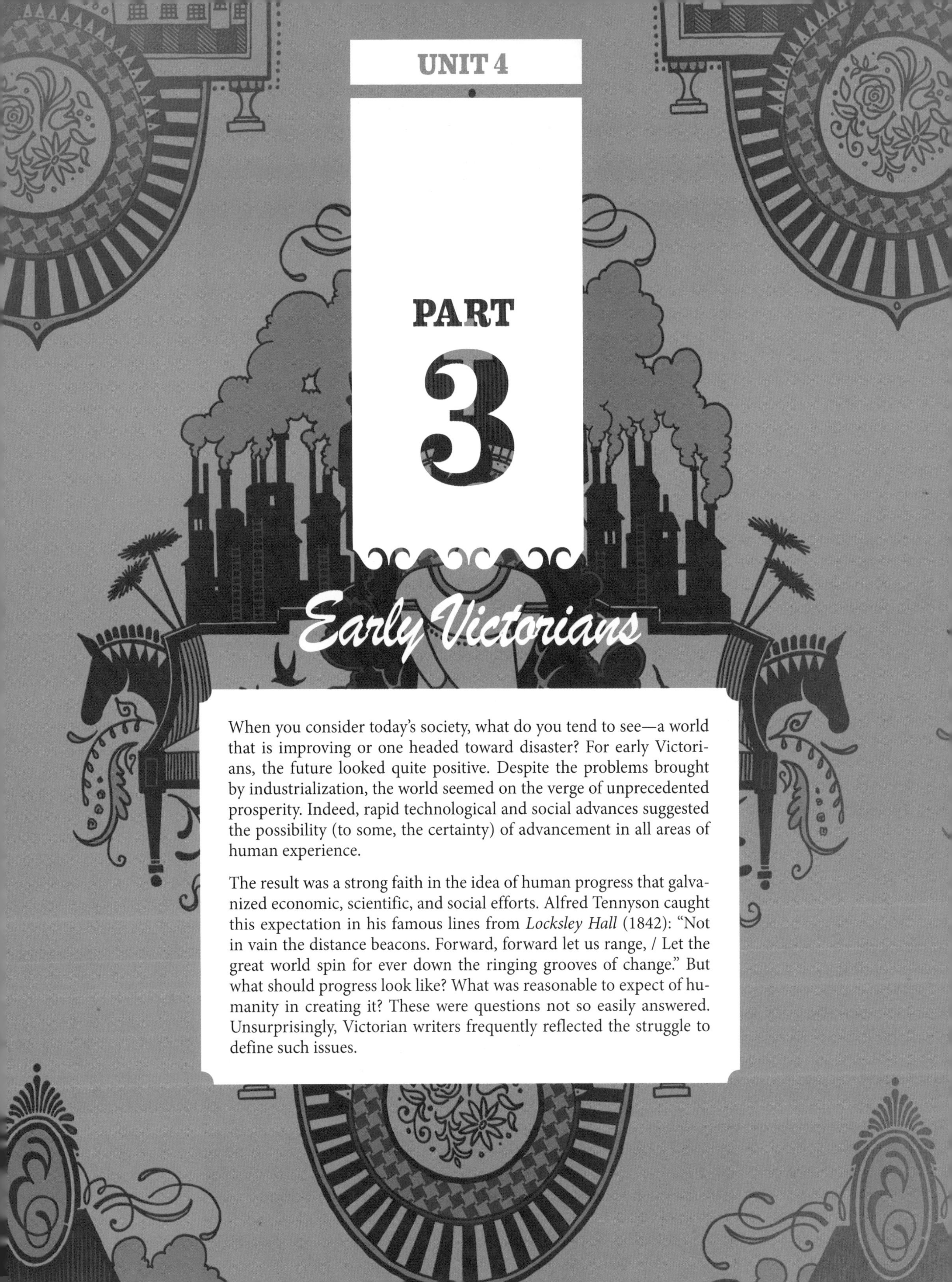

UNIT 4

PART 3

Early Victorians

When you consider today's society, what do you tend to see—a world that is improving or one headed toward disaster? For early Victorians, the future looked quite positive. Despite the problems brought by industrialization, the world seemed on the verge of unprecedented prosperity. Indeed, rapid technological and social advances suggested the possibility (to some, the certainty) of advancement in all areas of human experience.

The result was a strong faith in the idea of human progress that galvanized economic, scientific, and social efforts. Alfred Tennyson caught this expectation in his famous lines from *Locksley Hall* (1842): "Not in vain the distance beacons. Forward, forward let us range, / Let the great world spin for ever down the ringing grooves of change." But what should progress look like? What was reasonable to expect of humanity in creating it? These were questions not so easily answered. Unsurprisingly, Victorian writers frequently reflected the struggle to define such issues.

A strong strand of traditional Christianity remained in Victorian society and offered one perspective on progress. Many Christians believed that humanity's original stewardship purposes, renewed by the gospel, directed them to improve social conditions at home and abroad. Unlike some reformers, their optimism was often tempered by a knowledge of humanity's flaws and limitations. The poetry of Elizabeth and Robert Browning, both devout liberal Christians, reflects a traditional viewpoint on these matters in differing ways. Elizabeth wrote accomplished lyrical poetry that advocated for reform (e.g., in slavery, labor practices) and explored universal themes such as love and gender relations. Robert found his voice in dramatic narrative poetry that presented a psychologically complex view of humanity's great potential and deep flaws.

But many Victorians had unmoored themselves from Christian orthodoxies. Their worldview combined neoclassical, romantic, and Christian ideas to justify a belief in the perfectibility of society. However, they sometimes struggled to find an ethical rationale to support specific social goals or to deal with universal issues such as death. For example, the era's foremost poet, Tennyson, tried to salvage religious faith by blending Christianity with transcendentalism. Yet his works show that his hopes for the meaning of life and death were still weighed down by uncertainty and fear.

One solution for the lack of a set of secular ethics was offered by Jeremy Bentham (1748–1832), founder of utilitarianism. This philosophy posited that one could live happily by choosing behavior that produces the maximum of pleasure and the minimum of pain (considering long-term consequences and not just immediate effects). The goodness of an action was said to consist in the happiness it produced. Bentham thus discussed happiness in physically measurable terms and human relationships in coldly mechanistic fashion.

Literary writers debated utilitarian assessments of progress at length, with many despising Bentham's "moral arithmetic" (applied to politics, the greatest happiness for the greatest number) as lacking necessary heart. Perhaps the most widely read essayist, Thomas Carlyle questioned utilitarian values (among others) in his famous essay "On the Condition of England." Such was the power of his critique that it spawned a whole genre, the "Condition of England" novels, whose narratives depicted British society and its reform needs. The most famous of these novelists was undoubtedly Charles Dickens, who undertook to save society by restoring its moral and emotional nature.

Other novelists addressed social progress in different ways. The Brontë sisters—Charlotte, Emily, and Anne—all wrote novels of social commentary dealing with "the woman question" (Victorians' term for the debate on how women fit into ongoing social changes). Perhaps the most famous of these, Charlotte's *Jane Eyre*, transformed the gothic novel to offer intense psychological realism and thoughtful social commentary. Through the trials of her female protagonist, Brontë cuts to the heart of reform debates, arguing for the worth and dignity of every human and the need for extending genuine love and empathy in reform efforts rather than simply imposing rigid social expectations or dry moral demands.

The authors in this section express the diversity of viewpoints in Victorian literature. Two are women whose immense success was unprecedented. And several reflect the era's increased social mobility. Tennyson was born into a middle-class family and eventually knighted for his work; Charlotte Brontë's father was a rural curate; Carlyle rose from the Scottish working class to widespread fame and influence in society, and Dickens from an impoverished middle-class family to the same. Never before had class meant so little to literary success. As you read, consider how the topics, forms, or themes authors chose to use and the values they professed reflect various life experiences.

Alfred, Lord Tennyson (1809–92)

AT A GLANCE

- **1833** Experienced the tragedy of losing his friend, Arthur Hallam
- **1850** Published *In Memoriam*; appointed poet laureate
- **1852** Published "Ode on the Death of the Duke of Wellington"
- **1854** Published "The Charge of the Light Brigade"
- **1883** Made a peer of the realm
- **1885** Published completed *Idylls of the King* together

The poet Alfred Tennyson, more commonly known by his title Lord Tennyson, experienced a dark childhood. Although he eventually found emotional stability, he never resolved his lifelong struggle between religious faith and doubt. By portraying this struggle with a subtle, elegiac poetry, Tennyson perfectly captured the mood of Victorian England.

Early Years

Tennyson was born in Lincolnshire into a family that struggled with mental illness. His father battled with severe depression, and one of his brothers was confined to a mental hospital. Tennyson himself long feared that he had inherited a mental illness. His painful childhood formed the background for much of his poetry, which frequently portrays his struggles with doubt and suicide.

In 1827 Tennyson entered Cambridge, where he and the gifted young writer Arthur Hallam became fast friends. When Tennyson published his *Poems, Chiefly Lyrical* (1830), Hallam provided encouragement and enthusiastically reviewed the work in a literary magazine. Tragically, Hallam died of a stroke in the fall of 1833.

Years of Struggle and Success

Tennyson was already familiar with tragedy, but Hallam's death so shocked him that he refused to publish more poetry. In 1842, though, he published an edition of revised and new poems. Still struggling with grief and spiritual turmoil, Tennyson used poetry as an outlet. The result was his great lyrical work, *In Memoriam,* published in 1850 and dedicated to the memory of Hallam. The work is composed of one hundred thirty-three cantos (short poems in their own right) that vary considerably in topic. But broadly, the work grapples with Victorians' religious doubt in the wake of new scientific discoveries and the resulting struggle to effectively deal with life, death, and grief.

In Memoriam established Tennyson as the most significant poet of his generation. In the year of the poem's publication, Tennyson was named poet laureate; he also married Emily Sellwood, with whom he finally found a measure of personal peace. They moved to the Isle of Wight, where Tennyson spent much of the rest of his life with his wife and two sons. He is perhaps best known for the poems written during this period in his role as poet laureate. For example, his occasional works "Ode on the Death of the Duke of Wellington" (1852) and "The Charge of the Light Brigade" (1854) are among the most famous poems in English. They show the immense appeal of his work.

DID YOU KNOW ?

While at Cambridge, Tennyson belonged to a society called the Apostles.

Later Years and Legacy

In his later years, Tennyson continued to produce works of note. In 1883 he was made a peer of the realm, becoming the first person to receive the honor for poetic work. As the national poet, he explored Arthurian legend with the blank-verse cycle *Idylls of the King*, another masterwork. He also experimented (though with little success) in writing for the stage. He continued to write poetry, penning "Crossing the Bar" three years before his death.

In his lifetime, Tennyson was an international icon of the morals and taste of the Victorian era, and his poems have sometimes been associated with Victorian sentimentality. But his frank exploration of grief resonates with readers today. Furthermore, he mastered the sounds of English, and his poetry is often best read aloud. It has a flowing quality that has never been replicated. Despite the passage of time, readers still find his poetry readable and accessible today.

ANALYZE: *Meter and Sound Devices, Parallelism*

Tennyson, though sometimes criticized in his day for a lack of philosophical originality, had a talent for playing with language. He achieved great musicality in his poems, showing himself a master of blank verse (p. 184) in poems such as "Ulysses" and using iambic tetrameter to great effect in *In Memoriam*. As you read the poems that follow, notice the cadences he creates through **meter** and sound devices (e.g., **alliteration** and **assonance**, p. 465). How might these affect the flow or mood of each poem?

Additionally, Tennyson often structured his ideas using rhetorical devices. In particular, **parallelism** (p. 140) shows up in all three poems that follow. Parallelism can help emphasize key ideas or tie them together to highlight similarities or contrasts. This device is evident in *In Memoriam*, especially in the form of anaphora (p. 165). Which canto has the clearest examples of parallelism? How does the parallelism there help highlight ideas important to Tennyson's purpose? In "Crossing the Bar," the parallelism is especially subtle. Which of Tennyson's ideas about life might it highlight?

READ: *Compare and Contrast Texts*

The poems that follow include two **elegies** (p. 206) and one **dramatic monologue** (p. 298). The poems touch on multiple themes, but a look at their imagery reveals certain thematic similarities. First, Tennyson repeatedly references journeys and transitions from old to new. Where do these journeys begin and end? Who travels (or wants to travel) in each selection? What is the speaker's attitude toward his journeys? How might physical and spiritual journeys have resonated well with a Victorian audience?

Additionally, Tennyson frequently connects the image of a journey or transition with the use of boundaries as a symbol. The boundaries in "Ulysses" and "Crossing the Bar" are particularly clear. Ask yourself what these dividing lines separate. Why do the speakers cross them? Why are the boundaries problematic or helpful? What might they symbolize in context of each work's themes?

EVALUATE: *Author's View of Decline and Death*

The three selections deal with Tennyson's reflections on human decline, death, and grief. In these poems, he chronicles (sometimes indirectly) his own vacillations between spiritual doubt and faith. As you read, consider what Tennyson concludes about these topics and what beliefs about life and God he bases his conclusions on. For example, does he express hope despite the reality of human decline and death? If so, from what ideas does he gain comfort? How might his thoughts, like many other Victorians', reflect both romantic and Christian tendencies?

OBJECTIVES

- Identify the meter, sound devices, and parallelism of a work.
- Analyze a poet's use of meter, sound devices, and parallelism to support mood and theme.
- Compare and contrast an author's use of imagery, symbol, and theme across poems.
- Evaluate an author's view of decline and death from a biblical viewpoint.

VOCABULARY

stagnate (stăg′nāt′) *intr.v.* To be or become *stagnant* (*adj.* inactive or sluggish).

subserve (səb-sûrv′) *tr.v.* To serve to promote (an end); be useful to.

falter (fôl′tər) *intr.v.* To be unsteady in purpose or action, as from loss of courage or confidence; waver.

chaff (chăf) *n.* Trivial or worthless matter.

redress (rĭ-drĕs′) *n.* Satisfaction for wrong or injury; reparation.

mete (mēt) *tr.v.* To distribute or allot.

How do you make sense of OLD AGE *and* DEATH?

Modern American society is often accused of being obsessed with youth. From the realms of entertainment and celebrity to the workplace and everyday life, youth (or at least the appearance of it) is demonstrably prized. In contrast, the reality that every person ages and eventually dies is subtly pushed aside. Why is this attitude unhealthy? Why is it beneficial to think seriously about both topics? How can you be at peace with both realities in your own life?

The elegy In Memoriam *was prompted by Tennyson's grief after the death of his dear friend Arthur Henry Hallam. Inspired by this tragedy, the poem addresses a central concern of Victorian literature—the conflict of faith and doubt. Shaken by the contemporary idea that an impersonal Nature ruled material life, Tennyson sought to heal the breach between religion and science. The poem's central figure is a doubter, and the lyrics are sequenced to show his slow restoration of faith in divine purpose and human immortality. You can see this progression in the following selections if you read between the lines to recognize the speaker's thoughts and feelings. What initially causes the speaker's sense of doubt? What ideas does he eventually find comfort in? From whom or what does he glean these comforting ideas?*

PROLOGUE

Strong Son of God, immortal love,
Whom we, that have not seen thy face,
By faith, and faith alone, embrace,
Believing where we cannot prove;

Thine are these orbs of light and shade;[1]
Thou madest life in man and brute;
Thou madest death; and lo, thy foot
Is on the skull which thou hast made.

Thou wilt not leave us in the dust:
Thou madest man, he knows not why;
He thinks he was not made to die;
And thou hast made him: thou art just.

Thou seemest human and divine,
The highest, holiest manhood, thou:
Our wills are ours, we know not how;
Our wills are ours, to make them thine.

Our little systems[2] have their day;
They have their day and cease to be:
They are but broken lights of thee,
And thou, O Lord, art more than they. **A**

We have but faith: we cannot know;
For knowledge is of things we see;
And yet we trust it comes from thee,
A beam in darkness: let it grow.

Let knowledge grow from more to more,
But more of reverence in us dwell;
That mind and soul, according[3] well,
May make one music as before,

But vaster. We are fools and slight;
We mock thee when we do not fear:
But help thy foolish ones to bear;
Help thy vain worlds to bear thy light.

Forgive what seemed my sin in me;
What seemed my worth since I began;
For merit lives from man to man,
And not from man, O Lord, to thee.

Forgive my grief for one removed.
Thy creature, whom I found so fair.
I trust he lives in thee, and there
I find him worthier to be loved.

Forgive these wild and wandering cries.
Confusions of a wasted youth; **R**
Forgive them where they fail in truth,
And in thy wisdom make me wise.

7

Dark house, by which once more I stand
Here in the long unlovely street,
Doors, where my heart was used to beat
So quickly, waiting for a hand,

A hand that can be clasped no more—
Behold me, for I cannot sleep,
And like a guilty thing I creep
At earliest morning to the door. **R**

1. *orbs of light and shade:* sun and moon
2. *systems:* philosophies
3. *according:* working in agreement

Parallelism/Meter: In what lines so far can you find examples of anaphora? Combined with the regular meter (p. 182), what effect does this device have on the overall mood of the Prologue? What important ideas might these examples highlight as a whole? **A**

Compare/Contrast: In what ways does the speaker of *In Memoriam* request a transition from old to new in the Prologue? **R**

Compare/Contrast: What border does the poet approach but not cross? What might his inability to cross it symbolize within the context of his grief? **R**

He is not here; but far away
The noise of life begins again,
And ghastly through the drizzling rain
On the bald street breaks the blank day.

27

I envy not in any moods
The captive void of noble rage,
The linnet[4] born within the cage,
That never knew the summer woods:

I envy not the beast that takes
His license[5] in the field of time,
Unfettered by the sense of crime,
To whom a conscience never wakes;

Nor, what may count itself as blest,
The heart that never plighted troth,[6]
But **stagnates** in the weeds of sloth;
Nor any want-begotten rest.

I hold it true, whate'er befall;
I feel it, when I sorrow most;
'Tis better to have loved and lost
Than never to have loved at all. A

54

O yet we trust that somehow good
Will be the final goal of ill,
To pangs of nature, sins of will,
Defects of doubt, and taints of blood;

That nothing walks with aimless feet;
That not one life shall be destroyed,
Or cast as rubbish to the void,
When God hath made the pile complete;

That not a worm is cloven[7] in vain;
That not a moth with vain desire
Is shriveled in a fruitless fire,
Or but **subserves** another's gain.

Behold, we know not anything;
I can but trust that good shall fall
At last—far off—at last, to all,
And every winter change to spring.

So runs my dream: but what am I;
An infant crying in the night:
An infant crying for the light:
And with no language but a cry. E

55

The wish, that of the living whole
No life may fail beyond the grave,
Derives it not from what we have
The likest God within the soul?

Are God and Nature then at strife,
That Nature lends such evil dreams?

4. *linnet:* a type of songbird
5. *license:* Tennyson references two meanings: permission granted by an authority and the exercise of too much liberty.
6. *plighted troth:* promised faithfulness
7. *cloven:* past participle of "to cleave"; i.e., split by force

stagnate (stăg′nāt′) *intr.v.* To be or become *stagnant* (*adj.* inactive or sluggish).

subserve (səb-sûrv′) *tr.v.* To serve to promote (an end); be useful to.

Parallelism: What example of parallelism do you see in lines 71–72? What idea developed throughout canto 27 do these lines summarize and highlight? A

View of Death: How do the ideas about human life and death in canto 54 align with Scripture? E

So careful of the type she seems,
So careless of the single life;

That I, considering everywhere
Her secret meaning in her deeds,
And finding that of fifty seeds
She often brings but one to bear,

I **falter** where I firmly trod,
And falling with my weight of cares
Upon the great world's altar-stairs
That slope through darkness up to God,

I stretch lame hands of faith, and grope,
And gather dust and **chaff**, and call
To what I feel is Lord of all,
And faintly trust the larger hope.

106

Ring out, wild bells, to the wild sky,
The flying cloud, the frosty light:
The year is dying in the night;
Ring out, wild bells, and let him die.

Ring out the old, ring in the new,
Ring, happy bells, across the snow:
The year is going, let him go;
Ring out the false, ring in the true. **A**

Ring out the grief that saps the mind,
For those that here we see no more;
Ring out the feud of rich and poor,
Ring in **redress** to all mankind.

Ring out a slowly dying cause,
And ancient forms of party strife;
Ring in the nobler modes of life,
With sweeter manners, purer laws.

Ring out the want, the care, the sin,
The faithless coldness of the times;
Ring out, ring out my mournful rhymes,
But ring the fuller minstrel in.

Ring out false pride in place and blood,
The civic slander and the spite;
Ring in the love of truth and right,
Ring in the common love of good.

Ring out old shapes of foul disease;
Ring out the narrowing lust of gold;
Ring out the thousand wars of old,
Ring in the thousand years of peace.

Ring in the valiant man and free,
The larger heart, the kindlier hand;
Ring out the darkness of the land,
Ring in the Christ that is to be. **R**

130

Thy voice is on the rolling air;
I hear thee where the waters run;
Thou standest in the rising sun,
And in the setting thou art fair.

What art thou then? I cannot guess;
But though I seem in star and flower
To feel thee some diffusive power,
I do not therefore love thee less:

My love involves the love before;
My love is vaster passion now;
Though mixed with God and nature thou,
I seem to love thee more and more.

Far off thou art, but ever nigh;
I have thee still, and I rejoice;
I prosper, circled with thy voice;
I shall not lose thee though I die.

131

O living will that shalt endure
When all that seems shall suffer shock,
Rise in the spiritual rock,
Flow through our deeds and make them pure,

That we may lift from out of dust
A voice as unto him that hears,
A cry above the conquered years
To one that with us works, and trust,

With faith that comes of self-control,
The truths that never can be proved
Until we close[8] with all we loved,
And all we flow from, soul in soul. **R** **E**

8. *close:* to come together with

falter (fôl′tər) *intr.v.* To be unsteady in purpose or action, as from loss of courage or confidence; waver.

chaff (chăf) *n.* Trivial or worthless matter.

Sound Devices: Where can you see alliteration and assonance in stanza 1 of canto 106? How do stanzas 1 and 2 exemplify parallelism? What mood do these devices help create in canto 106 so far? **A**

redress (rĭ-drĕs′) *n.* Satisfaction for wrong or injury; reparation.

Compare/Contrast: What major transition in stanzas 1 and 2 creates the occasion for canto 106? List three other transitions Tennyson goes on to mention in the rest of the poem. **R**

Compare/Contrast: How does Tennyson's attitude in cantos 130–31 differ from his original state in canto 7? **R**

View of Death: What biblical or unbiblical religious tendencies does Tennyson seem to reflect in canto 131? **E**

The speaker in this dramatic monologue is Ulysses, hero of Homer's Greek epic, The Odyssey. *He has just returned to his kingdom of Ithaca after ten years fighting in the Trojan War and ten years wandering the Mediterranean, cursed by a goddess not to find his way home. Upon his return, he finds his wife Penelope besieged by suitors eager for her hand and control of Ithaca. With his now-grown son Telemachus (whom he knew only as a boy), Ulysses routs the suitors and retakes the kingdom. Finally, he is at peace. Or is he? The answer is the poem's central concern.*

VISUAL ANALYSIS
How does this portrait reflect the feelings of the speaker in "Ulysses"?

It little profits that an idle king,
By this still hearth, among these barren crags,
Matched with an aged wife, I mete and dole
Unequal laws unto a savage race,
That hoard, and sleep, and feed, and know not me.
I cannot rest from travel: I will drink
Life to the lees:[1] all times I have enjoyed
Greatly, have suffered greatly, both with those
That loved me, and alone; on shore, and when
Through scudding[2] drifts the rainy Hyades[3]
Vexed the dim sea: I am become a name; **A**
For always roaming with a hungry heart
Much have I seen and known; cities of men
And manners, climates, councils, governments,
Myself not least, but honored of them all;
And drunk delight of battle with my peers,
Far on the ringing plains of windy Troy.[4]
I am a part of all that I have met;
Yet all experience is an arch wherethrough
Gleams that untraveled world, whose margin fades
Forever and forever when I move.
How dull it is to pause, to make an end,

mete (mēt) *tr.v.* To distribute or allot.

Meter: What verse form is Tennyson using in this poem? How does "Ulysses" demonstrate the characteristics of this form? **A**

1. *to the lees:* to the very end of a cup, usually of wine
2. *scudding:* blown swiftly forward by the wind
3. *Hyades:* rain nymphs of Greek mythology
4. *Troy:* scene of the Trojan War, in which Ulysses fought for ten years, away from home

To rust unburnished,[5] not to shine in use!
As though to breathe were life. Life piled on life
Were all too little, and of one to me
Little remains: but every hour is saved
From that eternal silence, something more,
A bringer of new things; and vile it were
For some three suns to store and hoard myself,
And this gray spirit yearning in desire
To follow knowledge like a sinking star,
Beyond the utmost bound of human thought. R

This is my son, mine own Telemachus,
To whom I leave the scepter and the isle—
Well-loved of me, discerning to fulfill
This labor, by slow prudence to make mild
A rugged people, and through soft degrees
Subdue them to the useful and the good.
Most blameless is he, centered in the sphere
Of common duties, decent not to fail
In offices of tenderness, and pay
Meet adoration to my household gods,
When I am gone. He works his work, I mine.

There lies the port: the vessel puffs her sail:
There gloom[6] the dark broad seas. My mariners,
Souls that have toiled, and wrought, and thought with me— A
That ever with a frolic welcome took
The thunder and the sunshine, and opposed
Free hearts, free foreheads—you and I are old;
Old age hath yet his honor and his toil;
Death closes all: but something ere the end,
Some work of noble note, may yet be done, E
Not unbecoming men that strove with Gods.
The lights begin to twinkle from the rocks:
The long day wanes: the slow moon climbs: the deep
Moans round with many voices. Come, my friends,
'Tis not too late to seek a newer world.
Push off, and sitting well in order smite
The sounding furrows; for my purpose holds
To sail beyond the sunset, and the baths
Of all the western stars, until I die.
It may be that the gulfs will wash us down;
It may be we shall touch the Happy Isles,[7]
And see the great Achilles,[8] whom we knew.
Though much is taken, much abides: and though
We are not now that strength which in old days
Moved earth and heaven; that which we are, we are;
One equal temper of heroic hearts,
Made weak by time and fate, but strong in will
To strive, to seek, to find, and not to yield.

Compare/Contrast: What boundary does Ulysses wish to cross? What desire motivates his wish? R

Parallelism: Note the parallelism between lines 4 and 5 and lines 45 and 46. What does the parallelism reveal about Ulysses's priorities? A

View of Death: How does Ulysses view his own aging, decline, and eventual death? E

5. *unburnished:* unpolished
6. *gloom:* to be veiled in darkness
7. *Happy Isles:* Elysium, the Greek version of the afterlife reserved for the noble
8. *Achilles:* Trojan War hero who slew Hector

Crossing the Bar[1]

Sunset and evening star,
  And one clear call for me!
And may there be no moaning of the bar,[2]
  When I put out to sea,

But such a tide as moving seems asleep,[3]
  Too full for sound and foam,
When that which drew from out the boundless deep
  Turns again home.

Twilight and evening bell,
  And after that the dark!
And may there be no sadness of farewell,
  When I embark; **A**

For though from out our bourn[4] of time and place
  The flood may bear me far,
I hope to see my Pilot face to face
  When I have crossed the bar. **R**

1. *the bar:* border between the harbor and the ocean; a sandbar
2. *moaning of the bar:* beating of the tide on the sandbar
3. *a tide as moving seems asleep:* a tide that is headed out to sea and not crashing on the sandbar
4. *out our bourn:* out of our bounds

Parallelism: Identify one example of parallelism in the poem so far. What idea does this rhetorical device highlight? **A**

Compare/Contrast: What physical boundary is the speaker crossing? What might this boundary symbolize? **R**

VISUAL ANALYSIS
How does the atmosphere this painting projects match that of "Crossing the Bar"? How do you think the artist achieved this effect?

THINK AND DISCUSS

1. Identify one of the three poems as either an elegy or a dramatic monologue. Explain your answer.
2. In "Ulysses," how does the speaker's view of his youth contrast with his view of his old age?
3. In "Crossing the Bar," what is the speaker's expectation for what comes after he has crossed the bar?
4. Identify two lines from each poem that reference the theme of old age or death.
5. Identify and explain the major symbol in "Crossing the Bar."
6. How do images of voyaging and symbolic boundaries play a thematic part in "Ulysses" and "Crossing the Bar"?
7. Examine the different styles of *In Memoriam*. Which do you think is the most formal canto? Which is the least formal? Support your answer from the text.
8. What is a possible reason Tennyson has Ulysses speak in blank verse?
9. Choose one of the Tennyson selections and examine how parallelism emphasizes one of his messages.
10. Canto 106 of *In Memoriam* begs for the "ringing out" of many things. How do these "rung out" objects or actions reflect a Victorian mindset?
11. Describe Tennyson's attitude toward grief and death in the early cantos of *In Memoriam*. How has it changed by the poem's end? Support your answers from the text.
12. Evaluate the basis of Tennyson's renewed faith at the end of *In Memoriam* in a scriptural context.

Robert Browning (1812–89)

AT A GLANCE

- **1841–46** Published the volumes collectively entitled *Bells and Pomegranates*
- **1846** Married Elizabeth Barrett and moved to Italy
- **1855** Published *Men and Women*
- **1861** Returned to England after Elizabeth's death
- **1864** Published *Dramatis Personae*
- **1868–69** Published *The Ring and the Book*

Initially less well-known than his wife, the poet Elizabeth Barrett Browning (p. 517), Robert Browning came to be ranked as one of the greatest poets of his age. Though one of England's most learned poets, he did not linger in the abstract or elevated reaches of poetry, as Tennyson often did. Rather, Browning probed the shifting inner thoughts and feelings of his works' very human, very flawed narrators.

Beginnings

Browning was born in London to gifted parents. His mother, a talented pianist, had strong evangelical beliefs that influenced her son, while his father, a wealthy Bank of England clerk, loved art and scholarship. A brilliant child, Browning disliked classroom study and was educated primarily by his father and tutors. Fortunately, his father's library contained more than six thousand volumes, among which Robert's intellectual curiosity and imagination freely ranged.

Browning's parents were highly supportive of their son's literary aspirations and financed the publication of his initial plays and poetic volumes. Gaining little critical notice, Browning was forced to publish his next collection as a series of pamphlets. Known collectively as *Bells and Pomegranates*, these featured many poems in what became Browning's signature form: the dramatic monologue.

The dramatic monologue redirected Browning's interest in drama into poetry. Rather than representing characters' external actions in drama, he could represent their internal psychology through dialogue. In famous works such as "My Last Duchess," his speakers address an imagined audience in an informal, colloquial style and unwittingly reveal their inner natures. Frequently, they express unsavory motivations or self-contradictory thoughts or perceptions that readers are invited (through the resulting irony and dark humor) to judge. Browning polished this approach throughout his career, creating ever more vivid and realistically subtle characters.

Marriage

Bells and Pomegranates brought Browning to the attention of Elizabeth Barrett, then a well-known poet and homebound invalid. The two corresponded and fell in love. Because her controlling father wished none of his children to marry, they eloped to Italy in 1846. There Elizabeth recovered much of her health and gave birth to their son, Robert. The relationship mutually enriched the work of both poets. In fact, it was at Robert's encouragement that Elizabeth included her now famous love poetry in *Poems*. In 1855 Robert published *Men and Women* (dedicated to his wife), further exploring the dramatic monologue. When after several years of failing health Elizabeth died in Florence (1861), Browning returned permanently to England.

Literary Acclaim

After returning to London, Browning published more monologues in *Dramatis Personae* (1864), and for the first time earned widespread praise. Next, his portrayal of characters' complicated inner lives peaked in *The Ring and the Book* (1868–69), a murder mystery told in verse and from multiple perspectives. It quickly sold out and cemented his reputation. Browning spent the remainder of his life as a literary celebrity, even seeing the inauguration of The Browning Society (1881). By his death in 1889, his poetic reputation had outstripped Elizabeth's and rivaled Tennyson's. Influenced by his strongly Christian value system, his poetry presented a morally nuanced but optimistic view of humanity, refreshing to many. Twentieth-century poets would in turn value the vigorous but unconventional diction and innovative rhythms his monologues developed.

DID YOU KNOW ?

Browning died at his son's home in Venice, but his body was returned to England and buried in Westminster Abbey.

ANALYZE: *Dramatic Monologue, Persona, Plot*

Robert Browning is most famous for his use of **dramatic monologue** (p. 298), a poetic form in which a single character at a critical moment in his life speaks either to himself or to another character. In either case, readers are given only the speaker's words. Other characters' responses must be deduced from clues the speaker drops. This focus on the speaker is a distinctive of dramatic monologue, allowing the poet to explore the speaker's character as he or she unintentionally reveals it.

It is important to remember that the speaker of a dramatic monologue is a **persona**, a character the author creates and inhabits momentarily. The speaker may thus espouse viewpoints that the author disagrees with and subtly undercuts. For instance, he may contradict himself or use false reasoning on a point the author wants readers to question. As you read "Porphyria's Lover," pay close attention to such indirect characterization. What can you infer about the speaker's personality and state of mind? How does he develop in the poem? Is the author's tone accepting of his thoughts and actions or not? Finally, you may find it helpful to note the poem's compressed but distinct **plot** arc (p. 240), including an exposition, rising action, crisis, climax, falling action, and denouement. How might these coincide with the development of the persona character?

READ: *Annotate a Text*

For a complex poem such as "Porphyria's Lover," it may be helpful to annotate the text as you read it several times. For instance, on your first read through, note details early on that establish the **atmosphere** (p. 213) of the poem. What adjectives would you use to describe this mood? How might it foreshadow the poem's eventual end?

Additionally, tracking the subtleties of plot and characterization in "Porphyria's Lover" will be easier if you mark areas deserving further investigation as you read. Questions will undoubtedly spring to mind at times, the most obvious being *who* and *why* questions. Jot these in the text. As you reread, circle details from which you can draw inferences, ones that offer clues to flesh out the characterization of the speaker. Can you find a clear motive for his action? What does his thinking process unwittingly reveal about him? As you make these inferences, write them beside the text.

EVALUATE: *Aesthetic Effectiveness*

After you have read "Porphyria's Lover," ask yourself whether Browning is effective at engaging an audience. Do you find the poem compelling? Consider the tools Browning uses. He creates a definite atmosphere and a wildly imaginative plot to craft his portrait of the lover. Note how the plot structure builds and releases tension. Although there is not much external action, note the effective internal action. Why is the character so intriguing—so effective in pulling the audience in? Do the choice of genre—dramatic monologue—and the subsequent window into the mind of the persona contribute significantly to the audience's interest?

OBJECTIVES

- Annotate a text to support literary analysis.
- Determine the atmosphere and plot arc of a text.
- Analyze a dramatic monologue's development of a persona.
- Evaluate the artistic effectiveness of a text's use of literary elements.

VOCABULARY

sullen (sŭl′ən) *adj.* Gloomy or somber in tone, color, or portent.

vex (vĕks) *tr.v.* To irritate, bother, or frustrate.

warily (wâr′ə-lē) *adj.* Cautiously; carefully.

scorn (skôrn) *tr.v.* To consider or treat as contemptible or unworthy.

How do we DELUDE OURSELVES?

Have you ever listened to someone share details of an event or a conversation in which you had participated only to wonder where he got his version? If not intentionally lying, he had interpreted actions and words differently than you did. Do people ever see or hear only what they want to see or hear? Is self-delusion possible? When is it more likely? With a partner, discuss possible situations in which people might delude themselves.

VISUAL ANALYSIS
How does this portrait reflect the characters in "Porphyria's Lover" as they appear in stanzas 1–7? What do you expect will happen to these characters by the end of the poem?

Porphyria's Lover

1

The rain set early in tonight,
The sullen wind was soon awake,
It tore the elm-tops down for spite,
And did its worst to vex the lake,
I listened with heart fit to break. R

2

When glided in Porphyria; straight[1]
She shut the cold out and the storm,
And kneeled, and made the cheerless grate[2]
Blaze up, and all the cottage warm;
Which done, she rose, and from her form

3

Withdrew the dripping cloak and shawl,
And laid her soiled gloves by, untied
Her hat and let the damp hair fall,
And, last, she sat down by my side
And called me. When no voice replied,

4

She put my arm about her waist,
And made her smooth white shoulder bare,
And all her yellow hair displaced,
And, stooping, made my cheek lie there,
And spread, o'er all, her yellow hair,—

5

Murmuring how she loved me—she
Too weak, for all her heart's endeavor,
To set its struggling passion free
From pride, and vainer ties dissever,
And give herself to me forever. A

6

But passion sometimes would prevail,
Nor could tonight's gay feast restrain
A sudden thought of one so pale
For love of her, and all in vain:
So, she was come through wind and rain.

7

Be sure I looked up at her eyes
Happy and proud: at last I knew
Porphyria worshipped me; surprise
Made my heart swell, and still it grew
While I debated what to do. R

1. *straight:* immediately
2. *grate:* the fireplace

sullen (sŭl'ən) *adj.* Gloomy or somber in tone, color, or portent.

vex (vĕks) *tr.v.* To irritate, bother, or frustrate

Annotate a Text: Briefly describe the atmosphere Browning establishes in stanza 1. R

Persona: What picture of Porphyria do we get from the speaker? A

Annotate a Text: What questions do you have about the speaker's story so far? Does anything strike you as odd or out of place? R

8

That moment she was mine, mine fair,
  Perfectly pure and good: I found
A thing to do, and all her hair
  In one long yellow string I wound
Three times her little throat around,

9

And strangled her. No pain felt she;
  I am quite sure she felt no pain.
As a shut bud that holds a bee,
  I **warily** oped her lids: again
Laughed the blue eyes without a stain. **A**

warily (wâr′ə-lē) *adj.* Cautiously; carefully.

Plot/Persona: What important plot moment occurs in this stanza? What do readers realize about the persona at the same moment? **A**

10

And I untightened next the tress
  About her neck; her cheek once more
Blushed bright beneath my burning kiss:
  I propped her head up as before.
Only, this time my shoulder bore

11

Her head, which droops upon it still:
  The smiling rosy little head,
So glad it has its utmost will,
  That all it **scorned** at once is fled,
And I, its love, am gained instead!

scorn (skôrn) *tr.v.* To consider or treat as contemptible or unworthy.

12

Porphyria's love: she guessed not how
  Her darling one wish would be heard. **A**
And thus we sit together now.
  And all night long we have not stirred,
And yet God has not said a word!

Persona: What does the lover say about Porphyria? Is his opinion trustworthy? **A**

THINK AND DISCUSS

1. Identify the characteristics of a dramatic monologue. How does "Porphyria's Lover" qualify as an example?
2. Identify the atmosphere of "Porphyria's Lover" and analyze the way in which Browning creates it.
3. Identify the plot elements in "Porphyria's Lover" stanza by stanza.
4. Trace the development of the persona throughout "Porphyria's Lover."
5. Conjecture the motive in Porphyria's murder based on textual evidence.
6. What do you think the speaker means by the final line? What might Browning have meant by it?
7. Evaluate the aesthetic effectiveness of "Porphyria's Lover." How do genre and persona contribute in this regard in the poem?

Elizabeth Barrett Browning (1806–61)

Elizabeth Barrett Browning was a poet, literary critic, and translator whose poetry was widely celebrated during the Victorian Age. Although her reputation as a poet has since been eclipsed by that of her husband, Robert Browning, Elizabeth Barrett Browning (or "EBB," her favorite pen name) remains profoundly influential, having inspired authors such as George Eliot, Emily Dickinson, and Virginia Woolf.

Elizabeth Barrett was born in Durham into a family of wealthy landowners. She first wrote poetry at the age of four. At fifteen she began to experience the health problems that would dog her for the rest of her life. Despite being an invalid, she pursued a literary career, and her first mature book of poetry, *The Seraphim and Other Poems*, was published to acclaim in 1838.

After moving with her family to London in 1841, Elizabeth Barrett published *Poems* (1844), which was met with widespread enthusiasm. Included in the volume were several lines in praise of the young poet Robert Browning. He in turn wrote her a letter professing his love for her poetry and her person. After a lengthy correspondence and a dramatic courtship (commemorated in Elizabeth's cycle *Sonnets from the Portuguese*), the two eloped in 1846 to Italy, the place they would call home for the rest of her life.

In Italy Browning enjoyed family life, giving birth to her only son, Robert, in 1849. At the same time, she continued to pursue her poetic vocation. In 1856 she published *Aurora Leigh*, an epic verse-form novel that details a woman's struggle to succeed as a writer while addressing both class inequality and "the woman question" (p. 503) on issues such as education and vocation. *Aurora Leigh* was highly controversial but also incredibly successful, inspiring many women to follow in her footsteps. Much of Browning's other poetry from this period deals with political questions such as the abolition of American slavery and Italian reunification. By the end of the decade, however, her health was failing, and she died in Florence in 1861.

BEFORE READING

ANALYZE: *Imagery, Figurative Language, Theme*

Sonnet 43 relates a simple **theme**, love, but explores that theme with great richness and depth. Browning begins with a question and then answers it with a series of images and figurative expressions. Look for examples of **simile**, **metaphor**, and **hyperbole** (p. 240) in her answer. Also, note the combination of concrete **images** and abstract concepts she invokes. What do they together suggest about the scope of her love? Finally, how might your knowledge of Browning's life add to your understanding of some of the images she uses?

READ: *Annotate a Text*

To track the thematic development of Sonnet 43, annotate its imagery and structure. Circle each new image, and note how similar images are clustered and often form contrasts. Highlight these in different colors. How does the poem structure its content? For example, the images progress from present, to past, to future. Bracket these phases. Determine which sonnet structure Browning used, Italian or English (p. 185). How does her choice support the poem's developing theme?

CREATE: *Compare Texts*

Select one of the Renaissance sonnets you studied (pp. 187–91, 200) and compare it to Sonnet 43. What similarities and differences do you see? How does Browning echo these poems in some of her diction? Whom does each speaker address? How do the poems differ in attitude toward or message about love? Do you think Browning's gender made a difference in how she approached her theme? Which poem do you prefer? Why?

OBJECTIVES

- Annotate a text to identify its imagery and structure.
- Analyze how a text's imagery and figurative language develop its theme.
- Analyze how a text's structure promotes its theme.
- Compare the theme and literary elements of two sonnets.

How do you **MEASURE LOVE?**

Sonnet 43

Undoubtedly Browning's best-known work today, Sonnet 43 almost did not make it into print. The sonnet sequence from which it hails, Sonnets from the Portuguese, *was written while Browning was courted by her future husband, Robert. In her opinion, the poems revealed far too much of her feelings to be published for the public. Robert nonetheless convinced her to publish the work, but under a title that framed the poems as translations. And thus English poetry gained one of its most beloved lyrics on romantic love.*

How do I love thee? Let me count the ways.
I love thee to the depth and breadth and height
My soul can reach, when feeling out of sight
For the ends of Being and ideal Grace.
I love thee to the level of every day's
Most quiet need, by sun and candlelight.
I love thee freely, as men strive for Right;
I love thee purely, as they turn from Praise. **A**
I love thee with the passion put to use
In my old griefs, and with my childhood's faith.
I love thee with a love I seemed to lose
With my lost saints,—I love thee with the breath,
Smiles, tears, of all my life!—and, if God choose,
I shall but love thee better after death. **R**

Figurative Language: Identify an example of simile, metaphor, or hyperbole in lines 1–8. **A**

Annotate a Text: Which lines contain images that convey present, past, and future (p. 517)? **R**

THINK AND DISCUSS

1. How many "ways" of loving does the speaker count?
2. Explain what Browning means by the comparisons she draws to her past self in the images of lines 9–12b.
3. Identify and interpret an example of simile, of metaphor, and of hyperbole in the poem.
4. What does the wide-flung nature of the images in the poem suggest about the speaker's love?
5. Which sonnet form does Browning use? Justify your answer.
6. How does the skill and beauty with which this sonnet is constructed help communicate its truth and spur its readers to goodness?
7. Write a paragraph comparing Browning's sonnet with one of the Renaissance sonnets you studied. Consult the Create paragraph on page 517 for further ideas.

Thomas Carlyle (1795–1881)

AT A GLANCE

- **1818** Moved to Edinburgh to begin his literary career
- **1833–34** *Sartor Resartus* published in *Fraser's Magazine*
- **1837** Published *French Revolution*
- **1865** Completed a six-volume history of Frederick the Great of Prussia

Thomas Carlyle was a Scottish historian and essayist whose unique style and philosophy exerted tremendous influence over Victorian society. Although Carlyle began his adult life making incisive critiques of contemporary society, his outlook became increasingly authoritarian as he aged. Perhaps his greatest influence can be found in his personal relationships with countless British intellectuals.

DID YOU KNOW

Thinkers of the day flocked to the Carlyle home to speak with Thomas and Jane, both delightful conversationalists.

Unsettled Youth

Carlyle was born in rural Dumfriesshire, Scotland, into a family of devout, hard-working Calvinists. His parents encouraged the young Thomas to prepare for the ministry, first sending him to Annan Academy in Dumfries in 1805 and then to the University of Edinburgh in 1809 (he left in 1814 without taking a degree). But his studies unsettled his orthodox beliefs, and he became an atheist.

In 1818 Carlyle moved to Edinburgh to pursue a literary career, where he spent several desperate years in poor living conditions. There he experienced a religious conversion (later dramatized in his experimental novel *Sartor Resartus*) in which he turned away from materialism to a transcendental, deistic religion. In Edinburgh he also began to study German literature, which he introduced to the British public through a series of translations.

Radical Essayist

In 1826 he married Jane Welsh, with whom he would enjoy a fulfilling if sometimes difficult marriage. Through 1834 the two lived in rural Scotland while Carlyle wrote essays such as the influential "Signs of the Times," which defines the dawning Victorian era as the "Age of Machinery" (1829). He also worked on his masterpiece, *Sartor Resartus* (Latin for "the tailor retailored"). The novel, which presents itself as an English translation of an obscure German philosophical work, combines elements of personal autobiography with philosophical and scholarly satire in a searing, idiosyncratic prose. Appearing first in serial form throughout 1833–34, it was published as a complete novel in 1836.

Meanwhile, the Carlyles had moved to London in 1834, and Carlyle began work on *The French Revolution: A History*. Published in 1837, the history gave him instant financial and literary success. Now a celebrity, he continued weighing in on political subjects, famously outlining in *Chartism* (1840) the "Condition of England Question." The year 1841 saw the publication of his lectures *On Heroes*, in which he argues that only "great men" give shape to history, and that "hero worship" by their inferiors is not only natural but proper.

Traditionalist Historian

Implicit in *On Heroes*, and increasingly articulated in other works, is a belief that democracy is doomed to fail and that only government by great men can sustain civilization. This traditionalist attitude alienated some of Carlyle's contemporaries, but many also felt an affinity with his portrait of a European society verging on total collapse. In 1851 he devoted his life to writing a biography of Frederick the Great of Prussia, eventually producing a brilliant if somewhat hagiographic six-volume work (published from 1858–65). His efforts nearly broke his health and did break that of Jane, who died of heart failure in 1866. Carlyle was devastated, and he never recovered his literary voice. He died in London in 1881 and was buried at his birthplace.

In his time, Carlyle was both a polarizing figure and a profound influence. Among his vast set of friends were Ralph Waldo Emerson, the two Browning poets, and the art critic John Ruskin. His prose style inspired countless imitators and remains captivating to this day.

ANALYZE: *Argumentative Essay*

The Industrial Revolution brought many obvious and tangible benefits for British society; however, the problems that came with it had, by Carlyle's time, produced a subtle but pervasive anxiety about England's state of affairs. Concerned, Carlyle spoke and wrote to the public, seeking to diagnose the source of these problems and advocate for change. The two selections included here are both **essays**, brief nonfiction prose compositions that explore a subject or argue for a thesis regarding a particular subject. Both are also **argumentative** (p. 143), seeking to convince audiences to accept Carlyle's point of view.

As you read, look for Carlyle's main point (his thesis) and the ways in which he supports his position. Specifically, note how he develops his ideas using two main approaches. First, he broadly organizes both essays around a contrast between two ways of perceiving life and social change. Second, he frequently uses real-life examples to flesh out his ideas. These are especially evident in "The Condition of England." As you read each essay, observe the big ideas he discusses. What does he have to say about the current culture, both good and bad? What are his main supporting arguments? How do the paragraphs develop and prove them?

READ: *Paraphrase and Summarize*

Carlyle's content and style are very dense and complex. To help yourself understand his ideas and follow his train of thought, use the strategies of paraphrasing and summarizing. When you encounter a complicated sentence or highly developed thought, use paraphrasing to untangle syntax or restate ideas in relatable terms. If you start losing track of Carlyle's train of thought, reduce chunks of his thought to simpler, summary statements. Summarizing each paragraph, for instance, can help you more easily identify his main arguments and their supports.

Carlyle's prose is also very carefully crafted to highlight his ideas. Reading his work aloud may allow you to hear the emphasis he intentionally creates through rhythmic cadences. Similarly, it can draw attention to **rhetorical devices**, such as anaphora, parallelism, alliteration, allusion, and rhetorical questions. What ideas does he emphasize through such techniques?

EVALUATE: *Carlyle's Social Critique*

Carlyle lived at a time when the industrial society had brought about significant transformations in the way people lived. Many people lived with better clothing, housing, and food than had any previously in human history. Carlyle recognized these material benefits of industrialization. But his observations of British culture led him to conclude that some problems originating in the spirit had become more prevalent as well. The industrial society had become "mechanical in head and in heart." What does Carlyle mean by this phrase? How should a Christian think about his assessment of the Industrial Age? Is he correct in noting both benefits and problems in the Industrial Revolution (Gen. 1:28; 11:3–6)? Is he correct to severely criticize society for becoming "mechanical in head and in heart" (Job 28:9–15, 28; Psalm 20:7; Mark 7:21–23)?

OBJECTIVES

- Identify characteristics of essay in a text.
- Summarize or paraphrase a text to understand it.
- Analyze the thesis, main points, and supporting details of a text's argument.
- Evaluate an author's critique of social attitudes.

VOCABULARY

multifarious (mŭl′tə-fâr′ē-əs) *adj.* Having great variety; diverse.

fiat (fē′ət) *n.* An arbitrary order or decree.

arraign (ə-rān′) *tr.v. Law* To call (an accused person) before a criminal court to hear and answer the charge made against him or her.

plethoric (plĕ-thôr′ĭk) *adj.* Excessive in quantity; superabundant.

artisan (är′tĭ-zən) *n.* A person skilled in making a product by hand.

apparatus (ăp′ə-răt′əs) *n.pl.* An integrated group of materials or devices used for a particular purpose.

What can WEALTH *and* TECHNOLOGY *get us?*

How has technology affected our lives? Our education, our vocations, our transportation, our entertainment—practically every part of daily life is in some way affected by industry and technology. What good things have come out of these advances? What unintended negative effects have accompanied these conveniences? With a partner, brainstorm what results can come from the conveniences of wealth and technology.

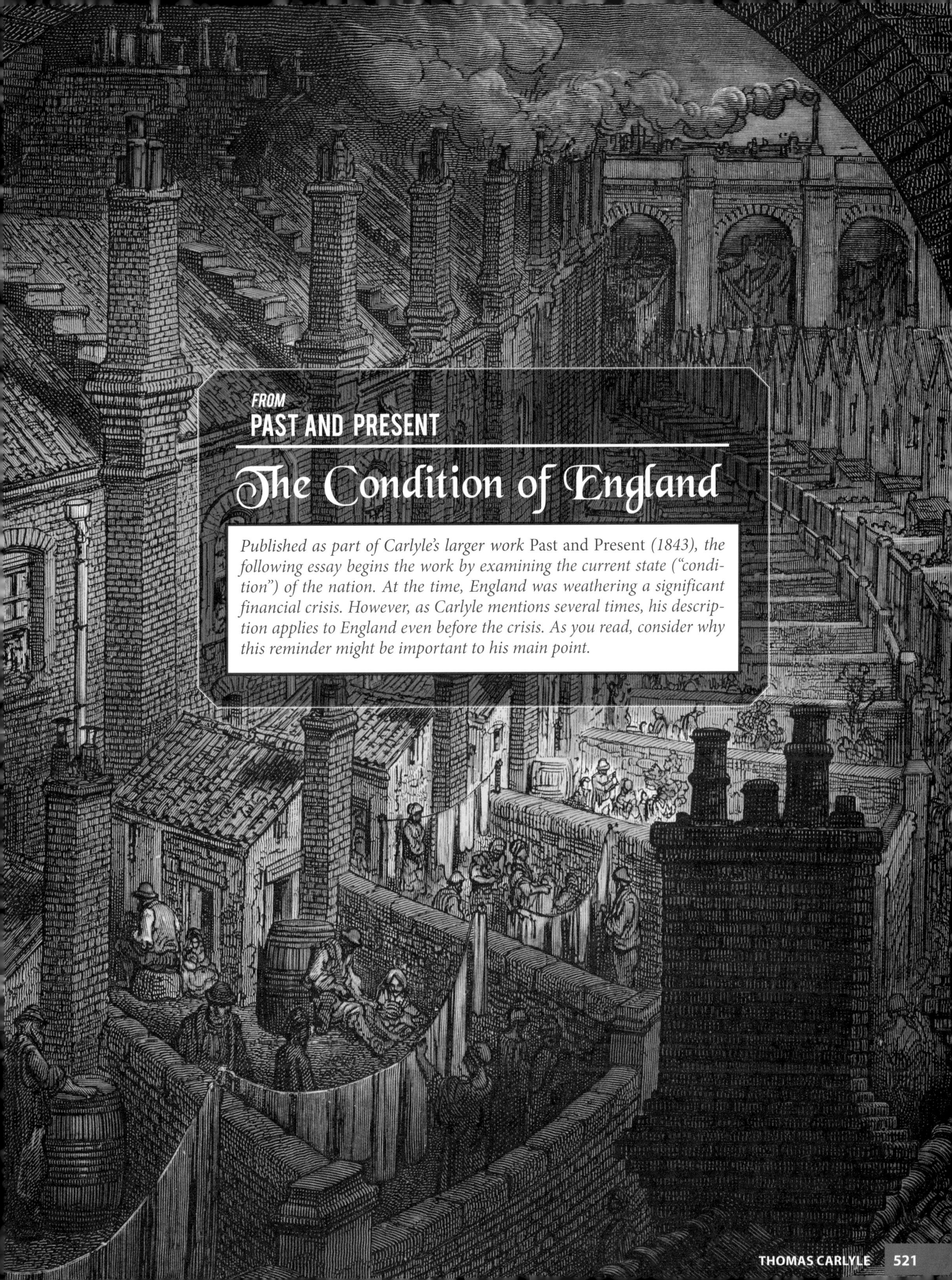

FROM
PAST AND PRESENT

The Condition of England

Published as part of Carlyle's larger work Past and Present *(1843), the following essay begins the work by examining the current state ("condition") of the nation. At the time, England was weathering a significant financial crisis. However, as Carlyle mentions several times, his description applies to England even before the crisis. As you read, consider why this reminder might be important to his main point.*

The condition of England, on which many pamphlets are now in the course of publication, and many thoughts unpublished are going on in every reflective head, is justly regarded as one of the most ominous, and withal one of the strangest, ever seen in this world. England is full of wealth, of **multifarious** produce, supply for human want in every kind; yet England is dying of inanition.[1] With unabated bounty the land of England blooms and grows; waving with yellow harvests; thick-studded with workshops, industrial implements, with fifteen millions of workers, understood to be the strongest, the cunningest and the willingest our earth ever had; these men are here; the work they have done, the fruit they have realized is here, abundant, exuberant on every hand of us: and behold, some baleful **fiat** as of enchantment has gone forth, saying, "Touch it not, ye workers, ye master-workers, ye master-idlers; none of you can touch it, no man of you shall be the better for it; this is enchanted fruit!" On the poor workers such fiat falls first, in its rudest shape; but on the rich master-workers too it falls; neither can the rich master-idlers, nor any richest or highest man escape, but all are like to be brought low with it, and made "poor" enough, in the money sense or a far fataler one. R

multifarious (mŭl′tə-fâr′ē-əs) *adj.* Having great variety; diverse.

fiat (fē′ət) *n.* An arbitrary order or decree.

Summarize: What is the state of England according to Carlyle? R

Of these successful skillful workers some two millions, it is now counted, sit in workhouses, Poor-Law prisons; or have "out-door relief" flung over the wall to them, the workhouse Bastille[2] being filled to bursting, and the strong Poor Law broken asunder by a stronger. They sit there, these many months now; their hope of deliverance as yet small. In workhouses, pleasantly so-named, because work cannot be done in them. Twelve hundred thousand workers in England alone; their cunning right-hand lamed, lying idle in their sorrowful bosom; their hopes, outlooks, share of this fair world, shut in by narrow walls. They sit there, pent up, as in a kind of horrid enchantment; glad to be imprisoned and enchanted, that they may not perish starved. The picturesque tourist, in a sunny autumn day, through this bounteous realm of England, descries[3] the union workhouse on his path. "Passing by the workhouse of St. Ives in Huntingdonshire, on a bright day last autumn," says the picturesque tourist, "I saw sitting on wooden benches, in front of their Bastille and within their ring-wall and its railings, some half hundred or more of these men. Tall robust figures, young mostly or of middle age; of honest countenance, many of them thoughtful and even intelligent-looking men. They sat there, near by one another; but in a kind of torpor,[4] especially in a silence, which was very striking. In silence: for, alas, what word was to be said? An Earth all lying round, crying, 'Come and till me, come and reap me'; yet we here sit enchanted! In the eyes and brows of these men hung the gloomiest expression, not of anger, but of grief and shame and manifold[5] inarticulate distress and weariness; they returned my glance with a glance that seemed to say, 'Do not look at us. We sit enchanted here, we know not why. The sun shines and the Earth calls; and, by the governing powers and impotences of this England, we are forbidden to obey. It is impossible, they tell us!' There was something that reminded me of Dante's hell[6] in the look of all this; and I rode swiftly away." R

Summarize: What does Carlyle notice about both the material and the spiritual state of those in England's work houses? R

1. *inanition:* malnutrition
2. *Poor Law prisons . . . Bastille:* As a result of the Poor Law Amendment Act of 1834, "Outdoor Relief," or government assistance, was mostly eliminated to prevent its abuse; government assistance for the poor still capable of working was limited to minimal support in Union workhouses only, in which the poor received basic provisions of food, clothing, and living quarters comparable to prisons. The Poor Law prisons were nicknamed the Bastille because of their resemblance to the fortress-like French prison.
3. *descries:* observes
4. *torpor:* dull stupor
5. *manifold:* diverse, plentiful
6. *Dante's hell:* an allusion to the *Inferno*, the classic Renaissance work by Italian poet Dante Alighieri, in which Dante describes nine circles of hell with individuals trapped and appropriately tormented for their sins

Sarin Images/Granger, NYC

So many hundred thousands sit in workhouses: and other hundred thousands have not yet got even workhouses; and in thrifty Scotland itself, in Glasgow or Edinburgh City, in their dark lanes, hidden from all but the eye of God, and of rare benevolence the minister of God, there are scenes of woe and destitution and desolation, such as, one may hope, the sun never saw before in the most barbarous regions where men dwelt. Competent witnesses, the brave and humane Dr. Alison,[7] who speaks what he knows, whose noble healing art in his charitable hands becomes once more a truly sacred one, report these things for us: these things are not of this year, or of last year, have no reference to our present state of commercial stagnation, but only to the common state. Not in sharp fever-fits, but in chronic gangrene[8] of this kind is Scotland suffering. A poor law, any and every poor law, it may be observed, is but a temporary measure; an anodyne,[9] not a remedy: rich and poor, when once the naked facts of their condition have come into collision, cannot long subsist together on a mere poor law. True enough: and yet, human beings cannot be left to die! Scotland too, till something better come, must have a Poor Law, if Scotland is not to be a byword among the nations. O, what a waste is there; of noble and thrice-noble national virtues; peasant Stoicisms,[10] Heroisms; valiant manful habits, soul of a nation's worth, which all the metal of Potosi[11] cannot purchase back; to which the metal of Potosi, and all you can buy with *it*, is dross and dust! ☑

Reading Check: How is the condition of the poor in Scotland worse than in England? ☑

Why dwell on this aspect of the matter? It is too indisputable, not doubtful now to anyone. Descend where you will into the lower class, in town or country, by what avenue you will, by factory inquiries, agricultural inquiries, by revenue returns, by mining-laborer committees, by opening your own eyes and looking, the same sorrowful result discloses itself: you have to admit that the working body of this rich English nation has sunk or is fast sinking into a state, to which, all sides of it considered, there was literally never any parallel. At Stockport Assizes,[12] and this too has no reference to the present state of trade, being of date prior to that, a mother and a father are **arraigned** and found guilty of poisoning three of their children, to defraud a "burial-society" of some £3 8*s*.[13] due on the death of each child: they are arraigned, found guilty; and the official authorities, it is whispered, hint that perhaps the case is not solitary, that perhaps you had better not probe farther into that department of things. . . . A

arraign (ə-rān′) *tr.v. Law* To call (an accused person) before a criminal court to hear and answer the charge made against him or her.

Argumentation: How do this and the previous two paragraphs' contents serve as examples of Carlyle's main idea in the essay's first paragraph? A

7. *Dr. Alison:* the Scottish writer of *Observations on the Management of the Poor in Scotland*; advocate for immunizations and government assistance for the poor
8. *gangrene:* medical condition in which tissue dies and may need to be removed; potentially fatal if untreated
9. *anodyne:* that which alleviates discomfort
10. *Stoicisms:* purely rational philosophy that disregards emotion
11. *Potosi:* Bolivian capital known for its huge silver deposit
12. *Stockport Assizes:* court which handled cases too difficult for the local county courts
13. *£3 8s:* an abbreviation for "three pounds, eight shillings"

Nor are they of the St. Ives workhouses, of the Glasgow lanes, and Stockport cellars, the only unblessed among us. This successful industry of England, with its **plethoric** wealth, has as yet made nobody rich; it is an enchanted wealth, and belongs yet to nobody. We might ask, Which of us has it enriched? We can spend thousands where we once spent hundreds; but can purchase nothing good with them. In poor and rich, instead of noble thrift and plenty, there is idle luxury alternating with mean scarcity and inability. We have sumptuous garnitures[14] for our life, but have forgotten to *live* in the middle of them. It is an enchanted wealth; no man of us can yet touch it. The class of men who feel that they are truly better off by means of it, let them give us their name! **A**

plethoric (plĕ-thôr′ĭk) *adj.* Excessive in quantity; superabundant.

Argumentation: Can you determine Carlyle's thesis for the essay yet? What do you think it is? **A**

Many men eat finer cookery, drink dearer liquors, with what advantage they can report, and their doctors can: but in the heart of them, if we go out of the dyspeptic[15] stomach, what increase of blessedness is there? Are they better, beautifuler, stronger, braver? Are they even what they call "happier"? Do they look with satisfaction on more things and human faces in this God's-earth; do more things and human faces look with satisfaction on them? Not so. Human faces gloom discordantly, disloyally on one another. Things, if it be not mere cotton and iron things, are growing disobedient to man. The master worker is enchanted, for the present, like his workhouse workman; clamors, in vain hitherto, for a very simple sort of "liberty": the liberty "to buy where he finds it cheapest, to sell where he finds it dearest." With guineas jingling in every pocket, he was no whit richer; but now, the very guineas threatening to vanish, he feels that he is poor indeed. Poor master worker! And the master unworker, is not he in a still fataler situation? Pausing amid his game preserves, with awful[16] eye, as he well may! Coercing fifty-pound tenants; coercing, bribing, cajoling; "doing what he likes with his own." His mouth full of loud futilities, and arguments to prove the excellence of his Corn Law;[17] and in his heart the blackest misgiving, a desperate half-consciousness that his excellent Corn Law is *in*defensible, that his loud arguments for it are of a kind to strike men too literally *dumb*.

To whom, then, is this wealth of England wealth? Who is it that it blesses; makes happier, wiser, beautifuler, in any way better? Who has got hold of it, to make it fetch and carry for him, like a true servant, not like a false mock-servant; to do him any real service whatsoever? As yet no one. We have more riches than any nation ever had before; we have less good of them than any nation ever had before. Our successful industry is hitherto unsuccessful; a strange success, if we stop here! In the midst of plethoric plenty, the people perish; with gold walls, and full barns, no man feels himself safe or satisfied. Workers, master workers, unworkers, all men, come to a pause; stand fixed, and cannot farther. Fatal paralysis spreading inwards, from the extremities, in St. Ives workhouses, in Stockport cellars, through all limbs, as if towards the heart itself. Have we actually got enchanted, then; accursed by some god? **R**

Rhetorical Devices: What rhetorical devices are evident in this paragraph? **R**

Midas longed for gold, and insulted the Olympians. He got gold, so that whatsoever he touched became gold, and he, with his long ears, was little the better for it. Midas had misjudged the celestial music-tones; Midas had insulted Apollo and the gods: the gods gave him his wish, and a pair of long ears,[18] which also were a good appendage to it. What a truth in these old fables! **A**

Argumentation: How does Carlyle's example of Midas support his main argument? **A**

14. *garnitures:* embellishments
15. *dyspeptic:* irritable
16. *awful:* watchful; poachers were harshly punished.
17. *Corn Law:* From 1815–46, there was a series of protectionist tariffs that limited grain imports and thus increased the cost of food.
18. *long ears:* In Greek mythology, Midas regretted the fulfillment of his wish for the golden touch. Because he preferred Pan's music to Apollo's, he was given the ears of a donkey.

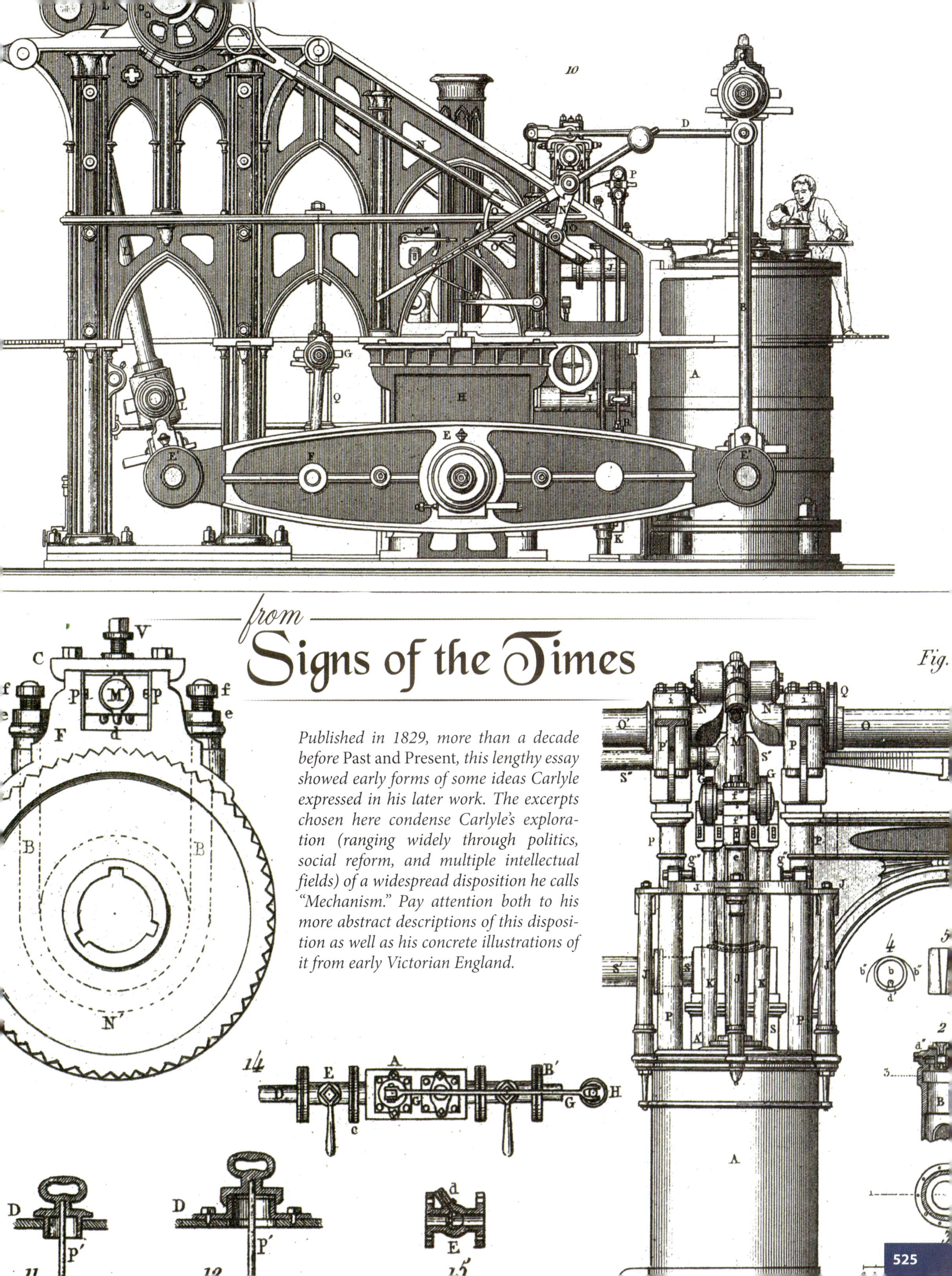

from

Signs of the Times

Published in 1829, more than a decade before Past and Present, *this lengthy essay showed early forms of some ideas Carlyle expressed in his later work. The excerpts chosen here condense Carlyle's exploration (ranging widely through politics, social reform, and multiple intellectual fields) of a widespread disposition he calls "Mechanism." Pay attention both to his more abstract descriptions of this disposition as well as his concrete illustrations of it from early Victorian England.*

Were we required to characterize this age of ours by any single epithet, we should be tempted to call it, not an Heroical, Devotional, Philosophical, or Moral age, but, above all others, the Mechanical Age. It is the Age of Machinery, in every outward and inward sense of that word; the age which, with its whole undivided might, forwards, teaches, and practices the great art of adopting means to ends. Nothing is now done directly, or by hand; all is by rule and calculated contrivance. For the simplest operation, some helps and accompaniments, some cunning, abbreviating process is in readiness. Our old modes of exertion are all discredited, and thrown aside. On every hand, the living **artisan** is driven from his workshop, to make room for a speedier, inanimate one. The shuttle[1] drops from the fingers of the weaver, and falls into iron fingers that ply it faster. The sailor furls his sail, and lays down his oar, and bids a strong, unwearied servant, on vaporous wings, bear him through the waters. Men have crossed oceans by steam; the Birmingham fire-king[2] has visited the fabulous East; and the genius of the Cape, were there any Camoens now to sing it, has again been alarmed, and with far stranger thunders than Gama's.[3] There is no end to machinery. Even the horse is stripped of his harness, and finds a fleet fire-horse yoked in his stead. Nay, we have an artist that hatches chickens by steam; the very brood-hen is to be superseded! For all earthly, and for some unearthly purposes, we have machines and mechanic furtherances; for mincing our cabbages; for casting us into magnetic sleep. We remove mountains, and make seas our smooth highway; nothing can resist us. We war with rude nature; and, by our resistless engines, come off always victorious, and loaded with spoils.

What wonderful accessions[4] have thus been made, and are still making, to the physical power of mankind; how much better fed, clothed, lodged, and, in all outward respects, accommodated, men now are, or might be, by a given quantity of labor, is a grateful reflection which forces itself on every one. What changes, too, this addition of power is introducing into the social system; how wealth has more and more increased, and at the same time gathered itself more and more into masses, strangely altering the old relations, and increasing the distance between the rich and the poor, will be a question for political economists, and a much more complex and important one than any they have yet engaged with. But leaving these matters for the present, let us observe how the mechanical genius of our time has diffused itself into quite other provinces. Not the external and physical alone is now managed by machinery, but the internal and spiritual also. Here, too, nothing follows its spontaneous course, nothing is left to be accomplished by old, natural methods. Everything has its cunningly devised implements, its pre-established **apparatus**; it is not done by hand, but by machinery. . . .

These things, which we state lightly enough here, are yet of deep import, and indicate a mighty change in our whole manner of existence. For the same habit regulates not our modes of action alone, but our modes of thought and feeling. Men are grown mechanical in head and in heart, as well as in hand.

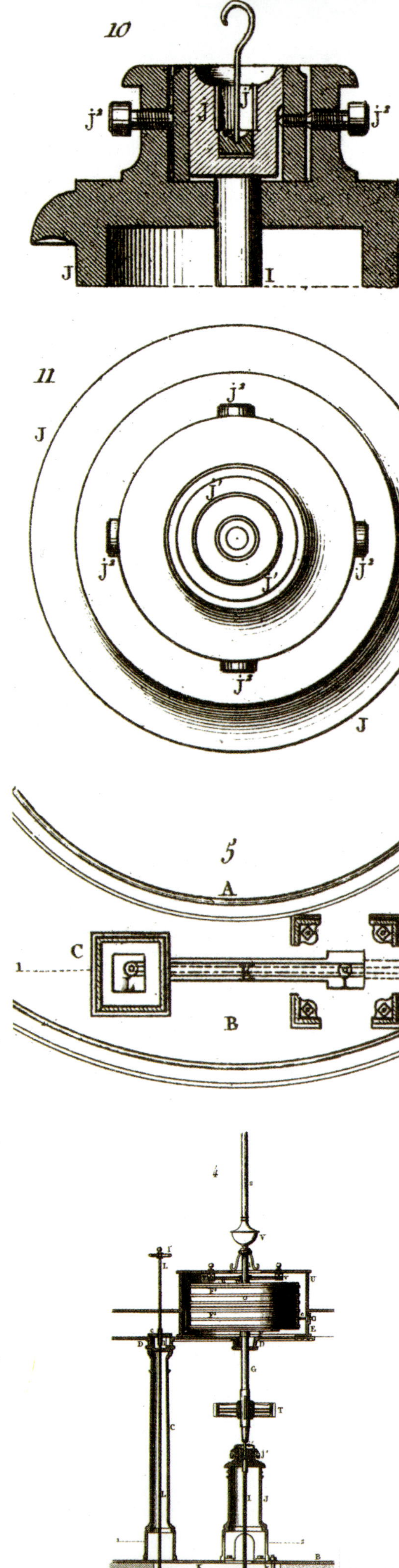

1. *shuttle:* weaving tool for moving the waft thread through the warp threads
2. *Birmingham fire-king:* Birmingham, a city of major industrial growth, was spreading ideas such as the use of steam and the steamship itself (the fire-king) to less developed areas.
3. *Camoens . . . Gama's:* Luís Vaz de Camões, a Portuguese poet, wrote about Portuguese explorer Vasco de Gama, the first to sail around Cape Verde to India.
4. *accessions:* enrichments

artisan (är′tĭ-zən) *n.* A person skilled in making a product by hand.

apparatus (ăp′ə-răt′əs) *n.pl.* An integrated group of materials or devices used for a particular purpose.

They have lost faith in individual endeavour, and in natural force, of any kind. Not for internal perfection, but for external combinations and arrangements, for institutions, constitutions, for mechanism of one sort or other, do they hope and struggle. Their whole efforts, attachments, opinions, turn on mechanism, and are of a mechanical character.

We may trace this tendency, we think, very distinctly, in all the great manifestations of our time; in its intellectual aspect, the studies it most favors, and its manner of conducting them; in its practical aspects, its politics, arts, religion, morals; in the whole sources, and throughout the whole currents, of its spiritual, no less than its material activity.

Consider, for example, the state of Science generally, in Europe, at this period. It is admitted, on all sides, that the Metaphysical and Moral Sciences are falling into decay, while the Physical are engrossing, every day, more respect and attention. In most of the European nations, there is now no such thing as a Science of Mind; only more or less advancement in the general science, or the special sciences, of matter. . . . In no nation but Germany has any decisive effort been made in psychological science; not to speak of any decisive result. The science of the age, in short, is physical, chemical, physiological, and, in all shapes, mechanical. . . .

. . . The metaphysical philosophy of this last inquirer[5] is certainly no shadowy or unsubstantial one. He fairly lays open our moral structure with his dissecting-knives and real metal probes; and exhibits it to the inspection of mankind, by Leuwenhoek microscopes and inflation with the anatomical blowpipe.[6] Thought, he is inclined to hold, is still secreted by the brain; but then Poetry and Religion (and it is really worth knowing) are "a product of the smaller intestines!" We have the greatest admiration for this learned doctor: with what scientific stoicism he walks through the land of wonders, unwondering; like a wise man through some huge, gaudy, imposing Vauxhall,[7] whose fire-works, cascades, and symphonies, the vulgar may enjoy and believe in,—but where he finds nothing real but the saltpetre, pasteboard, and catgut.[8] His book may be regarded as the ultimatum[9] of mechanical metaphysics in our time. . . .

This condition of the two great departments of knowledge—the outward, cultivated exclusively on mechanical principles; the inward finally abandoned, because, cultivated on such principles, it is found to yield no result—sufficiently indicates the intellectual bias of our time, its all-pervading disposition towards that line of inquiry. In fact, an inward persuasion has long been diffusing itself, and now and then even comes to utterance, that, except the external, there are no true sciences; that to the inward world (if there be any) our only conceivable road is through the outward; that, in short, what cannot be investigated and understood mechanically, cannot be investigated and understood at all. . . .

To speak a little pedantically,[10] there is a science of *dynamics* in man's fortunes and nature, as well as of *mechanics*. There is a science which treats of,

5. *this last inquirer:* a Dr. Cabanis, whose ideas Carlyle proceeds to satirize
6. *Leuwenhoek . . . blowpipe:* instruments used in biological dissections
7. *Vauxhall:* Vauxhall Gardens, a famous pleasure garden in London featuring everything from plays to concerts to dancing and food
8. *saltpetre . . . catgut:* specific materials used in these entertainments
9. *ultimatum:* "the extreme limit" (*OED*)
10. *pendantically:* scholarly in a showy way

Paraphrase: In your own words, explain what Carlyle means by the word *machinery* or *mechanism*.

Rhetorical Devices: Identify two rhetorical devices in this paragraph.

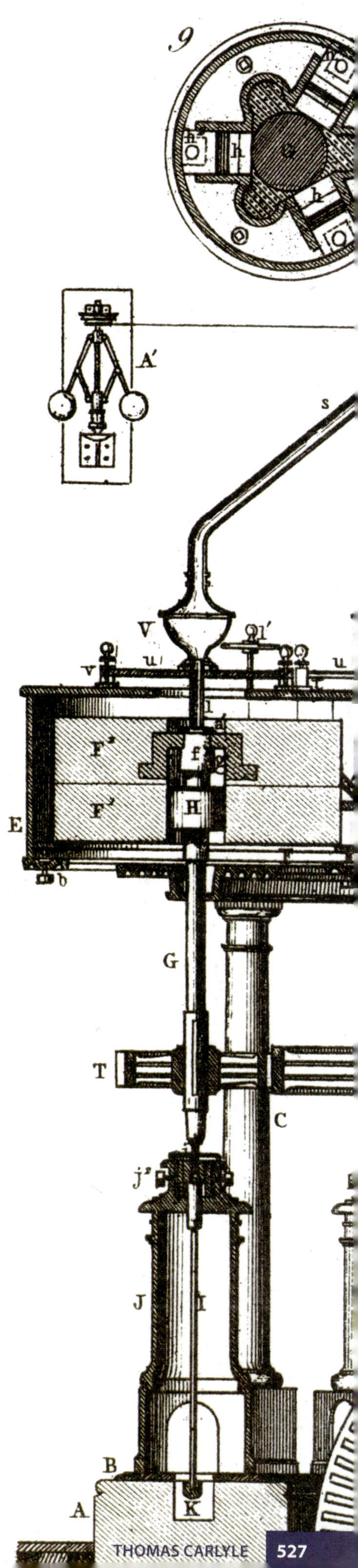

and practically addresses, the primary, unmodified forces and energies of man, the mysterious springs of love, and fear, and wonder, of enthusiasm, poetry, religion, all which have a truly vital and *infinite* character; as well as a science which practically addresses the finite, modified developments of these, when they take the shape of immediate "motives," as hope of reward, or as fear of punishment. **R**

Now it is certain, that in former times the wise men, the enlightened lovers of their kind, who appeared generally as moralists, poets, or priests, did, without neglecting the mechanical province, deal chiefly with the dynamical; applying themselves chiefly to regulate, increase, and purify the inward primary powers of man; and fancying that herein lay the main difficulty, and the best service they could undertake. But a wide difference is manifest in our age. For the wise men, who now appear as political philosophers, deal exclusively with the mechanical province; and occupying themselves in counting up and estimating men's motives, strive by curious checking and balancing, and other adjustments of profit and loss, to guide them to their true advantage: while, unfortunately, those same "motives" are so innumerable, and so variable in every individual, that no really useful conclusion can ever be drawn from their enumeration. But though mechanism, wisely contrived, has done much for man, in a social and moral point of view, we cannot be persuaded that it has ever been the chief source of his worth or happiness. Consider the great elements of human enjoyment, the attainments and possessions that exalt man's life to its present height, and see what part of these he owes to institutions, to mechanism of any kind; and what to the instinctive, unbounded force, which Nature herself lent him, and still continues to him. Shall we say, for example, that science and art are indebted principally to the founders of schools and universities? Did not science originate rather, and gain advancement, in the obscure closets of the Roger Bacons, Keplers, Newtons; in the workshops of the Fausts and the Watts; wherever, and in what guise soever Nature, from the first times downwards, had sent a gifted spirit upon the earth? Again, were Homer and Shakespeare members of any beneficial guild, or made poets by means of it? Were painting and sculpture created by forethought, brought into the world by institutions for that end? No; science and art have, from first to last, been the free gift of Nature; an unsolicited, unexpected gift: often even a fatal one. These things rose up, as it were by spontaneous growth, in the free soil and sunshine of Nature. They were not planted or grafted, nor even greatly multiplied or improved by the culture or manuring of institutions. Generally speaking, they have derived only partial help from these: often have suffered damage. They made constitutions for themselves. They originated in the dynamical nature of man, and not in his mechanical nature. . . . **E**

In fact, if we look deeper, we shall find that this faith in mechanism has now struck its roots deep into men's most intimate, primary sources of conviction; and is thence sending up, over his whole life and activity, innumerable stems, fruit-bearing and poison-bearing. The truth is, men have lost their belief in the invisible, and believe, and hope, and work only in the visible; or,

Summarize: According to Carlyle's arguments in the previous three paragraphs, how has science succumbed to mechanism? What two branches of human science does he propose in this paragraph? **R**

Social Critique: According to Carlyle, why are mechanisms insufficient to regulate human behavior or ensure human happiness and progress? **E**

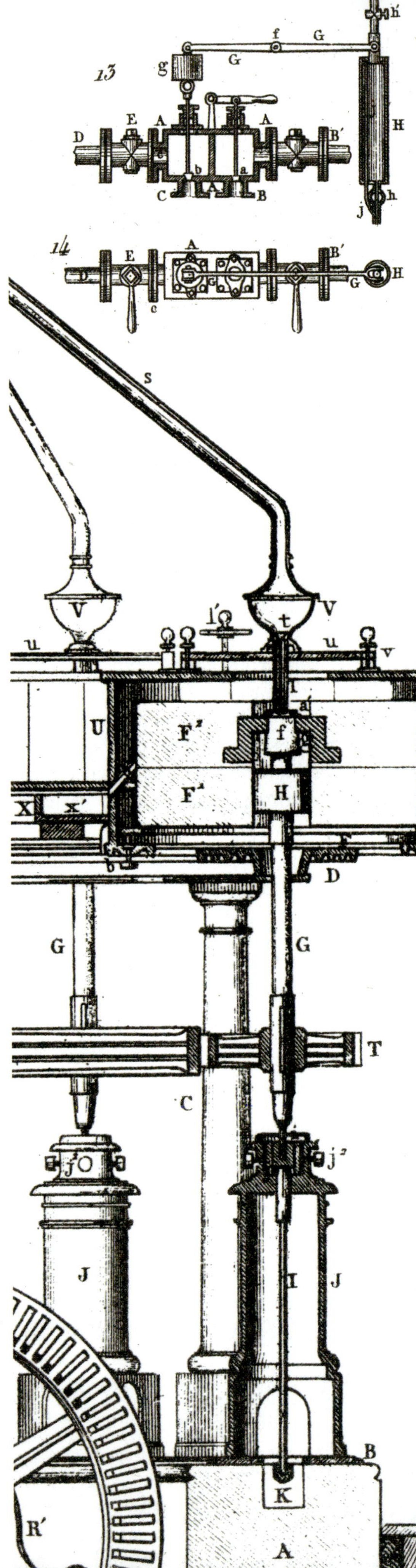

to speak it in other words, this is not a religious age. Only the material, the immediately practical, not the divine and spiritual, is important to us. The infinite, absolute character of virtue has passed into a finite, conditional one; it is no longer a worship of the beautiful and good; but a calculation of the profitable. Worship, indeed, in any sense, is not recognized among us, or is mechanically explained into fear of pain, or hope of pleasure. Our true deity is mechanism. It has subdued external Nature for us, and, we think, it will do all other things. We are giants in physical power: in a deeper than a metaphorical sense, we are Titans,[11] that strive, by heaping mountain on mountain, to conquer Heaven also.

The strong mechanical character, so visible in the spiritual pursuits and methods of this age, may be traced much farther into the condition and prevailing disposition of our spiritual nature itself. . . . Wonder indeed, is, on all hands, dying out: it is the sign of uncultivation to wonder. Speak to any small man of a high, majestic Reformation, of a high, majestic Luther to lead it, and forthwith he sets about "accounting" for it! how the "circumstances of the time" called for such a character, and found him, we suppose, standing girt and road-ready, to do its errand; how the "circumstances of the time" created, fashioned, floated him quietly along into the result; how, in short, this small man, had he been there, could have performed the like himself! For it is the "force of circumstances" that does every thing; the force of one man can do nothing. . . .

. . . Practically considered, our creed is fatalism: and, free in hand and foot, we are shackled in heart and soul, with far straighter than feudal chains. Truly may we say with the philosopher, "the deep meaning of the laws of mechanism lies heavy on us;" and in the closet, in the marketplace, in the temple, by the social hearth, encumbers the whole movements of our mind, and over our noblest faculties is spreading a nightmare sleep. E

11. *Titans:* parents of the Greek Olympian gods; associated strongly with primal natural forces

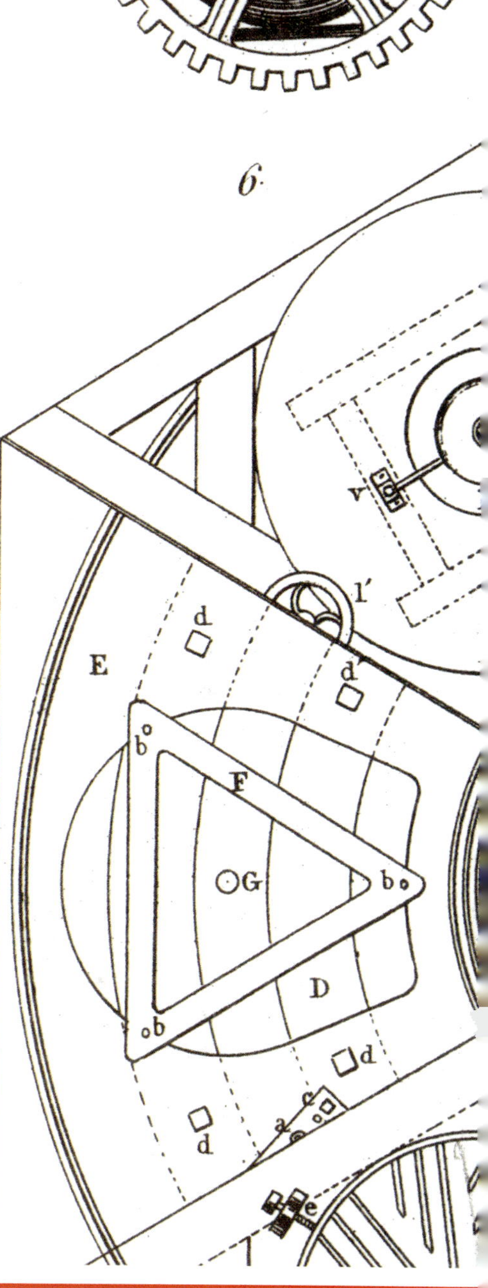

Social Critique: Based on the previous three paragraphs, what convictions or beliefs have resulted from the Industrial Revolution? What contrasting convictions does Carlyle say have been laid aside at the present? E

THINK AND DISCUSS

1. According to Carlyle, what are some improvements brought by the Industrial Revolution?
2. In "The Condition of England," what negative effects of the Industrial Revolution does Carlyle identify in the lower and upper classes?
3. Paraphrase Carlyle's thesis for "The Condition of England." Summarize one of his supporting arguments and give one example he uses to develop it.
4. How does "The Condition of England" qualify as an essay?
5. In "Signs of the Times," what does Carlyle mean by calling the era the "Age of Machinery"?
6. Describe what Carlyle calls the mechanical and dynamic human perspectives. What benefits or failures does he attach to each?
7. What is his thesis in the essay? How do these contrasting perspectives play a part in it?
8. Define two rhetorical devices that Carlyle uses and give two examples of each from the text. How do these effectively support his argument?
9. How do Carlyle's ideas about the spiritual state of Victorian England stack up against a biblical worldview? Consider his ideas about true wealth and his fear of becoming "mechanical in head and in heart" (p. 526). Incorporate some of the surrounding passages into your answer.

HARD TIMES

Charles Dickens

By the 1850s, Britain was in the throes of dramatic social change. The Industrial Revolution had transformed every aspect of life, yet Britain's social institutions seemed unwilling or unable to adjust to new conditions. In response, England's leading novelist took up his pen, seeking not only to expose dramatic injustices, but also to provide a way forward.

Charles Dickens and Victorian Society

That novelist was Charles Dickens. Dickens (1812–70) was born in Portsmouth and spent his formative years in London. When his father landed in debtor's prison in 1824, he was forced to secure work affixing labels to blacking (shoe polish) bottles for more than a year, giving him firsthand experience with industrial work. In 1827 another financial crisis in the family forced Charles back to work, this time as a legal clerk. His time in the law courts, as well as his subsequent career as a journalist, gave him an encyclopedic knowledge of contemporary English society.

Dickens's first novel, *The Pickwick Papers* (1836–37), brought him instant fame and success, and the newly made celebrity quickly went on to publish *Oliver Twist* (1837–39), *The Old Curiosity Shop* (1840–41), *A Christmas Carol* (1843), and *Martin Chuzzlewit* (1843–44), among others. While these early novels sympathize with the plight of the poor and deftly satirize hypocrisy in the middle class, they are all primarily comic in tone. By 1850, however, Dickens, like his contemporaries, was coming to see the importance of the "Condition of England Question," and his later novels are all concerned with systematic injustice. The second of his novels in this period, *Hard Times* (1854), was born after Dickens visited a weavers' strike in the industrial town of Preston, Lancashire.

Hard Times and the Condition of England

Hard Times explores the personal and moral consequences of what Dickens saw as the philosophy of "Facts." According to Dickens, this philosophy, which is embraced in the novel by both social utilitarians (p. 503) and laissez-faire capitalists (p. 415), reduces the complexity of human experience to the brute facts of economics. This brutal oversimplification is graphically rendered in the novel's setting, the fictional city of Coketown: "It was a town of red brick, or of brick that would have been red if the smoke and ashes had allowed it. . . . It contained several large streets all very like one another. . . . You saw nothing in Coketown but what was severely workful."

Against this harsh backdrop, it is no wonder that the wife of one character, worker Stephen Blackpool, is destroyed by substance abuse. But it does come as a surprise that an education in Facts destroys the humanity of its students; this is the novel's main concern. The book begins with the school superintendent, Mr. Gradgrind, proclaiming before his students, "You can only form the minds of reasoning animals upon Facts: nothing else will ever be of any service to them."

But as the novel progresses, this regimen of Facts proves insidious. Mr. Gradgrind's oldest daughter, Louisa, enters a loveless marriage and, as a consequence, is nearly seduced by a nihilistic aristocrat. Mr. Gradgrind's son Thomas devolves into a thieving gambler. By the end of the novel, the interior character of Mr. Gradgrind's pupils has come to mirror that of their bleak exterior environment, and it is only the intervention of working-class characters like Stephen Blackpool that saves Louisa and Thomas from utter moral disintegration.

If Facts can't save society, what can? Dickens insists that the solution is a return to traditional, humane values. Throughout *Hard Times*, when the brutality of Facts rips people's lives apart, it is only a quiet devotion to duty and love that brings healing to those wounds. For Dickens, neither unfettered capitalism nor trade-unionism can save society: only love can.

As you read the following excerpts from *Hard Times*, pay attention to how Dickens uses his descriptions of setting and characters and even names to communicate his thoughts about Facts and utilitarians' "moral arithmetic" (p. 503). What role does he imply literature can have in combatting such attitudes and fostering the right ones?

FROM CHAPTER 5

Coketown, to which Messrs. Bounderby and Gradgrind now walked, was a triumph of fact; it had no greater taint of fancy in it than Mrs. Gradgrind herself. Let us strike the key-note, Coketown, before pursuing our tune.

It was a town of red brick, or of brick that would have been red if the smoke and ashes had allowed it; but as matters stood it was a town of unnatural red and black, like the painted face of a savage. It was a town of machinery and tall chimneys, out of which interminable serpents of smoke trailed themselves forever and ever, and never got uncoiled. It had a black canal in it, and a river that ran purple with ill-smelling dye, and vast piles of building full of windows where there was a rattling and a trembling all day long, and where the piston of the steam-engine worked monotonously up and down, like the head of an elephant in a state of melancholy madness. It contained several large streets all very like one another, and many small streets still more like one another, inhabited by people equally like one another, who all went in and out at the same hours, with the same sound upon the same pavements, to do the same work, and to whom every day was the same as yesterday and tomorrow, and every year the counterpart of the last and the next. . . .

You saw nothing in Coketown but what was severely workful. . . . All the public inscriptions in the town were painted alike, in severe characters of black and white. The jail might have been the infirmary, the infirmary might have been the jail, the town-hall might have been either, or both, or anything else, for anything that appeared to the contrary in the graces of their construction. Fact, fact, fact, everywhere in the material aspect of the town; fact, fact, fact, everywhere in the immaterial. The M'Choakumchild school was all fact, and the school of design was all fact, and the relations between master and man were all fact, and everything was fact between the lying-in hospital and the cemetery, and what you couldn't state in figures, or show to be purchasable in the cheapest market and salable in the dearest, was not, and never should be, world without end, Amen.

A town so sacred to fact, and so triumphant in its assertion, of course got on well? Why no, not quite well. No? Dear me!

FROM CHAPTER 8

When she was half a dozen years younger, Louisa had been overheard to begin a conversation with her brother one day, by saying "Tom, I wonder"— upon which Mr. Gradgrind, who was the person overhearing, stepped forth into the light, and said, "Louisa, never wonder!"

Herein lay the spring of the mechanical art and mystery of educating the reason without stooping to the cultivation of the sentiments and affections. Never wonder. By means of addition, subtraction, multiplication, and division, settle everything somehow, and never wonder. Bring to me, says M'Choakumchild, yonder baby just able to walk, and I will engage that it shall never wonder. . . .

There was a library in Coketown, to which general access was easy. Mr. Gradgrind greatly tormented his mind about what the people read in this library: a point whereon little rivers of tabular statements periodically flowed into the howling ocean of tabular statements, which no diver ever got to any depth in and came up sane. It was a disheartening circumstance, but a melancholy fact, that even these readers persisted in wondering. They wondered about human nature, human passions, human hopes and fears, the struggles, triumphs and defeats, the cares and joys and sorrows, the lives and deaths, of common men and women. They sometimes, after fifteen hours' work, sat down to read mere fables about men and women, more or less like themselves, and about children, more or less like their own. They took De Foe to their bosoms, instead of Euclid, and seemed to be on the whole more comforted by Goldsmith than by Cocker. Mr. Gradgrind was forever working, in print and out of print, at this eccentric sum, and he never could make out how it yielded this unaccountable product.

Charlotte Brontë (1816–55)

AT A GLANCE

- **1821** Charlotte's mother died, the first of many family tragedies
- **1831** Left home to finish her education at Roe Head School
- **1842** Traveled to Brussels with her sister Emily
- **1846** Published *Poems* with Emily and Anne
- **1847** Published *Jane Eyre*
- **1849, 1853** Published *Shirley* and *Villette*

The poet and novelist Charlotte Brontë was one of three remarkable sisters (Charlotte, Emily, and Anne), all of whom wrote classic works of literature focused on women in Victorian England. Brontë's novels in general dramatize the conflict between the duty a woman owes herself and the duty she owes society. Through realistic depictions of the internal emotional states of women, her novels also challenged dominant Victorian assumptions about women's roles. These themes are communicated in an artistic prose with a keen, poetic eye for vivid details.

A Quiet, Tragic Childhood

The story of Charlotte's life is bound up with that of her unusual family. She was born in rural Yorkshire into the family of an Anglican rector. Tragedy haunted the household. Charlotte's mother died in 1821, and the unhealthy living conditions at their boarding school, Clergy Daughters' School at Cowan Bridge, led to the deaths of Charlotte's two older sisters in 1825. Charlotte and her younger sister Emily were quickly withdrawn from the school. Burdened with an eccentric and strict father, the remaining Brontë children (particularly Charlotte and her brother Branwell) spent the next five years creating their own imaginary world as an outlet. They populated it with fictional characters and developed around it an extensive literature of narratives and poetry. In 1831, however, Charlotte left home to finish her education at Roe Head School. There she formed one of the most important friendships of her life with Ellen Nussey. Charlotte later returned to teach at Roe Head in 1835.

DID YOU KNOW ?

Charlotte's father, Patrick, a redheaded Irishman from a poor family, changed his surname from Brunty to Brontë.

Adult Life and Early Work

Teaching at Roe Head School was unfavorable to Brontë's health. In 1838 she returned home to recover and to help her brother Branwell out of his debts. She worked as a governess in Rawdon, but Branwell could neither hold a job nor refuse the lure of opium. In 1842 Charlotte and Emily traveled to Brussels to study French and German with the goal of opening a girls' school upon their return. In Brussels, Charlotte formed another important attachment. Monsieur Constantin Heger ran the boarding school where Charlotte and Emily were studying, and Charlotte grew very fond of him. Though Charlotte was forced by Heger's jealous wife to leave Brussels, Constantin's friendship continued to influence Brontë for years. After Charlotte and Emily were both back on English soil, Charlotte discovered Emily's secret collection of poems. Charlotte encouraged her sister to publish, and the two sisters, along with their younger sister, Anne, published their collected *Poems* in 1846. They used the male pseudonyms Currer, Ellis, and Acton Bell.

Fame, Marriage, and Death

Having been driven by a lifelong literary ambition, Brontë found inspiration in the modest success of the publication. When she published *Jane Eyre* in 1847, the novel became an instant bestseller. But in 1848 tragedy quickly struck again, as first Branwell died of complications from substance abuse, and then Emily and Anne both quickly contracted and died of tuberculosis. Charlotte continued to pursue her literary work, publishing the novels *Shirley* (1849) and *Villette* (1853), but her newfound fame and sense of personal isolation drained her. After her father reluctantly consented, Brontë married the local curate Arthur Bell Nicholls in 1854, only to die from pregnancy complications, possibly exacerbated by severe morning sickness, the following year. She was only thirty-eight years old.

ANALYZE: *Gothic Novel, Theme, and Symbol*

Jane Eyre incorporates both Victorian and romantic themes, often in creative ways. Previously, Brontë had experimented with the **gothic** genre, which originated in sentimental literature (p. 359) and was popular with romantics (e.g., *Frankenstein*). Gothic works were often medieval in setting; gloomy, mysterious, and nightmarish in atmosphere; and suspenseful and often supernatural in plot. Brontë generously sprinkled *Jane Eyre* with gothic elements, but she often grounded them with more realistic elements. Where do imagination and the supernatural play a role in the chapters that follow? Can you identify the tensions between gothic content and a more realistic disposition in various scenes? Why might Brontë have included gothic elements at all?

As with most novels, *Jane Eyre* develops multiple complex **themes**. These ideas are often explored directly by Jane, who narrates her own story as autobiography (a development of the novel genre you can credit to Brontë). What big ideas does she talk about as she relates her thoughts and feelings and interprets the events of her life? Additionally, pay attention to Brontë's liberal use of **symbols** (p. 37) in the novel. What purpose do they achieve? Note that one key symbol in the following chapters highlights several of Brontë's themes at once, including her exploration of human isolation.

OBJECTIVES

- Identify romantic or Victorian themes and genres in a text.
- Analyze the connections between a text's characters, symbols, setting, and themes.
- Analyze a novel's use of psychological realism.
- Create a character's diary entry or drawing.

READ: *Draw Conclusions*

Brontë's novel forms an early example of **psychological realism**, realistic fiction that emphasizes characterization by focusing on characters' underlying thought processes and motivations. Brontë's choice to use Jane to narrate her own story thus makes her the key to unlocking the story's meaning. As you read, draw conclusions about Jane's character from what she reveals. What do you come to know about her? What does Jane understand about herself? What is she conflicted about? Additionally, consider how Jane's inner life intersects with other literary elements, such as the setting, symbols, and, of course, the story's themes. For example, how do the settings sometimes reflect Jane's more romantic disposition? How might her conflicts reflect the theme of "the woman question" (p. 503)? Draw conclusions about the other characters too. How does each highlight aspects of Jane's character and inner conflicts? Do they also reflect psychological realism?

VOCABULARY

efface (ĭ-fās′) *tr.v.* To remove or make indistinct.

officious (ə-fĭsh′əs) *adj.* Motivated by the desire to help others.

accost (ə-kôst′) *tr.v.* To approach and speak to, especially aggressively or insistently, as with a demand or request.

piquant (pē′kənt) *adj.* Appealingly provocative; charming.

rejoinder (rĭ-join′dər) *n.* An answer, especially to a reply.

celerity (sə-lĕr′ĭ-tē) *n.* Swiftness of action or motion; speed.

CREATE: *Character's Diary Entry or Drawing*

Pretend you are either Jane or Rochester, and put yourself in the meeting described in the selection. What impressions would either character have taken away about the other person after just two conversations? Create a diary entry recording or a drawing visualizing this scene from either Jane's or Rochester's point of view. Try to emulate the character's style of speech or artistic talent. Fill in details, like the emotions at play. Using your creativity, capture either Jane's or Rochester's way of viewing life.

What do people need to THRIVE?

When are you at the top of your game? Perhaps you can look back on a time of success, but can you identify your personality facets and the surrounding people and events that contributed to your triumph? What habits and people do you lean on so that you can experience long-term success? How do you think people around the world are alike in what it takes for them to thrive? List four or five things you think everyone needs to thrive.

from Jane Eyre

Jane Eyre, the novel's protagonist, begins her young life as an orphan at her Aunt Reed's house. Her aunt, cousins, and the servants mistreat Jane, mostly because her quietly passionate personality is unlike theirs. One day, when she is ten years old, her cousin John attacks her again, but this time she retaliates. Jane feels briefly liberated but is confirmed in her aunt's mind as a wicked child. Aunt Reed locks her in the "Red Room," where her uncle passed away and which Jane believes is haunted. Jane's imaginative temperament cannot handle the confinement, and she has a nervous collapse. Aunt Reed, eager to be rid of her, sends her to Lowood School, governed by the prejudiced and hypocritical Mr. Brocklehurst. There Jane suffers from malnourishment, cold, and rigidly strict expectations. Her best friend, Helen, tries to teach her to willingly accept hardship for her spiritual good, but Helen dies of consumption. Jane continues at Lowood as a student for six years and as a teacher for two years. She then seeks a governess position, and a Mrs. Fairfax hires her to tutor a little French girl named Adèle at Thornfield Hall, a rather gloomy manor in a remote rural area. Jane has not yet met the master of the house, but she works diligently at Adèle's education.

CHAPTER XII

The promise of a smooth career, which my first calm introduction to Thornfield Hall seemed to pledge, was not belied on a longer acquaintance with the place and its inmates. Mrs. Fairfax turned out to be what she appeared, a placid-tempered, kind-natured woman, of competent education and average intelligence. My pupil was a lively child, who had been spoiled and indulged, and therefore was sometimes wayward; but as she was committed entirely to my care, and no injudicious interference from any quarter ever thwarted my plans for her improvement; she soon forgot her little freaks, and became obedient and teachable. She had no great talents, no marked traits of character, no peculiar development of feeling or taste which raised her one inch above the ordinary level of childhood; but neither had she any deficiency or vice which sunk her below it. She made reasonable progress, entertained for me a vivacious, though perhaps not very profound, affection; and by her simplicity, gay prattle, and efforts to please, inspired me, in return, with a degree of attachment sufficient to make us both content in each other's society.

This, *par parenthèse*,[1] will be thought cool language by persons who entertain solemn doctrines about the angelic nature of children, and the duty of those charged with their education to conceive for them an idolatrous devotion: but I am not writing to flatter parental egotism, to echo cant,[2] or prop up humbug; I am merely telling the truth. I felt a conscientious solicitude for Adèle's welfare and progress, and a quiet liking to her little self; just as I cherished towards Mrs. Fairfax a thankfulness for her kindness, and a pleasure in her society proportionate to the tranquil regard she had for me, and the moderation of her mind and character.

Anybody may blame me who likes when I add further that now and then, when I took a walk by myself in the grounds, when I went down to the gates and looked through them along the road, or when, while Adèle played with her nurse, and Mrs. Fairfax made jellies in the storeroom, I climbed the three staircases, raised the trapdoor of the attic, and having reached the leads,[3] looked out afar over sequestered field and hill, and along dim skyline—that

VISUAL ANALYSIS
How might the woman in this portrait evoke the character of Jane Eyre?

1. *par parenthèse:* parenthetically; i.e., an aside by Jane (translations provided by Susanne Anderson)
2. *cant:* fashionable but empty sentiments or ideas on a topic
3. *leads:* the roof, from the practice of using lead panels in roofing

then I longed for a power of vision which might overpass that limit; which might reach the busy world, towns, regions full of life I had heard of but never seen: that then I desired more of practical experience than I possessed; more of intercourse with my kind, of acquaintance with variety of character, than was here within my reach. I valued what was good in Mrs. Fairfax, and what was good in Adèle; but I believed in the existence of other and more vivid kinds of goodness, and what I believed in I wished to behold. R

Draw Conclusions: What details do the first three paragraphs reveal about the narrator? R

Who blames me? Many, no doubt; and I shall be called discontented. I could not help it: the restlessness was in my nature; it agitated me to pain sometimes. Then my sole relief was to walk along the corridor of the third story, backwards and forwards, safe in the silence and solitude of the spot and allow my mind's eye to dwell on whatever bright visions rose before it—and, certainly, they were many and glowing; to let my heart be heaved by the exultant movement, which, while it swelled it in trouble, expanded it with life; and, best of all, to open my inward ear to a tale that was never ended—a tale my imagination created, and narrated continuously; quickened with all of incident, life, fire, feeling, that I desired and had not in my actual existence.

It is in vain to say human beings ought to be satisfied with tranquility: they must have action; and they will make it if they cannot find it. Millions are condemned to a stiller doom than mine, and millions are in silent revolt against their lot. Nobody knows how many rebellions besides political rebellions ferment in the masses of life which people earth. Women are supposed to be very calm generally: but women feel just as men feel; they need exercise for their faculties and a field for their efforts as much as their brothers do; they suffer from too rigid a restraint, too absolute a stagnation, precisely as men would suffer; and it is narrow-minded in their more privileged fellow creatures to say that they ought to confine themselves to making puddings and knitting stockings, to playing on the piano and embroidering bags. It is thoughtless to condemn them, or laugh at them, if they seek to do more or learn more than custom has pronounced necessary for their sex. . . . R

Draw Conclusions: Why do you think Jane is restless? What could be the results of this restlessness? R

October, November, December passed away. One afternoon in January Mrs. Fairfax had begged a holiday for Adèle because she had a cold; and, as Adèle seconded the request with an ardor that reminded me how precious occasional holidays had been to me in my own childhood, I accorded it, deeming that I did well in showing pliability on the point. It was a fine, calm day, though very cold; I was tired of sitting still in the library through a whole long morning: Mrs. Fairfax had just written a letter which was waiting to be posted, so I put on my bonnet and cloak and volunteered to carry it to Hay; the distance, two miles, would be a pleasant winter afternoon walk. Having seen Adèle comfortably seated in her little chair by Mrs. Fairfax's parlor fireside, and given her her best wax doll (which I usually kept enveloped in silver paper in a drawer) to play with, and a storybook for change of amusement; and having replied to her '*Revenez bientôt, ma bonne amie, ma chère Mdlle. Jeannette,*'[4] with a kiss, I set out.

The ground was hard, the air was still, my road was lonely; I walked fast till I got warm, and then I walked slowly to enjoy and analyze the species of pleasure brooding for me in the hour and situation. It was three o'clock; the church bell tolled as I passed under the belfry: the charm of the hour lay in its approaching dimness, in the low-gliding and pale-beaming sun. I was a

4. *Revenez bientôt . . . Mdlle. Jeannette:* Come back soon, my good friend, my dear Miss Jeannette.

mile from Thornfield, in a lane noted for wild roses in summer, for nuts and blackberries in autumn, and even now possessing a few coral treasures in hips and haws,[5] but whose best winter delight lay in its utter solitude and leafless repose. If a breath of air stirred, it made no sound here; for there was not a holly, not an evergreen to rustle, and the stripped hawthorn and hazel bushes were as still as the white, worn stones which causewayed the middle of the path. Far and wide, on each side, there were only fields, where no cattle now browsed; and the little brown birds, which stirred occasionally in the hedge, looked like single russet leaves that had forgotten to drop.

VISUAL ANALYSIS
How does this painting reflect the setting of this passage from *Jane Eyre*?

This lane inclined uphill all the way to Hay: having reached the middle I sat down on a stile[6] which led thence into a field. Gathering my mantle about me, and sheltering my hands in my muff, I did not feel the cold, though it froze keenly; as was attested by a sheet of ice covering the causeway, where a little brooklet, now congealed, had overflowed after a rapid thaw some days since. From my seat I could look down on Thornfield: the grey and battlemented hall was the principal object in the vale below me; its woods and dark rookery rose against the west. I lingered till the sun went down amongst the trees, and sank crimson and clear behind them. I then turned eastward.

On the hilltop above me sat the rising moon; pale yet as a cloud, but brightening momently:[7] she looked over Hay, which, half lost in trees, sent up a blue smoke from its few chimneys; it was yet a mile distant, but in the absolute hush I could hear plainly its thin murmurs of life. My ear too felt the

5. *hips and haws:* small, round, red fruits that develop from the blooms of roses and hawthorns
6. *stile:* a step or stairway for going over a fence
7. *momently:* all the time

flow of currents; in what dales and depths I could not tell: but there were many hills beyond Hay, and doubtless many becks[8] threading their passes. That evening calm betrayed alike the tinkle of the nearest streams, the sough[9] of the most remote. **A**

Theme: How have romantic and Victorian themes influenced Chapter 12 thus far? **A**

A rude noise broke on these fine ripplings and whisperings, at once so far away and so clear: a positive tramp, tramp; a metallic clatter, which effaced the soft wave-wanderings; as, in a picture, the solid mass of a crag, or the rough boles[10] of a great oak, drawn in dark and strong on the foreground, **efface** the aerial distance of azure hill, sunny horizon, and blended clouds, where tint melts into tint.

efface (ĭ-fās′) *tr.v.* To remove or make indistinct.

The din was on the causeway; a horse was coming; the windings of the lane yet hid it, but it approached. I was just leaving the stile; yet, as the path was narrow, I sat still to let it go by. In those days I was young, and all sorts of fancies bright and dark tenanted my mind: the memories of nursery stories were there amongst other rubbish; and when they recurred, maturing youth added to them a vigor and vividness beyond what childhood could give. As this horse approached, and as I watched for it to appear through the dusk, I remembered certain of Bessie's tales, wherein figured a North-of-England spirit, called a 'Gytrash,'[11] which, in the form of horse, mule, or large dog, haunted solitary ways, and sometimes came upon belated travelers, as this horse was now coming upon me.

It was very near, but not yet in sight, when, in addition to the tramp, tramp, I heard a rush under the hedge, and close down by the hazel stems glided a great dog, whose black and white color made him a distinct object against the trees. It was exactly one mask of Bessie's Gytrash, —a lion-like creature with long hair and a huge head: it passed me, however, quietly enough; not staying to look up, with strange pretercanine[12] eyes, in my face, as I half expected it would. The horse followed,—a tall steed, and on its back a rider. The man, the human being, broke the spell at once. Nothing ever rode the Gytrash: it was always alone; and goblins, to my notions, though they might tenant the dumb carcasses of beasts, could scarce covet shelter in the commonplace human form. No Gytrash was this,—only a traveler taking the short cut to Millcote. He passed, and I went on: a few steps, and I turned: a sliding sound and an exclamation of 'What the deuce is to do now?' and a clattering tumble, arrested my attention. Man and horse were down; they had slipped on the sheet of ice which glazed the causeway. The dog came bounding back, and seeing his master in a predicament, and hearing the horse groan, barked till the evening hills echoed the sound, which was deep in proportion to his magnitude. He snuffed round the prostrate group, and then he ran up to me; it was all he could do, there was no other help at hand to summon. I obeyed him, and walked down to the traveler, by this time struggling himself free of his steed. His efforts were so vigorous I thought he could not be much hurt; but I asked him the question:—"Are you injured, sir?"

I think he was swearing, but am not certain; however, he was pronouncing some formula which prevented him from replying to me directly. **A**

Gothic Novel: How does Brontë employ gothic elements and other factors to poke fun at gothicism in these last four paragraphs? **A**

"Can I do anything?" I asked again.

"You must just stand on one side," he answered as he rose, first to his knees, and then to his feet. I did; whereupon began a heaving, stamping,

8. *becks:* streams in mountainous countryside
9. *sough:* a rushing, wavelike sound
10. *boles:* trunks
11. *Gytrash:* dog of legend that symbolizes impending death
12. *pretercanine:* more than canine

clattering process, accompanied by a barking and baying which removed me effectually some yards' distance; but I would not be driven quite away till I saw the event. This was finally fortunate; the horse was re-established, and the dog was silenced with a "Down, Pilot!" The traveler now, stooping, felt his foot and leg, as if trying whether they were sound; apparently something ailed them, for he halted to the stile whence I had just risen, and sat down.

I was in the mood for being useful, or at least **officious**, I think, for I now drew near him again.

officious (ə-fĭsh'əs) *adj.* Motivated by the desire to help others.

"If you are hurt, and want help, sir, I can fetch someone either from Thornfield Hall or from Hay."

"Thank you; I shall do: I have no broken bones—only a sprain;" and again he stood up and tried his foot, but the result extorted an involuntary "Ugh!"

Something of daylight still lingered, and the moon was waxing bright: I could see him plainly. His figure was enveloped in a riding cloak, fur collared, and steel clasped; its details were not apparent, but I traced the general points of middle height, and considerable breadth of chest. He had a dark face, with stern features and a heavy brow; his eyes and gathered eyebrows looked ireful and thwarted just now; he was past youth, but had not reached middle age; perhaps he might be thirty-five. I felt no fear of him, and but little shyness. Had he been a handsome, heroic-looking young gentleman, I should not have dared to stand thus questioning him against his will, and offering my services unasked. I had hardly ever seen a handsome youth; never in my life spoken to one. I had a theoretical reverence and homage for beauty, elegance, gallantry, fascination;[13] but had I met those qualities incarnate in masculine shape, I should have known instinctively that they neither had nor could have sympathy with anything in me, and should have shunned them as one would fire, lightning, or anything else that is bright but antipathetic.

If even this stranger had smiled and been good-humored to me when I addressed him; if he had put off my offer of assistance gaily and with thanks, I should have gone on my way and not felt any vocation to renew inquiries: but the frown, the roughness of the traveler, set me at my ease: I retained my station when he waved to me to go, and announced:—"I cannot think of leaving you, sir, at so late an hour, in this solitary lane, till I see you are fit to mount your horse."

He looked at me when I said this: he had hardly turned his eyes in my direction before.

"I should think you ought to be at home yourself," said he, "if you have a home in this neighborhood: where do you come from?"

"From just below; and I am not at all afraid of being out late when it is moonlight: I will run over to Hay for you with pleasure, if you wish it; indeed, I am going there to post a letter."

"You live just below—do you mean at that house with the battlements?" pointing to Thornfield Hall, on which the moon cast a hoary gleam, bringing it out distinct and pale from the woods, that, by contrast with the western sky, now seemed one mass of shadow.

"Yes, sir."

"Whose house is it?"

"Mr. Rochester's."

"Do you know Mr. Rochester?"

"No, I have never seen him."

"He is not resident, then?"

13. *fascination:* ability to fascinate others

"No."

"Can you tell me where he is?"

"I cannot."

"You are not a servant at the hall, of course. You are—" He stopped, ran his eye over my dress, which, as usual, was quite simple; a black merino[14] cloak, a black beaver bonnet: neither of them half fine enough for a lady's maid. He seemed puzzled to decide what I was: I helped him.

"I am the governess."

"Ah, the governess!" he repeated; "deuce take me, if I had not forgotten! The governess!" and again my raiment underwent scrutiny. In two minutes he rose from the stile: his face expressed pain when he tried to move.

"I cannot commission you to fetch help," he said; "but you may help me a little yourself, if you will be so kind."

"Yes, sir."

"You have not an umbrella that I can use as a stick?"

"No."

"Try to get hold of my horse's bridle and lead him to me: you are not afraid!"

I should have been afraid to touch a horse when alone, but when told to do it I was disposed to obey. I put down my muff on the stile, and went up to the tall steed; I endeavored to catch the bridle, but it was a spirited thing, and would not let me come near its head; I made effort on effort, though in vain: meantime, I was mortally afraid of its trampling forefeet. The traveler waited and watched for some time, and at last he laughed.

"I see," he said, "the mountain will never be brought to Mahomet,[15] so all you can do is to aid Mahomet to go to the mountain; I must beg of you to come here."

I came. "Excuse me," he continued: "necessity compels me to make you useful." He laid a heavy hand on my shoulder, and leaning on me with some stress, limped to his horse. Having once caught the bridle, he mastered it directly, and sprang to his saddle; grimacing grimly as he made the effort, for it wrenched his sprain. **R**

Draw Conclusions: How does Jane's class affect her encounter with the traveler? **R**

"Now," said he, releasing his under lip from a hard bite, "just hand me my whip; it lies there under the hedge."

I sought it and found it.

"Thank you: now make haste with the letter to Hay, and return as fast as you can."

A touch of a spurred heel made his horse first start and rear, and then bound away; the dog rushed in his traces: all three vanished,

Like heath that, in the wilderness,
The wild wind whirls away.[16]

I took up my muff and walked on. The incident had occurred and was gone for me: it was an incident of no moment,[17] no romance, no interest in a sense; yet it marked with change one single hour of a monotonous life. My help had been needed and claimed; I had given it: I was pleased to have done something; trivial, transitory though the deed was, it was yet an active thing, and I was weary of an existence all passive. The new face, too, was like a new picture introduced to the gallery of memory; and it was dissimilar to all the

14. *merino:* wool from the merino sheep
15. *the mountain . . . to Mahomet:* This is a reference to Francis Bacon's saying in his 1625 *Essays*; the meaning is that if a person's will cannot achieve its end, another path must be taken.
16. *Like heath . . . whirls away:* quotation from Thomas Moore's poem "Fallen is thy throne, O Israel!"
17. *moment:* significance

others hanging there: firstly, because it was masculine; and, secondly, because it was dark, strong, and stern. I had it still before me when I entered Hay, and slipped the letter into the post office; I saw it as I walked fast downhill all the way home. When I came to the stile, I stopped a minute, looked round and listened, with an idea that a horse's hoof might ring on the causeway again, and that a rider in a cloak, and a Gytrash-like Newfoundland dog, might be again apparent: I saw only the hedge and a pollard willow before me, rising up still and straight to meet the moonbeams; I heard only the faintest waft of wind roaming fitful among the trees round Thornfield, a mile distant; and when I glanced down in the direction of the murmur, my eye, traversing the hall-front, caught a light kindling in a window: it reminded me that I was late, and I hurried on. **A**

Gothic Novel: How do you know that the events on the road to Hay are important to the narrator? **A**

I did not like re-entering Thornfield. To pass its threshold was to return to stagnation; to cross the silent hall, to ascend the darksome staircase, to seek my own lonely little room, and then to meet tranquil Mrs. Fairfax, and spend the long winter evening with her, and her only, was to quell wholly the faint excitement wakened by my walk, to slip again over my faculties the viewless fetters of an uniform and too still existence; of an existence whose very privileges of security and ease I was becoming incapable of appreciating. What good it would have done me at that time to have been tossed in the storms of an uncertain struggling life, and to have been taught by rough and bitter experience to long for the calm amidst which I now repined! Yes, just as much good as it would do a man tired of sitting still in a 'too easy chair' to take a

VISUAL ANALYSIS
How might this depiction of a mansion evoke Jane's feelings about Thornfield?

long walk; and just as natural was the wish to stir, under my circumstances, as it would be under his.

I lingered at the gates; I lingered on the lawn; I paced backwards and forwards on the pavement: the shutters of the glass door were closed; I could not see into the interior; and both my eyes and spirit seemed drawn from the gloomy house from the grey hollow filled with rayless cells, as it appeared to me to that sky expanded before me, a blue sea absolved from taint of cloud; the moon ascending it in solemn march; her orb seeming to look up as she left the hilltops, from behind which she had come, far and farther below her, and aspired to the zenith, midnight-dark in its fathomless depth and measureless distance: and for those trembling stars that followed her course; they made my heart tremble, my veins glow when I viewed them. Little things recall us to earth: the clock struck in the hall; that sufficed; I turned from moon and stars, opened a side door, and went in. **A**

Symbol: What is the major symbol in the two preceding paragraphs? Explain its significance to Jane's character. **A**

One of the first things Jane sees upon entering Thornfield is Pilot, the dog, near the hearth. Mrs. Fairfax informs Jane that Mr. Rochester has just arrived and that he had an accident on the road.

CHAPTER XIII

Jane and Adèle wait—Adèle very impatiently—to see Mr. Rochester, and they get their chance after he has received visitors in the library for most of the day. Mr. Rochester sends Mrs. Fairfax to invite his ward and her governess to tea at six o'clock. Mrs. Fairfax instructs Jane to put on her nice dress, and Jane, though feeling it strange, follows the order. Then the two ladies and Adèle enter the dining room.

Two wax candles stood lighted on the table, and two on the mantelpiece; basking in the light and heat of a superb fire lay Pilot—Adèle knelt near him. Half reclined on a couch appeared Mr. Rochester, his foot supported by the cushion; he was looking at Adèle and the dog: the fire shone full on his face. I knew my traveller with his broad and jetty eyebrows; his square forehead, made squarer by the horizontal sweep of his black hair. I recognised his decisive nose, more remarkable for character than beauty; his full nostrils, denoting, I thought, choler;[18] his grim mouth, chin, and jaw—yes, all three were very grim, and no mistake. His shape, now divested of cloak, I perceived harmonized in squareness with his physiognomy:[19] I suppose it was a good figure in the athletic sense of the term broad-chested and thin-flanked, though neither tall nor graceful.

Mr. Rochester must have been aware of the entrance of Mrs. Fairfax and myself; but it appeared he was not in the mood to notice us, for he never lifted his head as we approached.

"Here is Miss Eyre, sir," said Mrs. Fairfax, in her quiet way. He bowed, still not taking his eyes from the group of the dog and child.

"Let Miss Eyre be seated," said he: and there was something in the forced stiff bow, in the impatient yet formal tone, which seemed further to express, "What the deuce is it to me whether Miss Eyre be there or not? At this moment I am not disposed to accost her."

accost (ə-kôst′) *tr.v.* To approach and speak to, especially aggressively or insistently, as with a demand or request.

I sat down quite disembarrassed. A reception of finished politeness would probably have confused me: I could not have returned or repaid it by answering grace and elegance on my part; but harsh caprice laid me under no obligation; on the contrary, a decent quiescence,[20] under the freak of manner, gave

18. *choler:* term from medieval medicine; one of the four bodily humors, associated with irascibility
19. *physiognomy:* facial features
20. *quiescence:* attitude of quiet, lacking discord

me advantage. Besides, the eccentricity of the proceeding was **piquant**: I felt interested to see how he would go on.

piquant (pē′kənt) *adj.* Appealingly provocative; charming.

He went on as a statue would, that is, he neither spoke nor moved. Mrs. Fairfax seemed to think it necessary that someone should be amiable, and she began to talk. Kindly, as usual and, as usual, rather trite she condoled with him on the pressure of business he had had all day; on the annoyance it must have been to him with that painful sprain: then she commended his patience and perseverance in going through with it.

"Madam, I should like some tea," was the sole **rejoinder** she got. She hastened to ring the bell; and, when the tray came, she proceeded to arrange the cups, spoons, &c., with assiduous **celerity**. I and Adèle went to the table; but the master did not leave his couch.

rejoinder (rĭ-join′dər) *n.* An answer, especially to a reply.

celerity (sə-lĕr′ĭ-tē) *n.* Swiftness of action or motion; speed.

"Will you hand Mr. Rochester's cup?" said Mrs. Fairfax to me; "Adèle might perhaps spill it."

I did as requested. As he took the cup from my hand, Adèle, thinking the moment propitious for making a request in my favor, cried out: "N'est-ce pas, monsieur, qu'il y a un cadeau pour Mademoiselle Eyre, dans votre petit coffre?"[21]

"Who talks of cadeaux?" said he gruffly: "Did you expect a present, Miss Eyre? Are you fond of presents?" and he searched my face with eyes that I saw were dark, irate, and piercing.

"I hardly know, sir; I have little experience of them: they are generally thought pleasant things."

"Generally thought? But what do you think?"

"I should be obliged to take time, sir, before I could give you an answer worthy of your acceptance: a present has many faces to it, has it not? One should consider all before pronouncing an opinion as to its nature."

"Miss Eyre, you are not so unsophisticated as Adèle: she demands a 'cadeau,' clamorously, the moment she sees me: you beat about the bush."

"Because I have less confidence in my deserts than Adèle has: she can prefer the claim of old acquaintance, and the right too of custom; for she says you have always been in the habit of giving her playthings; but if I had to make out a case I should be puzzled, since I am a stranger, and have done nothing to entitle me to an acknowledgment."

"Oh, don't fall back on over-modesty! I have examined Adèle, and find you have taken great pains with her; she is not bright, she has no talents; yet in a short time she has made much improvement."

"Sir, you have now given me my 'cadeau'; I am obliged to you: it is the meed[22] teachers most covet; praise of their pupil's progress."

"Humph!" said Mr. Rochester, and he took his tea in silence.

"Come to the fire," said the master, when the tray was taken away, and Mrs. Fairfax had settled into a corner with her knitting; while Adèle was leading me by the hand round the room, showing me the beautiful books and ornaments on the consoles and chiffonnières.[23] We obeyed, as in duty bound; Adèle wanted to take a seat on my knee, but she was ordered to amuse herself with Pilot.

"You have been resident in my house three months?"

"Yes, sir."

"And you came from—?"

21. *N'est-ce pas . . . coffre?:* Is it not so, sir, that there is a gift for Miss Eyre, in your little chest?
22. *meed:* a reward that is deserved
23. *consoles and chiffonnières:* small work tables or end tables

"From Lowood school, in ______shire."

"Ah! a charitable concern. How long were you there?"

"Eight years."

"Eight years! You must be tenacious of life. I thought half the time in such a place would have done up any constitution! No wonder you have rather the look of another world. I marveled where you had got that sort of face. When you came on me in Hay Lane last night, I thought unaccountably of fairy tales, and had half a mind to demand whether you had bewitched my horse: I am not sure yet. Who are your parents?

"I have none."

"Nor ever had, I suppose: do you remember them?"

"No."

"I thought not. And so you were waiting for your people when you sat on that stile?"

"For whom, sir?"

"For the men in green: it was a proper moonlight evening for them. Did I break through one of your rings, that you spread that cursed ice on the causeway?"

I shook my head. "The men in green all forsook England a hundred years ago," said I, speaking as seriously as he had done. "And not even in Hay Lane, or the fields about it, could you find a trace of them. I don't think either summer or harvest, or winter moon, will ever shine on their revels more."

Mrs. Fairfax had dropped her knitting, and, with raised eyebrows, seemed wondering what sort of talk this was.

"Well," resumed Mr. Rochester, "if you disown parents you must have some sort of kinsfolk: uncles and aunts?"

"No; none that I ever saw."

"And your home?"

"I have none."

"Where do your brothers and sisters live?"

"I have no brothers or sisters."

"Who recommended you to come here?"

"I advertised, and Mrs. Fairfax answered my advertisement."

"Yes," said the good lady, who now knew what ground we were upon, "and I am daily thankful for the choice Providence led me to make. Miss Eyre has been an invaluable companion to me, and a kind and careful teacher to Adèle."

"Don't trouble yourself to give her a character," returned Mr. Rochester: "eulogiums will not bias me; I shall judge for myself. She began by felling my horse."

"Sir?" said Mrs. Fairfax.

"I have to thank her for this sprain."

The widow looked bewildered.

"Miss Eyre, have you ever lived in a town?"

"No, sir."

"Have you seen much society?"

"None but the pupils and teachers of Lowood; and now the inmates of Thornfield."

"Have you read much?"

"Only such books as came in my way; and they have not been numerous or very learned."

VISUAL ANALYSIS

Does the man in this portrait match your mental image of Rochester? Why or why not?

"You have lived the life of a nun: no doubt you are well drilled in religious forms; Brocklehurst, who I understand directs Lowood, is a parson, is he not?"

"Yes, sir."

"And you girls probably worshipped him, as a convent full of religieuses[24] would worship their director?"

"Oh, no."

"You are very cool! No! What! A novice not worship her priest! That sounds blasphemous."

"I disliked Mr. Brocklehurst; and I was not alone in the feeling. He is a harsh man; at once pompous and meddling: he cut off our hair; and for economy's sake bought us bad needles and thread, with which we could hardly sew."

"That was very false economy," remarked Mrs. Fairfax, who now again caught the drift of the dialogue.

"And was that the head and front of his offending?" demanded Mr. Rochester.

"He starved us when he had the sole superintendence of the provision department, before the committee was appointed; and he bored us with long lectures once a week, and with evening readings from books of his own inditing, about sudden deaths and judgments, which made us afraid to go to bed."

"What age were you when you went to Lowood?"

"About ten."

"And you stayed there eight years: you are now, then, eighteen?"

I assented.

"Arithmetic, you see, is useful; without its aid I should hardly have been able to guess your age. It is a point difficult to fix where the features and countenance are so much at variance as in your case. And now, what did you learn at Lowood? Can you play?" R

Draw Conclusions: How does the conversation in the last three pages achieve psychological realism? R

"A little."

"Of course: that is the established answer. Go into the library I mean, if you please. (Excuse my tone of command; I am used to say 'Do this,' and it is done: I cannot alter my customary habits for one new inmate.) Go, then, into the library; take a candle with you; leave the door open; sit down to the piano, and play a tune."

I departed, obeying his directions.

"Enough!" he called out in a few minutes. "You play a little, I see, like any other English schoolgirl: perhaps rather better than some, but not well."

I closed the piano and returned. Mr. Rochester continued:

"Adèle showed me some sketches this morning which she said were yours. I don't know whether they were entirely of your doing: probably a master aided you?"

"No, indeed!" I interjected.

"Ah! that pricks pride. Well, fetch me your portfolio, if you can vouch for its contents being original; but don't pass your word unless you are certain: I can recognize patchwork."

"Then I will say nothing, and you shall judge for yourself, sir."

I brought the portfolio from the library.

"Approach the table," said he; and I wheeled it to his couch. Adèle and Mrs. Fairfax drew near to see the pictures.

---

24. *religieuses:* similar to nuns; refers to females who have dedicated their lives to religious orders

"No crowding," said Mr. Rochester: "take the drawings from my hand as I finish with them; but don't push your faces up to mine."

He deliberately scrutinized each sketch and painting. Three he laid aside; the others, when he had examined them, he swept from him.

"Take them off to the other table, Mrs. Fairfax," said he, "and look at them with Adèle; —you" (glancing at me) "resume your seat, and answer my questions. I perceive these pictures were done by one hand: was that hand yours?"

"Yes."

"And when did you find time to do them? They have taken much time, and some thought."

"I did them in the last two vacations I spent at Lowood, when I had no other occupation."

"Where did you get your copies?"

"Out of my head."

"That head I see now on your shoulders?"

"Yes, sir."

"Has it other furniture of the same kind within?"

"I should think it may have: I should hope—better."

He spread the pictures before him, and again surveyed them alternately.

While he is so occupied I will tell you, reader, what they are: and first, I must premise that they are nothing wonderful. The subjects had, indeed, risen vividly on my mind. As I saw them with the spiritual eye, before I attempted to embody them, they were striking; but my hand would not second my fancy, and in each case it had wrought out but a pale portrait of the thing I had conceived.

These pictures were in watercolors. The first represented clouds low and livid, rolling over a swollen sea: all the distance was in eclipse; so, too, was the foreground; or, rather, the nearest billows, for there was no land. One gleam of light lifted into relief a half-submerged mast, on which sat a cormorant, dark and large, with wings flecked with foam: its beak held a gold bracelet, set with gems, that I had touched with as brilliant tints as my palette could yield, and as glittering distinctness as my pencil could impart. Sinking below the bird and mast, a drowned corpse glanced through the green water; a fair arm was the only limb clearly visible, whence the bracelet had been washed or torn.

The second picture contained for foreground only the dim peak of a hill, with grass and some leaves slanting as if by a breeze. Beyond and above spread an expanse of sky, dark blue as at twilight: rising into the sky was a woman's shape to the bust, portrayed in tints as dusk and soft as I could combine. The dim forehead was crowned with a star; the lineaments below were seen as through the suffusion of vapor; the eyes shone dark and wild; the hair streamed shadowy, like a beamless cloud torn by storm or by electric travail. On the neck lay a pale reflection like moonlight; the same faint luster touched the train of thin clouds from which rose and bowed this vision of the Evening Star.[25]

The third showed the pinnacle of an iceberg piercing a polar winter sky: a muster of northern lights reared their dim lances, close serried, along the horizon. Throwing these into distance, rose, in the foreground, a head, a colossal head, inclined towards the iceberg, and resting against it. Two thin hands, joined under the forehead, and supporting it, drew up before the lower features a sable veil; a brow quite bloodless, white as bone, and an eye hollow

25. *Evening Star:* the goddess Selene from Greek legend or the planet Venus; both associated with love

and fixed, blank of meaning but for the glassiness of despair, alone were visible. Above the temples, amidst wreathed turban folds of black drapery, vague in its character and consistency as cloud, gleamed a ring of white flame, gemmed with sparkles of a more lurid tinge. This pale crescent was "The likeness of a Kingly Crown"; what it diademed was "the shape which shape had none."[26] R

Draw Conclusions: What conclusions can you draw about Jane from her paintings? R

"Were you happy when you painted these pictures?" asked Mr. Rochester, presently.

"I was absorbed, sir: yes, and I was happy. To paint them, in short, was to enjoy one of the keenest pleasures I have ever known."

"That is not saying much. Your pleasures, by your own account, have been few; but I daresay you did exist in a kind of artist's dreamland while you blended and arranged these strange tints. Did you sit at them long each day?"

"I had nothing else to do, because it was the vacation, and I sat at them from morning till noon, and from noon till night: the length of the midsummer days favored my inclination to apply."

"And you felt self-satisfied with the result of your ardent labors?"

"Far from it. I was tormented by the contrast between my idea and my handiwork: in each case I had imagined something which I was quite powerless to realize."

"Not quite: you have secured the shadow of your thought: but no more, probably. You had not enough of the artist's skill and science to give it full being: yet the drawings are, for a schoolgirl, peculiar. As to the thoughts, they are elfish. These eyes in the Evening Star you must have seen in a dream. How could you make them look so clear, and yet not at all brilliant? for the planet above quells their rays. And what meaning is that in their solemn depth? And who taught you to paint wind? There is a high gale in that sky, and on this hilltop. Where did you see Latmos?[27] For that is Latmos. There, —put the drawings away!"

I had scarce tied the strings of the portfolio, when, looking at his watch, he said abruptly,—"It is nine o'clock: what are you about, Miss Eyre, to let Adèle sit up so long? Take her to bed." R

Draw Conclusions: What conclusions can you draw about Rochester from his response to Jane's paintings? R

Adèle went to kiss him before quitting the room: he endured the caress, but scarcely seemed to relish it more than Pilot would have done, nor so much.

"I wish you all good-night, now," said he, making a movement of the hand towards the door, in token that he was tired of our company, and wished to dismiss us. Mrs. Fairfax folded up her knitting: I took my portfolio: we curtseyed to him, received a frigid bow in return, and so withdrew.

"You said Mr. Rochester was not strikingly peculiar, Mrs. Fairfax," I observed, when I rejoined her in her room, after putting Adèle to bed.

"Well, is he?"

"I think so: he is very changeful and abrupt."

"True: no doubt he may appear so to a stranger, but I am so accustomed to his manner I never think of it; and then, if he has peculiarities of temper, allowance should be made."

"Why?"

"Partly because it is his nature and we can none of us help our nature; and, partly, he has painful thoughts, no doubt, to harass him, and make his spirits unequal."

26. *The likeness of a Kingly Crown . . . shape had none:* reference to Milton's *Paradise Lost*, Book 2; a description of death

27. *Latmos:* key location in the legend of Selene, goddess of the moon, and her mortal lover, Endymion

"What about?"

"Family troubles, for one thing."

"But he has no family."

"Not now, but he has had or, at least, relatives. He lost his elder brother a few years since."

"His *elder* brother?"

"Yes. The present Mr. Rochester has not been very long in possession of the property; only about nine years."

"Nine years is a tolerable time. Was he so very fond of his brother as to be still inconsolable for his loss?"

"Why, no perhaps not. I believe there were some misunderstandings between them. Mr. Bowland Rochester was not quite just to Mr. Edward; and, perhaps, he prejudiced his father against him. The old gentleman was fond of money, and anxious to keep the family estate together. He did not like to diminish the property by division, and yet he was anxious that Mr. Edward should have wealth too, to keep up the consequence of the name; and, soon after he was of age, some steps were taken that were not quite fair, and made a great deal of mischief. Old Mr. Rochester and Mr. Rowland combined to bring Mr. Edward into what he considered a painful position, for the sake of making his fortune: what the precise nature of that position was I never clearly knew, but his spirit could not brook what he had to suffer in it. He is not very forgiving: he broke with his family, and now for many years he has led an unsettled kind of life. I don't think he has ever been resident at Thornfield for a fortnight together since the death of his brother without a will left him master of the estate; and, indeed, no wonder he shuns the old place."

"Why should he shun it?"

"Perhaps he thinks it gloomy."

The answer was evasive—I should have liked something clearer; but Mrs. Fairfax either could not, or would not, give me more explicit information of the origin and nature of Mr. Rochester's trials. She averred they were a mystery to herself, and that what she knew was chiefly from conjecture. It was evident, indeed, that she wished me to drop the subject, which I did accordingly. **R**

Draw Conclusions: What conclusions can you draw about Rochester from the conversation between Jane and Mrs. Fairfax? **R**

THINK AND DISCUSS

1. Identify three gothic elements in the excerpt of *Jane Eyre*.
2. How is Jane conflicted at the beginning of the selection? Why does she feel her meeting with the rider on the road to Hay is a turning point for her?
3. Summarize the description of the road to Hay. How does it reflect Jane's personal character?
4. What are some similarities between the character of Rochester and the descriptions of his home, Thornfield Hall?
5. Compare Jane and Rochester. Characterize their general responses to each other in the selection.
6. Describe three elements in the selection that reflect or reveal Jane's romantic disposition.
7. Explain how two of Jane's experiences or inner conflicts develop themes associated with "the woman question."
8. Describe two ways in which these chapters touch on the Victorian concern with social class.
9. What dominant symbol in Chapters 12 and 13 represents the theme of human isolation?
10. Describe two elements of the novel (e.g., conflict, character, theme) that the switch between gothic and realistic elements seems to highlight.
11. How does the selection exemplify psychological realism? Support your answer from the text.
12. Briefly evaluate *Jane Eyre*'s treatment of romanticism, class, or "the woman question" from a biblical worldview.
13. Create either a diary entry or a drawing from either Jane's or Rochester's point of view. Be sure to capture something of the character's style of speech if you choose to write a diary entry. If you choose to create a drawing, employ textual details of the character.

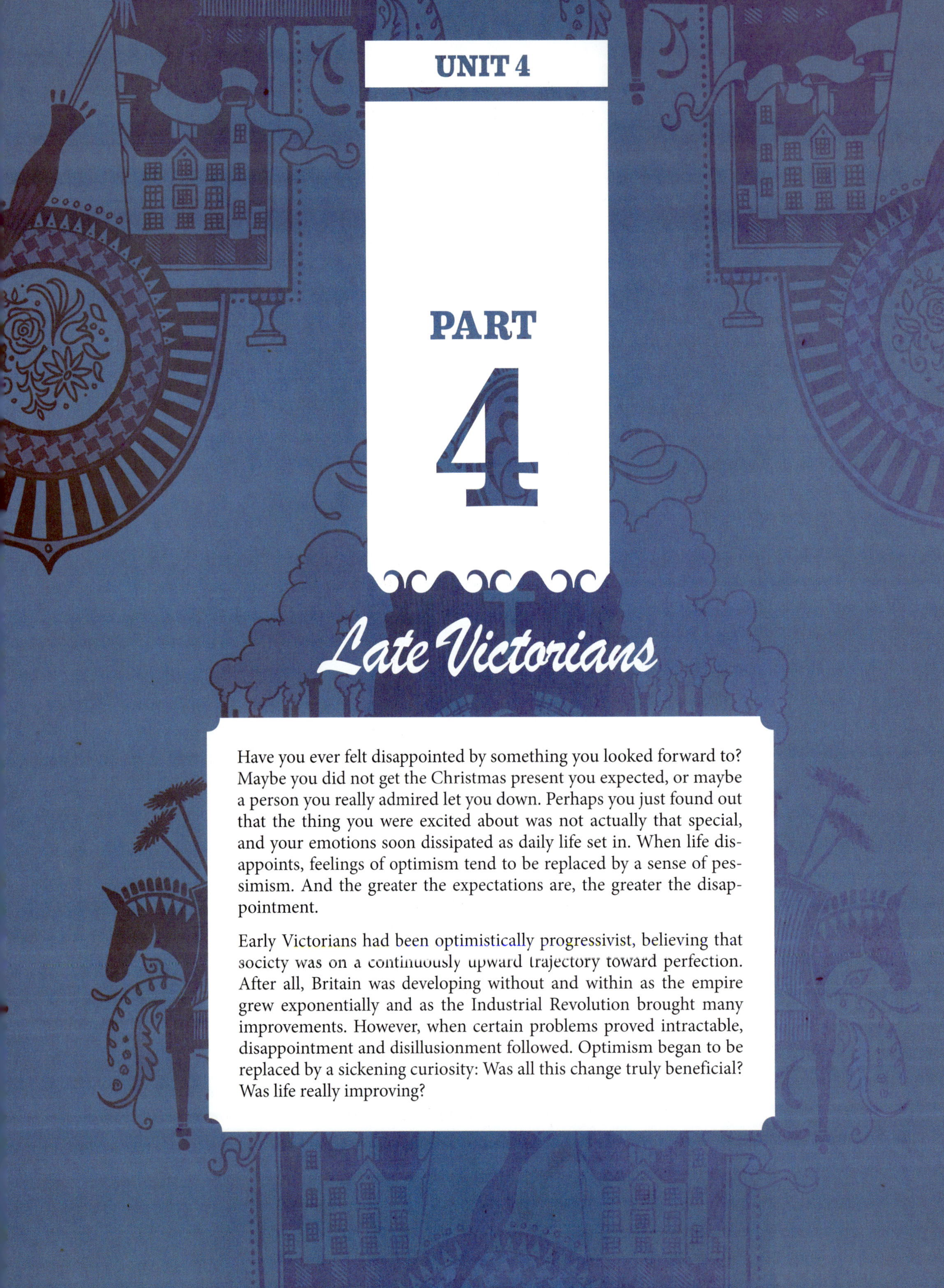

UNIT 4

PART 4

Late Victorians

Have you ever felt disappointed by something you looked forward to? Maybe you did not get the Christmas present you expected, or maybe a person you really admired let you down. Perhaps you just found out that the thing you were excited about was not actually that special, and your emotions soon dissipated as daily life set in. When life disappoints, feelings of optimism tend to be replaced by a sense of pessimism. And the greater the expectations are, the greater the disappointment.

Early Victorians had been optimistically progressivist, believing that society was on a continuously upward trajectory toward perfection. After all, Britain was developing without and within as the empire grew exponentially and as the Industrial Revolution brought many improvements. However, when certain problems proved intractable, disappointment and disillusionment followed. Optimism began to be replaced by a sickening curiosity: Was all this change truly beneficial? Was life really improving?

While early Victorian writers had offered a clear diagnosis and prescription for society's problems, late Victorians increasingly questioned whether any solution existed. Darwinism's advent lent credence to this pessimistic turn of thought, divorcing traditional faith and scientific understandings of the world. Men such as Thomas Henry Huxley believed that scientific reasoning demanded an agnostic worldview and promoted such thinking in public education. Herbert Spencer took the theory even further, applying its biological principles to human society in **social Darwinism**. He deemed natural selection evolution's keynote idea, framing it as "the survival of the fittest." While he believed in society's progression, according to him, no Creator or deity existed to govern this change; only the strongest would survive.

Such ideas undermined English society's traditional moral code and unleashed a cascade of crushing worldview issues: If no Creator exists and humans are only a product of natural selection, why do we exist? If only reproduction of the fittest really matters, are all of man's foundational concepts of self, God, and morality simply arbitrary, manmade constructs? And who are "the fittest" that should survive? What makes someone less or more evolved? Are such people still obligated to help those less fortunate than they?

These conflicts between faith and doubt were pivotal in literature as well. On the traditional end, some religious writers reacted conservatively to such changes. Anglicanism had grown into several groups—high-, mid-, and low-church—varying in doctrine and formal worship. Feeling that the Anglican Church was not serious enough about a variety of matters, writers like John Henry Newman and Gerard Manley Hopkins took part in the Tractarian Movement, advocating for Anglican reform toward high-church traditions.

Many eventually broke with the Anglican Church and converted to Catholicism's long tradition, seeking a sense of timeless certainty in an era of change. Other late Victorians became disillusioned with traditional beliefs. Writer and educator Matthew Arnold was reluctantly convinced by the new scientific theories and turned from evangelical beliefs to inner goodness as a bulwark against despair. He wished for, rather than believed in, a greater purpose to illumine the darkness. Meanwhile, **naturalism** extended Darwinism into literature. Realistic in style, naturalist literature depicted God (if He existed at all), nature, and society as indifferent to individuals, themselves mere animals whose hopes and dreams are at the mercy of forces they cannot control. The novelist Thomas Hardy, for instance, wrote fatalistically of characters forced by social circumstances to make terrible choices yielding tragic results.

With foundational beliefs and purposes eroded, many Victorian writers of the nineties seemed to flounder in decadence. Popular playwrights such as George Bernard Shaw composed flippant, nondidactic pieces in deliberate contrast to the serious tone of other late Victorians. Oscar Wilde, a flamboyant personality known for his humorous social satire, wrote plays and novels reflecting this premodern period. As part of the aesthetic movement, which created "art for art's sake," Wilde created plays and novels that wittily entertain and satirize Victorian conventions. Deceptively playful, they in fact often engaged in serious questions about the Victorian worldview.

Alongside these dichotomies grew another class of literature, that of empire. Although the era marked the British Empire's height, there were signs of controversy within. Writers such as Rudyard Kipling and Joseph Conrad addressed some of these. Having grown up in India, Kipling gives a practical perspective on colonialism and its inherent problems. While his perspective often demonstrates the common European sentiment of superiority, he also reflects a level of respect for India's complex and ancient culture. Conrad, meanwhile, laid bare some of imperialism's more chilling realities. The concerns of all three groups of writers would only escalate in the early twentieth century.

BIOGRAPHY

Matthew Arnold (1822–88)

Matthew Arnold was the son of Dr. Thomas Arnold, liberal clergyman and headmaster at Rugby School, and his wife, Mary. Although G. K. Chesterton later famously called him "perhaps the most serious man alive,"[1] Arnold was a bit mischievous as a child, standing behind his father and making faces while his father was speaking to the students. He attended Oxford University but did not excel to the level of his intelligence and preparation. Instead, he dressed as a dandy and socialized. To the horror of his friend and fellow poet Arthur Hugh Clough, Arnold finished his work as a second (a class of academic achievement) rather than a first. Nonetheless, he became a fellow and later a professor of poetry at Oxford and taught classics at Rugby.

Desiring an income that would support a wife and children, Arnold took the position of government school inspector. Shortly afterward, in 1851, he married Frances Lucy Wightman, with whom he had six children. For thirty-five years, he traveled throughout England and diligently examined teacher-preparation programs and primary schools (secondary education was not provided by the government at that time). This occupation allowed him close contact with middle-class people, some of whom, in his series of essays called *Culture and Anarchy*, he termed Philistines for their materialism, narrow-mindedness, conventional morality, and indifference to the arts. These flaws, he argued, were results of industrialization's moving people away from the land to stark factories and making their work a commodity. To counteract their effects, he advocated for a life of beauty and of the mind (for "sweetness and light").

Social consciousness marked both his prose and his poetry, for which he was equally well-known. Two notable pieces, "The Scholar Gipsy" and "Dover Beach," deal with both social issues and individual loneliness and alienation. Arnold, considered one of the best writers of the Victorian era, died in April 1888.

1. "Matthew Arnold," *The Bookman* 16, no. 2 (October 1902): 120.

BEFORE READING

ANALYZE: *Atmosphere*

In "Dover Beach" the **atmosphere** (the mood or emotion pervading a work, specifically when it is enhanced by a work's setting) is important to theme. Arnold creates this atmosphere primarily with imagery. For example, the initial physical setting sets a specific mood. The speaker observes the Strait of Dover: on one side stand the White Cliffs of Dover, and on the other side, twenty miles away, are the lights of Calais, France. What emotions do you feel as the speaker describes this setting? At what point in the poem does this feeling change? What other images does Arnold use to develop the poem's atmosphere?

READ: *Infer Meaning from Details*

Arnold leans on atmosphere, imagery, and figurative language to create his theme. But readers must infer the meaning that they together develop. As already noted, look for connections between the poem's images and atmosphere. How do specific sensory details (e.g., sounds, sights) infuse emotions? For instance, look for sound imagery (e.g., onomatopoeia, p. 465) that affects readers' emotions. Next, find any **metaphors** and **similes** (pp. 151, 212) Arnold uses. How do they help bring out the underlying meaning of the images? For example, what can you infer about the battle into which Arnold sweeps the reader at the poem's conclusion?

EVALUATE: *Author's Worldview*

"Dover Beach" sets forth Arnold's vision of the current state of the world. What specific aspect of humanity's state does Arnold narrow in on? Is he optimistic or pessimistic? Is his view accurate? Consider as you read how his vision compares with a biblical worldview.

OBJECTIVES

- Infer meaning from textual details.
- Determine the atmosphere in a text.
- Analyze how a poem's atmosphere, imagery, and figurative expressions develop theme.
- Evaluate an author's view of faith and the meaning of life.

VOCABULARY

tranquil (trăng′kwəl) *adj.* Free from commotion or disturbance.

tremulous (trĕm′yə-ləs) *adj.* Marked by trembling, quivering, or shaking.

turbid (tûr′bĭd) *adj.* Having sediment or foreign particles stirred up or suspended; muddy.

certitude (sûr′tĭ-to͞od′) *n.* Something that is assured or believed to be true.

DOVER BEACH

The sea is calm tonight.
The tide is full, the moon lies fair
Upon the straits;[1]—on the French coast the light
Gleams and is gone; the cliffs of England stand,
Glimmering and vast, out in the **tranquil** bay.
Come to the window, sweet is the night air!
Only, from the long line of spray
Where the sea meets the moon-blanched[2] land, **A**
Listen! you hear the grating roar
Of pebbles which the waves draw back, and fling,
At their return, up the high strand,[3]

1. *straits:* Strait of Dover, the narrowest section of the English Channel
2. *moon-blanched:* moon-whitened
3. *strand:* beach

tranquil (trăng′kwəl) *adj.* Free from commotion or disturbance.

Atmosphere: Give several adjectives to describe the atmosphere at the beginning of the poem. **A**

VISUAL ANALYSIS
How does this painting evoke the imagery and atmosphere in "Dover Beach"?

Begin, and cease, and then again begin,
With **tremulous** cadence slow, and bring
The eternal note of sadness in. R

Sophocles[4] long ago
Heard it on the Aegean, and it brought
Into his mind the **turbid** ebb and flow
Of human misery; we
Find also in the sound a thought,
Hearing it by this distant northern sea.

The Sea of Faith
Was once, too, at the full, and round earth's shore
Lay like the folds of a bright girdle furled.
But now I only hear
Its melancholy, long, withdrawing roar,
Retreating, to the breath
Of the night wind, down the vast edges drear
And naked shingles[5] of the world. R

Ah, love, let us be true
To one another! for the world, which seems
To lie before us like a land of dreams,
So various, so beautiful, so new,
Hath really neither joy, nor love, nor light,
Nor **certitude**, nor peace, nor help for pain;
And we are here as on a darkling[6] plain
Swept with confused alarms[7] of struggle and flight,
Where ignorant armies clash by night.

---

4. *Sophocles:* Greek dramatist who wrote tragedies, fifth-century BC
5. *shingles:* pebbly beaches
6. *darkling:* dusky, obscure
7. *alarms:* trumpet signals in battle

tremulous (trĕm′yə-ləs) *adj.* Marked by trembling, quivering, or shaking.

Infer Meaning: Find an example of onomatopoeia in lines 9–14. How might it affect the atmosphere so far? R

turbid (tûr′bĭd) *adj.* Having sediment or foreign particles stirred up or suspended; muddy.

Infer Meaning: What metaphor does stanza 3 develop? What is changing about the thing Arnold is describing? R

certitude (sûr′tĭ-to͞od′) *n.* Something that is assured or believed to be true.

THINK AND DISCUSS

1. Define *atmosphere.*
2. What is the initial atmosphere of "Dover Beach," and how does Arnold use imagery to convey it?
3. Identify the atmosphere that pervades most of "Dover Beach," and, citing two examples, explain how Arnold uses figurative language to develop it.
4. What is Arnold's theme in the poem?
5. How does the allusion in stanza 2 help to universalize the poem's theme?
6. Do you judge Arnold's view of the world to be accurate? Why or why not? Consider in your answer the events of Ecclesiastes 9:1–10, 12:13–14.

Thomas Hardy (1840–1928)

Thomas Hardy was born to a stonemason and his wife in the county of Dorset, one of the impoverished rural southwestern counties in England that he fictionalized as Wessex in his novels. Thought at first to be stillborn, he revived, but he grew to be only a little over five feet tall as an adult. He was at first educated at home, but at the age of eight, he began public school. His family could not afford higher education for him, so at sixteen, he became an apprentice to an architect. Hardy lived in London for about five years, where he worked in architecture, and then he moved back to his beloved home. He was married, widowed, and remarried, but he had no children.

Often considered a nineteenth-century novelist and twentieth-century poet, he is a transitional figure in the movement from the Victorian era to the modern era. He wrote a long poetic drama, two volumes of short stories, and fourteen novels, the best known being *Tess of the D'Urbervilles*, *The Mayor of Casterbridge*, *Far from the Madding Crowd*, *The Return of the Native*, and *Jude the Obscure*. The last was so dark and controversial that it essentially ended his career as a novelist. Among his hundreds of poems are "The Man He Killed," which questions why men engage in warfare, and "The Convergence of the Twain," which vividly describes the collision of the *Titanic* and the iceberg that sank it. Although he said that he believed that people could live happily, both his novels and poetry suggest otherwise, for they place humans at the mercy of chance and of physical and economic environments over which they have little or no control.

During his long life, which spanned great change in science, politics, and literature, he also influenced great modern poets such as Robert Frost and W. H. Auden. When he died in 1928, his ashes were placed in the Poet's Corner of Westminster Abbey; but his heart was buried in the same Dorset churchyard where his grandparents, parents, and first wife were buried.

BEFORE READING

ANALYZE: *Imagery, Figurative Language, Symbol*

Like many naturalist writers (p. 551), Hardy highlights nature, particularly the English countryside, in his work. Notice the way in which he imagines nature throughout "The Darkling Thrush." What features does he describe? What particular mood does he express through these **images** (p. 75)? Additionally, search for deeper meaning layered within these images. What **figurative language** (p. 129) does Hardy use to describe his subject? For example, pay attention to how personification hints at his message. Additionally, keep an eye out for universal **symbols** (p. 37) sprinkled throughout the poem. How might these allow the poem to be a commentary, not just on an outdoor scene, but on life in general?

READ: *Draw Conclusions About Tone and Theme*

Given his naturalistic worldview, readers expect a decidedly pessimistic tone from Hardy. Dark irony is strongly present in the poem. However, some critics see ambiguity in what Hardy is expressing. As you read, consider what Hardy seems to feel about what he is saying. Pay attention to the attitudes expressed through word choices, imagery, symbols, and figurative expressions. Does this tone change within the poem? If so, how might that change affect the theme that Hardy conveys?

EVALUATE: *Naturalism*

Reflect on the ideas of naturalism (p. 551) that the poem incorporates. Consider, for example, the poet's allusion to the "blessed hope" in the last stanza. How does Paul's use of the phrase in Titus 2:13 contrast with Hardy's attitude in context? How might a Christian respond to Hardy's perspective?

OBJECTIVES

- Identify and interpret a poem's major images, figurative expressions, and symbols.
- Analyze a text's development of tone and theme.
- Evaluate naturalism's perspective from a biblical worldview.

What makes you **ANXIOUS** *for the future?*

The Darkling Thrush

I leant upon a coppice gate[1]
  When Frost was specter-gray,
And Winter's dregs made desolate
  The weakening eye of day.
The tangled bine-stems[2] scored the sky
  Like strings from broken lyres,
And all mankind that haunted nigh
  Had sought their household fires. **A**

1. *coppice gate:* gate to a grove of trees
2. *bine-stems:* vine-stems

Imagery/Symbol: In stanza 1, what nature imagery do you find? What universal symbols have been incorporated as part of this imagery? **A**

The land's sharp features seemed to be
  The Century's[3] corpse outleant,[4]
His crypt the cloudy canopy,
  The wind his death-lament.
The ancient pulse of germ[5] and birth
  Was shrunken hard and dry,
And every spirit upon earth
  Seemed fervorless as I. **A**

At once a voice outburst among
  The bleak twigs overhead
In a full-hearted evensong[6]
  Of joy illimited;[7]
An aged thrush, frail, gaunt, and small,
  In blast-beruffled plume,
Had chosen thus to fling his soul
  Upon the growing gloom. **R**

So little cause for carolings
  Of such ecstatic sound
Was written on terrestrial things
  Afar or nigh around,
That I could think there trembled through
  His happy good-night air
Some blessed Hope, whereof he knew
  And I was unaware.

---

3. *The Century's:* nineteenth century's
4. *outleant:* stretched out, silhouetted
5. *germ:* a seed, bud, or spore
6. *evensong:* hymn sung at evening prayers
7. *illimited:* limitless

VISUAL ANALYSIS
How might the imagery and atmosphere of this painting correspond to the mood of the speaker in "The Darkling Thrush"?

Figurative Language: What is personified in stanza 2? **A**

Draw Conclusions: How does the thrush's appearance infuse a sense of irony into the poem's tone? **R**

THINK AND DISCUSS

1. List three examples of nature imagery from the poem.
2. How does the poem's nature imagery contribute to its mood and theme?
3. List one example of metaphor, of simile, and of personification from the poem.
4. Note and explain the meaning of a universal symbol used within the poem's nature imagery.
5. What is the poem's main symbol? What does it represent for Hardy?
6. Explain how situational or verbal irony contributes to Hardy's tone in the poem.
7. Note the speaker's allusion to Paul's "blessed hope" in Titus 2:13. What does Paul mean by the phrase? What does the speaker mean by and feel about this "hope" in context of the poem?
8. Explain the poem's theme. How does Hardy's tone add a sense of ambiguity to what he is saying? Support your answer from the text.
9. How does the poem support a naturalistic worldview (p. 551)? Offer a biblical response to at least one of these ideas.

Gerard Manley Hopkins (1844–89)

The poet-priest Gerard Manley Hopkins was the first child of Manley and Catherine Hopkins, high-church Anglicans who encouraged artistic development in their nine children. A marine-insurance adjustor, Manley provided the family a comfortable life and also published some poetry himself. Gerard studied at Oxford and, to his parents' dismay, followed key Victorian John Newman in converting to Roman Catholicism.

Rather than accepting a comfortable lifestyle, Hopkins chose that of an ascetic priest. Upon joining the Jesuits in 1868, he tried to humble himself by destroying all his poetry. Eventually, motivated by his superior, he began writing again but chose not to publish, keeping church work his priority and producing less poetry than some poets. He served as a parish priest in various cities, including the slums of the growing industrial cities Glasgow, Manchester, and Liverpool.

In his poetry, Hopkins sought to communicate the essential, specially created nature of a thing, purposefully designed for the glory of God. He communicated this idea (which he termed *inscape*) largely through his invented form, sprung rhythm. This flexible, unusual form inspired twentieth-century poets once Robert Bridges (poet laureate and Hopkins's friend) published Hopkins's poetry in 1918. Other lasting contributions include his playfulness with words; his creation of new, vivid vocabulary; and his invention of the curtal sonnet, a highly compressed sonnet form.

In 1884 Hopkins became a professor at University College in Dublin. The move took him away from friends and London to a place of political tumult and vocational challenges. Feeling disconnected from God, his poetic inspiration, he fought despair, as indicated by his "terrible sonnets." Eventually, he began writing from a more hopeful perspective again, and it was in this more positive frame of mind that he contracted typhoid and moved on to eternity.

BEFORE READING

ANALYZE: *Sprung Rhythm and Curtal Sonnet*

Like Anglo-Saxon verse, Hopkins's **sprung rhythm** is built on strong stresses. These may directly follow each other (see "rose-moles" in "Pied Beauty"), or they may be interrupted by one to three lesser stresses. The rhythm seems to quickly spring over the lesser stresses to reach the next strong one, tending to result in compact lines, a feature Hopkins extended in form as well. The form of "Pied Beauty" is his invention, the **curtal sonnet** (i.e., curtailed sonnet), in which he shortened the Italian sonnet's octave and sestet to 6 and 4.5 lines respectively. In contrast, "God's Grandeur" uses the Italian form's traditional extended structure.

READ: *Annotate a Text*

To help you grasp the rhythm and structured thought of both sonnets, annotate these elements in the texts. Read each poem aloud, listening for stressed syllables. Then annotate enjambment (p. 457) and stressed syllables to help you identify any sprung rhythm. Finally, notate each sonnet's overall structure and imagery. How might both imagery and structure support the theme's development?

CREATE: *Compose Poetry*

After your analysis, create your own stanza of sprung poetry, using "Pied Beauty" as a model. Begin by choosing one of your favorite things, something for which you can praise God, as your topic. Then consider how Hopkins uses lists to create sprung rhythm (e.g., in line 9, "swift, slow; sweet, sour; adazzle, dim"). Choose some key qualities of your topic, and use vivid descriptive adjectives that develop these qualities. Next, note how Hopkins frames these lists within sentences at the poem's beginning and end. Finally, using your notes and Hopkins's model, create a short praise stanza in sprung rhythm.

OBJECTIVES

- Define *sprung rhythm* and *curtal sonnet*.
- Examine a poem's rhythm and the way it helps support meaning.
- Analyze a poem's imagery and structure.
- Compose a short praise poem in sprung rhythm.

VOCABULARY

pied (pīd) *adj.* Patchy in color.

dappled (dăp′əld) *adj.* Spotted; mottled.

fallow (făl′ō) *n.* Ploughed land; arable land.

blear (blîr) *tr.v.* To blur; dim.

Pied Beauty

Glory be to God for **dappled** things—
For skies of couple-color as a brinded[1] cow;
For rose-moles all in stipple[2] upon trout that swim;
Fresh-firecoal chestnut-falls; finches' wings;
Landscape plotted and pieced—fold, **fallow**, and plough;[3]
And áll trádes, their gear and tackle and trim. A

All things counter, original, spare,[4] strange;
Whatever is fickle, freckled (who knows how?)
With swift, slow; sweet, sour; adazzle, dim;
He fathers-forth whose beauty is past change:
Praise him.

1. *brinded:* spotted or streaked
2. *stipple:* "a method of drawing, engraving, or painting using dots or short strokes" (*AHD*)
3. *Landscape . . . plough:* the patchwork of grazing land, untilled arable land, and cultivated land as seen from a height or a distance
4. *spare:* rare

pied (pīd) *adj.* Patchy in color.

dappled (dăp′əld) *adj.* Spotted; mottled.

fallow (făl′ō) *n.* Ploughed land; arable land.

Sprung Rhythm: Mark the stresses in the first stanza. Where is sprung rhythm clearly evidenced? A

VISUAL ANALYSIS

Examine Vincent van Gogh's paintings *Wheat Fields at Auvers Under Clouded Sky* (1890) on this page and *The Sower (Sower with Setting Sun)* (1888) on page 560. How do the artist's content and techniques (e.g., brush strokes, color choices) parallel some of the imagery in Hopkins's poems "Pied Beauty" and "God's Grandeur"?

GOD'S GRANDEUR

The world is charged with the grandeur of God.
It will flame out, like shining from shook foil;
It gathers to a greatness, like the ooze of oil
Crushed. Why do men then now not reck[1] his rod?
Generations have trod, have trod, have trod;
And all is seared with trade; **bleared**, smeared with toil;
And wears man's smudge and shares man's smell; the soil
Is bare now, nor can foot feel, being shod.[2] R

And for all this, nature is never spent;
There lives the dearest freshness deep down things;[3]
And though the last lights off the black West went
Oh, morning, at the brown brink eastward, springs—
Because the Holy Ghost over the bent
World broods with warm breast and with ah! bright
wings. A

1. *reck:* pay attention to, acknowledge
2. *shod:* past tense of *shoe*, as in the shod hooves of a horse
3. *deep down things:* deep down in things

blear (blîr) *tr.v.* To blur; dim.

Annotate: What change in the poem's imagery does the stanza break highlight? R

Sonnet: What characteristics of the Italian sonnet are present in the poem? A

THINK AND DISCUSS

1. How does the opening line of "God's Grandeur" demonstrate sprung rhythm?
2. Despite its shortened form, how does "Pied Beauty" demonstrate characteristics of a sonnet?
3. In what ways does "God's Grandeur" conform to and diverge from the Italian sonnet form?
4. In "God's Grandeur," what might the enjambment in lines 3–4 highlight in the stanza's line of thought?
5. Trace the imagery in "God's Grandeur." How does its progression support the speaker's theme?
6. How does the sprung rhythm in stanza 2 of "Pied Beauty" help emphasize the poem's message?
7. How does Hopkins use beauty in these poems to promote Truth and Goodness?
8. Using Hopkins's second stanza of "Pied Beauty" as a template, create your own stanza of sprung poetry. Consult the directions on page 558 for further detail.

Oscar Wilde (1854–1900)

AT A GLANCE

- **1890** Published *The Picture of Dorian Gray*, his only novel
- **1892** First performance of *Lady Windermere's Fan*
- **1893** Wrote *A Woman of No Importance*
- **1895** First performance of *An Ideal Husband* and *The Importance of Being Earnest*
- **1895–97** Incarcerated
- **1898** Wrote *The Ballad of Reading Gaol*

Early Life and Education

Oscar Fingal O'Flahertie Wills Wilde was born in Dublin to brilliant, bohemian parents. His father, Sir William Wilde, was an outstanding eye and ear doctor (also a witty conversationalist) who developed sophisticated treatments for ear maladies and conducted a medical census of Ireland. His mother, Lady Jane Elgee Wilde, was a nationalist poet who wrote under the pseudonym Speranza, dressed unconventionally, and mastered various languages.

Wilde was educated at Portora Royal School and then Trinity College, Dublin, where he fell in love with classical languages and won the award for the best student in Greek. He won a scholarship to attend Oxford, where he excelled as a student of the classics and also became involved in a growing movement, aestheticism (typified by the phrase "art for art's sake"). The movement reacted to the didacticism of much Victorian art by emphasizing the value of beauty in art, frequently above any moral, political, or social message it might offer.

DID YOU KNOW ?

Wilde wrote fairy tales, including "The Happy Prince," "The Nightingale and the Rose," and "The Selfish Giant," and often shared them at dinner parties.

Artistic Career

Wilde eventually moved to London (1878) and continued to publish poetry as he had since college. He became something of a society figure, cultivating a certain image as an artist. Unlike most men of the era, he dressed flamboyantly, favoring bright colors, silk stockings, furs, and velvet. With just the perfect word and turn of phrase, he was a master of conversation. Much like Mark Twain, he remains known for witty, satirical quotes such as these: "Women are meant to be loved, not to be understood."[1] "All women become like their mothers. That is their tragedy. No man does. That's his."[2] His flamboyance and aesthetic philosophy made him a satirical target. *Punch* magazine published a cartoon depicting him as an overweight dandy, and Gilbert and Sullivan in their comic opera *Patience*, may have based their character Bunthorne, "a fleshly poet," on him.

In 1882 Wilde spent a year touring America and speaking on aestheticism, in the process meeting literary notables such as Holmes and Longfellow, as well as Whitman, whom he particularly admired. He returned to spend a year touring Great Britain, speaking on art and on his experiences in America. Eventually, he resettled in London and married wealthy, socially prominent Constance Lloyd in 1884, with whom he had two sons.

Wilde led a varied writing career. He began as a poet, became a lecturer, expanded to writing essays (often literary criticism), and most memorably, wrote plays and a novel. *The Picture of Dorian Gray* (1890), first serialized in a magazine, remains a classic. But he is best known for his plays, including *The Importance of Being Earnest*, *Lady Windermere's Fan*, *A Woman of No Importance*, and *An Ideal Husband*. In these, as in many of his works, Wilde none so gently satirized Victorian social mores.

Incarceration and Death

His career came to a quick and unhappy end in 1895 when he was tried and convicted of homosexual behavior and sentenced to two years hard labor and prison. His poem *The Ballad of Reading Gaol* came from his experience in prison. He never fully recovered from having been in prison, nor did he ever regain his writing career. His wife divorced him and moved with their sons to another country, where they lived under a different surname. He spent his last few years in exile in France and Italy and died of meningitis in Paris in 1900.

1. *From "The Sphinx Without a Secret"*
2. *From act 1 of* The Importance of Being Earnest

ANALYZE: *Satire and Comedy of Manners*

As you have seen, **satire** (p. 85) is a powerful tool in the hand of an accomplished author like Chaucer (p. 86) or Swift (p. 345). The purpose of satire, whether gentle (p. 333) or harsh (p. 346), is to poke fun at something in order to make it better. Satire, in other words, is corrective ridicule. Wilde wielded the tool to critique the Victorian era, which he referred to wryly as the "age of ideals."

The Importance of Being Earnest is a comedy, a play with a happy ending, but more specifically it is a **comedy of manners**, a play that satirizes the social customs (the morals and manners) of a sophisticated society. A sense of decorum (a highly mannered code of etiquette and propriety) was extremely important in Victorian society; thus, Wilde's choice of genre is particularly apt. Wilde displays a good deal of **wit** and **repartee** (p. 445) to make his points, techniques that are characteristic of the genre and its violation of social conventions. As you read the excerpt from *The Importance of Being Earnest*, note where Wilde uses humor to reveal his thinking about Victorian society and its professed ideals.

READ: *Combine Strategies*

Oftentimes your best game plan in tackling a text is a combination of strategies. For *The Importance of Being Earnest*, you will first need to apply historical context to understand its satirical points. Some of the play's references that would have been familiar to audiences in Wilde's day are obscure to today's reader or audience member. Note the glosses. For example, specifically where was Ernest found? How might the setting and circumstances metaphorically connect the era's sense of physical and social mobility? Additionally, apply Victorians' ideas about social class and their strong sense of decorum when evaluating what you know and see of certain characters. What might each character represent in Victorian society?

Once you have applied historical background and noted Wilde's humor, you will need to draw conclusions about what he meant to say with such details. Note the way in which he uses **characters** satirically. For example, Jack is initially thought to be a suitable marriage partner for Gwendolen Fairfax. Why? What changes in the course of the excerpt, and how do other characters respond to that change? Additionally, look for examples of **irony** (p. 88) within the play's humor. What is the irony of Jack's assumed identity? Where else in the play does appearance contrast with reality? Use such details to draw conclusions about how Wilde viewed Victorian social structure and class distinctions.

EVALUATE: *Satiric Effectiveness*

As you read the excerpt, judge its effectiveness for yourself. *The Importance of Being Earnest* was immensely popular from its initial performance, outstripping Wilde's other plays, and continues to attract audiences even today. Why, in your opinion? What are the serious lessons to tease from his humorous satire? Do you personally find his points convincing?

OBJECTIVES

- Identify characteristics of the comedy of manners in a text.
- Apply historical context to understand a text's message.
- Analyze a text's use of wit, repartee, irony, and character to make a satirical point.
- Evaluate the effectiveness of a text's satire.

VOCABULARY

demonstrative (dĭ-mŏn′strə-tĭv) *adj.* Given to or marked by the open expression of emotion.

provincial (prə-vĭn′shəl) *adj.* Of or characteristic of people from the provinces; not fashionable or sophisticated.

indecorous (ĭn-dĕk′ər-əs) *adj.* Lacking propriety or decorum.

exact (ĭg-zăkt′) *tr.v.* To demand and obtain by force or authority.

immaterial (ĭm′ə-tîr′ē-əl) *adj.* Of no importance or relevance; inconsequential or irrelevant.

indiscretion (ĭn′dĭ-skrĕsh′ən) *n.* An *indiscreet* (*adj.* unwise or tactless) act or remark.

What can **HUMOR** *teach us?*

Rare is the person who does not enjoy a good laugh. In fact, humor is like a magnet, drawing people to its wielder. We like to laugh at the funny situations and foibles of others, and it is healthy to be able to laugh at our own mistakes and inconsistencies. Almost any lesson, even hard truths, can be made more palatable with a sprinkle of humor. What did humor last teach you? Write a paragraph to answer the question.

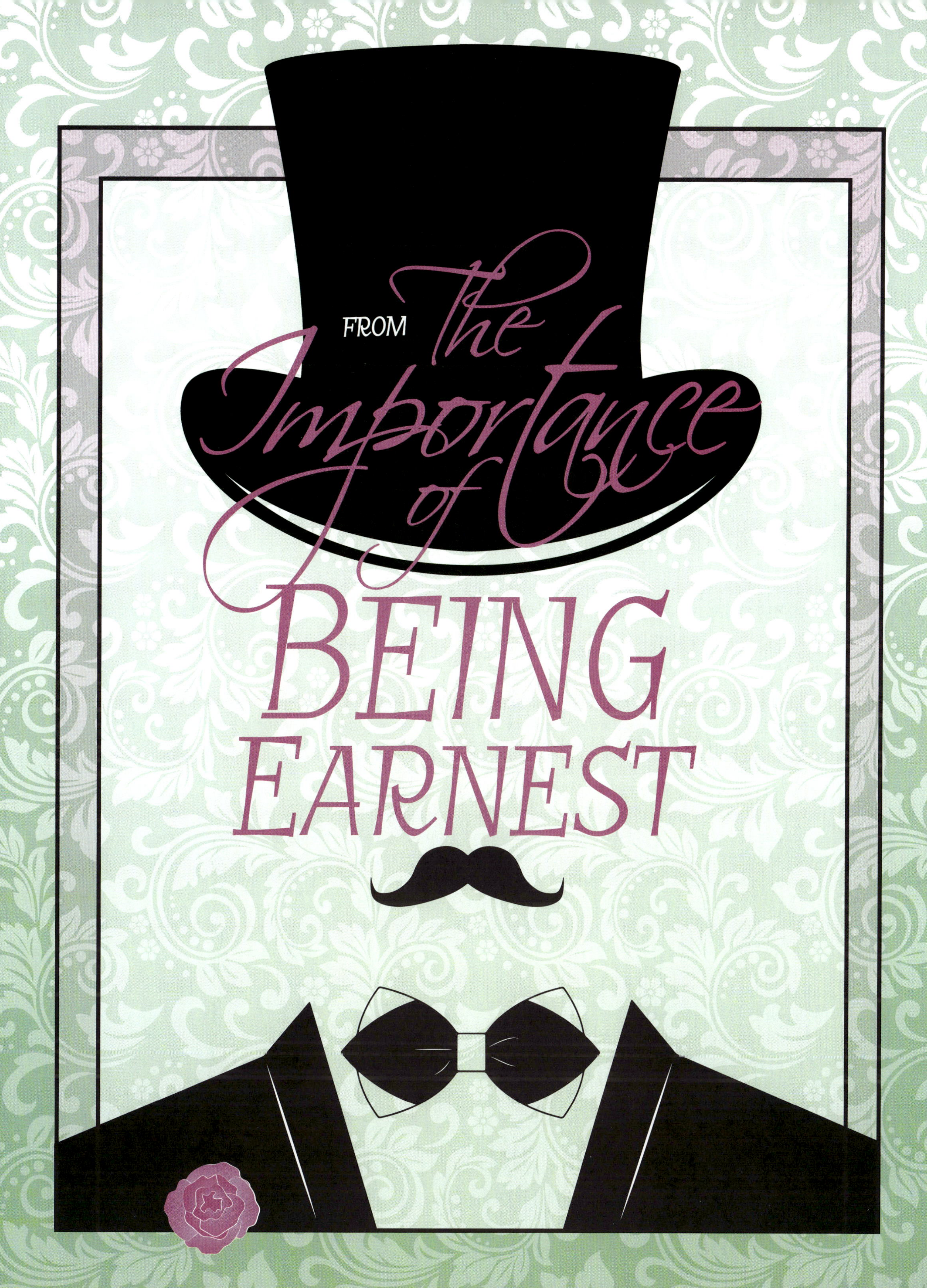
FROM The Importance of Being
BEING
EARNEST

from ACT I

Earlier in act 1 Algernon Moncrieff welcomes Ernest Worthing to his flat in town. Because of an inscription in his cigarette case, Ernest has to confess that his real name is Jack Worthing. Ernest is a name and identity that he assumes when in town. Similarly, Algernon confesses that he created a fictional invalid friend in the country, Bunbury, who enables him to escape there when he wants to avoid social engagements. Today Ernest is in town intent on proposing to Gwendolen Fairfax. Algernon agrees to help by getting Gwendolen's mother, Lady Bracknell, out of the way. When Lady Bracknell enters the room, she bows to Ernest with "icy coldness" because he is not on her list of eligible young men. In time Algernon is able to distract her in another room, leaving Ernest and Gwendolen alone.

JACK. Charming day it has been, Miss Fairfax.

GWENDOLEN. Pray don't talk to me about the weather, Mr. Worthing. Whenever people talk to me about the weather, I always feel quite certain that they mean something else. And that makes me so nervous.

JACK. I do mean something else.

GWENDOLEN. I thought so. In fact, I am never wrong.

JACK. And I would like to be allowed to take advantage of Lady Bracknell's temporary absence . . .[1]

GWENDOLEN. I would certainly advise you to do so. Mamma has a way of coming back suddenly into a room that I have often had to speak to her about.

JACK. (*Nervously.*) Miss Fairfax, ever since I met you I have admired you more than any girl . . . I have ever met since . . . I met you.

GWENDOLEN. Yes, I am quite aware of the fact. And I often wish that in public, at any rate, you had been more **demonstrative**. For me you have always had an irresistible fascination. Even before I met you I was far from indifferent to you. (JACK *looks at her in amazement.*) We live, as I hope you know, Mr. Worthing, in an age of ideals. The fact is constantly mentioned in the more expensive monthly magazines, and has reached the **provincial** pulpits I am told; and my ideal has always been to love someone of the name of Ernest. There is something in that name that inspires absolute confidence. The moment Algernon first mentioned to me that he had a friend called Ernest, I knew I was destined to love you. **A**

JACK. You really love me, Gwendolen?

GWENDOLEN. Passionately!

JACK. Darling! You don't know how happy you've made me.

GWENDOLEN. My own Ernest!

JACK. But you don't really mean to say that you couldn't love me if my name wasn't Ernest?

GWENDOLEN. But your name is Ernest.

JACK. Yes, I know it is. But supposing it was something else? Do you mean to say you couldn't love me then?

GWENDOLEN. (*Glibly.*) Ah! that is clearly a metaphysical speculation, and like most metaphysical speculations has very little reference at all to the actual facts of real life, as we know them.

demonstrative (dĭ-mŏn′strə-tĭv) *adj.* Given to or marked by the open expression of emotion.

provincial (prə-vĭn′shəl) *adj.* Of or characteristic of people from the provinces; not fashionable or sophisticated.

Satire: Gwendolen points out that they live in "an age of ideals." How would you characterize Gwendolen's ideal? **A**

1. *All suspension points (spaced dots indicating suspended speech) in the selection are from the original text.*

JACK. Personally, darling, to speak quite candidly, I don't much care about the name of Ernest. . .I don't think the name suits me at all.

GWENDOLEN. It suits you perfectly. It is a divine name. It has a music of its own. It produces vibrations.

JACK. Well, really, Gwendolen, I must say that I think there are lots of other much nicer names. I think Jack, for instance, a charming name.

GWENDOLEN. Jack? . . . No, there is very little music in the name Jack, if any at all, indeed. It does not thrill. It produces absolutely no vibrations. . . . I have known several Jacks, and they all, without exception, were more than usually plain. Besides, Jack is a notorious domesticity for John! And I pity any woman who is married to a man called John. She would probably never be allowed to know the entrancing pleasure of a single moment's solitude. The only really safe name is Ernest.

JACK. Gwendolen, I must get christened at once—I mean we must get married at once. There is no time to be lost.

GWENDOLEN. Married, Mr. Worthing?

JACK. (*Astounded.*) Well . . . surely. You know that I love you, and you led me to believe, Miss Fairfax, that you were not absolutely indifferent to me.

GWENDOLEN. I adore you. But you haven't proposed to me yet. Nothing has been said at all about marriage. The subject has not even been touched on.

JACK. Well . . . may I propose to you now?

GWENDOLEN. I think it would be an admirable opportunity. And to spare you any possible disappointment, Mr. Worthing, I think it only fair to tell you quite frankly beforehand that I am fully determined to accept you.

JACK. Gwendolen!

GWENDOLEN. Yes, Mr. Worthing, what have you got to say to me?

JACK. You know what I have got to say to you.

GWENDOLEN. Yes, but you don't say it.

JACK. Gwendolen, will you marry me? (*Goes on his knees.*)

GWENDOLEN. Of course I will, darling. How long you have been about it! I am afraid you have had very little experience in how to propose.

JACK. My own one, I have never loved anyone in the world but you.

GWENDOLEN. Yes, but men often propose for practice. I know my brother Gerald does. All my girlfriends tell me so. What wonderfully blue eyes you have, Ernest! They are quite, quite blue. I hope you will always look at me just like that, especially when there are other people present. (*Enter Lady Bracknell.*) **A**

LADY BRACKNELL. Mr. Worthing! Rise, sir, from this semi-recumbent posture. It is most **indecorous**.

GWENDOLEN. Mamma! (*He tries to rise; she restrains him.*) I must beg you to retire. This is no place for you. Besides, Mr. Worthing has not quite finished yet.

LADY BRACKNELL. Finished what, may I ask?

GWENDOLEN. I am engaged to Mr. Worthing, mamma. (*They rise together.*)

Satire: What do you conjecture that Wilde is poking fun at in Victorian society? **A**

indecorous (ĭn-dĕk′ər-əs) *adj.* Lacking propriety or decorum.

LADY BRACKNELL. Pardon me, you are not engaged to anyone. When you do become engaged to someone, I, or your father, should his health permit him, will inform you of the fact. An engagement should come on a young girl as a surprise, pleasant or unpleasant, as the case may be. It is hardly a matter that she could be allowed to arrange for herself. . . . And now I have a few questions to put to you, Mr. Worthing. While I am making these inquiries, you, Gwendolen, will wait for me below in the carriage.

GWENDOLEN. (*Reproachfully.*) Mamma!

LADY BRACKNELL. In the carriage, Gwendolen! (*GWENDOLEN goes to the door. She and Jack blow kisses to each other behind Lady Bracknell's back. Lady Bracknell looks vaguely about as if she could not understand what the noise was. Finally turns round.*) Gwendolen, the carriage!

GWENDOLEN. Yes, mamma. (*Goes out, looking back at Jack.*)

LADY BRACKNELL. (*Sitting down.*) You can take a seat, Mr. Worthing. (*Looks in her pocket for notebook and pencil.*)

JACK. Thank you, Lady Bracknell, I prefer standing.

LADY BRACKNELL. (*Pencil and notebook in hand.*) I feel bound to tell you that you are not down on my list of eligible young men, although I have the same list as the dear Duchess of Bolton has. We work together, in fact. However, I am quite ready to enter your name, should your answers be what a really affectionate mother requires. Do you smoke? **R**

Draw Conclusions: What social class does Lady Bracknell represent? What is ironic about her stated purpose here and the nature of the questions that follow? **R**

JACK. Well, yes, I must admit I smoke.

LADY BRACKNELL. I am glad to hear it. A man should always have an occupation of some kind. There are far too many idle men in London as it is. How old are you?

JACK. Twenty-nine.

LADY BRACKNELL. A very good age to be married at. I have always been of opinion that a man who desires to get married should know either everything or nothing. Which do you know?

JACK. (*After some hesitation.*) I know nothing, Lady Bracknell.

LADY BRACKNELL. I am pleased to hear it. I do not approve of anything that tampers with natural ignorance. Ignorance is like a delicate exotic fruit; touch it and the bloom is gone. The whole theory of modern education is radically unsound. Fortunately in England, at any rate, education produces no effect whatsoever. If it did, it would prove a serious danger to the upper classes, and probably lead to acts of violence in Grosvenor Square.[2] What is your income? **A**

Satire: What topic is Wilde using Lady Bracknell to satirize here? **A**

JACK. Between seven and eight thousand a year.

LADY BRACKNELL. (*Makes a note in her book.*) In land, or in investments?

JACK. In investments, chiefly.

LADY BRACKNELL. That is satisfactory. What between the duties expected of one during one's lifetime, and the duties **exacted** from one after one's death, land has ceased to be either a profit or a pleasure. It gives one position, and prevents one from keeping it up. That's all that can be said about land.

exact (ĭg-zăkt′) *tr.v.* To demand and obtain by force or authority.

JACK. I have a country house with some land, of course, attached to it, about fifteen hundred acres, I believe; but I don't depend on that

2. *Grosvenor Square:* a fashionable residential area of London where aristocracy lived and where Wilde himself lived for a time

for my real income. In fact, as far as I can make out, the poachers are the only people who make anything out of it.

LADY BRACKNELL. A country house! How many bedrooms? Well, that point can be cleared up afterwards. You have a town house, I hope? A girl with a simple, unspoiled nature, like Gwendolen, could hardly be expected to reside in the country.

JACK. Well, I own a house in Belgrave Square,[3] but it is let by the year to Lady Bloxham. Of course, I can get it back whenever I like, at six months' notice.

LADY BRACKNELL. Lady Bloxham? I don't know her.

JACK. Oh, she goes about very little. She is a lady considerably advanced in years.

LADY BRACKNELL. Ah, nowadays that is no guarantee of respectability of character. What number in Belgrave Square?

JACK. 149.

LADY BRACKNELL. (*Shaking her head.*) The unfashionable side. I thought there was something. However, that could easily be altered.

JACK. Do you mean the fashion, or the side?

LADY BRACKNELL. (*Sternly*) Both, if necessary, I presume. What are your politics?

JACK. Well, I am afraid I really have none. I am a Liberal Unionist.[4]

LADY BRACKNELL. Oh, they count as Tories. They dine with us. Or come in the evening, at any rate. Now to minor matters. Are your parents living?

JACK. I have lost both my parents.

LADY BRACKNELL. Both? . . . That seems like carelessness. Who was your father? He was evidently a man of some wealth. Was he born in what the Radical papers call the purple of commerce, or did he rise from the ranks of the aristocracy? **A**

Comedy of Manners: What characteristic of a comedy of manners does Lady Bracknell's dialogue illustrate? **A**

JACK. I am afraid I really don't know. The fact is, Lady Bracknell, I said I had lost my parents. It would be nearer the truth to say that my parents seem to have lost me . . . I don't actually know who I am by birth. I was . . . well, I was found.

LADY BRACKNELL. Found!

JACK. The late Mr. Thomas Cardew, an old gentleman of a very charitable and kindly disposition, found me, and gave me the name of Worthing, because he happened to have a first-class ticket for Worthing in his pocket at the time. Worthing is a place in Sussex. It is a seaside resort.

LADY BRACKNELL. Where did the charitable gentleman who had a first-class ticket for this seaside resort find you?

JACK. (*Gravely*) In a handbag.

LADY BRACKNELL. A handbag?

JACK. (*Very seriously.*) Yes, Lady Bracknell. I was in a handbag—a somewhat large, black leather handbag, with handles to it—an ordinary handbag in fact.

LADY BRACKNELL. In what locality did this Mr. James, or Thomas, Cardew come across this ordinary handbag?

3. *Belgrave Square:* another residential area for London's wealthy and aristocratic citizens

4. *Liberal Unionist:* a member of the Liberal Unionist Party, a faction of Liberals that split from the party when Gladstone (Liberal leader) chose to support Irish Home Rule (i.e., self-rule)

JACK. In the cloakroom at Victoria Station.[5] It was given to him in mistake for his own.

LADY BRACKNELL. The cloakroom at Victoria Station?

JACK. Yes. The Brighton line.[6]

LADY BRACKNELL. The line is **immaterial**. Mr. Worthing, I confess I feel somewhat bewildered by what you have just told me. To be born, or at any rate bred, in a handbag, whether it had handles or not, seems to me to display a contempt for the ordinary decencies of family life that remind one of the worst excesses of the French Revolution. And I presume you know what that unfortunate movement led to? As for the particular locality in which the handbag was found, a cloakroom at a railway station might serve to conceal a social **indiscretion**—has probably, indeed, been used for that purpose before now—but it could hardly be regarded as an assured basis for a recognized position in good society.

immaterial (ĭm′ə-tîr′ē-əl) *adj.* Of no importance or relevance; inconsequential or irrelevant.

indiscretion (ĭn′dĭ-skrĕsh′ən) *n.* An *indiscreet* (*adj.* unwise or tactless) act or remark.

JACK. May I ask you then what you would advise me to do? I need hardly say I would do anything in the world to insure Gwendolen's happiness.

LADY BRACKNELL. I would strongly advise you, Mr. Worthing, to try and acquire some relations as soon as possible, and to make a definite effort to produce at any rate one parent, of either sex, before the season is quite over.

JACK. Well, I don't see how I could possibly manage to do that. I can produce the handbag at any moment. It is in my dressing room at home. I really think that should satisfy you, Lady Bracknell.

LADY BRACKNELL. Me, sir! What has it to do with me? You can hardly imagine that I and Lord Bracknell would dream of allowing our only daughter—a girl brought up with the utmost care—to marry into a cloakroom, and form an alliance with a parcel? Good morning, Mr. Worthing! (*Lady Bracknell sweeps out in majestic indignation.*) A

Satire: What social attitude exhibited by Lady Bracknell is Wilde's humor satirizing? A

5. *Victoria Station:* London railway station that in Wilde's time had only two terminals, one going east and the other west

6. *The Brighton line:* the line traveling to the fashionable, upscale West and to Worthing, a coastal resort

THINK AND DISCUSS

1. Define *comedy*, *comedy of manners*, *wit*, and *repartee*.
2. Define *irony* and explain the irony in Jack's adoption of the name Ernest.
3. When Lady Bracknell first sees John Worthing, she treats him with "icy coldness" because he is not on her list of eligible young men. What is she later willing to do?
4. What segment of society does Lady Bracknell represent? Analyze Wilde's use of this character in order to satirize Victorian society.
5. Are the characters Jack and Gwendolen sympathetic to readers? What might they each satirize?
6. Reread Lady Bracknell's response to Gwendolen's announcement that she is engaged to Mr. Worthing (alias Ernest). Do you conjecture that Victorians approved or disapproved of arranged marriages? Do you think that Wilde approved or disapproved of arranged marriages? Why or why not?
7. Between what two characters do you see the best example of repartee? Who, in your opinion, wins at this verbal fencing?
8. Do you personally find the excerpt from *The Importance of Being Earnest* engaging? Do you want to read all of the play to know the outcome for the characters?
9. Is the play's satire effective? What lessons can you glean? Evaluate them in light of Scripture.

Rudyard Kipling (1865–1936)

AT A GLANCE

- **1878** Educated at the United Services College
- **1882** Began his formative India years as a journalist
- **1894** Published *The Jungle Book*
- **1901** Published *Kim*, considered his masterpiece
- **1907** Received the Nobel Prize for literature

Childhood in India and England

Rudyard Kipling was born in Bombay, India, to prominent English parents. His father, John, was an artist and head of the department of architectural sculpture at a school in Bombay. John was a likable man with a keen memory for what he had read. Kipling's mother, Alice, was known for her fiery wit. Kipling's early life in India exposed him to non-European religions and customs. Like many Anglo-Indian children, he had an Indian ayah, a nursemaid who cared for the children. These influences powerfully shaped his identity as a writer.

Because his parents wanted him to be educated in England, Kipling and his sister, Trix, lived in Southsea with a foster family, the Holloways, for several years. There Kipling was emotionally and physically abused, leading him to call the home "The House of Desolation." In 1877 Alice Kipling took her children out of the Holloway home, and Rudyard was enrolled in the United Services College in 1878.

Early Career and Family

In 1882 Kipling returned to India, where he worked as a journalist. He paid close attention to details of both Anglo-Indian and Indian life, and his conversations with people around him found their way into many of his tales. In 1889 he made his way, via Japan and the United States, back to London, where he debuted as a serious author. In 1892 he married American Carrie Balestier, and the couple lived in her home state of Vermont for four years. There he wrote *The Jungle Book* (1894) for their first child, Josephine, and its sequel in 1895. The Kiplings returned to England in 1896 (although visiting South Africa each winter) but sadly lost Josephine to illness in 1899, a tragedy that haunted Kipling. It was sadly compounded when their son, John, died in World War I, a war Kipling fervently supported but which he privately thought England ill-prepared for. After John's death, Kipling never wrote another children's piece.

DID YOU KNOW ?

Kipling's *Just So Stories* were originally stories Kipling made up to tell his daughter Josephine at bedtime.

Death and Literary Legacy

Although he turned down the position of poet laureate, Kipling became the first Nobel Prize winner in English-language literature in 1907 and continued to write for the rest of his life. He died in January of 1936, and his ashes are buried in the Poet's Corner of Westminster Abbey. Though his literary reputation had declined by his later years, the Kipling Society (1927) was well established before his death.

Kipling's range as a writer was unusually broad, including excellent poetry, novels, and short stories. A master of the short story, he wrote many detailing colonial life in India with ironic and humorous precision, among them the famous "The Man Who Would Be King." His poetry also enjoyed considerable acclaim. It ranges from the pleasantly inspiring poem "If," to rousing and often humorous ballads from the perspective of common British soldiers, to the (today racially fraught) work "The White Man's Burden," which offers a nineteenth-century view of Western imperialism. Today, Kipling's novels *The Jungle Book* and *Kim* are his best-known works. The latter is undoubtedly his prose masterpiece, managing to encompass both rousing adventure and nuanced commentary on the British Empire.

A friend to President Theodore Roosevelt, King George V, and Cecil Rhodes, Kipling was politically engaged and outspoken, especially on the topic of imperialism, which surrounded much of his work. His views have been particularly controversial, both in his own lifetime and since, for postcolonial critics. At the same time, literary greats such as T. S. Eliot respected him for his artistry and insight into the multifaceted British Empire.

ANALYZE: *Persona, Irony, and Imagery*

Kipling's short stories are usually immensely funny. In "The Conversion of Aurelian McGoggin" the humorous effect is achieved through the narrator. Similar to Kipling himself, the narrative **persona** (p. 513) gives vent to Kipling's tongue-in-cheek humor. What is the narrator's occupation, and what impression does he leave? What opinions does he express? Are these opinions clearly Kipling's as well?

You can approach an understanding of Kipling's opinions by analyzing the **irony** and **imagery** of the story. Who or what are the objects of sarcasm and understatement (forms of **verbal irony**, p. 240) in the story? How does Kipling create **situational irony** (p. 88)? Finally, examine how the story's central, recurring **image** (see the beginning poem) helps Kipling lay out his view of how life works in India. How is this line of imagery applied to Aurelian McGoggin? What other insights into characters, conflicts, and theme does the imagery help you gain?

OBJECTIVES

- Identify a text's central image.
- Apply historical context to interpreting a work.
- Analyze how narrative persona, imagery, and irony develop a work's theme.
- Evaluate characters' differing worldviews in light of Scripture.

READ: *Apply Historical Context*

Kipling was born into Anglo-Indian society, comprised of British citizens living in India, many as part of the British Raj (p. 422). Many came to India as young men (often with families) for the social and financial opportunities the Indian Civil Service offered. They encountered an environment and culture vastly different from England's and, responding to its demands, created a hybrid culture all their own. In *Plain Tales from the Hills* (the 1888 short-story collection that contains this selection), Kipling presented a "boots on the ground" perspective of this India for Britons who had only a vague notion of how the empire operated overseas.

Plain Tales also reflects a time of great philosophical upheaval. The legacy of deists, romantics, and now Darwinists had created major worldview questions: these centered on faith, doubt, reason, intuition, science, and the place of each in understanding and meeting life's problems. As you read, consider how the story draws on contemporary events that were then shaping government, colonialism, science, and industry. How do the various characters respond to these issues? What do they think and feel about how life is to be understood and its problems conquered? Does Kipling sympathize more with McGoggin or with the narrator and his colleagues? What conclusions does he want readers to draw from this story?

VOCABULARY

unmitigated (ŭn-mĭt′ĭ-gā′tĭd) *adj.* Without qualification or exception; absolute.

embellish (ĕm-bĕl′ĭsh) *tr.v.* To add ornamental or fictitious details to.

figment (fĭg′mənt) *n.* Something invented, made up, or fabricated.

amenable (ə-mē′nə-bəl) *adj.* Willing to accept a suggestion or submit to authority.

arrears (ə-rîrz′) *pl.n.* An unpaid, overdue debt or an unfulfilled obligation.

EVALUATE: *Characters' Worldviews*

The character of McGoggin arrives in India with the theories of Comte and Spencer floating around in his brain. These nineteenth-century philosophers asserted the importance of natural phenomena and the idea that biological evolution applied to human interactions. However, the other characters have worked long in India, some for decades, and have a very different approach to dealing with life. You can see their clash begin in the story's first paragraphs. Examine the challenges McGoggin faces as he tries to adhere to his theories in India. How do the narrator and his colleagues respond to McGoggin's attempts, and why do they think as they do? Most importantly, does either of their responses and views seem to reflect a generally biblical worldview?

How do our EXPERIENCES *shape who we are?*

No two people have the same life experiences. Some people grow up on military bases that are close-knit communities. Others live in towns like Dante, Virginia, that sprang up around coal seams. The variables of life experiences are endless. Discuss with your classmates how your own experiences have shaped your thinking and beliefs. How might understanding such connections help in your relationships with others, from friends to fellow citizens?

VISUAL ANALYSIS

Which characters in Kipling's story best match the people depicted in this engraving? How does this depiction reflect a certain attitude and style of living?

The Conversion of Aurelian McGoggin

Ride with an idle whip, ride with an unused heel,
But, once in a way, there will come a day
When the colt must be taught to feel
The lash that falls, and the curb that galls, and the sting of the rowelled steel.

—*Life's Handicap*

This is not a tale exactly. It is a Tract; and I am immensely proud of it. Making a Tract is a Feat.

Every man is entitled to his own religious opinions; but no man—least of all a junior—has a right to thrust these down other men's throats. The Government sends out weird Civilians[1] now and again; but McGoggin was the queerest exported for a long time. He was clever—brilliantly clever—but his cleverness worked the wrong way. Instead of keeping to the study of the vernaculars, he had read some books written by a man called Comte,[2] I think, and a man called Spencer.[3] [You will find these books in the Library.] They deal with people's insides from the point of view of men who have no stomachs. There was no

1. *Civilians:* British civil servants, specifically those in the Indian Civil Service
2. *Comte:* Auguste Comte founded the theory of positivism, which relies on natural phenomena for knowledge.
3. *Spencer:* Herbert Spencer was a follower of Comte and was known for promoting social Darwinism.

order against his reading them; but his Mamma should have smacked him. They fermented in his head, and he came out to India with a rarefied religion over and above his work. It was not much of a creed. It only proved that men had no souls, and there was no God and no hereafter, and that you must worry along somehow for the good of Humanity. E

Characters' Worldview: Summarize the basic tenets of McGoggin's philosophy. E

One of its minor tenets seemed to be that the one thing more sinful than giving an order was obeying it. At least, that was what McGoggin said; but I suspect he had misread his primers. A

Verbal Irony: Locate two instances of verbal irony in the story up to this point. Can you identify what the verbal irony is making fun of? A

I do not say a word against this creed. It was made up in Town where there is nothing but machinery and asphalt and building—all shut in by the fog. Naturally, a man grows to think that there is no one higher than himself, and that the Metropolitan Board of Works[4] made everything. But in India, where you really see humanity—raw, brown, naked humanity—with nothing between it and the blazing sky, and only the used-up, over-handled earth underfoot, the notion somehow dies away, and most folk come back to simpler theories. Life, in India, is not long enough to waste in proving that there is no one in particular at the head of affairs. For this reason. The Deputy is above the Assistant, the Commissioner above the Deputy, the Lieutenant Governor above the Commissioner, and the Viceroy above all four, under the orders of the Secretary of State who is responsible to the Empress. If the Empress be not responsible to her Maker—if there is no Maker for her to be responsible to—the entire system of our administration must be wrong. Which is manifestly impossible. At Home men are to be excused. They are stalled up a good deal and grow intellectually "beany."[5] When you take a gross, "beany" horse to exercise, he slavers and slobbers over the bit till you can't see the horns. But the bit is there just the same. Men do not get "beany" in India. The climate and the work are against playing bricks with words. A

Persona: Give three adjectives that describe the narrator's persona as it is portrayed so far. A

If McGoggin had kept his creed, with the capital letters and the endings in "isms," to himself, no one would have cared; but his grandfathers on both sides had been Wesleyan preachers, and the preaching strain came out in his mind. He wanted everyone at the Club to see that they had no souls too, and to help him to eliminate his Creator. As a good many men told him, he undoubtedly had no soul, because he was so young, but it did not follow that his seniors were equally undeveloped; and, whether there was another world or not, a man still wanted to read his papers in this. "But that is not the point—that is not the point!" Aurelian used to say. Then men threw sofa-cushions at him and told him to go to any particular place he might believe in. They christened him the "Blastoderm,"[6]—he said he came from a family of that name somewhere, in the prehistoric ages,—and, by insult and laughter strove to choke him dumb, for he was an **unmitigated** nuisance at the Club; besides being an offence to the older men. His Deputy Commissioner, who was working on the Frontier when Aurelian was rolling on a bed-quilt, told him that, for a clever boy, Aurelian was a very big idiot. And, if he had gone on with his work, he would have been caught up to the Secretariat in a few years. He was of the type that goes there—all head, no physique and a hundred theories. Not a soul was interested in McGoggin's soul. He might have had two, or none, or somebody else's. His business was to obey orders and keep abreast of his files, instead of devastating the Club with "isms." R

unmitigated (ŭn-mĭt′ĭ-gā′tĭd) *adj.* Without qualification or exception; absolute.

Apply Context: Describe an instance where Victorian-era ideas or Kipling's own experiences inform the story so far. Does this connection help you understand the story's humor? R

4. *Metropolitan Board of Works:* a body formed in 1855 to build and maintain London's infrastructure
5. *beany:* "full of beans"; unusually well nourished and energetic
6. *Blastoderm:* a name that mocks McGoggin's positivism and Darwinian beliefs

He worked brilliantly; but he could not accept any order without trying to better it. That was the fault of his creed. It made men too responsible and left too much to their honor. You can sometimes ride an old horse in a halter; but never a colt. McGoggin took more trouble over his cases than any of the men of his year. He may have fancied that thirty-page judgments on fifty-rupee cases[7]—both sides perjured to the gullet—advanced the cause of Humanity. At any rate, he worked too much, and worried and fretted over the rebukes he received, and lectured away on his ridiculous creed out of office, till the Doctor had to warn him that he was overdoing it. No man can toil eighteen annas in the rupee[8] in June without suffering. But McGoggin was still intellectually "beany" and proud of himself and his powers, and he would take no hint. He worked nine hours a day steadily.

"Very well," said the Doctor, "you'll break down, because you are over-engined for your beam." McGoggin was a little man.

One day, the collapse came—as dramatically as if it had been meant to **embellish** a Tract.

embellish (ĕm-bĕl′ĭsh) *tr.v.* To add ornamental or fictitious details to.

It was just before the Rains. We were sitting in the verandah in the dead, hot, close air, gasping and praying that the black-blue clouds would let down and bring the cool. Very, very far away, there was a faint whisper, which was the roar of the Rains breaking over the river. One of the men heard it, got out of his chair, listened and said, naturally enough, "Thank God!"

Then the Blastoderm turned in his place and said, "Why? I assure you it's only the result of perfectly natural causes—phenomena of the simplest kind. Why you should, therefore, return thanks to a Being who never did exist—who is only a **figment**—"

figment (fĭg′mənt) *n.* Something invented, made up, or fabricated.

"Blastoderm," grunted the man in the next chair, "dry up, and throw me over the *Pioneer*. We know all about your figments." The Blastoderm reached out to the table, took up one paper, and jumped as if something had stung him. Then he handed the paper.

"As I was saying," he went on slowly and with an effort— "due to perfectly natural causes—perfectly natural causes. I mean—'

"Hi! Blastoderm, you've given me the *Calcutta Mercantile Advertiser.*"

The dust got up in little whorls, while the tree-tops rocked and the kites whistled. But no one was looking at the coming of the Rains. We were all staring at the Blastoderm, who had risen from his chair and was fighting with his speech. Then he said, still more slowly—

"Perfectly conceivable—dictionary—red oak—**amenable**—cause—retaining—shuttle-cock—alone."

amenable (ə-mē′nə-bəl) *adj.* Willing to accept a suggestion or submit to authority.

"Blastoderm's drunk," said one man. But the Blastoderm was not drunk. He looked at us in a dazed sort of way, and began motioning with his hands in the half light as the clouds closed overhead. Then—with a scream—

"What is it?—Can't—reserve—attainable—market—obscure—"

But his speech seemed to freeze in him, and—just as the lightning shot two tongues that cut the whole sky into three pieces and the rain fell in quivering sheets—the Blastoderm was struck dumb. He stood pawing and champing like a hard-held horse, and his eyes were full of terror. **A**

Imagery: What does Kipling communicate about McGoggin here with the image of the horse? What lesson about life is McGoggin confronting? **A**

The Doctor came over in three minutes, and heard the story. "It's *aphasia*,"[9] he said. "Take him to his room. I knew the smash would come."

7. *fifty-rupee cases:* court cases over a small amount of money for the time
8. *eighteen . . . rupee:* This is two more annas than the rupee contains. Aurelian's effort is greater than the situation calls for.
9. *aphasia:* speech loss due to problems in the brain's control centers, sometimes associated with strokes

We carried the Blastoderm across in the pouring rain to his quarters, and the Doctor gave him bromide of potassium to make him sleep.

Then the Doctor came back to us and told us that *aphasia* was like all the **arrears** of "Punjab Head"[10] falling in a lump; and that only once before—in the case of a sepoy[11]—had he met with so complete a case. I have seen mild *aphasia* in an overworked man, but this sudden dumbness was uncanny—though, as the Blastoderm himself might have said, due to "perfectly natural causes."

arrears (ə-rîrz′) *pl.n.* An unpaid, overdue debt or an unfulfilled obligation.

"He'll have to take leave after this," said the Doctor. "He won't be fit for work for another three months. No; it isn't insanity, or anything like it. It's only complete loss of control over the speech and memory. I fancy it will keep the Blastoderm quiet, though."

Two days later, the Blastoderm found his tongue again. The first question he asked was—"What was it?" The Doctor enlightened him. "But I can't understand it!" said the Blastoderm. "I'm quite sane; but I can't be sure of my mind, it seems—my *own* memory—can I?"

"Go up into the Hills for three months, and don't think about it," said the Doctor.

"But I can't understand it," repeated the Blastoderm. "It was my *own* mind and memory."

"I can't help it," said the Doctor; "there are a good many things you can't understand; and, by the time you have put in my length of service, you'll know exactly how much a man dare call his own in this world." E

Characters' Worldviews: How does the Doctor's statement summarize the clash between Aurelian's views and the other characters'? E

The stroke cowed the Blastoderm. He could not understand it. He went into the Hills in fear and trembling, wondering whether he would be permitted to reach the end of any sentence he began.

This gave him a wholesome feeling of mistrust. The legitimate explanation, that he had been overworking himself, failed to satisfy him. Something had wiped his lips of speech, as a mother wipes the milky lips of her child, and he was afraid—horribly afraid.

So the Club had rest when he returned; and if ever you come across Aurelian McGoggin laying down the law on things Human—he doesn't seem to know as much as he used to about things Divine—put your forefinger to your lip for a moment, and see what happens.

Don't blame me if he throws a glass at your head. A

Situational Irony: How is McGoggin's aphasia an example of situational irony? A

10. *Punjab Head:* Europeans in India, unused to the climate, often experienced confusion of thought.
11. *sepoy:* "an Indian soldier serving under British command in India" (*AHD*)

THINK AND DISCUSS

1. Record two examples of verbal irony in the story.
2. Describe the narrator's persona in your own words.
3. Describe Aurelian McGoggin in your own words. How is the narrator different from McGoggin?
4. What makes the nature of McGoggin's collapse an example of situational irony?
5. What are two relationships between Kipling's own life and the events of the story?
6. Why do McGoggin's theories not work in India? How do his theories affect his thinking and behavior?
7. Does Kipling seem to object to McGoggin's theories?
8. What does Kipling seem to offer as a replacement to McGoggin's theories?
9. How does the horse imagery of the story relate to the characters and themes?
10. How does Kipling critique Victorian-era idiosyncracies in the story?
11. What does Kipling offer as truth in this story? Do you think the story's theme aligns with scriptural truth?

HEART OF DARKNESS

Joseph Conrad

In the first pages of Joseph Conrad's novella *Heart of Darkness*, a ship rests peacefully at anchor in the Thames. In it, a mariner named Marlow begins the tale of his journey down a different river, the Congo. The inspiration for this journey, he claims, was a childhood whim. Yet as Marlow's narrative progresses, his experiences in colonial Africa emerge not as a fulfillment of youthful dreams but rather as a powerful and terrifying reflection on the human condition.

The Author

Joseph Conrad (1857–1924) was born Józef Teodor Konrad Korzeniowski to Polish parents in Ukraine. By the time he was eleven, both were dead. At sixteen, he traveled to Marseilles to become a seaman, and in 1878 he entered the British merchant service. For the next sixteen years, Conrad traveled the globe, experiencing shipwreck and also perfecting his English. In 1890, to fulfill the same childhood whim as his narrator, Marlow, he commanded a steamboat up the Congo. His experiences in colonial Africa horrified him and broke his health, subjecting him to periodic fevers for the rest of his life.

In 1894 Conrad retired from sailing to pursue a literary career, establishing himself in Kent and publishing his first novel in 1895 under his famous pen name. Conrad's novels, with their exotic settings and seafaring adventures, found an instant public, and the retired seaman went on to write classics such as *Lord Jim* (1900), *Nostromo* (1904), and *The Secret Agent* (1907). *Heart of Darkness* itself was first published as a three-part serial in 1899. Conrad died of a heart attack in 1924.

The Work

Heart of Darkness anticipates modernist fiction in several regards, one being that the reader is not granted an objective viewpoint. Instead, the reader is forced to filter the story through the character of Marlow, an occasionally unreliable narrator whose perceptions of and reactions to his environment are the novella's focus. And as with other modernist works, the novella's plot casts considerable doubt on the soundness of European civilization. Although the Congo's colonizers proclaim themselves to be envoys of a superior culture, their moral conduct in Africa is demonstrably worse than that of the colonized Africans. In fact, the veneer of European civilization is shown to be a sham, as the isolation and crudity of the living conditions bring out the evil within the colonial functionaries that Marlow encounters.

One such functionary, Kurtz, serves as the fulcrum of the story. After arriving in Africa, Marlow is ordered to captain a ramshackle steamboat upriver and relieve Kurtz of his duties. As Marlow travels through the rugged African interior, he reflects on the terrifying nature of the external, material universe. But when Marlow finally confronts Kurtz, he discovers that he must also confront "the strange commingling of desire and hate" within himself.

Controversy and Influence

The novella endured some controversy in the twentieth century. In a landmark 1975 lecture, Nigerian novelist Chinua Achebe pointed out Conrad's default to European portrayals of native Africans as wild-eyed savages in a morally and civilly dark continent. He declared *Heart of Darkness* to be fundamentally racist, "an offensive and deplorable book." Critics still debate the question of Conrad's intentions and biases.

Nonetheless, since its publication, *Heart of Darkness* has become one of the most studied works in modern literature. Conrad's themes examining the evils of imperialism, including its dehumanizing effects on all parties, and the evils of the human heart itself remain worthy of study. They also foreshadowed twentieth-century anticolonialism. Many novelists adopted a similarly limited, unreliable narrator. And the work's central narrative—an explorer who, by navigating uncharted terrain, is forced to face his own personal flaws—recurs in countless films and books.

In the following passage, Marlow describes the goings-on of a colonial station in the Congo. It becomes obvious that the station community reflects in microcosm the broader social problems imperialism creates. Note these as you read.

I went to work the next day, turning, so to speak, my back on that station. In that way only it seemed to me I could keep my hold on the redeeming facts of life. Still, one must look about sometimes; and then I saw this station, these men strolling aimlessly about in the sunshine of the yard. I asked myself sometimes what it all meant. They wandered here and there with their absurd long staves in their hands like a lot of faithless pilgrims bewitched inside a rotten fence. The word "ivory" rang in the air, was whispered, was sighed. You would think they were praying to it. A taint of imbecile rapacity blew through it all like a whiff from some corpse. By Jove! I've never seen anything so unreal in my life. And outside, the silent wilderness surrounding this cleared speck on the earth struck me as something great and invincible, like evil or truth, waiting patiently for the passing away of this fantastic invasion.

Oh, these months! Well, never mind. Various things happened. One evening a grass shed full of calico, cotton prints, beads, and I don't know what else, burst into a blaze so suddenly that you would have thought the earth had opened to let an avenging fire consume all that trash. . . .

I strolled up. There was no hurry. You see the thing had gone off like a box of matches. It had been hopeless from the very first. The flame had leaped high, driven everybody back, lighted up everything—and collapsed. The shed was already a heap of embers glowing fiercely. A nigger[1] was being beaten nearby. They said he had caused the fire in some way; be that as it may, he was screeching most horribly. I saw him later on for several days, sitting in a bit of shade looking very sick and trying to recover himself. Afterwards he arose and went out—and the wilderness without a sound took him into its bosom again. As I approached the glow from the dark I found myself at the back of two men, talking. I heard the name of Kurtz pronounced, then the words, "take advantage of this unfortunate accident." One of the men was the manager. I wished him a good evening. "Did you ever see anything like it—eh? It is incredible," he said, and walked off. The other man remained. He was a first-class agent, young, gentlemanly, a bit reserved, with a forked little beard and a hooked nose. He was standoffish with the other agents, and they on their side said he was the manager's spy upon them. As to me, I had hardly ever spoken to him before. We got into talk, and by and by we strolled away from the hissing ruins. . . . The business entrusted to this fellow was the making of bricks—so I had been informed—but there wasn't a fragment of a brick anywhere in the station, and he had been there more than a year—waiting. It seems he could not make bricks without something, I don't know what—straw maybe. Anyways, it could not be found there, and as it was not likely to be sent from Europe, it did not appear clear to me what he was waiting for. An act of special creation perhaps. However, they were all waiting all the sixteen or twenty pilgrims of them—for something; and upon my word it did not seem an uncongenial occupation from the way they took it, though the only thing that ever came to them was disease—as far as I could see. They beguiled the time by backbiting and intriguing against each other in a foolish kind of way. There was an air of plotting about that station, but nothing came of it, of course. It was as unreal as everything else—as the philanthropic pretense of the whole concern, as their talk, as their government, as their show of work. The only real feeling was a desire to get appointed to a trading post where ivory was to be had, so that they could earn percentages. They intrigued and slandered and hated each other only on that account—but as to effectually lifting a little finger—oh, no.

1. *This term is now considered extremely offensive and is reproduced here only to represent the author's original work; its use highlights the racism pervading the narrator's colonial context.*

UNIT 4: PARTS 3 & 4 REVIEW

What Do You Know?

Understand the Background

1. Which two Victorian authors from Parts 3 and 4 employ dramatic monologues?
2. Name two major cultural issues addressed in Carlyle's essays. How does he support his call for reform?
3. What specifically Victorian issue is Charlotte Brontë known for addressing?
4. What late-Victorian attitude do Hardy and Arnold seem to share?
5. What nineteenth-century philosophies does Kipling reference in "The Conversion of Aurelian McGoggin"?

Apply the Concepts

6. Identify three instances of parallelism in Tennyson's works. Explain how each supports his message in context.
7. Using the text, describe the persona in "Porphyria's Lover." Is he trustworthy?
8. Interpret three images E. B. Browning uses to develop her theme in Sonnet 43.
9. Name at least two rhetorical devices used in Carlyle's arguments. How are they used effectively? Give two examples from the text to justify your answer.
10. Identify three instances in *Jane Eyre* that exemplify psychological realism. Explain your answers.
11. Analyze Arnold's use of the tide metaphor to communicate his message in "Dover Beach." How would you describe the tide's retreat and its effects? To what does Arnold liken the tide?
12. Identify two images Hardy develops in "The Darkling Thrush." How do these images support the poem's tone?
13. How does "Pied Beauty" illustrate sprung rhythm and the curtal sonnet form? Justify your answer with details from the text.
14. What does Hopkins's use of enjambment accomplish in the poems studied? Use an example from the text to illustrate your answer.
15. Explain the irony of Jack Worthing's adoption of the name *Ernest* as an alias in Wilde's work.
16. Analyze Wilde's use of the character Lady Bracknell in order to satirize Victorian society.
17. Describe the narrator and his point of view in "The Conversion of Aurelian McGoggin."
18. Identify one way *Heart of Darkness* anticipates modernist fiction.

Evaluate the Ideas

19. Evaluate Tennyson's conclusions about mortality from a biblical worldview.
20. How do Arnold and Hardy view the world similarly? Evaluate this worldview from a scriptural point of view.
21. Evaluate Kipling's characters' varying worldviews from a biblical perspective.

Write a Response

22. How do Carlyle's arguments against excessive mechanism speak to our modern age of technology?
23. Choose three authors from Parts 3 and 4 of this unit, and use their works to exemplify Victorians' varying responses to the conflict between faith and doubt.

Define each term and provide an example of each from a selection in Unit 4, Part 3 or 4.

TERMS

- elegy
- dramatic monologue
- persona
- essay
- argumentative essay
- gothic
- psychological realism
- social Darwinism
- sprung rhythm
- curtal sonnet
- comedy of manners

UNIT 5 OBJECTIVES

LITERARY ELEMENTS

- Analyze examples of the following genres: lyric poetry (e.g., aubade), short story, speech.
- Analyze the key elements of a short story (speakers, point of view, pacing, setting, mood, character, conflict, plot) and the ways they interact to develop its theme(s).
- Analyze an author's use of irony, black humor, imagery, symbolism, and stream of consciousness to develop modernist and contemporary perspectives.
- Analyze a work's use of techniques—from its sounds (e.g., rhythm, alliteration) and form to its figurative language, rhetorical devices, and rhetorical appeals—to support its theme(s).

READING STRATEGIES

- Make and check predictions about a text.
- Draw conclusions about a text.
- Use strategies in combination.

TEXT CRITICISM AND CREATION

- Evaluate from a biblical worldview the perspectives of authors on issues such as death, human relationships, prejudice, and life's uncertainties.
- Evaluate the truthfulness of an author's portrayal of human relationships.
- Evaluate the effectiveness of a writer's craft in a work.
- Compose texts in a variety of genres based on model works.

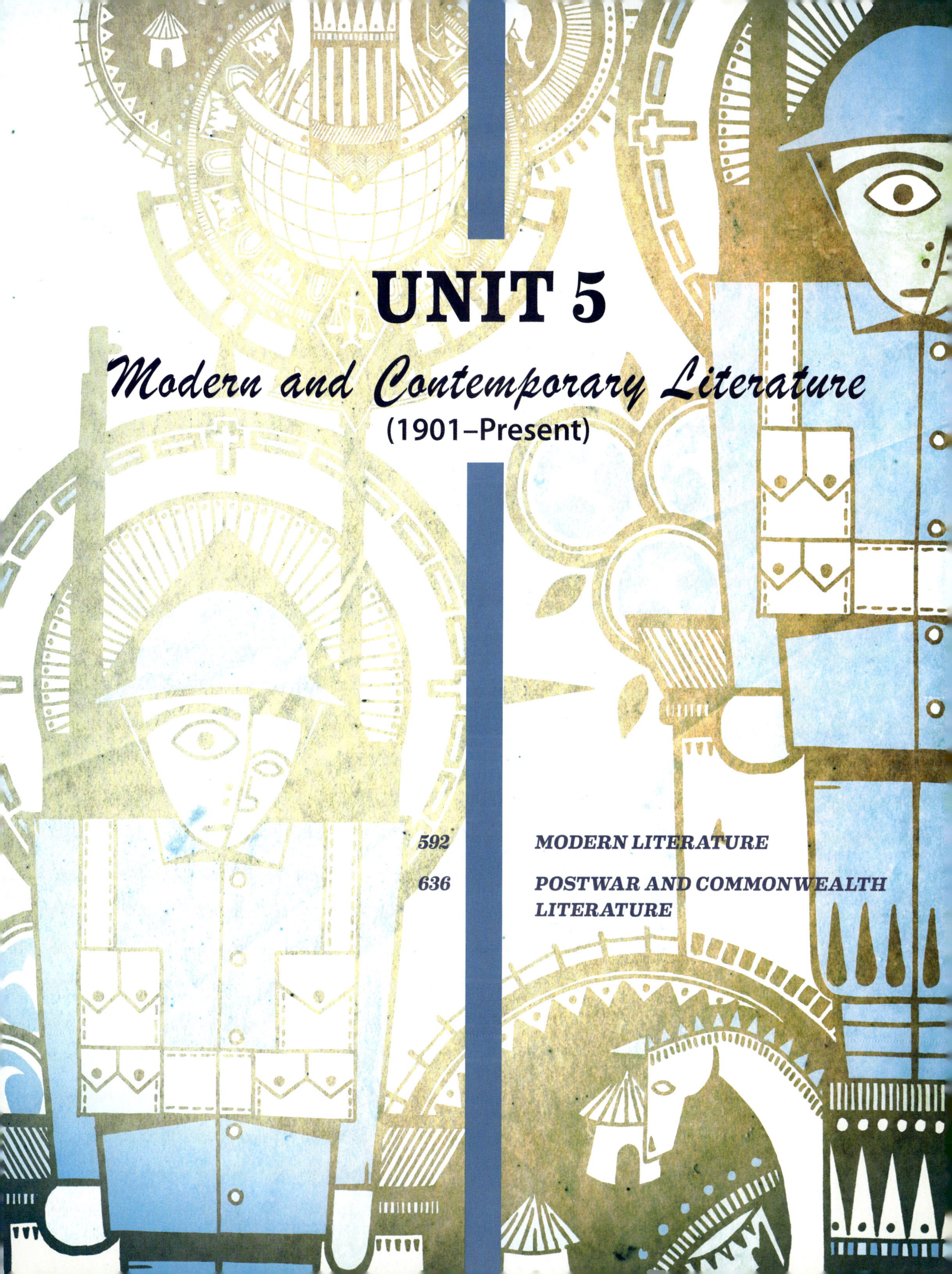

UNIT 5

Modern and Contemporary Literature

(1901–Present)

592 MODERN LITERATURE

636 POSTWAR AND COMMONWEALTH LITERATURE

Modern Britain

If the nineteenth century brought Britain world dominance, the twentieth showed how quickly the scales of power can tip. War, economic challenges, and, above all, rising democracy dealt British imperial power a succession of blows from which it would not recover. Meanwhile, cultural and political changes first heard rumbling in the Victorian era brought seismic changes to the nation at home. The latter part of the century showed a nation recovering from the crumbling of her empire and adjusting to a new social and economic order. Remarkably (and not without struggle), Britain has emerged resilient, evolving with the new realities of contemporary times. The nation's literature in the last century has reflected a similar path of upheaval, confusion, and renewal. Today, it shows the face of a vibrant and globalized Britain.

MODERN BRITAIN EMERGES

PREWAR BRITAIN

The years between Victoria's death (1901) and World War I (1914–18) remained stable on the surface. But underneath were roiling the problems late Victorians had begun to articulate. Abroad, the Second Boer War (1899–1902) punctured Britain's imperial prestige and certainty. Despite far superior resources and experience, British forces only barely defeated the Boer settlers. Moreover, some of their methods (e.g., the first concentration camps) damaged their sense of moral authority, further fueling a feeling of lost identity some Victorians had felt. Additionally, independence movements in colonies, particularly India, began gathering tremendous speed in the early century and would continue to rise through the coming decades.

At home, economic prosperity continued, but uncertainty crept in. Britain watched as Germany and America began to overtake it in speed of economic growth. More significantly, the extremes of rich and poor grew further apart. Many British citizens still existed in grinding poverty. Fueled by these inequalities and the resulting social problems, many people demanded a government with an expanded role, one that could ensure fair wages, better employment conditions, and governmental support for those in need (e.g., the unemployed, elderly, or disabled).

In politics, the new economic and social power of the working and middle classes continued to change the landscape. A key victory for the common man was the Parliament Act of 1911: the act stripped the House of Lords of its veto power, leaving the government's primary duties to elected officials. Additionally, universal suffrage seemed closer than ever. Even the women's suffrage movement gained traction as suffragettes became insistent (a few even violent) in their demands for a voice. And trade unions, adding organization and heft to the voices of working men and women, helped create the Labour Party, which eventually overtook the Liberals as one of Britain's two most powerful political parties. This volatile atmosphere was pushing England toward drastic social change when the assassination of the heir to the Austro-Hungarian Empire drew most of Europe into war.

THE IRISH QUESTION

Closer to home, the Irish, long under British rule, continued to demand home rule for themselves. A broadly nationalist movement arose in politics and the arts. The latter plumbed Ireland's cultural past and present to create a new, specifically Irish literature. The former sought political avenues to divest Ireland of British rule. Complicating the matter, a split arose between the northern counties (mostly Protestant descendants of British settlers) and the southern region (mostly Catholic Celts). Eventually, the southern region gained independence but not before Britain's suppression of the Easter Uprising in 1916, which united most of southern Ireland behind martyrs to the cause. By 1920 the Irish had become sufficiently troublesome for Britain to grant southern Ireland home rule and dominion status (as a member of the British Commonwealth, politically independent but allied to the British Crown) in 1921. Nonetheless, revolutionaries continued to pursue full autonomy.

A view of central London, including the river Thames, the Tower of London (ca. 1078–1399), Tower Bridge (1894), and modern skyscraper The Shard (2012).

WORLD WAR I AND ITS AFTERMATH

The Great War, the "war to end war," World War I—it is easy to overlook the horrifying scope of these now-familiar terms. Ironically, at its outset in the summer of 1914, most British citizens believed the conflict would be "over by Christmas." Thousands enlisted within months. But instead of martial glory, they found a brutal, dehumanizing, and seemingly pointless conflict. The war settled into a grinding stalemate in which, by 1917, British troops manned more than half the trenches of the Western Front in France.

By the war's end (1918), both sides had suffered terrible losses. British casualties numbered two-and-a-half million, including 750,000 dead, a whole generation of young men decimated. Civilians—in addition to losing family, friends, and neighbors—had been hit with food shortages and government crackdowns, including strict censorship, curfews, monitoring (sometimes detainment) of noncitizens, and industrial takeovers. The nation had lost more than a third of her merchant fleet and had accrued considerable debt. Made worse by war conditions, the Spanish flu epidemic spread around the world, killing over two hundred thousand in Britain alone.

The war was a blow to an already shaky traditional worldview and social order. Many Britons believed that the established order, from the ruling classes to traditional religion, had failed the country. Modern technology, in which Victorians had placed so much hope, had made war more inhumane than ever, and the traditional church seemed to offer few answers to the war's trauma. Similarly, Britain's war leadership had too often showed gross incompetence, costing soldiers' lives.

At the same time, the war effort had demanded enormous sacrifice from everyone, from soldiers to the working class. Even women had been called upon, replacing men in industrial and agricultural labor. After the government had lauded these contributions for four years, it could hardly expect people and their ways to return wholly to the prewar status quo.

THE 1920s AND '30s

The 1920s and '30s were thus a time of rapid social change. Real wages rose considerably for workers who found employment. Along with mass-produced goods, this new prosperity fueled rising standards of living and a consumer society. And while several depressions (including the Great Depression) hit England very hard in some sectors of the economy, their deepest effects were not quite as broad or as prolonged as in America and other parts of the world.

Simultaneously, social mores were undergoing rapid changes, both positive and less so. Women entered the workforce at greater rates than before. Education continued to expand the social and economic opportunities of many, and the vote was expanded to universal adult suffrage by government acts in 1918 and 1928. Modern conveniences and pop culture arrived, exercising a leveling effect in society as almost anyone could access them. Class distinctions in everyday life,

already undermined by total participation in the war effort, continued to crumble. Overall church attendance continued to decline, and Britain's social scenes developed their own fast crowd, parallel to America's decadent speakeasy and flapper culture.

These decades were also marked by economic struggle in some regions and further expansion of the government. Overall statistics aside, real economic hardship came to stay for some Britons, leading many voters toward a more socialistic view of their government's responsibilities. Unemployment rose as soldiers (particularly disabled veterans) returned after World War I to find jobs scarce. Then Britain's traditionally key industries experienced major depressions in the following decades. For example, in the early 1930s, iron and steel production and exports were reduced by half, and shipbuilding stopped entirely. Such conditions led to long-term high unemployment, poverty, and unrest in these sectors.

Workers began calling for unemployment insurance, housing subsidies, and other government interventions. Socialist ideas, from the gradual reformism of Fabianism to the revolutionary fervor of Marxism, gained popularity as a possible solution to these woes. Under these conditions, the 1930s saw increasing bureaucratic control of industry, utilities, transportation, and communication. Higher taxes, a natural result of these expansions, were more heavily levied on the extremely wealthy, further undermining traditional class distinctions.

WORLD WAR II

During the 1930s, Britain watched the rise of Nazism with mixed feelings. Some thought it had little to do with England. Others found themselves somewhat sympathetic to Hitler's message. A few, notably Winston Churchill, saw the danger early. The rise of Hitler threatened not only England's weak economy but also her political future. Still traumatized by the last war, England tried first to ignore, then to appease, the Nazi aggressors. But Hitler's invasion of Poland in September 1939 forced Britain to declare war.

Although initially driven from the Continent by German forces at Dunkirk in 1940, the British picked up the pieces and settled in for the long haul. In September 1940, Hitler ordered the saturation bombing of London and other civilian targets in order to break the will of the people. Now known as the Blitz, German air attacks on London lasted for two years. Air-raid warnings followed by thundering fiery devastation broke the daily and nightly routine of the British. Children were sent into the countryside, and almost every capable adult was mobilized in response. As the armed forces fought abroad, civilians resisted at home, while, as John F. Kennedy later observed, Churchill's eloquent speeches "mobilized the English language and sent it into battle."[1]

By the war's end (1945), British casualties totaled almost a million, of which more than a third were dead or missing and the rest disabled. Though the total loss of life was less than in World War I, the destruction came closer to home—indeed to the very doorsteps—with sixty thousand civilians killed and central London heavily damaged by bombing. The next years of transition from a wartime to a peacetime economy would require further sacrifice from the British.

1. *From a speech conferring honorary US citizenship on Sir Winston Churchill*

St. Paul's Cathedral during the Blitz, December 1940.

GEORGE VI AND ELIZABETH II

Drama in the royal family provided more indications of Britain's changing culture. The British witnessed the first voluntary abdication of a monarch in British history when George V's (1910–36) son and successor, Edward VIII, renounced the throne in 1936 to marry an American divorcée. Shocked, the nation instead turned to his brother, George VI (1936–52). Events proved him to be the better king. While historians have since noted Edward's sympathies with Nazi Germany, George VI, in contrast, proved an indefatigable leader during World War II. Along with his wife, Elizabeth, he remained in London during the Blitz, even after a bomb hit Buckingham Palace. Unfortunately, the war did little good for his health. Upon his death in 1952, his daughter was crowned (1953) in the first ever televised coronation ceremony as Elizabeth II. Like her father, she has proved a strong, steady, and beloved presence in her country through often unsteady times. In September 2015 she passed Queen Victoria to become the nation's longest-reigning monarch.

MODERNISM

NEW INTELLECTUAL INFLUENCES

Intertwined with this era of social upheaval were broad changes in how people perceived human beings and the world. Many of these changes began in the late Victorian era, but the devastations of the early 1900s gave them breadth and depth of influence. World War I was especially disillusioning as it both exposed weaknesses in Britain's society and brought a new generation face to face with man's inhumanity to man (a theme that would continue through the century). A traditional worldview seemed ever more naïve in the face of such failures in supposedly Christian societies.

This disillusionment opened the door to alternative ways of viewing the world. Victorian influences continued to spread. Darwinism persisted in widening the gap between science and religion and between modern and traditional thinking about spirituality. Its implication that humans were just another species of animal fundamentally challenged concepts of human morality. Meanwhile, the rise of anthropology and comparative cultural studies suggested to some that religion was simply a facet of human society, one created by humans and likely unnecessary.

Additionally, the new field of psychology began changing how people viewed the nature of human experience. People showed a keen interest in how the human mind perceived, interpreted, and structured reality. Especially influential were the psychoanalytic theories of Sigmund Freud. His concept of an unconscious mind that drives (and sometimes wars with) people's conscious desires, behaviors, and choices changed how people thought of themselves. He prioritized the unconscious over the conscious mind, posited that humans needed to express the pent-up emotional urges of the primal unconscious, and thus viewed moral constraints as a cause of unhappiness. Individual self-fulfillment became the way to satisfaction rather than self-restraint or conformity to outside standards.

Sigmund Freud.

Finally, socialism and Marxism were significant forces for social change in the first half of the century. The slow progress in breaking down rigid class systems, as well as the deep poverty and hardship from economic depressions, sent people searching for answers to society's inequities. Marxism's combination of idealistic hope for a fairer world, revolutionary fervor to bring justice to oppressors, and a seemingly rational plan to fix society caught the imagination of many for a time, especially in the 1930s. The news of Stalinist atrocities, however, dampened the enthusiasm of most.

MODERNIST LITERATURE

In literature, such changes in thought were explored by highly varied and individualistic writers known collectively as modernists. Beginning in the century's first decade, their writing critiqued British society and frequently offered visions of humanity and the world that starkly differed from a traditional worldview. While they sometimes differed in particulars, their works typically share the following characteristics.

First, most modernists continued the late Victorians' critique of conventional Victorian values, expressing disillusionment with modern life. Many used their literature to explore the realities and question the rightness of traditional class and gender roles, reflecting the continued diversity of voices in British literature. On a bleaker note, most modernists considered both the Victorian faith in human progress and the promises of organized religion to be hollow.

Also, motivating this disillusionment was a recognition that modern forces were fragmenting communities and alienating individuals within society. Class-fueled inequities and conflicts were partially at fault for this fragmentation. So also was the depersonalized nature of modern life and labor. Urban life, although crowded, lively, and busy, could be intensely lonely without real connections. And real connections between people seemed harder than ever to come by. Whom could you turn to in a city crowded with people but with no sense of community? What pride and connection could a person feel toward mechanized labor and mass-produced goods? Could the material conveniences and personal freedoms of modern life offer real fulfillment instead? These were questions modernists embodied in their texts.

Furthering this sense of alienation was the new focus on the individual and inner self that Freud had brought to modern culture. Modernist works tend to explore the inner lives of individuals and focus on creating psychological realism. Many of these characters struggle with a sense of disconnectedness, feeling that their inner struggles and desires are not truly known or acknowledged by themselves or those around them. Sometimes this isolation springs from characters' inner rejection of society's false values, a mindset that distances them from their peers. Thus, social conventions (of morality, class, gender, etc.) often become simply barriers to self-fulfillment and personal connection. In this, the modernists' characters sometimes mirror their own experiences.

Modernists' disillusionment and sense of alienation and fragmentation led to a search for meaning evident in many of their works. Indeed, the era is frequently known as one of questioning. Spiritually, the abandonment of a traditional worldview left many people at sea. Who or what could provide solace when the old spiritual truths were deemed unnecessary to modern, scientifically advanced humanity? Not all abandoned a stable worldview (for example, key modernist T. S. Eliot

VISUAL ANALYSIS

How does *The City Rises* (1910) by Umberto Boccioni reflect modernist experimentation with content and form?

was converted), nor did writers fully abandon spirituality. However, a number looked for alternative ways to frame and talk about it. For example, Irish poet W. B. Yeats, a leading modernist, replaced the broadly Christian worldview he had grown up in with Irish mythology and even occult spiritualist ideas. Others tried to piece together meaning on a more individual basis. Naturally, this individualism produced a splintering of consensus about life and its meaning.

These facets of the modernists' worldview—disillusionment, alienation and fragmentation, and a search for new meaning—seemed to demand the final characteristic of their art: experimentation. Many modernists cut their work loose from traditional content and form in some regard. Because they had something new to say, they wanted new ways to say it. Their poems and stories turned intentionally obscure at times, a deliberate reflection of the difficulty writers felt in making sense of the world or of humans' inner minds. Their characters' conversations and expectations became stilted or disconnected from each other. And sometimes a character's inner thoughts poured forth unorganized and unfiltered—fragments seemingly meaningless and often transgressive.

All of this experimentation was more than many readers wanted. Even literary writers themselves seemed to back away from radical experiments as the decades passed. The 1930s, for instance, saw a return to outward realism. But the more obscure works had already increased the divide most people believed separated high and low art. The effect was likely compounded by the simultaneous rise in literary criticism as a more defined discipline, with its own vocabularies and professionalized critics. Suddenly, a person had to be trained to have an opinion on literature. This high/low trend extended into the second half of the century and still affects reader expectations today.

VISUAL ANALYSIS

How does *Room in New York* (1932) by Edward Hopper help illustrate the modernist recognition of alienation and isolation?

From a Christian perspective, the bitter pessimism and moral uncertainty of much modern literature distance it from believers, just as its obscurity alienates most ordinary readers. Few knowledgeable readers would maintain that an explicit moral is essential to narrative (cf. the book of Ruth). Nor is the attempt to re-create real, tangled thought processes sinful (no matter how much it might confuse a reader). The Christian objection to much of modernist literature, therefore, is not to its unconventional techniques but rather to many of the messages it conveys.

POSTWAR BRITAIN

BRITAIN ABROAD

Britain emerged from World War II forever changed. In political, economic, and military spheres, she was now vastly overshadowed by American and Soviet power. Furthermore, she was unable to hold her empire, which began crumbling as native governments around the world asserted their independence. India officially broke ties in 1947 with the Indian Independence Act. The Ireland Act of 1949 formally broke off the Republic of Ireland (officially so declared in 1948) from Great Britain. Finally, Britain's African and Caribbean colonies largely declared independence during the 1960s and '70s.

Despite these losses, Britain maintained an outsized influence in world affairs. First, her past prestige and key participation in World War II gained her a seat on the UN's Security Council, while participation in organizations such as NATO and the European Economic Community (now the European Union) gave her access to the collective power of Europe. Second, the British Commonwealth (today the Commonwealth of Nations) offered mutually beneficial economic and cultural ties between Britain and

Viceroy Lord Louis Mountbatten announcing the independence and separation of India and Pakistan, August 1947.

many former colonies (expanding to more countries today). Finally, America and Britain, bound by strong historical and cultural ties, pursued an unofficial Special Relationship. This alliance has entailed cooperation in everything from trade agreements to military support and intelligence sharing (key during the Cold War and the War on Terror).

BRITAIN AT HOME

World War II devastated Britain economically. Her resources in material and human power had been depleted in the war effort. Her capital city was punctuated by ruins, and her economic ties to many foreign markets were broken. Rationing of food and other resources would, of necessity, continue into the mid-1950s.

In response, British society turned to a welfare state under the guidance of the Labour Party. The war efforts had led to a sense that the working class was owed for the tremendous sacrifices they had made. Additionally, to some it seemed that the economic state of affairs needed a strong hand at the wheel, and the government had already exerted such controls during the war. Industries such as gas and power were nationalized, and the government provided basic healthcare through a nationalized system. Educational opportunities were offered for a broader slice of society, and better wages were ensured through strong labor unions and government regulation. For a while, this system worked, and standards of living rose throughout the 1950s and '60s.

Socially, the first few decades after the war were a mix of good and bad. Class strictures continued to level out, producing a more socially and economically mobile society. On the other hand, a sense of spiritual malaise lingered, and church attendance dropped tremendously, never to recover. Then in the "Swinging Sixties," a new generation came of age and, as in America, brought on a cultural revolution. Traditional social ways were questioned while the country's pop-cultural influence in music, fashion, and film (known as the British Invasion) was felt around the globe.

Events of the 1970s punctured any economic and cultural optimism. Global events such as the oil crisis of 1973 destabilized the economy, and problems in the welfare state grew. The decade was marked by economic stagnancy and social unrest, including rioting. The Troubles, a conflict between Protestant Northern Ireland loyalists and Catholic Irish

The Beatles.

British Army troops confronting rioters in the streets of Londonderry, Northern Ireland, during the Troubles in August 1975.

republicans, increased the violence even in England, which was both a target and policeman for the conflict. At stake were equal rights for religious minorities on both sides as well as Northern Ireland's independence from the Irish Republic. The conflict drew in politicians, radical militants, and civilians, resulting in bombings, protests, segregated communities, and more. Unfortunately, a move toward peace did not occur until the Good Friday Agreement in 1998.

Furthermore, racism intensified as Britain's shrinking territory led many to define Britishness more exclusively by its roots in the British Isles. Significant nonwhite communities already existed in the nation. Many had grown as legal immigrants from Commonwealth nations (whose labor had fueled the economy in the previous two decades) settled down and had families. These were perceived by some white Britons as an economic and cultural threat. Underlying this conflict was a struggle to construct a new British identity that persists to the present.

LANGUAGE

The twentieth and twenty-first centuries have once again brought widespread changes to British English. With greater democracy and diversity of voices came a wider acceptance of English vocabulary, grammar, and pronunciation previously deemed nonstandard. For example, Received Pronunciation (p. 425) no longer carries the social weight it once did and, in fact, can sometimes be material for satire. Instead, the proliferation of other voices in television, radio, and music has normalized a wide variety of regional and ethnic variations, many of which have enriched broader British vocabulary.

Also, today more than ever, British English reflects the globalization of modern societies. Like most other languages, it has acquired the vocabulary of new technology (e.g., digital technology) and scientific advancements. It reflects the influence of American pop culture as well as facets of many other cultures (e.g., food names, fashions, and cities). Additionally, the flourishing of English around the world (e.g., in America, India, the Caribbean) has led to the concept of World Englishes, versions of English that have their own significant variations in rules and standards. As these new forms grow and affect each other, the evolution of British English will only accelerate.

REBIRTH

Margaret Thatcher.

Its confidence at a low ebb, the country found an alternative approach in the 1980s with the rise of Thatcherism. Named for Margaret Thatcher, its main proponent and Britain's first female prime minister, Thatcherism was a political ideology that advocated for a return to a more market-driven economy. Under Thatcher's leadership, many national industries were sold to private investors, and government bureaucracy shrank.

While historians disagree about the success of Thatcherism itself, the decade was a turning point for the United Kingdom. London began to reemerge as one of the globe's key centers for finance and banking, a position that has only strengthened today. Additionally, the nation seemed to regain some of its confidence in rising levels of patriotism. However, this economic success led to a widening financial gap between upper and lower classes that has been the source of increased economic and social tensions.

AN EVOLVING BRITAIN

Recent decades have brought significant changes to British identity. The late 1990s saw the devolution of the United Kingdom when the Scotland and Northern Ireland Act (1998) gave each country its own parliament, resulting in greater political independence. Additionally, the country has begun the process of embracing a broader concept of Britishness, one that encompasses its many ethnically diverse, nonwhite communities that had previously been sidelined politically, economically, and culturally.

Foreign affairs are also in flux as the British struggle over who they wish to be in the world. For instance, many Britons are ambivalent about the War on Terror, an attitude that has added tension to Britain and America's traditional Special Relationship. More recently, voters controversially, and by razor thin margins, approved Britain's withdrawal from the European Union. Negotiations for the secession (colloquially termed *Brexit*) will affect Britain's future economic and diplomatic affairs significantly. The country seems poised once again to reinvent its position in world affairs.

CONTEMPORARY LITERATURE

British literature since World War II has taken a number of different paths. The full nature, significance, and lasting power of some of these are not yet apparent. What is clear is that literature, contrary to some predictions after the rise of popular media such as radio and television, has not lost its power in contemporary times. It has merely diversified. As the reach of education continues to expand, literacy and familiarity with literary analysis continue to rise. In addition, the increased convenience and affordability of modern publishing (print and digital) have continued a centuries-long trend of growing access to literature. Markets now exist for a wide variety of literary points of view and genres. As you will see, this diversity is reflected in the changing face of Britain's literary poetry, prose, and drama.

In the decades following World War II, however, some feared that writers in Britain had run out of new ideas. In some ways, it seemed that they were still reacting to the forces that the modernists had encountered. Like World War I, the Second World War, with its horrifying Holocaust and introduction of atomic weaponry, caused widespread disillusionment. Additionally, the war and its economic aftermath further fueled distrust of the bureaucracy and the social status quo. Issues such as class mobility, social equity, and gender roles and sexuality remained primary topics for exploration. For instance, in the 1950s and '60s, works written in a mode called kitchen sink realism painted in stark detail the anger, stress, and worry of the British working class during economically difficult times.

A scene from a 2009 production of *Endgame* by Samuel Beckett. Notice the nontraditional staging and lower-class characters.

As fewer found the realities of organized religion compelling, the search for meaning continued. Instead, existentialism, which had been rising in popularity before the war, gained new momentum. Based on the idea that there is no factual evidence for God or a larger spiritual meaning to human life, **existentialism** posits that people nonetheless require meaning and so must rise above despair over life's absurdity to create their own meaning for their existence. To do this, they must have freedom to choose their own meaning while acknowledging full responsibility for those choices. Only this way, proponents say, can humanity make a solution to man's inhumanity to man. Existentialism surfaced in a variety of literature, from the modernist theater of the absurd in the 1950s to the writings of later postmodern writers.

Still, there were significant differences between modernist and postwar literature. Many new writers overtly rejected the more experimental and obscure aspects of modernist writing as alienating to most readers. Instead, the poetic school known as the Movement spearheaded a return to more traditional uses of form and more ordinary uses of language and imagery. While it soon faded, other movements of the era continued to emphasize an approach and a use of language relevant to the everyday working-class person. Generally speaking, experimentation in poetry and prose returned in greater measure only with the rise of postmodernist writers and their use of elements such as parody, pastiche, metanarrative, and magical realism.

In contrast, the era's drama early on saw an uptick in nontraditional approaches to its subjects. For centuries, drama in Britain had been censored, subject to the approval of the Lord Chamberlain's Office. Relatively few outstanding dramatists had appeared in the last century. After the war, playwrights began resisting traditional constraints. They experimented with absurdist drama and unconventional staging and pushed the envelope in traditionally acceptable content. Groups such as the kitchen sink realists challenged class conventions while the theater of the absurd challenged the notion that life has clear meaning. Finally, the Theatres Act of 1968 abolished the practice of censorship. Today British theater continues to employ experimentation to challenge viewers.

BRITISH IDENTITY AND LITERATURE

Another thread in contemporary British literature began early after the war with the implosion of the British Empire. Previously, almost anyone born within the empire's territories was considered a British subject. Thus Katherine Mansfield (a writer from New Zealand) and W. B. Yeats (a poet born in Ireland) were both considered British writers. Today, such a broad notion of Britishness clearly no longer applies politically, but leftover cultural connections remain. These have led to a broader conception of British literature than other nationalities might encompass.

As the empire faded in the 1950s and '60s, the United Kingdom was receiving an influx of immigrants. Some came to study in Britain's world-class universities, some came to find work and opportunities, and others came to escape troubles in their previous homes. Those who stayed brought their own heritage to mingle with older British culture. While this commingling has sometimes met with great resistance, these immigrants and their descendants have enriched British culture and literature with their new perspectives. Among some of the most famous such writers are Nobel Prize–winning Kazuo Ishiguro, postmodernist novelist Salman Rushdie, and contemporary prose writer Zadie Smith.

The question of identity has been a controversial aspect of literature not just in Britain. A new cohort of writers of English literature has arisen from an unexpected corner—the Commonwealth nations. These Commonwealth authors do not claim British nationality. However, they extend the heritage of British literature in the aftermath of colonial independence in ways unique to their particular cultures. Commonwealth writers hail from around the globe, from Canada, India, Nigeria, South Africa, and more.

The choice to write in English has come with controversy for some of these, particularly in countries where people wish to reassert their original indigenous culture. But these writers have frequently turned to English-language literature to reflect and address the reality that colonialism has left a permanent cultural mark. Often called postcolonial literature, their work explores these lingering effects in their own countries even after the countries have achieved independence. They point out where colonization has affected the country's cultural dynamics, for instance creating clashing value systems or hybridized customs and attitudes. These writers thus tell part of Britain's story as well and enrich the British tradition with their unique perspectives.

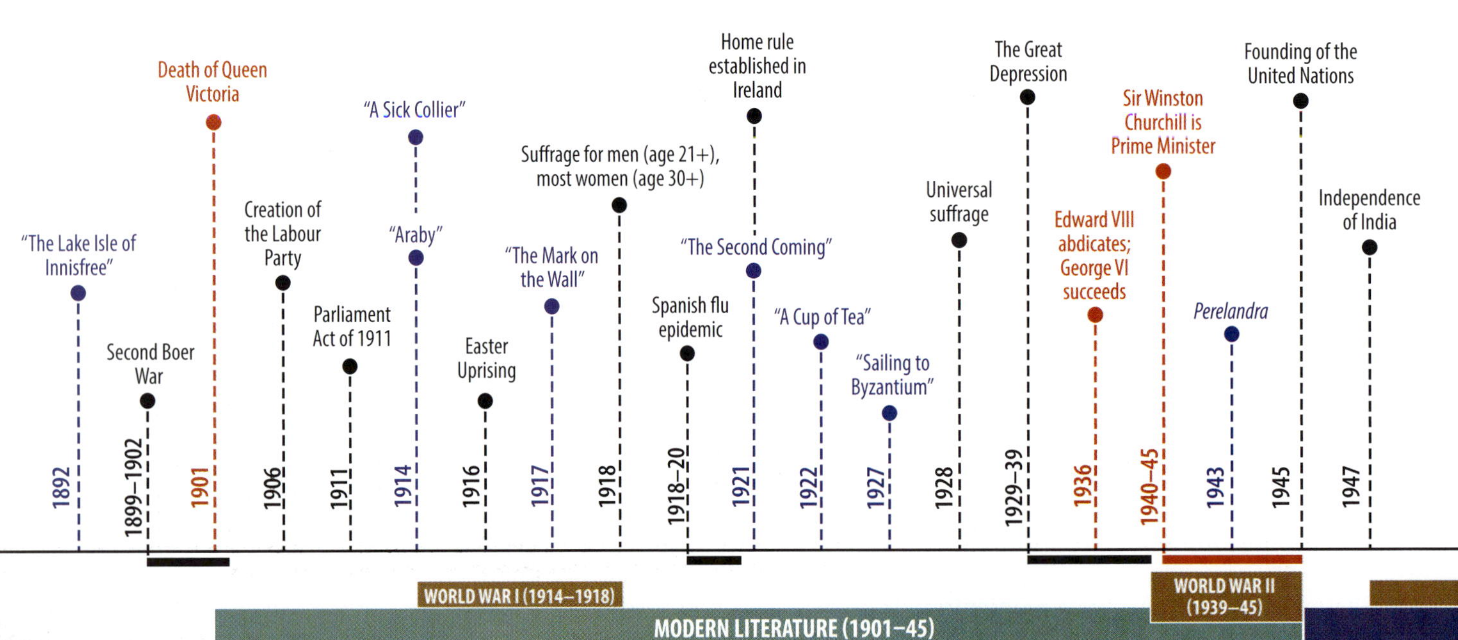

SUMMARY

The heritage of British literature now stretches back over a millennium. And interestingly enough, it has circled back to where it first began (in *Beowulf* and Arthurian legend) as a literature that transcends purely national borders. As in every age that followed—Renaissance, Enlightenment, Romantic, Victorian, Modernist—the literature continues to form a conversation about what humans value, where they fail in those ideals, and how they can improve and move forward.

For the Christian especially, the literature of the modern era serves as a warning and a reminder. At its worst, it warns of the confusion that follows when people abandon the foundational truths God has shared in His Word. Such confusion reminds believers of the deep need of humanity for salvation. At its best, it shows forth the image of God that yet remains in broken humanity—recognizing the value of other human beings, treasuring the beauty of creation and of creating, and endeavoring to create a better future.

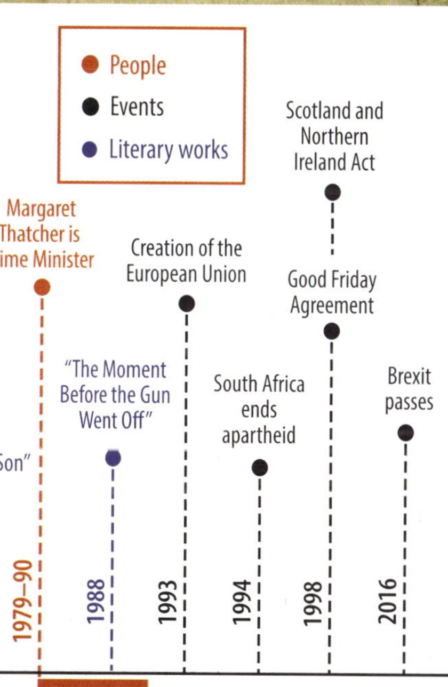

- People
- Events
- Literary works

1949 Ireland Act

1951–55 Sir Winston Churchill is Prime Minister

1952 Elizabeth II's reign begins

1952 *Waiting for Godot* (in French)

1954 *Waiting for Godot* (in English)

1957 "The Thought-Fox"

1957 "Not Waving but Drowning"

1958 *Things Fall Apart*

1960 Independence of Nigeria

1966 "Follower"

1968–98 The Troubles

1968–98 Theatre Act (1968) abolishes censorship

1973 UK joins the European Economic Community

1973–74 Oil crisis

1977 "Aubade"

1978 "A Devoted Son"

1979–90 Margaret Thatcher is Prime Minister

1988 "The Moment Before the Gun Went Off"

1993 Creation of the European Union

1994 South Africa ends apartheid

1998 Scotland and Northern Ireland Act

1998 Good Friday Agreement

2016 Brexit passes

COLD WAR (1947–91)

WAR ON TERROR (2001–Present)

CONTEMPORARY LITERATURE (1945–PRESENT)

UNIT 5

PART 1

Modern Literature

Have you ever interacted at length with someone who is unsettled, angry, or upset? Though you may care about this person, there is only so much conflict you can handle. In a similar way, modernists expressed a lot of disappointment, frustration, anger, and confusion. They also wrote in ways that can seem (and sometimes were) intentionally obscure. Although reading their literature can be challenging, doing so is an investment in understanding humanity and the effects of modernism on contemporary culture.

Modernists continued late Victorians' dissatisfaction with British society, which felt hypocritical and stagnant. This disillusionment pervades much of what you will read in this section. It is often expressed through a strong use of irony. Furthermore, determinism—the idea that people are trapped by conditions imposed on them by human nature, society, and the world—is a common thread. The characters of both D. H. Lawrence and James Joyce frequently search for greater happiness and security but are stymied by these forces. At most they achieve only greater self-knowledge.

Modernists frequently traced the intertwined forces of fragmentation and alienation to society's unjustified expectations or false barriers. Many of their characters experience a deep sense of personal alienation. For example, Virginia Woolf's female characters depict the alienation and marginalization felt by women, especially those suffering from mental illness. Katherine Mansfield frequently portrayed relationships influenced, usually for the worse, by gender and class barriers.

Fundamentally, though, modernists' alienation seems to originate with a search for meaning. Absent a coherent and shared sense of the world, it seemed unlikely that people could connect. But modernists were often less certain of how to replace the values they had rejected. Some, like the Irish poet W. B. Yeats, tried to construct their own worldview (in his case, made of ancient Celtic mythology and a cyclical view of history). Others focused simply on solving a few major concerns. But as you will see, while modernists tended to successfully identify and portray human and social problems, they struggled to provide a comprehensive and lasting answer to these problems.

Experimentation with literary form and technique naturally grew out of such questioning. Two trends in this tinkering emerged. First, combining Freud's interest in the individual mind and their own personal attempts to make sense of life, modernists primarily explored individual experiences and perspectives. The conflicts of these individuals typically involved the difficult (sometimes impossible) search for self-knowledge, connection with others, and ultimate meaning in life. These explorations were often unusually frank for the time, reflecting both the writers' goal of psychological realism and their rejection of conventional norms.

In portraying the individual, Joyce and Woolf took a particularly radical approach early on in the twentieth century. Inspired by psychology's exploration of how human consciousness perceives realities and constructs them into a meaningful whole, they tried to represent such human thought processes. The resulting stream-of-consciousness narratives emphasized an individual's (and the readers') attempt to impose meaning on an often chaotic jumble of observations, experiences, and subconscious attitudes or desires.

Another key trait of modernist literature is indirectness, beginning with a rejection of the heavy-handed didacticism in Victorian popular literature. Modernists believed the world should speak through a writer, rather than the writer imposing his views on the world. This attitude, combined with a focus on individual minds, led modernists to favor the indirect and subjective in their work. Themes emerge from their works by readers' inferences. Symbols frequently convey complex meanings in ways ambiguous or unique to particular authors. Additionally, some authors used obscure or fragmented allusions, valuing difficulty of interpretation over ease of access. For instance, Joyce sometimes incorporated newly coined words and a unique blending of sixty or more languages. The impenetrability of such texts ingeniously conveyed the modernists' sense of alienation, fragmentation, or confusion.

While modernists dominated the era's literature, they were by no means representative of its whole. Some of the period's most popularly successful writers maintained a traditional, conventional ideology and writing style. For example, C. S. Lewis emerged as a key defender of a Christian worldview. During this tumultuous time, his novels, essays, and radio addresses reflected the power of real Truth and Goodness. Additionally, when Britain was once again in crisis (World War II), it was the clear moral vision and traditional rhetoric of Prime Minister Winston Churchill's speeches that rallied Britain to continue fighting. Modernist literature offered a realistic perspective on life and human nature itself, but without Christ, it lacked a balm for the trials of the human heart. ❁

William Butler Yeats (1865–1939)

AT A GLANCE

- **1889** Published *The Wanderings of Oisin and Other Poems*
- **1899** Published *The Wind Among the Reeds*
- **1904** Helped found Abbey Theatre in Dublin
- **1917** Married Georgie Hyde-Lees
- **1923** Was awarded the Nobel Prize in Literature
- **1928** Published *The Tower*

William Butler Yeats, widely considered the greatest lyric poet of the twentieth century, was a radical traditionalist. While deeply involved in the politics of his time, he wrote poetry that challenged later generations to focus on concrete images and spare diction. Yeats found universal themes in local concerns and individualistic independence amid ancient cultural roots.

Early Life

Yeats was born in County Dublin, Ireland, into the privileged life of a ruling family. Ireland was still part of the United Kingdom, and Yeats's father, a descendant of the English who had colonized the country, was a successful lawyer and painter. Yeats was given the best education available, spending most of his youth studying or writing in England. But it was during his childhood vacations in County Sligo that he fell in love with the beauty of the Irish landscape and the simplicity of its people.

Irish Literary Renaissance

In 1885 he met the Irish revolutionary John O'Leary, who inspired the young poet to investigate Irish traditional culture. His 1889 meeting with another revolutionary, Maud Gonne, was equally pivotal. Yeats fell hopelessly in love with Gonne, who refused his repeated proposals. Nevertheless, Yeats quickly threw himself into the Irish Literary Renaissance, a movement that sought to create an authentically Irish national art. In 1889 he published a volume of poetry celebrating Irish myths, *The Wanderings of Oisin and Other Poems*, and in 1893 he brought out *The Celtic Twilight*, a collection of folktales and folklore. The full flowering of his nationalistic poetry came in 1899 with *The Wind Among the Reeds*.

Yeats's passion for Ireland can also be found in his diction. More than perhaps any of his contemporaries, Yeats concentrated on the music of his verse, introducing Gaelic sounds and rhythm into his English poetic lines. His passion also led him to reject traditional Christianity in favor of what he viewed as a deeper, truer paganism latent in Irish culture. Pagan motifs and themes are central to both his early and mature poetry.

His ambition to speak directly to the Irish people led him to help found the Abbey Theatre in 1904, a national theater in Dublin that still seeks to perform and support Irish drama. Yeats both managed the theater and penned many of its early plays.

Mature Life

In 1917 Yeats married Georgie Hyde-Lees, who shared his interest in pagan spiritualism. He also brought out a new, refined technique in *The Wild Swans at Coole*, a style that he developed into full maturity in *The Tower* and *The Winding Stair and Other Poems* (1933). Yeats's mature style reflects the influence of imagist poets such as Ezra Pound, whom he met in 1913. Yeats's later work features concrete images and spare diction, employing nouns, verbs, and adjectives to the near exclusion of adverbs. Yet Yeats also rejected the heavy reliance on allusion found in the poetry of T. S. Eliot. And while his contemporaries abandoned traditional poetic devices such as rhyme and meter, Yeats found innovative ways to harness them. His brushes with danger during the Irish Civil War (1922–23) also helped him produce a tough tone not found in other modernists.

Yeats was awarded the 1923 Nobel Prize in Literature for "preserving contact with his people while upholding the most aristocratic artistry." He died in France in 1939 and was reburied after World War II in County Sligo, Ireland, in 1948. The epitaph on his tombstone comes from "Under Ben Bulben," one of his final poems, and expresses the defiance that often characterized Yeats in life: "Cast a cold eye / On life, on death. / Horseman, pass by!"

DID YOU KNOW ?

Unable to win Maud Gonne, Yeats proposed to her daughter Iseult, who also rejected his proposal.

ANALYZE: *Lyric Poetry, Allusion, Symbol*

Although innovative in content, the form of Yeats's poetry is typically traditional. For example, he often wrote **lyric poems** (p. 183). One of the characteristics of lyric poetry that Yeats employed is musicality. He created this musicality, especially in his early poems, through sound devices, including **alliteration**, **assonance**, and **consonance** (p. 465). As you read, watch for sound devices and consider their effects in the poem. Additionally, note Yeats's frequent use of **end rhyme** (rhymes at the ends of lines). What does it accomplish? If it is absent, might there be a thematic reason for its being left out?

Yeats created multiple layers of meaning in his poems, often using traditional figures of speech. He used carefully selected **allusions** (p. 129), for example, to bring the past into the present. What allusions can you find in his poems, and how do they contribute to a poem's theme? Yeats is also famous for his use of **symbols** (p. 37), which both compress his ideas and imaginatively suggest larger meanings. His interest in the spiritual world often colors his choice of symbols. One of his favorites, the gyre, appears in both "Sailing to Byzantium" and "The Second Coming." Look up the word's dictionary definition and, as you read, consider what Yeats used it to express beyond this literal meaning. What other symbols can you identify in these poems? How do they contribute to each poem's theme?

READ: *Draw Conclusions About Modernism*

As you read these poems, draw conclusions about Yeats's modernism. How do his poems qualify as modern literature? For example, consider whether his poetry reflects the disillusionment and alienation prevalent in modern literature. Do his poems demonstrate a search for meaning, or do they offer a solution to the fragmentation of his era? What do Yeats's poems have to say about religion? Look for allusions, symbols, and other images that recur in a particular poem or from poem to poem. Do any of his poems exhibit evidence of experimentation? Look for evidence of traditional poetic qualities and for evidence of innovation. How does your knowledge of Yeats and his worldview affect your understanding of his poetry?

EVALUATE: *Worldview*

In "The Second Coming," as in some of his other poems, Yeats takes biblical topics and uses them for his own purposes. Find the biblical allusions in the poem and determine their meaning to Yeats. What is the significance of these allusions? How do they reveal or reinforce the theme of the poem? Consider the effect of Yeats's worldview on his poetry. Where does his poem agree with Scripture? Which ideas are contrary to the Bible? Consult Micah 5:2, Matthew 2:1–6, Revelation 13, and Revelation 19:20 as you consider these questions.

OBJECTIVES

- Identify a poet's allusions in a text.
- Apply background knowledge to a text.
- Analyze a poet's use of imagery and symbolism.
- Evaluate a poem's message from a biblical worldview.

VOCABULARY

commend (kə-mĕnd′) *tr.v.* To express approval of; praise.

artifice (är′tə-fĭs) *n.* An artistic device or convention.

anarchy (ăn′ər-kē) *n.* Political disorder and confusion.

conviction (kən-vĭk′shən) *n.* A fixed or strong belief.

What makes someone a VISIONARY?

Those who know the past and can anticipate the future provide perspective for the rest of the world. Whom do you think of as a visionary? Do you know one personally? Consider leaders such as William Wilberforce, Martin Luther, and Martin Luther King Jr. What characteristics do they have in common? With a classmate, come up with a description of a visionary and an example of this type.

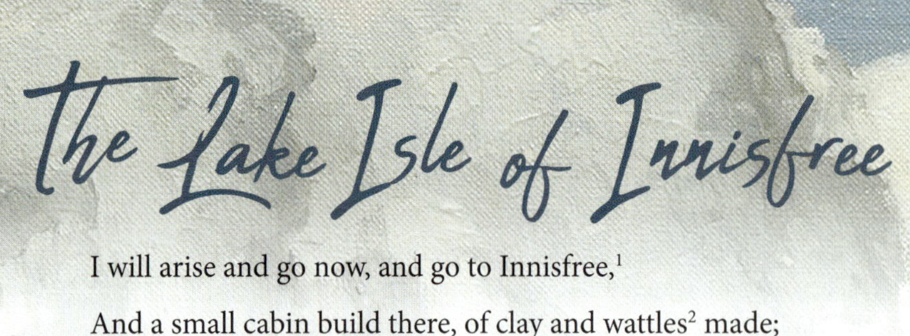

I will arise and go now, and go to Innisfree,[1]
And a small cabin build there, of clay and wattles[2] made;
Nine bean rows will I have there, a hive for the honey bee, **A**
And live alone in the bee-loud glade.

And I shall have some peace there, for peace comes dropping slow,
Dropping from the veils of the morning to where the cricket sings;
There midnight's all a glimmer, and noon a purple glow,
And evening full of the linnet's wings.[3]

I will arise and go now, for always night and day
I hear lake water lapping with low sounds by the shore;
While I stand on the roadway, or on the pavements gray, **A**
I hear it in the deep heart's core. **R**

1. *Innisfree:* a little island on Lake Lough Gill in County Sligo, Ireland
2. *wattles:* twigs or branches woven with poles or rods into a lattice-like structure for use in construction
3. *linnet's wings:* finch's wings

Lyric Poetry: What sound devices can you find in line 3? **A**

Lyric Poetry: What does the end rhyme accomplish in this poem? **A**

Draw Conclusions: What does the poet say he remembers hearing? What sound imagery is present in this poem? How does the theme presented through these images reflect modernism? **R**

VISUAL ANALYSIS
How does the painting *Sunshine in Kerry* by Irish artist Paul Henry suit the content of Yeats's "The Lake Isle of Innisfree"?

Sailing to Byzantium

I

That is no country for old men. The young
In one another's arms, birds in the trees
—Those dying generations—at their song,
The salmon-falls, the mackerel-crowded seas,
Fish, flesh, or fowl, **commend** all summer long
Whatever is begotten, born, and dies.
Caught in that sensual music all neglect
Monuments of unaging intellect. A

II

An aged man is but a paltry thing,
A tattered coat upon a stick, unless
Soul clap its hands and sing, and louder sing
For every tatter in its mortal dress,
Nor is there no singing school but studying
Monuments of its own magnificence;
And therefore I have sailed the seas and come
To the holy city of Byzantium.[1] A

III

O sages standing in God's holy fire
As in the gold mosaic of a wall,
Come from the holy fire, perne in a gyre,[2]
And be the singing-masters of my soul.
Consume my heart away; sick with desire
And fastened to a dying animal
It knows not what it is; and gather me
Into the **artifice** of eternity. A

IV

Once out of nature I shall never take
My bodily form from any natural thing,
But such a form as Grecian goldsmiths make
Of hammered gold and gold enamelling
To keep a drowsy Emperor awake;
Or set upon a golden bough to sing
To lords and ladies of Byzantium
Of what is past, or passing, or to come. R

commend: (kə-mĕnd′) *tr.v.* To express approval of; praise.

Symbol: What does the speaker imply through the contrasting symbols of music and monuments in this stanza? A

Lyric Poetry: What sound devices does the poet employ in lines 15 and 16? What effect do they produce? A

artifice (är′tə-fĭs) *n.* An artistic device or convention.

Symbol: What does the gyre symbolize in this stanza? What does Yeats desire from the ancient wise men? A

Draw Conclusions: What recurring idea is represented in this line, pointing to the poem's theme? How is modernism reflected here? R

1. *Byzantium:* formerly the Roman capital Constantinople; currently known as Istanbul
2. *perne in a gyre:* spiral in a whirling motion

THE SECOND COMING

Turning and turning in the widening gyre
The falcon cannot hear the falconer;
Things fall apart; the center cannot hold;
Mere **anarchy** is loosed upon the world,
The blood-dimmed tide is loosed, and everywhere
The ceremony of innocence is drowned;
The best lack all **conviction**, while the worst
Are full of passionate intensity.

Surely some revelation is at hand;
Surely the Second Coming is at hand.
The Second Coming! Hardly are those words out
When a vast image out of *Spiritus Mundi*[1]
Troubles my sight: somewhere in sands of the desert
A shape with lion body and the head of a man, [A]
A gaze blank and pitiless as the sun,
Is moving its slow thighs, while all about it
Reel shadows of the indignant desert birds.
The darkness drops again; but now I know
That twenty centuries of stony sleep
Were vexed to nightmare by a rocking cradle,
And what rough beast, its hour come round at last,
Slouches towards Bethlehem to be born?

anarchy (ăn′ər-kē) *n.* Political disorder and confusion.

conviction (kən-vĭk′shən) *n.* A fixed or strong belief.

1. *Spiritus Mundi:* Latin for "spirit world"

Allusion: What allusion is found in line 14? [A]

Caption for above image: Félix Vallotton painted *Verdun* (1917) to convey through art what he had witnessed during a visit to the front lines of World War I.

THINK AND DISCUSS

1. How does Yeats's use of symbol contribute to theme in "Sailing to Byzantium"?
2. Compare and contrast Yeats's use of sound devices in "The Lake Isle of Innisfree" and "The Second Coming." How might any differences be connected to their differing themes?
3. How is the 1921 poem "The Second Coming" reflective of modernism? Have any of Yeats's predictions proved correct?
4. Consider Yeats's allusions regarding one coming to Bethlehem. What lines in the poem accurately represent Scripture? In what ways is his vision different from biblical prophecy? Consider Micah 5:2, Matthew 2:1–6, Revelation 13, and Revelation 19:20.
5. How does Yeats use beauty to communicate his message in "The Second Coming"? Evaluate this message according to the principles of Goodness and Truth. What does the poet get right? What would you disagree with, based on a biblical worldview?

Katherine Mansfield (1888–1923)

Kathleen Mansfield Beauchamp, better known by her pen name, Katherine Mansfield, is widely considered a great master and innovator of the short-story form. Through a style that combines realistic insight with symbolic significance, her works reveal an acute perception of the frailties and ambiguities of human nature.

Mansfield was born to a prosperous merchant family in New Zealand. Receiving her early education in Wellington, she then traveled with her two sisters to study in England. After a two-year stint back in New Zealand, she returned to London in 1908 to pursue a literary career. There she lived a disordered life, engaging in several romantic relationships and even marrying and then leaving a music teacher in the same day. In 1909 her mother intervened by taking Mansfield away from London and installing her in a German sanitorium. Mansfield's experiences there inspired her first collection of short stories, *In a German Pension* (1911).

Mansfield returned to London in 1910, where she became involved in a literary set that included D. H. Lawrence. She also met Virginia Woolf. The women came to admire and emulate each other's work. In 1915 her brother, an officer training to fight in France, died in an accident. Fraught with grief, Mansfield sought solace in the French Riviera, a setting that would inspire many of her stories. Her brother's death also motivated her to explore in her writing her childhood memories of New Zealand. She spent much of the remainder of her life in either the Riviera or London.

When the Great War ended, Mansfield was just beginning to write her best fiction, publishing *The Garden Party and Other Stories* in 1922. Tragically, however, her health was deteriorating from the effects of gonorrhea and tuberculosis. She died in an artistic community in France.

In each of Mansfield's best stories, insights into the natural environment are juxtaposed against the thoughts of the characters, creating a focus on the characters' perceptions, particularly as related to class. These characters, although frequently emotionally fragile women, are always complex, full of internal contradictions and transcendent yearnings.

BEFORE READING

ANALYZE: *Character, Point of View, Setting*

In her short stories, Mansfield tends to focus on one main **character**, carefully exploring his or her thoughts, emotions, and choices in a given situation. In "A Cup of Tea," how might her use of **third-person limited point of view** (in which the narrator stands outside the story, refers to characters in the third person, and "gets inside" only one character's head) heighten this focus? How might it color readers' perceptions of the characters? Additionally, Mansfield vividly evokes the era's **setting**, especially upper-class manners and values. Pay attention to how characters, setting, and point of view interact. For example, both characters' class and their gender are significant to their character.

READ: *Make and Check Predictions*

The narration focuses on the character of Rosemary. Her responses, emotions, and choices are important to what Mansfield wants to say. As you read, try to predict how Rosemary will choose to act next. Note which people, events, and beliefs influence her decisions throughout the story. For example, how do Rosemary's social position and gender affect her choices? Compare the story's conclusion to your predictions. Did anything surprise you?

EVALUATE: *Compare Characters*

The premise of this story holds much in common with Christ's story of the Good Samaritan (Luke 10:25–37). As you read, compare Rosemary's actions and character to the Samaritan's. How are their motivations similar or different?

OBJECTIVES

- Identify characteristics of third-person limited point of view in a text.
- Make predictions about a character's choices.
- Analyze an author's use of point of view, character, and setting to convey theme.
- Evaluate the main characters' values and actions according to a biblical worldview.

A Cup of Tea

Rosemary Fell was not exactly beautiful. No, you couldn't have called her beautiful. Pretty? Well, if you took her to pieces . . .[1] But why be so cruel as to take anyone to pieces? She was young, brilliant, extremely modern, exquisitely well dressed, amazingly well read in the newest of the new books, and her parties were the most delicious mixture of the really important people and . . . artists—quaint creatures, discoveries of hers, some of them too terrifying for words, but others quite presentable and amusing.

Rosemary had been married two years. She had a duck of a boy. No, not Peter—Michael. And her husband absolutely adored her. They were rich, really rich, not just comfortably well off, which is odious and stuffy and sounds like one's grandparents. But if Rosemary wanted to shop she would go to Paris as you and I would go to Bond Street. If she wanted to buy flowers, the car pulled up at that perfect shop in Regent Street, and Rosemary inside the shop just gazed in her dazzled, rather exotic way, and said, "I want those and those and those. Give me four bunches of those. And that jar of roses. Yes, I'll have all the roses in the jar. No, no lilac. I hate lilac. It's got no shape." The attendant bowed and put the lilac out of sight, as though this was only too true; lilac was dreadfully shapeless. "Give me those stumpy little tulips. Those red and white ones." And she was followed to the car by a thin shop girl

1. *All suspension points in the selection are from the original text.*

staggering under an immense white paper armful that looked like a baby in long clothes. . . . **A**

Character: Based on the narration, what is your initial impression of Rosemary? **A**

One winter afternoon she had been buying something in a little antique shop in Curzon Street. It was a shop she liked. For one thing, one usually had it to oneself. And then the man who kept it was ridiculously fond of serving her. He beamed whenever she came in. He clasped his hands; he was so gratified he could scarcely speak. Flattery, of course. All the same, there was something . . .

"You see, madam," he would explain in his low respectful tones, "I love my things. I would rather not part with them than sell them to someone who does not appreciate them, who has not that fine feeling which is so rare. . . ." And, breathing deeply he unrolled a tiny square of blue velvet and pressed it on the glass counter with his pale fingertips. **A**

Character/Setting: What can you discern about Rosemary's and the shop man's character from these paragraphs? How do they reflect an awareness of class? **A**

Today it was a little box. He had been keeping it for her. He had shown it to nobody as yet. An exquisite little enamel box with a glaze so fine it looked as though it had been baked in cream. On the lid a minute creature stood under a flowery tree, and a more minute creature still had her arms around his neck. Her hat, really no bigger than a geranium petal, hung from a branch; it had green ribbons. And there was a pink cloud like a watchful cherub floating above their heads. Rosemary took her hands out of her long gloves. She always took off her gloves to examine such things. Yes, she liked it very much. She loved it; it was a great duck. She must have it. And, turning the creamy box, opening and shutting it, she couldn't help noticing how charming her hands were against the blue velvet. The shop man, in some dim cavern of his mind, may have dared to think so too. For he took a pencil, leaned over the counter, and his pale bloodless fingers crept timidly towards those rosy, flashing ones, as he murmured gently, "If I may venture to point out to madam, the flowers on the little lady's bodice."

"Charming!" Rosemary admired the flowers. But what was the price? For a moment the shop man did not seem to hear. Then a murmur reached her. "Twenty-eight guineas, madam."

"Twenty-eight guineas." Rosemary gave no sign. She laid the little box down; she buttoned her gloves again. Twenty-eight guineas. Even if one is rich . . . She looked vague. She stared at a plump teakettle like a plump hen above the shop man's head, and her voice was dreamy as she answered, "Well, keep it for me—will you? I'll . . ."

But the shop man had already bowed as though keeping it for her was all any human being could ask. He would be willing, of course, to keep it for her forever.

The discreet door shut with a click. She was outside on the step, gazing at the winter afternoon. Rain was falling, and with the rain it seemed the dark came too, spinning down like ashes. There was a cold bitter taste in the air, and the new-lighted lamps looked sad. Sad were the lights in the houses opposite. Dimly they burned as if regretting something. And people hurried by, hidden under their hateful umbrellas.

Rosemary felt a strange pang. She pressed her muff to her breast; she wished she had the little box, too, to cling to. Of course, the car was there. She'd only to cross the pavement. But still she waited. There are moments, horrible moments in life, when one emerges from shelter and looks out, and it's awful. One oughtn't to give way to them. One ought to go home and have an extra special tea. But at the very instant of thinking that, a young girl, thin, dark, shadowy—where had she come from?—was standing at Rosemary's elbow and a voice like a sigh, almost like a sob, breathed, "Madam, may I speak to you a moment?" **A**

"Speak to me?" Rosemary turned. She saw a little battered creature with enormous eyes, someone quite young, no older than herself, who clutched at her coat collar with reddened hands, and shivered as though she had just come out of the water.

"M-madam," stammered the voice. "Would you let me have the price of a cup of tea?"

"A cup of tea?" There was something simple, sincere in that voice; it wasn't in the least the voice of a beggar. "Then have you no money at all?" asked Rosemary.

"None, madam," came the answer.

"How extraordinary!" Rosemary peered through the dusk, and the girl gazed back at her. How more than extraordinary! And suddenly it seemed to Rosemary such an adventure. It was like something out of a novel by Dostoevsky, this meeting in the dusk. Supposing she took the girl home? Supposing she did do one of those things she was always reading about or seeing on the stage, what would happen? It would be thrilling. And she heard herself saying afterwards to the amazement of her friends, "I simply took her home with me," as she stepped forward and said to that dim person beside her, "Come home to tea with me."

The girl drew back startled. She even stopped shivering for a moment. Rosemary put out a hand and touched her arm. "I mean it," she said, smiling. And she felt how simple and kind her smile was. "Why won't you? Do. Come home with me now in my car and have tea."

"You—you don't mean it, madam," said the girl, and there was pain in her voice.

"But I do," cried Rosemary. "I want you to. To please me. Come along." **A**

The girl put her fingers to her lips and her eyes devoured Rosemary. "You're—you're not taking me to the police station?" she stammered.

"The police station!" Rosemary laughed out. "Why should I be so cruel? No, I only want to make you warm and to hear—anything you care to tell me."

Hungry people are easily led. The footman held the door of the car open, and a moment later they were skimming through the dusk.

"There!" said Rosemary. She had a feeling of triumph as she slipped her hand through the velvet strap. She could have said, "Now I've got you," as she gazed at the little captive she had netted. But of course she meant it kindly. Oh, more than kindly. She was going to prove to this girl that—wonderful things did happen in life, that—fairy godmothers were real, that—rich people had hearts, and that women *were* sisters. She turned impulsively, saying, "Don't be frightened. After all, why shouldn't you come back with me? We're both women. If I'm the more fortunate, you ought to expect . . ."

But happily at that moment, for she didn't know how the sentence was going to end, the car stopped. The bell was rung, the door opened, and with a charming, protecting, almost embracing movement, Rosemary drew the other into the hall. Warmth, softness, light, a sweet scent, all those things so familiar to her she never even thought about them, she watched that other receive. It was fascinating. She was like the little rich girl in her nursery with all the cupboards to open, all the boxes to unpack.

"Come, come upstairs," said Rosemary, longing to begin to be generous. "Come up to my room." And, besides, she wanted to spare this poor little

Point of View: How does Mansfield's chosen point of view offer readers important information at this point in the story? **A**

Character: What seems to be motivating Rosemary to help a stranger? **A**

thing from being stared at by the servants; she decided as they mounted the stairs she would not even ring for Jeanne, but take off her things by herself. The great thing was to be natural! R

Make Predictions: How does Rosemary feel about helping this girl? How do you think she will affect this stranger? R

And "There!" cried Rosemary again, as they reached her beautiful big bedroom with the curtains drawn, the fire leaping on her wonderful lacquer furniture, her gold cushions and the primrose and blue rugs.

The girl stood just inside the door; she seemed dazed. But Rosemary didn't mind that.

"Come and sit down," she cried, dragging her big chair up to the fire, "in this comfy chair. Come and get warm. You look so dreadfully cold."

"I daren't, madam," said the girl, and she edged backwards.

"Oh, please,"— Rosemary ran forward—"you mustn't be frightened, you mustn't, really. Sit down, and when I've taken off my things we shall go into the next room and have tea and be cozy. Why are you afraid?" And gently she half pushed the thin figure into its deep cradle.

But there was no answer. The girl stayed just as she had been put, with her hands by her sides and her mouth slightly open. To be quite sincere, she looked rather stupid. But Rosemary wouldn't acknowledge it. She leaned over her, saying, "Won't you take off your hat? Your pretty hair is all wet. And one is so much more comfortable without a hat, isn't one?"

There was a whisper that sounded like "Very good, madam," and the crushed hat was taken off.

"Let me help you off with your coat, too," said Rosemary.

The girl stood up. But she held on to the chair with one hand and let Rosemary pull. It was quite an effort. The other scarcely helped her at all. She seemed to stagger like a child, and the thought came and went through Rosemary's mind, that if people wanted helping they must respond a little, just a little, otherwise it became very difficult indeed. And what was she to do with the coat now? She left it on the floor, and the hat too. She was just going to take a cigarette off the mantelpiece when the girl said quickly, but so lightly and strangely, "I'm very sorry, madam, but I'm going to faint. I shall go off, madam, if I don't have something." A

Point of View/Setting: How do Rosemary's internal perceptions of the girl in this passage highlight their differing life experiences? A

"Good heavens, how thoughtless I am!" Rosemary rushed to the bell.

"Tea! Tea at once! And some brandy immediately!"

The maid was gone again, but the girl almost cried out. "No, I don't want no brandy. I never drink brandy. It's a cup of tea I want, madam." And she burst into tears.

It was a terrible and fascinating moment. Rosemary knelt beside her chair.

"Don't cry, poor little thing," she said. "Don't cry." And she gave the other her lace handkerchief. She really was touched beyond words. She put her arm round those thin, birdlike shoulders.

Now at last the other forgot to be shy, forgot everything except that they were both women, and gasped out, "I can't go on no longer like this. I can't bear it. I shall do away with myself. I can't bear no more."

"You shan't have to. I'll look after you. Don't cry any more. Don't you see what a good thing it was that you met me? We'll have tea and you'll tell me everything. And I shall arrange something. I promise. *Do* stop crying. It's so exhausting. Please!" A

Character: What do we learn about Rosemary through her manner of comforting? A

The other did stop just in time for Rosemary to get up before the tea came. She had the table placed between them. She plied the poor little creature with everything, all the sandwiches, all the bread and butter, and every time her cup was empty she filled it with tea, cream, and sugar. People always said sugar was so nourishing. As for herself she didn't eat; she smoked and looked away tactfully so that the other should not be shy.

And really the effect of that slight meal was marvelous. When the tea table was carried away a new being, a light, frail creature with tangled hair, dark lips, deep, lighted eyes, lay back in the big chair in a kind of sweet languor, looking at the blaze. Rosemary lit a fresh cigarette; it was time to begin.

"And when did you have your last meal?" she asked softly.

But at that moment the door handle turned.

"Rosemary, may I come in?" It was Philip.

"Of course."

He came in. "Oh, I'm so sorry," he said, and stopped and stared.

"It's quite all right," said Rosemary smiling. "This is my friend, Miss—"

"Smith, madam," said the languid figure, who was strangely still and unafraid. **A**

Character/Setting: How has Rosemary helped the girl? Why do you think that until this moment, she has neither introduced herself nor asked the girl's name? **A**

"Smith," said Rosemary. "We are going to have a little talk."

"Oh, yes," said Philip. "Quite," and his eye caught sight of the coat and hat on the floor. He came over to the fire and turned his back to it. "It's a beastly afternoon," he said curiously, still looking at that listless figure, looking at its hands and boots, and then at Rosemary again.

"Yes, isn't it?" said Rosemary enthusiastically. "Vile."

Philip smiled his charming smile. "As a matter of fact," said he, "I wanted you to come into the library for a moment. Would you? Will Miss Smith excuse us?"

The big eyes were raised to him, but Rosemary answered for her. "Of course she will." And they went out of the room together.

"I say," said Philip, when they were alone. "Explain. Who is she? What does it all mean?"

Rosemary, laughing, leaned against the door and said, "I picked her up in Curzon Street. Really. She's a real pickup. She asked me for the price of a cup of tea, and I brought her home with me."

"But what on earth are you going to do with her?" cried Philip.

"Be nice to her," said Rosemary quickly. "Be frightfully nice to her. Look after her. I don't know how. We haven't talked yet. But show her—treat her—make her feel—"

"My darling girl," said Philip, "you're quite mad, you know. It simply can't be done."

"I knew you'd say that," retorted Rosemary. "Why not? I want to. Isn't that a reason? And besides, one's always reading about these things. I decided—"

"But," said Philip slowly, and he cut the end of a cigar, "she's so astonishingly pretty."

"Pretty?" Rosemary was so surprised that she blushed. "Do you think so? I—I hadn't thought about it."

"Good Lord!" Philip struck a match. "She's absolutely lovely. Look again, my child. I was bowled over when I came into your room just now. However . . . I think you're making a ghastly mistake. Sorry, darling, if I'm crude and all that. But let me know if Miss Smith is going to dine with us in time for me to look up *The Milliner's Gazette*." **A**

Character: How does Philip successfully get his wife to change her mind? Why does he do so? **A**

"You absurd creature!" said Rosemary, and she went out of the library, but not back to her bedroom. She went to her writing room and sat down at her desk. Pretty! Absolutely lovely! Bowled over! Her heart beat like a heavy bell. Pretty! Lovely! She drew her check book towards her. But no, checks would be no use, of course. She opened a drawer and took out five pound notes, looked at them, put two back, and holding the three squeezed in her hand, she went back to her bedroom. R

Half an hour later Philip was still in the library, when Rosemary came in.

"I only wanted to tell you," said she, and she leaned against the door again and looked at him with her dazzled exotic gaze, "Miss Smith won't dine with us tonight."

Philip put down the paper. "Oh, what's happened? Previous engagement?"

Rosemary came over and sat down on his knee. "She insisted on going," said she, "so I gave the poor little thing a present of money. I couldn't keep her against her will, could I?" she added softly.

Rosemary had just done her hair, darkened her eyes a little, and put on her pearls. She put up her hands and touched Philip's cheeks.

"Do you like me?" said she, and her tone, sweet, husky, troubled him.

"I like you awfully," he said, and he held her tighter. "Kiss me."

There was a pause.

Then Rosemary said dreamily, "I saw a fascinating little box today. It cost twenty-eight guineas. May I have it?"

Philip jumped her on his knee. "You may, little wasteful one," said he.

But that was not really what Rosemary wanted to say.

"Philip," she whispered, and she pressed his head against her bosom, "am I *pretty*?" A

VISUAL ANALYSIS
How might the woman in this painting (*The Red Ribbon* by Frederick Carl Frieseke) suggest the character of Rosemary?

Check Predictions: Did you predict Rosemary's final decision? What was correct or incorrect about your reasoning? R

Character: What does Rosemary's final conversation tell you about her and her relationship with her husband? A

THINK AND DISCUSS

1. Define *third-person limited point of view*. In "A Cup of Tea," which character's thoughts can the narrator perceive? Give an example from the text.
2. Briefly describe Rosemary, the girl, and Philip.
3. What aspects of Rosemary's character were demonstrated early on, foreshadowing the story's conclusion? Justify your answer with textual details.
4. How does the third-person limited narrator affect readers' understanding of the characters? Consider the narrator's access to information and tone toward each. Use the text to support your answers.
5. Using details from the text, explain two ways that class affects the thoughts or actions of each main character.
6. Choose one additional characteristic of modernist writing and explain how the story illustrates it.
7. In what ways does Rosemary's character illustrate unhealthy social strictures and expectations for women that authors such as Wollstonecraft pointed out? Consider Rosemary's insecurity and her interactions with her husband. How might a biblical perspective on love view and address her situation?
8. Evaluate Rosemary's treatment of Miss Smith. How does Rosemary compare to the Good Samaritan (Luke 10:25–37)? How might Mansfield be promoting Goodness in portraying Rosemary's attempt at charity?

James Joyce (1882–1941)

AT A GLANCE

- **1898** Enrolled at University College
- **1914** Published *Dubliners*
- **1914** Published *A Portrait of the Artist as a Young Man*
- **1922** Published *Ulysses*
- **1939** Published *Finnegans Wake*

Although Irish author James Joyce exiled himself from his homeland, his experimental fiction put Ireland at the center of the modernistic movement. In his work Joyce plays with language, fights conventions, and plumbs the depths of the subconscious, all the while reflecting a broken yet beautiful Ireland.

Early Life and Work

Joyce was born into a relatively prosperous family in a Dublin suburb. When he was fourteen, Joyce seriously considered preparing for the Catholic priesthood. At the same time, however, the young Joyce was dabbling in gross immorality. He came to view Christianity as being too narrow to express the full range of human experience, and after graduating from University College in Dublin, he decided to become a writer.

Feeling constricted by colonial politics and traditional Irish society, he left Ireland for good in 1904 with his future wife, Nora Barnacle. He would return only three brief times, spending his early years abroad working variously as an English teacher and a banker.

DID YOU KNOW ?

The word for a subatomic particle, *quark*, was taken from the seabirds' cheer in *Finnegans Wake*.

But his fiction is set exclusively in Ireland, and it often minutely recreates Irish ways and geography.

His first significant work is a collection of masterfully written short stories titled *Dubliners* (1914). Each story is a vignette of ordinary Dublin life that dwells on a moment of personal limitation or failure in the life of a central character. In 1914 Joyce began publishing his autobiographical novel, *A Portrait of the Artist as a Young Man,* in serial form. This novel's experimental language (which grows in complexity as its narrator ages) brought Joyce to the attention of the modernist avant-garde. With the encouragement of established figures such as Ezra Pound, Joyce began work on the novel *Ulysses*, which was published in Paris in 1922.

Revolutionary Fiction

Ulysses is a sharp break from literary convention. Although the novel is more than seven hundred pages long, its events all occur in the space of one day, June 16, 1904. The novel focuses on the interior thoughts and perceptions of its characters. Its only organization derives from the ways in which its protagonist's wanderings through Dublin parallel Odysseus's adventures in Homer's *Odyssey*. The book's obscene content led to its being banned from publication in England and the United States until the 1930s.

Encouraged by the success of *Ulysses* and now free of financial difficulties, Joyce spent the remainder of his life struggling against his fading eyesight and failing health to compose *Finnegans Wake*. This novel, finally published in 1939, pushes the revolutionary tendencies of *Ulysses* to their extremes. The only readily discernible structure in *Finnegans Wake* is its circularity: the novel's first sentence is broken halfway, ending at the beginning of the book and beginning at the end. The novel seeks to embody the diversity and cyclical nature of the universe itself. Unfortunately for Joyce, the book was panned by critics. Grieving over his failure and his daughter, Lucia, who was committed to an insane asylum in 1935, Joyce died of an ulcer in Zurich in 1941.

Literary Influence

Joyce's literary legacy is controversial. While *Ulysses* is often considered one of the greatest novels ever written, it is also, in Joyce's own words from *Finnegans Wake*, "usylessly unreadable." What is not controversial is that in both *Ulysses* and *Finnegans Wake* Joyce fully developed the stream-of-consciousness technique, which would become a staple of modern fiction. And at its best, Joyce's work abounds in psychological insight and dazzling linguistic virtuosity.

ANALYZE: *Stream of Consciousness and Epiphany*

In "Araby" Joyce tells the story through the eyes of a youth growing up in Dublin. He uses the **stream-of-consciousness technique** (a type of writing in which the author attempts to reproduce the flow of thoughts in a character's mind with little attention to grammar or logic) to reveal the thoughts and feelings of the boy as they occur. This style of writing reflects the modernistic emphasis on the inner self and allows the reader to experience what the boy experiences along with him. At the end of his tale, the boy—and the reader—has an **epiphany** (a sudden revelatory insight into some aspect of life or reality that springs from an ordinary person, object, or event). What does he realize about his life in Dublin, his relationships, and his dreams?

READ: *Draw Conclusions About Theme*

In addition to using the stream-of-consciousness technique, Joyce relies heavily on **symbolism** (p. 37) as he intertwines story elements to recreate this account of self-discovery. By examining the story elements and interpreting the symbolism, a reader can uncover the theme of the story. As you read, consider the modernistic emphases on disillusionment, alienation, and fragmentation. Try to identify symbols that portray the boy's feelings toward his reality. For example, the narrator begins by describing the Dublin setting in which he places the boy. What atmosphere (p. 213) do these details create? How do you think the boy feels about his environment? What do Mangan's sister and Araby symbolize to the boy? What conflict do they create for him? What does he learn from his epiphany?

EVALUATE: *Author's Perspective*

Interpreting the author's purpose for this tale is not as simple as it may appear. Full interpretation of the boy's actions requires the reader to understand the writer's opinion of the Roman Catholic Church, which dominated his town and his life. To reveal his opinion, he begins by highlighting the Church's domination of the boy's world. Then he uses the lens of religion to reveal the boy's thought processes. What references does the boy make to the Church? What role does religion play in his life? What attitude does he seem to have toward the Church? Do you think his attitude is justified? Would it be justified if it were applied to all churches? Do people today have similar attitudes toward churches? Ephesians 4:11–16 says that the church is a body in which every part helps every other part become more like Christ, the head of the body, through showing love—especially speaking the truth in love. Use these verses to evaluate your conclusions about Joyce in the preceding questions.

OBJECTIVES

- Identify stream of consciousness.
- Analyze the author's use of story elements and stream of consciousness to convey theme.
- Draw conclusions about theme.
- Evaluate the author's adult perspective as a result of experience.

VOCABULARY

imperturbable (ĭm′pər-tûr′bə-bəl) *adj.* Unshakably calm and collected.

impinge (ĭm-pĭnj′) *intr.v.* To collide or strike against something.

annihilate (ə-nī′ə-lāt′) *tr.v.* To destroy completely.

amiability (ā′mē-ə-bil′ə-tē) *n.* Lovableness.

garrulous (găr′ə-ləs) *adj.* Given to excessive and often trivial or rambling talk.

Is ANTICIPATION *half the fun?*

How long does it take to open presents on Christmas morning? How long does it take to ride a roller coaster? Both events are over in a flash. You will probably agree—anticipation is half the fun. Buying and wrapping presents or traveling and standing in lines build excitement for the actual event. It is also possible to anticipate something and be disappointed. Write a paragraph about a personal experience with anticipation.

ARABY

North Richmond Street, being blind,[1] was a quiet street except at the hour when the Christian Brothers' School set the boys free. An uninhabited house of two stories stood at the blind end, detached from its neighbors in a square ground. The other houses of the street, conscious of decent lives within them, gazed at one another with brown **imperturbable** faces. E

The former tenant of our house, a priest, had died in the back drawing room. Air, musty from having been long enclosed, hung in all the rooms, and the waste room behind the kitchen was littered with old useless papers. Among these I found a few paper-covered books, the pages of which were curled and damp: *The Abbot,* by Walter Scott, *The Devout Communicant* and *The Memoirs of Vidocq*. I liked the last best because its leaves were yellow.

imperturbable (ĭm′pər-tûr′bə-bəl) *adj.* Unshakably calm and collected.

Author's Perspective: What do you think the narrator, as an irreligious adult, is implying about Catholicism in this first paragraph? E

1. *blind:* dead-end street

The wild garden behind the house contained a central apple tree and a few straggling bushes under one of which I found the late tenant's rusty bicycle pump. He had been a very charitable priest; in his will he had left all his money to institutions and the furniture of his house to his sister.

When the short days of winter came dusk fell before we had well eaten our dinners. When we met in the street the houses had grown somber. The space of sky above us was the color of ever-changing violet and towards it the lamps of the street lifted their feeble lanterns. The cold air stung us and we played till our bodies glowed.[2] Our shouts echoed in the silent street. The career[3] of our play brought us through the dark muddy lanes behind the houses where we ran the gauntlet[4] of the rough tribes[5] from the cottages, to the back doors of the dark dripping gardens where odors arose from the ashpits, to the dark odorous stables where a coachman smoothed and combed the horse or shook music from the buckled harness. **R** When we returned to the street light from the kitchen windows had filled the areas. If my uncle was seen turning the corner we hid in the shadow until we had seen him safely housed. Or if Mangan's sister came out on the doorstep to call her brother in to his tea we watched her from our shadow peer up and down the street. We waited to see whether she would remain or go in and, if she remained, we left our shadow and walked up to Mangan's steps resignedly.[6] She was waiting for us, her figure defined by the light from the half-opened door. Her brother always teased her before he obeyed and I stood by the railings looking at her. Her dress swung as she moved her body and the soft rope of her hair tossed from side to side. **R**

Draw Conclusions: What atmosphere does the setting create? What does the narrator imply about the boy's future? **R**

Draw Conclusions: Note the contrast of light and darkness in this paragraph. What do you think each symbolizes? How does the contrast contribute to the theme? **R**

Every morning I lay on the floor in the front parlor watching her door. The blind was pulled down to within an inch of the sash[7] so that I could not be seen. When she came out on the doorstep my heart leaped. I ran to the hall, seized my books and followed her. I kept her brown figure always in my eye and, when we came near the point at which our ways diverged, I quickened my pace and passed her. This happened morning after morning. I had never spoken to her, except for a few casual words, and yet her name was like a summons to all my foolish blood.

Her image accompanied me even in places the most hostile to romance. On Saturday evenings when my aunt went marketing I had to go to carry some of the parcels. We walked through the flaring[8] streets, jostled by drunken men and bargaining women, amid the curses of laborers, the shrill litanies[9] of shop boys who stood on guard by the barrels of pigs' cheeks, the nasal chanting of street singers, who sang a *come-all-you* about O'Donovan Rossa, or a ballad about the troubles in our native land. These noises converged in a single sensation of life for me: I imagined that I bore my chalice[10] safely through a throng of foes. Her name sprang to my lips at moments in strange prayers and praises which I myself did not understand. My eyes were often full of tears (I could not tell why) and at times a flood from my heart seemed to pour itself out into my bosom. I thought little of the future. I did not know whether I would ever speak to her or not or, if I spoke to her, how I

2. *glowed:* had "a bright, warm, usually reddish color" (*AHD*)
3. *career:* rapid course
4. *ran . . . gauntlet:* continued while under attack
5. *tribes:* "a group of people forming a community" (*OED*)
6. *resignedly:* unresisting acceptance of something as inescapable
7. *sash:* "a frame, usually of wood, rebated and fitted with one or more panes of glass forming a window or part of a window" (*OED*)
8. *flaring:* "glaring, showy, gaudy, extravagant" (*OED*)
9. *litany:* a continuous repetition or long enumeration resembling those of repetition prayers
10. *chalice:* a cup used at Holy Communion during the mass

could tell her of my confused adoration. But my body was like a harp and her words and gestures were like fingers running upon the wires. **E**

One evening I went into the back drawing room[11] in which the priest had died. It was a dark rainy evening and there was no sound in the house. Through one of the broken panes I heard the rain **impinge** upon the earth, the fine incessant needles of water playing in the sodden beds. Some distant lamp or lighted window gleamed below me. I was thankful that I could see so little. All my senses seemed to desire to veil themselves and, feeling that I was about to slip from them, I pressed the palms of my hands together until they trembled, murmuring: *"O love! O love!"* many times.

At last she spoke to me. When she addressed the first words to me I was so confused that I did not know what to answer. She asked me was I going to *Araby*. I forget whether I answered yes or no. It would be a splendid bazaar,[12] she said she would love to go.

"And why can't you?" I asked.

While she spoke she turned a silver bracelet round and round her wrist. She could not go, she said, because there would be a retreat that week in her convent. Her brother and two other boys were fighting for their caps and I was alone at the railings. She held one of the spikes, bowing her head towards me. The light from the lamp opposite our door caught the white curve of her neck, lit up her hair that rested there and, falling, lit up the hand upon the railing. It fell over one side of her dress and caught the white border of a petticoat, just visible as she stood at ease. **R**

"It's well for you," she said.

"If I go," I said, "I will bring you something."

What innumerable follies laid waste my waking and sleeping thoughts after that evening! I wished to **annihilate** the tedious intervening days. I chafed against the work of school. At night in my bedroom and by day in the classroom her image came between me and the page I strove to read. The syllables of the word *Araby* were called to me through the silence in which my soul luxuriated and cast an Eastern enchantment over me. I asked for leave to go to the bazaar on Saturday night. My aunt was surprised and hoped it was not some Freemason[13] affair. I answered few questions in class. I watched my master's face pass from **amiability** to sternness; he hoped I was not beginning to idle. I could not call my wandering thoughts together. I had hardly any patience with the serious work of life which, now that it stood between me and my desire, seemed to me child's play, ugly monotonous child's play. **R**

On Saturday morning I reminded my uncle that I wished to go to the bazaar in the evening. He was fussing at the hall stand, looking for the hat brush, and answered me curtly:

"Yes, boy, I know."

Author's Perspective: What religious symbolism do you see? What do you think the narrator is saying about the boy's feelings for Mangan's sister? **E**

impinge (ĭm-pĭnj′) *intr.v.* To collide or strike against something.

Draw Conclusions: Why do you think this girl is not named? What conflict do you see developing? **R**

annihilate (ə-nī′ə-lāt′) *tr.v.* To destroy completely.

amiability (ā′mē-ə-bil′ə-tē) *n.* Lovableness.

Draw Conclusions: Why does the boy feel discontent? **R**

11. *drawing room:* "a large room in which guests are entertained" (*AHD*)
12. *bazaar:* "a market consisting of a street lined with shops and stalls" (*AHD*)
13. *Freemason:* pertaining to a secret society

As he was in the hall I could not go into the front parlor and lie at the window. I left the house in bad humor and walked slowly towards the school. The air was pitilessly raw and already my heart misgave me.[14]

When I came home to dinner my uncle had not yet been home. Still it was early. I sat staring at the clock for some time and, when its ticking began to irritate me I left the room. I mounted the staircase and gained the upper part of the house. The high cold empty gloomy rooms liberated me and I went from room to room singing. From the front window I saw my companions playing below in the street. Their cries reached me weakened and indistinct and, leaning my forehead against the cool glass, I looked over at the dark house where she lived. I may have stood there for an hour, seeing nothing but the brown-clad figure cast by my imagination, touched discreetly by the lamplight at the curved neck, at the hand upon the railings and at the border below the dress. **A**

Stream of Consciousness: How does this paragraph illustrate stream of consciousness? **A**

When I came downstairs again I found Mrs. Mercer sitting at the fire. She was an old **garrulous** woman, a pawnbroker's widow, who collected used stamps for some pious purpose. I had to endure the gossip of the tea-table. The meal was prolonged beyond an hour and still my uncle did not come. Mrs. Mercer stood up to go: she was sorry she couldn't wait any longer, but it was after eight o'clock and she did not like to be out late, as the night air was bad for her. When she had gone I began to walk up and down the room, clenching my fists. My aunt said:

garrulous (găr′ə-ləs) *adj.* Given to excessive and often trivial or rambling talk.

"I'm afraid you may put off your bazaar for this night of Our Lord."

At nine o'clock I heard my uncle's latchkey in the hall door. I heard him talking to himself and heard the hall stand rocking when it had received the weight of his overcoat. I could interpret these signs. When he was midway through his dinner I asked him to give me the money to go to the bazaar. He had forgotten.

"The people are in bed and after their first sleep now," he said.

I did not smile. My aunt said to him energetically:

"Can't you give him the money and let him go? You've kept him late enough as it is."

My uncle said he was very sorry he had forgotten. He said he believed in the old saying: "All work and no play makes Jack a dull boy." He asked me where I was going and, when I had told him a second time he asked me did I know *The Arab's Farewell to his Steed*. When I left the kitchen he was about to recite the opening lines of the piece to my aunt. **R**

Draw Conclusions: What literal and figurative roadblocks have kept the boy from going to the bazaar? What might they foreshadow about the boy's quest? **R**

I held a florin[15] tightly in my hand as I strode down Buckingham Street towards the station. The sight of the streets thronged with buyers and glaring with gas recalled to me the purpose of my journey. I took my seat in a third-class carriage of a deserted train. After an intolerable delay the train moved out of the station slowly. It crept onward among ruinous houses and over the twinkling river. At Westland Row Station a crowd of people pressed to the carriage doors; but the porters moved them back, saying that it was a special train for the bazaar. I remained alone in the bare carriage. In a few minutes the train drew up beside an improvised wooden platform. I passed out on to the road and saw by the lighted dial of a clock that it was ten minutes to ten. In front of me was a large building which displayed the magical name.

I could not find any sixpenny entrance and, fearing that the bazaar would be closed, I passed in quickly through a turnstile, handing a shilling to a

14. *misgave me:* made me suspicious
15. *florin:* an older British coin equivalent to two shillings

weary-looking man. I found myself in a big hall girdled[16] at half its height by a gallery.[17] Nearly all the stalls were closed and the greater part of the hall was in darkness. I recognized a silence like that which pervades a church after a service. I walked into the center of the bazaar timidly. A few people were gathered about the stalls which were still open. Before a curtain, over which the words *Café Chantant* were written in colored lamps, two men were counting money on a salver.[18] I listened to the fall of the coins.

Remembering with difficulty why I had come I went over to one of the stalls and examined porcelain vases and flowered tea sets. At the door of the stall a young lady was talking and laughing with two young gentlemen. I remarked their English accents and listened vaguely to their conversation.

"O, I never said such a thing!"

"O, but you did!"

"O, but I didn't!"

"Didn't she say that?"

"Yes. I heard her."

"O, there's a . . . fib!"

Observing me the young lady came over and asked me did I wish to buy anything. The tone of her voice was not encouraging; she seemed to have spoken to me out of a sense of duty. I looked humbly at the great jars that stood like eastern guards at either side of the dark entrance to the stall and murmured:

"No, thank you."

The young lady changed the position of one of the vases and went back to the two young men. They began to talk of the same subject. Once or twice the young lady glanced at me over her shoulder.

I lingered before her stall, though I knew my stay was useless, to make my interest in her wares seem the more real. Then I turned away slowly and walked down the middle of the bazaar. I allowed the two pennies to fall against the sixpence in my pocket. I heard a voice call from one end of the gallery that the light was out. The upper part of the hall was now completely dark.

Gazing up into the darkness I saw myself as a creature driven and derided by vanity; and my eyes burned with anguish and anger. **A**

Epiphany: What is the boy's epiphany? From whose point of view is it written? How can you tell? **A**

16. *girdled:* surrounded
17. *gallery:* "a roofed promenade, especially one extended along the wall of a building and supported by arches or columns on the outer side; a long enclosed passage, such as a hallway or corridor" (*AHD*)
18. *salver:* tray used to present food or other objects

THINK AND DISCUSS

1. Describe the story's setting.
2. Identify two examples where the text illustrates stream-of-consciousness writing. Describe the characteristics of each passage that mark it as an example of the stream-of-consciousness technique.
3. Discuss the narrator's use of symbolism when describing the setting and the boy's feelings toward his setting.
4. What conflicts for the boy do Mangan's sister, Dublin, and Araby represent?
5. Evaluate the narrator's tone. How do the religious references support this tone? What message do you think the narrator is communicating?
6. What is the boy's epiphany?
7. Why do you think Joyce was disillusioned with the Roman Catholic Church? Do you think any of his complaints are justified? Why or why not?
8. Evaluate your conclusions in question 7 in light of Ephesians 4:11–16.

D. H. Lawrence (1885–1930)

AT A GLANCE

- **1913** Published *Sons and Lovers*
- **1914** Married Frieda Weekley
- **1915** Published *The Rainbow*
- **1920** Published *Women in Love*
- **1928** Published *Lady Chatterley's Lover*

D. H. Lawrence was an English novelist, short-story writer, essayist, and poet whose work, although perhaps best known for its sexual themes, constitutes an extended meditation on the shifting, fragmented nature of human experience.

Early Life

The son of a coarse, almost illiterate coal miner and a refined schoolteacher, David Herbert "Bert" Lawrence was born in a mining town in Nottinghamshire. Lawrence's mother was ambitious to lift her children out of a working-class environment. In his early home environment, Lawrence witnessed family conflicts that shaped his character and writing. He was clearly gifted and was able to obtain a formal education, first at the local high school (having won a scholarship) and then at University College, Nottingham (1906–8), where he earned a teacher's certificate. The successful publication of his first two novels, written while he was a teacher, convinced Lawrence to abandon teaching in favor of a literary career.

In 1912 he met a German aristocrat, Frieda Weekley, then the wife of Lawrence's former professor. Lawrence and Frieda, who left her three young children, eloped to the Continent and were eventually married after she obtained a divorce in 1914. Their marital life, however, was turbulent. In 1917 the Lawrences were accused of sending signals to German submarines and were expelled from their home in Cornwall as a result of this unfounded suspicion. Disgusted with England, they left the country in 1919 for a life of globetrotting, living variously in Italy, the United States, Mexico, and France. Lawrence returned to England only twice for brief visits.

DID YOU KNOW ?

Lawrence was given a 160-acre ranch in Taos, New Mexico, in exchange for a manuscript of *Sons and Lovers*. His ashes were taken there in 1935.

Professional Life

In 1913 Lawrence published his semiautobiographical novel, *Sons and Lovers,* to general critical acclaim. The circumstances of its main character, Paul, mirror those of Lawrence in early life. For example, Paul's father is a coal miner who drinks. The mother has married below her social and economic class, is unhappy, and frequently fights with her husband. She looks to her sons for love, particularly the oldest, and is devastated when he dies. Lawrence's older brother also died, and the close relationship between Paul and his mother reflects Lawrence's personal situation. Paul loses his mother just as Lawrence did his. In these and other ways, the novel reflects Lawrence's personal situation. His short-story collection *The Prussian Officer and Other Stories* (1914), which includes "A Sick Collier," also draws from his family and social background.

In 1915 one of Lawrence's experimental novels, *The Rainbow,* was banned by the government. While abroad, Lawrence wrote prolifically, notably publishing *Women in Love* in 1920 and *The Plumed Serpent* in 1926. Lawrence's final return to England inspired *Lady Chatterley's Lover* (1928), a sexually explicit novel that remained banned in England until 1960.

By 1924 Lawrence had contracted tuberculosis, and though he spent time in a sanatorium in the south of France, the disease claimed his life in 1930. Although most famous for his novels, Lawrence was also an accomplished poet (employing the free verse of Walt Whitman after initially beginning with traditional forms) and short-story writer. His work, while never as experimental in style as that of his modernist contemporaries, reflects the period in its Freudian psychoanalysis and freedom of expression in controversial content.

ANALYZE: *Conflict, Character, Plot, and Theme*

The action of "A Sick Collier" centers on several **conflicts** (p. 213) surrounding two major **characters** (p. 213), a coal miner and his wife. As you read, identify the key differences in these characters and analyze other major sources of conflict. What motivates each character as he or she makes choices? What forces must they defeat in order to survive? Which of the two characters provides a lens from which readers can access the story? Finally, decide which one is **sympathetic** (p. 394) and which one is **unsympathetic** (p. 394).

To understand what an author means to say with the elements of conflict and character, readers must examine how they develop over the course of the story's plot structure. Each stage of the plot generally coincides with significant character conflicts and choices. Trace these plot elements in "A Sick Collier." Begin by noting the **exposition**, where you are introduced to the characters and setting. What is the **inciting incident**, the event initiating the conflict? Which elements constitute **rising action**, leading to the **crisis**, the major turning point for the protagonist? Determine the **climax**, the moment of highest emotional intensity. Identify the **falling action**, leading to the narrative's conclusion, or **denouement**, when the loose ends are tied up. How does the story, including the resolution, reflect modernist themes? Try to state the story's **theme** (p. 229) in your own words.

READ: *Make Predictions*

Lawrence provides clues throughout the story that **foreshadow** (hint at events that will occur later within the story) future events. For example, what is unusual about the description of the coal miner's head? What is his relationship to his job like? How does his marriage affect him? As you read, predict what the outcomes of the various conflicts will be. For example, how will the conflict between the coal miner and his wife conclude? Do you think their marriage will flourish in spite of their differences? How will outside influences, such as the workers' strikes, affect their relationship? What are the clues on which you based your predictions? Can you make use of Lawrence's modernist outlook in order to make predictions? At the story's conclusion, check your predictions. Does Lawrence answer all the questions you had? Revisit the clues to detect what led (or misled) you.

CREATE: *Alternative Ending to the Story*

Given Lawrence's complex arrangement of setting, characters, and conflicts, there are several plausible (and many exciting, implausible) ways in which this short story could conclude. After asking yourself why Lawrence chose the conclusion he did, create a new ending to the story. How can you remain true to Lawrence's themes and modern angst while applying your unique perspective to the situation? For example, will your ending create new problems for the characters? Will you designate one of the characters to resolve the story's dilemmas? Starting with the last line of the story, write at least one page of a new ending. Try your hand at imitating the regional dialect Lawrence employs. Be ready to explain how your conclusion works within the plot, characters, and conflicts Lawrence has provided.

OBJECTIVES

- Identify conflicts in a short story.
- Identify sympathetic and unsympathetic characters.
- Analyze how plot and conflict help to develop theme.
- Create an alternative ending to the story.

VOCABULARY

flaunt (flônt) *tr.v.* To exhibit ostentatiously or shamelessly.

demur (dĭ-mûr′) *intr.v.* To voice opposition; object.

entice (ĕn-tīs′) *tr.v.* To attract (someone), usually to do something, by arousing hope, interest, or desire.

contrive (kən-trīv′) *tr.v.* To plan with cleverness or ingenuity; devise.

subside (səb-sīd′) *intr.v.* To become less intense, active, or severe; abate.

How do OUTSIDE FACTORS *contribute to your identity?*

Most of us assume that our family backgrounds, communities, and nationalities exert influence on our identities. Some of you may indicate the type of school or church you attend as a factor that influences your identity. Certainly friends and extracurricular activities shape you too. How do you think a long-term relationship or your future choice of career makes you who you are? What are the limitations of outside influences in defining you? Can you choose who you will be?

A SICK COLLIER[1]

She was too good for him, everybody said. Yet still she did not regret marrying him. He had come courting her when he was only nineteen, and she twenty. He was in build what they call a tight little fellow; short, dark, with a warm color, and that upright set of the head and chest, that **flaunting** way in movement recalling a mating bird, which denotes a body taut and compact with life. Being a good worker he had earned decent money in the mine, and having a good home had saved a little.

flaunt (flônt) *tr.v.* To exhibit ostentatiously or shamelessly.

She was a cook at "Uplands," a tall, fair girl, very quiet. Having seen her walk down the street, Horsepool had followed her from a distance. He was taken with her, he did not drink, and he was not lazy. So, although he seemed a bit simple, without much intelligence, but having a sort of physical brightness, she considered, and accepted him. R

Make Predictions: Do you think the marriage will succeed or fail? Why? R

When they were married they went to live in Scargill Street, in a highly respectable six-roomed house which they had furnished between them. The street was built up the side of a long, steep hill. It was narrow and rather tunnel-like. Nevertheless, the back looked out over the adjoining pasture, across a wide valley of fields and woods, in the bottom of which the mine lay snugly.

1. *Collier:* a coal miner

He made himself gaffer[2] in his own house. She was unacquainted with a collier's mode of life. They were married on a Saturday. On the Sunday night he said:

"Set th' table for my breakfast, an' put my pit-things afront o' th' fire. I s'll be gettin' up at ha'ef pas' five. Tha nedna shift thysen not till when ter likes."

He showed her how to put a newspaper on the table for a cloth. When she **demurred**:

demur (dĭ-mûr′) *intr.v.* To voice opposition; object.

"I want none o' your white cloths i' th' mornin'. I like ter be able to slobber if I feel like it," he said.

He put before the fire his moleskin trousers, a clean singlet, or sleeveless vest of thick flannel, a pair of stockings and his pit boots, arranging them all to be warm and ready for morning.

"Now tha sees. That wants doin' ivery night."

Punctually at half-past five he left her, without any form of leave-taking, going downstairs in his shirt. **A**

Character/Conflict: What type of man is the coal miner? How is he different from his wife? **A**

When he arrived home at four o'clock in the afternoon his dinner was ready to be dished up. She was startled when he came in, a short, sturdy figure, with a face indescribably black and streaked. She stood before the fire in her white blouse and white apron, a fair girl, the picture of beautiful cleanliness. He "clommaxed" in, in his heavy boots.

"Well, how 'as ter gone on?" he asked.

"I was ready for you to come home," she replied tenderly. In his black face the whites of his brown eyes flashed at her.

"An' I wor ready for comin'," he said. He planked[3] his tin bottle and snap-bag[4] on the dresser, took off his coat and scarf and waistcoat, dragged his arm-chair nearer the fire and sat down.

"Let's ha'e a bit o' dinner, then—I'm about clammed,"[5] he said.

2. *gaffer:* a man of authority or deserving of respect
3. *planked:* placed or set down
4. *snap-bag:* lunch bag
5. *clammed:* starved

"Aren't you goin' to wash yourself first?"

"What am I to wesh mysen for?"

"Well, you can't eat your dinner—"

"Oh, strike a daisy,[6] Missis! Dunna I eat my snap i' th' pit, wi'out weshin'?—forced to."

She served the dinner and sat opposite him. His small bullet head was quite black, save for the whites of his eyes and his scarlet lips. It gave her a queer sensation to see him open his red mouth and bare his white teeth as he ate. His arms and hands were mottled[7] black; his bare, strong neck got a little fairer as it settled towards his shoulders, reassuring her. There was the faint indescribable odor of the pit in the room, an odor of damp, exhausted air. **R**

Make Predictions: What do you think Lawrence is foreshadowing with the "small bullet head" description of the miner? **R**

"Why is your vest so black on the shoulders?" she asked.

"My singlet? That's wi' th' watter droppin' on us from th' roof. This is a dry un as I put on afore I come up. They ha'e gre't clothes-'osses,[8] an' as we change us things, we put 'em on theer ter dry."

When he washed himself, kneeling on the hearthrug stripped to the waist, she felt afraid of him again. He was so muscular, he seemed so intent on what he was doing, so intensely himself, like a vigorous animal. And as he stood wiping himself, with his naked breast towards her, she felt rather sick, seeing his thick arms bulge their muscles.

They were nevertheless very happy. He was at a great pitch[9] of pride because of her. The men in the pit might chaff[10] him, they might try to **entice** him away, but nothing could reduce his self-assured pride because of her, nothing could unsettle his almost infantile satisfaction. In the evening he sat in his arm-chair chattering to her, or listening as she read the newspaper to him. When it was fine, he would go into the street, squat on his heels as colliers do, with his back against the wall of his parlor, and call to the passers-by, in greeting, one after another. If no one were passing, he was content just to squat and smoke, having such a fund of sufficiency and satisfaction in his heart. He was well married.

entice (ĕn-tīs′) *tr.v.* To attract (someone), usually to do something, by arousing hope, interest, or desire.

They had not been wed a year when all Brent and Wellwood's men came out on strike. Willy was in the Union, so with a pinch they scrambled through. The furniture was not all paid for, and other debts were incurred. She worried and **contrived**, he left it to her. But he was a good husband; he gave her all he had. **R**

contrive (kən-trīv′) *tr.v.* To plan with cleverness or ingenuity; devise.

Make Predictions: Will their marriage survive if Willy loses his job? Is his wife or his job more important to him? **R**

The men were out fifteen weeks. They had been back just over a year when Willy had an accident in the mine, tearing his bladder. At the pit head the doctor talked of the hospital. Losing his head entirely, the young collier raved like a madman, what with pain and fear of hospital.

"Tha s'lt go whoam,[11] Willy, tha s'lt go whoam," the deputy said.

A lad warned the wife to have the bed ready. Without speaking or hesitating she prepared. But when the ambulance came, and she heard him shout with pain at being moved, she was afraid lest she should sink down. They carried him in.

"Yo' should 'a' had a bed i' th' parlor, Missis," said the deputy, "then we shouldna ha' had to hawkse[12] 'im upstairs, an' it 'ud 'a' saved your legs." **A**

Plot: Describe the movement of the plot arc thus far in the story. Can you identify the inciting incident or any other plot elements? **A**

But it was too late now. They got him upstairs.

6. *strike a daisy:* an imprecation expressing slight exasperation
7. *mottled:* spotted or smeared
8. *clothes-'osses:* clothes-horses; racks for drying clothes
9. *pitch:* the greatest height
10. *chaff:* tease
11. *s'lt go whoam:* shall go home
12. *hawkse:* lift, hoist

"They let me lie, Lucy," he was crying, "they let me lie two mortal hours on th' sleck[13] afore they took me outer th' stall. Th' peen, Lucy, th' peen; oh, Lucy, th' peen, th' peen!"

"I know th' pain's bad, Willy, I know. But you must try an' bear it a bit."

"Tha munna carry on in that form, lad, thy missis'll niver be able ter stan' it," said the deputy.

"I canna 'elp it, it's th' peen, it's th' peen," he cried again. He had never been ill in his life. When he had smashed a finger he could look at the wound. But this pain came from inside, and terrified him. At last he was soothed and exhausted.

It was some time before she could undress him and wash him. He would let no other woman do for him, having that savage modesty usual in such men.

For six weeks he was in bed, suffering much pain. The doctors were not quite sure what was the matter with him, and scarcely knew what to do. He could eat, he did not lose flesh, nor strength, yet the pain continued, and he could hardly walk at all.

In the sixth week the men came out in the national strike. He would get up quite early in the morning and sit by the window. On Wednesday, the second week of the strike, he sat gazing out on the street as usual, a bullet-headed young man, still vigorous-looking, but with a peculiar expression of hunted fear in his face.

"Lucy," he called, "Lucy!"

She, pale and worn, ran upstairs at his bidding.

"Gi'e me a han'kercher," he said.

"Why, you've got one," she replied, coming near.

"Tha nedna touch me," he cried. Feeling his pocket, he produced a white handkerchief.

"I non want a white un, gi'e me a red un," he said.

"An' if anybody comes to see you," she answered, giving him a red handkerchief.

"Besides," she continued, "you needn't ha' brought me upstairs for that."

"I b'lieve th' peen's commin' on again," he said, with a little horror in his voice.

"It isn't, you know it isn't," she replied. "The doctor says you imagine it's there when it isn't."

"Canna I feel what's inside me?" he shouted.

"There's a traction-engine[14] coming downhill," she said. "That'll scatter them. —I'll just go an' finish your pudding." **A**

Character: At this point in the story, do you sympathize more with Lucy or with Willy? Explain your answer. **A**

She left him. The traction-engine went by, shaking the houses. Then the street was quiet, save for the men. A gang of youths from fifteen to twenty-five years old were playing marbles in the middle of the road. Other little groups of men were playing on the pavement. The street was gloomy. Willy could hear the endless calling and shouting of men's voices.

"Tha'rt skinchin'!"[15]

"I arena!"

"Come 'ere with that blood-alley."[16]

"Swop us four for't."

"Shonna, gie's hold on't."[17]

---

13. *sleck:* mud
14. *traction-engine:* a steam engine built to pull heavy loads across land instead of on rails
15. *skinchin':* cheating
16. *blood-alley:* a type of marble
17. *gie's hold on't:* give it up (over) or give up your claim to it

He wanted to be out, he wanted to be playing marbles. The pain had weakened his mind, so that he hardly knew any self-control.

Presently another gang of men lounged up the street. It was pay morning. The Union was paying the men in the Primitive Chapel. They were returning with their half-sovereigns.

"Sorry!" bawled a voice. "Sorry!"

The word is a form of address, corruption probably of "Sirrah." Willy started almost out of his chair.

"Sorry!" again bawled a great voice. "Art goin' wi' me to see Notts play Villa?"

Many of the marble players started up.

"What time is it? There's no treens, we s'll ha'e ter walk."

The street was alive with men.

"Who's goin' ter Nottingham ter see th' match?" shouted the same big voice. A very large, tipsy man, with his cap over his eye, was calling.

"Com' on—aye, com' on'!" came many voices. The street was full of the shouting of men. They split up in excited cliques and groups.

"Play up, Notts!" the big man shouted.

"Plee up, Notts!" shouted the youths and men. They were at kindling pitch. It only needed a shout to rouse them. Of this the careful authorities were aware. **A**

Conflict: What conflict of the story does this paragraph hint at? **A**

"I'm goin', I'm goin'!" shouted the sick man at his window.

Lucy came running upstairs.

"I'm goin' ter see Notts play Villa on th' Meadows ground," he declared.

"You—*you* can't go. There are no trains. You can't walk nine miles."

"I'm goin' ter see th' match," he declared, rising.

"You know you can't. Sit down now an' be quiet."

She put her hand on him. He shook it off.

"Leave me alone, leave me alone. It's thee as ma'es th' peen come, it's thee. I'm goin' ter Nottingham to see th' football match."

"Sit down—folks'll hear you, and what will they think?"

"Come off'n me. Com' off. It's her, it's her as does it. Com' off."

He seized hold of her. His little head was bristling with madness, and he was strong as a lion.

"Oh, Willy!" she cried.

"It's 'er, it's 'er. Kill her!" he shouted, "kill her." **A**

Conflict: Whom or what is Willy fighting? **A**

"Willy, folks'll hear you."

"Th' peen's comin' on again, I tell yer. I'll kill her for it."

He was completely out of his mind. She struggled with him to prevent his going to the stairs. When she escaped from him, who was shouting and raving, she beckoned to her neighbor, a girl of twenty-four, who was cleaning the window across the road.

Ethel Mellor was the daughter of a well-to-do check-weighman.[18] She ran across in fear to Mrs. Horsepool. Hearing the man raving, people were running out in the street and listening. Ethel hurried upstairs. Everything was clean and pretty in the young home.

Willy was staggering round the room, after the slowly retreating Lucy, shouting:

"Kill her! Kill her!"

18. *check-weighman:* one who checks the weight of each load of coal as it is sent up from the mines

"Mr. Horsepool!" cried Ethel, leaning against the bed, white as the sheets, and trembling. "Whatever are you saying?"

"I tell yer it's 'er fault as th' pain comes on—I tell yer it is! Kill 'er—kill 'er!" **A**

"Kill Mrs. Horsepool!" cried the trembling girl. "Why, you're ever so fond of her, you know you are."

"The peen—I ha'e such a lot o' peen—I want to kill 'er."

He was **subsiding**. When he sat down his wife collapsed in a chair, weeping noiselessly. The tears ran down Ethel's face. He sat staring out of the window; then the old, hurt look came on his face.

Conflict: Which people or groups are alienated from each other in this scene? **A**

subside (səb-sīd′) *intr.v.* To become less intense, active, or severe; abate.

"What 'ave I been sayin'?" he asked, looking piteously at his wife.

"Why!" said Ethel, "you've been carrying on something awful, saying, 'Kill her, kill her!'"

"Have I, Lucy?" he faltered.

"You didn't know what you was saying," said his young wife gently but coldly.

His face puckered up. He bit his lip, then broke into tears, sobbing uncontrollably, with his face to the window.

There was no sound in the room but of three people crying bitterly, breath caught in sobs. Suddenly Lucy put away her tears and went over to him.

"You didn't know what you was sayin', Willy, I know you didn't. I knew you didn't, all the time. It doesn't matter, Willy. Only don't do it again."

In a little while, when they were calmer, she went downstairs with Ethel.

"See if anybody is looking in the street," she said.

Ethel went into the parlor and peeped through the curtains.

"Aye!" she said. "You may back your life Lena an' Mrs. Severn'll be out gorping,[19] and that [. . .][20] Mrs. Allsop."

"Oh, I hope they haven't heard anything! If it gets about as he's out of his mind, they'll stop his compensation, I know they will."

"They'd never stop his compensation for *that*," protested Ethel.

"Well, they *have* been stopping some—"

"It'll not get about. I s'll tell nobody."

"Oh, but if it does, whatever shall we do? . . ."

19. *gorping:* gawking
20. *[. . .]:* This ellipsis was inserted by the publisher. Suspension points are in the original.

THINK AND DISCUSS

1. Characterize Willy and Lucy. Are they sympathetic or unsympathetic characters?
2. What instances of foreshadowing does Lawrence include? Were any of your predictions about the end of the story correct?
3. Identify three conflicts occurring in the story. Which would you consider to be the story's primary conflict?
4. How did Willy change or remain the same after his accident?
5. Identify the climax of the story. How does Lawrence wrap up the plot's loose ends?
6. What do Lucy and Ethel think will happen to Willy if the mine owners find out he has been acting insane?
7. How does the story reflect Lawrence's modernist tendency to explore the topic of alienation?
8. Consider the relationship between conflict and theme in "A Sick Collier." Try to state the theme of the story in a sentence.
9. Do Willy and Lucy have a good marriage? Use textual details to support your answer.
10. Create a one-page original ending to "A Sick Collier."

Virginia Woolf (1882–1941)

AT A GLANCE

- **1904** Helped establish the Bloomsbury Group
- **1912** Married Leonard Woolf
- **1915** Published *The Voyage Out*, her first novel
- **1925** Published her best-known novel, *Mrs. Dalloway*
- **1941** Took her own life

Virginia Woolf was an English novelist, essayist, and publisher whose fiction experimented with modernist forms while exploring feminist themes. Her work vividly portrays the profound but unspoken moments in everyday life. As a publisher and essayist, Woolf also exerted a monumental influence on both literary modernism and modern feminism.

Early Life

Woolf was born Adeline Virginia Stephen in London to an intellectual family. Her father was a literary luminary, and his daily tutoring as well as his extensive library provided most of her education. But her early life was also characterized by tragedy and abuse. Both parents died when she was in her early teens, and she was repeatedly molested by a half-brother. By age thirteen, Virginia was hearing voices and had developed severe depression. She was twice committed to a sanatorium.

In 1904 Virginia and her sister Vanessa moved into their own lodgings in Bloomsbury, London, where they assembled a literary set later known as the Bloomsbury Group. The group was characterized by its blatant disregard for Victorian mores and its commitment to the artistic avant-garde. In 1912 Virginia married the writer Leonard Woolf, but continuing psychological instability led her to attempt suicide in 1913. For the rest of her life, Virginia found much-needed emotional support both in her husband and in her relationships with women such as the aristocrat and novelist Vita Sackville-West. In fact, the latter inspired the titular character of Woolf's famous novel *Orlando*.

In 1910 Woolf and several friends disguised themselves and boarded the *Dreadnought* as Abyssinian royals.

Publisher and Author

During the prewar period Woolf had been working on her first novel, *The Voyage Out*, which was published in 1915. In 1917 the Woolfs founded the Hogarth Press, which quickly became a leading publisher of modernist work. The press would go on to print the work of T. S. Eliot and Katherine Mansfield, as well as that of the Woolfs themselves. The 1920s saw Virginia Woolf producing some of her finest literary work in the experimental novels *Jacob's Room* (1922), *Mrs. Dalloway*, and *To the Lighthouse* (1927). According to Woolf, her goal was to portray people as "splinters & mosaics; not, as [previous thinkers] used to hold, immaculate, monolithic, consistent wholes."[1]

Although as a woman she was not allowed to hold a full degree from Cambridge, Woolf delivered a series of lectures at the university in 1928. These were later revised into *A Room of One's Own* (1929). In the lectures, Woolf argues that conservative moral and legal codes prevent women from fully developing their intellectual abilities. She further developed this theme in *Three Guineas* (1938), which contends that patriarchy is the basis of economic and military oppression.

Later Life and Influence

Throughout her life, Woolf was a prolific essayist, publishing three volumes of critical essays and writing about four hundred essays altogether. As both an essayist and publisher, she was a key advocate for literary modernism and for second-wave feminism. But World War II overturned Woolf's previously stable life, with the bombing of her London home in 1940. Disturbed by the threat of German invasion and by the return of voices in her head, Woolf drowned herself in March 1941.

Woolf's fiction is widely recognized as among the finest stream-of-consciousness work of her era. In her prose, Woolf deploys a rich, poetic language to capture meaningful moments within women's lives, showing how commonplace events and details may have extraordinary significance. Woolf is also revered as a feminist icon, celebrated for her sexual radicalism and vigorous polemics against patriarchy, and it is as the great modernist feminist that she remains most popular today.

1. *The Diary of Virginia Woolf*, ed. Anne Olivier Bell (New York: Harcourt Brace Jovanovich, 1978), 2:314.

ANALYZE: *Interior Monologue and Symbol*

If you spoke your inner thought process into a microphone while alone in a room, you would come close to Woolf's mode of delivery in "The Mark on the Wall." Woolf creates an **interior monologue**, a type of stream-of-consciousness narration in which the speaker's inner thoughts tumble onto the page seemingly just as they do inside his or her head. As you read the story, ask yourself how Woolf gives the impression that she is recording thoughts as they occur. How is this mode different from a soliloquy (p. 210) or dramatic monologue (p. 298)?

The story's emphases circulate around Woolf's development of a **symbol**. But Woolf is so indirect in developing this symbol (the titular "mark on the wall") that you may have difficulty identifying what she means it to suggest. More important than the mark's physical identity are the narrator's thoughts surrounding it. Her inner ponderings on its identity imbue it with meaning beyond itself. As you read, list the concrete guesses the narrator makes. Next, list the ideas and conflicts that follow each guess. How do the contents of each list differ in nature? What broad problem does the mark come to represent for the narrator?

READ: *Draw Conclusions About Themes*

Drawing conclusions about Woolf's themes in the story is not easy. The narrator's professed focus, the mark, repeatedly gives way to digressions, personal memories, and philosophical speculations, displaying the modernist love of obscurity and indirectness. As you read, reflect on how Woolf's story might subtly reflect characteristic modernist concerns and attitudes (pp. 592–93).

First, examine the narrator's topics and tone. What images or ideas recur? Toward which does the narrator convey strong emotions? What does she contrast or critique, embrace or discard? Second, pay attention to the interior monologue that Woolf shapes. Describe the speaker's thought processes. Are they well structured, logical, and confident? Do objective facts or personal impressions dominate? How might the narrator's purpose reflect in a small way the quest of modernist writers?

EVALUATE: *Author's View of Uncertainty in Life*

Like most modernists, Woolf grappled with a sense of disillusionment. When "The Mark on the Wall" was written, World War I was an ugly reality, and Victorian conventions were dying. New philosophies and attitudes vied for authority. These changes exposed both the ugly and the beautiful in human nature and left uncertainty in their wake. This story conveys in part Woolf's struggle with various uncertainties, especially those caused by the war, whose ongoing reality hovers silently in the background of this piece. The narrator seems unsure of many things, from society's values to her own beliefs. Within her own mind, what does she admit she finds unknowable? Does she affirm any certainties? How might Woolf's portrayal of her thoughts reflect Beauty, Goodness, or Truth, and where might it ignore the comfort and instruction of Scripture?

OBJECTIVES

- Identify characteristics of interior monologue in a text.
- Draw conclusions about a work's themes.
- Analyze a work's use of symbolism and interior monologue.
- Evaluate an author's beliefs about life's uncertainties.

VOCABULARY

haphazard (hăp-hăz′ərd) *adj.* Dependent upon or characterized by mere chance.

vigilant (vĭj′ə-lənt) *adj.* On the alert, as for danger or error; watchful.

prominent (prŏm′ə-nənt) *adj.* Immediately noticeable; conspicuous.

attrition (ə-trĭsh′ən) *n.* A rubbing away or wearing down by friction.

quiescent (kwē-ĕs′ənt) *adj.* Quiet, still, or inactive.

What is the value of INTROSPECTION?

Similar to romantics, the modernists were intrigued by, and often wrote about, individual minds and ways of perceiving the world. Do you ever reflect on your own patterns of thought and feeling? Perhaps someone in your life has encouraged you to engage in self-reflection. Does such introspection frustrate or inspire you? What intellectual, emotional, and spiritual benefits might it bring? What does James 1:23–25 offer as a process for introspection?

VISUAL ANALYSIS
How might *The Window* (1916) by Henri Matisse, like Woolf's stream-of-consciousness technique, reflect modernist interest in how people perceive reality?

THE MARK ON THE WALL

Perhaps it was the middle of January in the present year that I first looked up and saw the mark on the wall. In order to fix a date it is necessary to remember what one saw. So now I think of the fire; the steady film of yellow light upon the page of my book; the three chrysanthemums in the round glass bowl on the mantelpiece. Yes, it must have been the winter time, and we had just finished our tea, for I remember that I was smoking a cigarette when I looked up and saw the mark on the wall for the first time. I looked up through the smoke of my cigarette and my eye lodged for a moment upon the burning coals, and that old fancy of the crimson flag flapping from the castle tower came into my mind, and I thought of the cavalcade[1] of red knights riding up the side of the black rock. Rather to my relief the sight of the mark interrupted the fancy, for it is an old fancy, an automatic fancy, made as a child perhaps. The mark was a small round mark, black upon the white wall, about six or seven inches above the mantelpiece.

How readily our thoughts swarm upon a new object, lifting it a little way, as ants carry a blade of straw so feverishly, and then leave it. . . . If that mark was made by a nail, it can't have been for a picture, it must have been for a miniature[2]—the miniature of a lady with white powdered curls, powder-dusted cheeks, and lips like red carnations. A fraud of course, for the people who had this house before us would have chosen pictures in that way—an old picture for an old room. That is the sort of people they were—very interesting people, and I think of them so often, in such queer places, because one will never see them again, never know what happened next. They wanted to leave this house because they wanted to change their style of furniture, so he said,

1. *cavalcade:* a procession or a group moving in order
2. *miniature:* a small painting of someone's face done with careful detail

and he was in process of saying that in his opinion art should have ideas behind it when we were torn asunder, as one is torn from the old lady about to pour out tea and the young man about to hit the tennis ball in the back garden of the suburban villa as one rushes past in the train.

But as for that mark, I'm not sure about it; I don't believe it was made by a nail after all; it's too big, too round, for that. I might get up, but if I got up and looked at it, ten to one I shouldn't be able to say for certain; because once a thing's done, no one ever knows how it happened. Oh dear me, the mystery of life! The inaccuracy of thought! The ignorance of humanity! To show how very little control of our possessions we have—what an accidental affair this living is after all our civilization—let me just count over a few of the things lost in our lifetime, beginning, for that seems always the most mysterious of losses—what cat would gnaw, what rat would nibble—three pale blue canisters of book-binding tools? Then there were the bird cages, the iron hoops, the steel skates, the Queen Anne coal-scuttle, the bagatelle board, the hand organ—all gone, and jewels too. Opals and emeralds, they lie about the roots of turnips. What a scraping paring affair it is to be sure! The wonder is that I've any clothes on my back, that I sit surrounded by solid furniture at this moment. Why, if one wants to compare life to anything, one must liken it to being blown through the Tube[3] at fifty miles an hour—landing at the other end without a single hairpin in one's hair! Shot out at the feet of God entirely naked! Tumbling head over heels in the asphodel meadows[4] like brown paper parcels pitched down a shoot in the post office! With one's hair flying back like the tail of a racehorse. Yes, that seems to express the rapidity of life, the perpetual waste and repair; all so casual, all so **haphazard**. . . . **A**

haphazard (hăp-hăz′ərd) *adj.* Dependent upon or characterized by mere chance.

Interior Monologue: Where and how does the story already illustrate stream of consciousness? **A**

But after life. The slow pulling down of thick green stalks so that the cup of the flower, as it turns over, deluges one with purple and red light. Why, after all, should one not be born there as one is born here, helpless, speechless, unable to focus one's eyesight, groping at the roots of the grass, at the toes of the Giants? As for saying which are trees, and which are men and women, or whether there are such things,[5] that one won't be in a condition to do for fifty years or so. There will be nothing but spaces of light and dark, intersected by thick stalks, and rather higher up perhaps, rose-shaped blots of an indistinct color—dim pinks and blues—which will, as time goes on, become more definite, become—I don't know what. . . . **R**

Draw Conclusions: What common modernist themes has Woolf already evoked? **R**

And yet the mark on the wall is not a hole at all. It may even be caused by some round black substance, such as a small rose leaf, left over from the summer, and I, not being a very **vigilant** housekeeper—look at the dust on the mantelpiece, for example, the dust which, so they say, buried Troy[6] three times over, only fragments of pots utterly refusing annihilation, as one can believe.

vigilant (vĭj′ə-lənt) *adj.* On the alert, as for danger or error; watchful.

The tree outside the window taps very gently on the pane. . . . I want to think quietly, calmly, spaciously, never to be interrupted, never to have to rise from my chair, to slip easily from one thing to another, without any sense of hostility, or obstacle. I want to sink deeper and deeper, away from the surface, with its hard separate facts. To steady myself, let me catch hold of the first idea that passes. . . . Shakespeare. . . . Well, he will do as well as another. A man who

3. *Tube:* the London subway or underground
4. *asphodel meadows:* according to Greek mythology, fields of flowers in paradise
5. *As for saying . . . there are such things:* This is an allusion to the philosopher Plato's Cave allegory about humans' imperfect perceptions of reality. In fact, the allusion begins in the title of this short story. In Plato's allegory, chained prisoners face a wall of a cave on which only shadows of people and objects passing behind them can be seen. The shadows are indistinct, so the prisoners cannot tell what the shadows represent.
6. *Troy:* setting of the Trojan War, buried several times over from the city's multiple collapses

sat himself solidly in an armchair, and looked into the fire, so—a shower of ideas fell perpetually from some very high heaven down through his mind. He leaned his forehead on his hand, and people, looking in through the open door—for this scene is supposed to take place on a summer's evening—but how dull this is, this historical fiction! It doesn't interest me at all. I wish I could hit upon a pleasant track of thought, a track indirectly reflecting credit upon myself, for those are the pleasantest thoughts, and very frequent even in the minds of modest mouse-colored people, who believe genuinely that they dislike to hear their own praises. They are not thoughts directly praising oneself; that is the beauty of them; they are thoughts like this: **A**

Interior Monologue: According to the narrator, what does she want her thoughts to become like? Do you think she's successful so far? **A**

"And then I came into the room. They were discussing botany. I said how I'd seen a flower growing on a dust heap on the site of an old house in Kingsway.[7] The seed, I said, must have been sown in the reign of Charles I.[8] What flowers grew in the reign of Charles I?" I asked—(but I don't remember the answer). Tall flowers with purple tassels to them perhaps. And so it goes on. All the time I'm dressing up the figure of myself in my own mind, lovingly, stealthily, not openly adoring it, for if I did that, I should catch myself out,[9] and stretch my hand at once for a book in self-protection. Indeed, it is curious how instinctively one protects the image of oneself from idolatry or any other handling that could make it ridiculous, or too unlike the original to be believed in any longer. Or is it not so very curious after all? It is a matter of great importance. Suppose the looking glass smashes, the image disappears, and the romantic figure with the green of forest depths all about it is there no longer, but only that shell of a person which is seen by other people—what an airless, shallow, bald, **prominent** world it becomes! A world not to be lived in. As we face each other in omnibuses[10] and underground railways we are looking into the mirror; that accounts for the vagueness, the gleam of glassiness, in our eyes. And the novelists in future will realize more and more the importance of these reflections, for of course there is not one reflection but an almost infinite number; those are the depths they will explore, those the phantoms they will pursue, leaving the description of reality more and more out of their stories, taking a knowledge of it for granted, as the Greeks did and Shakespeare perhaps—but these generalizations are very worthless. The military sound of the word is enough. It recalls leading articles, cabinet ministers—a whole class of things indeed which as a child one thought the thing itself, the standard thing, the real thing, from which one could not depart save at the risk of nameless damnation. Generalizations bring back somehow Sunday in London, Sunday afternoon walks, Sunday luncheons, and also ways of speaking of the dead, clothes, and habits—like the habit of sitting all together in one room until a certain hour, although nobody liked it. There was a rule for everything. The rule for tablecloths at that particular period was that they should be made of tapestry with little yellow compartments marked upon them, such as you may see in photographs of the carpets in the corridors of the royal palaces. Tablecloths of a different kind were not real tablecloths. How shocking, and yet how wonderful it was to discover that these real things, Sunday luncheons, Sunday walks, country houses, and tablecloths were not entirely real, were indeed half phantoms, and the damnation which visited the disbeliever in them was only a sense of illegitimate freedom. What now takes the place of those things I

prominent (prŏm′ə-nənt) *adj.* Immediately noticeable; conspicuous.

7. *Kingsway:* a then recently opened road in central London, named for Edward VII, who planned the road
8. *Charles I:* monarch of England during the English Civil War
9. *catch . . . out:* a predominantly British idiom meaning to realize a mistake
10. *omnibuses:* horse-drawn or motorized buses typically designed with two decks for seating

wonder, those real standard things? Men perhaps, should you be a woman; the masculine point of view which governs our lives, which sets the standard, which establishes Whitaker's Table of Precedency,[11] which has become, I suppose, since the war half a phantom to many men and women, which soon, one may hope, will be laughed into the dustbin where the phantoms go, the mahogany sideboards and the Landseer prints,[12] gods and devils, hell and so forth, leaving us all with an intoxicating sense of illegitimate freedom—if freedom exists. . . . E

Uncertainty: What modern changes in society does the speaker touch on in this passage? How does this last sentence reveal a mixed reaction to them? E

In certain lights that mark on the wall seems actually to project from the wall. Nor is it entirely circular. I cannot be sure, but it seems to cast a perceptible shadow, suggesting that if I ran my finger down that strip of the wall it would, at a certain point, mount and descend a small tumulus,[13] a smooth tumulus like those barrows on the South Downs which are, they say, either tombs or camps.[14] Of the two I should prefer them to be tombs, desiring melancholy like most English people, and finding it natural at the end of a walk to think of the bones stretched beneath the turf. . . .There must be some book about it. Some antiquary[15] must have dug up those bones and given them a name. . . .What sort of a man is an antiquary, I wonder? Retired colonels for the most part, I daresay, leading parties of aged laborers to the top here, examining clods of earth and stone, and getting into correspondence with the neighboring clergy, which, being opened at breakfast time, gives them a feeling of importance, and the comparison of arrowheads necessitates cross-country journeys to the county towns, an agreeable necessity both to them and to their elderly wives, who wish to make plum jam or to clean out the study, and have every reason for keeping that great question of the camp or the tomb in perpetual suspension, while the colonel himself feels agreeably philosophic in accumulating evidence on both sides of the question. It is true that he does finally incline to believe in the camp; and, being opposed, indites a pamphlet which he is about to read at the quarterly meeting of the local society when a stroke lays him low, and his last conscious thoughts are not of wife or child, but of the camp and that arrowhead there, which is now in the case at the local museum, together with the foot of a Chinese murderess, a handful of Elizabethan nails, a great many Tudor clay pipes, a piece of Roman pottery, and the wine glass that Nelson[16] drank out of—proving I really don't know what.

VISUAL ANALYSIS
How might the viewer's first impression of *Woman in a Purple Coat* (1937) by Henri Matisse be similar to the reader's of the narrative in *The Mark on the Wall*? What similar effects do their experimental approaches create?

11. *Whitaker's Table of Precedency:* In Woolf's day, as in ours, hosts and hostesses at social gatherings needed to know the order in which their guests should be introduced or shown in to dinner. This table, included in *Whitaker's Almanack*, lists all the nobility and wealthy in their order of authority or prominence so that there is no excuse for a social faux pas.

12. *Landseer prints:* Edwin Landseer, romantic artist, was known for his animal paintings and for the lion sculptures in Trafalgar Square.

13. *tumulus:* a mound, sometimes covering a grave for a ceremonial purpose

14. *barrows . . . camps:* There are various archeological remains from the Roman times on the South Downs, which are hills of mostly chalk in the southeastern part of England.

15. *antiquary:* one who pursues archeology or who collects relics as a hobby or profession

16. *Nelson:* Lord Horatio Nelson is best remembered for his victories in the Napoleonic Wars.

No, no, nothing is proved, nothing is known. And if I were to get up at this very moment and ascertain that the mark on the wall is really—what shall we say?—the head of a gigantic old nail, driven in two hundred years ago, which has now, owing to the patient **attrition** of many generations of housemaids, revealed its head above the coat of paint, and is taking its first view of modern life in the sight of a white-walled fire-lit room, what should I gain? Knowledge? Matter for further speculation? I can think sitting still as well as standing up. And what is knowledge? What are our learned men save the descendants of witches and hermits who crouched in caves and in woods brewing herbs, interrogating shrew-mice and writing down the language of the stars? And the less we honor them as our superstitions dwindle and our respect for beauty and health of mind increases . . . Yes, one could imagine a very pleasant world. A quiet spacious world, with the flowers so red and blue in the open fields. A world without professors or specialists or housekeepers with the profiles of policemen, a world which one could slice with one's thought as a fish slices the water with his fin, grazing the stems of the water-lilies, hanging suspended over nests of white sea eggs. . . . How peaceful it is down here, rooted in the center of the world and gazing up through the grey waters, with their sudden gleams of light, and their reflections—if it were not for Whitaker's Almanack—if it were not for the Table of Precedency! R

attrition (ə-trĭsh′ən) *n.* A rubbing away or wearing down by friction.

Draw Conclusions: How does the narrator critique Victorian expectations for new knowledge in her tale of the colonel and her resentment of *Whitaker's Almanack*? How does her preferred world differ from theirs? R

I must jump up and see for myself what that mark on the wall really is—a nail, a rose-leaf, a crack in the wood?

Here is Nature once more at her old game of self-preservation. This train of thought, she perceives, is threatening mere waste of energy, even some collision with reality, for who will ever be able to lift a finger against Whitaker's Table of Precedency? The Archbishop of Canterbury[17] is followed by the Lord High Chancellor;[18] the Lord High Chancellor is followed by the Archbishop of York.[19] Everybody follows somebody, such is the philosophy of Whitaker; and the great thing is to know who follows whom. Whitaker knows, and let that, so Nature counsels, comfort you, instead of enraging you; and if you can't be comforted, if you must shatter this hour of peace, think of the mark on the wall.

I understand Nature's game—her prompting to take action as a way of ending any thought that threatens to excite or to pain. Hence, I suppose, comes our slight contempt for men of action—men, we assume, who don't think. Still, there's no harm in putting a full stop to one's disagreeable thoughts by looking at a mark on the wall.

Indeed, now that I have fixed my eyes upon it, I feel that I have grasped a plank in the sea; I feel a satisfying sense of reality which at once turns the two Archbishops and the Lord High Chancellor to the shadows of shades. Here is something definite, something real. Thus, waking from a midnight dream of horror, one hastily turns on the light and lies **quiescent**, worshipping the chest of drawers, worshipping solidity, worshipping reality, worshipping the impersonal world which is proof of some existence other than ours. That is what one wants to be sure of. . . . A Wood is a pleasant thing to think about. It comes from a tree; and trees grow, and we don't know how they grow. For years and years they grow, without paying any attention to us, in meadows, in forests, and by the side of rivers—all things one likes to think about. The cows swish their tails beneath them on hot afternoons; they paint rivers so green

quiescent (kwē-ĕs′ənt) *adj.* Quiet, still, or inactive.

Symbol: According to the narrator, in what three situations might thoughts of the mark offer a remedy? What help does it seem to offer in each case? A

17. *Archbishop of Canterbury:* highest-ranking bishop and leader of the Church of England
18. *Lord High Chancellor:* first-ranked officer of the state
19. *Archbishop of York:* second-ranked bishop in the Church of England

that when a moorhen dives one expects to see its feathers all green when it comes up again. I like to think of the fish balanced against the stream like flags blown out; and of water-beetles slowly raising domes of mud upon the bed of the river. I like to think of the tree itself: first the close dry sensation of being wood; then the grinding of the storm; then the slow, delicious ooze of sap. I like to think of it, too, on winter's nights standing in the empty field with all leaves close-furled, nothing tender exposed to the iron bullets of the moon, a naked mast upon an earth that goes tumbling, tumbling all night long. The song of birds must sound very loud and strange in June; and how cold the feet of insects must feel upon it, as they make laborious progresses up the creases of the bark, or sun themselves upon the thin green awning of the leaves, and look straight in front of them with diamond-cut red eyes. . . . One by one the fibers snap beneath the immense cold pressure of the earth, then the last storm comes and, falling, the highest branches drive deep into the ground again. Even so, life isn't done with; there are a million patient, watchful lives still for a tree, all over the world, in bedrooms, in ships, on the pavement, lining rooms, where men and women sit after tea, smoking cigarettes. It is full of peaceful thoughts, happy thoughts, this tree. I should like to take each one separately—but something is getting in the way. . . . Where was I? What has it all been about? A tree? A river? The Downs? Whitaker's Almanack? The fields of asphodel? I can't remember a thing. Everything's moving, falling, slipping, vanishing. . . . There is a vast upheaval of matter. Someone is standing over me and saying—

"I'm going out to buy a newspaper."

"Yes?"

"Though it's no good buying newspapers. . . . Nothing ever happens. Curse this war[20] [. . .][21]! . . . All the same, I don't see why we should have a snail on our wall."

Ah, the mark on the wall! It was a snail. **E**

Uncertainty: In the final passage, how does the narrator respond when she loses track of the mark? How does she react when she finds out what it is? **E**

20. *this war:* World War I
21. *[. . .]:* This ellipsis was added by the publisher. All suspension points are in the original.

THINK AND DISCUSS

1. From your reading of this text, describe one way in which interior monologue differs from a soliloquy or a dramatic monologue. Identify two examples where the text illustrates stream-of-consciousness writing.
2. Name two things that the narrator suggests the mark on the wall might be.
3. How is the other character in the story different from the narrator? Why do you think this second person comes to a conclusion about the mark so quickly?
4. Give two examples in which the narrator contrasts the conventional or concrete with a less defined view of the world.
5. What is the narrator's attitude toward knowledge? Does she take a more Victorian or modernist approach? Explain your answer using textual details.
6. Give two examples in which the narrator questions Britain's traditional ways. How does her questioning of society's mores seem to affect her mental and emotional state? Support your answer from the text.
7. How do the work's form (interior monologue) and content both reflect the modernist search for meaning?
8. As is typical of modernist symbols, the meaning of the mark is highly specific to this work and hard to pin down. List the meanings Woolf wants it to suggest.
9. Why do you think the revelation of the mark's identity comes at the very end of the story? Do you think this revelation will affect the narrator's views in any way? Support your answer from the text.
10. Evaluate one of the narrator's criticisms of her society. Which of her values align(s) with biblical definitions of Truth, Goodness, and Beauty?
11. Evaluate the narrator's ambivalent feelings about reality and uncertainty from a biblical worldview. Rely on both Scripture and the story to support your answer.

PERELANDRA

C. S. Lewis

While both world wars led many intellectuals to abandon their faith in humanity and Western civilization, others vigorously disagreed. These intellectuals found the source of the West's ills not in its Christian heritage but rather in its abandonment of Christianity. Among these, perhaps the most broadly influential was the Irish novelist, poet, theologian, and literary critic C. S. Lewis.

Life and Work

Clive Staples Lewis (1898–1963), known to family and friends as Jack, was born in Belfast, Ireland, to a book-loving, middle-class family. A sensitive and imaginative child, he was unimpressed by his parents' empty adherence to religious formalities, and by his teens he considered himself an atheist. He matriculated into Oxford in 1916, joined the army, was wounded in combat in 1918, and in 1919 returned to Oxford. There his academic success was dazzling—he took three degrees in only four years. In 1925 he began tutoring as a fellow at Magdalen College, Oxford, where he worked until accepting Cambridge's chair of Medieval and Renaissance Literature in 1954.

At Oxford Lewis met brilliant people, such as J. R. R. Tolkien, who professed Christianity. Under their influence, he grudgingly began to accept rational arguments for the Christian faith, and in 1931 he converted to Anglicanism. Lewis quickly took to Christian apologetics, publishing an allegorical account of his conversion in *The Pilgrim's Regress* (1933). In both *Regress* and his later apologetic work, Lewis argues that many have rejected Christianity because they have not sufficiently understood it and that a return to Christian tradition is the only salvation from the modern predicament.

In 1938 Lewis published the first novel (*Out of the Silent Planet*) in his Space Trilogy, of which *Perelandra* (1943) is the second installment. During World War II, he gave a series of radio broadcasts on Christianity, later collected in *Mere Christianity* (1952), one of the twentieth century's most influential works of popular apologetics. The war prompted the internationally bestselling satire *The Screwtape Letters* (1942). And Lewis's experiences hosting refugees from the London Blitz led to his allegorical children's series about the magical land of Narnia, beginning with *The Lion, the Witch, and the Wardrobe* (1950).

In 1950 Lewis began corresponding with American writer Joy Davidman, and in 1956 the two were married, despite her ongoing treatments for cancer. After a two-year remission, Joy died in 1960. In life, she inspired Lewis to write his most critically celebrated novel, *Till We Have Faces* (1956). Her death beget *A Grief Observed* (1961), Lewis's powerful and intensely personal meditation on grief. Lewis himself died from complications of renal failure in 1963.

The Novel

Although a work of science fiction, *Perelandra* defies easy categorization. The story does feature interplanetary travel but is almost entirely dedicated to theological themes. The protagonist, Elwin Ransom, is a linguist sent to the planet Perelandra to prevent the devil from successfully tempting the planet's new humanoid life. What follows is both a riveting adventure and a meditation on the nature of good and evil.

Being a traditionalist, Lewis does not take up the modernist trend of the fragmented narrative in *Perelandra* but instead deploys a luxuriant, poetic style. Again, unlike his contemporaries, he does not see evil as merely a product of the human mind. Rather, his devil is a ruthless, terrifyingly real character who forces the reader to confront the sordid nature of evil itself. But against this figure of supreme evil, Lewis does not, like many modernists, wallow in despair. Instead, he offers the glorious possibilities of the sinless life, giving the reader not just something to fight but something to fight for.

In the following excerpt, the Green Lady, who rules Perelandra, is engaged in a debate with Weston, a human from Earth whose body has been possessed by the devil. God ("Maleldil") has commanded that no one live on Perelandra's one Fixed Island (the rest of the islands float continuously). The Green Lady speaks first, Weston answers, and the dialogue continues in this manner until Ransom joins the conversation. As you read, consider what biblical event this scene parallels. What theological point is Lewis thus making through the debate?

"How can I step out of His will save into something that cannot be wished? [. . .][1] To walk out of His will is to walk into nowhere."

"That is true of all His commands except one."

"But can that one be different?"

"Nay, you see of yourself that it is different. These other commands of His—to love, to sleep, to fill this world with your children—you see for yourself that they are good. And they are the same in all worlds. But the command against living on the Fixed Island is not so. [. . .] If it were really good, must He not have commanded it to all worlds alike? For how could Maleldil not command what was good? There is *no* good in it. Maleldil Himself is showing you that, this moment, through your own reason. It is mere command. It is forbidding for the mere sake of forbidding."

"But why . . . ?"

"In order that you may break it. What other reason can there be? [. . .] It stands between you and all settled life, all command of your own days. Is not Maleldil showing you as plainly as He can that it was set up as a test—as a great wave you have to go over, that you may become really old, really separate from Him."

"But if this concerns me so deeply, why does He put none of this into my mind? It is all coming from you, Stranger. There is no whisper, even, of the Voice saying Yes to your words."

"But do you not see that there cannot be? He longs—oh, how greatly He longs—to see His creature become fully itself, to stand up in its own reason and its own courage even against Him. But how can He *tell* it to do this? That would spoil all. Whatever it did after that would only be one more step taken *with* Him. This is the one thing of all the things He desires in which He must have no finger. Do you think He is not weary of seeing nothing but Himself in all that He has made? If that contented Him, why should He create at all? To find the Other—the thing whose will is no longer His—that is Maleldil's desire."

"If I could but know this—"

"He must not tell you. He cannot tell you. The nearest He can come to telling you is to let some other creature tell it for Him. And behold, He has done so. Is it for nothing, or without His will, that I have journeyed through Deep Heaven to teach you what He would have you know but must not teach you Himself?"

"Lady," said Ransom, "if I speak, will you hear me?"

"Gladly, Piebald."

"This man has said that the law against living on the Fixed Island is different from the other Laws, because it is not the same for all worlds and because we cannot see the goodness in it. And so far he says well. But then he says that it is thus different in order that you may disobey it. But there might be another reason."

"Say it, Piebald."

"I think He made one law of that kind in order that there might be obedience. In all these other matters what you call obeying Him is but doing what seems good in your own eyes also. Is love content with that? You do them, indeed, because they are His will, but not only because they are His will. Where can you taste the joy of obeying unless He bids you do something for which His bidding is the *only* reason? When we spoke last you said that if you told the beasts to walk on their heads, they would delight to do so. So I know that you understand well what I am saying."

"Oh, brave Piebald," said the Green Lady, "this is the best you have said yet. This makes me older far: yet it does not feel like the oldness this other is giving me. Oh, how well I see it! We cannot walk out of Maleldil's will: but He has given us a way to walk out of *our* will. And there could be no such way except a command like this. Out of our own will. It is like passing out through the world's roof into Deep Heaven. All beyond is Love Himself. I knew there was joy in looking upon the Fixed Island and laying down all thought of ever living there, but I did not till now understand."

1. *[. . . .]:* This and other ellipses were added by the publisher. The suspension points in paragraph five are in the original.

Sir Winston Churchill (1874–1965)

Most people know Sir Winston Leonard Spencer Churchill for his gifted leadership and powerful oratory during the dark days of World War II. But he was also a prolific writer who produced works on a variety of subjects, most notably history.

Born into a storied, aristocratic family, Churchill was the son of an American heiress and an English lord. Though a gifted scholar, he followed tradition and entered the military as a young man. He participated in several colonial wars (most famously the South African Boer War) as a soldier and war correspondent and returned to England a war hero.

Like his father, he entered politics and rose rapidly in office, becoming First Lord of the Admiralty in 1911. But the disastrous 1915 Gallipoli campaign in Turkey (for which he had strongly advocated) appeared to finish his political career. He spent the interwar years primarily working on celebrated histories, such as a history of the Great War, *The World Crisis* (1923–31), and a biography of his ancestor, the first Duke of Marlborough (1933–38).

As Nazi Germany grew in strength, Churchill repeatedly, and unsuccessfully, warned of its danger. His prescience, combined with early failures of the British government in World War II, led political leaders to choose Churchill as the next prime minister. On May 10, 1940, just before the British army's defeat at Dunkirk, Churchill took office. In his first speech to Parliament, he delivered his famous rallying cry, "I have nothing to offer but blood, toil, tears, and sweat."

Churchill's steady optimism and confident speeches inspired the British people during what he called "their finest hour." With the end of the war, however, Churchill was swept out of office by a public seeking social reforms. While he did again serve as prime minister from 1951–55, he spent much of his remaining years writing histories, his most famous being *The Second World War* (1948–53) and the multivolume *A History of the English-Speaking Peoples* (1956–58). In 1953 he was both knighted by the queen and awarded the Nobel Prize for his lifetime literary achievements. After a period of deteriorating health, the old hero died at the age of ninety. Befitting his contributions, he was honored with one of the largest state funerals in history.

BEFORE READING

ANALYZE: *Rhetorical Devices, Connotation*

In constructing his speeches, Churchill carefully framed his ideas using rhetorical devices such as **repetition**, **parallelism**, **antithesis** (p. 179), and **rhetorical questions** (p. 403). Identify examples of these as you read. Second, he paints the conflict in value-laden terms by employing **connotative language** (p. 403) and images that let him powerfully evoke audience beliefs and emotions. As you read, notice the implications of the words he chose for key moments.

READ: *Combine Strategies*

As you read, draw conclusions about the purpose of the speech. What was Churchill trying to accomplish in his audience? Consider the historical context: he had just taken office, and news from the front was alarming. Also annotate any **rhetorical appeals** (p. 129) he used, noting which kind (logos, pathos, ethos) dominates. Infer meaning from this choice. Why would he have used this appeal most?

EVALUATE: *Rhetorical Effectiveness*

Finally, consider how (and how well) Churchill accomplished his purpose. What effects did his rhetorical devices create on listeners? Would the speech have been less effective without them? Pay attention to the beliefs about the morality of the conflict and its participants that Churchill expresses directly and indirectly. How might his values have resonated well with his audience? Are his rhetorical appeals sound?

OBJECTIVES

- Identify examples of rhetorical devices in a piece.
- Combine reading strategies to understand a text's purpose.
- Analyze the author's use of rhetorical devices and appeals in a text.
- Evaluate a speaker's effective use of rhetoric.

VOCABULARY

formidable (fôr′mĭ-də-bəl) *adj.* Arousing fear, dread, or alarm.

invincible (ĭn-vĭn′sə-bəl) *adj.* Incapable of being overcome or defeated; unconquerable.

indomitable (ĭn-dŏm′ĭ-tə-bəl) *adj.* Unyielding; stubbornly persistent or resolute.

bludgeoned (blŭj′ənd) *adj.* Struck down or wounded with or as with a *bludgeon* (*n.* a short stout stick or club).

"BE YE MEN OF VALOR"

with Introduction by David Cannadine

In the early hours of 10 May, the Germans invaded Holland and Belgium, and within four days they had broken through the French defenses at Sedan. On 15 May, Holland surrendered, and Churchill flew to Paris to confer with the French leaders. It soon became clear that French resistance would not long continue, and that the position of the British troops on the Continent was perilous. At a meeting of the War Cabinet on 18 May, Chamberlain urged the Prime Minister to broadcast to the nation, to indicate "that we were in a tight fix, and that no personal considerations must be allowed to stand in the way of the measures necessary for victory."

On the following day, after only three hours in which to compose it, Churchill broadcast this speech live, his first as Prime Minister. He held out the hope that France might continue to resist, warned his listeners that a German assault on Britain might be imminent, and made plain his resolve "to call forth from our people the last ounce and the last inch of effort of which they are capable."

It seems clear that this broadcast caught the nation's imagination. Anthony Eden told Churchill he had never "done anything as good or as great." The Evening Standard *thought it a speech "of imperishable resolve." Even Lord Halifax considered it "worth a lot." Churchill's war of words had begun in earnest.*

VISUAL ANALYSIS

In this work, *The Combat*, what two forces are in conflict? What does the artist, using visual language, convey about the nature of each and about the state of the conflict?

BBC, London, 19 May 1940

I speak to you for the first time as Prime Minister in a solemn hour for the life of our country, of our Empire, of our Allies, and, above all, of the cause of Freedom. A tremendous battle is raging in France and Flanders. The Germans, by a remarkable combination of air bombing and heavily armored tanks, have broken through the French defenses north of the Maginot Line, and strong columns of their armored vehicles are ravaging the open country, which for the first day or two was without defenders. They have penetrated deeply and spread alarm and confusion in their track. Behind them there are now appearing infantry in lorries,[1] and behind them, again, the large masses are moving forward. The regroupment of the French armies to make head against, and also to strike at, this intruding wedge[2] has been proceeding for several days, largely assisted by the magnificent efforts of the Royal Air Force. **A**

We must not allow ourselves to be intimidated by the presence of these armored vehicles in unexpected places behind our lines. If they are behind our Front, the French are also at many points fighting actively behind theirs. Both sides are therefore in an extremely dangerous position. And if the French Army, and our own Army, are well handled, as I believe they will be; if the French retain that genius for recovery and counterattack for which they have so long been famous; and if the British Army shows the dogged endurance and solid fighting power of which there have been so many examples in the past—then a sudden transformation of the scene might spring into being.

It would be foolish, however, to disguise the gravity of the hour. It would be still more foolish to lose heart and courage or to suppose that well-trained, well-equipped armies numbering three or four millions of men can be overcome in the space of a few weeks, or even months, by a scoop, or raid of mechanized vehicles, however **formidable**. We may look with confidence to the stabilization of the Front in France, and to the general engagement of the masses, which will enable the qualities of the French and British soldiers to be matched squarely against those of their adversaries. For myself, I have **invincible** confidence in the French Army and its leaders. Only a very small part of that splendid army has yet been heavily engaged; and only a very small part of France has yet been invaded. There is good evidence to show that practically the whole of the specialized and mechanized forces of the enemy have been already thrown into the battle; and we know that very heavy losses have been inflicted upon them. No officer or man, no brigade or division, which grapples at close quarters with the enemy, wherever encountered, can fail to make a worthy contribution to the general result. The Armies must cast away the idea of resisting behind concrete lines or natural obstacles, and must realize that mastery can only be regained by furious and unrelenting assault. And this spirit must not only animate the High Command, but must inspire every fighting man. **A**

In the air—often at serious odds—often at odds hitherto thought overwhelming—we have been clawing down three or four to one of our enemies; and the relative balance of the British and German Air Forces is now considerably more favorable to us than at the beginning of the battle. In cutting down the German bombers, we are fighting our own battle as well as that of France. My confidence in our ability to fight it out to the finish with the German Air Force has been strengthened by the fierce encounters which have taken place and are taking place. At the same time, our heavy bombers are striking nightly at the taproot of German mechanized power, and have already inflicted serious damage upon the oil refineries on which the Nazi effort to dominate the world directly depends.

We must expect that as soon as stability is reached on the Western Front, the bulk of that hideous apparatus of aggression which gashed Holland into ruin and slavery in a few days, will be turned upon us. I am sure I speak for all when I say we are ready to face it; to endure it; and to retaliate against it—to any extent that the unwritten laws of war permit. There will be many men, and many women, in this island who when the ordeal comes upon them, as come it will, will feel comfort, and even a pride that they are sharing the perils of our lads at the Front—soldiers, sailors and airmen, God bless them—and are drawing away from them a part at least of the onslaught they have to bear. Is not this the appointed time for all to make the utmost

1. *lorries:* British word for trucks
2. *intruding wedge:* a configuration created from a body of people moving forward in a triangular formation; also called a flying wedge

Rhetorical Devices: What connotative words does Churchill use to project both crisis and confidence? **A**

formidable (fôr′mĭ-də-bəl) *adj.* Arousing fear, dread, or alarm.

invincible (ĭn-vĭn′sə-bəl) *adj.* Incapable of being overcome or defeated; unconquerable.

Connotation: Reread paragraphs 2 and 3. What feeling does Churchill want the British citizens to have about the French and British armies? What words does he use to create that feeling? **A**

exertions in their power? R If the battle is to be won, we must provide our men with ever-increasing quantities of the weapons and ammunition they need. We must have, and have quickly, more aeroplanes, more tanks, more shells, more guns. There is imperious need for these vital munitions. They increase our strength against the powerfully armed enemy. They replace the wastage of the obstinate struggle; and the knowledge that wastage will speedily be replaced enables us to draw more readily upon our reserves and throw them in now that everything counts so much.

Our task is not only to win the battle—but to win the War. After this battle in France abates its force, there will come the battle for our island—for all that Britain is, and all that Britain means. That will be the struggle. In that supreme emergency we shall not hesitate to take every step, even the most drastic, to call forth from our people the last ounce and the last inch of effort of which they are capable. The interests of property, the hours of labor, are nothing compared with the struggle for life and honor, for right and freedom, to which we have vowed ourselves.

I have received from the Chiefs of the French Republic, and in particular from its **indomitable** Prime Minister, M. Reynaud, the most sacred pledges that whatever happens they will fight to the end, be it bitter or be it glorious. Nay, if we fight to the end, it can only be glorious. A

Having received His Majesty's commission, I have found an administration of men and women of every party and of almost every point of view. We have differed and quarreled in the past; but now one bond unites us all—to wage war until victory is won, and never to surrender ourselves to servitude and shame, whatever the cost and the agony may be. This is one of the most awe-striking periods in the long history of France and Britain. It is also beyond doubt the most sublime. Side by side, unaided except by their kith and kin[3] in the great Dominions and by the wide Empires which rest beneath their shield—side by side, the British and French peoples have advanced to rescue not only Europe but mankind from the foulest and most soul-destroying tyranny which has ever darkened and stained the pages of history. Behind them—behind us—behind the armies and fleets of Britain and France—gather a group of shattered States and **bludgeoned** races: the Czechs, the Poles, the Norwegians, the Danes, the Dutch, the Belgians— upon all of whom the long night of barbarism will descend, unbroken even by a star of hope, unless we conquer, as conquer we must; as conquer we shall.

Today is Trinity Sunday.[4] Centuries ago words were written to be a call and a spur to the faithful servants of Truth and Justice: "Arm yourselves, and be ye men of valor, and be in readiness for the conflict; for it is better for us to perish in battle than to look upon the outrage of our nation and our altar. As the Will of God is in Heaven, even so let it be."[5] E

3. *kith and kin:* relatives and acquaintances
4. *Trinity Sunday:* the first Sunday after Pentecost, honoring the holy Trinity
5. *Churchill's quotation is found in 1 Maccabees 3:58–60.*

Rhetorical Appeal: What kind of rhetorical appeal does Churchill use in the preceding sentences? How does he make this appeal? R

indomitable (ĭn-dŏm′ĭ-tə-bəl) *adj.* Unyielding; stubbornly persistent or resolute.

Rhetorical Devices: Which rhetorical devices can you find in this and the previous paragraphs? A

bludgeoned (blŭj′ənd) *adj.* Struck down or wounded with or as with a *bludgeon* (*n.* a short stout stick or club).

Rhetorical Effectiveness: Skim over the last two paragraphs. How does Churchill directly and indirectly emphasize a sense of moral conflict? E

THINK AND DISCUSS

1. Identify an example of antithesis, parallelism, and rhetorical question in the speech.
2. Identify an example of each type of rhetorical appeal in the speech.
3. Which type of appeal dominates in the speech? What does this fact tell you about Churchill's purpose for the speech?
4. Select three words or phrases and analyze their connotative meanings.
5. Write a detailed analysis of paragraph 5, specifically addressing Churchill's use of rhetorical devices, appeals, and connotative words.
6. Examine Churchill's overall message to the British citizenry. Explain why you do or do not think it was effective. Consider his use of rhetorical devices and appeals in your answer.

UNIT 5

PART 2

Postwar and Commonwealth Literature

Have you ever encountered a situation so drastically different from what you had expected that you floundered while trying to determine an appropriate response? Did you find yourself speechless? Depending on the situation, did you become angry? Maybe you laughed; maybe you cried. Or maybe your mind immediately went into problem-solving mode. You expect life to bring changes, but how do you react when your whole world seems to change?

After World War II, Britons found themselves in an unexpected situation. Their country rapidly contracted from the largest empire in the world to just the British Isles. And internal fractures appeared even within that core. Britain also went from being one of the world's economic centers to claiming only a fraction of that status as she struggled economically and was supplanted by American business. Politically, she also diminished from a primary world power to a secondary one in the shadow of two warring superpowers. All this change occurred as Britons (and the world) were still coping with the war's traumas, including the brutal Holocaust and terrifying introduction of atomic weaponry.

Postwar writers were burdened with these compounding issues. The resulting uncertainty offered fertile ground for a continuation of modernists' disillusionment and search for meaning. Underneath much of the literature of the next few decades runs a current of darkness and despair.

Postwar theater especially reflected a struggle to find meaning. Playwrights such as Samuel Beckett dramatized modern man's paradoxical mix of despair and hope and attempts to create meaning where there seemed to be none. His tragicomedy *Waiting for Godot* (1955) blends despair and comedy to force audiences to wrestle with the meaning of existence.

In poetry, Stevie Smith, Philip Larkin, Ted Hughes, and Seamus Heaney each offered a different angle on the struggle for meaning and hope. Smith and Larkin notably explored themes of isolation and loss. Smith's poetry at first appears simple, full of playfulness and parallels to nursery rhymes. Yet it reveals hidden thematic depths of deep irony, even welcoming death as a friend. Like Smith, Larkin typically used traditional forms and a relatable voice. Larkin's themes, however, are usually developed very directly and rationally. Unfortunately, they tended toward disillusionment, fatalism, and loss of hope, reflecting pervasive feelings of cultural stagnancy.

Ted Hughes and Seamus Heaney took a different tack toward the problems of modern man. Hughes was deeply affected by both world wars. Although not without hope, his works display profound misgivings about man's nature and modern situation, exploring the subconscious and humanity's place in the world. His poems incorporate a grander, more symbolic style than Smith's or Larkin's and offer almost mythic visions of natural forces and the animal kingdom, depicting their power, beauty, and impersonal violence.

Meanwhile, the works of Northern Irish poet Seamus Heaney perhaps depict the beginning of British poetry's emergence from despair. They likewise incorporate the beauty and violence of the natural and mythological worlds. Heaney's poetry also grapples at times with the Troubles (p. 650). Nonetheless, Heaney tends to be gentler than Hughes and more hopeful than Larkin and Smith. In his most famous poetry, Heaney tends toward relatable diction and imagery and uses highly musical language to explore universal human relationships and to communicate a sense of wonder at life's daily miracles.

While writers in Britain were struggling against despair, Commonwealth nations abroad were dealing with the continued fallout of colonialism. Known as the Father of African Literature, Chinua Achebe wrote moving stories depicting the intersection of his Nigerian heritage and British colonial culture. Despite frequent criticism that he wasn't being "African enough," Achebe wrote in English and presented both the negative and positive leftovers from colonial influence. His famous novel *Things Fall Apart* stands as a clear testament to his insight and desire that Nigeria move forward, creating for itself a new identity by incorporating the positive from both cultural influences.

In South Africa, Nadine Gordimer grappled with the effects of colonialism embodied in the racist policies of apartheid (p. 654). In her novels and short stories, she frequently plays with narrative perspectives and audience expectations, juxtaposing love and the effects of racism in a way that changed readers' minds. Her stories were influential in the fight against apartheid.

Finally, Indian author Anita Desai examines the extensive influence of Britain's long presence in her country. Her novels, novellas, and short stories create memorable, realistic characters. Their struggles typically embody both universal themes about family relationships and the conflict in Indian culture between westernized modern values and a traditional Indian worldview. These themes often intersect as different generations clash in a family.

Contemporary British literature is marked by a tremendous range of topics and voices. And the tradition of British literature continues to grow.

Philip Larkin (1922–85)

AT A GLANCE

- **1943** Graduated from St. John's College, Oxford
- **1946** Published *Jill*
- **1964** Published *Whitsun Weddings*, establishing his popularity
- **1974** Published *High Windows*
- **1977** Published the poem "Aubade"
- **1983** Published *Required Writing*, a book of literary criticism

Philip Larkin was an English poet whose work reflected the prevailing sense of despair in postwar Britain. A convinced atheist, Larkin bemoaned the bitterness and viciousness of life. At the same time, Larkin eulogized the passing of the traditional values and countryside of England. His work commemorates the commonplace, and his depressive note has earned him the reputation of a graveyard poet.

DID YOU KNOW ?

One of Larkin's hobbies was playing the saxophone. He was also a recognized jazz critic, publishing *All What Jazz*, a collection of his jazz reviews.

Early Life and First Publications

Larkin was born in Coventry to a middle-class family. Philip's father, Sydney Larkin, was overly authoritarian and was sympathetic to the Nazi cause; he went so far as to take Philip to Germany while Hitler was in power. The young Philip wrote poems in imitation of W. H. Auden and T. S. Eliot, and his studies at Oxford continued to develop his deep interest in English literature. After graduating, Larkin was unable to serve in the military because of his poor eyesight, so he took up work as a college librarian in Hull, Shropshire. It was in this dingy, working-class village that Larkin published his first book of poetry as well as his two novels (*Jill* and *A Girl in Winter*). In 1950 Larkin moved to Belfast, Northern Ireland, where he began writing poetry in his mature style. Larkin published these poems in *The Less Deceived* (1955), which brought him to national prominence. That year Larkin also began working as the head librarian at the University of Hull, where he served for the rest of his life.

Established Poet and Critic

Larkin was rigorously critical of his own work, and he did not bring out a new edition of poems until *The Whitsun Weddings* in 1964. This collection established a widespread popularity, which was strengthened by *High Windows* in 1974. By this time, however, Larkin was feeling a decline in his poetic powers, a decline that coincided with his mother's failing health. His last major poem, "Aubade," was published in a magazine in 1977, the same year his mother died. Larkin was also a gifted critic, publishing a collection of literary criticism, *Required Writing*, in 1983. He was responsible for directing academic critical attention to Thomas Hardy's poetry. Larkin's last years were characterized by his deepening depression, anti-social persona, and reliance on alcohol. He died of throat cancer in 1985.

Poetic Style and Themes

Strongly influenced by Auden, Yeats, and Hardy, Larkin employed traditional poetic forms as display cases for the musical qualities of everyday English. With his profound interest in the meaning and meaninglessness in normal life, his sometimes racist and misogynistic attitudes, and a disdain for high-brow literary criticism, Larkin perfectly captured a widespread sense of national decline. In his time he was considered by many to be the unofficial poet laureate.

ANALYZE: *Aubade, Mood, and Irony*

An **aubade**—a form that dates back to the twelfth century and that was used by the likes of Chaucer, Donne, and Shakespeare—is a lyric poem or song greeting the dawn and often expressing the regret of two lovers at parting. Aubades are usually exuberant expressions of joy in a new day, revels in life's beauties. Given this history of the form, what would you expect the **mood** (emotion pervading a work) of Larkin's "Aubade" to be? Do you think these emotions reflect feelings the speaker has experienced only once, or are these feelings habitual? How is the speaker's view of the world reflected in the mood?

"Aubade" is replete with levels of **irony** (p. 88) that begin with Larkin's choice of an aubade to deliver his content. To unpack the irony in this poem, examine where the speaker is, what he is doing, and what his subject matter is. For example, consider what is ironic about the speaker's thought process in the context of the time of day. Does Larkin accept the ideals of love and life on which the aubade was founded? How does "Aubade" fit in the postwar world that had come unraveled by its response to tragedy?

READ: *Draw Conclusions About Style*

Do you remember learning from the study of Samuel Johnson that every author has a **style**—a mode of writing formed by a combination of elements such as syntax, diction, figurative language, imagery, tone, and voice? Larkin's style in the following poem reflects the cold disillusionment of postwar Britain with a biting nihilism, a rejection of hope. Consider the cultural, intellectual, and religious factors at work during the time Larkin was writing. For instance, in what ways are Larkin's sterile rationalism and rejection of highbrow literary trappings reflected in the poem's style? In addition, think about where and with whom Larkin worked for most of his adult life. How does his poem's **figurative language** (p. 129), such as the similes and personification, reference the environment and people around Larkin? How does Larkin employ a particular style to contribute to the overall mood of the poem and to communicate his theme?

EVALUATE: *Author's View of Approaching Death*

Several authors you have read in this textbook have dealt with death in their works. Think back to Tennyson's "Ulysses," in which an old man decides to make the most of the opportunities left to his waning years. When Larkin wrote "Aubade," his mother had just died. Larkin's obsession with death intensified after this loss, and his motivation to live spiraled downward significantly. How does he reckon with the fact that all men are mortal and will face the grave? The apostle Paul describes a Christian's death in 1 Thessalonians 4:13–14. Compare Larkin's view to this passage. Does Larkin view the afterlife similarly? What worth does he ascribe to his life in light of approaching death?

OBJECTIVES

- Identify the characteristics of an aubade in the poem.
- Analyze the irony of the poem.
- Draw conclusions about the style of the poem.
- Evaluate the author's view of approaching death from a biblical worldview.

VOCABULARY

dispel (dĭ-spĕl′) *tr.v.* To break up, drive away, or cause to disappear.

specious (spē′shəs) *adj.* Having the ring of truth or plausibility but actually fallacious.

anesthetic (ăn′ĭs-thĕt′ĭk) *n.* An agent that causes loss of sensation with or without the loss of consciousness; something likened to this in effect.

What gets YOU OUT OF BED *in the morning?*

Do you often spring out of bed in the morning? Or is it difficult to get up? Are you among those who tackle life only after a cup of coffee? What motivates you to get up? Do you look forward to seeing your friends? Finishing the book that left you on a cliffhanger the previous night? Competing in a volleyball game? Do you have a life purpose that motivates you to start a new day?

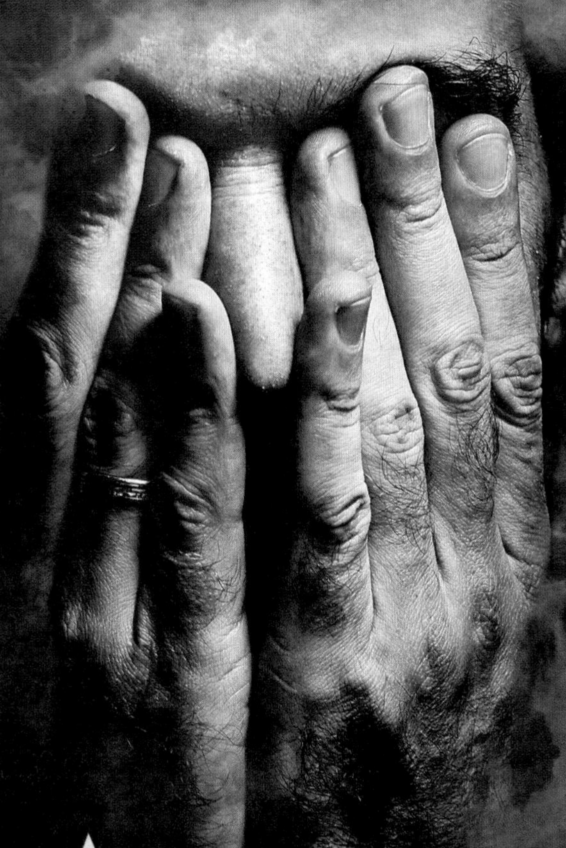

AUBADE

I work all day, and get half-drunk at night.
Waking at four to soundless dark, I stare.
In time the curtain-edges will grow light.
Till then I see what's really always there:
Unresting death, a whole day nearer now,
Making all thought impossible but how
And where and when I shall myself die.
Arid interrogation: yet the dread
Of dying, and being dead,
Flashes afresh to hold and horrify. **A**

The mind blanks at the glare. Not in remorse
—The good not done, the love not given, time
Torn off unused—nor wretchedly because
An only life can take so long to climb
Clear of its wrong beginnings, and may never;
But at the total emptiness forever,
The sure extinction that we travel to
And shall be lost in always. Not to be here,
Not to be anywhere,
And soon; nothing more terrible, nothing more true. **A**

VISUAL ANALYSIS
How might the visual background for "Aubade" reflect the speaker's state of mind and the poem's overall mood? How does it emphasize the irony of the poem's title?

Mood: What emotions are habitual for the speaker? **A**

Aubade and Irony: How do the poem's content and title demonstrate irony thus far? **A**

This is a special way of being afraid
No trick **dispels**. Religion used to try,
That vast moth-eaten musical brocade
Created to pretend we never die,
And **specious** stuff that says *No rational being*
Can fear a thing it will not feel, not seeing
That this is what we fear—no sight, no sound,
No touch or taste or smell, nothing to think with,
Nothing to love or link with,
The **anesthetic** from which none come round.

And so it stays just on the edge of vision,
A small unfocused blur, a standing chill
That slows each impulse down to indecision.
Most things may never happen: this one will,
And realization of it rages out
In furnace-fear when we are caught without
People or drink. Courage is no good:
It means not scaring others. Being brave
Lets no one off the grave.
Death is no different whined at than withstood. E

Slowly light strengthens, and the room takes shape.
It stands plain as a wardrobe, what we know,
Have always known, know that we can't escape,
Yet can't accept. One side will have to go.
Meanwhile telephones crouch, getting ready to ring
In locked-up offices, and all the uncaring
Intricate rented world begins to rouse.
The sky is white as clay, with no sun.
Work has to be done.
Postmen like doctors go from house to house. R

dispel (dĭ-spĕl′) *tr.v.* To break up, drive away, or cause to disappear.

specious (spē′shəs) *adj.* Having the ring of truth or plausibility but actually fallacious.

anesthetic (ăn′ĭs-thĕt′ĭk) *n.* An agent that causes loss of sensation with or without the loss of consciousness; something likened to this in effect.

View of Death: How does the speaker handle his fear of death? E

Draw Conclusions: How would you describe Larkin's style? How do his diction and figurative language in the last stanza convey his message? R

THINK AND DISCUSS

1. Identify four uses of figurative language in the poem.
2. List five phrases, images, or instances of figurative language that convey the poem's mood.
3. Why does the speaker have difficulty getting out of bed in the morning? Do you think he gets out of bed in this instance? Why or why not?
4. What do the last two lines of the poem convey about the speaker's attitude toward death?
5. How is Larkin's poem an atypical aubade?
6. How does the poem's style convey the bleakness of the speaker's outlook?
7. In two or three sentences, explain the irony of the poem. Defend your answer with textual details.
8. Evaluate from a biblical perspective how the speaker views death. Reference at least one Bible passage and details from the text of the poem in your answer.

Ted Hughes (1930–98)

AT A GLANCE

- **1957** Won first place for *The Hawk and the Rain* in the New York City Poetry Center's First Publication Award
- **1960** Published *Lupercal*
- **1968** Published the children's book *The Iron Man*
- **1984** Appointed Britain's poet laureate
- **1998** Published *Birthday Letters*

Ted Hughes was an English poet, children's author, and literary critic whose earthy, sometimes violent poetry revolutionized English verse. By pairing insights into the natural world with mythological symbols, Hughes developed a rich poetry that explores the mystery of humanity's relationship with the universe. And by working extensively as an educator, Hughes inspired generations of future poets.

Early Life and Radical Poet

Edward "Ted" James Hughes was born into a working-class family in Yorkshire. As a boy he spent many hours exploring the neighboring countryside, developing a lifelong love for nature. By the age of sixteen, Hughes was determined to be a poet, and his marked ability enabled him to attend Cambridge, from which he graduated in 1954.

DID YOU KNOW?

Although Hughes won a scholarship to Cambridge for studies in English language, he eventually changed his major to anthropology and archeology.

In 1956 Hughes met the American poet Sylvia Plath. Plath instantly recognized his talent and encouraged him to submit a collection of his poems (which she personally edited) to a prestigious poetry competition. The collection, *The Hawk and the Rain*, won first prize—publication by Harper and Row—and instant critical recognition. Plath and Hughes were married just four months after they met, and they traveled between the United States and Great Britain for the next few years. In 1960 Hughes published *Lupercal*, which cemented his reputation.

By 1962 Hughes and Plath had two children and a troubled marriage. Hughes's open adultery with one of their friends, Assia Wevill, led to the married couple's separation. In early 1963 Plath committed suicide. Although Hughes dedicated himself to publishing Plath's writing, his destruction of some of her journals prompted accusations of censorship. It also led to suspicion, and for the rest of his life Hughes was accused of having driven Plath to her death. These suspicions only deepened when Wevill killed both herself and their four-year-old daughter in 1969.

Later Life and Poet Laureate

Grieving over these two shocks, Hughes published *Crow: From the Life and Songs of the Crow* (1970), a cycle of mythological poems that depict a crow's journey toward spiritual healing. In 1970 Hughes married Carol Ann Orchard, whose father was a farmer in Devon. Two years later Hughes himself purchased a farm in Devon, and the experience of working his own land led to *Season Songs* (1975) and *Moortown Diary* (1979). In 1984 he was made poet laureate, and in 1998 he published *Birthday Letters*, a collection of poems exploring his relationship with Plath.

Hughes had a lifelong concern for education. In addition to writing poetry and books for children (his most famous being *The Iron Man*, 1968), Hughes organized writing workshops and gave frequent readings in schools. He also compiled two poetry anthologies to be used in the classroom. He died of colon cancer.

Style and Influence

Hughes's early poetry marked a sharp break from contemporary convention. His verse was inelegant and often marked by violent imagery. Seeing humanity as firmly rooted in the natural world, Hughes employed animal imagery to express the vibrant and sometimes horrifying nature of human existence. Following Yeats, Hughes was also attracted to pagan mythology. Hughes inspired many younger poets while also instilling in them his poetic goals and technique. It is in his dual role as both poetic iconoclast and educator that he became one of the most important poets of the twentieth century.

ANALYZE: *Setting, Mood, Extended Metaphor*

Hughes begins the following poem within an indirectly described **setting** for his speaker. As you read the first two stanzas, determine what this speaker's physical setting is. What do you think the speaker is attempting to do? In addition, what **mood** (p. 639) is set for the scene? Consider how this mood develops throughout the rest of the poem.

The speaker's mind wanders into another scene as well, one which reflects Hughes's love of nature imagery. Hughes overlays this imaginary scene on the original setting, building an **extended metaphor** (p. 151) between the speaker's real and imagined scenarios. As you read, consider the parallel images between these scenes—for instance, the darkness present in each. Additionally, decide what becomes the central image of this new scene. Trace its movements (conveyed in small glimpses) to help interpret its metaphorical meaning. Where does Hughes connect it into the original setting? What does he mean the image to represent in that broader context?

OBJECTIVES

- Determine the setting and mood of a poem.
- Combine reading strategies to understand and analyze a poem.
- Analyze the connections between a poem's extended metaphor, pacing, and theme.
- Compose an extended metaphor.

READ: *Combine Strategies*

Hughes's poem can be somewhat difficult to follow. His sentences are sometimes fragmented and tangled, overlapping between stanzas. You may wish to follow your first reading by paraphrasing his thoughts to better understand them. Reading the poem aloud can also help you recognize the connections between various phrases and clauses.

Hughes's fragmented syntax is not a mistake. In fact, he uses the syntax to push and pull the poem's pace, slowing it when the syntax gets especially difficult or unusual. For the same reason, he avoids meter or perfect rhyme, which can force poems into a steadier pace. Unsurprisingly then, enjambment and caesura occur frequently in the poem. Pay attention to the overall progression of the poem's pacing. Does it get slower or faster as it moves on? How might this pacing mimic the movement of the metaphor's central image and the revealing of it to both the speaker and the readers? What might this connection help you infer about the meaning of the extended metaphor?

CEATE: *Extended Metaphor*

In "The Thought-Fox," Hughes makes use of an extended metaphor. The psalmist David also uses an extended metaphor in Psalm 23. In this model, he compares his Lord to a shepherd and himself to a sheep and continues to weave this comparison through the psalm. For instance, in verses two and three, David says that just as the shepherd provides nourishment, comfort, and tranquility for his sheep, so the Lord does for him. Think of a biblical metaphor or devise one of your own. Make a list of related ideas that extend this metaphor. Now write a paragraph or poem beginning with your chosen metaphor, and then extend it with your related ideas.

Do you still use your IMAGINATION?

Children often engage in imaginative play, creating fanciful worlds and creatures. Perhaps you once had your own make-believe world. Now that you are older, do you ever let your imagination run wild? You might not think about dark forests and ferocious beasts, but you might imagine things the way you wish they could be. Or perhaps you imagine what your future might be. What "wild" things do you imagine now?

THE THOUGHT-FOX

I imagine this midnight moment's forest:
Something else is alive
Beside the clock's loneliness
And this blank page where my fingers move.

Through the window I see no star:
Something more near
Though deeper within darkness
Is entering the loneliness: [A]

Cold, delicately as the dark snow,
A fox's nose touches twig, leaf;
Two eyes serve a movement, that now
And again now, and now, and now

Sets neat prints into the snow
Between trees, and warily a lame
Shadow lags by stump and in hollow
Of a body that is bold to come

Across clearings, an eye,
A widening deepening greenness,
Brilliantly, concentratedly,
Coming about its own business [R]

Till, with a sudden sharp hot stink of fox
It enters the dark hole of the head.
The window is starless still; the clock ticks,
The page is printed. [A]

VISUAL ANALYSIS
How does the composition and style of *Foxes* (1913), painted by expressionist Franz Marc, reflect the way Hughes constructs his main image in this poem?

Mood: What mood do you feel in the opening scene? What words lead you to that conclusion? [A]

Combine Strategies: Where has the poet used enjambment so far? [R]

Extended Metaphor: Given this last line, what do you think the speaker is describing with his metaphor? [A]

THINK AND DISCUSS

1. Paraphrase the scene in lines 9–20.
2. Compare your paraphrase to the original lines. How does their pacing differ from yours? Identify two instances where Hughes's syntax, enjambment, or caesura speeds or slows the pace.
3. Describe the speaker and setting at the poem's beginning and end. What is the speaker trying to do?
4. Describe the mood of the opening scene. How does this mood shift in the second setting? Explain your answers.
5. What is the second scene's central image? How does Hughes connect it to the original setting?
6. What is similar about both settings? Given where they reconnect, what might the second represent about the speaker and his task?
7. Briefly summarize how the central image's movements help flesh out the extended metaphor's meaning.
8. Write a paragraph or poem extending a biblical metaphor.

WAITING FOR GODOT

Samuel Beckett

In 1953 an obscure Parisian theater performed a French-language play written the previous year by an equally obscure Irish writer. Soon the English version of that play—translated by the author himself in 1954—had exploded into a worldwide phenomenon, changing English drama forever. That play was *Waiting for Godot*.

The Playwright

The author of this epoch-making play was Samuel Beckett (1906–89). Beckett was born in County Dublin to a solidly middle-class family. After a brilliant career in Ireland as a student, in 1928 Beckett moved to Paris, which he would call home for the rest of his life. While in Paris, he met his fellow Irishman James Joyce, whose creative language both inspired and inhibited the younger man's development. When Nazi Germany invaded France, Beckett participated in the resistance. After the war, Beckett discovered his literary mission: to be an author who flourished "in impoverishment, in lack of knowledge and in taking away."[1] Though his knowledge of English literature was extensive, Beckett began writing in French to limit his language. By 1949 he had finished the French version of *Waiting for Godot*. After the smashing success of *Godot*, Beckett wrote many more experimental novels and plays, such as *Endgame* (1957) and *Krapp's Last Tape* (1958). He was awarded the Nobel Prize in Literature in 1969. He died from emphysema-related complications in 1989.

1. James Knowlson, *Damned to Fame: The Life of Samuel Beckett* (New York: Simon & Schuster, 1996), 319.

The Play

Much of the power of *Waiting for Godot* lies in its ambiguity. While the play repeatedly references philosophy, literature, and Christian theology, it also consistently undermines any attempts to construct meaning from these references. This ambiguity is perhaps most puzzling in the relationship of the two main characters, Vladimir and Estragon, to the titular Godot. Neither Vladimir nor Estragon personally knows Godot, although another character (the boy) does. Yet when the curtain opens, Vladimir and Estragon are expecting Godot's arrival, and they spend the entire play amusing themselves and annoying each other while waiting for Godot, who, despite the boy's assurances that he will come "tomorrow," famously never comes at all.

Some critics have seen Godot as a symbol for God and consequently have interpreted the play as a dramatization of the failure of religion. But although Vladimir and Estragon appear to believe that Godot will "save" them, it is not clear how they imagine he will do so or precisely what they think he will save them from. Nor does Godot appear to have any supernatural characteristics. On the contrary, the boy appears to know him personally.

The seeming meaningfulness of the play—set upon a nearly empty stage with only a bare tree in the background—combines with its mysteriousness to foil any attempt at interpretation. The audience members appear invited to join with Vladimir and Estragon in creating meaning out of a strange situation. The play's strangeness is compounded by its tone, one of intense gloominess punctuated by comedy.

The Influence

Waiting for Godot revolutionized English theater. With its minimalist set and obscure message, Godot stripped drama down to the bone, freeing playwrights to pursue radical new forms. Many of the practices and goals of contemporary English-language theater can be traced back to *Godot*.

The play also served as an important popularizer of philosophical existentialism. Although Beckett was not familiar with the work of existentialist thinkers such as Jean-Paul Sartre, Beckett had thought his way to similar conclusions, and the play is their perfect artistic representation. With its systematic rejection of definitive interpretation, *Godot* represents the absurdity of the world, and when the mind (in this case, the audience member's) confronts this absurdity, it is forced to create meaning for itself.

As you read, pay attention to what the characters say about the mysterious Godot. What is the significance of the message Vladimir sends to him?

This photograph of a staged scene from Beckett's work depicts the characters of Vladimir, Lucky, Pozzo, and Estragon.

VLADIMIR. Was I sleeping, while the others suffered? Am I sleeping now? To-morrow, when I wake, or think I do, what shall I say of to-day? That with Estragon my friend, at this place, until the fall of night, I waited for Godot? That Pozzo passed, with his carrier, and that he spoke to us? Probably. But in all that what truth will there be? *(Estragon, having struggled with his boots in vain, is dozing off again. Vladimir looks at him.)* He'll know nothing. He'll tell me about the blows he received and I'll give him a carrot. *(Pause.)* Astride of a grave and a difficult birth. Down in the hole, lingeringly, the grave-digger puts on the forceps. We have time to grow old. The air is full of our cries. *(He listens.)* But habit is a great deadener. *(He looks again at Estragon.)* At me too someone is looking, of me too someone is saying, He is sleeping, he knows nothing, let him sleep on. *(Pause.)* I can't go on! *(Pause.)* What have I said?

He goes feverishly to and fro, halts finally at extreme left, broods. Enter Boy right. He halts. Silence.

BOY. Mister . . . (Vladimir turns.) Mister Albert . . .

VLADIMIR. Off we go again. (Pause.) Do you not recognize me?

BOY. No Sir.

VLADIMIR. It wasn't you came yesterday.

BOY. No Sir.

VLADIMIR. This is your first time.

BOY. Yes Sir.

Silence.

VLADIMIR. You have a message from Mr. Godot.

BOY. Yes Sir.

VLADIMIR. He won't come this evening.

BOY. No Sir.

VLADIMIR. But he'll come to-morrow.

BOY. Yes Sir.

VLADIMIR. Without fail.

BOY. Yes Sir.

Silence.

VLADIMIR. Did you meet anyone?

BOY. No Sir.

VLADIMIR. Two other . . . *(he hesitates)* . . . men?

BOY. I didn't see anyone, Sir.

Silence.

VLADIMIR. What does he do, Mr. Godot? *(Silence.)* Do you hear me?

BOY. Yes Sir.

VLADIMIR. Well?

BOY. He does nothing, Sir.

Silence.

VLADIMIR. How is your brother?

BOY. He's sick, Sir.

VLADIMIR. Perhaps it was he came yesterday.

BOY. I don't know, Sir.

Silence.

VLADIMIR. *(softly)*. Has he a beard, Mr. Godot?

BOY. Yes Sir.

VLADIMIR. Fair or . . . *(he hesitates)* . . . or black?

BOY. I think it's white, Sir.

Silence.

VLADIMIR. Christ have mercy on us!

Silence.

BOY. What am I to tell Mr. Godot, Sir?

VLADIMIR. Tell him . . . *(he hesitates)* . . . tell him you saw me and that . . . *(he hesitates)* . . . that you saw me. *(Pause. Vladimir advances, the Boy recoils. Vladimir halts, the Boy halts. With sudden violence.)* You're sure you saw me, you won't come and tell me to-morrow that you never saw me! *Silence. Vladimir makes a sudden spring forward, the Boy avoids him and exits running. Silence. The sun sets, the moon rises. As in Act 1, Vladimir stands motionless and bowed.*

Stevie Smith (1902–71)

As Britain underwent dramatic social transformations in the mid-twentieth century, many Britons were left feeling isolated and purposeless, a feeling that was perfectly captured by the poet and novelist Stevie Smith. Smith was born Florence Margaret Smith in Hull, Yorkshire. In 1906 her father left his family to find work, and Florence, along with her mother and older sister, moved to the London suburb of Palmers Green, which became Florence's lifelong home. After attending high school and college, in 1922 Smith began work as a secretary, where her boyish appearance earned her the nickname "Stevie."

Smith found her secretarial work meaningless and dull, but she read widely in her spare time and began writing. Her first collection of poems was rejected by a publisher, who in the notice advised her to write fiction. This she immediately set out to do, publishing her first novel in 1936 and two other novels later in life. The success of her novels led to the successful publication of her poetry, with her first volume, *A Good Time Was Had by All,* coming out in 1937.

Although Smith regularly published poetry and enjoyed friendships with literary luminaries such as George Orwell, she grew increasingly depressed with her work and attempted suicide in 1953. After retiring that year, she began to concentrate on her writing, going on to publish her well-received volumes *Not Waving but Drowning* (1957) and *The Frog Prince* (1966). In the 1960s she began to give popular readings of her poetry. She died of brain cancer in 1971.

Smith's poetry is idiosyncratic. On the surface, her poetry has a childlike simplicity, frequently employing traditional meter and rhyme. Editions of her poetry also include complementary, primitivistic line drawings that seem to underscore her simplistic style. But Smith is a sophisticated poet—her work abounds in literary allusions—and she deploys her seeming innocence to explore mature themes of isolation and loss, including her loss of faith in the Christian God. Because Smith could neither deny God's existence nor accept Christianity's picture of Him, she fashions a god in which she could believe.

BEFORE READING

ANALYZE: *Speaker, Irony, and Black Humor*

Typically, a poem has only one **speaker** (p. 298). How many does "Not Waving but Drowning" have? Identify what makes each distinct. How do the speakers contribute to the poem's **dramatic irony** (p. 240)? Additionally, notice the poem's title. Underlying its obvious meaning lies a deeper symbolic message developed within the poem. As you read, consider how Smith communicates that message. The situation the title describes illustrates **black humor**. Black humor is a form of shock humor derived from treating grotesque, serious, or morbid situations comically. How does Smith's use of black humor reflect contemporary attitudes?

READ: *Infer Meaning*

The brevity of poetry drives readers to closely analyze each word to infer meaning. In this poem Smith has something to say about the death of the person who drowns. She draws parallels between his death experience and life experience through key **symbols** (p. 37), which point to the theme. What does she imply about his life, particularly his experience with relationships?

EVALUATE: *Theme*

As you read, observe what the dead and the living say after the drowning. What do you think Smith is saying about the effectiveness of communication in life? What problem does Smith identify in human relationships? Is her concern valid? Evaluate the speakers' perspectives according to a biblical worldview. How does the Bible instruct believers to support one another? Consider these verses: John 13:34–35, Ecclesiastes 4:9–10, James 1:19, Proverbs 27:9–10, and Philippians 2:4.

OBJECTIVES

- Identify the speakers in this poem.
- Infer meaning from a text's details.
- Analyze a poem's use of dramatic irony, black humor, and symbol to communicate theme.
- Evaluate a poet's view of human relationships.

Not Waving but Drowning

Nobody heard him, the dead man,
But still he lay moaning:
I was much further out than you thought
And not waving but drowning. A

Poor chap, he always loved larking
And now he's dead
It must have been too cold for him his heart gave way,
They said.

Oh, no no no, it was too cold always
(Still the dead one lay moaning)
I was much too far out all my life
And not waving but drowning. A R

Black Humor: How is stanza 1 representative of black humor? A

Irony: How is the dead speaker's communication ironic? A

Infer Meaning: What two states of mind do waving and drowning symbolize? R

VISUAL ANALYSIS

The illustrator here copied Smith's practice of drawing stick figures to illustrate her poems. How does the image's style match the poem's? How might it highlight the work's humor?

THINK AND DISCUSS

1. How does the speakers' communication illustrate dramatic irony?
2. How does black humor reflect postwar thought?
3. Using two examples from the poem, explain how irony and black humor point to the theme.
4. Other than "waving" and "drowning," what symbols can you identify? How do the symbols relate to the theme?
5. How is the poem's theme relevant for postwar writers?
6. Does Smith communicate Beauty and arrive at a universal Truth? Defend your answer using details from the poem.

Seamus Heaney (1939–2013)

AT A GLANCE

- **1965** Married Marie Devlin
- **1966** Published *The Death of a Naturalist*, his first major volume of poems
- **1975** Published *North*
- **1985–2006** Taught at Harvard University
- **1995** Published *The Redress of Poetry*; received the Nobel Prize in Literature
- **1999** Published a best-selling translation of *Beowulf*

Seamus Heaney was an Irish poet, translator, and literary critic whose work explores history, myth, and language. Drawing on his upbringing in rural Northern Ireland, Heaney's poetry celebrates the common miracles of life. In his translations, he has also given classic literature contemporary relevance.

Roots and Career

Heaney was born into a farming family in County Derry, Northern Ireland. As a child, he experienced not only the earthy beauty of the farm but also the tragedy of war—he personally witnessed Allied soldiers training for the Normandy invasion. At school, Heaney developed a love for language, studying Latin and Irish at his secondary school and Old English later at university. After graduating from Queen's University in Belfast in 1961, he took a diploma in teaching in 1962 and began a lifelong career as a teacher. In 1965 he married fellow teacher Marie Devlin, who shared his interest in writing and who later published a volume on Irish mythology.

DID YOU KNOW

Seamus was the oldest of nine Heaney children. The accidental childhood death of one of his brothers occasioned the poem "Mid-Term Break."

Poet and Translator

In 1966 Heaney published his first volume of poems, *The Death of a Naturalist.* In this work Heaney memorialized the economic transitions in County Derry while giving them a timeless cast. *Door into the Dark* (1969) continued these themes, but in 1972 Heaney's poetry took a darker turn, as he began reflecting on the ongoing political tragedy in Northern Ireland, a period known as the Troubles. Both *Wintering Out* (1972) and *North* (1975) are meditations on the age-old problems within humanity as well as the violence that Ireland was then undergoing.

In 1975 Heaney moved permanently to the Republic of Ireland (ultimately making his home in Dublin), as he identified himself more with Ireland than with Great Britain. When he discovered that his work had been included in a 1982 anthology of British literature, he protested with the poem "An Open Letter," explaining that "my passport's green." In 1985 Heaney became a tenured professor at Harvard. As a professor, Heaney was also an accomplished literary critic, with his collection of lectures *The Redress of Poetry* (1995) summarizing his views on the value and function of poetry.

Remaining a prolific poet throughout his career, Heaney began publishing translations in 1982 with his rendering of a medieval Irish poem. *The Cure at Troy* (1991) and *The Burial at Thebes* (2004) are widely acclaimed versions of plays by Sophocles, and his translation of *Beowulf* (1999) became a bestseller. Heaney was awarded the Nobel Prize in Literature in 1995. He died in Dublin in 2013.

Legacy

Unlike much modern poetry, Heaney's poetry generally avoids experiments with form and syntax. Instead, Heaney utilizes the rhythms of everyday speech, rhythms infused with Irish cadences and the earthiness of Anglo-Saxon sounds. While much modern poetry tends toward complex imagery, Heaney's poems are often deceptively simple, developing the sensory impact of a moment from life, history, or myth. The complexity of a Heaney poem lies in the many ambiguities of life itself.

Heaney was particularly interested in the impact of history upon the present, and his poetry and translations frequently explore how the present both mirrors and differs from the past. By both celebrating and scrutinizing our historical inheritance, Heaney has inspired many contemporary authors to connect their work with history. And by meditating on timelessly profound truths with accessible language, Heaney has found a wide readership.

ANALYZE: *Sound Devices and Rhythm*

Part of Heaney's artistry lies in his deft use of sound devices. The following poem exhibits rhyme, both perfect and slant (i.e., partial). **Perfect rhyme** is simply the agreement of words' sounds from the last stressed vowel sound onward. **Slant rhyme** occurs when words come close to perfect rhyme but do not fully achieve it: usually they agree in significant consonant sounds but disagree in vowel sounds, or they agree in the vowel sounds but not the consonants (e.g., toll/sell or sun/chum). Three other **sound devices** appear in "Follower": alliteration, consonance, and assonance. Review their definitions and see if you can spot them in the poem.

Finally, note how Heaney deftly manipulates the poem's flow, using **enjambment** (p. 457) and **caesura** (p. 457). When you read poetry, you tend to pause at the end of a line or at a natural syntactical break. Enjambment carries a sentence's syntax past a line's end, pushing a reader into the next line in order to find this break. Caesura, if you recall, creates a pause or stop in the middle of a line of poetry. As you read, look for these poetic techniques.

OBJECTIVES

- Identify a poem's devices of sound and rhythm.
- Draw conclusions about how a poem's sound and rhythm enhance its meaning.
- Analyze a poem's central theme.
- Evaluate a poem's theme biblically.

READ: *Draw Conclusions About a Poem's Flow*

As you find examples of sound devices and altered rhythm, ask yourself what effects they might have on the poem's overall flow and message. How might these affect the poem's meaning? For example, consider how a caesura might draw attention to nearby content. And can you recognize where enjambment visually mimics an action described in the poem? In a similar way (but more subtly), perfect and slant rhyme affect a poem's flow. Done evenly and consistently, perfect rhyme tends to create a steady rhythm. Readers begin to hear it as a kind of vocal punctuation to line ends. How might the effect of slant rhyme differ?

Finally, pay attention to individual words and their sounds as well. Note that some sounds roll easily off the tongue (e.g., vowels, consonants such as *l*, *r*, *n*). Others slow speech, requiring you to stop the flow of breath (e.g., *k*, *g*, *t*) or to close your lips or teeth (e.g., *b*, *ch*, *j*). Why might Heaney have chosen to use particular words based on how their sounds affect the poem's pacing? Draw conclusions about how all these artistic choices might support the poem's message.

EVALUATE: *Theme*

The images (p. 75) as well as the sound devices in "Follower" work together to communicate the poem's **theme** (p. 229). After you have read the poem, describe the boy's attitude toward his father and the father's toward his son. What aspect of the parent/child relationship does the poem highlight? What concrete images vividly depict this topic? How does Heaney feel about his subject? Having discovered Heaney's theme, evaluate it from a biblical perspective. What, according to Scripture, do we know about the parent/child relationship that might apply to Heaney's insight? Consider the following passages: Exodus 20:12, Proverbs 1:8–9, Proverbs 23:22, and Ephesians 6:1–3. Does Heaney's attitude agree or conflict with Scripture?

WHO *has blazed a trail for you?*

When you hear trailblazer *or* pathfinder, *do you think of a vehicle or of a pioneer? Either way you get the idea of traversing new territory. Blazes are actual markers put on a trail or path to guide those who follow. Who has provided guidance for you on the path of life? Has someone provided "markers," perhaps internal, that signal the direction to take or that reassure you that you are on track? Write about that person in one well-developed paragraph.*

FOLLOWER

My father worked with a horse-plough,
His shoulders globed like a full sail strung
Between the shafts[1] and the furrow.
The horses strained at his clicking tongue.

An expert. He would set the wing
And fit the bright steel-pointed sock.[2]
The sod rolled over without breaking.
At the headrig,[3] with a single pluck [A]

Of reins, the sweating team turned round
And back into the land. His eye [A]
Narrowed and angled at the ground,
Mapping the furrow exactly.

I stumbled in his hob-nailed wake,
Fell sometimes on the polished sod;
Sometimes he rode me on his back
Dipping and rising to his plod.

I wanted to grow up and plough,
To close one eye, stiffen my arm.
All I ever did was follow
In his broad shadow round the farm.

I was a nuisance, tripping, falling,
Yapping always. But today
It is my father who keeps stumbling
Behind me, and will not go away. [E]

Sound Devices: Identify rhymed words in stanzas 1 and 2 and label the kind of rhyme they illustrate. [A]

Rhythm: What technique is illustrated in lines 8–10? How might it visually reinforce the poem's content? [A]

Theme: What comes as a surprise at the poem's end? [E]

1. *shafts:* i.e., the plough shafts
2. *wing . . . sock:* parts of a plow that slice through and turn the soil
3. *headrig:* where the horse and plow turn back to create the next furrow

THINK AND DISCUSS

1. Describe Heaney's boyhood relationship with his father. How does the imagery of "Follower" convey this relationship?
2. Where and why does the poem exhibit an obvious shift?
3. Identify an example of enjambment, caesura, perfect rhyme, and slant rhyme from "Follower."
4. Identify the specific sound devices illustrated in the following lines: "His shoulders globed like a full sail strung / Between the shafts and the furrow. / The horses strained at his clicking tongue." Give examples of each sound device.
5. Analyze the possible purpose and effect of slant rhyme in "Follower." How do these differ from perfect rhyme?
6. How did Heaney use caesura and enjambment effectively in stanzas 2 and 3 of the poem?
7. Analyze Heaney's use of alliteration in stanza 1 compared to his use of consonance in line 13. How do the sounds illustrate the content of the poem?
8. Evaluate Heaney's relationship with his father in "Follower" from a biblical worldview. How does he exhibit a window into Truth?

Nadine Gordimer (1923–2014)

Nadine Gordimer was a South African novelist and short-story writer whose fiction depicts her homeland's tangled racial dynamics. Although she was born into a white family that benefited from South Africa's racial caste system, Gordimer's search for truth led her to uncover that system's dehumanizing effects. Even after racial injustice became entrenched by apartheid in 1948, she continued to advocate against apartheid until its demise.

Gordimer was born in Springs in northeast South Africa. She was considered a sickly child and received little formal schooling. But she read widely and, at fifteen, published her first short story. Her first book was a short-story collection, *Face to Face* (1949). In 1948 she moved to Johannesburg, the country's capital, which became her home for the rest of her life. There her stories gained increasing international attention.

In 1960 Gordimer responded to government violence by actively involving herself in the anti-apartheid movement. Although she didn't consider her writing political, her depictions of life under apartheid furthered the anti-apartheid cause. Her accurate documentary led to the government's banning three of her novels. Heedless of the bans, she wrote critically acclaimed novels such as *The Conservationist* (1974), *Burger's Daughter* (1979), and *July's People* (1981). After apartheid fell in 1991—the same year she was awarded the Nobel Prize in Literature—she continued to document the complexity of South African life. She died in 2014.

Rather than present apartheid-era whites in a wholly negative light, Gordimer examines the ambiguities of the white experience, detailing how whites are often blind to their role in oppression. And while Gordimer portrays how apartheid dehumanizes nonwhite members of the community, she also celebrates that they find human dignity despite a crushing regime and that South Africans from all races are bound to each other by the threads of shared existence.

BEFORE READING

ANALYZE: *Point of View*

Gordimer was writing during a time when two groups in South Africa had radically different desires for their culture. It is against this backdrop that her story employs a unique **point of view** (p. 394). Gordimer's narrative style both reflects her artistic goals and underscores the theme of the story. Is the narrator omniscient or limited? Is he detached from the thoughts and feelings of the protagonist? Does the narrator stay aloof from other characters?

READ: *Make and Check Predictions*

One reading skill that allows you to focus on the plot of a story is making and checking predictions. In the following story, Gordimer's political aims play a role in directing the story's events, and her characters do not escape the influence of systemic prejudice. Predict how the protagonist will act in the political struggle. What impact will his decisions have? Are there any events in the story that you did not predict or that violated your expectations (**situational irony**, p. 88)? If so, how does this irony communicate Gordimer's theme? How do you think the story's conflicts will resolve? If the conflicts do resolve, who will benefit the most?

EVALUATE: *Effects of Prejudice*

Gordimer observed the effects of prejudice all around her in South Africa. Though she did not claim to adhere to Christianity, her perspective does echo some biblical teachings. For instance, what does she say about people's duties to each other? How does her message compare to that of Galatians 3:23–29? How do her implied solutions uphold biblical Truth and Goodness?

OBJECTIVES

- Describe the narrator's point of view.
- Make and check predictions about the story.
- Infer how irony conveys the story's theme.
- Evaluate from a biblical worldview the author's message about the effects of prejudice.

VOCABULARY

domestic (də-mĕs′tĭk) *adj.* Of or relating to the family or household.

mishap (mĭs′hăp′) *n.* An unfortunate accident.

infiltrator (ĭn-fĭl′trāt-ər) *n.* One who *infiltrates* (*v.* to penetrate with hostile intent).

negligence (nĕg′lĭ-jəns) *n.* Failure to use the degree of care appropriate to the circumstances, resulting in an unintended injury to another.

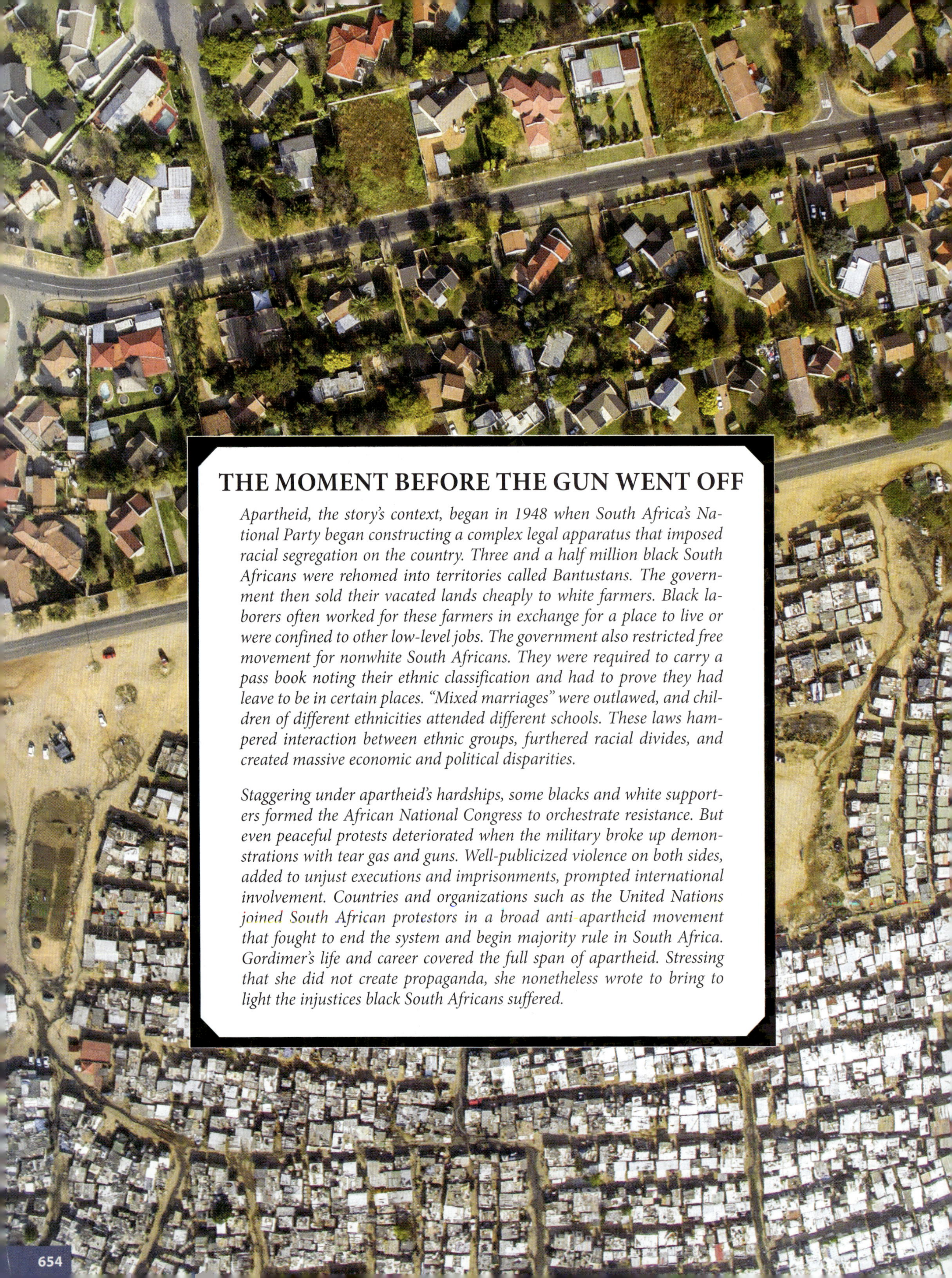

THE MOMENT BEFORE THE GUN WENT OFF

Apartheid, the story's context, began in 1948 when South Africa's National Party began constructing a complex legal apparatus that imposed racial segregation on the country. Three and a half million black South Africans were rehomed into territories called Bantustans. The government then sold their vacated lands cheaply to white farmers. Black laborers often worked for these farmers in exchange for a place to live or were confined to other low-level jobs. The government also restricted free movement for nonwhite South Africans. They were required to carry a pass book noting their ethnic classification and had to prove they had leave to be in certain places. "Mixed marriages" were outlawed, and children of different ethnicities attended different schools. These laws hampered interaction between ethnic groups, furthered racial divides, and created massive economic and political disparities.

Staggering under apartheid's hardships, some blacks and white supporters formed the African National Congress to orchestrate resistance. But even peaceful protests deteriorated when the military broke up demonstrations with tear gas and guns. Well-publicized violence on both sides, added to unjust executions and imprisonments, prompted international involvement. Countries and organizations such as the United Nations joined South African protestors in a broad anti-apartheid movement that fought to end the system and begin majority rule in South Africa. Gordimer's life and career covered the full span of apartheid. Stressing that she did not create propaganda, she nonetheless wrote to bring to light the injustices black South Africans suffered.

Marais Van der Vyver shot one of his farm laborers, dead. An accident, there are accidents with guns every day of the week—children playing a fatal game with a father's revolver in the cities where guns are **domestic** objects, nowadays, hunting **mishaps** like this one, in the country—but these won't be reported all over the world. Van der Vyver knows his will be. He knows that the story of the Afrikaner[1] farmer—regional Party[2] leader and Commandant of the local security commando[3]—shooting a black man who worked for him will fit exactly *their* version of South Africa, it's made for them. They'll be able to use it in their boycott and divestment campaigns,[4] it'll be another piece of evidence in their truth about the country. The papers at home will quote the story as it has appeared in the overseas press, and in the back-and-forth he and the black man will become those crudely drawn figures on anti-apartheid banners, units in statistics of white brutality against the blacks quoted at the United Nations[5]—he, whom they will gleefully be able to call "a leading member" of the ruling Party. **A**

domestic (də-mĕs′tĭk) *adj.* Of or relating to the family or household.

mishap (mĭs′hăp′) *n.* An unfortunate accident.

Point of View: For what group or individual is the narrator speaking in this paragraph? **A**

People in the farming community understand how he must feel. Bad enough to have killed a man, without helping the Party's, the government's, the country's enemies, as well. They see the truth of that. They know, reading the Sunday papers, that when Van der Vyver is quoted saying he is "terribly shocked," he will "look after the wife and children," none of those Americans and English, and none of those people at home who want to destroy the white man's power will believe him. And how they will sneer when he even says of the farm boy (according to one paper, if you can trust any of those reporters), "He was my friend, I always took him hunting with me." Those city and overseas people don't know it's true: farmers usually have one particular black boy they like to take along with them in the lands; you could call it a kind of friend, yes, friends are not only your own white people, like yourself, you take into your house, pray with in church and work with on the Party committee. But how can those others know that? They don't want to know it. They think all blacks are like the big-mouth agitators in town. And Van der Vyver's face, in the photographs, strangely opened by distress—everyone in the district remembers Marais Van der Vyver as a little boy who would go away and hide himself if he caught you smiling at him, and everyone knows him now as a man who hides any change of expression round his mouth behind a thick, soft mustache, and in his eyes by always looking at some object in hand, leaf of a crop fingered, pen or stone picked up, while concentrating on what he is saying, or while listening to you. It just goes to show what shock can do; when you look at the newspaper photographs you feel like apologizing, as if you had stared in on some room where you should not be. **E**

Prejudice: Who has shown prejudice toward someone else in the story thus far? **E**

There will be an inquiry; there had better be, to stop the assumption of yet another case of brutality against farm workers, although there's nothing in doubt—an accident, and all the facts fully admitted by Van der Vyver. He made a statement when he arrived at the police station with the dead man in his bakkie.[6] Captain Beetge knows him well, of course; he gave him brandy. He was shaking, this big, calm, clever son of Willem Van der Vyver, who

VISUAL ANALYSIS

This 2016 aerial view of two Johannesburg neighborhoods, one traditionally white and one traditionally black, shows how racial divides linger in post-apartheid South Africa. What results of legalized discrimination does it reveal? What emotional response does it evoke from you, the viewer?

1. *Afrikaner:* a South African white person who speaks Afrikaans; usually of Dutch descent
2. *Party:* the National Party (the white government's party) in power from 1948–94
3. *Commandant . . . commando:* Units organized and run by the community and used by the government to police hard-to-reach rural farm areas. The system predated apartheid but was inevitably affected by it.
4. *boycott . . . campaigns:* anti-apartheid campaigns, especially relating to international sanctions; included protests on US college campuses
5. *United Nations:* The United Nations played a key role in bringing sanctions against South Africa in order to pressure the National Party to end apartheid.
6. *bakkie:* a farm vehicle, probably similar to a pickup truck

inherited the old man's best farm. The black was stone dead, nothing to be done for him. Beetge will not tell anyone that after the brandy Van der Vyver wept. He sobbed, snot running onto his hands, like a dirty kid. The Captain was ashamed, for him, and walked out to give him a chance to recover himself. R

Predictions: How do you think an inquiry into the tragedy would affect Van der Vyver? His community? His farm? R

Marais Van der Vyver left his house at three in the afternoon to cull a buck[7] from the family of kudu[8] he protects in the bush areas of his farm. He is interested in wildlife and sees it as the farmers' sacred duty to raise game as well as cattle. As usual, he called at his shed workshop to pick up Lucas, a twenty-year-old farmhand who had shown mechanical aptitude and whom Van der Vyver himself had taught to maintain tractors and other farm machinery. He hooted, and Lucas followed the familiar routine, jumping onto the back of the truck. He liked to travel standing up there, spotting game before his employer did. He would lean forward, braced against the cab below him.

Van der Vyver had a rifle and .300 ammunition beside him in the cab. The rifle was one of his father's, because his own was at the gunsmith's in town. Since his father died (Beetge's sergeant wrote "passed on") no one had used the rifle and so when he took it from a cupboard he was sure it was not loaded. His father had never allowed a loaded gun in the house; he himself had been taught since childhood never to ride with a loaded weapon in a vehicle. But this gun was loaded. On a dirt track, Lucas thumped his fist on the cab roof three times to signal: look left. Having seen the white ripple-marked flank of a kudu, and its fine horns raking through disguising bush, Van der Vyver drove rather fast over a pot hole. The jolt fired the rifle. Upright, it was pointing straight through the cab roof at the head of Lucas. The bullet pierced the roof and entered Lucas's brain by way of his throat. R

Predictions: Why do you think the title of the story is "The Moment Before the Gun Went Off"? Do you think Lucas's killing will turn out to be truly accidental? R

That is the statement of what happened. Although a man of such standing in the district, Van der Vyver had to go through the ritual of swearing that it was the truth. It has gone on record, and will be there in the archive of the local police station as long as Van der Vyver lives, and beyond that, through the lives of his children, Magnus, Helena and Karel—unless things in the country get worse, the example of black mobs in the towns spreads to the rural areas and the place is burned down as many urban police stations have been. Because nothing the government can do will appease the agitators and the whites who encourage them. Nothing satisfies them, in the cities: blacks can sit and drink in white hotels, now, the Immorality Act[9] has gone, blacks can sleep with whites . . . It's not even a crime any more.

Van der Vyver has a high barbed security fence round his farmhouse and garden which his wife, Alida, thinks spoils completely the effect of her artificial stream with its tree ferns beneath the jacarandas.[10] There is an aerial soaring like a flag pole in the back yard. All his vehicles, including the truck in which the black man died, have aerials that swing their whips when the driver hits a pot hole: they are part of the security system the farmers in the district maintain, each farm in touch with every other by radio, twenty-four hours out of twenty-four. It has already happened that **infiltrators** from over the border have mined remote farm roads, killing white farmers and their families out on their own property for a Sunday picnic. The pot hole could have set off a land mine, and Van der Vyver might have died with his farm

infiltrator (ĭn-fĭl′trāt-ər) *n.* One who *infiltrates* (*v.* to penetrate with hostile intent).

7. *cull a buck:* hunting terminology for removing an inferior deer from the population for the purpose of improving the rest of the herd
8. *kudu:* a type of antelope
9. *Immorality Act:* Passed in 1950, the law forbade marriage and any sexual relations between black people and white people; the ban was lifted in 1985.
10. *jacarandas:* tall trees with blue or white flowers

boy. When neighbors use the communications system to call up and say they are sorry about "that business" with one of Van der Vyver's boys, there goes unsaid: it could have been worse.

It is obvious from the quality and fittings of the coffin that the farmer has provided money for the funeral. And an elaborate funeral means a great deal to blacks; look how they will deprive themselves of the little they have, in their lifetime, keeping up payments to a burial society so they won't go in boxwood to an unmarked grave.[11] The young wife is pregnant (of course) and another little one, wearing red shoes several sizes too large, leans under her jutting belly. He is too young to understand what has happened, what he is witnessing that day, but neither whines nor plays about; he is solemn without knowing why. Blacks expose small children to everything, they don't protect them from the sight of fear and pain the way whites do theirs. It is the young wife who rolls her head and cries like a child, sobbing on the breast of this relative and that. E

Prejudice: How is the black community described in this paragraph? Is any prejudice involved in the tone? E

All present work for Van der Vyver or are the families of those who work; and in the weeding and harvest seasons, the women and children work for him, too, carried—wrapped in their blankets, on a truck, singing—at sunrise to the fields. The dead man's mother is a woman who can't be more than in her late thirties (they start bearing children at puberty) but she is heavily mature in a black dress between her own parents, who were already working for old Van der Vyver when Marais, like their daughter, was a child. The parents hold her as if she were a prisoner or a crazy woman to be restrained. But she says nothing, does nothing. She does not look up; she does not look at Van der Vyver, whose gun went off in the truck, she stares at the grave. Nothing will make her look up; there need be no fear that she will look up at

11. *burial society . . . unmarked grave:* Death played an important role in South Africans' cultural values. Burial society membership, often linked to church membership, helped alleviate the funeral expenses for the families of the deceased and allowed for a funeral fairly free of white cultural influences.

him. His wife, Alida, is beside him. To show the proper respect, as for any white funeral, she is wearing the navy-blue-and-cream hat she wears to church this summer. She is always supportive, although he doesn't seem to notice it; this coldness and reserve—his mother says he didn't mix well as a child—she accepts for herself but regrets that it has prevented him from being nominated, as he should be, to stand as the Party's parliamentary candidate for the district. He does not let her clothing, or that of anyone else gathered closely, make contact with him. He, too, stares at the grave. The dead man's mother and he stare at the grave in communication like that between the black man outside and the white man inside the cab the moment before the gun went off. **A**

Point of View: Does the narrator adopt the same point of view in this paragraph that he had in the first paragraph of the story? If not, how is the perspective in this paragraph different? **A**

The moment before the gun went off was a moment of high excitement shared through the roof of the cab, as the bullet was to pass, between the young black man outside and the white farmer inside the vehicle. There were such moments, without explanation, between them, although often around the farm the farmer would pass the young man without returning a greeting, as if he did not recognize him. When the bullet went off what Van der Vyver saw was the kudu stumble in fright at the report and gallop away. Then he heard the thud behind him, and past the window saw the young man fall out of the vehicle. He was sure he had leapt up and toppled—in fright, like the buck. The farmer was almost laughing with relief, ready to tease, as he opened his door, it did not seem possible that a bullet passing through the roof could have done harm.

The young man did not laugh with him at his own fright. The farmer carried him in his arms, to the truck. He was sure, sure he could not be dead. But the young black man's blood was all over the farmer's clothes, soaking against his flesh as he drove.

How will they ever know, when they file newspaper clippings, evidence, proof, when they look at the photographs and see his face—guilty! guilty! they are right!—how will they know, when the police stations burn with all the evidence of what has happened now, and what the law made a crime in the past. How could they know that *they do not know.* Anything. The young black callously shot through the **negligence** of the white man was not the farmer's boy; he was his son. **R**

negligence (nĕg′lĭ-jəns) *n.* Failure to use the degree of care appropriate to the circumstances, resulting in an unintended injury to another.

Predictions: Is this the ending you had expected? If not, how is it different? **R**

THINK AND DISCUSS

1. Now that you know the end of the story, list two instances of foreshadowing (p. 614). Were any of your predictions for the story's end correct?
2. Explain one reason the ending was surprising to you. If you were not surprised, explain how the ending functions as a surprise ending or plot twist.
3. Which group—apartheid or anti-apartheid—is correct about Van der Vyver? Explain your answer.
4. Is the story's narrator limited or omniscient? Defend your answer with textual details.
5. Name the group for which the narrator predominantly speaks. Can Van der Vyver share the truth with this group of people? With their political opponents?
6. Identify two statements in the story that stem from a character or group's attitude of racial prejudice. How does Gordimer discredit that attitude?
7. Analyze the significance of the title. Why does Gordimer emphasize the moment *before* the gun's discharge?
8. What is the central example of situational irony in the story? How does this irony convey a message for South Africa?
9. Evaluate from a biblical worldview Gordimer's message about the effects of prejudice.

Anita Desai (b. 1937)

The technological revolutions of the twentieth century brought with them a profound sense of dislocation. As mass media and rapid transit made the globe an increasingly smaller place, languages and cultures disappeared, leaving behind a sense of alienation and loss. Perhaps one of the best novelists of this modern dislocation is the Indian writer Anita Desai.

Desai was born Anita Mazumdar in Mussoorie, India, the daughter of a Bengali engineer and a German mother. Growing up in colonial India, she became fluent in English, Hindi, and German. A lifelong lover of books, she wrote her first story at age nine. She earned a degree in English literature from the University of Delhi in 1957. In 1958 she married Ashvin Desai, with whom she had four children and whose career would repeatedly move the family across India.

Despite constant displacement and the demands of family life, Desai continued writing, always in English, publishing her first novel in 1963. In 1977 she published *Fire on the Mountain*, a stylized, imagistic novel that brought her critical attention. She followed this achievement in 1978 with the short-story collection *Games at Twilight*. Desai's growing literary stature led to a professorship in the United States, where she moved in 1987. The following year she published an homage to her German heritage in *Baumgartner's Bombay*. Since then she has continued to publish a steady stream of critically acclaimed novels, novellas, and short stories.

Desai's mature fiction explores the quiet struggles and sense of loss felt by those caught in the swirling tides of the modern world, often between conflicting cultural forces. These dilemmas frequently lead to personal tragedies. For Desai, cultural dislocation produces misunderstanding and pain, but her fiction also shows how the sufferings of modern life can be borne with fortitude and grace.

BEFORE READING

ANALYZE: *Conflict and Character*

"A Devoted Son" exhibits **conflict** (p. 213), essential to good fiction. Although the conflict may initially appear to be between merely two characters, the plot reveals a larger conflict at work between two major forces. As you read, identify the forces working against each other. Which of the characters caught up in the conflict is **static**, remaining essentially the same throughout the story, and which is **dynamic**, undergoing change as the story progresses? Whom would you personally label as **sympathetic** (p. 394)? What about **unsympathetic** (p. 394)? What kind of resolution does Desai provide for their conflicts?

READ: *Make Predictions*

The inciting incident is the event that sets the conflict in motion. As you read, identify the point in the story when something happens to initiate conflict. Try to predict its effect. As you continue reading, what do you foresee happening in the family? What do you think, if anything, will change? Do any of the events undermine your predictions, perhaps illustrating **irony** (p. 88)?

EVALUATE: *Navigating Human Relationships*

Storytellers aim to mirror some aspect of real life in their fiction. As you read, examine how Desai represents the psychology of human relationships. For example, consider her portrayal of Varma and his wife, and then, of Rakesh and of his relationship with his parents. What motivates each character to behave as he or she does? Does a consideration of motive alter how you view the characters and their relationships? Also, consider biblical principles helpful in navigating complicated human relationships and their conflicts.

OBJECTIVES

- Identify examples of irony in a story.
- Make predictions about plot.
- Analyze a story's development of conflicts and characters.
- Evaluate the truthfulness of an author's portrayal of human relationships.

VOCABULARY

filial (fĭl′ē-əl) *adj.* Of, relating to, or befitting a son or daughter.

rancor (răng′kər) *n.* Bitter, long-lasting resentment; deep-seated ill will.

complaisant (kəm-plā′sənt) *adj.* Exhibiting a desire or willingness to please; cheerfully obliging.

decrepit (dĭ-krĕp′ĭt) *adj.* Weakened, worn out, impaired, or broken down by old age, illness, or hard use.

adamantly (ăd′ə-mənt-lē) *adv.* Unwaveringly, resolutely; in a manner which suggests one will not be persuaded to change one's mind.

A Devoted Son

When the results appeared in the morning papers, Rakesh scanned them, barefoot and in his pajamas, at the garden gate, then went up the steps to the veranda[1] where his father sat sipping his morning tea and bowed down to touch his feet.[2]

"A first division, son?" his father asked, beaming, reaching for the papers.

"At the top of the list, Papa," Rakesh murmured, as if awed. "First in the country."

Bedlam broke loose then. The family whooped and danced. The whole day long visitors streamed into the small yellow house at the end of the road, to congratulate the parents of this *Wunderkind*,[3] to slap Rakesh on the back and fill the house and garden with the sounds and colors of a festival. There were garlands and *halwa*,[4] party clothes and gifts (enough fountain pens to

1. *veranda:* a balcony or porch on the outside of a building
2. *touch his feet:* In India this gesture signals respect for an elder.
3. *Wunderkind:* a person achieving great success early in life
4. *halwa:* a carrot-based sweet dessert pudding often served in Indian homes

VISUAL ANALYSIS

What is the significance of the action being depicted in this picture? How does it reflect the traits of these two characters?

last years, even a watch or two), nerves and temper and joy, all in a multicolored whirl of pride and great shining vistas newly opened: Rakesh was the first son in the family to receive an education, so much had been sacrificed in order to send him to school and then medical college, and at last the fruits of their sacrifice had arrived, golden and glorious.

To everyone who came to him to say, "*Mubarak,*[5] Varmaji, your son has brought you glory," the father said, "Yes, and do you know what is the first thing he did when he saw the results this morning? He came and touched my feet. He bowed down and touched my feet." This moved many of the women in the crowd so much that they were seen to raise the ends of their saris[6] and dab at their tears while the men reached out for the betel leaves and sweetmeats that were offered around on trays and shook their heads in wonder and approval of such exemplary **filial** behavior. "One does not often see such behavior in sons any more," they all agreed, a little enviously perhaps. Leaving the house, some of the women said, sniffing, "At least on such an occasion they might have served pure *ghee* sweets,"[7] and some of the men said, "Don't you think old Varma was giving himself airs? He needn't think we don't remember that he comes from the vegetable market himself, his father used to sell vegetables, and he has never seen the inside of a school." But there was more envy than **rancor** in their voices and it was, of course, inevitable—not every son in that shabby little colony at the edge of the city was destined to shine as Rakesh shone, and who knew that better than the parents themselves? E

And that was only the beginning, the first step in a great, sweeping ascent to the radiant heights of fame and fortune. The thesis he wrote for his MD brought Rakesh still greater glory, if only in select medical circles. He won a scholarship. He went to the USA (that was what his father learned to call it and taught the whole family to say—not America, which was what the ignorant neighbors called it, but, with a grand familiarity, "the USA") where he pursued his career in the most prestigious of all hospitals and won encomiums from his American colleagues which were relayed to his admiring and glowing family. What was more, he came *back*, he actually returned to that small yellow house in the once-new but increasingly shabby colony, right at the end of the road where the rubbish vans tipped out their stinking contents for pigs to nose in and rag-pickers to build their shacks on, all steaming and smoking just outside the neat wire fences and well-tended gardens. To this Rakesh returned and the first thing he did on entering the house was to slip out of the embraces of his sisters and brothers and bow down and touch his father's feet.

As for his mother, she gloated chiefly over the strange fact that he had not married in America, had not brought home a foreign wife as all her neighbors had warned her he would, for wasn't that what all Indian boys went abroad for? Instead he agreed, almost without argument, to marry a girl she had picked out for him in her own village, the daughter of a childhood friend, a plump and uneducated girl, it was true, but so old-fashioned, so placid, so **complaisant** that she slipped into the household and settled in like a charm, seemingly too lazy and too good-natured to even try and make Rakesh leave home and set up independently, as any other girl might have done. What was more, she was pretty—really pretty, in a plump, pudding way that only gave

filial (fĭl′ē-əl) *adj.* Of, relating to, or befitting a son or daughter.

rancor (răng′kər) *n.* Bitter, long-lasting resentment; deep-seated ill will.

Truth: Do the human relationships painted here—between Rakesh's family, between them and the neighbors—ring true to life so far? How or how not? E

complaisant (kəm-plā′sənt) *adj.* Exhibiting a desire or willingness to please; cheerfully obliging.

5. *Mubarak:* a traditional Muslim greeting meaning "blessed"
6. *sari:* a form of Indian traditional dress for women
7. *ghee sweets:* sweets made with clarified butter

way to fat—soft, spreading fat, like warm wax—after the birth of their first baby, a son, and then what did it matter? **A**

For some years Rakesh worked in the city hospital, quickly rising to the top of the administrative organization, and was made a director before he left to set up his own clinic. He took his parents in his car—a new, sky-blue Ambassador with a rear window full of stickers and charms revolving on strings—to see the clinic when it was built, and the large sign-board over the door on which his name was printed in letters of red, with a row of degrees and qualifications to follow it like so many little black slaves of the regent.[8] Thereafter his fame seemed to grow just a little dimmer—or maybe it was only that everyone in town had grown accustomed to it at last—but it was also the beginning of his fortune for he now became known not only as the best but also the richest doctor in town.

However, all this was not accomplished in the wink of an eye. Naturally not. It was the achievement of a lifetime and it took up Rakesh's whole life. At the time he set up his clinic his father had grown into an old man and retired from his post at the kerosene dealer's depot at which he had worked for forty years, and his mother died soon after, giving up the ghost with a sigh that sounded positively happy, for it was her own son who ministered to her in her last illness and who sat pressing her feet at the last moment—such a son as few women had borne.

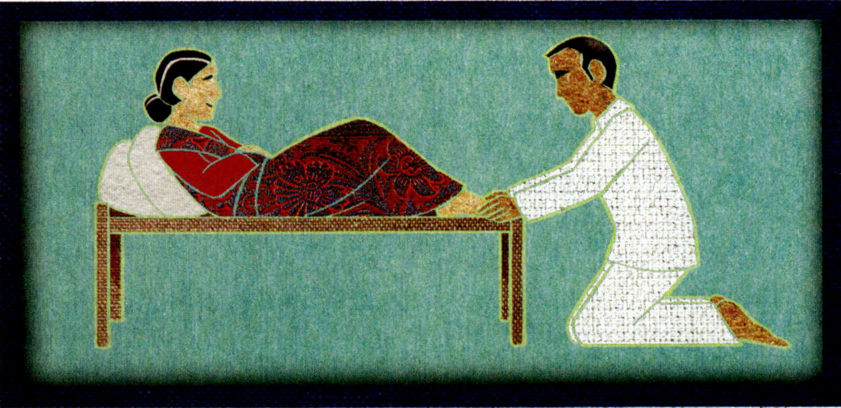

For it had to be admitted—and the most unsuccessful and most rancorous of neighbors eventually did so—that Rakesh was not only a devoted son and a miraculously good-natured man who contrived somehow to obey his parents and humor his wife and show concern equally for his children and his patients, but there was actually a brain inside this beautifully polished and formed body of good manners and kind nature and, in between ministering to his family and playing host to many friends and coaxing them all into feeling happy and grateful and content, he had actually trained his hands as well and emerged an excellent doctor, a really fine surgeon. How one man—and a man born to illiterate parents, his father having worked for a kerosene dealer and his mother having spent her life in a kitchen—had achieved, combined and conducted such a medley of virtues, no one could fathom, but all acknowledged his talent and skill. **A** **R**

It was a strange fact, however, that talent and skill, if displayed for too long, cease to dazzle. It came to pass that the most admiring of all eyes eventually faded and no longer blinked at his glory. Having retired from work and having lost his wife, the old father very quickly went to pieces, as they say. He developed so many complaints and fell ill so frequently and with such mysterious diseases that even his son could no longer make out when it was something of significance and when it was merely a peevish whim. He sat huddled on his string bed most of the day and developed an exasperating habit of stretching out suddenly and lying absolutely still, allowing the whole family to fly around him in a flap, wailing and weeping, and then suddenly sitting

Character: What important trait seems to be a defining characteristic of Rakesh so far? **A**

Character: Would you label Rakesh as a sympathetic or an unsympathetic character at this point? **A**

Make Predictions: Do Rakesh's good qualities seem genuine? Do you think they will change over time? **R**

8. *regent:* ruling administrator of a country

up, stiff and gaunt, and spitting out a big gob of betel juice as if to mock their behavior.

He did this once too often: there had been a big party in the house, a birthday party for the youngest son, and the celebrations had to be suddenly hushed, covered up and hustled out of the way when the daughter-in-law discovered, or thought she discovered, that the old man, stretched out from end to end of his string bed, had lost his pulse; the party broke up, dissolved, even turned into a band of mourners, when the old man sat up and the distraught daughter-in-law received a gob of red spittle right on the hem of her new organza[9] sari. After that no one much cared if he sat up cross-legged on his bed, hawking and spitting, or lay down flat and turned gray as a corpse. Except, of course, for that pearl amongst pearls, his son Rakesh.

It was Rakesh who brought him his morning tea, not in one of the china cups from which the rest of the family drank, but in the old man's favorite brass tumbler, and sat at the edge of his bed, comfortable and relaxed with the string of his pajamas dangling out from under his fine lawn night-shirt, and discussed or, rather, read out the morning news to his father. It made no difference to him that his father made no response apart from spitting. It was Rakesh, too, who, on returning from the clinic in the evening, persuaded the old man to come out of his room, as bare and desolate as a cell, and take the evening air out in the garden, beautifully arranging the pillows and bolsters on the divan in the corner of the open veranda. On summer nights he saw to it that the servants carried out the old man's bed onto the lawn and himself helped his father down the steps and onto the bed, soothing him and settling him down for a night under the stars. **A**

Character: Would you consider Varma to be a sympathetic or an unsympathetic character at this point? **A**

All this was very gratifying for the old man. What was not so gratifying was that he even undertook to supervise his father's diet. One day when the father was really sick, having ordered his daughter-in-law to make him a dish of *soojie halwa*[10] and eaten it with a saucerful of cream, Rakesh marched into the room, not with his usual respectful step but with the confident and rather contemptuous stride of the famous doctor, and declared, "No more *halwa* for you, Papa. We must be sensible, at your age. If you must have something sweet, Veena will cook you a little *kheer*,[11] that's light, just a little rice and milk. But nothing fried, nothing rich. We can't have this happening again."

The old man who had been lying stretched out on his bed, weak and feeble after a day's illness, gave a start at the very sound, the tone of these words. He opened his eyes—rather, they fell open with shock—and he stared at his son with disbelief that darkened quickly to reproach. A son who actually refused his father the food he craved? No, it was unheard of, it was incredible. But Rakesh had turned his back to him and was cleaning up the litter of bottles and packets on the medicine shelf and did not notice while Veena slipped silently out of the room with a little smirk that only the old man saw, and hated. **R**

Halwa was only the first item to be crossed off the old man's diet. One delicacy after the other went—everything fried to begin with, then everything sweet, and eventually everything, everything that the old man

Make Predictions: What do you think will happen as a result of Rakesh's decision? Will he relent and defer to his father's wishes? **R**

9. *organza:* a kind of fine, lightweight sheer fabric, traditionally made from silk
10. *soojie halwa:* an Indian dessert made with saffron and cashews
11. *kheer:* Indian rice pudding

enjoyed. The meals that arrived for him on the shining stainless steel tray twice a day were frugal to say the least—dry bread, boiled lentils, boiled vegetables and, if there were a bit of chicken or fish, that was boiled too. If he called for another helping—in a cracked voice that quavered theatrically—Rakesh himself would come to the door, gaze at him sadly and shake his head, saying, "Now, Papa, we must be careful, we can't risk another illness, you know," and although the daughter-in-law kept tactfully out of the way, the old man could just see her smirk sliding merrily through the air. He tried to bribe his grandchildren into buying him sweets (and how he missed his wife now, that generous, indulgent and illiterate cook), whispering, "Here's fifty *paise*"[12] as he stuffed the coins into a tight, hot fist. "Run down to the shop at the crossroads and buy me thirty *paise* worth of *jalebis*,[13] and you can spend the remaining twenty *paise* on yourself. Eh? Understand? Will you do that?" He got away with it once or twice but then was found out, the conspirator was scolded by his father and smacked by his mother and Rakesh came storming into the room, almost tearing his hair as he shouted through compressed lips, "Now Papa, are you trying to turn my little son into a liar? Quite apart from spoiling your own stomach, you are spoiling him as well—you are encouraging him to lie to his own parents. You should have heard the lies he told his mother when she saw him bringing back those *jalebis* wrapped up in filthy newspaper. I don't allow anyone in my house to buy sweets in the bazaar, Papa, surely you know that. There's cholera in the city, typhoid, gastro-enteritis[14]—I see these cases daily in the hospital, how can I allow my own family to run such risks?" The old man sighed and lay down in the corpse position. But that worried no one any longer. **A**

Conflict: What conflict has developed between father and son? Who do you think is in the right? **A**

There was only one pleasure left the old man now (his son's early morning visits and readings from the newspaper could no longer be called that) and those were visits from elderly neighbors. These were not frequent as his contemporaries were mostly as **decrepit** and helpless as he and few could walk the length of the road to visit him any more. Old Bhatia, next door, however, who was still spry enough to refuse, **adamantly**, to bathe in the tiled bathroom indoors and to insist on carrying out his brass mug and towel, in all seasons and usually at impossible hours, into the yard and bathe noisily under the garden tap, would look over the hedge to see if Varma were out on his veranda and would call to him and talk while he wrapped his *dhoti*[15] about him and dried the sparse hair on his head, shivering with enjoyable exaggeration. Of course these conversations, bawled across the hedge by two rather deaf old men conscious of having their entire households overhearing them, were not very satisfactory but Bhatia occasionally came out of his yard, walked down the bit of road and came in at Varma's gate to collapse onto the stone plinth built under the temple tree. If Rakesh were at home he would help his father down the steps into the garden and arrange him on his night bed under the tree and leave the two old men to chew betel leaves and discuss the ills of their individual bodies with combined passion.

decrepit (dĭ-krĕp′ĭt) *adj.* Weakened, worn out, impaired, or broken down by old age, illness, or hard use.

adamantly (ăd′ə-mənt-lē) *adv.* Unwaveringly, resolutely; in a manner which suggests one will not be persuaded to change one's mind.

"At least you have a doctor in the house to look after you," sighed Bhatia, having vividly described his martyrdom to piles.[16]

"Look after me?" cried Varma, his voice cracking like an ancient clay jar. "He—he does not even give me enough to eat."

12. *paise:* plural of *paisa*, "a unit of currency equal to 1/100 of the rupee in India" (*AHD*)
13. *jalebis:* "an Indian sweetmeat made by frying a coil of batter and then steeping it briefly in syrup" (*OED*) [Note: the word is plural, but the definition is singular.]
14. *cholera . . . gastro-enteritis:* infectious diseases
15. *dhoti:* traditional loincloth worn by Hindi men
16. *piles:* hemorrhoids

"What?" said Bhatia, the white hairs in his ears twitching. "Doesn't give you enough to eat? Your own son?"

"My own son. If I ask him for one more piece of bread, he says no, Papa, I weighed out the *ata*[17] myself and I can't allow you to have more than two hundred grams of cereal a day. He *weighs* the food he gives me, Bhatia—he has scales to weigh it on. That is what it has come to."

"Never," murmured Bhatia in disbelief. "Is it possible, even in this evil age, for a son to refuse his father food?"

"Let me tell you," Varma whispered eagerly. "Today the family was having fried fish—I could smell it. I called to my daughter-in-law to bring me a piece. She came to the door and said No . . ."

"Said No?" It was Bhatia's voice that cracked. A *drongo*[18] shot out of the tree and sped away. "*No?*"

"No, she said no, Rakesh has ordered her to give me nothing fried. No butter, he says, no oil—"

"No butter? No oil? How does he expect his father to *live*?"

Old Varma nodded with melancholy triumph. "That is how he treats me—after I have brought him up, given him an education, made him a great doctor. Great doctor! This is the way great doctors treat their fathers, Bhatia," for the son's sterling personality and character now underwent a curious sea change. Outwardly all might be the same but the interpretation had altered: his masterly efficiency was nothing but cold heartlessness, his authority was only tyranny in disguise. **A**

Conflict: Do you share Varma's assessment of his son's character? What larger conflicts might underlie the father's and son's differing views of this situation? **A**

There was cold comfort in complaining to neighbors and, on such a miserable diet, Varma found himself slipping, weakening and soon becoming a genuinely sick man. Powders and pills and mixtures were not only brought in when dealing with a crisis like an upset stomach but became a regular part of his diet—became his diet, complained Varma, supplanting the natural foods he craved. There were pills to regulate his bowel movements, pills to bring down his blood pressure, pills to deal with his arthritis and, eventually, pills to keep his heart beating. In between there were panicky rushes to the hospital, some humiliating experiences with the stomach pump and enema, which left him frightened and helpless. He cried easily, shriveling up on his bed, but if he complained of a pain or even a vague, gray fear in the night, Rakesh would simply open another bottle of pills and force him to take one. "I have my duty to you, Papa," he said when his father begged to be let off.

"Let me be," Varma begged, turning his face away from the pills on the outstretched hand. "Let me die. It would be better. I do not want to live only to eat your medicines."

"Papa, be reasonable."

"I leave that to you," the father cried with sudden spirit. "Let me alone, let me die now, I cannot live like this."

"Lying all day on his pillows, fed every few hours by his daughter-in-law's own hands, visited by every member of his family daily—and then he says he does not want to live 'like this,'" Rakesh was heard to say, laughing, to someone outside the door.

"Deprived of food," screamed the old man on the bed, "his wishes ignored, taunted by his daughter-in-law, laughed at by his grandchildren—*that* is how I live." But he was very old and weak and all anyone heard was an incoherent croak, some expressive grunts and cries of genuine pain. Only once,

17. *ata:* Indian wheat flour
18. *drongo:* a bird, usually black, that lives in Africa, Australia, and Asia

when old Bhatia had come to see him and they sat together under the temple tree, they heard him cry, "God is calling me—and they won't let me go."

The quantities of vitamins and tonics he was made to take were not altogether useless. They kept him alive and even gave him a kind of strength that made him hang on long after he ceased to wish to hang on. It was as though he were straining at a rope, trying to break it, and it would not break, it was still strong. He only hurt himself, trying.

In the evening, that summer, the servants would come into his cell, grip his bed, one at each end, and carry it out to the veranda, there setting it down with a thump that jarred every tooth in his head. In answer to his agonized complaints they said the Doctor Sahib[19] had told them he must take the evening air and the evening air they would make him take—thump. Then Veena, that smiling, hypocritical pudding in a rustling sari, would appear and pile up the pillows under his head till he was propped up stiffly into a sitting position that made his head swim and his back ache. "Let me lie down," he begged. "I can't sit up any more."

"Try, Papa, Rakesh said you can if you try," she said, and drifted away to the other end of the veranda where her transistor radio vibrated to the love-sick tunes from the cinema that she listened to all day.

So there he sat, like some stiff corpse, terrified, gazing out on the lawn where his grandsons played cricket, in danger of getting one of their hard-spun balls in his eye, and at the gate that opened onto the dusty and rubbish-heaped lane but still bore, proudly, a newly touched-up signboard that bore his son's name and qualifications, his own name having vanished from the gate long ago. **A**

Character: At this point do you view Varma as a sympathetic or an unsympathetic character? Why? **A**

At last the sky-blue Ambassador arrived, the cricket game broke up in haste, the car drove in smartly and the doctor, the great doctor, all in white, stepped out. Someone ran up to take his bag from him, others to escort him up the steps. "Will you have tea?" his wife called, turning down the transistor set, "or a Coca-Cola? Shall I fry you some *samosas*?"[20] But he did not reply or even glance in her direction. Ever a devoted son, he went first to the corner where his father sat gazing, stricken, at some undefined spot in the dusty yellow air that swam before him. He did not turn his head to look at his son. But he stopped gobbling air with his uncontrolled lips and set his jaw as hard as a sick and very old man could set it.

"Papa," his son said, tenderly, sitting down on the edge of the bed and reaching out to press his feet.

Old Varma tucked his feet under him, out of the way, and continued to gaze stubbornly into the yellow air of the summer evening.

"Papa, I'm home."

Varma's hand jerked suddenly, in a sharp, derisive movement, but he did not speak.

"How are you feeling, Papa?"

Then Varma turned and looked at his son. His face was so out of control and all in pieces, that the multitude of expressions that crossed it could not make up a whole and convey to the famous man exactly what his father thought of him, his skill, his art.

"I'm dying," he croaked. "Let me die, I tell you."

19. *Sahib:* similar to *sir*, a term of respect in India
20. *samosas:* traditional Indian stuffed pastries that are fried or baked

"Papa, you're joking," his son smiled at him, lovingly. "I've brought you a new tonic to make you feel better. You must take it, it will make you feel stronger again. Here it is. Promise me you will take it regularly, Papa."

Varma's mouth worked as hard as though he still had a gob of betel in it (his supply of betel had been cut off years ago). Then he spat out some words, as sharp and bitter as poison, into his son's face. "Keep your tonic—I want none—I want none—I won't take any more of—of your medicines. None. Never," and he swept the bottle out of his son's hand with a wave of his own, suddenly grand, suddenly effective.

VISUAL ANALYSIS
Compare this depiction of father and son to the one on page 660. How do the differences in their positions and actions reflect the changes that have occurred in their relationship?

His son jumped, for the bottle was smashed and thick brown syrup had splashed up, staining his white trousers. His wife let out a cry and came running. All around the old man was hubbub once again, noise, attention.

He gave one push to the pillows at his back and dislodged them so he could sink down on his back, quite flat again. He closed his eyes and pointed his chin at the ceiling, like some dire prophet, groaning, "God is calling me—now let me go." E

Truth: What, if any, resolution does Desai provide for the main conflict? Does her ending seem true to how human relationships work? E

THINK AND DISCUSS

1. Briefly describe the characters of Rakesh and Varma.
2. How does their relationship change in the story?
3. What kind of irony might this change illustrate? Explain your answer.
4. Describe the initial conflict in "A Devoted Son." What broader conflicts might this small one develop in the story?
5. Classify Varma and then Rakesh as a static or as a dynamic character. Support your answer from the text.
6. Is Rakesh a devoted son? Defend your answer, using evidence from the text.
7. Whose side does Desai take in the conflict? What truths about personal relationships did you glean from this fictional story?
8. Give three biblical principles germane to the conflict in "A Devoted Son," the application of which could have improved the situation.

THINGS FALL APART

Chinua Achebe

Nineteenth-century colonialism had forever changed many African societies, importing European culture and establishing new national boundaries. The latter often arbitrarily united diverse, sometimes competing, cultures under one colonial state. Independence later gained, these states were faced with a profound question: Should they reject the now-familiar English culture and language imposed by their colonizers or adopt these for unity's sake and risk abandoning their own rich traditions? In 1958 the novelist and poet Chinua Achebe (1930–2013) proposed a startling answer.

The Author

Born Albert Chinualumogu Achebe in British Nigeria, Achebe was the son of Christian evangelists and grew up feeling alienated from the local Igbo culture he deeply loved. His education was highly Eurocentric. Only while studying literature at the University of Ibadan did he realize that European literature had been leading him to despise his own race. Thus, he set out to tell stories from the perspective of his own Igbo people and, despite significant resistance, published his first novel, *Things Fall Apart.*

An instant success, the work became the bestselling African novel of all time. Achebe wrote four more widely acclaimed novels, including *Arrow of God* (1964) and *Anthills of the Savannah* (1987). He also achieved renown as a literary critic and educator, teaching at institutions such as the University of Massachusetts and Brown University. In 1990 a car wreck in Lagos, Nigeria, paralyzed him, and he was forced to spend the rest of his life in the West. He died in 2013, widely considered the Father of African Literature.

The Work

Things Fall Apart is a clear-eyed depiction of life in the Igbo village of Umuofia—and of the irreversible changes that British colonization brought. Fearlessly honest, the novel records both the sophistication of the Igbo people and cultural failures such as ritual infanticide. And while Christian missionaries are portrayed as well-meaning and occasionally noble believers, they are also depicted as narrow-minded and subservient to British colonial power.

The novel's protagonist is Okonkwo, a village leader whose devotion to manly strength and traditional values ultimately proves to be his undoing. When Okonkwo sets himself against the British colonizers, he ultimately finds himself dealing with cultural and economic forces beyond his control. In Okonkwo, Achebe tenderly depicts the strengths and shortfalls of traditional Igbo culture while also dramatizing the clash of civilizations.

The white man . . . has won our brothers, and our clan can no longer act like one. He has put a knife on the things that held us together and we have fallen apart.

Putting Things Back Together

Things Fall Apart is about personal and societal collapse. But the novel also suggests a model for cultural growth. Postcolonial Africa, Achebe avers, can never be restored to its precolonial state. Instead, he argues that young African nations forge a future by unsparingly confronting their history and drawing on the rich inheritance of both traditional and colonial cultures. His other fiction and his literary criticism suggest the same pragmatic approach.

In addition, the novel pioneers a uniquely African prose. Against the advice of many contemporaries, Achebe wrote in English, thus affirming its role as the *lingua franca* of Nigeria and other former colonies. But Achebe enriches his English with the cadences and imagery of Igbo. *Things Fall Apart*, then, refuses a false dichotomy, insisting instead that British influence and traditional culture can together form a dynamic whole.

UNIT 5 REVIEW

What Do You Know?

Understand the Background

1. Identify two authors who were personally affected by the rise of Nazi Germany.
2. Compare and contrast Joyce's and Heaney's attitudes toward Ireland. Use examples from their biographies and writings to support your conclusions.
3. Which Unit 5 author is a representative of postcolonialism?
4. List characteristics of modernism.

Apply the Concepts

5. Choose either "The Lake Isle of Innisfree" or "The Second Coming" and explain how Yeats's use of symbolism points to theme.
6. How does the third-person narrator in "A Cup of Tea" present Rosemary? What value does the use of third-person narrator offer as opposed to first-person?
7. Choose one of the stream-of-consciousness pieces. Use examples to explain how this approach differs from normal story narration and how it reflects modernist attitudes within your chosen work.
8. Identify and give examples of several rhetorical devices Churchill used in "Be Ye Men of Valor."
9. What primary method of rhetorical appeal did Churchill use? Why was this method dominant? Give several examples from his speech.
10. Give examples of how either Lawrence or Woolf is representative of modernism.
11. How do Smith and Larkin exemplify postwar attitudes in their poems?
12. Larkin, Hughes, and Heaney all use enjambment to great effect in their poetry. Choose one of their poems and explain how enjambment affects the poem.
13. Describe how Hughes develops an extended metaphor around his central image in "The Thought-Fox."
14. Identify and analyze the key conflict in "A Devoted Son."

Define each term and provide an example of each from a selection in Unit 5.

TERMS

- end rhyme
- third-person limited point of view
- stream of consciousness
- epiphany
- foreshadowing
- interior monologue
- aubade
- mood
- black humor
- perfect rhyme
- slant rhyme

Evaluate the Ideas

15. Evaluate the theme of either "Sailing to Byzantium" or "A Sick Collier" according to a biblical worldview. How are Truth and Beauty reflected?
16. Evaluate Mansfield's attitude toward human nature. Does she present a truthful reflection? How could Scripture inform her point of view?
17. Evaluate Joyce's depiction of religion from a biblical worldview.
18. Why does the speaker in "Aubade" say he is horrified of death but not remorseful for his mistakes? Evaluate his view of death from a biblical worldview.
19. Evaluate the contrasting perspectives of the drowned man and his acquaintances in "Not Waving but Drowning."

Write a Response

20. What is Gordimer's message in "The Moment Before the Gun Went Off"? How does the story interact with domestic and international politics of the day?
21. Compare Heaney's treatment of the father/son relationship with Desai's. Especially consider the development of character and conflict.

A

act. A major division in the action of a play.

aestheticism. A devotion to beauty, and therefore to art, as the highest human concern.

allegory. A story with a literal and an implied level of meaning. The implied level of meaning may suggest actual persons, places, events, and situations (as in historical allegory) or a set of ideas (as in conceptual allegory). A parable, a brief story told to illustrate or clarify a truth, is a form of allegory.

alliteration. Repetition of initial consonant sounds.

alliterative verse. Unrhymed poetry that uses alliteration to structure its lines.

allusion. A reference within a work of literature to something outside it, usually history or another artistic work. A **biblical allusion** refers to people, places, events, or passages from the Bible. A **classical allusion** refers to the writings of ancient Greece or Rome.

analogy. A detailed comparison of one thing to another dissimilar thing.

anapest. A **poetic foot** consisting of three syllables, two unstressed followed by a stressed.

anaphora. The repetition of words or phrases at the beginnings of lines or grammatical units.

anecdote. A short narrative of a single interesting or amusing incident.

antagonist. A force or character who opposes the protagonist.

antihero. The central character of a narrative who lacks traditional heroic traits (e.g., largeness, goodness, truth) and is instead predominantly flawed (e.g., weak, bumbling, thoughtless, dishonest).

antithesis. The use of syntactical parallelism in two adjacent phrases or clauses to emphasize their contrasting meanings.

aphorism. A short, pithy statement to express a serious truth.

apostrophe. An address to an absent person, abstraction, or inanimate object as if it were able to reply.

argumentation. The process of presenting claims and providing reasons to support those claims.

aside. A brief disclosure made by one actor in the presence of other actors who, by convention, are thought not to hear him.

assonance. The repetition of the same vowel sound in nearby stressed syllables.

atmosphere. The mood or emotion pervading a work, specifically when it is enhanced by a work's setting. See also **mood.**

aubade. A lyric poem or song greeting the dawn and often expressing the regret of two lovers at parting.

audience. The person or group of people to whom an author writes or a speaker delivers an address.

autobiography. A work of nonfiction in which an author tells his own life story.

B

ballad. A narrative poem often derived from folklore and originally intended to be sung or recited. **Folk ballads** are characteristically impersonal, compressed, dramatic (in use of dialogue and absence of transitions), ritualistic in effect (through various devices of repetition), and simple in stanza form. Common **ballad stanza** consists of quatrains of alternating four- and three-stress lines, usually rhyming *abcb*. This stress pattern is often termed **ballad meter**. Ballad meter is frequently iambic pentameter.

beast fable. A brief, fanciful tale that embodies a moral and in which animals act like humans.

bias. Personal preferences or viewpoints that inhibit one from seeing the potential value of others' judgments or rendering events or ideas impartially.

biography. A nonfiction account of the life events of a real person other than the author.

black humor. Also known as *black comedy*. A form of shock humor derived from treating grotesque, serious, or morbid situations comically.

blank verse. Unrhymed iambic pentameter.

Byronic hero. Named for Lord Byron and characterized as an unrepentant rebel rendered godlike, mysterious, and grandly aloof—an anguished but arrogant figure of impenetrable thought.

C

cacophony. The use of words that are harsh and discordant in sound.

caesura. A pause in the middle of a line of poetry, usually indicated by a mark of punctuation.

carpe diem. A Latin phrase meaning "seize the day."

catalog. A formal list of persons, objects, or attributes in poetry. Such lists are often associated with oral poetry and give a ritualistic effect to the passages in which they appear. See also **epic conventions**.

character. A person or being who performs the action of the story. A **major character** is portrayed more fully by the author; a **minor character** is portrayed less fully. A **round character** is distinguished physically and psychologically as an individual. A **flat character** has little individuality (few distinguishing physical or psychological details). A **sympathetic character** is one with whom the reader identifies or for whom he has favorable feelings; an **unsympathetic character** is one with whom the reader cannot identify or for whom he has strong feelings of dislike. A **static character** remains essentially the same throughout the story; a **dynamic character** (also called *developing character*) changes or develops as the story progresses.

characterization. The art of portraying a character in a narrative either directly (through telling) or indirectly (through showing). **Direct characterization** uses explicit statements to tell the reader about the character; **indirect characterization** reveals the qualities of a character by showing them through dialogue, description, or action.

chiasmus. A reversal in word order of the second of two parallel phrases, clauses, or sentences.

Christ figure. A character who resembles Jesus Christ in characterization or function; a form of biblical allusion drawing parallels between Christ's life and the character.

chronicle. A record of a place's or group's history chronologically by year, listing significant facts and events and often weaving all into an overall narrative.

climax. See **plot**.

comedy. Drama that focuses on light-hearted matters such as courtship and love and that may also be satirical.

comedy of manners. A kind of comedy that satirizes the social customs (the morals and manners) of a sophisticated society and often has love as its subject.

comitatus. In Anglo-Saxon tribal social tradition, a relationship of mutual respect and friendship in which a tribal leader protected and provided for his followers, who in turn pledged their loyalty and support in battle.

common meter. A standard hymn meter composed of quatrains of iambic lines typically alternating between tetrameter and trimeter (denoted in a hymn book as *8.6.8.6*).

conceit. A metaphor, often extended, that draws a parallel between highly dissimilar objects or concepts. In **metaphysical conceits** (see also **metaphysical poet**), these comparisons tended to reference more intellectually complex imagery and highlight shared qualities (rather than physical traits) in two very dissimilar things.

conflict. The opposition of two or more characters or forces; the three main conflicts are *man against a greater force*, *man against man*, and *man against himself*. Conflict may be **external** (between characters or between a character and his environment, whether society or nature) or **internal** (between a character and his own emotions or duties, or both).

connotative language. Language that conveys the meaning of a word with its implications and emotional associations.

consonance. The repetition of terminal consonant sounds and, more rarely, of internal consonants, that creates extra emphasis on the words involved.

couplet. A pair of rhymed lines. A **heroic couplet** is a pair of rhymed lines in iambic pentameter.

crisis. See **plot**.

cultural context. The beliefs, customs, and thoughts characteristic of the time and place in which a work of literature was created.

curtal sonnet. A curtailed version of the Italian sonnet. It reduces the octave to six lines and the sestet to four and a half lines. The invention of Gerard Manley Hopkins. See also **sonnet**.

D

dactyl. A **poetic foot** that contains one stressed and then two unstressed syllables.

deductive reasoning. Reasoning from a general truth to a specific conclusion.

deism. A rationalistic religious view prevalent during the eighteenth century. Deists tended to favor natural over revealed theology and to minimize the supernatural. Although their doctrinal positions varied considerably, many denied revelation and miracles and believed in an impersonal, distant Creator; the essential goodness of man, whose faults may be corrected by education; and an afterlife in which vice will be punished and virtue rewarded.

denotative language. Language that reflects the exact definition of a word as found in a dictionary.

denouement. See **plot**.

devotional literature. Literature, the purpose of which is to encourage individuals to deepen their devotion to God.

dialect. The manner of speech characteristic of a certain area or class. Dialectal differences may appear in vocabulary, grammatical constructions, and pronunciation.

dialogue. A conversation between characters. In a play, the text the actors will speak aloud on stage.

diary. An informal daily record of a person's life.

didactic. Literature that is instructive.

dimeter. See **meter**.

drama. Literature written to be acted.

dramatic monologue. A lyric poem in which a character (not the author) speaks to a silent audience about a critical moment in his life. The poem focuses on the character of the speaker, which is revealed entirely and unintentionally by what he says.

dramatic poetry. Poetry meant to be acted out.

dramatis personae. A list at the beginning of a script that identifies the roles or characters in the play.

E

elegy. Originally any poem of solemn meditation. Now traditionally *elegy* refers to a longer, formal poem lamenting the loss of a particular person (or loss in a more general sense) or meditating on the subject of death itself; in contemporary poetry, however, an elegy may designate any poem dealing with death or loss.

end-stopped lines. Poetic lines that end with a natural break or pause such as the end of a sentence or phrase, typically indicated by punctuation (the opposite of enjambed lines).

enjambment. A poetic device in which lines flow past the end of one verse line and into the next, breaking up a grammatical unit such as subject and verb or verb and object, with no punctuation at the end of the first verse line.

epic. A long, stylized narrative poem celebrating the deeds of a great national or ethnic hero of legend. **Folk** (or traditional) **epics** originate as oral poems (e.g., *Beowulf*) and reflect the customs, rituals, and ideals of their tribal society. A **literary epic** is written by an author from a literate society in imitation of the style and conventions of folk epics. The **mock epic** ridicules a subject by treating it in high heroic terms while allowing its triviality to appear (e.g., Chaucer's description of Chanticleer).

epic conventions. Traditional characteristics of epic poems. Typical conventions included a hero larger than life, a setting broad in scope, a supernatural element, a necessary journey or battle, and themes addressing topics central to human existence. Specific stylistic features included beginning **in medias res** with a statement of theme and an invocation to a muse (i.e., asking for inspiration), incorporating long, formal speeches that interrupt the poem's actions, and using devices such as **epic similes**, **catalogs**, and **stock epithets**.

epic simile. A **simile** in which the comparison is extended and elaborate. See also **epic conventions**.

epigram. A type of short poem from classical poetry that dealt with one subject and was noted for its wit, pithiness, and balanced, polished style.

epiphany. A sudden, revelatory insight into some aspect of life or reality that springs from an ordinary person, object, or event.

epithet. See **stock epithet**.

essay. A nonfiction prose composition (usually of shorter length) that explores a subject or argues for a thesis (**argumentative essay**) but that is not intended to address a subject in its entirety.

ethos. See **rhetorical appeal**.

euphony. The use of words whose sounds are pleasant and musical to the ear.

exposition. See **plot**.

F

falling action. See **plot**.

farce. A type of broad, highly exaggerated comedy.

fiction. A work that contains events and characters and sometimes settings invented by the author.

figurative language. An artful deviation from literal speech or normal word order (cf. metaphor, simile, personification, apostrophe, antithesis).

first-person narrator. See **point of view**.

flashback. A technique in which the author relates events that occurred before the action of the main story.

foil character. A character used to emphasize another character's opposing traits within a work.

foot. See **poetic foot**.

foreshadow. To hint at events that will occur later within the story.

frame tale. A group of tales unified by a central situation.

free verse. Also called *open form*. Poetry with no set **rhyme** or **meter**.

G

genre. A type or category of literature.

gothic. A term applied to a particular genre of works (most often novels) that are generally medieval in setting; gloomy, mysterious, and nightmarish in atmosphere; and suspenseful and often supernatural in plot.

H

hagiography. A biography of a saint.

heptameter. See **meter**.

hexameter. See **meter**.

historical narrative. An account of a historical event with characters who are real people.

Homeric epithet. See **stock epithet**.

humanist. During the Middle Ages a student of the humanities (subjects dealing with the human experience and culture).

hymn. A lyric poem of praise or thanksgiving to God.

hyperbole. Obvious overstatement or exaggeration intended to make a point.

I

iamb. A **poetic foot** consisting of one unstressed followed by one stressed syllable.

iambic pentameter. Ten-syllable poetic lines consisting of five iambic feet (unstressed-stressed). One of the most common meters in English poetry. See also **blank verse**.

imagery. Descriptive words or phrases that appeal to sense perceptions (visual, tactile, auditory, etc.) to create an impression.

inciting incident. See **plot**.

inductive reasoning. Reasoning from specific evidence to general principles.

in medias res. Latin phrase meaning "in the middle of things." See also **epic conventions**.

interior monologue. See **stream of consciousness**.

irony. The use of language to convey meaning other than what is stated or a contradiction in what is expected to happen and what actually happens. **Verbal irony** occurs when a speaker's meaning differs from what he expresses in words. **Situational irony** occurs when the story's events violate normal expectations. **Dramatic irony**, an application of situational irony, occurs when the reader or audience is aware of a plot development of which a character in the story is unaware.

K

kenning. A metaphoric compound of two words, peculiar to Germanic oral poetry.

L

legend. An ostensibly historical story that is popularly believed but that lacks factual evidence.

literary criticism. The practice of establishing criteria for and engaging in the analysis, interpretation, and evaluation of works of literature.

litotes. A type of understatement in which something is affirmed by denying its contrary.

logos. See **rhetorical appeal**.

lyric poetry. Originally denoting verse to be sung accompanied by a lyre, the term refers to poems that are typically brief, personal, and emotional, presenting the speaker's thoughts and feelings from his own perspective.

M

metaphor. An imaginative comparison consisting of the stated or implied equivalence of two dissimilar things. A metaphor consists of a **tenor**—its subject—and a **vehicle**—the image to which the subject is compared. An **extended metaphor** is developed beyond a single sentence or comparison.

metaphysical poet. A seventeenth-century English poet who explored intellectual and theological subjects ("metaphysics"), such as love and faith, through the use of intellectual poetic devices, such as **conceit** and **paradox**.

meter. The regular pattern of stressed and unstressed syllables in a line of poetry. Meter is labeled based on the number of poetic feet (see **poetic foot**) a line contains. One foot per line is called **monometer**; two feet, **dimeter**; three feet, **trimeter**; four feet, **tetrameter**; five feet, **pentameter**; six feet, **hexameter**; seven feet, **heptameter**; and eight feet, **octameter**.

miracle play. A drama portraying a story from the life of a church saint.

monometer. See **meter**.

mood. The emotion pervading a work. See also **atmosphere**.

morality play. An allegorical drama representing a spiritual theme or truth, the best example of which is *Everyman*.

motif. An element—object, image, description, or theme—that repeats throughout a specific work or a group of works.

mystery play. One of a cycle of short plays depicting biblical stories and meant to be performed together.

N

narrative poetry. Poetry that tells a story.

narrator. The individual telling the story to the reader.

naturalism. An outgrowth of realism applying Darwinism to literature. Naturalism emphasized three main ideas: that God (if He exists at all), nature, and society are indifferent to individuals (i.e., cosmic chill); that humans are mere animals; and that they are at the mercy of forces they cannot control (i.e., the trap of social circumstances).

neoclassicism. A movement (1660s–1700s) that emulated the aesthetics of ancient Greece and Rome with an adherence to the rules of genre and an emphasis on clarity, order, decorum, the rule of reason, and didacticism.

nonfiction. Prose that tells of real people and events.

novel. An extended work of fictional prose.

novella. A prose work of medium length, longer than a short story yet shorter than a novel.

novel of sensibility. See **sensibility**.

O

octameter. See **meter**.

octave. A stanza of eight lines.

ode. A long lyric poem elevated in style and written in a complex stanza on a serious theme and often for a specific occasion.

onomatopoeia. The use of words that imitate the sounds being described (e.g., *hiss*, *buzz*).

oral tradition. The audible means by which much cultural knowledge was transferred from generation to generation before the prevalent use of written language.

P

pamphlet. A short publication that includes arguments and information on a single (often controversial) subject.

paradox. A statement that seems to be self-contradictory yet actually makes sense when understood in the right context.

parallelism. Similarity in the structure of two or more phrases, clauses, or sentences.

parody. A special form of **satire** that mocks its subject by incongruous imitation of its style.

pastoral. Refers to literary works that idealize the simple life close to nature, especially that of shepherds. The tradition descended from classical times and occurs frequently in Renaissance poetry.

pathos. See **rhetorical appeal**.

pentameter. See **meter**.

persona. The person created by the author to tell the story, affecting the way a story is told.

personification. Giving human characteristics to something, such as an inanimate object or abstract concept, that is not human.

perspective. The author's mental view or outlook that influences his account of a story.

play. See **drama**.

plot. A connected series of events arranged to produce a definite sense of movement toward a specific goal. The **exposition** introduces the reader to the setting, the characters, and the situation. The **inciting incident** is the event that introduces the **conflict** and sets it in motion. The events that follow the inciting incident and lead up to the crisis compose the **rising action**. The **crisis** is the major turning point for the protagonist, the point at which something happens that affects the outcome of the story and determines the future of the main character. The point at which the plot reaches the moment of highest emotional intensity for the reader is the **climax**, which may or may not be the same moment as the crisis. The events that unfold the results of the crisis and lead to the conclusion compose the **falling action**. The final outcome of a story and the last element of the plot in which the major complications are explained or settled is called the **denouement**, or *resolution*.

poetic diction. Diction meant to elevate important genres by using refined words (archaisms, Latinisms), and elaborately rephrased ideas to avoid everyday language.

poetic foot. The predominantly repeated unit in a poetic line: a specific combination of two or three stressed and/or unstressed syllables. See also **iamb**, **trochee**, **anapest**, **dactyl**, **spondee**, and **pyrrhic**.

poetry. Artfully compressed thought resulting in the elevated expression of ideas.

point of view. The perspective or angle from which a story is told. In **first-person point of view** the narrator, as one of the story's characters, refers to himself as *I* throughout the piece. In **third-person point of view** the narrator stands outside the story and refers to the characters with pronouns such as *he*, *she*, or *they*. The third-person point of view may be **limited** (the narrator "gets inside" only one character) or **omniscient** (the storyteller "knows all").

proscenium. A three-walled stage at one end of a room separating the audience from the action by an arched invisible "wall" behind which a curtain is often hung. This kind of stage dominated in the late seventeenth century and is common today.

prose romance. Also called *romance novel*. A romance without the lines and other conventions of poetry but with the usual romance content. See also **romance**.

protagonist. The main character of a story.

psychological realism. Realistic fiction that emphasizes characterization by focusing on underlying thought processes and motivations.

purpose (authorial). The purpose for which an author wrote a work (e.g., to describe, to explain).

pyrrhic. A **poetic foot** consisting of two unstressed syllables.

Q

quatrain. A four-line stanza, one of the most common stanzas in English poetry.

R

rationalism. The belief that human reason rather than divine revelation or human authority is the source of all knowledge and the only valid basis for action.

realism. A literary style that seeks to reflect life accurately in subject matter and in depiction. Also, the literary movement of the nineteenth century that reacted against romanticism to present life as it was, not as it should be.

refrain. A line or group of lines repeated throughout a poem or song.

repartee. Besting another's remark or turning it to one's own advantage in a contest of wits.

repetition. The act of creating patterns or emphasis by repeating elements (e.g., sounds, words, lines, meter, or syntax).

rhetoric. The effective use of language for persuasive purposes (e.g., through analogy, rhetorical appeals, and rhetorical devices).

rhetorical appeal. An appeal in argumentative and persuasive writing to logic, emotion, or credible authorities (i.e., **logos**, **pathos**, or **ethos** respectively).

rhetorical devices. A deviation from the standard use of language—mainly in syntactical arrangement (word order)—to achieve a special effect. See also **parallelism**, **repetition**, **chiasmus**, **antithesis**.

rhetorical question. A question asked, not to receive an answer, but to achieve an effect.

rhyme. Two or more words having identical sounds in the last stressed vowel and all the sounds following that vowel. **Perfect rhyme** is the agreement of sounds from the last stressed vowel sound onward, with a difference in the immediately preceding consonant sounds (e.g., *came*, *shame*). When the rhyming sounds consist of only one syllable, the rhyme is known as masculine (e.g., *came*, *shame*). When the rhyming sounds include more than one syllable, the rhyme is called feminine (e.g., *hiring*, *firing*). **Imperfect rhyme** includes partial rhyme and eye rhyme. **Slant** (or **partial**) **rhyme** shows agreement in terminal consonant sounds (see **consonance**) but disagreement in the preceding vowel sounds (e.g., *held*, *build*) or agreement in the vowel sounds (see **assonance**) but disagreement in the succeeding consonant sounds (e.g., *in*, *trim*). **Eye rhyme** is based on similarity of sight rather than sound and consists of identical spelling (e.g., *laughter*, *daughter*). Rhyme is distinguished also by its location: **end rhyme** refers to rhymes at the ends of lines; **internal rhyme** to rhymes within a line.

rhyme scheme. The pattern of rhyme sounds in a poem or in a stanza of poetry, described by assigning to each rhyme sound successive letters of the alphabet.

rhythm. A more or less regular pace or beat. As rhythm approaches regularity in poetry, it becomes **meter**. Usually looser, prose rhythm involves syllable groups of varying length and patterning and occurs sporadically.

rising action. See **plot**.

romance. A poetic narrative that focused on courtly life and the knightly code of chivalry rather than the heroism of a tribal warrior found in the epic (which it overtook in popularity).

romanticism. In Britain, a reaction against neoclassicism that emphasized *individual* over group perceptions and judgments, preferred *imagination* and intuition to reason as a way of perceiving truth, and looked to *nature* for inspiration. It valued the emotionally dynamic over the rationally controlled and exalted man in nature over man in society. Literary romantics thought themselves *visionaries*, intuiting and communicating a new future. In their work, they preferred the natural to the artificial (e.g., common diction and imagery), stressed the importance of originality, and invoked *the sublime* by referencing *the distant* in time and place and by incorporating the supernatural.

S

sarcasm. A type of verbal irony in the form of mock praise or mock assent (the expression's literal meaning is a contradiction of its implied meaning).

satire. Corrective ridicule in literature, or a work that is designed to correct an evil by means of ridicule. **Horatian satire** is genial and generally lighthearted, while **Juvenalian satire** is biting, savage, and more serious in intent. **Social satire** points its critiques at a society.

scansion. The process of identifying the two major features of meter (metrical unit and foot) in a particular poem.

scene. In a drama, a subdivision of an act that does not typically contain a change of time or place.

sensibility. An eighteenth-century emphasis on emotion, reacting against neoclassicism's emphasis on reason and anticipating some aspects of romanticism. The ability to sympathize with others and to appreciate beauty is seen as evidence of goodness, which such literature often meant to encourage. Sometimes called **sentimentality**. The **novel of sensibility** induces audience sympathy for characters who triumph over difficult situations through such goodness.

sensory details. Descriptions appealing concretely to the five senses.

sentimental comedy. Drama which featured relatable middle-class protagonists who used goodness to defeat vice and which often elicited audience tears to create sympathy for their themes. See also **sensibility**.

sentimentality. See **sensibility**.

sestet. A stanza of six lines.

setting. The time, place, and way of life in which the action of a story occurs.

short story. A brief work of prose fiction.

signal words. Verbal cues that guide readers through the writer's train of thought.

simile. A comparison of two unlike things using *like* or *as*.

slave narrative. An autobiographical account of the author's experience as a slave.

social Darwinism. The belief that certain biological principles (e.g., natural selection) applied not only to plants and animals but also to humans and their society.

soliloquy. A speech in which a character expresses his thoughts directly to the audience. A soliloquy is spoken by an actor who is alone or thinks he is alone on stage.

sonnet. A lyric poem of fourteen lines in iambic pentameter conventionally rhyming according to one of two patterns. The **Italian** (or **Petrarchan**) **sonnet** consists of an octave, rhyming *abbaabba*, followed by a sestet, rhyming variously with two or three new rhymes (e.g., *cdecde, cdccdc,* or *cdedce)*. Popularized by the Italian poet Petrarch (1304–74), the form was introduced into England by Sir Thomas Wyatt (1503–42) and widely cultivated in England during the Renaissance. The **English** (or **Shakespearean**) **sonnet** consists of three quatrains with a concluding couplet, the whole rhyming *abab cdcd efef gg*. The English sonnet was improvised from the Italian by the Earl of Surrey (ca. 1517–47) and refined by Shakespeare (1564–1616).

speaker (in poetry). The character or person who voices a poem. See also **persona**.

speech. An oral, public communication that can be used for various purposes.

Spenserian stanza. A nine-line stanza, rhyming *ababbcbcc* with eight iambic pentameter lines followed by a line of iambic hexameter. Devised by Edmund Spenser, it was popular among romantic poets.

spondee. A **poetic foot** that consists of two stressed syllables.

sprung rhythm. An invention of Gerard Manley Hopkins, sprung rhythm is a variation of strong-stress meter. Strong stresses may directly follow each other or be interrupted by one to three lesser stresses.

stanza. Division of a poem based on thought, meter, or rhyme, usually recognized by the number of lines it contains and distinguished in print by spacing.

stock epithet. A stock phrase inserted to describe or rename a particular person or thing that recurs in a poem, generally in an epic. Also termed *Homeric epithet*.

stream of consciousness. A type of writing in which the author attempts to reproduce the flow of thoughts in a character's mind with little attention to grammar or logic. **Interior monologue** is a type of stream of consciousness narration.

style. The author's manner of expression in prose or verse, in written or oral discourse. Style is formed by a combination of elements such as syntax (word order), diction (word choice), **figurative language**, **imagery**, **tone**, and **voice**.

sublime, the. A momentary emotional experience in which readers transcend everyday living and briefly grasp ultimates of beauty, horror, time, or grandeur. See also **romanticism**.

symbol. A person, place, or thing within a narrative or poem that means something in addition to itself.

T

tenor. See **metaphor**.

tercet. Also known as *triplet*. A **stanza** of three lines that usually share the same rhyme.

terza rima. A verse form in which three-line stanzas (**tercets**) interlock in the following rhyme pattern: *aba, bcb, cdc, ded*, etc.

tetrameter. See **meter**.

text structure. The organization of a text's contents.

theater-in-the-round. A stage design in which the audience completely surrounds an open stage and is on the same level or slightly elevated. This arrangement, which harks back to ancient Greece and Rome, gives the audience a feeling of engagement with the actors.

theme. A recurring or emerging idea in a work of literature. A work may have many themes. Its major theme is its main point, similar to the thesis of an essay. A theme may be **explicit** or **implicit**. Theme serves a didactic purpose by embodying and emphasizing a work's message and serves an aesthetic purpose by providing coherence.

thrust. The most common Elizabethan stage design, which protruded out into an open air courtyard from the thatch-roofed backstage area.

tone. The attitude of an author toward the subject. Tone is the emotional view of the subject (indignation, awe, compassion, derision, etc.) the reader is meant to share with the author.

tragedy. Drama in which the protagonist experiences tremendous suffering, resulting in a catastrophe, or disastrous conclusion. Considered by Renaissance culture to be a higher form than comedy and thus frequently featured kings and nobles whose actions affect national destinies. Renaissance tragedies reflected Aristotelian conceptions of the hero and plot. The **tragic hero** is the play's protagonist (usually someone of importance) who is not inherently bad but makes bad decisions. The **tragic flaw** is the character flaw that triggers his downfall. The **tragic plot** comprises the action surrounding this regrettable decision leading to the hero's reversal of fortunes and ruination. These events were meant to evoke audience pity and fear.

transcendentalism. A movement originating among the German disciples of Immanuel Kant (1724–1804) that sought a higher religious view than Christianity and a higher artistic ideal than neoclassicism. Its god is a World Spirit inhabiting all. Its bible is nature and the human heart. Access to truth is through intuition rather than through reason or revelation.

tricolon. The repetition of three parallel phrases or clauses of equal length within a sentence, often building with emphasis (e.g., *I came; I saw; I conquered*).

trimeter. See **meter.**

trochee. A **poetic foot** that contains a stressed and then an unstressed syllable.

U

unities, the. The unities consist of unity of action, unity of place, and unity of time. These refer to the belief that a play should have only one major plot line and should take place in one setting over the course of only one day. The unities originated with Aristotle and heavily influenced Renaissance drama in particular.

utopia. A genre of fictional writings about ideal societies.

V

variation. New grammatically parallel phrases to elaborate on something just stated.

vehicle. See **metaphor**.

verisimilitude. The inclusion of minute, even superfluous details to create an allusion of actuality.

verse epistle. A minor neoclassical poetic genre in which a poem, usually of high moral seriousness, takes the form of an address to a friend.

voice. The unique imprint of an author's personality on a work. In considering the characters, incidents, style, and particularly tone, the reader forms an impression of the creator of a work.

W

wit. Brief verbal expressions that amuse listeners through clever yet unexpected turns of phrase or connections between ideas.

worldview. The philosophical viewpoint from which a person examines the world and draws conclusions.

wyrd. Fate.

PUBLIC DOMAIN WORKS

UNIT 1

70–72 Sir Arthur Quiller-Couch, ed. *The Oxford Book of Ballads*. Oxford: Clarendon, 1910. **73** *Sumer is icumen in*, 2nd Ed. London: Novello, 1914. **73** Sir Arthur Quiller-Couch, *The Oxford Book of English Verse: 1250–1918*. 1900. Reprint, New York: Oxford UP, 1955. **83** John Strong Perry Tatlock, ed. *Representative English Plays: From the Middle Ages to the End of the Nineteenth Century*. New York: Century, 1917.

UNIT 2

141–42 Albert S. Cook, ed. *The Defense of Poesy*. Boston: Ginn, 1890. **144–45** *Salve Deus Rex Judaeorum*. London: Valentine Simmes, 1611. **148–50** Charles W. Eliot, ed. *Essays, Civil and Moral and The New Atlantis*. Vol. 3. New York: P. F. Collier, 1909. **152–54** *Observations upon Experimental Philosophy*. London: Maxwell, 1666. (Early English Books Online and The Huntington Library, San Marino, CA). **155** *Poems and Fancies*. London: J. Martin and J. Allestrye, 1653 (Early English Books Online and The Huntington Library, San Marino, CA). **159** *The 1662 Book of Common Prayer*. Cambridge: John Baskerville, 1762. **161–63** *The Acts and Monuments of John Foxe*. Vol. 8. London: Seeley, Burnside and Seeley, 1849. **166** John Wycliffe, trans. *The New Testament*. 1388. Reprint, Oxford: Clarendon, 1879. **166** William Tyndale, trans. *The New Testament*. 1534. Reprint, Cambridge: Cambridge UP, 1938. **167** *The Geneva Bible*, 1560. Reprint, Peabody, MA: Hendrickson Publishers, 2007. **167–68** Authorized Version of The Holy Bible, 1611. **171–78** George Armstrong Wauchope, ed. *Spenser's The Faerie Queene*. Book 1. London: Macmillan,1903. **189** *Sonnets and Poems (Selected)*. London: John Long, 1906. **190–91** W. J. Rolfe, ed. *Shakespeare's Sonnets*. New York: American Book, 1905. **194–95** A. H. Bullen, ed. *England's Helicon: A Collection of Lyrical and Pastoral Poems*. London: Lawrence & Bullen, 1899. **198–200** E. K. Chambers, ed. *The Poems of John Donne*. Vol. 1. London: Lawrence & Bullen, 1896. **202–3** Arthur Waugh, ed. *The Poems of George Herbert*. London: Oxford UP, 1907. **205–6** *Plays and Poems*. London: George Routledge, 1895. **214–80** Janie Caves McCauley, ed. *The Tragedy of Macbeth*. 1606. Reprint, *British Literature for Christian Schools Teacher's Guide*, 2nd Ed. Greenville, SC: BJU Press, 1984.

UNIT 3

297 Edward Everett Hale, Jr., ed. *Selections from the Poetry of Robert Herrick*. Boston: Ginn, 1895. **297** *Songs and Sonnets*. New York: R. H. Russell, 1901. **299–300** *The Poetical Works of Andrew Marvell*. Boston: Little, Brown, 1857. **303–4** Laura E. Lockwood, ed. *Selected Essays of Education, Areopagitica, The Commonwealth*. Boston: Houghton Mifflin, 1911. **305** Charles W. Eliot, ed. *The Complete Poems of John Milton*. Vol. 4. New York: P. F. Collier, 1909. **307–13** Albert Perry Walker, ed. *Selections from Paradise Lost*. Book 1. Boston: D. C. Heath, 1897. **315–19** Henry B. Wheatley, ed. *The Diary of Samuel Pepys*. Vols. 4 and 5. London: George Bell, 1894–95. **323–31** *The Life and Adventures of Robinson Crusoe*. Boston: D. Lothrop, 1884. **334–35** *The Tatler*. Philadelphia: M. Wallis Woodward, 1835. **336–37** Alexander Chalmers, ed. *The Spectator*. Vol. 1. New York: D. Appleton, 1853. **340–41** A. M. Van Dyke, ed. *The Rape of the Lock and An Essay on Man*. New York: American Book, 1898. **342–44** W. C. Armstrong, ed. *The Complete Poetical Works of Alexander Pope*, 4th Ed. Vol. 1. Hartford: Silas Andrus, 1848. **347–56** G. Ravenscroft Dennis, ed. *The Prose Works of Jonathan Swift*. Vol. 8: *Gulliver's Travels*. London: George Bell, 1905. **362–63** *Johnson's Dictionary of the English Language*. Vol. 1 (A–K). London: J. Johnson, 1799. **364** *Johnson's Dictionary of the English Language*. Vol. 2 (L–Z). London: J. Johnson, 1799. **365–66** Arthur Murphy, ed. *The Works of Samuel Johnson: A New Edition in Twelve Volumes*. Vol. 2. London: F. C. and J. Rivington, 1823. **368–73** *Boswell's Life of Johnson*. Vol. 1. London: Henry Frowde, 1904. **375–79** Austin Lane Poole, ed. *The Poetical Works of Gray and Collins*. London: Oxford UP, 1917. **385–90** *The Pilgrim's Progress*. London: J. M. Dent, 1910. **392** G. Burder, ed. *The Psalms and Hymns of the Rev. Isaac Watts*. London: Whittingham, 1806. **393** *Hymns and Devotional Poetry*. New York: Protestant Episcopal Society for the Promotion of Evangelical Knowledge, 1858. **404–7** *The Life of Olaudah Equiano, or Gustavus Vassa, the African*. Boston: Isaac Knapp, 1837. **408–10** *The Speech of William Wilberforce, Esq., Representative for the County of York, on Wednesday the 13th of May, 1789, on the Question of the Abolition of the Slave Trade*. London: Logographic, n.d.

UNIT 4

429–30, 434 F. W. Farrar, ed. *With the Poets: A Selection of English Poetry*. New York: Funk & Wagnalls, 1883. **431** *The Poems and Songs of Robert Burns*. Vol. 6. New York: P. F. Collier, 1909. **435** John Sampson, ed. *The Poetical Works of William Blake*. London: Oxford UP, 1914. **436** John Sampson, ed. *The Poems of William Blake*. London: Chatto & Windus, 1921. **438–43** Miriam Brody, ed. *A Vindication of the Rights of Woman*. 1792. Reprint, London: Penguin Books, 1975. **446–53** *Pride and Prejudice*. 1908. Reprint, David M. Shapard, ed. *The Annotated Pride and Prejudice*. New York: Anchor Books, 2004. **458–59** Ernest Rhys, ed. *The Shorter Poems of William Wordsworth*. London: J. M. Dent, 1907. **460–63** *The Poetical Works of William Wordsworth*. Vol. 2. London: Edward Moxon, 1849. **466–78** James Weber Linn, ed. *Poems by Wordsworth, Coleridge, Shelley, and Keats*. New York: Henry Holt, 1911. **481–85** *Childe Harold and Other Poems*. New York: D. Appleton, 1899. **486** Matthew Arnold, ed. *Selected Poems of Lord Byron*. New York: Thomas Y. Crowell, 1893. **489–94** W. J. Alexander, ed. *Select Poems of Shelley*. Boston: Ginn, 1898. **497, 499** Laurence Binyon, ed. *The Poetical Works of John Keats*. Edinburgh: Turnball and Spears, 1916. **498** *Poems*. London: George Bell, 1897. **506–10** *Poems of Tennyson, Poet Laureate*, New Revised Ed. Boston: James R. Osgood, 1877. **511** Henry Van Dyke, ed. *Poems of Tennyson*. New York: Charles Scribner's Sons, 1920. **515–16** *Poems of Robert Browning*. New York: A. L. Burt, 1872. **518** *Poems*, 4th Ed. Vol. 3. London: Chapman & Hall, 1856. **521–24** *Past and Present*. New York: Charles Scribner's Sons, 1897. **525–29** *The Modern British Essayists*. Vol. 5. Philadelphia: Carey & Hart, 1852. **530–31** *Hard Times*. Vol. 1. Cambridge: Riverside, 1869. **535–49** *The Life and Works of the Sisters Brontë*. Vol. 1 New York: Harper & Brothers, 1899. **553–54** *Poems*. Vol. 2. London: Macmillan, 1903. **556–57** *Wessex Poems and Other*

Verses. London: Macmillan, 1908. **559–60** W. H. Gardner, ed. *Poems of Gerard Manley Hopkins*, 3rd Ed. London: Oxford UP, 1918. **563–68** *The Plays of Oscar Wilde*. Vol. 2. Boston: John W. Luce, 1905. **571–74** *Plain Tales from the Hills*. Garden City, NY: Doubleday, Page, 1922.

UNIT 5

596 *The Poetical Works of William B. Yeats*. Vol. 1. Lyrical Poems. New York: Macmillan, 1920. **598** *Later Poems*. London: Macmillan, 1922. **600–5** *The Doves' Nest and Other Stories*. New York: Alfred A. Knopf, 1923. **608–12** *Dubliners*. London: Grant Richards, 1914. **615–21** *The Prussian Officer and Other Stories*. London: Duckworth, 1914. **624–29** *Monday or Tuesday*. 1921. Reprint, London: Hesperus, 2003.

ILLUSTRATORS

All unit and part openers: Jon Andrews

UNIT 1 INTRODUCTION

Map of Britain: Sarah Lompe

UNIT 1 PART 1

***Beowulf*:** Justin Gerard

***The Anglo-Saxon Chronicle*:** Freda Sue

***Sir Gawain and the Green Knight*:** Justin Gerard

Thomas Malory biography: Zach Franzen

***Le Morte d'Arthur*:** Zach Franzen

UNIT 1 PART 2

***Caedmon's Hymn*:** Sandy Mehus

Popular Genres ("Sir Patrick Spens"): David Lompe

Popular Genres ("Get Up and Bar the Door"): David Lompe

Popular Genres ("The Cuckoo Song"): David Lompe

Popular Genres ("I sing of a maiden"): David Lompe

***Revelations of Divine Love*:** Courtney Wise

UNIT 1 PART 3

***The Canterbury Tales* (selection title page and border throughout):** Jon Andrews

***The Canterbury Tales* (characters throughout):** Zach Franzen

"The Nun's Priest's Tale" (header): Jon Andrews

"The Nun's Priest's Tale" (illustrations): Zach Franzen

UNIT 2 PART 1

***Utopia*:** Jon Andrews

***An Apology for Poetry* (header):** Jon Andrews

***Essays* (header):** Jon Andrews

***Observations upon Experimental Philosophy*:** Jon Andrews/Sandy Mehus

"A World Made by Atomes": Jon Andrews/Sandy Mehus

UNIT 2 PART 2

Beatitudes: Chris Koelle

1 Corinthians: Chris Koelle

***The Faerie Queen*:** David Lompe

UNIT 3 PART 1

***Areopagitica* (header):** Jon Andrews

Sonnet 19 (header): Jon Andrews

***Paradise Lost* (header):** Jon Andrews

***Paradise Lost* (last illustration):** Jon Andrews

UNIT 3 PART 2

***Robinson Crusoe*:** Aaron Miller

***The Tatler* No. 25.:** Zach Franzen

***The Spectator* No. 34.:** Zach Franzen

***An Essay on Man*:** Marc Scheff

***An Essay on Criticism*:** Marc Scheff

***Gulliver's Travels*:** Jonathan Bartlett

UNIT 3 PART 3

***Elegy Written in a Country Churchyard*:** Jeremy Wilson

UNIT 3 PART 4

***The Pilgrim's Progress*:** Michael Wimmer

Hymnody: Marc Scheff

***Oroonoko*:** Simon Carr

***The Life of Olaudah Equiano, or Gustavas Vassa, the African*:** Del Thompson

UNIT 5 PART 1

"A Sick Collier": Bryndon Everett

UNIT 5 PART 2

"A Devoted Son": Courtney Wise/Sarah Lompe

Key: (t) top; (c) center; (b) bottom;
(l) left; (r) right; (bg) background

FRONT MATTER

xiil "Three Ladies Adorning a Term of Hymen" by Sir Joshua Reynolds/Wikimedia Commons/Public Domain; **xii**r Pictorial Press Ltd/Alamy Stock Photo

UNIT 1

PART 1

2–3 stevekeall/iStock Editorial/Getty Images Plus; **4**l "Bewcastle Cross, Plate of Runes" by Cook, Albert S. 1912. The Date of the Ruthwell and Bewcastle Crosses. Yale University Press./Wikimedia Commons/Public Domain; **4**r Print Collector/Hulton Archive/Getty Images; **5** Print Collector/Hulton Archive/Getty Images; **6–7**bg Loop Images/Universal Images Group/Getty Images; **7**t De Agostini/A. Dagli Orti/De Agostini Picture Library/Getty Images; **8** "De Grey Hours f.28.v St. Thomas of Canterbury"/The National Library of Wales/Wikimedia Commons/Public Domain; **9** Emile Signol/Getty Images; **10**t "Holbein Danse Macabre 37"/Die imposante Galerie/Wikimedia Commons/Public Domain; **10**b "Holbein Danse Macabre 15"/Die imposante Galerie/Wikimedia Commons/Public Domain; **11** "Map-Wars of the Roses"/Wikimedia Commons/Public Domain; **12** "God Speed" by Edmund Leighton/Wikimedia Commons/Public Domain; **13** Walker Art Library/Alamy Stock Photo; **16–17**bg, **22–23**bg Nopporn Subyen/Shutterstock.com; **17**b, **19, 20, 22**b, **23**t, **25, 27, 28, 30** Illustrations by Justin Gerard; **36–37** Muessig/Shutterstock.com; **38, 40–46, 48–51** siam sompunya/Shutterstock.com

PART 2

65–67bg Nopporn Subyen/Shutterstock.com; **68** "Pieter Brueghel the Younger - The Peasant Wedding - Google Art Project"/Wikimedia Commons/Public Domain; **74** "St Julian's Church, Norwich, 2009 by Charles Hutchins from London, United Kingdom"/Wikimedia Commons/CC By-SA 2.0; **82**t Ron Dahlquist/Photodisc/Getty Images; **82**t Ron Dahlquist/Photodisc/Getty Images; **82**b imageBROKER/Superstock; **83** Public Domain

PART 3

86–87bg Dmitry Naumov/Shutterstock.com; **86**t Stock Montage/Archive Photos/Getty Images; **116** Culture Club/Hulton Archive/Getty Images

UNIT 2

PART 1

120–21bg © Areinwald | Dreamstime; **120** (portrait) "Workshop of Hans Holbein the Younger - Portrait of Henry VIII - Google Art Project"/Wikimedia Commons/Public Domain; **120** (frame) Karina Bakalyan/Shutterstock.com; **121** (portrait) "Maria Tudor1"/Wikimedia Commons/Public Domain; **121** (frame) Det-anan/Shutterstock.com; **122, 127** Public Domain; **123** World History Archive/Superstock; **124** North Wind Picture Archives/Alamy Stock Photo; **125**t North Wind Picture Archives/Alamy Stock Photo; **125**b Joao Virissimo/Shutterstock.com; **126**l (portrait) "James I of England" by Daniel Mytens/Wikimedia Commons/Public Domain; **126**l (frame) Prokrida/Shutterstock.com; **126**r (portrait) "King Charles I after original" by van Dyck/Wikimedia Commons/Public Domain; **126**r (frame) LiliGraphie/Shutterstock.com; **130** "Hans Holbein, the Younger - Sir Thomas More - Google Art Project"/Wikimedia Commons/Public Domain; **140** "Sir Philip Sidney from NPG"/Wikimedia Commons/Public Domain; **143** "Nicholas Hilliard 010"/Wikimedia Commons/Public Domain; **144** Everett - Art/Shutterstock.com; **146** "Francis Bacon, Viscount St Alban from NPG (2)"/Wikimedia Commons/Public Domain; **151** "Margaret Cavendish, Duchess of Newcastle" by Peter Lely/Wikimedia Commons/Public Domain; **152–55**bg siam sompunya/Shutterstock.com

PART 2

158–59bg Aisle/Alamy Stock Photo; **160** "John Foxe from NPG cleaned"/Wikimedia Commons/Public Domain; **161**bg "Foxe's Book of Martyrs title page"/Wikimedia Commons/Public Domain; **163** Pictorial Press Ltd/Alamy Stock Photo; **164–65**bg © iStock.com/dennisvdw; **169** (portrait) ART Collection/Alamy Stock Photo; **169** (frame); Kuznetcov_Konstantin/Shutterstock.com; **179** "Darnley stage 3"/Wikimedia Commons/Public Domain; **180** "Spanish Armada"/Wikimedia Commons/Public Domain

PART 3

184l "Portrait of Francesco Petrarca" by Altichiero/Wikimedia Commons/Public Domain; **184**tr Chronicle/Alamy Stock Photo; **184**br FALKENSTEINFOTO/Alamy Stock Photo; **186** (painting) Art Collection 2/Alamy Stock Photo; **186** (frame) tomertu/Shutterstock.com; **188** Gift of J. Pierpont Morgan, 1917, metmuseum.org; **189** LAURA_VN/Shutterstock.com; **190** (locket) © Aperturesound | Dreamstime; **190**l "Self-portrait with a Sunflower" by Anthony van Dyck/Wikimedia Commons/Public Domain; **190**r "Portrait of a young woman" by Nicolaes Maes/Wikimedia Commons/Public Domain; **191** © iStock.com/NoDerog; **192**t GL Archive/Alamy Stock Photo; **192**b "Portrait of Sir Walter Raleigh" by Nicholas Hilliard/Wikimedia Commons/Public Domain; **194, 203** (painting), **206** (painting) Public Domain; **195** "The Shepherdess of Rolleboise" by Daniel Ridgway Knight/Wikimedia Commons/Public Domain; **196** "John Donne" by Isaac Oliver/Wikimedia Commons/Public Domain; **198, 199** © Rajesh Misra | Dreamstime; **200** Nejron Photo/Shutterstock.com; **201** Classic Vision/Media Bakery; **202** donatas1205/Shutterstock.com; **203** (frame) MikhailSh/Shutterstock.com; **204** "Benjamin Jonson" by Abraham van Blyenberch retouched/Wikimedia Commons/Public Domain; **205** © iStock.com/duncan1890; **206**bg Ovidiu Stoica/Shutterstock

.com; **206**t Lana Veshta/Shutterstock.com; **206** (frame) valkoinen/Shutterstock.com

PART 4

210 Sam Vaudrey/Alamy Stock Photo; **211** "Shakespeare"/ Wikimedia Commons/Public Domain; **212** Public Domain; **214–15, 217–18, 221, 223, 225–27, 230, 232, 234, 237–38, 241, 244, 246–47, 251–52, 255, 258, 260–62, 264–65, 270–72, 274–79** (metal plaque images) donatas1205/Shutterstock.com; **214, 218**b, **221**t, **227**t, **232**b, **237**c, **238**t, **246**t, **249, 255**t, **258**c, **259, 261**t, **264**t, **265**b, **271**t, **279**t, BJU Photo Services; **223**t stocker1970/Shutterstock.com, **224** Vince Reilly/Shutterstock.com, **230**t Damian Gil/Shutterstock.com; **241**t Nella/Shutterstock.com; **268** michelaubryphoto/Shutterstock.com; **275**t LouieLea/Shutterstock.com; **277**t Lukas Juocas/Shutterstock.com

UNIT 3

PART 1

284–85b Kiev.Victor/Shutterstock.com; **285**t "Oliver Cromwell" by Samuel Cooper/Wikimedia Commons/Public Domain; **286**t "Arrival of Charles II, King of England, in Rotterdam, 24 May 1660" by Lieve Pietersz Verschuier/Wikimedia Commons/Public Domain; **286** (portrait) "Charles II" by John Michael Wright/Wikimedia Commons/Public Domain; **286** (frame) Various-Everythings/Shutterstock.com; **287** (portrait) "Double-portrait of William II (1626-1650), Prince of Orange, and his wife Mary Stuart (1631-1660)" by Gerard van Honthorst/Wikimedia Commons/Public Domain; **287** (frame) Kittibowornphatnon/Shutterstock.com; **287**c "India1765and1805b"/Edinburgh Geographical Institute/Wikimedia Commons/Public Domain; **287**b, **288**t North Wind Picture Archives/Alamy Stock Photo; **288–89**b Digital Image Library/Alamy Stock Photo; **289**t "John Wesley preaching outside a church. Engraving. Wellcome V0006868"/Wikimedia Commons/CC by SA-4.0; **290**t Piotr Wawrzyniuk/Shutterstock.com; **290–91**b AlexeiLogvinovich/Shutterstock .com; **291**t "Nicolas de Largillière, François-Marie Arouet dit Voltaire (vers 1724-1725) -002-transparent"/Wikimedia Commons/Public Domain; **291**c "Voltaire Philosophy of Newton frontispiece"/Wikimedia Commons/Public Domain; **292** "Three Ladies Adorning a Term of Hymen" by Sir Joshua Reynolds/Wikimedia Commons/Public Domain; **293** Pictorial Press Ltd/Alamy Stock Photo; **296**t "Richard Lovelace" by William Dobson/Wikimedia Commons/Public Domain; **296**b UniversalImagesGroup/Getty Images; **297** Maria Stezhko/ Shutterstock.com; **298** Culture Club/Hulton Archive/Getty Images; **299–300**bg Oaurea/Shutterstock.com; **300**b Nataliia K/Shutterstock.com; **301** UniversalImagesGroup/Getty Images; **309** © iStock.com/THEPALMER; **310** © iStock.com/ bauhaus1000; **314** "Samuel Pepys" by John Hayls/Wikimedia Commons/Public Domain; **315** Lordprice Collection/ Alamy Stock Photo; **315–17**bg, **318–19**bg Mark Carrel/ Shutterstock.com; **317** Lebrecht Music and Arts Photo Library/Alamy Stock Photo; **318** GL Archive/Alamy Stock Photo

PART 2

322 "Daniel Defoe Kneller Style"/Wikimedia Commons/Public Domain; **332** "The Reader" by Jean-Honoré Fragonard/ Wikimedia Commons/Public Domain; **333**t DEA PICTURE LIBRARY/De Agostini/Getty Images; **333**b "Sir Richard Steele" by Jonathan Richardson/Wikimedia Commons/Public Domain; **338** "Alexander Pope" by Michael Dahl/Wikimedia Commons/Public Domain; **345** National Portrait Gallery/ SuperStock; **334–37**bg McLura/Shutterstock.com

PART 3

360 Heinz-Dieter Falkenstein/age fotostock/SuperStock; **362** hddigital/Shutterstock.com; **363**bg Paladin12/Shutterstock.com; **363–64** Jakub Krechowicz/Shutterstock.com; **365–66**bg McLura/Shutterstock.com; **365, 366** DeMih/ Shutterstock.com; **367** "James Boswell, 1740-1795. Diarist and biographer of Dr Samuel Johnson" by George Willison/ Wikimedia Commons/Public Domain; **369** Print Collector/ Hulton Fine Art Collection/Getty Images; **370–71** Print Collector/Hulton Archive/Getty Images; **374** Portrait of Thomas Gray (engraving), Eccardt, John Giles (fl.1740-79) (after)/ Private Collection/Bridgeman Images

PART 4

382 Heinz-Dieter Falkenstein/age fotostock/SuperStock; **384, 386, 388** Illustration by Mike Wimmer, www.mikewimmer.com; **394** "Aphra Behn" by Peter Lely/Wikimedia Commons/Public Domain; **402**t "Olaudah Equiano - Project Gutenberg eText 15399"/Wikimedia Commons/Public Domain; **402**b Rischgitz/Stringer/Hulton Archive/Getty Images; **408** Lebrecht Music and Arts Photo Library/Alamy Stock Photo; **409** Peter Righteous/Alamy Stock Photo

UNIT 4

PART 1

414–15bg Jon Arnold Images Ltd/Alamy Stock Photo; **416** Peterloo Massacre, published by Richard Carlile, 1st October 1819 (coloured engraving), English School, (19th century)/ Manchester Central Library, UK/Bridgeman Images; **417–18** Public Domain; **419** Heritage Image Partnership Ltd/Alamy Stock Photo; **420**t Anti universal suffrage cartoon in the lead up to the 1867 Reform Act (engraving), English School, (19th century)/Private Collection/© Look and Learn/Peter Jackson Collection/Bridgeman Images; **420**b © iStock.com/ ilbusca; **421** World History Archive/Alamy Stock Photo; **422**t Dinodia Photos/Alamy Stock Photo; **422**b "Imperial Federation, Map of the World Showing the Extent of the British Empire in 1886 (levelled)"/Wikimedia Commons/Public Domain; **423**t Art Collection 2/Alamy Stock Photo; **423**tr "The Boy's Own Paper, front page, 11 April 1891"/Wikimedia Commons/Public Domain; **423**cl "1832 PennyMagazine Oct27 London"/Wikimedia Commons/Public Domain; **423**cr "The Strand Magazine, bound volume 1894"/Wikimedia Commons/Public Domain; **423**b "Illustrated London News - front page - first edition"/Wikimedia Commons/Public Domain; **424** "The Lady of Shalott" by John William Waterhouse/Wikimedia Commons/Public Domain; **428** Ian G Dagnall/Alamy Stock Photo; **429**t "Ploughing Scene in Suffolk" by John Constable/Wikimedia Commons/Public Domain; **429**b prapann/Shutterstock.com; **431** (portrait)**, 432** Public Domain; **431** (frame) Atstock Productions/Shutterstock .com; **434** The Metropolitan Museum of Art, Rogers Fund, 1917, www.metmuseum.org; **435** 'The Tyger'/British Library, London, UK/© British Library Board. All Rights Reserved/ Bridgeman Images; **436** Artokoloro Quint Lox Limited/ Alamy Stock Photo; **437** Art Collection 2/Alamy Stock Photo; **438, 440** (frame design)**, 441, 442** (frame)**, 446, 448, 450** © iStock.com/tatarnikova; **440** World History Archive/Alamy Stock Photo; **442** "Portrais in the Characters of the Nine Muses in the Temple of Apollo" by Richard Samuel/Wikimedia Commons/Public Domain; **444** Pictorial Press Ltd/Alamy Stock Photo; **447** illustration from 'Pride and Prejudice' by Jane Austen (colour litho), Brock, Charles Edmund (1870-1938)/British Library, London, UK/Bridgeman Images; **451** illustration from 'Pride and Prejudice' by Jane Austen (colour litho), Brock, Charles Edmund (1870-1938)/British Library, London, UK/Bridgeman Images

PART 2

456 "William Wordsworth"/Wikimedia Commons/Public Domain; **458** The Poppy Field near Giverny, 1885 (oil on canvas), Monet, Claude (1840–1926)/Musee des Beaux-Arts, Rouen, France/Bridgeman Images; **459** Cliff at Varengeville, 1882 (oil on canvas), Monet, Claude (1840-1926)/Private Collection/Photo © Lefevre Fine Art Ltd., London/Bridgeman Images; **460, 463** (detail) Art Collection 2/Alamy Stock Photo; **464** "Portrait of Samuel Taylor Coleridge" by Peter Vandyke/Wikimedia Commons/Public Domain; **466–67, 469, 471–72, 475–76, 478** © iStock.com/duncan1890; **466** (border design) © iStock.com/tatarnikova; **479, 482** Public Domain; **481** classicpaintings/Alamy Stock Photo; **484** DEA/E. LESSING/De Agostini/Getty Images; **486**bg Ozz Design/Shutterstock.com; **486** (portrait) "The Lady with the Veil (the Artist's Wife)" by Alexander Roslin/Wikimedia Commons/Public Domain; **486** (mirror) Eric Isselee/Shutterstock .com; **487** "Percy Bysshe Shelley" by Alfred Clint/Wikimedia Commons/Public Domain; **489** A Caravan caught in the Sinum wind near Gizah (oil on canvas), Frey, Johann Jakob (1813-65)/Private Collection/Photo © Christie's Images/ Bridgeman Images; **490** Lebrecht Music and Arts Photo Library/Alamy Stock Photo; **492** Artepics/Alamy Stock Photo; **492** (border)**, 493–94** Niagara705/Shutterstock.com; **495** "John Keats" by William Hilton/Wikimedia Commons/Public Domain; **497** Yale Center for British Art, Paul Mellon Collection; **498** North Wind Picture Archives/Alamy Stock Photo; **499** Anna Kutukova/Shutterstock.com; **500** IanDagnall Computing/Alamy Stock Photo

PART 3

504 Bettmann/Getty Images; **506** A black border Victorian memorium card, c.1880 (monochrome), English School, (19th century)/Private Collection/Photo © David Pearson/ Bridgeman Images; **507** I am the Resurrection and the Life, or The Village Funeral, 1872 (oil on canvas), Holl, Frank (1845-88)/Leeds Museums and Galleries (Leeds Art Gallery) U.K./Bridgeman Images; **509** (portrait) Public Domain; **509** (pillars) Rakic/Shutterstock.com; **511** The Traeth Mawr, Moonlight, 1872-73 (oil on canvas), Moore, Henry (1831-95)/Private Collection/Photo © The Maas Gallery, London/ Bridgeman Images; **512** Peter Horree/Alamy Stock Photo; **514** (detail) Painter's Honeymoon, c.1864 (oil on canvas), Leighton, Frederic (1830-96)/Museum of Fine Arts, Boston, Massachusetts, USA/Charles H. Bayley Picture and Painting Fund/Bridgeman Images; **517, 530** Public Domain; **518** The Pride of Dijon, 1879, Hennessy, William John (1839-1917)/ Private Collection/Cooley Gallery, Old Lyme, Connecticut, USA/Bridgeman Images; **519** Time Life Pictures/The LIFE Picture Collection/Getty Images; **521** Lebrecht Music and Arts Photo Library/Alamy Stock Photo; **523** Sarin Images/ Granger, NYC; **525–29** © iStock.com/bauhaus1000; **531–32** World History Archive/Alamy Stock Photo; **534** A Lady in Grey, 1859 (oil on canvas), Macnee, Daniel (1806-82)/National Galleries of Scotland, Edinburgh/Bridgeman Images; **537** And All the Air a Solemn Silence Holds, c.1900 (oil on canvas), Farquharson, Joseph (1846-1935)/Walker Art Gallery, National Museums Liverpool/Bridgeman Images; **541** An October Afterglow, 1871 (oil on canvas), Grimshaw, John Atkinson (1836-93)/Private Collection/Photo © Christie's Images/Bridgeman Images; **545** Sir Charles Edward Trevelyan, 1st Bt (1809-1886), Eddis, Eden Upton (1812-1901)/Wallington Hall, Northumberland, UK/National Trust Photographic Library/Bridgeman Images

PART 4

552 Rischgitz/Hulton Archive/Getty Images; **553** The Reef, St Ives Bay, Cornwall (oil on canvas), Olsson, Albert Julius (1864-1942)/Blackburn Museum and Art Gallery, Lancashire, UK/Bridgeman Images; **555** "Thomas Hardy" by Herbert Rose Barraud/Wikimedia Commons/Public Domain; **556** Winter Scene, 1990, Knyazef, Yuri (b.1927)/Private Collection/Roy Miles Fine Paintings/Bridgeman Images; **558** Hulton Archive/Getty Images; **559–60** PAINTING/Alamy Stock Photo; **561** "Oscar Wilde portrait" by Napoleon Sarony/Wikimedia Commons/Public Domian; **563** Alexander Reprintsev/Shutterstock.com; **563**bg, **564–68**r RODINA OLENA/ Shutterstock.com; **565–66** Robbie Jack/Corbis Entertainment/Getty Images; **569** ullstein bild Dtl./Getty Images; **571** Chronicle/Alamy Stock Photo; **575** Hulton Deutsch/Corbis Historical/Getty Images; **576** © iStock.com/duncan1890

UNIT 5

PART 1

580–81 jgolby/Shutterstock.com; **582**t Paul Popper/Popperfoto/Getty Images; **582**c World History Archive/Alamy Stock Photo; **582**b Keystone/Hulton Archive/Getty Images; **583**tl Lordprice Collection/Alamy Stock Photo; **584**t Lisa Sheridan/Hulton Royals Collection/Getty Images; **583**bl Eddie Gerald/Alamy Stock Photo; **583**br Shawshots/Alamy Stock Photo; **585** "The City Rises" by Umberto Boccioni/Wikimedia Commons/Public Domain; **584**b "Sigmund Freud, by Max Halberstadt (cropped)"/Wikimedia Commons/

Public Domain; **586**t © 2018 Heirs of Josephine Hopper / Licensed by VAGA at Artists Rights Society (ARS), NY; Room in New York, 1932 (oil on canvas), Hopper, Edward (1882-1967) / Sheldon Museum of Art, University of Nebraska, Lincoln, USA / Bridgeman Images; **586**b Bettmann/Getty Images; **587**tl Shawshots/Alamy Stock Photo; **587**tr The Advertising Archives/Alamy Stock Photo; **587**c CBS Photo Archive/Archive Photos/Getty Images; **587**b Alain Le Garsmeur "The Troubles" Archive/Alamy Stock Photo; **588**l David Levenson/Alamy Stock Photo; **588**r Anthony Collins/Alamy Stock Photo; **589**t Alex Segre/Alamy Stock Photo; **589**b Geraint Lewis/Alamy Stock Photo; **590** niroworld/Shutterstock.com; **591** Marco Rubino/Shutterstock.com; **594** Pictorial Press Ltd/Alamy Stock Photo; **596–97** © 2018 Estate of Paul Henry / Artists Rights Society (ARS), New York / IVARO, Dublin; Sunshine in Kerry, c.1939-40 (oil on canvas), Henry, Paul (1877-1958) / Private Collection / Photo © Christie's Images / Bridgeman Images; **598, 605** (painting), **624** Public Domain; **599** World History Archive/Alamy Stock Photo; **600** (painting) "Unter den Linden" by Lesser Ury/Wikimedia Commons/Public Domain; **600, 605** (frame) Magenta10/Shutterstock.com; **606** Science History Images/Alamy Stock Photo; **608** (image), **613** Bettmann/Getty Images; **608** (frame) Peshkova/Shutterstock.com; **610** Roman Nerud/Shutterstock.com; **622** "Virginia Woolf 1927"/Wikimedia Commons/Public Domain; **624–29**bg HorenkO/Shutterstock.com; **627** © 2018 Succession H. Matisse / Artists Rights Society (ARS), New York; Woman in a Purple Coat, 1937 (oil on canvas), Matisse, Henri (1869-1954) / Museum of Fine Arts, Houston, Texas, USA / Museum purchase funded by Audrey Jones Beck / © 2018 Succession H. Matisse/DACS, London / Bridgeman Images; **630** Wolf Suschitzky/The LIFE Images Collection/Getty Images; **631** Foliage I (oil on canvas), Abel, Catherine/Private Collection/Bridgeman Images; **632** IanDagnall Computing/Alamy Stock Photo; **633** PUNCH Magazine Cartoon Archive

PART 2

638, 642 © estate of Fay Godwin/British Library/National Portrait Gallery, London; **640** krsmanovic/Shutterstock.com; **640**bg KongNoi/Shutterstock.com, Chizhenkova Svetlana/Shutterstock.com; **646** Louis MONIER/Gamma-Rapho/Getty Images; **647** Geraint Lewis/Alamy Stock Photo; **648** Hulton Deutsch/Corbis Historical/Getty Images; **649** triocean/Shutterstock.com; **650** Seamus Heaney, 1996 (photo)/Private Collection/Photo © Mark Gerson/Bridgeman Images; **652** SantaLiza/Shutterstock.com; **653** Ulf Andersen/Hulton Archive/Getty Images; **654** Johnny Miller/Millefoto/REX/Shutterstock; **657** Shoula/Photonica/Getty Images; **659** Agence Opale/Alamy Stock Photo; **668** Jonathan Sherrill/Alamy Stock Photo

Entries in SMALL CAPITALS refer to artists and authors. Entries in *italics* refer to titles of paintings and literary selections. Entries in **bold** refer to literary terms.

A

Abolition Speech, 1789, 403, 408–10
ACHEBE, CHINUA, 668
Acts and Monuments of the English Martyrs, The, 160, 161–63
ADDISON, JOSEPH, 333
aestheticism, 496
allegory, 170, 383
alliteration, 193, 296, 465, 505, 595
alliterative verse, 18, 36, 64
allusion, 129, 383, 595
Ambassadors, The, 122
Amoretti, 185, 189
analogy, 140, 151
anaphora, 165, 403, 433
anecdote, 367
Anglo-Saxon Chronicle, The, 31, 32–35
Anglo-Saxon riddles, 68, 69, 70
antithesis, 179, 212, 632
aphorism, 147
Apology for Poetry, An, 140, 141–42
apostrophe, 201, 433
Araby, 607, 608–12
Areopagitica, 302, 303–4
argumentation, 143, 437, 520
ARNOLD, MATTHEW, 552
aside, 210
assonance, 465, 505, 595
Astrophil and Stella, 185, 188
atmosphere, 213, 513, 552
  See also **mood**
aubade, 639
Aubade, 639, 640–41
AUSTEN, JANE, 444

B

BACON, SIR FRANCIS, 146
ballad, 68, 70–72, 465
  ballad meter, 296
  ballad stanza, 69
  folk ballad, 68, 69
Batter my heart, three person'd God, 197, 200
Bayswater Omnibus, The, 423
beast fable, 105
Beatitudes, The, 165, 166–67
BECKETT, SAMUEL, 646
BEDE, 64
BEHN, APHRA, 394
Behold the Man!, 391, 393
Beowulf, 16, 17, 18, 19–30
Bewcastle Cross, 4
Be Ye Men of Valor, 632, 633–35
bias, 31
biography, 367
black humor, 648
BLAKE, WILLIAM, 432
blank verse, 184, 254, 306
BOCCIONI, UMBERTO, 585
Book of Common Prayer, The, 158, 159
BOSWELL, JAMES, 367
BRONTË, CHARLOTTE, 532
BROWNING, ELIZABETH BARRETT, 517
BROWNING, ROBERT, 512
BUNYAN, JOHN, 382
BURNS, ROBERT, 428
BYRON, LORD (GEORGE GORDON), 479
Byronic hero, 455, 480

C

cacophony, 496
caesura, 457, 651
Canterbury Tales, The, 87, 88, 89–115
CARLYLE, THOMAS, 519
carpe diem, 193
catalog
  See **epic conventions**
CAVENDISH, MARGARET, 151
character, 213, 465, 562, 599, 614
  characterization, 88
  —direct characterization, 88, 445
  —indirect characterization, 88, 445
  dynamic character, 465, 659
  static character, 465, 659
  sympathetic character, 394, 445, 614, 659
  unsympathetic character, 394, 445, 614, 659
CHAUCER, GEOFFREY, 86
chiasmus, 212
Childe Harold's Pilgrimage, 480, 481–85
Christ figure, 53
chronicle, 31
CHURCHILL, SIR WINSTON, 632
City Rises, The, 585
climax
  See **plot**
COLERIDGE, SAMUEL TAYLOR, 464
comedy of manners, 562
comitatus, 15
conceit, 184, 197
  metaphysical conceit, 183, 197
Condition of England, The, 520, 521–24
conflict, 213, 614, 659
connotative language, 403, 632
CONRAD, JOSEPH, 575
consonance, 465, 595
Conversion of Aurelian McGoggin, The, 570, 571–74
Corinthians, I, 13: 1–13, 165, 168
couplet, 185
  heroic couplet, 339
crisis
  See **plot**
Crossing the Bar, 505, 511
Cuckoo Song, The, 69, 73
Cup of Tea, A, 599, 600–05
curtal sonnet, 558
  See also **sonnet**

D

Dance of Death, 10
Darkling Thrush, The, 555, 556–57
DARLY, MATTHEW, 293
deductive reasoning, 147
DEFOE, DANIEL, 322
deism, 289
denouement
  See **plot**
DESAI, ANITA, 659
Devoted Son, A, 659, 660–67
devotional literature, 75
dialect, 428
dialogue, 367, 445
diary, 314
Diary of Samuel Pepys, The, 314, 315–19
DICKENS, CHARLES, 530
Dictionary of the English Language, A, 290, 361, 362–64
didactic, 18
DONNE, JOHN, 196
Dover Beach, 552, 553–54
dramatic monologue, 298, 505, 513
dramatic poetry, 183
dramatis personae, 210

INDEX

E

Ecclesiastical History of the English People, An, 64, 65–67
elegy, 206, 505
Elegy Written in a Country Churchyard, 374, 375–79
ELIZABETH I, QUEEN, 179
England in 1819, 488, 491
English Bible, The, 164, 165, 166–68
enjambment, 457, 651
epic, 16, 18
  literary epic, 170, 306
  mock epic, 105
epic conventions, 306
  catalog, 170
  epic simile, 170
  epithet, 64
  in medias res, 16, 306
epic simile
  See **epic conventions**
epigram, 204
epiphany, 607
epithet
  See **epic conventions** (*see also* **stock epithet**)
EQUIANO, OLAUDAH, 402
essay, 147, 520
Essay on Criticism, An, 339, 342–44
Essay on Man, An, 339, 340–41
Essays (Bacon), 147, 148–50
ethos
  See **rhetorical appeals**
euphony, 496
Everyman, 83
Eve's Apology in Defense of Women, 143, 144–45
exposition
  See **plot**

F

Faerie Queene, The, 170, 171–78
falling action
  See **plot**
farce, 82
Farewell, Love, and all thy laws forever, 185, 187
figurative language, 129, 555, 639
first-person narrator
  See **point of view**
foil character, 445
Follower, 651, 652
foreshadow, 614
Form of Solemnization of Matrimony, The, 159
FOXE, JOHN, 160
Foxe's Book of Martyrs
  See The Acts and Monuments of the English Martyrs
frame tale, 87
Frankenstein: Or, The Modern Prometheus, 500

G

Get Up and Bar the Door, 69, 72
Go and catch a falling star, 197, 198
God Speed, 12
God's Grandeur, 558, 560
GORDIMER, NADINE, 653
gothic, 533
GRAY, THOMAS, 374
Gulliver's Travels, 346, 347–56

H

hagiography, 64
Hard Times, 530, 531
HARDY, THOMAS, 555
Having this day my horse, my hand, my lance, 185, 188
HEANEY, SEAMUS, 650
Heart of Darkness, 575, 576
HERBERT, GEORGE, 201
HERRICK, ROBERT, 296, 297
historical narrative, 160
HOLBEIN, HANS, THE YOUNGER, 10, 122
Holy Sonnet 14, 197, 200
HOPKINS, GERARD MANLEY, 558
HOPPER, EDWARD, 586
HOWARD, HENRY, EARL OF SURREY, 184
How do I love thee? Let me count the ways, 517, 518
HUGHES, TED, 642
humanist, 9
hymn, 391
hyperbole, 240, 517

I

iambic pentameter, 185
  See also **blank verse**
idealism, 416
image, 428, 465, 517, 555, 570
imagery, 75, 229, 570
Importance of Being Earnest, The, 562, 563–68
inciting incident
  See **plot**
inductive reasoning, 147
in medias res
  See **epic conventions**
In Memoriam, 505, 506–8
interior monologue
  See **stream of consciousness**
irony, 562, 570, 639, 659
  dramatic irony, 240, 648
  situational irony, 88, 570, 653
  verbal irony, 88, 240, 445, 570
I sing of a maiden, 69, 73
I wandered lonely as a cloud, 457, 458

J

Jane Eyre, 533, 535–49
JOHNSON, SAMUEL, 290, 360
JONSON, BEN, 204
Jordan (2), 201, 202
JOY, GEORGE WILLIAM, 423
JOYCE, JAMES, 606
JULIAN OF NORWICH, 74

K

KEATS, JOHN, 495
kenning, 18, 64
KIPLING, RUDYARD, 569

L

Lake Isle of Innisfree, The, 595, 596
Lamb, The, 433, 434
LANGLAND, WILLIAM, 116
LANIER, AMELIA, 143
LARKIN, PHILIP, 638
LAWRENCE, D. H., 613
legend, 53
LEIGHTON, EDMUND, 12
Le Morte d'Arthur, 53, 54–60
Let me not to the marriage of true minds, 185, 191
LEWIS, C. S., 630
Life of Olaudah Equiano, or Gustavas Vassa, the African, The, 403, 404–7
Life of Samuel Johnson, The, 367, 368–73
Lines Composed a Few Miles Above Tintern Abbey, 457, 460–63
literary criticism, 140, 361
litotes, 18
logos
  See **rhetorical appeals**
London, 433, 436
Love (3), 201, 202
LOVELACE, RICHARD, 296, 297
lyric poetry, 183, 595

M

Macbeth, 213, 214–80
MALORY, THOMAS, 52
MANSFIELD, KATHERINE, 599
Mark on the Wall, The, 623, 624–29
MARLOWE, CHRISTOPHER, 192, 194
MARVELL, ANDREW, 298
medieval lyrics, 68, 73
metaphor, 151, 517, 552
  extended metaphor, 151, 643
meter, 182, 505
  common meter, 391
  tetrameter, 391
Methodism, 289
MILTON, JOHN, 301
miracle play, 82
Moment Before the Gun Went Off, The, 653, 654–58
mood, 639, 643
  See also **atmosphere**
morality play, 82
MORE, SIR THOMAS, 130
Most glorious Lord of life! that, on this day, 185, 189
motif, 254, 383
My mistress' eyes are nothing like the sun, 185, 191
mystery play, 82

N

narrative poetry, 183
narrator, 346
naturalism, 551
neoclassicism, 292
Not Waving but Drowning, 648, 649
novel of sensibility
  See **sensibility**
Nun's Priest's Tale, The, 105, 107–15
Nymph's Reply to the Shepherd, The, 193, 195

O

Observations upon Experimental Philosophy, 151, 152–54
octave, 185
ode, 488, 496
Ode on a Grecian Urn, 496, 498
Ode to the West Wind, 488, 492–94
Of Atheism, 147, 149–50
Of Studies, 147, 148
Old Royal Naval College, The, 285
One day I wrote her name upon the strand, 185, 189
On My First Son, 204, 206
onomatopoeia, 465
Oroonoko, 394, 395–401
Our God, Our Help in Ages Past, 391, 392
Ozymandias, 488, 489

P

pamphlet, 302
Paradise Lost, 306, 307–13
paradox, 165, 197
parallelism, 140, 179, 433, 505, 632
parody, 105
Passionate Shepherd to His Love, The, 193, 194
Past and Present, 520, 521–24
pastoral, 183, 193
pathos
  See **rhetorical appeals**
PEARL POET, 36
PEPYS, SAMUEL, 314
Perelandra, 630, 631
persona, 513, 570
personification, 201
perspective, 31
philosophes, 290–91, 321
Pied Beauty, 558, 559
Piers Plowman, 116
Pilgrim's Progress, The, 383, 385–90
plot, 240, 513
  climax, 240, 614
  crisis, 240, 614
  denouement, 240, 614
  exposition, 240, 614
  falling action, 240, 614
  inciting incident, 240, 614
  rising action, 240, 614
Poems and Fancies, 155
poetic diction, 374
point of view, 653
  first-person, 394, 403
  third-person, 394
  third-person limited, 599
POPE, ALEXANDER, 338
popular genres, 68, 70–73
Porphyria's Lover, 513, 515–16
Preface to *A Dictionary of the English Language,* 361, 362–63
Preface to *Observations upon Experimental Philosophy,* 151, 152–54
Pride and Prejudice, 445, 446–53
primitivism, 417
progressivism, 417
Prologue to *The Canterbury Tales, The,* 88, 89–104
proscenium, 210
prose romance, 53
  See also **romance**
psychological realism, 533
Pulley, The, 201, 203
purpose (authorial purpose), 160

Q

quatrain, 185

R

RALEIGH, SIR WALTER, 192, 195
Rambler, The, 361, 365–66
rationalism, 284
Red, Red Rose, A, 428, 431
refrain, 69
repartee, 445, 562
repetition, 433, 632
Revelations of Divine Love, 75, 76–81
REYNOLDS, JOSHUA, 293
rhetorical appeals, 129, 140, 437, 632
  ethos, 140, 179, 403
  logos, 140, 403
  pathos, 140, 179, 403
rhetorical devices, 129, 140, 520
  See also **parallelism, repetition, chiasmus, antithesis**
rhetorical question, 403, 433, 632
rhyme, 296
  end rhyme, 595
  internal rhyme, 465
  perfect rhyme, 651
  slant rhyme, 651
rhyme scheme, 185
riddles, Anglo-Saxon, 68, 69, 70
Ridiculous Taste or the *Ladies Absurdity,* 293
Rime of the Ancient Mariner, The, 465, 466–78
rising action
  See **plot**
Robinson Crusoe, 322, 323–31
romance, 36, 170
romanticism
  distant, the, 455
  imagination, 455
  individual, 455
  nature, 455
  sublime, the, 455, 480
  visionary, 454
Room in New York, 586

INDEX

S

Sailing to Byzantium, 595, 597
Salve Deus Rex Judaeorum, 144
sarcasm, 240
satire, 85, 562
  Horatian satire, 333
  Juvenalian satire, 346
  social satire, 131
Second Coming, The, 595, 598
sensibility, 359, 374
  novel of sensibility, 332, 359
  sentimentality, 359
sensory details, 314, 403, 433
sentimental comedy, 359
sentimentality
  See **sensibility**
sestet, 185
setting, 213, 599, 643
SHAKESPEARE, WILLIAM, 184, 211–212
She Walks in Beauty, 480, 486
SHELLEY, MARY, 500
SHELLEY, PERCY BYSSHE, 487
Sick Collier, A, 614, 615–21
SIDNEY, SIR PHILIP, 140, 184
signal words, 75
SIGNOL, ÉMILE, 9
Signs of the Times, 520, 525–29
simile, 212, 517, 552
Sir Gawain and the Green Knight, 37, 38–51
Sir Patrick Spens, 69, 70–71
slave narrative, 403
SMITH, STEVIE, 648
social Darwinism, 551
soliloquy, 210
Song, 197, 198
Song to Celia, 204, 205
sonnet, 184, 302
  English (Shakespearean) sonnet, 185
  Italian (Petrarchan) sonnet, 185
Sonnet 19 (Milton), 302, 305
Sonnet 43 (Browning), 517, 518
Sonnets (Shakespeare)
  Sonnet 73, 185, 190
  Sonnet 116, 185, 191
  Sonnet 130, 185, 191
Sonnets (Sidney)
  Sonnet 31, 185, 188
  Sonnet 41, 185, 188
Sonnets (Spenser)
  Sonnet 68, 185, 189
  Sonnet 75, 185, 189
sound devices, 505, 651
speaker (in poetry), 298, 648
  See also **persona**
Spectator, The, 333, 336–37
speech, 403
Speech to the Troops at Tilbury, 179, 180
SPENSER, EDMUND, 169, 184
Spenserian stanza, 480
sprung rhythm, 558
STEELE, RICHARD, 333
Still to be neat, 204, 205
stock epithet, 18
stream of consciousness, 607
  interior monologue, 623
style, 339, 361, 374, 639
SWIFT, JONATHAN, 345
symbol, 37, 229, 433, 465, 533, 555, 595, 607, 623, 648

T

Taking of Jerusalem by the Crusaders, 15th July 1099, 9
Tatler, The, 333, 334–35
TENNYSON, ALFRED, LORD, 504
terza rima, 488
text structures, 75
That time of year thou mayst in me behold, 185, 190
theater-in-the-round, 210
theme, 229, 428, 517, 533, 614, 651
Things Fall Apart, 668
Thought-Fox, The, 643, 645
thrust, 210
To a Mouse, 428, 429–30
To Autumn, 496, 497
To His Coy Mistress, 298, 299–300
To Lucasta: Going to the Wars, 296, 297
tone, 88, 131, 160, 433
To the Virgins, To Make Much of Time, 296, 297
tragedy, 209
  tragic flaw, 209, 269
  tragic hero, 209, 269
  tragic plot, 209, 269
transcendentalism, 416
transitional phrases, 31
tricolon, 147
trimeter, 391
Tyger, The, 433, 435

U

Ulysses, 505, 509–10
unities
  unity of action, 209
  unity of place, 209
  unity of time, 209
utopia, 131
Utopia, 131, 132–39

V

Valediction Forbidding Mourning, A, 197, 199
variation, 18, 64
verisimilitude, 322, 332
verse epistle, 340
Vindication of the Rights of Woman, A, 437, 438–43
voice, 361

W

Waiting for Godot, 646, 647
WATTS, ISAAC, 391
WESLEY, CHARLES, 391
When I consider how my light is spent, 302, 305
When I have fears that I may cease to be, 496, 499
WILBERFORCE, WILLIAM, 402
WILDE, OSCAR, 561
wit, 445, 562
With how sad steps, O moon, thou climb'st the skies, 185, 188
WOLLSTONECRAFT, MARY, 437
WOOLF, VIRGINIA, 622
WORDSWORTH, WILLIAM, 456
world is too much with us, The, 457, 459
World Made by Atomes, A, 151, 155
WREN, SIR CHRISTOPHER, 285
WYATT, SIR THOMAS, 184
wyrd, 18

Y

YEATS, WILLIAM BUTLER, 594